Y0-BIP-760

INTERNATIONAL THEOLOGICAL LIBRARY.

AN INTRODUCTION

TO THE

LITERATURE OF THE NEW TESTAMENT.

BY

JAMES MOFFATT, B.D., D.D.

NEW YORK
CHARLES SCRIBNER'S SONS
1921

SENATVI · VNIVERSITATIS · SANCTI · ANDREAE

QVI · ME · S·S· THEOLOGIAE · DOCTOREM

CREANDVM · DECREVIT

HOC · OPVS · QVANTVLVMCVMQVE

DEDICO

GRATA · MEMORIA

"Without doubt, some of the richest and most powerfu and populous communities of the antique world, and some of the grandest personalities and events, have, to after and present times, left themselves entirely unbequeath'd. Others have arrived safely, as from voyages over wide, century-stretching seas. The little ships, the miracles that have buoy'd them, and by incredible chances safely convey'd them (or the best of them, their meaning and essence) over long wastes, darkness, lethargy, ignorance, etc., have been a few inscriptions—a few immortal compositions, small in size, yet compassing what measureless values of reminiscence, contemporary portraitures, manners, idioms and beliefs, with deepest inference, hint and thought, to tie and touch for ever the old, new body, and the old, new soul! These! and still these! bearing the freight so dear—dearer than pride—dearer than love. All the best experience of humanity, folded, saved, freighted to us here. Some of these tiny ships we call Old and New Testament. . . ."

WALT WHITMAN, *Democratic Vistas.*

"A book that is really old and really valuable has nothing to fear from the critic, whose labours can only put its worth in a clearer light, and establish its authority on a surer basis. In a word, it is the business of the critic to trace back the steps by which any ancient book has been transmitted to us, to find where it came from and who wrote it, to examine the occasion of its composition, and search out every link that connects it with the history of the ancient world and with the personal life of its author."

W. ROBERTSON SMITH, *The Old Testament in the Jewish Church* (Lect. I.).

"From the first the living stream of christian experience, though holding that onward course of which the successive flood-marks are the epistle to the Romans and the gospel ascribed to St. John, had been stagnating by the way into pools formed on the one side by Judaism, on the other by philosophic systems. The popular habit of regarding the writings of the NT as a body of doctrine pitched into the world all at once, has caused this fact to be generally overlooked. Yet an examination of these writings themselves might satisfy us that they came into being as successive assertions of the fulness of christian life against a cotemporaneous stiffening of it either into Jewish ordinance or gentile philosophy."

T. H. GREEN, *Works* (vol. iii. p. 170).

PREFACE

SINCE this manual is designed primarily for the use of students, most of whom need to be reminded that if the first commandment of research is, 'Thou shalt work at the sources,' the second is, 'Thou shalt acquaint thyself with work done before thee and beside thee,' I have agreed to notice, as far as the limits of my space and knowledge permit, the views of scholars who for various reasons are led to occupy positions which differ from those adopted in the following pages. The literary criticism of the New Testament still contains a large number of unsettled problems, and it is only fair, in a handbook of this kind, that facilities should be given for comparing the ramifications of argument and argument. Among other things, I have tried to draw up sifted lists of references to the relevant literature for the convenience of those who desire to find their way about in the world of more or less recent opinion upon the subject. The bibliographies have to be read in the light of what Eusebius wrote at the close of the ninth book of his *Præparatio Euangelica*: καὶ πολὺς δὲ ἄλλος μαρτύρων ἡμῖν ὄχλος παλαιῶν τε καὶ νέων συγγραφέων ἐπιρρεῖ, τὴν ὁμοίαν τοῖς τεθεῖσι ψῆφον ἐπισφραγιζομένων, ὧν τὰς φωνὰς, λόγου προνοούμενοι συμμετρίας, τοῖς φιλομαθέσι ζητεῖν τε καὶ διερευνᾶν ἀπολείψαντες, ἐπὶ τὴν λείπουσαν αὐτοὶ μεταβησόμεθα ἐπαγγελίαν. I could have wished to make the lists as well as the arguments ampler at several points. Still, they will perhaps serve, for all their defects, to give some clue to the main divergences of critical research from the track which has been outlined in the present volume.

JAMES MOFFATT.

BROUGHTY-FERRY, *August 12th*, 1910.

CONTENTS

CHAPTER II.

THE HISTORICAL LITERATURE.

CHAPTER III.

HOMILIES AND PASTORALS.

CHAPTER IV.

CHAPTER V.

HISTORICAL TABLES: TO ILLUSTRATE THE HISTORY AND LITERATURE BETWEEN 230 B.C. AND 370 A.D.

B.C.	Rome and the East.	Jewish Literature.		Greek and Latin Literature.	
230	Ptolemy III. (Euergetes), 247–222. First diplomatic relations between Greece and Rome, 229. Celts, invasion and defeat of, 225.	Gk. version of Pentateuch (by c. 250).	Close of prophetic canon.	Cleanthes (died 232). Eratosthenes. Antigonus of Carystos. Chrysippus (–207). Archimedes (287–212). Apollonius Rhodius (238–188).	L. Andronicus (284–204). Nævius (264–194).
	Gallia Cisalpina, a Roman province, 222.				
220	Second Punic War (218–202). War over Palestine between Antiochus the Great and Ptolemy IV.–V., 218–197. Battle of Raphia, 217.	Simon II., high priest (219–199). Epistle of Aristeas?		Euphorion fl. Macho (com.). Rhianus (eleg.).	
210	Independence of Parthia. Scipio in Africa. Ptolemy Epiphanes, 205–182. Battle of Zama, 202.	Demetrius (hist.)? Ecclesiastes?		Zeno of Tarsus. Sotion of Alexandria.	Q. Fabius Pictor (Gk.). Plautus (254–184 c.).
200	First Macedonian war (200–197). Greece declared free. Rosetta Stone, 196. Celtic revolt.	Antigonus of Socho. Enoch (1–36), before 170.		Hermippus. Alcæus of Messenia (poet).	Ennius (239–169). Cato (234–149).

HISTORICAL TABLES—(*continued*).

B.C.	Rome and the East.	Jewish Literature.	Greek and Latin Literature.	
190	Conquest of Galatae in Asia Minor.		Aristophanes of Byzantium (257–180).	Cincius, 'de re militari.'
		Joseph ben Joezar.	Polemon of Ilium.	
	Sumptuary legislation in Rome.	" " Jochanan.		
180	Ptolemy Philometor, 182–146.	Ecclesiasticus (*c.* 180).	Aristarchus.	Carcilius Statius.
		Prayer of Manasseh.		
	Hellenising of Judea.	Eupolemus (hist.).	Aristobulus (phil.).	Pacuvius (220–130).
170	Second Macedonian war, 171–168.	Aristobulus (phil.), 170–150 fl.	Polybius (207–122).	Titinnius (com.).
	First public library in Rome, 167.	Maccabean Psalms.		Terence (195–159).
	Antiochus Epiphanes (176–165).			"Origines" of Cato.
	Maccabean revolt.		Demetrius of Scepsis.	
	Purification of Temple, 165.	Daniel.	Gk. phil. and rhetor. expelled from Rome, 161.	
160	Judas Maccabæus (166–161 fl.).		Carneades (213–128).	
	Jonathan Maccabæus (160–144).			Sempronius Asellio.
	Embassy of philosophers to Rome (155).	Gk. version of Daniel (–150).	Hipparchus (astron.).	
			Diogenes of Seleucia.	
	First stone bridge in Rome (179–142).			M. Brutus.
			Postumius Albinus.	
150	Third Punic war (149–146).		Nicander.	A. Postum. Albinus (Gk. hist.), 150 *c.*
	Ptolemy Physkon, 146–117.	Esther (150–130).	Moschus fl.	Attius (dram.).
	Simon Maccabæus (143–135).	Jason of Cyrene.	Ammonius (critic, 145 *c.*).	
	Destruction of Corinth and Carthage (146).	Psalter complete, *c.* 140.	Antipater of Tarsus.	

140	Greece, a Roman province (145). Letters from Rome to East in favour of Jews, 138–137. Jewish independence.	Artapanus (hist.), περὶ Ἰουδαίων.		Panætius of Rhodes (phil.), 150–120 fl.	Lucilius (148–103).
		Sibylline Or. (iii. 97–817), *c.* 140.	Philo (epic)?		
	The Gracchi (164–121). John Hyrcanus (135–107). Conquest of Spain.	3 Esdras (170–100). Gk. version of Ecclesiasticus.		Apollodorus of Athens, Χρονικά.	Q. Mucius Scævola, *Annales Maximi* (133).
130	Sempronian laws (133–123). Destruction of temple on Mount Gerizim. Edom merged in Judea.	Jehoshua, Matthai } 140–110.	Theodotus (poet)?	Dionysius Thrax (130 *c.*).	Hostius, *de bello Istrico* (125). Sextus Turpilius (com.). L. Cælius Antipater.
	Marius (155–86).	Chronicles of Hyrcanus.			
120	Gallia Narbon., R. province. Sumptuary laws (115). Sulla (138–78). Cimbrian war (113–102).	Cleodemus (Malchus). Judith (130–105). Enoch: chs. 83–90.	Ezekiel (dram.)?	Apollonius Molon (*c.* 120), Συσκευὴ κατὰ Ἰουδαίων. Agatharcides (geogr.). Clitomachus. Theodosius (math.).	
110	Jugurthine war (111–106). Numidia, R. province (106). Alex. Jannæus (106–79).	Jubilees, 135–105? Gk. Additions to Daniel (–90). Test. XII Patriarchs (groundwork, before 100).		Antipater of Sidon.	M. Æm. Scaurus.
100	Cilicia, R. province (102). Jewish capture of Philistia. Schools of oratory in Rome. Tyranny and overthrow of Pharisees.	Jehuda.		Philo of Larissa (147–80). Bion? Hero (math.)?	C. Licinius Macer.

HISTORICAL TABLES—(*continued*).

B.C.	Rome and the East.	Jewish Literature.	Greek and Latin Literature.
		Enoch: chs. 91–104 (between 134 and 95).	Accius (trag.). Lucius Afranius.
	Jews revolt against Jannæus (95–86).		
90	Social war in Italy.	1 Mac. ± 90. 2 Mac. 150–50?	Scymnus (geogr.). Parthenius.
	Sulla captures Athens (86).		
		Wisdom of Solomon?	Antiochus of Askalon (phil.). Auctor ad Herennium.
	Alexander's campaign east of Jordan.		
			Gk. art and sc. in Rome.
	Sertorius in Spain (83–72).		Valerius Cato.
80	Pharisaic reaction under Salome, 79–69.	Schimeon ben Shetach.	Posidonius (phil.), 110–50 fl. Claudius Quadrigarius.
		Activity of Scribes.	Diotimus (Stoic). Q. Hortensius (114–50).
		Letter of Jeremiah? Enoch (Similitudes=37–70), 95–65.	Apollodorus of Pergamon (105–33). Philoxenus. Sisenna (hist.). Coll. of Sibyll. Oracles.
70	Aristobulus II., 69–63.	Alexander Polyhistor (80–40), περὶ Ἰουδαίων.	Meleager (eleg.).
	Catilinarian conspiracy (65–63). Sadducees dominant.		Lysimachus (anti-Semite). Cornelius Nepos (99–54).
	Syria, R. province (65).	Pseudo-Phocylides?	

	Interference of Rome in Jewish dissensions.			T. Pomponius Atticus.
		Greek additions to Esther?	Tyrannion (elder), 115–25.	Nigid. Figulus (phil.).
60	Pompey takes Jerusalem (63). Jewish exiles at Rome.	Psalter of Solomon (63–48).	Andronicus (phil.).	Lucretius, *de rerum natura* (56).
	Cyprus, R. province (57). Cæsar in Gaul (58–51), in Britain (55–54). Cleopatra (69–30).		Artemidorus (geogr.).	Catullus (87–54).
	Jewish revolts against Roman power, suppressed by Gabinius.	Hyrcanus II. (63–40).	Metrodorus.	Quintus Cicero. Decius Laberius.
		Book of Jannes and Jambres?	Menippus.	Bibaculus (83–24). Cicero (106–43).
	Gaul, R. province (50).			Cæsar.
	Crassus plunders temple.	Schemaiah, Abtalion } 65–35.	Philodemus.	Sallust (86–35). Varro.
50	Cæsar crosses Rubicon, 49.	Tobit (before 25).		Dellius (hist.). Cornelius Gallus.
	Battle of Pharsalia, 48. Cæsar befriends Antipater.	Book of Noah?	Castor ('Chronicle').	M. Junius Brutus.
	Murder of Cæsar, 44. Antipater poisoned.	Apocalypse of Elijah?	Didymus of Alexandria.	Q. Sextius (phil.).
40	Pollio's library in Rome. Herod the Great, King of Judea, with aid of Romans, 37–4.	Sibyll. Orac. iii. 36–92 (*c.* 40).	Sosigenes (phil.).	Aulus Hirtius. P. Syrus. Vergil (73–19). L. Varius Rufus.
		Menachem.	Antipater of Tyre.	

HISTORICAL TABLES—(*continued*).

B.C.	Rome and the East.	Jewish Literature.	Greek and Latin Literature.	
	Battle of Actium, 31.	Hillel (70 B.C.–6 A.D.).		C. Asinius Pollio.
	Egypt, R. province (30).			
30	Augustus (30–Aug. 19, 14 A.D.).		Timagenes (hist.).	Tibullus.
	Rise of Herodians.			Propertius.
	Pantheon built in Rome, 27.		Diodorus Siculus (hist.).	
	Hellenising of Judea.			Horace.
	Galatia and Pamphylia, R. provinces, 25.	Shammai.	Conon (mythogr.).	
	Social reforms, *c.* 21.			
	Building of Cæsarea, 22–10.			Æmilius Macer.
20	Augustus visits Syria.	Philo born.	Juba.	
	Rebuilding of Temple at Jerusalem.			
	Secular games, 17.	Commentaries of King Herod?	Nicolaus Damascenus.	Messalla (–9 A.D.).
	Rhætia and Noricum, R. province 15.			Vitruvius Pollio, *de archit.* (14).
			Hypsikrates.	Livy (59–17 A.D.).
10	Drusus in Germany (12–9).		Dionysius Halicarn., 'Roman Archæol.,' 8 B.C.	Trogus Pompeius.
				M. Corvinus (hist.).
	Seneca born, *c.* 4.			Germanicus.
	Jesus born, ± 6.		Theodorus of Rhodes (rhet.), 6 B.C.–2 A.D. fl.	Ovid, *Ars Amor.* (2–1).

A.D. 1	Herod Antipas (B.C. 4–A.D. 39).	Popular revolt under rabbis Judas and Matthias (4).		
	Philip tetrarch („ –A.D. 34).			**Hyginus.**
	Census of Quirinius, 6–7.	**Annas high priest (6–15).**	**Lesbonax.**	
	Judas the Galilean, revolt and defeat of Zealots.			
		Assumptio Mosis?	**Dionysius Periegetes.**	**Fenestella (hist.).** Albinovanus.
	Rebellion of Arminius (9–19).			
				Monum. Ancyranum.
10	**Pannonia, R. province.**		**Strabo (54 B.C.–24 A.D.).**	
	Germanicus (14–19).			
		Slavonic Enoch (1–50 A.D.).		**Manilius, *Astronomica*?**
	Census (14).			
	Tiberius (Aug. 19, 14 A.D.–March 16, 37 A.D.).	Ptolemy of Ascalon, *Life of Herod*?	**Apollonius Sophista.**	
	Parthian dissensions.			Antonius Musa (med.).
	Earthquake in Asia, 17.			
20	Power of Sejanus (–31).	Caiaphas high priest (18–36).	**Theon.**	Cn. Lentulus Gætulicus.
	Reign of terror at Rome.			Celsus (med.).
	Mission of John	the Baptist (25–26).		
	Pilate procurator (26–36).		Apion.	Valerius Maximus.
	Tiberius at Capreæ (26–37).	Hananja ben Hiskia (ed. of Ezekiel).	Philippus of Thessalonika.	
				Afer Domitius (orat.).
	Crucifixion of	Jesus (29–30).	Xenocrates (med.).	
30		Gamaliel I. (30–40).		
	Power of Macro.			Phædrus (30–40 fl.).
	Herod Agrippa	I., king (37–44).		
	Caligula (March 16, 37–Jan. 24, 41).	3 Maccabees?		Velleius Paterculus.
	Persecution of Jews in	Alexandria (38).		

HISTORICAL TABLES—(*continued*).

A.D.	The Roman Empire.	Jewish and Christian Literature.	Greek and Latin Literature.	
	Nero born, 37.	Apion lectures through Greece on Homer.		Lucan.
	Josephus born, 37–38.		Babrius?	
	Apion in Rome.			Q. Asconius Pedianus.
40	Claudius (41–Oct. 13, 54).	Philo, *contra Flaccum*.	Cornutus.	Pomponius Secundus.
	Romans in Britain.	*Legatio ad Caium*.		
	Lycia, R. province.			
	Revolt of Theudas.			Seneca (4 B.C.–65 A.D.).
	Judaism in Adiabenê.			Aufidius Bassus.
	Thrace, a R. province, 45.		Heliodorus.	
	Messalina fl.			
	S. Britain, R. province, 47.			
	Census (48)	Abba Chilkijja.		Scribonius Largus.
	London founded by Aulus Plautius (47).	Abba Scha'ul.		
50	Jews banished from Rome.	Agrippa II. (50–100).	Nikomachus Gerasenus.	
	Turbulence in Palestine.	Paul's missions.		Pomponius Mela.
	Felix procurator.			
	Nero (54–June 9, 68).		Onosander (milit.).	Persius (34–62).
				Q. Remmius Palæmon.
	Josephus among Essenes (53–56).		Antipater of Thessalonika.	
				Cæsius Bassus.

60	Josephus joins Pharisees	(57).		Chaeremon (phil.).	Petronius Arbiter.
	Festus procurator.		Arrest of Paul.		Thrasea Pætus.
	James of Jerusalem, d. c. 60.	Josephus in Rome.		Dioskorides (med.). Pamphilê.	Columella of Gades.
	64, burning of Rome, persecution of Christians.		Paul's prison epistles (Rome).		
	Revolt of Boadicea in Britain.		First Peter?	Heraclides (gramm.).	
	Gessius Florus, proc.			Erotianus.	Calpurnius Siculus.
	Outbreak of war in Palestine. Siege and capture of Jerusalem.	Eleazar ben Jacob.		Leonidas of Alexandria. Sextius (phil.).	"Aetna."
	False Nero in East (c. 69).			Musonius Rufus (phil.). Ammonius.	M. Valerius Probus.
		Birth of Polykarp.			
70	Flavia Neapolis founded. Stoics banished from Rome.	Onias (±70).	Gospel of Mark (±70).	Aretæus (med.). "Periplus Maris Erythræi."	M. Cluvius Rufus (hist.). Vipstanus Messala.
	Vespasian's *Fiscus Judaicus* (72).				
	Judea, separate province. Abolition of Sanhedrim.	Eleazar ben Azarja (	-82).		Q. Curtius. Vespasian's "Memoirs."
	Colosseum built (70–80).	Josephus, *Wars of Jews*.	Gospel of Matthew, 75–90.		Anton. Julianus.
	Epictetus in Rome.	Predominance of Pharisees and rabbis.			Epaphroditus (gramm.).
	Titus (June 23, 79–Sept. 13, 81).		Hebrews, ± 80.	Demetrius.	Pliny, *Nat. Hist.* (77).
	False Nero on Euphrates. Hercul. and Pompeii destroyed, 79.				C. Val. Flaccus, *Argonautica*.

HISTORICAL TABLES—(*continued*).

A.D.	The Roman Empire.	Jewish and Christian Literature.	Greek and Latin Literature.
80	Domitian (Sept. 81–Sept. 18, 96). Agricola in Britain (78–85). Josephus in Rome (70–100). Domitian's triumph in Gaul (83). Defeat of Caled. at Mons Grampius. False Nero on Euphrates. Severe policy towards Jews and Christians.	Rabbinic school at Jamnia. Rabbi ben Asai (70–100). ,, Jochanan. ,, Josse. Justus of Tiberias (hist.). Gospel acc. Hebrews (before 100). 4 Esdras? Synod of Jamnia, OT canon fixed (*c.* 90).	Dio Prusæus. Fabius Rusticus. Silius Italicus. Verginius Rufus. Sext. J. Frontinus. Papinius Statius. Niketas of Smyrna. Martial, *Epigrammata* (83–101).
90	Secular Games (88). Philosophers expelled from Rome, 94. Persecution of Christians. Nerva (Sept. 96–Jan. 25, 98).	John the presbyter. Josephus, *Antiquities* (93–93). Eleazar ben Hyrkanos, at Lydda. The Apocalypse of John. Clem. Rom. *c.* 96. Gamaliel II. at Jamnia. Luke's writings (*c.* 100). Eleazar ben Zadok. Cerinthus. ,, ,, Arach.	Epictetus at Nikopolis, 89. Arruntius Stella. Juvenal. Plutarch (48–120). Quintilian *Instit.*, 93 ± Tacitus, *Agricola* (97–98). Æmilius Asper.
100	Trajan (Jan. 98–Aug. 9, 117).	Elischa ben Abuja. Menander. Origin of Massoretic text of OT. Fourth Gospel (100–115).	Isæus (sophist). Siculus Flaccus. Tacitus, *Historiæ*.

	Conquest of Dacia (101–106). ,, Nabatean realm (106).		First epistle of John. Pastoral epistles (90–115).	Calv. Taurus (phil.).	Pliny younger, *Letters*. Terent. Maurus.
	Martyrdom of Symeon.	(107).		Nikarchus.	Annæus Florus.
			Rise of gnostic literary activity.		
		Ascensio Isaiæ (6^1–11^1 11^{23-40}). Book of Elxai (?).	Naaseni.	Ælianus. Aristides Quintilianus (mus.).	Flavius Caper.
110	Column of Trajan, 113.	Roman Symbol?	Gospel of Egyptians (before 130).		111–113, Pliny's correspond. with Trajan on Christians.
	Jews revolt in Cyrene, Cyprus, etc.	Letters of Ignatius.	Simonians.	Dio Chrysost.	Tacitus, *Annales* (115–117).
	Roman Empire at largest extent.		Ophites.	Mesomedes.	
	Hadrian (Aug. 117–July 10, 138).	Epistle of Polykarp.	Saturninus.	Moschio.	Hyginus.
	Jews of Palestine revolt.	Irenæus born, 115.	Ebionitic gospel of the Twelve?	Apollodorus Poliorketes.	
	Hadrian in Britain, 119.				Priscus Neratius.
		Didachê (100–150).			
120	Hadrian in Athens, 123–126. Hadrian's Rescript.	Quadratus (apol.). R. Tarphon (*c.* 120).	Basilides in Alexandria (Ἐξηγητικά).	Draco (gramm.).	Suetonius, *Vit. Cæs.*
	War with Picts and Scots, 120–138.	Aquila (version of OT)? R. Ishmael ben Elischa.	Satornil in Antioch.	Phlegon ('Chronica').	Q. Ter. Scaurus.
	Polykrates of Ephesus, born, *c.* 125.	Protevangelium Jacobi? Preaching of Peter (100–130).	Isidor, son of Basilides.	Renaissance of Gk. literature.	Jabolenus Priscus (jurist).
	Florinus born.	Sibyll. Or. v. 1–51?	Carpokrates.		Annianus.

HISTORICAL TABLES—(*continued*).

A.D.	THE ROMAN EMPIRE.	JEWISH AND CHRISTIAN LITERATURE.		GREEK AND LATIN LITERATURE.	
130	Second tour of Hadrian (129–134).	Death of Rabbi Joshua (131).	Epist. Barnabas (130?). Παραδόσεις Ματθίου.	Artemidorus.	C. Sulp. Apollinaris.
	Hadrian rebuilds Jerusalem, 130f.		Hermas, ± 130?	Herennius Philo.	
	Insurrection of Bar-kokhba, 132–135. Bloodshed in Judea.	Death of R. Akiba (95–135 fl.).	*Protevangelium Jacobi* (before 160).	Byblius, περὶ Ἰουδαίων.	
	Apotheosis of Antinous, 133. Ælia Capitolina, 136. Marcus, bish. Jerusalem.	Justin in Ephesus (conversion of). *Rest of Words of Baruch* (Jewish?).		Zenobius. Favorinus (phil.). Proclus.	Sextus Pomponius. Aulus Gellius (125–175 c.).
	Antonius Pius (July 10, 138–March 7, 161).	Papias' *Exposition* (?).	Valentinus and Cerdo in Rome: epp., pss., homilies.	Arrian.	M. Corn. Fronto.
	Hyginus, bish. R. (136–140).	Epist. Diognetus (i.–x.)?		Herodes Atticus.	
40		Apology of Aristides.	Marcion in Rome.	Demetrius.	L. Ampelius ('liber memorialis')?
	Wall of Anton., Forth to Clyde, begun, 142.	2 Clement.		Appian.	
	Pius, bish. R. (140–155).	Apoc. Peter (before 150?). Aristo of Pella (c. 145).		Cassius Longinus.	"Pervigilium Veneris"?
	M. Aurelius converted to philos., 145.	Second ep. Peter (?).	Ptolemæus.	Marcellus Sidetes.	
	M. Aurelius co-regent, 147–161.	Marcion's NT canon.	Herakleon (comm.). Tatian in Rome.	Apollonius Dyscolus.	Salvius Julianus.

			Marcosians.	Aetius.	
150	**Primus, bish. Corinth.**	Tatian, *Oratio ad Græcos.*	Epiphanes, son of Carpokrates.	Cl. Ptolemæus.	Granius Licinianus (annal.).
	Irenæus in Rome (150–160).	Justin's *Apologia* (i.).			
	Hegesippus in Rome.	Gospel of Peter?		Hephæstio (gram.).	Cælius Aurelianus (med.).
		Gk. Apoc. Baruch (after 140).			
	Anicetus, bish. R. (155–166).	Martyrdom of Polykarp?	Sect of Carpokrates flourishes.		Junius Rusticus.
		Hegesippus (150–180 fl.).	Ptolemæus, ὑπομνήματα.	Polyænus of Macedonia (milit.).	Luc. Appuleius of Madaura.
		Justin's *Dialogue with Trypho.*	Rise of Montanism.		Fulgentius.
	Revolution in Palestine, 161.	"Dialogue" of Aristo (130–170).		Ælius Aristides.	Gaius, 'Institutes.'
160	Marcus Aurelius (March 7, 161–March 17, 180).	*Acts of John, c.* 160.	Coptic gnostic treatises.		
		Clem. Hom.? Musanus (anti-Encratite).			
	Soter, bish. Rome (166–174).	*Acts of Paul?*	Julius Cassianus fl.	Lucian.	
	Martyrdom of Justin.	*Acts of Paul and Thekla* (before 190).			
	Pestilence, 166.	Dionysius of Corinth (*epp.*).	Asterius Urbanus (Mont.).	Antoninus Liberalis	Terent. Maurus.
	Conquest of Parthia.	Apology of Miltiades.			
		Melito (160–190 fl.).	Themison's cath. epist. (Mont.).	Herodianus.	
		Symmachus, comm. on Matthew? (Eus. *H. E.* vi. 17).		Oppianus.	
170	**Wars with Marcomanni (167–180).**	Athenagoras.	Hegesippus, Ὑπομνήματα.	M. Aurelius.	Q. C. Scævola.
		Philip of Gortyna (anti-Marcionite).			

HISTORICAL TABLES—(*continued*).

A.D.	The Roman Empire.	Jewish and Christian Literature.	Greek and Latin Literature.
	Eleutherus, bish. R. (175–189).	Apollinaris of Hierapolis (anti-Montanist).	Celsus, Ἀληθὴς Λόγος (177–180).
		Alogi? Modestus.	
	Persecution in Gaul, martyrdom of Pothinus (Lyons).	Minucius Felix (?). *Acts of Carpus, Papylus, and Agathonike.* Symmachus (version of OT)? Rhodon.	Ptolemæus. Pausanias.
	Irenæus in Lyons.	*Epistle of Lyons and Vienne churches.*	
180	Commodus (March 19, 180–Jan. 1, 192).	Irenæus, *adv. Haer.* (180–190).	Alciphron.
	Martyrs of Scili, 180.	Pantænus in Alexandria.	Phrynichus.
	Martyrdom of Apollonius.	Tertullian (160–220 *c.*). Apelles, συλλογίσμοι, φανερώσεις.	Galen (130–200).
	Origen born, 185.		Boethus.
	Victor, bish. Rome (189–199).	First writer in theological Latin, Theophilus.	Numenius of Apameia.
		Theodotion (version of OT)?	Maximus of Tyre.

A.D.	Rome and the East.	Christian Literature.	Greek and Latin Literature.
		Acts of Apollonius.	
190	Narcissus, bish. Jerus. (190–213).	Paschal Controversy. Florinus?	Hermogenes.
		Clement of Alexandria.	Pollux (archæol.).
	Pertinax (193).	Muratorian Canon.	Sextus Empiricus (*c.* 190).
		Polykrates of Ephesus (epist. 195).	

	Sept. Severus (193–211). Parthian outbreak put down (195). Rabbi Juda.	Bardesanes in Edessa. 'Correspondence of Jesus and Abgar of Edessa.'	Dio Cassius (155–240).
		Demetrius of Alexandria (correspondence). Tertullian's *Apology* (197).	Alex. Aphrodisiensis.
200	Zephyrinus, bish. R. (199–217). Persecution of Christians.	Serapion of Antioch (192–209 fl.). *Evangelion da-Mepharreshê* (*c.* 200). *Passio Perpetuæ et Felicitatis.*	Athenæus (180–230 fl.). Callistratus (jurist).
	Ammonius Saccas at Alexandria.	Apollonius (anti-Mont.). Tertullian turns Montanist.	Decay of Gk. and Latin literature.
	Campaigns in Britain, 208–211.	*Acts of Peter* (200–210). Hermogenes (180–210).	
		Sextus Julius Africanus. Hermias, διασύρμος. Gaius (anti-Mont.).	Papinian (jurist).
		Origen at Alexandria.	Pseudo-Dositheus
210	**Caracalla** (211–April 8, 217). Persecution in Alexandria.	Hippolytus. Proklus (Montanist). Tertullian, *de corona* and *de fuga* (211–212).	Diogenes Laertius. Pseudo-Oppian, *Cynegetica.*
	Asclepiades, bish. Antioch (211–217).	'Dialogue of Gaius and Proklus' (200–217).	Ulpian (jurist).
			Acro.
	Alexander, bish. Jerus. (213–250).	Tertullian, *ad Scapulam.*	Ælian (nat. hist.).
	Philetus, bish. Antioch (217–230).	Epistle to Laodiceans?	Porphyrio (schol. on Horace).
	Elagabalus (218–March 10, 222).	Book of Elkesai published (at Rome?).	
220	Calixtus, bish. R. (217–222).	Tertullian, *aduersus Praxean.* Χρονογραφίαι of Africanus.	Ammonius Saccas.
	Urbanus, bish. R. (222–230).		Philostratus (215–245 fl.).

HISTORICAL TABLES—(*continued*).

A.D.	ROME AND THE EAST	CHRISTIAN LITERATURE.	GREEK AND LATIN LITERATURE.	
	Alex. Severus (222–March 19, 235). Overthrow of Parthian, rise of Persian, Empire.	Beryllus of Bostra (218–244 *c.*).	Apsines (rhet.)?	Solinus (epitome of Pliny). Q. Sammonicus Severus.
230	Zebinus, bish. Antioch (230–240).	Pseud. Clem. *Epp. de uirginitate* (?). Firmilian of Cæsarea.		Julius Paulus (jurist).
	Pontianus, bish. R. (230–235).	*Acts of Thomas* (after 232)?	Philostratus II.	Censorinus, *de die natali* (chron.).
	Heraklas, bish. Alexandria (231–247).			
	Max. Thrax (235–238). Anterus, bish. Rome (235–236).	Dionysius of Alexandria, head of local school (232 f.).		Marius Maximus?
	Fabianus, bish. Rome (236–250).			Herennius Modestinus (jurist).
	Philip Arab. (238–248).			
240	Babylas, bish. Antioch (240–250).	Novatian.		
	Barbarian invasions.	Nepos (Egypt), ἔλεγχος ἀλληγοριστῶν.	Rise of Neo-Platonism.	
		Origen { Hexapla (by 245). κατὰ Κέλσου. Comm. on Matthew.		Commodianus (poet).
	Dionysius, bish. Alexandria (247–264).	Cyprian (210–258), bishop of Carthage.	Plotinus (205–270).	
	Secular games.	Noetus (*c.* 250).		

250	Goths invade Empire, 250.			
	Decius (249–summer of 251). Persecution of Christians.	Gregory Thaumaturgus (213–270 *c.*).		Junius Cordus (hist.), *c.* 250.
		Cyprian, *de lapsis* (251). 5 Esdras?		
	Gallus, Volusianus (sum. 251–May 253).	Commodianus (poet). *Carmen apologeticum adv. Judæos et Gentes.*	Herodian.	
	Cornelius, bish. R. (251–253).			
	Lucius, bish. R. (253–254).	Death of Origen in Tyre.		
	Valerian, Gallienus (253–March 4, 268).		Minucianus (rhet.), *c.* 260.	
	Pestilence at Rome.	*Pistis Sophia* (250–300).	Longinus, 220–273.	
	Barbarian inroads.			
	Edict of toleration.			
260	Greece ravaged by barbarians.	Paul of Samosata, 260 fl.		
	Dionysius, bish. R. (259–268).			
	Porphyry in Rome.		Porphyry, 233–300.	
	Rabbah b. Abuha, R. Nahman b. Jacob at Mahoza.			
	Goths ravage Greece and Asia.			
	Maximus, bish. Alexandria (264–282).			

HISTORICAL TABLES—(*continued*).

A.D.	The Roman Empire.	Christian Literature.	Greek and Latin Literature.	
	Claudius (March 4, 268–April 270). Defeat of Goths.	Anatolius, bish. of Laodicea (268 f.). 6 Esdras?		
270	Aurelian (270–275). Zenobia's reign.		Menander (rhet.).	
	Tacitus (Sept. 25, 275–April 276). Eutychianus, bish. R. (275–283)	Victorinus of Pettau (comm. Apocalypse).		
	Probus (April 276–282).		Timæus (gramm.).	
	Successful campaign in Gaul.	Theognostus of Alexandria ὁ ἐξηγητής.		Calpurnius?
280	Carus, Carinus, Numerian (Oct. 282–Sept. 284).	Methodius of Olympus (d. 311).	Aristides Quintilianus. Heliodorus.	Spartianus.
	Caius, bish. R. (283–296).	Lucian of Samosata (d. 312), ed. of LXX.		Nemesianus, *Cynegetica*.
	Diocletian (Sept. 17, 284–March 305).			
		Pierius of Alexandria.		Vulcatius Gallicanus.
290	Independence of Britain.	Theonas of Alexandria (282–300). Alexander of Jerusalem.		Julius Capitolinus.
	Marcellinus bish. R. (296–304).	Pamphilus of Cæsarea (martyred 309).		L. Ampelius.
	R. ben Huna, head of academy of Sura.	Hesychius?		Mamertinus.
300	Council of Elvira (306).	Petrus, bish. of Alexandria (300–312).		Trebellius Pollio.

	Persecution of Christians begins.	Arnobius, *adv. Nationes.*		
		Attempted destruction by Romans of Scriptures.		Eumenius of Autun.
	Maxentius, emperor at Rome.	*Pseudo - Adamant. Dialogue.* Eustathius of Antioch (-337).		Vopiscus.
	R. ben Nahmani (270–330), head of academy of Pumbedita.	Eusebius of Cæsarea (-339).		
	Galerius' edict of toleration.			
310	Edict of Milan (312).	Lactantius (260–340), "the Christian Cicero."	Iamblichus (280–330 *c.*).	
	Death of Diocletian, 313.	Theodotus of Laodicea (310–340).		Ælius Lampridius.
	R. Joseph b. Raba (280–352), at Maḥoza.	Coptic version?		
	Sylvester I., bish. R. (314–336).			
		Alexander, bish. of Alexandria (313–326).		Rhemnius Fannius.
		Athanasius, *de Incarnatione Verbi* (318).		
	Constantine's German campaign.	*De Mortibus Persecutorum* (?).	Aphthonius.	
320	Rise of Egyptian Monasticism, under Pachomius.	Eusebius, *Ecclesiastical History* (*c.* 324).		Revival of Latin literature.
	Constantine, emperor, 324.	Eusebius of Emesa (-359).		
	Constantinople founded, 326.			
	Nicene Council (325).	Athanasius, bish. of Alexandria.		Completion of *Historia Augusta.*
	Queen Helena's visit to Palestine.	Theodore of Heraclea (-355).		
	S. Antony in Egypt.			
330		Sahidic version (?).	Ulpian.	Juvencus (Christian poet).

HISTORICAL TABLES—(*continued*).

A.D.	THE ROMAN EMPIRE.	CHRISTIAN LITERATURE.		GREEK AND LATIN LITERATURE.	
	Marcus I., bish. R. (336–337). Death of Arius, 336 Julius I., bish. R. (337–352).	Codex Vaticanus = B (fourth cent.). Codex Sinaiticus = ℵ (fourth cent.).		Dexippus. Philostratus III. Proæresius.	Tiberianus.
340	Defeat and death of Constantine. Constans prohibits pagan sacrifices. Council of Antioch, 345. " Sardica, 347. " Jerusalem, 349.	Gregory Nazianzen (–389). Macarius (Egypt), *Homilies*. Ephraem Syrus (–373). Ulfilas (tr. of Bible into Gothic).	Jerome born. Chrysostom born (347). Augustine born (354).	Aristænetus (erot.). Firm. Maternus. Libanius (314–393).	Ælius Donatus.
350	Constantius, emperor. Council of Sirmium, 351. " Arles, 353. Julian at Athens. Council of Antioch, 358.	Acacius of Cæsarea (–366). Titus of Bostra (–370). Hilary of Poictiers (300–370). Athanasius (–373). Epiphanius. Basil of Cæsarea (–379). Reticius of Autun.	Diodorus of Tarsus.	Themistius. Himerius.	Avienus. Sextus Aurelius Victor. Prudentius (Christ. poet, 348–410).

360	Julian (361–363). The pagan reaction.	Apollinarius of Laodicea (-393).	Theon.	Eutropius.
		Council of Laodicea, 364.		
	Jerome in Rome.	Cyril of Jerusalem (-386). 'Ambrosiaster' (366–384, Rome).	Hesychius (lexicogr.).	
	Jovian (363).	Martin of Tours (316–397).		Sextus Rufus.
	Valentinian and Valens (364–374).	Didymus of Alexandria (-395).		Paulinus of Nola (Christ. poet).
		Gregory of Nyssa (-395).		**Ausonius (Christian poet).**
		Evagrius of Pontus (-398).		
		Ambrose of Milan (-397).		
		Theodore of Mopsuestia (-429).		

ABBREVIATIONS

AA. . . . The Apostolic Age, History of:
Weizsäcker's *das apostolische Zeitalter*^{3} (1902, Eng tr. of second edition, 1894).
A. C. McGiffert (Internat. Theol. Library, 1897).
J. V. Bartlet (in 'Eras of Christian Church,' 1900).
J. H. Ropes, *The Apostolic Age in the Light of Modern Criticism* (1906).

ACL. . . . Harnack and Preuschen, *Geschichte der altchristlichen Litteratur bis Eusebius.* i. *Die Ueberlieferung und der Bestand* (1893); ii. *Die Chronologie* (1 = 1897, 2 = 1904).
Ehrhard's *die altchristliche Litteratur u. ihre Erforschung seit 1880* (part i. 1894).

AJT. . . . *The American Journal of Theology* (Chicago).

ARW. . . . *Archiv für Religionswissenschaft* (Berlin, ed. Dieterich and Achelis).

BFT. . . . *Beiträge zur Förderung christl. Theologie* (ed. Schlatter).

BL. . . . Schenkel's *Bibel-Lexicon.*

BLE. . . . *Bulletin de Litt. ecclésiastique* (Paris).

BNT. . . . Harnack's *Beiträge zur Einleitung in das NT* (i. *Lukas der Arzt*, 1906, Eng. tr. 1907; ii. *Sprüche u. Reden Jesu*, 1907, Eng. tr. 1908; iii. *die Apgeschichte*, 1908, Eng. tr. 1909).

BZ. . . . *Biblische Zeitschrift.*

CB. . . . *The Century Bible* (London, Eng. text and notes).

CGT. . . . *The Cambridge Greek Testament for Schools and Colleges.*

Chron. . . . W. Brückner, *die chronolog. Reihenfolge in welcher die Briefe des NT verfasst sind* (1890).

CQR. . . . *The Church Quarterly Review.*

CRE. . . . Sir W. M. Ramsay, *The Church in the Roman Empire*^{8} (1904).

DB. . . . Hastings' *Dictionary of the Bible* (1898–1904).
Smith's *Dictionary of the Bible.*
Vigoroux's *Dictionnaire de la Bible* (Paris).

DCB. . . . Smith's *Dictionary of Christian Biography* (1877–1887).

DCG. . . . Hastings' *Dictionary of Christ and the Gospels* (1906–1908).

Diat. . . . E. A. Abbott's *Diatessarica* (London, A. and C. Black): (i.) *Clue, A Guide through Greek to Hebrew Scripture* (§§ 1–272); (ii.) *The Corrections of Mark adopted by Matthew and Luke* (§§ 273–552); (iii.) *From Letter to Spirit* (§§ 553–1149); (iv.) *Paradosis* (§§ 1150–1435); (v.) *Johannine Vocabulary* (§§ 1436–1885); (vi.) *Johannine Grammar* (§§ 1886–2799); (vii.) *Notes on NT Criticism* (§§ 2800–2999); (viii.) *The Son of Man* (§§ 3000–3635).

EB. . . . *The Encyclopaedia Britannica* (small superior numbers denote the edition).

EBi. . . . *The Encyclopaedia Biblica* (London, 1899–1903; ed. J. S. Black and T. K. Cheyne).

EGT. . . . *The Expositor's Greek Testament* (ed. Sir W. R. Nicoll, 1897–1910).

Einf. . . . Nestle's *Einführung in das Griechische NT*[3] (1899, Eng. tr. under title, 'An Introduction to the Textual Criticism of the Greek New Testament').

Einl. or INT. . R. Simon's *Histoire critique du texte du NT* (Rotterdam, 1689 f.)*, *Histoire critique des versions du NT* (1690), and *Nouvelles observations sur le texte et les versions du NT* (Paris, 1695);[1] J. W. Rumpæus, *Commentatio critica in libros NT* (1757); J. D. Michaelis, *Einleitung in die göttl. Schriften des neuen Bundes*[4] (1788; Eng. tr. by Marsh, 1793, Fr. tr. by Chenevière, 1822); A. Hänlein, *Handbuch d. Einl. in die Schriften des NT*[2] (Erlangen, 1801–1809); J. G. Eichhorn, *Einl. in das NT* (1804–1827)*; J. E. C. Schmidt, *Historisch-krit. Einl. in's NT*[2] (Giessen, 1818); L. Bertholdt, *Historisch-krit. Einleit. in sämmtliche kanon. u. apokry. Schriften des A. u. N. T.* (1813–1819); H. E. F. Guericke's *Beiträge zur Einl. in das NT* (Halle, 1828 f., against de Wette);[2] A. B. Feilmoser, *Einl. in die Bücher des neuen Bundes für die öffentlichen Vorlesungen*

[1] The Protestant reply to Simon was J. H. Mai's *Examen Historia Criticæ N. T. a R. Simone Vulgatæ* (1694) rather than the Lutheran Pritius' *Introductio in lectionem NT* (1704, etc.); the Roman Catholic, Kleuker's *Untersuchungen der Gründe für die Echtheit u. Glaubwürdigkeit der schriftlichen Urkunden des Christenthums* (1788). I have not seen the English version of Simon's first two works (London, 1689 f.). For an estimate of Simon's contribution to NT criticism, see Margival in *RHL.*, 1899, 139–216.

[2] The fifth ed. (1848) of de Wette's *Lehrbuch der hist.-kritischen Einleitung* (Berlin, 1826) was translated into English by Frothingham (U.S.A., 1858).

(Tübingen, 1830[3]); H. A. Schott, *Isagoge historico-critica in libros N. Foederis sacros* (Jena, 1830); Schneckenburger, *Beiträge zur Einl. in's NT* (1832); K. A. Credner's *Einl. in das NT* (Halle, 1836, with his *Das NT nach Zweck, Ursprung, u. Inhalt*, 1843)*; C. G. Neudecker, *Lehrbuch der historisch-kritischen Einl. in das NT mit Belegen aus den Quellenschriften u. Citaten aus der älteren u. neuen Litteratur* (Leipzig, 1840); J. M. A. Scholz (1845 f.); Schleiermacher's[1] posthumous *Einl. in das NT** (Berlin, 1845, in vol. i. of his collected works, ed. G. Wolde); J. L. Hug's *Einl. in die Schriften des NT*[4] (1847, Fr. tr. by Cellerier, 1823, Eng. tr. of third ed. Andover, 1836)*; Daniel Haneberg (1850, fourth ed. 1876); Ad. Maier (1852); Joseph Dixon, *A General Introd. to Sacred Scriptures* (1852); F. X. Reithmayr's *Einl. in die kanon. Bücher des NT* (Regensburg, 1852); J. H. Scholten, *Kritische Inleiding tot de Schriften des NT*[2] (1856); de Wette's *Einl.*[6] (ed. Messner and Lünemann, 1860)*; H. de Valroger (*Introd. hist. et critique*, 1861); G. A. Freytag, *die heilig. Schriften des NT* (Berlin, 1861); Neander, *Pflanzung u. Leitung d. christl. Kirche*[5] (1862, Eng. tr. 1842, 1865)*; Günther (*Introductio*, 1863); J. B. Glaire, *Introd. Historique et Critique aux Livres de l'ancien et du Nouveau Testament*[4] (1865, Italian tr. 1846); Bleek[3] (1866, Eng. tr., Edin. 1883); Lamy (*Introd. in sacras scripturas*, 1866–1867, against Scholten); Guericke's *Isagogik*[3] (1868); Joseph Langen, *Grundriss der Einl. in das NT* (Freiburg im B. 1868; second ed. 1873); Grau's *Entwickelungsgeschichte d. NTlichen Schriftthums* (1871–1872); Immer's *Hermeneutik* (1873); Reuss, *die Geschichte d. heilig. Schriften des NT*[5] (1874, Eng. tr. 1884)*; A. Hilgenfeld, *Historisch-Kritische Einl. in das NT* (Leipzig, 1875)*; M. Aberle (1877); Horne's *Introd.*[10] (ed. Tregelles, 1875); von Hofmann (*die heilige Schrift NT*, ix., ed. Volck, 1881); Mangold (ed. of Bleek's *Einleitung*, 1886)*; B. Weiss, *Einl. in das NT* (third ed. 1897, Eng. tr. of second ed. 1886); L. Schulze (in Zöckler's *Handbuch der theol. Wiss.* 1883–1889); M. A. N. Rovers, *Nieuw-testamentliche letterkunde*[2] (1888); Leblois, *Les livres de la nouvelle alliance* (Paris, 1889); U. Ubaldi, *Introd. in sacram Scripturam NT*[4] (Rome, 1891); H. J.

---

[1] Critical estimate in J. Conradi's *Schleiermacher's Arbeit auf dem Gebiete der NT Einleitungswissenschaft* (Leipzig, 1907).

Holtzmann, *Lehrbuch d. historisch-kritischen Einl. in das NT*[3] (1892) *; S. Davidson[3] (1894); Godet, *Introd. au NT* (1893–1899, unfinished; Eng. tr. 1894, 1899); R. Cornely, *Introd. specialis in singulos NT libros*[2] (Paris, 1897); G. Salmon[8] (1897); F. S. Trenkle (1897); Th. Zahn, *Einl. in das NT* (1897, Eng. tr. of third ed. 1909) *; Aloys Schäfer (1898); W. F. Adeney, *A Biblical Introduction* (1899), pp. 275 f.; B. W. Bacon (1900); J. M. S. Baljon, *Geschiedenis van de boeken des Nieuwen Verbonds* (1901) *; J. E. Belser, *Einleitung in das NT*[2] (1902); A. Jülicher's *Einl. in das NT*[6] (1906) *; E. Jacquier, *Histoire des Livres du NT* (1903–1908); von Soden's *Urchristliche Literaturgeschichte* (*die Schriften des NT*), 1905 (Eng. tr. 1906); Wrede, *die Entstehung d. Schriften des NT* (1907, Eng. tr. 1909); Barth, *Einleitung in das NT* (1908); C. R. Gregory (*Einleitung in das NT*, 1909); A. S. Peake, *Critical Introduction to the NT* (1909)—besides the popular manuals by E. H. Plumptre (*Introd. to NT*, 1883); M. Dods[2] (*Introd. to NT*, London, 1894); M'Clymont, *The New Testament and its Writers* (London, 1893), and Gutjahr (*Einleitung . . . Leitfaden zunächst für Studierende der Theologie*, Graz, 1896), along with Weingarten's ed. (Berlin, 1872) of Hertwig, *Die Einleitung in's NT im tabellarischer Uebersicht*[4]; P. Fargues, *Introd. au Nouveau Testament* (Paris, 1902), and L. Kunze's *Einführung in das NT* (Berlin, 1906). Hug, Feilmoser, Günther, Haneberg, Scholz, Maier, Reithmayr, Langen, Aberle, Lamy, Cornely, Ubaldi, and Schäfer, represent the older, Trenkle and Belser and Jacquier the modern school of Roman Catholic criticism.

ERE. . . Hastings' *Encyclopaedia of Religion and Ethics* (1909 f.).

ESR. . . Lichtenberger's *Encyclopédie des Sciences Religieuses* (1877 f.).

ET. . . *The Expository Times* (ed. J. Hastings, Edinburgh).

Exp. . . *The Expositor* (ed. Sir W. R. Nicoll, London; small superior numbers denote the series).

GGA. . . *Götting. Gelehrte Anzeigen*.

GHD. . . *The Gospels as Historical Documents*, by V. H. Stanton (Oxford); i. (1903); ii. (1909).

GK. . . (i.) Zahn's *Geschichte des NT Kanons* (1888 f.); (ii.) Leipoldt's *Gesch. des NT Kanons* (1907–1908).

Hausrath . . *A History of the NT Times* (*The Times of the Apostles*); Eng. tr. 1895.

HBNT. . . *Handbuch zum NT* (Tübingen, 1906 f., ed. Lietzmann).

HC. . . *Hand-Commentar zum NT* (Freiburg i. B.).

HD. . . . Harnack's *Dogmengeschichte* (Eng. tr. in seven volumes, 'The History of Dogma,' 1894 f.).

H. E. . . . Eusebius, *Eccles. Historia* (ed. Schwartz and Mommsen).

HJ. . . . *The Hibbert Journal* (London).

HJP. . . . Schürer's *Geschichte des jüd. Volkes* (Eng. tr. of second ed. under the title, 'A History of the Jewish People in the Time of Jesus Christ.' The fourth German edition is occasionally quoted as *GJV*).

HNA. . . . Hennecke's (i.) *Neutestamentliche Apokryphen*, and (ii.) *Handbuch zu den neutest. Apokryphen* (Tübingen, 1904).

HNT.[1] . . . Moffatt, *The Historical New Testament*[2] (Edinburgh, 1901).

HS. . . . Sir John C. Hawkins' *Horæ Synopticæ* (1899; second ed. 1909).

ICC. . . . *The International Critical Commentary* (Edinburgh).

JBL. . . . *The Journal of Biblical Literature.*

JC. . . . Hort's *Judaistic Christianity* (1896); G. Hoennicke's *Das Judenchristentum* (1908).

JPT. . . . *Jahrbücher für protestantische Theologie.*

JQR. . . . *The Jewish Quarterly Review* (London).

JTS. . . . *The Journal of Theological Studies.*

Keim . . . Eng. tr. in six volumes of Keim's *Geschichte Jesu von Nazara.*

LC. . . . *Literarisches Centralblatt.*

LXX . . . The Septuagint, cited from Swete's manual edition (Cambridge).

MAC. . . . Harnack's *die Mission und Ausbreitung des Christenthums*[2] (1906; Eng. tr. 1908).

Meyer . . . Meyer's *Kommentar zum NT* (latest editions).

NKZ. . . . *Neue kirchliche Zeitschrift.*

NTA. . . . *The New Testament in the Apostolic Fathers* (Oxford, 1905).

NTTh. . . . *The Theology of the New Testament*:

Reuss, *Histoire de la théologie chrétienne au siècle apostolique* (Eng. tr. of third ed. 1872).

B. Weiss[7] (Eng. tr. of third ed. 1888).

Bovon's *Théologie du NT* (1893).

Beyschlag (Eng. tr. 1896).

H. J. Holtzmann (1897).

G. B. Stevens (Internat. Theol. Library, 1899).

E. P. Gould (1900).

P. Feine (1910).

---

[1] Occasionally one or two sentences are reproduced from this earlier volume, on the principle defended by Isokrates in his fifth oration (93): Καὶ μηδεὶς ὑπολάβῃ με βούλεσθαι λαθεῖν ὅτι τούτων ἔνια πέφρακα τὸν αὐτὸν τρόπον ὅνπερ πρότερον. ἐπιστὰς γὰρ ἐπὶ τὰς αὐτὰς διανοίας εἱλόμην μὴ πονεῖν γλιχόμενος τὰ δεδηλωμένα καλῶς ἑτέρως εἰπεῖν.

NZ. . . .	Schwegler, *das nachapostolische Zeitalter in den Hauptmomenten seiner Entwickelung* (Tübingen, 1846). R. Knopf, *das nachapost. Zeitalter* (1905).
OCL. . . .	W. C. van Manen, *Handleiding voor de Oudchristelijke Letterkunde* (1900).
Philo . . .	Cohn and Wendland's edition (Berlin, 1896 f.).
PM. . . .	*Protestantische Monatshefte* (ed. Websky).
PRE. . . .	*Real-Encyclopädie für protest. Theologie u. Kirche*[3] (ed. Hauck, 1896–1909).
RB. . . .	*Revue Biblique internationale* (Paris).
Renan . . .	Renan's *Histoire des Origines du Christianisme* (1863 f.,. (i.) Vie de Jésus ; (ii.) Les Apôtres ; (iii.) S. Paul , (iv.) L'antéchrist ; (v.) Les évangiles ; (vi.) L'église chrétienne.
RHL. . . .	*Revue de l'histoire et de littérature religieuses* (Paris).
RHR. . . .	*Revue de l'histoire des religions* (Paris, ed. J. Réville).
RS. . . .	*Revue Sémitique* (Paris).
RTQR. . . .	*Revue de Théologie et des Quest. Religieuses* (ed. Bois. Montauban).
SB. . . .	*Studia Biblica* (Oxford).
SBAW. . . .	*Sitzungsberichte der kais. Akademie der Wissenschaften zu Wien.*
SBBA. . . .	*Sitzungsberichte der königlich Preuss. Akad. d. Wissenschaften zu Berlin.*
SK. . . .	*Studien und Kritiken* (Gotha).
SNT. . . .	*Die Schriften des NT* (1905 f., ed. J. Weiss).
SPT. . . .	Ramsay's *St. Paul the Traveller and the Roman Citizen*[7].
Strauss . . .	Strauss' *Leben Jesu* (George Eliot's version, ed. of 1892).
ThA. . . .	*Theologische Abhandlungen C. von Weizsäcker gewidmet* (Freiburg, 1892).
ThSt. . . .	*Theologische Studien Herrn Prof. B. Weiss dargebracht* (1897).
TLZ. . . .	*Theologische Literaturzeitung.*
TQ. . . .	*Theologische Quartalschrift* (Tübingen).
TR. . . .	*Theologische Rundschau* (ed. Bousset).
TS. . . .	*Texts and Studies* (Cambridge).
TT. . . .	*Theolog. Tijdschrift* (Haarlem).
TU. . . .	*Texte und Untersuchungen zur Geschichte der altchristlichen Literatur* (ed. von Gebhardt, Harnack, and C. Schmidt).
Urc. . . .	Hilgenfeld's *das Urchristenthum in den Hauptwendepunkten seines Entwickelungsganges* (1855). Spitta's *Zur Geschichte u. Litter. des Urchristenthums* (i. 1893 ; ii. 1896 ; iii. 1903). Heinrici's *das Urchristenthum* (Göttingen, 1902). Wernle's *die Anfänge des Christentum* (Eng. tr. under title, 'The Beginnings of Christianity,' 1903 f.). Pfleiderer's *das Urchristenthum*[2] (1903, Eng. tr. 1906 f.).

von Dobschütz's *die urchristlichen Gemeinden* (1902; Eng. tr. 'Christian Life in the Primitive Churches,' 1904).

Raffaele Mariano's *Il Cristianesimo nei primi secoli* (Firenze, 1902).

WC. . . . *The Westminster Commentaries* (London: Eng. text and notes).

WH. . . . Westcott and Hort, *The New Testament in Greek.*

ZK. . . . *Kommentar zum NT* (Erlangen, ed. Zahn).

ZKG. . . . Brieger's *Zeitschrift für Kirchengeschichte.*

ZNW. . . . Preuschen's *Zeitschrift für die neutest. Wissenschaft und die Kunde des Urchristenthums.*

ZSchz. . . . *Theologische Zeitschrift aus der Schweiz* (ed. Meili).

ZTK. . . . *Zeitschrift für Theologie und Kirche.*

ZWT. . . . Hilgenfeld's *Zeitschrift für Wissenschaftliche Theologie.*

N.B.—In the bibliographies an asterisk is appended to works which possess special importance, historical or intrinsic, in the criticism of the subject.

PROLEGOMENA.

I.

COLLECTION OF NT WRITINGS INTO A CANON: METHOD AND MATERIALS OF NT INTRODUCTION.

THE early Christian writings which form the New Testament fall within a period which covers, roughly speaking, a single century. Jesus died about A.D. 30. He wrote none of the works treasured by the church. He wrote once, but it was on the dust; like Socrates, he remained an authority, not an author, for his adherents. The subsequent literature which gathered round his name and cause embraced accounts of his own life or of the movement which he inaugurated, as well as compositions occasioned by exigencies and emergencies in the life of the Christian societies throughout the Roman empire. The last of these writings (2 Peter) dates not much later than about one hundred years after the crucifixion. By the end of the second century all our present canonical NT writings are known to have been in existence, while the majority existed as a sacred collection which was being used for ecclesiastical purposes. The problem set to the literary critic is to examine the rise and growth of these writings one by one, to estimate their historical object, to discuss their inter-relations, and to analyse their structure.

An introduction* to any literature, ancient, mediæval, or

* The Libri Introductorii referred to by the sixth-century aristocratic and scholarly monk, M. Aurelius Cassiodorus, in his *Institutio diuinarum lectionum* (Migne, *patr. lat.* lxx. 1105 f.), appear to have been mainly occupied with biblical exegesis and hermeneutic, and the Εἰσαγωγὴ εἰς τὰς θείας γραφάς of Hadrianus (fifth century, ed. Gössling, Berlin, 1887) does not differ essentially from the sources used by the Abruzzi scholar. The lost Key to

modern, is concerned primarily with literary problems, and with other questions only as these impinge upon the central issue, namely, the literary genesis and growth of the writings under review. The study of the documents as documents is its *métier*. The origin and the objects of these documents in their own age form its special business. Yet, as literature rises from life, and as any writing not only is shaped by, but itself helps to shape, events in history, literary criticism is repeatedly obliged to wade into the waters of historical investigation; the imperial policy of Rome, *e.g.*, is as germane to the criticism of the Apocalypse of John as is the policy of Philip to the discussion of Demosthenes' Olynthiac orations. Literary criticism and historical criticism are therefore auxiliary sciences. The historian, whether of life or thought, requires to be able to presuppose the results of investigation into the date, authenticity, and form of the relevant documents; while the literary critic, in order to place his documents, leans on the results of the historian's survey. But neither science can be isolated. Literary judgments frequently depend upon some presupposition as to the course of history, and the very data for this presupposition are often in their turn drawn largely from the documents in question. This is not arguing or working in a circle. The moment theory is deserted for practice, the difficulties tend to solve themselves; they are really difficulties of method, and if the literary critic and the historian keep their respective flags flying, they need not scruple to cross their allotted borders when occasion demands.

Much of the historical significance which attaches to certain writings would remain hidden from us if we did not happen to know that certain events were fresh in the minds of writers and readers alike. *Paradise Lost* is not a political pamphlet, much less a religious treatise; but it is impossible to miss in its dialogues and descriptions either the theology of current Puritanism, with its controversies and abstractions, or the republican tendencies by which the author's conceptions of government were shaped, or, finally, his instinctive distrust for the intellectual passion awakened by the Renaissance. Similarly—to take one instance out of hundreds from ancient literature—the *Prometheus Vinctus* and the *Septem contra Thebas* are unintelligible apart from the aspirations of the Athenian τύραννοι and Themistokles. The literary and historical criticism of the NT has a corresponding duty of unravelling the various threads of influence

---

the Interpretation of the Scriptures, by Melito of Sardis (Ἡ κλεῖς), probably belonged to the same class.

which tie a writing to some period. It is essential here as elsewhere to ascertain the mental and moral latitudes in which an author worked, to use his work in conjunction with other aids for the discovery and illustration of these latitudes, and again to use these for the further elucidation of the book itself. The latter is moved more or less, according to its character, by recent and contemporary events, just as the period in its turn is set off and rendered more vivid by the contemporary literature—

"Like as the wind doth beautify a sail,
And as a sail becomes the unseen wind."

As the early Christian literature was not national, however, such synchronisms* yield less for the NT than for almost any other group of ancient writings. We should expect, *e.g.*, that an event like the fall of Jerusalem would have dinted some of the literature of the primitive church, almost as the victory at Salamis has marked the *Persæ*. It might be supposed that such an epoch-making crisis would even furnish criteria for determining the dates of some of the NT writings. As a matter of fact, the catastrophe is practically ignored in the extant Christian literature of the first century. Beyond slight traces in the synoptic, especially the Lucan, version of the eschatological predictions made by Jesus, and a possible echo in one of the sources underlying the Apocalypse, no vibrations of the crisis can be felt.

Literary criticism and textual criticism are also bound to overlap at many points; but each has a sphere of its own. The boundary question here is theoretically simpler than between the historian and the literary critic. The place of investigation into early Christian tradition is more difficult to determine. An ancient writing often lies in a matrix of later information upon its origin or its author, and it is necessary to examine such materials in order to ascertain whether or how far they are the result of later fancy wearing unreliable reports around an honoured literary product, or the outcome of a genuine tradition which goes back in subterranean fashion to the very period at which and for which the author wrote.

From such difficulties, arising out of the content and the form of documents, it is not to be expected that a critical Introduction to the literature of the NT can be exempt. Volumes on this subject have often been planned and executed along lines which overlapped into the sphere of works upon early church history, New Testament theology, and textual criticism. In the hands of some older writers, like Horne and

* A *Contemporary History of the New Testament* is to form a special volume of the International Theological Library.

Glaire, NT Introduction was equivalent to an encyclopædia or biblical dictionary, in which all topics relative to the contents as well as to the form of the NT writings were elaborately discussed, whether historical, literary, textual, or archæological. The escape from this ideal of a Juvenalian farrago was only a matter of time. With the development of historical criticism and the increasing specialisation which it demanded, such a conception of Introduction became more and more impracticable. It is now recognised that while a NT Introduction handles the materials of volumes on the language and text of the NT writings as well as on the apostolic age, it is differentiated from these by a controlling reference to the literary problem as such, which determines roughly the amount of space assigned to questions of chronology, theology, archæology, and textual criticism.

Naturally it is impossible, *e.g.*, to discuss Paul's epistle to the Christians of Galatia without some reference to the narrative of Acts and the geographical data of the provinces in Asia Minor, or to pronounce on the authenticity of the second epistle to the Thessalonians without checking the results of recent inquiry into the eschatological currents flowing through Judaism and primitive Christianity. Textual criticism also bears directly upon several problems in the literary criticism of the documents, as, *e.g.*, in the case of the Bezan text of Acts, or of the pericopê in the Fourth gospel, or of the appendix to Mark's gospel. The new attention paid to the Old Latin and Syriac versions, which promise to throw light on the Greek text prior to the rise of the great uncials, is destined to affect NT Introduction as well as exegesis in the near future. But it is the problem of tradition which is most crucial. It assumes a much more serious character in NT Introduction than is usual elsewhere in the literary criticism of classical or Oriental literature. The problem of tradition is, in one aspect, a phase of investigation in early church history; but, in another, it is bound up with the special question of the Canon *—a question which, by its unique significance, imposes specific difficulties upon the literary criticism of the NT. As the very term *New Testament* suggests, these writings are extant in a special collection. The idea and

* The right of historical criticism to examine the origin and authority of the NT Canon was first stated by Semler in his *Abhandlung von freier Untersuchung des Kanons* (1771–1775).

the history of this collection belong to the province of church history and to the special department of the Canon; but it would be unscientific to treat NT Introduction as if it were entirely insulated from contact with all such problems. The (i.) very process of collecting and arranging the various documents has not been without its effect upon the shape, the order, and even the contents of the documents themselves; and (ii.) the various strata of ecclesiastical tradition during the second and the first half of the third century—after which time little or no valuable information need be looked for—preserve several items of interest and importance about the primitive documents, which, like lumps of quartz, need to be carefully washed if they are to yield any specks of golden, authentic tradition.

This view of the method and functions of NT Introduction may appear comparatively obvious, but it has only been held within fairly recent years. Indeed, with the possible and partial exception of Junilius,* a royal official of Constantinople during the first half of the sixth century, whose *Institutio regularia diuinæ legis* (ed. Kihn, Freiburg, 1880) incorporated the substance of lectures given by Paul of Nisibis upon the authorship, authority, and contents of the Scriptures, nothing worthy of the name of a NT Introduction was written till the sixteenth century, unless we stretch the term far enough to include the Muratorian Canon, which gives a few words upon several of the NT writings, the *Church History* of Eusebius, which gathers up many current traditions, the books mentioned on p. 1, and subsequent treatises such as the twelfth century *de eruditione didascalia* and *de scriptura et scriptoribus prænotatiunculæ* by Hugo of St. Victor, and the fourteenth century *Postillæ perpetuæ in uniuersa biblia* of Nicolas the Franciscan of Lyra. Even in the sixteenth century, historical criticism of the Scriptures was hardly born within the church, as is plain from the so-called Introductions by the Dominican friars Santes Pagninus (*Isagogæ ad sacras litteras liber unus*, Lyons, 1536) and Sixtus of Siena, whose important *Bibliotheca sancta* (Venice, 1566), in eight books, was dominated by the recent decision of the Council of Trent upon the Canon. The influence of Sixtus is visible in the Jesuit Salmeron's *Prolegomena in uniuersam scripturam* (Madrid, 1597). No real advance was made by the various Roman Catholic writers of the seventeenth century in Spain or Germany. Dogmatic interests were equally strong within the Reformed churches, meanwhile, as almost every page of the *Isagoge* of Andreas Rivetus and the *Enchiridion biblicum* (1681) of J. H. Heidegger makes clear.

With the writings of Richard Simon, the French Oratorian priest, a new day dawned for the science of NT Introduction. Among the numerous good services which modern research owes to this great scholar

* He was a friend of Primasius, the bishop of Hadrumetum, who commented on the Apocalypse; cf. Kihn's *Theodor von Mopsuestia und Junil. Africanus* (1879), pp. 213 f.

are the separation for the first time * of the OT from the NT, the application of literary criticism to the writings, and the employment of textual criticism as a factor in the process of appreciating the various documents. The translation of Simon's essays into German, and the publication of Michaelis' *Introduction* (Göttingen, 1750 f.), started a prolonged series of really critical works in Germany, of which the most notable were de Wette's, Credner's, and Schleiermacher's; the most popular, from the Roman Catholic side, was Hug's. The rise of the Tübingen school marked the next epoch in the history of the science. Although Baur himself wrote no actual Introduction, his interpretation of the apostolic age and its writings exercised a powerful influence, attractive as well as antagonistic, upon all who were seriously engaged in NT research.† The outstanding contribution of the Tübingen movement to NT Introduction ‡ was its emphasis on the close relation between history and literature; it failed to make due allowance for the pre-dominantly religious interest of the apostolic age as distinguished from polemic, but it assigned each document to some phase or another of a historical evolution within the early church. The value of this principle was independent of the particular application made of it by Baur and his followers. A debt of gratitude is further due to "the sincerity and courage of the Tübingen school . . . Not only were the facts emphasised by them, however exceptional, important, and unduly neglected; not only did they do justice to the ideal which underlies the concrete; but truth, and therefore piety, can permanently only be the gainer by the results of free investigation, with ample consideration of the strength and weakness of every rational hypothesis" (Dr. A. Robertson, *Regnum Dei*, p. 83). While Baur's particular positions in NT criticism were frequently supported in detail, the publication of Ritschl's *Entstehung der altkatholischen Kirche* (2nd ed. 1857) and of Hilgenfeld's *Einleitung* showed that the general thesis could not be worked out over the field of the NT literature. This has been confirmed not so much by opponents of Baur like Guericke, Salmon, and von Hofmann, as by the independent treatises of Reuss, Mangold, and above all H. J. Holtzmann, whose standard work represents quite a modified form of Baur's hypothesis. At present, workers in the science of NT Introduction may be divided into three groups. The radical wing is represented by Havet in France, and especially by van Manen and Rovers in Holland. The liberal wing numbers not only Holtzmann, but Jülicher (his crisp, first rate manual is rather less radical than even Holtzmann's), von Soden, Bacon, and Baljon. The

---

* Not for the last time, unfortunately. The collocation of the two survives in popular or semi-critical volumes like J. K. Huber's *Einleitung in die sämmtlichen Bücher d. heil. Schrift*[3] (1840), Gilly's *Précis* (1867–1868). A. Schlatter's *Einleitung in die Bibel* (1889), Cornely's *Compendium* (1889), F. W. Weber's *Kurzgefasste Einleitung in die heil. Schriften AT und NT*[9] (ed. Deinzer, 1891), and Franz Kaulen's *Einleitung in die heilige Schrift Alten u. Neuen Testaments*[5] (1905).

† A sympathetic and critical sketch of Baur's great services to NT Introduction is given by Holtzmann (*New World*, 1894, 207–218).

‡ So far as method was concerned, the effect was less salutary; it tended to resolve NT Introduction into the history of the Canon.

conservative wing includes, besides all the Roman Catholic writers, B. Weiss, Godet, and Zahn; the latter's volumes are conspicuous for their massive learning. Apart from S. Davidson, whose point of view approximated generally to that of Hilgenfeld, the few English writers on this subject are predominantly conservative (Adeney with some modifications), with the recent and brilliant exception of Peake.

Amid the varieties of critical opinion during last century, however, there was a prevailing adherence to the method first laid down in full by de Wette, who showed in practice how NT Introduction could be cleared from extraneous and heterogeneous elements. He and Reuss brought out the literary function of Introduction. It was now seen pretty generally that the science must devote itself more than ever to the problems clustering round the origin and growth of the NT writings, taken individually and in groups, whilst the final phase of their historical setting lay in their gradual incorporation into the Canon. Thus, while the canonical environment of the writings lent a certain unity to the studies bearing upon their contents and career, the extension of interest to the domain of their literary and historical environment invested the science with an unwonted elasticity. Its task was "to take that section of early Christian literature which has been allotted the rank of a classical literature for Christendom, thanks to the conception of the Canon, and apply thereto the laws of literary and historical criticism which cover the writings in question, when treated as literary products at any rate—and this apart altogether from the further question whether the outcome of such a subsumption of the NT under the general category of literary growth must end in the confirmation, or supersession, or modification of the dogma of the Canon" (Holtzmann, *Einl.* p. 13).

This modern conception, which is due to the rise of the historical method, was first stated definitely by Hupfeld in his essay, *Über Begriff u. Methode der sogen. biblischen Einleitung* (Marburg, 1844). Many critics still clung to the idea that an Introduction to the NT literature corresponded more or less to a critical account of the Canon,* and that the business of the science was to investigate a book's title to the predicate of canonical; but, on the whole, the conception of NT Introduction as a history of the NT literature had now fairly won its footing. Literary problems, in the light of historical research, were recognised to be paramount. One result has been that, instead of dwelling on the ecclesiastical function of the writings or on their reception into the Canon, critics have turned to devote more attention to the rise and shape of the individual writings, studying each either by itself or in the group to which its inner affinities, not necessarily its canonical position, would assign it.

At the same time a NT Introduction is not equivalent to a collection of such brief introductions as might be prefixed to separate editions of the books

* So even Baur (*Theol. Jahrb.*, 1850, pp. 474 f.), though his historical sense led him to define "Introduction" finally as "the theological science which has to investigate the origin, primitive situation, and characteristics of the canonical writings." Compare Hupfeld's criticism in *SK.* (1861, pp. 1 f.), and Baur's further exposition in *Theol. Jahrb.*, 1851, pp. 70 f., 222 f., 291 f.

in question. The science of NT Introduction deals with each writing not merely as it stands by itself, but as it is correlated to the other volumes of its special group or of the canonical collection in general, endeavouring to set each book in its relative literary position, marking its place in the development of the whole, and indicating the later processes of ecclesiastical rearrangement by which often it was shifted from its original position to a more or less alien place in the collection. It is only by the pursuit of this historical and genetic line that NT Introduction escapes from the reproach of being largely concerned with "isolated points which have no connection among themselves," * or of leaving upon the mind the impression of a literature which lies unrelated and accidental, resembling either

"A lonely mountain tarn,
Unvisited by any stream,"

or a series of deep scattered pools, one book or group of books coming after another in a more or less haphazard fashion. It is indispensable to detect the running stream of life that winds steadily, for all its eddies and backwaters, between and through these varied writings; and this is impossible till the critic stands beside the life which they presuppose and out of which they rise. He can do this and at the same time keep in view the fact, of which the Canon serves as a reminder, that the NT writings not only sprang out of history but had a history of their own, and that apart from the second and third century literature they would often be misinterpreted, if not unintelligible in more ways than one.

In a note to the first chapter of *The Fair Maid of Perth*, discussing the magnificent view of the Tay valley which may be gained from the Wicks of Baiglie, Scott quotes what a local guide said, on reaching a bold projecting rock on Craig Vinean —"Ah, sirs, this is the decisive point." One of the first objects of the literary historian, in attempting the survey of any period, is to secure the decisive point from which he may command the lie of the country, and see it as fully as possible in its natural proportions. Such a vantage-ground lies usually at some distance from the particular literature. That is one reason why the decisive point of elevation from which to scan the primitive Christian literature is to be found in the traditions which begin to rise by the second half of the second century, when writings of the primitive age had begun to be gathered into a sacred collection. This starts a further question, however. The primitive canon does not correspond exactly to the contents of the modern NT, but the idea is the same, viz., that of a selection made for ecclesiastical purposes. This idea, as well as the very name of "New Testament," is later than the writings which have

* Dr. M. W. Jacobus, *A Problem in NT Criticism* (1900), p. 49.

gravitated into the Canon. The large majority of these writings originated in a period when there was no "New Testament," and no thought of any such collection. None of them was written for a canonical position, and it is therefore an anachronism for literary and historical criticism to attach the predicate of "canonical" to them, or to treat them as if they had possessed from the first a privileged and unique character. The NT Canon represents a dogmatic selection from the literature of primitive Christianity. In accepting this selection for the purpose of literary criticism, is there not a danger, it may be asked, of isolating the writings unhistorically under the influence of what was the postulate of a later generation? This contention does not necessarily cast any reflection upon the instinct which led the early church to draw up such a collection; it does not mean that the unity of the New Testament is a purely factitious characteristic which has been imposed upon its contents by the ecclesiastical interests of a subsequent age.* "No one is called upon to deny that the ancient church in her New Testament brought together *upon the whole* what was of most value from the religious standpoint, and also *upon the whole* all that was oldest and therefore, from a documentary standpoint, most important, not only in the literature known to us, but in the current literature of the period" (Wrede, *Ueber Aufgabe und Methode der sogenannten Neutestamentlichen Theologie*, 1897, p. 11).† The pith and justice of the argument lie in its protest against introducing *a priori* conceptions of unity and uniqueness into the historical criticism of the religious ideas and the literary form of the New Testament writings. It has less bearing, in any case, upon the literary criticism than upon the theological study of the NT.‡ Strictly speaking, the method of the former should

* Cf. on this Denney's *Death of Christ* (1902), pp. 1–4, and Sanday in *ERE.* ii. 576–577.

† The opening pages of Wrede's essay (pp. 8–17, cp. *GGA.*, 1896, 525 f.), G. Krüger's pamphlet on *Das Dogma vom Neuen Testament* (1896), and his pages in *ARW.*, 1902, 258 f., 267 f., represent this position most effectively. The credit of starting it originally belongs to the two Dutch scholars, van Manen (cf. *EBi.* 3471 f.) and Baljon. On the general principle, see Preuschen's paragraphs in *ZNW.* (1900), pp. 10 f.

‡ As early as Clement of Rome and Ignatius there is a retrospective recognition of an authority in religious tradition which belonged to the apostles; but this was not confined to extra-canonical writers, and it did not necessarily imply a literary record or expression of that authority.

include the non-canonical compositions which are contemporary with the canonical, as is done, *e.g.*, by Schwegler and Pfleiderer, by Reuss and van Manen, and in G. Krüger's *Geschichte d. altchrist. Litteratur.* Practical considerations, however, determine otherwise. Since the present series is a "theological" library,—implying that the inclusion of the New Testament writings denotes their canonical character,—and since Dr. C. R. Gregory's volume has outlined the process by which they attained this position in the church, the present volume is perforce confined to the earlier history of the Christian writings which have thus become canonical; only, it is written from the standpoint which views them not as canonical but as products of the primitive Christian movement, and it attempts primarily to read them in the light not of what they afterwards became or did, but of what they were to the age and circle of their origin. The question practically renders itself into one of method. So long as inquiries into the literature of the NT are prosecuted apart from any dogmatic assumptions upon the priority or superiority of that literature to the other writings of the period, no breach of scientific principle is committed. The dependence of the Fourth gospel, *e.g.*, upon Justin or even the Leucian Acts, may be denied, but not for the *a priori* reason that the one is canonical and the others are not. Criticism, again, may place certain NT writings in the same period as others which are

> "Contemporaneous,
> No question, but how extraneous
> In the grace of soul, the power
> Of hand."

This description, however, must be deduced from the internal evidence of the books in question, not from any consideration of the canonical prestige which attaches to one or other of them Thus, even when the immediate scope of the inquiry is confined to a selection from the early Christian literature, the principles on which the investigation proceeds need not and must not be narrowed in such a way as to exclude from the purview of the critic any relevant data furnished by the form and contents of any contemporary literature which is extant. So far as literary morphology is concerned, *e.g.*, no valid distinction can be drawn between the so-called "NT" literature and the early Christian writings of the first or the second century.* The same forms appear; epistles continue to be written; apocalypses start up; acts are compiled; and even gospels continue to rise above the surface. Each *genre* has an earlier example within the NT collection, but the later productions are by no means merely imitative in form or contents; the derivative element is frequently lost amid the vigorous and independent creations of apologist or romancer. Besides, some (*e.g.* Clemens Romanus, perhaps Barnabas) are prior to, and others at least (Ignatius) contemporaries of, one or two writings which are now included in the Canon. No line of demarcation can be drawn even in time any more than in form.

(*a*) Unless the literary criticism of early Christian writings is to become merely a subordinate branch of dogmatic theology † or of church history, it must apparently forego its rights to use the title of "NT Introduction except upon the grounds of practical convenience. From the logical and historical point of view there is no such thing as a science of NT Introduction, unless "NT" is regarded as equivalent to the NT Canon, and the origin of the various NT writings treated merely as a prelude to their subsequent history in the church. But while the scientific ideal would undoubtedly be an Introduction to the early Christian literature, which abstains on principle from crowning any members of the primitive company with a posthumous halo, just as conscientiously as a modern philologist would refuse to treat the language of the NT writers as an isolated island in the sea of the profaner κοινή, the NT is with us, and it will be with us to the end. Partly owing to intrinsic, partly owing to extrinsic qualities, its contents have acquired a vogue shared by no other early Christian writings,‡ and there are practical considerations in favour of continuing to treat this selection of choice documents as a separate whole, in the light of its wider literary environment. Most writers on NT Introduction add to their discussion of the separate NT writings not only a section on the Canon, but also some account of the uncanonical literature. But this is to swell the size of a NT Introduction without adequately avoiding its unscientific bias. Even when a NT Introduction is confined to a discussion

* See F. Overbeck's essay, 'Über die Anfänge der patristischen Literatur' in *Historische Zeitschrift* (1882), pp. 417–472, especially pp. 428 f.

† Or of apologetic, as, *e.g.*, A. G. Rudelbach (*Zeitschrift für lutherische Theologie u. Kirche*, 1848, pp. 1 f.) and Aberle (*Einl.* pp. 3 f.) held quite frankly.

‡ "The books did not come together by chance. They are not held together simply by the art of the bookbinder. It would be truer to say that they gravitated towards each other in the course of the first century of the church's life, and imposed their unity on the Christian mind, than that the church imposed on them by statute . . . a unity to which they were inwardly strange" (Denney, *The Death of Christ*, 1902, p. 3).

of the NT books, the scientific demands of literary criticism may be met by following a method which actually, though not formally, treats the canonical writings not as canonical but as early Christian documents, eschewing any factitious or fortuitous grouping due to a later period, and steadily keeping in view their relations to the so-called uncanonical document of the first and second centuries. This, it must be confessed, is a makeshift. But it manages to conserve the rights of historical criticism.

(*b*) The name is older than the subject. Exposition and inspiration (*i.e.* the problems of canonical authority) rather than literary criticism occupied the earlier works which may be grouped under the title of Introduction,* from Adrianus to Santes Pagninus and Rivetus. Such treatises grouped the OT and the NT together. Latterly, their interest in the canonical authority of the scriptures led to an increasing emphasis upon the question of the text, which the investigations of Simon and Mill soon forced into prominence. The former of these scholars, though none of his works is called an Introduction, is the real founder of the modern science. In point of fact, even prior to Simon, the most relevant materials of Introduction were furnished by works which bore other names, from the Muratorian Canon and the writings of Jerome (especially the *de uiris inlustribus*, which had so powerful an influence on mediæval thought §) down to the Dominican Sixtus and M. Walther (*Officina Biblica*, 1636). There have been three distinct stages in the development of NT Introduction. The first is marked by R. Simon's works, which emphasised the duty of investigating the pre-canonical origin of the literature. The second synchronises with the discussions upon the relation of the science to the NT Canon, which are associated with the names of Hupfeld and Baur, especially the former. By this time NT Introduction had realised to some degree its vocation in literary and historical criticism alike. The third stage, inaugurated by Overbeck and worked out by the scholars above noted (p. 9), is still in progress. At first sight it appears to spell the death of the science, resolving it into the larger discipline of an Introduction to the early Christian literature; but there is less practical justification for this † than for the allied purpose to replace "NT theology" by "The history of religious ideas in primitive Christianity."

The fullest study of the history of NT Introduction is Zahn's article in *PRE.* v. 261–274; the English student will find materials in Bleek's *INT.* i. pp. 7–38, and Weiss (*INT.* §§ 1–4), as well as in H. S. Nash's *History of the Higher Criticism of the New Testament*, and G. H. Gilbert's *Interpretation of the Bible* (1908); although the latter, like R. Simon's exhaustive *Histoire critique des principaux commentateurs du NT depuis le commencement du Christianisme jusques à nôtre temps* (1693), deals with exegesis rather than Introduction proper.

---

* On Jerome's influence upon the Canon of the Western Church, see Sir H. Howorth in *JTS.* x. 481 f.

† Cf. J. Weiss, *Die Aufgaben der Neutestamentlichen Wissenschaft* (1908), pp. 32, 48 f.

II.

ARRANGEMENT OF NT WRITINGS.

Do the traditions underlying the various early canonical arrangements of the NT throw any reliable light upon the origin and relative position of the latter? This question must be asked and answered before the canonical order is set aside by literary criticism. It involves an inquiry into the sequence and contents of the various sections in the NT Canon (cp. Zahn's *GK.* ii. 343–383; S. Berger, *Histoire de la Vulgate* (1893), pp. 301 f., 331 f.; Moffatt, *HNT.* pp. 107–117; Jülicher's *Einl.* § 46; Nestle's *Einf.* 127–128).

In the following lists, early Christian writings like the Apocalypse of Peter and Hermas, which are frequently ranged with the canonical, have been omitted for the sake of clearness. Heb. is ranked with the Pauline epp., except where otherwise noted. It is obvious that the relative order of the sections cannot be earlier than the third or fourth century, when the whole of the NT came to be written as a single codex, and that even the order of books in the separate sections seldom goes further back than the period when the collection of gospels or epistles was first made.

(*a*) The order (cp. Credner's *GK.* pp. 390 f.; Barth's *Einl.* pp. 387 f.; Gregory's *Canon and Text of NT*, pp. 467–469) of the component sections of the Canon occupies the first place in this preliminary inquiry; but, although the results are fairly clear, their value for the historical appreciation of the writings is of subordinate importance. As the reader will notice from the appended tables (expanded from *HNT.* pp. 108 f.), the gospels almost invariably come first, though in the synopsis of Chrysostom, as in D, they follow Paul, owing to liturgical reasons. The Apoc, again, is as invariably last, though in the Decretum Gelasii (which otherwise tallies with B), as in the Fleury palimpsest and in the Catalogus Mommsenianus (which otherwise tallies with A), it precedes the catholic epistles, while in the oldest Armenian MS (Venet., *c.* 1220 A.D.), which otherwise tallies with B, Paul follows the Apoc.

The usual position of Acts, before or after the catholic epistles, and the explicit title of the former, *Actus Apostolorum* (Iren. *adv. Hær.* iii. 13. 3, etc.) or *Acta omnium Apostolorum* (Murat.), though erroneous, denote the catholicizing tendency of the early church. Philastrius (4th cent., *Hær.* lxxxviii.) observes that the catholic epistles "actibus apostolorum conjunctæ sunt"; this is the order in A, E, F, and G, their priority (in E and F) over Paul being due to the influence of Gal 1^{17} (τοὺς πρὸ ἐμοῦ ἀποστόλους). Acts was of special value not only as an introduction upon the one hand to Paul's epistles, but as a witness, on the other hand, to the twelve apostles (as represented by the catholic epistles); in this way it seemed to prove the unity of the early church. Its position immediately after the gospels was due to the feeling that the historical books should go together.

A	B*	C	D	E	F	G†
Epiph.: Jerome: ℵ: Codex Fuldensis, etc.	Council of Carthage: Amphilochius: Philastrius: Rufinus: Syriac Canon (om. Cath. and Apoc.), etc.	Chrysostom.	Apost. Constit. (ii. 57).	Codex Alexandrinus: Athanasius: Cyril: Leontius (6th cent.): Cassiodorus: Nicephorus (om. Apoc.), etc.	Council of Laodicea: Cyril of Jerusalem: John of Damascus, etc.	Augustine: Innocent I.: Isidore of Spain (7th cent.), etc.
Evv Paul Acts Cath Apoc	Evv Acts Paul Cath Apoc	Paul Evv Acts Cath	Acts Paul Evv	Evv Acts Cath Paul Apoc	Evv Acts Cath Paul	Evv Paul Cath Acts Apoc

(*b*) More interest attaches to the order of the writings included in these sections. With regard to the gospels (cp. Nestle's *Einf.* pp. 127 f.; Zahn's *GK.* ii. 364 f., 1014), the main data may be tabulated as follows:—

A	B	C	D	E	F	G‡
Murat. Canon: Irenæus: Syrsin: Jerome: Greg. Naz.: Augustine: ℵ A B: Athanasius, etc.	Ambrosiaster.	Catalogus Mommsenianus (4th cent.): Syrcur: Theophilus.	Apost. Constit.: Codex Bezæ: ℵ: Gothic version. Many old Latin MSS (Vercellensis, Palatinus, etc.).	Catalogus Claromontanus (3rd cent. ?).	Chrysostom (in Migne's *Patr. Gr.* lvi. 317).	Bohairic version: Sahidic version (R, an Egyptian Codex of 6th cent., has Jn, Lk, Mk, Mt).
Mt Mk Lk Jn	Mt Lk Mk Jn	Mt Mk Jn Lk	Mt Jn Lk Mk	Mt Jn Mk Lk	Jn Mt Lk Mk	Jn Mt Mk Lk

* So Greg. Naz., omitting Apoc. The order of B ("item ordo Scripturarum NT quem sancta catholica Romana suscipit et ueneratur ecclesia," Decret. Gelasii) was adopted finally by the Council of Trent.

† So Apost. Canons, omitting Apoc, and Catalogus Claromontanus (4th cent.), placing Apoc before Acts. The original order of Codex Bezæ (cp. Dom Chapman in *Exp.*[6] July 1905, 46–53) seems to have been Evv, Apoc, Cath (1–3 Jn), Acts.

‡ Minuscule 19 has Jn, Mt, Lk, Mk; minuscule 90 has Jn, Lk, Mt, Mk. Here, as in D and F, Mk is put last on the score of its size. Corroboration of this order was probably found (as by Irenæus and Victorinus) in Apoc 4^7, where John was identified with the lion, Luke with the calf, Matthew with the man, and Mark with the eagle. The more common arrangement

A, which was adopted by the Council of Laodicea (A.D. 363), reflects an early tradition preserved by Origen (Eus. *H. E.* vi. 25. 3), who learnt ἐν παραδόσει that Mt was written first of all, then Mk (on the basis of Peter's preaching), thirdly Lk (referred to in Ro 2^{16}, 2 Ti 2^{8}), ἐπὶ πᾶσιν τὸ κατὰ Ἰωάννην (so *In Jesum Nave hom.* vii. 1). It is reproduced by the large majority of manuscripts and versions. B is another early arrangement, reported by Clement (Eus. *H. E.* vi. 14, 5–7) as a παράδοσις περὶ τῆς τάξεως τῶν εὐαγγελίων which he had received from τῶν ἀνέκαθεν πρεσβυτέρων. The tradition thus goes back to the middle of the second century at least, if it is not earlier; there are even traces of it in Irenæus. But the principle of arrangement is that priority belongs to the gospels which contain genealogies; Mark's gospel reflects the subsequent preaching of Peter at Rome, while John's is the spiritual gospel which crowns and supplements all three. Otherwise (except in D and F) Mk as the Petrine gospel precedes the Pauline Lk. Irenæus, indeed, gives a chronological basis for A (cp. Eus. *H. E.* v. 8. 2), but the traditions which he preserves fall to be discussed in connexion with the gospels of Matthew and Mark (see below). The gradual (C–G) elevation of Jn from the fourth place to the first or second was due to the theory that the directly apostolic gospels (Mt, Jn) were in a position of priority as compared with those which were merely composed by apostolic subordinates (Mk, Lk),* perhaps also to the idea † that Jn was written when the circle of the apostles was still unbroken (cp. Schwartz, *Der Tod d. Söhne Zebedaei*, pp. 26 f.), and possibly to a desire for emphasis on the gospels which connected Jesus directly with the OT. G certainly reflects a pre-Origen order current in the Egyptian church. The monarchian prologues to the four gospels, which represent on the other hand a Roman tradition slightly later than the Muratorian Canon (cp. Corssen in *TU.* xv. 1), place Mt first, as written before the others in Judæa; then Jn ("qui etsi post omnes euangelium scripsisse dicitur, tamen dispositione canonis ordinati post Matthæum ponitur"); then Lk and Mk, though the latter (written in Italy) chronologically preceded the former.‡ The prologues

---

of the symbols (cp. Swete's *Mark*, pp. xxxvi f.), which allied the figures respectively to Mark, Luke, Matthew, and John, does not seem to have influenced the chronological order, but in the old Latin codex Bobiensis Mk precedes Mt.

* See Tert. *adv. Marc.* iv. 2 ("nobis fidem ex apostolis Johannes et Matthæus insinuant, ex apostolicis Lucas et Marcus instaurant, iisdem regulis exorsi").

† This notion, which underlies the Muratorian Canon's account of the Fourth gospel's origin, probably explains the subsequent allusion in the same Canon to the priority of the Apocalypse over Paul ("cum ipse beatus apostolus Paulus sequens prodecessoris sui Johannis ordinem non nisi nominatim septem ecclesiis scribat)."

‡ The remark that Mk "non laborauit natiuitatem carnis, quam in prioribus uiderat, dicere," seems to contradict this, whether *in prioribus* (sc. *euangeliis*) refers to Mt and Lk (Corssen), or to Mt and Jn (see the words immediately above, "initium carnis in domino et dei aduenientis habitaculum"). Zahn's attempt to explain the phrase as a translation of ἐν τοῖς πρὸ τούτων or ἐν τοῖς ἔμπροσθεν, is quite improbable.

thus witness to the order of A as that of the composition of the four, but for ecclesiastical reasons they reproduce D. The Western order of D also occurs in the newly discovered (Egyptian) Freer MS. Here as elsewhere Mk's size was probably one reason for Lk's priority. A is probably the oldest tradition extant upon the order; it is drawn from several early ecclesiastical traditions connected with the apostolic authorship or origin of the gospels. Mt, as composed by Matthew the taxgatherer for the Jewish Christians of Palestine, is supposed to precede Mk, which was associated with Peter's subsequent preaching at Rome, just as Lk was connected with Paul's preaching. C represents an order of the Western church, and there is internal evidence to suggest that the archetype of Codex Bezæ had the gospels in this order, its present order (D) being due to a later scribe (cp. Dom Chapman in *ZNW.*, 1905, 339–346).

The division and arrangement of the gospels thus appear to have been determined partly on chronological grounds, partly from considerations of internal value or even of size, partly from ecclesiastical ideas of the author's rank, and partly from arbitrary fancies—or, at any rate, from what seem arbitrary and unintelligible to a modern. All these features are further illustrated in the disposition of the Pauline and catholic epistles.

(*c*) The Pauline epistles are arranged as follows:—

A*	B	C†	D	E	F
Marcion (cf. Tert. *adv. Marc.* iv. 5).	Muratorian Canon.	Jerome: Athanasius: Council of Laodicea: Amphilochius of Ikonium: Nicephorus (Stichometry): John of Damascus: Freisingen fragm. of old Latin (with Heb after 1 Ti), etc.	Catalogus Claromontanus.	Decretum Gelasii.	Victorinus (on Rev 1[20]).
Gal	Corr	Rom	Rom	Rom	Rom
Corr	Eph	Corr	Corr	Corr	Corr
Rom	Phil	Gal	Gal	Eph	Gal
Thess	Col	Eph	Eph	Thess	Eph
Laod	Gal	Phil	...	Gal	Thess
Col	Thess	Col	...	Phil	Phil
Phil	Rom	Thess	Tim	Col	Col
Phlm	Phlm	Tim	Tit	Tim	[" postea singularibus personis scripsit, ne excederet numerum septem ecclesiarum "]
	Tit	Tit	Col	Tit	
	Tim	Phlm	Phlm	Phlm	

* The order Gal, Co, Ro seems to have also prevailed, possibly after Marcion, in the early Syriac canon (as in Efraem).

† Athanasius and Council of Laodicea, like ℵA, insert Heb between Thess and Tim; in the Bohairic version it also follows 2 Th, though the Fayyumic and Sahidic (perhaps on account of its size) place it after 2 Co. Augustine, like Isidore of Spain (7th cent.), puts Col between Thess and Tim; and Cassiodorus, reversing the order of Eph and Phil, also places Heb between Thess and Tim.

The position of Philem after Col in A and D is natural, but the distinction * of ecclesiastical and private epistles, which dominates B, C, E, and F, tended to throw Philem not only near but after Tim and Tit on account of its brevity (as in C, E). Thus it is uncertain whether Marcion's order put Philem after Phil (so Tert. *adv. Marc.* v.) or before it (Epiph. *hær.* xlii.). The priority of Rom in C, D, and E was due partly to its size, partly to the prestige of the Roman church.

The position of Hebrews within the Pauline *corpus* is usually † between the ecclesiastical and the private epistles (Eastern Church) or after the latter (Western Church). Luther threw Heb, Jas, Judas, and Apoc to the end of his bible with the curt remark: "bisher haben wir die rechten gewissen hauptbücher des NT gehabt, diese vier nachfolgende aber haben vor zeytten ein ander ansehen gehabt."

(*d*) The canonical arrangement of the catholic epistles throws even less light on their origin, or even upon the traditions which grew up round them in the early church. They were tabulated in order as follows:—

A	B	C‡	D	E	F§
ℵ A B: Council of Laodicea (363 A.D.): Cyril of Jerusalem (4th cent.): John of Damascus (8th cent.): besides Epiphanius, Athanasius, Greg. Naz., Nicephorus, etc.	Council of Carthage (397 A.D.): Apostolic Canons, etc.	Catalogus Claromontanus (3rd cent. ?): Gelasii Decretum: Codex ψ.	Augustine (*de doctr. Christ.* ii. 12): Philastrius (4th cent.): Cassiodorus.	Rufinus (*Expositio in symbolum apost.* 37).	Innocent I. (405 A.D.).
Jas 1 Pt 2 Pt 1 Jn 2 Jn 3 Jn Judas	1 Pt 2 Pt 1 Jn 2 Jn 3 Jn Jas Judas	1 Pt 2 Pt Jas 1 Jn 2 Jn 3 Jn Judas	1 Pt 2 Pt 1 Jn 2 Jn 3 Jn Judas Jas	1 Pt 2 Pt Jas Judas 1 Jn 2 Jn 3 Jn	1 Jn 2 Jn 3 Jn 1 Pt 2 Pt Judas Jas

* It is explicitly stated in Murat. Canon and by Victorinus that Paul wrote to seven churches, as John did, the seven representing the one catholic church.

† Occasionally, however, after 2 Co and before Gal (so, *e.g.*, Sahidic version) or Eph (Theodore Mops.).

‡ Pope Damasus I. (4th cent.), who follows this order, distinguished 2 and 3 Jn as "alterius Johannis presbyteri epistolæ."

§ Catalogus Mommsenianus (4th cent.), which follows F, omits Judas and Jas. The "una sola," which is appended in one of its MSS to Jn and Pt, represents an early gloss which protests against the canonicity of 2–3 Jn and 2 P, not a comment upon Jas and Judas, which have been accidentally omitted (Belser, *Einl.* 727). See Gregory's *Canon and Text of NT*, 271–272.

Owing to the length of time which elapsed before the seven catholic epistles succeeded in winning ecclesiastical recognition, and owing to the variety of their authors as well as to the obscurity which besets the origin of almost all in the traditions of the church, no tradition of their respective order or chronological arrangement is either early or reliable. Thus, the priority of Peter in B is due to hierarchical reasons (Jerome, acc. to Cassiod. *Inst. Div. Litt.* 11, put the Petrine epp. before the Pauline, next to the gospels). B passed into the Roman church through the Council of Trent. A represents a common and even earlier Eastern arrangement. For the priority of Jas, cp. Eus. *H. E.* ii. 23, 24 (οὗ ἡ πρώτη τῶν ὀνομαζομένων καθολικῶν ἐπιστολῶν εἶναι λέγεται); but the order (Jas, Pt, Jn) probably is no more than an ecclesiastical reflection of Gal 2^9, and it possesses as little independent historical value as B.

By the time of Eusebius, who first mentions *the seven so-called catholic epistles* (*H. E.* ii. 23, cp. vi. 14), the Eastern church in particular had reserved the term *catholic*, as a literary designation, for a group of seven early Christian writings which, with more or less unanimity, had been accepted as apostolic and canonical. The sense of the term, in this connection, is equivalent to encyclical or general. As distinguished from Paul's epistles, these were supposed to be addressed either to Christendom in general or to a wide circle of Christian churches. The second century anti-Montanist Apollonius (as cited in Eus. *H. E.* v. 18. 5) describes how Θεμίσων . . . ἐτόλμησεν, μιμούμενος τὸν ἀπόστολον, καθολικήν τινα συνταξάμενος ἐπιστολήν, κατηχεῖν μὲν τοὺς ἄμεινον αὐτοῦ πεπιστευκότας, συναγωνίζεσθαι δὲ τοῖς τῆς κενοφωνίας λόγοις, βλασφημῆσαι δὲ εἰς τὸν κύριον καὶ τοὺς ἀποστόλους καὶ τὴν ἁγίαν ἐκκλησίαν. Themison was a Montanist leader at Cumane, but we have no further information about his ecclesiastical or literary career. It is plain, however, that καθολική in this connection means neither canonical nor orthodox, but œcumenical or general.

The extant fragment of the Latin version of Clement's *Hypotyposes* (see Zahn's *Forschungen*, iii. pp. 134 f.) proves that, while he reckoned Clemens Romanus and Barnabas * as apostolic, he only commented on four of the catholic epistles, viz. 1 P, Judas, 1 Jn and 2 Jn. These four represent the nucleus of the corpus catholicum. The latter three alone are included in the Muratorian Canon, while Irenæus knew 1 P, 1 Jn, and 2 Jn, and Tertullian 1 P, 1 Jn, and Judas. Tertullian's silence on 2 Jn may be as accidental as that of Irenæus upon Judas; but even Origen, the first of the church fathers to vouch for all the seven catholic epistles, puts 2 and 3 Jn, Judas, 2 P, and Ja, into the second class of ἀντιλεγόμενα or ἀμφιβαλλόμενα.

More than once the further question rises, did the formation of the Canon exert any influence upon the original form and text of the early Christian writings which were thus gathered into a collection of sacred books for the purposes of the church? Did the canonical process involve any editing? and if so, where, and to what extent? Higher criticism and textual criticism interlace, in problems of this nature. Rohrbach's hypothesis about the lost

* Origen also reckoned this a καθολικὴ ἐπιστόλη (*c. Cels.* i. 63), and so did the Catalogus Claromontanus.

ending of Mark, Harnack's on the titles of the catholic epistles, and the widespread theories on Romans and 2 Corinthians, are instances in point. It is also a fair question, whether the text of Paul's epistles may not have been slightly "catholicised" for the purpose of the canon These problems, however, fall to be noticed below, in connection with the respective writings. All that can be premised is that the canonical editing, which added titles to several of the writings, may quite well have gone further in the interests of liturgical edification.

As the plan of this volume departs from the canonical arrangement, it will be useful at this point to outline the course followed in grouping the various documents.

The literature dating from the early decades of the Christian movement may be called "Epichristian"—to borrow a convenient term from de Quincey.* As it happens, the extant fragments of this literature consist almost entirely of letters written by the apostle Paul. The period includes, however, the rise of the primitive evangelic material, which afterwards was worked up into the synoptic gospels. Collections of logia may in some cases be traced even within Paul's epistles; one of them, the Q-source of Matthew and Luke, certainly is contemporaneous with him. Though none has survived in its original form, it would be an unbalanced estimate of the epi-christian period and its literature which would identify the latter with the correspondence of the great apostle.

In form, at any rate, the historical literature stands by itself. The use of the epistle for religious purposes did not originate with Paul, though he was the first to popularise it within Christianity. The special traits of a gospel, however, as we find them in the synoptic writers, are not anticipated in the earlier biographical memoirs or monographs or ἀρεταλόγαι of ancient literature. On this account alone the four books of the historical literature demand a chapter to themselves. From

* In his essay on the Essenes he invents the adjective in order to describe primary elements and movements in Christianity which first matured in the generation immediately succeeding the lifetime of Jesus Christ. "That particular age or generation (of twenty or thirty years, suppose) which witnesses the first origin of any great idea, system, discovery, or revelation, rarely indeed witnesses the main struggle and opening rush of its evolution. Exactly as any birth promises vast results for man, it may be expected to slumber silently. Then suddenly kindling, and spreading by ratios continually accelerated, it rushes into the fulness of life with the hurry of a vernal resurrection in Sweden."

the standpoint of literary criticism, they represent a new departure. As they followed Paul's correspondence chronologically, they may be studied next to the apostle's letters and epistles, the more so that the origin and the significance of the so-called Pauline elements which they contain constitute one of the problems which beset the task of estimating the extent to which the gospels reflect the common Christianity of the primitive church in reproducing the sayings and deeds of Jesus.

So far as the NT is concerned, this period, *i.e.* the half century after A.D. 70,* has also thrown up a number of compositions which the later church, in framing its Canon, grouped either as Pauline or as "catholic" epistles. It is customary in most manuals of Introduction to treat the former under the Pauline correspondence, even when they are recognised to be sub-Pauline, and to discuss the latter separately. This method may be defended on the score of practical convenience; but even when adopted in order to facilitate reference and to avoid confusion, it has grave drawbacks. It is better to regard all these sub-Pauline writings, from the standpoint of literary criticism, under the general title of pastorals and homilies. The introduction of a classification such as that of the "catholic epistles" is a much later and artificial arrangement.

Any disposition of these homilies and pastorals is more or less provisional. Their chronological succession, their literary relationships, and even the schools of thought or localities to which they might be referred, are too insecure to afford any basis for an arrangement which would correspond to the little that is known about their situation. I have put Judas and 2 Peter immediately after 1 Peter, since, although Judas differs from 1 Peter, 2 Peter depends on both, and Judas lies chronologically between the two. A second subdivision is headed by Ephesians, which is also allied to 1 Peter; in its wake we may range the three epistles to Timotheus and Titus, since they, too, bear Paul's name. Hebrews again, like Ephesians, breathes an atmosphere in which the Pauline ideas are being transmuted

* It is totally unhistorical to describe the age between the death of the apostles and the middle of the second century as an unproductive period, whose practical tasks resembled those of the post-Reformation era, when it was men's chief business, as Martin Chemnitz put it, *parta tueri*.

into a form approximating to the later transformation in the Fourth gospel. With it the homily or tract of James may be placed, for lack of any more appropriate position. Finally, the two little pastorals written by John the presbyter lead up naturally to the Apocalypse. In literary form, the Apocalypse is partly allied to the pastorals and homilies, but the uniqueness of its contents justifies the special position assigned to it as the only one of the early Christian apocalypses which eventually managed to retain a foothold inside the Canon. The Fourth gospel has formal affinities both to the pastorals and to the historical literature; here again, however, the distinctive characteristics of the document merit isolated treatment. The anonymous homily or pastoral which bears the canonical title of "First John" will be discussed, for the sake of convenience, in the wake of the Fourth gospel, with which its affinities are closest, instead of in its proper class.

The chief complete commentaries on the NT are:—Beza's *Annotationes* (1565); Aretius, *Commentarii* (Paris, 1607); Grotius, *Annotationes* (1644); Alberti's *Observationes philologicæ in sacros Noui Fœderis libros* (1725); Hardouin's *Commentarius* (1741); de Beausobre's *Remarques historiques, critiques, et philologiques sur le NT* (1742); Bengel's *Gnomon* (1742); Rosenmüller's *Scholia* (1777); H. E. G. Paulus (1800–1804), J. O. Thiess (1804–1806), Kuinoel (1807–1818), S. T. Blomfield's *Greek Testament* (London, 1829); J. Gossner (Berlin, 1827–1830); E. Burton's *Greek Testament* (Oxford, 1831); Alford; C. Wordsworth; and A. Bisping's *Handbuch* (1867–1876).

III.

LITERARY SOURCES OF NT.

A New Testament* implies an Old. The New Testament writings, even separately, presuppose the authority no less than the existence of the older γραφή of the Jews, by means of which Paul justified the principles of the Gentile mission, and the evangelic tradition enriched as well as verified its outline of Jesus the messiah. It was the analogy of the OT which contributed, together with the growing prestige of early Christian apostolic

* Tertullian, using *instrumentum* in its juristic sense of a written authority or proof, distinguishes the OT, as *instrumentum Judaicæ literæ*, from the NT as the *instrumentum prædicationis* or *Christianæ literæ* (Rönsch, *Das NT Tertullians*, 1871, 47–49).

writings as apostolic* (cp. Köppel in *SK.*, 1891, 123 f.), to the formation of a NT.

Eusebius recognises a providential circumstance in the composition of the LXX. Had it not been for this version, he observes, "we should not have got from the Jews those oracles (τὰ παρ' αὐτοῖς λόγια, cp. Ro 3^2), which they would have hidden away from us in jealousy" (Eus. *Praep. Evang.* 349 c). The argument is that since the OT prophecies were to prove essential to the preaching of Christ throughout the world, God had thus arranged for the accurate translation and wide diffusion of oracles which would witness incontrovertibly to his Son. This standpoint was that of the early church as a whole. To the OT they appealed for proofs of their doctrine of Jesus Christ. Their earliest theoretic interest was the demonstration from OT prophecies that Jesus was the true messiah. In the case of Paul, the author of Matthew, and the writer of Hebrews, the extent to which the original Hebrew text was employed in quotations becomes a problem for exegesis, but in the main the LXX was more convenient. More than once, *e.g.* in Hebrews and Paul, the argument turns upon some pivot in the LXX text. Several times, *e.g.* in Matthew, Barnabas, and Justin, the so-called proofs are simply illustrations, and not always very happy illustrations, of the doctrine in question, while the OT text could also furnish upon occasion material for the stories as well as for the sayings in the gospels. The main point is, however, that the early church steadily clung to the OT, despite the hostility of the Jews, the contempt of the Marcionites and certain gnostic sects who repudiated the OT, and the difficulties in which its interpretation often plunged the Christian teacher and apologist.

On the strong influence of the LXX upon the Greek world outside Judaism, and its value as an instrument of the Christian propaganda, see Harnack. *SBBA.*, 1902, 508 f., *MAC.* i. 279 f., 284 f. ; and Deissmann, *Neue Jahrbücher für das klass. Alterthum* (1903), 161 f. (on 'die Helleniesierung des semit. Monotheismus').

---

* The impulse to keep up communication of some sort with the apostolic base was not confined to Catholic Christians. The Gnostics shared this instinct. It found expression in their repeated efforts (*a*) to attach themselves to the traditions of some apostle or apostolic disciple, (*b*) to interpret allegorically (and edit) some apostolic writing, and to compose (*c*) gospels of their own (cp. Eus. *H. E.*, iii. 25. 6–7).

Ignatius (*ad Phil.* 8[2]) declares he once heard some people saying (ὅτι Ἐὰν μὴ κτλ.), "If I do not find it ἐν τοῖς ἀρχείοις, I do not believe (it) ἐν τῷ εὐαγγελίῳ." When he replied, "It *is* written," they retorted, "That is just the question (πρόκειται)." Τὰ ἀρχεῖα (ἀρχαῖα) here means the OT, which Ignatius claims to be in line with the gospel. It is unnecessary and awkward to put ἐν τῷ εὐαγγελίῳ in apposition to τοῖς ἀρχείοις, taking πιστεύω in an absolute sense (so Zahn, Funk), or to follow the ingenious emendation of A. N. Jannaris (*Class. Rev.*, 1903, 24–25), who prefers to read ὅ,τι ἐὰν for ὅτι Ἐὰν, and πρόσκειται (=προστέθειται) for πρόκειται, so that the passage would run: "For I heard certain persons saying, Whatever I find not in the records, in the gospel, I believe not. And when I said to them, It is written, they answered, It is added." The latter interpretation would refer to the corruption of the gospel text. But the comparison of the OT and the Christian propaganda is inherently more probable.

Three considerations have to be borne in mind in this connection:

(i.) Even the LXX was not employed literally. The early church used the OT in many cases not as it lies before the modern reader, but in the light of the luxuriant midrashic interpretation which gathered round it during the later Judaism. Allowance has to be made repeatedly for this factor, in estimating the form and contents of early Christian traditions.* There is a partial analogy in the influence of Milton upon the later interpretation of Genesis; but even this gives no adequate idea of the extent † to which, not simply in the field of eschatology and apocalyptic, the letter of the OT was embellished and modified by midrashic speculations.

(ii.) The composite OT quotations in the NT as well as in the early Christian literature from Barnabas and Melito to Cyprian's *Testimonia* especially, render it highly probable that *florilegia* and *catenae* of OT passages were in circulation. A pre-Christian origin for such excerpts is not impossible; the size of the OT would make it convenient for short manuals of this kind to be drawn up for the purpose of teaching and propaganda. But this need would be intensified when the

* On the midrashic elements, *e.g.*, in Stephen's speech (Ac 7), see *EBi.* 4791; the traces in Josephus are collected by Bloch (*Die Quellen des Flavius Josephus*, 1879, pp. 20–51), the Philonic by L. Treitel in *Monatsschrift für Geschichte und Wiss. des Judentums* (1909), 28 f., 159 f.

† Thus the tradition of the Asiatic elders (Iren. v. 33. 3–4) about the fertility of the earth in the latter days transferred to Jesus a midrashic prophecy, perhaps from Apoc. Bar. (2S[3]) 29[5], or from a source common to that apocalypse and Papias (a Hebrew midrash on the Blessing of Isaac, J. R. Harris, *AJT.*, 1900, 499; cp. Hennicke's *HNA.* ii. 21).

controversy between Jews and Christians turned largely on the OT proof that Jesus was the true messiah. Following the contemporary habit, the early Christian propaganda would produce, or adapt for its own purpose, short collections of extracts, messianic and otherwise, for the use of those who had to argue from the OT. The internal evidence of the early Christian composite quotations, with their sequence of texts (*e.g.* Is 8^{14} and 28^{16} in Ro $9^{32\text{-}33}$ and 1 P $2^{6\text{-}8}$), their special textual forms (*e.g.* 1 Co 2^{9}), their editorial comments, and their occasional errors in the attribution of authorship (*e.g.* Mk $1^{2\text{-}3}$, Mt $27^{9\text{-}10}$), converge on the conclusion that such manuals were in use even during the first century. The evidence of Barnabas, Justin Martyr, and Clement of Alexandria throws light back upon their predecessors in this respect. It is possible that early Christian writers occasionally used not only Greek *testimonia* of this kind, but their Aramaic originals. Thus if, as is most likely, the combination of citations in Mk $1^{2\text{-}3}$ is derived from a book of *testimonia*, that book was compiled upon rabbinic principles, and probably written in Hebrew or Aramaic. Rabbinic combinations of texts were made from a sense of similarity in words as well as in ideas, and it is only in the original of the Malachi and Isaiah passages that the clue to their association here is seen, viz. the unique phrase פנה דרך (cp. Abrahams in *Cambridge Biblical Essays*, 1909, 179). In any case the deliberate and composite character of a number of early Christian quotations suggests that they are secondary, taken not from the originals, but from collections of proof-texts upon different subjects which were arranged in order, *e.g.*, to illustrate topics like "the forerunner," "the sufferings of messiah," "the call of the Gentiles," etc. (cp. Harnack, *HD.* i. 175; Moffatt, *HNT.* 351, 617; and the author of *The Logia of Papias*, 1894, pp. v–vii).

The existence of such *testimonia* explains, *e.g.*, the OT citations in Matthew (Allen, Stanton: *GHD.* ii. 344 f.) as well as in Paul. The hypothesis, stated by Credner (*Beiträge zur Einl.* ii. 318 f.) and Hatch (*Essays in Biblical Greek*, 1889, 203–214), has been raised to the level of strong probability by the repeated proofs led by Rendel Harris * (cp. *e.g.* *Exp.*[7] ii.

* Dr. Harris even finds in Ac 26^{23} the headlines of such *testimonia*, awkwardly incorporated in the text. On the whole subject, cp. Elter's essay, 'de gnomologiorum historia,' in *Byzant. Zeitschrift*, vii. 445 f. The later use of such excerpts in theological discussion is traced by Theodor Schermann in *Die Geschichte der Florilegia vom V–VIII Jahrhundert* (1904).

385–409, vii. 63 f.: *Gospel of Peter*, 86; *Contemp. Review*, Aug. 1895), and is widely accepted, *e.g.* by Westcott (*Hebrews*, 476 f.), Vollmer (*Die Alttest. Citate bei Paulus*, pp. 38 f.), Clemen (*Paulus*, i. 96), Swete (*Introd. to OT in Gk.* 252), Jacquier (*INT.* iii. 253–254), Sanday and Headlam (*Romans*, pp. 264, 282), and Drummond (*Character and Authorship of the Fourth Gospel*, p. 365, "it is conceivable that there may have grown up, whether in writing or not, an anthology of passages useful in controversy, which differed more or less from the correct Greek translation" of the OT).

(iii.) The religious life of a community is always enriched by the use of sources wider than the mere letter of their sacred codex. It is difficult to ascertain the precise limits of the Jewish OT Canon at this period, or to be sure how far they as well as the early Christians * employed extra-canonical writings; but, apart from this, the primitive Christian literature, including the NT, shows ample traces of dependence on written sources which lay outside the OT. In some cases direct quotation can be proved, though in the majority of instances the evidence does not warrant so direct a filiation.

(*a*) "The influence of Enoch on the New Testament has been greater than that of all the other apocryphal and pseudepigraphical books taken together" (Charles, *The Book of Enoch*, pp. 41–49, where the evidence is summarised). It is only quoted directly in Judas $^{14-15}$ (=En 1^{9} 5^{4} 27^{2}), as by name in Barn 4^{3} (cp. 16^{4} ἡ γραφή=En $89^{56.66}$; cp. Veil in *HNA.* ii. 212, 228), but there are verbal echoes, *e.g.*, in Hebrews (4^{13}=En 9^{5}, cp. 11^{5}), Mt 19^{28} (=En 62^{5}) and 26^{24} (=En 38^{2}), Lk 16^{9} (=En 63^{10}), Jn 5^{22} (=En 69^{27}), Paul (1 Th 5^{3} =En 62^{4} etc.), 1 P 3^{19-20} (=En $10^{4-5\ 12-13}$),† and the Apocalypse (*passim*). The powerful influence of Enoch upon the eschatological traditions of pre-Christian Judaism naturally affected the early Christian literature along this line to an extent which no collection of parallels can fully bring out. For the use and prestige of the book in the early church during the first two centuries, see Harnack, *ACL.* i. 852, ii. 1. 563 f. The slighter *Book of the Secrets of Enoch*, a later but pre-Christian apocalypse, also helped to popularise conceptions such as that of the seven heavens (cp. Charles and Morfill's edition, pp. xxxi f.), but it is not quoted by name in the early Christian literature. (*b*) Flakes of Ecclesiasticus, read as an edifying religious treatise,

---

* On the early Christian use and editing of uncanonical Jewish literature, cp. E. Grafe's *Das Urchristenthum u. das Alte Testament* (1906), pp. 39 f., and Budde's *Der Kanon des AT*, pp. 73 f.

† Dr. Rendel Harris (*Exp.*[6] iv. 194–199) adds 1 P 1^{12a} (=En 1^{2} *οὐκ εἰς τὴν νῦν γενεὰν διενοούμην ἀλλ' ἐπὶ πόρρω οὖσαν ἐγὼ λαλῶ*), conjecturing *διενοοῦντο* for *διηκόνουν* in the former passage, as well as (*Exp.*[6] iv. 346–349) Ἐνώχ after ἐν ᾧ καί (ΕΝΩΚΑΙ [ΕΝΩΧ] ΤΟΙϹ) in 1 P 3^{19}; cp. Clemen in *Exp.*[6] vi. 316 f., on "The first epistle of Peter and the Book of Enoch," and Hühn's *die alttest. Citate u. Reminiscenzen im NT*, ii. pp. 125 f., 291. For a *caveat* on Paul and the Gospels, see Abbott's *Diat.* 3353–3354.

lie far and wide over the surface of the church's literature during the first two centuries, from James and Hermas to Origen and Clement of Alexandria (cp. Bleek, *SK.*, 1853, 344 f.; Werner, *TQ.*, 1872, 265 f.). Not only does Clemens Romanus quote it (60^{1}=Sir 2^{11}), like the Didachê (4^{5}=Sir 4^{31}) and Barnabas (19^{9}), but there are data in the gospels which prove "that both Wisdom and Sirach were known to Matthew, Luke, John, or to collectors of *logia* of Jesus earlier than those gospels; that Sirach especially was used by the author of the *Magnificat* [*e.g.* 1^{17}=Sir 48^{10}, 1^{52}=Sir 10^{14}], and that our Lord seems to have made use of both books, Sirach more probably than Wisdom" (Adeney in *DCG.* i. 101a; see, further, J. H. A. Hart's *Ecclesiasticus, The Gk. Text of Codex* 248, 1909). One of the most interesting and significant cases is that of Mt 11^{28-30}, which contains more than one reminiscence not only of the OT, but of Sirach (*e.g.* $51^{1.\,10-12.\,17.\,23}$, 24^{19-22}, 6^{24-25}, 51^{26-27}, 6^{29}); see Brandt's *Evang. Geschichte und der Ursprung des Christenthums*, 576 f., with Loisy's note in *Les Evangiles Synoptiques*, i. p. 913, and Harnack's *BNT.* ii. 304 f. Further cases occur in 4^{4}=Mt 5^{42}, 4^{10}=Lk 6^{35}, 7^{14}=Mt 6^{7}, 11^{19}=Lk 12^{19}, 13^{9-10}=Lk 14^{7-10}, 28^{2}=Mt 6^{14}, in John (6^{35}=Sir 24^{21}, 14^{23}=Sir 2^{15}), and in Paul (*e.g.* 7^{34}=Ro 12^{15}, 8^{5}=Gal 6^{2}, $13^{17f.}$=2 Co 6^{14}, 14^{2}=Ro 14^{22}, 16^{20}=Ro 11^{33}, 3^{20-24}=Ro $12^{3.\,16f.}$, 25^{24}=1 Ti 2^{14}). Ecclesiasticus was used not only by Jewish writers like Philo, the authors of The Testaments of the Twelve Patriarchs and The Psalms of Solomon, as well as in the rabbinic literature (see Schechter, *JQR.*, 1891, 682–706),* but by Christian writers in the primitive and early church, alike in the East and in the West (cp. T. André's *Les apocryphes de l'ancien Testament*, 1903, pp. 290–297); Clement of Alexandria commented on it as an OT scripture. (*c*) Next to Enoch and Sirach, no writing of the later Judaism had such a vogue within the early church as the Wisdom of Solomon, which, even by those who, like Origen and Augustine, doubted its Solomonic authorship, was almost invariably regarded as a divine and prophetic scripture (cp. Schürer, *GJV.*³ iii. pp. 381 f.). It is ranked with the catholic epistles in the Muratorian Canon,† which also bears witness to the early (Jerome: "nonnulli scriptorum ueterum hunc esse Judæi Philonis affirmant") belief that it was composed by Philo; the words ("*ab amicis* Salomonis in honorem ipsius scripta") are probably a mistranslation of ὑπὸ Φίλωνος. Proofs of its use and authority drift right across the early Christian literature. The earliest are in Paul (cp. Bleek, *SK.*, 1833, pp. 340–344, and E. Grafe's essay on "das Verhältniss d. paulin. Schriften zur Sapientia Solomonis," in *ThA.* pp. 251–286), whose ideas upon predestination, the nature of idolatry, and heathenism, in Ro $1^{20f.}$ and $9^{19f.}$ especially, reveal a study of this book‡ (cp. Resch, *Paulinismus*, pp. 608–609; Sanday and Headlam's "Romans," *ICC.* pp. 51 f., 266 f.). Echoes of it are audible in Hebrews (1^{3}=Sap $7^{25f.}$, $3^{3f.}$=Sap $13^{3f.}$, 4^{12}=Sap $7^{23f.}$ etc.), 1 Peter (1^{4}=Sap 3^{13} 4^{2} 8^{20}, 1^{7}=Sap 3^{6} etc.), and James, while Clemens Romanus twice alludes to passages from it (3^{4}=Sap 2^{24}, 27^{5}=Sap 11^{22} 12^{12}). Beyond a

---

* For Akiba, see Graetz's *Gnosticismus und Judenthum*, pp. 119 f.

† The conjecture *ut* for *et* is improbable.

‡ For another literary derivation of Ro 1^{29-31}, see Rendel Harris, *The Teaching of the Apostles* (1887), pp. 82–87.

phrase or two—*e.g.* 15^{8} (*τὸ τῆς ψυχῆς ἀπαιτηθεὶς χρέος*) = Lk 12^{20}—there is no clear trace of Sap in the synoptic gospels. But 9^{1} (*ὁ ποιήσας τὰ πάντα ἐν λόγῳ σου*) = Jn 1^{3} may be a reminiscence, as also 8^{19-21} = Jn 1^{13}. We may compare also the functions of the Spirit in 16^{8} (*ἐλέγξει τὸν κόσμον περὶ ἁμαρτίας καὶ περὶ δικαιοσύνης καὶ περὶ κρίσεως*) with Sap 1^{3-8} (*δοκιμαζομένη τε ἡ δύναμις ἐλέγχει τοὺς ἄφρονας . . . ἅγιον γὰρ πνεῦμα ἐλεγχθήσεται ἐπελθούσης ἀδικίας*), the reiteration of *ἔλεγχος* as the doom of the wicked (Sap 1^{8} 4^{20} 18^{5} = Jn 3^{20}), the reproof of an uneasy conscience by goodness (Sap 2^{14} *ἐγένετο ἡμῖν εἰς ἔλεγχον ἐννοιῶν ἡμῶν. βαρύς ἐστιν ἡμῖν καὶ βλεπόμενος . . . καὶ ἀλαζονεύεται πατέρα θεόν* = Jn 3^{20} and 7^{7} also 5^{18} *ἐζήτουν οἱ Ἰουδαῖοι ἀποκτεῖναι αὐτόν, ὅτι . . . πατέρα ἴδιον ἔλεγεν τὸν θεόν*), the collocation of death and the devil (Sap 2^{24} = Jn 8^{44}), the inscrutability of heavenly things (Jn $3^{12f.}$ = Sap 9^{16} *τὰ δὲ ἐν οὐρανοῖς τίς ἐξιχνίασεν ;*), the claim of the righteous to know God (Sap 2^{13} *ἐπαγγέλλεται γνῶσιν ἔχειν θεοῦ* = Jn 8^{55} 7^{29}), the safety of the righteous in God's hand (Sap 3^{1} = Jn 10^{28-30}), the knowledge of the truth (Sap 3^{9} = Jn 8^{31}), the authority of evil magistrates ($6^{3f.}$ = Jn 19^{10-11}), love and obedience (Sap 6^{18} of wisdom, *ἀγάπη δὲ τήρησις νόμων αὐτῆς* = Jn $15^{10.14}$, 14^{15} = 1 Jn 5^{3} *αὕτη ἐστιν ἡ ἀγάπη τοῦ θεοῦ, ἵνα τὰς ἐντολὰς αὐτοῦ τηρῶμεν*), knowledge of God equivalent to eternal life (15^{3} = Jo 17^{3}), and knowledge of divine things as an endowment of the Spirit (9^{13-17} = Jn 16^{12-14}). Ewald, an excellent judge in matters of style, felt in the nervous energy of the author of Wisdom, as well as in the depth of some of his conceptions, a certain premonition of the Fourth gospel, "like a warm rustle of the spring, ere its time is fully come." (*d*) The use of Philo in Barnabas (cp. Heinisch, *Der Einfluss Philos auf die älteste christliche Exegese*, 1908, pp. 36 f.) is not quite so clear as in Clemens Romanus and Josephus,* but the reminiscences in Hebrews (cp. especially Siegfried's *Philo von Alex. als Ausleger des AT*, 321 f. ; Pfleiderer, *Urc*. ii. 198 f. ; von Soden, *HC*. iii. 5–6 ; Ménégoz, *La Théologie de l'épître aux Hébreux* (1895), 197 f. : Rendall, *Theology of Hebrew Christians*, pp. 58–62, and Büchel in *SK*., 1906, 572 f.) are obvious ; *e.g.* the same use of the allegorical method, the same belief in the verbal inspiration of the LXX, and the same phraseology about the Logos † (though the conception is naturally different). By a characteristically Philonic method (cp. Siegfried's *Philo*, pp. 179 f.) the writer finds a religious significance in the very silence of the OT ; thus the absence of any allusion to the parents of Melchizedek (7^{3}) is as pregnant to him as the similar lack of any reference to Sarah's mother is to the Alexandrian thinker (*quis rerum div. hær*. 12 ; *de ebrietate*, 14), and the titles of Melchizedek suggest religious truths to him no less than to Philo (*leg. alleg*. iii. 25) and to Josephus (*Bell. Jud*. vi. 10, *Ant*. i. 10. 2). The quotation in 13^{5} occurs only, in this form, in *de Conf. Ling*. 32 ; and there are verbal echoes, *e.g.*, in 3^{1} (= *de Somniis*, i. 38, *ὁ μὲν δὴ μέγας ἀρχιερεύς*), 3^{2} (= *de plant*. 16 *ad finem*), 3^{5} (= *leg. alleg*. iii. 81, *Μωσῆς μαρτυρούμενος ὅτι ἐστὶ πιστὸς ἐν ὅλῳ τῷ οἴκῳ*), 5^{8} (= *de Somniis*, ii. 15, *ὁ παθὼν ἀκριβῶς ἔμαθεν*), 5^{9} (= *de agric.*

* Cp. Harnack, *ACL*. i. 1. 859 f. ; Windisch, *Die Frömmigkeit Philos und ihre Bedeutung für das Christentum* (1909), pp. 96–135.

† On the transference of the Philonic Logos-predicates to Christ, see Aal's *Der Logos*, ii. pp. 38 f.

22, *ἑτέροις αἴτιος σωτηρίας γενόμενος*), 7^{1-2} [*] (=*leg. alleg.* **iii. 25**), and 10^{3} *ἀνάμνησις ἁμαρτιῶν* (=*de plant.* 15, *de vit. Mos.* iii. 10). The allegorical method of interpretation (cp. Holtzmann in *ARW.*, 1900, 341 f., and Leipoldt, *GK.* i. pp. 20 f.) which received a powerful impetus from the Alexandrian Judaism, presupposed a keen appreciation of the letter of the ancient Scriptures, which was not confined to Hebrews; cp. *e.g.* the haggadic and genuinely Philonic touches in the haggada of 1 Co 10^{1-11}, 2 Co 3^{7-18}, Gal 4^{22-25}, the pressing of the singular in Gal $3^{16.\ 19}$ (cp. Ro $4^{13.\ 16f.}$ 9^{8}) in the Philonic spirit of attaching significance to numbers, and a passage like 1 Co 9^{9-10} (cp. Philo, *de vict. offer.* 1, *οὐ γὰρ ὑπὲρ τῶν ἀλόγων ὁ νόμος, ἀλλ' ὑπὲρ τῶν νοῦν καὶ λόγον ἐχόντων*). Room must be left, however, for the possibility that in Hebrews, as even in Paul, this allegorical method of treating the OT may have been due as much to the well-known predilections of contemporary Stoicism as to Philonism or rabbinism. (*e*) The possibility that Josephus has been used by some NT writers is raised in connection with 2 Peter, the Fourth gospel, and Luke. (i.) In the preface to the *Antiquities* (§ 4) he observes that Moses considered it of primary importance Θεοῦ *φύσιν κατανοῆσαι* (2 P 1^{4}) in order to promote the virtue of his readers (*εἰς ἀρετῆς λόγον*, cp. 2 P 1^{5}). While other legislators followed myths (*τοῖς μύθοις ἐξακολουθήσαντες*=2 P 1^{16} *οὐ μύθοις ἐξακολουθήσαντες*), Moses held that God possessed perfect virtue (*τὴν ἀρετὴν ἔχοντα τὸν θεόν* = 2 P 1^{3}), so that the Pentateuch contains nothing *πρὸς τὴν μεγαλειότητα τοῦ θεοῦ ἀνάρμοστον* (= 2 P 1^{16}). Similarly in the last address of Moses (iv. 8. 2), besides isolated expressions and phrases like *τοιάδε* (= 2 P 1^{17} *τοιᾶσδε*), *μνήμην* (= 2 P 1^{15}), *νομίμων τῶν παρόντων* (= 2 P 1^{12}), *εὐσέβεια* (= 2 P 1^{6} 3^{11}), *καταφρονεῖν* (= 2 P 2^{10}), and *κοινωνοί* (= 2 P 1^{4}), Moses declares *δεῖ με τοῦ ζῆν ἀπελθεῖν* (= 2 P 1^{14}) . . . *οὐ μέλλω* (= 2 P 1^{12}) *βοηθὸς ὑμῖν ἔσεσθαι* . . . *δίκαιον ἡγησάμην* (= 2 P 1^{13} *δίκαιον δὲ ἡγοῦμαι*), warns them against the abuse of *ἐλευθερία* (2 P 2^{19}), and uses *ἔξοδος* and *ἀνάμνησις* and *βεβαία* close together (cp. 2 P $1^{10.\ 12.\ 15}$). Compare further *εὐάλωτοι* with *ἅλωσιν* (2 P 2^{12}), *Bell. Jud.* vii. 8. 7 with 2 P 1^{1-3}, ii. 9. 1 with *λήθην λαβών* (2 P 1^{9}), iii. 9. 3 (*τολμηταὶ καὶ θανάτου καταφρονοῦντες* = 2 P 2^{10}), *Antiq.* iv. 6. 7–8 with 2 P 2^{3} 2^{20}, and xi. 6. 12 (*οἷς καλῶς ποιήσετε μὴ προσέχοντες*) with 2 P 1^{14} (*ᾧ καλῶς ποιεῖτε προσέχοντες*); while 2 P $3^{5f.}$ explicitly alludes to the Jewish legend (cp. *Antiq.* i. 2. 2; Bousset in *ZNW.*, 1902, 45) that Adam predicted the twofold destruction of the world by the deluge and by fire. Further linguistic proofs are led by Krenkel (*Josephus u. Lucas*, pp. 348 f.) and Dr. E. A. Abbott (*Exp.*[2] iii. 49–63, *Diat.* 1116 f.), and rejected by Warfield (*Southern Presbyterian Review*, 1882, pp. 45 f., 1883, pp. 390 f.), Salmon (*INT.* 497 f.), Chase (*DB.* iii. 814), Zahn (*INT.* ii. 291), and Mayor (*Jude and 2 Peter*, pp. cxxvii–cxxx). Farrar (*Exp.*[2] iii. 401–423, *Exp.*[3] viii. 58–69), who recognises a literary connexion, inclines to place the dependence on the side of Josephus. The occurrence in Josephus of several unusual words and phrases which are characteristic of 2 Peter would not of itself be decisive, as some also occur in Philo and elsewhere. Even the common use of midrashic traditions does not involve literary filiation. But

---

[*] Of the brazen serpent's effect on the beholders (*τοῖς θεασαμένοις*, cp Jn 3^{14}).

a number of the coincidences of language and style occur not only in the compass of two short paragraphs of Josephus, but in a sequence and connection which is not dissimilar; and, even after allowance is made for the widespread use of rhetorical commonplaces, these coincidences can hardly be dismissed as fortuitous. Their weight tells in favour of the hypothesis that the author of 2 Peter was familiar with Josephus,—an inference which is the more plausible as in any case the epistle belongs to the second century. (ii.) One indication of the connection between Josephus and the Fourth gospel occurs in Jn 4 (cf. Krenkel, *op. cit.* 347 f.). Josephus (*Ant.* ii. 11. 1, developing Ex 2^{15}) describes Moses as arriving at a city, καθεσθεὶς ἐπί τινος φρέατος ἐκ τοῦ κόπου καὶ τῆς ταλαιπωρίας ἠρέμει, μεσημβρίας οὔσης, οὐ πόρρω τῆς πόλεως, uses in the immediate context the term θρέμματα (Jn 4^{12}), and (*Ant.* ii. 15. 3) employs the phrase ὑπὸ τῆς ὁδοιπορίας κεκοπωμένων (cp. Jn 4^{6} κεκοπιακὼς ἐκ τῆς ὁδοιπορίας). Cf., further, Jos. *Ant.* xii. 1–10 and xiii. 3. 4 with Jn 4^{20}. The curt tone of the discussion in $11^{48f.}$ also answers to the tradition preserved by Josephus (*B. J.* ii. 8. 14), that "the behaviour of the Sadducees to one another is rather rude, and their intercourse with their own party is as brusque as if they were talking to strangers"; and in *Antiq.* ix. 14. 3 (cf. Jn 4^{17}), Josephus not only explains that each of the five nations of 2 K $17^{30f.}$ who settled in Samaria brought a god of its own (ἕκαστοι κατ' ἔθνος ἴδιον θεὸν εἰς τὴν Σαμάρειαν κομίσαντες, πέντε δ' ἦσαν κτλ.), but that they denied the right of a Jew to expect any favour at their hands (=Jn 4^{9}). The words of 4^{20} also recall *Ant.* xii. 1. 1 (the Jerusalemites τὸ παρ' αὐτοῖς ἱερὸν ἅγιον εἶναι λεγόντων . . . τῶν δὲ Σαμαρειτῶν εἰς τὸ Γαριζεὶν ὄρος κελευόντων) and xiii. 3. 4 (the quarrel of the Alexandrian Jews with the Samaritans οἱ τὸ ἐν Γαριζεὶν ὄρει προσεκύνουν ἱερὸν οἰκοδομηθὲν κτλ.). The coincidence between 10^{22-23} and Jos. *B. J.* i. 21. 10, where the street of Antioch in Syria is described as equipped πρὸς τὰς τῶν ὑετῶν ἀποφυγὰς ἰσομήκει στοᾷ, is of no importance, though Kreyenbühl (ii. 498 f.) makes use of it as a local touch to prove his theory that the gospel was composed by Menander of Antioch; the same may be said, *e.g.*, of 19^{23}=*Ant.* iii. 7. 4 (the high priest's robe οὐκ ἐκ δυοῖν περιτμημάτων . . . φάρσος δ' ἐν ἐπίμηκες ὑφασμένον κτλ.). (iii.) It is in relation to the Lucan writings, however, that the problem has been most keenly agitated (first by J. B. Ott, *Spicilegium seu excerpta ex Flavio Josepho ad NT. illustrationem*, 1741, and J. T. Krebbs, *Observationes in NT. e Flavio Josepho*, 1755). Apart from resemblances in vocabulary and style, which are not of primary significance, one or two of the statements common to both are worth noticing. Luke, *e.g.* dates the opening of John's mission (3^{1-2}) in A.D. 28 or 29 by Λυσανίου τῆς Ἀβιληνῆς τετρααρχοῦντος; but as Lysanias had been executed in 36 B.C., the alternatives are to postulate the existence of some younger Lysanias (so, *e.g.*, Schürer, *HJP.* i. 2. 335 f., after Wieseler's *Beiträge zur Wurdigung d. Evangelien*, 1869, 194 f., and S. Davidson, *INT.* i. 214 f.), or to assume a chronological inaccuracy on the part of Luke. In the latter case, the error may be explained from the fact that the territory of Lysanias retained his name even after his death (so, *e.g.*, Wellhausen); or from Josephus, who in *Ant.* xx. 7. 138, relates that in A.D. 53, Agrippa II. acquired among other territories (including Trachonitis) Abila, Λυσανίου δ' αὕτη ἐγεγόνει τετραρχία. As in A.D. 37 it had been given to Agrippa I. (*Ant.* xviii. 6. 10), the theory is that Luke (whose language resembles *Ant.* xviii. 4. 6) inferred from Josephus that it was the tetrarchy of Lysanias when John the Baptist came forward. Apart from some such hypothesis, it is difficult to account for the mention of Lysanias and Abilene at all in this connection. The passage in Josephus, on the other hand, explains its collocation with Trachonitis and also the anachronism about Lysanias. So Keim, ii. 384 f., Krenkel (*Josephus u. Lucas*, 1894, 95–98), Schmiedel (*EBi.* 2840–2844), Burkitt (*Gospel History and its Transmission*, pp. 109 f.), and Holtzmann (*HC.* i. p. 325: "der 3. Evglst sich einigermaassen im Josephus umgesehen habe, ohne aber im Stande gewesen zu sein, aus den zahllosen Notizen der weitläufigen Schriften desselben ein klares Bild von der politischen Lage Palästinas zur Zeit Jesu zu gewinnen"). There may have been another Lysanias, but his existence is at best conjectural, and Josephus certainly knew nothing of him. In Ac $5^{36f.}$ again, Luke makes Gamaliel speak thus to the council: *in days gone by* (*πρὸ τούτων τῶν ἡμερῶν*) *ἀνέστη Θευδᾶς λέγων εἶναι τινα ἑαυτὸν . . . ὃς ἀνηρέθη καὶ πάντες ὅσοι ἐπείθοντο αὐτῷ διελύθησαν . . . μετὰ τοῦτον ἀνέστη Ἰούδας ὁ Γαλιλαῖος ἐν ταῖς ἡμέραις τῆς ἀπογραφῆς καὶ ἀπέστησεν λαὸν ὀπίσω αὐτοῦ.* The parallel passages in Josephus (*Ant.* xx. 5. 1: When Fadus was procurator of Judæa, a charlatan named Θευδᾶς *πείθει τὸν πλεῖστον ὄχλον . . . προφήτης γὰρ ἔλεγεν εἶναι.* Fadus, however, dispatched a squadron of cavalry *ἥτις . . . πολλοὺς . . . ἀνεῖλεν*; and *Ant.* xx. 5. 2, *πρὸς τουτοῖς δὲ καὶ οἱ παῖδες Ἰουδᾶ τοῦ Γαλιλαίου ἀνήχθησαν τοῦ τὸν λαὸν ἀπό Ῥωμαίων ἀποστήσαντος Κυρινίου τῆς Ἰουδαίας τιμητεύοντος*) leave little reasonable doubt that both stories relate to the same Theudas, and, unless recourse is had to the desperate expedient of conjecturing that the name in Josephus (Blass) or in Acts (B. Weiss) is a later interpolation, it is highly probable that Luke's acquaintance with the passage in Josephus led him to mention Theudas and Judas loosely in an order which is not only inverted but out of keeping with the situation, since the revolt of Theudas did not take place till about at least ten years after Gamaliel is supposed to have spoken. The order in Josephus is natural; Luke's is an inaccurate reflection of it,* as even the phraseology suggests, for the coincidences are too remarkable to be accidental in this case. "Non facile adducimur ut casui tribuamus Theudæ Judæque apud utrumque scriptorem junctam commemorationem" (Blass). Why Luke remembered the order and some of the phrases and yet attributed to Judas the fate of his sons, we can no longer explain; but this difficulty does not invalidate the hypothesis. A third Lucan instance has been found in Ac $11^{28f.}$ = *Ant.* xx. 5. 2.

JOSEPHUS.	LUKE.
ἐπὶ τούτοις δὲ καὶ τὸν μέγαν λιμὸν κατὰ τὴν Ἰουδαίαν συνέβη γενέσθαι, καθ' ὃν καὶ ἡ βασίλισσα Ἑλένη πολλῶν χρημάτων ὠνησαμένη σῖτον ἀπὸ τοῦ Αἰγύπτου διένειμε τοῖς ἀπορουμένοις.	*Ἄγαβος ἐσήμανεν . . . λιμὸν μεγάλην μέλλειν ἔσεσθαι ἐφ' ὅλην τὴν οἰκουμένην, ἥτις ἐγένετο ἐπὶ Κλαυδίου τῶν δὲ μαθητῶν καθὼς εὐπορεῖτο τις κτλ.*

---

* So Krenkel (*op. cit.* pp. 162–174), Schmiedel (*EBi.* 5049–5056), and Burkitt (*Gospel History and its Transmission*, 109 f.), besides Wendt and H. J. Holtzmann in their editions of Acts (cp. Sonntag, *SK.*, 1837, 622–652).

The verbal resemblances here, however, are not significant. Descriptions of famine relief, as of revolt, must employ similar language. But if the former case of dependence be granted, there is a likelihood that Luke also preserves in this story another reminiscence of his younger contemporary. Other parallels occur, *e.g.*, in the account of the disappearance of Moses in a cloud (*Ant.* iv. 8. 38) = Ac $1^{5f.}$, the prologue Lk 1^{1-4} = *Apion.* i. 10, Lk 2^{46-47} = *Vita* 2, Lk $19^{41f.}$ = *B. J.* vii. 5 (Titus bemoaning the fate of Jerusalem), Ac 16^{8-10} = *Ant.* xi. 8 (Alexander's vision), Ac $20^{20f.}$ = *B. J.* ii. 16 (Agrippa's speech to the Jews). The whole question is argued, in favour of Luke's dependence, by Keim (*Aus dem Urchristentum*, 1878, i. 1–21), Krenkel, Holtzmann (*ZWT.*, 1873, 85 f., 1877, 535 f., 1880, 121 f.), Jüngst (*Quellen d. Apgeschichte*, 201 f.), Schmiedel (as above), Clemen (*SK.*, 1895, 335 f., also *Die Apostelgeschichte*, 1905, pp. 15–21), and Burkitt; see, further, Cassel in *Fortnightly Review* (1877), 485–509, and *SR.* 605 f. The opposite position is held by Schürer (*ZWT.*, 1876, 574 f.), Gloel (*Die jüngste Kritik d. Galaterbriefes*, 64 f.), Belser (*TQ.*, 1895, 634 f., 1896, 1–78), Blass (*SK.*, 1896, 459 f.), Ramsay (*Was Christ born at Bethlehem?* 1898, pp. 252 f.), J. A. Cross (*ET.* xi. 538–540), Zahn (*INT.* § 61), Jacquier (*INT.* iii. 101–108), and Stanton (*GHD.* ii. 263 f.). The last-named inclines to admit the case for a knowledge of the *Jewish War* (273–274). (*f*) That a pre-Christian Apocalypse of Elijah (cp. Schürer's *GJV.*[3] iii. 267 f.; Harnack, *ACL.* i. 853 f.; Ropes, *Sprüche Jesu* pp. 19 f.) was quoted in 1 Co 2^{9} and Eph 5^{14}, has been known since Origen's (*in Matth.* 27^{9}, "In nullo regulari libro hoc positum inuenitur, nisi in Secretis Eliæ prophetæ") allusion to the former passage (cp. Jerome on Is 64^{4} and *Epp.* 57^{9}) and the remark of Epiphanius (*haer.* 42, p. 478), πόθεν τῷ ἀποστόλῳ τὸ· διὸ καὶ λέγει· ἀλλὰ ἀπὸ τῆς παλαιᾶς δῆλον διαθήκης; τοῦτο δὲ ἐμφέρεται παρὰ τῷ Ἡλίᾳ) on the latter, for in 1 Co 2^{9} Paul is not loosely citing Is 64^{4} (65^{16}) (cf. Vollmer's *Alttest. Citate bei Paulus*, 44–48, and *NTA.* 42–44), and it is impossible (cf. *ACL.* ii. 1. 571–572) to suppose with Zahn (*GK.* ii. 801 f.) that the patristic references are to a second century writing which was fabricated in order to clear up the ambiguous Pauline quotations. It is this apocalypse, and not 1 Co 2^{9}, which is further quoted in *Asc. Isa.* 11^{34}, Clem. Rom. 34^{8} and Clem. Alex. *Protrept.* x. 94. A fresh fragment has been discovered recently by de Bruyne (*Revue Bénédictine*, 1908, pp. 149 f.) embedded in an apocryphal epistle of Titus (eighth cent. MS). The fragment begins as follows: "Denique testatur propheta Helias uidisse. Ostendit, inquit, mihi angelus domini conuallem altam quæ uocatur gehenna, ardensque sulphore et bitumine; et in illo loco sunt multæ animæ peccatorum et taliter ibi cruciantur diuersis tormentis" (whereupon follows a Dantesque description of the future punishments assigned to various classes of sinners, on the general lines of the Apocalypse of Peter). It is impossible to determine whether Paul (in 1 Co 2^{9}) regarded this apocalypse as γραφή, or simply quoted its language as that of a current religious writing, or cited it as canonical by an error of memory. The occurrence of a cognate citation in the Latin (and Slavonic) versions of *Asc. Isa.* 11^{34} explains Jerome's statement that the "testimonium" of 1 Co 2^{9} was contained in the *Ascensio Isaiæ* as well as in the *Apocalypsis Eliæ*. (*g*) Eph 5^{14} has been variously referred to an apocryphon of Jeremiah (Euthalius), to an apocryphal book cited inadvertently as γραφή (Meyer), to a paraphrase of Is $60^{1. 19-20}$, or to a

Christian hymn. The last hypothesis (suggested by Theodoret, and advocated, *e.g.*, by Bleek and Storr) is plausible, on the score of the rhythmical structure of the lines. But ὁ Χριστός (=the messiah) would not be improbable in a Jewish writing, and, even if it were, it might be conjectured that the writer of Ephesians substituted it for the ὁ θεός of the original (Harnack). (*h*) Hermas (*Vis.* ii. 3. 4) quotes the book of Eldad and Modad (ἐγγὺς Κύριος τοῖς ἐπιστρεφομένοις, ὡς γέγραπται ἐν τῷ Ἐλδὰδ καὶ Μωδάτ, τοῖς προφητεύσασιν ἐν τῇ ἐρήμῳ τῷ λαῷ), and the προφητικὸς λόγος cited in 2 Clem. 11^{2-4} (Clem. Rom. 23^{3}) is probably from the same source (so, *e.g.*, Lightfoot, Spitta, Holtzmann), perhaps also the γραφή reproduced in Jas 4^{5-6}. To these have been added, though on precarious grounds, the citations in Clem. Rom. 46^{2} (γέγραπται γάρ· κολλᾶσθε τοῖς ἁγίοις, ὅτι οἱ κολλώμενοι αὐτοῖς ἁγιασθήσονται) and 17^{6} (καὶ πάλιν [Moses] λέγει, Ἐγὼ δέ εἰμι ἀτμὶς ἀπὸ κύθρας, cp. Jas 4^{14}), the latter of which Hilgenfeld prefers to assign to the lost conclusion of the *Assumptio Mosis*. It was a book of 400 στίχοι, which Nicephorus ranked with Enoch, etc., among the ἀπόκρυφα of the OT. According to rabbinic tradition (reproduced in the Palestinian Targums), Eldad and Modad (Nu 11^{24-29}) were humble men who received a greater measure of grace directly from God than the seventy elders; their prophetic gift was more lasting and far-reaching (it foresaw the attack of Gog and Magog), and, unlike the seventy, they reached the promised land. If this tradition represents the spirit of the midrashic prophecy in question, the contents of the latter may be taken to tally with the above citations in the early Christian literature, as Spitta argues (*Urc.* ii. 121–123; see, further, Weinel, *HNA*. i. 208 f., 229, and M. R. James, *TS*. ii. 3. 174 f.). (*i*) The earliest quotation from Tobit is in 2 Clem. 16^{4} where 12^{8-9} is reproduced, though even closer citations occur in Polykarp, *ad Phil.* 10^{2} (=To 4^{10} 12^{9}) and Did 1^{2} =To 4^{15}). Origen and Clement of Alexandria quote it more than once by name as γραφή. Its presence in the Greek Bible helped to popularise it, together with other writings of this class, such as Judith (first referred to in early Christian literature by Clem. Rom. 55), among the early Christians, Catholic and Gnostic alike, though the Palestinian Jews appear to have excluded it from their Canon in the second century (Origen, *ad Afric.* 13: Ἑβραῖοι τῷ Τωβίᾳ οὐ χρῶνται οὐδὲ τῇ Ἰουδήθ· οὐδὲ γὰρ ἔχουσιν αὐτὰ ἐν ἀποκρύφοις ἑβραϊστί). (*j*) 2 Maccabees was evidently in the library of the author of Hebrews, as is plain from a passage like He $11^{34f.}$; cp. *e.g.* ^{34}=2 Mac 8^{24}, ^{35} (ἄλλοι δὲ ἐτυμπανίσθησαν κτλ.)=$6^{19.28}$ (ἐπὶ τὸ τύμπανον) and 6^{30} $7^{9.14}$, ^{36}=$7^{1.10}$, ^{38}=5^{27} 6^{11} 10^{6}, also 10^{31}=2 Mac 6^{26}, 12^{7}=2 Mac 6^{12}, 13^{6}=2 Mac 10^{30} etc. It was also known to Hermas (*Vis.* i. 3. 4, *Mand.* xii. 4. 2). (*k*) The *Assumptio Mosis* has not only preserved the legend mentioned in Jude ^{9}, but supplied some of the phrases in v.^{16} of that epistle (cp. 5^{5} erunt illis temporibus mirantes personæ, 7^{7} quærulosi, 7^{9} et manus eorum et mentes immunda tractantes et os eorum loquetur ingentia); for other coincidences, cp. *e.g.* 17=2 Co 11^{14}. (*l*) The uncertainty attaching to the date and origin of the Διαθήκη Ἰώβ renders any inferences from its use in or of the NT problematical. The probabilities, however, favour a pre-Christian period for its composition (so, *e.g.*, Kohler in *Semitic Studies in honour of Kohut*, 1897, 264–338, and Spitta, *Urc.* iii. 2. 141–206), with echoes in the epistle of James, *e.g.* 1^{13}=Test. Job 4, 1^{9-12}=Test. Job 32–33, 41, 1^{17}=Test. Job 33, ἡ δόξα αὐτοῦ ἐν τῷ αἰῶνί ἐστιν τοῦ ἀπαραλλάκτου), 5^{2}=Test. Job 43, 5^{4}= Test. Job 12 (*ἐργάτης εἶ ἄνθρωπος προσδοκῶν καὶ ἀναμένων σου τὸν μισθόν· ἀνάγκην ἔχεις λαβεῖν· καὶ οὐκ ἐῶν μισθὸν μισθωτοῦ ἀπομεῖναι*), 5^{11}=Test. Job 1 and 26 (also 4), and 5^{13}=Test. Job 16, 14 (*καὶ ἔψαλλον αὐταῖς κτλ.*). The evidence for the use of this midrash elsewhere in the NT is slight. The most striking coincidences perhaps are Lk 2^{7}=Test. Job 40, Apoc 2^{10} (*γίνου πιστὸς ἄχρι θανάτου, καὶ δώσω σοι τὸν στέφανον τῆς ζωῆς*)=Test. Job 4–5 (where, to the angel's promise of a *στέφανος* for his endurance, Job replies: *ἄχρι θανάτου ὑπομείνω καὶ οὐ μὴ ἀναποδίσω*), Apoc 7^{2-3}=Test. Job 5 (Job sealed by the angel before the devil attacks him), the occurrence of *ἀκωλύτως* as final (Ac 28^{31}= Test. Job 45), of *τὰ βάθη τοῦ κυρίου* in Test. Job 37, and of *τὰ ἐπουράνια* in Test. Job 36, 38 (= Eph 1^{3} etc.), Test. Job 27 (Satan says, *ἐγὼ δὲ εἰμὶ πνεῦμα*)= Eph 6^{12}, Test. Job 48 (*καὶ ἀνέλαβεν ἄλλην καρδίαν, μηκέτι τὰ τῆς γῆς φρονεῖν*)= Col 3^{2}, Test. Job 37 (where Job confesses his hope is not in riches but *ἐπὶ τῷ θεῷ τῷ ζῶντι*)=1 Ti 6^{17}; the analogy between the synoptic temptation-narratives (and the visit of the magi) and the older midrash is naturally close at several points, and there are occasional verbal identities which are more than fortuitous (*e.g.* Jn 3^{12}=Test. Job 38, Jn 13^{27}=Test. Job 7, *ὃ ποιεῖς ποίησον*, cp. context). (*m*) The post-exilic book from which the quotation in Lk 11^{49-51} (*καὶ ἡ Σοφία τοῦ θεοῦ εἶπεν κτλ.*) is taken (cp. 7^{35}, Sap 7^{27} etc.) has not survived. That the words are originally a citation, and not meant (so recently Grill, *Untersuchungen über d. Entstehung d. vierten Evangeliums*, 179 f.) to represent Jesus speaking of himself as the Wisdom of God, is fairly plain from v.^{51b} where *ναί, λέγω ὑμῖν, ἐκζητηθήσεται κτλ.* take up the foregoing *ἐκζητηθῇ*. Luke, in putting the words into the mouth of Jesus, has altered the original *σοφοὺς καὶ γραμματεῖς* (Mt 23^{34}) into *ἀποστόλους*, but the background of a Wisdom-cycle (Bacon, *DCG.* ii. 827 f.) is still visible, and the quotation probably came from some Jewish writing of the Wisdom-group which is no longer extant (so, *e.g.* Ewald, Bleek, Paulus, Weizsäcker, Pfleiderer, Scholten, J. Weiss). (*n*) The *γραφή* quoted in Jn 7^{38} (*ὁ πιστεύων εἰς ἐμέ, καθὼς εἶπεν ἡ γραφή, ποταμοὶ ἐκ τῆς κοιλίας αὐτοῦ ῥεύσουσιν ὕδατος ζῶντος*) cannot be explained satisfactorily from any of the OT parallels or rabbinic traditions, and probably was derived from an apocryphal source no longer extant (so, *e.g.*, Whiston, Semler, Weizsäcker, Ewald). A. J. Edmunds (*Buddhist Texts quoted as Scripture by the Gospel of John*, 1906, pp. 9 f.) finds the original in the Buddhist Paṭisambhidā, i. 53 ("What is the Tathāgato's knowledge of the twin miracle? In this case, the Tathāgato works a twin miracle unrivalled by disciples; from his upper body proceeds a flame of fire, and from his lower body proceeds a torrent of water"), but the citation is drawn in all likelihood from the same Wisdom-literature as that employed in Lk $11^{49f.}$ (cp. Bacon, *DCG.* ii. 829). (*o*) The origin of the allusion in Mt 2^{23} (*ὅπως πληρωθῇ τὸ ῥηθὲν διὰ τῶν προφητῶν ὅτι Ναζωραῖος κληθήσεται*) has not yet been identified in any pre-Christian writing, canonical or uncanonical (Resch). The use of the plural (*προφητῶν*) might suggest * a loose summary of OT prophecies (so, recently, Clemen, *Religionsgeschichtliche Erklärung des NT*, 238–239), though the use of *ὅτι* in 26^{54} is hardly a parallel. In this

* So Jerome (ostendit se non uerba de scripturis sumpsisse sed sensum) as at 26^{64}.

case Ναζωραῖος is substituted for Ναζαρηνός by a kind of pious paranomasia in order to suggest the messianic term (נֵצֶר, נְצוֹרֵי) of Is 11^{1}, and the paranomasia was probably mediated by the Aramaic equivalent (נִצְרָא) for "branch" or "shoot" (cp. Box, *DCG.* ii. 235–236, and Jeremias, *Babylonisches im NT*, 1905, pp. 46–47). The alternative is to refer the citation to the prophecy of Samson's birth in Jg 13^{5} (Ναζίρ [ἡγιάσμενον Ναζιραῖον, A] θεοῦ ἔσται τὸ παιδάριον κτλ., cp. Mt 1^{21}). (*p*) Halévy, arguing (in *RS.*, 1902, pp. 13–60) that the correct place of the Temptation is after Mk 8^{33} (= Mt 16^{23}), finds that many of the traits in the synoptic narrative are modelled upon the midrash of the *Martyrdom of Isaiah*; but the proofs are not convincing. Even though Tyre and Sidon in that midrash are the refuge of prophets (pp. 44 f.), this would not prove that Mk $7^{24f.}$ was filiated to it. (*q*) The Aḥiḳar-cycle of stories and traditions,* however, has left traces in the NT,† *e.g.* in the parable of the fruitless fig-tree (Lk 13^{6-8}), which contains echoes of the passage in Aḥiḳar: "My son, said Ahikar, be not like the tree which grew near the water and bore no fruits, and when its owner would have cut it down, said, Plant me in another spot, and then, if I bear no fruit, cut me down. But the owner said, Thou art close to the water and yet bearest no fruit; how then wilt thou bear if thou art set elsewhere?" Similarly the parable of the wicked servant (Mt 24^{45-51}) is modelled in part on the legend of the wicked Nadan, who, after gathering his disreputable associates, begins to eat and drink with them, and to maltreat the men and maidservants, till suddenly his uncle Aḥiḳar reappears—whereupon Nadan, detected and rebuked, "swelled up immediately and became like a blown-out bladder. And his limbs swelled, and his legs and his feet and his side, and he was torn, and his belly burst asunder, and his entrails were scattered, and he perished and died. And his latter end was destruction, and he went to hell."‡ The very punishment of flogging (Lk 12^{47}) is the same, for Nadan is bound and then given a thousand lashes on the shoulder and a thousand more on the loins; but the parable (like some later versions of the tradition) modifies the legend by substituting διχοτομεῖν for the conventional, ghastly ending. "As the story was clearly popular, and is also pre-Christian, it would be no very strange thing if the Parable had borrowed a trait or two from it" (M. R. James, *Apocrypha Anecdota*, ii., 1897, p. 158; J. Rendel Harris in *The Story of Aḥikar*, pp. x f.). Such data tend to show that some of the sayings and stories in the evangelic tradition were not simply ætiological in origin or based on OT prophecy, but derived part of their matter as well as of their form occasionally from earlier folk-lore no less than from midrashic models, outside the letter of the OT. Behind the

---

* On their early origin, prior to Tobit, cp. R. Smend's *Alter u. Herkunft des Achikar-Romans* (in *Beihefte zur Zeitschrift für die alt. Wiss.* xiii. 1908).

† Cp. Halévy in *RS.* (1900) pp. 61 f., (1901) pp. 255 f. His arguments in favour of parallel reasoning in the case of Jesus and his adversaries and Aḥiḳar and his enemies are not cogent, but the Aḥiḳar-tale may certainly be allowed to form "one of those interesting Jewish products of the Greek period which facilitated the transformation of the Hebrew Haggada in both of its main growths, rabbinic and Christian."

‡ Or, as To 14^{10} (B) has it, "went down to darkness" (cp. Mt 22^{13} 25^{30}).

early Christian accounts of the death of Judas,* who was, like Nadan, characterised by black ingratitude and treachery (cp. Jn 13^{18}), the Aḥiḳar-tradition may be also conjectured to stand, especially when the manner of Nadan's death (see p. 34) is compared with Ac 1^{18} and with the tale of Papias about Judas's body swelling up. "We need not be surprised if Aḥikar should furnish the key to the genesis of the Judas legends" (Harris, *op. cit.* p. lxv),† particularly if, as in the Armenian, πρησθεὶς be substituted for the awkward πρηνὴς γενόμενος in Ac 1^{18}. Folk-lore of this kind, however, is not the only clue to the Judas stories. Thus, after describing a scoffer at the Hebrew scriptures, Philo adds that he presently committed suicide (*de mut. nomin.* 8, ἐπ' ἀγχόνην ᾖξεν, ἵν' ὁ μιαρὸς καὶ δυσκάθαρτος μηδὲ καθαρῷ θανάτῳ τελευτήσῃ) by hanging, a death appropriate to a polluted person. (*r*) One or two minor and casual citations from ancient literature may be noted in conclusion.‡ The λόγος quoted in Jn 4^{37} (ἄλλος ἐστὶν ὁ σπείρων καὶ ἄλλος ὁ θερίζων) is a loose citation of the common proverb, which occurs also in Pseudo-Diogenes, ii. 62 (cp. Wendland in *Neue Jahrb. f. d. klass. Alt.*, 1902, p. 6 n.). The παροιμία cited in 2 P 2^{22} is either from the Aḥiḳar-cycle (cp. Halévy in *RS.*, 1900, p. 66) or from Herakleitus (cp. Wendland, *SBBA.*, 1898, 788–796); the sow-proverb is quoted also by Clem. Alex. *Protrept.* x. 92. 4, etc., who is closer to the original form (ὕες ἥδονται βορβόρῳ μᾶλλον ἢ καθαρῷ ὕδατι). The sarcastic description of the Cretans in Tit 1^{12} (Κρῆτες ἀεὶ ψεῦσται, κακὰ θηρία, γαστέρες ἀργαί) is a hexameter apparently drawn from the περὶ χρησμῶν of the local philosopher, Epimenides (cp. Diels in *SBBA.*, 1891, 387–403, and J. R. Harris in *Exp.*^{7} ii. 305–317), who attacked the Cretan claim that Zeus lay buried in Crete. Callimachus quotes the first three words. The famous apologue of Men. Agrippa was probably in Paul's mind when he wrote 1 Co 12^{12-27}, and the iambic trimeter in 1 Co 15^{33} φθείρουσιν ἤθη χρήσθ' ὁμιλίαι κακαί) originally lay either in Euripides or Menander; but the hexameter in Ja 1^{17} (πᾶσα δόσις ἀγαθὴ καὶ πᾶν δώρημα τέλειον), where ἀγαθή and τέλειον are unconvincingly taken by Fischer (*Philologus*, 1891, 377–379) as predicates (*sc.* ἐστίν), is of unknown origin. On the other hand, the line of poetry put into Paul's mouth at Athens, in Ac 17^{28} (ὡς καί τινες τῶν καθ' ὑμᾶς ποιητῶν εἰρήκασιν· τοῦ γὰρ καὶ γένος ἐσμέν), is probably from his fellow-countryman Aratus (cp. Hoole, *The Classical Element in the NT*, pp. 82–84, and Blass' note), if not from the hymn of Cleanthes.

---

* The connection of the Judas stories with the Aḥiḳar tradition is decidedly closer than the filiation which Halévy prefers (*RS.*, 1902, 46 f.) to find between them and the machinations of Bechira, the Samaritan accuser of Isaiah in the midrash. His explanation of Ἰσκαριώτης as a corruption of Σιχαριώτης (a native of the Samaritan Sichor) is highly precarious.

† Cp., further, *AJT.*, 1900, 490–513, for proof that Mt $27^{3f.}$ and Ac $1^{16f.}$ rest on the Aḥiḳar-legend (*EBi.* 2627). The historicity of both stories is upheld by Schlatter in his *Zur Topographie und Geschichte Palästinas* (1893), 217 f.

‡ Further materials for the influence of Jewish apocalypses on the NT and on early Christian literature in general are collected by Prof. R. H. Charles in his editions of *The Apocalypse of Baruch* (1896), *The Assumption of Moses* (1897), *The Ascension of Isaiah* (1900), *The Book of Jubilees* (1902), and the

IV.

STRUCTURE AND COMPOSITION OF NT.

"Time's glory," according to the Shakespearean line, "is to blot old books and alter their contents." This is not a glory in which the literary critic can be expected to rejoice. It has imposed on him the task of reconstructing the original form of several ancient documents, and of allowing for processes of interpolation, displacement, and compilation.*

(i.) Interpolation † means the addition of passages to an original composition, or the incorporation of later verses, sections, and even words, in a writing which has come down from some earlier period, either (*a*) at the hands of the author himself, or (*b*) by subsequent editors of the volume, after the writer's death, or (*c*) by scribes (or editors) of the text. Like other fragments of ancient literature, ‡ the early Christian records were liable to such handling, though the dimensions of this form of textual corruption were restricted by the ecclesiastical scrutiny which before long came to be exercised over documents of the apostolic faith within the archives of the church.

(*a*) Instances of editorial addition, by the author himself, are to be found, *e.g.*, if tradition be reliable, in the *Persæ* of Æschylus, in Herodotus, and in the *Georgics*—Vergil having cut out the original ending of the fourth Georgic and inserted another, after the death of Gallus. Juvenal revised and rewrote some of his Satires, while Martial appears to have reissued the tenth book of his epigrams, altered and adopted to the requirements of the reign of

---

Testaments of the Twelve Patriarchs (1908); on the NT quotations from the last-named book, see his articles in *HJ.*, 1905, 558–573, and *Exp.*[7] vii. 111 f.

* Cf. *HNT.* 608 f., for a fuller discussion of these points. The following paragraphs are simply meant to pave the way for later references under the successive NT books.

† Hermann, the famous Homeric critic, used the term to denote not only the insertion of verses, but, in accordance with strict etymology, the refurbishing of an older writing (cp. the pref. to his edition of the Homeric hymns, p. viii).

‡ In his chapter on "Interpolation in Thucydides" (*The Fourth Book of Thucydides*, 1889, pp. xxxi f.), Dr. W. G. Rutherford, after discussing the question of these glosses and scholia, or interpolated adscripts, declares that "nothing could have prevented the importation into the text of any author of a great deal of what was properly comment." The general theory and practice is well put by A. Gercke in *Neue Jahrb. für das klass. Altertum* (1901), pp. 3 f.

Trajan. Several passages in the *De Rerum Natura* (*e.g.* ii. 165–183) are also to be explained most naturally as additions made by Lucretius himself to the original draft, and in the case of the Third gospel or its sequel it is not unlikely that Luke may have re-edited (*ἀνασκευασθέν, διασκευασθέν*) his work. (*b*) Editorial additions are much more numerous, as, *e.g.*, in the well-known instances of Jer 17^{19-27} (a later insertion), 31^{35-40} 33^{17-26} (om. LXX), Is 66^{21-24} etc., and in the Catalogue of the ships (Hom. *Iliad*, $2^{484-877}$). The last-named fragment must be pronounced not simply an originally independent document from the Hesiodic school in Boeotia, but itself interpolated. The Homeric *διασκευασταί* are supposed to have worked thus on the *Iliad* and *Odyssey* with the view of smoothing out and harmonising it (cp. the list of passages in Jebb's *Homer*, p. 163); the famous passage in the *Antigone* (904–920) is almost certainly to be regarded as an interpolation, perhaps by the son of Sophocles, in the original; and stage interpolations, as might be expected, were especially frequent in the text of the Athenian dramatists. Later works even in literature and philosophy were not exempt from the intrusion of such alien matter, which, it is hard, in some cases (*e.g.* in Lucretius, iii. 806–818 and i. 44–49), to attribute certainly to (*b*) or (*c*), though internal evidence suggests that passages like *Iliad* $2^{180-183}$, 20^{75-353} and Herod. $6^{121-124}$ were added by a later hand. The corresponding source of interpolation in early Christian literature was the liturgical use of the documents in the worship of the churches (cp. Apocalypse); the Fourth gospel, among the NT writings, offers the clearest case of a document which has been edited by some later reviser, but Romans and 2 Corinthians present substantially the same phenomenon, though their canonical form was due in all probability to the interests of the Pauline Canon itself. Mark's gospel is supposed by some critics to have been written before A.D. 70, but to have received (from the author?) one or two touches after that date. A modern instance of this procedure is furnished by *Northanger Abbey*, which was first composed by Jane Austen in 1798. In the fifth chapter, however, we have an illusion to Miss Edgeworth's *Belinda*—a novel which did not appear until 1801. This proves that Miss Austen's work lies before us in a revised form; the first draft was gone over by the authoress before its final publication some years later. The third class of interpolations (*c*) cannot be strictly differentiated from (*b*), but it also is amply verified in ancient literature by the evident freedom exercised by copyists and editors of a text.* Glosses, such as Herod. 1^{82} $2^{117.145}$ 4^{32}, would creep in from the margin, or be incorporated (*e.g.* Jer $25^{13b.26b}$, Is 50^{10-11}) in order to straighten out a passage or bring it up to date. The possibility of such treatment is familiar to all students of the ancient texts; and such phenomena as the LXX rearrangement of Proverbs, or the Noachian interpolations in the Book of Enoch, indicate the frequency of the practice in the circles among which primitive Christianity arose. The evidence for (*a*) and (*b*) is either drawn from tradition or from internal evidence, but (*c*) offers a class of instances which naturally are more obvious, where the discrepancies of MSS at once reveal sutures of the text. Even

---

* Cp. S. Reinach's *Manuel de Philologie Classique*² (1904), i. pp. 43, 50 f. The extant letters of Epicurus have been swollen by the intrusion of marginal glosses, which are part of the text as given by Diogenes Laertius.

where the extant text does not suggest any break, the possibility of interpolations cannot be denied outright; the distance between the oldest MSS, or even the oldest versions, and the date of composition, leaves ample room for changes to have taken place in the interval between the autograph and the earliest known text.* Thus sheer internal evidence comes into play as a valid factor in the critical analysis.

The extent of interpolations varied from a word or two to a paragraph, and the motives for it varied equally from sinister to naive. During the second century the less reputable reasons for interpolation sprang from the growing prestige of the Christian scriptures, which were being appealed to in controversies. Heretical remodelling was rife, and the practice of alteration and omission was not entirely confined to one side. Origen charged the Valentinians with it; Eusebius blamed Tatian; Celsus retorted upon the Christians the charge of having interpolated in their own interests the Sibylline oracles; while Dionysius of Corinth, *c.* 170 A.D., was disgusted to find that his own epistles were being tampered with. The early Christians themselves seem to have had no hesitation in treating the LXX text with a certain freedom, inserting here and there phrases to fill out the messianic predictions of Jesus.

So far as the gospels were concerned, the most natural motives for interpolation were the harmonising bias † and the disinclination of copyists—whose powers, it must be remembered, amounted occasionally to almost editorial functions—to allow useful material, floated within reach by the oral tradition, to pass away. Expansion was more natural than abbreviation, though omissions were not uncommon, in cases where utterances seemed either contradictory or unedifying in some special degree.‡ The liberties occasionally taken with the text of the gospels are shown, *e.g.*, by the revision of Luke contained in Codex Bezæ, the work of Marcion, the use made of Mk by Mt and Lk, and numerous scribal or editorial touches in the MSS (contrast D and the other uncials) and versions. "There are abundant traces in the MSS and other authorities for the text of the gospels, that they were copied at first with great freedom. Possessors of copies did not hesitate to add little items of tradition, often oral, in some cases perhaps written, which reached them. . . . Much of this may be due to the fact that these early copies were probably to a large extent the works, not of professional copyists but of private individuals, whose interest was strong in the subject-matter of what they wrote, and who were glad to record any stray sayings or act of Christ which came in their way, even though it was not found in the copy before them" (Sanday, *Inspiration*^{2}, 1894, 294, 297).

---

* The pseudo-Adamantian Dialogue was interpolated within twenty or thirty years after it was composed. For Galen, see Rutherford's *A Chapter in the History of Annotation* (1905), p. 57.

† This was not confined to the gospels. One of the classical instances is the conformation of Verg. *Ecl.* 5^{37} in the majority of MSS to *Georg.* 1^{154}.

‡ *e.g.* the omission of 2 K 18^{14-16} (Hezekiah's submission) in Is 36–39, the omission by the LXX of the headings prefixed to various collections in Proverbs in order to bring the whole under the ægis of Solomon, and the Homeric omissions of Aristarchus (Athen. v. 180–181 D).

(ii.) It is also a fair question whether a document may not contain genuine but misplaced passages. Any application of the hypothesis of a displacement in the text requires to be checked by a hesitation about attributing too exact and systematic a character to a volume, especially when no MS evidence is available. But in itself the hypothesis is legitimate. Whether due to carelessness in copying, or to the misplacement of leaves of papyri (cp. Blau's *Studien zur alt-Hebräischen Buchwesen*, 1902, pp. 23 f.), or to some material mishandling of a codex,* inverted order is by no means an uncommon feature of ancient documents. One classical instance is furnished by the canonical order of the Nikomachean Ethics; Aristotle's original order was undoubtedly bks. i.–iii., vii.–viii., vi.–v. In the OT Jer 3^{6-18} 9^{23-26} and 10^{1-16} are, even if genuine, misplaced; Zec 4^{6-10} comes too late; Isa 41^{6-7} is conjectured, by an attractive argument of Marti, to have lain originally between 40^{19} and 40^{20}, and Hab 1^{5-11} may be supposed to have followed 2^4 in the autograph. Similarly, in the pseudo-Philonic treatise *de incorruptibilitate mundi*, according to Bernays, the present confusion of the traditional text is best accounted for by the conjecture that some leaves have been misplaced.

Carelessness on the part of copyists (cp Gercke, pp. 81 f.) was a common source of disorder, *e.g.* Hor. *Epp.* i. $15^{38f.}$ (cp. H. A. J. Munro's *Lucretius*, i. 28 f.). Verses were often misplaced, or even whole paragraphs. In several of the biblical instances (James, Fourth Gospel, Acts, Apocalypse, etc.), such displacements are due to the common practice of scribes or copyists who wrote in "narrow columns, after the fashion of what was on the papyrus strips; two, three, or even four columns being on each page. If a scribe, through inadvertence or interruption, happened to omit a phrase, he would write it either on the margin or in the space between two of the columns, with a suitable mark in the text to indicate where it ought to be" (A. S. Lewis, *ET*. xii. 519). The next copyist, who incorporated his predecessor's marginal note in the text, might easily misunderstand the reference marks, and thus insert the passage in the wrong column.

---

* As in the case of Aristotle; cp. Tredelenburg, *Hist. Beiträge zur Philos.* iii. 413 f.; Ueberweg, *Hist. Phil.* i. 147. For other dislocations, see the *Politics*, i. 11. 7, iii. 4. 11 f.; Dr. H. Jackson's edition of the Nikomachean Ethics, bk. v., where (pp. xiv f.) the dislocated canonical text is rearranged, and Susemihl and Hicks' ed. of the *Politics* (1894, pp. 78 f.), where the possibility is admitted that the textual phenomena may be due to two parallel versions. The minor phenomenon of words displaced by a copyist (cp. W. Headlam, *Class. Rev.* 1902, 243–256) falls under textual criticism.

(iii.) Compilation, or the incorporation of earlier sources without acknowledgment, is too obvious, especially in the historical literature, to require any detailed notice (cp. *HNT.* 615–619). The literary historian usually worked over his sources. Hebrew chronographers were often content to transcribe, leaving the strata of their sources fairly obvious. Greek or Roman authors, however, felt too strongly the claims of form and literary finish to allow any mere transliteration of some earlier document to stand.* So far from being inconsistent with historical accuracy, this practice obtained among the most scrupulous writers. It was a canon and convention of the time, and the credit of Tacitus has not been impaired even for moderns by the discovery that the original speech of Claudius, *de iure honorum Gallis dando*, differs materially from the words put by the historian into the emperor's lips. Thucydides, so far as we can check his methods, rewrote his sources in his own style. His authorities were moulded by his own diction and conceptions, and writers of his school and spirit would have curtly dismissed as mere *ὑπομνήματα* any collection of earlier sources or work in which previous materials had not been artistically recast.† The apocalypse of John, like most other apocalypses, is also an example of how older fragments were brought up to date and reset by a later writer; the small apocalypse of the synoptic gospels is one of such fragments.

(iv.) It is in the criticism of apocalyptic literature that the question of pseudonymity is also started (cp. *HNT.* 619 f.; G. H. Putnam, *Authors and their Public in Ancient Times*[2], 1894, pp. 67 f., 202 f.). The apocalypses of the later Judaism were pseudepigrapha almost invariably. Such writings, by a recognised literary custom, were issued under the name of some older prophet or hero, whose name lent sanction and authority to the contents of the prophecy.

Throughout the Judaism of Alexandria,‡ subsequent to the Ptolemies, the practice developed in several directions. The older Jewish literature reveals the tendency to group literature round great names of the past, from Moses to David and Solomon; and, long before Daniel had started the line of pseudonymous apocalypses, the book of Deuteronomy showed that this literary device was quite compatible with religious and moral motives of the highest order. One development of the practice in Alexandrian Judaism, that of circulating works under the ægis of some pagan authority, historical or mythological, was naturally foreign to the early Christian literature. The Sibyl, Hekatæus, and Aristeas play a rôle in pre-Christian Judaism to which there is nothing exactly corresponding in the primitive church. But when

* Cp. Nipperdey's *Opuscula* (1877), pp. 418 f.

† Cp. Lucian, *de hist. conscrib.* 16; Cic. *ad Att.* ii. 1. 1 f.; Dio Cassius spent twelve years in rewriting materials which it had taken him ten years to collect.

‡ Susemihl, *Geschichte d. Griech. Literatur in d. Alexandrinerzeit*, ii. 597 f., 601 f.

pseudonymity expanded to include epistles, as it did in Greek literature long before it did in Judaism, the way was prepared along which some early Christians * essayed to serve their age (Susemihl, ii. pp. 589 f.). Like boulders on a mountain-slope, most of the great personalities came to be covered with the moss of a more or less extensive correspondence, and the rise of a literature which included the Solomonic correspondence, written by Eupolemus, or the so-called "epistle of Jeremiah" (preserved at the close of the book of Baruch), indicates how congenial and innocent the practice was in pre-Christian Judaism.

(*a*) The range of pseudonymous literature was wider, however, in Greece and Rome, and although "the entire classical period of Greek literature furnishes us with no authentic instance of a literary fraud," † the centuries preceding and following the rise of Christianity were marked by a fairly extensive use of the pseudepigraphic method in philosophy, religion, and literature. The inducements to employ the names and characters of illustrious men varied in quality. One was the desire for pecuniary gain, which undoubtedly operated during the period in which Ptolemy Philadelphus was forming his library (cf. Bentley's *Dissert. on Phalaris*, pp. 80 f.); this cannot be traced within the early Christian literature. The higher motives for such compositions sprang from the innocent admiration and naive sympathy which prompted a disciple to reproduce in his own language the ideas, or what he conceived to be the ideas, of his master, and yet forbade him, out of modesty, to present these under his own name. Conscious of the master's influence, disciples viewed their own writings as an extension of his spirit. In them, through their pages, he spoke, not they. Αὐτὸς ἔφα. What they wrote was not so much a private venture or independent outburst of their own, as the propagation of his mind and spirit. Hence it became a point of unselfish piety to give up all claims to personal glory, and attribute their writings to the master himself. Such was the practice of the later Pythagoreans (Zeller, *Pre-Socratic Philosophy*, i. pp. 311 f.). This throws light upon the ethos of NT writings like Ephesians and the Pastorals. While 2 Peter represents in the NT Canon a pseudonymous epistle, pure and simple, the pastoral epistles, on the other hand, were composed by a Paulinist who must have had access to certain notes or papers of the great apostle, which he incorporated in his own writings. A similar instance, in Greek literature, is furnished by the Fourth Philippic and the speech περὶ συντάξεως, which, though appearing under the name of Demosthenes, were in all likelihood composed, not long after the orator's death, by a writer who possessed some genuine notes of his predecessor

---

* Cp. K. R. Köstlin (*Theol. Jahrb.* 1851, 149–221, "der pseud. Literatur der ältesten Kirche, Ein Beitrag zur Geschichte der Bildung des Kanons").

† Gudemann, in *Classical Studies in honour of H. Drisler* (New York, 1894), pp. 52–74. One rare instance of a malicious motive is pointed out in the case of Anaximenes of Lampsacus (Paus. vi. 18. 2 f.), who imitated the style of Theopompus to the latter's discredit. For the later Augustan epistolography, see Peter, *op. cit.* (below), pp. 171 f. Epicurus also suffered, according to Diog. Laertius (x. 3), from pseudonymous epistles.

and used these as the basis or nucleus of these orations (cp. Blass, *die Attische Beredsamkeit*, iii.[1] pp. 382 f.).

(*b*) Another tendency which fostered pseudonymous epistles was the recognised device, employed by ancient historians, of composing epistles in order to lend vividness and point to their narratives. Though some of these epistles may be genuine,* as in the case of one or two of Sallust's in the *Catiline*, the large majority, however true to the general spirit of the situation and the supposed writer, were undoubtedly due to the creative imagination of the author himself (cp. Westermann, *de Epistol. Script. Graecis*, i. pp. 4 f.). Of the two examples in Luke's second volume (Ac $15^{23f.}$ 23^{26-30}), the former suggests some historical nucleus, the latter is more independent. To this feature may be added that of composing the dedication or preface in the form of an epistle, as is often the case in modern books, although the extension of the practice to historical works is confined to writers like Aulus Hirtius and Velleius for the most part, among Roman authors of the classical period, and to Josephus among Jewish.

(*c*) It is further obvious that from the historian composing not only a letter but a speech in the name of some historical figure, it was only a short step to the composition of a pseudonymous epistle, in all good faith, which was designed to edify and instruct. The practice of composing speeches, which was perfectly consonant with the ancient historian's canons of veracity, varied from a free invention of such addresses to the conservation of salient points in an oral or written piece of tradition. The latter is not infrequent in Tacitus; he feels at perfect liberty to construct speeches like that of Germanicus on his death-bed, but he appears to exercise less freedom in his condensation, rearrangement, and rewriting of the emperor's addresses and letters to the senate (cp. Furneaux's *Annals of Tacitus*, i. pp. 23 f.). Consequently, the fact that ancient historians assumed and were allowed this licence does not *ipso facto* bar out the hypothesis that in certain cases the writer may have wrought upon the outline or substance of an authentic speech transmitted by tradition. This would be more credible when speeches were composed in *oratio obliqua*, as is generally the case with Cæsar, whose historical credibility in this matter is to be ranked high, in spite of obvious temptations to literary effect and political tendency.†

The rhetorical element in ancient historiography naturally adopted the method of (ἠθογραφῆσαι) bringing out the character of a person or the salient features of a situation by means of speeches. The author composed such a speech as appeared to him suitable for the occasion, drawing perhaps upon any materials of oral or written tradition that lay to his hand, but casting the speech into such forms as were apt to the setting chosen. The rival methods of indirect speech or of psychological analysis were open, but they were at once less dramatic and less easy. Tacitus commonly preferred the

---

* Or elaboration of a genuine nucleus (cp. W. Vischer's *Kleine Schriften*, i. pp. 429 f.). See further on this point, Hermann Peter's *die Scriptores Historiæ Augustæ* (sechs litteratur-geschichtliche Untersuchungen, 1892), pp. 153 f.

† Cp. Fabia's essay, *de orationibus quæ sunt in Comm. Cæs. de Bello Gallico* (1889), pp. 91 f.

latter process, and there are cases of conscientious preference for the former; but the public life of the ancients, where so much of importance was transacted in and by speeches, led the majority of historians to adopt the method of composing speeches for their *dramatis personæ* as the most intelligible and popular method of giving plastic expression to historical truth.* The speech served as an analysis of character. It revealed the speaker, and rayed light on the situation more effectively than paragraphs of comment or analysis. Thucydides is the master of this school of historians;† Theopompus and Sallust are his leading successors. The speeches in the NT literature consist of (*a*) compositions made up from previous materials, usually genuine in the main; and (*b*) more or less free compositions, which, without being purely rhetorical exercises,‡ represent what the writer's historical sense judged appropriate to the situation. This judgment may have been guided by tradition in some cases. But the general type of the second class of speeches, which includes the majority of those in Acts,§ corresponds to the speeches of Thucydides or Cæsar, Polybius or Josephus. Occasionally, as, *e.g.*, in Livy, vii. 30, x. 6 f., and xxxiv. 54, or in Aulus Gellius even, a speech may possess historic value as the reflection or reproduction of some older source,‖ instead of being, like the work of Dionysius Halicarnassus in this department, purely imaginative. Historians of the Gracchi period, like Fannius, proved invaluable to subsequent writers in this respect. Their annals incorporated genuine speeches of contemporary statesmen, now and then almost verbally, upon which both Cicero and Plutarch drew. Consequently later speeches which rest on such authentic fragments acquire a historical weight out of all proportion to their extant shape and setting.¶ The longer speeches in the gospels are partly based upon such earlier sources (*e.g.* Matthew), but they are partly (as in the Fourth gospel) due to prophetic and homiletical expansions of authentic logia. The inspired prophet, speaking in the Lord's name, is not far from the preacher who develops a homily (*e.g.* Mt $25^{31f.}$); preaching, in its higher phases, is almost lyric, and this creative process, in which a mind brooding on some gospel

---

* See C. Nipperdey's *Opuscula* (1877), pp. 415 f.

† "I have put into the mouth of each speaker the sentiments proper to the occasion, expressed as I thought he would be likely to express them, while at the same time I endeavoured, as nearly as I could, to give the general purport of what was actually said" (i. 22, tr. Jowett). Cp. Ivo Bruns, *das lit. Idealporträt* (1896), pp. 24 f.

‡ Or compositions written with a deliberate purpose, like most if not all of the speeches in Cæsar, which, while apposite and vivid, are intended to colour the whole situation.

§ E. Curtius (cp. *Exp.*[7] iv. 436–455) puts in a vigorous plea for the speech at Athens. "Whoever disputes the historical value of the account of St. Paul in Athens, tears one of the most important pages from the history of the human race."

‖ Cp. Soltau, *neue Jahrbücher f. d. klass. Alterthum* (1902,) pp. 23 f.

¶ *i.e.* if the source be trustworthy. But when Appian (v. 39–45) draws on the commentaries of Augustus, the unreliable nature of the latter deprives the later historian of any right to credibility on this score.

word brings out an edifying monologue or dialogue, accounts for some passages in the synoptists as well as in the Fourth gospel more naturally than the hypothesis of deliberate literary inventiveness.

(v.) The question of translation (*HNT.* 605 f.), with regard to any early Christian writing, covers a wider tract of interest than the problem of its date. Undoubtedly, translation implies, as in the case of Ecclesiasticus, a gap of years between the composition of the original and the issue of the version; but it also implies problems relating to the authorship and contents. Thus, in the case of the Matthæan logia, it is too common to assume that the various Greek translations were practically verbatim. They partook of the nature of recensions. The particular recension which was fused with Mk in order to form the canonical Matthew may have been almost as far as the Greek recension of Josephus' *Wars* from the Aramaic original. "For Greek and Roman readers it would need to be materially recast. . . . Very probably the *résumé* of Jewish history from the time of Antiochus Epiphanes to the death of Herod (bk. i.) was first prefixed in the Greek; the greater part of the seventh book was doubtless added at the same time" (G. F. Moore, *EBi.* 2091). Matthew is not a translation, but it is a fair conjecture—so far as literary canons go—that in Mt 1–2 glosses might have been added by an editor,* whether from a special source or sources or from personal access to Palestinian traditions, when the Aramaic draft (beginning with 3^1?) was translated.

V.

SOME LITERARY FORMS IN NT.

The gospel was the new † form of literature developed by Christianity. The embryonic stages of this literary product were not wholly novel, however; the λόγια, or collections of sayings of the Master, resembled the collections of apophthegms current among the disciples of philosophic teachers; and even among the Christians themselves ἀπομνημονεύματα,‡ not εὐαγγέλια, was a primitive term in use for their gospels.

* Jacoby (*NT Ethik*, 1899, pp. 410 f.) puts down $5^{18.19}$ 23^8 and 24^{20} to this exposition which blended with the text.

† The ancient conception of depicting a character, subjective and objective, as illustrated by Polybius, Livy, and Tacitus, are discussed by Ivo Bruns in *die Persönlichkeit in der Geschichtschreibung der Alten* (1898).

‡ The ἀπομνημονεύματα of Moiragenes, which were subsequently combined with the ὑπομνήματα of Damis (*i.e.* extracts from diaries) to form the bio-

Aristotle draws a distinction between his *ἐξωτερικοὶ* or *ἐκδεδομένοι λόγοι* (published works) and his *ἀκρόασεις*. The latter were private summaries or abstracts, resembling a *précis* for his audience of students. We thus get a distinction between *τὰ ἀνεγνωσμένα* and *τὰ ἀνέκδοτα* which throws light on writings like the Ur-Marcus * and Q, both of which would resemble the former But even in these, and still more clearly in the canonical gospels, the material assumes forms which have partial analogies in ancient literature.

(*a*) The chief of these is the dialogue. At first sight the philosophical development of literature among the disciples of Socrates is unlike the primitive Christian literature in one important respect: the faith and reverence of the disciples of Jesus prevented them from composing literary dialogues in which their Master was made to answer problems of thought and conduct. But it is not accurate to suggest (so R. Hirzel, *Der Dialog, ein literar-historischer Versuch*, Leipzig, 1895, ii. 367) that the first efforts in this line made by the early Christians are to be found in writings like the Pistis Sophia and the fabricated correspondence of Jesus. Examples of the dialogue-method lie earlier in the literature of the church. For one thing, the composition of several sections in the synoptic gospels was prompted by the rise of questions about conduct. How were Christians to bear themselves in preaching the gospel? or when attacked? or towards the Jewish authorities? How did Jesus behave towards the priests? What was his attitude to the law? These and similar questions were the nuclei round which several reminiscences of the evangelic tradition gathered. The outcome, as it lies in the gospels, was in many cases made up of genuine recollections and authentic logia; but there was also an element of composition. Even oral tradition could not hand down logia invariably as they were spoken. A plus of preaching inevitably attached to them. Furthermore, the setting was ultimately the work of an author, who, as is plain, *e.g.*, from Matthew's gospel, worked often on principles of schematism

graphy of Apollonius of Tyana, resembled πράξεις. Reitzenstein (*Hellenistische Wundererzählungen*, 1906, 40 f.) thinks the former must have been a sort of prototype of the gospels (especially the Fourth), the latter a parallel to the we-sections in Acts.

* Abbott (*Diat.* 996) speaks of Mk's "note-book gospel." The phrase suits the Ur-Marcus even better than the canonical Mark.

and with certain ideas and tendencies in his mind which were not without influence upon his materials. Each evangelist had his conception of Jesus; he had also his own idiosyncrasies, and he was face to face with the special needs of his audience or age. The conjoint influence of these led to such literary dialogues as the synoptic tradition includes in its narrative of Jesus. But the earliest and closest approach furnished by Christianity to the classical dialogue-form of literature is to be found in the middle sections of the Fourth gospel, where Jesus and the Jews are made to debate in a thoroughly controversial fashion. This marks the passage of early Christianity into its dogmatic stage, when it was confronted with rival systems, Jewish, Gnostic, and pagan (cp. P. Gardner, *Exploratio Evangelica*, pp. 164–165; Moffatt, *HNT.* 34 f.); it is the first phase of the dialogue in Christian hands as an instrument of anti-Jewish propaganda.

Later instances of this dialogue-form in anti-Jewish and anti-pagan propaganda multiply from the Dialogue of Jason and Papiscus and Justin onwards; it naturally became, as in the old philosophic style, a literary weapon in the controversies between one school of Christian and another (*e.g.* Bardesanes, Jerome, pseudo-Adamantius, etc.).

(*b*) A cognate form of the dialogue, the *diatribê*, has also passed into the early Christian literature, although the NT writings contain merely a few rudimentary traces of its vogue and influence. The διατριβή was a dialogue transformed into a monologue, in which the imaginary opponent appears by way of φησίν (*inquit*). He is cited, only to be refuted; his words are quoted in order to form the text of a fresh outburst on the part of the speaker. When the method is skilfully managed, as, *e.g.*, in Arrian's descriptions of Epictetus, the effect is vivacious and telling. The interest of the *diatribê* was primarily ethical; hence its popularity among the later Stoics and even among Jewish Christian (Philo) and early Christian (Clem. Alex.) writers on religion.* One trace of the διατριβή-style is to be detected in

* Cp. Wendland, *Philo und die Kynisch-Stoische Diatribê* (1895), p. 7, "Wenn neutestamentlichen Schriften manche Begriffe und Ideen, Stilformen und Vergleiche mit der philosophischen Litteratur gemeinsam sind, so ist es nicht ausgeschlossen, dass die Diatribe schon auf Stücke der urchristlichen Litteratur einen gewissen Einfluss ausgeübt, den man sich nicht einmal litterarisch vermittelt zu denken braucht." The last clause is important. A number of the diatribe-forms spring naturally from the moral tension and spiritual conflict set up by the new faith. Cp. Heinrici's *Die litter. Charakter der NT Schriften* (1908), 11 f., 47, 66.

Paul's habit of quoting some phrase of his opponents in order to refute their arguments. Introduced by *φησίν*, just as in Epictetus, these citations lend vivacity to the style; they also suggest the genetic relations between the dialogue and the epistle, between the spoken language of discussion and the epistolary idiom.

(*c*) The address, based usually on the older scriptures, and therefore to a large extent exegetical as well as hortatory, was described* in philosophic language (Lucian, *Tim.* 10; Ælian, *v. hist.* 3[19]) as ὁμιλία (cp. Ac 20[11] 24[16]; Ignat. *ad. Polyk.* 5), and afterwards as διάλεξις or *disputatio.* It differs from the διατριβή in being less conscious of an opponent; what it presupposes is an audience to be convinced, rather than a single adversary to be refuted. This literary form underlies the homilies of the gospels and most of the later epistles.

(*d*) The epistle and the oral address were of kindred origin. Long before the rise of Christianity the rhetorical schools had been in the habit of throwing their ideas into the form of epistles, and the obvious similarity between the audience who heard an address and the readers of an epistle, the frequent use of the second person in exhortation, and the presence of a flowing, flexible element in the argument, helped to develop the use of the epistolary form for ends which were wider than those of private correspondence.† It is often a real problem to determine whether a given writing is a λόγος or an ἐπιστολή. In many cases the epistolary form is little more than a literary device. One speech of Demosthenes actually came to be published under the title of ἐπιστολὴ Δημοσθενοῦς, and it was natural that later writers, addressing a wide public, should adopt, for the sake of dramatic effect and point, the epistolary form of composition as the nearest to that of the oration. Furthermore, a speech did not require to have been spoken in order to be published; and, as a matter of fact, it was the custom even of historians‡ to write for *hearers*—the form in this case being all the more natural as the readers would read the volume aloud.§

* See Hilgenfeld's *Ketzergesch. d. Urc.* II.

† Cp. Aristides, xii. p. 148 D, ὅπερ γε καὶ ἐν ἀρχῇ τῆς ἐπιστολῆς εἶπον ἢ ὅτι βούλεσθε καλεῖν τὸ βιβλίον.

‡ Cp. Rohde, *Griech. Roman*, pp. 304 f.

§ Lucian, *adv. indoct.* 2 (ἀναγινώσκεις ἔνια πάνυ ἐπιτρέχων φθάνοντος τοῦ ὀφθαλμοῦ τὸ στόμα).

The epistle had been bound up in its earlier stages in Greek literature with the dialogue.* The philosophical discussions which were native to the genius of the latter had acquired fresh literary form in epistolography; † the epistle, said Artemon (the editor of Alexander the Great's correspondence in the second century), is a sort of semi-dialogue. Consequently a personal note pervaded it. A treatise might be, and often had to be, abstract and impersonal, but the affinity of the epistle to the oral address on the one hand and the dialogue upon the other, naturally tended to present in it the question and answer, the play of sentiment, and the dialectic movement inevitable to any reproduction of personal intercourse. The treatise dealt in a more or less systematic way with some philosophic subject; ‡ it conveyed instruction directly and didactically. But the epistle rose alongside of it to reach circles or groups of people in a less formal fashion; and when philosophic scholars multiplied and the world of culture grew less restricted than before, the epistle acquired a special vogue as a channel for conveying instruction to people whose common interests united them in some pursuit or science. The correspondence of Epicurus marks a distinct stage in this literary evolution. His letters to philosophers and private individuals had in some cases only a semi-private object (cp. Hirzel, *der Dialog*, i. pp. 355 f.); they discussed such topics as natural philosophy and astronomy, besides ethical themes, and his scholars continued the practice. Epistles became not merely the ties knitting like-minded scholars

* The various materials and phases are collected in Hercher's *Epistolographi græci*. See, further, Peter, *op. cit.* (below) pp. 213 f., on "der Brief als Einkleidung für Flugschriften, wissenschaftliche und litterarische Erörterungen, Mahnungen, Widmungen," and especially Rudolf Hirzel's *der Dialog*, i. pp. 353 f., ii. pp. 8 f.

† The changes made by Paul and other early Christians in the formulæ, *e.g.*, of the introductory address, are noticeable. It is only in Ac 15^{23} (23^{26}) and Ja 1^{1} that the ethnic ὁ δεῖνα τῷ δεῖνι χαίρειν is employed; the former is not a Christian letter, while in the latter, by a literary device like that in the third and eighth of the Platonic epistles, the opening is linked to what follows. The origin of the χαίρειν formula was connected with the news (εὐαγγέλιον) of victory, according to tradition (Lucian, *de lapsu in salutando*, 3; cp. G. A. Gerhard's "Untersuchungen zur Geschichte des griechischen Briefes," i., in *Philologus*, 1905, 27–65).

‡ For what follows, see especially Hermann Peter's *der Brief in der römischen Litteratur* (1901), pp. 16 f., and Wehofer, "Untersuchungen zur altchristlichen Epistolographie" (*SBAW*, 1901, pp. 102 f.).

together, but means of instruction, defence, and debate. In the treatment of scientific questions the epistle thus acquired a new rôle of its own. It accompanied and promoted the popularising of knowledge. Letters, or rather epistles, for example, were written on the Copais sea by Crates of Chalkis (cp. Westermann, *de epist. græc.* iv. pp. 9 f.), on mathematics (cp. Susemihl, i. pp. 419 f.), and antiquities (by Polemon of Ilion); and an equally didactic character attached to the letters of Augustus.

The soil was thus prepared for the growth of epistles and epistolary homilies within the sphere of early Christianity. The philosophic epistle had long been acclimatised among the Greeks and Romans. *Hortationes ad philosophiam* were composed by Augustus as well as by less princely authors (Suet. *Aug.* lxxxv.), and epistles of consolation are frequent in the correspondence of the age (*e.g.* that of Sulpicius Severus, Cic. *ad Fam.* iv. 5). The letters of Seneca to Lucilius, as has been often noted (cp. *e.g.* Peters, pp. 228 f.), are in reality designed for the young world of Rome, and merely dedicated to Lucilius;* the personal address and air are retained, but the object is to furnish all and sundry with exhortations and admonitions which may take the place of some philosophic friend at hand.† Several even of Seneca's so-called dialogues might be described as epistles. The epistolary literature of the early Christians, in fact, almost exemplifies the threefold division ‡ made by Cicero into (*a*) epistles or letters which convey instruction or information, (*b*) playful and familiar notes to one's friends, and (*c*) letters of consolation. The nearest approach to the personal letter, unstudied and spontaneous, is Paul's note to Philemon or 3 John. Personal or semi-personal letters, however (like Galatians and 1 Thessalonians), might contain matter of some permanent interest. They might be contributions to some controversy,

* Luke's two books, dedicated to Theophilus, are a NT analogy.

† Cp. Martha, *les moralistes sous l'empire Rom.* pp. 3 f., 23 f. The Seneca-letters to Lucilius, as Lord Bacon saw, were simply "dispersed meditations, though conveyed in the form of epistles."

‡ *e.g.* in his letter of September, 46 B.C., to Trebianus in exile (*ad Fam.* vi. 10. 4), or more explicitly in *ad Fam.* iv. 13. 1 and ii. 4 ("letters, as you are well aware, are of many kinds. One is undeniable, the original cause of letter-writing indeed, viz., to acquaint the absent with anything which it is to their interest or to the writer's interest that they should know. . . . Two other kinds of letters there are, which mightily please me: the one familiar and sportive, the other grave and serious").

like the letters of Antony to which Tacitus (*Ann.* iv. 34) and Suetonius (*Aug.* 63) allude; or discussions of various questions, like the epistles of Varro,* Capito, and M. Valerius Messalla. The epistolary form, in short, was employed more and more to give a vivid and semi-literary dress to dissertations upon criticism, jurisprudence, and even science, among the Greeks and Romans. Thus partly by the circulation of really personal letters, and partly by the adoption of the epistolary form for public or semi-public ends, the transition was made from the private letter to the epistle or epistolary homily. The NT epistles vary between both; † the former was transmuted into the shape of a letter addressed to some church for which the writer (Paul) felt a strong personal affection; ‡ the latter passed, in the sub-Pauline period, into writings which were for the most part epistolary in form only (1 John, James, 2 Peter).

VI.

THE CIRCULATION OF THE NT WRITINGS. §

Paul and some other early Christian writers ‖ dictated, not because, like Charles the Great, they could not write, but for purposes of speed and convenience. A letter might be either written with one's own hand or dictated to a scribe or secretary (ταχυγράφοι, *librarii*, *notarii*). In one case, the amanuensis of Paul ¶ inserts a greeting from himself in the midst of the apostle's

* Cp. Ritschl's *Opuscula*, iii. pp. 476 f.

† Deissmann's valuable but too narrow antithesis (*Bible Studies*, pp. 1–60) is reproduced by W. Soltau (*neue Jahrbücher für d. klass. Alterthum*, 1906, 17–29).

‡ Similarly 3 John and the letters of Ignatius prove that a real letter could be written to a church. This fact of Christian intercourse prevents the category of "letter or epistle" from applying, without qualification, to early Christian correspondence.

§ Cp. *HNT*. 123 f.; Gregory, *Canon and Text of NT*, 299 f.; and Sir W. M. Ramsay, *Letters to the Seven Churches* (1904), pp. 23 f., "The Christian Letters and their Transmission."

‖ Ignatius (see Lightfoot on Ro 10[1]), Origen (Eus. *H. E.* vi. 23. 2), and others; cp. Pliny's *epp.* ix. 36. 2, and Jerome's *epp.* 21. 42. On the later use of *dictare* = to compose, see Norden, ii. 957 f.

¶ Tertius was a *scriba literarius* of Paul, for the time being, who took down, as a private secretary, what the apostle had to say (cp. Marquardt's *Das Privatleben der Römer*, i.[2] pp. 151 f.), and made copies of it if necessary. Such *notarii* were frequently stenographers.

salutations (Ro 16^{22}); but as a rule the author speaks throughout. It was apparently Paul's ordinary custom to dictate his correspondence, though, to authenticate a letter, he might add a salutation in his own handwriting (2 Th 3^{17}, 1 Co 16^{21}, Col 4^{18}). Such letters and epistles were written either on wax-covered tablets with a stilus, or with a reed-pen and ink on parchment (cp. 2 Co 3^{3}, 2 Jn ^{12}, 3 Jn ^{13}). If Paul's remark in Gal 6^{11} means that he himself wrote part of the epistle personally,* it is likely that the latter method was employed. His handwriting, like that of Cicero, "on *charta* with a pen would have been much more easily recognised than his initials carved with a *stilus* on wax. Moreover, the use of pen and paper would be so obviously more suitable for long letters." †

The shape and the size ot some of the recently discovered papyri at Oxyrhynchus indicate that even for religious, as well as for literary purposes, the papyrus *codex* was in use throughout Egypt before the third century A.D. Instead of the papyrus in roll form, the papyrus in book form was more widely and more early used than has hitherto been suspected.‡

For various reasons, partly owing to the uncertainties of communication, letters of special moment were copied§ before being dispatched; and more than one copy was sometimes sent, lest one of them should go astray (cp. *e.g.* Cic. *ad Fam.* ix. 16. 1). The carelessness and dishonesty of letter-carriers were thus checkmated to some extent (*ad Fam.* iv. 4. 1). This consideration has some bearing on the literary characteristics of 2 Thessalonians and Ephesians. Furthermore, the same letter might be sent to different persons, as was the practice of Epicurus.‖ "I have wanted," writes Cicero to Cornificius, "a

* The sender occasionally wrote part himself, if he wished to be particularly confidential (Cic. *ad. Att.* xi. 24).

† Tyrrell's *Correspondence of Cicero*, vol. i. p. lv. Quintilian's advice, in favour of wax tablets (*Instit. Orat.* x. 31 f.) for jottings or notes (Lk 1^{63}), is due to the fact that erasures were more easily made on wax than on parchment. Illustrations of wax tablets are given by W. Schubart (*Das Buch bei den Griechen u. Römern*, 1907, 16 f.).

‡ Cp. Grenfell and Hunt, *The Oxyrhynchus Papyri*, ii. (1899) pp. 1–3, and W. Schubart, *Das Buch bei den Griechen und Römern*, 1907, pp. 107 f.

§ Not by the author, however. "Quis solet eodem exemplo pluris dare, qui sua manu scribit?" (*ad Fam.* xviii. 2).

‖ So, too, Seneca (*ad Lucil.* xvi. 99. 1: "epistulam, quam scripsi Marullo, cum filium paruulum amisisset et diceretur molliter ferre, misi tibi").

letter from you addressed to my very own self" (*ad Fam.* xii. 30. 3). Even without the alteration of the address, a letter could be copied and scattered broadcast for a wider audience (so Cic. *ad Att.* viii. 9. 1), in which case the epistle became almost a tract or pamphlet. Such must have been the method with epistolary homilies like Galatians, 1 Corinthians, and 1 Peter, as well as with the Apocalypse.

In the case of the NT, the autographs themselves perished at an early date. That they were no longer in existence in the second quarter of the second century is evident from the fact that Marcion could be charged with falsifying their text. Had the autographs been available, the accusations of Tertullian and others would have been superfluous; the editors and correctors of the text would have been refuted simply by the production of the autograph itself. Within less than a century the autograph of the apocalypse, *e.g.*, had disappeared; a number of copies existed which were no longer uniform.* This is hardly to be wondered at; for, once a document was copied, there would not be the same interest in preserving the *ἰδιόγραφον*. Tertullian seems in one passage to appeal to the originals: "percurre ecclesias apostolicas, apud quas ipsæ adhuc cathedræ apostolorum suis locis præsident, apud quas ipsæ *authenticæ literæ* eorum recitantur, sonantes uocem et repræsentantes faciem uniuscuiusque" (*præscr. hæret.* 36). But the phrase italicised probably means no more than "originals," in the sense of uncorrupted, genuine copies, as opposed either to translations or to interpolated (or mutilated) editions, such as those issued by Marcion. If he really meant autographs, the passage would require to be set down to his rhetorical temperament.†

Naturally the wear and tear was felt primarily at the opening and at the end of a manuscript. Well-known instances of opening sentences having been lost are to be found in Plutarch's *Vita Themistoclis* and three of the books of the elder Seneca's *Controuersiae*. This is what underlies the theories about Hebrews having lost its original address, and Mark its original ending, by accident. The errors of copyists in the body of the work explain the variations in Apoc 13[18] (Iren. v. 30. 1, *ἐν πᾶσι τοῖς σπουδαίοις καὶ ἀρχαίοις ἀντιγράφοις κτλ.*), etc., as well as the primitive corruptions which must have

---

* Origen (in Mt 19[19]) similarly attests the widespread diversities in the copies of the gospels.

† Cp. Cobet and Kuenen's *NT ad fidem Codicis Vaticani* (1860), pp. 26 f.

arisen very early, since there is no ripple of variation in the MSS or versions. A clear case of the latter occurs in Ac 2[9], where Ἰουδαίαν, between Μεσοποταμίαν and τε καὶ Καππαδοκίαν, is certainly wrong. The alternatives are to omit it altogether (so, *e.g.*, Harnack, *BNT.* iii. 65 f.), or to regard it as a corruption of Συρίαν (Jerome on Is 11[10], Blass), Λυδίαν (Bentley), Ἀδιαβαίαν (Nestle, *ZNW.*, 1908, 253–254), Ἀρμενίαν (Tert. *adv. Jud.* 7; Aug. *Contra Fund.* 9), Ἀραμαίαν (W. H. P. Hatch, *ZNW.*, 1908, 255–256), Ἰωνίαν (as in 1 Mac 8[8]; Cheyne, *EBi* 2169), Ἰνδίαν (Erasmus, Schmid, Zahn), Ἰδυμαίαν (Bentley, Barth, Spitta), or Βιθυνίαν (cp. below, 'First Peter,' § 3, note).

When an epistle of Paul was received by a local church, it would be laid up in the archives of the community (*scrinia*, κιβώτιον, κίστη), just as private letters were collected in a family,* or public epistles in the pre-Christian Jewish synogogues. Copies † would be taken and issued to the various churches embraced in the address. In a town of any size, where there were several house-churches (Col 4[15]), an epistle would be probably copied, even though it was not a circular letter; but from Col 4[16] we may infer that the exchange of letters between churches was not yet a matter of course. A church would retain its own letter, normally. Was it taken out from time to time for purposes ‡ of discussion or reference? or did the church read the epistle regularly at worship? The incidental reference of Pliny (*ep.* x. 98) is silent on any ἀνάγνωσις, and the evidence of Justin shows that it was the gospels and books of the OT prophets which were read weekly. But the growing prestige of the apostles must have led during the early part of the second century to the reading of their epistles as a part of public worship, though the process of their elevation to the rank of scriptures remains obscure. Eventually, the church authorities became responsible for what was thus read, as we see from the well-known case of Serapion.§ The distinguishing characteristic of canonical writings was that they were read aloud in the worship of the churches. Subsequently a distinction was drawn between writings which were read on Sundays and writings

* Cp. Peter, *Der Brief*, pp. 33 f.

† Cp. Dziatzko in Pauly-Wissowa's *Real-Encyclopädie der class. Altertumswissenschaft*, iii. 966 f.

‡ Perhaps also to let individual members copy out parts of it for their own purposes.

§ The growing unity of the church, and the need of safeguarding Christians from heretical scriptures, led to the rapid diffusion of the NT writings; but this was by no means uniform, as the evidence of the Canon in various churches is enough to prove, except in the case of the gospels.

which, though used for edification, did not attain to this rank. But the primitive age of Christianity knew nothing of this classification.

The allusions to reading in the early Christian literature almost invariably (Mk 13^{14}, Apoc 1^{3}, 1 Ti 4^{13}) denote the public reading of the scriptures in the churches.* How far the early Christians, and even the apostles, were able to read, is uncertain. The accomplishment was not universal, and although the education of the average Christian in the primitive church need not be ranked so low as, *e.g.*, by Paul Glaue in his monograph on *Die Vorlesung heiliger Schriften in Gottesdienste* (Teil i., 1907), pp. 13–30, still, the fact that many members were comparatively uneducated, and that even when they were not the spoken word was preferred in worship—this, together with the expense of copies, corroborates the view that the large majority of early Christians knew their scriptures mainly by the hearing of the ear.

The practice of reading aloud one's own compositions was a corollary to the earlier habit of reciting the works of dead authors. In the former case the object was sometimes to benefit the audience; reading thus resembled the modern lecture (cp. Epict. *Diss.* iii. 23. 7 f.). But more often an author recited his work to a chosen audience in order to get their critical opinion. "The audience at recitations may be compared with the modern literary reviews, discharging the functions of a preventive and emendatory, not merely of a correctional tribunal. Before publication a work might thus become known to more hearers than it would now find readers: in the same way specimens of a forthcoming work are now made known through popular magazines. After publication † it might still be recited, not only by the author, but by others, with or without his leave, in the country or the provinces as well as in the city, before public or private assemblies" (Mayor on Juv. 3^{9}). It is the latter practice which throws light on the propagation and circulation of the early Christian scriptures, which were not written for any literary ends. This applies even to literary epistles like James and Ephesians, which were pastorals, written for no definite audience. The homily, cast in the form of an epistle, was a recognised literary feature among Jewish and Greek, as well as Roman,‡ circles, before the early

---

* The recitation of the gospel-stories in the Antioch church was probably a source of information, *e.g.*, for Luke (cp. Salmon's *Human Element in Gospels*, pp. 26 f.).

† On the meaning of 'publication,' see G. H. Putnam's *Authors and their Public in Ancient Times*[2] (1894), pp. 78 f.

‡ Cicero's letter to Lentulus Spinther (*ad Fam.* i. 9), *e.g.*, approximates to a philosophical discourse or a speech, and the famous *Commentariolum petitionis* is as much an essay on political methods as anything else. For further examples of the epistolary *εἰσαγωγή* in Roman literature, see Norden in *Hermes* (1905), pp. 524 f.

Christians began to write. Even though it was marked, for the sake of vividness, by appeals to *hearers* and the like, it was designed originally and directly for readers. The early Christian homily shared these characteristics of form, but it was ultimately designed to reach audiences not individuals, and the channel was public reading in gatherings for worship.

VII.

SOME LITERARY CHARACTERISTICS OF THE NT WRITINGS.

This practice of reading aloud the scriptures, even before they were scriptures in the canonical sense of the term, helped to determine insensibly their literary form. It was a pre-natal influence. The profound effect which Plato ascribes to Homer in Hellenic education and politics was due to hearing rather than to reading. It was the solemn and didactic recitation of the poems by ῥαψῳδοί, who sought to bring home not only the words but the spirit of Homer, which enabled the audience to sustain its feeling of kinship with the original. The influence of the early Christian writings, particularly the gospels, operated under similar conditions. The large majority of Christians only listened to them in worship or learnt their contents in the catechetical instruction of the church. Both letters and gospels, as well as the tracts which we know as homilies and pastorals, were written for the most part with this end in view; their close connection with the address and the dialogue (see above, pp. 48 f.) determined their adherence to the forms and spirit of a rhetoric which corresponded to the needs of actual life.

The so-called metrical prose, or prose which recognised the use of a certain *clausula*, passed from the Asiatic school of rhetoric with some of the Roman authors, such as Seneca, Pliny, and Cicero, who managed to preserve ease and freedom under a more or less conscious recognition of certain general but unwritten laws of rhythm and diction. The existence of this rhythmic element need not be supposed to impair necessarily the spontaneity of a writing. Ancient standards of composition admitted, even in writings of fresh and apparently unstudied grace, such as Cicero's letters of consolation,* a scrupulous

* Zielinski's *Das Clauselgesetz in Cicero's Reden* (1904) is discussed by A. C. Clarke (*Class. Rev.*, 1905, 164 f.), and Bornecque's *La Prose Metrique dans la Correspondance de Cicéron*, by Prof. Tyrrell (*Hermath.*, 1905, 289 f.).

attention to the niceties of rhythm, cadence, and accent, and a care for laws of sound in style which may seem strained and hyper-ingenious to modern tastes. Modern theorists often state it in extravagant forms. But, fanciful methods apart, if the ancients really read with their ears as well as with their eyes,* it is quite intelligible how even prose style, as Cicero and Quintilian maintain, could observe certain poetical canons; without being metrical, as Aristotle put it,† prose style must not be wholly unrhythmical. History, said Quintilian, is next to poetry; it is *quodam modo carmine solutum*, and Luke's writings show how effective cadences and easy rhythms could be present to the mind of an ancient writer whose aim was to convince and impress, not to display the finish and mastery of his own style, nor to observe hard and fast canons of rhythm. Thus it is with early Christian writings like Hebrews just as with some of the most effective prose-orations of antiquity; they were composed by men trained in this spirit of artistic symmetry. In the minds of those who composed or read the early Christian books there was no primary thought of intellectual entertainment. None, with the partial exceptions of the two Lucan writings and Hebrews, can be described as a literary product. Faith was their germ and their design. They were composed and employed to edify the Christian communities for which they were originally written, and among which they came to circulate. But some at least of them, like many earlier works in classical literature, are instances of how style and fervour were not incompatible, and how they were meant to catch the hearer's heart, as the Christian message fell effectively upon his ears.

The presence of this rhetorical element in the early Christian writers is felt in reminiscences of figures common to the Greek prose of the day,‡ and in the construction of sentences and even larger sections, as, *e.g.*, in an epistle like Hebrews. The former is illustrated by plays on words like λιμοί-λοιμοί,

* Some of Paul's epistles, like those of Ignatius, gain incredibly in emphasis when read aloud. Public reading must have brought out their point and charm, in many passages.

† In ch. viii. of his *Rhetoric* (bk. 3) he handles the need and structure of rhythm in literary prose. Cp. G. L. Hendrickson in *Amer. Journ. of Philology* (1904), 126 f., and the general discussion in Norden, i. 92 f., 134 f.

‡ Cp. the collection of Pauline instances in J. F. Böttcher's essay, *de paronomasia finitimisque ei figuris Paulo apostolo frequentatis* (Leipzig, 1824), and R. Bultmann's *Stil der Paul. Predigt u. die kynisch-stoische Diatribe* (1910).

ἔμαθεν-ἔπαθεν, φθόνου-φόνου (Ro 1^{29}),* ἀσυνέτους-ἀσυνθέτους (1^{31}), πολλοῖς πολλάκις (2 Co 8^{22}), etc. The parallelism of the Greek prose (παρίσωσις) and of later Latin writers like Apuleius, however, is one of form rather than of thought † (so Norden, *op. cit.* ii. 816 f.); the Semitic parallelism, like that of the Finnish Kalevala, develops an idea in two or more strophes, and this is specially characteristic of the strophes and anti-strophes in the gospels It is in Paul, particularly, that the style, for all its rabbinic dialectic, shows traces of the Hellenic element, due to the widespread influence of rhetoric on pre-Christian prose, especially in Asia Minor; it is denoted by the presence of balanced periods ‡ and a clearly marked evolution of strophic formations, with themes, refrains, etc. Special attention was paid to the sequence of accents in a sentence. As the writing was often written to be read aloud, it was composed by one whose ear was sensitive to the harmony of the style, the fall of the antithesis, and the music of the period. More than once in Paul it becomes an open question whether he is quoting from an early Christian hymn, or developing half-unconsciously the antitheses of his glowing thought. A good case in point is furnished by 1 Co 15^{42-43}:

σπείρεται ἐν φθορᾷ,
ἐγείρεται ἐν ἀφθαρσίᾳ·
σπείρεται ἐν ἀτιμίᾳ,
ἐγείρεται ἐν δόξῃ·
σπείρεται ἐν ἀσθενείᾳ,
ἐγείρεται ἐν δυνάμει.

Elsewhere, however, the genuine rhetoric § of the speaker is

* Further exx. in Ro 2^{1} 5^{16} 12^{8} 14^{23}.

† Cp. E. du Méril's *Essai philosophique sur le principe et les formes de la versification* (1841), pp. 47 f.

‡ Cp. J. Schmidt on 'das rhythmische Element in Cicero's Reden' (*Wiener Studien*, 1893, pp. 209 f.), with Blass on rhythm in the Attic orators (*Neue Jahrb. für das klass. Altertum*, 1900, 416–431), and H. Peter (*ibid.*, 1898, pp. 637–654, 'rhetorik u. Poesie im klass. Alterthum'; *Der Brief*, pp. 25 f., on rhythmic element in epistolography).

§ Cp. J. Weiss, *Beiträge zur paulinischen Rhetorik* (reprint from *ThSt.*), *die Aufgaben d. neutest. Wissenschaft* (1908), pp. 11 f., Heinrici (— Meyer, *2 Cor.*^{8} 436 f.), and U. von Wilamowitz in *Der Kultur der Gegenwart*, i. 8, pp. 156 f. Blass (*Die Rhythmen der asian. und röm. Kunstprosa*, 1905, *SK.*, 1906, 304 f.) has pushed this theory to extremes, which involve an arbitrary treatment of the Pauline text and an unreal estimate of the apostle's literary ambitions (cp. Deissmann, *TLZ.*, 1905, 231 f.; W. G. Jordan, *Theol. Litteratur-Blatt*, 1905, 481 f., and Norden, *GGA.*, 1901 felt through the written words; they show unpremeditated art of the highest quality, as, *e.g.*, in passages like the hymn to love (1 Co 13), or the great apostrophe and exulting pæan of Ro $8^{31ff.}$. "How such language of the heart must have penetrated the souls of people who were accustomed to listen to the silly rigmaroles of the Sophists! In such passages the diction of the apostle rises to the heights of Plato in the *Phædrus*" (Norden, ii. 506). In short, with Christianity "the language of the heart was born again. Since the hymn of Cleanthes nothing at once so heart-felt and magnificent had been written in Greek as Paul's hymn to love" (*ibid.* ii. 459).

Elsewhere in the NT fragments of hymns can be definitely found, *e.g.* in 1 Ti 3^{16}:

ὃς ἐφανερώθη ἐν σαρκί,
ἐδικαιώθη ἐν πνεύματι,
ὤφθη ἀγγέλοις,
ἐκηρύχθη ἐν ἔθνεσιν,
ἐπιστεύθη ἐν κόσμῳ,
ἀνελήμφθη ἐν δόξῃ.

This is a piece of early Christian hymnody (cp. Col 3^{16}, Eph 5^{14}; Pliny's *Ep.* x. 98), written in short cola with ὁμοιοτέλευτα (cp. Norden, *Antike Kunstprosa*, ii. 852 f.), which probably served as a semi-liturgical confession of faith (Klöpper, *ZWT.*, 1902, 336 f.). The early church, for all its defects, had not yet lost sight of the truth that any creed worthy of acceptance should be fit for use in the praise and worship of believing men. A similar five-lined stanza, on the birth of Jesus, is inserted in the nineteenth ode of Solomon (cp. *TU.* xxxv. 4, p. 51). 2 Ti 2^{11-12} is another fragment of an early hymn:

εἰ γὰρ συναπεθάνομεν, καὶ συνζήσομεν·
εἰ ὑπομένομεν, καὶ συνβασιλεύσομεν·
εἰ ἀρνησόμεθα, κἀκεῖνος ἀρνήσεται ἡμᾶς·
εἰ ἀπιστοῦμεν, ἐκεῖνος πιστὸς μένει.

The hymns in the Apocalypse and possibly the songs in Lk 1–2 are further instances of early Christian song. It was not until later that verse included polemic (cp. Iren. i. 15. 6).

593 f.). For other literary forms, *e.g.* the παραβολή, the παροιμία, the ἀπορία, and the allegory, see pp. 77 f., 313 f. of König's *Stylistik, Rhetorik, Poetik in Bezug auf die biblische Litteratur* (1900), *PRE.* vi. 688 f. and xvii. 733 f., and *ERE.* i. 328 f.

CHAPTER I.

THE CORRESPONDENCE OF PAUL.

LITERATURE.—The patristic commentaries (cp. C. H. Turner, *DB*. v. 484-530, and *JTS* iv. 134f.) on Paul's epistles are more valuable for exegesis than for historical criticism; their outstanding contributions are the early homilies of Chrysostom and 'Ambrosiaster' (fourth century), the editions of Theodore of Mopsuestia (ed. Swete, Cambridge, 1880–2), Theodoret of Cyrus, Pelagius, and Euthalius, from the fifth century, followed by John of Damascus (eighth century), Maurus of Mayence (ninth century), Oecumenius (tenth century), Theophylact, Peter the Lombard, and Euthymius Zigabenus (twelfth century), with the thirteenth century *expositio* of Thomas Aquinas, Nicolas of Lyra's *perpetua postilla* (fourteenth century), and the fifteenth century *Annotationes* of Laurentius Valla. The sixteenth century witnessed a slight increase of attention to the historical environment of the epistles, although dogmatic prepossessions still controlled the large majority of commentators, Roman catholic (*e.g.* Erasmus, *Annotationes*, 1510, *Paraphrases in omnes epistolas Pauli*, 1521; Catharinus, 1551; Gregorius, 1564; Maldonatus; Estius; Cornelius a Lapide, 1635 [best ed. by Padovani, Rome, 1908f.], and Leander, *Commentaria in epist. omnes S. Pauli*, Paris, 1663) and Protestant (*e.g.* Bugenhagen's *Annotationes*, 1524; N. Hemminge, 1571; Zwingli's *Adnotationes* [Zürich, 1539, pp. 518-39]; Calvin; H. Bullinger's *Commentarii* [Zürich, 1544, 498–551]; Zanchi's *Commentarius* 1594, and Beza). The most notable contributions from the seventeenth century, in the shape of complete editions, are the works of J. Piscator (*Analysis logica epp. Paul.* 1638), Conrad Vorstius, Grotius (1641), Balduin (1655), Cappellus (1658), Chemnitz (1667), Locke (1684), M. Pole, *Synopsis* (vol. iv., 1694), and Hammond (1699). The eighteenth century produced the R. C. expositions of Bernardinus a Piconio (1703), Alexandre Noel (Rouen, 1710), Hardouin the Jesuit, and Ant. Remy (1739), together with Bengel's great *Gnomon* (1742), besides the *Curæ philologicæ et criticæ in x posteriores S. Pauli epistolas* of J. C. Wolf (1734), Kypke's *Observationes sacræ in Novi Testamenti libros* (1755), J. D. Michaelis, *Paraphrasis und Anmerkungen über die Briefe Pauli*[2] (1769), Rosenmüller's *Scholia* (1777), and J. B. Koppe's edition of the NT (second ed. 1791).

The nineteenth century has produced several more or less complete editions of the Pauline epistles, notably those of J. F. Weingart (*Commentarius perpetuus in decem apostoli Pauli quas uolgo dicunt epistolas minores*, Gotha, 1816), T. Belsham (London, 1823), Alford (*Greek Testament*, ii.–iii.), Hofmann (1862f.), and Wordsworth[6] (1871), with Scholz (1830), Winser (1834), de Wette (1835f.), Olshausen (1840f.), Turnbull (1854), Blomfield's *Greek Testament* (1855), Ewald (*Sendschreiben des Paulus*, 1857), Bisping's *Exegetische Handbuch zu den Briefen Pauli* (1855f.), Reuss (*Les épîtres*

Paulin., 1878, in the third volume of his NT Section of *La Bible*), Heydt (*Exeget. Commentar zu 9 Briefen*, Elberfeld, 1882), Manoury (Paris, 1878–82), P. Rambaud (Paris, 1888), L. Bonnet (Lausanne, 1892), J. van Steenkiste (*Commentarius in omnes S. Pauli epistolas*, Bruges, 1899), B. Weiss (vol. ii. of his *Das NT Handausgabe*, 1902), and A. Lemonnyer (*Épîtres de S. Paul*[2], Paris, 1905).

Separate introductions to the Pauline epistles have been issued by H. Böttger (*Beiträge zur Einleitung in die paulin. Briefe*, Göttingen, 1837 f.), P. J. Gloag (Edinburgh, 1874), and Dr. R. D. Shaw[3] (Edinburgh, 1909). The epistles are also commented on in several of the special monographs on Paul, *e.g.* those in English by Lewin, Conybeare and Howson, and Farrar, in French by Renan, and in German by Clemen and Schrader.

When the Scillitan martyrs were asked what they had in their satchel or chest, their leader Speratus replied: 'libri [αἱ καθ' ἡμᾶς βίβλοι, *i.e.* the gospels] et epistulæ Pauli uiri iusti.' This was in A.D. 180. But the unique position assigned by the church to Paul's epistles can be traced back to the age preceding Marcion. Marcion drew up an edited collection of the apostle's letters. The church's collection may have been occasioned, in self-defence, by this action, but the probability is (cp. C. H. Turner in *JTS.* x. 357 f.) that as Marcion's edition of Luke was constructed out of the church's third gospel, so his Pauline canon was 'a similar réchauffé of an existing Pauline collection in the church.' Whether this *corpus Paulinum* can be dated as early as the age of Ignatius, or even earlier (as Zahn argues), is a question which can only be asked, in the paucity of the available evidence. It is hardly likely that the idea of such a collection occurred to Paul or to any one during his lifetime,* but if the church at Philippi was anxious to possess any extant letters of Ignatius (Polyk. *ad Phil.* 13), it is reasonable to infer that a similar desire must have already prompted local collections of Paul's letters, long before there was any thought of ranking them with the scriptures (2 P 3^{16}). This would be rendered possible by the close communications † between churches, not only in one district but abroad. What is certain is that the early Christian literature begins for us with Paul's correspondence.

Genesis, says Tertullian in the fifth book of his treatise against Marcion, *Genesis promised me Paul long ago.* For, he adds (playing on a Latin rendering of Gn 49^{27}), *when Jacob was pronouncing typical and prophetic blessings upon his sons, he*

* He had not the literary self-consciousness of Cicero (*Att.* xvi. 5. 5).

† Cp. Harnack, *MAC.* i. 369 f.

turned to Benjamin and said, 'Benjamin is a ravening wolf; in the morning he shall devour his prey, but towards evening he shall provide food.' He foresaw that Paul would spring from Benjamin, 'a ravening wolf, devouring his prey in the morning': that is, in early life he would lay waste the flocks of God as a persecutor of the churches; then towards evening he would provide food: that is, in his declining years he would train the sheep of Christ as a teacher of the nations. This fanciful exegesis of the African Father brings out the fact that Paul did not begin to write the letters by which he is best known until he had been a Christian for about twenty years. So far as it can be reconstructed from the extant sources, the activity of Paul as a Christian evangelist and apostle falls into two main periods or passages.* The first of these, (*a*) covering about seventeen years, includes his work in *τὰ κλίματα τῆς Συρίας καὶ τῆς Κιλικίας*, with Tarsus and Antioch as his headquarters (Gal $1^{21f.}$, Ac 9^{30} $11^{25f.}$), and Barnabas as his main coadjutor. The second (*b*) dates from the crisis at Jerusalem, which impelled him to go further afield (Ac $15^{36f.}$ $16^{6f.}$); after hesitating about his route and sphere, he started upon the great mission to Asia Minor, Macedonia, and Achaia, which occupied him for six or seven years (Ac 19^{21}, cp. Ro 15^{23}). His coadjutors now were principally Silas and Timotheus. Thereafter he was evidently planning a mission to Spain. The Southern Mediterranean he probably passed by, as Egypt was being already evangelised,† but in the Western Mediterranean he hoped to break fresh ground, and *en route* to Spain he arranged to pay a long-deferred visit to the church at Rome. Meantime, he had to discharge his duty to the church at Jerusalem, by handing over the proceeds of the collection made by the Christians of Macedonia and Achaia on behalf of the poor saints in the Jewish capital. The untoward result of his visit is well known He left Jerusalem a prisoner, was confined for two years at Cæsarea, and finally reached Rome in custody. So far as we can see, he did not regain his freedom. The projected tour to Spain had to be abandoned, and he never revisited Asia Minor.

* The older scheme of three mission-tours is to be abandoned in favour of this division of his activity into two mission-spheres (cp. von Dobschütz, *Probleme des apostolichen Zeitalters*, 1904, pp. 58 f.).

† See Harnack, *MAC.* i. 73 f.; Zahn, *Skizzen aus dem Leben d. alten Kirche* ² (1898), 143 f.; Moffatt, *Paul and Paulinism* (1910), pp. 24–26.

The extant letters of the apostle fall within or after the second period, that is, in the late afternoon of his career. If he wrote any letters previous to the crisis at Jerusalem, they have perished. The letters to the churches of Thessalonika, Galatia, Corinth, and Rome date from (*b*); the rest of the epistles, so far as they are genuine, are the correspondence of a prisoner, and were composed either at Cæsarea or more probably at Rome. Their relative order can be determined with approximate accuracy, but their exact dates are bound up with chronological calculations based on Tacitus and Josephus, as well as on early Christian tradition, which are still matters of dispute. The following table (cp. *HNT.* 121 f.), reflecting usually the old schematism of the three journeys, will give some idea of the variety of critical opinion upon the chronology of the apostle's life:

	C. H. Turner.[1]	Neteler.[2]	O. Holtzmann.[3]	Bartlet.[4]	Cornely.[5]	Harnack.[6]	McGiffert.[7]	Zahn.[8]	Ramsay.[9]
Crucifixion of Jesus	29	29	29	29	29	29/30	30	30	30
Conversion of Paul	35/36	30	29	31/32	34	30	31/32	35	32
First visit to Jerusalem	38		32	34/35	37	33	34/35	38	34
Second visit to Jerusalem (Ac $11^{27f.}$ 12^{25})	46	44		46	42	[44]	45	44	45
First mission tour	47	44/45		47	46	45	bef. 45	50–51	46–48
Council at Jerusalem	49	47	46	49	51	47(46)	45	52	50
Second mission tour	49	47	47	49	51	47(46)	46	52	50–53
Third mission tour	52	51	49	52	55	50	49	54	53 57
Arrest in Jerusalem	56	55	53	56	59	54(53)	53	58	57
Arrival in Rome	59	57	56	59	62	57(56)	56	61	60
Death of Paul	64/65	67	64	61/62	67	64	58	66/67	67
Death of Peter	64/65	67			67	64	64	64	

1 *DB.* i. 415-425; *JTS.* iii. 120–128.

2 *Untersuchungen neut. Zeitverhältnisse* (1894).

3 *Neutest. Zeitgeschichte* (1895), §§ 15–17; differently in second ed. 1906.

4 *AA.* pp. xiii-xiv, etc.

5 Similarly Laurent (*NT Studien*, 67–91), placing the second visit in 47, however, the first tour in 47–50, and the second in 52–55.

6 *ACL.* ii. 1. 233–239.

7 *AA.* 164, 172, etc.

8 *PRE.* xv. 61–88, and *INT.* iii. 450 f.

9 *SPT.* 363 f., as revised in *Pauline and other Studies* (1906), 345 f.

A word may be added on the problem of the authenticity[a] of the Pauline letters. Their criticism has passed through a

[a] 'Authentic,' in this connection as elsewhere in the criticism of the NT, "has reference to the origin only, not to the contents; to say that a document is authentic is merely to say that its origin is certain, not that its contents are free from error" (C. V. Langlois and C. Seignobos, *Introduction aux études historiques*, Eng. tr. 1898, p. 159).

phase corresponding, for example, to that which has occurred in the artistic estimate of Giorgione's pictures: after successive verdicts which unreasonably reduced the number of the genuine to a minimum, the application of a less rigid and more accurate standard has at last revealed the existence of a larger number of authentic canvases in the one case and of epistles in the other. This shift of critical opinion has been brought about, for the most part, by a gradual recognition of the fact that writers and painters do not always work at the same pitch of excellence. The progress of historical criticism on Acts and, to a less degree, on the sources of the gospels, together with the recent researches into the *κοινή*, gnosticism, and contemporary Judaism, has also helped to determine the authenticity of several Pauline letters which were suspected half a century ago. "It has been the

Lightfoot.[10]	Wendt.[11]	Renan.	Bornemann.[12]	Clemen.[13]	Gilbert.[14]	Weiss.[15]	Sabatier.[16]	Jülicher.[17]	Findlay.[18]	Farrar.[19]	Belser.[20]	Steinmann.[21]	Hoennicke.[22]
[30]	31(29)	33	33										30–33
34	35	38	34	31	32	35	35	35	36	37	33	36/37	33–35
37	38	41	37	34	35	38	38	38	39	39	36	39/40	36–38
45					(44)	44				44	46	44	45–46
48	45–50	bef. 51	44f.		45–47		50/51		46	45	46	45	49?
51	52	51	51	48	48	52	52	52	49	51	50	50/51	50–52
51	52	51	51	49–52	49–51	52	52–55	52	49	51	50–53	51	
54	55	54		53–59	52·56	55	55	55	53	54	53–57	64	
58	59	58	58	59	56	59	58/59	59/60	57	58	58	58	
61	62	61	60/61	62	59	62	61/62	61	60	60	61		60–62
67	64	64	63/64	64	65–68			[64]	67	68	67		
64		64									67		

10 *Biblical Essays* (pp. 215–233). Similarly Aberle, *BZ.* (1903) 256 f., 372 f., (1905) 371–400.

11 *Acts* (Meyer), pp. 53–60.

12 *Thessalonians* (Meyer), pp. 17–18. Similarly von Dobschütz.

13 *Paulus*, i. 411.

14 *Student's Life of Paul*, pp. 242–259.

15 *INT.* i. pp. 154 f.

16 *Paul*, pp. 13 f.

17 *Einl.* 31 f.

18 *DB.* iii. 696–731.

19 *Paul* (appendix, vol. ii. pp. 623 f.).

20 *TQ.* (1896) 353 f., *Einl.* 190.

21 *Abfassungszeit des Galaterbriefes* (1906), p. 189.

22 *Die Chronologie des Paulus* (1903), cp. *NKZ.* (1902) 569–620.

mission of the nineteenth century to prove that everybody's work was written by somebody else, and it will not be the most useless task of the twentieth to betake itself to more profitable inquiries" (Saintsbury, *History of Criticism*, p. 152). The epistles to Timotheus and Titus, together with Ephesians, are probably Pauline rather than Paul's; they belong to the class of literary ἀδέσποτοι in early Christianity. Otherwise[1] it may be assumed that the letters which are grouped under Paul's name in the canon were written by him, whatever processes of editing they may have passed through before their incorporation into the sacred collection of the church.

(A) *CORRESPONDENCE WITH THESSALONIKA.*

(*a*) Editions—Georgius Major (*Enarratio duarum epp. ad Thess. prælecta*, 1561); Musculus (*Comment. in Phil. Col. Thess. Tim.*, 1565 f.); R. Rollock (Edinburgh, 1598); J. A. Gleiche's *Erklärung* (1729); J. A. Turretin's posthumous *Comment. theoretico-practicus in epp. ad Thess.* (1739); P. J. Müller (1784); F. A. W. Krause (1790); Schleiermacher (1823); T. C. Tychsen[3] (1823); J. F. Flatt, *Vorlesungen über die briefen an die Phil. Col. Thess.* (Tübingen, 1829); Ludwig Pelt (*Epistolae P. apostoli ad Thess. perpetuo illust. commentario*, Greifswald, 1830)*; H. A. Schott, *Epistolae P. ad Thess. et Galatas* (Leipzig, 1834); Baumgarten-Crusius (*Commentar über Phil. und Thessal.* 1848); Olshausen (1840, Eng. tr. 1851); J. Lillie (New York, 1856); Ewald, *Sendschreiben des Paulus* (1857); de Wette[3] (1864); Meyer[3] (1867); Hofmann[2] (1869); Eadie (1877); A. J. Mason (in Ellicott's NT, 1879); Reuss (1878–9); Ellicott[4] (1880)*; H. Reinecke (Leipzig, 1881); Alexander (*Speaker's Com.* 1881); Marcus Dods (in *Schaff's Comment.* 1882); Hutchison (Edin. 1883); Lünemann[4] (— Meyer, Eng. tr. 1884); Gloag (1887); Zöckler (in *Strack und Z.'s Comm.* 1888–95); A. Schäfer (1890); Schmiedel[2] (*HC.* 1892)*; Zimmer (in *Denkschrift des theol. Seminars Herborn*, 1891, and *Theol. Comment. z. d. Thess.* 1894)*; Padovani (1894); Jowett, *St. Paul's Epp. to Thess. Gal. and Romans*[3] (1894); Bornemann (— Meyer, 1894); Lightfoot (*Notes on Epp. of St. Paul*, 1895, pp. 1–92); J. Drummond (*Internat. Hdbks to NT*, 1899); Gutjahr, *Briefe des Paulus. I. Thess. Gal.* (1900); Adeney (*CB.*, n. d.); G. G. Findlay (*CGT.* 1904)*; W. Lueken (*SNT.*[2] 1907); J. M. S. Baljon (1907); G. Milligan (1908)*; Wohlenberg[2] (*ZK.*, 1908); von Dobschütz (— Meyer, 1909)*; Moffatt (*EGT.* 1910); R. Mackintosh (Westminster NT, 1910).

(*b*) Studies—(i.) general:—P. Schmidt, *der erste Th. brief neu erklärt, nebst einen Exkurs über d. 2 gleichn. Brief* (1885); L. Monnet, *Les épîtres aux Thess. étude biblique* (1889); Sabatier (*ESR.* xii. 123 f.); Hausrath, iii. 209 f.; Lightfoot (Smith's *DB.* iii. 1477–84)*; E. de Faye, *de vera indole Pauli ap. ad Thessal. dissertatio critica* (Paris, 1892); Denney (*Expositor's Bible*, 1892); McGiffert, *AA.* 250 f.; Bartlet, *AA.* 110 f.; Pfleiderer, *Urc.* i. 125–143;

[1] Most doubt attaches to 2 Thessalonians, less to Colossians. A similar dubiety prevails, *e.g.*, with regard to the two fragments of the epistles which are supposed to have been written by Cornelia, the mother of the Gracchi; the problem of their authenticity divides scholars like Nipperdey, Mommsen, Hubel, and M. Schlelein from those who, like Mercklin and E. Meyer, deny their genuineness.

von Dobschütz, *Urc.* 81 f.; F. Trautzsch, *Die mündliche Verkündigung des Ap. Paulus* (1903); E. Ullern, *S. Paul, évangeliste et pasteur des Thessaloniciens. Étude* (Nimes, 1903); C. Bruston (*RTQR.*, 1905, 160 f., 369 f.); Senstius, *die Abfassungszeit der Thess. Briefe* (1908); R. Scott, *The Pauline Epistles* (1909), 215–233; Lütgert, *BFT.* xiii. 6 (1909), pp. 55–102 (on errorists); Harnack, *Das Problem des Zweiten Thessalonicherbriefs* (1910, *SBBA.* 560–578).

(ii.) on the text:—John Phillips, *The Greek of the First Ep. to the Thess.* (London, 1751); Zimmer, *Der Text der Thessal. Briefe* (1893); Baljon, (*Theol. Studiën*, 1888, 347–352); Blass, *Rhythmen der asian. u. röm. Kunstprosa* (1905), pp. 196 f.

(iii.) against Pauline authorship:—Baur in *Theol. Jahrb.* (1855), pp. 141–168, and in *Paul* (ii. 341 f., Eng. tr. ii. 314–340); van der Vies, *de beide brieven aan de Th.* (1865); Steck (*JPT.*, 1883, 509–524); Pierson and Naber (*Verisimilia, laceram conditionem NT exhibentia*, 1886, 3–25).

(iv.) for Pauline authorship:—Grimm (*SK.*, 1850, 780 f.); Hilgenfeld (*ZWT.*, 1862, 225 f., 1866, 295 f.); Lightfoot (*Biblical Essays*, 251–269, and in Smith's *DB.*); Sabatier, *Paul*, pp. 106 f.; Askwith, *Introd. to Thess. epp.* (1902)*; Lock (*DB.* iv. 743–749); A. C. McGiffert (*EBi.* 5036–5046); Zahn, *Einl.* §§ 14–16; Clemen, *Paulus*, i. 111 f.

1 Thessalonians.

In addition to the general literature already cited, the (*a*) editions by Calixtus (1654); W. Sclater (*Exposition with notes*, London, 1619); A. S. Paterson (Edin. 1857); A. Koch[2] (1855)*; Röhm (Passau, 1885); Johannes, *Kommentar zum ersten Th. Brief* (Dillingen, 1898)*: (*b*) studies by J. Martinus (*Analysis epistolae prioris ad Thess.*, Groningen, 1663); Lipsius (*SK.*, 1854, 905 f., "über Zweck u. Veranlassung des 1 Th.," a reply to Baur); J. J. Prins, "de eerste brief van Paulus aan de Thessalonikers" (*TT.*, 1885, 231 f.); von Soden (*SK.*, 1885, 263–310)*; Brückner's *Chron.* 193–199.

2 Thessalonians.

In addition to the above general literature: (*a*) against the Pauline authorship—Kern (*Tübing. Zeits. für Theol.*, 1839, 145 f.); J. E. C. Schmidt, (*Einl.* 256 f.); Hilgenfeld (*ZWT.*, 1862, 242–264); van Manen, *onderzoek naar de echtheid van Paulus' tweeden brief aan de Thess.* (Utrecht, 1865); Michelsen (*TT.*, 1876, 70–82); Bahnsen (*JPT.*, 1880, 681–705); Spitta, *Urc.* i. 109–154; Weizsäcker (*AA.* i. 295 f.); C. Rauch (*ZWT.*, 1895, 457–465); H. J. Holtzmann (*ZNW.*, 1901, 97–108); Pfleiderer (*Urc.* i. 95–101); Wrede (*TU.*, Neue Folge, ix. 2, 1903)*; Hollmann (*ZNW.*, 1904, 28–38); von Soden (*INT.* 324–333).

(*b*) for the Pauline authorship—Reiche, *authent. posterioris ad Thess. epistolæ* (1829; against Schmidt); Schneckenburger (*Jahrb. für deutsche Theol.*, 1859, 405–467); Renan (iii. 248–255); Westrik, *de echtheid van II Thess.* (1879); Klöpper in part 8 (pp. 73–140) of *Theol. Stud. u. Skizzen aus Ostpreussen* (1889)*: Titius, *der Paulinismus* (1900), 49 f.; G. G.

Finlay (*Exp.*[6], Oct. 1900, 251–261); G. W. Garrod (London, 1900) Kolmodin, *Pauli andra tess.-bref* (Stockholm, 1901); Moffatt, *HNT.* 142–149; Brüning, *der Echtheit d. 2 Thess. Briefes* (1903); E. Vischer. *Paulus-briefe* (1904) 70 f.; Wernle (*GGA.*, 1905, 347 f., review of Wrede); Jülicher (*Einl.* § 5); R. J. Knowling, *The Testimony of St. Paul to Christ* (1905), 24 f.; Jacquier (*INT.* i. 94 f.); Barth (*Einl.* § 6); A. S. Peake (*INT.*, 1909, 12 f.); Grüner, 'Besteht zwischen d. 2 und 1 Briefe an die Gemeinde von Thess. eine literar. Abhängigkeit?' (*Weidenauer Studien*, ii. 419 f., against Wrede).

§ 1. *Contents and character of 1 Thess.*—The Christians of Thessalonika were mainly Greeks by birth and training (1^{9} 2^{14}), who had been won over from paganism by the efforts of Paul, Silvanus, and Timotheus. The mission had only lasted for a month or two. After preaching for three weeks in the local synagogue, the evangelists continued their work till they were prematurely driven from the city by the intrigues of the local Jews. They left a vigorous church behind them, however, and the central position of Thessalonika upon the Via Egnatia at the head of the Thermaic gulf presented excellent opportunities for the diffusion of the new faith (1^{7-8} 4^{10}).*

The narrative of Acts 17^{1-9}, though admitting that the large majority of the converts were proselytes (17^{4}),† ignores any work outside the synagogue, and restricts the term of the mission apparently to three weeks. This account is inadequate. As Baronius once said, *epistolaris historia est optima historia.* The membership and influence of the church, its reputation throughout Macedonia and even Achaia, to say nothing of Paul's allusions to a period of training (1 Th $2^{5f.}$), imply the lapse of a considerable interval between the apostle's arrival and departure. Besides, his stay must have been prolonged, if he had occasion not only to support himself (1 Th 2^{8-11} $^{17-20}$ 3^{5-10}) by his trade, but to receive gifts of money (Ph 4^{16}) from his friends at Philippi, a hundred miles away. It was the last-named fact which, among other things, gave rise to the imputation of mercenary motives ($2^{5.\ 9}$). The primary charge against Paul and his friends before the local authorities had been treason and sedition (Ac 17^{6-8} βασιλέα ἕτερον); in his enforced absence through the success of this manœuvre, charges against his personal character were circulated. Naturally he refers to the former subject quite incidentally (1 Th 2^{12} *God's own kingdom*); the latter dominates his mind.

---

* These passages cover not only Philippi and Berea (Lightfoot, *Biblical Essays*, pp. 237 f.), but a somewhat extensive work by Paul, as well as by the Thessalonians, which may have reached as far west as Illyrikum (Ro 15^{19}).

† This, together with the religious training of the synagogue, helps to explain—what is otherwise rather remarkable—the unusually rapid growth of the local church (Wynne, *Exp.*[7] iv. 364–377).

His primary reason for writing to the Christians of Thessalonika was anxiety on their behalf. It was the first community of any importance which he had been able to found in Europe; and the exemplary character, the exceptional opportunities, and the influence of its members had already produced a wide impression on the surrounding district. To this Paul alludes (1^{7-8}) with a pardonable touch of hyperbole * (cp. Ro 1^8, Ph 1^{18}). From no church was he torn with such evident reluctance. But the urgent claim of the church on his solicitude was the suffering to which it had been exposed even during his stay, and especially since he had left. Concerned for his friends' stability, and unable to return in person, † he had dispatched Timotheus, as the younger of his companions, from Athens in order to rally and confirm their faith. Meanwhile events had driven him from Athens across to Corinth (1^{7-8}), where Timotheus brought him the glad tidings (a real gospel—note the rare use of *εὐαγγελισάμενου* in 3^6) of the Thessalonians' affection and constancy. He at once proceeds to send this informal letter, written (i.) out of warm personal affection, which he rejoices to find returned, and (ii.) in order to convey instructions upon some points of Christian belief and conduct.

For an ingenious attempt to prove that 1 Thess. answers a letter brought by Timotheus from the Thessalonians themselves, see Rendel Harris in *Exp.*[6] viii. 161 f., 401 f., and Bacon's *INT.* 73 f. (*Story of St. Paul*, 235 f.). The hypothesis is tenable, but the evidence is elusive: *καὶ* in 2^{18} and 3^6 cannot be pressed into a proof of this, nor can *οἴδατε* (='you have admitted in your letter'); and *ἀπαγγέλλετε*, though attractive, is not a necessary reading in 1^9.

---

* The rhetorical phrase *ἐν παντὶ τόπῳ* is not to be pressed (as by Zahn, *Einl.* i. 146 f.) into a proof that the news of the Thessalonian mission had time to reach the Asiatic Christians, whose congratulations came back to Paul before he wrote.

† Why? Because, in Oriental phrase, *Satan hindered us* (2^{18})—an enigmatic remark which probably means either sickness (2 Co 12^7) or pressure of local circumstances at Corinth. To refer it to a guarantee exacted by the Imperial authorities from Jason and his associates that peace would be kept, and Paul kept away (Ramsay, *SPT.* 228 f.; Woodhouse, *EBi.* 5047; and Finlay), conflicts with the idea of the Empire in 2 Th $2^{2f.}$. Besides, the Thess. would have easily known in that case why Paul could not come back. That Paul had any intention of returning to Thessalonika by sea, after he was driven out of Berea, is a precarious inference from 2^{18}, though the idea occurred at an early stage of the Christian tradition, as is plain from the insertion of the Bezan editor in

The former (i.) consideration emerges in a series of allusions to malignant suspicions of his conduct, especially of the purity of his motives and methods, circulated by local outsiders ($2^{3f.\ 18}$ etc.). This does not mean that he had reproached himself with having appeared to leave his friends in the lurch; such cannot be the entire explanation (so Spitta, pp. 115–116) of the phrases. A self-defence of this kind would be sadly *post factum*. The language undoubtedly implies that insinuations to his discredit were current in Thessalonika; they struck at the church through the apostle; and because the peace and faith of the Thessalonian Christians were so intimately bound up with confidence in his integrity, he vindicates their trust by showing how, in an age in which impostors, religious, medical, and philosophical, flourished by crooked methods, he had not worked for mercenary ends, nor set up high pretensions, nor made exacting demands on his followers, nor left them meanly in the lurch. He appeals to his record in Thessalonika, and shows that his absence was neither voluntary nor equivalent to a slackening of his interest or affection. Such malicious calumnies, circulated mainly or at least primarily by the Jews,* Paul further meets by unbaring his very heart. He reveals his throbbing interest in the church (2^{8} $3^{6.\ 10}$), tells them of the joy and pride their loyalty afforded him (see the praise of other Macedonians in Ph 4^{1}), and expands previous oral admonitions (2^{12} $4^{1\text{-}2.\ 6.\ 10\text{-}12}$) in a series of written counsels.

(ii.) The second and supplementary part of the letter, passing from this personal and apologetic aspect, warns them against such perils as (περὶ ἁγιασμοῦ, $4^{3\text{-}8}$) sensuality, (περὶ φιλαδελφίας,

Ac 17^{15} (παρῆλθεν δὲ τὴν Θεσσαλίαν· ἐκωλύθη γὰρ εἰς αὐτοὺς κηρύξαι τὸν λόγον), which, like the equally inferior reading in 17^{4} (σεβ. καὶ Ἑλλ.), is due to the harmonising tendencies of the second century.

* So Hilgenfeld (*Einl.* 241), Lipsius, Sabatier (pp. 107, 110), Schmidt (25 f., 96), Renan, G. G. Finlay, Weiss, etc. In the nature of things, as already (*e.g.* Ac 14^{19} etc.), Paul's principal detractors would be Jews, angry at this renegade's success; besides, the transition from $2^{9\text{-}12}$ to $2^{13\text{-}16}$ and back to $2^{17f.}$ rather points to Semitic agitation. Others (*e.g.* Hofmann, von Soden, *SK.*, 1885, pp. 302, 306 f., Schmiedel, and Zahn) think of pagans (cp. Clemen, *NKZ.*, 1896, 151 f.). In any case the references are too keen and detailed to be merely prophylactic. Probably the charges were started by Jews and caught up by pagans; they were not directed (as in Galatia) against his apostolic authority, but more subtly against his personal character. Passages like $2^{3.\ 18}$ $4^{11\text{-}12}$ (cp. 2 Th $2^{2f.}$ $3^{8f.}$) do not justify the theory (Lipsius) that a Judaistic party was at work within the church.

$4^{9f.}$) selfishness, and noisy indolence, due as much to a misapprehension of their faith as to pagan surroundings. The occurrence of some deaths had raised uncertainties about the Lord's Second coming, and Paul briefly handles this with reference to (*a*) the dead (4^{13-18} περὶ τῶν κοιμωμένων), who are declared not to have forfeited their place in the messianic realm of the age to come; and (*b*) to the living (5^{1-11} περὶ τῶν χρόνων καὶ τῶν καιρῶν), who are exhorted to moral alertness in view of this great event, which may be expected at any moment (5^{3}), as well as to an ethical steadiness * unaffected by unsettling expectations of the end. This need of mutual exhortation (5^{11}) naturally leads to a word on subordination and obedience to the local church authorities ($5^{12f.}$), and with some general counsels the letter ends. While it would be actually put into the hands of the local leaders (5^{12}), it was addressed, and was to be read, to all the members of the church, not to any exclusive section of them (5^{27}).† Apparently it did its work, so far as Paul's character was concerned.

The perils indicated in this writing belong to an inexperienced and unconsolidated Christianity; they have no connection with any Judaising propaganda on the part of Paul's opponents, as was the case in Corinth. The saving quality of the Thessalonians' religion was its generous and widespread (1^{3} $3^{6.12}$ $5^{8.13.15}$) charity (traces of this later in 2 Co 7–9), combined with an enthusiasm which survived depressing trials and isolation alike. Their faith required completion rather than correction (3^{10}). They were on the right path; what they chiefly needed was stimulus and direction (3^{12} $4^{1.10}$). Consequently there was no occasion for Paul to introduce what are elsewhere enunciated as cardinal principles of his theology. For the same reason the letter is not marked by passion and agitation. There is an outpouring of relief, but no fierce outburst of indignation or alarm or wounded dignity; what reproof Paul has to give is delicately conveyed, as usual, in the wake of praise.

§ 2. *Authenticity of 1 Thess.*—As the letter is included not only in the Muratorian Canon but in Marcion's strictly Pauline collection (Tert. *adv. Marc.* v. 15; Epiph. *haer.* xlii. 9; cp. Zahn's *GK.* ii. 520 f.), it was known and circulated by the first quarter of the second century. Definite quotations, however, chiefly of

* After his own example ($2^{9f.}$). "La modèle qu'il concevait était un artisan rangé, paisible, appliqué à son travail" (Renan, iii. 246).

† As some previous letter had been? cp. 3 Jn ^{9}. To delete 5^{27} as a marginal gloss, added by some second-century reader when the apostolic letters were coming into prominent use (Hitzig, Schmiedel, J. Weiss: *SK.*, 1892, 261 f.), is gratuitous, in view of this natural explanation.

the eschatological passages, emerge for the first time in Irenæus (*adv. hær.* v. 6. 1 = 5^{23}, v. 30. 2 = 5^{3}) and Tertullian (*de resurr. carnis*, xxiv. = 5^{1} and $1^{9\text{-}10}$), while both Clement of Alexandria and Origen employ the epistle (for Dionysius of Corinth, see Eus. *H. E.* iv. 23). The so-called allusions in the apostolic fathers are scanty and vague, for the most part; but it is probable that there is a reminiscence of 5^{13} in Hermas (*Vis.* iii. 9. 10. εἰρηνεύετε ἐν αὑτοῖς), and—if the reading were certain—of 5^{17} in Ignat. *Eph.* x. 1 (ἀδιαλείπτως προσεύχεσθε), of 1^{6} in *Eph.* x. 3 (μιμηταὶ δὲ τοῦ Κυρίου σπουδάζωμεν εἶναι, different context), and 2^{4} in *Rom.* ii. 1 (οὐ θέλω ὑμᾶς ἀνθρωπαρεσκῆσαι, ἀλλὰ Θεῷ); cp., too, 4^{9} = Barn. 21^{6} γίνεσθε δὲ θεοδίδακτοι (different context). The general similarity of outline between $4^{14\text{-}16}$ and Did. xvi. 6 (revelation of the Lord, trumpet, resurrection) is too vague to denote any literary filiation.

These traces are not early enough to preclude the possibility that the epistle is pseudonymous, and a post-Pauline origin has occasionally been claimed for it on various grounds. (i.) The resemblances between it and the Corinthian epistles (Baur) are no argument against its originality; whatever 1 Thess. may be, it is a decided error of literary criticism to pronounce it a mere copy and echo of 1 and 2 Corinthians. (ii.) The discrepancies between its account of the Thessalonian mission and that of Acts are not serious enough to invalidate the epistle (Schrader, Baur, etc.; see p. 66). A few months were enough to raise the problem of Christians dying before the παρουσία. The favourable soil for the gospel at Thessalonika, partly among proselytes, must have led to a rapid development of the church, and Paul was too careful a missioner to leave his converts without a rudimentary but effective local organisation. Unless, therefore, Acts is taken as a rigid standard, 1 Thess. can be naturally set in the situation presupposed by the former, although a comparison of Ac $17^{1\text{-}5}$ and 1 Th 1–2 shows that the former narrative requires to be supplemented and corrected by the details of Paul. Luke was not a member of the party at Thessalonika, and in any case it was not his purpose to describe the inner development of the Pauline churches. As a rule, he is content to narrate how Paul and his companions got a foothold in any city, and how they had to leave it. From Luke we fail to understand that the local church was recruited mainly from the pagan population, that the mission lasted for some time, and that the evangelists kept in touch with the local church after their enforced departure. But all this tells strongly in favour of the epistle, whose incidental allusions are not only coherent but natural. It is capricious to pronounce the epistle a colourless imitation, if it agrees with Acts, and unauthentic if it disagrees. "Die Art wie Paulus in 1 Thess. die unmittelbar vorhergegangenen Begebenheiten in Philippi und die Rückkehr des Timotheus (vgl. 1 Th 3^{1-6} und Ac 17^{14} 18^{5}) erwähnt, beweist theils, dass dies nicht künstlich aus der Apgeschichte gemacht ist, weil dort eine Aussendung des Timotheus nach Thessalonika nicht erwähnt ist, theils dass der Brief nicht lange nachdem Timotheus wieder zu Paulus gestossen ist, kann geschrieben sein, weil die kleinen Umstände sonst nicht vorkommen würden. Diese Uebereinstimmung ist nun von der Art, dass sie die Aechtheit der Briefes beweist, so dass wir nach innern Merkmalen weiter nicht zu fragen haben" (Schleiermacher, *Einl.* 150). (iii.) The vocabulary of 1 Thess. presents no features which can fairly be described as necessarily unPauline, except when an arbitrary standard of Pauline thought and style is constructed from Gal., Cor., and Romans. A few words occur, as in any letter of Paul, which do not happen to be used elsewhere by him (*e.g.* *θεὸς ἀληθινός* 1^{9}, *ἀναμένειν* 1^{10}, *ὁ πειράζων* 3^{5}, *σαίνεσθαι* 3^{3}, *ἄγειν* in sense of 4^{14}, *ἀνιστάναι* 4^{14-16} of the resurrection of Jesus and men, *λόγος κυρίου* 4^{15}, *ἁρπάζειν* 4^{17}, *νεφέλαι* and *ἀπάντησις* 4^{17}, *λόγοι* of apostolic injunctions 4^{18}, *ἀκριβῶς* 5^{2}, *ὑπερεκπερισσοῦ* (cp. Eph 3^{20}) 5^{13} and 3^{10}, *ἡγεῖσθαι ἐν* 5^{13}; but the general language of the letter is thoroughly Pauline, and the style bears no trace of a later hand. When set side by side with the rest of the Pauline letters, 1 Thess. invites the judgment passed by von Soden on 1 Th 5^{4-11} as compared with Ro $13^{11f.}$: "the similarities of the passages show their kinship; the differences exclude any question of imitation." It is almost superfluous to add that the letter was dictated in Greek. The idea (cp. Bertholdt's *Einl.* 3488 f.) that it represents a translation by Silvanus and Timotheus from the original Aramaic is a sheer *jeu d'esprit.* (iv.) It is more difficult to explain the lack of any allusion, even where such might be expected, to the characteristic Pauline ideas of the law, forgiveness in relation to the death of Christ, and the union of the Christian with Christ and the Spirit. One line of explanation may be set aside decisively. Paul had been a Christian, and a Christian preacher, for nearly twenty years when he wrote this letter, and the ordinary catechetical instruction, such as he was now giving at Corinth (1 Co 1^{23} 2^{1} 15^{8}), certainly included a much fuller account of the death of Jesus in relation to forgiveness than happens to be mentioned in 1 Thessalonians. Behind him lay the struggle with Jewish Christian traditionalism at Antioch and Jerusalem,* which had already compelled him to define his principles and think out the deeper aspects of his gospel. It is therefore historically and psychologically impossible to read the Thessalonian epistles as if they represented a primitive stage in the apostle's thought, when he had not yet developed dogmatic Paulinism. If his gospel centres here round the Coming † rather than the Cross of Jesus Christ, and if he seems to argue that men were to be sanctified by hope rather than justified by faith, the explanation must be sought in the special circumstances which determined the composition of the letter. There was apparently nothing to call out any discussion of the Law or any theorising on forgiveness (cp. Feine's *Gesetzesfreie Evglm d. Paulus*, 169–181). The clue to the comparative absence of technical terms and theories is probably to be found in Paul's desire to educate the Thessalonian Christians in the rudiments of their faith. He fed them, as he was feeding the Corinthians, with elementary principles (1 Co 3^{2} γάλα ὑμᾶς ἐπότισα). *Paruulos nutrix fouet: proficientes uero pater instituit* (Pelagius). And Paul was both nurse and father to them, as he himself affectionately reminded them ($2^{7.\ 11}$). In any case, a later Paulinist writing in his master's name would probably have introduced some reference to the distinctive dogmas of Paulinism. Their absence from 1 Thess. is a difficulty, but it is not a proof of unPauline origin. "Das dogmatische System des Apostels wird in diesem Briefe selbstverständlicherweise nicht entfaltet, sondern nur gestreift, dies aber in durchaus original-paulinischer Art und Weise" (P. Schmidt, *op. cit.* p. 78). (v.) Another real difficulty may be removed by recourse to the hypothesis of an interpolation. "When it is

* Unless, of course, Acts is held to have ante-dated (so Spitta and Weizsäcker) the Jerusalem Council, which ought to be subsequent to Paul's dispute with Peter at Antioch. In this way (cp. Ménégoz, *le Péché*, 4) room might be found for the Thess. epistles as an expression of unformulated, primitive Paulinism; but even so, we should have to imagine that Paul's mind did not begin to work upon his religion till the exigencies of controversy forced him to construct a theology.

† Every paragraph runs out into the future (1^{9} $2^{12.\ 16.\ 19\text{-}20}$ 3^{13} $4^{6ff.}$ $5^{10.\ 23}$).

said that after the Jews have continually filled up the measure of their sins, ἔφθασε δὲ ἐπ' αὐτοὺς ἡ ὀργὴ εἰς τέλος, what does this suggest to us more naturally than the punishment that came upon them in the destruction of Jerusalem?" (Baur, *Paul.* ii. 88). The words (2^{16b}) are a reminiscence of Test. Levi vi. 11. It is unnecessary to suspect 2^{14-16} as a later interpolation (cp. *HNT.* pp. 625–626), but 2^{16b} must be admitted to have all the appearance of a marginal gloss, written after the tragedy of A.D. 70 (so, *e.g.*, Spitta, Pfleiderer, Schmiedel, Teichmann: *die paul. Vorstellungen von Auferstehung u. Gericht*, 83; Drummond, etc.). The recent massacres, revolutions, and famines in Palestine, to say nothing of the edict of Claudius, *de pellendis Judæis* (P. Schmidt, 86 f.), might be considered to afford a suitable background for the verse, but the definite sense assigned to ὀργή, which is more than mere judicial hardening (cp. Dante's *Paradiso*, vi. 88–93), tells in favour of the reference to the horrors of A.D. 70. Instead of relegating the entire epistle to this period, it is better to regard the words as a Christian reader's gloss upon 2^{16a}. (vi.) The attempt of Steck (*JPT.*, 1883, 509–524) to prove that $4^{15f.}$ is a quotation from 4 Es 5^{41-42} is hopelessly forced (cp. Schmidt, 107–110; Bornemann, 310 f.). Paul's reference is, probably, not to some ἄγραφον, but to a prophetic revelation vouchsafed to himself or possibly to Silvanus (cp. Ac 15^{32}) in a vision (see *EGT.* iv. 37). Even if the passage were a quotation, it would be from oral tradition or from some early collection of evangelic logia. The point of the saying is opposed to that of 4 Esdras, and the parallel, such as it is, is too far-fetched to denote the post-Pauline origin of the epistle.

The ἡμεῖς κτλ. of $4^{15f.}$ (cp. 1 Co $15^{51f.}$) must not be evaporated into a general and hypothetical sense, as, *e.g.*, by those who hesitate to attribute a miscalculation to Paul, or by those who at the opposite extreme (like Steck, *PM.*, 1905, 449–453) deny that such expressions form any barrier to the theory that the epistles of Paul were composed as late as the second century.

§ 3. *Place and period of composition.*—The letter was written from Corinth (Ac 18^{11}), as the reference to Achaia (1^{7-8}) is enough to prove.* The words ἐν Ἀθήναις (3^{1}) do not necessarily mean that Paul was not there when he wrote (cp. 1 Co 15^{32} 16^{8}), but they are insufficient to prove that Athens was the place of the letter's composition,—a theory advocated from Theodoret and

* Böttger (*Beiträge*, 1837, 28) thinks of some town in Achaia.

Pelagius (cp. the subscription of A B K L, πρὸς Θεσσαλονικεῖς πρώτη ἐγράφη ἀπὸ Ἀθηνῶν) to Schrader (*Apostel Paulus*, pp. 90 f.), the latter placing it during the period of Ac $20^{2f.}$, mainly on the ground that πρεσβύτεροι (cp. 1 Ti 3^{6}) could not exist in a church of neophytes which had only been founded for a few months, and that deaths (4^{13-18}) could not have already occurred. J. F. Kohler (*Abfassungszeit der epistolischen Schriften im NT*, 1830, p. 112) dated it even later (after A.D. 66), on the ground that 2^{14-16} implied the death of James, the Lord's brother, and the outbreak of the Jewish rebellion.

The narrative of Acts requires further correction at this point. According to Luke (Ac 18^{5}), Silas and Timotheus, who had remained at Berea with orders to rejoin Paul as soon as possible, did not reach him till he had arrived at Corinth. Since Timotheus had meanwhile visited Thessalonika (1 Th 2^{17}–3^{6}), we must assume (*a*) either that he hurried to Athens himself, was sent back by Paul to Thessalonika, and on his return picked up Silas at Berea, or (*b*) that both men joined Paul at Athens and were dispatched on different missions, Silas perhaps to Philippi, and Timotheus certainly to Thessalonika. Otherwise Paul left Silas behind at Athens (cp. Ac 18^{5}), if the plural in 1 Th 3^{1} is not the *pluralis auctoris*. In any case the natural sense of 1 Th 3^{1-2} is that Paul sent Timotheus from Athens, not (so, *e.g.*, von Soden) that he merely sent directions from Athens that his colleague should leave Berea and betake himself to Thessalonika (*EBi.* 5076–5077).

§ 4. *Contents and setting of 2 Thess.*—After congratulating the Thessalonian Christians on their brotherly love and faith and patience (1^{1-4}), Paul addresses himself to the situation which had specially called into exercise the last-named virtue. (*a*) The trials and troubles under which they are now suffering (1^{4-12}) are simply a prelude to the relief and vindication which will be theirs at the coming of Jesus. (*b*) As the anticipation of this, however, had already produced a morbid fanatical excitement in certain quarters, owing to the fact of some people, apparently from a misunderstanding of his instructions, having failed to recollect that the παρουσία, while near, could not happen till after the appearance and overthrow of a hostile power, Paul proceeds (2^{1-12}) to reiterate his oral teaching on this point. He then concludes (2^{13-17}) with an expression of confidence in them, an appeal for loyalty to his teaching, and a brief prayer for their constancy and comfort. Asking their prayers, in turn, for himself, he renews his expression of confidence and interest (3^{1-5}), whereupon, after a word on the maintenance of discipline and industry, the epistle closes (3^{6-18}).

Assuming both letters to have come from Paul,* we need not hesitate to place 1 Thessalonians prior to 2 Thessalonians, in opposition to the reverse hypothesis of Grotius (based mainly on an antiquated chronology), Bunsen, Renan (iii. 235 f.), Ewald (*Sendschreiben*, pp. 15 f.), and Laurent (*SK.*, 1864, pp. 497 f.; *NT Studien*, pp. 49 f.). There is no reason why such a criterion of genuineness as 2 Th 3^{17} should have appeared in the earliest of Paul's letters; in view of 2^{2} its appearance, after the composition of 1 Thess. and even other letters, is psychologically accurate. It is unnatural to find a reference to 2 Th 3^{6-16} in 1 Th 4^{10-11}; besides, as Bornemann points out (p. 495), if 2 Thess. is held to betray all the tone of a first letter (Ewald), what about 2 Th 2^{16}? The comparative absence of allusions in 2 Thess. to 1 Thess. (cp., however, 2 Th 2^{1} = 1 Th 4^{17} etc.) is explained by the fact that in the second epistle Paul goes back to elaborate part of his original oral teaching in view of fresh needs which had appeared since he wrote 1 Thess. Finally, while 1 Th 2^{17}–3^{6} does not exclude the possibility of a previous letter, it cannot be made to presuppose one of the character of 2 Thess., least of all when written from Berea (Ac 17^{10}, Laurent and Ewald).

Paul is still with Silvanus and Timotheus (1^{1}) at Corinth (3^{2} = Ac 18, 1 Th $2^{15f.}$); he is writing presumably not long † after the dispatch of the former epistle (2^{15}), having heard (3^{11}) ‡ of the mischief caused by local misunderstandings of what he had taught on the course of the Last Things. To repudiate misconceptions and thereby to calm the mind of the church amid its anabaptist perils, is the apostle's aim. What he has to communicate by way of instruction is practically a re-statement, firmer and more detailed, of teaching already orally imparted ($2^{5.15}$), not a discussion of novel doubts and difficulties. If any change

* On the hypothesis that both are sub-Pauline, Baur and van der Vies (*op. cit.* pp. 128–164) argue for the priority of 2 Thessalonians, the latter separating the two by the fall of Jerusalem. The arguments against them are stated by van Manen (*Onderzoek*, 11–25), and the evidence in favour of the canonical order is best arrayed by Hofmann (pp. 365 f.), Lünemann (160 f.), Bornemann (pp. 492 f.), and Johannes (124 f.), in their respective editions. The problem is not so gratuitous as it may appear. A similar difficulty vexes critics of the Olynthiac orations; some (*e.g.* Whiston, Flathe, Grote, and Thirlwall) hold, on internal evidence, that Demosthenes must have delivered the second speech first, and the question has excited keen debate, especially since Petrenz's defence of the edited order.

† The *terminus ad quem* is his next visit to Thessalonika (Ac 20^{1-2}). Corinth is the only place that we know of, where the three men were together at this period.

‡ The channel of information is not specified, but possibly Paul had been appealed to by the leading men to lend his authority against the spurious 'spiritual' developments at Thessalonika (3^{14}). The situation demanded explicit written counsels; evidently no visit of Silvanus or Timotheus would have sufficed, even had they been able to leave Corinth.

in the situation has taken place, it has been to shift the centre of gravity from fears about the dead to extravagant hopes cherished by the living, and to aggravate the restlessness of some pietistic members. Hence, for one thing, the general similarity of structure and atmosphere in both epistles, and, on the other hand, the sharper emphasis in the second upon Paul's authority.

Both of these features, together with the singular eschatology and the style, have roused suspicion as marks of a sub-Pauline period.

§ 5. *Authorship and aim of 2 Thess.*—Is the literary relation between 1 Thess. and 2 Thess. more intelligible if they are taken as written successively by Paul, or if the second is composed by a later Paulinist working on the basis of the first? The latter theory draws its strength from the remarkably close and continuous similarities between the two epistles in style and content and arrangement (apart from 2^{1-12}, the fresh material of 2 Thess. occurs mainly in 1^{5-12} 2^{15} $3^{2.\,13-14.\,17}$). These similarities can hardly be explained by the mere fact that Paul was once more (in 2 Thess.) writing to the same people; for while any writer's correspondence shows an almost unconscious reproduction of the same ideas and terms in letters written, even to different people, during a given period when his mind was full of similar conceptions, the literary phenomena in the present case are rather too numerous and detailed to permit of any explanation save one which presupposes either (cp. Zahn's *INT.* § 16, note 6) that Paul read over a copy (see above, p. 51) of 1 Thess. before writing 2 Thess., or that the author of the latter had the former before him.

The latter theory, which regards the Epistle as a pseudonymous writing composed by some Paulinist, on the basis chiefly of 1 Thess. and the Corinthian* Epistles, in order to win Pauline sanction for its eschatological conceptions, has been worked out along two lines † in the main, one (i.) dating it in the latter part of

* A little salt of common sense would evaporate some of the arguments used by van Manen and Völter. who find even 1 Th 3^{1-8} suspicious because it resembles 2 Co 7^{6-7}. This implies that similar circumstances must not recur in a man's lifetime, and that, if he wishes to describe the mission of one friend to a church, he must eschew language, however natural, which he had employed on a previous occasion. 1 Th 1^{3} and 2 Th 1^{3-4} are, of course, mere imitations of 1 Co 13^{13}!

† An intermediate date, in various forms, was advocated by Kern (who

the seventh decade (*e.g.* Baur and Schmiedel), the other (ii.) going further down towards the end of the first (Wrede, von Soden) or the beginning of the second century (Hilgenfeld, *Einl.* 642 f.; Hase, *Kirchengeschichte*[10], p. 69; Bahnsen, Pfleiderer, Rauch, Holtzmann, Hollmann, Brückner: *Chron.* 253–256; N. Schmidt, *Prophet of Nazareth*, p. 196 = *c.* 110 A.D.) during Trajan's reign. The latter group of theories, in so far as it traces an anti-Gnostic polemic in the epistle (self-deification being a Gnostic trait, cp. Jude $^{8.10}$, 2 P 2^{10-12}; Justin's *Apol.* i. 26, etc.), has been undermined by modern investigations into the cycle of eschatological traditions upon antichrist, which put it beyond doubt that the language of 2^{3-12} need not, and indeed cannot, be taken in a symbolic sense as the delineation of doctrinal errors. The references to internal apostasy in Mt $24^{10f.}$ (Pfleiderer) * are by no means so realistic or detailed as here, and no hypothesis of this kind has yet succeeded in giving a coherent account of the restraining force. The allusion to the temple (2^4) is a particular difficulty in the way of all theories which date the writing after A.D. 70; upon the other hand, as Wrede candidly allows, the case for a date *c.* 70 A.D. (as put, *e.g.*, by Schmiedel) is largely hypothetical, not only on account of the impossible Neronic interpretation which it involves, but because it is extremely difficult to understand how a pseudonymous letter could get into circulation at so early a period, unless it were addressed to the church at large. 2 Thess. is addressed to a specific church, and though this may be held to have been merely a piece of drapery, the hypothesis lacks any basis in reality.

The nearest analogy to the apocalyptic speculations of 2^{3-12} lies in the later Apocalypse of John. Both writings reflect the traditional conceptions of self-deification and blasphemy (2 Th $2^{4f.}$ = Apoc $13^{2f.}$ etc.); both, as was natural, view the sufferings of the saints under the category of a future retribution (2 Th $1^{6f.}$ = Apoc $6^{10f.}$ etc.); both distinguish the antichrist-figure from Satan, though Paul, unlike the later prophet, says nothing of the doom of Satan, confining himself to the fate of the devil's agents and victims (2 Th $2^{8f.}$, cp. Apoc $20^{10f.}$); both anticipate a climax of evil ere the end, though 2 Thess. lacks any reference to the Nero redivivus myth. But this neither involves a con-

---

took the restrainer to be Vespasian or Titus, the antichrist to be Nero redivivus, and the author to be a Paulinist of the eighth decade) and Havet (*Origines*, iv. 373), who regarded Vespasian as ὁ κατέχων (2^7), and Domitian as the ἄνομος.

* These do not justify any theory of literary dependence on the part of 2 Thess. (R. Scott; cp. H. A. A. Kennedy, *St. Paul's Conceptions of the Last Things*, 55 f., 96 f.).

temporary origin, nor the dependence of the one writing upon the other. To Paul the empire is the restraining power, which for a while is able to hold in check the antichrist or pseudo-messiah. His view of it is religious. To John the empire itself, with its worship of the emperor, is the antichristian force in politics. The latter outlook lay far beyond the horizon of Paul, and the similarities of conception which underlie this difference run back to the common eschatological tradition which had been flowing since Daniel. Since the outbreak of Antiochus Epiphanes, self-deification and the seduction of men had been notes of the final enemy; any vivid expectation of the end, such as that cherished by ardent Jewish Christians like Paul, instinctively seized on these traits in order to depict the false messiah; it required no historical figure like Nero, or even Caligula, to suggest them (cp. *EGT.* iv. 14 f., and M. Dibelius, *die Geisterwelt im Glauben des Paulus*, 1909, 57–61).* Paul, in 2 Th $2^{3f.}$, is simply operating with a familiar Beliar-saga, which is too realistic to be a second-century description of Gnosticism, and too early to require a date in the seventh decade of the first century.

In both epistles, but especially in the second, we can see the torch of apocalyptic enthusiasm, streaming out with smoke as well as with red flame, which Paul and many Jewish Christians in the early church employed in order to light up their path through the dark providences of the age. Paul is prophesying—none the less vividly and effectively that he does so ἐκ μέρους. The chief element of novelty which he introduces in 2 Thess. from Jewish tradition (cp. Dn 11^{36}) into the primitive Christian eschatology, is the conception of a supernatural antagonist, a final pseudo-messiah or antichrist, who shall embody all that is profane and blasphemous, and who shall be welcomed, instead of repudiated, by Jews as well as pagans.

When the Pauline authorship is doubted, upon other grounds, the eschatological stratum of 2 Thess. is differently viewed. According, *e.g.*, to Wrede,† the ablest representative of this view, 2 Thess. was written by one who desired to counteract the eschatological views encouraged throughout the church by Paul's epistles, and who took 1 Thess. for his starting-point, since that

* So R. H. Charles (*Ascension of Isaiah*, pp. lxii f.: 'in no case could 2 Th 2^{1-12} have been written after A.D. 70. This section, whether of Pauline authorship or not, is in its main features a Christian transformation of a current Judaistic myth').

† Two of the weak points in Wrede's clever reconstruction are (*a*) the unsatisfactory reason given why such a writer should have fixed on 1 Thess, and if so, why he should have elaborated his arguments into the peculiar shape of 2 Thess.; (*b*) why he made his eschatological correction in such ambiguous terms. The very obscurity of 2 Th 2^{1-12} tells in favour of, rather than against, the Pauline authorship (cp. Mackintosh in *Exp.*[7] ii. 427–433).

letter contained the most notable outline of this eschatology. The sole foothold for such theories is the acceptance of 1 Thess. as genuine, in which case 2 Thess. would be an attempt to conserve the substance of the earlier epistle, bringing it up to date with warnings against contemporary fanaticism and pietistic enthusiasm, and restating the Pauline eschatology, for the benefit of a later generation, in terms of a wider historical prospect. For this general view of the document an excellent case may be stated, when the features of style and spirit, the special eschatological motives, the absence of special traits in the situation of the Thessalonians, and even allusions like 2^{2} and 3^{17}, are put together. The argument, however, is at best cumulative, and, for all the difficulties of the epistle, it is fair to say that almost every one of the features which seem to portray another physiognomy from that of Paul can be explained, without straining the evidence, upon the hypothesis that he wrote the epistle himself (so most recent editors). It is upon the resemblances to, and the discrepancies with, 1 Thess. that most recent critics of the Pauline authorship (Weizsäcker, Holtzmann, Hollmann, Wrede) are content to rest their case, arguing that 2 Thess. is connected with 1 Thess. as Ephesians with Colossians. The following are the main points in debate:—

(*a*) Of the ten *ἅπαξ εὑρημένα*, one or two, *e.g.* (1^{9}) *δίκη*=punishment (Sap 18^{11} etc., cp. Judas[7]), *ἐγκαυχάομαι* (1^{4}, Pss), *τίνω* (1^{9}, cp. Pr 27^{12}), *ἀποστασία* (2^{3}), *σέβασμα* (2^{4}, Sap 14^{20}), may be fairly ascribed to the predominant influence of the LXX upon the writer's mind; others, like *κρίσις* (1^{5}) and *θροοῦμαι* (2^{2}), though absent from the other genuine epistles of Paul, are too common in the primitive Christian vocabulary to admit of much importance being attached to their solitary appearance here. The appearance of *ἐπιφάνεια*, which only recurs in the Pauline pastorals (see on this term E. Abbot in *JBL.*, 1881, 16–18, Milligan's ed. 148 f.), is surprising, and the absence of *ἄν*, together with the use of *αἰώνιος* as an adj. of three terminations, is almost suspicious. Still, as Nägeli (*Wortschätz des Apostels Paulus*, 1905, 80) concludes, "im ganzen ergeben die lexikographischen Verhältnisse dieses Briefes weder für die Bejahung noch für die Verneinung der Echtheitsfrage etwas Wesentliches." (*b*) But if the vocabulary by itself would not be sufficient to excite comment, the style of the letter is remarkable. In addition to a certain formality or official tinge, there is a curious poverty of expression and even a lack of point. In the treatment of a subject like this, it was inevitable that one or two phrases and terms should recur fairly often, *e.g.* the *θλῖψις*-group ($1^{4\text{-}6}$), the *πίστις*-group ($1^{4.\,10\text{-}11}$ $2^{11\text{-}13}$ $3^{2\text{-}3}$), *ἐργάζεσθαι* and allied terms (1^{11} 2^{17} $3^{8.\,10\text{-}12}$), *παραγγέλλω* ($3^{4.\,6.\,10.\,12}$), and *εἰρήνη* (1^{2} 3^{16}). Still, it may be confessed that elsewhere, *e.g.* in the description of God and Christ ($1^{1\text{-}2}$ 2^{16} 1^{12}), the giving of thanks (1^{3} 2^{13}), and the repetition of παράκλησις, etc. (2^{16-17} 3^{12}), there is a stereotyped adherence to certain forms of expression or terms which admittedly is unusual in Paul. In parts the style resembles nothing to be met elsewhere in the letters of Paul. This is particularly the case in passages like 1^{6-11}, where, it must be allowed, "the language is broad and inflated, and also digressive to an extent foreign to Paul's manner" (Weizsäcker). But, after some allowance is made for the influence of the subject on the vocabulary and spirit of the author, as well as for the possible co-operation * in parts of Silvanus, himself a prophet and in all likelihood the amanuensis of Paul (cp. 1 P 5^{12}), this feature assumes proportions which are not incompatible with the hypothesis that Paul dictated the letter as a whole.†

J. Weiss (*SK.*, 1892, 253 f.) attributes both letters to the Silvanus who wrote 1 P. R. Scott similarly dates them between A.D. 70 and 80, the apocalyptic parts by Silvanus (*i.e.* 1 Th 4–5, 2 Th 1–2), the rest composed and the whole edited by Timotheus.

As for the discrepancies ‡ which have been alleged—the larger emphasis on the apostle's teaching (2^{15}) and example (3^7, cp. 1 Th 1^6) does not imply that some suspicion of his authority must have sprung up at Thessalonika. The severe tone (3^{6-15}) is now as necessary for the Thessalonians' benefit as it was to be soon for the welfare of the Corinthians (1 Co 4^{21} 5^{3-5}); the time had come for plain-speaking and warning addressed to them as it was to come for the Galatians (Gal 4^{17} 5^{3-12}). The different reasons alleged for working at his trade in order to support himself are by no means psychologically incompatible. The motive of independence given in 1 Th $2^{9f.}$ may quite well have been Paul's primary thought; but this does not exclude the secondary motive of wishing to set an example, which might be adduced when necessary. Greater difficulty attaches to the apparent change of front towards the second advent, which in 1 Th 5^2 is sudden while in 2 Th $2^{3f.}$ it is the climax of a development. But this is mainly a difference of emphasis. Such a discrepancy (cp. Clemen, *TLZ.*, 1902, 523 f.) is native to almost all the primitive Christian conceptions of the end; to be instantaneous and also to be heralded by a historical prelude were eschatological traits of the second advent which were constantly left side by side. On this point the variations of the two Thessalonian letters are explicable as proceeding from one man's mind under the stress of different practical religious needs;

---

* "The difficulties of structure and expression marking 2 Th 1^{6-10} indicate the introduction by the original writer of some non-Pauline, and probably liturgical, sentences" (Findlay, p. lvii; cp. McGiffert, *EBi.* 5054). The rhythmical swing of 2^{7b-10} suggests a reminiscence or quotation of some early Christian hymn, perhaps one of the ψάλμοι which he heard at Corinth (1 Co $15^{15. 26}$).

† "Dass II Th in keinem Sinn ein grosses Buch ist, wird man zugestehen . . . aber Paulus kann auch einmal aus einer gewissen Verlegenheit heraus einen Brief geschrieben haben, welcher den Eindruck macht, den seine Gegner sonst seinem persönlichen Auftreten nachsagten (2 Co 10^{10}) . . . *Wenn wir I Th nicht besässen, würden wir II Th nicht beanstanden*" (Jülicher, 56).

‡ The alleged inconsistency of 1^8 with 1 Th 3^{10}, as Jowett shows, is not "so great as the difference in tone of 1 Co 1^{5-9} and the rest of the epistle."

they do not oblige us to posit any revision or correction of Paul's ideas by a later writer who felt moved to reconcile the apparent postponement of the advent with the eager primitive hope. Baur, who makes both letters post-Pauline, frankly admits that the same writer could have viewed the παρουσία from different points of view, and expressed himself in such different ways as these epistles indicate. If this is so, there is less reason to hesitate about ascribing both to Paul, particularly when the evidence of style and vocabulary is found to present no insuperable difficulty.

§ 6. *Integrity of 2 Thess.*—Attempts have been made to solve the problem by finding in the epistle (*a*) a Pauline nucleus which has been worked over, or (*b*) a Pauline letter which has either suffered interpolation, or (*c*) incorporated some earlier fragment perhaps of Jewish origin. (*a*) Starting from the alleged incompatibility of 2^{1-2} with the eschatology of 1 Thess., P. Schmidt postulated a genuine Pauline epistle in 1^{1-4} 2^{1-2a} 2^{13}–3^{18}, which was edited and expanded by a Paulinist in A.D. 69. Apart, however, from the absence of any adequate literary criterion for this distinction, the passages assigned to Paul are not free from the very feature which Schmidt considers fatal to the others, viz. similarity to 1 Thess. Besides, little is really gained by postulating such a restricted activity on the part of the editor. For his purpose it would have been as simple and more effective to compose an entire epistle, and the section 2^{1-12} is so cardinal a feature of the canonical writing that the latter may be said to stand or fall with it. As a matter of fact, Hausrath's conjecture that the whole epistle is a later scaffolding built round the original Pauline passage in 2^{1-12}, is even preferable to any theory like that of Schmidt. (*b*) The strongly retributive cast, and the emphatic OT colouring, of 1^{6-10} might suggest the possibility of this passage having been interpolated (McGiffert, *EBi.* 5044), the εἰς ὃ of v.[5] connecting with v.[11]. This is, at any rate, more plausible than the older idea that 2^{1-12} represented a Montanist interpolation (J. E. C. Schmidt, *Bibliothek für Kritik u. Exegese des NT.*, 1801, 385 f.), or 2^{1-9} a Jewish Christian piece of apocalyptic (Michelsen, *TT.*, 1876, 213 f.). (*c*) Finally, in 2^{2-12} Spitta (*op. cit.* pp. 139 f.) detects a Caligula-apocalypse,* though it is not quite clear how far Timotheus, the supposed author of the epistle, has simply reproduced its leading features or transcribed part of it. More elaborately but less convincingly

* The figure of Caligula, with his impious self-deification, is seen by other critics behind this passage; cp. *e.g.* Grotius, Renan, ii. 193 f., iii. 254 f., and Hausrath.

a pre-Christian Jewish apocalypse is found by Pierson and Naber (*op. cit.* pp. 21 f.) in 1^{5-10} 2^{1-12} $3^{1-6. 14-15}$, which was worked over by the unknown second-century Paul whom the Holland critics find so prolific and indispensable. The literary criteria, however, are as unreliable here as in the cognate attempts to apportion various sections of John's apocalypse to Jewish and to Christian belief; such theories ignore the large amount of common ground between primitive Christians and their Jewish compatriots, especially in the sphere of eschatology. In 2^{1-12} the Jewish basis is no more plain than the Christian superstructure.

The enigmatic *μήτε δι' ἐπιστολῆς ὡς δι' ἡμῶν*, which has frequently been used to prove the sub-Pauline date, may refer to something Paul had written (either in 1 Thess.* or in a lost letter), or it may denote some misrepresentation of his ideas in a pseudonymous letter, purporting to emanate from himself or one of his companions. In any case, the expression does not conclusively point to a post-Pauline origin; neither does 3^{17}, which, while conceivably† due to the premeditated endeavour of a Paulinist to win authority for his work by an appeal to Paul's signature, may just as reasonably indicate a natural precaution of the apostle in view of suspected pseudonymous epistles.‡ Furthermore, in view of passages like 1 Co 11^{23} 15^{5}, it is needless to read a second-century emphasis on oral apostolic tradition (Hilgenfeld) into the language of 2^{15} 3^{6}.

§ 7. *Earliest traces of 2 Thess.*—The acquaintance of Polykarp with the epistle (1^{4} in Pol. xi. 3, and 3^{15} in xi. 4 = et non sicut inimicos tales existimetis), and the echoes of the eschatological section in Justin Martyr, *dial.* xxxii., cx., cxvi., together with its inclusion in Marcion's Canon, prove the existence of the writing early in the second century, and therefore tell against any theory of its composition between A.D. 100 and 120. Later, like the first epistle, it occurs in the Muratorian Canon; it is explicitly quoted by Tertullian (*Scorp.* xiii., *resurr. carnis*, xxiv.), Irenæus (*adv. hær.* iii. 7. 2, v. 25. 1), and Clem. Alex. (*Strom.* v. 3), whilst Origen appears to have commented on it as well as on 1 Thess. (cp. *DB.* v. 496^{a}). The echoes in Barnabas (2^{6} = xviii. 2, 2^{8} = iv. 9, $2^{8. 12}$ = xv. 5, *ὅταν ἐλθὼν ὁ υἱὸς αὐτοῦ καταργήσει τὸν καιρὸν τοῦ ἀνόμου καὶ κρινεῖ τοὺς ἀσεβεῖς*) seem to indicate rather more than a common basis of popular tradition (so Rauch in *ZWT.*, 1895, 458 f.), and, like the Apocalypse of John, 2 Thess. appears to have been circulated in Gaul (cp. the epistle of Lyons and Vienne, Eus. *H. E.* v. 1).

---

* According to Pfleiderer, it indicates a desire on the part of the writer to discredit 1 Thess. in favour of his own composition.

† Hitzig (*Monatsschrift d. wissenschaftl. Vereins in Zürich*, 1856, 57–68) considered that 3^{17b} in this epistle, and $5^{10. 27}$ in the first, were all the unauthentic elements to be found. Wrede saw behind it, as behind Polykarp, a *corpus Paulinum*.

‡ Some (*e.g.* Weisse, *Beiträge zur Kritik d. Paul. Briefe*, p. 9; Spitta, and J. Weiss) hold it is a marginal note.

(B) *GALATIANS.*

LITERATURE.—(*a*) Editions—(for the numerous patristic and mediæval commentaries, see Lightfoot's ed. pp. 227 f.). Luther's epoch-making *In Epistolam Pauli ad Galatas commentarius* (Latin, 1519, etc.; German, 1525 f.; English, 1575 f.); J. Bugenhagen, *Adnott. in Galatas*, etc. (1527); Cajetan, *Literalis expositio* (Rome, 1529); J. Gagnæus, *Brevissima Scholia* (Paris, 1543); W. Musculus, *Comm. in epistolas P. ad Galat. et Ephes.* (1561); John Prine (Oxford, 1567); Pierre Barahona's *Expositio* (Salamanca, 1590); Salmeron (Cologne, 1602); R. Rollock, *Analysis Logica* (London, 1602); B. Battus, *Commentarii* (Greifswald, 1613); D. Pareus (Heidelberg, 1621); Crellius (1628); Ferguson (1659); Cocceius (1665); S. Schmid (1690); T. Akersloot, *De sendbrief van Paullus an de Galaten* (Leiden, 1695, Germ. tr. 1699); Struensee (Flensburg, 1764); S. J. Baumgarten, *Auslegung der Briefe P. an die Galat. Eph. Phil. Coloss. Phlm. und Thessal.* (Halle, 1767); Chandler (1777); Mayer (Vienna, 1788); Carpzov (1794); S. F. N. Morus, *Acroases in epistolas P. ad Galat. et Ephesios* (1795); Hensler (1805); Borger's *Interpretatio* (Leyden, 1807); von Flatt, *Vorlesungen über d. Brief an die Galat.* (1828); H. E. G. Paulus, *Des Apostel Paulus Lehrbriefe an die Galater u. Römerchristen*, etc. (1831); Matthies (Greifswald, 1833); Rückert (Leipzig, 1833); L. Usteri (Zürich, 1833); H. A. Schott (1834)*; Sardinoux (*Commentaire*, Valence, 1837); Olshausen (1840); F. Windischmann (Mayence, 1843); de Wette[3] (1845); Hilgenfeld (*der G.-brief übersetzt, in seinem gesch. Beziehungen untersucht u. erklärt*, Leipzig, 1852); John Brown (Edin. 1853); S. H. Turner (New York, 1856); G. J. Jatho (1856); H. J. T. Bagge (London, 1857); K. Wieseler (Göttingen, 1859)*; G. B. Winer[4] (1859); C. Holsten, *Inhalt u. Gedankengang d. Briefes an die G.* (1859); Messmer's *Erklärung* (Brixen, 1862); Meyer[4] (1862); Bisping[2] (1863); G. J. Gwynne (Dublin, 1863); Vömel (1865); G. W. Matthias (1865); F. X. Reithmayr (1865); Sir Stafford Carey (London, 1867); Ellicott[4] (1867)*; Eadie (1869); Drach (Paris, 1871); F. Brandes (1871); Hofmann[2] (1872); Reuss (1878); G. W. Flügge (1878); Sanday (in Ellicott's *Comm.* 1879); Schaff (1881); Philippi (1884); Huxtable (*Pulpit Comm.* 1885); Beet[5] (1885); D. Palmieri (1886); G. G. Findlay (*Exp. Bible*, 1888); A. Schäfer (1890); Schlatter (1890); E. H. Perowne (Camb. Bible, 1890); Lipsius[2] (*HC.* 1892); Cornely (1892); Seidenpfenning (Munich, 1892); Lightfoot[11] (1892)*; J. Drummond, *The Ep. of St. Paul to the Gal., explained and illustrated* (London, 1893); Kähler[2] (1893); Jowett[3] (1894); Zöckler[2] (1894); J. Dalmer (1897, Gütersloh); Sieffert (Meyer,[9] 1899)*; J. Drummond (*Intern. Hdbk. NT*, 1899); Gutjahr (1900); Ceulemans, *Pauli ad Rom., 1 et 2 Co., ad Galatas* (1901); O. Schmöller (in Lange's *Bibel-Werk*, 1901); F. Rendall (*EGT.* 1903); Adeney (*CB.* n. d.); Bousset[2] (*SNT.* 1907); Niglutsch[2] (*Brevis Commentarius*, 1907); Zahn[2] (*ZK.* 1907)*; R. Wulff (1908); B. W. Bacon (New York, 1909); Lietzmann (*HBNT*, 1910); A. L. Williams (*CGT.* 1910).

(*b*) Studies—(i.) historical:—G. Hermann's *De P. epist. ad Gal. tribus primis capitibus dissertatio* (1834); Baur's *Paulus* (Eng. tr. i. 109 f., 260 f.)*; Hilgenfeld, 'Zur Vorgeschichte des Gal.' (*ZWT.*, 1860, 206 f., 1866, pp

301 f., 1884, pp. 303 f.); Volkmar, *Paulus von Damaskus bis zum Galaterbrief* (1887); Holtzmann, *BL.* ii. 316–318; Sabatier (*ESR.* v. 359–364); Kappeler (*Prot. Kirchenzeitung*, 1892, pp. 714 f., 746 f., 763 f.); Schmiedel (*EBi.* 1617–1626); Jacquier (in Vigouroux, *DB.* iii. 61–77). (ii.) on the text: Klostermann's *Probleme im Aposteltext* (1883); Baljon, *de tekst der brieven van Paulus aan de Romeinen, de Corinthiërs, en de Galatiërs* (1884), and *Exegetisch-kritische verhandeling over den brief v. P. a. d. Gal.* (1889); Cramer, *de brief van Paulus aan de Galatiërs in zijn oorspronkelijken vorm hersteld en verklaard*, 1890; and Völter (*die Composition der paulin. Hauptbriefe I. Der Römer- und Galaterbrief*, 1890); Sulze (*Protest.-Kirchenzeitung*, 1888, 981 f.), with Zimmer, *Zur Textkritik d. Galaterbriefes* (*ZWT.*, 1881, pp. 481 f., 1882, pp. 129 f.). (iii.) on Gal 2 and Ac 15, C. Bertheau, *Einige Bemerkungen über die Stelle Gal. 2 und ihr Verhältniss zur Apgeschichte*, (Hamburg, 1854, a reply to Baur); Zimmer's *Galat. und Apostelgeschichte* (1887); M. Thomas, *Mélanges d'histoire et de litterature religieuse* (Paris, 1899), pp. 1–195; R. Mariano, *Urc.* (1902) i. pp. 111 f.; Völter, *Paulus und Seine Briefe*, 1905, pp. 253–273; Bacon, *Story of St. Paul*, pp. 116 f., and in *AJT.* (1907) 454 f.; J. Kreyenbühl (*ZNW.*, 1907, 89 f.). (iv.) general: Chemnitz, *Collegium theologicum super Ep. P. ad Gal.* (Jena, 1656); Semler, *Paraphrasis* (1779); F. J. A. Schütze, *Scholia in Epist. ad Galatas* (1784); Mynster, *Einl. in d. Brief an die Gal.* (1825); W. S. Wood, *Studies in St. Paul's Ep. to the G.* (1887); Belser, *die Selbstvertheidigung des hl. Paulus im Galat.* 1^{11}–2^{21} (1896); A. B. Bruce, *St. Paul's Conception of Christianity* * (1894), 37 f.; W. M. Ramsay, *Historical Commentary* (1899); M. Dods in *DB.* ii. 93–98; Haupt's introductory studies in *Deutsche Evang. Blätter* (1904), 1–16, 89–108, 161–183, 238–259; R. D. Shaw, *The Pauline Epistles*[3] (pp. 60 f.); von Dobschütz (*Urc.* 99 f.); and R. Scott, *The Pauline Epistles* (1909), 103–116.

§ 1. *Occasion.*—Although the Galatian epistle was written after Paul had visited Thessalonika, the Galatian churches were founded during a mission which he had undertaken some time before he crossed from Asia to Europe. From the more or less direct reminiscences of which the letter happens to be full, it is possible to reconstruct a preliminary outline of his relation to these churches, without calling in evidence from Acts which is disputable and which falls to be considered separately in the first instance.

Paul had visited the Galatian churches twice.* On the former of these visits (4^{13} τὸ πρότερον), though broken down by illness (? 2 Co 12^{7-9}), he had been enthusiastically and hospitably welcomed (4^{13-15}); many had been won over from polytheism and idolatry (4^{8-9}) to the knowledge of God, *i.e.* (as at Thessalonika) to faith in Christ the crucified (3^{1}), whose death † meant their

* This must be maintained resolutely against all attempts, especially in the interests of a theory, to make τὸ πρότερον = πάλαι or iampridem.

† The emphasis in Galatians upon the death of Jesus was due to the

deliverance from slavish ignorance and the present evil world (1^{4} 3^{13}). The immediate result of the mission was an outburst of religious fervour (3^{1-5} $4^{4f.}$). The local Christians, who were predominantly Gentile by birth, made a promising start (5^{7}). On his second visit (4^{13} 1^{7} 5^{21}), Paul found in many of them a disheartening slackness, due to discord and incipient legalism. His plain speaking gave offence (4^{16}) in some quarters, though it was not wholly ineffective. Otherwise, the second visit (1^{9} 5^{3}) is left in the shadow.* So far as it was accompanied by warnings, these were rather general than elicited by the presence of any definite and imminent peril to the churches.

Not long after this visit, some Judaising opponents † of the apostle, headed by one prominent, and evidently powerful individual (5^{10}), made their appearance among the Galatians, with disturbing and unsettling effects (3^{1}). Their 'gospel' was not freedom from, but fidelity to, the Law (1^{6-10}), which Paul's 'gospel' was alleged to contradict and invalidate. Arguing from the OT, they represented Paul's gospel as an imperfect message which required to be supplemented by legal exactitude,‡ including ritual observances (4^{10}) and even circumcision.§ As a corollary of this, Paul's apostolic position was

exigencies of the local controversy; the Judaising propaganda had naturally forced this point into prominence. Yet it must have been so from the opening of the mission; Paul had begun there as at Corinth by 'depicting' the crucified (3^{1}). The sole explicit allusion to the resurrection of Jesus is due to the fact that Paul desires to indicate his commission as the direct and divine gift of the reigning Christ ($1^{1.\ 15}$), not of an earthly Jesus known in the flesh.

* It is not quite clear whether the traces of the Judaistic agitation were found by Paul on this visit (so especially Hemsen, Schott, Reuss, Credner, Sieffert, Lipsius, Holsten, Weiss, Pfleiderer, Weizsäcker, and Zöckler), or whether they sprang up only after he had left (so, *e.g.*, Bleek, Philippi, Renan, Hofmann, Zahn). The tone of surprise which marks the opening of the epistle tells on the whole in favour of the latter theory.

† The contemptuous anonymity of *τινες* (1^{7}) resembles that of Col $2^{4f.}$. They were emissaries of the Jerusalem-church, like the high churchmen of Ac 15^{1}, Gal 2^{12}, reactionaries of James' party.

‡ Apparently, however, they withheld from the deluded Galatians the inference that the entire law had to be obeyed (5^{3}).

§ This rite, they alleged (5^{11}), Paul had himself employed (in the case of Timotheus?). As some of the Galatians (6^{13}) had been carried away by the propaganda, which appealed at once to higher and to lower motives, promising a complete possession thereby of the privileges of God's Israel (6^{16}) and also exemption from persecution at the hands of Jews (5^{11} 6^{12}), *My* brands or wounds, says Paul, are those of Jesus, not of legal circumcision (6^{17}).

depreciated. His authority, the Galatians were told, was derived from the apostles at Jerusalem, and consequently his teaching must be checked and tested by the orthodox standard which these emissaries claimed to embody. In short, the admission of pagans to the true church and promises ($3^{6-9. 16}$) of God required the observance of the Mosaic law, which formed the sole valid charter of divine privilege and messianic inheritance. This, and the consequent disparagement of the apostle * as an unauthorised agent, formed probably an easy relapse for people who, like other Christians, may have felt the depth and inwardness of Paul's spiritual gospel too much for their average powers, particularly when the dominating influence of his personality was removed.

The mischief done by this propaganda alarmed Paul. Matters evidently had not yet gone too far to be remedied; only a few had been circumcised. Consequently as he was unable (or unwilling) for some reason to revisit them, he wrote this trenchant letter in order to shame them out of their levity and retrograde superstitions, by reiterating and expanding the spiritual principles of his gospel as divinely authoritative † and morally adequate. How the information of the Galatian lapse reached him, it is not possible to say. ‡ There is no trace of any letter sent by the Galatians (Hofmann, Ramsay). But the gravity of the situation renders it unlikely that he delayed for any length of time in writing to counteract his opponents, and to judge from allusions like those in 1^6 (ταχέως and μετατίθεσθε—the lapse still in process), the interval between the reception of the news and the composition of the letter must have been comparatively brief.

§ 2. *Outline.*—The epistle is one of the books militant in ancient literature. After a brief introduction (1^{1-5}), Paul, instead

* Implied in their catchword, *those of repute* (οἱ δοκοῦντες, 2^6). Other echoes of their terminology can be overheard in such phrases as *we are Abraham's seed* (3^{16}), and *Jerusalem which is our mother* (cp. 4^{26}), as well as in their charges against Paul of *seeking to please men* (1^{10}), and *preaching circumcision* (5^{11}). For the phrase *sinners of Gentiles* (2^{15}), cp. Jub 23^{23-24}.

† Οὐδὲ ἐγώ (1^{12}), any more than the original apostles. Paul, too, believed by revelation, not by relation.

‡ Lightfoot's suggestion that a messenger brought news of the disaffection and also of the lack of heartiness in responding to the financial appeal (1 Co 16^1 = Gal $6^{7ff.}$), is as plausible as any. It need not imply, however, that Galatians was not composed till after 1 (and 2) Corinthians (see below).

of opening with his usual word of commendation, dashes into a personal and historical vindication of his independence as a Christian apostle; this, developed negatively and positively, forms the first of three great sections in the epistle (1^{6}–2^{21}).

These opening pages, especially, justify the comparison of Galatians to a torrent ("one continuous rush, a veritable torrent—of genuine and inimitable Paulinism, like a mountain stream in full flow, such as may often have been seen by his Galatians," J. Macgregor. "Unfinished phrases, daring omissions, parentheses which leave us out of sight and out of breath, rabbinical subtleties, audacious paradoxes, vehement apostrophes pour on like surging billows," Sabatier); cp. P. Farel, 'Exegèse du Gal 1^{1-10}' (*RTQR.*, 1910, 332-338).

The address (1^{2} *ταῖς ἐκκλησίαις τῆς Γαλατίας*) is singularly curt, and Paul associates no one by name with himself. The unique *οἱ σὺν ἐμοὶ πάντες ἀδελφοί* (1^{2}), to which Ph 4^{21} is only a partial parallel, implies no more than a group of Christians who sympathised with his gospel. There is nothing in the words to suggest either that he was on a journey, away from any settled church, or, on the other hand, that he backs up his admonition by the authority of a church like Antioch.

In 2^{15-21} he passes from a hasty * account of his interview with Peter into a sort of monologue † upon the incompatibility of the Mosaic law with the Christian gospel, which starts a fresh rush of expostulation and appeal (3–5^{12}) upon the alternatives of Law and Spirit. Faith dominates this section, faith in its historical career and as the vantage-ground of Christianity. The genuine *sons of Abraham* are not legalistic Jewish Christians, but those who simply possess faith; the much-vaunted Law is a mere provisional episode culminating in Christianity (3^{7-28}) as the religion of filial confidence and freedom (3^{29}–4^{11}).‡ A passionate appeal to the Galatians follows ($4^{12f.}$); then, harping still on Abraham, the apostle

* "He is far too quick a thinker to be a master of mere narrative; the question of Christian freedom was too hot in his heart to leave him free for reminiscence, and the matter is not very clear" (Glover, *Conflict of Religions in Early Roman Empire*, 1909, p. 168). This applies to the Antioch story as well as to the preceding narrative.

† 2^{16-17} is an indirect summary of what he actually said; in 2^{18-21} the passion wakened by the memory of the situation carries him straight forward into the situation of his readers. Years had passed since the crisis, but he lived it over again as he recollected how he had fought for people like the G., who were exposed to a similar danger of religious compromise (cp. Gercke, *GGA.*, 1894, 576 f.). On the thought of the whole passage, see T. H. Green's *Works*, iii. 186 f.

‡ On 3^{15}–4^{7} cp. Max Conrat in *ZNW.* (1904) 204–227 ('Das Erbrecht im Galaterbrief').

essays, with fresh rabbinic dialectic (on 4^{20-31} see Linder's essay in *ZWT.*, 1900, 223–226), to establish spiritual Christianity over legalism as the religion that is both free and final, applying this to the moral situation of the Galatians (5^{1-12}). The mention of freedom * leads him to define the moral responsibilities of the faith (5^{13}–6^{10}), in order to prevent misconceptions and to reinforce the claims of the gospel upon the individual and social life of the Galatians. The epilogue (6^{11-21}) reiterates, in a series of abrupt, emphatic sentences, the main points of the epistle.

Another scheme of the epistle (so, *e.g.*, Holsten, Sabatier, Sieffert, and Lipsius) is to find in 1^{6}–2^{21} 3^{1}–4^{11} 4^{12}–6^{10} three successive arguments upon (*a*) the divine origin of Paul's gospel, (*b*) the complete right of Gentile Christians to the messianic inheritance, and (*c*) the vital connection between the Christian Spirit and the moral life.

6^{11-18} is an emphatic postscript or summary, written by Paul himself. For similar instances of ancient letters containing autographic conclusions, after the main body of the letter had been dictated,† see Cic. *ad Attic.* viii. 1. 1, and Aug. *Epist.* 146, with the remark of Julius Africanus (*Rhet. Latin. min.*, ed. Halmel, 448^{27}): "obseruabant veteres, carissimis sua manu scribere vel plurimum subscribere." This leaves it an open question whether ἔγραψα (cp. Abbott, *Diat.* 2691) does not refer to the entire epistle (so, *e.g.*, Mill, Ewald, Hofmann, Eadie, Zöckler, Clemen, and Zahn, quoting from a letter of Ambrose [i. 3] to the Emperor Gratian: "scripsisti tua totam epistolam manu, ut ipsi apices fidem tuam pietatemque loquerentur'); probably, however, it is the epistolary aorist (cp. Philem ^{19}),‡ and 6^{11-18} is to be classified with 2 Th 3^{17}, 1 Co 16^{21-24}, and Col 4^{18}. In any case, γράμματα means not 'epistle' but the characters of the handwriting. On placards (cp. 3^{1} προεγράφη) and public inscriptions (cp. Sieffert, p. 349; Ramsay, 466), large letters were employed at the end or at the beginning in order to catch the eye (Lucian, *Hermot.* 11, *Gymn.* 22). Plutarch (cp. Field's *Otium Norvicense*, iii. 191) narrates that Cato wrote histories for his son ἰδίᾳ χειρὶ καὶ μεγάλοις γράμμασιν.

§ 3. *The text.*—Galatians, for all its unpremeditated vigour, is composed § not only with some care for language, but even with

* In spite of coincidences like 1^{16}=Mt 16^{15-17}, $4^{14b.}$=Mt 10^{40}, $5^{10.\ 18}$= Mk 12^{40} (Lk 20^{47}), 5^{14}=Mk 12^{31}, 6^{13}=Mt 23^{4} (Lk 11^{46}), and the apparent similarity of $5^{4.\ 11.\ 22}$ to Lk 13^{6-9} (cp. 6^{10}=Lk 13^{8}), it is hazardous to admit more than the bare possibility that Paul had in mind some sayings of Jesus against legalism (Feine, *Jesus Christus und Paulus*, 70 f.).

† "Exact analogies to this may be found in many Egyptian papyri, where the body of a document is written by a friend or clerk, and the principal appends his ratification in a large hand at the close" (Kenyon, *Hdbk to Textual Criticism of NT*, 1901, p. 26). See above, p. 51.

‡ For ἔγραψα in this sense, cp. Xen. *Anab.* i. 9. 25; Thuc. i. 129. 3; Ezra 4^{14} (LXX), and Lucian, *Dial. Meretr.* 10.

§ Cp. the minute analysis of the whole epistle in Blass's *die Rhythmen der* a rhythmical flow which recalls in several places the methods of contemporary rhetorical prose. In this respect it agrees with 1 Thessalonians (Blass, *op. cit.* pp. 61 f., 196–204), 1 Corinthians (*op. cit.* pp. 53 f., 76 f.), Ro $3^{19f.}$ 11^{28-33} etc. (*op. cit.* pp. 68 f.), and Philippians (*op. cit.* 66 f., 73 f.),* all of which are more or less marked by rhythmical features; whereas in 2 Corinthians, for example, the indications of rhetorical structure are much less prominent. How far Paul was conscious of such traits of composition and style, it is impossible to say. Their presence is due doubtless to his early training in the schools; probably they had become a second nature to him (see above, p. 57). But they are sufficient to prove that he wrote with some care and rhetorical finish,† even in epistles which appear, on a superficial examination, to have been written under an overmastering freshet of emotion.

The extant text, however, is not free from serious difficulties. Its frequent roughnesses have suggested the hypothesis that marginal glosses and interpolations have become incorporated here and there in the original; but in most cases‡ the evidence is far from cogent, as, *e.g.*, for the conjecture *τεσσάρων* for *δεκατεσσάρων* (2^1, *e.g.* Grotius, Semler, Keil, Böttger, Reiche, Michelsen, Baljon: pp. 168–9),§ the omission of 2^{10} (Michelsen, Weisse, van Manen, Baljon: pp. 172–174) or of 3^{19-20} (Weiss, Cramer: 3^{19b-20}, Baljon: pp. 175–178),‖ and the hypothesis of a marginal gloss in 6^1 (Laurent). On the other hand, if 4^{25a} (*τὸ γὰρ Σινᾶ ὄρος ἐστὶν ἐν τῇ Ἀραβίᾳ*) is correctly read, it probably represents the explanatory and prosaic marginal note of a later editor (Mill, Holsten, Schott, Cramer, Prins, Baljon, p. 185), as many scholars have seen, since the days of Bentley (*opuscula philologica*, 1781, 533 f.). The transposition of 2^{3-5} to a place after 2^1 (so J. Weiss, *SK.*, 1893, pp. 504 f.) clears up the movement of the whole passage, but it must not be defended on the ground that the incident of 2^{3-5} could not have taken place in

---

asianischen u. römischen Kunstprosa (1905), pp. 43–53, 204–216, where the text is perversely handled in the interests of the theory.

* In 3^1 (*ἐμοὶ μὲν ὤν ὀκνηρόν, ὑμῖν δ' ἀσφαλές*) the comic trimeter may well be, like that in 1 Co 15^{33}, a reminiscence of Menander.

† D. H. Müller's strophic theory of prophetic prose has been applied by Wehofer to the epistolography of the early Christian fathers (*SBAW.* cxliii., 1901), but unsuccessfully upon the whole.

‡ See the essay by Prins (*TT.*, 1887, 70 f.). Jowett's apt remark that "in a writer at once so subtle and so abrupt as St. Paul, obscurity is not a strong ground of objection," is often forgotten in criticism of this kind.

§ The considerable support once given to this supposed change of δ' into ιδ' (from Capellus to Bertholdt, Guericke, Schott, and Wurm, in last century) was due to chronological prepossessions.

‖ Michaelis (*Einl.* p. 745) and Lücke (*SK.*, 1828, pp. 101 f.) are among those who take 3^{20} as a marginal gloss.

Jerusalem, though παρείσακτοι would fit Syrian Antioch in some respects better than the capital. The reading and rendering of 2[5] (οἷς οὐδὲ πρὸς ὥραν εἴξαμεν τῇ ὑποταγῇ) was debated as early as the second century (cp. Zahn's excursus in his edition, pp. 287–296, and K. Lake in *Exp.*[7], March 1906, 236–245); the omission not only of οἷς (so Marcion, Syr[pesh], and some Gk. MSS) but also of οὐδέ (Gk. MSS, D, old Latin, archetype of G, etc.) has early and strong support (so, *e.g.*, Semler, Michaelis, Klostermann: *op. cit.* 55–58, Völter, J. Weiss: *SK.*, 1893, 504 f., and Lake). The dubiety about a negative is not unexampled in ancient literature; a similar problem arises over the insertion of *non* by most modern editors in Cicero's criticism of Lucretius (*Q. Fr.* ii. 9. 4, cp. also *ad Att.* xiv. 1–2). In Gal. the matter is complicated by the exegesis of 2[3]. Was Titus circumcised, and was this brought up against Paul (cp. 5[11], so Spitta), who defends himself by replying that he was not *compelled* to be circumcised? Is 2[5], therefore, the confession of a momentary lapse of judgment, which the later church sought to smooth over by the insertion of the negative? The internal probabilities seem to point the other way, but the problem can scarcely be said to be settled satisfactorily one way or another, owing to our ignorance of the facts at issue.

§ 4. *The destination.*—The problems of Galatians belong to historical and theological rather than to literary criticism. It is impossible, however, to discuss its destination or date without some reference to the questions raised by the Lucan narrative in Acts (especially of Ac 11–16), which describes, from a different point of view, most of the incidents presupposed or mentioned in the epistle.

The geographical situation of the Galatian Christians has led to a debate as warm and intricate as that waged over the problem of Hannibal's route across the Alps. Two rival hypotheses hold the field. The matter in dispute is the meaning of Γαλατία in 1[2] (cp. 1 Co 16[1]). Is it (*a*) the large Roman province of that name, including the southern townships of Derbe, Lystra, Ikonium, and Pisidian Antioch, besides part of Phrygia; or (*b*) the smaller region of Galatia proper, in the ethnographical sense of the term, lying north-east in Asia Minor?

The latter view belongs to the North Galatian or traditional theory, which is advocated by editors of Acts like H. J. Holtzmann, Wendt, Blass, Hilgenfeld, and Knopf; by editors of Galatians like Windischmann, Holsten, Wieseler, Reithmayr, Holsten, Lightfoot (cp. *Colossians*, 24 f.), Howson (*Speaker's Comm.* 1881), Rückert, Jowett, J. Dalmer, Lipsius, Sieffert, Zöckler (also *SK.*, 1895, pp. 51–102)*, G. G. Findlay, Lietzmann, Bousset, and Williams; and by general critics like Godet, Trenkle (*Einl.* 21), Salmon, S. Davidson, Schäfer (*Einl.* 88 f.), Jülicher, Haupt (*SK.*, 1906, 144–146), Hoennicke (*Chronologie des Paulus*, 32 f.), von Dobschütz, Vischer (*Die Paulusbriefe*, 1904, 30 f.), Mommsen (*ZNW.*, 1901, 86), Schürer (*JPT.*, 1892, 460 f.), Gheorghiu, G. H. Gilbert (*Student's Life of St. Paul*, 1902, pp. 260-

272), Chase (*Exp.*[4] viii. 401 f., ix. 331 f.)*, and Barth (*Einl.* § 7). Two thoroughgoing presentations of this theory are now accessible in Schmiedel's article (*EBi.* 1596–1616), and A. Steinmann's essays on *Die Abfassungszeit des Galaterbriefes* (1906) and *Der Leserkreis der Galaterbriefes* (1908), which discuss with minute scholarship every relevant point, exegetical or historical. Schmiedel's attitude towards Acts is much less conservative than Steinmann's, and the latter's sweep of argument is wider (embracing Weber especially, in addition to Ramsay); but the two statements supplement each other admirably, and together they constitute by far the most adequate plea for the North Galatian hypothesis.

The South Galatian hypothesis was first popularised by Perrot (*De Galatia provincia Romana*, 1867, pp. 43 f.), and then restated, with a wealth of geographical learning, by Prof. Sir W. M. Ramsay in a masterly series of articles and volumes (e.g. *Historical Geography of Asia Minor*, 1890; *Exp.*[4] ii. 1–22, ix. 43 f., 137 f., 288 f., etc.; *SB.* iv. 15–57; *CRE.* 8 f., 74 f., 97 f.; *DB.* ii. 81 f.; *The Cities of St. Paul*, 1907; as well as in his commentary). The theory is accepted, though with many modifications and for varying reasons, by editors of Acts like Bartlet (cp. also his *AA.* 71 f., 84 f.), Jacobsen, Rackham, and Forbes; by editors of Galatians like Steck, Zahn, Adeney, Gutjahr, Bacon (cp. also *Exp.*[5] vii. 123 f., x. 351 f.), and Rendall (cp. also *Exp.*[4] ix. 254–264); and by general critics like Niemeyer (*de tempore quo epistola ad Gal. conscripta sit accuratius definiendo*, Göttingen, 1827), Renan (iii. 311 f.), Hausrath (iii. 146–199), Weizsäcker (*Jahrb. f. deutsche Theol.*, 1876, 606 f., and *AA.* i. 252 f.), Pfleiderer (*Urc.* i. 191–210), E. H. Gifford (*Exp.*[4] x. 1–20), McGiffert (*AA.* 178 f., 221 f.), O. Holtzmann (*ZKG.*, 1894, 336–346; *ZNW.*, 1905, 102–104), von Soden (*INT.* 56 f.), Woodhouse (*EBi.* 1592 f.), J. Weiss (*PRE.* x., 1901, pp. 554–560, 'Kleinasien'), D. Walker (*ET.* xiii. 511–514), Belser, Clemen, and Askwith (*Date and Destination of Ep. to Galatians*, 1899); it is worked out most compactly and thoroughly in exegesis by Zahn (see also his Introduction, § 11), and from a special standpoint by Prof. Valentin Weber in a long series of ingenious articles (cp. especially *Katholik*, 1898, pp. 193 f., 301 f., 412 f., 1899, pp. 45 f., 1900, pp. 339 f., 481 f.) and monographs.*

---

* Especially *Der heilige Paulus vom Apostelübereinkommen bis zum Apostelkonzil* (1901), and *Die Abfassung des Galaterbriefs vor dem Apostelkonzil* (1900); the third section of the latter is reprinted in *Der Galaterbrief aus sich selbst geschichtlich erklärt* (1902). His main contentions are supported by Belser (*TQ.*, 1901, 285 f.), Rohr (*Allgem. Lit. Blatt.*, 1901, 226 f.), and Gutjahr (in his ed. of Thess. and Gal., 1904), and rejected not only by Jülicher (*TLZ.*, 1901, 469–472) and Holtzmann (*GGA.*, 1902, 1 f.) but by Steinmann. Weber is right in demurring to the undue sharpening of the differences between Acts and Galatians, but he goes to the other extreme in minimising them. His general scheme is as follows:—Paul's first visit to Jerusalem (Gal 1^{18-20} = Ac 9^{26-28}) followed by missionary activity from Tarsus (Ac 9^{30}) and Antioch (Ac 11^{25-26}, Gal 1^{21-24}); his second visit (Ac 11^{30} 12^{25} = Gal 2^{1-10}), with the double object of conveying the money (only hinted at in Gal 2^{10}) and securing the rights of his gospel (in private conference, Gal $2^{3f.}$); then the first tour (Ac 14^{21-23} = Gal 4^{23}), with a double visit to S.

According to Weber, the visit of Gal 2^{1-10} is not that of Ac 15 but that of Ac 11^{30}, after which, but before the Council of Jerusalem, Paul composed Galatians (Antioch, A.D. 49; cp. Ac 14^{28}). This implies that the opposition of Peter and the Judaisers could not have taken place after the Council, and that the church of Jerusalem did not interfere with Paul's method of ignoring the law in his Syrian and Cilician churches, though his practice was well known to them. But such a hypothesis is quite improbable. Gal 1^{23} simply states that they knew the bare fact of his activity in preaching, not that they tacitly approved of his methods till their hand was forced by the Judaistic party in the church. Furthermore, the theory is open to the same objections as similar forms of the S. Galatian hypothesis, that it arbitrarily makes the burning question of circumcision for Gentile Christians emerge in an acute shape some time before the period of Ac 15—a view for which there is no evidence in Acts (cp. Steinmann's *Abfassungzeit*, 170 f.), and against which the probabilities of the general situation tell heavily. Finally, it involves the incredible idea that Paul circumcised Timotheus (Ac 16^{3}) after he had written Gal 5^{2}.

Weber's reconstruction is rejected by Zahn, who also differs in his view of Ac 16^{6} and on some other details from Ramsay; the latter scholar's interpretation of the Lucan passages, of the date, and of several passages in the epistle, is challenged by many of the South Galatian theorists themselves, so that, beyond the general contention that Galatians was written to the church of Derbe, Lystra, Ikonium, etc., there is seldom much unity in their ranks.

An intermediate hypothesis, advocated by Mynster, Cornely (*Einl.* iii. 415 f.), Jacquier (*INT.* i. 171 f.), and (temporarily) Zahn, which has been described as Pan-Galatian, views the churches of Galatia addressed by Paul as at least including some to the N. of Southern Galatia. This modification attempts to do justice to the plain sense of Ac 16^{6}, but it fails to bring out the evident homogeneity of the churches addressed in Galatians, and involves more difficulties than it solves (cp. Gilbert, *op. cit.* 266 f., and Steinmann's *Abfassungszeit*, 166 f.).

Twice in Acts, Luke alludes to a mission which appears to coincide with the Galatian enterprise presupposed in this epistle. The first of these passages is Ac $16^{6f.}$.

Αἱ *μὲν οὖν ἐκκλησίαι ἐστερεοῦντο τῇ πίστει καὶ ἐπερίσσευον τῷ ἀριθμῷ καθ' ἡμέραν*. *But they* (*i.e.* Paul, Silas, and Timotheus) *traversed* (διῆλθον δέ, in contrast to the South Galatian mission just concluded:* not recapitulating 1–4, but marking a fresh departure) τὴν Φρυγίαν καὶ Γαλατικὴν χώραν, *since they had been forbidden* † *by the holy Spirit to preach the word in Asia* (explaining

Galatia, after which the Antioch-outburst (Gal $2^{11f.}$) so affected the Galatian converts that the epistle had to be written.

* The purpose of 15^{36} (*let us visit the brothers in every city where we proclaimed the word of God*) had been accomplished ($16^{1.\,4\text{-}5} = 14^{21}$); cp. N. J. D. White in *Hermathena*, 1903, 128 f.

† The S. Galatian hypothesis, as advocated by Ramsay, implies that κωλυθέντες is a ptc. of subsequent action; the natural and grammatical sense,

why, instead of turning west,* they pushed north). *And when they came opposite Mysia* (κατά, up as far as: striking it well to the north of Phrygia, in the neighbourhood of Dorylæum or Cotyæum) *they tried to enter Bithynia* (north of Phrygia), *but the Spirit of Jesus would not permit them. So, ignoring Mysia* (as part of the prohibited Asia), *they went down to Troas* (*i.e.* due west). Then Luke comes upon the scene himself, and Paul plunges into the European mission.

Every phrase of this summary paragraph has had pages of discussion poured over it. To the present writer it seems that the disputed words τὴν Φρυγίαν καὶ Γαλατικὴν χώραν can only mean, in the light of passages like 19^{21} (διελθὼν τὴν Μακεδονίαν καὶ Ἀχαΐαν) and 27^{5} (κατὰ τὴν Κιλικίαν καὶ Παμφυλίαν), *Phrygia and the region of Galatia.* Φρυγίαν, here at any rate (as in 2^{10} 18^{23}), is not an adjective, and καί does not mean *or.* The phrase therefore is not an equivalent for Phrygia-Galatica, or for the borderland between Eastern Phrygia and Western Galatia: it denotes not one district but two. As Luke uses Pamphilia (13^{13}), Pisidia (13^{14}), and Lykaonia (14^{6}) in their geographical sense, it is fair to infer that he does so in 16^{6} unless there is good reason to the contrary.

The South Galatian theorists ask why he did not write Γαλατίαν outright. Probably because it would have been misleading; the great province of ἡ Γαλατία or ἡ Γαλατικὴ ἐπαρχία included the Lykaonian and Phrygian townships already mentioned. In order to emphasise the new departure, Luke uses *the region of Galatia, i.e.* the district inhabited by the Galatians proper, lying beyond Phrygia. The terminology therefore really supports the North Galatian interpretation. It is a periphrasis, like χώρα τῆς Ἰουδαίας (Ac 10^{39} 26^{20}, cp. *EBi.* 1602). Per contra, if Luke had viewed Derbe, Lystra, and the rest of Paul's earlier mission-field as belonging to Γαλατία proper, it is inexplicable why the name should not occur in Ac 13–14. Furthermore, Derbe and Lystra belonged to Lykaonia (Ac $14^{6.\,11}$), not to Phrygia, so that the South Galatian view, that Ac 16^{6} is recapitulatory, breaks down at the outset. Harnack (*BNT.* iii. 58) suggests that Luke spoke of ἡ Γαλατικὴ χώρα "because Galatia was poor in cities, and because in official terminology the word 'regiones' was also used of this province. It follows, therefore, that in the much debated question where the Galatia of Paul is

---

on the contrary, implies that it refers either to an antecedent or at best to a synchronous experience (cp. Schmiedel, *EBi.* 1599; Moulton's *Grammar of NT Greek*, i. 132 f.). It was apropos of this forced construction of διῆλθον . . . κωλυθέντες that Chase wrote, "the South Galatian theory is shipwrecked on the rock of Greek grammar."

* Ἀσία here = the coast-land round Ephesus, as in 2^{9} (where Phrygia is also distinguished from it, by a popular use of the geographical term) and 27^{2}.

to be found, we may not claim Luke as a witness in favour of the South-Galatian theory; rather we must regard him as a witness to the contrary."

Luke's usage, it may be retorted, is not decisive for Paul. This is perfectly true, but Paul's use of Γαλατία corresponds to the inferences from Acts. It is a rather precarious conclusion that because he was a Roman citizen, he must have confined himself to the Roman provincial titles, and that therefore Γαλατία in Gal 1^2 means the province, not the country, of the Galatæ. No fixed rule of this kind can be attributed to him; not even Asiatics like Strabo and Dio Cassius adhered to such a practice. In Gal 1^{21} Paul himself does not speak in this way about Syria and Cilicia, and even in Gal 1^{22} (cp. 1 Th 2^{14}) it is not necessary to suppose that he alluded to Judæa in anything except the popular or geographical sense (cp. Steinmann's *Leserkreis*, 76 f., 103, and Schmiedel, *op. cit.* 1604 f.). Furthermore, in Ac 2^9, Asia and Pontus denote districts, not provinces, and the same is probably true of Cappadocia, as of Pontus, Galatia, Cappadocia, and Asia in 1 P 1^1. "Of the vast province of Galatia the part to be visited [by the bearer of 1 P] between Pontus and Cappadocia could be only Galatia proper, the Galatia of St. Paul's epistles" (Hort, *1 Peter*, pp. 183 f.).

Paul and his companions had no definite sphere in view when they left Lykaonia; certainly neither Troas nor Bithynia was their objective. Luke's narrative, or rather summary, at this point becomes singularly curt and rapid. Apparently he was not interested in the Northern Galatian mission. His engrossing aim is to get Paul across to Europe; and the approach of the Macedonian mission, in which he himself first joined the apostle, leads him to hurry over the movements of the apostles in the interior of Asia Minor. It does not follow, however, that these movements were a series of purposeless journeys in which the evangelists were casting about in vain for a sphere and were finally shut up to make for Troas. On the contrary, what the N. Galatian view involves is that during this journey Paul took advantage of his enforced detention, owing to sickness, in order to evangelise in the western * part of Galatia. "It is sufficient to suppose that during his illness, or during his convalescence, Paul founded a few churches, none of them very far apart, and all situated in the W. of North Galatia" (*EBi.* 1606–1607). The possibility of this is admitted not only by Zahn (*INT.* i. 189 f.) but by J. Weiss, one of the most cautious and careful of the South Galatian theorists ("Natürlich kann man sich denken, dass die Missionäre etwa von Amorium (oder von Nakoleia

* The alternative form of the N. Galatian theory (so, *e.g.*, Lightfoot) is to regard Ancyra, Tavium, and Juliopolis, as also and chiefly evangelised by Paul. Zöckler's modification (as above) seems preferable.

über Orkistos, Ramsay, *Geogr.* p. 230) aus den Versuch gemacht hätten, in Pessinus und Germa zu predigen, und als sie die Verhältnisse dort ungunstig oder den Erfolg gering fanden, sich nach Doryläum wandten," *op. cit.* pp. 558 f.). The evidence of Galatians shows, however, that this mission was more than a possibility and by no means an unsuccessful venture. There is little doubt that διέρχεσθαι in 16[6], taken along with 18[23], implies preaching-activity, not simply travelling (cp. Ramsay's article in *Exp.*[5] 1896, May).*

Two or three years later, Paul paid a second visit to Galatia (Ac 18[23]).† *After spending some time there* (*i.e.* at Antioch), *he went off on a tour through the region of Galatia and Phrygia* (διερχόμενος καθεξῆς τὴν Γαλατικὴν χώραν καὶ Φρυγίαν), *establishing all the disciples.* This time he moved from east to west, reversing the route of 16[6], and reaching Ephesus viâ Asian Phrygia. In contrast to the settled churches of S. Galatia (16[5]), the North Galatian Christians were as yet scattered and unorganised; they were naturally more liable, on this account, to be unsettled by Judaistic agitators from the far south than communities like those of Ikonium, Lystra, and Antioch, which were closer to the centre, and also in possession of the decrees (16[4]). Furthermore, Paul tells the Galatians about the controversy as if it were a novelty. There is no οἴδατε δέ (Holtzmann). This suits the N. Galatians rather better than the S. Galatians (Ac 16[4]), who must have learned of the matter for themselves at an early date.

Such is, on the North Galatian hypothesis, the Lucan narrative of the Galatian mission. It remains to notice one or two objections on exegetical or geographical grounds.

(*a*) The title *Galatians* (Gal 3[1]) is alleged to be more suitable to the inhabitants of Southern Galatia than to those of N. Galatia. Sir W. M. Ramsay (*Hist. Comm.* 137 f.) finds that the N. Galatian theorists, who deny this, show "no sign" of having "specially studied the use and implication of

---

* The admission that Paul did preach in N. Galatia (in Ac 18[23]) makes it extremely unlikely that, on the S. Galatian hypothesis, the epistle was written after this, since Γαλατία would then include N. Galatia, and the close unity of the readers' situation forbids this (see above).

† Here again the historian's allusion is brief and bare. Galatia lay off the line of his European interests; even the great mission at Ephesus (19[10]) is dismissed in a sentence, so that the treatment of the Galatian mission is not singular. "Can it be that the historian gladly drew a veil over the infancy of a church which swerved so soon and so widely from the purity of the gospel?" (Lightfoot, *Galatians*, p. 21; so Schmiedel, *EBi.* 1607).

political titles amid the contending forces that were then causing the development of society in Central Asia Minor." Such a study, he reiterates (cp., especially, *op. cit.* 318 f.), would prove to these amateurs that the people of Antioch, Ikonium, Lystra, etc., could be addressed very aptly as *Galatians*. Unluckily, this confident assertion is flatly denied by one whose authority upon the subject is based upon years of special study. "In my opinion," says Mommsen (*ZNW.*, 1901, p. 86), "it is inadmissible to take the 'Galatians' of Paul in anything except the distinct and narrower sense of the term. The provinces which were combined with Galatia under a legatus, as, *e.g.*, Lykaonia certainly had been under Claudius, were by no means incorporated into that province. Still less could the inhabitants of Ikonium and Lystra be named Galatians in the common speech of the day." Thus it remains open to argue that Γαλάται, instead of being specially appropriate to the Lykaonians and Phrygians, would have ignored their national characteristics (cp. Gheorghiu, *op. cit.* pp. 49 f.). There is no reason, in the term itself, to suppose that it denoted any save the inhabitants of Galatia proper. and there is not enough historical evidence (cp. Steinmann's *Leserkreis*, 53–60) to show that the S. Galatians were reckoned in the κοινὸν τῶν Γαλατῶν.

(*b*) While S. Galatia is represented by Gaius and Timotheus,* North Galatia, it is contended, is not represented by any delegates in the company who met at Troas (Ac 20[4]) to accompany Paul and hand over the collection at Jerusalem. But it is more than doubtful if this was the sole object of the gathering. Even if it were, there is no representative from Corinth, or Philippi, or Achaia. Besides, the Galatian contribution may have been sent independently (so Weber, *Addressaten*, p. 52).

(*c*) Paul's references to Barnabas do not necessarily imply that he was personally known to the readers (who were therefore, it is alleged, in South Galatia; cp. Ac 13–14); the apostle speaks of B. also to the Corinthians, though he had never visited Corinth; and the allusions to B. in Galatians imply no more than the references to Peter (who had not been in N. Galatia).

(*d*) The phrase, ἵνα ἡ ἀλήθεια τοῦ εὐαγγελίου διαμείνῃ πρὸς ὑμᾶς (2[5]), does not necessarily imply that the Galatian churches were in existence when the controversy at Jerusalem broke out. Paul merely says he was fighting the battle on behalf of all Gentile Christians who should believe. He tells the Galatians that they belonged to the converts in whose interests he had been contending (cp. John 17[20]).

(*e*) It is further argued that Luke devotes far more attention to the South Galatian churches, and that Galatians is more likely to have been addressed to them than to Christians in an out-of-the-way, unimportant district like North Galatia. This is one of the most plausible pleas which are advanced by the South Galatian theorists, but it is inconclusive. (i.) Luke, according to

---

* This assertion is precarious, however. Timotheus was Paul's companion primarily, and Gaius may be mentioned for the same reason. Besides, as Schmiedel acutely points out, "it would have been quite irrational to convey monies from S. Galatia to Jerusalem by way of Macedonia, and run all the risks (2 Co 11[26]) of such a journey" (*EBi.* 1612).

the North Galatian theory, does mention these churches twice (16[6] 18[23]); so do Peter (1 P 1[1]) and Paul himself (1 Co 16[1]). They are more prominent than even the Roman church, to which Paul wrote a letter, but of whose founding Luke says nothing. Luke is indifferent to Paul's early and long and important mission to Syria and Cilicia; * he ignores the work in Dalmatia and Illyria; and there is not a word of the church at Colossæ, to which the apostle afterwards wrote a letter.† These, together with the silence upon the stormy relations between Paul and the Corinthian church, are sufficient to disprove any argument against the North Galatian theory which is drawn from the silence of Acts. Luke's predilections, which led him to ignore several Pauline spheres, explain themselves. (ii.) North Galatia was by no means inaccessible by road; on the contrary, it was touched by several open routes (cp. Ramsay, *Hist. Geography of Asia Minor*, 237 ff.). Ancyra, ἡ μετρόπολις τῆς Γαλατίας (south as well as north), was connected by roads with the surrounding districts; ‡ while Tavium, as a military station and road-centre, was probably (cp. J. Weiss, *PRE*. x. 559 f.) linked even with Pisidian Antioch. There is no real difficulty, from a geographical standpoint, in understanding how Paul could reach N. Galatia; it would not take him over any more difficult country than his route from Perga to Antioch over the Taurus (Ac 13[14]; cp. Ramsay, *CRE*. 24 f., *DB*. v. 391[a]). (iii.) It is time that some critics stopped depreciating the condition of N. Galatia. On this point it is sufficient to refer to Sir W. M. Ramsay's own brilliant pages (*Gal.* 128–164) upon the civilisation of the province of Northern Galatia. Ancyra was "one of the greatest and most splendid cities of Asia Minor" (Ramsay, *Exp.*, 1898, viii. 233; cp. Steinmann's *Leserkreis*, 50 f.), and the Roman sway had long since permeated the country with civilising influences.§

* Sir W. M. Ramsay (*Cities of St. Paul*, 81) concludes from the slight and vague allusions to Syria and Cilicia that Luke had no personal knowledge of these regions. Exactly the same inference follows from his scanty reference to N. Galatia. On the same page he confesses that "even about the Galatian cities he [*i.e.* Luke] has not very much to relate that is detailed or picturesque."

† If it is argued that surely Paul would have written an epistle to such important churches as those of Derbe, Lystra, Ikonium. etc., the obvious reply is that (i.) extant letters do not represent all that the apostle wrote; (ii.) that no letter was written by him, as far as we know, even to so central a church as that of Ephesus.

‡ "There were regular roads from either Ikonium or Antioch to Pessinus. Moreover, the apostle, who was accustomed to 'perils of robbers, perils of rivers, perils in the wilderness' (2 Co 11[26]), and who preferred walking from Troas to Assos (Ac 20[13]) while his companions sailed, would not be deterred by any rough or unfrequented paths" (Lightfoot, *Colossians*, 26–27).

§ Cp. Professor Anwyl in *Mansfield College Essays* (1909), pp. 158 ("Galatia was rapidly penetrated by the civilisation of the Mediterranean area") and 160 ("whether the epistle to the Galatians was addressed to them or not, there is no evidence that in the apostolic age they were conspicuously more backward than the inhabitants of other parts of Asia Minor").

In any case the Galatians were capable of being converted,* and Paul was an evangelist, not a lecturer. The proportion and influence of the local Jews exactly correspond to the insignificant position they seem to have occupied in the churches, judged by the epistle. Finally, it may be pointed out that "the Galatian cities were in far closer relations with the cities of Bithynia-Pontus than of Asia" (Ramsay, *Gal.* p. 143); which supports the contention that Paul, after his work in N. Galatia, naturally thought of Bithynia. Any historical evidence which is available does not imply that the civilisation of N. Galatia, during the first century A.D., was Romano-Gallic rather than Hellenic; as the inscriptions and coins indicate, the Anatolian culture which predominated throughout the province did not exclude either the impression of Greek religious ideas or of the Greek language. It is therefore beside the mark to dismiss the North Galatian theory on the ground that it implies a degree of Greek culture which was foreign to the Galatians. Besides, when the evidence of the epistle itself is examined, the amount of acquaintance which it presupposes with Greek usages and conceptions (*e.g.* in 4^{2}) does not appear to preclude the possibility of the Northern Galatians having been familiar with such elementary Græco-Asiatic culture. The Hellenic ideas used in Galatians might have been perfectly intelligible to the Galatians of the northern province, so far as any reliable evidence is at our command (cp. Burton in *AJT.*, 1901, 152–153). At any rate, Greek was not only the official but the trading language. Unless we exaggerate the so-called Hellenism of Paul and the barbarism of Galatia, there is no cogent reason why any argument employed in Galatians would have been inappropriate to inhabitants of Northern Galatia. It did not require any special contact with the Græco-Roman culture of the age, such as is claimed for S. Galatia, in order to understand what Paul wrote about slavery, adoption, or wills. This is frankly admitted by Dr. Dawson Walker in his essay on "The Legal Terminology in the Epistle to the Galatians" (*Gift of Tongues*, etc., pp. 127 f.). "Whether the Christian communities to which the epistle was sent were situated in North or in South Galatia, there would be a sufficiently strong Roman environment to make such general allusions as St. Paul makes to Roman civil law quite intelligible. We therefore conclude that the legal allusions in the epistle are indecisive. There is nothing in them that bears so directly on the question of the locality of the Galatian Churches as to enable us to say decisively whether the epistle was sent to North or to South Galatia" (*op. cit.* 174 f.).

(*f*) Once more, the South Galatian argument that Paul always sought out important centres in which to carry on his propaganda is sadly shattered

---

* Another phase of this argument is that the N. Galatian churches remain unimportant in early church history, and that not till the end of the second century is there much light upon their existence. But even so, what of the South Galatian churches? "All the more strange," on account of the marked success of the preaching at Antioch (Ac $13^{44.48f.}$), "is the subsequent unimportance of the South Galatian churches" (*EBi.* 184). This is candidly written by Mr. Woodhouse, who adheres to the South Galatian hypothesis. The Syriac martyrology even points to martyrdoms at Ancyra before the reign of Trajan (cp. *ET.* xxi. 64 f.).

by the fact that Derbe and Lystra were quite second-rate cities, with very little in common between them and the Roman world. The former "was one of the rudest of the Pauline cities, education had made no progress in it." Sir W. M. Ramsay even wonders how so rustic and sequestered a spot as Lystra came to be visited by Paul. "How did the cosmopolitan Paul drift like a piece of timber borne by the current into this quiet backwater?" (*The Cities of St. Paul*, 408). Since he did evangelise such places, we may perhaps be spared the argument that North Galatia would have been beneath his notice. Even apart from the case of Derbe and Lystra, the common assertion that Paul invariably sought out important imperial centres is not justified by the evidence. Paul, like Wesley, was an evangelist who had a passion for the regions beyond (2 Co 10^{15-16} *εἰς τὰ ὑπερέκεινα ὑμῶν εὐαγγελίσασθαι*; cp. Ro $15^{19f.}$); North Galatia lay on the line of his circle from Jerusalem, and his procedure elsewhere makes the enterprise in that country not simply credible but probable.

Many internal arguments used on both sides to prove the character of the people addressed in the epistle are of little independent value. No stress can be laid, *e.g.*, on the so-called Celtic fickleness, in the interests of the N. Galatian hypothesis. On the other hand, it is as irrelevant to discover anything characteristically S. Galatian in 6^{1-5} (so Ramsay, *Hist. Comm. Gal.* 454 f.), as if the pitiless temper were specially Phrygian! If any local colour is to be sought, the allusion in 6^{17} suggests the custom of marking slaves by scars and cuts, which was notoriously a practice of the North Galatians (cp. Ramsay, *Hist. Comm. Gal.* 82 f.). The alleged coincidences between Galatians (cp. 4^{4}) and Paul's address in the South Galatian Pisidian Antioch (Ac 13^{16-24}) are interesting (cp. *op. cit.* 399 f.), but they are not confined to this address, and represent the primitive Christian outlook rather than Paul's specific views.

The South Galatian theory has several attractive features, but it lies open to objections of more or less cogency. *E.g.*, (i.) if the opening of the South Galatian mission is so fully described in Ac 13–14, why is there no mention of the illness which Paul specially mentions in Gal 4^{13}? Again, (ii.) the Galatians received Paul *ὡς ἄγγελον θεοῦ, ὡς Χριστὸν Ἰησοῦν* (Gal 4^{14}), in spite of his illness—a very different thing from hailing him in full health as the pagan Hermes (Ac 14^{12})! There is not (iii.) a hint in the epistle of any persecution or suffering endured by him in his evangelisation of Galatia, whereas his South Galatian mission was stormy in the extreme (Ac 13–14, 2 Ti 3^{11}). Once more (iv.), if Paul had evangelised S. Galatia prior to the Council, it is not easy to understand why he did not say so in Gal 1^{21}. None of these objections is satisfactorily met by the S. Galatian theory, in any of its forms.

On both sides, but especially on the S. Galatian, there is too great a tendency to tamper with the text of Acts in order to bring it into line with the requirements of a theory. Thus Weber and Ramsay, as well as Lightfoot (*Biblical Essays*, 237 f.), prefer the inferior v.l. *διελθόντες* in Ac 16^{6}; Blass in 16^{8} substitutes the equally inferior *διελθόντες* for *παρελθόντες*, and reads, on the sole authority of a thirteenth cent. Latin MS, *τὰς Γαλατικὰς χώρας* in 16^{6}; even Belser is driven (*Einl.* 423), like Weber and J. Weiss, to regard the reference to Γ. χ. in the latter verse as corrupt, possibly a harmonising gloss from 18^{23}.

This opens up the complex problem of the relationship between Galatians and the narrative of Acts. (*a*) As to the various journeys of Paul to Jerusalem, neither theory entirely escapes the familiar difficulties; the S. Galatian hypothesis, in one or two forms, succeeds in evading them, but only by conjectural alterations of the order of the narratives (see below). A more important question (*b*) relates to the Council of Jerusalem. Here the identity of Gal 2^{1-10} with Ac 15 must be maintained. In the former passage Paul is certainly giving his own version of what Luke subsequently described from a later and a different standpoint. The narrative of Acts, whatever be the historical value or site of the decree, is the counterpart of Gal 2^{1-10}. Since the object of the two visits in Ac 11^{27-30} and Gal 2^{1-10} is different, and since 11^{27-30} can hardly be regarded as a variant account of 15, the only alternative is to regard Ac 15 and Gal 2^{1-10} as referring to the same incident. This hypothesis is not wrecked by the patent difference of motive noticed in the two narratives, as there is nothing inconsistent in Paul emphasising the inward impulse, under the circumstances, and Luke recalling the joint-action of the church. The omission of any reference to Titus or the private conference is strange but not unparalleled in Acts, and, on the other hand, both narratives agree (and this is fundamental) is making the object of the journey a desire to settle the relation of Gentile Christians to the law; both imply two conferences. resulting in the recognition of Gentile Christians, and the refusal, on the part of the apostles, to sanction the orthodox demand for universal circumcision. Ac 15 certainly presents a modified, and even in some respects an unhistorical, account of what had been a very serious crisis in the early church. With characteristic tact, Luke passes over the friction between Paul and the three pillar-apostles, as well as the difference of opinion which yielded but slowly to Paul's remonstrances; he also represents both James and Peter * as in essential harmony with the apostle of the Gentiles from the first. This irenical purpose helps to explain Luke's subsequent silence upon the bitter anti-Pauline movement of the Judaisers †

---

* For the odd attempt of some Roman Catholic scholars to prove that Cephas and Peter are different persons (as Clement of Alexandria was the first to suggest), cp. Pesch in the *Zeitschrift für kath. Theol.* (1883) pp. 456–490, with Vigoroux, *Les Livres Saints et la critique rationaliste*, vol. v. pp. 456–476. Another curiosity of ancient interpretation was the view popularised by Chrysostom, Jerome, and alleged to go back to Origen, that the dispute was a got-up scene. The patristic attitude towards the dispute is sketched by Overbeck in his *Auffassung des Streits des Paulus mit dem Apostel Petrus bei den Kirchenvätern* (Basel, 1877), and Lightfoot (*Gal.* pp. 128–132).

† Upon the North Galatian theory, the Judaistic agitation in Galatia was a recrudescence of the movement against Gentile Christianity which the Council had temporarily checked. The counter-mission was cleverly carried into far-off districts where people were less well acquainted with the proceedings at Jerusalem and Antioch, and as adroitly the reactionary party took advantage of Paul's absence to undermine his authority. The burning question was circumcision as it had been at Jerusalem. On the S. Galatian hypothesis, this question had arisen prior to the Council, and Paul simply took advantage

and the Corinthian dissensions, as well as upon (*c*) the dispute between Paul and Peter at Antioch. The natural impression made by 2^{11-16} is that Peter's visit to Antioch followed the events narrated in 2^{1-10}, and there is no reason, historical or grammatical, to reverse this opinion.* That Peter's inconsistency was only possible before the Council (Weber, Belser, van Bebber) is an arbitrary hypothesis, which depends on the erroneous idea that the Council's decree regulated the social intercourse of Jewish and Gentile Christians. The reconstruction certainly tends to modify the unfavourable impression made by Peter's vacillating conduct; but in $2^{11f.}$ Paul is not harking back, in defence of his apostolic authority, to an episode which preceded that of 2^{1-10}. The point of $2^{11f.}$ lies in its historical sequence (cp. Steinmann's *Abfassungszeit*, pp. 132 f.; Clemen's *Paulus*, i. 41 f.). The principle successfully upheld at the negotiations in Jerusalem had to be vindicated practically at Antioch soon afterwards. "When we follow Paul's account, the growing excitement with which he unmistakably records the event at Antioch is sufficient to prove that, in his view, it was there that the crisis was reached" (Weizsäcker, *AA.* i. 176). In a word, Gal 2^{11-16} forms the climax, from Paul's point of view, in his triumphant assertion of the free Christian rights belonging to Gentile converts.

That the Antioch collision took place before Paul left (Ac 15^{36}), and not during the visit of Ac 18^{23} (Renan, Neander, Sabatier, Godet), is also the natural inference from the narrative; it is corroborated by the fact that after $15^{36f.}$ Barnabas was never alongside of Paul, as is implied in Gal 2^{13}.

§ 5. *The date.*—The division of opinion upon the destination has led to an even greater variety of conjectures as to the date of the epistle's composition. On the North Galatian hypothesis the letter cannot have been written before the period of Ac 18^{23}; but it may have been composed either (i.) on the way from Galatia to Ephesus (Hug, Rückert); or (ii.) during Paul's stay at Ephesus (Ac $19^{1.10}$), perhaps during one of his journeys in the vicinity; or (iii.) on his way from Ephesus to Corinth

of the collection for the Jewish poor to enlist the sympathies and win the confidence of the Jewish Christians in the capital. But both implications are improbable, especially the second; neither Luke nor Paul says anything about this motive, and the use supposed to have been made of the collection is the outcome of imagination rather than the reflection of history.

* As is done by C. H. Turner (*DB.* i. 423 f.), R. A. Falconer (*ET.* xi. 487–490), Williams, and Zahn (*NKZ.*, 1894, 435 f.; *Gal.* 110 f.), after Calvin, Schneckenburger (*Zweck der Apgeschichte*, 109 f.), etc., all of whom place the Antioch-episode prior to Ac 15^{1}, either between Ac 12^{25} and 13^{1} or between 14^{26} and 15^{4}. Ramsay, who formerly held the latter view (*SPT.* 158 f.), now inclines to think that Peter's visit to Antioch (Gal $2^{11f.}$) "preceded the first missionary journey of Paul and Barnabas, and that he was sent from Jerusalem as far as Syrian Antioch to inspect and report on this new extension of the church, just as he had been sent previously to Samaria along with John on a similar errand" (*Cities of St. Paul*, 302–303).

cp. Moffatt, *HNT.* 127 f.). There is not much to choose between (ii.) and (iii.), but upon the whole the more probable hypothesis is that the epistle was written from Ephesus (Ac 19[1]), soon after Paul had left Galatia (Ac 18[23]) for the second time; so, *e.g.*, Wieseler, Credner, Hofmann, Godet, Alford, Reuss, Meyer, H. J. Holtzmann, Lipsius, Sieffert, Schmiedel, Steinmann, etc. This was the traditional view as early as Victorinus ('epistula ad G. missa dicitur ab apostolo ab Epheso') and earlier; the only real alternative is Paul's stay in Macedonia or Corinth, during the period covered by Ac 20[1f.] (so especially Lightfoot, after Conybeare and Howson, with Bleek, Salmon, von Dobschütz, etc.).

One of the charges made against Paul at Thesssalonika was that he had left his converts in the lurch. He had to meet this insinuation by showing that he had been unable, not unwilling, to return. No such calumny is mentioned in Galatians. The tone of 4[20] implies that the Galatians recognised he could not visit them in person. Why, we do not know. Galatia was accessible from Ephesus, but there may have been reasons why he could not leave the latter place at the moment. Otherwise, we may suppose he was either on the point of starting for Corinth or on his way there, when the news of the Galatian relapse reached him. Luke unfortunately has no more to tell us about Paul's relations with the backward Galatæ than about Paul's contemporary troubles with the recalcitrant Corinthians.

The South Galatian hypothesis, upon the other hand, permits of a much earlier date. The majority tend to put it first of all the extant epistles (cp. Miss E. G. Briggs, *New World*, 1900, 115 f.; C. W. Emmet, *Exp.*[7] ix. 242 f.). Some even place it prior to the Council of Jerusalem; so, *e.g.*, Calvin (on 2[1] "ac ne satis quidem constat, quo tempore scripta fuerit epistola: nisi quod Græci missam Roma diuinant, Latini Epheso. Ego autem non tantum scriptam ante fuisse arbitror, quam Paulus Romam uidisset, uerum antequam habita fuisset illa consultatio et de ceremoniarum usu pronuntiassent apostoli") and Beza, followed by Ulrich and Böttger. This involved the identification of the journey in Ac 11[30] with that of Gal 2[1f.],—a view which has subsequently found favour with several of the South Galatian advocates in their manipulation of the Lucan narratives

Galatians occupied the first place in Marcion's list of the Pauline letters; but, as Thessalonians is put after Romans, it is obvious that Marcion either arranged the epistles unchronologically, or had no sure tradition upon their

relative position. The former is probably the true solution (cp. Tert. *adv. Marc.* v. 2). Galatians was put in the forefront as Paul's battle-cry against the Judaism which Marcion detested (see above, p. 16).

Bartlet (*op. cit.*) holds that Galatians was written by Paul on his way to Jerusalem (Ac 15^{3}; Gal 2^{1-10} being identified with a visit unknown to Luke, and a second visit being denied in Gal 4^{13}). A less complex view is represented by W. A. Shedd (*ET.* xii. 568) and Douglass Round (*Date of St. Paul's Ep. to the Galatians*, 1906), who identify Gal 2^{1-10} with Ac 11^{30}, and date the epistle from Antioch before Paul went to Jerusalem for the Council of Ac 15. This theory, however, does not avoid the difficulties encountered by the similar attempt of Weber (see above) to place the epistle prior to the Council. These difficulties are most ingeniously met by McGiffert, who, identifying Gal 2^{1-10} with Ac 11 = 15 (all referring to the same incident), places the composition of Gal. in Antioch prior to the second tour of Ac 16^{6}. This involves the interpretation of Ac 16^{3} as unhistorical (against this cp. the present writer's article in *EBi.* 5076 and Bacon's *Story of St. Paul*, 148 f.). But it is the very circumcision of Timotheus which lends point to the charges underlying Gal 1^{10} and 5^{11}. Again, the failure to mention Barnabas as the co-founder of the churches is not intelligible except after the rupture, and to identify the second visit with the mere return journey from Derbe is hardly adequate to the impression made by the epistle, which suggests that the visit in question was paid to the province as a whole, instead of to one or two particular cities and their churches.

Even when the epistle is admitted to be subsequent to the Council of Ac 15, there is no agreement on its period. Thus Hausrath dates the epistle from Macedonia during the second tour, in the autumn of A.D. 53, mainly upon the erroneous ground that 4^{8-11} alludes to the sabbatical year. Albrecht (*Paulus*, 1903, pp. 114 f.) and Clemen (*Paulus*, i. 396 f.) choose Athens, identifying the οἱ σὺν ἐμοὶ πάντες ἀδελφοί of 1^{2} with Christians who had accompanied Paul from Berea! This is supposed to explain the absence of Timotheus and Silas from the greeting. For similar reasons, many adherents of the S. Galatian hypothesis come down to the opening period of Paul's residence at Corinth (so, *e.g.*, Mynster, Zahn, Bacon, and Rendall). But the hyperbole of 1 Th 1^{8-9} does not imply that the news of the

Thessalonians' conversion had reached Galatia; and there is not enough time to allow for the exchange of news between Paul and that country. Besides, it is rather fanciful to regard Galatians as having temporarily checked the Judaising movement which, after a lull (reflected in Thessalonians), burst out again in Corinthians and Romans. Volkmar (*op. cit.* 37 f.) dates Gal. from Antioch at the close of the second tour (Ac 18^{23}), while Renan and Ramsay * (*SPT.* 189–192) prefer to date the epistle from Syrian Antioch during the period of Ac 18^{23}, prior to the third tour,—a theory which has naturally proved a stumbling-block to most of those who share the S. Galatian view. It offers no satisfactory explanation, *e.g.*, of why Paul omitted any reference to his third visit to Jerusalem (Ac 15), still less of Luke's failure to note any interruption (on the second visit to Galatia) of the harmony between Paul and the local churches. Furthermore, the obvious meaning of Gal 4^{20} (ἤθελον δὲ παρεῖναι πρὸς ὑμᾶς ἄρτι) is that Paul cannot visit them. There is not the slightest indication in the epistle that he was planning a visit very soon, and that the messenger who carried the letter took news of this to the churches. The same arguments (cp. Round, *op. cit.* 48 f.) tell as heavily against the hypothesis (*e.g.* Askwith and Pfleiderer and D. Walker) that the epistle was written (so Jacquier hesitatingly) by Paul from Macedonia or Achaia during the third tour.

These latter variations of the S. Galatian theory really tally, so far as the date is concerned, with the N. Galatian hypothesis; and occasionally the same arguments are employed to defend them, viz. from the affinities of thought and style between Galatians and the other *Hauptbriefe.* Galatians may be (i.) prior to Corinthians; so, especially, Baur (*Paul,* i. 260 f.), Havet, *les Origines du Christ.* iv. 101 f.; Hilgenfeld (*Einl.* 249 f.; *ZWT.*, 1883, 303–343), Sabatier (*Paul,* 137–155), B. Weiss, Godet, Renan, H. J. Holtzmann, Jülicher, Sieffert, Holsten (in *Short Protest. Comm.*[3], Eng. tr. 1883, ii. 254–320), Lipsius, Ramsay (*SPT.* 189 f.), Bovon (*NTTh.* ii. 73 f.), Sanday and Headlam ("Romans," *ICC.* pp. xxxvi–xxxvii), Warfield (*JBL.*, 1884, 50–64), Schäfer (*Einl.* 87 f.), etc. The case for this relative order rests rather on a detailed examination of each writing by

* In his review of Weber (*ET.* xii. 157–160), however, he says he has never felt clear on the point, "and have often doubted in the last few years whether the early date should not after all be preferred."

itself than upon any attempt to trace a dogmatic or controversial evolution in Paul's mind. The ἄλλοις of 1 Co 9[2] may be an allusion to Galatians (cp. 1 Co 9[1f.] with Gal 5[6-8]), and Gal 2[4-5] may give us the clue to *Am I not free?* in 1 Co 9[1]; but such threads are too slight to bear any weight of conclusions about the relative order. As a matter of fact, this process of reasoning has led some to exactly the opposite result, viz., that (ii.) Galatians is subsequent to 2 Corinthians and next to Romans in order. So Hartmann (*ZWT.*, 1899, 187–194), arguing from 2 Co 12[2] and Gal 2[1], but especially Bleek, Howson, Credner, Salmon (Smith's *DB.*[2] i. 1108 f.), and Lightfoot (pp. 36–56), followed by Farrar, S. Davidson (*INT.* i. 73–83), W. Brückner (*Chron.* 174 f.), Hort, Findlay, M. W. Jacobus (*A Problem in Criticism,* 1900, pp. 113 f.), Resch (*Paulinismus,* 475 f., very emphatically), Askwith (chs. vii.–viii.), Adeney, and Williams. The argument is that the net resemblances of thought and language imply a grouping of Galatians and Romans close together; that the Judaism combated in 2 Cor. is less matured than in Galatians; and so forth. But there is no reason to suppose that the Judaistic agitation developed uniformly. Such reasoning assumes erroneously "that the Judaising heresy had reached at the same point of time the same stage of development everywhere. So soon as we remember that some of these epistles were written to enlightened Corinth and others to barbarous Galatia, all these nice arrangements are seen to be the growth of misunderstanding" (Warfield, *JBL.*, 1884, p. 52). The similarity of attitude in Gal. and Rom. yields no safe inference as to their period of composition. The latter epistle carries forward the conceptions outlined in the former, after a brief lapse of time, during which other and more pressing questions (*e.g.* 1 and 2 Cor.) had engrossed the writer's mind. The comparative absence of doctrinal controversy (in 2 Cor.) with the Judaistic emissaries proves, not that the conflict with them was still in some inchoate stage which is reflected in Gal., but simply that the particular conditions at Corinth demanded special treatment. The exposure of these agitators in 2 Cor. is not inconsistent with a previous refutation of their principles such as is flung out in Galatians. See further on this point, Rendall (*Exp.*[4] ix. 260), C. H. Turner (*DB* i. 423), Zahn (*INT.* i. pp. 200–201), Peake (*INT.* pp. 27 f.), and especially Sieffert's essay in *ThSt.* (332–357). W. S. Wood

(*Studies in Gal.* pp. 2 f.) specially controverts Lightfoot, in the interests of a date at least synchronous with Thessalonians.

It is important to avoid this ultra-logical and literary method* of treating Paul's correspondence,—as if he could not return to any given topic from a later standpoint,—since it is often used not only (*a*) to support *a priori* views of their dates, but also (*b*) to discredit their authenticity.

(*a*) One instance of the former error is presented by the patristic tradition (Eusebius of Emesa, Jerome, Theodoret, Oecumenius, etc.), reflected in the subscription of one or two later uncials (ἐγράφη ἀπὸ Ῥώμης), and prevalent in some circles of the Eastern church, which has occasionally been revived by critics (*e.g.* Schrader, *der Apostel Paulus*, 1830, i. 216 f.; Köhler, *Versuch über die Abfassungszeit der epistolischen Schriften im NT*, 1830, pp. 125 f.; Halmel, *Röm. Recht im Galaterbrief*, 1895, pp. 30 f., and R. Scott), who actually place Galatians in the Roman imprisonment. The reasons alleged for this curious date are quite unconvincing. The argument led from its affinities with Romans has been already met (cp. pp. 104 f.). The notion (Halmel) that it implies a knowledge of Roman law which involves a residence in Italy is out of the question: Paul was a Roman citizen himself, and any such acquaintance with Roman legal procedure as the epistle may be held to presuppose was quite possible throughout a province like Galatia (see above, pp. 97–98). Finally, the fancied allusions to imprisonment evaporate under examination. Had Paul been in prison, he would have referred plainly to it, *e.g.*, at 4^{20} (cp. Ph 1^{7} $4^{10f.}$ etc.).

It is no improvement on this theory to place the epistle during Paul's last voyage to Palestine (perhaps at Troas, Ac 20^{6}; so Mill, *NT Prolegomena*, 4), on the ground that 2^{10} refers to the collection (Ro 15), or (so Kühn, *NKZ.*, 1895, 156 f., 981 f.) in the Cæsarean imprisonment, when Paul could not get away (4^{21}) to revisit his friends, and when he had been maltreated by the Jews (6^{17} = Ac 21^{33}).

§ 6. *Authenticity.*—It is this relationship to Romans which also (*b*) started the theories of Galatians as a second-century product (see below, under "Romans"), composed upon the basis of Romans and Corinthians, in order either to oppose the milder conception of Paul in Acts, or to promulgate a broader form of Christianity, or to emphasise the rupture between Judaism and Christianity. The ablest statement of the theory was R. Steck's *der Galaterbrief nach seiner Echtheit untersucht, nebst kritischen Bemerkungen zu den paulinischen Hauptbriefen* (Berlin, 1888), written in a phase of reaction against the Tübingen identification of the four *Hauptbriefe* with the genuine Paul. J. Friedrich's

* Thus, in his essay on *Die Ursprunglichkeit des Galaterbriefes* (Leipzig, 1903), Hermann Schulze tries to prove the filiation of the later NT literature to Galatians, in a way which lands him in repeated exaggerations.

die Unaechtheit des Galaterbriefs (Halle, 1891) is less original. The hypothesis is no longer anything but a curiosity of criticism, like Père Jean Hardouin's relegation of most of the classics to the fourteenth century, and Edwin Johnson's discovery that the primitive Christian literature was forged in the Renaissance and Reformation periods (*Antiqua Mater*, London, 1887). All that requires to be said against such vagaries has been put by Schmiedel (*LC.*, 1888, 1697 f.; *EBi.* 1617–1623), Kappeler (*Z. Schw.*, 1889, 11–19), Sieffert (*op. cit.* pp. 26 f.), Lindemann (*die Aechtheit der paulinischen Hauptbriefe*, 1889), Gloël (*die jüngste Kritik des Galaterbriefs auf ihre Berechtigung geprüft*, 1890), C. H. van Rhijn (*Theol. Studiën*, 1890, 363 f.). Wohlenberg (*NKZ.*, 1893, 741 f.), Zahn (*Einl.* § 9), R. J. Knowling (*Witness of the Epistles*, 133 f., and *Testimony of St. Paul to Christ*, 1905, 34 f.), and Clemen (*Paulus*, i. 18 f.).

(*a*) No weight or worth attaches to the attempts made to disentangle a Pauline nucleus from later editorial accretions, as, *e.g.*, by Cramer, who detects unauthentic interpolations all through (*e.g.* 1^{7a} 2^{2-4} etc.), but notably in $3^{16-20.\ 26-29}$ 4^{24-27} 5^{5-6} $6^{1-6.\ 9-10}$. Even Völter, who applies this method to the other Pauline epistles, recognises that Galatians is practically a literary unity, although that does not prevent him from relegating it to a post-Pauline date (*Paulus u. seine Briefe*, pp. 229–285). Van Manen's attempt (*TT.*, 1887, 400 f., 456 f.) to prove that Marcion's text was more original than the canonical, is answered at length by Baljon (*op. cit.* pp. 1–101) and Clemen (*Einheitlichkeit d. Paul. Briefe*, 1894, 100 f.).

(*b*) The earliest reference to Galatians by name, is the notice of its inclusion in Marcion's *Apostolicon*; but almost verbal echoes of 3^{10-18} occur in Justin's *Dial.* xciv.–xcv. (as of 4^{9} in Athenag. *Leg.* 16, and of 4^{10} in Diogn. 10) and *Orat.* 5 (of Gal 4^{12}), and the epistle was almost certainly known to Polykarp, as the quotations in 5^{1} (from Gal 6^{7}) εἰδότες οὖν ὅτι Θεὸς οὐ μυκτηρίζεται and 3^{3} (from Gal 4^{26}) πίστιν, ἥτις ἐστὶν μήτηρ πάντων ἡμῶν, and the allusions in 3^{3} (Gal 5^{14}), 5^{3} (Gal 5^{17}), 9^{2} (Gal 2^{2}) prove. Apart from *Phil.* 1^{1} (οὐκ ἀφ' ἑαυτοῦ οὐδὲ δι' ἀνθρώπων = Gal 1^{1}), the traces of the epistle in Ignatius (2^{21} = *Trall.* 10^{1}, 5^{11} = *Eph.* 18^{1}, 5^{21} = *Eph.* 16^{1}, 6^{14} = *Ro* 7^{2}) are faint, as is also the case with Clem. Rom. (2^{1} = Gal 3^{1}, 5^{2} = 2^{9}). As the second century advances, the evidence of the epistle's popularity multiplies on all sides, from Ptolemæus and the Ophites to Irenæus and the Muratorian Canon (cp. Gregory, *Text and Canon of NT*, 201–203).

The inferiority of its early attestation, as compared, *e.g.*, with that of 1 Cor. or of Rom., may be due to the remote situation of the churches in which it was originally circulated (*i.e.* on the North Galatian hypothesis), or to its polemical tone. Celsus observed that Christians, despite their shameful quarrels and divisions, could all be heard saying, 'The world is crucified to me, and I to the world.' Origen (*c. Cels.* v. 64) declares this is the only sentence which Celsus ever quoted from Paul (Gal 6^{14}).

(C) *PAUL'S CORRESPONDENCE WITH CORINTH.*

LITERATURE.[1]—(*a*) Editions:—Cajetan (Venice, 1531); Morton (1596); Cornelius à Lapide (1614); Crellius (1635); Lightfoot (1664); Grotius (1644); Semler's *Paraphrasis* (1770–6); Morus (1794); J. G. F. Billroth (1833, Eng. tr. by W. L. Alexander, 1837–8); Rückert (Leipzig, 1836–7); de Wette (1841); Peile (London, 1848); Olshausen[2] (1840, Eng. tr. 1851); J. H. Thom (1851); Hodge (1857–60); A. Maier (1857); Neander (*Ausleg. d. beiden Briefe*, ed. Beyschlag, 1859); Burger (1859–60); Kling (1861, Eng. tr. 1866); C. Wordsworth[4] (1866); Hofmann[2] (1874–7); Braune[3] (1876); Meyer[5] (1870, Eng. tr. 1877); Stanley[6] (1882); Bisping (1883); Beet[3] (1885); Ellicott (1887); Schnedermann (in *Strack u. Zöckler*, 1887); W. Kay (1887); Göbel (1887); Schmiedel[2] (*HC.* 1892)*; Cornely (Paris, 1892); J. Drummond (*Intern. Hdbks. NT*, 1899); Ceulemans (1901); Couard[2] (1901); B. Weiss[2] (1902); A. Schäfer (1903); Massie (*CB.* n. d.); Bousset[2] (*SNT.* 1907): Gutjahr (1907); A. Schlatter (1907); J. Niglutsch[2] (*Brevis Commentarius*, 1907); Lietzmann (*HBNT.* 1907).

Of 1 Cor. alone:—D. Pareus (Heidelberg, 1621); Krause (1792); Heydenreich (Marburg, 1825–7); Osiander (1849); A. Maier (1857); Evans (*Speaker's Comm.* 1881)*; Heinrici* (1880); T. C. Edwards (London, 1885)*; Ellicott (1887); Godet* (1887, Eng. tr.); Farrar[4] (*Pulpit Comm.* 1888); Siedenpfennig (1893); Lias (*CGT.* 1895); Lightfoot (*Notes on Epp. of St. Paul*, 1895; on 1^1–7^{40}); Heinrici (— Meyer[8], 1896); G. G. Findlay, (*EGT.* 1901)*; Goudge (*WC.* 1903); Bachmann (*ZK.* 1905)*; J. Weiss (— Meyer[9], 1910).

Of 2 Cor. alone:—Mosheim (*Erklärung des zweiten Briefe des heiligen apostels Paulus an die Gemeinde zu Cor.* 1762); J. G. F. Leun (1804); Emmerling (1823); Scharling (1840); Osiander (1858); Klöpper* (1874); Waite (*Speaker's Comm.* 1881); Farrar (*Pulpit Comm.* 1883); Heinrici* (1887); Heinrici (— Meyer[8], 1900); Plummer (*CGT.* 1903); J. H. Bernard (*EGT.* 1903)*; F. Langheinrich[2] (1905); R. Cornely (*Comm. in S. Pauli epp. ad Cor. alteram et Galatas*, Paris, 1907); Bachmann (*ZK.* 1909)*.

(*b*) Studies:—(i.) of 1 Cor. alone—Petrus Martyr. (*Commentarii*, ed. 1551); Gibaud's *Introd. à la première épître aux Cor.* (Thèse de Strasb. 1835); Straatman's *Kritische studien over den 1 Kor.* (1863); Holsten, *Evangelium des Paulus*, i. (1880); M. Dods (*Expos. Bible*, 1889); G. Wahle (*NKZ.*, 1898, 540 f., 605 f.); C. H. van Rhijn, "het opschrift van der eersten Brief aan de K." (*Theol. Stud.*, 1900, 357 f.); E. Kühl, *Erläut. Umschreibung*, etc., 1905). (ii.) of 2 Cor. alone.—T. Heshusius (*Explicatio*, 1572); H. Royaards, *Disputatio inauguralis de altera P. ad C. epistola* (1818); K. F. A. Fritzsche, *de nonnullis posterioris Pauli ad Corinthios Epistolæ locis dissertationes duæ* (1824); M. Wirth, *Altes und neues über d. zweiten Brief an die Korinth.* (1825); Roux, *Analyse de la deux. épître aux Cor.* (1836); Klöpper, *Exegetische-kritische Unters. über den zweiten Brief des Paulus an die Gemeinde zu Korinth* (1869)*: Denney (*Expos. Bible*, 1894)*; G. Barde, *Paul l'apôtre, études sur la 2*

[1] For the ancient and mediæval literature, from Chrysostom to Calvin, see T. C. Edwards' edition, pp. xxvi–xxxii.

épître aux C. (1906). (iii.) of 2 Cor. favourable to intermediate Letter hypothesis (see further below, p. 121); Hausrath, *der Vier-Capitel Brief des Paulus an die Corinthier* (1870); Hagge (*JPT.*, 1876, pp. 481–531); Völter (*TT.*, 1889, pp. 294–325); Brückner (*Chron.* 177–180); König (*ZWT.*, 1897, pp. 482–554); J. H. Kennedy (*Exp.*[5], 1897, pp. 231 f., 285 f., 1899, pp. 182 f.; *The Second and Third Letters of St. Paul to the Corinthians**, 1900; and *Hermathena*, 1903, 340–367); R. Mackintosh (*Exp.*[7] vi. 77 f., 226 f., 336 f.); G. H. Rendall, *The Epistles of St. Paul to the Corinthians* (1909). Unfavourable: Gabler, *De capp. ult. ix.-xiii. posterioris epist. P. ad Cor. ab eadem haud separandis* (Göttingen, 1782; reply to Semler); Hilgenfeld (*ZWT.*, 1899, pp. 1–19); N. J. D. White (*Exp.*[5] vii. 113 f.; reply to Kennedy; so *Hermathena*, 1903, pp. 79–89). (iv.) of both epp.—G. T. Zachariae's *Erklärung* (1769); J. F. Flatt's *Vorlesungen* (1827); Le Fort, *Rapports de S. Paul avec l'église de Corinth* (1836); Schenkel, *dissertatio de eccles. Corinthi primæva factionibus turbata* (Basel, 1838); J. G. Müller, *de tribus P. itineribus Corinthum susceptis de epistolisque ad eosdem non deperditis* (Basel, 1831); Eylau, *zur Chronologie der Kor.-Briefe*, (1873); Räbiger, *Kritische Untersuchungen über d. Inhalt d. beiden Briefe d. Apostels P. an die Kor. Gemeinde*[2] (1886)*; A. Sabatier's *Paul* (Eng. tr.) 156–184; Krenkel's *Beiträge zur Aufhellung der Geschichte u. der Briefe des Paulus* (1890); van Manen, *De brieven aan de Korinthiers* (1896); Sanday (*EBi.* 899–907); A. Robertson (*DB.* i. 483–498); W. Schmidt, (*PRE.* xi. 369 f.); Jacquier (Vigoroux' *DB.* ii. 983–1005); Rohr, *Paulus u. die Gemeinde von Korinth auf Grund d. beiden Korintherbriefe* (Freiburg, 1899); Ermoni (*RB.*, 1899, 283–289); Holsten (*ZWT.*, 1901, pp. 324–369); W. M. Ramsay (*Exp.*[6] i.–iii., 'historical commentary')*; G. Hollmann, *Urchristenthum im Corinth* (1903); Clemen's *Paulus* (1904), i. pp. 49–85; von Dobschütz, *Urc.* pp. 11 f.; C. Munzinger, *Paulus in Korinth. neue Wege zum Verständniss d. Urchristenthum* (1907)*; W. Lütgert, *Freiheitspredigt und Schwarmgeister in Korinth* (*BFT.* xii. 3, 1908); R. Scott, *The Pauline Epistles* (1909), 61–95.

§ 1. *Outline of the correspondence.*—Paul's correspondence with the Christians of Corinth, so far as traces of it are extant, included four letters from him. (*a*) The earliest (1 Co 5^{9} ἔγραψα ὑμῖν ἐν τῇ ἐπιστολῇ μὴ συναναμίγνυσθαι πόρνοις κτλ.) has not been preserved, unless, as is very probable, 2 Co 6^{14}–7^{1} is one fragment of it. This letter must have been written after Ac 18^{18} and prior to (*b*) 1 Cor., which was sent (possibly by Titus among others; cp. Lightfoot's *Biblical Essays*, 281 f.) from Ephesus ($16^{5-9. 19}$), during the period of Ac 19^{1}–20^{1}, in reply to a communication, conveyed perhaps[1] by Stephanus, Fortunatus, and Achaicus (1 Co 16^{17-18}), from the Corinthian Christians themselves (1 Co 7^{1} περὶ δὲ ὧν ἐγράψατε). The subsequent visit referred to in 4^{19-21} (ἐλεύσομαι δὲ ταχέως πρὸς ὑμᾶς . . . ἐν ῥάβδῳ

[1] Not necessarily, however. These men may have come independently (cp. Lemme in *Neue Jahrb. für deutsche Theologie*, 1895, 113 f.).

ἔλθω; cp. 11^{34} 16^{7}) was probably paid; at least this is a fair inference from the language of 2 Co 2^{1} 12^{14} (ἰδοῦ τρίτον τοῦτο ἑτοίμως ἔχω ἐλθεῖν, cp. 13^{1}). After this brief, disciplinary visit he returned to Ephesus, saddened and baffled (2 Co $2^{5f.}$). But what he had been unable (2 Co 10^{10} 12^{21}) to effect personally, he tried to carry out by means of (*c*) a letter (2^{4} 7^{8}) written ἐκ πολλῆς θλίψεως καὶ συνοχῆς καρδίας διὰ πολλῶν δακρύων, and preserved in part in 2 Co 10^{1}–13^{10}. It was evidently carried by Titus (2 Co 2^{13} $7^{6.\ 13\text{-}14}$). Finally, in a fourth letter (*d*), written from Macedonia shortly after he had left Ephesus to meet Titus on his return journey from Corinth, Paul (2 Co 1–9) rejoices over the good news which his envoy had brought, and seeks to bury the whole controversy. Titus and two other brothers (2 Co $8^{16\text{-}23}$) carry this irenicon to Corinth, and Paul promises to follow before long (2 Co 9^{4}, cp. Ac 20^{2}).

The scantiness of the data upon the visits, not only of Paul but of Titus and Timotheus to Corinth, renders it almost impossible to reconstruct any scheme of events which is not more or less hypothetical at various points. For the movements of Titus and Timotheus, see Lightfoot's *Biblical Essays*, 273 f.; Schmiedel, 82 f., 267–269; A. Robertson (*DB.* i. 492–497), Rendall (41–42), the articles on both men in Hastings' *DB.* (Lock) and *EBi.* (the present writer), and Kennedy (*op. cit.* pp. 69–77, 115 f.). That Titus had at least two missions to Corinth is more than probable. Much depends on whether he is made the bearer of 1 Co and 2 Co 10–13, and whether the mission of 2 Co 12^{18} is identified with the former visit.

The precise dates of the various letters vary with the chronological schemes (see above, pp. 62–63); all that can be fixed, with any approximate accuracy, is their relative order. Sabatier's scheme (which is substantially that of Clemen) is—the letter of 1 Co 5^{9}=end of 55; 1 Co=spring of 56; intermediate visit =autumn of 56; intermediate letter=spring of 57; 2 Co=autumn of 57. Zahn's arrangement is—the letter of 1 Co 5^{9}=end of 56 (or begin. of 57); 1 Co=spring of 57; 2 Co=(Nov. Dec.) 57. Most (*e.g.* Baur, Renan, Weiss, Lightfoot, Plummer, Barth, Farrar) still put both forward into A.D. 57–58 (Alford=57). Others, however, throw them back into 54–55 (Rendall) or even 54 (Bacon), Harnack into 53 (52), and McGiffert into 51–52. As for 1 Co, T. C. Edwards chooses the spring of 57; Bachmann (cp. his discussion of the date, pp. 480 f.), like Findlay, among recent editors, the spring of 56 (so Jülicher, Belser, Ramsay); Goudge=the spring of 55 (so C. H. Turner, *DB.* i. 424); Ramsay=autumn (October) of 55. The allusions to Apollos (1 Co 16) show that 1 Co was not written till after the period of Ac $19^{1f.}$, and the remark of 1 Co 16^{8} serves as a further *terminus ad quem* for the composition of the letter within whatever year is selected.

§ 2. *The unrecorded letter.*—Our canonical First Corinthians was not the first written communication which passed between Paul and the church of Corinth. In it he alludes (5^{9}) to a previous letter in which, among other things* perhaps, he had charged them to withdraw from social intercourse with openly immoral members of the church—a counsel which they had misinterpreted. When and why this letter was written, remains a matter for conjecture. Evidently it soon perished, for Clement of Rome (xlvii. 1) knows nothing of it.

In 5^{9} *ἔγραψα*, as the context shows, cannot be the epistolary aorist (as in 9^{15}). To delete *ἐν τῇ ἐπιστολῇ*, as Blass proposes (*BFT.* x. 1. 60 f.), in order to avoid the necessity of assuming that a Pauline letter was lost, is justified neither by considerations of rhythm nor by the apparent absence of the words from the text of Chrysostom. Had an editor wished to emphasise the fact that Paul was alluding to the present letter, he would have written *ἐν ταύτῃ τῇ ἐπιστολῇ*. The use of the plural in 2 Co 10^{10-11} at least corroborates the inference from 1 Co 5^{9} that the canonical First Corinthians was not the only letter which had been sent from Paul to the local church, and the context of the latter passage indicates that the unrecorded letter would fairly be reckoned among the *βαρεῖαι καὶ ἰσχυραὶ ἐπιστολαί*.

§ 3. *The first* (*canonical*) *epistle.*—The construction of 1 Co is simple and its course is straightforward. The Corinthian or rather the Achaian Christians were confronted with a series of problems, arising mainly from their social and civic relationships, which were forced upon them as they realised that Christianity meant not a mere ethical reform, but an absolutely new principle and standard of morality. These problems Paul discusses seriatim. The question of the cliques is first taken up (1^{10}–4^{21}), because it formed the most recent news received by the writer. After handling this ecclesiastical abuse, he passes to a question of incest (5^{1-13}), and thence † to the problem of litigation between Christians in pagan courts ($6^{1-9a.}$), finally ‡ turning back to the topic of fornication (6^{10-20}). He then (7^{1} *περὶ δὲ ὧν ἐγράψατε*) takes up the various points on which the Corinthians had consulted him in their letter, one after another: marriage and its problems (*περὶ δὲ τῶν παρθένων*, 7^{25}), including celibacy (7^{2-40}), the wisdom or legitimacy of using foods offered to idols (*περὶ δὲ τῶν εἰδωλοθύτων*, 8^{1}–11^{1}), and public worship and its problems—including rules for women (11^{2-16}), the administration

* An announcement of his next visit? A word on the collection (16^{1})?

† The transition is mediated partly by the double sense of *judge* in $5^{3.\ 12-13}$, partly by the fact that the remarks about the outside world ($5^{10f.}$) would naturally suggest another and a cognate aspect of the subject.

‡ The plea of the Corinthians quoted in 6^{12} (*all things are lawful for me*) carries forward Paul's warning against ethical sophistry in 6^{9} (*Be not deceived*)

of the Lord's Supper (11^{17-34}), and the spiritual gifts (περὶ δὲ τῶν πνευματικῶν, 12^{1}–14^{40}). Finally, in reply to some Christians whose Hellenic prejudices cast doubt upon the possibility of a bodily resurrection for the dead saints, Paul argues * that such a rejection of the resurrection of the dead implied the rejection of that historical resurrection of Christ (15^{1-19}), which not only is the source and staple of the apostolic preaching, but also (15^{20-28}) the pivot of the Christian eschatological hope, and the only explanation of contemporary Christian conduct (15^{29-34}). He then gives a positive account of the resurrection body (15^{35-57}). A brief paragraph follows on the collection for the poor saints of Jerusalem (περὶ δὲ τῆς λογίας, 16^{1-4}), after which the letter closes (16^{5-24}), as it had opened (1^{1-9}), with personal details (περὶ δὲ Ἀπολλώ, 16^{12}) and injunctions.

(*a*) The contents of the epistle present several problems of historical and theological importance, viz., the parties in the local church, the man and his ward or daughter (7^{36-38}), the narrative of the Lord's Supper, the glossolalia, and the argument upon the resurrection.† But comparatively few problems of literary criticism are started. Occasionally the reader can detect echoes of what the Corinthians had written in their letter. Thus Paul takes up now and then phrases of theirs as a text or pivot for what he has to say; *e.g.* πάντα μοι ἔξεστιν (6^{9}), τὰ βρώματα τῇ κοιλίᾳ καὶ ἡ κοιλία τοῖς βρώμασιν (6^{13}), πάντες γνῶσιν ἔχομεν (8^{1}), οὐδὲν εἴδωλον ἐν κόσμῳ, οὐδεὶς θεὸς ἕτερος εἰ μὴ εἷς (8^{4}), πάντα ἔξεστιν (10^{23}), ἀνάστασις νεκρῶν οὐκ ἔστιν (15^{12}, cp. 15^{35}). Further attempts to reconstruct this letter are made by Lewin (*St. Paul*, i. 386), Lock (*Exp.*[5] vi. 127 f.), Findlay (*Exp.*[6] i. 401 f.), and P. Ewald (*Neue Jahrb. f. deutsche Theologie*, 1894, 194–205).

(*b*) The language of 4^{13} (ὡς περικαθάρματα τοῦ κόσμου ἐγενήθημεν, πάντων περίψημα) is drawn from the rites of the Thargelia (cp. Usener in *SBAW.* cxxxvii. 139 f.), in which only the off-scourings of humanity played the rôle of victims, and 5^{11} (τῷ τοιούτῳ μηδὲ συνεσθίειν) recalls the well-known saying of the Aḥikar-cycle, *My son, do not even eat bread with a shameless man* (cp. Ep. Aristeas, 142). If 9^{10b} is a citation, it may be from the same source as 2^{9} (see above, p. 31). The use of written evangelic sources has been conjectured in $11^{23f.}$ (*e.g.* by Resch, *Agrapha*, 105 f., 178 f.; *TU.* x. 3. 627–638), and in 15^{3-7} (*e.g.* by Brandt, *Evang. Geschichte*, 414 f.); and one or two (*TLZ.*, 1900, 661) Philonic echoes are heard, *e.g.*, in 3^{2} (cp. Philo,

* Cp. van Veen, *Exegetisch-kritisch onderzoek naar 1 Co 15^{1-10}* (1870). It is possible, though there is no trace of it in the context, that ch. 15 was occasioned by news of some local difficulties and doubts at Corinth. The connection of $16^{1f.}$ with $14^{34f.}$ is logically close, but letters are not written by logic, and there is no reason to suspect that 15 was subsequently inserted.

† The Christians at Corinth and in Achaia, unlike those at Thessalonika, were free from persecution at this period; their troubles were internal.

de agricult. 9, etc.), 3^{10} (cp. also Epict. ii. 15. 8–9),* 8^{4} 15^{30} 14^{21} (= *de decalogo*, 105), and the exegetical principle in $9^{9f.}$ (cp. Philo, *de spec. leg.* περὶ θυόντων 1, οὐ γὰρ ὑπὲρ ἀλόγων ὁ νόμος ἀλλὰ τῶν θυόντων).

§ 4. *Its structure.*—The evenness of style and the genuine epistolary stamp of the letter are so well marked that, in spite of Kabisch's hesitation (*die Eschatologie des Paulus*, pp. 31 f.), its unity hardly requires detailed proof. The most drastic hypotheses to the contrary have been furnished by Hagge and Völter (*Paulus u. seine Briefe*, pp. 1–73, 100–134, superseding his earlier essays). The former distinguishes three epistles: A, in 1^{1-8} 11^{2-34} 7^{1}–8^{13} 9^{19}–11^{1} 12–14 16^{1-9} 4^{16-20} $16^{10-21.\ 24}$; B, in 1^{9}–$4^{15.\ 21}$, 2 Co 10^{1}–11^{4} 1 Co 15, 2 Co 11^{5b} 1 Co 9^{1-18}, 2 Co 11^{7}–12^{21} 1 Co 5–6, 2 Co 13^{1-10} 1 Co $16^{22f.}$; and C, in 2 Co 1–7. 9. 13^{11-13}, while 2 Co 8 is taken as a separate note written by some non-Macedonian church along with Paul.

Völter's analysis distinguishes an original epistle in 1–2^{5} $3^{1-9.\ 16-23}$ $4^{1-16.\ 18-21}$ $5^{1-2.\ 6-13}$ $7^{1-6.\ 8-24}$ $8^{1-5a.\ 6a.\ 7-13}$ $9^{1-12.\ 19-20a}$ 10^{23-33} $11^{1.\ 17-22.\ 29-34}$ $12^{1-12.\ 14-31}$ $14^{2-33a.\ 37-40}$ $15^{1-6.\ 8-22.\ 29-31.\ 32b-44.\ 46-50.\ 53-55.\ 57-58}$ 16, to which a later editor † has added sections containing more developed ideas of the person of Christ, the sacraments, justification, and so forth. Pierson and Naber, as usual, discover numerous fragments of Jewish and of second-century Christian origin (*Verisimilia*, pp. 50 f.), for which the curious may consult their pages and those of Lisco (*Paulus Antipaulinus. Ein Beitrag zur Auslegung d. ersten vier Kap. d. 1 Korintherbriefes*, 1894).

Such wholesale theories hardly merit even a bare chronicle, but it is a legitimate ‡ hypothesis that small passages here and there may have been interpolated, creeping in from their position as marginal glosses, or being inserted by editors to smooth out or supplement the text. Such, *e.g.*, are:

ἐγὼ δὲ Χριστοῦ (1^{12}, so Bruins and Heinrici; Rhijn conjectures Κρίσπου!), 9^{24-27} (Schmiedel, pp. 145–146), $14^{33b-35\ (36)}$ (Straatman, pp. 134–138; Holsten, *das Evang. Paul.* i. 495 f.; Schmiedel, Hilgenfeld, Michelsen,

* Among other striking parallels with Epictetus, cp. 6^{13} = iv. 1 (one of the frequent Stoical touches in Paul), 7^{35} = iii. 22, 14^{24} = iii. 23 (οὕτω πρὸ ὀφθαλμῶν ἐτίθει τὰ ἑκάστου κακά), 15^{33} = iii. 24. 93.

† Or editors; for 10^{1-22} and 11^{23-28} seem to Völter to represent divergent views of the Lord's Supper, as do 3^{10-15} and 15^{23-28} etc. of eschatology (pp. 131 f.).

‡ Findlay (*EGT.* i. p. 754) admits this as an 'abstract possibility,' though he finds none of the instances proven. For the latter, see Bruins (*TT.*, 1892, pp. 381 f., 471 f.). R. Scott detects in 1^{16} + 16^{13-18} 3^{16-17} and 15^{20-34} interpolations probably by Silas, the general editor of the whole correspondence.

Pfleiderer: *Urc.* i. 119 n., Baljon, Moffatt: *HNT.* pp. 170, 627-628; Heinrici and Bousset: pp. 123–124 = vv.$^{34-35}$),* and the exegetical gloss in 15^{56} (Straatman, Völter, Schmiedel, von Soden: *TLZ.*, 1895, 129; Heinrici, Drummond, Moffatt, J. Weiss, *Beiträge zur paul. Rhetorik*, 170; M. Dibelius, *die Geisterwelt im Glauben des Paulus*, 1909, 116–117).

Much less probable is the excision of 1^{2a} (see above, p. 19) as an editorial addition, of 1^{7} as a gloss (Michelsen: refuted by Baljon, *op. cit.* pp. 40 f.), or 1^{16} (Holsten, *das Evang. Paul.* i. 461; Völter, 2), or 3^{10-15} (Bruins, *TT.*, 1892, 407 f.; Völter), or 3^{16} (Michelsen; but see Baljon, pp. 48–49), or 7^{17-22} (Straatman, Baljon), or 11^{10} (Straatman, Holsten, Baljon), or 11^{23-29} (Straatman, pp. 38 f.; Bruins, p. 399; Völter, pp. 41 f.), or 12^{13-14} (Straatman, pp. 87 f.; Völter, p. 55), or 15^{23-28} (Michelsen, *TT.*, 1877, pp. 215 f.; Bruins, pp. 391 f.; Völter, pp. 64 f.; but cp. Baljon, pp. 109 f., and Schmiedel, pp. 195 f.), or 15^{32a} (Völter), or 15^{45} (Straatm., Völter), or 16^{22} (a Jewish Christian gloss: Bruins; Rovers, *INT.* p. 37; Baljon, pp. 134 f.; Holsten)—to name only some of the suspected texts. For the various conjectures of a marginal gloss in 4^{6}, see Clemen's *Einheit.* p. 30; Baljon, pp. 49–51; van Manen's *Paul.* iii. 188–189, and Heinrici's note; the fairest verdict is Clemen's "es bleibt also nur übrig, hier ähnlich wie 2^{9} ein Apokryphon angeführt zu sehen, wodurch sich vielleicht auch die Unebenheit in der Konstruction erklärt."† The transposition of 14^{34-35} to a place after 14^{40} (so D E F G, 93, d e f g, etc.) is plausible, that of 7^{17-24} to between 7^{40} and 8^{1} (Beza) is unconvincing. In the latter case,‡ while 7^{16} and 7^{25} connect well, the *εἰ μή* of 7^{17} does not follow 7^{40} with anything like smoothness; its present position is on the whole as likely to have been original as any other,—a verdict which applies also to 16^{22} (transferred by Hagge to a position after 2 Co 13^{10}).

§ 5. *Its attestation.*—First Corinthians has strong and early attestation (cp. Knowling's *Testimony of St. Paul to Christ*, 51 f.) in Clement of Rome, Ignatius, and Polykarp, to all of whom it appears to have been familiar. The figure of the body and its members ($12^{12.\ 14.\ 21}$) emerges in Clem. Rom. xxxvii. 5, while the language and ideas of 13^{4-7} reappear in xlvi. 5 (*ἀγάπη πάντα ἀνέχεται, πάντα μακροθυμεῖ κτλ.*);§ but as the epistle is actually referred to (1^{11-13}) in xlvii. 1 (*ἀναλάβετε τὴν ἐπιστολὴν τοῦ μακαρίου Παύλου τοῦ ἀποστόλου. τί πρῶτον ὑμῖν ἐν ἀρχῇ τοῦ εὐαγγελίου ἔγραψεν; ἐπ' ἀληθείας πνευματικῶς ἐπέστειλεν ὑμῖν περὶ ἑαυτοῦ τε καὶ Κηφᾶ τε*

* Zscharnack, *der Dienst der Frau in d. ersten Jahrh. der Christl. Kirche*, 1902, 70 f.

† Lietzmann's reason for rejecting any hypothesis of interpolation here ("Voll verstehen können wir die Stelle nicht, eben weil wir einen Privatbrief intimster Art vor uns haben") is untrue to the character of 1 Co.

‡ While this passage cannot (as, *e.g.*, by Straatman and Baljon) be assigned to the second century, it may, like $14^{35f.}$, belong to the pre-canonical epistle to the Corinthians.

§ On the freedom with which Clement really paraphrases Paul, cp. Westcott's *Canon of the NT.* pp. 49–50.

καὶ Ἀπολλώ, διὰ τὸ καὶ τότε προσκλίσεις ὑμᾶς πεποιῆσθαι), it is needless to do more than note the repeated echoes in **xxiv.** 1 (15^{20-23}), xxiv. 4–5 (15^{36-37}), xxxvii. 3 (15^{23}), xxxviii. 2 (16^{17}), xlvi. 7 (6^{15}), and xlviii. 5 (12^{8-9}).* The use of the epistle by Ignatius is even more distinct and copious; *e.g.* 2^{10} = *Phil.* vii. 1 (τὸ πνεῦμα . . . τὰ κρυπτὰ ἐλέγχει), 6^{9-10} (μὴ πλανᾶσθε· οὔτε πόρνοι . . . οὔτε μοιχοί . . . βασιλείαν Θεοῦ κληρονομήσουσι) with 3^{17} = *Eph.* xvi. 1 (μὴ πλανᾶσθε, ἀδελφοί μου· οἱ οἰκοφθόροι βασιλείαν Θεοῦ οὐ κληρονομήσουσι) and *Phil.* iii. 3, 9^{15} = *Rom.* vi. 1 (καλόν μοι ἀποθανεῖν διὰ Ιησοῦν Χριστὸν ἤ κτλ.), 10^{16-17} = *Phil.* iv. 1 (μία γὰρ σὰρξ τοῦ Κυρίου ἡμῶν Ἰησοῦ Χριστοῦ, καὶ ἓν ποτήριον εἰς ἕνωσιν τοῦ αἵματος αὐτοῦ). Numerous other reminiscences occur: 3^{10-17} = *Eph.* ix. 1 (λίθοι ναοῦ), 5^{7} = *Magn.* x. 3 (the old and evil leaven), 7^{22} = *Rom.* iv. 3 (ἀπελεύθερος Ἰ. Χριστοῦ), 9^{27} = *Trall.* xii. 3 (ἵνα μὴ ἀδόκιμος εὑρεθῶ), 12^{12} = *Trall.* xi. 2, 15^{58} = *Eph.* x. 2, xx. 1, 16^{18} = *Eph.* ii. 2, etc. (cp. *NTA.* pp. 64–67: "Ignatius must have known this epistle almost by heart"). Polykarp, like Clement, actually quotes the epistle (xi. 2, aut nescimus quia sancti mundum iudicabunt? Sicut Paulus docet = 6^{2}); alone, among the apostolic fathers, he uses οἰκοδομεῖν, a favourite term of 1 Cor., and more than once his language reflects the earlier writing —*e.g.* iii. 2–3 = 13^{13}, iv. 3 (οὔτε τι τῶν κρυπτῶν τῆς καρδίας) = 14^{25}, v. 3 = 6^{9}, and xi. 4 = 12^{26}—though his employment of it is less explicit than that of Ignatius. No stress can be laid on the occasional coincidences between 1 Cor. and Hermas (*Sim.* v. vii. = 3^{16-17}), *Mand.* (iv. iv. 1–2 = 7^{39-40}), 2 Clem. (vii. 1 = 9^{24-25}, ix. 3 = 3^{16} 6^{19}), Barnabas (iv. 11, vi. 11 = $3^{1.\,16.\,18f.}$), or the Didachê (x. 6, μαρὰν ἀθά = 16^{22}). With 2 Cor., it appears in Marcion's Canon and in the Muratorian, besides being used by the Ophites and Basilides, quoted almost verbally in Justin (*dial.* xxxv. = $11^{18f.}$, *cohort.* xxxii. = 12^{7-10} etc.) and *Diognet.* v. (= 4^{12}) and xii. (= 8^{1}), and cited by Irenæus † (*adv. haer.* iv. 27. 3 = 10^{1-12}, v. 36 = 15^{25-26}), Athenagoras (*de resurr. mortis*, 61 = 15^{54}), Tertullian (*praescr. haer.* xxxiii.), and Clement of Alexandria (*Paed.* i. 33, etc.). Tertullian once (*de monog.* 3) asserts that it was written about one hundred and sixty years ago; although his language is loose, it proves, as Harnack points out, that by the

* Cp. *NTA.* 40–44, where the occurrence of the same quotation in 1 Co 2^{9} and Clem. Rom. xxxiv. 8 (*Mart. Polyk.* ii.), is explained by the independent use of a pre-Christian source (see above, p. 31).

† Quoting the earlier testimony of an elder.

beginning of the third century an interest was taken by some Carthaginian Christians in the chronology of Paul's letters.

§ 6. *The unrecorded visit.*—Previous to the composition of 1 Cor., Paul does not seem to have visited Corinth after his first mission, when the local churches were founded (Ac 18^{4-11}). The silence, not only of Acts but of 1 Cor. itself,* tells against the hypothesis (*e.g.* of Billroth, Reuss, B. Weiss, Schmiedel: 51 f., Holsten, Denney, G. G. Findlay, and Zahn) that this diffident and successful visit (1 Co 2^{2}) was followed by another, prior to the letter of 1 Co 5^{9}, which has remained unrecorded (Alford, Lightfoot, Sanday, Waite, and Bernard, after Klöpper and Räbiger; cp. Hilgenfeld in *ZWT.*, 1888, 171 f.). His recent knowledge of the church, at the time when 1 Cor. was composed, rested on information given him by οἱ ἐκ Χλόης (1^{11}, cp. 5^{1} 11^{18}), and on the letter forwarded to him by the church itself (7^{1}); the communications between himself and the Christians of Corinth, since he left, had been entirely epistolary (5^{9}). The sole visit implied in 1 Co (cp. 2^{1} 3^{2} 11^{2}) is that which led to the establishment of the church; and, although Paul may have mentioned it in the letter of 1 Co 5^{9}, while the new developments drove it into the background afterwards, it is not easy to suppose that if he had revisited the church during the interval he would have spoken, as he does in 1 Cor., about his personal relations with the local Christians.

While 1 Cor. does not presuppose a second visit, however, it foreshadows one. The tone of 2 Co 2^{1} (*ἔκρινα δὲ ἐμαυτῷ τοῦτο, τὸ μὴ πάλιν ἐν λύπῃ πρὸς ὑμᾶς ἐλθεῖν*), where *πάλιν* most naturally goes closely with *ἐν λύπῃ*, implies that, since writing 1 Cor. he had paid a visit which left painful memories.† The *λύπη* was not the depression of 1 Co 2^{3}; it was a later sorrow, probably occasioned by unworthy members of the church itself, but we can only conjecture (from references like 2 Co 12^{21}) its origin. Why did Paul hurry over to Corinth? To vindicate in person his authority against the machinations of Judaistic agitators who had been discrediting his gospel and his character? To enforce the discipline of the incestuous person (1 Co 5^{3}), which the local Christians were perhaps unwilling to carry through? Or to maintain discipline more generally (cp. 2 Co 12^{21})? The choice probably lies among the two latter; the occasion of

* 1 Co 16^{7} cannot be pressed into the support of this view, for ἄρτι points forward, not backward.

† So formerly Belser (*TQ.*, 1894, 17–47).

the visit was moral laxity rather than the emergence of cliques in the local church. This view is almost necessary when the intermediate visit is placed prior to the letter of 1 Co 5^9, but it fits in with the theory which inserts that visit between 1 Cor. and the intermediate letter, although our lack of information about the origin of the cliques at Corinth prevents any reconstruction from being more than hypothetical.

Grammatically, the language of 2 Co 12^{14} and 13^1 might be taken to denote not his actual visit, but simply his intentions (so *e.g.* Paley, Baur, de Wette, Davidson, Hilgenfeld, Renan, Farrar, Ramsay, G. H. Gilbert: *Student's Life of Paul*, pp. 160 f., Robertson). The context and aim of the epistle must decide, and the evidence seems strongly in favour of the former view. Against people who suspected his consistency and goodwill, it would have been of little use to plead that he had honestly intended to come, that he had been quite ready to visit them. His actions, not his wishes, were the final proof desiderated by the Corinthians, and the passages in question (cp. 13^2 where *παρὼν τὸ δεύτερον καὶ ἀπὼν νῦν* answers to *εἰς τὸ πάλιν*) gain immensely in aptness when they are taken to imply that Paul was on the point of paying a third visit in person.

In any case the key to 2 Cor. is not so much its affinity of style and language to 1 Cor. as the change which has come over the situation. New elements of strain have entered into the relations between Paul and the church, and one of these, which lies on the face of 2 Cor., is a suspicion of his character. This was occasioned, among other things, by an alteration which he had felt himself obliged to make in his plans for revisiting the church. The details of this new situation, so far as they can be made out, are one of the main proofs for the thesis that 2 Cor. cannot be explained simply out of 1 Cor.

In 1 Co 16^{5f} Paul promises to pay them what he hopes will be a long visit, on his way south from Macedonia. At present (*ἄρτι*), he would only have time for a flying visit (*ἐν παρόδῳ*): besides, the pressure of work at Ephesus will keep him there till Pentecost. The critical state of matters at Corinth forced him, however, to pay a rapid visit. When he writes the intermediate letter, he anticipates a third visit, but says nothing about its details, except to protest that he would take no money for his support ($12^{14f.}$), and that he would be as strict, if necessary, as on his second disciplinary visit ($13^{2f.}$). But either in the lost part of this letter,* or more probably orally (on

* The *γράφομεν* of 1^{13} is often used to support this view; but it may quite well refer simply to the present letter.

the occasion of his rapid visit; König, *ZWT.*, 1897, pp. 523 f.), he must have led the Corinthians to believe that on this occasion he would pass through Corinth on his way to Macedonia, and then return to Corinth on his way to Judæa (2 Co $1^{16f.}$; his destination is now more definite than when he wrote 1 Co 16^6 *οὗ ἐὰν πορεύωμαι*). It was his desire thus to give them the benefit of a double visit (*δευτέραν χάριν*).* Cicumstances, however, led him to alter his plans. Instead of crossing to Corinth, in the wake of Titus, he hurried anxiously to meet the latter on his return journey (2 Co $2^{12f.}$) via Macedonia, and 2 Co 1^{15}–2^{13} is his explanation of the reasons which led to this change of plan. He defends himself against any suspicion of insincerity, explaining that he could not trust himself to come at once to them under the circumstances; he could not have spared them (2 Co 1^{23}, an allusion to 13^2), and it was kinder to keep away. This implies that the Corinthians had heard not only of the promised double visit but of its abandonment,† and that therefore they suspected him of *ἐλαφρία*. If he was not coming at all, they argued, he had grown indifferent to them; and even if he was taking the round-about route via Macedonia, he had broken his promise to take them first.

The competing view that the plan authorised in 2 Co $1^{15f.}$ was his original idea, and that 1 Co $16^{5f.}$ represents the change which the suspicious Corinthians misinterpreted to his discredit, reads into the latter passage a motive which is not there, and fails to account for the fear of *λύπη* which (according to 2 Co 1^{23}–2^3) was his real motive for altering the programme (cp. Schmiedel, p. 69). The change of plan therefore falls later than the dispatch of 1 Cor.

K. Hoss (*ZNW.*, 1903, 268–270) argues it was by his second visit that Paul practically altered the programme of 1 Co 16^{5-7}. He meant then to go on to Macedonia and return to Corinth, but the local troubles in the latter church drove him either straight back to Ephesus, or, more probably, on first of all to Macedonia, where the receipt of bad news (2 Co 1^{23}) made him abandon any thought of return in the meantime, and forced him back to Ephesus. In 2 Co $1^{13f.}$ he justifies this course of action. The theory is plausible, and would be strengthened by Krenkel's view that *ἔρχεσθαι* is generally used in the sense of 'return' by Paul, as by other Greek writers (pp. 202 f.).

Luke was as indifferent to the subsequent relations of Paul with the Corinthian as with the Thessalonian Christians, but the lacunæ of his outline in Ac 18–19 are not seriously felt until we pass from 1 Cor. to 2 Cor. The latter writing presupposes a

* On this view *δευτέραν* refers to the return visit on this tour, not to the second of his three visits (12^{14} 13^1), the *καί* clauses being epexegetic of *χάριν*. The variant *χαράν* corresponds excellently to 1^{24} (*συνεργοί ἐσμεν τῆς χαρᾶς ὑμῶν*), but may have been introduced from that very passage.

† Halmel (*Der Zweite Kor. Brief*, 48 f.), Dr. Kennedy (*op. cit.* pp. 34 f.), and Plummer all deny this; but the passage (2 Co 1^{15-16}) seems deprived of its force if it is reduced to a defence against the charge of *ἐλαφρία*, on the ground that he really wanted to visit them "if only he could do so without having to exercise severity," or that he had simply delayed to pay his promised visit as he had intended.

stormy interlude, upon which Acts throws no light and 1 Cor. very little; the painful situation has to be reconstructed from allusions in 2 Cor. itself. Either Luke was ignorant of the details or, as is more likely, he chose to pass over so unedifying and discreditable a local episode. In any case it did not come within the scope of his work to sketch the development of the Gentile Christian churches founded by the apostle Paul, or to chronicle every later visit paid by the missioners to a church.

§ 7. *The intermediate letter* (= 2 Co 10^{1}–13^{10}).—From this visit Paul returned to Ephesus, saddened and baffled (2 Co $1^{23f.}$). His mission had been fruitless and unpleasant. *I decided,* he tells the Corinthians, *that I would not visit you again in sorrow*; instead of a visit, which would have only led to pain, *I wrote to you out of much distress and misery of heart with many tears* (2^{4} 7^{8}). This distress and passion made Paul's letter so sarcastic and severe that the recollection of the language he had used afterwards caused him some qualms of conscience ($2^{4f.}$), although its threats and appeals were intended to lance a tumour.

Unless this letter has been lost,* like the first one sent by Paul to Corinth, it must be identified either (*a*) with 1 Corinthians or (*b*) with 2 Co 10–13. The former (*a*) hypothesis† surely breaks down when 1 Cor. is compared with the object of the intermediate letter as defined in 2 Co $1^{15f.}$ $2^{3f.}$ $7^{8f.}$. Even such passages in 1 Cor. as vibrate with irony and passion (*e.g.* $4^{8f. 14f.}$) are not only inadequate to account for Paul's anxiety about the pain he had caused his friends, but also too few and too little characteristic of the epistle as a whole to be regarded as likely to stamp themselves specially either on the mind of the Corinthians or on the memory of the apostle. 1 Cor. is permeated by a spirit of calm, practical discussion, whose occasional outbursts of emotional tension (*e.g.* in 5–6) could not have caused Paul even a momentary twinge of compunction. His language in 2 Co 2^{4} and 7^{8} is too definite to be explained as the mere recollection of one or two isolated sentences in an epistle of the size and general character of 1 Cor., and a solitary postscript like 1 Co 16^{24} cannot be adduced as proof of the ἀγάπη recalled in 2 Co 2^{4}. The alternative is to suppose (*b*) that this letter of disturbed feeling has been preserved, in whole or part, in the closing section (10^{1}–13^{10}) of our canonical 2 Corinthians, an hypothesis which is favoured by the spirit, contents, and style of these chapters. They are written out of the tension felt by one who was not yet sure of his ultimate success in dealing with a difficult

---

* So especially Bleek (*SK.*, 1830, 625–632), Credner (*Einl.* i. 371), Olshausen, Ewald (*Sendschreiben d. Paulus*, 227 f.), Godet, Neander (293 f.), Sabatier, Klöpper (*Untersuchungen*, 24 f.), Robertson, Drummond, Findlay in *DB.* iii. 711 f.; Jacquier, Lietzmann, and Barth (*INT* 49–50).

† Advocated by Meyer, Ellicott, B. Weiss, Sanday, Denney, Zahn, and Bernard, amongst others.

situation. They vibrate with anger and anxiety. Paul's authority and actions had been called in question by a Jewish Christian party of intruders whose teaching also constituted a real peril for his converts. To meet these dangers, due to the same overbearing party who had gained a footing in the church (11^{20}), possibly headed by some ringleader (*ὁ τοιοῦτος, τις*, 2^{6} 7^{12}), Paul retorts upon his detractors. It is possible, and even evident, that they had been able to inflict some severe and public humiliation upon him by means of charges of unscrupulous dealing, overbearing conduct, unfounded pretensions to the apostolic ministry, and so forth. At any rate their success roused his anger. Not on personal grounds merely, but because, as at Thessalonika (see above), an attack on his character and authority involved his very gospel, Paul eagerly rushes to defend himself against slander and censure on the part of his opponents and suspicion on the part of his converts. He proceeds to exhibit his own titles to credit and honour as an apostle of Christ. Self-exaltation is the keynote: *καυχᾶσθαι δεῖ.* Paul's aim is to defend his character, with which his gospel was bound up, against slander and depreciation. He exhibits, with a mixture of pride and reluctance, his indefeasible titles to credit as an apostle of Jesus Christ. In chs. 1–9 the sense of *καύχησις, καύχημα*, and *καυχᾶσθαι* (a group of words especially characteristic of 2 Cor.) is, except once (1^{12}), entirely complimentary to the Corinthians, and indeed confined to them, whereas the nineteen instances in 10–13 are permeated by a hot sense of personal resentment against disloyal suggestions and criticisms at Corinth. Psychologically this tone is entirely suitable to the occasion. "In great religious movements the leaders are often compelled to assert themselves pretty peremptorily, in order that their work may not be wrecked by conceited and incapable upstarts" (Drummond, pp. 171–172). Paul follows here much the same method as in his first letter to the Thessalonians, although the latter had not been carried away like the Corinthians by the insinuations of outsiders against their apostle. He endeavours to expose the shamelessness and futility of such attacks upon him, in order to discredit the influence of such opponents upon his converts. It is painful, he protests, to be obliged to assert his apostolic authority (10^{1-6}, cp. an excellent paper by V. Weber in *BZ.*, 1903, 64–78), but authority he has (10^{7-18}) as well as his rivals, these superlative apostles of the Judaising party. If he must parade his apostolic claims (11^{1-6}) to the Corinthians, let him remind them that he had merely foregone his claim to maintenance out of disinterested consideration (11^{7-15}), not—as his opponents malignantly insinuated—because he felt he dared not ask the support which every legitimate apostle was entitled to demand. After a fresh, half-ironical apology (11^{16-21}), he goes on proudly to match his merits against those of his rivals (11^{21-23}), and to claim superiority in actual services and sufferings for the cause of Christ (11^{24-33}).* Finally, he gives an autobiographical outline of his claim to have visions and revelations (12^{1-10}). After a summary of these arguments (12^{11-13}), he reiterates his honesty and authority in view of a third visit (12^{14}–13^{10}).

It is to this intermediate letter, as much as to Romans or Galatians, that

* On the insecurity and danger of travelling, see Miss A. J. Skeel's *Travel in the First Century after Christ, with special reference to Asia Minor* (1901), pp. 70 f.

Jerome's famous description of Paul's style applies: 'quam artifex, quam prudens, quam dissimulator sit eius quod agit, uidentur quidem uerba simplicia, et quasi innocentis hominis ac rusticani . . . sed quocunque respexeris, fulmina sunt. hæret in causa, capit omne quod tetigerit, tergum uertit ut superet, fugam simulat ut occidat.' This tallies not merely with his employment of OT citations, but with his argument and invectives. The abruptness of the opening words (αὐτὸς δὲ ἐγὼ Παῦλος) shows that 10^{1}–13^{10} represents in all likelihood only a fragment of the original. It is more probable that the entire letter was written by Paul (the earlier part, no longer extant, perhaps in his own name and in that of Timotheus) than that the extant portion was appended originally to a circular letter from other Christian leaders at Ephesus. 13^{10} does echo 10^{10}, but this does not prove that the latter passage represents the original opening of the epistle. From $10^{1f.}$ we might conjecture that the lost context included a reference to the apostle's detractors at Corinth, but in any case there is no logical or psychological antithesis between 9^{15} and $10^{1f.}$.

The incongruity of 10–13 as a sequel to 1–9 was seen as far back as the eighteenth century by Semler, who tentatively suggested that 10–13 represented a later and separate epistle, or that portions of them (*e.g.* 12^{14-21}, 13^{1-10}) were misplaced from 1 Co 2^{3} 5^{9-13}; and by M. Weber (*de numero epist. ad Corinth. rectius constituendo*, 1798), who separated 1–9, 13^{10-13} from 10–13^{10}, a construction still advocated on varying grounds by critics like Krenkel (*Beiträge*, pp. 308 f.) and Drescher (*SK.*, 1897, pp. 43–111). The latter portion, on this theory, was written after Titus and his party had come back from Corinth. The further step of relegating 10–13 to an earlier period than that of 1–9 was first taken by Hausrath in his momentous essay, whose general conclusions have been ratified and restated by an increasing cohort of scholars, including (besides those named above on p. 109) Paulus, Weisse (*Philos. Dogmatik*, i. 145), Wagenmann (*Jahrb. deut. Theol.*, 1870, p. 541), Michelsen (*TT.*, 1873, 424), Lipsius (*JPT.*, 1876, pp. 530 f.), Steck, Seufert (*ZWT.*, 1885, p. 369), Schmiedel, Cramer, Cone (*Paul, The Man, The Teacher, and the Missionary*, pp. 47, 125), McGiffert (*AA.* 313–315), Adeney (*INT.* 368 f.), Moffatt (*HNT.* pp. 174 f.), Bacon (*INT.* 93 f., *Story of St. Paul*, pp. 284 f.), Clemen (*Paulus*, i. 79 f.), Plummer, Pfleiderer (*Urc.*, Eng. tr., i. 144 f.), von Soden (*INT.* 46–56), Völter, R. Scott, G. H. Rendall, and A. S. Peake (*INT.* 35 f.). Schmiedel's treatment has given a new rank and impressiveness to the theory, but Kennedy and Rendall are its ablest advocates in English. The internal evidence for 10^{1}–13^{10} as prior to 1–9 has been already outlined, and it remains only to point out how often in the latter letter the former is echoed (*e.g.* 13^{2} in 1^{23}, 13^{10} in 2^{3}, 10^{6} in 2^{9}, the self-assertion of $11^{5.18.23}$ in $3^{1}=5^{12}$), how incidental phrases like εἰς τὰ ὑπερέκεινα ὑμῶν (10^{16}=Rome and Spain, cp. Ro $15^{24.28}$) and οἱ ἀδελφοὶ ἐλθόντες ἀπὸ Μακεδονίας (11^{9}) suit Ephesus better than Macedonia as the place of composition, and finally how the two letters came to be united in an order which was the reverse of the chronological one.

When the Pauline letters came to be edited for the purposes of the Canon, the earlier of the two extant letters to Corinth was stripped of its opening and added to the later and larger one. Both made up a single writing similar in size to 1 Cor. Instances of this inverted order, in the editing of letters, are known in the case, *e.g.*, of Cicero's correspondence. The finalê, 13^{11-13}, which does not come naturally * after 13^{10}, was probably shifted to that position from its original site at the end of 9 (note the characteristic play on words in χάρις and χαίρετε, 9^{15} 3^{11}, and the aptness of 13^{11-13} as a finalê to 9, where the collection on behalf of the Palestinian relief fund is treated as a bond of union and an opportunity of brotherly kindness). Here, as elsewhere in ancient literature, the reasons for such editorial handling elude the modern critic. Possibly, as Kennedy suggests, the copyist or editor of the two letters welded them together in this order, since ch. 9 promised a visit and ch. 10 apparently referred to it. "It is indeed a visit of a very different kind. There is an apparent resemblance concealing a deep-seated difference, but this is precisely the complexion of things which would be likely to mislead a copyist."

Objections have been tabled to the identification of 10^1–13^{10} with the intermediate and painful letter, (*a*) such as the lack of any reference to the case of the local offender (2 Co 2^5 7^{12}), which was not yet settled.† But 10^1–13^{10} is not necessarily the whole of the original letter, and in any case the apostle probably leaves the offender alone because his mind was concentrated on the broader issue of which this man's case formed only part. The case had now fallen to the Corinthians to deal with. Possibly, too, the matter was left out of the final recension, as it had ended satisfactorily. (*b*) 10^{10} need not refer to the painful intermediate letter; the allusion fits the letter of 1 Co 5^9 and 1 Co itself quite admirably. (*c*) 1^{23} does not imply that the painful letter was in lieu of a visit. As 2^1 shows, the painful visit had been made.

The alternative to this rearrangement of 10–13, 1–9, is to account for the abrupt alteration of tone in $10^{1f.}$ by conjecturing, *e.g.*, (*a*) that since writing 1–9, Paul had unexpectedly received unfavourable news from Corinth, which led him to break out upon his disloyal church with fresh reproaches. This is possible, but it is pure guesswork. There is no word of it in 10–13, as there surely would have been in order to account for the rapid change of tone. The supposition (*b*) that in the last four chapters he suddenly turns to a special and recalcitrant faction in the church is equally forced. They are addressed to the church as a whole (cp. 13^2), not to any turbulent

---

* The sequence of 13^{10} and 13^{11} is plainly editorial (cp. especially Krenkel, pp. 358 f.). "So does no man write. The tragedy of King Lear, passing into an idyllic dance of peasants—such is the impression of the paragraph as it stands. It is an absolute *non sequitur*" (Mackintosh, p. 338).

† It should no longer require to be proved that this offender is not the incestuous person of 1 Co 5^1, but some one who had wronged Paul himself (ὁ ἀδικηθείς). The indulgent consideration of 2 Co $7^{8.11}$ refers to a situation which did not exist when 1 Cor. was written (cp. Weizsäcker, *AA.* pp. 341–353), and Timotheus could not be ὁ ἀδικηθείς, except as Paul's representative. The person who insulted Paul might conceivably be the offender of 1 Co 5^1, but the likelihood is that he was another Corinthian who took umbrage, or rather voiced the feelings of those who took umbrage, at Paul's domineering methods of discipline. Had the misconduct been due to a private quarrel between two members of the local church (Krenkel, 304 f.), it could hardly have become so significant as to involve the apostle.

minority. It is in the opening of the later epistle that Paul distinguishes the majority ($2^{5f.}$) from a section of disaffected members, and the ὑπακοή of $2^9 = 7^{15-16}$ is much more intelligible after than before 10^6. The sharp warning of 12^{21} upsets the (*c*) view that in 1–9 Paul is praising the church for its repentance, while in 10–13 he is blaming it for still siding with his opponents. Finally (*d*), the view of Drescher and Klöpper, that Paul wrote 1–9 under a sanguine misapprehension of the real state of affairs at Corinth, as reported by Titus incorrectly, and that 10–13 represents his rebound to the opposite extreme of denunciation, lies open to the same objection as (*a*). In short, all theories which place 10–13 after 1–9, either as part of the same epistle or as a later letter, involve the hypothesis that the Corinthian trouble, after all that had happened, broke out again in the same acute form as before. This difficulty besets even the presentment of the case for the canonical structure of the epistle (recently urged, with ability, by Weiss, *AJT.* i. 355–363; Klöpper, Rohr, A. Robertson, Zahn, *INT*, §§ 19–20; Denney, Bachmann, 414 f., and Bernard), which defends its integrity mainly on the general ground that the closing four chapters represent not a fresh situation, but an emotional and argumentative climax, the last charge, as it were, of Paul's dialectic, which was carefully kept in reserve until it could sweep out to complete the victory already gained in part (1^{14}). Some critics further argue that 2 Cor. is emphatically a letter of moods,* which was not composed at a single sitting, and that strong cross-currents of feeling are to be expected under the circumstances. But the variations in 1–9 and 10–13 are too decisive to be explained upon the mere supposition that Paul was a busy man who stopped now and then, as he dictated, or hurried from one subject to another. On any hypothesis there is a residuum of obscurity owing to the extremely intricate and subtle character of the relations between Paul and the Corinthian church; but this residuum is decidedly less upon the theory just advocated than upon the view that after writing 2 Co 1–9 the apostle relapsed, for no obvious reason,† into the temper of scathing animosity and indignation from which he had just emerged, resuscitating an old quarrel after it had been almost buried. There is a psychological inconsequence on the latter theory which it is difficult to credit, even in a man of Paul's passionate temperament.

§ 8. *2 Co 1–9.*—The effect of this sharp letter was favourable. Titus returned from Corinth to greet Paul in Macedonia with the glad news that the church had regained her loyalty and vindicated him at the expense of his opponents (2^{13} 7^{13}).

This happy intelligence found Paul (at Philippi?) tossing on a sea ‡ of troubles (1–2), partly raised by recent experiences in

* This invalidates the parallel (brought forward by Cornely, after Hug and Rückert) with the *De Corona*, the first part of which is calm and moderate, while in the later sections Demosthenes breaks out deliberately into a violent polemic against his opponent.

† The *reductio ad absurdum* of this hypothesis is surely reached in Lietzmann's naive remark (p. 204): 'mir genugt z. B. die Annahme einer schlaflos durchwachten Nacht zwischen c. 9 und c. 10 zur Erklärung.'

‡ Cp. the description of 2 Cor. by L. Davies (*Exp.*[4] iv. 299–300): "The

Asia Minor, partly by anticipations of the future. Driven from his old anchorage at Ephesus, he was still uncertain whether Corinth, his former harbour, would admit him. The information brought by Titus banished this anxiety, and out of the glad sense of relief* he wrote a fresh epistle (1–9), breathing delight and affectionate gratitude, irenical in tone, designed to re-establish mutual confidence and to obliterate all memories of the past bitter controversy. To forgive and to forget is its keynote. The sky is once more clear, so far as the apostle is concerned. Indeed, after pouring out his heart to the Corinthians, he even ventures at the close to renew his appeal on behalf of the collection (8–9). These two chapters are not an anticlimax (see below), and "there is no good reason for treating them as a separate epistle. As such the semi-apologetic tone would make it poor and unconvincing; while, as an appendage to 1–7, the tone adopted is appropriate, natural, and in perfect good taste. It is a happy parallel to the epistle to Philemon, and the same note of Christian chivalry, courtesy, and delicacy pervades both" (Rendall, p. 73).

The epistle opens with an invocation of God as the comforter, which leads Paul to speak about his own recent experiences of deliverance (1^{3-11}) in Asia Minor. He then passes on ($1^{12f.}$) to explain his change of plans,† his reasons for writing instead of travelling to them (1^{23}–2^{11}), and his journey to Macedonia (2^{12-17}). This suggests a general vindication of his ministry and preaching (3^{1}–4^{6}), with all its sufferings (4^{7}–5^{10}) and methods of appeal (5^{11}–6^{10}). Then, after a quick outburst of appeal to the Corinthians themselves for frank confidence in him (6^{11-13} 7^{2-4}), the apostle harks back to the contrast between their past trouble and this present happiness ($7^{5f.}$), thanking them for their kind reception of Titus his envoy ($7^{13f.}$), and using the example of the Macedonian churches' liberality to incite them to proceed with the business of the Palestinian relief fund or collection for the poor saints of Jerusalem (8–9) —a task which Titus himself‡ would superintend in person. With a hearty farewell (13^{11-13}) the letter then closes.

---

letter exhibits a tumult of contending emotions. Wounded affection, joy, self-respect, hatred of self-assertion, consciousness of the authority and importance of his ministry, scorn of his opponents, toss themselves like waves, sometimes against each other, on the troubled sea of his mind. Strong language, not seldom stronger than the occasion seems to warrant, figurative expressions, abrupt turns, phrases seized and flung at his assailants, words made up, iterated, played upon, mark this epistle far more than any other of the apostle's letters."

* Note the repetition of παράκλησις (eleven times).

† On $1^{6.\ 8-10.\ 15-17.\ 23}$ 2^{1}, cp. Warfield in *JBL.* (1886) 27 f.

‡ The old identification of the anonymous brother (τὸν ἀδελφόν) of 8^{18} and 12^{18} with Luke is carried a step further by Souter (*ET.* xviii. 285, 325–336), who takes the words in their literal sense.

The course of the letter is determined by the unpremeditated movements of the writer's mind, working on the practical situation of the Corinthians. It is too artificial to find, with Heinrici, any rhetorical scheme in the disposition of its contents, as if it presented a *προοίμιον* (3^{1-6}), *πρόθεσις* and *ἀπόδειξις* (3^{7-18}), *λύσις* (4^{1-15}), *egressus in causa* (4^{16}–5^{21}) *ἐπίλογος* (6^{1}–7^{4}), and *ἀνατροπὴ μεθ' ὑπερβολῆς* (10–13). For one thing this covers at once too much (10–13) and too little (1–2) of the epistle, and, while such artistic schematism may be applicable to Hebrews (see below), it seems irrelevant in the case of this genuine letter.

(*a*) The paragraph 6^{14}–7^{1} probably is a fragment interpolated from some other epistle, in all likelihood from the lost letter written first of all to the Corinthian church (see above, p. 109).* In its present situation it looks like an erratic boulder, and although no MSS evidence can be adduced for the hypothesis, the internal evidence is fairly conclusive (so Emmerling, Schrader: *der Apostel Paulus*, 1835, 300 f.; Straatman, pp. 138 f.; Ewald; Hilgenfeld; A. H. Franke, *SK.*, 1884, pp. 544–583; S. Davidson, *INT.* i. 63; Holsten, *zum Ev. des Paulus u. Petrus*, p. 386: Sabatier's *Paul*, pp. 177–178; Hausrath, iv. 55 f.; Renan, iii. lxii–lxiii; Rovers, Baljon, Cremer, Clemen, Pfleiderer: *Urc.* i. 134; McGiffert, p. 332; Moffatt, *HNT.* pp. 628–629; von Soden, Bacon, Halmel, etc.). The connection of 6^{11-13} and 7^{2} is good: † *we keep nothing back from you, O Corinthians; our heart is wide open. Your constraint lies not in us, it lies in your own hearts. Now one good turn deserves another* (*to speak as to my children*), *be you wide open too. Take us into your hearts.* On the other hand 6^{13} fits on as roughly to 6^{14} as 7^{1} to 7^{2}, and the ordinary explanations of the canonical order are singularly strained. Thus Godet (*INT.* i. 321–323) makes Paul's demand for strict abstinence the reason why the Corinthians were holding back from him; but the constraint of which he is conscious lies surely in the personal feelings left by the recent strain between them and himself. "Much of the coldness towards Paul" was, no doubt, "the result of an unworthy deference to heathen sentiment and practice" (Drummond); but of this particular cause there is no hint in the context or even in the letter (for 13^{2} belongs to an earlier epistle).‡

---

* So Hilgenfeld, Franke, Sabatier, Lisco, von Dobschütz (*Urc.* pp. 29, 45), and von Soden; cp. Whitelaw, *Class. Review* (1890), pp. 12, 248, 317. Other conjectures suppose it has drifted from a later apostolic epistle (Ewald), or that it originally lay after 1 Co 10^{22} (Hausrath, Blass: *BFT.* x. 1, 51–60), if not 1 Co 6 (Pfleiderer). The letter mentioned in 1 Co 5^{9} contained the very advice given in 2 Co 6^{14}–7^{1} (cp. *ἐξελθεῖν*, 1 Co 5^{10} = *ἐξέλθατε*, 2 Co 6^{17}).

† Lisco's intercalation of 12^{11-19} between 6^{13} and 7^{2} is hopelessly wrong.

‡ Weizsäcker's theory (*AA.* i. 363) is that the outburst of 6^{14}–7^{1} is semi-apologetic, but the language does not suggest a desire on the part of the apostle to assert his opposition to pagan vices by way of meeting Judaistic reflections on his character and gospel. For Lütgert's ingenious but equally unconvincing view, see *ET.* xx. 428–429. Recent explanations of its present position as part of the original epistle are offered by Bachmann (289 f.) and Windisch (*Taufe u. Sünde im Urchristenthum*, 149 f.).

Neither the language nor the ideas justify a suspicion of the genuineness of the passage,* as though it emanated from Jewish Christians, with a narrow repulsion to 'unclean things' (6^{17}), or from a Puritan Christian of the second century (Straatman, i. pp. 138–146; Baljon, pp. 147–150, and others, including Schrader; Bakhuyzen; Holsten; Michelsen, *TT.*, 1873, 423; Rovers, *INT.* pp. 37–38; Halmel, 115 f.; Krenkel, *Beiträge*, 332; and R. Scott, *The Pauline Epistles*, 236–237). The sole feature which is at first sight out of keeping with Paul's normal thought is, as Schmiedel admits (pp. 253 f.) after an exhaustive discussion, the allusion to the *defilement of flesh and spirit* (7^1); but † *flesh* here is used in a popular sense (cp. 1 Co 7^{34} *holy in body and spirit*) almost as an equivalent to *body*, while *spirit* is to be read untechnically in the light of a passage like 1 Th 5^{23}.

(*b*) A second instance of extraneous matter in the canonical letter is furnished by the brief paragraph 11^{32-33}, describing Paul's escape from Damascus; this interrupts the sequence of thought in 11^{30-31} 12^{1-5} (exulting and weakness) so violently as to rouse suspicions of its right to stand here (so Holsten, *ZWT.*, 1874, 388 f., and van Leeuwen, *de joodsche achtergrond van der Brief aan de Romeinen*, 1894, p. iii., adding 12^{1a}; Hilgenfeld, Schmiedel, and Baljon, adding 12^1; Michelsen, *TT.*, 1873, pp. 424 f., adding $12^{1.7a}$; and Rovers, *INT.* 38, adding $12^{1.11b-12}$). 'The historicity of the paragraph need not be doubted' (Schmiedel), the two real difficulties being the precise date of the incident and the manner in which the paragraph drifted into its present position. On the latter point, the alternatives are to suppose (with Rovers, *ZWT.*, 1881, 404, and others) that it was inserted by a scribe who failed to find any illustration ‡ of ἀσθένεια (11^{30}) in the context, or that it is a marginal addition by Paul himself, properly belonging to the parenthesis $11^{24f.}$ (so Wendt, *Acts*, p. 35), or that it originally belonged to some other letter (Bacon, *Story of St. Paul*, pp. 87–88). The last-named scholar dates the occurrence after A.D. 38, in the period of Gal. 1^{22-24} (cp. 2 Co 12^2).

§ 9. *The structure of 2 Cor.*—Beyond the relegation of 6^{14}-7^1 to an earlier epistle, and of 10–13^{10} to the intermediate letter, it is hardly possible to push the analysis. 2 Co 1–8 and even 1–9 hang together too closely to be resolved into more than one letter (cp. Clemen in *TLZ.*, 1897, 560 f.; Rohr, pp. 102 f.), but it is the supposed difference of situation between 8 and 9 which started not only Semler's theory (9 = a separate letter to the Christians of Achaia), but more recently A. Halmel's § drastic

* Cp. Clemen's discussion, *Einheitlichkeit*, pp. 58 f., and *Paulus*, i. 77–78.

† So Sokolowski emphatically (*Die Begriffe Geist u. Leben bei Paulus*, 1903, pp. 126 f., 144 f.), and M. Dibelius (*Die Geisterwelt im Glauben des Paulus*, 1909, 62 f.).

‡ Those who defend the passage in its present position take this line of interpretation, as if Paul were frankly confessing an experience which savoured to some of cowardice (so especially Heinrici).

§ Cp. Holtzmann's review in *GGA.* (1905) 667 f., of his *Der zweite Korintherbrief des Apostels Paulus. Geschichtliche und Literaturkritische* reconstruction of three letters: A = 1^{1-2} 1^{8}–2^{13} 7^{5}–8^{24} 13^{13}, B = 10^{1}–13^{10}, and C = 1^{8-7} 2^{14}–7^{4} 9. 13^{11-12}, A and C being put together about A.D. 100, when 6^{14}–7^{1} 3^{12-18} and $4^{3-4.\ 6}$ were editorially added, whilst B was not incorporated until afterwards. The deletion of the two latter passages as non-Pauline (allied to the ep. of Barnabas) is fatal to this theory. The discovery of a flaw in the juxtaposition of 2^{13} and $2^{14f.}$ is due to prosaic exegesis, and the failure to see that $1^{15f.}$ implies a second visit obliges the author to posit this visit between the composition of A and B, in fulfilment of the promise made in $1^{15f.}$. C was written immediately prior to the apostle's last visit. Some of the obvious difficulties in this complicated scheme (B = the appendix* to a letter from the Macedonian churches which the Corinthians took as an ἐπιστολὴ συστατική, cp. $3^{1f.}$!) are avoided by Völter (*Paulus und seine Briefe*, pp. 74 f.), who advocates the identification of 10–13^{10} with the Intermediate Letter, but *acutius quam verius* eliminates 1^{21-22} 2^{16b}–4^{6} 4^{16}–5^{11} 5^{16} 6^{14}–7^{1}, and 8^{9} from 1–9, 13^{11-13} as matter due to a later editor or editors (see above, p. 113). The criticism of Halmel would apply even more stringently to Lisco's keen attempt on similar lines (*Die Enstehung des zweiten Korintherbriefes*, Berlin, 1896) to find three separate epistles in A = 10–13^{10} with 6^{14}–7^{1} between 12^{10} and 12^{20}, B = 1^{1}–6^{13} with 12^{11-19} and 7^{2-3} 9, 13^{11-13}, and C = 7^{4}–8^{24}, an attempt which, in his *Judaismus Triumphatus: Ein Beitrag zur Auslegung der vier letzten Kapitel des zweiten Corintherbriefes* (1896), rightly identifies A with the sharp letter presupposed in B, but makes C the letter entrusted to Titus, while, more elaborately still, in his *Vincula Sanctorum, Ein Beitrag zur Erklärung der Gefangenschaftsbriefe des Apost. Paulus* (1900), for reasons as precarious in exegesis as they are

Untersuchungen (1904), which presents a revised form of his earlier monograph on *Der Vierkapitelbrief im zweiten Korintherbrief* (1894), reviewed by J. Weiss in *TLZ.*, 1894, 513 f. Halmel appeals (pp. 8 f.) to a Dutch critic, E. J. Greve, who in the third volume (1804) of his *De brieven van den Apostel Paulus, uit het Grieksch vertaald, met Aanmerkingen*, argued that Titus left for Corinth without Paul's letter, which was written as far as 2 Co 8^{16}, and that the rest was added by the apostle on receipt of fresh news from Corinth. J. Weiss' attempt to detect the intermediate letter in 1. 2^{14}–7^{4} 10^{1}–13^{10} fails to prove the connection between the two latter sections, or to justify the separation of $2^{14f.}$ from its context.

* Hausrath had made it the appendix to a letter from the Ephesian church (Aquila?).

ill-supported in tradition, he places the prison epistles in some Ephesian captivity of the apostle; after A (as above) come Titus, Colossians, and Ephesians, previous to the trial, followed by 2 Timothy and Philippians, and then B C (as above) with 1 Co 15 written after his release. Some basis for such a reconstruction may be found in history, but none exists for Pierson and Naber's (*Verisimilia*, pp. 108 f.) deletion of $1^{1-10a. 15-18. 23f.}$ $2^{1. 4}$ 4^{7-12} 5^{12} 7^{2-4} 11^{1}–$13^{2. 10-13}$. The significance of Halmel and Völter in the criticism of the Corinthian correspondence mainly consists in their recoil from the results of the aberration which some years ago led a Dutch school of writers to regard even 2 Cor. as a romance of the second century (cp. *e.g.* van Manen, *OCL.* 38–41).

Several more or less plausible cases of transposition or interpolation may be seen in the traditional text. 2^{12-13} probably has been displaced from its original setting after 1^{22} (Van de Sande Bakhuyzen) or better after 1^{16}, where chronologically its contents belong; so Laurent (*NT Studien*, pp. 24–28), Michelsen, and Baljon (pp. 142–143). This leaves an admirable and characteristic juxtaposition between 2^{11} (Satan's machinations) and 2^{14} (God's overruling providence).* Upon the other hand, the attempts to isolate 8 as a separate note (Hagge, p. 482 f.), written later than 9 (Baljon, pp. 150–152), or as part of the Intermediate Letter (Michelsen, *TT.*, 1873, 424; Hagge), break down for much the same reasons as the cognate hypothesis that 9 itself was a subsequent letter sent to the Achaian churches (9^{2}, so Semler). The unity of the situation presupposed in 8 and 9 is too well-marked to justify any separation of the chapters either from one another or from the letter 1–9, whose natural conclusion they furnish (cp. Völter, pp. 92–94; Schmiedel, pp. 267–269, as against Halmel's arguments in *der zweit. Kor.* pp. 11–22). In 9^{1} Paul is really explaining why he needs to say no more than he has said in 8^{24}. Instead of being inconsistent with what precedes, 9^{1} clinches it, and 9^{5-7} simply shows that he felt a difficulty, not unnatural under the circumstances, about saying either too much or too little on the delicate topic of collecting money.† On the other hand, 11^{32}–12^{1} has all the appearance of a marginal addition (cp. Wendt on Ac 9^{24-25}), which has been misplaced from $11^{24f.}$, or of a gloss interrupting the sequence (so Holsten, Hilg. *ZWT.*, 1888, 200; Schmiedel, Baljon, cp. *HNT.* 629–630), although the order $11^{30. 32. 33. 31}$ would partially ease the somewhat jolting transition (see above, p. 126).

* This helps to meet Halmel's vehement objection (pp. 58 f.) to the position of 2^{14}–7^{4} in the canonical epistle.

† With 8^{20} compare Byron's remark to Moore (in 1822): "I doubt the accuracy of all almoners, or remitters of benevolent cash." The precautions taken with regard to the conveyance of the temple-tribute are noted by Philo in *De Spec. Legibus*, i. (περὶ ἱεροῦ, § 3), *καὶ χρόνοις ὡρισμένοις ἱεροπομποὶ τῶν χρημάτων ἀριστίνδην ἐπικριθέντες, ἐξ ἑκάστης οἱ δοκιμώτατοι, χειροτονοῦνται, σώους τὰς ἐλπίδας ἑκάστων παραπέμψοντες.*

§ 10. *Attestation of 2 Cor.*—2 Cor. is quoted by the same authors as is 1 Cor. (see above, p. 114), after Marcion (cp. *Diognet.* v. 12 f. = 6^{9-10}), but its earlier attestation is not equally strong. In two passages of Polykarp (iv. 1, vi. 2) the language recalls Romans rather than 2 Cor. (see below, p. 148), and vi. 1, like 8^{21} and Ro 12^{17}, probably goes back to Pr 3^{4} (LXX) rather than to either of these Pauline passages; on the other hand, ii. 2 (ὁ δὲ ἐγείρας αὐτὸν ἐκ νεκρῶν καὶ ἡμᾶς ἐγερεῖ) may echo 4^{14} (ὁ ἐγείρας τὸν Κύριον Ἰησοῦν καὶ ἡμᾶς σὺν Ἰησοῦ ἐγερεῖ). In Ignatius there are apparent, though far from distinct, reminiscences of 6^{16} (= *Eph.* xv. 3, αὐτοῦ ἐν ἡμῖν κατοικοῦντος, ἵνα ὦμεν ναοὶ καὶ αὐτὸς ἐν ἡμῖν θεός) and 4^{14} (= *Trall.* ix. 2), possibly, too, of 1^{12} 11^{9-10} 12^{16} (= *Philad.* vi. 3). The contents of Clem. Rom. v. 5–6 are inadequate to prove the use of 11^{23-27}, and xxxvi. 2 can be explained apart from 3^{18}, as can Barn. iv. 11–13 (5^{10})* and vi. 11 f. (5^{17}). The indifference of Clem. Rom. to 2 Cor., taken together with his appeal to 1 Cor., is all the more striking as the former epistle would have served his own purposes of exhortation with telling effect. It is perhaps a fair inference that, in its canonical form, 2 Cor. was not as yet circulated throughout the churches (cp. Kennedy, pp. 142 f.; Rendall, 88 f.); possibly it had not as yet been thrown into its present form.

§ 11. *The apocryphal correspondence.*—The Syrian, Armenian, and even some of the Latin churches, admitted for some time to their NT Canon (in Efraim's commentary between 2 Cor. and Gal., elsewhere after Hebrews) an apocryphal letter of Paul to the Corinthians which originally belonged to the *Acta Pauli*,† and was translated into Latin and Syriac during the third century. Stephanas and others ask Paul's advice upon the teaching of two Gnostics, Simon and Cleobius, who have arrived at Corinth. Paul, who is imprisoned at Philippi, replies from the standpoint of the genuine apostolic tradition. This so-called third epistle to the Corinthians (translated by Byron, cp. Moore's *Life of Byron*, vi. 269–275) was once defended as authentic by Whiston and W. F. Rinck (*Das Sendschreiben d. Kor. an der Apostel Paulus u. dritte Sendsch. P. an die Korinther*, 1823), but the correspondence is obviously composed‡ on the basis of 1 Co 5^{9} and 7^{1} by

* Cp. *NTA.* 11–12, where Bartlet suggests a common source.

† Vetter (*TQ.*, 1895, 622 f.) conjectures in addition a rabbinic midrash on the resurrection. The original site of the correspondence in the *Acta Pauli* was first proved definitely by C. Schmidt (*Neue Heidelb. Jahrb.*, 1897, 117 f., *Acta Pauli aus der Heidelberger koptischen Papyrushandschrift Nr. 1 herausgegeben*, 1904, 125 f.).

‡ Just as 2 Co 12^{4} was made the text and occasion of an ἀναβατικὸν Παύλου, according to Epiphanius (*Haer.* xviii. 12).

an author who stood no nearer to Paul than did the composer of the Thekla legends, and who wrote with reference to the doctrine of Bardesanes (cp. Berendts' essay on the Christology of the correspondence, in *Abhandlungen A. von Oettingen zum 70 Geburtstag gewidmet*, 1898).

For text and literature, see P. Vetter's Tübingen programme, *Der Apokryphe dritte Korintherbrief* (1894); Lietzmann's *Kleine Texte* (12, 1905); Zahn's *GK*. ii. 592–611; Harnack in *SBBA*., 1905, 3–35, and *ACL*. i. 37–39, ii. 1. 506–508; and Rolffs in *HNA*. i. 362 f., 378 f., ii. 360, 388 f. The Latin version, discovered in 1890, was published by S. Berger and Carrière (*La correspondance apocryphe de S. Paul et des Corinthiens. Ancienne version latine et traduction du texte Arménien*, 1891); cp. Harnack and Bratke in *TLZ*., 1892, 7–9, 585–588, Deeleman in *Theol. Studiën* (1909) 37–56.

(D) *ROMANS.*

LITERATURE.—(*a*) Editions[1]—Locke, *Paraphrase and Notes* (1733); G. T. Zachariä's *Erklärung* (1788); Semler's *Paraphrasis* (1769); C. F. Boehme's *Comment. perpetuus* (1806); Belsham (London, 1822); R. Cox (*Horae Romanae*, London, 1824); Flatt's *Vorlesungen* (1825); Klee (1830); H. E. G. Paulus (1831); Benecke (1831); Reiche (*Versuch einer ausführl. Erkl.* etc. 1833–4)*; Hodge (1835); Olshausen (1835); Fritzsche (1836–43)*; Rückert[2] (1839); R. Haldane (1842); Maier (1843); Rasmus Nielsen (Leipzig, 1843); Baumgarten-Crusius (1844); Reithmayr (1845); Kreyhl (1845); de Wette[4] (1847); R. Knight (1854); A. A. Livermore (Boston, 1854); van Hengel (1854–9); Beelen (1854); Purdue (Dublin, 1855); Tholuck[5] (1856, Eng. tr. 1842); Nielsen (Denmark, 1856); F. W. K. Umbreit (*der Brief an die Römer, auf dem Grunde des AT ausgelegt*, 1856); Ewald (1857); Dr. John Brown (Edinburgh, 1857); G. F. Jatho (1858–9); S. H. Turner (New York, 1859); Dr. David Brown (Glasgow, 1860); Colenso (*St. Paul's ep. to Rom. Ed. from a mission. point of view*, 1863); S. L. A. Ortloph (Erlangen, 1865–6); Hofmann (1868); J. Forbes (Edinburgh, 1868); F. Delitzsch, *Brief a. d. Römer aus dem griech. Urtext in das Hebraische uebersetzt u. aus Talmud u. Midrasch erläutert* (1870)*; Bisping (1870); H. A. W. Meyer[5] (1872); Volkmar (1875); Moses Stuart[2] (1876); Reuss (1878); Moule (*Cambridge Bible*, 1879); Klofutar (1880); Godet (1879–80, Eng. tr. 1888)*; Oltramare (1881 f.); E. H. Gifford (in *Speaker's Comm.* 1881)*; H. Reinecke (1884); F. Zimmer (1887); Kleinschmidt (1888); C. J. Vaughan[7] (1890); Barmby (*Pulpit Comm.* 1890); C. W. Otto[2] (1891); A. Schäfer (1891); Lipsius[2] (*HC.* 1892); Jowett[3] (1894); Lightfoot (*Notes on Epp. St. Paul*, 1895, on 1^1–7^{25}); Philippi[4] (Frankfurt, 1896); Cornely (*Commentarius*, Paris, 1897); J. M. Stifler (New York, 1897); Th. Heusser (1898); J. Drummond (1899); Weiss[9] (— Meyer, 1899)*; W. G. Rutherford (tr. and analysis, 1900); Ceulemans (1901); J. Agar Beet[9] (1901); Denney (*EGT.* 1901)*; Garvie (*CB.* 1901); Schlatter[4] (1901); Schat-Petersen

[1] On the patristic and mediæval commentaries, see Sanday and Headlam, pp. xcviii–cii; on the pre-Lutheran, Denifle's *Luther u. Luthertum*, i. ii. (1905), besides the conspectus in Meyer's ed. (Eng. tr., W. P. Dickson, Edin. 1873–1874) and in Grafe's monograph.

(*Paulus Briev til Romerne*, 1902); J. van Andel (*Briev aan de Romeinen*, Kampen, 1904); Sanday and Headlam[5] (*ICC.* 1905)*; Lietzmann (*HBNT.* 1906); Jülicher (*SNT.*[2] 1907); G. Richter (1907); J. Niglutzsch[2] (*Commentarius*, 1907); Zahn (*ZK.* 1910).

(*b*) Studies.—H. E. G. Paulus, *de originibus Pauli epistolæ ad Rom.* (Jena, 1801); Baur (*Tübing. Zeitschr. f. Theol.*, 1836, 59 f.)*; R. Rothe, *Brief P. an die R. erklärt* (1852); Th. Schott, *der Römerbrief, seinem Endzweck und Gedankengang nach ausgelegt* (1858); W. Mangold, *der Römerbrief u. die Anfänge der röm. Gemeinde* (1866); Beyschlag (*SK.*, 1867, pp. 627 f.); Schenkel (*BL.* v. 106–116); Baur's *Paulus* (Eng. tr. i. 321 f.); Weizsäcker in *Jahrb. deutsche Theol.* (1876) 248 f.; M. Arnold, *St. Paul and Protestantism* (1876, ch. i.); Keble, *Studia Sacra* (1877, 45–147 on 1^{1}–6^{14}); Holsten (*JPT.*, 1879, 95 f., 314 f., 680 f.)*; Grafe, *über Veranlassung u. Zweck d. Römerbriefs* (1881)*; A. Klostermann's *Korrekturen z. bisher. Erklärung d. Römerbriefes* (Gotha, 1881); W. Mangold, *der Romerbrief u. seine gesch. Voraussetzungen* (1884); Lorenz, *das Lehrsystem im Römerbrief* (1884); Schürer (*EB.*[9]); van Manen, *de brief aan de Romeinen* (1890); Hilgenfeld (*ZWT.*, 1892, 296–347); Liddon, *Explanatory Analysis* (1893); Hort, *Romans and Ephesians* (1895)*; A. C. Headlam (*ET.* 1894–5); M. W. Jacobus, *A Problem in NT Criticism* (1900), 237 f.; Denney (*Exp.*[6] iii.–v., 'The Theology of the Epistle to the Romans')*; A. Robertson (*DB.* iv. 295–306); Feine, *der Römerbrief* (1903); G. Semeria, *il pensiero die S. Paolo nella littera ai Romani* (Roma, 1903); Pfleiderer, *Urc.* i. 149 f. (Eng. tr. i. 211 f.); Bahnsen (*PM.*, 1904, 26–31); von Dobschütz, *Urc.* pp. 121 f.; D. Völter, *Paulus u. seine Briefe* (1905), pp. 135–228; Hupfeld, *der Römerbrief*[2] (1905); R. J. Knowling, *Testimony of St. Paul to Christ* (1905, pp. 60 f., 311 f., 465 f.); Zahn (*Einl.* §§ 21–24); G. Richter's *Kritische-polemische Untersuchungen* (*BFT.*, 1908, xii. 6.).

§ 1. *Contents and outline.*—Special literature: C. F. Schmid (*De epist. ad R. consilio*, Tübingen, 1830); Kiene, *Das Römerbrief u. das Joh. Evglm* (1868), pp. 1–42; E. Walther, *Inhalt und Gedankengang d. Römerbriefs* (1897).

After a brief introduction (1^{1-7}), Paul explains why he had never been able as yet to visit the Roman church, although he had hoped and still hoped to do so, in the course of preaching the gospel. Meanwhile, he proceeds to state that gospel as the exhibition of God's δικαιοσύνη ἐκ πίστεως εἰς πίστιν (1^{8-17}) for all men. This forms the theme of what follows.[1] In 1^{18}–3^{20} the need of such a δικαιοσύνη is proved by the fact that Gentiles (1^{18-32})[2] and Jews (2^{1}–3^{20}) alike had missed it. But, just as the apostle's religious philosophy of history has dipped into almost

[1] On 3, cp. Dr. Jas. Morison's monograph (1866), and G. W. Matthias' *Exegetische Versuch* (Cassel, 1857); on 1–3, E. Weber's essay (*BFT.*, 1905, ix. 4) on 'die Beziehungen von Röm 1–3 z. Missionspraxis des Paulus.'

[2] For the Alexandrian traits of 1^{18-20} cp. Schjött in *ZNW.*, 1903, 75–78.

unrelieved gloom, it is brightened by the positive fact * that in Jesus Christ (3^{21-31}) God had revealed his δικαιοσύνη to the faith of man, whether Gentile or Jew. Faith, however, had been in the world before Christ, and so had revelation, particularly within the sphere of the Jewish Law; Paul therefore turns for a moment to show how the Christian gospel of δικαιοσύνη by faith, instead of being at variance with the spiritual order of the OT, was identical in principle with the very faith of Abraham upon which the Jew prided himself (4^{1-25}). Returning to the positive and blissful consequences of the universal δικαιοσύνη revealed in Jesus Christ (5^{1-11}), he throws these into relief against the sombre results of the fall of Adam; life had now superseded death, grace had triumphed over sin. But the supersession of the Law, so far from relaxing the moral bonds of life, only laid higher obligations on the soul of the believing man ($6^{1f.}$). This leads the apostle to describe the struggle of the soul between the Law's demands and the thwarting power of sin, a conflict between the spirit and the flesh ($7^{1f.}$) which can only be resolved by the interposition of Jesus Christ.† The faith which identifies man with him invests life with the divine Spirit ($8^{1f.}$), which is the sole guarantee of a sound life in the present and of security in the future.

At this point there is a certain break in the argument. Hitherto he has been mainly engaged in a positive statement of his gospel, prompted by the charges, which were liable to be brought against it, of being ethically mischievous or ineffective. The following section reverts to the thought underlying passages like $2^{17f.}$ 4^{1}. The gracious fellowship enjoyed by Christians with their God through Jesus Christ ($8^{35f.}$) sadly reminds him, as a warm-hearted Jew, of the fact that the very people who should have been in the direct line of this δικαιοσύνη were standing as a nation outside it (9^{1-5}). How was this unbelief of Israel, the ancient people of God, to be reconciled with the justice and promises of God? Paul addresses himself ‡ to this problem in

* For an argument that 3^{22b-26} originally lay, instead of 1^{17}, after 1^{16}, and was followed by 5–6, see D. Völter in *ZNW.* (1909) 180–183.

† Cp. Engel's exhaustive monograph, *Der Kampf am Röm vii* (1902).

‡ The antinomy of this patriotic outburst (partly due to the feeling that the motives of a renegade might be suspected), or divergence into a nationalistic outlook, is one of the most characteristic features in Paul. His religious philosophy of history is suddenly shot across by a strong personal emotion. Hausrath has somewhere remarked that if Paul had not spent

9–11. He begins by pointing out, as he had already done in Gal $4^{7f.}$ (cp. Ro 2^{28-29}), that even in the OT there were traces of God discriminating between the bodily children of the patriarchs ($9^{6f.}$), and that mere physical descent had never entitled a Jew to the promises. Besides, he adds (9^{14-29}), nettled at the idea of Jewish pride and presumption daring to charge God with unfaithfulness or injustice, cannot God do as He pleases? Is not His freedom sovereign? "Here, to speak plainly, Paul's argument has got into an *impasse*. He is not able to carry it through, and to maintain the sovereign freedom of God as the whole and sole explanation of human destiny, whether in men or nations" (Denney, *EGT.* ii. 664). He breaks away by quoting from the LXX in order to prove that God's apparently harsh methods with the Jews had a larger end in view, viz., the election of a people, Jewish and Gentile, on the score of faith, so that the doom of the Jews was their own fault, consisting in a stubborn refusal to enter into God's greater plan (9^{22-29}). They are to blame, not God (9^{30}–10^{21}). He had made righteousness by faith open and accessible to all; Israel could not plead lack of opportunity and warning. Finally, Paul tries to sees a ray of light in the dark tragedy thus enacted. Israel's unbelief, he contends, is only partial (11^{1-10}) and ($11^{11f.}$) temporary; it may have a providential purpose (so that the Gentiles need not boast over their less favoured neighbours, 11^{13-24}; cp. Ramsay's *Pauline and other Studies*, 1907, 219 f.) in stirring them up ultimately ($11^{25f.}$) to claim their heritage in the messianic kingdom. *For God has shut up all under disobedience, that upon all He may have mercy.* The vision of this glorious consummation stirs the apostle to an outburst of solemn adoration (11^{33-36}), with which the whole section fitly closes.*

himself in the service of Jesus, he would have shed his blood with some other natives of Tarsus on the walls of Jerusalem in A.D. 70; and this passage shows how his religious patriotism flickered up inside his Christian outlook, even in spite of the treatment he received from Jews and Judaists alike. Cp. the present writer's *Paul and Paulinism* (1910), pp. 66 f.

* 11^{32-36} rounds off 1–11, as well as 9–11 (cp. Bühl in *SK.*, 1887, 295–320). What Paul has in mind is not a Judaising tendency among the Jewish Christians at Rome in particular, but the general and perplexing question of Judaism in relation to the new faith of the gospel. On the dialectic of the whole passage, see Gore's paper in *SB.* iii. ('The argument of Rom ix.–xi.'). The literature, up to 1897, is summarised in H. J. Holtzmann's *NTTh.* ii. 171 f.

Applying (οὖν) the thought of God's mercy and its obligations (12^{1-2}), Paul now sketches the ethic of Christians as members of the church (12^{3-21}) * and of society, and as members of the State (13^{1-7}); love is to be the supreme law (13^{8-10}), and the nearness of the end the supreme motive to morality (13^{11-14}).

These thoughts of mutual charity and of the impending judgment are still before the apostle (14^{3-10}) as he leaves the plane of general ethical counsels for that of a special practical problem which was vexing the Roman church, viz., the question of abstinence or non-abstinence from food offered to idols. Sheer anxiety about personal purity (13^{13-14}) was leading some † to be over-scrupulous at Rome, while the stronger Christians were prone to judge such sensitive brothers hastily and harshly, and to live without due consideration for weaker members of the church who might be offended by their serene indifference to such scruples. After laying down the general principle of individual responsibility (14^{1-12}), in order to rebuke censoriousness, he appeals nobly to the majority, who were strong-minded, for consideration and charity towards the weaker minority (14^{13}–15^{6}). Towards the close, the plea broadens into a general ‡ appeal for Christian forbearance and patience (15^{1-6}), which finally streams out into an exhortation (15^{8-13}) to all, Gentile and Jewish Christians alike, to unite in praise of God's mercy to them in Christ.

In a brief epilogue ($15^{14f.}$), Paul justifies himself for having written thus to the Roman Christians, by alleging his apostolic vocation; he tells them ($15^{22f.}$) of his future plans, which include a visit to Rome on his way from Jerusalem to Spain; then with an appeal for their prayers and a brief benediction the letter closes (15^{30-33}).

§ 2. *The sixteenth chapter.* — Special literature: — Keggermann (*de duplici epistolae ad Rom. appendice*, 1767); Semler's *Paraphrasis*, pp. 277–311; D. Schulz (*SK.*, 1829, 609 f.); Spitta's *Urc.* iii. 1, pp. 6 f.; Moffatt, *HNT.* 209 f.

* For παντὶ τῷ ὄντι ἐν ὑμῖν (12^{3}) read π. τῷ ὄντι τι ἐν ὑμῖν (cp. Ac 5^{36} λέγων εἶναί τινα ἑαυτόν), with Baljon and Vollgraff (*Mnemosyne*, 1901, 150).

† They were vegetarians and total abstainers. The former practice (cp. von Dobschütz, *Urc.* pp. 396 f.) was not confined to Jews: the neo-Pythagoreans and the Orphic societies favoured it. But the high estimate of the sabbath (14^{5}) suggests that these weaker brethren were Jewish Christians.

‡ There is no hint that in $15^{1f.}$ Paul is turning (so Paulus and Bertholdt) to address the leaders of the church. Paul does not address the ἐκκλησία of Rome, and 15^{14} implies the general body of the local Christians.

Since the questions of the nature and needs of the church to which the epistle was written depend upon, rather than determine, the problem of its literary structure, it will be convenient to discuss the latter first. In order to clear the way, it is necessary to recognise the evidence for the hypothesis that ch. 16 did not belong to the original epistle; (*a*) 16^{25-27} represents a later conclusion, added by some Paulinist editor (so Reiche, Kreyhl, Mangold: pp. 44 f., Schürer, Hilgenfeld, de Wette, Volkmar, Lucht, Lipsius, von Soden, Pfleiderer, Holtzmann, W. Brückner: *Chron.* pp. 184–185, Weizsäcker: *AA.* i. 382, Baljon: pp. 37–40, Völter, Jülicher, R. Scott, Corssen, etc.); and (*b*) 16^{1-23} is a special note addressed to the church of Ephesus.

(*a*) 16^{25-27} is not simply an irrelevant (Bacon, *JBL.* 1899, 167–176) but an un-Pauline finale, evidently (cp. Jud $^{24f.}$) modelled on some stereotyped Jewish form of benediction (cp. Mangold, pp. 44–81), and breathing the atmosphere of the later epistles to Timotheus and Titus (and of Ephesians). The addition of such a doxology is as unexampled in Paul's correspondence as the definition of God as *the only wise* or *eternal* and of the scripture as *prophetic*; while the silence upon the *μυστήριον* during *times eternal* outdoes expressions like Col 1^{26} and is hardly consonant with Ro 1^2 3^{21}. Corssen (*ZNW.*, 1909, 32 f.) probably goes beyond the mark in assigning its origin to Marcionitism, but at any rate it does not betray Paul's mind.

(*b*) That Ro 16^{1-23} contains a note which did not originally belong to Paul's Roman epistle is a widely, though not universally,* accepted hypothesis which has been under discussion for nearly a century and a half. Most probably the note begins, not with v.^{3} (Schulz, Ritschl, Ewald, pp. 428–430; Schürer, Reuss, Laurent, van Rhijn, Pfleiderer, Mangold: *der Römerbrief*, pp. 136 f.), but with v.^{1} (Eichhorn, Weiss, Renan, Lucht, Lipsius, Völter, von Soden, etc.); it ends, not with v.^{20} (Eichhorn, Ewald, Schulz, Reuss, Renan, Mangold, Lucht, Weiss, Lipsius, Völter, von Soden, Richter) nor even earlier (some critics, *e.g.* Laurent and Hitzig, breaking off at v.^{16} or at v.^{16}, as Hausrath, Pfleiderer, Krenkel, Schmiedel), but with v.^{23} (so Weizsäcker, McGiffert and Jülicher, Holsten and R. Scott needlessly omitting vv.$^{17-20}$).† While vv.$^{21-23}$ might well go with Ro 15^{33}, it is not Paul's way to

* For all that can be said on the other side, consult Schlatter's article (*SK.*, 1886, pp. 587 f.), the discussions of Jacquier (i. pp. 277 f.), and Zahn (*Einl.* i. 272 f.), the remarks of Sanday and Headlam (*op. cit.* pp. xciii f., 416 f.), and Mair in *Exp.*^{4} vii. 75 f.

† "It is generally assumed that the men referred to [in vv.$^{17-20}$] were Jewish Christians, simply because Paul's antagonists generally belonged to that class; but there is nothing in the passage itself to suggest this. The plausible and eloquent talk, the love of good feeding, and the implied assumption of wisdom, point rather to Greek adventurers, who, when they had failed elsewhere, sought to impose on the simplicity of the Christians" (Dr. J. Drummond, p. 352).

add salutations after a final Amen, and the passage connects even better with 16^{1-20}, though it may have originally lain (Koennecke, Jülicher) between v.^{16} and v.^{17}. It is needless to regard v.^{19} as a marginal note of Paul to v.^{16} (Laurent), or to put ^{19a} (omitting ἡ γάρ) after ^{16} (Baljon, pp. 35–36), though v.^{20} is more likely to have crept in from the margin (Grotius, Laurent) than to have been displaced from after v.^{23} (Blass and Baljon, p. 37).

Whilst the letter is not expressly directed to Ephesus, there is much in its contents which points to that city and church as its original destination. When all is said, it is inconceivable that Paul could have intimately known so many individuals, and been acquainted with their local circumstances and histories, in a church like that of Rome to which he was as yet personally a stranger. The tone of Romans militates against such an idea. In Ro 1–15 the apostle has been writing as a stranger to strangers, without betraying —even at points where such a reference would have been telling and suitable— any trace of personal friendship with the members of the church or first-hand knowledge of their local environment and situation. Occasionally, it is true, he does evince some knowledge of the general course of events (*e.g.* in 14–15) within the Roman community, but never more than what would percolate to him through the ordinary channels of hearsay and report. Such incidental familiarity with the Roman situation by no means implies the presence of friends upon the spot who had supplied him with information. Upon the other hand, the wealth of individual colour and detail in 16^{1-20} presupposes a sphere in which Paul had resided and worked for a considerable time. He knows the people. He can appeal to them, and even speak authoritatively to them. Now, as he wrote probably from Corinth, the only other city which answers aptly to this description is Ephesus, where Paul had had a prolonged and varied experience; indeed, several of the names in this note are connected more or less directly with that city or with Asia Minor: *e.g.* Epaenetus (v.^{5} ἀπαρχὴ τῆς Ἀσίας), and Aquila and Prisca (v.^{3}), who were at Ephesus immediately before Romans was written (Ac $18^{18.\ 26}$, cp. 1 Co 16^{19}), and apparently were there (2 Ti 4^{19}) not long afterwards. These are the first mentioned in the note, and the reference in 1 Cor. and here to the house-church of Aquila and Prisca tells against the likelihood of a sudden migration on the part of this devoted pair.

Furthermore, the sharp warning against heretics and schismatics (vv.$^{17-20}$) suits Rome at this period less well than Ephesus, where, then as afterwards (1 Co 16^{8-9}, Ac $20^{29f.}$, Apoc $2^{2f.}$), trouble of this kind was in the air. There is no evidence, even from Romans itself, to indicate the existence of *διχοστασίαι* and *σκάνδαλα* among the Roman Christians of that day. Controversy against false teachers is conspicuously absent from Romans, and it is extremely difficult to reconcile this outburst of Paul with the traits of Ro 1–15, even when we identify the errorists with Greek adventurers rather than Jewish Christian antagonists. Least convincing of all is the suggestion (Zahn) that Paul's language here resembles that of Gal 1^{9} 5^{3}, Ph $3^{1f.}$; these warnings are not genuine prophylactic counsels, inasmuch as the trouble had already begun in Galatia—which, as even Zahn admits, was not the case in Rome when the apostle wrote — while the intimate relations between Philippi and Paul differentiate Philippians materially from an epistle like Romans Nor, again, is it likely that the apostle was vaguely warning the Roman Christians against errorists who were already troubling other churches and might at some future date make mischief in the capital. The whole point of the counsel is lost if the readers did not know the facts and persons in question. How else could they mark and turn away from them? In short, the tenor of these words marks not an occasion which might possibly arise, but a peril already present, just such a situation as was in force in Ephesus, where intrigues and divisions (Ac 20[19, 29f.]) were so rife that the apostle was determined to follow his usual method, in such cases, of avoiding any personal intercourse with the local church. Hence he writes this note of warning, incorporating his counsel in Phœbe's letter, whose lack of address probably indicates that she might visit other communities in the district. Set in this light, the letter assumes a truly historical place. For while the distant tone of even a passage like 15[20f.] shows that the apostle was not on such terms of close intimacy with the Roman church as would prompt the pointed language of 16[19], these words, when addressed to Ephesus, are entirely apposite. This is borne out by the consideration, accepted by many critics (so, in addition to those already mentioned, Farrar, *St. Paul*, ch. xxxvii; Laurent, *NT Studien*, pp. 32–38; Holtzmann, *Einl.* 242–246; Adeney, *INT.* pp. 379–380; O. Holtzmann, *NT Zeitgeschichte*, p. 132; Cone, *St. Paul*, pp. 12 f.; Purchas, *Johannine Problems and Modern Needs*, 47 f.; and Haupt, *SK.*, 1900, pp. 147–148), that the note is a note of recommendation for Phœbe (*ἐπιστολή συστατική*); for Paul would naturally introduce a person to a circle or circles in which he exercised some influence. The value of such a recommendation would mainly consist in the writer's title to respect and obedience from those whom he addressed, and it is obvious that this footing of intimacy obtained at Ephesus rather than at Rome.

It may be urged, on the opposite side, that these Christians might have migrated to Rome, as there was constant communication between that city and the provinces of the empire. In the abstract, this is quite possible. But the point is that when Paul wrote Romans, no such migration had occurred. All evidence for it is awanting, and the probabilities tell against such a wholesale influx of Paul's friends to the capital. At a later date, in the course of time, it is conceivable that they gradually migrated to Rome in his footsteps, as Aquila and Prisca did perhaps. Asiatics constantly betook themselves thither, and it is therefore far from remarkable—and by no means a final argument against the above theory of Ro 16[1-20]—that almost all of the names mentioned in this note have been found by archæologists (cp. Lightfoot, *Philippians*, pp. 171 f.) within the Roman *Corpus Inscriptionum*. Most of the names are fairly common throughout the Roman world (cp. Lietzmann, p. 73), whilst half are found in the Greek* *Corpus Inscriptionum* for Asia Minor (so, *e.g.*, Epaenetus, Hermes, and Hermas). So far as any weight can be attached to the significance of names like Prisca, Ampliatus, Nereus, and Apelles, in the subsequent history of primitive Christianity at Rome, it is practically irrelevant to the present question; even though the bearers of these names could be safely identified in every case with those mentioned by Paul in this note, it would be a far from

* In the Ephesian Gnostic *Acta Johannis* (*c.* A.D. 160) the house of Andronicus (Ro 16[7]) is one centre of activity.

valid inference that because they are found to have sojourned afterwards * in Rome they must have been there when Paul wrote Romans, or that such a combination of names, Greek, Roman, and Jewish, was impossible outside the mixed lower population of the capital.

Gifford (pp. 27–30) regards 16^{3-20} as part of a second letter written by Paul after his release from the first Roman imprisonment. This theory (partially anticipating Spitta's) gets over the difficulty which arises on the canonical view, that Paul could hardly have had so many personal friends in Rome before he had reached the capital, but it is not more probable than the view which has been just outlined. Similarly Erbes (writing in *ZKG.*, 1901, pp. 224–231) finds in 16^{1-16a} a note written by Paul to Rome during his last voyage as a prisoner, and forwarded by some Ephesian Christians who were free (yet cp. 16^{7}), in order to let the Roman Christians know of his arrival (Ac 28^{15}). These envoys hurried on, undelayed by the exigencies of the apostle's voyage, and were themselves among the persons to be greeted in the note. Of all this, however, there is no hint in the note itself, and the theory † is really no improvement on that of Semler, who regarded 16^{3-16} as designed for Paul's friends outside Rome, to introduce the bearers of the epistle. One point of such hypotheses is to explain how the note came to be attached to Romans, but this can be done otherwise. Eichhorn (*Einl.* iii. 243 f.) took 16^{1-20} as addressed to Corinth, while Schenkel less probably regarded it as intended for all the churches which Phœbe was to visit. Still more drastic but equally unsatisfying is Ryder's conjecture (*JBL.*, 1898, 184–198) that, since *ἔγραψα ὑμῖν* (15^{15}) and *ὁ γράψας τὴν ἐπιστολήν* (16^{22}) have the same subject, and since the latter phrase indicates a weightier function than that of an amanuensis, chs. 15^{1}–16^{24} are a fragment written by Tertius himself not later than A.D. 64 before the Neronic persecution. If any theory of the epistle's composition is sought along these lines, Spitta's is more ingenious (see below).

Once this note is detached from Romans, its date is no longer dependent upon that of the larger epistle, except when it is regarded as part of some larger Ephesian letter which has been incorporated in the canonical Romans (see below). Taken by itself, it offers no secure evidence of its date or place of writing, beyond the fact that, when vv.$^{21-23}$ are included in it, the mention of Gaius (cp. 1 Co 1^{14}) probably points to Corinth as the church from which Paul wrote (cp. Cenchreæ, 16^{1}). If, as is otherwise likely, the immediate destination of the note was Ephesus, with its local circuit of churches, the fact of Paul sending greetings and warnings is entirely consonant with the situation presupposed in Ac 20 (see above). The description of Andronicus and Junias as *fellow-prisoners* (16^{7}) does not imply that Paul

---

* Yet, in the letters subsequently written by Paul from Rome, not one of these Christians is ever mentioned.

† In a further study (*ZNW.*, 1909, 128–147, 195–218, 'Zeit und Ziel d. Grüsse Röm 16^{3-25} und der Mittheilungen 2 Ti 4^{9-21}'), Erbes developes this theory by arguing that 2 Ti 4^{16} (*ἐν τῇ πρώτῃ μου ἀπολογίᾳ οὐδείς μοι παρεγένετο, ἀλλὰ πάντες με ἐγκατέλιπον*), which contradicts the hypothesis that Paul had such loyal supporters in the Roman church as Ro 16^{1-20} (on the ordinary theory) assumes, really refers to his earlier trial in Palestine.

was in captivity when he wrote the letter,* but merely that these Christians like himself, perhaps with himself on some occasion (at Ephesus or elsewhere; cp. 2 Co 11^{23}; Clem. Rom. v.), had been incarcerated.

The obscurity which besets the editing of the Pauline epistles for canonical purposes prevents us from doing more than conjecture how this letter came to be appended to Romans. Perhaps, when the first collection was drawn up at Ephesus, this local note was preserved by being put in the wake of the larger epistle, especially if the latter was last in the list. Also, it contained the names of several who afterwards became prominent in the church of Rome (*e.g.* Ampliatus).

§ 3. *Structure and integrity.*—Special literature:—Riggenbach (*neue Jahrb. f. deutsche Theol.*, 1892, 498–525); Lightfoot and Hort's essays in the former's *Biblical Essays* (287–374); Wabnitz (*RTQR.*, 1900, 461–469); Moffatt (*HNT.* 630 f.); Harnack, (*ZNW.*, 1902, 83 f., on 1^7); Godet, *INT.* i. 395–407: Zahn's *Einl.* § 22; R. Steinmetz (*ZNW.*, 1908, 177–189, 'Text-kritische Untersuchung zu Röm 1^7); P. Corssen (*ZNW.*, 1909, 1–45, 97–102); R. Scott, *The Pauline Epistles* (1909), 96 f.; K. Lake (*Exp.*^{7} x. 504-525).

The textual phenomena of 16^{25-27} (apart from any question of their authorship) are sufficient by themselves to start the further problem, whether the canonical form of Romans does not represent a process of more or less extensive editing. The insertion of Ro 16^{1-23} proves that the epistle as it stands did not come from Paul and his amanuensis at Corinth, but we cannot even be sure that $1–15^{33}$ is equivalent to the original letter. It is plain that when the Romans came to be incorporated in the Pauline canon, editorial changes were made either then or (perhaps also) at a subsequent period. The question is, whether such internal phenomena as can be noted (partly from the textual condition of the epistle) were due to Paul himself or to a later hand.

The doxology (16^{25-27}) is found (see Lucht, *op. cit.* pp. 43 f., 49 f.) not only (i.) in its present canonical position (so most MSS and vss), but (ii.) either after 14^{23} alone (so L, many cursives, Chrysostom and Theodoret, etc., with the Gk. lectionaries), or (iii.) there in addition to its position after 16^{24} (so AP, arm.), whilst (iv.) F^{gr} (with vacant space after 16^{24}) and G (with vacant space after 14^{23}) omit it entirely. According to Origen (vii. 453, Lommatzsch),†

---

* As, *e.g.*, Lisco assumes, on his peculiar hypothesis of an imprisonment at Ephesus, during which Paul wrote several epistles, including this one (*Vincula Sanctorum*, 1900).

† "Caput hoc (*i.e.* 16^{25-27}) Marcion, a quo scripturæ euangelicæ atque apostolicæ interpolatæ sunt, de hac epistula penitus abstulit: et non solum (hic ?)

(i.) was its normal place in his day; but even in some codices which did not reflect Marcion's edition (ii.) was to be found—apparently in consequence of an edition having been drawn up for reading in the churches, for which purpose the details of 15–16 would be irrelevant. This probably explains the fact that the capitulations of Codex Fuldensis and Codex Amiatinus, the major (sixth century) MSS of the Vulgate, reflect a similar edition (see, further, de Bruyne in *Revue Bénédictine*, Oct. 1908, 423 f.). But it does not carry us very far back; for while an ecclesiastical edition might contain $1–14^{23}$ + 16^{25-27}, it is extremely unlikely (in spite of all arguments to the contrary) that Paul would stop at 14^{23}, even if 16^{25-27} were genuine. The latter is not a doxology like $11^{33f.}$, and it does not lead to $15^{1f.}$ as Eph 3^{20-21} does by closing a section. It is one thing that $15–16^{24}$ should be omitted for church-purposes, and quite another for the author himself, with the natural sequel 15^{1-13} before him, to break off at 14^{23} and append the doxology, unless we are to assume that there was room for no more on the sheet of papyrus. There is a strong inherent improbability, therefore, against all theories which attribute to Paul, at any rate, any issue of Romans ceasing with 14^{23}. Even were 16^{25-27} admitted to have been written by the apostle, its position after 14^{23} affords no secure basis for any theories of an edition of Romans from his own hand which ended there. It may be questioned, indeed, whether the reasons usually given for an ecclesiastical transference of the doxology to the close of ch. 14 are adequate. Modern ideas of what an early Christian church would or would not have found edifying, are apt to be too narrow. On the same principle we should expect to find traces of 1 Co $16^{21f.}$ having been put after 15^{57-58}, and no textual evidence for such a transference is forthcoming. But, in the case of Ro 16^{25-27}, such textual evidence is clear and early. The only question is, Does Origen's charge imply that Marcion actually mutilated the epistle, or that he found an exemplar in use which did end with $14 + 16^{25-27}$? The former theory depends on the probability that the contents of Ro 15–16 would prove obnoxious to Marcion; but this hardly appears likely, for the OT quotations would not discredit the passage to Marcion, any more than they did the gospel of Luke. The latter view assumes that an ecclesiastical recension of the epistle existed by the beginning of the second century, which omitted 15–16 as less suitable for public reading (so, *e.g.*, Hort and Godet) and appended 16^{25-27} to 14. Still, it may be accidental that Clement of Alexandria and Origen are the only Ante-Nicene fathers who quote from Ro 15–16. The personal contents of 16, like those of 1 Co 16, may have prevented any widespread allusions to it.

---

hoc, sed et ab (? in) eo loco ubi scriptum est *omne autem, quod non est ex fide, peccatum est* [*i.e.* 14^{23}] usque ad finem cuncta dissecuit. In aliis uero exemplaribus, id est in his quæ non sunt a Marcione temerata, hoc ipsum caput diuerse positum inuenimus: in nonnullis etenim codicibus post eum locum quem supra diximus, hoc est, *omne autem, quod non est ex fide, peccatum est*, statim cohærens habetur *ei autem qui potens est uos confirmare*; alii uero codices in fine id, ut nunc est positum, continent." It is disputed (cp. Zahn's *GK.* ii. 519 f.) whether 'dissecuit,' in this version of Rufinus, means 'removed' (='abstulit') or 'cut up.' Against Zahn, see Corssen in *ZNW.*, 1909, 13 f., who argues for the former (=διέτεμεν).

The omission of ἐν Ῥώμῃ in $1^{7. 15}$ by G (Gk. and Lat. text), and in 1^7 further by g Ambrosiaster (πᾶσιν τοῖς οὖσιν ἐν ἀγάπῃ Θεοῦ, κλητοῖς ἁγίοις), appears to indicate that these words were absent, if not from an early recension of the epistle, at least from a number of early copies (including the text used by Origen). As the variation is too significant and widespread to have been due to a transcriptional error, it must be explained as due either (*a*) to the same motive as is alleged for the excision of ἐν Ἐφέσῳ in Eph 1^1, *i.e.* an ecclesiastical or liturgical desire (cp. Tert. *adv. Marc.* v. 17; Ambrosiaster on Col 4^{16}; Apollonius in Eus. *H. E.* v. 18. 5) to mark the epistle's catholicity of reference; or (*b*) to Marcion's revision (cp. Corssen, de Bruyne, Sanday and Headlam, pp. xcvii–xcviii), the latter motive covering the excision of 15–16 as well. (*a*) seems on the whole preferable (so, *e.g.*, Steinmetz and Schmiedel). Zahn's contention, that the original text of 1^7 did not contain ἐν Ῥώμῃ (so W. B. Smith, *JBL.*, 1901, pp. 1–21; cp. Harnack, *ZNW.*, 1902, 83 f.), but that 1^{15} did, is based on inadequate textual evidence, as R. Steinmetz and Corssen have shown. The former critic agrees with those who regard the position of the doxology after 14 as the result of liturgical reading. "Man las den Römerbrief bis Kap. 14 und setzte dorthin die Doxologie. Man wagte dabei aber nicht, einen so grossen Abschnitt wie Kap. 15 und 16 einfach ganz zu beseitigen, wie man das mit den Worten ἐν Ῥώμῃ in 1^7 und in 1^{15} ohne Bedenken tat" (*ZNW.*, 1908, 188). Corssen's intricate arguments lead him to refer all the phenomena of the shorter recension of Romans to Marcion. A further conjecture (*c*) is that the words were omitted (together with 15–16) in a special edition of the epistle issued by Paul himself (so variously from Rückert to Lightfoot). This edition-hypothesis (Renan, iii. pp. lxiii f., 461 f.; Sabatier, Denney, etc.) assumes usually that $1–14+16^{1-20}$ represented the edition sent to Ephesus, whilst $1–14+16^{21-24}$ and 1–11+15 were copies of the circular forwarded to the churches of Thessalonika and Rome respectively. Spitta carries forward this conjecture in *Urc.* iii. 1 (1901), holding *acutius quam uerius* (cp. Bahnsen in *PM.*, 1902, 331–336) that $12^1–15^7+16^{1-20}$ represent a short letter written after Ac 28^{30} (A.D. 63–64) during a tour among the Gentile Christian churches, while $1^{18}–11^{10}+15^{14-33}$ were written earlier (at the crisis over the Council of Jerusalem) for believing Jews, to justify the Gentile mission, and re-adapted by the apostle for Gentile-Christian readers with the addition, *e.g.*, of 11^{11-30} and 15^{8-13}. Lightfoot's simpler view posited a double recension, the original draft ($1–16^{23}$) being addressed to the Roman church, the second (omitting ἐν Ῥώμῃ in $1^{7. 15}$ and 15–16, but adding 16^{25-27}) being designed for a wider circle; subsequently the doxology was transferred to its present position in the original and earlier recension, represented by the canonical epistle. Attempts have been made on broader lines to disentangle in whole or part a larger letter to Ephesus, *e.g.* in 12–14+16 (Straatman, *TT.*, 1868, 25 f.), $12–15^6+16^{3-20}$ (Schultz, *Jahrb. für deutsche Theol.*, 1876, 104 f.), and 9–11+16 (Weisse's *Beiträge*, 46 f.); cp. J. Weiss in *TLZ.*, 1893, 395, and *ThSt.* 182–184. None of these, however, works out at all well in detail.

Apart from the doxology (16^{25-27}), when a note to Ephesus is found in 16^{1-23} it becomes superfluous to discuss the theory, once held by Baur, Schwegler (*NZ.* ii. pp. 123 f.), and some others (recently, W. B. Smith, *JBL.*, 1901, 129–157) that 15–16 are totally, or even partially (Lucht), spurious, as well as composite.* There is little or nothing in 15 to justify the supposition that it was not composed by Paul (see on this especially Mangold, pp. 81 f.); the bold expressions of $15^{8.16}$ are as likely to have come from the apostle as from any one else, and none of the other points alleged, *e.g.* by Lipsius, is decisive against the Pauline authorship (cp. *HNT.* 630). The close connection of 15 with 14 tells against the view (Schenkel) that 15 represents a postscript to the original letter. The balance of probability is upon the whole in favour of the hypothesis that 1^{1}–15^{33} represents substantially the original epistle; that 16^{1-23} was added to it, when the Pauline canon was drawn up at Ephesus; that 16^{25-27} represents an editorial climax to this composite production; and that the omission of ἐν Ῥώμῃ in 1^{7} and the relegation of 16^{25-27} to a place after 14 were due to subsequent liturgical procedure.

Evanson's arguments against the Pauline authorship (*Dissonance of the Four Generally Received Evangelists*², 1805, 306–312) were as unable to attract the attention of scholars as those independently advanced by Bruno Bauer half a century later (*Kritik der paulin. Briefe*, 1852, iii. 47–76; *Christus und die Caesaren*, 1877, 371–380). The denial of Paul's existence, which is bound up with such theories, was developed by Loman in his 'Quæstiones Paulinæ' (*TT.*, 1882–1883, 1886), and the fool's cap was placed unconsciously on them by Steck's attempt (see above, p. 73) to show that Romans depended on Seneca, as well as upon Philo, the Assumptio Mosis, and Fourth Esdras. Van Manen's arguments answer themselves; if the methods he employs (cp. *EBi.* 4127–4145) are valid, then not merely biblical but literary critics must allow that their occupation is gone. The reproduction of similar views by W. B. Smith (cp. *HJ.* i. 309–334) led to a patient and careful refutation by P. W. Schmiedel (*HJ.* i. 532–552), after or against which there is little to be said. For other criticisms in detail, see R. J. Knowling's *The Witness of the Epistles*, pp. 133 f., and Clemen's *Paulus*, i. pp. 85 f. The futility of these wholesale theories was soon felt by Völter, who attempted to posit an authentic epistle underneath extensive interpolations, separating the original genuinely Pauline letter ($1^{1.\ 5b-7.\ 8-17}$ $5^{1-12.\ 15-19.\ 21}$ $6^{1-13.\ 16-23}$ 12–13 14^{1}–15^{6} $15^{14-16.\ 23b-33}$ 16^{21-24}) written to the Gentile Christian church of Rome, from interpolations by an editor who sought to Hellenise Paul's teaching with the help of Stoic and Platonic ideas derived in part from the Wisdom of Solomon, Philo, and Seneca, and to controvert not Jewish Christians, but Jews of his own day. In addition to this editor's contributions, further glosses are visible in 2^{14-15} 3^{21-26} 7^{25b} 11^{11-36} $15^{7-13.\ 17-23a}$ $16^{7-20a.\ 25-27}$ from the pen of one who also omitted ἐν Ῥώμῃ in $1^{7.\ 15}$ in order to generalise the epistle for the use, primarily, of the church at Ephesus.

While the criteria for such hypotheses are too subjective to deserve attention, the canonical text of the epistle here and there has been more justly suspected of incorporating glosses. Thus (*a*) the awkward construction of 2^{13-16}, where v.^{16} seems to follow vv.$^{12-13}$ rather than $^{14-15}$ or the whole

* R. Scott (*op. cit.* 237–246) makes 12–15 practically all non-Pauline, while the original epistle (1–11 + 15^{25-28}) is regarded as the slow elaboration of two or three distinct essays (*e.g.* 1–5, 6–8, 9–11).

paragraph, has suggested (cp. Lietzmann's note, pp. 14–15) either that $^{14-18}$ represent a marginal gloss (so Wilke, *die Neutest. Rhetorik*, pp. 216–228; Laurent, *NT Studien*, 17–19, 32 f.; Blass; Völter, 141–142; J. Weiss,* *Beiträge zur paul. Rhetorik*, 56–57), or less probably that v.^{16} should be taken as an interpolation (Weisse, Baljon, pp. 4–6), if not put after v.^{12} (Michaelis, Wilke, Wassenbergh) or v.^{29} (Hitzig). Otherwise v.^{13} might be a marginal insertion of Paul (Eichhorn), though not the later addition of an editor (from Ja 1^{22}; so Weisse, Michaelis adding ^{11}, and van Manen adding $^{14-15}$). (*b*) 5^{7} is a natural parenthesis rather than a break in the argument, and need not be taken as a gloss (as by Semler, Weisse, Michelsen, Lipsius, Koennicke, and Jülicher $= {}^{7b}$), or as two (Naber, *Mnemosyne*, 1881, 287 f.). Nor (*c*) is 5^{12b} καὶ διὰ τῆς ἁμαρτίας ὁ θάνατος to be suspected as a scribal gloss (van Manen, Straatman, Baljon), though 5^{13-14} (Weisse, *Beiträge*, p. 35; Völter, *op. cit.* pp. 147 f., for exegetical reasons) has an illogical appearance.† (*d*) 7^{25b} (ἄρα οὖν αὐτὸς ἐγὼ τῷ μὲν νοΐ δουλεύω νόμῳ θεοῦ, τῇ δὲ σαρκὶ νόμῳ ἁμαρτίας) may readily have been misplaced by a scribe from its true place before v.^{24} (Venema, Wassenbergh, Keil, van Hengel, Lachmann, Koennicke, *BFT.* xii. 1. 24–25; Blass, Lietzmann, etc.); to delete it entirely (Michelsen, Reiche, Weisse, Baljon, pp. 17–18; Völter, pp. 157–8) is to leave no room for an explanation of how it ever came to be inserted.‡ (*e*) As the διὰ παντός of 11^{9-10} is, strictly speaking, inconsistent with the thought of what follows, it has been conjectured (*e.g.* by Holsten, *ZWT.*, 1872, 455; Michelsen, Rovers, van Manen, and Lipsius) that this passage is a marginal gloss written, like 1 Th 2^{16}, after the fall of Jerusalem, to emphasise the final exclusion of the Jews from the messianic kingdom. Against this it is rightly urged that the metaphor of v.^{11} would follow awkwardly after that of v.^{8}. But surely not more so than that of v.^{9} in its present site. (*f*) Apart from those who reject the entire chapter as un-Pauline, various critics have felt obliged to regard one or two passages in $15^{14f.}$ as later glosses; Straatman, *e.g.*, deletes vv.$^{14.\ 17-24}$; van Manen, vv.$^{16.\ 19-24.\ 27.\ 30-32}$; Völter, vv.$^{17-23a}$ (altering ἔχων to ἔχω in ^{23b}) and Lipsius, vv.$^{19b.\ 20b.\ 23-24}$. The reasons for such a hypothesis do not seem justified by literary or historical criticism (cp. Feine's *Römerbrief*, 138 f.). Thus a mission to Illyria is quite within the bounds of probability, during one of Paul's residences in Macedonia; and

---

* Adding 2^{26-27} as another gloss from the same hand, since the γάρ of ^{28} reaches back to ^{25}, while the οὖν of ^{26} does not connect well with the context.

† The same critics, with Michelsen, find 6^{14-15} an interpolated gloss, with as little reason as leads them (with Volkmar and Baljon, pp. 14–15) to delete 7^{19-20}.

‡ To suppose (with Völter, p. 226) that some scribe, failing to grasp the connection between 7^{24a} and 8^{1}, added this recapitulatory comment as a bridge, is surely a *tour de force*. See Jülicher's note (*SNT.* ii. p. 48), and Clemen's *Einheitlichkeit*, pp. 84 f. (cp. his *Paulus*, i. 99–100). On the other hand, τοῖς στοιχοῦσιν (4^{12}) is plainly an instance of textual primitive corruption, while οὔτε δυνάμεις (8^{38}) must precede logically (as in K L, etc.) οὔτε ἐνεστῶτα κτλ., unless it is to be deleted (as by van Hengel, Baljon, Tholuck, Koennicke, and others).

the silence of Galatians does not necessarily preclude some preaching at Jerusalem, even granting that Jerusalem here should not be taken in a colloquial and geographical sense. At all events it is hardly fair to object to the one statement because it conflicts with the silence, to the other because it seems to disagree with the statements, of Acts (cp. Clemen, *TLZ.*, 1902, 230 f.). The expression (*fully preached the gospel*, v.[19]) is rhetorical; Paul, as often, is using a natural hyperbole (Curtius, *SBBA.*, 1893, 929, quotes an apt verbal parallel from Aristoph. *Knights*, 642 f.), and [20b] is not inconsistent with [23f.], for the apostle's visit to Rome (cp. 1^{11-13}) is as much for his own sake as for theirs; in any case Rome is to him but the point of departure for a further tour, not the object of independent mission-work. Finally, as even Völter (p. 178) admits, there is nothing suspicious about the reference to this Spanish mission; after his death it would have hardly been attributed to him.

Such detailed difficulties in the contexture of the epistle do not amount to any proof that it is a patchwork of different writings. Its composition must have taken some time. "We must try to comprehend the position of such a man when, perhaps in the midst of his handicraft, he dictated on difficult matters in which his thoughts pressed one upon another, in order to judge truly to what degree he would be likely to fail in good connexion and orderly progress of thought" (P. W. Schmiedel, *HJ.*, 1903, 549). This consideration, taken along with the internal evidence, is enough to disprove any rigid theory of heterogeneous composition. Paul was many-sided, and more than one side of his nature came out in this epistle, a fact which is missed when attempts are made to trace a rectilinear dialectic throughout the successive chapters.

§ 4. *Date and aim.*—When $15^{14f.}$ is accepted as genuine, the date of the epistle is fixed towards the close of Paul's mission in Achaia (Ac $20^{2f.}$); it was written from Corinth,* on the eve of his departure for Jerusalem. The collection, which forms so prominent a feature of the Corinthian correspondence, is now finished, and Paul is on the point of conveying the money to the Palestinian Christians on whose behalf it has been raised. The precise year depends on the view taken of the apostolic chronology (see above, p. 62); most editors fix on ± A.D. 58; but the general period of the epistle's composition is at any rate plain, as well as its relative position after the Corinthian correspondence.

The purpose of the letter is less plain, and any characterisation of it depends on the relative importance assigned to its general and its specific elements. Those who emphasise the former, view the epistle as a compendium of the Pauline gospel (so from Luther, Melanchthon, Reiche, and de Wette to Weiss

* Paulus inferred from 15^{19} that it was composed in some town of Illyrikum. The facilities of communication point to Corinth, however (cp. Paley's *Horae Paulinae*, ed. Birks, 1852, pp. 8 f.).

and Godet), but the absence of definite teaching upon such questions as the Lord's Supper, the church, eschatology, and the resurrection, is sufficient to disprove the theory. Others find a much more specific and personal object in the epistle. But its aim is not simply to secure in the church of Rome a vantage-ground for further propaganda in the West (so, *e.g.*, Schott, Beyschlag, and Riggenbach, exaggerating the weight of passages like 1^{10} and 15^{24}), much less to justify Paul against a supposed charge of neglecting so important a church (Hofmann); it is rather to state, for the primary benefit of the Roman Christians, the *χάρισμα πνευματικόν* which Paul was conscious of possessing in his knowledge of the gospel, and which he imparts in writing, *ἀπὸ μέρους, ὡς ἐπαναμιμνήσκων ὑμᾶς διὰ τὴν χάριν τὴν δοθεῖσάν μοι ἀπὸ τοῦ θεοῦ* (15^{15}, cp. $1^{11f.}$). The feature of the gospel which is chiefly before his mind is its universal range, as the divine *δύναμις εἰς σωτηρίαν παντὶ τῷ πιστεύοντι*. It is a gospel for *τὰ ἔθνη* (cp. 1^{5} 15^{16} etc.), and as such it involves a supersession of Jewish praxis and principle. This outlook explains the course of 1^{18}–11^{36}; 9–11 falls into its proper place, not as the centre and pith (Baur) of the letter, but as a specific, historical application of the principles already laid down in 1–8.

Baur argues that Paul would not have devoted so important a part of his letter as 9–11 to the problem of Judaism in relation to Hellenism, "had he not had close at hand some special material reason for doing so, and this was afforded him by the circumstances of the local church" (*Paul*, i. 329), but the problem had been raised by his past experience in the long mission throughout Asia and Greece. It is not even enough to argue that the object of Romans was to counteract the Jewish Christian propaganda in the Roman church (so Weizsäcker); one would expect in this event to find the christological problem more prominent. It is more plausible to detect the conciliatory motive (Pfleiderer) of reconciling the Gentile Christian majority with the Jewish Christian minority, by expounding more fully Paul's gospel as a deeper and broader exposition of the faith than either party had yet reached. This aspect is enforced by those who (like Bleek, Hodge, Hilgenfeld, Volkmar, and Holsten) variously lay stress upon the irenical tone of Paul's dialectic. A more polemical view is taken by scholars like Aberle (*Einl.* 205 f.) and Feine, who find that Paul is opposing unbelieving Jews, though it is not easy to see why he should do so in an epistle to Rome especially, and in an epistle primarily addressed to Gentile Christians. Judaism as the enemy is the view also underlying both Ewald's and Grafe's theories; the former regards the epistle (culminating in 13^{1-6}) as an attempt to disentangle Christianity from any compromising association with the Judaism whose fate he saw impending at the hands of the Roman power; Grafe (*op. cit.* pp. 54 f.), on the other hand, hears in the epistle a desire to establish Paul's free gospel against the influences of local Jews who were corrupting the Roman Christians with legalistic sympathies.

These conflicting or complementary views open up the intricate problem of the readers to whom the epistle was addressed. Here we face apparently diverging statements, some of which imply Gentile Christians, while others point to Jewish Christians. The former passages include $1^{5f. 13}$ 11^{13} and $15^{15f.}$ which are perfectly explicit; they reckon the Roman Christians as among the Gentiles, and none of the counter-references is strong enough to overbear the force of such allusions. The use of the first person plural in 3^{9} 4^{1} and 9^{10}, which seems to rank Paul with a Jewish Christian audience, means no more than the similar allusion in 1 Co 10^{1}; and the connection of his readers with the Law in 7^{1-6} etc. is on all-fours with the tone of the argument in Gal 4^{1-9} (to Gentile Christians). The obscurity which wraps the origin of the Roman church, or churches, prevents us from checking the internal evidence of the epistle by any external traditions of historical value, but the probabilities are that a Jewish Christian nucleus was surrounded by a Gentile Christian majority, perhaps drawn in part from the local proselytes.* Thus the view that the Roman church was predominantly Gentile Christian (so, *e.g.*, Schott, Weizsäcker, Pfleiderer, Schürer, von Soden, Feine, Jülicher, Denney, Belser,

* "The labours of St. Paul himself and his associates, first in Asia Minor and then in Macedonia and Greece, must have started many little waves, as it were, of Christian movement, some of which could hardly fail to reach as far as Rome. The Christianity they carried would as a matter of course be the Christianity of St. Paul himself . . . and if it found at Rome a pre-existing Christianity of a more Jewish type, the old might either pass into the new or remain unchanged. There was no necessity or likelihood that any violent antagonism should arise between them, unless a fresh element should be introduced in the shape of Jewish emissaries deliberately sent from the East to counterwork Paul" (Hort, *Romans and Ephesians*, p. 16). Of such a counter-movement there is no clear evidence in the epistle.

Peake, and especially Hoennicke, *JC.* 161 f.) is, so far as the evidence of the epistle goes, preferable to the hypothesis that it was predominantly Jewish Christian (so, *e.g.*, Baur, Lipsius, Reuss, and Zahn). There is no topic in the letter which can be said to be foreign to the interests of the former, and no method of argument which can be pronounced off the line of legitimate appeal to them. Paul may have had in mind a Gentile Christian community in which there was a minority (= *the weak* of 14^1–15^{13}) of Jewish Christians (cp. E. Riggenbach's essay in *SK.*, 1893, 649–678), probably including a number of proselytes,* but the primary aim of the writer is not to adjust the relations of these parties (so especially Holsten and Hilgenfeld). This would be to make 14^1–15^{13} the climax of the foregoing pages, instead of a supplement to them. The purpose of the apostle is rather to re-state, in the light of his experience during the long mission now closing, and in view of the fresh propaganda which he contemplated in the West, the principles of his gospel for the Gentiles in its relation to Judaism. All he knew of the internal condition of the Roman church was from hearsay. He did not write on account of any special trouble there, and it is artificial to suppose, with Pfleiderer and others, that he keeps one eye on the Jewish Christian and another upon the Gentile Christian portion of his audience. Romans is more of a treatise than any other of Paul's epistles. Its structure is not determined by any local questions suggested to him, and, unlike all the preceding letters which are extant, this is not addressed to a church which he had founded. It is not written in the air. Paul is not composing in order to clear up or to express his own mind. But neither is he writing with a direct reference to the Roman Christians at every turn. "The letter does not attack Jewish Christianity, but Judaism —the Israelitish religion—standing over against Christianity as a distinct, independent entity which casts its shadow over the path of the new religion. Though he formulates objections in order to refute them, we must not imagine that persons pressing such objections really existed in the Roman church; St. Paul

* Beyschlag's arguments in favour of a proselyte-element have been independently worked out by Völter in his *Die älteste Predigt aus Rom* (1908). Kattenbusch (*das Apost. Symbol*, ii. 450) rightly observes that Romans is inexplicable apart from the fact that the majority of its readers were originally proselytes.

simply adopts the customary style for such discussions,—a style which was especially in accord with the lively genius of one so disposed to dialectic development of his thought" (von Soden, *INT.* 80–81). "If Paul was going to write to the Romans at all, no matter from what immediate impulse,—though it should only have been to announce his approaching visit,—it would be natural that his communication, in proportion as he realised the place and coming importance of the church at Rome, should assume a catholic and comprehensive character" (Denney, *EGT.* ii. 569). Psychologically, the breadth and general scope of the epistle are thus intelligible. A partial analogy in literature is furnished by Burke's *Reflections on the Revolution in France*, which were begun as a private letter to a gentleman in Paris. As Burke went on, however, the matter so grew and gained upon him that its importance and bulk demanded wider consideration than could be given in a mere letter. He therefore widened his scope, but adhered to the semi-private form of address. "I wish," he says at one point to his correspondent, "to communicate more largely what was at first intended only for your private satisfaction. I shall still keep your affairs in my eye, and continue to address myself to you. Indulging in the freedom of epistolary intercourse, I beg leave to throw out my thoughts, and express my feelings, just as they arise in my mind, with very little attention to formal method."

§ 5. *Traces in early Christian literature.*—Echoes of Romans occur in 1 Peter, and probably in Hebrews and James as well. Like 1 Cor., it was undoubtedly used by Clement of Rome, as is plain from the following passages, amongst others:—1^{21}=xxxvi. 2, *ἡ ἀσύνετος καὶ ἐσκοτωμένη διάνοια* (cp. li. 5, *τὰς ἀσυνέτους καρδίας*), 1^{29-32}=xxxv. 5–6, 2^{24}=xlvii. 7, 4^{7-9}=l. 6–7 (perhaps), 6^{1}=xxxiii. 1 (cp. context), 9^{4-5}=xxxii. 2, and 13^{1}=lxi. 1. It is thus a component part of the Pauline group which Clem. Rom. proves to have been in circulation by the last quarter of the first century. The echoes in Ignatius are indubitable, also, if less distinct. Καινότης ζωῆς (6^{4}) recurs in *Eph.* xix. 3, 1^{3-4} underlies *Smyrn.* i. 1 (*ἐκ γενοῦς Δαυεὶδ κατὰ σάρκα, υἱὸν Θεοῦ κατὰ θέλημα καὶ δύναμιν*, cp. *Eph.* xviii. 2), and striking coincidences occur in *Magn.* vi. 2 (=6^{17}), ix. 1 (=7^{6}), *Trall.* ix. 2 (=8^{11}), *Eph.* ix. (=9^{23}) etc. Polykarp's knowledge of the epistle is fairly certain (cp. iii. 3=13^{8}, x.=12^{10}), though twice the allusion might be to 2 Cor. instead (vi. 2=$14^{10, 12}$ cp. 2 Co 5^{10}, and iv. 1=13^{12} 6^{13} cp. 2 Co 6^{7}). The familiarity of Justin with Romans is patent; cp. *e.g.* *Dial.* xxiii.=$4^{3f.}$, xxvii.=3^{11-17}, xliv.=9^{7}, xlvii.=2^{4} etc. (with *Apol.* i. 40=10^{18}), as is that of Athenagoras (*Leg. pro Christ.* xiii.=12^{1}, xxxiv.=1^{27}). On the other hand, κολλώμενοι ἀγαθῷ (v. 2) is too slender a basis to establish a use of the epistle 12^{9}) in the Didachê, and the solitary glimpse in Hermas (*Mand.* x. ii. 5=

8^{26-27}) proves next to nothing. The epistle appears, however, in the Canon of Marcion and in the Muratorian Canon; while it is expressly cited by Irenæus (quoting an elder, *adv. hær.* iii. 16. $3 = 1^1\ 9^6$ etc.), Clem. Alex. (*Paedag.* $70 = 11^{22}$ etc.), and Tertullian (e.g. *adv. Praxeam*, xiii. $= 1^7\ 9^5$). According to Hippolytus, it was employed also by several Gnostic or semi-Gnostic sects, including the Ophites or Naasseni, and by the Valentinians (cp. Iren. *adv. haer.* i. 8. 3, i. 3. 4).

(E) *COLOSSIANS.*

LITERATURE. — (*a*) Editions — Bugenhagen (1527); Melanchthon's *Enarratio epist. Pauli ad Coloss.* (1559); W. Musculus (*Comm. in epp. ad Phil. Col.* etc., 1865); J. Grynæus (*Explicatio*, 1585); R. Rollock (Edinburgh, 1600); Thomas Cartwright (London, 1612); Bishop Davenant (Cambridge, 1627); P. Bayne (London, 1634); N. Byfield (London, 1649); G. Calixtus (*Expositio litt. in Eph. Col.* etc. 1664–6); J. H. Suicer (*in epist. S. Pauli ad Col. comment. crit. exeget. theol.* 1669)*; J. Alting, *Analysis exegetica in Ep. ad Coloss.* (Amsterdam, 1687); P. J. Spener's *Erklärung* (1706); Hazevoet's *Verklaering* (Leyden, 1720); S. van Til (Amsterdam, 1726); Roell, *Epistolæ Pauli ad Coloss. exegesis* (1731); Baumgarten's *Auslegung* (Halle, 1767); J. D. Michaelis[2] (1769); G. C. Storr's *Dissertatio exegetica* (Tübingen, 1783–7, Eng. tr. Edin. 1842)*; F. Junker, *Historisch-krit. und philolog. Comm.* (München, 1828)*; J. F. von Flatt's *Vorlesungen* (1829); C. F. Bähr, *Comment. über d. Brief P. an die Kol. mit Berücksichtigung d. ältern u. neuern Ausleger* (Basel, 1833); Mannheim (1833); Steiger, *der Brief Pauli an die Colosser; Uebersetzung, Erklärung, einleitende u. epikritische Abhandlungen* (Erlangen, 1835); Böhmer (*Theol. Auslegung*, Breslau, 1835); Huther (1841); Dan. Wilson (1845); Baumgarten-Crusius (1847); de Wette[2] (1847); Wiesinger (in Olshausen's *Comm.* 1850); Bisping's *Erklärung* (1855); Ewald (1857); Ellicott (1857, etc.); Dalmer (Gotha, 1858); Messner's *Erklärung* (1863); Meyer[3] (1865); Bleek's *Vorlesungen über die Briefe an die Col., den Philemon, u. die Epheser* (ed. Nitzsch, 1865); Schenkel (in Lange's *Bibel-Werk*[2], 1867; Braune (*ibid.*, Eng. tr. 1870); Hofmann (1870 f.); A. Klöpper (1882)*; J. Eadie[2] (Edin. 1884)*; J. Ll. Davies[2] (*Eph. Col. and Philemon*, 1884); J. A. Beet (1890); Lightfoot[9] (1890 and later)*; Oltramare, *Commentaire sur les ép. de S. Paul aux Col. Eph. et à Philémon* (1891 f.)*; H. C. G. Moule (*Cambridge Bible*, 1893); von Soden[2] (*HC.* 1893); Wohlenberg (in Strack-Zöckler's *Comm.* 1895); Findlay (*Pulpit Commentary*, 1895)*; T. K. Abbott (*ICC.* 1897); G. W. Garrod (1898); Maurer[2] (1900); Haupt (— Meyer[8], 1902)*; G. C. Martin (*CB.*, n. d.); Peake* (*EGT.* 1903); P. Ewald (*ZK.* 1905); Lueken[2] (*SNT.* 1907); J. M. S. Baljon (1907); A. L. Williams (*CGT.* 1907); P. Bijsterveld (*de briev van P. aan de Col.* (1908); G. Alexander (New York, 1910).

(*b*) Studies—against the standard treatise of H. J. Holtzmann, *Kritik der Epheser- und Kolosserbriefe* (1872*), see J. Koster, *de echtheid van de brieven aan de Kolossers en aan de Ephesiërs* (1877) and von Soden (*JPT.* 1885, pp. 320 f., 407 f., 672 f.). Partly on Holtzmann's lines, J. Weiss (*TLZ.*, 1900, 553–556); Soltau (*SK.*, 1905, 521–562, 'die ursprüngliche Gestalt des Kolosserbriefs), and Michelsen (*TT.*, 1906, 159 f., 317 f.); (i.) against the Pauline authorship:—Baur's *Paulus*, 417 f. (Eng. tr. ii. 1–44); Schwegler, *NZ.* ii. 325 f.; Planck (*Theol. Jahrb.*, 1847, 461 f.); Mayerhoff, *der Brief an die Kolosser mit vornehenlicher Berücksichtigung der Pastoralbriefe* (1838); Hoekstra (*TT.*, 1868, 559 f.); Hilgenfeld (*ZWT*, 1870, pp. 245 f.); Weizsäcker (*AA.* ii. 240 f.); Brückner (*Chron.* 41 f., 257 f.); Cone, *The Gospel and its Interpretations* (pp. 249–255). (ii.) for:—Schenkel (*Christusbild d. Apostel*, pp. 83–86); Renan (iii., ix.–xii.); Hort, *Judaistic Christianity* (pp. 116 f.); Sanday in Smith's *DB.* i. 624–631 (1893); Weiss (*AJT.* i. 371–377); Sabatier's *Paul* (pp. 229 f.) and in *ESR.* iii. 272–275, McGiffert (*AA.* 366–374); E. H. Hall (*Papias*, 1899, 283 f.); Jülicher (*EBi.* i. 860 f.); Pfleiderer, *Urc.*[2] i. 258 f.; Clemen, *Paulus*, i. pp. 122 f.; Moffatt, *HNT.* 214 f.; Bacon, *Story of St. Paul* (1905), 303 f., 330 f.; Jacquier in Vigoroux' *DB.* ii. 866–876. (iii.) general:—C. G. Hofmann (*Introductio in lect. epistolae P. ad Coloss.* 1739); Storr (*dissertatio in epist. P. ad Coloss.* 1786); Boehmer's *Isagoge* (Berlin, 1829); L. Montet, *Introductio in epistolam ad Coloss.* (Montauban, 1841); J. Wiggers, 'das Verhältniss des Ap. Paulus zu der christlichen Gemeinde in Kol.' (*SK.*, 1838, pp. 165 f.); Schenkel (*BL.* iii. 566–571); J. O. F. Murray (*DB.* i. 454–456); K. J. Müller, *Ueber d. Gedankengang d. Apostels Paulus in Kol.* (1905); M. Rohr, *Les épîtres de l'apôtre Paul aux Col. et aux Eph.* (1905). (iv.) on the errorists:—Schneckenburger's *Ueber das Alter d. jüd. Proselyten-Taufe, nebst einer Beilage über die Irrlehrer zu Colossae* (Berlin, 1828); Rheinwald (*de pseudo-doctoribus Colossensibus*, 1834); Osiander in *Tüb. Zeitschrift* (1834), pp. 96 f.; J. Barry (*les faux docteurs de Colosses*, Montauban, 1846); Hilgenfeld (*ZWT.* xiii. 233 f.); Neander's *Planting of Christian Church* i. 319 f., M. Dibelius, *Die Geisterwelt im Glauben des Paulus* (1909), 151–155.

§ 1. *Analysis.*—Like Romans, this epistle was written to a church which the author only knew by hearsay. Paul had neither founded nor even visited ($1^{4.\ 7\text{-}9.\ 23}$ 2^{1}) the Christian community at Colossê, a Phrygian township on the left bank of the Lycus; but, as their founder, Epaphras (1^{7} $4^{12f.}$), was probably a disciple of his, and certainly a Gentile Christian like themselves ($1^{21.\ 27}$ 2^{13} $4^{11f.}$), the apostle evidently regarded the Colossian Christians as belonging to his mission-sphere. His authority to address them was plainly unquestioned, and the letter shows traces of a warm, mutual interest ($4^{2\text{-}18}$).

After a brief greeting, in which he associates Timotheus with himself ($1^{1\text{-}2}$), he assures them of his constant thankfulness for their fine Christian character ($1^{3\text{-}8}$), and of his equally constant prayers for their steady growth in the knowledge and service ($1^{9f.}$) of God who had redeemed them by Jesus Christ, the head alike of the creation ($1^{15\text{-}17}$) and of the church ($1^{18\text{-}23}$), according to Paul's gospel, at any rate ($1^{23\text{-}29}$). To prevent them and others like them in Asia Minor from being misled on this cardinal matter ($2^{1f.}$), he reiterates the need of adherence to the simple and sufficient faith of Christ ($2^{6f.}$),* as opposed to any extraneous theosophy and ritual system ($2^{16f.}$) with ascetic obligations. The risen life with Christ is above either such severities ($2^{20f.}$) or the lax conduct which they vainly oppose. This leads Paul to sketch the true Christian ethic in general ($3^{5f.}$), negatively † and positively; also specifically for wives and husbands ($3^{18\text{-}19}$), children and parents ($3^{20\text{-}21}$), slaves and masters (3^{22}–4^{1}). With some brief words of general counsel ($4^{2\text{-}6}$) and personal details ($4^{7\text{-}17}$), the letter then closes.‡

Colossians is an example of great prose being addressed to a very little clan. Colossê was a second-rate township, inferior to its (4^{13}) powerful neighbours Laodicea and Hierapolis; and the local church was of no importance in early Christianity. The occasion of the epistle was the arrival of Epaphras (1^{8}) with news of the church, which was in some perplexity over a specious theosophy recently promulgated, and which perhaps—if we are to read between the lines—had expected or did expect a visit from Paul ($2^{1f.}$). At the moment he is imprisoned § and cannot come to them, nor does he appear to anticipate any opportunity for a visit; ‖ the reasons of this they are to learn orally from Tychicus and Onesimus ($4^{7\text{-}9}$), who bring the epistle. All he can do personally is to write. The letter reciprocates their prayers (1^{9} *καὶ ἡμεῖς*), assures them of his keen interest and pride in them ($2^{1f.}$), and invites their interest in his own mission-work (4^{3}); but its dominant aim is to restate the absolute adequacy of Jesus in relation to the world and to the church, to show how faith in him requires no outside philosophy or esoteric cult in order to perfect itself, and to expose the absurdity (*κενη ἀπάτη*) of any mystical supplement to the Christian experience of Jesus as redeemer. Apparently Epaphras and his fellow-teachers were unable to cope with the ramifications of the local theosophy, and Paul interposes with this letter on their behalf. The predominance of abstract teaching over personal reference in it

---

* The point of the apparently irrelevant clause *περισσεύοντες ἐν εὐχαριστίᾳ* (2^{7}) is very fine; to be thankful to God for all he has done and is to us in his Son, involves a thoughtful and hearty realisation of these benefits which is the best antidote to any hesitation about his power of meeting the needs of the soul. Gratitude to God, as Paul implies, means a firmer grasp of God (cp. 4^{2}).

† With Col 3^{11} contrast the tone of the thanksgivings in Plutarch's *Marius*, 46, § 1; Diog. Laert. i. 33, and the Talmudic-Berachoth ("Rabbi Judah taught that a man should say every day, Blessed be God for not creating me a pagan, nor foolish, nor a woman").

‡ Does the phrase, *περὶ οὗ ἐλάβετε ἐντολάς* (4^{10}), refer to a letter previously sent to the Colossians by Paul, or simply to oral instruction?

§ This would not necessarily follow from 4^{10} (*ὁ συναιχμάλωτός μου*), which might mean no more than Ro 16^{7}, but 4^{3} (*δέδεμαι*) puts it beyond doubt.

‖ Epaphras, too, is unable to return, but the Colossians and the other local Christians are not to fear he has lost his interest in them ($4^{12\text{-}13}$).

is natural when one recollects that the readers were not directly converts of the apostle, and that the letter was intended to be supplemented by Tychicus' oral information (4^7) upon the writer's situation and prospects.

§ 2. *Object.*—The dangers felt by Paul in the situation of the Colossian Christians were due to something at once more serious and definite than mere shortcomings of the practical religious life. The presence of errorists with semi-Gnostic tendencies is revealed by the warnings against a spurious φιλοσοφία, arbitrary ἐντάλματα, and an erroneous διδασκαλία. It is improbable that any definite system was being propagated. The likelihood is rather that the local Christians were being affected by a syncretistic, eclectic movement of thought, fostered by esoteric tendencies in the local Judaism (cp. Hoennicke's *JC.* 122 f.) Paul's references to the movement naturally are confined to the special points at which it threatened to impinge upon the true faith of Jesus Christ, and we do not possess any outside independent evidence upon the subject; but the tenets indicate a local phase of some syncretistic theosophy (so recently Jacquier, Haupt, and Dibelius), a blend of disparate elements rife within the popular religion of Phrygia, together with notions and practices current among Jewish circles which were sensitive to semi-Alexandrian influences.

That a Jewish element entered into the theosophy is evident from the allusions to circumcision and the sabbath ($2^{11f.\ 16}$), but it was a subtler form of legalism than had crept into the Galatian churches. The Law was no longer opposed to grace; no attempt was made to enforce the ceremonial practices of Judaism upon the Gentile Christians, and the errorists do not seem to have attacked Paul personally. Their claim was to lead men from a mere faith in Christ to an esoteric γνῶσις which admitted the initiated into the mysteries of an angelic hierarchy and thereby into a higher and a fuller religious experience. These intermediate beings contain the divine fulness, and therefore are to be worshipped (cp. Lueken's *Michael*, 4 f., 62–91) by all who would attain to the power and insight of the perfected life (1^{28}). Such personal spirits play a cosmic rôle also, as τὰ στοιχεῖα τοῦ κόσμου (2^8); their functions are not only creative but also providential, in a sense, resembling those of the saints in Roman Catholicism. Finally, this type of theosophy tended to foster asceticism ($2^{21f.}$) and exclusiveness (3^{11}). The latter was then, as afterwards, the inevitable accompaniment of movements which emphasised speculative attainments, mystical or otherwise; pretensions and prerogatives were the badge of all their tribe. As for asceticism, or the abstinential side of practical ethics, it was the natural result of any φιλοσοφία, as Philo and Josephus chose to describe their Judaism, which sharply contrasted the material and the spiritual, making attainments in the knowledge of the divine being depend upon the eschewing, as far as possible, of contact with gross matter. The universe was composed of angelic στοιχεῖα. Man was part of them (cp. Philo, *de vict. offerentibus*, 2), and therefore owed them the same sort of reverence as the Mithraic initiate owed to the spirits or angels (cp. Dieterich's *Mithras-Liturgie*[2], pp. 52 f.),—a reverence which partly consisted in keeping one's higher self pure from all earthly corruptions. In this way, as Dibelius points out, angel-worship * and asceticism form the foci of the ellipse.

The compass has been pretty well boxed in the endeavour to ascertain the direction of Paul's refutation in Colossians. The errorists have been identified as Jews with theosophic or Alexandrian tendencies (Eichhorn, Junker, Schneckenburger), as pagans with Pythagorean (Grotius) or Oriental (Hug) affinities, or as Christians tinged with Essene ideas (Mangold, Klöpper, Weiss); the φιλοσοφία has been assigned to a definite source such as Mithraism (A. Steinmann in *Strassburg. Diözesanblatt*, 1906, 105–118) or Cerinthus (Mayerhoff, R. Scott, after Nitzsch). The affinities with Essenism, emphasised by Thiersch, Ewald, Lightfoot, and Godet amongst others, do not amount to very much; the parallel on angel-worship breaks down, the practice of asceticism differs, and other traits of the Colossian errorists do not correspond exactly to those of the Essenes (cp. Hort's *JC.* 116 f., and Junker's ed. pp. 24 f.). Michaelis thought of disciples of John the Baptist; the Tübingen critics, followed by Sabatier, S. Davidson, and Pfleiderer, detected the physiognomy of gnostic Ebionites.

§ 3. *Authenticity.*—The reasons which led the Tübingen school to regard Colossians as sub-Pauline (see above, especially Weizsäcker, *AA.* ii. 240–245; and Brückner, *Chron.* pp. 41–56, 138 f.) were in the main (*a*) too rigid a view of Paul's mind, based on the Corinthian, Galatian, and Roman epistles; and (*b*) a belief that the epistle presupposed the full-blown gnostic systems of the second century. Subsequent researches into the presuppositions of gnosticism in Orientalism and in the later phases of Jewish speculation have, however, disclosed the existence, in more or less developed forms, of widely scattered conceptions and practices of a semi-speculative tendency, which render it quite possible that such a religious temper as that controverted in Colossians could have prevailed during the first century. The contact of Orientalism with Judaism on its speculative and popular sides, in the Diaspora, is independent of and

* "Im übrigen ist die Engellehre dasjenige Gebiet des Paulinismus, welches von der Logia Jesu am wenigsten beeinflusst ist" (Resch, *Der Paulinismus*, 161).

prior to the rise of Christianity, and the germs of what was afterwards gnosticism can be detected in various quarters during the earlier half of the first century. At any time after A.D. 40, early Christianity was upon the edge of such speculative tendencies; and while a discussion such as that of Colossians is unprecedented, so far as Paul's epistles are concerned, it is a long way from being historically a prolepsis.

(*a*) The traces of Colossians in the earlier half of the second century literature are both dim and dubious. In Barn. xii. 7 (*ἐν αὐτῷ, sc.* Jesus, *πάντα καὶ εἰς αὐτόν*) $1^{16f.}$ (*τὰ πάντα δι' αὐτοῦ καὶ εἰς αὐτὸν ἔκτισται . . . καὶ τὰ πάντα ἐν αὐτῷ συνέστηκε*) may be echoed (cp. *κατ' εἰκόνα*, $3^{9f.}$ = vi. 12 f.), and the occurrence of *ἀγὼν ὑπέρ* (2^{1}) in Clem. Rom. ii. 4 is noticeable; but neither here nor in Polykarp (i. 2 = 1^{5-6}, x. 1, firmi in fide et immutabiles = 1^{23}, cp. 1 Co 15^{58}) can stress be laid on the coincidences, though Pol. xi. 2 = 3^{5}, were it not for Eph 5^{5}, would be a certain reminiscence. The practice of Ignatius in confining *σύνδουλος* to deacons (*Eph.* ii., *Magn.* ii., *Phil.* iv., *Smyrn.* xii.), may, however, as Lightfoot suggests, be a reflection of Col 1^{7} 4^{7} (where alone Paul employs the term, and both times with *διάκονος*) and the other parallels (2^{14} = *Smyrn.* i. 2, *καθηλωμένους ἐν τῷ σταυρῷ*, 1^{16} = *Trall.* v. 2, *ὁρατὰ καὶ ἀόρατα*) serve to corroborate upon the whole the likelihood that the epistle was known to Ignatius. In Hermas, the description of Christ as *ἡ ζωή* (*Vis.* II. ii. 8), if it be accurate, might reflect Jn 14^{6} as much as Col 3^{4}, the more so as the reference to 'denying the law' in the context points to passages like Mt 10^{33}; and *Sim.* IX. xii., with its definition of God's Son as *πάσης τῆς κτίσεως αὐτοῦ προγενέστερος* (2) and its allusion to Christ's salvation of angels (15), indicates the spread of the ideas of Colossians rather than a definite acquaintance with its text. The inclusion of the epistle in Marcion's Canon proves, however, that it was well known at Rome as elsewhere during this period, and the inference to be drawn from the scanty use of it as compared with the richer traces of Ephesians is that the latter writing, by its superior size and value, must have tended to attract more notice from those who were in sympathy with the ideas voiced by both. Like the other Pauline letters, it is definitely cited by Irenæus (*adv. haer.* iii. 14. 1 = 4^{14}), Tertullian (e.g. *de praescr. haer.* vii. = 2^{8}), and Clem. Alex. (*Strom.* i. 1, etc. = 1^{28}), besides being included in the Muratorian Canon and employed by Origen (*c. Cels.* v. 8 = 2^{18-19}). The allusions in Justin to Christ as the *πρωτότοκος πάσης κτίσεως* (*Dial.* lxxxv., cp. lxxxiv., and *Cohort. ad Graecos*, xv.), and to the *περιτομή* (*Dial.* xli., xliii.), probably flow from Col $1^{16f.}$ and $2^{11f.}$, while gnostic sects like the Peratici used it, as well as Basilides and Ptolemæus (according to Hippolytus).

(*b*) The vocabulary presents no features which necessarily involve a sub-Pauline author. When account is taken of the fact that Paul is writing upon a new subject to a strange church, in which no objection had been taken to his apostolic authority or gospel, the proportion of *hapax heuromena* is not unnatural. Several characteristic Pauline terms are lacking, *e.g.* *ἀποκάλυψις, δύνασθαι, εἰ μή, εἴ τις, εἰ καί, εἴπερ, κοινωνία, λοιπός, μᾶλλον, οὐκέτι, πείθειν*; but, on the other hand, *δικαιοσύνη* is also absent from 1 Thess., a large number (including δικαίωσις, δόκιμος, κοινός, σωτηρία, ὑπακοή) are also absent from Gal., δικαιοῦν never occurs even in 1 Thess., 2 Cor., and Phil., νόμος is absent from 2 Cor., σωτηρία from 1 Cor., and σταυρός from Romans. Genitival constructions and composite forms are unusually frequent, but they do not constitute any primary argument against the Pauline authorship.

The style is perhaps slower and loftier than that of the earlier epistles; clauses are linked to one another by participles and relatives, often in a loose connection (*e.g.* 1^{28c}), which contrasts with Paul's ordinary use of particles like ἄρα, διό, and διότι. There are anacoloutha, but the dialectic is less rapid and pointed, especially in the opening sections of the epistle. "Die Ausdrücke sind weicher, voller, feierlicher, die Gedanken sind breiter ausgesponnen, vgl. $2^{6f.}$. Man könnte den Stil einen liturgischen nennen, wie wir ihn etwa auf Ehrendekreten für Augustus finden" (Nägeli, *Wortschätz des Paulus*, 84). This, however, may be due to the absence of any personal opponent. The circumstances were not such as to provoke the agitation and the sharp argumentative method which characterise, *e.g.*, Galatians and Corinthians.

(*c*) The speculative advance constitutes a more serious difficulty. Christ is ($1^{15f.}$) the principle of creation, but this is implied in 1 Co 8^{6} and due to the elaboration of his pre-existence as a heavenly Man. His cosmical significance (1^{17} τὰ πάντα ἐν αὐτῷ συνέστηκεν) is a corollary of this, and the doctrine of his person as the object of creation (1^{16} τὰ πάντα εἰς αὐτὸν ἔκτισται) is no more opposed to 1 Co 15^{28}, Ro 11^{36} than is 1 Co 8^{6} to Ro 11^{36}. The triumph of the redeemer over hostile spirits ($2^{8f.}$, cp. 1^{20}) is also presupposed in 1 Co $2^{6f.}$ and Phil $2^{5f.}$; the former passage, in fact, indicates that there were elements in Paul's theosophy which were more central than the exigencies of the extant letters suggest. Often, as at Thessalonika and Corinth, they had to be ignored in his ordinary preaching; but all along Paul had his cosmic speculations, and Colossians is an example of how he developed them when an occasion offered for expressing them in certain applications. In meeting the Colossian heresy, he naturally drew largely upon the vocabulary and ideas of the σοφία which he was in the habit of imparting to the τελείοι. Furthermore, he probably used several technical terms employed by the errorists themselves. These considerations may help to show how the advanced christology of this epistle, especially when it is taken along with Philippians, does not—even in its cosmic extension of the redemptive death and in its organic relation of Christ to the church—represent a position which would have been necessarily impossible for Paul to occupy.

Recent proofs of the Pauline character of this christology may be found in Denney's *Jesus and the Gospel* (1909), pp. 34 f., and in M. Dibelius, *die Geisterwelt im Glauben des Paulus* (1909), pp. 125–151. The latter critic, after an exhaustive discussion of Pfleiderer's arguments, concludes that "neither the language nor the contents of Col 1–2 render the Pauline authorship impossible."

§ 4. *Integrity.*—Meditating hypotheses have more than once been suggested in order to explain here, as in the case of the pastorals, the apparent mixture of Pauline and sub-Pauline elements. Thus Ewald (*Sendschreiben*, pp. 466 f.) attributed the form of the epistle to Timotheus (1^{1}), as Spitta did afterwards with 2 Thessalonians, whilst Hitzig (*Zur Kritik paulin. Briefe*, 1870, pp. 22 f.) regarded the epistle as a genuine Pauline note worked up for later and dogmatic purposes, and R. Scott (*The Pauline Epistles*, 300 f.) attributes its composition entirely to Timotheus. When the stylistic data are fairly weighed, however, the necessity for such hypotheses largely disappears. More might be said, perhaps, for the supposition that the epistle contains some interpolations in its canonical text (cp. Weisse, *Beiträge zur Kritik paul. Briefe*, pp. 22 f., 59 f.). The possibility of such changes being made during the second century is to be admitted, especially as scribes had always the temptation of conforming Colossians to Ephesians. When the latter is taken as sub-Pauline, any glosses in Col. may be referred (i.) either to the author of Eph., or (ii.) to subsequent editors. For the former hypothesis (Holtzmann, cp. *TLZ.*, 1877, 109 f., 1892, 37 f.; Hausrath, iv. 122 f., and Soltau) see further below. The latter is more convincing because less rigorous, although the working out of the hypothesis carries us often behind any textual evidence.

Editorial handling has been suspected, *e.g.*, in (*a*) 1^{15-20} (the christological section) in whole or part (om. ^{16} Marcion, $^{16b-17}$ von Soden, $^{18ab+20}$ Weisse, $^{18-20}$ Holtzmann and Clemen) * owing to its faulty connection and the difficulty of harmonising the reconciling of *τὰ . . . οὐρανοῖς* with the view of $2^{13f.}$, or even with the Pauline doctrine elsewhere (cp. Baljon, *Theol. Studiën*, 1885, 316–329); in (*b*) 1^{23} (*οὗ ἠκούσατε . . . οὐρανόν*, J. Weiss); in (*c*) 2^{1} (*καὶ ὅσοι . . . σαρκί*), which might be a catholicising gloss (so Weisse, J. Weiss). The corrupt state of the text in 2^{17-23} has also led to attempts at emendation † and hypotheses of interpolation ($^{16-17}$ *θέλων . . . ἐμβατεύων*, $^{18.\ 23}$, Weisse; $^{17.\ 18ab.\ 19}$, *πάντα* and *κατὰ κτλ.* ^{22}, *ἅτενα . . . τινί* ^{23}, Hitzig; $^{17-18b.\ 19.\ 22b}$ *τινα . . . τινί* ^{23}, Holtzmann). "This epistle, and more especially its second chapter, appears to have been ill-preserved in ancient times" (WH. ii. 127), but such interpolations or glosses as may reasonably be conjectured do not point to any far-reaching process of editing, least of all upon the part of the author (or under the influence) of Ephesians.

In $1^{15f.}$ under the speculative christology there vibrates a doctrine similar to that of the Alexandrian Judaism which reappears in Philo,‡ according to

* *Einheitlichkeit*, pp. 127 f.; *Paulus*, i. pp. 127 f.

† Θέλων (2^{18}) seems to be either a gloss (Bakhuysen, Baljon) or a corruption of some primitive reading like *ἐλθών* (Junius, Toup, Linwood), *θέλγων* (Clericus). In v.^{14} *ὃ ἦν ὑπεναντίον ἡμῖν* is probably a marginal gloss on *καθ' ἡμῶν*.

‡ "Christ was not a lay figure that Paul could drape as he chose in the finery of Palestinian apocalyptic or of Alexandrian philosophy. He is not exhibiting Christ as divine or quasi-divine, by investing him in the wavering

which the Logos as God's shadow (σκία) was employed as the organ of God at creation (*leg. alleg.* iii. 31), the Logos also being prior to all creation (*leg. alleg.* iii. 61). But there is not the slightest reason for conjecturing (as Norden does, *Antike Kunstprosa*, ii. 475) a lost source, treating of the Logos from the OT standpoint, behind Philo, the author of Colossians, and Theophilus of Antioch, simply because the same term, πρωτοτόκος πάσης κτίσεως, is applied in Col 1^{15} to the Son of God as is used by Philo and Theophilus (*ad Autol.* ii. 21) for the Logos,—Theophilus never elsewhere using the Pauline epistles.

Holtzmann's ingenious and complicated theory postulates an original Pauline epistle, directed against the legal and ascetic tendencies of the Colossians; this was worked up by the *autor ad Ephesios*, first of all, into the canonical Ephesians, as a protest against a Jewish-Christian theosophy, and afterwards remodelled separately into the canonical Colossians. Such filagree-criticism has failed to win acceptance; the literary criteria are too subjective, and the evidence for bisecting the error attacked in Colossians is not convincing. Soltau postulates an original Colossian epistle, its framework visible in Col $1^{1-5.\ 7-8.\ 10-18}$ and 4^{10-18}, with its main contents in a threefold division: (*a*) a section independent of Eph., viz. 2^{1}–3^{4} (with interpolations in $2^{2.\ 7.\ 9.\ 11b.\ 13.\ 15.\ 19.\ 22a}$), (*b*) a christological section 1^{21-29}, and (*c*) the table of household duties, 3^{5}–$4^{4.\ 7-9}$. This was worked over by a later editor using the epistle to the Laodiceans, whose original form may be reconstructed perhaps from Col 1^{21-29} 3^{5}–$4^{4.\ 7-10}$ (with an address modelled on Col 1^{1-2}, Eph 1^{1-2}). Then came the composition of Eph., based in part also on the epistle to Laodicea, after which Col. suffered further accretions, largely due to an interpolator who used Eph. But this hypothesis is not preferable to Holtzmann's. It assumes that the original Colossians was not circulated at all widely; that it suffered a twofold process of homiletical and dogmatic expansion to a degree unparalleled in the history of early Christian literature; and, finally, that the ministry which Archippus is to fulfil (4^{17}) is to look after the interests of Onesimus! On general grounds this explanation of the relationship between Col. and Eph. has nothing more in its favour than most of its rivals; and, above all, the criteria employed to detect later glosses in the original text,

and uncertain glories of the Alexandrian Logos; he is casting upon all creation and redemption the steadfast and unwavering light of that divine presence of which he was assured in Christ, and for which the Alexandrians had groped in vain" (Denney, *Jesus and the Gospel*, 36–37).

and to separate the two forms of the epistle, are often arbitrary. That glosses may have crept in from the margin into this, as into other epistles of Paul, is perfectly possible; but the reasons adduced in the present instance for such interpolations are not convincing. Soltau seems to assume that wherever parallel passages occur, one or other must be secondary; which rests on an entirely *a priori* conception of style, especially in an epistle, and on an erroneous estimate of Paul's style in particular. Thus no adequate grounds can be alleged why one writer should not refer three times to Christ as ἡ κεφαλή, or why the repetition of almost synonymous terms, like (2^7) ἐρριζωμένοι and τεθεμελιωμένοι, should be held un-Pauline. Furthermore, the supposed aim of the original Colossian epistle, viz., to oppose the φιλοσοφία of Philo, involves too restricted a meaning of φιλοσοφία.

Michelsen's theory is even more elaborate. Pfleiderer, who also postulates a Pauline original, more prudently declines to reconstruct it out of the canonical epistle, which he regards as a subsequent adaptation or resetting of the genuine letter; but this is little improvement on the Holtzmann-Soltau view.

§ 5. *Place and Period.*—To the period of imprisonment under Felix at Cæsarea, some, if not all, of the captivity-epistles have been assigned: Col., Eph., and Philemon by D. Schultz (*SK*, 1829, pp. 616–617), after Beza and Thiersch, with Schott (§ 66), Böttger (*Beiträge*, ii. 47 f.), Wiggers (*SK.*, 1841, pp. 436–450), Meyer, Laurent, Schenkel, Hausrath (iv. 118–119, Col. and Philemon), Sabatier (pp. 225–249), Reuss, Weiss, and Haupt; and even Philippians by O. Holtzmann (*TLZ.*, 1890, p. 177; *NT Zeitgeschichte*, pp. 133–134), Spitta (*Apgeschichte*, 281; *Urc.* i. 34), and Macpherson (*Ephesians*, pp. 86–94). Philemon* and Philippians (see below) must certainly be dated in the Roman imprisonment, however, and there is not evidence

* "Paul's expectations of release were more natural at Rome than at Cæsarea. During the latter part of his imprisonment at Cæsarea he knew that he was going to Rome. It would be necessary then to place the letter in the earlier part. But it does not well suit this, for Paul had been for a long time anxious to see Rome, and it is most unlikely that he should think of going to Colossæ first" (Peake, *EGT.* iii. 491–492). The arguments against the Cæsarean period are succinctly put by Bleek (*Einl.* §§ 161, 165) and Hort (*Romans and Ephesians*, 101–110). For the other side, see E. L. Hicks (*The Interpreter*, April 1910: "Did St. Paul write from Cæsarea?").

enough to prove the contrary for Colossians. Had it been written from Cæsarea (so von Dobschütz, *Urc.* 102), some greeting from Philip (Ac 21[8-14]) would have been included, or, at any rate, some mention of him among the apostle's friends and companions (4[11]). The two years in Cæsarea are certainly a blank, and as certainly Paul must have been active during this interval, but we are not entitled, without adequate evidence, to fill up this blank by placing Colossians or any other epistle within its limits. There is no reason to break away from the ordinary view that Colossians was composed during Paul's imprisonment at Rome. As Philippians was certainly the last letter he wrote, Colossians falls earlier; it is earlier than Ephesians, even when the letter is ascribed to Paul (so especially Hönig, *ZWT.*, 1872, 63 f., followed by Weiss, *AJT.* i. 377 f.; Sabatier, *ESR.* iv. 439 f.; and Godet, *INT.* 475–490), though Coleridge (*Table-Talk*, May 25, 1830) thought otherwise. "The Epistle to the Ephesians is evidently a catholic epistle addressed to the whole of what might be called St. Paul's diocese. It is one of the divinest compositions of man. . . . The epistle to the Colossians is the overflowing, as it were, of St. Paul's mind upon the same subject." This priority of Ephesians is upheld by Eichhorn, Böhmer, Hug, Credner, Anger, Schneckenburger, Matthies, Reuss, Guericke, T. K. Abbott, and P. Ewald amongst others, who advocate its Pauline authorship, mainly on the ground that it is the epistle referred to in Col 4[16] (and therefore written previously). Mayerhoff, among critics of the opposite school, is almost alone in putting it prior to Colossians.

§ 6. *The Laodicean epistle.*—The enigmatic reference to an epistle ἐκ Λαοδικίας (4[16]) has given rise to a swarm of hypotheses,* identifying the writing in question either with one or another of the extant Pauline letters, *e.g.* Ephesians (so, further, Grotius, Huth, Mill, Wetstein, Paley, Hofmann, Mangold, Holzhausen),† or 1 Tim. (John of Damascus, Theophylact), or Philemon (Wieseler, *Comment. de epistola Laodicena quam vulgo perditam putant*, 1844), or else with Hebrews (Schulthess, Schneckenburger,

* Special monographs by K. Rudrauff (*de epistola Laodicensium*, Giessen, 1680), C. J. Huth (*Epist. ad Laod. in encyclic. ad Eph. adservata*, Erlangen, 1751), R. Anger (*Ueber den Laod.-Brief*, Leipzig, 1843)*, A. Sartori (*Ueber den L.-Brief*, 1853); see, further, Zahn (*GK.* i. 277 f., ii. 83 f., 566 f., 583 f.).

† Especially by Laurent (*Jahrb. für deutsche Theol.*, 1866, 129 f.) and Klostermann (*ibid.*, 1870, 160 f.).

etc.).* The Ephesian hypothesis has won some favour in the form of a conjecture that ἐν Λαοδικίᾳ was in one of the copies of the circular letter now known as Ephesians (so, *e.g.*, Usher, Matthies, Conybeare and Howson, Credner, Michaelis, Eichhorn, Schrader, Olshausen, Wiggers, Neander, Anger, Harless, Bleek, Lightfoot, Salmon, Abbott); under the title προς Λαοδικεας, it is argued, Marcion placed Ephesians in his Canon (see below, under Ephesians). The hypothesis of Theodore of Mopsuestia, Calvin, Beza, Erasmus, Cornelius à Lapide, Estius, and others, that the epistle was one from the Laodicean church to Paul (or Epaphras, or Colossê), not from Paul to them, is needless grammatically, as ἐκ has the pregnant force of *from* and *out of*, and intrinsically improbable, as Paul was much more likely to give directions about a letter which he had written to the neighbouring church of Laodicea than about one which that church had written or was to write to him. The context plainly implies (καὶ ὑμεῖς) that the Colossians and the Laodiceans stood in the same relation to the two letters in question.

No trace of this epistle is to be found, and it must be regarded as having perished at an early date after its composition. It was in order to avoid this conclusion that an epistle of Paul could have been lost, attempts were made to identify it with 1 Tim., at the close of which the words εγραφη απο λαοδικειας (*i.e.* L. = place of composition) are added in several MSS (Zahn, *GK.* ii. 567 f.), just as occasionally at the close of one or other of the Thessalonian epistles. But Paul had never been at Laodicea. Probably it was the same motive which prompted the cognate explanation of ἐκ Λ. as "sent from Laodicea to Paul" (see above). But the letter could have been neither written by Paul at Laodicea (a place he had never evangelised) nor composed by the Laodiceans themselves.

It is plain from Col 2^1 that Paul's letter to the church of Laodicea was, like Colossians, addressed to Christians who were strangers to him. The apostle orders the two churches, being on the same footing towards himself, to exchange copies of their respective epistles. The latter point bears incidentally on the circulation of apostolic epistles. The first injunction (cp. 1 Th 5^{27}) was to get an epistle read to all the members of the church addressed, instead of to any coterie or circle; the next

* Philastrius (*Haer.* lxxxix.) mentions this opinion as held by some who attributed its composition to Luke.

was to promote in certain cases the circulation of a given epistle among neighbouring churches. The Colossian Christians were not only to salute the Christians at Laodicea (Col 4^{15}), but to communicate Colossians to them and secure "Laodiceans" from them, or rather to read it when they received it in due course. The most natural meaning of τὴν ἐκ Λαοδικίας (= the letter you are to receive from Laodicea) implies that Paul had either given oral instructions (to Tychicus?) to have a copy of Laodiceans sent to the neighbouring church of Colossê, or inserted in that letter an injunction corresponding to Col 4^{15-16}. He gives no reason for this procedure, and it does not follow that Laodiceans, any more than Colossians, was a circular pastoral intended for several churches. The probability is that, like Colossians, it had individual traits, whereas the canonical Ephesians contains none of these.

The pseudo-Pauline *Epistola ad Laodicenses* is a much later forgery, dating from the second (Zahn) or more probably the fourth century; cp. Harnack, *ACL.* i. pp. 36–37, and Lightfoot's *Colossians* (pp. 272 f.).[1] Four fresh Spanish MSS are noticed in *JBL.* (xxiii. pp. 73 f.), and a transcription of one in Madrid is given by Prof. E. J. Goodspeed in *AJT.* (1904) pp. 536–538. The epistle was not only read in some circles of the early church ("legunt quidam et ad Laodicenses, sed ab omnibus exploditur," Jerome, *de uir. inlustr.* 5), but widely circulated in the mediæval period. For over nine centuries "this forged epistle hovered about the door of the sacred Canon, without either finding admission or being peremptorily excluded. At length the revival of learning dealt its death-blow to this as to so many other spurious pretensions" (Lightfoot, p. 297).

(F) *PHILEMON.*

LITERATURE.—(*a*) Editions—Besides most edd.[2] of Colossians, see the special edd. by R. Rollock (Geneva, 1602); W. Jones (London, 1635); L. C. G. Schmidt (1766); G. C. Storr (1781); Hagenbach (Basel, 1829); J. K. I. Demme, *Erklärung d. Phil. Briefes* (1844); H. A. Petermann, *ad fidem versionum . . . cum earum textu orig. græce* (Berlin, 1844); Rothe, *Pauli ad Phil. epistolae interpretatio historico-exegetica* (Bremen, 1844)*; Koch (Zürich, 1846); Wiesinger (in Olshausen's *Comm.* 1850); F. R. Kühne (1856); Bleek (Berlin, 1865); van Oosterzee (Eng. tr., New York, 1868);

[1] The Latin text of the epistle is printed by Lightfoot (with a Gk. rendering), Westcott (*Canon of the NT,* appendix E), and Wohlenberg in his edition of the Pastoral epistles (pp. 339 f.).

[2] Especially those by Meyer, Ellicott, Lightfoot, Oltramare, and Haupt. It is edited by some others (*e.g.* Wiesinger and M. R. Vincent) along with Philippians, by a few (*e.g.* G. T. Zachariä and M. F. Sadler) along with the Pastoral epistles.

M. R. Vincent (*ICC.* 1897, 'Philippians and Philemon'); Lueken (*SNT.*[1] 1906); A. H. Drysdale (1906); A. Schumann (1908); Oesterley (*EGT.* 1910).

(*b*) Studies—J. G. C. Klotzsch, *de occasione et indole epistolae ad Philem.* (1792); D. H. Wildschut, *de vi dictionis et sermonis elegantia in epistola ad Philem.* (1809); Schenkel (*BL.* iv. 531–532); Holtzmann (*ZWT.*, 1873, pp. 428 f., 'der Brief an Philemon kritisch untersucht'); J. P. Esser, *de Brief aan Philemon* (1875)*; S. Davidson, *INT.* i. 153–160; Steck (*JPT.*, 1891, 570–584); Z. Weber's *Der Brief an d. Philemon, Ein Vorbild für die christl. Behandlung socialer Fragen* (1896); C. Roth (*ZSchw.*, 1897, 1–13); von Dobschütz, *Urc.* 115 f.; J. H. Bernard (*DB.* iv. 832–834); van Manen (*OCL.* 59 f.; *EBi.* 3693–3697).

The occasion of this note is as follows: Onesimus, a slave, had run away from his master, a prosperous and influential citizen of Colossê (cp. Col 4[9]), either owing to some harshness on the latter's part (Col 4[1]), or because he took advantage of his master's Christian forbearance (Col 3[22f.]). Paul never hints at the former reason in his note. On the other hand, vv.[11. 18-19] suggest that Onesimus had robbed as well as deserted Philemon, and for either offence he was liable to be crucified. We have no information as to how or why he came across Paul, voluntarily (Bengel, Haupt, cp. Lightfoot, 310–311) or accidentally. This little note simply shows the erstwhile δραπέτης in the apostle's company as a Christian, and on the point of being sent back to his master, for whose forbearance the apostle pleads in a few charming, tactful lines. After greeting Philemon, Apphia his wife, and Archippus (possibly his son), with the Christians who met for worship at Philemon's house (v.[2]), Paul begins with a *captatio benevolentiæ* of praise for Philemon's kindly Christian character ([4-7]), which encourages him to make a winning appeal on behalf of the unworthy Onesimus ([8-21]), now returning (Col 4[9]) along with Tychicus to Colossê, as a penitent and sincere Christian, in order to resume his place in the household of Philemon and Apphia. With a line or two of personal detail ([22-25]) the note then closes. Possibly (cp. v.[19] ἐγὼ Παῦλος ἔγραψα τῇ ἐμῇ χειρί) it was an autograph; if it was dictated, v.[19] was probably written by Paul himself on the margin of the note when finished, and the parenthesis of v.[5] may have a similar origin.

As Paul evidently had some hope of a speedy release from his imprisonment ([1. 22-23]), and as Aristarchus and Luke ([24], cp. Col 4[10. 14]) were with him, Cæsarea might conceivably be the place from which this note was sent (so, *e.g.*, Hilgenfeld and Hausrath); but Paul's eyes were towards Rome during his captivity under Felix, and at Cæsarea the conditions were less favourable than at Rome (Ac 28^{30-31} ἀπεδέχετο πάντας τοὺς εἰσπορευομένους πρὸς αὐτόν) for an outsider like Onesimus getting access to the apostle. Rome, too, was the natural refuge of runaway slaves (*fugitivarii*), who could the more easily escape detection by plunging into its seething population. Both Aristarchus and Luke were also with Paul at Rome (Ac 28^{16}). In all likelihood, therefore, the note was written during Paul's confinement in the capital (cp. Phil 2^{24}). This is corroborated by the similarity of style and contents between it on the one hand and Colossians and Philippians on the other, both written at this period: cp. *e.g.* συνέργος and συστρατιώτης ($^{1-2}$, Phil 2^{25}), ἐπιγνώσει (^{6}, Phil 1^{9}, Col 1^{9-10}), ἀνῆκον (^{8}, Col 3^{18}), συναιχμάλωτος (^{23}, Col 4^{10}), ἀπέχω (^{15}, Phil 4^{18}), and ἀδελφὸς ἀγαπητός (^{16}, Col 4^{7}), besides the fact that all three are written by Paul as a prisoner and as associated with Timotheus, whilst Col. and Philem. in addition contain greetings to Archippus and associate Luke, Mark, Aristarchus, and Demas in the closing salutations.*

(*a*) The inclusion of καὶ Τιμόθεος ὁ ἀδελφός in v.^{1} seems at first sight a semi-official tinge, but Timotheus may have been a friend of Philemon and his family; there is no obvious reason for suspecting that the words are an editorial addition during the period of the letter's reception into the Canon, although the v.l. ἔσχομεν (or ἔχομεν) in v.^{7} represents an early effort to bring out the fact of Timotheus as Paul's associate. It is extremely unlikely that Paul added his name in order to adduce a second witness (cp. 2 Co 13^{1}) to the slave's reformed character (Zahn, Belser).

(*b*) Philemon's residence has been variously assigned to Laodicea (so, *e.g.*, Wieseler†), Ephesus (Holtzmann), and Colossê (Hilgenfeld, Bleek, etc.). Even if Archippus belonged to Laodicea (so Lightfoot on Col 4^{15-17}), it would not follow that Philemon's residence must also have been there; the two towns lay not far from one another. Paul cannot (Col 2^{1}) have converted Philemon at Colossê; they may have met at Ephesus, but even if the Ephesian Onesimus of Ignatius (*ad Eph.* ii.) were supposed to be the Onesimus of this note, it would not prove that Philemon stayed there. The probabilities, such as they are, point on the whole to Colossê. No credence, however, can be given to the statement of *Apost. Constit.* vii. 46, which turns all three into bishops, Archippus of Laodicea, Philemon of Colossê, and Onesimus of Berea.

* To complete the parallelism of names in Col 4^{10-14} = Philemon $^{23-24}$ Amling (*ZNW.*, 1909, 261–262) proposes to read Ἰησοῦς (=Ἰοῦστος) for Ἰησοῦ in the latter passage, or Ἰησοῦ, Ἰησοῦς.

† On the ground that this note is that referred to in Col 4^{16} (*Chron.* 450 f.).

(*c*) The note is not strictly private. It is addressed not only to Philemon (primarily), but to Apphia his wife (ἀδελφή, as often in this sense). Unless 2 Jn is addressed to an individual, this note is the only extant letter in the NT literature which is even partially addressed to a woman, although Phoebe (see above, pp. 137 f.) had one written on her behalf. For letters of ancient philosophers to women (*e.g.* Epicurus and Seneca to their mothers. Ptolemæus to Flora, and Porphyry to Marcella), see J. Geffcken in *Preuss. Jahrbücher* (1905), 427–447.

The seven Pauline ἅπαξ εὑρόμενα in this note (ἀναπέμπειν, ἀποτίνειν, ἄχρηστος, ἐπιτάσσειν, ξενία, ὀνίνασθαι, and προσοφείλειν) are all current in the κοινή (as the papyri prove), and most occur elsewhere in the LXX or in the NT itself. "Wenn uns eine Schrift des NT von der zwanglosen hellenistischen Unterhaltungsprache eine Vorstellung zu geben mag, so ist es der anmutige Philemonbrief" (Nägeli, *der Wortschätz des Apostel Paulus*, 82). The play on the name of Onesimus ([20] ἐγώ σου ὀναίμην ἐν κυρίῳ) happens to recur in Ignat. *ad Ephes.* ii.; but it is too common and obvious (even when supported in Ignat. *ibid.*, by ἀναπαύω in sense of Philemon [7. 20]) to indicate that Ignatius had this note in mind. Philemon, however, which is twice quoted as Pauline by Origen (its first commentator), was included in Marcion's Canon (cp. Tert. *adv. Marc.* v. 21 = soli hinc epistolæ breuitas sua profuit, ut falsarias manus Marcionis euaderet) as well as in the Muratorian; but its private character, its brevity, and its lack of dogmatic teaching threw it into positive disfavour with many Christians, especially throughout the Syrian church, where the first tardy recognition of it occurs in the Catalogus Sinaiticus. Jerome, in his preface (A.D. 388), had to defend it against widespread depreciation ('a plerisque ueteribus repudiatam'). A good account of this is given in Zahn's *GK.* i. 268 f., ii. 997 f., and in Leipoldt's *GK.* i. 208–213. In modern times the note has had to run the gauntlet of a doctrinaire criticism which regarded it as a pseudonymous little pamphlet, composed as a pendant to the un-Pauline Colossians and modelled on Pliny's well-known letter to Sabinianus (so from Baur to Steck and van Manen).* More moderately, but unconvincingly (cp. Schenkel's *BL.* iv. 531–532, and Clemen's *Paulus*, i. 128 f.), interpolations have been suspected (*e.g.* by Holtzmann, Hausrath, iv. 122–123, and Brückner, *Chron.* 200 f.) in vv.[1] (καὶ Τιμόθεος ὁ ἀδελφός μου, with ἡμῶν), [5-6] (the chiasmus), and [19]. A Frenchman is usually worth attention upon questions of literary style, and two French critics have summed up on the letter to Philemon with admirable insight. "Peu de pages," says Renan, (iv. 96) "ont un accent de sincérité aussi prononcé. Paul seul a pu écrire ce petit chef-d'œuvre." "Ce ne sont que quelque lignes familières," Sabatier (*l'apôtre Paul*, 234, Eng. tr. p. 226) adds, "mais si pleines de grâce, de sel, d'affection sérieuse et confiante que cette courte épître brille comme une perle de la plus exquise finesse,

---

* As Hausrath observes (iv. 122 f.), "the thought that Christianity unites in a higher sphere things severed in this world, and teaches them mutual love, cannot be maintained against the plain realism of the document. This is a reunion in which Onesimus obviously fears a too speedy acquaintance with the lash, and the object of the epistle is simply to save him from this fate." "Simply" is not quite accurate, but otherwise Hausrath's judgment is correct

dans le riche trésor du Nouveau Testament. Jamais n'a mieux été réalisé le précepte que Paul lui-même donnait à la fin de sa lettre aux Colossiens (4[6])."

(G) *PHILIPPIANS.*

LITERATURE.—(*a*) Editions—besides the older commentaries of Calvin (1539), Estius (1614), and Henry Airay (1618), Michaelis, *Paraphrasis*[2], etc. (1769); G. C. Storr (1783); Rheinwald (1827, 1834); Flatt's *Vorlesungen* (1829); M. Eastburn (New York, 1833); T. Passavant (1834); H. S. Baynes (London, 1834); Matthies (1835); van Hengel (*Comment. perpet.*, Leyden, 1838); Hölemann (Leipzig, 1839); A. Rilliet (Geneva, 1841)*; de Wette[2] (1847); Baumgarten-Crusius (1848); Wiesinger in Olshausen's *Commentar* (1850, Eng. tr. 1851); Neander (Eng. tr. 1851, Edinburgh); Beelen (Louvain, 1852); G. F. Jatho (1857); Weiss, *der Philipperbrief ausgelegt u. die Geschichte seiner Auslegung kritisch dargestellt* (1859)*; Meyer[3] (1865); Bisping[2] (1866); Schenkel (1867); Hofmann (1871); Braune[2] (Lange's *Bibel-werk*, 1875); Reuss (1878); H. Maurer (1880); Reinecke (1881); Eadie[2] (1884); C. J. Vaughan (1885); Franke (— Meyer[5], 1886); Ellicott[5])1888)*; J. Gwynn (*Speaker's Comm.* 1889); M. F. Sadler (1889); J. Agar Beet (1890); Lightfoot[6] (1891, etc.)*; Padovani (1892); Lipsius[2] (*HC.* 1892)*; A. Klöpper (1893)*; Wohlenberg (*Kurzgefasst. Comm.* 1895); Weiss (1896); Moule (*CGT.* 1897); M. R. Vincent (*ICC.* 1897); K. J. Müller (Freiburg, 1899); J. Drummond (*Intern. Hdbks. to NT*, 1899); Haupt (— Meyer[8], 1902)*; G. C. Martin (*CB.* n. d.); H. A. A. Kennedy* (*EGT.* 1903); Baljon (1904); von Soden[2] (1906); von Huene (1907); W. Lueken (*SNT.*[2] 1907); P. Ewald (*ZK.* 1908).

(*b*) Studies—(i.) against Pauline authorship—Baur's *Paulus* (Eng. tr.), ii. pp. 45 f., and in *Theol. Jahrb.*, 1849, 501 f., 1852, 133 f.; Hinsch (*ZWT.*, 1873, pp. 59 f.); Hoekstra (*TT.*, 1875, pp. 416 f.); Holsten* (*JPT.*, 1875, pp. 425 f., 1876, pp. 58 f., 282 f.); Schwegler (*NZ.* ii. 133 f.); Straatman, *de Gemeente te Rome* (1878), pp. 201 f., after Hitzig (*Zur Kritik d. paulin. Briefe*, 1870) and B. Bauer (*Christus u. die Caesaren*, 373 f.); van Manen *OCL.*; 49–51, 82–84. *EBi.* 3703–3713.

(ii.) For Pauline authorship—Lünemann (*Pauli ad Philipp. ep. contra Baurium defensa*, 1847); Ernesti (*SK.*, 1848, 858–924, 1851, pp. 591–632); B. Brückner (*Ep. ad Philipp. Paulo auctori vindicata contra Baurium*, 1848); Resch, *de l'authent. de l'épître aux. Ph.* (1850); Grimm (*ZWT.*, 1873, pp. 33 f.); Sabatier (*ESR.* x. 569–573); Weizsäcker (*AA.* i. 218 f., 279 f.); P. W. Schmidt, *NTliche Hyperkritik* (1870, 54 f., against Holsten); Hilgenfeld (*ZWT.*, 1884, pp. 498 f.); Mangold (*der Römerbrief*, pp. 256 f.); Pfleiderer (*Urc.*, Eng. tr. i. 248–257); W. Brückner (*Chron.* 218–222); Clemen, *Paulus*, i. 130–138.

(iii.) General—A. F. Busching's *Introductio in epistolam ad Philipp.* (Halle, 1746); Hoog, *de coetus christ. Phil. conditione primaeva* (1825); Schinz, *die christl. Gemeinde Ph.* (1833); C. Müller, *Commentatio de locis quibusdam Ep. ad Philipp.* (1844); Hasselmann, *Analyse pragmatique de l'ép. aux Phil.* (1862); Schenkel, *BL.* iv. 534–538; Hatch (*EB.*[9]); R. R. Smith, *The Epistle of St. Paul's First Trial* (1899); J. Gibb, *DB.* iii. 840–844; F. Költzsch (*Der Phil. Brief wie er zum ersten Male verlesen und gehört ward*, 1906); Lütgert, 'Die Vollkommenen im Philipperbrief u. die Enthusiasten in Thessalon.' (*BFT.* xiii. 6, 1906).

(iv.) On 2^{5-11}—Tholuck's *Disputatio Christologica de loco Pauli Phil.* 2^{6-9} (1847); H. J. Holtzmann (*ZWT.*, 1881, 101–107); Weiffenbach, *Zur Auslegung d. Stelle Phil.* 2^{5-11} (Karlsruhe, 1884)*; A. B. Bruce, *Humiliation of Christ*[8] (1889), 15 f., 357 f.; E. H. Gifford, *The Incarnation* (reprint from *Exp.* 1896); J. Kögel (*BFT.* xii. 2).

§ 1. *Contents.*—Paul's last epistle is written to the first church which he founded in Europe. After a brief address (1^{1-2}), Paul assures the Philippians of his thankfulness for their κοινωνία in the gospel ἀπὸ τῆς πρώτης ἡμέρας ἄχρι τοῦ νῦν (1^{3-8}), and of his prayers for the maturing (1^{9-11}) of their ἀγάπη. He then relieves their anxiety about himself; the recent turn in his affairs had really helped, instead of hindering (as they had feared), the prospects of the gospel (1^{12-18}); furthermore, he had even the prospect of being set free and of revisiting[1] Philippi (1^{19-26}). Meantime, however, they are to show a united front[2] to their adversaries (1^{27-30}), μιᾷ ψυχῇ συναθλοῦντες τῇ πίστει τοῦ εὐαγγελίου. Suffering must not daunt them, nor disintegrate them. Against the latter danger Paul urges (2^{1-11}) the duties of harmony and fellow-feeling (τὴν αὐτὴν ἀγάπην ἔχοντες, σύνψυχοι) which flow from a humility like that of Jesus Christ, and he reiterates[3] ($2^{12b} = 1^{27b}$) his appeal for brotherly love (2^{12-18}). As his own movements are uncertain, he promises to send Timotheus before long (2^{19-24}, cp. 1^{1}), and also bespeaks a hearty welcome for their delegate, Epaphroditus, after his illness (2^{25-30}).

The letter swerves at this point into a philippic against Jews or Jewish Christian agitators[4] (3^{2-21}). Paul tries to safeguard the Philippian church in advance against their intrigues by recalling his own character and gospel as the true norm of Christianity, but the danger of internal friction is still present to his mind ($3^{15f.}$), and he proceeds to warn gently some

[1] Jatho (pp. 7–8) finds this already in v.[9], where he takes τοῦτο as referring to an ἐλθεῖν implied in ἐπιποθῶ. This backward aspect of τοῦτο is possible (*e.g.* Demosth. *de Corona*, § 26, and Xen. *Mem.* ii. 2. 4, cp. Thuc. vi. 39), but hardly so natural here as the prospective sense.

[2] The occurrence of πολίτευμα in 3^{20} suggests that πολιτεύεσθε here retains some of its communal associations.

[3] In 2^{1} (πληρωσατέ μου τὴν χαράν, positive motive), in 2^{16} (ὅτι οὐκ εἰς κενὸν ἔδραμον, negative motive); the former is resumed in 2^{17-18}.

[4] They have nothing to do with the evangelists mentioned in $1^{15f.}$; the latter preach Christ truly; it is their motives, not the content of their gospel, to which Paul takes exception.

prominent individuals in the church against it (4^{1-7}) in a passage which is partly recapitulatory (cp. *χαίρετε* in $4^{1.4}$ as already in 2^{18} 3^1; *συνήθλησαν*, $4^3 = 1^{27}$; and *στήκετε* 4^1, as in 1^{27}), but which flows over into the closing appeal of 4^{8-9} ($4^9 = 3^{17}$) for harmony. In a parenthesis, he then thanks them (4^{10-20}) for a fresh present of money which Epaphroditus had brought, and with some brief salutations (4^{21-23}) the letter ends.

Timotheus is associated with Paul in the address (1^1), owing to his local associations (2^{22} = Ac $16^{8.12f.}$); but the apostle writes in the first person throughout (even in 4^{21}), and indeed speaks of his companion as distinguished from himself (2^{19-24}). The only exception is in 3^{17} (*ἡμᾶς*).

The text presents few difficulties,* apart from the interpolations which have been conjectured (see below) in 1^1 and 2^{6-7}. The transposition in 1^{16-17} (for the chiasmus, see Ro 2^{6-12}) is one of the few which have left traces in the textual material. Other conjectures of glosses (cp. Weisse's *Beiträge zur Kritik d. Paul. Briefe*, 56 f.), *e.g.* in 1^{16-17} 1^{22} (*εἰ δὲ . . . καρπὸς ἔργου*), 2^{30} 3^{18-19} (marginal gloss, Laurent), 3^{21} (Brückner), 4^{3-5} and 4^{18-19} are due to inadequate exegesis for the most part. The style and vocabulary, viewed in the light of research into the *κοινή*, present no real obstacles to the acceptance of the epistle as Pauline. The most noticeable feature, according to Nägeli (*Wortschätz des Apostels Paulus*, 80 f.), is a tendency to employ several expressions, *e.g.* *ἐγείρειν*, *ἐξομολογεῖσθαι*, *τὰ ἔμπροσθεν*, in a sense closer to that of literary Greek than to that of the LXX as heretofore. "Paulus scheint sich also im Verkehr mit den Griechen nach und nach zu gunsten des in der höhern *κοινή* bevorzugten Gebrauches von der einen und andern bei den LXX beliebten Wortbedeutung emanzipiert zu haben." The use of *ἀρετή* is a case in point; † so is the absence of any OT citation.

The iambic trimeter in 3^1 (*ἐμοὶ μὲν οὐκ ὀκνηρόν, ὑμῖν δ' ἀσφαλές*) is not the only instance of rhythmical structure in the epistle. 2^{5-10} is specially important in this connection, as the balance of clauses bears on the exegesis of this carefully modulated section (J. Weiss, *Beiträge zur paul. Rhetorik*, 28 f.):—

1. (*a*) *ὃς ἐν μορφῇ θεοῦ ὑπάρχων οὐχ ἁρπαγμὸν ἡγήσατο τὸ εἶναι ἴσα θεῷ*
   (*b*) *ἀλλὰ ἑαυτὸν ἐκένωσεν μορφὴν δούλου λαβών*
   (*c*) *ἐν ὁμοιώματι ἀνθρώπων γενόμενος καὶ σχήματι εὑρεθεὶς ὡς ἄνθρωπος*
   (*d*) *ἐταπείνωσεν ἑαυτόν, γενόμενος ὑπήκοος μέχρι θανάτου, θανάτου δὲ σταυροῦ.*
2. (*a*) *διὸ καὶ ὁ θεὸς αὐτὸν ὑπερύψωσεν*
   (*b*) *καὶ ἐχαρίσατο αὐτῷ ὄνομα τὸ ὑπὲρ πᾶν ὄνομα*
   (*c*) *ἵνα ἐν τῷ ὀνόματι Ἰησοῦ πᾶν γόνυ κάμψῃ κτλ.*
   (*d*) *καὶ πᾶσα γλῶσσα ἐξομολογήσηται ὅτι κύριος Ἰησοῦς Χριστός.*

---

* In 3^{14} *τῆς ἄνω κλήσεως* apparently was read by Tertullian as *τῆς ἀνεγκλήσεως* and by Origen as *τῆς ἀνεγκλησίας*.

† In this passage, $4^{8f.}$, "it is as if one heard the ripple of the waves at the meeting of the two streams which have their source in Zion and the Parthenon" (von Soden, p. 114).

The balancing of the clauses against one another, and the reiteration of the same word in the same or in successive clauses, are noticeable.

§ 2. *Occasion and date.*—Communications had already passed between the Christians of Philippi and Paul, not only during his residence at Thessalonika (4^{15-16}), but at some subsequent period (4^{18}), when Epaphroditus had brought him a present of money. It is possible that the gift was accompanied by a letter. At any rate, the extant epistle is the reply to one received subsequently from the Philippians, who had evidently desired information about his prospects and health (1^{12}), assured him of their prayers (1^{19}), wondered whether he, their καύχημα, would return to them ($1^{25f.}$), expressed their anxiety about the health of Epaphroditus (2^{26}), and possibly apologised for not sending money to him sooner ($4^{10f.}$). The latter point emerges in passages like $2^{17.\ 25.\ 30}$, as well as in $4^{10f.}$, where Paul is apparently trying to remove some fear which had been expressed by the Philippian Christians lest he should have been dissatisfied with "the smallness and the tardiness of their last remittance" (cp. Zahn, *INT.* § 30).

The epistle was written toward the close of the διετία ὅλη of Ac 28^{30}, not in the earlier part of the imprisonment. Paul is on the eve and edge of the final decision, with (1^{12-13}) a period behind him during which considerable progress has been made in the local preaching and extension of the gospel, and his language does not imply that this new departure in the propaganda was stimulated by the mere novelty of his arrival. This argument is not affected by the fact that when Paul reached Rome, he already found a considerable body of Christians. He traces the flourishing character of the local church in no small measure to the stimulating effect produced by his own imprisonment. Furthermore, the relations between Philippi and Paul presuppose an interval of time which cannot be fairly compressed within a few months. News of his arrival must have had time to reach the church; money was collected (2^{25} 4^{18}) and then sent by Epaphroditus, who fell sick after he reached the capital; news of this again floated back to Philippi, and Paul subsequently heard of the Philippians' concern (2^{26}). Not till then did he compose the present letter. Luke and Aristarchus were apparently (2^{20}) no longer with him.

This setting of the epistle (so, *e.g.*, Godet, *INT.* 427 f.; Sabatier's *Paul*, 250 f.; Reuss, Lipsius, Klöpper, Gwynn, Ramsay, *SPT.* 357 f.; McGiffert,

AA. 364–393; Bovon, *NT Theol.* ii. 73–120; Bartlet, *AA.* 178 f.; Schäfer, *Einl.* 133–146; H. A. A. Kennedy, *ET.* x. 22 f.; Gibb, Clemen, Bacon, Jacquier, Barth, Peake), which ranks it later than the other epistles of the Roman imprisonment has been challenged by three * rival hypotheses.

(*a*) The attempt of several scholars (from Paulus, D. Schulz, Böttger's *Beiträge*, ii. 46 f., Rilliet, and Thiersch, to Spitta and Macpherson, *Ephesians*, 86 f.) to place its composition at Cæsarea (Ac 23^{23}–26^{32}) is to be set aside,† not only on account of the positive evidence ‡ pointing to Rome (1^{13} 4^{22}), but because the uncertain critical outlook of the apostle does not correspond to the situation at Cæsarea when he was in no immediate danger of death. Not until he reached Rome did his life come into real peril at the hands of the Roman authorities. Besides, the large number of local preachers of the gospel (1^{17}) accords much better with the capital than with the provincial town of Cæsarea; the latter cannot be said to have been a centre of vigorous Christian propaganda. Delays in a trial were perfectly natural in Rome, for the wheels of procedure did not always run the swifter as they neared the headquarters of the law. It required no such recent experience of Jewish agitators as that of Ac $21^{27f.}$ to make Paul flash out into the language of Ph $3^{2f.}$. Timotheus is not known to have visited Rome, but this is an argument from silence which, in the scantiness of our available data for the period, is of little or no weight. Finally, the plea (Spitta, *Apgeschichte*, 281) that the cupidity of Felix (Ac 24^{26}) was aroused by the arrival of the money from Philippi (Ph 4^{10}), belongs to imaginative fiction rather than to historical reconstruction. Of the two other views which have been taken of the epistle's date, apart from the Cæsarean hypothesis, one (*b*) is that the terms of $1^{13f.}$ (compared with Col 4^{11}) imply that the comparatively free διετία was over, and had been replaced by a stricter durance (so, *e.g.*, Alford,§ Hofmann, Wohlenberg, Zahn, and Belser). This throws Phil. still later, but the lack of other evidence upon the course of the trial renders it impossible to be certain whether the apostle had exchanged his *custodia libera* for one of closer restraint.‖ (*c*) Others again place the epistle earlier, in the opening period of the διετία

---

* Four, if the epistle (cp. M. Albertz, *SK.*, 1910, 551–594, 'ueber die Abfassung des Philipperbriefes des Paulus zu Ephesus) could be placed in an Ephesian imprisonment, to which a few (*e.g.* Deissmann, *Licht vom Osten* [2], pp. 171 f.) would give the other prison-epistles.

† Even Schenkel, Meyer, and Reuss, who put Col. Eph. and Philemon into the Cæsarean period, emphatically relegate Philippians to Rome.

‡ Πραιτώριον might mean the π. τοῦ Ἡρώδου of Ac 23^{35}, but the probabilities lie between the prætorian guard and the *praefecti praetorio* or judicial authorities of the imperial court.

§ Summer of 63; early in 63 (W. T. Bullock, Smith's *DB.*[1] ii. 839–843).

‖ If a genuine fragment or tradition lies below 2 Ti $4^{6f.}$, it might corroborate the setting of Phil. towards the end of Paul's confinement: cp 2 Ti 4^{5}=Col 4^{17}, 2 Ti 4^{6}=Ph 2^{17} and 1^{23}, $4^{9f.}$=Ph $2^{20f.}$; only, by the time Timotheus reached him (on this theory), Luke had gone. Both Krenkel (*Beiträge*, 424 f., 442 f.) and Kreyenbühl (*Evang. d. Wahrheit*, i. 213 f.), like Erbes, refer 2 Ti 4^{16} to Paul's defence before Felix. These hypotheses fall, however, with the case for the Cæsarean site of the epistle.

(so Bleek, Ewald, Lightfoot, pp. 30–46; Farrar, *St. Paul*, ch. xlvi.; Moule; Beyschlag; Sanday; Smith's *DB.*[2] i. 627; Hort, *JC.* 115–129; Trenkle, *Einl.* 49–50; Lock, *DB.* i. 718–719), partly for reasons already met by anticipation (see above, p. 168), partly because Philippians represents a less advanced stage in the development of the church than Colossians (and Ephesians). The latter fact may be granted, but the influence must be disputed. Neither to place Philippians among the later, nor Galatians among the earlier, epistles, is it sufficient to lay stress upon resemblances of style and a systematic evolution of thought. "The tone of *Col.* and *Ephes.* is determined by the circumstances of the churches addressed. The great cities of Asia were on the highway of the world, which traversed the Lycos valley, and in them development took place with great rapidity. But the Macedonians were a simple-minded people in comparison with Ephesus and Laodicea and Colossai, living further away from the great movements of thought. It was not in Paul's way to send to Philippi an elaborate treatise against a subtle speculative heresy, which had never affected that church" (Ramsay, *SPT.* 359). The predominance of dogmatic teaching in Col. (and Eph.) and the resemblances between Rom. and Phil. do not necessarily imply that Phil. lay between Rom. and Col. (Eph.) in a chronological and logical sequence. Such characteristics are due to the variety of objects and interests which confronted the apostle as he turned to the Asiatic and the Macedonian churches. To arrange the epistles in the order and for the reasons suggested, *e.g.*, by Lightfoot, is to confuse the parade-ground with the battle-field, where quick phases and unexpected transitions often drive the general to fight twice on the same ground and to develop sudden movements in order to checkmate crises which were unforeseen. It is much more true to life to take each of the prison-epistles upon its own merits, as an outcome of Paul's mood and duty at the time being, than to classify them, for reasons of style and matter, in plausible but unnatural groups. The priority of Col. to Phil. is therefore unaffected by the fuller theology of the former. When Eph. is reckoned post-Pauline, this becomes all the more clear, but even when it is attributed to Paul himself, the place of Phil. as the climax of the Pauline correspondence remains upon the whole more true than any other re-arrangement of the epistles to the data of the period. The time is too short for such a development as Lightfoot's theory would postulate.

§ 3. *Authenticity.*—Doubts upon the Pauline authorship were voiced during last century, on four accounts: (*a*) alleged traces of imitation in the epistle, (*b*) ecclesiastical anachronisms, (*c*) gnostic controversies, and (*d*) doctrinal discrepancies between the epistle and the other Pauline letters, especially Gal., Cor., and Romans. (*a*) The literary argument is barely worth refuting. The style and vocabulary (see above) offer no real difficulty, and the epistle is marked by the genuinely Pauline traits of courtesy and affection, by the blending of humility and authority, the digressions, the warm. swift touches of feeling, and the devout passion for Christ. which are the water-marks of Paul's mind. It is true that a passage like 1[18] breathes "a certain resignation to which we are not accustomed in the author of Galatians and 2 Corinthians. But resignation is the general characteristic of these last writings, wherein his moods are strangely mingled" (Hausrath, iv. 167). Neither in this respect nor in any other is the epistle unnatural under the circumstances, much less unworthy of the Paul we know. Baur, indeed, found the epistle "characterised by a monotonous repetition of what has been already said, by a want of any profound and masterly connection of ideas, and by a certain poverty of thought," whilst van Manen dubbed it nebulous, unintelligible, and high-flown. So did Johnson judge of Gray.

The perverse interpretation of 4[2-3] as a series of references to parties in the early church is now abandoned upon almost all hands, though the γνήσιε σύνζυγε of 4[3] baffles explanation. If Σύνζυγε is a proper name, as is most likely, it is needless to interpret σύνζυγε of Lydia or Paul's wife (which would require γνησία), or even of Epaphroditus, Timotheus, etc.

(*b*) The words σὺν ἐπισκόποις καὶ διακόνοις in 1[1] are admittedly strange. No other epistle of Paul mentions any officials in its address, while ἐπίσκοποι and διάκονοι are not only collectively but singly absent from his writings. The former may here be used in the sense of Ac 20[28], the latter in that of Ro 12[7], and their specific mention may be due to the gifts received by Paul, which would come through the hands of the officials in charge of the local finance; but there is at least a case for regarding the words as a gloss inserted by some second-century editor, when the epistle came into use as part of the Canon in the services of the church (so Schmiedel, *EBi.* 3147–3148, after Brückner and Völter). This is, at any rate, better than to keep them and throw suspicion on the entire epistle, or to emend them into ἐπισκόπῳ καὶ διακόνοις (Linwood). If such catholicising glosses are to be admitted anywhere in the NT, this is as obvious a place as any.

(*c*) Recent research has found the background of the categories in 2[5f.], not in the Valentinian gnosis, as Baur and Hoekstra * imagined, but in the earlier religious speculations †

* Pfleiderer (see below) still adheres to this notion of "a reference to the myth in the Ophite and Valentinian gnosis of the Sophia which desired to unite itself on equal terms with the primal Deity of the Father, or of the subordinate demiurge Jaldabaoth, who attempted to misuse his god-like power of lordship in order to put himself in the place of the highest God."

† Cp. Clemen's *Religionsgeschichtliche Erklärung des NT*, 122 f.; M. Dibelius, *die Geisterwelt im Glauben des Paulus* (1909), 10 f., and Bousset's *Hauptprobleme der Gnosis*, 160 f.

upon a pre-existent original Being or *Urmensch* in heaven which are preserved, *e.g.*, in Poimandres (cp. 12 f., where the divine μορφή is also attributed to this Man, who ἀθάνατος ὢν καὶ πάντων τὴν ἐξουσίαν ἔχων τὰ θνητοῦ πάσχει ὑποκείμενος τῇ εἱμαρμένῃ· ὑπεράνω γὰρ ὢν τῆς ἁρμονίας ἐναρμόνιος γέγονε δοῦλος) and the *Ascensio Isaiæ* ($10^{29f.}$), where the Lord "descended into the firmament where dwelleth the ruler of this world," but where, although his form was like that of the spirits, the latter refused to do homage to him, since "they were envying one another and fighting" (cp. Charles' ed. p. 74: contrast οὐχ ἁρπαγμόν κτλ.). Some analogous phrases in *Test. XII Patr.*, *e.g.* Zab 7^{8} (ὄψεσθε θεὸν ἐν σχήματι ἀνθρώπου) and *Benj.* 10^{7} (ἐν μορφῇ ἀνθρώπου ἐν ταπεινώσει) are probably Christian interpolations.

(*d*) The weakness of the attempt to find gnosticism in $2^{5f.}$ and typical or second-century allusions in 4^{2-3} (γνήσιε σύνζυγε = Peter, etc.), was promptly acknowledged by Holsten, whose difficulties centred on the supposed inconsistencies of the epistle with Paul in regard to the conceptions of Christ and salvation. He still shared the tendency to see in 4^{2-3} a subtle effort to reconcile by way of allegory the Jewish and the Gentile Christians, but he felt most some apparent discrepancies between Phil. and the *Hauptbriefe.*

Holsten's general theory of the epistle's origin, however, is even more improbable than Baur's, since it is extremely difficult to imagine how such an epistle could have been accepted by the church shortly after Paul's death, had it been composed by a Paulinist who desired to write and encourage the local Christians after their great founder had passed away. His particular objections to the christology of $2^{5f.}$ as un-Pauline (cp. 2 Co 8^{9} where the so-called christological reference is also adduced for practical purposes), on the score of its inconsistency with the pre-existent heavenly Man of Ro 8^{3} etc., depend on too narrow an exegesis (cp. Schmidt, *op. cit.* 54 f.; Weiffenbach, *op. cit.* 64 f.; and Holtzmann, *NT Theologie*, ii. 88 f., "somit haben wir kein Grund, die christologische Darstellung Ph 2^{6-11} als incompatibel mit derjenigen der Hauptbriefe aus dem paulin. Lehrbegriff auszuscheiden").* Brückner (ἐν μορφῇ θεοῦ . . . ὡς ἄνθρωπος), Weisse (τὸ εἶναι ἴσα θεῷ and μορφὴν δούλου . . . ἐταπείνωσεν ἑαυτόν), Schmiedel (om. ἀλλά in 2^{7}, all of 2^{8} except ὅς, and ἐπουρανίων . . . καταχθονίων in 2^{10}), and Pfleiderer (i. 321–323) all omit more or less of 2^{6-7} as interpolated, but for no cogent reasons. Their procedure, however, suggests a fresh set of hypotheses with regard to the unity of the epistle.

§ 4. *Integrity.*—These hypotheses either distinguish between a Pauline nucleus and editorial matter, or between two Pauline

* This is all the more obvious when Colossians is accepted as Pauline.

notes. Both, but especially the latter, start from the abrupt turn in 3^{1} (τὰ αὐτὰ γράφειν ὑμῖν κτλ.). It is a fair inference from these words that Paul had written * already to the Christians of Philippi (so, *e.g.*, Haenlein, Bertholdt, Lünemann, Flatt, Bleek, Wiesinger, Ewald, Jatho, Schenkel, Meyer, Mangold, Bisping, Hilgenfeld, Hofmann, Meyer, etc.); the various attempts to explain τὰ αὐτά from the context and contents of the canonical epistle are more or less strained. Paul had not spoken so often or so amply of rejoicing (1^{4} 2^{28}), that his hearers would feel it irksome to have χαίρετε ἐν Κυρίῳ repeated to them. Some more serious and vital topic is required. Δικαιόσυνη is not sufficiently emphatic in the following paragraph to make it probable that Paul was half apologising for speaking of it (Holsten), and the least unlikely solution is that either the danger of dissensions (Lightfoot) or the errorists are in his mind. Against the latter he may have had occasion previously to warn them,† out of his mournful experiences in Asia and Achaia ($3^{1} = 3^{18}$ οὓς πολλάκις ἔλεγον ὑμῖν). The readiest explanation of $3^{1f.}$ is to suppose (with Ewald, Schenkel, Reuss, etc.) that Paul started to complete or supplement what he had already written, possibly because some fresh tidings from Philippi had reached him in the interval. There is nothing specifically un-Pauline even in $3^{1f.}$ to justify the hypothesis ‡ that the extant epistle consists of a genuine and a later letter, which some editor of the second century has patched together.

The use of the plural in Polykarp's letter to the Philippians (iii.), where he speaks of Paul having written ἐπιστολάς εἰς ἃς ἐὰν ἐγκύπτητε, δυνηθήσεσθε οἰκοδομεῖσθε εἰς τὴν δοθεῖσαν ὑμῖν πίστιν, is indecisive; ἐπιστολαί like *litterae*, might be used of a single

* Without pressing γράφειν unduly, one may say that the scope of the expression would cover more than merely oral communications from Paul himself or through his delegates. Ewald found traces of such written communications somewhat precariously in 2^{12} and 3^{18}.

† Völter (*Paulus u. Seine Briefe*, 319 f.) thinks that the editor must have had in his mind the warning of 2 Co $11^{18f.}$.

‡ Schrader (*der Apostel Paulus*, v. 233 f.) took 3^{1}–4^{9} as an unauthentic interpolation; Völter (*TT.*, 1892, 10–44, 117–146) separated a genuine Pauline note (1^{1-2} exc. σ. ἐπισκ. κ. διακ. $1^{3-7.\ 12-14.\ 18b-26}$ $2^{17-20.\ 22-30}$ $4^{10-20.\ 21.\ 23}$) from material ($1^{8-11.\ 27-30}$ 2^{1-16} $3^{1b.\ 21}$ $4^{1-9.\ 22}$) dating from the reign of Trajan or Hadrian, the redactor being responsible for $1^{1.\ 15-18a}$ 2^{21} 3^{1a}; but he now (*Paulus und Seine Briefe*, 286 f.) detects the Pauline original in 1^{1-2} (except σὺν ἐπ. κ. διακόνοις), $1^{3-7.\ 12-20}$ (except καὶ ἐπιχορ. τοῦ πνευμ. Ἰ. Χ. and εἴτε δ. ζ. εἴτε δ. θ.), 1^{25-26} $2^{17-18.\ 25-30}$ 4^{10-21}.

dispatch. Yet elsewhere in Polykarp (cp. ch. xiii.), as in the NT itself (1 Co 16^3 etc.), the distinction between singular and plural in the use of the term is carefully observed; nor would the use of *epistolae* in the Lat. version of ch. xi. of Polykarp's epistle (in quibus laborauit beatus Paulus, qui estis in principio epistolae eius) invalidate this argument, since *epistolae* there is not genit. sing * but nom. plur. (cp. 2 Co 3^2). The probabilities therefore are that Polykarp knew of more than one Pauline letter to Philippi, and the alternatives are to suppose (i.) that some other previous letter (or letters) to that church did not survive, or (ii.) that Polykarp was referring loosely to 2 Thessalonians, which was also written to a neighbouring Macedonian church. In favour of (i.) it may be pointed out that if its contents were similar, as *ex hypothesi* they must have been, to those of the canonical epistle, there would be less chance of it surviving. If it be argued that such a fate would be unlikely, when it had survived to the age of Polykarp, the answer is that Polykarp's language does not necessarily imply more than that the church had in the earlier period of its history (4^{16}) received more than one letter from the apostle. (ii.) More probably, however, the reference covers the Thessalonian epistles (or 2 Thessalonians), of which the Philippian church would possess a copy; for in addressing the Philippians themselves (xi. 3) he actually uses language (de uobis etenim gloriatur in omnibus ecclesiis) which is palpably a reminiscence of 2 Thessalonians (cp. 1^4), as if the latter epistle were somehow associated in his mind with Philippi. Tertullian (*ad Scorp.* 13) similarly quotes Phil. as if it were addressed to Thessalonika, and the three Macedonian epistles seem to have been often grouped together in the archives of the early church (Zahn). The ἐπιστολαί of Polykarp are most readily to be understood in this sense, *i.e.*, as a collection of Pauline epistles, including not only Philippians but those addressed to the neighbouring church of Thessalonika (cp. Harnack in *TU.*, 1900, v. 3. 86 f., and Wrede in *TU.*, 1903, 94 f.).

Unlike 1 Co 5^9 and Col 4^{16}, the allusion in Ph 3^1 did not prompt any writer in the early church to produce an apocryphal letter to the Philippians. The existence of such a letter may be inferred from the Syriac Catalogus Sinaiticus (cp. Mrs. Lewis in *Studia Sinaitica*, i. 11 f., and W. Bauer, *Der Apostolos der Syrer*, 1903, pp. 34 f., 37 f.), which mentions two Philippian

* Nestle's conjecture, ἀποστολῆς for ἐπιστολῆς in the original (cp. Zahn, *INT*. i. 536), is ingenious but unnecessary.

epistles; but, as it omits 1 Tim., its evidence is not trustworthy, and no clear trace of any such apocryphon has been preserved. The language of Polykarp does not yield any proof, while the casual remark of Georgius Syncellus (*Chron.*, ed. Dindorf, i. 651: τούτου [*i.e.* Clement of Rome] καὶ ὁ ἀπόστολος ἐν τῇ πρὸς Φιλιππησίους μέμνηται πρώτῃ ἐπιστολῇ) may be an oversight.

The internal evidence fails upon the whole to add any valid proof for a partition-theory, even as advocated by Hausrath (iv. 162 f.) and especially by Bacon (*The Story of St. Paul*, pp. 367 f.), both of whom put 3–4 earlier than 1–2, as a separate Pauline letter; but 2^{21} is not necessarily incompatible with 1^{14} and 4^{21}; in 2^{21} Paul vents, with some exaggeration, his annoyance at finding it impossible to persuade any of his local coadjutors to undertake the mission to Philippi, and accuses them of selfishness and worldliness (so in 2 Ti 4^{10}). The errorists of $3^{2f.}$, as has been already noted, are not mentioned in 1^{18}. And, although this hypothesis relieves the epistle of the unwieldly postscript ($3^{1f.}$), it does not work out with anything like the same plausibility* as the similar view of 2 Co 10–13. Still more unconvincing is the earlier theory of Heinrichs (*Comment. über Philipp.*, 1810) and Paulus (*de tempore scriptae prioris ad Tim. atque ad Philipp. epist. Pauli*, 1799), elaborated from a hint of S. Le Mayne's *Varia Sacra*, ii. 332 f. (1685), which discovered in 3^1–4^{20} a special letter addressed either to an esoteric circle of the apostle's friends or the authorities of the local church (in spite of 4^{10}!), the rest of the canonical epistle (*i.e.* 1^1–3^1 4^{21-23}) being intended for the local church in general (so Paulus, *Heidelberg. Jahrbücher*, 1812, 702 f., confining the special letter to 3^1–4^9). Psychologically, the change of tone from $2^{19f.}$ with its farewell note, to $3^{2f.}$ with its sudden outburst, is quite credible in a writer like Paul, who is composing not a treatise but an informal letter, probably amid many interruptions. The hiatus is striking, but it need not denote the place at which two notes have been joined.† The least violent explanation would be to conjecture (with Ewald) that 3^1–4^1 and

* Cp. Belser's *Einl.* 555 f., and Clemen's *Paulus*, i. 130 f. (where he retracts the earlier view of his *Einheitlichkeit d. paul. Briefe*, 133 f.). Each of the letters postulated by the partition-theories must have been mutilated; furthermore, as Pfleiderer points out, "the first lacks any expression of thanks for the gift of the Philippians, which (2^{25}) must have already been made."

† Thus the phrase τὸ λοιπόν approximates to οὖν (cp. Mt 26^{45}, Ac 27^{20}, 1 Th 4^1, 2 Ti 4^8 etc.); it need not have a final sense.

$4^{2f.}$ represent a couple of postscripts which were appended to the original letter. $4^{10f.}$, however, is hardly an after-thought; it rather rounds off the topics interrupted by the disgression of $3^{1f.}$. 4^{10} (ἐχάρην δὲ ἐν Κυρίῳ μεγάλως) and 3^{1a} (χαίρετε ἐν Κυρίῳ) is a good sequence, but in a letter it is not affected by the intervening passage. It is doubtful, therefore, if the attempts to analyse the epistle have proved much more satisfactory than the similar movements of literary inquiry into the first Philippic of Demosthenes, where criticism has swung back in the main to a conservative position (see A. Baran's article in *Wiener Studien*, 1884, 173–205).

§ 5. *History in early church* (cp. *NTA.* 53 f., 71 f., 94 f.; R. J. Knowling's *Testimony of St. Paul to Christ*, 111 f., and Gregory's *Canon and Text of NT.* 205 f.).

The first indubitable echoes of the epistle occur in Polykarp; cp. i. 1 συνεχάρην ὑμῖν μεγάλως ἐν Κυρίῳ = 2^{17} χαίρω καὶ συγχαίρω πᾶσιν ὑμῖν, 4^{10} ἐχάρην δὲ ἐν Κυρίω μεγάλως; ii. 1 ᾧ [*i.e.* Christ] ὑπετάγη τὰ πάντα ἐπουράνια καὶ ἐπίγεια = 2^{10} 3^{21}; ix. 2, οὗτοι πάντες οὐκ εἰς κενὸν ἔδραμον = 2^{16} (rather than Gal 2^{2}, where the context is different); xii. 3, et pro inimicis crucis = 3^{18} τοὺς ἐχθροὺς τοῦ σταυροῦ τοῦ Χριστοῦ, and the allusion in iii. 2 to Paul, ὃς καὶ ἀπὼν ὑμῖν ἔγραψεν ἐπιστολάς. The earlier allusions in Ignatius are less distinct, yet probably reliable: *Smyrn.* iv. 2, πάντα ὑπομένω αὐτοῦ με ἐνδυναμοῦντος = 4^{13}, the occurrence of κατ' ἐρίθειαν and κατὰ κενοδοξίαν ($2^{3.5}$) in *Philad.* i. 1, viii. 2, and *Smyrn.* xi. 3, τέλειοι ὄντες τέλεια καὶ φρονεῖτε = 3^{15} ὅσοι οὖν τέλειοι, τοῦτο φρονῶμεν. In Clem. Rom. xxi. 1 (ἐὰν μὴ ἀξίως αὐτοῦ πολιτευόμενοι κτλ., cp. iii. 4), till we have better evidence for the phrase being common, it is fair to admit a trace of 1^{27} (μόνον ἀξιῶς τοῦ εὐαγγελίου τοῦ Χριστοῦ πολιτευέσθε), and the same may be said of xlvii. 2, where Clement speaks of the Corinthians receiving Paul's epistle ἐν ἀρχῇ τοῦ εὐαγγελίου, his own phrase in Phil 4^{15}. In the Martyrdom of Polykarp (i. 2), 2^{4} is quoted, and in Diognet. v. 9 (ἐπὶ γῆς διατριβοῦσιν, ἀλλ' ἐν οὐρανῷ πολιτεύονται) there may be an allusion to 3^{20}. The epistle was used also by Theodotus the Valentinian and the Sethites; it is quoted in the epistle from Lyons and Vienne (Eus. *H. E.* v. 2. 2 = 2^{6}). Earlier it appeared in Marcion's ἀπόστολος, as at a later period in the Muratorian Canon, whilst Irenæus (iv. 18. 4 = 4^{18}), Clem. Alex. (repeatedly), and Tertullian cite its contents.

CHAPTER II.

THE HISTORICAL LITERATURE.

(A) THE SYNOPTIC PROBLEM.

LITERATURE.—(*a*) Editions of synoptic gospels:—J. Brent (***Commentarii in Matthæum, Marcum et Lucam***, Tübingen, 1590); H. E. G. Paulus, *Exegetisches Handbuch über die drei ersten Evglien* (Heidelberg, 1830–3); Baumgarten-Crusius (Jena, 1844–5); G. H. A. Ewald, *Die drei Evglien* (Göttingen, 1850); F. Bleek, *Synoptische Erklärung d. drei ersten Evglien* (1862); H. Sevin, *Die drei ersten Evglien synoptisch zusammengestellt* (Wiesbaden, 1866); L. Bonnet[2] (Lausanne, 1896); G. L. Cary (New York, 1900); A. B. Bruce (*EGT.*[2] 1901); H. J. Holtzmann (*HC.*[3] 1901)*; Salmon, *The Human Element in the Gospels. A Commentary upon the Synoptic narrative* (posthumous, London, 1907); A. Loisy, *Les Évangiles Synoptiques** (1907–8); J. Weiss (*SNT.*[2] 1907); C. G. Montefiore, *The Synoptic Gospels, edited with an Introduction and a Commentary* (1909).

(*b*) Studies—Lessing, *neue Hypothese über die Evglisten als bloss menschliche Geschichtschreiber betrachtet* (1778); Koppe, *Marcus non epitomator Matthaei* (1782); Griesbach, *Commentatio quâ Marci evangelium totum e Matthaei et Lucæ commentariis decerptum esse monstratur* (1790 f.);[1] G. C. Storr, *De Fonte evangeliorum Mt. et Lucæ*[2] (1794); Gieseler, *Historisch-krit. Versuch über die Entstehung u. die frühesten Schicksale der schriftlichen Evglien* (1818, oral tradition); Principal Campbell, *On the Gospels* (Edin. 1821); Hug (*Einl.*[3] ii. 1–243, 1826); Knobel, *De origine Marci* (1831); Schleiermacher (*SK.*, 1832, 735–768)*; Lachmann (*SK.*, 1835, 570 f.)*; C. G. Wilke, *der Urevangelist, oder exeg.-kritische Untersuchung über das Verwandtschaftsverhältniss der drei ersten Evglien* (1838); E. F. Gelpke, *Ueber die Anordnung der Erzählungen in den synoptischen Evglien* (1839); F. J. Schwartz, *Neue Untersuchungen über d. Verwandtschaftsverhältniss der syn. Evglien* (1844); Bruno Bauer, *Kritik d. evangelische Geschichte d. Synopt.*[2] (1846); F. C. Baur, *Kritische Untersuchungen über die kanonischen Evglien* (1847); A. Norton, *Evidences of the Genuineness of the Gospels* (1847); Ritschl, *Theol. Jahrb.* (1851), 481–538 ("On the present position of Synoptic Criticism"); Smith, *Dissertation on the Origin and Connection of the Gospels* (1853); K. R. Köstlin, *Der Ursprung und die*

---

[1] The first vigorous appearance of this unlucky and prolific dandelion, which it has taken nearly a century of opposition (led by Storr, Knobel, Lachmann, Wilke, Weisse, B. Weiss, Holtzmann, Weizsäcker, and Wendt) to eradicate.

Komposition d. synoptischen Evglien (Stuttgart, 1853); A. Hilgenfeld, *Die Evglien nach ihrer Entstehung und geschichtlichen Bedeutung* (1854); C. H. Weisse, *der Evglienfrage in ihrem gegenwärtigem Stadium* (1856); Plitt, *de compositione evang. synopt.* (1860); G. d'Eichthal, *Les Évangiles* (Paris, 1863); H. J. Holtzmann, *die Synoptische Evglien* (1863)*; Weizsäcker, *Untersuchungen über die evangelische Geschichte* (1864, second ed. 1901)*; Jahn, *Beiträge zur Kritik d. syn. Evglien* (1866); Sabatier, *Sources de la Vie de Jésus* (Paris, 1866); Scholten, *das ältest. Evglm* (1869, Eng, tr. of *Het oudste Evglm*, 1868); G. Volkmar, *die Evglien, oder Marcus und die synopse. . .*[2] (1876); Bruno Bauer, *Christus und die Caesaren* (1877, pp. 356 f., orig. gospel imbedded in Mark and Marcion's Luke); G. Wetzel, *Die synoptischen Evglien* . . . (1883, oral tradition); A. Jacobsen, *Untersuchungen über die evang. Geschichte* (1883); Holsten, *die synoptischen Evglien nach der Form ihrer Inhalts* (1885); Wendt (*Lehre Jesu*, 1886; second ed. 1901); Schulze, *Evangelientafel*[2] (1886); W. Brückner, *die vier Evglien* (1887); Fillion, *Introd. générale aux évangiles* (1889); F. H. Woods (*SB.* ii. 59 f.)*; Westcott, *Introduction to Study of Four Gospels*[7] (1889); A. Wright, *The Composition of the Gospels* (1890); W. Sanday (*Exp.*[4] iii. 81 f., 177 f., 302 f., 345 f., 411 f.); F. P. Badham, *The Formation of the Gospels*[2] (1892); Alexander, *Leading Ideas of Gospels* (new ed. 1892); Resch, *Aussercanonische Paralleltexte* (i. 1893, ii. 1894, iii. 1895, in *TU.*)*; H. von Soden 'das Interesse d. apost. Zeitalters an d. evang. Geschichte' (*ThA.* 1892); Gloag, *Introduction to Syn. Gospels* (Edin. 1895); A. J. Jolley, *The Synoptic Problem for English Readers* (1893); Roehrich, *La Composition des évangiles* (1897); Harnack, *ACL.* ii. 1. 651–700; Resch, *Die Logia Jesu* (Leipzig, 1898); McGiffert (*AA.* 479 f.); Wernle, *die Synoptische Frage* (1899)*; P. Calmes, *Comment se sont formés les évangiles* (Paris, 1899); W. Soltau, *Eine Lücke d. synoptischen Forschung* (1899), *Unsere Evglien* (1901); V. H. Stanton (Hastings' *DB.* ii. 234–249); Abbott[1] and Schmiedel (*EBi.* 1761–1839, 1840–96)*; U. Fracassini, 'La critica del vangeli nel secolo xix' (*Studi Religiosi*, 1901, 30–52, 309–331); Moffatt (*HNT.*,[2] 1901, 11 f., 258 f., 635 f.); A. Loisy, *Études evangéliques* (Paris, 1902); J. A. Robinson, *The Study of the Gospels*[3] (1903); J. Halévy, *Études evangéliques* (Paris, 1903); Bonaccorssi, *I tre primi Vangeli el la critica letteraria* (1904); H. von Soden, *Die wichtigsten Fragen im Leben Jesu* (1904); E. D. Burton, (*Introduction to Gospels*, Chicago, 1904); E. D. Burton, *Some Principles of Literary Criticism and their Application to the Synoptic Problem* (Decennial Publications of Chicago University, vol. v., 1904)*; E. Mangenot (Vigoroux' *DB.* ii. 2058–2097); J. Wellhausen, *Einleitung in die drei ersten Evglien** (1905); N. J. D. White (*DCG.* i. 663–671); Bosanquet and Wenham (*Outlines of the Synoptic Record*, 1905); Jacquier (*INT.* ii., 1905); Loisy, *Morceaux d'exégese* (1906); Jülicher, *Neue Linien in die Kritik d. Evang. Uberlieferung* (1906); J. E. Carpenter, *The First Three Gospels*[4] (London, 1906); C. E. Scott Moncrieff, *St. Mark and the Triple Tradition* (1907); P. Feine (*PRE.* xix. 277–381); Blass, *ET.* xviii. ('Origin and Character of our Gospels'); G. H. Müller, *Zur Synopse* (*Untersuchung über die*

[1] See the discussions in *Contemp. Review* (vol. xiii.) between Jannaris (pp. 37–40, 532–539) and Abbott (249–254).

Arbeitsweise des Lk. u. Mt. und ihre Quellen), 1908; F. Nicolardot, *Les procédés de Rédaction des trois premiers Évangélistes* (Paris, 1908)*; T. Nicol, *The Gospels in the Earliest Church History* (1908); J. R. Cohu, *The Gospels in the Light of Modern Research* (1909); E. Wendling, 'Synoptische Studien' (*ZNW.*, 1907, 256 f., 1908, 96 f., 1909, 46 f., 219 f.); W. Flinders Petrie, *The Growth of the Gospels as shown by Structural Criticism* (1910).

(*c*) Surveys[1] of recent criticism :—A. Menzies (*Review of Theology and Philosophy*, iv. 757 f., v. 1–17; J. Weiss (*TR.*, 1908, 92 f., 122 f.); Wendling (*ZWT.*, 1908, 135 f.); B. W. Bacon (*Harvard Theol. Review*, 1908, 48–69); H. L. Jackson (*Cambridge Biblical Essays*, 423 f.).

(*d*) The best synopsis of the textual data is Rushbrooke's *Synopticon* (1880), but smaller and convenient manuals are published in English by W. A. Stevens and E. D. Burton (Boston, 1894); A. Wright (*Synopsis of the Gospels*[2], 1903); Colin Campbell (*First Three Gospels in Greek*[2], 1899), and J. M. Thompson (*The Synoptic Gospels*, 1910); in German by Veit (*Die Synoptische Parallelen*, 1897); Heineke (*Synopse der drei ersten Evglien*, 1898), and Huck (*Synopse der drei ersten Evglien*[4], 1910). The older literature of synopses (usually=harmonies), includes Tatian's 'Diatessaron' [cp. *The Earliest Life of Christ ever compiled*, by Dr. J. H. Hill, Edin. 1894]*; Ammonius (third century); Augustine (*de consensu evangelistarum*, cp. H. J. Vogels in Bardenhewer's *Biblische Studien*, xiii. 5); A. Bruich (*Monotessaron breve ex quat. evang.*, Cologne, 1539); Salmeron (*Comment. in evang. historiam*, Madrid, 1598); Calvin; Osiander; Chemnitz (*Harmonia*, 1704); Bengel's *Harmonie* (1736); M'Knight, *Harmony of the Gospels* (1763); Planck, *Entwurf einen neuen synopt. Zusammen.* (1809); Roediger's *Synopsis* (1829); H. N. Clausen, *Quatt. evang. tabulæ synopticae* (Copenhagen, 1829); J. S. Thompson, *A Monotessaron* (Baltimore, 1828–9); Gresswell, *Harmonia evangelica* (Oxford, 1830); R. Chapman, *Gk. Harmony of Gospels* (1836); Lant Carpenter[3] (*A harmony or syn. arrangement of the gospels*, 1838); De Wette and Lucke's *Synopsis*[2] (1842); Gehringer (1842); Wieseler, *Chron. Synopsis der vier Evglien* (1843, Eng. tr., Cambridge, 1864); Robinson (Boston, 1845, ed. Riddle, 1892); R. Anger, *Synopsis Evang. Mt. Mk. Lucae* (1852); Patrizi, *De Evangeliis* (1852); W. Stroud, *A new Gk. Harmony of the four Gospels* (London, 1853); Sevin (1866); Gardiner (Andover, 1871); E. Salmon, *Analysis of the Four Parallel Gospels* (1876), also *The Parallel Gospels* (London, 1876); Fillion, *Synopsis evangelica* (Paris, 1882); Tischendorf, *Synopsis Evangelica*[6] (1891); C. C. James, *A Harmony of the Gospels* (1892); J. A. Broadus, *A Harmony of the Gospels in the Revised Version*[5] (New York, 1898), and J. C. Rambaud, *Harmonia et synopsis*[3] (Paris, 1898).

§ 1. *The documentary hypothesis.*—*Felix qui potuit rerum cognoscere causas.* This felicity has not yet been the portion of investigators into the literary origin of the synoptic gospels, but the subtle and exhaustive processes of criticism, which

[1] Historical sketches of research in Gloag, *op. cit.* pp. 44 f.; Meignan, *Les évangiles et la critique au XIXe siècle* (Paris, 1864); Feine (*op. cit.*) Jacquier (*INT.* ii. 284–355), and Zahn (*INT.* § 50).

have been applied to the synoptic problem since Schleiermacher, have at last resulted in (*a*) the conclusion that the problem is primarily one of literary criticism. The gospels are books made out of books; none of them is a document which simply transcribes the oral teaching of an apostle or of apostles. Their agreements and differences cannot be explained except on the hypothesis of a more or less close literary relationship, and while oral tradition is a *uera causa*, it is only a subordinate factor in the evolution of our canonical Greek gospels. (*b*) Secondly, the priority of Mark to Matthew and Luke no longer requires to be proved. Whatever modifications and qualifications it may be necessary to introduce into this general thesis, the starting-point of research is the working hypothesis that the order and outline of the second canonical gospel lay before the writers of Matthew and Luke, who employed it more or less freely as a framework into which they introduced materials from other sources.

(*a*) The oral hypothesis (Westcott, Godet, Wetzel, Veit, Wright) assumes that the gospel was officially drawn up by the primitive apostles or by one of them (Peter, Matthew), and that, by dint of repetition, the various cycles of narrative and discourse became stereotyped before passing into written form. "The common element of our three synoptic gospels was not a mere cento of sayings of Jesus, or of anecdotes of His actions, but an oral Gospel which gave a continuous history of His life, from His baptism by John to His crucifixion" (Salmon, *Human Element in the Gospels*, pp. 27 f.). It further requires a definite order of teachers or catechists who made it their business to teach this oral gospel. The necessity of a recourse to such assumptions is even less favourable than the impossibility, upon this theory, of giving any rational account of how the large sections in Mt. and Lk., which Mk. omits, ever came into existence and into the special places which they occupy.* No appeals to the Oriental memory, with its extraordinary power of retentiveness (cp. Margoliouth in *Christian Apolegetics*, 1903, 48 f.)† will suffice to explain the intricate variations and coincidences in the synoptic gospels, without involving artificial reconstructions of the early church's attitude to the sayings of Jesus. The detailed proof of this, with a thoroughgoing refutation of the oral hypothesis, is led by Zahn (*INT.* ii. 408 f.), Chavannes (*Revue de Théologie et Philosophie*, 1904, 138–160), and Stanton (*GHD.* ii. 17 f.), more briefly by Schmiedel (*EBi.* 1845–6) and Peake (*INT.* 104 f.).

---

* Even a resolute adherent of the theory, like Dr. Wright (*ET.* xxi. 211 f.), now admits that documents were in use from the first, for catechetical purposes. To call the documents 'temporary' does not conceal the collapse of the oral hypothesis.

† See also G. H. Putnam's *Authors and their Public in Ancient Times*³ (1894), pp. 106 f.

One objection to the oral hypothesis—viz. the gospel's preservation in Greek instead of Aramaic—is removed by the cognate hypothesis of a primitive Semitic gospel upon which the synoptists have all drawn (Resch, Abbott, Briggs); but, although the theory helps to account for one or two Greek variants by pointing out the possibility that they may go back to the omission, confusion, or transposition of consonants in the Hebrew original, as a complete explanation of the textual phenomena it fails. There is perhaps no antecedent improbability in Hebrew being still written between A.D. 40 and 50 in Palestine; the newly discovered fragments of Ecclesiasticus show that a Jew could write in fair Biblical Hebrew long after it had ceased to be spoken generally. But why should an evangelist of Jesus? If any Semitic gospel is to be postulated, Aramaic (so, *e.g.*, Lessing, Eichhorn) is much more likely than Hebrew to have been its language, and all the relevant facts of the case can be met by allowing for Aramaic sources behind the gospels and for the Aramaic background of their oral tradition. Misconception by Greek translators of a Semitic phrase is indeed a *uera causa* in the interpretation, *e.g.*, of some passages from Q, the common source of Mt. and Lk., which probably existed in different recensions. To quote a modern example, when we find in some translations of Don Quixote (part ii. ch. xxxiv.) *the Greek Commentator*, and in others *the Greek Commander*, it is obvious that these represent the wrong and the correct renderings of *El Commendador Griego*. The synoptic variant renderings of a common Semitic original, it must be allowed, usually give a good sense; it may not be the exact sense of the original, but it is intelligible, and generally it is consonant with the characteristic aims and traits of the gospel in which it occurs. The latter phenomenon, indeed, prevents us from supposing that the particular rendering was invariably accidental. On the other hand, this theory, when pushed to its full limits, reduces the inventive and independent element in the synoptic writers, by laying stress on the possibilities of error and alteration which were involved in the transition from a Hebrew original to various Greek translations. The synoptic variations are referred to different conceptions of Hebrew words and phrases rather than to the editorial freedom of writers, who omitted, added, and altered details in a source before them, for the sake of producing a special impression of Jesus as the Son of God or the fulfiller of ancient prophecy. "We do not often find very early apocryphal evangelists, and never the canonical ones, deliberately inventing new traditions. It is generally possible to detect, even now, some basis of fact or ancient tradition for what appears at first sight to be a mere fiction; and it is a reasonable inference that if we had before us all the 'narratives' of the 'many' authors mentioned by Luke, and all the written interpretations of Matthew's Logia handed down by those who, as Papias says, 'interpreted them each to the best of his ability,' we should find the paucity of invention almost equal to the magnitude of accretion" (*Diat.* 552). This is much too strongly put. It is to press matters too far if we undervalue the inventiveness of the primitive tradition, and miss the varied motives which led to the production of edifying apologues within the evangelic tradition. We have no business to assume that a writer, who had (say) Mark or some other primitive written source before him, would not feel comparatively free to diverge from its exact terminology, to tell a story in his own way, or to reproduce a saying in the light of his own religious prepossessions. Furthermore, the 'telegram'* theory—that the primitive gospel was written in an elliptic, condensed style, whose ambiguities and brevity explain the later gospels—fails often to render the primitive source intelligible. "The result of eliminating all words which are not common to all the evangelists is often to make the narrative unintelligible without the help of one of the existing Gospels to throw light on it" (Salmon, *The Human Element in the Gospels*, p. 15).

(*b*) The latter theory is not incompatible with the recognition of Mark as prior to the other two synoptists; as a matter of fact, one of the most searching and minute statements of the evidence for Mark's priority is in Dr. Abbott's *Diat.* 314–330 (with table, 542–544, of corrections made by Mt. and Lk. on Greek text of Mk.—the latter being regarded as a Greek version, 'with a good many errors, conflations, and additions,' of the Hebrew Ur-Evangelium). Even Pfleiderer (*Urc.* ii. 284 f. 392 f.), who adheres to a primitive Aramaic gospel-source, admits that it was first used by Mark among many others (Lk 1^1), then by Luke who also used Mk.; as Mk. and Lk. represented the Gentile Christian church, while the original gospel continued to be used independently (with legendary expansions) by the Palestinian and Syrian churches,† Mt. was written to fuse together both the Gentile and Jewish Christian traditions. One of the weakest points in this theory is the necessity of supposing that all the discourse and narrative material common to Lk. and Mt. lay originally in Mark's basis, the Aramaic gospel, from which it was derived by these writers through the medium of a Greek translation. A recent modification of this view,‡ by Scott-Moncrieff, similarly postulates a Foundation-document used by all three evangelists, but assumes it must have been written by Mark; Mt. and Lk. used not Mk. but this earlier draft (practically = an Ur-Marcus); Mk. 'in the more literary atmosphere' of Rome revised his original MS (based on Petrine reminiscences) and published it for the benefit of the Roman church.

It is the extravagant claims occasionally made on behalf of Mk. as a Petrine gospel and as free from secondary elements, which have led to a double reaction not only against the Petrine tradition (see below under 'Mark') but against Mark's priority to Matthew (so especially Hilgenfeld, Badham, Belser, and Merx, after Hug, Keim, and many others). The latter theory is inadequate, even with the ingenious modifications proposed by Zahn (*INT.* §§ 54–56), who, following the lead of Grotius and Michaelis, places the original (Hebrew) Matthew prior to Mark, and the canonical Greek Matthew

* Cp. Abbott and Rushbrooke, *The Common Tradition of the Synoptic Gospels* (1884), p. xi: "It is possible that for some time the Evangelistic records were handed down not in writing, but by means of oral tradition, like the Mishna of the Jews."

† Hence the origin of the apocryphal gospels, especially the gospel *καθ' Ἑβραίους*, which was a collateral branch from the parent stem of the original Aramaic gospel.

‡ B. Bonkamp (*Zur Evangelien-Frage*, 1909, 53 f.), on the other hand, agrees with those who make Mk. a compilation, and Mt. and Lk. dependent on the Aramaic Ur-evangelium.

(as a translation of the Ur-Matthæus) subsequent to Mark; Mark, in short, used the Hebrew Matthew and was in turn used by the Greek Matthew.

The documentary hypothesis (cp. *HNT.* 615 f.) goes back not only to the habits of Oriental historiography, which permitted a writer to incorporate a source *literatim* or to alter it for his special purpose, instead of rewriting it, but to ancient praxis in general. "Critical investigation into the sources of the ancient historians has shown beyond a question that, when they were dealing with times not within their own memory, they handled their authorities according to methods very different from those pursued in modern times. Not only materials, but the form in which these materials were worked up, were taken from predecessors usually without acknowledgment, and clearly without fear of any charge of plagiarism" (Hardy, *Plutarch's Galba and Otho*, 1890, p. xliv). This was all the more feasible in the case of a book like Mark, which was not written with any literary object. It was the common property of Christians, and neither Matthew nor Luke had any scruple in adapting it at a later period.* In the abstruse problem of the synoptic embryology, the Ur-Marcus and Q represent the work of artisans, who compiled and wrote the raw materials, which the artists, *i.e.* the authors of the canonical gospels, afterwards worked up into shape.†

The documentary hypothesis is further corroborated by the methods of Tatian in compiling his Diatessaron during the last quarter of the second century. An examination ‡ of the structure of this harmony, which was based on the four

* The fusion of Mk. with Q and other sources is shown by the presence of the doublets (cp. *HS.* 80–107). These do not invariably denote different sources (cp. Badham's *Formation of Gospels*[2], 12 f.); still in the main they point, not to different occasions on which Jesus uttered the same kind of word, but to variant traditions of the same saying or deed.

† A very suggestive analogy to the processes of idealisation, treatment of the miraculous, and influence of later church tendencies upon the tradition, has been outlined by Gardner (*Explor. Evangelica*, 174 f.) and R. B. Drummond (*Papers of Society of Historical Theology*, Oxford, 1907, 37 f.) in the Franciscan literature.

‡ See A. A. Hobson's scholarly essay, *The Diatessaron of Tatian and the Synoptic Problem* (Chicago. 1904), which carefully investigates the evidence afforded by Tatian's methods for the documentary theory of the synoptic gospels and their origin. The relation of such methods to the documentary analysis of the Pentateuch is discussed by G. F. Moore in *JBL.* ix. 201–215, and Lofthouse (*ET.* xiii. 565 f.).

canonical gospels, reveals the practice not only of freely altering, for purposes of edification and greater clearness as well as for the sake of literary effect, the order of words, sentences, and entire paragraphs, but also of arranging and fusing materials drawn from different sections in order to present a continuous and full account. All this is consonant with a certain scrupulous fidelity on the part of Tatian. His work shows, *e.g.*, a comparative absence of rewritten or omitted paragraphs. The bearing of his methods of composition on those of the synoptic evangelists lies in the twofold direction of showing (*a*) how earlier Christian sources could be dealt with in a fairly free fashion by later writers, without any lack of reverence; and (*b*) how alterations by a later author do not require in all cases a special tendency, but merely literary habits, in order to account for their origin and extent. The former consideration is important. If Tatian, writing after the idea of the canon had taken shape, could compose a Diatessaron with some freedom from the four gospels, it is highly probable that the writers of these gospels, prior to the formation of the canon, would exercise not less liberty in their treatment of available sources, "which they nevertheless regarded as historically trustworthy, and whose historical testimony they endeavoured substantially to preserve" (Hobson, p. 80). The second (*b*) inference supports what has been already said upon the need of eschewing an ultra-documentary bias in the study of the synoptic problem. One of the obstacles raised by the documentary hypothesis has been the inadequate place assigned by many of its upholders to the place and function of oral tradition as an element in the process; and it will help to render that hypothesis more tenable and attractive, if it is shown to include such a reason for variation as literary habit or individual idiosyncrasy. In a semi-literary work like one of the early Christian gospels, it is artificial to imagine that the author had some conscious ulterior purpose in every change he made. Although tendencies may be visible over the broad surface of his work, and although the general purpose of his composition may be plain, this does not exclude a certain freedom of literary choice, an artlessness, and the play of individual fancy and taste. No theory which fails to allow for such an element is true to the facts of the case. On the principles alike of literary criticism and of common sense, this consideration vindicates itself as a reasonable criterion in the examination and explanation of the synoptic variations, and it is amply borne out by a consideration of the phenomena presented by the Diatessaron. The latter shows a series of changes which are not due to any rigid or specific purpose. It reflects, as the synoptic variations in Matthew and Luke must in all fairness be held to reflect, a much wider variety of motives underneath such alterations than is yielded by any theory which would determine a writer's movements simply by some earlier sources and some controlling tendency of his own mind or circle. Consequently, we may argue, the failure to account for every single variation in the synoptic gospels does not discredit the documentary hypothesis, except when the latter is stated in some ultra-academic form.

The earliest traditions extant upon the origin of the gospels, *i.e.* the fragmentary remarks of John the presbyter quoted from Papias by Eusebius, show that no stereotyped official gospel was known to the memory of the sub-apostolic age. The first shapes which loom out in the mist are two documents roughly corresponding to the gospels of Mark and Matthew. What is their nature, and what is their relation to the documentary hypothesis?

§ 2. *The Papias-traditions.*—The earliest clue furnished by tradition is the evidence of Papias, bishop of Hierapolis in Phrygia during the first half of the second century. The two quotations from his "Expositions of the Lord's Λόγια," in five συγγράμματα (Eus. *H. E.* iii. 39. 15–17), are very brief, and we have no clue to their context. Even the date of this Exposition is uncertain. As Papias was an ἀρχαῖος ἀνήρ to Irenæus, and as, on the other hand, he looked back to his connection with the oral tradition of the presbyters as an old episode when he composed his book, the date of that volume cannot be put much earlier than *c.* A.D. 120. If the De Boor fragment (*TU.* v. 2. p. 170), which makes him mention people who, after being raised from the dead by Jesus, lived till the age of Hadrian, is really a quotation, the date would have to be carried down at least another decade; but it is not a quotation,* and the *terminus ad quem* for this writing's composition is not later than *c.* A.D. 160. It may be dated in 140(5)–160

* Philip Sidetes, who preserves the quotation, was excerpting from Eusebius at this point, and the likelihood is that he made a mistake in attributing to Papias a similar remark of Quadratus which the historian happens to narrate (*H. E.* iv. 3. 2).

(Harnack), 140–150 (Westcott), 130–140 (Lightfoot), or *c.* 125 (Zahn). As he got his information from John the presbyter, when he was gathering materials for the book, the date of the latter authority is carried back to the opening of the second century.

For discussions of Papias, his date, authorities, and writings, cp. especially Zahn (*SK.*, 1866, 649–696, 1867, 539–542, *Acta Joannis*, pp. cliv-clxxii, *GK.* i. 2. 849 f., ii. 2. 780 f.); Weiffenbach, *Die Papiasfragmente* (1878); Lipsius (*JPT.*, 1885, 174 f.); Holtzmann (*ZWT.*, 1880, 64–77); Hilgenfeld (*ZWT.*, 1875, 231–270, 1886, 257–291); with *SR.* (pp. 277 f.) and Lightfoot's invaluable articles (*Cont. Review*, 1867, 1875); Salmon (*DCB.* iv. 185–190); Westcott (*Canon of NT.*[6] pp. 69 f.); Link (*SK.*, 1896, 435 f.); Harnack (*ACL.* ii. 1. pp. 335 f., 356 f.); Abbott (*EBi.* ii. 1809 f.); Goetz on "Papias u. seine Quellen," in *Sitzungsberichte d. philos.-histor. Klasse d. Königl. bayr. Akademie d. Wiss.* (1903) 267–320; Schwartz (*Ueber den Tod der Söhne Zebedaei*, Berlin, 1904, pp. 18 f.), and Ehrhard (*ACL.* 112 f.).

To the bearing of Papias upon the problem of the apostle John's residence in Asia Minor and the origin of the Fourth gospel, it will be necessary to return later on. Meantime, we must look at his evidence upon the synoptic gospels of Mark and Matthew, or, at any rate, upon what Papias believed to be the origin of these canonical scriptures.

καὶ τοῦθ' ὁ πρεσβύτερος ἔλεγεν:

Μάρκος μὲν ἑρμηνευτὴς Πέτρου γενόμενος, ὅσα ἐμνημόνευσεν, ἀκριβῶς ἔγραψεν, οὐ μέντοι τάξει, τὰ ὑπὸ τοῦ Χριστοῦ ἢ λεχθέντα ἢ πραχθέντα. οὔτε γὰρ ἤκουσεν τοῦ Κυρίου, οὔτε παρηκολούθησεν αὐτῷ, ὕστερον δέ, ὡς ἔφην, Πέτρῳ· ὃς πρὸς τὰς χρείας ἐποιεῖτο τὰς διδασκαλίας, ἀλλ' οὐχ ὥσπερ σύνταξιν τῶν κυριακῶν ποιούμενος λόγιων, ὥστε οὐδὲν ἥμαρτεν Μάρκος, οὕτως ἔνια γράψας ὡς ἀπεμνημόνευσεν. ἑνὸς γὰρ ἐποιήσατο πρόνοιαν,

This also the presbyter said:

'Mark, who was[*] Peter's interpreter,[†] wrote down accurately, though not in order,[‡] all that he recollected of what Christ had said or done.[§] For he was not a hearer of the Lord, nor a follower of his; he followed Peter, as I have said, at a later date,[‖] and Peter adapted his instructions to practical needs, without any attempt to give the Lord's words systematically. So that Mark was not wrong in writing down some

---

* "had been" would give the sense more accurately.

† = מְתוּרְגְּמָן (cp. Schlatter in *BFT.*, 1899, iii. pp. 51 f.)?

‡ On this phrase, see below.

§ The quotation from the presbyter may end here, the rest (*as I have said*) being Papias' reproduction of the primitive tradition.

‖ Not, after having followed Paul, but after the lifetime of Jesus.

τοῦ μηδὲν ὧν ἤκουσεν παραλιπεῖν ἢ ψεύσασθαί τι ἐν αὐτοῖς.

Ταῦτα μὲν οὖν ἱστόρηται τῷ Παπίᾳ περὶ τοῦ Μάρκου. περὶ δὲ τοῦ Ματθαίου ταῦτ' εἴρηται· Ματθαῖος μὲν οὖν Ἑβραΐδι διαλέκτῳ τὰ λόγια συνεγράψατο,* ἡρμήνευσεν δ' αὐτὰ ὡς ἦν δυνατὸς ἕκαστος.

things in this way from memory, for his one concern was neither to omit nor to falsify anything he had heard.'

Such is Papias' account of Mark; this is what he says about Matthew: 'So then Matthew composed the Logia in the Hebrew language, and every one interpreted them as he was able.'

As these traditions are preserved by Papias from the presbyter John, and as they go back not only to a period previous to the final composition of the *Exposition*, but apparently to the time when Papias was merely collecting oral testimony, the problem of the date of the book from which they are now cited becomes comparatively insignificant. These explanations of Mark and Matthew must have been in circulation by the end of the first century. The beginning of the second century is the latest period at which we can assume they came to Papias. Furthermore, they are not inventions of his own. Their authority is the presbyter John, who was in close contact with the cycles of primitive apostolic tradition, and there is no reason to suppose that these two particular traditions suffered accretion or corruption in passing through the channel of Papias' memory. Doubtless they were exposed to the atmosphere of sub-apostolic desire to connect all canonical writings, directly or indirectly, with some apostolic authority, but the atmosphere did not create them. Their motive is unambiguous. By the time that Papias wrote, if not much earlier, difficulties were evidently felt about the differences in the four gospels, which implies that they had begun to be read together or, at any rate, laid side by side. The divergence, *e.g.*, between Mark's *τάξις* and that of the Fourth gospel seems to have occasioned surprise. Papias writes in an explanatory tone. He quotes the presbyter in order to defend Mark against a certain depreciation, and his defence presupposes that the authority of the Fourth gospel was so strong in certain local circles that it served as a standard for estimating the style and shape of earlier.

A further point urged by Papias in these quotations from the presbyter is the difference of language.† Both the Petrine oral

* *συνετάξατο*, the variant reading (preferred by Schwartz), does not alter the sense materially, though *συνεγράψατο* brings out more clearly the fact that it was a writing.

† There is also an implicit side-reference to the gnostic circle of Basilides,

teaching and the Matthæan book of the Logia were in Aramaic, but while Mark's gospel fixed the former in Greek shape, the latter was for some time circulated without any such definitive editing. It is implied that this phase of things was past by the time not only of Papias but of his informant, and that the need of such independent off-hand translations no longer existed. Why, we can only conjecture, for no further information from Papias is extant. But the obvious answer is that some definitive recension of the Matthæan Logia had superseded the numerous earlier translations.

The translating or interpreting to which Papias alludes cannot be explained (so Schlatter and Salmon, *Human Element in the Gospels*, 27 f.) as part of the worship of the churches. In the Jewish synagogues the lesson from the Hebrew scriptures, read by the rabbi, was followed by the interpretation or rendering of it into the popular tongue; but the latter task fell to a 'meturgeman,' or interpreter. Even though the rabbi knew both languages, he confined himself to one, *i.e.* to the older and more sacred speech. But the use of the Matthæan Logia to which Papias alludes was not restricted to Christian worship (cp. *GHD.* i. 55 f.). He is thinking, as the context shows, about writings, and the presbyter's words denote also independent, probably paraphrastic versions of the Logia made for catechetical and missionary purposes. It is improbable, therefore, although plausible, to hold that *ἑρμηνευτής* as applied to Mark and *ἡρμήνευσεν* as applied to the early Christian teachers or missionaries who used the Matthæan writing, denote the same sort of work, except that in the one case the translating or interpreting followed the oral Aramaic teaching of Peter, with its reminiscences of the Lord's words and deeds, while in the other the basis of the interpretation lay in Matthew's written Aramaic record. When the informant of Papias reports that "every one translated (or interpreted) the Logia as best he could," the reference must include various Greek versions (Resch, *Agrapha*, pp. 54 f.); it cannot mean simply the worship and work of the early Christian mission, where at first any one who used the Matthæan collection had to give a Greek equivalent upon his own responsibility and from his own resources.

Two minor points of some importance remain. (*a*) One is the meaning of *οὐ μέντοι τάξει*. In the light of the well-known passage from Lucian (*de hist. conscrib.* 16 f.), *τάξις* seems here to imply not order or consecutiveness in the modern sense of the term, so much as the artistic arrangement and effective presentation of the materials. The latter, in their unadorned and artless sequence, are *ἀπομνήματα*. Set *ἐν τάξει* they are orderly, harmonious. The criticism passed by Papias on Mark refers to the style, then, rather

---

who claimed that the *διδάσκαλος* of the latter was Glaukias, the interpreter of Peter (Clem. *Strom.* 7. 106). Papias points out that the true Petrine tradition was conveyed by Mark, and that, instead of being a secret kabbala, it was published in a gospel (cp. Schwartz, 11, 20 f.).

than to the chronological sequence.* What Mark wrote down was the ἀπομνημονεύματα or recollections of Peter, which were simply delivered πρὸς τὰς χρείας, and the literary result was not a ἱστορία. It had not τάξις enough for that. A simple record, as exact and complete as possible, was what came from Mark's pen, just such notes as might be described under Justin's title of apostolic ἀπομνημονεύματα. When τάξις is translated 'order,' therefore, the reference is to 'orderliness' rather than to historical sequence. "Ce que l'on entend par 'ordre' n'est pas la chronologie . . c'est la bonne distribution des matières" (Loisy, i. 26). (*b*) Does the phrase τὰ λόγια mean the works and words of Jesus, a practical equivalent for τὸ εὐαγγέλιον? Or does it mean primarily utterances? The former view has been strongly supported,† particularly by those who desired to identify these Aramaic logia as closely as possible with the contents of the canonical Greek Matthew, but the context, together with the historical probabilities, indicates that the phrase here means *effata*, utterances or discourses or commands of the Lord. These sayings, of course, must have included often a piece of narrative. Many of the Lord's most striking words were associated with some event or incident. When they were plucked from the soil of the ἄγραφος μνήμη in the primitive tradition, they would come up with some historical details of time and place clinging to them, like earth to the roots of a plant. The frequent exchange of question and answer in the extant conversations of Jesus necessitates some context of circumstances,‡ and Matthew's gospel more than once appears to record an incident for the purpose of a saying which it sustained. Furthermore, in his own book, the Ἐξήγησις λογίων κυριακῶν, we know that Papias included some stories and narratives of the life of Jesus, for the purposes of his exposition. On the other hand, the differentiation of τὰ λόγια τοῦ Κυρίου and τὸ μαρτύριον τοῦ σταυροῦ in Polyk. *Phil.* 7, tells against the identification of Matthew's τὰ λόγια in Papias with any work similar to Mark or even Matthew. Papias is certainly lax in his use of the term, for, in the Marcan notice, he seems to describe indifferently the substance of Mark as τὰ ὑπὸ τοῦ Χριστοῦ ἢ λεχθέντα ἢ πραχθέντα and as κυριακοὶ λόγοι or κυριακὰ λόγια. But the analogy of the OT prophets, where *the words of Jeremiah*, *Hosea*, etc., include narrative as well as sayings and speeches, bears out the view that while the Matthæan Logia of Papias were not a gospel-narrative, they were not a mere collection of sayings.

A fair exegesis of the Papias-traditions forbids us then to infer that any sharp distinction was drawn between the contents of the Marcan gospel and the writing of Matthew. The latter could not have been confined to sayings, any more than could the former, or any similar narrative of Jesus, to incidents and deeds. The distinction intended by Papias (if not by his informant) was drawn elsewhere. Mark's gospel was evidently

* So, after Norden, Corssen (*GGA.*, 1899, pp. 317 f.).

† From Lücke, Baur, and Keim, to Hilgenfeld, Zahn, and Belser.

‡ Thus Eusebius (*H. E.* iii. 245) observes that Matthew and John alone have left us τῶν τοῦ κυρίου διατριβῶν ὑπομνήματα.

felt by many to be incomplete, as compared with Matthew, besides being disorderly, as compared with John. The presbyter explains the reason of the former defect. The exigencies of its composition prevented Mark's gospel from giving a συντάξις of the Lord's utterances; Mark was not able to provide this. But it was furnished by Matthew, a hearer and follower of the Lord. He composed or compiled τὰ λόγια, and his account, it is implied, was adequate, so far as contents went. This distinction, together with that of the language, may be regarded as uppermost in the Papias-traditions.

While the harvest from Papias is thus scanty, it is not unimportant. We learn that there had been an Aramaic gospel-writing by Matthew, which Papias at any rate connected somehow with the canonical Matthew. How far he believed the latter to represent a version of it, we have no information. On Mark, again, the testimony is ampler. It is uncertain what was, or what Papias believed to be, the relation between the canonical gospel of Mark and this Petrine record of Mark, but the latter was not composed, apparently, until Mark had ceased to be Peter's ἑρμηνευτής, whether owing to some change of circumstances or to Peter's death. The latter view is that of Irenæus (*ap.* Euseb. *H. E.* v. 8. 3), who puts the composition of Mark's gospel subsequent to the decease of Peter, but the mist which shrouds the later history of the apostle prevents us from checking the truth of this remark, and another tradition, vouched for in two different ways by Clement of Alexandria (*H. E.* ii. 15. 2, and vi. 14. 6), asserts that Mark wrote when Peter was still alive.* The unanimous tradition of the second and third centuries upon the connection of Mark, as the author of the gospel, with Peter (cp. Swete, pp. xviii f.), probably is little more than a prolonged echo of the Papias-tradition, combined with inferences, more or less fictitious, from 1 P 5^{13}. These later testimonies add little or nothing of independent historical value to the tradition which has just been discussed, and the latter must now be set side by side with the canonical gospel. It is only after an examination of Mark as we have it, that it is possible to ascertain how far the notice preserved by Papias is an adequate and trustworthy piece of criticism. And

* This is evidently the product of later reflection in the church, stimulated by a desire to claim spiritual authority and a Petrine guarantee for Mark's narrative (cp. Schwartz, pp. 18 f.).

the same holds true of Matthew. The results upon which the following sections converge may be outlined at this point, for the sake of convenience. The two writings mentioned by John the presbyter lie at the back of Mk. and Mt. respectively; they correspond to the Ur-Marcus and the Q source,* which the internal criticism of these gospels has succeeded in feeling if not in laying bare underneath the strata of the canonical texts. There are insuperable difficulties in the way either of rejecting † the Papias-tradition or of identifying the two writings of this fragment with the canonical Mark and Matthew, and the solution is to suppose that the former represents a later edition ‡ of the original Mark (which resembled a κήρυγμα Πέτρου), while the latter represents the work of a Jewish Christian writer, with catholic interests, who employed in his work not only Mk. but the Matthæan Logia. Luke's gospel, like Matthew's, draws upon (possibly a different text of) the Ur-Marcus and upon Q or the logia-source (probably in a different translation); but, unlike Matthew's, it embodies subsidiary sources, one of which at least ranked of such importance that the author more than once preferred it even to Mk. and Q.

§ 3. *Mark and the Ur-Marcus.*—The relation of Mark to Peter is described in the opening words of the Muratorian fragment on the Canon, *quibus tamen interfuit et ita posuit.* If *quibus* is taken to have been originally *aliquibus* (*i.e.* certain incidents or episodes in the life of Jesus), the author would mean that although Mark was not an eye-witness of the life of Jesus, still he was present at one or two occasions in it (*e.g.* Mk 14^{51}?). But *quibus* probably referred to a preceding *colloquiis Petri*, and the sense

* The common discourse-material is best explained as due to the use of some such source A similar literary problem arises in connection with Plutarch's and Tacitus' accounts of Galba. Here, too, the hypothesis of absolute independence is precluded by the close agreements, and the alternatives are to suppose that Plutarch used Tacitus, or to conjecture that both had access to some common authority such as the elder Pliny's *Histories* or *Cluvius Rufus.*

† On the ground that it might be no more than an inference from 1 P $5^{1.13}$, an ill-informed guess which Papias or his informant made (cp. *e.g.* Loofs, *Die Auferstehungsberichte*, pp. 22 f.).

‡ "Eine vermehrte Ausgabe, in welcher der überlieferte Text möglichst respektiert werden sollte" (Wendling, *Entstehung des Marcus-Evgliums*, p. 2). "Il y a eu un Prôto-Marc dont en résumé notre second évangile est comme une réédition quelque peu retouchée" (Réville, *Jésus de Nazareth*, i. 477).

of the incomplete conclusion to the sentence is that Mark set down what he had heard from Peter. This tallies with the earlier evidence of John the presbyter, as reported by Papias, whether it is a mere echo or an independent corroboration. Now the canonical Mark, after an analysis of its literary structure, shows distinct traces of editorial work upon a source (see below under 'Mark'); it is not the naive transcript or precipitate of oral tradition, but arranged upon a definite, chronological plan, with a definite aim. Upon the other hand, the materials which form its basis show a distinctly Palestinian and even Petrine colour. "Dass der älteste Evangelist nicht der erste Aufzeichner ist, sondern bereits Sammler und Redaktor; dass er nicht mehr bloss aus der freifliessenden mündlichen Ueberlieferung schöpft, sondern bereits festgeformte Massen gruppiert und mit seinem Missionarsgeist durchdringt, das ist ein Ergebnis, das nicht mehr verloren gehen kann" (J. Weiss, *TR.*, 1908, 133). It is a fair hypothesis, therefore, to identify not the canonical Mk. but the rougher notes of the Ur-Marcus with the source to which the Papias-tradition refers (so, *e.g.*, Schleiermacher, Renan, Scholten, S. Davidson, Wendt, von Soden).* The fact that the canonical gospel was based on this Marcan work was responsible for Mark's name being attached to it.

Several critics (so, *e.g.* Weisse, Schenkel, Réville) have argued that the Ur-Marcus must have been (*a*) larger than the present Mk., since Mt. and Lk. repeatedly agree in matter which Mk., telling the same story, omits. Unless, as is improbable, Lk. used Mt. or *vice versa*, or unless the coincidences be due to the harmonising tendencies of copyists, these common additions of Mt. and Lk., so far as they are not trivial, would seem to show that both had access to a form of Mk. fuller than the canonical. But other explanations of this phenomenon are not only possible but more probable, and the theory involves the great difficulty of supposing that Mk. deliberately omitted a good deal of available material. It is much more likely that the Ur-Marcus was (*b*) smaller than the present Mk. (so, *e.g.*, P. Ewald, Reuss, J. Weiss, von Soden, Wendling), especially when the Papias-tradition of

* The Ur-Marcus theory, with or without a reference to the Papias-tradition, has been held by Credner, Reuss, Köstlin, A. Réville, Schmiedel, J. Weiss, and Loisy. It is ably controverted in Burkitt's *Gospel History and Its Transmission* (1906), 40 f.

the former is accepted. As for the further question, whether Mt. and Lk. used the shorter Ur-Marcus or the canonical Mk. (in substantially its present form), the evidence tells strongly in favour of the latter view (so, *e.g.* Wernle, Wellhausen, Jülicher, Burkitt, Loisy). Their omissions can be partly accounted for by tendency, and in part they do not need to be accounted for at all. In several instances * it can be shown that they knew parts of Mk. which they omitted (cp. Badham's proof for Luke in *ET.* vii. 457–459).

This fact, that both Matthew and Luke † omit a certain amount of material in Mk. which, *ex hypothesi*, lay before them, opens up the two alternatives, viz. (*a*) that the omissions were deliberate, or (*b*) that such sections, though extant in our canonical Mk., were not added to Mk. until after its use by the later synoptists. On the latter hypothesis, the amount of matter in Mk. which is absent from Mt. and Lk. must have been added to Mk. after Mt. and Lk. had used it; or, at any rate, they must have employed a copy of the Marcan source different from that which formed the nucleus of the canonical Mk. In other words, where Mt. and Lk. agree in omitting a Marcan passage or, more generally, as against Mk., the latter is presumed not to have lain before them, unless adequate reason can be given for such omissions. But is a literary criterion of this kind absolutely valid? Surely, some obvious *caveats* at once occur to the mind. For one thing, it is an extremely delicate and hazardous task for a modern, Western mind to determine the precise motives which may have induced a later synoptic writer to omit or abbreviate a source which lay before him. Even although the omission of passages like Mk 4^{26-29} 7^{33-37} 8^{22-26} $11^{11.\,26}$ 12^{33-34} 13^{33-37} and $14^{51f.}$ may be difficult to explain, it would be hasty to conclude that such passages did not lie before Mt. and Luke. The desire to be as full as possible may be granted; it is natural to suppose that neither would wish to leave out anything of vital importance. But, after all, a writer must be allowed some freedom. It is not to be taken for granted that a later writer of the gospel story would incorporate whatever lay before him in an earlier source, even if these materials were consonant with his special purpose; such a canon of criticism, which is tacitly assumed in many quarters, requires to be seriously revised and qualified. Completeness would as a rule be an end and object with the writer of any gospel. His work was to circulate by itself; he could rarely if ever presuppose, in his audience, acquaintance with other evangelic writings which might supplement gaps in his own; indeed,

* One of the clearest is in Luke's change (17^{6}) of the logion preserved in Mt 17^{20b}. Luke has nothing corresponding to Mk $11^{12-15a.\,19-27a}$; but, as this reminiscence proves, he knew the incident of the cursing of the fig-tree.

† Furthermore, John occasionally sides in such circumstances with Mk., as he sides again (*Diat.* 1806 f.) with Mk. and Mt. against Luke's deviations or omissions (*Diat.* 1282 f., 1309 f., 1344, 1373, 1730 f.).

in the case of Luke, we have a historian whose aim was to supersede many inferior and defective records in circulation throughout the churches. But completeness of this kind is always relative to the writer's special aim, and even apart from the range of that aim his individual taste would be sure to operate—to say nothing of considerations of space and symmetry. Such implications tell against the view that Mt. and Lk. must have used a shorter form of Mark. They may also be held to disprove the view that Mark did not use Q, but this conclusion rests upon independent grounds (cp. § 5).

§ 4. *Matthew's gospel and Q* (=*Matthaean Logia*).—The style and contents of Matthew show that it is neither the translation of an Aramaic source nor composed by an apostle. For these and other reasons it is impossible to identify it with a translation of the Logia-source mentioned by Papias. But the large amount of discourse-material which Mt. has incorporated with Mk. permits the identification of this special source with the Matthæan Logia of Papias (so from Schleiermacher to McGiffert, Burton, Allen, Peake, and Stanton).* This explains, more satisfactorily than any other theory, the traditional authorship of the gospel. Matthew's gospel (εὐαγγέλιον κατὰ Ματθαῖον) was so called, not because it was the first to make use of the Matthæan source, but because it embodied this σύνταξις τῶν λόγιων with special thoroughness. The most notable feature in its composition was the use made of this source. Matthew was too obscure an apostle to be associated by later tradition with a gospel, unless there was good ground for it; and, as he cannot have written the canonical gospel, the natural inference is that he was responsible for the primary logia-source which characterised it.

This is more satisfactory than to identify the Logia of Matthew, to which Papias alludes, with a florilegium of messianic proof-texts made in Hebrew by Matthew the tax-gatherer (Hart, *Exp.*[7], July 1906, 78 f.; Burkitt, *Transmission*, 126 f.; K. Lake, *Review of Biol. and Phil.* iii. 483 f.). A collection of such *testimonia* would not be important enough either to justify the tradition or to lend Matthew's name to a gospel which employed them, apart altogether from the fact that a midrashic anecdote like Mt 2 [13-15] could hardly have formed part of a source emanating from an apostolic eye-witness, and that τὰ λόγια could not denote OT extracts *per se* (cp. Stanton, *GHD.* ii. 48).

On the other side, a comparison of Mt. and Lk. shows the common use of a discourse-source, Q. The problem is to

* Harnack (*BNT.* ii. 248 f.) only admits "a strong balance of probability that Q is the work of Matthew." "From the so-called charge to the apostles we can only conclude that behind the written record there stands the memory of an apostolic listener."

connect Q with the Matthæan Logia, and this may be solved by identifying the latter with the substantial nucleus of the former. For all practical purposes, they may be considered one and the same source. If so, this has an important bearing upon the determination of Q as reproduced in Mt. and in Lk. (*a*) The general opinion is that the latter's setting of the Logia is in many, perhaps in most, cases superior to Mt.'s. This may well be, from the historical point of view, but Lk.'s arrangement of them (*e.g.* of the Lord's Prayer) need not represent a close reproduction of them as they lay in Q. It is argued that Mt. is more likely to have massed the sayings together than Lk. to have broken them up, but, in view of Lk.'s dramatic (as distinguished from historic) framework, this argument is not convincing. It is a good working hypothesis that the grouping of the Logia in Q, as distinguished from their spirit (which Lk., for all his greater stylistic changes, has kept upon the whole more closely), is preserved substantially in Mt. Where Lk. differs from the latter in his arrangement of the Logia, and where that arrangement is historically valid (which is not the case, *e.g.*, with $13^{34\text{-}35}$), is due to the fact that he found the basis for his re-setting in some other source,* or possibly now and then in oral tradition. Elsewhere, the Lucan *mise en scène* is due to the writer's imagination. (*b*) The Q source must also have been more Jewish Christian in character than Lk.'s gospel would suggest. Mt. retained, *e.g.*, the 'particularistic' logia for archaic reasons; he was more conservative in the use of his source than Luke. Where the latter either omitted or modified, Mt. was content to preserve, adding broader logia of his own.

The verbal coincidences of Mt. and Lk. do not necessarily imply that they used the same Greek version of the Matthæan Logia. Translations of such sayings would inevitably have a great deal in common; the scope for variations is necessarily restricted; and the literary identities of Mt. and Lk. in their common parts are explicable without either the hypothesis that the latter used the former, or even that both had the same Greek recension of Q before them. Occasional variations of rendering (cp. Wellhausen, *Einl.* 36 f.)† corroborate the view that they used different versions of the original Aramaic; *e.g.* Mt $5^{11\text{-}12}$ = Lk $6^{22\text{-}23}$ (where, in the latter verse, the Matthæan τοὺς πρὸ ὑμῶν

* This implies that some of Q's logia were in circulation in other forms—a view which is decidedly to be upheld (cp. pp. 205 f.).

† It does not meet the full data of these passages to argue (Harnack, Loisy: *RHR.*, 1907, 441 f.) that the changes are due to the free development of the writer's thought as exhibited in the context.

and the Lucan *οἱ πατέρες αὐτῶν* go back to the Aramaic variants *daq' damaikôn* and *daq' damaihôn*), Mt 5^{48} = Lk 6^{36} (where *τέλειοι* and *οἰκτίρμονες* are variants of שְׁלֵם), Mt 23^{23} = Lk 11^{42} (cp. Nestle, *ET.* xv. 528; *ZNW.*, 1906, 260–261), and Mt 23^{26} = Lk 11^{41} (where Matthew's *καθάρισον* and Luke's *δότε ἐλεημοσύνην* go back to the Aramaic *dakkau* and *zakkau*). Sometimes both versions reproduce the same error (*e.g.* *πολλῶν* for *πολλῷ* in Mt 10^{31} = Lk 12^{7}, cp. Wellhausen's note); but this is the exception (cp. above, p. 181).

At the same time, this recognition of a specifically Matthæan character in Q does not involve the abandonment (so, *e.g.*, Burton, Allen) of the latter as a common source for Mt. and Lk. Lk. possibly knew it in a special recension; * but even this hypothesis is not necessary in order to explain the differences of setting and spirit in the corresponding Lucan Logia. The first clue for the reconstruction of Q lies in the common materials of Mt. and Lk. But this implies that the latter, *e.g.*, could only have access to the Q-sayings in their Q-form, that both writers reproduced Q almost entirely, and that practically † nothing which is only preserved in one or the other originally belonged to Q. None of these assumptions can be granted. Furthermore, the analogy of Mk. is a warning against over-precise reconstructions of this common source (cp. Robinson's *Study of Gospels*, 91 f., and Burkitt in *JTS.*, 1907, 454 f.). If Mk. had to be picked out of Mt. and Lk., on the same principles as Q, many of its most striking characteristics would be awanting, *e.g.* 12^{41-44}. "In comparison with the real Mk. it would be a headless, armless torso." These considerations do not invalidate the attempt to fix approximately the outlines and general characteristics of Q,—especially when we accept the additional clue to its origin furnished by the Papias-tradition,—but they are a check upon detailed analyses which profess to regain the exact stylistic and religious characteristics of a source which neither writer may have preserved in its entirety and which both have worked over.

If the formula (*καὶ ἐγένετο ὅτε ἐτέλεσεν ὁ Ἰησοῦς κτλ.*), which recurs five times in Mt. (7^{28} 11^{1} 13^{53} 19^{1} 26^{1}), was taken over

* As distinct from a special translation. It is not probable that Mt.'s Jewish Christian idiosyncrasies were due to a similar recension of Q, which lay before him, though there is every likelihood that a work like Q would pass through stages of accretion (cp. Pfleiderer, *PM.*, 1907, 117–139, and Schott's analysis of Mt 10, in *ZNW.*, 1906, 140–150).

† Thus Harnack (*BNT.* ii. 26 f., 185) only admits the parable of the mustard-seed, which occurs in Mk. (4^{30-32})

from Q, as is inherently likely (cp. *HS.* 165), this is a fresh proof that the latter source—so far as form goes—approximated to the successive masses of logia preserved in Mt., and also that they were connected by fragments of narrative. The fivefold division was not uncommon in Jewish and early Christian literature, and Q may have been compiled, like the exposition of Papias (Eus. *H. E.* iii. 39), in five parts. The following list of passages may be taken to represent approximately the Q-source, as it can be felt vibrating in Matthew:

3^{7-12} (baptism of John, etc.; strictly speaking, introductory sayings about Jesus),* 4^{3-11} (temptation), $5^{3-12.\ 13-17.\ 20-24.\ 25-30.\ 31-48}$ $6^{1f.}$ $7^{1-12.\ 15-23.\ 24-27}$ (sermon), 8^{5-13} (centurion of Kapharnaum), 8^{19-22} 9^{13a} $10^{5f.\ 17-38\ (42)}$ $11^{2-19.\ 20-30}$ $12^{5-8.\ 11-13.\ 25-45}$ $13^{14-15.\ 16-17.\ 24-29.\ 33-35.\ 36-43.\ 44-52}$ (group of parables), $15^{12-14.\ 23-24}$ $16^{17-19\ (?)}$ $17^{19-20.\ (24-27\ ?)}$ $18^{3-5.\ 10.\ 12-14.\ 15-20.\ 23-35}$ $19^{6-12.\ 28}$ 20^{1-16} $21^{14-17.\ 31b.-32.\ 28-31a}$ $22^{1-10.\ 11-14}$ 23^{1-39} (seven woes), $24^{(9).\ 10-12\ 26-27.\ 37-41.\ 42-44.\ 45-51}$ $25^{1-30.\ (31-46\ ?)}$ 26^{52-54}.

The passages in black type represent for the most part the material which is also used by Luke more or less closely (22 and 25 containing scattered parallels); passages like 4^{13-16} and 12^{16-21} came from a messianic florilegium. We have hardly any criteria for determining how far any pieces of Luke's *Sondergut* should be added to this list, owing to the greater variety of sources upon which he drew. But, even as it stands, this outline of the Matthæan Logia is both coherent and distinctive. It is not a heterogeneous mass of logia, but a collection moulded by catechetical and homiletical processes, with sayings on the Kingdom grouped together for the purposes of edification and apologetic, strongly marked by eschatological traits, and shaped, more than once, by polemical interests. The outstanding features are the grouping of the sayings (which is not simply the work of Mt.'s editor) and the emphatically Jewish Christian cast of some sections.

The variety and the consensus of opinion upon the contents of Q will be evident from a glance, first of all, at eight reconstructions† which aim at reproducing the outline as well as the contents of the source.

(*a*) Albert Réville (*Jésus de Nazareth*, i. pp. 299, 469–470) groups the

---

* Their presence in Q is due either to the connection of the baptism with the temptation, or to the need of explaining subsequent references to John.

† In the following analyses, the verbal minutiæ have been generally omitted, for the sake of space and clearness.

material in a sevenfold arrangement: * (i.) the new law Mt 5^{3}–7^{27}=Lk $6^{20f.}$ 11^{33}, 8^{16} 14^{34} 16^{17}, 12^{58-59} 16^{18}, 6^{29-36} 11^{2-4}, 12^{33-34} 11^{34-36}, 12^{22-31} 16^{13}, $6^{37. 41f.}$ 11^{9-13}, 6^{31} 13^{24-27}, 6^{47-49}; (ii.) apostolic instructions, Mt 9^{37-38} $10^{5-16. 23-42}$=Lk $10^{2. 4-12. 3}$, 6^{40} 8^{17} 12^{2-9}, 12^{51-53} 14^{26-27}, 17^{33} 10^{16}; (iii.) in defence of the kingdom, Mt $11^{7b-19. 21-24. 25b-30}$ $12^{22-26. 28-30. 37. 39. 41-45}$=Lk 7^{24-28}, 16^{16} 7^{31-35}, $10^{13-15. 21-22}$, 12^{10} 6^{43-45}, $11^{29-32. 24-26}$; (iv.) parables of the kingdom, Mt 13^{24-52}=Lk $13^{19. 21}$; (v.) members of the kingdom. Mt 18^{2b-35} 20^{1-16}, 21^{23-27} $22^{1-6. 8-14}$=Lk 17^{1-2} 15^{4-7}, 17^{3-4} 14^{16-24}; (vi.) woes, Mt 23^{2-39}=Lk $11^{46. 52. 42. 39. 44. 49-51}$, 13^{34-35}; (vii.) the coming of the kingdom, Mt $24^{11-12. 26-28. 37-51}$, 25=Lk $17^{23. 37. 26-30}$, 12^{35-40}, 19^{12-27}. (*b*) Barnes (see below under 'Matthew') further proposes to find in this source the actual document mentioned by Papias, "a complete treatise on the teaching of Christ concerning the new kingdom . . . a manual of the new law for the use of the church at large," but confines his investigations to the non-Marcan materials of Mt., and discovers the substance of the Lord's teaching in five books: viz. (i.) the new law (Mt 5–7), (ii.) the rulers of the new kingdom (Mt 10), (iii.) parables of the new kingdom (Mt 13. 22), (iv.) relations between members of the kingdom (Mt 18), and (v.) the coming of the king (Mt 24–25). (*c*) Similarly Burton † finds the Matthæan Logia-source (not used by Lk.) in Mt 3^{14-15} $5^{4. 7-10. 13a. 14. 16-17. 19-24. 27-28. 31. 33-39a. 41-43}$ $6^{1-7. 10b. 13b. 15-18. 34}$ $7^{6. 12b. 15-22}$ 9^{13a} $10^{5. 6. 8b. 23. 25b. 36. 41}$ 11^{28-30} $12^{5-7. 11-12a. 34}$ $13^{14. 15. 24-30. 35-53}$ $15^{12-14. 23-24}$ 16^{17-19} 17^{24-27} $18^{4. 10. 14. 16-20. 23-34}$ $19^{10-12. 28}$ 20^{1-15} $21^{14-16. 28-32. 43}$ 22^{1-14} $23^{2. 3. 5. 7b-10. 15-22. 24. 28. 32}$ $24^{10-12. 30a}$ $25^{1-11a. 13. 14-46}$ 26^{52-53}. (*d*) Wernle (*Synopt. Frage*, pp. 224 f.) submits a detailed outline: (*a*) historical introduction Mt 3^{7-12}=Lk $3^{7-9. 16f.}$, Mt 4^{3-10}=Lk 4^{3-12}; (*b*) rules for Christians and missionaries, Mt 5^{3-48} 7^{1-6} 12^{12-27}=Lk 6^{20-49} 11^{33} 12^{58-59} 16^{17}, Mt 8^{5-13}=Lk 7^{2-10} 13^{28-30}, Mt 8^{19-22} 9^{37-38} $10^{5-16. 23-25. 40-42}$ 11^{20-27} 13^{16-17}= Lk 9^{57-62} $10^{1-16. 21-24}$; (*c*) sayings of a more polemical nature, Mt 11^{2-19}= Lk 7^{18-35} 16^{16}, Mt 12^{22-37}=Lk 11^{14-23} 12^{10}, Mt 12^{38-45}=Lk $11^{29-32. 24-26}$, Mt 23^{1-39}=Lk 11^{39-52} 13^{34-35}; and (*d*) instructions for the Christian life, especially in view of the second advent, Mt 6^{9-13} 7^{7-11}=Lk $11^{2-4. 9-13}$, Mt 6^{19-34} =Lk 12^{22-34} 11^{34-36} 16^{13}, Mt $13^{31-33. 44-46}$=Lk 13^{18-21}, Mt 10^{26-39}=Lk $12^{2-12. 51-53}$ 14^{26-27}, Mt $18^{7. 12-22}$=Lk 15^{3-10} 17^{1-4}, Mt 22^{1-14}=Lk 14^{16-24}, Mt $24^{26-28. 37-51}$=Lk 17^{23-37} 12^{39-46}, Mt 25^{14-30}=Lk 19^{12-27}. (*e*) Von Soden, considering the Lucan tradition the more original ‡ of the two, postulates a systematic collection of sayings grouped as follows:—(*a*) the appearance and reception of Jesus, including (i.) words on right mutual conduct (Lk 6^{20}–7^{1}, cp. Mt 5–7), (ii.) the Gentile centurion (7^{2-10}=Mt 8^{5-13}), and (iii.) the Jewish baptist (7^{18-35}=Mt 11^{2-19}); (*b*) sayings on (i.) offers of discipleship (9^{57-62}=Mt 8^{19-22}), (ii.) the vocation of d. (10^{1-24}=Mt 10^{1-15} 11^{20-27}), (iii.) and the prayers of d. (11^{1-13}=Mt 6^{9-13} 7^{7-11}); (*c*) sayings on adversaries, including (i.) the calumnies of the Pharisees (11^{14-36}=Mt $12^{22-30. 43-45. 38-43}$ $6^{22f.}$), (ii.) the condemnation of the Pharisees (11^{37-54}=Mt 23), and (iii.) behaviour towards such opponents (12^{1-12}=Mt 10^{26-33} 12^{32} $10^{19f.}$); (*d*) sayings on the world, including (i.) the

---

* He adds a few logia scattered throughout the Marcan framework, *e.g.* 8^{11-13} $13^{12. 16}$ 15^{13b-14} and 16^{2-3}.

† His document is printed in full and discussed in detail (pp. 23 f., 361 f.) by H. B. Sharman in *The Teaching of Jesus about the Future* (Chicago, 1909)

‡ So, *e.g.*, Wright and Robinson (*Study of Gospels*, 77 f.).

attitude of disciples towards worldly possessions (12^{22-34} introduced by 12^{13-21} = Mt 6^{20-33}), (ii.) the experiences of disciples in the world (12^{35-39} = Mt 24^{42-51} 25^{1-13} 10^{34-36} $16^{2f.}$ $5^{25f.}$), and (iii.) signs of the coming storm and finale ($13^{1-5.\ 6-9.\ 18-21}$ = Mt 21^{19} 13^{31-33}); with (*e*) omens of the end in (i.) denunciation (13^{22-35} = Mt $7^{13f.}$ $25^{11f.}$ $7^{22f.}$ $8^{11f.}$ 19^{30} 23^{37-39}), (ii.) warnings for disciples ($14^{15-27(-33)\ (-35)}$ 15^{4-7} 17^{1-4} = Mt 22^{2-10} $10^{37f.}$ $18^{12-14.\ 6f.\ 21f.}$), and (iii.) words on the end of the world (17^{20-37} = Mt 24). (*f*) Stanton (*GHD.* ii. 70 f.) outlines the contents of the source thus: ushering in of ministry of Christ = preaching of Baptist (Lk $3^{2.\ 7-9a.\ 16b.\ 17}$ = Mt $3^{5.\ 7-12}$), baptism of Jesus (Lk 3^{21-22} = Mt $3^{13.\ 16-17}$), temptation of Jesus (Lk 4^{1-13} = Mt 4^{1-11a}); first stage in preaching of gospel = discourse on heirs of the kingdom (Lk 6^{17-49}), centurion (Lk 7^{1-10} = Mt $8^{5-10.\ 13}$), John and Jesus (Lk $7^{18-28.\ 31-35}$ = Mt $11^{2-11.\ 16-19}$); extension of gospel = tour of Jesus (Lk 8^{1} = Mt 9^{35}), warnings to aspirants (Lk 9^{57-60} = Mt 8^{19-22}), saying on harvest (Lk 10^{2} = Mt 9^{37-38}), directions for preachers (Lk 10^{3-12} = Mt $10^{5a.\ 7-16.\ 40}$); rejection and reception of divine truth = Woe of Lk 10^{13-15} (Mt 11^{21-23}), thanksgiving of Lk 10^{21-22} (Mt 11^{25-27}), beatitude of Lk 10^{23-24} (Mt 13^{16-17}); instruction on prayer = Lord's prayer (Lk 11^{2-4} = Mt 6^{9-13}), on earnestness (Lk 11^{9-13} = Mt 7^{7-11}); Jesus and his opponents = lawyer (Lk 10^{25-28} = Mt 22^{34-40}), accusation of Lk $11^{14-15.\ 17-23}$ (Mt 12^{22-30}), saying of Lk 11^{24-26} (Mt 12^{43-45}), demand for sign (Lk $11^{16.\ 29-32}$ = Mt 12^{39-42}), on lamp of body (Lk 11^{34-36} = Mt 6^{22-23}), denunciation of Lk 11^{38-52}; exhortations to disciples = confessing Christ (Lk 12^{2-10} = Mt 10^{26-33} 12^{32}), trust in Providence (Lk 12^{22-34} = Mt $6^{25-34.\ 19-21}$), watching (Lk 12^{39-40} = Mt 24^{43-44}), prudence (Lk 12^{42-46} = Mt 24^{45-51}), thoroughness (Lk 12^{51-53} 14^{26-27} = Mt 20^{34-38}), two parables of Lk 13^{18-21} (Mt 13^{31-33}), offences (Lk 17^{1-4} = Mt $18^{5-7.\ 15.\ 21-22}$), power of faith (Lk 17^{5-6} = Mt 17^{19-20}); doom of Jerusalem, etc. = Lk 13^{34-35} (Mt 23^{37-39}) and Lk 17^{22-37} (Mt $24^{26-28.\ 37-41}$). (*g*) Barth (*Einl.* 225 f.) divides his sayings-source into five sections: *introduction* = John the Baptist and his preaching (Mt 3^{1-12} etc.), baptism and temptation of Jesus (Mt 4^{1-11} etc.), appearance of Jesus in Galilee (Mt 4^{12-17} etc.); *Jesus' preaching on the kingdom* = righteousness (Mt $5^{1-12.\ 17-22.\ 27-48}$ $6^{1-6.\ 16-18}$ $7^{1-6.\ 12.\ 15-20.\ 24-27}$ = Lk 6^{20-49}), reconciliation (Mt 5^{23-26} = Lk 12^{58-59}), prayer (Mt 6^{7-15} 7^{7-11} = Lk 11^{1-13}), riches (Mt 6^{19-34} = Lk 12^{22-34} 16^{13}), childlikeness (Mt $18^{1-6.\ 10.\ 14}$ etc.); *against the world* = message of Baptist (Mt 11^{2-19} = Lk 7^{18-35}), Beelzebub sayings (Mt $12^{22-32.\ 43-45}$), on signs (Mt 12^{38-42} = Lk 11^{29-32}), against the Pharisees (Mt 23^{2-36} etc.), parable of lost sheep (Mt 18^{11-13} = Lk 15^{4-7}), revelation (Mt 11^{25-27} = Lk 10^{21-22}), parable of sower (Mt $13^{3-15.\ 18-23}$ etc.), woe (Mt 11^{21-24} = Lk 10^{13-15}), wail over Jerusalem (Mt 23^{37-39} = Lk 13^{34-35}), parable of feast (Mt 22^{1-14} = Lk 14^{16-24}); *calling of disciples* = Kapharnaum-centurion (Mt 8^{5-10} = Lk 7^{1-10}), felicitation of disciples (Mt 13^{10-17} = Lk 10^{23-24}), three aspirants (Mt 8^{19-22} = Lk 9^{57-62}), counsels to disciples (Mt 10^{37-39} = Lk 14^{26-27}), disciples as light (Mt 5^{15-16} 6^{22-23} etc.), disciples on salt (Mt 5^{13} etc.), mission of disciples (Mt 10^{5-15} etc.), promise of divine help (Mt 10^{16-33} = Lk 12^{2-12}), discord (Mt 10^{34-36} = Lk 12^{49-53}), offences (Mt $18^{6-9.\ 15-22}$ etc.), faith (Mt 17^{20} etc.), seed and leaven (Mt 13^{31-33} etc.); *the future* = rejection of unworthy disciples (Mt $7^{13-14.\ 21-23}$ etc.), on loyalty (Mt 24^{42-51} etc.), sudden coming of Son of man (Mt 24^{37-41} = Lk 17^{20-37}), use of talents (Mt 25^{14-30} = Lk 19^{12-27}), speech on Parousia (Mt 24^{4-36} etc.). Finally (*h*), Allen's (*Matthew*, pp. lvii f.) analysis of the Matthaean Logia ("a collection of Christ's sayings containing isolated sayings, sayings grouped into discourses and parables"), based on Mt like that of Barnes, includes:—$5^{3-12.\ 13-16.\ 17-48}$ 6^{1-33} 7^{1-27} 8^{11-12} $9^{13a.\ 37-38}$ $10^{5b-8.\ 23}$ 10^{24-41} (not in this connection) 11^{2-30} (not necessarily in this order) 12^{5-12} 12^{25-45} (not necessarily in this order) $13^{16-17.\ 24-30.\ 33\ (?).\ 31-52}$ $15^{12-14.\ 24}$ 16^{17-19} 17^{20} $18^{3-4.\ 10.\ 12-35}$ $19^{10-12.\ 28}$ 20^{1-16} $21^{16.\ 28-32.\ 43}$ $22^{1-14.\ 35-40}$ 23 (not necessarily in this order) $24^{10-12.\ 23-27.\ 30a.\ 37-41.\ 43-51}$ $25^{1-13.\ 14-30.\ 31-46\ (?)}$ $26^{52-54\ (?)}$.

With these eight outlines eight others, which enter into rather closer parallel details, may be compared.

(*a*) O. Holtzmann (*Leben Jesu*, Eng. tr. pp. 25 f.).

Mt	3^{7-12}	4^{1-11}	$5^{3}-7^{27}$	8^{5-13}	11^{2-19}	8^{19-22}	10^{5-42}	11^{20-24}	11^{25-27}	6^{9-13}
Lk	$3^{7-9.\ 16f.}$	4^{1-13}	6^{20-49}	7^{2-10}	7^{18-35}	9^{57-60}	10^{2-16}		10^{21-24}	11^{1-4}

Mt	7^{7-11}	$12^{43-45.\ 38-42}$	$6^{22f.}$	23^{1-39}	$10^{26f.}$	$6^{25-33.\ 19-21}$	$24^{43f.}$	10^{34-36}	$16^{2f.}$	$5^{25f.}$
Lk	$11^{9-13.\ 24-32.\ 34-36}$			11^{39-52}	$12^{2-9.\ 22-31.\ 33f.}$		$12^{39-46.\ 51-56}$			$12^{58f.}$

Mt.	13^{31-33}	$7^{13f.\ 22f.}$	23^{37-39}	12^{11}		23^{12}		22^{1-14}	$10^{37f.}$	18^{12-14}
Lk	$13^{18-21.\ 24-30}$		$13^{34f.}$	13^{15}	14^{5}	14^{11}	18^{14}	14^{15-24}	$14^{26f.}$	15^{4-7}

Mt	6^{24}	$11^{12f.}$	5^{18}	18^{7}	$18^{15.\ 21f.}$	17^{20}	24^{26-28}	25^{14-30}	19^{28}
Lk	16^{13}	16^{16}	16^{17}	$17^{1f.}$	$17^{3f.}$	$17^{5f.}$	17^{22-37}	19^{12-26}	$22^{29f.}$

(*b*) Harnack (*BNT.* 127 f., 253 f., Gk. text and discussion).*

Mt	$3^{5.\ 7-12}$	4^{1-11}	$5^{1-4.\ 6.\ 11-12}$	$5^{39-40.\ 42.\ 44-48}$	7^{12}	7^{1-5}	15^{14}
Lk	$3^{7-9.\ 16-17}$	4^{1-13}	$6^{17.\ 20-23}$	$6^{29.\ 30.\ 27-28.\ 35b.\ 32-33.\ 36}$	6^{31}	$6^{37-38.\ 41f.}$	6^{39}

Mt	10^{24-25}	$7^{16-18f.}+12^{33}$	$7^{21.\ 24-27}$	$7^{28}+8^{5-10.\ 13}$	11^{2-11}	11^{16-19}	10^{7}	
Lk	6^{40}	6^{43-44}	6^{46-49}	7^{1-10}	7^{18-28}	7^{31-35}	9^{2}	$10^{9.\ 11}$

Mt	8^{19-22}	9^{37-38}	10^{16a}	10^{12-13}	10^{10b}	10^{15}	11^{21-23}	10^{40}	11^{25-27}	13^{16-17}
Lk	9^{57-60}	10^{2}	10^{3}	10^{5-6}	10^{7b}	10^{12}	10^{13-15}	10^{16}	10^{21-22}	10^{23b-24}

Mt	6^{9-13}	7^{7-11}	$12^{22-23.\ 25.\ 27-28.\ 30.\ 43-45}$	$12^{38-39.\ 41-42}$	5^{15}	6^{22-23}	$23^{4.\ 13.\ 23}$
Lk	11^{2-4}	11^{9-13}	$11^{14.\ 17.\ 19.\ 20.\ 23-26}$	$11^{16.\ 29-32}$	11^{33}	11^{34-35}	$11^{46.\ 52.\ 42.}$

Mt	$23^{25.\ 27.\ 29.\ 30-32.\ 34-36}$	10^{26-33}	12^{32}	6^{25-33}	6^{19-21}	24^{43-51}	10^{34-36}
Lk	$11^{39.\ 44.\ 47-52}$	12^{2-9}	12^{10}	12^{22-31}	12^{33-34}	$12^{39-40.\ 42-46}$	$12^{51.\ 53}$

Mt	5^{25-26}	13^{31-33}	7^{13-14}	8^{11-12}	23^{37-39}	23^{12}	10^{37}	10^{38}	5^{13}	18^{12-13}
Lk	12^{58-59}	13^{18-21}	13^{24}	13^{28-29}	13^{34-35}	14^{11}	14^{26}	14^{27}	14^{34-35}	15^{4-7}

Mt	6^{24}	11^{12-13}	5^{18}	5^{32}	18^{7}	$18^{15.\ 21-22}$	17^{20b}	$24^{26-28.\ 37-41}$	10^{39}
Lk	16^{13}	16^{16}	16^{17}	16^{18}	17^{1}	17^{3-4}	17^{6}	$17^{23-24.\ 37.\ 26-27.\ 34-35}$	17^{33}

Mt	25^{29}	19^{28}
Lk	19^{26}	$22^{28.\ 30}$

(*c*) Wellhausen.

Mt	3^{1-12}	4^{1-11}	$5^{1-12.\ 38-48}$	6^{19-34}	$7^{1-6.\ 7-11.\ 15-27}$			8^{5-13}	10^{5-15}	11^{1-19}
Lk	3^{1-7}	4^{1-15}	$6^{20-23.\ 27-36}$	12^{22-34}	6^{37-42}	11^{9-13}	6^{43-49}	7^{1-10}	10^{1-12}	7^{18-35}

* Special criticism of this reconstruction by Burkitt (*JTS.*, 1907, 454–459); Windisch (*ZWT.*, 1908, 135 f.); Emmet (*ET.* xix. 297 f., 358 f.), and W. C. Allen (*ET.* xx. 445–449).

Mt 11^{20-30} 12^{22-42} (22^{1-14} 23^{13-39} 24^{1-51} 25^{14-30})

Lk 10^{13-24} 11^{14-32} (14^{16-24} 11^{37-52} 13^{34-35} 17^{20-35} 12^{35-46} 19^{11-27})

(*d*) Roehrich.

Mt $3^{1-12\ (14-15\ ?)}$ 4^{1-11} 5–7 $8^{5-13.\ 18-22}$ $9^{32-34.\ 37-38}$ $10^{5-15.\ 26-41}$

Lk 3^{1-20} 4^{1-13} 6^{20-49} 7^{1-10} 9^{57-60} 11^{14-15} 10^{9-16} $12^{2-9.\ 49-53}$ 14^{26-27}

Mt 11^{1-15} 11^{16-30} $12^{22-23.\ 27-28.\ 30.\ 33-45}$

Lk 17^{33} 10^{16} 7^{18-28} 7^{31-35} $10^{13-15.\ 21-22}$ $11^{19.\ 23}$ 6^{43-45} $11^{24.\ 29-32}$

Mt $13^{16-17.\ 24-30.\ 33.\ 44-50}$ $16^{1-4.\ 17-20}$ 17^{24-27} $18^{7.\ 10-11.\ 13-15}$ 20^{1-16} $21^{14-16.\ 28-32}$

Lk 10^{23-24} 13^{20} 12^{54} 17^{6} 17^{1} 15^{1-7} (17^{4})

Mt 22^{1-14} $23^{1-12.\ 13-39}$ $24^{26-28.\ 37-41.\ 43-51}$ 25^{1-13} $25^{14-30.\ 31-46}$

Lk ($14^{16\,f.}$) 20^{45} $17^{23-24.\ 37.\ 26-27.\ 35}$ $12^{39-40.\ 42-46}$ (19^{12-27})

(*e*) Wendt.

Mt 3^{7-12} 5–7 (pt.) 8^{5-13} 11^{2-19} 21^{28-35} 8^{19-22} 9^{37-38}

Lk $3^{7-9.\ 16-17}$ 6^{20-49} 16^{17-18} 7^{2-10} 7^{18-35} 16^{16} 7^{36-50} 8^{1-3} 9^{57-62} 10^{1-16}

Mt $10^{1-16.\ 40-42}$ 11^{20-24} 11^{25-30} 13^{16-17} 6^{7-15} 7^{7-11} 9^{32-34} 12^{22-45} 16^{4} $6^{22\,f.}$ 23^{1-4}

Lk 10^{17-42} 11^{1-13} 11^{14-32} 6^{45} 11^{33-54}

Mt 10^{24-33} 12^{32} 6^{19-34} 24^{43-51} 25^{1-12} 10^{34-39} 5^{13} $16^{2\,f.}$ $5^{25\,f.}$

Lk 12^{1-12} 6^{40} 12^{13-34} 12^{35-46} 13^{25} 12^{49-53} 14^{25-35} 17^{33} 13^{1-9} 12^{54-59} 13^{10-17}

Mt 13^{31-33} $7^{13\,f.\ 22\,f.}$ $8^{11\,f.}$ 22^{1-14} 23^{37-39} $12^{10\,f.}$ 25^{14-30}

Lk 13^{18-30} 14^{15-24} 13^{31-35} 14^{1-6} 14^{7-14} $15^{3.\ 8-32}$ 16^{1-13}

Mt 6^{24} 18^{6-35} 17^{20} $24^{26-28.\ 37-41}$

Lk 19^{11-27} 12^{47-48} 16^{14-31} 18^{9-14} 17^{1-4} 15^{4-7} $17^{5-6.\ 7-21}$ $17^{22-35.\ 37}$ 18^{1-8}

Mt $21^{15\,f.}$ 21^{44} 19^{28} 5^{14b} 7^{6}

Lk 19^{11-27} 21^{34-36} 4^{16-30} 5^{39} 19^{1-10} 19^{37-44} 20^{18} $22^{14-17.\ 26-32.\ 35-38}$

Mt 9^{27-30} 12^{5-7} $13^{24-30.\ 47-50}$ $13^{44-46.\ 52}$ 16^{17-18} 17^{24-27} 18^{19-20} 19^{10-12} 20^{1-16}

Lk

Mt 23^{1-12} 25^{31-46}

Lk

(*f*) Hawkins (*HS.* 107 f.).

Mt 3^{7-10} 3^{12} 4^{3-11} $5^{1-4.\ 6.\ 11-12.\ 18.\ 25-26.\ 39-40.\ 42.\ 44-48}$ $6^{9-13.\ 20-24}$

Lk 3^{7-9} 3^{17} 4^{3-13} 6^{20-23} 16^{17} 12^{58-59} $6^{27-30.\ 32-36}$ 11^{2-4} 12^{33b-34} 11^{34-35} 16^{13}

Mt 6^{25-33} $7^{1-2.\ 3-5.\ 7-14.\ 21-27}$ 8^{5-10}

Lk 12^{22-31} $6^{37.\ 38.\ 41-42}$ 11^{9-13} 6^{31} $13^{23-24\ (?)}$ 6^{46} $13^{25-27\ (?)}$ 6^{47-49} $7^{1-3.\ 6-9}$

Mt $8^{11-12.\ 19-22}$ 9^{37-38} $10^{7.\ 8a.\ 10.\ 11-13.\ 15-16a.\ 24-25a.\ 26-38.\ 40}$

Lk 13^{28-29} 9^{57-60} 10^{2} $10^{9b.\ 9a.\ 4.\ 7b.\ 8.\ 5-6.\ 12.\ 3}$ 6^{40} $12^{2-9.\ 51-53}$ $14^{(26-27)}$ 10^{16}

Mt $11^{2-3.\ 4-13.\ 16-19.\ 21-27}$ $12^{22-23.\ 27-28}$ $12^{30.\ 33-35.\ 38-39}$

Lk $7^{18-19.\ 22-28}$ 16^{16} 7^{31-35} 10^{12-15} 10^{21-22} $11^{14.\ 19-20}$ $11^{23.\ 16.\ 29-32.\ 24-26}$

Mt $12^{41-42.\ 43-45}$ $13^{16-17.\ 33}$ 15^{14} 17^{20} $18^{7.\ 12-14.\ 15.\ 21-22}$ 19^{28}

Lk 6^{43-45} 10^{23-24} 13^{20-21} 6^{39} $17^{6\ (?)}$ 17^{1} $15^{4-5.\ 7}$ 17^{3-4} $22^{28.\ 30\ (?)}$

Mt $23^{4. 12-14. 23. 25-27. 29-31. 34-39}$ $24^{27-28. 37-41. 43-51a}$

Lk 11^{46} 14^{11} $11^{52. 42. 39. 41. 44 (?). 47-51}$ 13^{34-35} $17^{24. 37}$ $17^{26-27. 34-35}$ $12^{39-40. 42-46}$

(*g*) J. Weiss (*SNT.*[2] 1906).

Mt 3^{7-10} 3^{12} 4^{1-11} $5^{1b-6. 10. 13. 15. 18. 20-48}$ $(6^{1-9\,?})$ 6^{10-13}

Lk 3^{7-9} $3^{17f.}$ 4^{1-13} 11^{33} 14^{34-35} $16^{16f.}$ $16^{18\,?}$ 11^{2-4}

Mt $(6^{14-15\,?})$ 6^{19-33} $7^{1-5. 7-13. 17-22a. 24-28}$ $8^{5-13. 19-22}$

Lk 16^{13} $12^{33f.}$ 11^{34-35} 12^{22-31} 11^{9-11} $13^{23-24f.}$ 6^{47-49} $7^{1-3. 7-10}$ 9^{57-60}

Mt 9^{37-38} $10^{7-8a. 10\,?. 11a. 12-13. 14\,?. 15-16a. 17-22\,?. 24-25a. 26a-40}$

Lk 13^{28-30} $10^{2f.}$ 12^{11-12} 14^{26-27} 10^{16} $12^{2-8\,?. 51f.}$

Mt $11^{3-9. 11. 16-19. 21-27}$ $12^{11. 23-24. 27-28. 33. 35. 38-39. 41-45b}$ $13^{16-17. 31-33\,?}$

Lk $7^{18-26. 28-35}$ $10^{13f. 21-22}$ $11^{15f.}$ 12^{10} 11^{29-31} 11^{24-26} 10^{23-24} 13^{18-21}

Mt $18^{7. 12f. 15. 22}$ $21^{32a. b}$ 22^{1-10} $23^{4. 6-7\,?. 13-15. 23a. b. 25. 27. 29-31. 34-39}$

Lk $17^{1f.}$ 15^{3-7} 17^{5-6} $18^{13. 15f.}$ 14^{16-23} 11^{39-52} 14^{11} 10^{25-27}

Mt $24^{26-28. 37-41. 42-44\,?}$ 24^{45-51} $25^{1-13\,?}$

Lk 13^{34-35} $17^{23-24. 26-27. 31. 33b. f.}$ 12^{39-40} 12^{41-46} 13^{25} $22^{22-23\,?. 24f.\,?}$

(*h*) B. Weiss (*Quellen d. Syn. Ueberlieferung*, pp. 1–96, Greek text and discussion).

Mt 3^{3-10} 3^{11-12} 3^{13-17} 4^{1-11} 8^{2-4} 9^{1-8} 12^{3-8} $7^{3f. 13-20}$ 8^{5-13}

Lk 3^{1-9} $3^{15f.}$ $3^{21f.}$ 4^{1-13} 5^{12-16} $5^{17-26 (?)}$ 6^{3-5} 6^{39-45} $7^{1-10 (?)}$

Mt $11^{5-19. 21. 31f.}$ 13^{1-9} 12^{46-50} $10^{1. 9-14 (?)}$ $14^{13-21 (?)}$ $16^{13-19 (?)}$ $10^{32f. (?)}$

Lk 7^{22b-35} $8^{4-8 (16f. ?)}$ $8^{19f.}$ $10^{4-11 (?)}$ $9^{10b-17 (?)}$ $9^{23f. (?)}$

Mt $17^{1-20 (?)}$ 8^{18-22} $9^{37f.}$ $10^{5f.}$ $10^{7f.}$ 10^{15} 11^{20-24} 11^{25-30} $13^{16f.}$ 22^{35-40}

Lk $9^{28-42 (?)}$ 9^{57-60} 10^{2} 10^{3-8} $10^{9f.}$ $10^{12-16. 17-20}$ 10^{21-24} 10^{25-28}

Mt $6^{7f.}$ 7^{6-11} $9^{32f.}$ 11^{25-37} $12^{38f.}$ 10^{26-33} $12^{31f.}$ $6^{25f.}$ 24^{43-51} $5^{25f.}$

Lk 11^{1-13} $11^{14f.}$ $11^{16-26. 29-36 (37-52 ?)}$ $12^{2-9. 10-32 (33-34 ?). 39-48. 54-59}$

Mt $13^{31f.}$ $7^{13f. 22f.}$ $20^{16. 37f.}$ 5^{13} $18^{12f.}$ $11^{12f.}$ $5^{18. 32}$ $18^{6f.}$

Lk 13^{18-35} . $14^{34f.}$ 15^{4-10} 16^{1-13} 16^{16-18} $17^{1-2. 20-end}$

Mt $24^{26f. 37f.}$ $21^{33-44 (?)}$ $24^{4-8 (?)}$ $24^{15f. (?)}$ 24^{32-35} $19^{28f.}$

Lk $18^{1-8 (28f. ?)}$ $20^{9-18 (?). 45-47 (?)}$ $21^{8-11 (?)}$ $21^{20-28 (?)}$ 21^{29-33} $22^{24-30. 35-38}$

If Q was a gospel, *i.e.* an attempt to present notable sayings of Jesus in a biographical outline of his life, the inclusion of John the Baptist's preaching is as intelligible at the beginning as the omission of the passion-story at the end is unintelligible. Furthermore, when it is identified with the Matthæan Logia (or with some form of these), it is not easy to understand how it could have been a narrative of the life of Jesus, since Luke ($1^{1f.}$) implies that no such narrative was drawn up by an eye-witness. Finally, if Q is assumed to have ended without any account of the death or resurrection, it can hardly have been composed very soon after the resurrection (K. Lake, *Exp.*[7] vii. 494–507).* It is difficult to suppose that at any time between 30 and 50 A.D. the death and resurrection of Jesus were so unimportant to Christians, in view of the speedy return of Messiah, that a gospel could be written which ignored them. These difficulties do not compel the introduction of a passion-narrative into Q, much less its relegation to the lifetime of Jesus, but they reinforce the hypothesis that it was not a gospel at all.

When the Matthæan Logia are identified with Q, the date of the latter (at any rate in its original form) is not later than the seventh decade of the first century; so far as the internal evidence goes, it may even fall within the sixth. It is thus an apostolic Aramaic treatise which has every likelihood of having been composed prior not only to Mark, but to the Ur-Marcus; it reflects the faith and mission and sufferings of the primitive Jewish Christian church of Palestine, long before the crisis of 70 A.D. began to loom on the horizon.†

Wellhausen's (*Einl.* 65 f., 73 f.) attempt to prove that Q is not only later than, but for the most part inferior to, Mark, rests on an undue depreciation of the former (see the careful proofs of Bousset in *TR.*, 1906, 5–14, 43 f.; Harnack, *BNT.* ii. 193 f.; with Jülicher's less certain protests in *Neue Linien*, 43 f., and Denney's *Jesus and the Gospel*, 194 f.), an assumption that the projection of early Christian christology was larger in the case of the sayings than of the narratives, and an idea that Mark harvested the best of the available sayings which were authentic ("if, unintentionally, this or that saying escaped his notice, nevertheless the gleaning of old and genuine material which he left for others cannot have been incomparably richer than his own harvest," *Einl.* 86). But Q is not a humble Ruth in the field of the logia; Mark did not aim, as Luke did, at completeness; and it is to reverse the probabilities of the case, to discredit the tradition of the sayings of Jesus in favour of the narratives.‡ Both grew under the spirit of the church, but

---

* "No date after the Passion seems impossibly early" (p. 503). "Every year after 50 A.D. is increasingly improbable for the production of Q" (p. 507). Resch (*Der Paulinismus u. die Logia Jesu*; *TU.* xiii. 1904), who thinks, like J. Weiss, that Paul knew Jesus on earth, explains the Pauline references by conjecturing that the apostle got a copy of the Logia from Ananias; but the proofs are much too speculative.

† Cp. Bousset, *TR.*, 1906, 46 ("Jedenfalls lehnt die Gemeinde, die diese Worte überlieferte [*i.e.* 17^{6} $10^{5f.}$ 10^{23}], es ab, ihrerseits Heidenmission zu treiben, wie die Urapostel nach Gal 2^{9}").

‡ Contrast Wundt's recent remark (cited by Montefiore) in his *Völkerspsychologie*, ii. 3, 1909, p. 528: 'No unprejudiced person, even tolerably familiar with the formation of myths, and fairly well acquainted with the

the former are not inferior in historicity to the latter. It is doubtful if the words υἱοῦ Βαραχίου stood originally in Q (Mt 23^{35}); but, even if they did, they are not a historical anachronism which proves that Q (or this part of it) was written after 68 (70) A.D. (Wellhausen, *Mt.* 119–121). The reference is to the Zechariah of 2 Ch 24^{20}, not to the wealthy and pious Zechariah who (Josephus, *BJ.* iv. 5. 4) was assassinated by the Zealots in the temple. Wellhausen has made a sad and rare slip in describing the former as "quite an obscure man." He was, on the contrary, a hero of Jewish tradition (cp. B. Sanhedr. 96b; Gittin, 57b; J. Taanith, 69a), whose midrashic elaborations of 2 Ch 24^{19-25} go back to an early date (cp. Nestle, *ET.* xiii. 582, *ZNW.*, 1905, 198–200; G. F. Moore, *Journal of the American Oriental Society*, xxvi. 317 f.; Allen, *DCG.* i. pp. 171–172). It is the legendary fame of Zechariah ben Jehoiada, and of the bloody expiation exacted by God for his death, which underlies the logion; from Abel to Zechariah means from the first to the last book of the canonical OT (*i.e.* 2 Chronicles, where Z. is the last martyr mentioned); and this collocation of the two martyrs is much more natural for an early Christian than the other. The logion (cp. Lk 11^{49-51}) may be a quotation from a Wisdom source, or it may directly reflect, like many other passages of the NT, the midrashic atmosphere which surrounded the OT for early Christians, but it has not any bearing on the date of Q.

The subsequent fortunes of Q are unknown, unless traces of it can be found in some of the apocryphal gospels (*e.g.* the gospel καθ' Ἑβραίους). It suffered a sea-change, when it was employed by Matthew; but this incorporation did not destroy its independent circulation. John the presbyter seems still to have known it at the beginning of the second century, and, if Luke wrote then, he is another witness to its existence as a separate document during the last decades of the first century.

§ 5. *Q and Mark.*—Any reconstruction of Q exhibits a certain amount of parallelisms (cp. list in Burkitt's *Transmission*, 147–166) between it and Mk., which may be held to imply a literary dependence of Mk. on Q. So, *e.g.*, B. Weiss,* van Rhijn (*Theol. Studiën*, 1897, 432 f.), Titius (*ThSt.* 284–331), Resch (*Paulinismus*, pp. 544 f.), Badham, Jolley (*op. cit.* pp. 113 f.), Bousset, Barth, J. Weiss, O. Holtzmann, Loisy, von

growing light thrown on the sources of ancient Oriental myths, can doubt any longer that, except for a few incidents in the narratives of the Passion which probably possess adequate historical attestation, the outward life of Jesus is a tissue of legends. But what these legends leave untouched, and what is never found in their mythological counterparts and predecessors, is the series of sayings and speeches of Jesus handed down to us in the synoptic gospels."

* The rejection of the Ur-Marcus theories usually leads to the conclusion that Mark employed Q (cp. B. Weiss, *Quellen des Lukas-Evglims*, 134 f., 190).

Soden, Bacon, Nicolardot, and Montefiore (i. pp. xxxvi f.).* This hypothesis, however, even with the qualifications which Loisy and others have introduced into Weiss' statement, is upon the whole to be rejected. (*a*) The theory assumes that Q had a monopoly of such sayings. But the tradition of the churches was far too widespread to permit any such restriction of logia. Sayings of Jesus, such as come into question here, must have been circulating in many directions; it is contrary to all probabilities that they were drawn into the single channel or canal of Q, so that any other writer had to derive them from this source. In the nature of the case there must have been a considerable amount of material common to the Petrine tradition and the Matthæan Logia; it is to adopt an ultra-literary method if we explain any parallels (*e.g.* 4^{21-22} 6^{7-13} $9^{37. 42f.}$ $10^{42f.}$ 11^{22-25}) between the reproduction of the former in Mark and the latter by the hypothesis of borrowing, especially as Q itself must have gone back partially to the Petrine tradition of the sayings (cp. Loisy, i. 114). (*b*) No satisfactory explanation is offered why Mark made such scanty use of Q. Several of its sayings would have been perfectly relevant to his purpose; we can hardly imagine a Christian evangelist ignoring words like those of Mt 11^{27}, or assuming that because his readers already possessed Q, it was superfluous to repeat its contents, and even the hypothesis that he only knew a shorter form of Q fails to meet this objection. (*c*) In no instance is it absolutely necessary, either on the score of substance or of style, to assume that Mk. borrowed from Q. Thus passages like $1^{7-8. 10-11. 12-13}$ may quite as well be summary echoes of oral tradition as of Q (cp. Wernle, *Syn. Frage*, 208–212; Scott-Moncrieff, *Mark*, 78–83; Stanton, *GHD.* ii. 109 f.). It is very doubtful if stories like 1^{40-45} 2^{1-12} $9^{14f.}$ and sayings like $7^{1f.}$ really go back to Q at all; certainly the small apocalypse of $13^{5f.}$ does not. In some passages (*e.g.* $3^{22f.}$) it is even possible that the canonical Mk. has been affected by Mt. or Lk.,†

* Jülicher (*Einl.* 229–323) admits that the common element of Mk. and Q is extremely scanty, and hesitates to dogmatise, on the ground that the compositeness and accretion of Q—at once older and younger than Mk.—render any judgment on the latter's indebtedness extremely precarious. Harnack, who used to be sound on this matter (cp. *BNT.* ii. 225 f.), has recently made slight concessions to B. Weiss (cp. *TLZ.*, 1908, 463 f., "at least Mark knew the circle in which Q, or large portions of it, existed orally, before it was committed to writing, and existed substantially in the same form").

† So Wellhausen for $8^{11-12. 15}$.

while in others (*e.g.* the parables $4^{1-20.\ 26f.}$ with $5^{21f.}$ $9^{48f.}$ 10^{10-12}) Mt. and Lk. may have borrowed directly from Mk. instead of from Q. When allowance is made for these factors or possibilities, as well as for accidental coincidences, the data for any literary relation between Mk. and Q practically disappear. The abstract possibility must indeed be left open, that the author of Mk. (though not the Ur-Marcus) was acquainted with some form of Q; he could hardly fail to be.* Perhaps even he intended, by his re-editing of the ur-Marcus, to supplement Q, just as the author of Mt. afterwards fused Mk. and Q into a more rounded unity. Otherwise, it would not be easy to understand why he casually quoted it, perhaps from memory —which is the very utmost that can be inferred from the relevant data.

When the Matthæan Logia are regarded as composed solely of sayings couched in the form of the Semitic Wisdom lore, to the exclusion not only of historical narrative but also of the parables and larger discourses or Halacha of Jesus (Briggs, *JBL.*, 1904, 191–210), it is naturally easier to find traces of their use in Mark, *i.e.* in passages, *e.g.*, $2^{21-22.\ 28-29}$ 4^{21-25} 9^{1} 9^{41-50}, which have been added to the original Mk. by the later editor. But this limitation of Q's scope is untenable.

§ 6. *Matthew and Luke.*—There is no reason *a priori* why Mt. should not have been one of Lk.'s sources as well as Mk. Chronologically,† this is possible. Still, the coincident variations of Lk. and Mt., as against Mk., and especially their agreements, are not to be explained by their use of the Ur-Marcus (see above, pp. 192 f.), nor by Lk.'s use of Mt., but for the most part by the operation of the same desire to smooth out the Marcan text. In some cases they are accidental coincidences; in others, they are due to oral tradition; a large number came from Q (especially the parts more or less parallel to Mk.) or from common sources; and finally, allowance has to be made for later conformations‡

* The later Mark is dated, especially as the edition of an ur-Marcus, the more difficult it is to deny the possibility, and even the probability, that the writer knew Q, and to explain how it could be merely a subsidiary source.

† On the theory that Mt. is later, Lk. has even been held to form one of its sources (Hitzig, Volkmar, Pfleiderer).

‡ Assimilation took place between the texts of Mt. and Lk., during the period preceding the εὐαγγέλιον τετραμόρφον, more readily than in the case of Mk., which did not circulate with equal popularity (cp. Lake in *TS.* vii. 3, p. lvii, and—for a discussion of later harmonistic corruptions—Burgon and Miller's *Causes of Corruption of Tradit. Text of Gospels*, 1896, pp. 89 f.).

of the text (*e.g.* Lk 22^{62}). The infancy-narratives are independent (see below), and the passion-story in Luke does not exhibit any traces of adherence to the specifically Matthæan narrative. The data in the intervening sections are upon the whole fairly covered by the common use of Q and by the presence of Luke's special source (sources). The hypothesis is not to be dismissed hastily, but a scrutiny of the evidence leads to a verdict of "non proven." At most, the claim is * that Mt. was merely a subsidiary and secondary source; but even this is less probable than the similar relationship urged between Mk. and Q.

Fullest recent statement of the case for Lk.'s use of Mt., by E. Simons, *Hat der dritte Evangelist den kanonischen Matthäus benutzt?* (Bonn, 1880). Similarly Stockmeyer (*ZSchw.*, 1884, 144 f.), E. Y. Hincks (*JBL.*, 1891, 92–156), Holtzmann, Wendt, Halévy, Soltau (*PM.*, 1907, 185 f.), etc. The opposite case is put best by Wernle (*Syn. Frage*, 40–61), Roehrich (*op. cit.* 179–184), B. Weiss (*Die Quellen des Lukas-Evglms*, pp. 30 f., 39, 56, 61 f., 73, 222, etc.), Burton (pp. 30 f.), Stanton (*GHD.* ii. 140 f.), and Zahn (*INT.* iii. 107 f.), followed by Schmiedel (*EBi.* 1860–1862), Harnack, Jülicher, etc.

§ 7. *Other sources of the Synoptic Gospels.*—(*a*) A written (ὁ ἀναγινώσκων νοείτω, Mk 13^{14} = Mt 24^{15}) fly-leaf of early Christian apocalyptic prophecy, or 'small apocalypse,' consisting of material set in the ordinary triple division common to apocalyptic literature (cp. Apoc 9^{12} 11^{14}):

ἀρχὴ ὠδίνων: Mk 13^{7-8} = Mt 24^{6-8} = Lk 21^{9-11}.
θλίψις: Mk 13^{14-20} = Mt 24^{15-22} = (Lk 21^{20-24}).
παρουσία: Mk 13^{24-27} = Mt 24^{29-31} = (Lk $21^{25-27.\ 28}$).

The details of the re-constructed apocalypse are not quite certain,† but its general contour is unmistakable: it parts, as a whole, readily from the context and forms an intelligible unity, whatever were its original size and aim. If the introductory passage Mk 13^{5-6} (= Mt 24^{4-5}) is added (with Weiffenbach, Keim, and others), probably Mk 13^{21-23} (= Mt 24^{23-25}) should also be incorporated (as, *e.g.*, by Keim, Weizsäcker, and Spitta),

* "Seine Berücksichtigung des Mt. ist also keine systematische, planvolle, durch bestimmte Gesichtspunkte geregelte; vielmehr müssen wir unsere Auffassung dahin formuliren, dass der kanonische Mt. für Lc. ein Nebenquelle" (Simons, *op. cit.* p. 108).

† Wendt (Mk $13^{7-9a.\ 14-20.\ 24-27.\ 30\,f.}$), Weiffenbach and Pfleiderer (Mk $13^{7-9a.\ 14-20.\ 24-27}$), Loisy (Mk $13^{6-8.\ 14.\ 17-20.\ 24-31}$), Schmiedel (Mk $13^{7-9a.\ 14-20.\ 24-27.\ 30}$), Wellhausen (Mk $13^{7-8.\ 12.\ 14-22.\ 24-27}$), Holtzmann (Mk $13^{5-9.\ 14-20,\ 24-27}$).

since Mk 13^{21} takes up Mk 13^{6}. In Mk. it stands apart from even the parabolic collection in 4 as the only long speech put into the mouth of Jesus; Mt seems to preserve it in a more primitive or archaic form,* though he uses part of it (10^{17-22}) in an earlier connection; while Luke has coloured it by the light of the Roman siege of Jerusalem, and the delay in the Parousia.† Luke, however, seems only to have known it as a component part of Mk. Whatever may be the historic value of the sayings in the apocalypse, it is a literary product, not the record of what Jesus said on this or any other occasion, but a tract of the apocalyptic propaganda. "In a private conversation with two or three disciples, Jesus would not speak in a sustained style of eschatological commonplace." ‡

The period of the apocalypse is the seventh decade, when the approaching fall of Jerusalem seemed to herald the end. The fly-leaf is not a *uaticinium ex euentu*, for the Christians of the capital did not fly to the mountains, but across the Jordan to Pella (*κατά τινα χρησμόν*, Eusebius declares, *H. E.* iii. 5. 3); no appearance of false messiahs or prophets is known to have taken place then, and the Danielic prediction of the *βδέλυγμα τῆς ἐρημώσεως* is coloured not by contemporary incidents, but by eschatological tradition. The apocalypse was probably written by a Palestinian Jewish Christian (so, *e.g.*, Colani, Renan,

* The Matthæan (24^{3}) definition of *τὸ σημεῖον* (*τῆς σῆς παρουσίας καὶ συντελείας τοῦ αἰῶνος*) is quite in keeping with the eschatological programme of this gospel.

† Spitta (*SK.*, 1909, 384–401), with his usual predilection for Luke, reconstructs the eschatological speech of Jesus entirely from the Lucan version, where, he holds (like Goguel, *L'évangile de Marc*, 228 f.), it is most accurately preserved (in Lk $21^{5-9.\ 12-15.\ 18-24.\ 10-11.\ 25b-27.\ 29-31}$). Those who, like B. Weiss and Bacon, reject the "small apocalypse" theory outright, make the whole speech an agglutination of sayings from Q and editorial insertions,—a theory which does not work out naturally, even in its less analytic forms (Stevens, *NTTh.* 152 f.; Briggs, *Messiah of Gospels*, 132–165; Fiebig, *PM.*, 1904, 24 f.; Zimmermann, *Hist. Wert der ältesten Ueberlieferung von der Gesch. Jesu im Marcusevglm*, 1905, 138 f.). The alternative view, that the whole speech is a later composition, is re-stated by Clemen in his review (*TLZ.*, 1902, 523–525) of Weiffenbach's recent essay on *Die Frage der Wiederkunft Jesu nochmals kurz erörtert* (1901). The fullest account of the retrospective element in Luke's treatment of the tradition, after A.D. 70, is given in Sharman's *Teaching of Jesus about the Future* (1909), pp. 150 f.

‡ Muirhead, *The Terms Life and Death in the Old and New Testament* (1908), 123 f. Dr. Muirhead's adhesion to this theory is notable, as in his earlier work on *The Eschatology of Jesus* (1904) he had refused to accept it.

Hausrath, Holtzmann, Keim, Wernle, Wendt, Stanton); its incorporation in the evangelic tradition was due to the existence of genuine eschatological sayings which received a fresh accent and emphasis at the period, and to the vivid zest for apocalyptic ideas in the Palestinian church of that age.

Started by Colani (*Jésus Christ et les Croyances messianiques de son Temps*,[2] 1864, pp. 201 f.) and Weiffenbach (in *Der Wiederkunftsgedanke Jesu*, 1873, pp. 69 f., 135 f.), this hypothesis of the small apocalypse has been adopted by writers on the messianic consciousness of Jesus, like Baldensperger and Schwartzkopff, as well as by numerous editors and critics of the synoptic gospels, including Vischer (*TU.* ii. 3, p. 9 n.), Jacobsen,* Pfleiderer (*Jahrbuch für deutsche Theol.*, 1868, 134–149, *Urc.*[2] i. 379 f.), Simons (p. 74), Mangold, Weizsäcker (*Untersuch.* 121 f., *AA.* ii. 22 f.), Renan (iv. chs. iii. and xii., v. pp. 123–125), Carpenter (*First Three Gospels*, pp. 222, 322), Cone (*Gospel Criticism*, pp. 282 f.), O. Schmiedel, and N. Schmidt (*Prophet of Nazareth*, pp. 132 f.). It is now a *sententia recepta* of synoptic criticism, as may be seen from the expositions by Wendt (*Lehre Jesu*, i. 10 f.), Spitta (*Urc.* ii. 178 f.), Hausrath (iv. 246 f.), Keim (v. 235 f.), Holtzmann (*HC.* i. 96 f., 167 f., *NTTh.* i. 327–328), Menzies (*Earliest Gospel*, 232 f.), O Holtzmann (*Leben Jesu*, Eng. tr. 456 f.), Charles (*Crit. History of Eschatology*, 324 f.), Wernle (*Syn. Frage*, pp. 212–214), Klostermann, Loisy (ii. 393 f.), and Montefiore. Among recent adherents are to be named Steudel (*Der religiöse Jugendunterricht*, 1896), Cheyne (*EBi.* i. 21–23), Schweitzer (*Das Abendmahl*, ii. 95), Wellhausen, Muirhead (*Life and Death in the Old and New Test.* 124 f.), Schmiedel (*EBi.* ii. 1857), and Stanton (*GHD.* ii. 116 f.). Further details in G. L. Cary (*op. cit.* pp. 274 f.), Jülicher (*Einl.* 282 f.), Burkitt (*Gospel History and its Transmission*, 62 f.), and Moffatt (*HNT.* 637–640).

(*b*) The hypothesis of a special source for the birth-narratives in Mt. and Lk. has no basis in the internal evidence. Three hypotheses of literary criticism are open: the two narratives are either (i.) derived from a common pre-canonical source; or (ii.) dependent on each other, the one correcting and amplifying the other; or (iii.) of independent origin. The superiority of (iii.) to (ii.) is discussed below. As for (i.), the serious objections to any form of it which has been hitherto adduced, whether by Resch (*Kindheitsevglm nach Lucas u. Matthaeus* in *TU.* x. 5, Leipzig, 1897; Gk. version of a Hebrew original) or by L. Conrady (*die Quelle der kanonischen Kindheitsgeschichte Jesu*, 1900: source = Gk.

* Jacobsen (*Protest. Kirchenzeitung*, 1886, 536 f.) and N. Schmidt contend that this apocalypse was the medium through which the term *Son of Man*, as a messianic title, passed into Mark. The latter critic (*op. cit.* 85 f., 132 f., 231 f.) ascribes the small apocalypse and the ground-work of Mt 23^{34-39} $25^{31f.}$ to a *Wisdom of God* (Lk 11^{49}) or Aramaic apocalypse.

version * of Heb. *Protevangelium Jacobi*), are the sharp divergence of the genealogical tables, and the fact that, apart from the tradition of the virgin-birth, the agreement of the narratives (*e.g.* the birthplaçe, names of parents, Nazareth residence, and Davidic descent) require only the data of the synoptic tradition to account for their origin. Where Mt. and Lk. agree elsewhere, the contour of the agreements is much closer than can be made out in their birth-narratives. Furthermore, the prolix and fanciful *Protevangelium Jacobi* betrays, to any trained literary sense, the later elaborations of the Christian imagination, with its somewhat crude and even coarse expansion of details in the canonical descriptions. As for Resch's theory of a Hebrew *book of the generations of Jesus the messiah* (cp. Mt 1[1] βίβλος γενέσεως Ἰ. Χ.), furnished with a genealogy like the book of Ruth, which, when translated into Greek, formed the source of both Matthew and Luke (the latter omitting, owing to haste and lack of space, what Mt. had already included), the differences between the two canonical narratives are enough to upset any such arguments, and the whole hypothesis is beset by fanciful and arbitrary presuppositions, such as the use of the source in the Prologue to the Fourth gospel (*op. cit.* pp. 243 f.) and its employment, in a different Gk. recension, by Justin. The earliest traces of extra-canonical sources are to be found in the fancy of the star in Ignatius, and in Justin's allusion to the birth of Jesus in a cave near Bethlehem (*Dial.* 78), the latter trait occurring in the Gospel of James. Justin's access † to extra-canonical sources of information is evident from *Apol.* 1[33] (ὡς οἱ ἀπομνημονεύσαντες πάντα τὰ περὶ τοῦ σωτηρος ἡμῶν Ἰησοῦ Χριστοῦ ἐδίδαξαν), but it is more probable that the bizarre conception of the cave was a trait added from contemporary mythology to the canonical tradition, than that the latter was modified from an ampler and more circumstantial account. The simple precedes the elaborate in the evolution of tradition, and the Gospel of James has the

* Based on the Egyptian myth of Isis, cast in a Hebraised form (cp. *SK.*, 1889, 728–784). He (*SK.*, 1904, 176–226) also regards Mt 2[13f.] as an excerpt from some independent account (moulded on pagan lines) of the flight to Egypt, which the apocryphal gospels have preserved more fully.

† Justin admits that those who rejected the virgin-birth were still Christians (ἀπὸ τοῦ ἡμετέρου γένους, *Dial.* 48); but this does not necessarily imply that the idea was as yet a comparative novelty (Hillmann in *JPT.* 1891, pp. 255 f.).

stamp neither of originality nor of unity, despite Conrady's pleadings to the contrary (pp. 207 f.).*

While most of the apostolic fathers ignore the virgin-birth, even when it naturally lay in their way to use it in treating the incarnation, Ignatius and Aristides (in the Syriac version) allude to it as an accepted article of the Christian belief, the former in a series of passages (*Eph.* 18^2 19^1, *Magn.* ^{11} etc.) which plainly presuppose a gospel-source corresponding to our present Matthew (cp. Smyrn. 1^1 with Mt 3^{17}),† the latter also in a sentence which implies the use of the canonical birth-stories (*Apol.* 2: "God came down from heaven, and from a Hebrew virgin assumed and clothed himself with flesh; and the Son of God lived in a daughter of man. This is taught in the gospel, as it is called, which a short time ago was preached among them" [*i.e.* Christians]). Both Ignatius and Aristides, like Melito afterwards, seem to fuse the Johannine idea of the incarnation with the synoptic birth-stories.‡

The employment of a Wisdom-source has been already noticed (p. 33); but, apart from this and the small apocalypse, the other sources of Mt. and Lk. are simply the special documents which, in the latter particularly, may be detected by the processes of literary analysis.

§ 8. *Date of Gospels* (*EBi.* 1826–1840; A. Wright, *Composition of Gospels*, 128 f.).—The earliest tradition upon the date of the gospels is that of Irenæus (iii. 1. 1; Eus. *H. E.* v. 8. 2–3), who means to give chronological information on the point.§ In this passage (cp. pp. 15 f.) ἔξοδον, unless it is due to a misinterpretation of 2 P 1^{15} (Blass, *Acta Apost.* p. 5), refers to the death of Peter and Paul, not (Grabe, Harvey, Cornely) to their departure from Rome. The allusion is significant; for, as tradition tended to throw back the origin of apostolic writings as far as possible, the words of Irenæus give a *terminus a quo* for the composition of

* Cp. Hilgenfeld's exhaustive refutation (*ZWT.*, 1901, 186 f.), with the criticisms of Holtzmann (*TLZ.*, 1901, 135 f.) and T. A. Hoben (*The Virgin Birth*, Chicago, 1905, pp. 12 f., also his articles on the ante-Nicene conception, etc., in *AJT.*, 1902, 473 f., 709 f.).

† The attempts of Hillmann to explain away the language of Ignatius as inconsistent with Lk 1^{34-35} 3^{23}, or to regard γεγεν. ἐκ παρθένου (Smyrn. 1^1) as interpolated, are unavailing. The virgin-birth undoubtedly belonged to the *Kerugma* reproduced by Ignatius, though it is impossible to infer the details of the historical tradition which he presupposed.

‡ Hence the difficulty of agreeing with Usener (*Relig. Untersuchungen*, i. 92 f.) that Carpokrates and the Ebionites denied the virgin-birth because it was absent from the gospels in their possession.

§ This is denied by Dom Chapman (*JTS.*, 1905, 563–569), but on insufficient grounds. The clause, τοῦ Πέτρου καὶ τοῦ Παύλου ἐν Ῥώμῃ εὐαγγελιζομένων κτλ., is a simultaneous reference.

Mk. and Mt. It is corroborated by the fact that both writers incorporate 'the small apocalypse,' which cannot well be dated earlier than the seventh decade of the first century. Apart from this, the evidence is purely internal.

(*a*) As the logion of Mk 9^1 is substantially reproduced in Mt 16^{28} and Lk 9^{27}, it does not necessarily imply that Mk. was written during the first generation of disciples. On the other hand, the editing of the small apocalypse shows that the crisis of the siege was recent, and that the writer wishes to distinguish between this seeming end and the real end. *The gospel must first be preached to all nations* (13^{10}); then, and then only, would the Parousia arrive. Meantime, the original *husbandmen of the vineyard* had been destroyed, and the vineyard given *to others*. The internal evidence of Mk. thus corroborates upon the whole the view that it represents a final version of the Ur-Marcus composed shortly after the events of A.D. 60–70.

(*b*) Since Mt. used not the Ur-Marcus but Mk. in substantially its present form, the *terminus a quo* of its composition is A.D. 70. The phrase in 27^8 and 28^{15} (ἕως τῆς σήμερον, μέχρι τῆς σήμερον) tallies with the general impression that a considerable interval has elapsed since the days of Jesus, during which the church has become organised and belief developed. The archaic character of the main source and the strongly marked eschatology of the gospel are of less moment for the question of its date than the final editor's anticipation of a prolonged period (cp. 28^{20}) during which the Gentile mission was to proceed apace. Mt. falls then between A.D. 70 and 110, since it was certainly known to Ignatius (passages and proofs in *GHD*. i. 27 f.; *NTA*. 76 f.), although the fact that Ignatius employs and quotes another evangelic source with equal belief, shows how far our canonical gospels yet were from a position of undisputed authority within the churches. The dubious nature of the supposed allusions in Hermas is generally recognised (cp. *GHD*. i. 72 f.; *NTA*. 117 f.), but in any case the *terminus ad quem*, as fixed by the traces of the gospel in the second century, is *c*. A.D. 110.

Efforts are still made to date Mt. earlier than A.D. 70, but without success. It is a mistake, for example, to suppose that there would be no point in preserving eschatological predictions like those of the small apocalypse after A.D. 70. Many Christians in the second century and later looked forward to a literal fulfilment, *e.g.*, of a prophecy like that of Mt 24^{15} (cp. Iren. *adv. Haer*. v. 25. 2). Belser, again, uses the anti-Pharisaic element to prove that the gospel was composed under the stress of the hard times which befell Palestinian Christianity, when Herod Agrippa I. made common cause with the Pharisees (Ac 12[1f.]). But even if the historical influence were proved, it would not determine the date of the gospel as contemporary; the sharp

A.D.	BEFORE 70.	BETWEEN 70 AND 100.	AFTER 100.
Mark*	Belser (*c.* 44), Birks (*c.* 48), Schenkel (45–58), Hitzig (55–57), Gloag (–55), Mill (63). 64–67: Bartlet, Schäfer, Küppers, Schanz, Robinson (65), Zimmermann (66), Zahn, J. Weiss. 65–70: Abbott, Alford, Allen, W. Brückner, Stanton, Swete, Salmond, Wendt, Weiss, Harnack, Maclean, Barth, Peake.	*c.* 70: Carpenter, Menzies. 70–80: Volkmar (73), Renan (76), Beyschlag, Wright, Wernle, Bacon, Wellhausen, von Soden, Burkitt, Loisy (75), O. Schmiedel (80), Goguel (75–85), Montefiore. 80–90: Holsten, Hilgenfeld. Rovers (*c.* 90), Bleek.	Hoekstra (100), Köstlin (100–110). Keim (115–120). S. Davidson (120). Usener (120–130). Baur (130 f.).
Matthew†	40–50: Grotius, Cornely. 55–60: Roberts, Gloag. *c.* 60: Belser (Gk.), Mill, Michaelis. *c.* 63: Zimmermann, Solger. *c.* 65: Hug, Maier, Schanz. 66: Barnes. 68 ±: Bleek, Meyer, Adeney, Bartlet, Godet, Jacquier, Keim. 60–70: Batiffol, Hug, Rose, Schanz.	70–80: Holsten, Hilg., Reuss (after 75), Weiss, Wright, Harnack (?), Sanday, Bruce, Baljon, Allen (65–75), J. Weiss (70–100), Barth. 80–90: Rovers (*c.* 80), Köstlin, Renan, W. Brückner, Réville, Jülicher (–96), Zahn (in Gk.), McGiffert, Bacon, Stanton (*c.* 80). 90–100: Carpenter (?), Wernle, Burkitt, O. Schmiedel (90–120?), Montefiore.	Loisy (*c.* 100). S. Davidson (*c.* 105), Carpenter. Holtzmann (–110). Volkmar. Soltau (110). Schmiedel (–130). Baur, Pfleiderer (–140).
Luke‡	Blass (54–56), Küppers (53–57). 58–60: Alford, Schaff, Gloag, Belser (61–62), Cornely (59–63). 63–64: Horne, Michaelis, Guericke, Fillion, Resch. 65–70: Godet, Hahn, Schanz, Schäfer, Batiffol. 60–70: Jacquier.	70–80: Bleek, Beyschlag, Weiss, Adeney, Bartlet, Bovon, Plummer, Sanday, Wright, Zahn. 80–90: Köstlin, Mangold, Abbott, Carpenter, J. Weiss, Bacon, McGiffert, Jülicher (–120), Harnack, Briggs, Barth (75–90). 90–100: Keim, Renan, Soltau, Wernle, Knopf, Burkitt, Loisy, Peake, Montefiore.	*c.* 100: Holsten, Scholten, Pfleid., J. Weiss, O. Schmiedel. 100–110: Volkmar, Rovers, Holtzmann, S. Davidson, Hilgenfeld, Weiss, Hausrath, Schmiedel. *c.* 130: Baur.

* The patristic hypothesis of (*a*) A.D. 43 (Jerome), and (*b*) A.D. 64–67 (Iren., Clem. Alex.), are still maintained by some Roman Catholic writers, *e.g.* (*a*) by Patrizi, Bisping, Schegg, and Reithmayr; (*b*) by Hug, Maier, Schanz, and Jacquier.

† J. H. Wilkinson (*Four Lectures on Early History of Gospels*, 1898) places Mt. in A.D. 70–75 (Mk. = 65–70, Lk. = 78–93), with an editing of all three in Asia Minor (A.D. 106–115).

‡ In *Horæ Evangelicæ* (ed. 1892, pp. 49–179, 252 f.), T. R. Birks dates Luke in A.D. 51 and Matthew (pp. 292 f.) in A.D. 42.

memories of it might have lingered and reappeared decades later. Belser's corroborative arguments do not amount to much, *e.g.* the reliance on the tradition that Matthew left Jerusalem in A.D. 42 and published his gospel before his departure, when the misconceptions of Christians in the church who were more Pharisees and Jews than anything else (Ac $11^{1f.}$ $15^{1f.}$) still formed the primary object of the gospel. Allen (*ET.* xxi. 439–444) similarly tries to show that the alleged 'catholic' and ecclesiastical allusions are not incompatible with its composition at Antioch *c.* A.D. 50, but the literary dependence on Mk. is by itself sufficient to disprove all such hypotheses.

(*c*) Luke's date depends not only on his use of Mk., which is certain, and his use of Mt., which is extremely uncertain, but on the relations between his work and Josephus, on which see pp. 29–31. The above table will give some idea of the various periods which are assigned to it and to the other two gospels.

While the gospels of Mark and Matthew, together with the two volumes by Luke, which make up the historical literature within the NT Canon, were not composed till the last quarter of the first century, and while all of them, particularly the synoptic gospels, are composite, their sources reach back to the period prior to A.D. 70. This covers not simply their traditions but their written materials. Q, or the common source of Mt. and Lk., was certainly composed by the seventh decade of the century, probably even earlier; Mk., in its original shape and source, dates from the former period. Thus the roots of the historical literature lie in the same period as the correspondence of Paul, though the flowers bloom side by side with the later pastorals and homilies. It is of still more importance that the two main roots of the subsequent evangelic tradition are deep in the primitive Palestinian circle, and that neither shows any distinct influence of Pauline tendencies.

The primitive epistolary literature of the early church was, like the primitive ceramic art of Hellas, comparatively private. Upon vases intended for the household's use, painting first lavished its grace and skill; and in letters for the quieter purposes of intercourse, the literary spirit was employed by Christians before the aim and scope of it became enlarged. In the nature of things, the use of epistles, taken over from Judaism, especially Alexandrian Judaism (*e.g.* Jer $29^{1.\,25.\,31}$, epp. of Jerem. and Baruch, also 2 Mac $1^{1.\,10}$),* preceded evangelic

* The famous epistle of Aristeas to Philokrates has been called "a predecessor, in form, of the larger NT epistles."

narratives.* The former were occasional and immediate in character, the latter—λόγια, διηγήσεις, ἀπομνημονεύματα—imply a rather more advanced epoch, when the early advent of Jesus was no longer a momentary expectation, and when his life had assumed greater importance and prominence. Nevertheless, by A.D. 50 at least, such notes and collections may have begun to exist in rough form. The current was, at any rate, setting unmistakably in that direction. By the time of Paul's later literary activity, written evangelic narratives were in existence here and there, especially within the primitive Palestinian churches. The primary need for these is to be found in the fact that a new generation was rising, who were dependent for their acquaintance with the history of Jesus upon a fast-diminishing company of eye-witnesses, in the rapid extension and consolidation of the Christian communities, and even in the mission activities of the Palestinian disciples.† To these impulses there must also be added another which sprang from them before long, namely, the need of translating the tradition from the original Aramaic vernacular into Greek. That attempts must have been soon made to meet such requirements is inherently probable, and it is corroborated by the surviving gospels. Even the earliest of them leaves no impression of tentativeness on the mind; there is very little of that comparative lack of precision and definite outline which is often felt in the pioneers of any department in literature. They represent the midsummer, not the spring, of their literary cycle. The subject had been already—perhaps often—handled, even before Mark's gospel took its present shape, although these earlier narratives, like the sources and authorities of Tacitus in the *Annales*, have disappeared. Luke's preface proves that our first three gospels are 'first' for us, not absolutely 'first.' They were the best, but they were

* The collections of parables, stories, and sayings in the gospels find their nearest analogy, upon the other hand, in the midrashic literature of Palestinian Judaism. "Die Evangelien, die wir besitzen, sind in griechischer Sprache bearbeitete Midrashim" (G. Klein, *ZNW.*, 1904, 144 f., 'Zur Erläuterung der Evglien aus Talmud und Midrasch'). Parts of them certainly are closer in form and spirit to midrashic pieces than to Epictetus or Plutarch. This is the burden of P. Fiebig's pamphlet on 'Die Aufgaben der neutestamentlichen Forschung in der Gegenwart' (1909, especially pp. 10 f.).

† Cp. Heinrici, *Der litterarische Charakter der neutest. Schriften* (1908), pp. 23 f., and Sanday in *EKE.* ii. 573 f.

neither the only nor the earliest narratives. It is probable that the literature, of which they are the survivors, and which they seem to have speedily antiquated, began to rise as far back as the sixth decade; and, upon any reasonable criticism of the synoptists, their sources must have partially existed in written form by the opening of the seventh decade. "Mox etiam libros de Jesu compositos esse puto, vel in eosdem usus vel Theophilis (qui profecto multi fuerunt) destinatos, ut intra viginti fere annos a Christi excessu jam copia quædam talium librorum exstaret. Erat enim ætas illa litterarum plena, novaque religio minime intra illiteratam plebem manebat" (Blass, *Acta Ap.* p. 5). There is evidence sufficient, at any rate, to prove that during the Pauline period, prior to the homilies and pastorals, the early church contained the embryonic phases of what eventually was shaped into the canonical gospels.

The subsequent composition of the gospels, which were contemporary with the later homilies, had the same ends of edification in view, and this helps to explain their structure and general characteristics. Euclides in the *Theatetus* (143) describes the way in which he recorded the conversations between Socrates and Theatetus. On returning from Athens, he jotted down at once some notes of what Socrates had told him (ἐγραψάμην ὑπομνήματα), and subsequently wrote on from memory. Finally, whenever he re-visited Athens, he would ask Socrates about anything he had forgotten, and then make corrections in his manuscript. None of the synoptic gospels can claim any such direct relation to Jesus. The earliest of the sources upon which they draw were not composed till about twenty years after he died, and no one took down the words of Jesus during his lifetime. Retentiveness of memory, however, and the needs of the Christian halacha in the churches, helped to carry many of these words through the preliminary period of oral tradition. But even when the earliest literary products rose, *e.g.* Q and the Ur-Marcus, they were not biographical. Still less were the subsequent gospels.* None of them is the direct transcript of an apostle's memories, even by another hand. Their *genre* is not that of biographies so much as of memoirs which were written ἐκ πιστέως εἰς πίστιν, in order to convey and apply certain Christian beliefs about the person of the Lord Jesus, the

* Cp. Harnack, 'die Evangelien' (*Preuss. Jahrb.*, 1904, cxv. pp. 209 f.)

main literary[1] difference being that the gospels, unlike, *e.g.*, the *Memorabilia* of Xenophon, preserve an impersonal tone. The writer does not come forward in the course of the narrative. Even in the case of the Third gospel, where tradition has done most, not only for the question of the authorship, but also for the personal traits and character of the author, the standpoint is hardly less objective than in its predecessors. This apparent absence of personal colouring points back to one cause. It is not due to the overmastering impression of the contents, nor even to the literary self-suppression which Aristotle praises in Homer. The authors' names are not concealed as were those of the Gottes Freunde in the fourteenth century, lest pride of authorship should form a spiritual peril. These anonymous gospels[2] represent to a large extent the final shape given to collections of evangelic matter which had been previously composed by and for members belonging to the general body of the Christian societies. They are communal in spirit and shape—even Luke's is; they resemble the pastorals and epistles in this, that they are a direct outcome of living intercourse and mutual service within the Christian communities. Παράδοσις and *μαρτύριον* are the two words that characterise their contents, for all the free handling of their materials and the creative pressure, naive and deliberate, of their tendencies.

(B) *MARK.*

LITERATURE.—(*a*) Editions (for the patristic and mediæval, cp. Swete, pp. cxiv f.)—P. Poussin's *Catena* (Rome, 1673); Elsner (*Commentarius*, 1773); Matthæi's *Catena* (Moscow, 1775); K. Fritzsche (Leipzig, 1830); Olshausen (1853, Eng. tr. 1863); J. A. Alexander[3] (New York, 1863); Lange (1861, Eng. tr. 1866); Petter (London, 1861); A. Klostermann (1867); F. C. Cook (*Speaker's Comm.* 1878); E. H. Plumptre (*Ellicott's Com.* 1879); P. Schanz (1881)*; Fillion (Paris, 1883); T. M. Lindsay (Edin. n. d.); J. Morison, *A Practical Commentary* (Edin. 1889); Maclear (*CGT.* 1893); Knabenbauer (Paris, 1894); Tiefenthal (Münster, 1894); E. P. Gould (*ICC.* 1896);

[1] Justin's phrase (*ἀπομνημονεύματα*) for the gospels is the term used by Moiragenes for his work on Apollonius (Origen, *c. Cels.* vi. 41); on its applicability to the Christian gospels, *e.g.*, see Usener's *Relig. Untersuchungen*, i. 95 f.; Hirzel's *Der Dialog*, i. 141 f., and above (p. 44 f.).

[2] For some early difficulties (quod nec ab ipso scriptum constat nec ab eius apostolis, sed longo post tempore a quibusdam incerti nominis uiris) raised by this feature of the gospels, see the interesting correspondence of Augustine and Faustus (especially epp. xxxii., xxxiii.).

B. Weiss (— Meyer[9], 1901); A. Menzies, *The Earliest Gospel* (1901)*; S. D. F. Salmond (*CB.* n. d.); Wellhausen (1903)*; V. Rose (Paris, 1904); A. Merx, *Die Evglien Markus u. Lukas* (1905); W. P. Drew (Boston, 1905); Du Buisson (London, 1906); Baljon (1906)*; E. Klostermann (*HBNT.* 1907); W. Kelly (ed. 1907); H. B. Swete[2] (1908)*; B. W. Bacon, *The Beginnings of Gospel Story* (1909)*; Wohlenberg (*ZK.* 1910).

(*b*) Studies (i.) general:—Saunier, *Ueber die Quellen d. Evgliums des Marcus* (1825); Michelsen, *Het Evangelie van Markus* (1867); P. Rohrbach, *Der Schluss der Markusevglms, der Vier-Evglien Kanon und die kleinasiatischen Presbyter* (Berlin, 1894)*; Du Buisson, *The Origin and Peculiar Characteristics of the Gospel of St. Mark* (1896); Hadorn, 'die Entstehung des Mk-Evglms auf Grund der syn. Vergleichung aufs neue untersucht' (*BFT.* ii., 1898); S. D. F. A. Salmond (*DB.* iii. 248–262); J. Weiss, *das älteste Evglm, ein Beitrag zum Verständniss des Markus-Evglms und der ältesten evang. Ueberlieferung**; (1903); Jülicher (*PRE* xii. 295 f.); K. F. A. Lincke, 'Jesus in Kapernaum' (*Ein Versuch zur Erklärung des Markus-Evglms,* 1904; dual account, historical and legendary, in 1^{21-28}); Loisy (*RHL.*, 1904, 513–527); E. D. Burton, *Studies in Gospel of Mark* (1904); A. S. Barnes (*Monthly Review,* Sept. Oct. 1904, *JTS.*, 1905, 187 f., 356 f.); R. A. Hoffmann, *Das Marcus-Evglm und seine Quellen* (Königsberg, 1904); B. Weiss, *die Geschichtlichkeit des Markus-Evglms* (1905); E. Wendling, *Ur-Markus, Versuch einer Wiederherstellung der ältest. Mitteilungen des Lebens Jesu* (1905); A. Müller, *Geschichtskerne in den Evglien nach moderner Forschungen,* 1905 [Conservative reply to Wernle, Wrede, and J. Weiss]; H. Zimmermann, *Der Historischer Wert d. älteste Ueberlieferung von der Geschichte Jesu im Marcus-Evglim* (1905); A. J. Maclean (*DCG.* ii. 120–138)*; E. Wendling, *Die Entstehung des Marcus-Evglms: Philologische Untersuchungen* (1908); M. Goguel, *L'évangile de Marc et ses rapports avec aux de Mathieu et de Luc* (Paris, 1909); (ii.) on special points:—C. L. Reboul (*Paulula, oder Einiger Wenige zur genauenen Erforschung d. Marcus-Evglm,* Gotha, 1876); Bakhuyzen, van Manen, and Callenfels, *Beoordeling van de conjecturen Mk. en Lk.* (1885); Blass, 'Textkritische Bemerkungen zu Markus' (*BFT.*, 1899, 3); W. Wrede, *Des Messiasgeheimnis in der Evglien, Zugleich ein Beitrag zum Verständnis des Marcus-Evglms* (1901)*; Spitta, 'Lücken im Markus-evangelium' (*Urc.* iii. 2. 109–138); Burkitt, *Gospel History and its Transmission* (1906), pp. 33–104; H. J. Holtzmann, *ARW.* x. 18–40, 161–200 ('Die Marcus-Controverse in ihrer heutigen Gestalt')*, and B. W. Bacon (*JBL.*, 1910, 41–60).

§ 1. *Outline.*—The gospel[1] opens with a brief summary (1^{1-13}) of John the Baptist's mission, introducing the baptism and temptation of Jesus. Then begins the first of the two large sections of narrative, describing the Galilean (1^{14}–9^{50}) and the Judæan (10–13) ministry. The former is divided into an account of the

[1] On the score of the opening words, Blass (*BFT.* iii. 3, p. 52) denies that Mk. is a literary work at all. "The book is not a σύγγραμμα, but a ὑπόμνημα, *i.e.* a *Commentarius,* like Cæsar's *Commentarii.*"

work in Eastern Galilee (1^{14}–7^{23}), of which Kapharnaum usually forms the headquarters, and a briefer description of work in Northern Galilee (7^{24}–9^{50}). Returning from the latter district to Kapharnaum ($9^{33f.}$), Jesus then passes southward into Judæa (10–13); and this section closes with his triumphal entry into Jerusalem (11^{1-27}), his controversies with the local authorities (11^{27}–12^{44}), and his final message of doom and judgment on the city and nation (13^{1-37}).

Mark's gospel plunges at once *in medias res.* No account of the birth either of John or of Jesus is furnished at the outset; all we get is a brief and even meagre notice (1^{1-13}) of John's ministry ἐν τῷ ἐρήμῳ and his baptism of Jesus, followed by a mention of the subsequent temptation of our Lord. The writer hurries on to depict the Galilean ministry.

(*a*) No new section of the gospel is to be found at $8^{27f.}$, which is merely the prelude to $8^{31f.}$ $9^{2f.}$ $9^{30f.}$, *i.e.* to the close of the Galilean ministry; and the confession of Peter at Cæsarea Philippi does not occupy in Mark the large and pivotal place which Mt. and Lk. both assign to it. (*b*) It is unnecessary to suppose that the writer has blurred (in $6^{14f.}$) a vital crisis in the fortunes of Jesus, as though Herod's hostility to Jesus, as to John (in Josephus), really drove him into a safe retirement (so Rauch, *ZNW.*, 1902, 303–308; Wellhausen, *Einl.* 48 and on Mark 6^{33}, and Loisy, i. 90). In this event, the evangelist would have obliterated the flight of Jesus before Herod. Rauch corroborates his view by adducing the Syriac text of Mk 6^{30} which connects the 'messengers' with the disciples of John, the course of things being that Jesus and John's adherents retired together ($6^{29-31a.\ 45f.}$). But Mt.'s treatment of Mk. at this point (14^{12}) is too artificial to be claimed as a witness to some more primitive tradition, and the general reconstruction is too hypothetical to be trustworthy.

The second part of the gospel (10^{1}–13^{37}) describes the Judæan ministry, undertaken with the shadow of his death at Jerusalem resting upon his soul (9^{31}). The route taken lies on the eastern side of the Jordan, and Jesus passes through Jericho to Bethany (11^{11}). Hitherto he has only met the Jewish authorities defensively in controversy, but now he takes the initiative, following up his triumphal entry into the capital by driving the money-changers and traders out of the temple ($11^{15f.}$). Further controversy with the authorities follows (11^{27}–12^{12} 12^{13-17} 12^{18-27} 12^{28-37}); then a prophetic prediction of the future (13^{1-37}) marks the close and climax of his public teaching. The remaining part of the book narrates mainly the circumstances of his arrest, trial, crucifixion, and burial (14^{1}–15^{47}), breaking off abruptly with an account of how two women, coming to anoint his corpse, found the tomb empty and saw an angel who bade them and the rest of the disciples return to Galilee: *there shall you see him, as he told you* (16^{1-8}).

(*a*) The closing words are explained by Abbott (*Diat.* 527 f.) from the misrendering of the Hebrew original, as though Mk.'s *said nothing* and Mt. and Lk.'s *carried word to* rest on a confusion between לא and לו such as is found in LXX of Jer 18^{19}, while *they feared* (= Mt. and Lk.'s *beheld*) implies a similar and equally natural (cp. LXX Job 37^{24}, Is 16^{12} etc.) confusion between ירא and ראה. This is plausible, but it is not the only possible explanation, and the other evidence for a Hebrew original is not cogent.

(*b*) The chronological sequence of the gospel is better marked in its large sections than in details. The mission of John the Baptist is described without any note of its period ($1^{4f.}$),* but it closed (1^{14}) before the mission of Jesus began. Even in what follows, apart from the reiterated *εὐθύς* and *καί* (sometimes both together), Mk.'s arrangement is neither consecutive nor coherent (cp. $6^{18f.}$); occasionally he dates a saying or incident on the Sabbath (1^{21} 2^{23} 6^{2}), and twenty-four hours† cover 1^{21-39}, but the healing of the leper ($1^{40f.}$) is undated, the return to Kapharnaum takes place *δι' ἡμερῶν* (2^{1}), and the succeeding incidents are narrated one after another without any attempt at chronological order, the rare notes of sequence being quite vague (*e.g. ἐν ἐκείναις ταῖς ἡμέραις πάλιν κτλ.*, 8^{1}). How long the Galilean mission lasted, or the sudden visit to the territory of Tyre ($7^{24f.}$), we are not told. The two exceptions are the transfiguration (six days after the previous conversation, 9^{2}) and the passion-week ($11^{1f.}$). The various days of the latter are noted ($14^{1, 12}$ 16^{1-2}). Here the tradition evidently was fairly exact and precise (even to hours, 15^{33}), and the same primitive quality attaches to the *μετὰ ἡμέρας ἕξ* of 9^{2} (reproduced by Mt. but altered by Lk. into the vague *ὡσεὶ ἡμέραι ὀκτώ*),‡ which is probably equivalent to 'one week,' reckoned from Sabbath to Sabbath (cp. Keim, iv. 308). The tradition is too early and naive to render it likely that this chronology is artificial, due to the exigencies of public worship (O. Holtzmann, *Leben Jesu*, Eng. tr. p. 344).

§ 2. *Analysis.*—The abbreviated and cursory character of the prologue (1^{1-13}; cp. Bacon, *JBL.*, 1908, 84–106) as compared with the detailed fulness of the following passages in the gospel, has suggested three solutions. It has been held to point, (*a*) in common with other structural phenomena of the book, to the editing of an Ur-Marcus; or (*b*) to Mark's use of Q, the common source of Matthew and Luke, which he generally abridges; or (*c*) to Mark's dependence upon either or both of these gospels

* The 'forty' days of the temptation (1^{12-13}) is symbolic, as in Ac 1^{3} (cp. *DCG.* ii. 250).

† Other little groups of a day's doings, in (2^{2-17}?) $4^{1-35f.}$ $5^{21f.}$ $6^{31f.}$ $9^{2f.}$ 11^{1-11} 11^{12-19} $11^{20f.}$ $14^{12f.}$ $15^{1f.}$ $16^{1f.}$.

‡ The similar phrase in Job 20^{28} (*μεθ' ἡμέρας ὀκτώ*) is more definite; but in neither case is it necessary to think of the eight-day week of the Roman calendar (Mommsen, *Röm. Chronologie*², p. 228).

(so especially Hilgenfeld and Badham). The first-named is decidedly superior to the other two theories, and is borne out by the subsequent traces of editorial revision throughout the gospel. No attempt (*e.g.* von Soden, J. Weiss) to disentangle the precise Petrine traditions or source is convincing,* but the work of the editor in combining Mark's record with logia (*e.g.* in $9^{30f.}$ 11^{25} and 13), in inserting summary links, and in re-arranging the materials, can be seen from $1^{1-13\,(15)}$ onwards. "It is as though the type of Petrine narrative gospel had been already too firmly fixed to admit of radical re-casting, and the new material had been added in adaptation only, and for the most part in the form of memoriter interpolations and supplements" (Bacon, p. xxi).

(*a*) The unrealities into which an ultra-literary criticism of the gospels slips are illustrated by the conflicting views taken of a passage like Mk 1^{1-13}. It is as arbitrary to make Mt. and Lk. expansions of Mk. as to see in Mk. little more than an abbreviation of the large narrative in Q upon which Mt. and Lk. subsequently drew. Q's use of Mk. and Mk.'s use of Q (even in a primitive form) are equally superfluous here. Throughout the whole section one has the impression of a writer who is outlining rapidly a familiar story, in order to reach the point at which either his characteristic contribution or more probably the source before him first begins. There is no reason why the facts of $1^{1-13\,(15)}$ should have been only accessible in Q or in any other document. In that primitive Christian world even Q had no monopoly of such traditions; and although Q were prior to Mk., there would not be the slightest necessity to postulate any documentary source from which the latter must have drawn the contents or even the form † of the summary in 1^{1-13}. Spitta, who regards *ἀρχη τοῦ εὐαγγελίου Ἰησοῦ Χριστοῦ (υἱοῦ θεοῦ)* as a title, further conjectures that about a page of the original autograph has been lost before 1^2, since *καθὼς γέγραπται κτλ.* cannot be supposed to introduce a sentence, much less a paragraph. This introductory page must have described the advent of the Baptist, together with the genealogy and birth of Jesus; but the reasons for this 'must' are as slender as those for similar omissions between 1^6 and 1^7, in 1^{13}, and at 3^{21} (*ZNW.*, 1904, 305 f.; *Urc.* iii. 2, pp. 122–138).

(*b*) In the following section, which belonged to the Ur-Marcus, 1^{28} is plainly proleptic. Mark ‡ dwells on the widespread impression made throughout Galilee by the expulsion of the unclean spirit; but even an immediate impression (*εὐθύς*) of this kind is not made in a few minutes, whereas he goes on in v.[29] to describe what Jesus did after leaving the

---

* On the other hand, it is hypercritical to reject not only the Petrine tradition preserved in Papias, but the possibility of finding any definite Petrine basis for the stories in Mk., as M. Brückner does (*ZNW.*, 1907, 48 f.).

† In 1^{13} it goes back to Test. Napht. 8: *ὁ διάβολος φεύξεται ἀφ' ὑμῶν, καὶ τὰ θηρία φοβηθήσονται ὑμᾶς, καὶ οἱ ἄγγελοι ἀνθέξονται ὑμᾶς.*

‡ *i.e.* for convenience the composer of the gospel, as distinguished from the Mark of the Ur-Marcus.

synagogue on that very day. 1^{21-38} certainly hangs together; the picture of a single day's activity is a historical and literary unity. But 1^{40-45}, though evidently meant to follow 1^{39} (as a specimen of the exorcisms there mentioned) in order to explain Christ's avoidance of the cities (1^{45}), scarcely introduces $2^{1f.}$, which probably existed in the Ur-Marcus in a detached form.* $2^{13f.}$ seems to echo $1^{16f.}$, but the call of Levi is remembered principally for the sake of the famous reply of Jesus to the scribes of the Pharisees (2^{16-17}). The following set of sayings upon fasting (2^{18-22}) are merely topically connected with the preceding context; it is impossible to be sure that the order is consecutive, or even that both debates (or either) occurred at so early a period, for though both Mt. and Lk. emphasise the chronological order, this only proves that they had no other outline to fall back upon. The cycle of conflict-stories is then rounded off by two (2^{23-28} 3^{1-6}) which are set in very vague connections of time, while 2^{28} seems hardly to have lain originally next 2^{27}. The encounter with the Pharisaic authorities, which naturally arose from the free observance of the Sabbath and the synagogue-ministry of Jesus (3^{1-6}), closes with an allusion to the Pharisees and Herodians (3^{6}) which again is proleptic (cp. 12^{13}). But the fact that Jesus had already raised the suspicions of the authorities explains the inquisitorial visits of the Jerusalem-scribes in 3^{22} and 7^{1}. Meantime Mark adds a short general paragraph to sum up the increasing popularity of Jesus not merely in Galilee, but far beyond its confines (3^{7-12}).

(*c*) This paragraph forms a transition between the opening section of the gospel (where it throws the popular enthusiasm into relief against the malevolent criticism of the authorities) and the following section (3^{13}–6^{13}) which begins by describing how Jesus began to provide for the future, in view of the demands and the dangers of the work, by organising his disciples. Twelve are chosen (3^{12-19}) to preach and to cast out demons, not to heal sicknesses—a function which Mark, unlike Matthew (10^{8}) and Luke (9^{2}), reserves for Jesus himself.† But no mission is assigned them till the close of the section (6^{6b-11}), and Mark again fills up his record with materials which are both vaguely located (cp. 3^{20}) and loosely connected. The first of these is the defence of Jesus against a charge of insanity brought against him by the scribes from Jerusalem, whose interference is topically set in an account of a similar interference by his own family (3^{21-35}). The lake-side teaching is then resumed (4^{1}, cp. 2^{13} $3^{7f.}$); but instead of describing as usual the effect, Mark now gives a specimen of its contents (not necessarily borrowed from Q). What Jesus taught in the synagogues is not explicitly reported (but cp. Lk 4^{21-27}). On the other hand, a selection from the parables spoken to the open-air audiences is presented, containing three parables ($4^{3-9.\ 26-29.\ 30-32}$), with a discussion of the parabolic method in general (4^{10-12}) and an explanation of the first parable (4^{13-20}). Interpolated between this and the second parable is a saying upon the Lamp, apropos of the duty of openness for a disciple (4^{21-25}). As his hearers, after v.^{10}, are the disciples, it almost follows that vv.$^{26-32}$ (cp. the *αὐτοῖς* of v.^{33}), which presuppose the crowd,

* The scribes and Pharisees do not pursue Jesus over the country; they wait till he finishes a tour or journey (cp. $3^{22f.}$ $7^{1f.}$ $8^{10f.}$).

† As a matter of fact, however, they do heal, when the time comes (6^{12-13}).

originally followed vv.$^{1-9}$. This cycle of sayings is now closely linked chronologically to a cycle of miraculous deeds (4^{35}–5^{43}; cp. $4^{1}=4^{36}$, the second busy day's proceedings narrated by Mark), depicting the power of Jesus over the forces of nature (4^{35-41}), unclean spirits (5^{1-20}), sickness (5^{25-34}), and death ($5^{21-24.\ 35-43}$). These incidents are closely and chronologically set. But his sceptical reception at Nazareth (6^{1-6a}) is an erratic boulder,* like the subsequent account of the commission of the twelve, which took place during some preaching tour (6^{6b-13}).

(*d*) The fame of Jesus on this tour reaches the ears of Herod Antipas, whose conscience is troubled by the appearance of one whom he takes to be John the Baptist *redivivus* (6^{14-29}); but Mark has nothing to say of any precautions taken by Herod, or even of what Jesus said or did during the absence of the disciples. He simply proceeds to narrate a couple of miracles ($6^{30-44.\ 45-52}$) which happened immediately after their return, and to note the unabated popularity of Jesus as a healer of diseases (6^{53-56}). Then follows a cluster of sayings on true purity as opposed to ceremonial, occasioned by a visit of the Pharisees and scribes from Jerusalem (7^{1-23}). No motive is assigned for the next move north into the Tyrian country (7^{24-30}), and only one incident is recorded—the cure of a Syrophœnician woman's daughter.† On the way back,‡ or possibly after his return, a deaf and dumb man is cured (7^{31-37}); but the incident is not fixed to any time or place. The next section (8^{1-26}) not only opens vaguely (8^{1}), but contains material which is parallel to, or a duplicate of, $6^{32f.}$, viz. a miracle of feeding ($8^{1-10}=6^{32f.}$) in an out-of-the-way spot, followed by an encounter with the Pharisees ($8^{11f.}$, cp. $7^{1f.}$), and a cure ($8^{22f.}$, cp. $7^{31f.}$). The characteristic traits of the separate stories are probably due to oral tradition; their agreements, which outweigh their differences, seem to denote a common, single type; their juxtaposition is literary rather than the result of oral tradition.

(*e*) The following fragment of teaching delivered on the way north to Cæsarea Philippi marks a more private and tragic phase in the gospel ($8^{27f.}$); the fate of Jesus as the Christ implies a resolute renunciation and confession on the part of his disciples, to whom he now imparts special instruction. But as the term τὸν ὄχλον in 8^{34} shows, $8^{34f.}$ does not belong to this particular cycle of teaching; it is one of the intercalations of the editor who elsewhere (7^{14}) introduces a crowd (though not necessarily from Lk 14^{25}). A certain roughness of arrangement or dislocation of the natural order is evident indeed in the whole of 8^{27}–9^{13}, where $8^{27f.}$ seems to be resumed § in 9^{11-13} after the break of 9^{2-10}; but source and editor are not easily disentangled

---

* Its position next to $6^{6bf.}$ is meant to bring out the contrast between Christ's rejection by his own people and the success of his disciples abroad.

† Here only, by a foreigner, is Jesus called κύριος in Mk., and here only does the writer represent him as healing at a distance from the patient.

‡ Unless we are to suppose that Jesus took a long and apparently purposeless circular tour north and east and south, it is better, with Wellhausen, to regard *Sidon* as an erroneous rendering of צידן (Saidan = Bethsaida); cp. 8^{22} and Mt 11^{21}.

§ The suggestion that 9^{11-13} should read $9^{11.\ 12b.\ 12a.\ 13}$ certainly clears up the passage, and is preferable to deleting $9^{12b.\ 13c}$ (Wernle) as a gloss.

Bacon (*AJT.*, 1898, pp. 541 f., 1902, pp. 236 f.) regards 9^{2-10} as practically a duplicate of 8^{27}–9^{1}, 9^{11-13}, which it interrupts with its vision-incident much as Ac 9^{30}–11^{18} precedes 13–15; Loisy (*RHR.*, 1904, pp. 386 f., 1907, p. 446) assigns 8^{27-30} $9^{1.\ 11-13}$ to a primitive separate source; and Schweitzer (*Das Abendmahl*, ii. 58 f.) puts 8^{34}–9^{29} back into the Bethsaida-period (6^{31-56}). On Wellhausen's arbitrary characterisation of 8^{27}–10^{45} (*Einl.* 81 f.) as a reflection of the later Christian consciousness, cp. Denney, *Jesus and the Gospel*, 181 f.

The twofold apologetic motive of the transfiguration-story is fairly obvious: viz. to meet the objection raised by the Elijah-tradition (cp. Justin, *Dial.* 49), and to explain how the crucified Jesus could be the Christ of God. The former is emphasised by Mark; the latter is specially brought out by Mt. and Luke. It has been conjectured that the transfiguration * originally represented an appearance of Jesus six days after death (Wellhausen on Mk 9^{13} 'vielleicht der älteste in den Evangelien,' cp. Loisy, *Évang. Syn.* ii. 39–40) to the disciples in Galilee (Mt 28^{16}); but though Peter is prominent here (9^{5} cp. 8^{29}), this is hardly enough by itself to prove that the vision tallies with that of 1 Co 15^{5}. On the other hand, in 2 P 1^{14-18} the prophetic announcement by Jesus of Peter's death (cp. Jn $21^{18f.}$) is followed by an allusion to the vision and voice on the holy mountain which (Hofmann, cp. Spitta's monograph, pp. 89 f.) might refer to a post-resurrection vision like this, as is plainly the case in *The Apocalypse of Peter* (§§ 2 f.), where the twelve on a mountain with the risen Lord see two departed saints in radiant form *ἐμπροσθεν τοῦ κυρίου.*

(*f*) The account of the transfiguration (9^{2-13}) is followed by the expulsion of an evil spirit from a boy (9^{14-29}), the last miracle in Galilee thus belonging to the same class as the first ($1^{23f.}$). The closing paragraph on the Galilean mission consists of some fragments from the private conversation of Jesus and his disciples (9^{30-50}), which the editor has inserted without any close links. Jesus is no longer preaching or healing; his whole attention is concentrated on the inner circle of his adherents. 9^{36-37} seems rather isolated, especially if the curious v.^{35} (calling the twelve, when he was already with them!), which is partly omitted by D, is taken as an editorial link between $^{33-34}$ and $^{36-37}$ (Wellhausen). 9^{38-40} certainly belonged originally to another site; its present position is due to the topical mention of the Name ($9^{37.\ 39}$), and 9^{42} is the most natural sequel, at any rate, to 9^{37}. In 9^{49-50} the discourse apparently becomes still more disconnected and obscure, but the closing note (9^{50}) is on the same key as the opening ($9^{33f.}$).

(*g*) The final departure of Jesus from Galilee (10^{1-2}) marks the beginning of the Judæan ministry (10–13). The details of this are scanty and vague until he reaches Jerusalem, when the record becomes suddenly richer. Thus the discussion with the Pharisees on divorce (10^{2-12}) apparently occurs in the open-air (cp. v.^{10}), but the setting of the incident is ambiguous. Two incidents of travel follow ($10^{13-16.\ 17-31}$), after which the narrative becomes vivid ($10^{32f.}$), though the request of James and John ($10^{35f.}$) comes abruptly

---

* O. Schmiedel (*Hauptprobleme d. Leben-Jesu-Forschung*², 81 f.) postulates a similar origin for the synoptic stories of the feeding of the 5000 and the walking on the sea (Mk $6^{31f.}$ etc.).

after what precedes.* The cure of the blind beggar outside Jericho (10^{46-52}) was evidently a fixed point in the primitive tradition; it is the only cure wrought by Jesus outside Galilee, and it marks, by the beggar's acclamation of Jesus as *the Son of David*, the opening stage of his messianic entry into the capital (11^{1-11}). The site of the subsequent dialogues and discourses is the temple (cp. 11^{11}), where he spends the day but not the night; his headquarters are at Bethany ($11^{11.\ 20}$). The cleansing of the temple (11^{15-18}) is inserted in the symbolic story of the blighted fig-tree ($11^{12-14.\ 20f.}$), to which Mark has, as usual, attached several disparate sayings ($11^{23f.}$). In a series of encounters, Jesus silences and outwits the official parties one after another. The climax of these is the admission of a scribe † that Jesus is a true teacher ($12^{32f.}$), whereupon Jesus takes the initiative ($12^{35f.}$) by attacking the teaching and conduct ($12^{38f.}$) of the scribes, to the delight of the people. Since 10^{46} Jesus has been teaching not his disciples but the public; in 13^{1-37}, however, which forms the close of the Judæan ministry and the climax of his relations with the temple, the editor, by using the small apocalypse, represents him as instructing the inner circle of his disciples privately upon the future destruction of the temple and the prospects of his own cause.

(*h*) The story of the Passion now begins ($14^{1f.}$), the account of the treachery of Judas being interrupted by that of the anointing at Bethany (14^{3-9}), and followed by that of the celebration of the passover (14^{12-25}). While 14^{12-16} is rejected as unhistorical by critics like Brandt and Wellhausen, it is deleted by Spitta (*Urc.* i. 266 f.) on grounds that are hardly more solid than those on which Rauch (*ZNW.*, 1902, 308–314) bases his theory that 14^{12-17} forms a later gloss, intended to make the meal a passover-supper. Only when vv.$^{12-16}$ are omitted, does the absence of *εἰς* Ἰεροσόλυμα in v.^{17} seem suspicious (cp. v.^{16}), as though the supper had been perhaps eaten at Bethany (so, *e.g.*, Wendling). $14^{13.\ 16}$ is not an unhistorical duplicate of 11^{1-4}, and there is nothing in the style of the passage to warrant any suspicion of later editorial handling. O. Holtzmann (*Leben Jesu*, ch. xiii.), who places Jn 7^{53}–8^{11} before Mk 12^{35}, regards Christ's verdict on this woman as an incident at the beginning of the Monday when he ate the passover evening meal with his disciples, and argues that as neither Jesus nor his disciples can have been busy with preparations for that meal, the elimination of Mk 14^{12-16} would involve the loss of any tradition relating to the earlier part of that day,—a loss which would be incredible, since the disciples were far from likely to forget the last day they spent in the company of their Master. This is subtle, but not untrue to the history or psychology of the situation. For the theory that the time-references in Mark's story of the passion-week were not in the Ur-Marcus, cp. J. Weiss (*DCG.* ii. 323–324); for detailed criticism of the trial-stories, see Moffatt, *DCG.* ii. 749–759.

§ 3. *Structure.*—This survey (i.) shows that, while the general scheme is clear, Mark's arrangement of materials is often topical

* Here 10^{42-45} is secondary, as compared with the Lucan version (22^{25-27}).

† Neither 12^{28-34} nor even 12^{18-27} is closely related to this period, and probably Lk. (10^{25-28}) is right in placing the former at an earlier phase of the ministry.

rather than historical. Sayings and incidents are grouped in a way which suggests not so much chronological sequence as similarity of subject-matter. Hence the criticism of Papias is justified, if it referred to order. Compared with the Fourth gospel, whose carefully marked sequences were familiar and popular in Asia Minor in the opening of the second century, the narrative of Mark would appear irregular. In the second place (ii.), Mark's gospel is plainly a composition, not in the sense in which Mt. and Lk. are, but still in a noticeable degree of its own. It is not an artless transcript of oral reminiscences. The author has had before him various materials, not only oral but also written sources, which he has occasionally re-arranged.* The narratives betray unevenness at certain points; gaps and breaks occur, and more than one current of opinion or tradition may be detected. The problem of literary criticism which results from these data is, whether there is adequate evidence to prove that more than one hand need be traced in the composition of the gospel, or whether such editorial manipulation as can be unbared may not have been the work of John Mark himself, to whom the first draft of the Petrine reminiscences was due. There are two *a priori* reasons for hesitation in attempting an analysis of Mark into an original edition which has been revised or amplified by a later writer. (*a*) We cannot assume that what appear to be secondary elements were not already present to some extent in the Petrine tradition which formed the basis of the original gospel; by the time that Mark took down the reminiscences of Peter there was ample time for the oral tradition of the primitive churches to have filled out some of the sayings of our Lord, and for elements of reflection and distortion to have crept in. (*b*) The uniformity of language, both in style and vocabulary constitutes a second reason; but, although Wendling has driven the linguistic and stylistic argument to the verge of unreality, there are nevertheless traces of strata, and such uniformity as may be found is as likely to be the work of the final editor. These

* "Dans une œuvre aussi peu littéraire, le défaut de cohésion n'est pas une preuve de rédaction multiple. Mais l'incoherence qu'on pourrait appeler positive, le désaccord entre les morceaux juxtaposés qui procèdent de courants d'idées très différents, l'accumulation de données disparates qui se laissent reconstituer en groupes homogènes, caractérisés chacun par une inspiration distincte, les doubles emplois peuvent attester, ici comme ailleurs, la combinaison des traditions ou des sources écrites et la complexité du travail redactionnel" (Loisy, i. 85–86).

reasons, therefore, suggest hesitation not in the acceptance but in the working out of the hypothesis that the canonical Mark, written shortly after A.D. 70, is based for the most part on Mark's draft of the Petrine reminiscences.

The hypothesis that our canonical Mark represents the later edition of an earlier document, or that it can be analysed into two or more different sources, may be based either upon considerations drawn from the internal structure of the gospel itself (so, *e.g.*, P. Ewald, Wendling, Wellhausen), or from a comparison of its contents with those of Mt. and Luke (so, *e.g.*, J. Weiss, Réville, von Soden). It has undergone various vicissitudes. Advocated formerly by Holtzmann, it was worked out by Schenkel, Weiffenbach, Wittichen and others, especially by Sevin, Jacobsen, and Mangold. Weizsäcker then pushed the analysis of Mk. still further, and more recent attempts at a pre-canonical source or sources are to be seen in the essays of Beyschlag (*SK.*, 1881, pp. 565 f.), Feine (*JPT.*, 1886–1888), and J. Weiss (*SK.*, 1890, pp. 555 f., 1891, pp. 289 f.). One motive which actuated some of these critics was the desire to reconstruct the original Mark of Papias; but, independently of this, others have worked out a series of secondary features, Pauline or apostolic, which have overlaid the primitive materials of the Petrine story (cp. recently Schmiedel in *EBi.* 1844 f.). Thus Wendling actually traces two different sources, in addition to an editor, throughout the gospel. M^1, an Aramaic source, represents the primitive, realistic impression of Jesus the teacher, conveyed by Peter. This was translated into Greek by M^2 with poetical and artistic additions of his own to bring out the supernatural powers of Jesus the divine messiah, the Son of Man who makes a mystery of his person. Finally, a redactor (= Ev), whose dogmatic interests overrode his historical sense, inserted some passages (*e.g.* 1^{1-3} $3^{6f. 22f.}$ etc.) and edited others (*e.g.* $8^{31f.}$ $11^{12f. 19f.}$ and 12^{38-44}). But this, apart from the lack of sufficient criteria in style, implies too rigid and *a priori* a conception of the developments of primitive Christology. Even an incidental allusion like that of 1^{24} shows that Jesus was more than a teacher in the earliest source, and many of Wendling's special results are too subjective and dogmatic to command assent (cp. Menzies, *Review of Theology and Philosophy*, ii. pp 3–6). The over-elaboration of the theory will be seen from the following outline :—

M^1 1^{16-34a} $^{35-39a}$ $^{40-44}$ 2^{1-13a} $^{16b-17.}$
M^2 1^{4-14a}
Ev 1^{1-3} $^{14b-15}$ ^{34b} ^{39b} ^{45} $2^{13b, 16a,}$ ^{18a}

M^1 $2^{18b. 19a}$ ^{21}–3^5 $^{20-21}$ ^{31}–4^9 $^{26-29}$ ^{33}
M^2
Ev 2^{19b-20} 3^{6-19} $^{22-30}$ 4^{10-25} $^{30-32}$ ^{34}

M^1 6^{32-34} 8^{27-30a}
M^2 4^{35}–5^{42} ^{43b} 6^{14} $^{17-29}$ $^{35-44}$
Ev 5^{42a} 6^{1-13} $^{15-16}$ $^{30-31}$ ^{45}–8^{26}

M^1 8^{33b} $^{36-37}$ 10^1 $^{13-23}$ ^{28}
M^2 9^{2-8} $^{14-27}$
Ev $8^{30b-33a}$ $^{33c-35}$ ^{38} 9^1 $^{9-13}$ $^{28-50}$ 10^{2-12} ^{24}

M^1		10^{31-32a}		35-37		41-44				15-17	
M^2								$10^{46}–11^{10}$			
Ev	10^{26-30}		32b-34		38-40		45		11^{11-14}		18-23. 27a

M^1	$11^{27b}–12^{14a}$		14c-31		34b-37 13^{1-2}		28-29		33-36		14^{1-7}	
M^2												
Ev		12^{14b}		32-34a		3-27		30-32		37		14^{8-9}

M^1	14^{10-11}			22-25								43-46		48-50			
M^2		14^{12-20}			26-35a		36-37		39-41a		42		47		51-56		60-62a
Ev			14^{21}			35b		38		41b						57-59	

M^1			14^{65}		15^{1-15}		21-22		24a		26-27		31-32		34a	
M^2		14^{63-64}		66-72		15^{16-20}		23		24b-25		29-30		33		34b-36
Ev	14^{62b}															

M^1	15^{37}							
M^2		15^{38}		40-43		$15^{46}–16^{7a}$		8
Ev			15^{39}		44-45		16^{7b}	

R. A. Hoffmann's scheme postulates two Aramaic editions of Mk., one written by Mark for Jewish Christians and used by Mt., the other (a larger and longer work) employed by the canonical Mk. and Lk. In this way the occasional superiority of Mt. to the others is explained, but the agreements of all three are left in the dark (cp. Schmiedel, *LC.*, 1904, 154 f.), and the theory of an Aramaic original for Mk. is not convincing.

Wendling's analysis is rivalled, in point of elaboration, by Bacon's recent theory that R, the final editor, who was an anti-Jewish Paulinist, used not only Q (chiefly in the Lucan recension) and P (the primitive Petrine tradition, as outlined in Ac 10^{37-38}) but X (an unknown source). R's hand appears in $1^{1.\ 3-6.\ 24-28.\ 34b}$ $2^{19b-20.\ 27-28}$ $3^{6.\ 20-21}$ $4^{33-34.\ 39f.}$ $5^{1-21.\ 37}$ $6^{1-3.\ 5-6.\ 16-29.\ 45.\ 52b.\ 56}$ $7^{3-4.\ 8.\ 18}$ $8^{10.\ 13.\ 16-21}$ $9^{6.\ 12b.\ 30-32.\ 41.\ 50b}$ $10^{1.\ 12.\ 32-34.\ 41f.}$ $11^{16.\ 17\ (?).\ 18}$ 12^{12} $13^{3f.\ 10f.\ 24f.}$ $14^{8-9.\ 12f.\ 26.\ 28.\ 41.\ 55f.}$ 15^{2-5}, but he also edited Q in $1^{2.\ 7.\ 12-13.\ 14-15}$ $2^{5b-10.\ 15-16.\ 18-19a}$ $3^{1-5.\ 8-19.\ 22-25.}$ $4^{2-8.\ 11-12.\ 21-25}$ $6^{30-31.\ 53-55}$ $7^{1.\ 5.\ 14-17.\ 20-23.\ 31-37}$ $8^{11-12.\ 14-15\ (?).\ 22f.}$ 8^{30-34} $9^{37.\ 40.\ 42.\ 43f.\ (?)\ 50}$ $10^{10-11.\ 28f.}$ $11^{9-10.\ 12-14.\ 20-21}$ $12^{1-11.\ 38-40}$ $13^{9.\ 14f.\ 28f.}$ $14^{17f.\ (?)}$ 15^{40-41}, and P in $4^{35f.}$ 6^{14-15} $9^{11-12a.\ 13-17.\ 19f.\ 24f.\ 33-35}$ $10^{46f.\ (?)}$ $11^{1f.\ 11.\ 19.\ 27f.}$ $14^{27.\ 32f.\ 53}$ $15^{1.\ 6f.\ 39}$, as well as X in 1^{40-45} 3^{7} $8^{36-37\ (?)}$ $9^{36.\ 38-39}$ $10^{13-16.\ 24f.}$ 12^{35-37} $15^{16f.\ 22f.\ 34f.\ 42f.}$. There are more or less complete fragments of P in $1^{16-23.\ 29-34a.\ 35-39}$ $2^{1-5.\ 11-14}$ (4^{1}?) $5^{22-36.\ 38-43}$ $7^{24f.\ (?)}$ $8^{1-9\ (?).\ 27-29}$ 9^{1} $11^{15f.}$ 12^{13} $14^{1f.\ 10-11.\ 22f.\ 29f.\ 43f.\ 65f.}$ 15^{73}, of X in $1^{8.\ 9-11}$ $2^{17.\ 21-26}$ $4^{9-10.\ 13-20}$ $6^{4\ (?).\ 32-45\ (?).\ 46-52a}$ 7^{6-7} 9^{49} $10^{2-9\ (?).\ 17-23.\ 35f.}$ $12^{13f.\ 41f.}$ 13^{1-2} 14^{3-7} $15^{21.\ 33.\ 38}$, and of Q in $4^{26-32\ (?)}$ $6^{4\ (?).\ 7-13}$ 7^{9-13} 8^{35-38} $9^{2-5\ 7-10.\ 18.\ 23}$ 10^{22-25}. It is obvious that this analysis reduces P to a minimum and raises R to a maximum; the criteria for distinguishing Q and X are rarely cogent, and a large amount of matter assigned to either, as well as to R, might well be grouped under P.

Solger's (*Urc.* 64 f.) "Ur-Marcus" consists of 1^{4-45} $2^{1-20.\ 23-28}$ $3^{1-26.\ 31-35}$ $4^{1-10.\ 13-27.\ 36-41}$ $5^{1-7.\ 9-43}$ $6^{1-13.\ 30}$ $7^{1-2.\ 5-14.\ 16-36}$ $8^{1-17.\ 21-30.\ 32-35.\ 38}$ $9^{17-30.\ 33-37}$ $10^{1-31.\ 46-52}$ $11^{1-24.\ 27-33}$ $12^{1-9.\ 12-44}$ $13^{1-9.\ 11-22.\ 24-30.\ 32-37}$ $14^{12-13.\ 16-22.\ 26.\ 32.\ 34-35.\ 40.\ 50-53.\ 55.\ 60-64}$ $15^{1-15.\ 22.\ 25-28.\ 30-32.\ 34.\ 37.\ 39.\ 42-46}$, composed *c.* A.D. 38 by John Mark (cp. Ac 12^{12}). Both Scholten and Jacobsen had already advocated this view of the authorship of the source, which is also held by A. Müller (the source being

Aramaic), and which is much nearer to the data of the gospel and of the primitive tradition than any of the analyses just noticed,* or than that of a critic like J. Weiss, who holds rigidly that the Ur-Marcus contained little or nothing which cannot be found in Mt. and Lk., and in whose hands this primitive source loses its graphic colouring and circumstantial detail, since most of the salient features of the canonical Mark are ascribed to the redactor.

The difficulty of determining what is primary and what is secondary is illustrated, *e.g.*, by such a minor linguistic point as the use of the semi-proverbial formula, *he who has ears* (*to hear*) *let him hear* (cp. *HS.* 106–107). This denotes a pregnant reminder to the reader or hearer; but it may quite well have been used by Jesus (*e.g.* in Mk $4^{9.\ 23}$) in some of the connections preserved in the gospels. The Joh. apocalypse's use of it (2^{7} etc. 13^{9}) is hardly normative, and the call to note a deeper sense in the adjoining context is not to be referred exclusively to the age of the Epigoni, when the sayings of Jesus were becoming the subject of devout allegorising (so M. Dibelius in *SK.*, 1910, 461–471).

(*a*) The opening paragraph (1^{1-4}) starts two special problems: one upon the meaning of 1^{1} (ἀρχὴ τοῦ εὐαγγελίου Ἰησοῦ Χριστοῦ, υἱοῦ θεοῦ), and one upon the relation of the OT citation in 1^{2-3} to the rest of the context. The former passage is the title of the prologue. In v.[4] the writer begins his narrative proper of the life of Jesus with the remark that Jesus came into Galilee preaching τὸ εὐαγγέλιον τοῦ θεοῦ. The different sense of εὐαγγέλιον in v.[1]—where the words Ἰησοῦ Χριστοῦ are not subjective (so Zahn), as if it were the gospel which Jesus preached, but objective—indicates a conscious play upon the term. The ἀρχή of the Christian dispensation lay in the prophetic mission of John, who summed up the previous order of things (cp. Mt 11^{13}) and prepared the way for the new. Hence the twofold citation in 1^{2-3}. The editor in v.[2] explains how the ἀρχή was not Jesus himself but some one else, the divinely predicted forerunner (= ἐγένετο Ἰωάννης κτλ.), while in v.[3] he explains how the very sphere of the forerunner's mission had also been prophesied (= ἐν τῷ ἐρήμῳ, v.[4]).

Although ἀρχή here is not equivalent to *summa rei* (so Herklotz in *BZ.*, 1904, pp. 77 f., 1905, pp. 408 f.), it might be a misrendering of the *incipit*

* P. Ewald (*Das Hauptproblem der Evglienfrage und der Weg zu seiner Lösung*, 1890, pp. 178 f.) gives the redactor little more than 1^{1-3} 1^{24}–8^{26} 16^{9-20}; du Buisson assigns him a few linguistic changes (*e.g.* in 13), one or two details, and some context supplements (*e.g.* in $2^{15.\ 16.\ 18}$ 6^{35} 7^{19} 8^{1} 9^{37} 10^{27} $12^{15\ 21.\ 28}$ 14^{16}).

prefixed to Mark when the gospels were written in one manuscript (so Nestle in *Exp.*[4] x. 458–460; *Einl.* pp. 130 f., Eng. tr. 163; *Philol. Sacra*, pp. 45–46); the heading of the book would thus become the opening of the text. But if ἀρχή is an unparalleled opening for an early Christian writing, καθώς (especially introducing a quotation) is equally abnormal. None of the cases quoted in *ACL.* i. 996 is really analogous at all points to Mk 1^{1-3}, and, as it seems clumsy and contrary to Mark's style to connect v.[1] with v.[4] grammatically, the alternative is to regard the OT citation as due to an editorial hand, whereas, in the original, v.[1] was the heading or description either of the opening section or of the whole book. In the latter case, the object of the gospel would be to portray the start and origin (cp. Ac 1^1, He 2^3, Jn 15^{27}) of the gospel of Jesus in his lifetime on earth (so Zahn, *Skizzen aus dem Leben der alten Kirche*, p. 240). This would gain in likelihood if one accepted the hypothesis (see below) that Mark wrote another treatise (which underlies the opening chapter of Acts) to describe the progress and advance of the gospel whose opening his first book had depicted. But in view of the precariousness of this theory, it is safer to confine the scope of v.[1] to the opening section of the gospel itself. Otherwise, ἀρχή κτλ. might be taken with ἐγένετο in v.[4], the intervening verses being a lengthy parenthesis (so, *e.g.*, Hilgenfeld, *ZWT.*, 1906, 196–199, and Goguel, *op. cit.* 36)—a hypothesis which Chajes utilises in favour of his Semitic * original for the gospel by conjecturing that ἀρχή is really a misinterpretation of קֹדֶם=קֳדָם (πρὶν), though Halévy prefers to think of תחלת (cp. Hos 1^2 LXX). But such Semitic hypotheses † are generally precarious, and, in this instance, they are superfluous.

The awkwardness of the whole passage, whether [2-3] is taken as a parenthesis or [1-3] as an anacolouthon, suggests irresistibly that the OT references at least are inserted by an editorial hand from some book of florilegia (p. 24). Some primitive disturbance or corruption of the original text is almost certain, and, as no evidence is to be found in MSS, it occurred probably in the process of editing the Ur-Marcus. Deleting [2b] (ἰδοὺ ἐγὼ . . . σοῦ), Weiffenbach opens what he considers to be a "beautiful and grand portal to the gospel" (*JPT.*, 1882, 668–680; similarly Soltau, *Eine Lücke*, pp.

---

* Hebrew. W. C. Allen similarly falls back on an Aramaic original, regarding the prophetic references, together with the mistranslation, as the work of the Greek translator. Wellhausen (*Einl.* 53–57) even pushes his revised edition of the Ur-Marcus earlier than its translation into Greek.

† That Mark is the translation of an Aramaic original is held, *e.g.*, by H. P. Chajes (*Markus Studien*, 1889), Halévy (*RS.*, 1900, 115–149), W. C. Allen (*ET.*, 1902, 328–332; *Exp.*[6] i. 436–443), Blass (*Philology of Gospels*, 190–218), R. A. Hoffmann, Zimmermann (*SK.*, 1903, 287 f.), and Wellhausen (*Einl.* 14 f., 43 f.). Zimmermann's (*SK.*, 1901, 415–458) analysis makes all three synoptists (Mark before A.D. 66) translate AQ, the primitive Aramaic gospel; while neither Mt. nor Lk. used Mk., Lk. had access to a special source (LQ); but his birth-story is drawn from AQ in order to counteract Mt.'s legendary narrative (see below), and his resurrection cycle of stories is based on another special source (Semitic) extending into Acts.

1–7, and Holtzmann in *HC.*): but it is better, with Lachmann (*SK.*, 1830, p. 844), P. Ewald, Weizsäcker, Scholten, Wellhausen, and others, to take [2-3] as an editorial gloss. Spitta (*ZNW.*, 1904, 305–308), who rightly takes v.[1] as the title (cp. J. Weiss, *das älteste Evglm*, pp. 24 f.), regards [2a+3] as the original of the opening passage; but he complicates this by declaring that some previous introductory narrative must have lain in the original text (see above, p. 221).

If the fusion of the citations is not due to Mark himself, it is probable that he was indebted for it to a *florilegium* of messianic proof-texts which was circulated among the churches, for the benefit of those who were exposed to controversy with the Jews. The Malachi-citation, grouped under Isaiah in Mk 1^2, occurred in a subsequent passage of Q (Mt 11^{10} = Lk 7^{27}) which is absent from Mark's narrative. If Mt. and Lk. had Mk. 1^{2-3} before them, they probably preferred the more correct situation of Mk 1^2. But even if they had not, it would be unnecessary to fall back on either of the three hypotheses just mentioned, as though Mk. or the editor of the Ur-Marcus deliberately fused together the separate citations which he found in Q or in Mt. and Lk.

The other OT reminiscences are scanty and unimportant; for the most part they are conformed to the LXX (cp. W. C. Allen, *ET.* xii. 187–189).

(*b*) The position of the conflict-section in Mk 2^1–3^6 suggests doubts of its chronological setting. The uniform colour of the five incidents ($2^{1-12, 13-17, 18-22, 23-28}$, 3^{1-6}), the notice of a plot of the Herodians and Pharisees against his life at this early stage (3^6), the proleptic occurrence of the messianic* *Son of Man* (cp. $8^{29. 38f.}$), and the general unlikelihood of such an immediate and rapid succession of encounters—these considerations point to the antedating of the incidents in question, or at least to the fact that some of them (excluding the call of Levi, 2^{14}), like 3^{1-6}, have been drawn into this early group through the influence of associations. The probability is that they belonged to a special source incorporated either by Mark or by the final editor at this point† (so Wendt, *Lehre Jesu*, i. 23 f.; Baldensperger, Dalman,

* It cannot well be equivalent to the generic *bar nasha* in 2^{10}, any more than in $2^{28f.}$, Lk 22^{48}, Mt 10^{23} 26^{45}. That Jesus used it as a non-messianic self-designation is over-subtle; neither here nor elsewhere is it possible to explain the title as an equivalent for *man* (*the man*), the first person singular, or *some one* (cp. Mt 11^9). Even the alternative, that Jesus used it as an incognito, to provoke thought, is unsatisfactory (cp. Abbott's *Diat.* 3152 f.).

† The source is resumed at 12^{15} (cp. Wendt, pp. 25 f.).

etc.). Similarly 3^{22-30} is misplaced from after 7^{23} (the Jerusalemite scribes do not appear on the scene till after 7^{1}),* and the editorial hand appears in 3^{6-19} (Wellhausen, Wendling).

(*c*) In passages like 4^{1-34} (cp. *EBi.* 1866–1867) $9^{33f.}$ and 13, the impression of editorial work upon a source, not simply on oral tradition, deepens; *e.g.* $4^{10f.}$ is secondary to its context (cp. J. Weiss and Wendling), which lies more level to 2^{1}–3^{6}. Without carrying the analysis further, we may therefore outline the process by which Mk.'s gospel reached its present form, thus: notes of Peter's reminiscences written down by Mark † (hence the Aramaic colouring and vivid detail of certain sections) were afterwards edited by a (Roman?) Christian who used not only the small apocalypse but some other logia of Jesus (not necessarily Q). The gospel is not a gospel of Peter, but it contains a cycle of traditions for which Peter is the authority and in which he plays a prominent rôle. The first person mentioned in the narrative of Christ's mission ($1^{14f.}$) is Simon; his call ($1^{16f.}$) is followed ere long ($1^{29f.}$) by the cure of his mother-in-law. Simon *καὶ οἱ μετ' αὐτοῦ* (1^{36}) form the inner circle (cp. $9^{2f.}$ 3^{3} 14^{33}) of the first disciples (2^{15}); he is named first in the list of the twelve ($3^{16f.}$); he first hails Jesus openly as the Christ ($8^{29f.}$), and is evidently the leader and spokesman of the twelve (8^{33} 10^{28} 11^{21} *καὶ ἀναμνησθεὶς ὁ Πέτρος λέγει αὐτῷ*,‡ 14^{7} 16^{7}), though now and then speaking (14^{29}) and acting (14^{47}) impetuously for himself (cp. $14^{54. 66f.}$). One slight feature, which emphasises not only the prominence of Peter but the leading position next him of the sons of Zebedee, is the way in which the latter, after $1^{16. 29}$, are mentioned between Simon and his less famous brother Andrew (cp. $3^{16f.}$ 13^{3} with $9^{2f.}$ $10^{35f.}$ $14^{33f.}$). The connection of the Ur-Marcus with Peter accounts for the

* The inaccuracies of Mk $7^{1f.}$ upon Jewish purifications also show that the source here has been edited by some Gentile Christian, who, unlike Peter and John Mark, was unfamiliar with local religious customs (cp. Büchler in *ET.* xxi. 34–40).

† Cp. above, pp. 190 f. Salmon's verdict (*Human Element in Gospels*, 21) sums up the case moderately, "I do not believe that St. Peter had any share in the composition of St. Mark's gospel, or that he was in any way responsible for its contents. But I consider that critical study would lead us to believe that some of the evangelist's statements were derived directly or indirectly from that apostle, and therefore I would not hastily reject the tradition that there had been personal intercourse between the two."

‡ Mt. (21^{20}) generalises this into *οἱ μαθηταί*.

historical nucleus at the bottom of the Marcan stories. Several of the latter are more than circumstantial; they reveal the man who was there. The secondary features of the gospel are adequately accounted for by the process of editing, which has left the gospel something very different from the naive transcript of an eye-witness's reminiscences, even when the latter had passed into the form of preaching material πρὸς τὰς χρείας.

Scattered throughout the book are editorial touches due partly to catechetical influences, such as the addition of Ἰησοῦ Χριστοῦ (+υἱοῦ θεοῦ?) to εὐαγγελίου (1^{1}), of* καὶ πιστεύετε ἐν τῷ εὐαγγελίῳ to μετανοεῖτε (1^{15}), of καὶ τοῦ εὐαγγελίου in 8^{35} (as in 10^{29}), of ὅτι Χριστοῦ ἐστέ (9^{41}) and μετὰ διωγμῶν in 10^{30}, the incidental description of the twelve as *apostles* (6^{30}), the observations in 6^{52} (cp. πωρώσις in Eph 4^{18}) and 13^{37}, reflections of the apostolic age. as, *e.g.*, in the description of John's baptism (1^{4}, cp. Ac 2^{38}), editorial glosses like καθαρίζων πάντα τὰ βρώματα (7^{19}, showing how the author viewed the Antioch controversy in the apostolic church), and other additions which are either marginal glosses, or insertions of an early copist, καὶ ἆρον τὸν κράβαττόν σου (2^{9}), τὸ καινὸν τοῦ παλαιοῦ (2^{21}), τὸν ἐσχηκότα τὸν λεγιῶνα (5^{15}), ὁ γὰρ καιρὸς οὐκ ἦν σύκων (11^{13}, so Bakhuyzen, Baljon, Wernle, and others), μὴ καταλιπὼν σπέρμα (12^{21}), τοῦ Ἰησοῦ (14^{67}), καὶ ἀλέκτωρ ἐφώνησεν (14^{68}), etc. Even the repeated εὐθύς does not necessarily belong to the Ur-Marcus; in several places textual criticism indicates that it was inserted subsequent to the use of the Ur-Marcus by Mt. and Luke.†

§ 3. *Religious Characteristics.*—The primary aim of Jesus, according to Mk., was to proclaim the good news of the kingdom (1^{14} κηρύσσων), at first by teaching in the synogogues ($1^{21f.}$). What aroused wonder and admiration was the powerful and authoritative character of his words. This at once involved him in encounters with unclean spirits; the new teacher became inevitably the exorcist ($1^{23f.}$), while another side of his mission was that of healing the sick. Mark brings out, in his first chapter, how what Jesus conceived to be his proper mission, viz. preaching (1^{38} εἰς τοῦτο γὰρ ἐξῆλθον, referring to his divine commission, not to the house of v.^{35}, which he had left not to preach but to pray), was handicapped ‡ by his very popularity as an exorciser

* On the secondary character of Mk. here, as compared with Mt. and Lk., cp. J. Weiss, *Die Predigt Jesu*², p. 69. The *gospel of God* was an expression first popularised, if not coined, by Paul, so far as we know (cp. Resch, *Paulinismus*, p. 380).

† Cp. Weiss' exhaustive study in *ZNW.* (1910, 124–133); he finds εὐθύς certainly original in $1^{18.\ 42}$ 2^{12} 4^{17} 5^{42} 10^{52} 14^{72} probably original in 4^{5} 6^{50} 5^{29}.

‡ Hence the more difficult reading ὀργισθεὶς (1^{41}) of D a ff² as a complement to the ἐμβριμησάμενος of 1^{43}, not an echo of it, is preferable to the smoother σπλαγχνισθεὶς, which was probably introduced for motives of

and healer (cp. 1^{45}). To Mark, Jesus is above all things the preacher and teacher, in Galilee ($2^{2.13}$ $4^{1-2.33f.}$ $6^{2.6}$ with 10^{1}), where his true work is interrupted by appeals for cures which his compassion could not refuse.

The emphasis laid by Mark (cp. *Diat.* 3624–3625) on the power exerted by Jesus over evil spirits, denotes an early Christian tendency or tradition which found evidence for his messianic claims in this sphere of authority. What the eschatological messiah had been expected by some circles to accomplish, that Jesus had done—and more. The first experience of Jesus, after his endowment with the messianic spirit, is a prolonged conflict with Satan, in which he is supported or surrounded by an angelic retinue (1^{10-13}). The results of this encounter are at once visible, Jesus exorcises the evil spirits ($1^{23-27.34}$). They repeatedly own his authority (cp. 3^{11}), but he refuses to accept their wild witness. His popularity ($3^{7f.}$) and unpopularity ($3^{20f.}$) alike are attributed to this power; the most heinous sin is that of attributing it to a trafficking with the evil spirits themselves ($3^{22.30}$). Satan or Beelzebub with his realm of demons is set over against the divine realm inaugurated by Jesus. It is not, however, correct to argue * that the exorcising of demons by Jesus forms an important feature in the synoptic use of the term "Son of Man." So far as Mk. is concerned, this term is never connected with the expulsion of evil spirits (cp. $2^{10.28}$). It is as God's Son (cp. 1^{11}), the holy one of God (1^{24}, cp. 3^{29}), the Son of the most high God (5^{7}), that Jesus of Nazara casts demons out of men. Consequently, while the Marcan (and indeed the synoptic) accounts of demon-expulsion must be read in the light of contemporary superstitions (cp. W. O. E. Oesterley in *DCG.* i. 440–443), they cannot be regarded as imaginative illustrations of an element in messianic prophecy. Whatever be their historical nucleus, these naive popular traditions derive from a definite set of apostolic reminiscences.† Thus, even though the words υἱοῦ θεοῦ in 1^{1} are a gloss, they are a correct gloss. The unclean spirits hail their exorciser as the *Son of God* (3^{11}, cp. 5^{7}); Jesus is God's Son (1^{11}, cp. 13^{32}) from first to last, and the last testimony paid him is this unconscious homage from a pagan's lips (15^{39}).

But, while the valuation of Jesus as the Christ is the determining factor of any gospel, critics like Köstlin, Keim, M. Schulze (*ZWT.*, 1894, pp. 332 f.) and Wrede (pp. 71 f.) go to uncritical extremes in exaggerating the superhuman, mysterious, and even metaphysical traits of the Marcan Jesus at the expense of the human element. Mark does note *the spirit* of Jesus more

reverence (cp. Nestle's *Philolog. Sacra*, 26, and *Einf.* 219–220, Eng. tr. p. 262). Rauch (*ZNW.*, 1902, 300–303) is one-sided in regarding $1^{41a.43}$ and 1^{44} (ὅρα . . . εἴπῃς) as editorial glosses introduced to glorify Jesus.

* As Volz does (*Jüdische Eschatologie*, p. 215).

† To this position Wrede was driven back (cp. *ZNW.*, 1904, 169–177) by critics of his brilliant but one-sided *Messiasgeheimnis*; he admitted that the Marcan interpretation was rooted ultimately in actual occurrences of exorcism (*e.g.* in $1^{23f.}$ $5^{1f.}$) as the soil of the later schematism.

than once (1^8 1^{10} where Lk.'s τὸ πνεῦμα τὸ ἅγιον is probably more correct, 2^8 8^{12}), but there is no tendency to represent this in any dogmatic form as a sheer supernatural force, any more than to ignore or depreciate the limitations of his supernatural power and knowledge (cp. 13^{32}). Upon the contrary, it was the frank recognition of these human limitations which led both Mt. and Lk. to modify several of the Marcan sayings (cp. *e.g.* 1^{34} with Mt 8^{16} and Lk 4^{40}, 3^{21} with Mt 12^{47} and Lk 8^{20}). If the Jesus of Mk. is not a humanitarian rabbi or sympathetic prophet, he is still less the pictorial representation of a divine energy in history.

Although it is no longer possible to argue, with the Tübingen theorists (*e.g.* Holsten, *Die Synopt. Evglien*, 1885, pp. 179 f.), that Mk.'s gospel was composed by a Paulinist in order to justify the preaching of the Pauline gospel in opposition to the Petrine manifesto of Mt., much less that it was designed to be a counterblast to the Apocalypse of John (Volkmar), there are traits (cp. *e.g.* 1^{14-15} = Gal 4^4, 4^{10-12} = 1 Co $14^{21f.}$ Ro $9^{18f.}$ 10^{16-21}, 8^{38} = Ro 1^{16}, 9^{2-8} = 2 Co 3^7–4^6) which serve as watermarks of an age when elements of the Pauline gospel had had time to affect the writer's environment. The specifically Pauline elements in Mk. are discussed especially by von Soden (*ThA.* 143 f., 150 f.), Titius (*ThSt.* 325 f.), W. Brückner (*PM.*, 1900, 426 f.), Menzies (*The Earliest Gospel*, 1901, 38 f.), J. Weiss (*Das älteste Evglm*, 42 f.), and Bacon (*Beginnings of Gospel Story*, pp. xxvii f., xxxiv f.). The last-named scholar attributes the radical Paulinism of the book to its redactor, but there is no conscious or radical 'Paulinism' in Mk. The gospel has traces of the apostolic age; both in language and spirit it reflects naturally its environment, and the Pauline gospel had entered into that environment. But Mark was not a Paulinist.* His emphasis on the proof from miracles and his theory of the resurrection-appearances diverge from Paul; Paul never uses the favourite Marcan title of the Son of Man; and Mark's christology has interests to which Paul was indifferent. The theory of the parables in 4^{10-12} betrays the influence of views

* "Auf alle Fülle gehört es in den paulinischen Kreis hinein, womit doch keineswegs gesagt ist, dass sein Verfasser als ein paulinischer Christ, sei es auch nur in dem sehr bedingten Sinne, wie solches ja von vielen neutestamentlichen Schriftstellern gilt, zu betrachten sei" (Holtzmann, *ARW.* x. 40; cp. Bousset, *TLZ.*, 1904, 682).

such as Paul urged in 1 Co 14^{21-22} and Ro 9^{18-29} 10^{16-21} 11^{8-10}; in spite of the considerations which may be urged to the contrary (cp. *e.g.* P. Fiebig's *Altjüdische Gleichnisse und die Gleichnisse Jesu*, 1904, 146 f.; Knoke, *NKZ*, 1905, 137–164; P. Lagrange in *RB.*, 1910, pp. 5–25; and Feine, *Jesu Christus und Paulus*, 135–149), it is not easy to deny that these words, in their present form, bear the impress of the Pauline theory of Israel's rejection (cp. Jülicher's *Gleichnisreden Jesu*, i. 120–148), and 10^{45} is generally reckoned as another instance. But the challenging logia of 2^{27-28} $7^{15f.}$ and 12^{32-34}, the avoidance of νόμος, and the universalism of 11^{17} and 13^{10} (cp. 14^{9}) are primitive Christian, not specifically Pauline, and it is to make a tether out of a hair when the story of 9^{38-39} and the refusal of the request of the sons of Zebedee are supposed to be inserted in Paul's interests, or when references to the cross and suffering are attributed to Paulinism (as if the latter monopolised these in the primitive church), or when a saying like that of 14^{38} is run back to the Pauline category of the flesh and the spirit. On the other hand, some of the allegorical or symbolical touches, *e.g.*, in the story of the fig-tree and in 15^{38}, are significantly Pauline.

§ 4. *Origin.*—That the gospel, in its present form, was intended for an audience outside Palestine is plain not only from Mk.'s omission of much Jewish detail that is preserved in the ordinary synoptic tradition, but from his careful explanations of customs (*e.g.* $7^{3-4.\ 11}$ 15^{42}), phrases (5^{41} 7^{34}), and names (*e.g.* 3^{17} 10^{46}) which would be unfamiliar to Christians of Gentile birth throughout the empire. The fact that the gospel was written in Greek does not, of course, invalidate the hypothesis that it was written in or for the Roman church, since Greek was widely known at this period (cp. Caspari's *Quellen zur Gesch. d. Taufsymbols*, iii. 267 f.), but the occasional Latinisms merely prove at most that the writer was in touch with the Latin language.* The wide range of the Empire made this possible in many countries of the East, and no linguistic feature of this kind can be assumed to have any local significance. The presence of such Romanised forms might even be held to corroborate the ancient tradition that Mark was connected with Alexandria; in the κοίνη of Egypt, where the civilisation and culture of Rome spread so widely

* On the NT 'Latinisms,' see Hahn's *Rom und Romanismus im griech.-röm. Osten* (1906), 257 f.

during the first century * B.C., many Latin terms may still be traced, including military terms † like λεγιών and κεντυρίων (cp. P. Meyer's *Heerwesen*, pp. 131 f.). But the Latinisms belong to Mk.'s colloquial style, and, beyond the vague inferences which may be drawn from his connection with Peter and the latter's connection with Rome, there is no evidence, internal or external, to suggest the church for which, or the place at which, the gospel was composed. Even if the Rufus of 15^{21} were the Rufus of Ro 16^{13}, this would not necessarily point to a Roman circle (see above, p. 137), and the bearing of 7^{1-23} (things clean and unclean) is too general to be confined to the Roman church (Ro 14, He 13^{9}).

§ 5. *Style*.—Mark has no special style; his book has not the Biblical tinge of Mt. nor the literary art of Luke; it is written usually (cp. J. B. Pease, *JBL.*, 1897, 1–16) in terse, vivid Greek, of a popular and even a colloquial order (cp. the use of terms like *κράββατος* and *σφύρις*); the occasional looseness of construction and roughness of phrasing is due to a vigorous emphasis (*e.g.* in 2^{22} 7^{2} 8^{2} 11^{31-32} 13^{33-34}). This accounts in part for some of his idiosyncrasies, such as his fondness for double negatives (*e.g.* 1^{44} 2^{2} 3^{27} 5^{3} 11^{14} etc.), and diminutives like *θυγάτριον*, *ἰχθύδια*, *κοράσιον*, *κυνάριον*, *παιδίον* (*παιδία*), *παιδίσκη*, *πλοιάριον*, *ψιχία*, and *ὠτάριον*; his predilection for *εὐθύς*, *πάλιν*, and *πολλά* (adverbial); his addiction to the historic present—a mark of the anecdotist—and *καί* in narrative connections. The so-called Aramaisms are sometimes not real Aramaisms (*e.g.* the double *δύο*); when sifted, they prove an Aramaic background for the tradition, not an Aramaic document which has been translated, nor even a cast of style which can be described as particularly Hebraistic.

But, while Mark as a whole is shorter than Mt. or Luke, in his descriptions he is frequently elaborate and ample. Many of what may be termed his "extra-touches" are, no doubt, due to his vivid and circumstantial imagination, possibly working upon the oral reminiscences of Peter and others; but more than once his narrative has a redundant and even heavy form which

* The papyri show the later spread of the Latin element (cp. Wessely's paper on 'die latein. Elemente in der Gräzitat der ägypt. Papyrusurkunden,' *Wiener Studien*, 1902, pp. 99–151).

† Mk.'s explanation of Greek terms by Latin (12^{42} 15^{16}) is perhaps the one exception which turns the scale in favour of a church whose members knew Latin.

Mt. and Luke, with larger books to write, have carefully **avoided** Salient instances of this may be seen, *e.g.*, in 1^{32} (ὀψίας δὲ γενομένης ὅτε ἔδυσεν ὁ ἥλιος), where Mt. omits ὅτε κτλ. (8^{16}) and Lk. ὀψίας δὲ γενομένης (4^{40}); in 14^{30} (σήμερον ταύτῃ τῇ νυκτί), where Mt. omits (26^{34}) and Lk. retains alone (22^{34}) σήμερον; in passages like 2^{25} (= Mt 12^{3}, Lk 6^{3}) and 14^{43} (= Mt 26^{47}, Lk 22^{47}), where Mt. and Lk. agree in omitting the same clause or phrase in a Marcan duplicate expression, and elsewhere (cp. the collection of material in *HS.* 110–113). This pleonastic method of composition is frequent enough in Mk. to be regarded as a predominant feature. He loves to linger over details, and to bring out clearly and profusely the *mise en scène*, or the feelings of Jesus and his circle. More than once, indeed, his account of some incident is actually longer than the corresponding narrative or narratives in Mt. and Lk. (cp. Menzies, *The Earliest Gospel*, pp. 34 f.); after $11^{1f.}$ the tendency generally is to be less compressed.

§ 6. *The Conclusion* ($16^{9\text{-}20}$).—The gospel breaks off abruptly at 16^{8}, in the middle of a sentence, like the first edition of Sidney's *Arcadia*. The words ἐφοβοῦντο γάρ might indeed be taken, like ἦν γὰρ μέγας σφόδρα (16^{4}), as merely a stylistic negligence; but even so it is not possible, in spite of all that can be urged to the contrary (*e.g.* by P. W. Schmidt, *Gesch. Jesu*, 1904, p. 49; Wellhausen, and B. Weiss),* to imagine that the author intended his book to end thus. (i.) That he was prevented by some emergency from finishing it, is possible. (ii.) That he did finish it, although the conclusion was lost or suppressed, is not less probable. (i.) The former hypothesis in one form (Zahn, *GK.* ii. 928 f.) accounts for the circulation of copies lacking $16^{9\text{-}20}$ by assuming that Peter's death prevented Mark from completing the volume at once, and that, before he could do so, copies of it were made by some of his friends. There is a partial parallel in the literary fortunes of the notes written by Arrian of the lectures of Epictetus, which, like the first edition of the *Religio Medici*, were at first published surreptitiously, or at least without the connivance of the author. Otherwise, accident or death may be held to have prevented the author from ever finishing his treatise. (ii.) The original conclusion may also have perished, how

* Jacoby (*NT Ethik*, 1899, 413) argues that though the close is accidental, it "admirably reflects the feeling which fills the evangelist as he stands before Jesus. Jesus is to him the sacred mystery of humanity," with his power over dæmons, etc.

ever, not by the accidental mutilation of the autograph, but because it was suppressed soon after the gospel was written. The possibility of this is not to be denied on *a priori* grounds. The gospel was short; it lacked the special features of Mt. and Lk., in which the bulk of it had been incorporated, and its slow circulation in the sub-apostolic age, reflecting its initial literary fortunes (cp. Burkitt, *Two Lectures on the Gospels*, pp. 32 f.), serves to explain how all trace of the original conclusion perished. At one time there must have been practically only a single copy in existence, and that *minus* the closing leaf. A plausible reason for its removal (Rohrbach) was that it gave, like the lost (suppressed?) part of the Gospel of Peter, a Galilean account of the Resurrection-appearances which did not tally with the Asiatic traditions of the Elders, who favoured Luke (cp. Lk 24^{8} with Mk 16^{8}) and John, or else (Réville) that it was too brief and unconventional to suit the needs of the later church. The compilation of the canon (especially and primarily of the four gospels) then led to the addition of 16^{9-20} with its generalised and conventional statement of the resurrection-appearances.

In a region where nearly every step is a surmise, this is as plausible as any hypothesis yet offered, but it leaves two questions open: (*a*) What of the original conclusion? Can any trace of it be discovered? (*b*) And what of the later second-century supplement or appendix (16^{9-20})?

(*a*) Obviously the Marcan epilogue included an appearance of Jesus to Peter (so Paul and Luke), probably in Galilee (cp. Melzer, *PM.*, 1902, 147–156)—which suggests a connection between it and the Gospel of Peter. More detailed reconstructions (cp. T. S. Rördam, *HJ.*, 1905, 769–790) are precarious, though we may fall back provisionally,* with Blair (*Apostolic Gospel*, 372–385), on Lk $24^{9. 11-13}$, and, with E. J. Goodspeed (*AJT.*, 1905, 484–490; cp. W. C. Allen, *ICC.* 302 f.),† on Mt 28^{9-20} (or rather on Mt $28^{7-10. 16-20}$), than which, as Mt. usually enlarges his sources, the Marcan appendix can hardly have been longer. Goodspeed's version of the supposed original is as follows: *And behold Jesus met them, saying, Hail. And they came and took hold of his feet and worshipped him. Then saith Jesus to them, Be not afraid, go, tell my brethren to depart into Galilee, and there shall they see me. And the eleven disciples went into Galilee unto the mountain where Jesus had appointed them. And Jesus came to them, and when they saw him they worshipped him, but some doubted. And he spake unto them, saying, All authority hath been given unto me in heaven and upon earth. Go ye therefore and make disciples of all the nations, teaching them to observe all things whatsoever I have commanded you. And lo, I am with you alway, even unto*

* The objections are noticed by K. Lake, *The Resurrection of Jesus Christ* (1907), 81 f., and Rördam (pp. 770 f.).

† Cp. Wright, *NT Problems*, 122 f.

the end of the world. In this case, the loss of the ending would more probably be accidental than deliberate.

(*b*) It is no longer necessary * to spend time in leading the cumulative and overwhelming proof from textual criticism (Tischendorf's *NT.*[8] i. 403–407; WH. ii. 28–51; Zahn, *GK.* ii. 910–938), stylistic considerations (cp. Swete, xcvi f.), and internal contents, that this condensed and secondary fragment was not the Marcan conclusion of the gospel. But this negative certainty does not lead to many positive results upon its character, date, or authorship. It is just possible that it originally existed in independent form before it was incorporated in its present place, like the Homeric catalogue of the troops in *Iliad*, $2^{484-877}$, or that it represents the close of some narrative of the resurrection, based upon inferior tradition, the opening of which has been irretrievably lost. Attempts have also been made, but unsuccessfully, to connect it with the Teaching or Preaching of Peter (Zahn, *GK.* i. 922 n.; von Dobschütz, *TU.* xi. 1. 75–79). Probably the clue to its origin is to be sought in the opening decades of the second century, when, according to Rohrbach's theory, the gospel was furnished with its unauthentic conclusion by those who edited the first canon of the gospels, and when the appendix was added to the Fourth gospel. There is no adequate evidence for Rohrbach's idea (so H. Schmidt, *SK.*, 1907, 489–513) that Mk 16^{9-20} is used in Jn 21, but otherwise his reconstruction fits in with the main data of the problem.

This process is assumed by Rohrbach to have taken place in Asia Minor.† Now, the volume of expositions or illustrations of Christ's words which Papias compiled (Eus. *H. E.* iii. 39. 8 f.) during the first part of the second century, contained many traditions and διηγήσεις of the Lord's sayings handed down by Aristion, among them apparently a story of Justus surnamed Barsabas (Ac 1^{23-24}) having drunk some deadly poison with impunity. This would tally with Mk 16^{18b} excellently. Furthermore, an Aristo(n) of Pella is known (Eus. *H. E.* iv. 6. 3) to have lived and written after A.D. 135, whom Resch (*TU.* x. 2. 449–456; *ThSt.* 109–110; *Paulinismus*, 395–398) takes to have edited (*c.* A.D. 140) the first canon of the gospels,—the archetype of Codex Bezæ,—and whom Hilgenfeld (*ZWT.*, 1883, 13, 1894, 627) openly identifies with the Aristion of Papias. 'Αρίστων is certainly the more common form of 'Αριστίων, and both are apt to be confused; but Eusebius

---

* All that can, together with a good deal that cannot, be said on its behalf may be seen by the curious in Burgon's well-known and incisive treatise (*The Last Twelve Verses of the Gospel according to St. Mark*, 1871) and in *The Traditional Text of the Holy Gospels* (1896), pp. 298 f. Belser still (*Einl.* 100 f.) holds that it was added by Mark (*c.* A.D. 63–64) to the original gospel which he wrote about twenty years earlier, while J. P. van Kasteren (*RB.*, 1902, 240 f.) makes Mark add it after the appearance of Lk.'s gospel, and Hilgenfeld singularly maintains the authenticity of the passage. Further discussions in *DB.* iii. 252–3, and *HNT.* 550–555.

† Even if Mk 16^{15} were held to be reflected in Hermas (*Sim.* ix. 25. 1–2), this would not imply necessarily that Mk 16^{9-20} emanated also from the Roman church (so Stanton, *GHD.* i. 45–46), for it could easily have reached Rome from Asia Minor, and would naturally do so, under the circumstances.

plainly regarded the disciple and the Jewish Christian historian as different persons, so that we are thrown back upon conjectures. Conybeare's discovery of a tenth-century Armenian codex with (Ἀριστῶνος πρεσβυτέρου) "from the presbyter Aristo" opposite Mk 16^{9-20} between vv.$^{8.9}$ (*Exp.*^{4} viii. 241 f.; *Exp.*^{5} ii. 401 f.), seemed at first to clear up matters, by revealing a tradition (trustworthy though late) which viewed the passage as a διηγήσις (Lk 1^1) of Aristion the Lord's disciple. Aristion's contributions to Papias were oral, it is true; no written memoranda are mentioned by Eusebius. But he may have been an author as well as John the presbyter, and he may have written a brief narrative of Jesus and the apostles (16^{20} seems to open out into a record like that of Ac 1), for διήγησις in Lk 1^1 covers a written source as well as an oral. "It may be further remarked that if Aristion was a disciple of the Lord, or even a fellow and companion of the apostles, he was probably an inhabitant of Palestine; and this agrees well with the patristic statement already noticed [Victor of Antioch] that the ancient Palestinian copy of Mark included these twelve verses." Conybeare's conjecture * has been widely accepted, *e.g.* by Harnack, Nestle, Swete, Lisco (in *Vincula Sanctorum*), Eck (*Preuss. Jahrb.*, 1898, pp. 42–43, as by Theologus in the same journal for 1897, p. 227), Mader (*BZ.*, 1905, 269 f.), Rohrbach, Sanday (*DB.* ii. 638–639), and Chapman (*Revue Bénéd.*, 1905, 50 f.). But it is not certain whether Aristo of Pella, who wrote an account of Judæa's revolt against Hadrian, is the same as the Christian elder Aristion who formed one of Papias' sources of information (*H. E.* iii. 39), or even whether the former wrote *The Dialogue of Jason and Papiscus*. His period is almost too late to permit of him being called a disciple of the Lord. Furthermore, Aristion is not definitely called 'the presbyter' by Papias or Eusebius, though this objection is perhaps not serious. The possibility of the Armenian gloss being an error must, of course, be admitted; but some valid account of how the error arose is necessary, and to suppose it was due to the Armenian scribe confusing Aristion or Ariston with Moses of Chorene's Ariston, the secretary of Bishop Mark (?) in Jerusalem after A.D. 135, seems hazardous, despite Prof. Bacon's ingenious arguments (*Exp.*^{6} xii. 401 f.; *DCG.* i. 114–118). The Armenian historian's evidence is not enough to prove that he knew about Ariston independently of Eusebius. Upon the whole, then, while Conybeare's theory cannot be said to have furnished the final solution of the problem, it offers a not unimportant hint upon the composition of this passage.† If Aristion was not its author, he may have been its source or one of its sources (for 16^{14-18} perhaps). At any rate, the passage appears to have existed

---

* Cp. Ehrhard, *ACL.* i. pp. 115 f., and Zahn's *Forschungen*, vi. 219 f. The criticisms of Resch and Zahn, which substantially favour Conybeare's main contention, are reproduced in *Exp.*^{4} x. 219–232.

† The secondary as well as legendary character of the passage is obvious (vv.$^{9-11}$ reflecting Lk 8^2 + John 20^{1-10}, vv.$^{12-13}$ being an echo of Lk $24^{13f.}$, vv.$^{17-18}$ of Ac 2^{1-13} 28^{3-6}, and vv.$^{19-20}$ of Lk 24^{50-51}, Ac 1^{9-11}). Besides the reference (v.^{17}) to the glossolalia, cp. vv.$^{12-19}$ = 1 Ti 3^{16}, v.^{15} = Col 1^{23}, v.^{16b} = 2 Th 2^{12}, v.^{17} = Ac 16^{18}, and v.^{20} = Heb 2^4—evidence which is, of course, far from justifying the thesis of H. H. Evans' monograph, *St. Paul the Author of the Last Twelve Verses of the Second Gospel* (1886).

originally in a longer and larger form, to judge from Jerome's (*c. Pelag.* ii. 15; cp. Harnack, *TU.* xii. 1, and Zahn's *Forschungen*, vi. 219) quotation of a passage which lay between v.[14] and v.[15]. This quotation has been recently corroborated by the discovery of a new papyrus. Jerome's words are: *In quibusdam exemplaribus et maxime in Græcis codicibus iuxta Marcum in fine eius euangelii scribitur: 'postea quum accubuissent undecim, apparuit eis Iesus et exprobauit incredulitatem et duritiam cordis eorum, quia his, qui uiderant eum resurgentem, non crediderunt, et illi satisfaciebant dicentes: sæculum istud iniquitatis et incredulitatis sub satana est, qui non sinit per immundos spiritus ueram dei apprehendi uirtutem; idcirco iam nunc reuela iustitiam tuam.'* Rohrbach (pp. 20 f.) attempted to reconstruct the Greek original of this passage, but it has now been discovered in the so-called Freer-logion (cp. Sanders, *Bibl. World*, 1908, 138–142; E. J. Goodspeed, *ibid.* 218–226, with the critique of C. R. Gregory, *das Freer-Logion*, 1908) of an uncial (fifth century) manuscript of the gospels which, between Mk 16[14] and 16[15], runs thus:—*κἀκεῖνοι ἀπελογοῦντο λέγοντες· ὅτι ὁ αἰὼν οὗτος τῆς ἀνομίας καὶ τῆς ἀπιστίας ὑπὸ τὸν Σατανᾶν ἐστιν ὁ μὴ ἐῶν τὰ ὑπὸ τῶν πνευμάτων ἀκάθαρτα τὴν ἀλήθειαν τοῦ θεοῦ καταλαβέσθαι δύναμιν· διὰ τοῦτο ἀποκάλυψον σοῦ τὴν δικαιοσύνην ἤδη. ἐκεῖνοι ἔλεγον τῷ Χριστῷ. καὶ ὁ Χριστὸς ἐκείνοις προσέλεγεν· ὅτε πεπλήρωται ὁ ὅρος τῶν ἔτων τῆς ἐξουσίας τοῦ Σατανᾶ, ἀλλὰ ἐγγίζει ἄλλα δεινά· καὶ ὑπὲρ τῶν ἁμαρτησάντων ἐγὼ παρεδόθην εἰς θάνατον, ἵνα ὑποστρέψωσιν εἰς τὴν ἀλήθειαν καὶ μηκέτι ἁμαρτήσωσιν, ἵνα τὴν ἐν τῷ οὐρανῷ πνευματικὴν καὶ ἄφθαρτον τῆς δικαιοσύνης δόξαν κληρονομήσωσιν. ἀλλὰ πορευθέντες κτλ.*

In the light of this, it becomes probable that the source from which Mk 16[9-20] was taken was some early apocryphal gospel; that the passage was not written (cp. Warfield, *Textual Crit. of NT*, 199 f.) for its present position, and that when it was borrowed, it was not borrowed in complete form. At an early date, however, some sentences which had originally lain between 16[14] and 16[15] were transcribed on the margin of at least one Greek codex of the gospel, and eventually found their way into the text. Jerome quotes a part of them; the Freer-logion preserves the whole of the excerpt. It is still an open question whether the passage is or is not allied to the Palestinian presbyter-traditions, which are preserved by Papias (so Harnack, *TLZ.*, 1908, 168–170). The *terminus ad quem* for its date is about the second quarter of the second century; for, while echoes of the passage can hardly be heard in Clem. Rom. and Barnabas (so Dr. C. Taylor, however, in *Exp.*[4] viii. 71–80), much less in Hebrews (van Kasteren), it was known to Tatian and the *Acta Pilati*, if not to Justin Martyr (*Apol.* i. 45), and a Syriac version may be postulated by *c.* A.D. 150 (Chase, *Syriac Element in Codex Bezæ*, 150–157).

(C) *MATTHEW.*

Literature.—(*a*) Editions—Luther (1538); W. Musculus (*In Evangelistam Matthaeum Commentarii . . . digesti*, etc. (1548); Ferus (*Annotationes*, 1577); Danæus (1583); Jansenius (Leyden, 1589); Alphonse Avendaño (*Commentaria in Ev. D. Matt.*, Madrid, 1592–3); Maldonatus (1596); Kirstenius (*Notæ in M. Evangelium*, 1610); Paræus (1641); J. B. Lightfoot (*Horæ Hebraicæ*, 1658); J. Gerhard (*Annotationes*, 1663); Elsner (*Commentarius*, ed. Stosch, 1767); De Beausobre et Lenfant (*A new version of the gospel acc. to St. Matthew, with Comm. on all the difficult passages*, Eng. tr. 1779, Cambridge, U.S.A.); Wakefield (1781); Aloys Gratz, *Kritisch-histor. Commentar* (1821–1823); Fritzsche (1826); J. E. K. Kauffer (1827); Glöckler (Frankfort, 1835); de Wette[3] (1838); Baumgarten-Crusius (ed. Otto, 1844); Peter Schegg (1856–8); M. Arnoldi (Trier, 1856); T. J. Conant (New York, 1860); J. A. Alexander (New York, 1861); Lange[3] (1868, Eng. tr., Schaff, 1864); R. F. Grau (1876); Wickelhaus (ed. Zahn, 1876); Meyer[6] (1876, Eng. tr., Edin. 1877); J. L. Sommer (1877); Keil (Leipzig, 1877); Fillion (1878); Mansel (*Speaker's Comm.* 1878); Schanz (1879); J. A. Broadus (New York, 1887); Kübel (1889); J. Morison[8] (London, 1890); Knabenbauer's *Commentarius* (Paris, 1892); Carr (*CGT.* 1894); J. Niglutsch (*Brevis Comment. in usum clericorum*, 1896); Nösgen[2] (1897); *The gospel of Jesus according to S. Matthew as interpreted to R. L. Harrison by the light of the godly experience of Sri Parânanda* (London, 1898); B. Weiss (— Meyer[9], 1898); Baljon, *Commentaar op het Evglie van Mt.* (1900)*; Slater (*CB.* 1901); Blass, *Evglium sec. Matthæum cum variæ lectionis delectu* (1901); Zöckler (Lange's *Bibel-Werk*[5], 1902); A. Merx, *Die vier kan. Evglien nach ihr. ält. bekannte Texte. Matthäus* (1902, Syriac version, tr. and annotated)*; V. Rose (Paris, 1904); Wellhausen (1904)*; Zahn[2] (*ZK.* 1905)*; C. A. Witz-Oberlin (ed. 1905, Stuttgart); J. Weiss[2] (*SNT.* 1906); W. C. Allen (*ICC.* 1907)*; E. E. Anderson (Edinburgh, (1909); E. Klostermann and Gressmann (*HBNT.* 1909); Plummer[2] (1910).

(*b*) Studies—Besides such patristic studies as the commentaries of Origen, Hilary, and Jerome, Augustine's *Quæstiones*, Chrysostom's *Homilies* (ed. Field, Cambridge, 1839), Theophylact's *Commentary* (ed. W. G. Humphrey, Cambridge), Peter of Laodicea's (cp. Heinrici's *Beiträge*, v., 1908), Poussin's *Catena* (Toulouse, 1646), and the Venerable Bede's edition (ed. 1647), reference may be made to F. G. Mayer (*Beiträge zur Erklärung des Ev. Mt.*, 1818); Klener, *Recentiores quæstiones de authentia evang. M.* (1832); Schneckenburger, *Ursprung des ersten kanon. Evglms* (1834); G. C. A. Harless, *de compositione evang. quod M. tribuitur* (Erlangen, 1842); Delitzsch, *Untersuchungen über die Entstehung u. Anlage des Mt. Evglms* (1853); J. S. Knowles, *The gospel attributed to S. Matthew the record of the whole original apostlehood* (1855); C. Luthardt, *de compositione Ev. M.* (1861); A. Réville, *études critiques sur l'Ev. selon S. Matthieu* (Leyden, 1862); Ibbeken, *Das Leben Jesu nach der Darstellung des Matthæus* (1866); Lutteroth, *Essai d'interprétation de quelques parties de l'évang. selon S. Mt.* (1876); Barhebræus (*Scholia*, ed. Spanuth, 1879); B. Weiss, *das Matthäus Evglm und seine Lucas-parallelen erklärt* (Halle, 1876)*; Renan, v. chs. x. xi.; Massebieau, *Examen des citations de l'ancien Testament dans l'évangile* *selon Matthieu* (Paris, 1885); Gla, *Die Original Sprache des Mt. Evglms* (1887, Aramaic); F. Gardiner (*JBL.*, 1890, 1–16, Mt. wrote discourses in Aramaic, had them tr. into Gk., and added Gk. narrative); Kübel (*Bibl. World*, 1893, 194 f., 263 f., 'Fundamental Thought and Purpose of Matthew'); T. Naville, *Essai sur l'évangile selon S. Matthieu* (Lausanne, 1893); Harman (*JBL.*, 1895, 114–124; 'The Judaism of the First Gospel'); A. B. Bruce, *With Open Face* (1896), pp. 1–24; Jülicher (*PRE.* xii. 428–439); Haussleiter, 'Probleme des Matthäus-Evglms' (*BFT.*, 1900, vi., on virgin-birth and Lord's prayer specially); V. Bartlet (*DB.* ii. 296–305); Blass, 'Text-kritische Bemerkungen zu Matthäus' (*BFT.* iv. 4); Pfleiderer, *Urc.* ii. 301–395; A. S. Barnes (*JTS.*, 1905, 187–203); A. Carr (*Exp.*[7], 1907, 339–349, 'Authenticity and Originality of First gospel'); Burkitt, *Gospel History and its Transmission*, pp. 184 f.; W. C. Allen (*DCG.* ii. 143–150); Hawkins (*HS.* 154–178); D. H. Müller, *die Bergpredigt im Lichte d. Strophentheorie* (1908).

§ 1. *Plan and outline.*—It is essential, at the outset, to feel the massive unity of this book, if any justice is to be done to it either from the literary or from the religious standpoint. Jesus the true messiah, born and trained under the Jewish law, and yet Lord of a church whose inward faith, organisation, procedure, and world-wide scope transcended the legal limitations of Judaism—this is the dominant conception of Matthew's gospel from beginning to end. The book is compiled from at least two sources, and their different nuances are more than once unmistakable; but these discrepancies and variations do not blur the final impression made by the writer's clear-cut purpose (cp. Renan, v. pp. 209 f.). He wishes to show that, in spite of the contemporary rupture between Judaism and Christianity, there has been a divine continuity realised in the origin and issues of faith in Jesus as the Christ. (*a*) *Thou shalt call his name Jesus: for he shall save his People from their sins.* That People is no longer Israel (cp. 21^{43}), but a wider community. (*b*) *A greater than the temple is here*, one who is also (*c*) the promulgator of a new Law which transcends the old (cp. $5^{17f.}$ 28^{20}). The three sacred possessions of Judaism have thus passed into higher uses, as a result of the life of Jesus the Christian messiah. It is Mt.'s aim to justify this transition by showing from the life of Jesus how it was not the claim of a heretical sect who misread the Bible by the light of their own presumptuousness, but the realisation of a divine purpose and the verification of divine prophecies in the sphere of history.

The opening section (1^1–4^{11}) describes the preparation of Jesus for his work, his birth-roll (1^{1-17}), birth (1^{18}–2^{23}), baptism at the hands of John (3^{1-17}), and temptation (4^{1-11}). The arrest of John marks his retiral and return to Galilee, where Kapharnaum became the headquarters of his Galilean mission (4^{12}–18^{35}). A summary or introduction ($4^{23f.}$ περιῆγεν . . . διδάσκων . . . καὶ κηρύσσων . . . καὶ θεραπεύων) lays stress * upon his preaching or teaching, then upon his healing powers. Hence we get first of all a cycle of teaching (5–7, the so-called Sermon on the Mount), followed by a cycle of incidents in his healing work (8^{1}–9^{34}, mainly miracles). † The summary or introduction is then repeated ($9^{35f.}$), in order to pave the way for the wider mission of the twelve (10^{1-42}) and a general survey of the relation of his own work to that of John, as well as of its Galilean results (11^{1-30}). ‡

Hitherto the deeds and disciples of Jesus have occupied the foreground of the gospel. Now the evangelist describes in more detail (cp. $9^{11f.}$) the nature of the opposition which he had to encounter from the Pharisees ($12^{1-9.\ 10-21.\ 22-37.\ 38-45}$), while a series of excerpts from his parables (13^{1-52}) is set within a brief account of his strained relations with his family (12^{46-50}) and townsfolk (13^{53-58}). These conflicts develop into a crisis. The murder of John the Baptist (14^{1-12}) drives Jesus to safer quarters ($14^{13f.}$), where his mission is interrupted twice by encounters with the Pharisees and scribes ($15^{1f.}$) and the Pharisees and Sadducees (16^{1-12}). This foreshadows only too clearly the end, and Peter's confession at Cæsarea Philippi (16^{13-20}) is therefore followed by a revelation of the coming tragedy at Jerusalem, in word and deed ($16^{21f.}$ $17^{1f.}$). Before closing his narrative of the Galilean mission, however, the evangelist adds a number of sayings (17^{24}–18^{35}).

The Judæan ministry really falls into two parts, one a brief record of some incidents and sayings on the way to Jerusalem (19^{1}–20^{34}), the other an account of the triumphal entry (21^{1-17}) and the subsequent teaching given by Jesus partly to his disciples in private, partly to the crowd in public (in the temple), and partly in controversy with the religious authorities ($21^{18f.}$). § The period is summed up characteristically with a long, passionate invective against the scribes and Pharisees (23) and an apocalyptic forecast of the future (24), followed by a cycle of parables (25). The final story of the Passion (26^{1}–27^{66}) describes the circumstances of the arrest (26^{1-56}), the trial (26^{57}–27^{31}), the crucifixion (27^{32-56}), and the burial (27^{57-66}). Two appearances of Jesus after death are then chronicled, one in Jerusalem to the women, one in Galilee to the eleven disciples, and the ministry of Jesus ends as it began with a commission spoken from a Galilean hill ($28^{1-10.\ 11-15.\ 16-20}$).

---

* Cp. 4^{17} with 4^{23} and 5^{1}.

† Cp. Sir J. C. Hawkins on 8–9, in *ET.* xii. 471 f., xiii. 20 f.

‡ Note how 11^{5} summarises the preceding section, *the blind regain their sight* (9^{27-31}), *the lame walk* (8^{5-13} 9^{1-8}), *the lepers are cleansed* (8^{1-4}), *the deaf hear* (9^{32-34}), *the dead are raised up* ($9^{18-19.\ 23-26}$), *and the poor have the gospel preached to them* (9^{35} 10^{7} 11^{1}).

§ Halévy (*RS.*, 1902, 305 f.) is right in preferring Mt.'s version of the parable in $22^{1f.}$ to Luke's as being more pointed (cp. Hilgenfeld, *ZWT.*, 1893, 126–143); he is less happy in arguing that 22^{1-7} and $22^{1.\ 8-13}$ are different redactions of the same story, and that the latter is modelled on a parable of R. ben Zakkai, a Sadducean teacher at Jamnia in the first century A.D. (quoted in Shabbath, 153*b* and based on Ecclus 7^{8}, Isa 65^{13-14}).

From the point of view of effect, the work is clearly and coherently arranged; the successive paragraphs have a comprehensive sweep which unfolds the leading ideas in the author's mind, even when it ignores the historical perspective of the subject. It is this constructive literary power which characterises Mt. among the synoptics. "S'il ignorait l'art de peindre, comme Luc, ou de buriner, comme Marc, il avait pourtant, lui aussi, son talent de bon ouvrier. Il possédait l'imagination ordonnatrice de l'architecte" (Nicolardot, p. 113).

§ 2. *Matthew's treatment of Mk.*—(Cp. F. H. Woods, *SB.* ii. 63 f.; Wernle, *Syn. Frage*, 124–178; Schmiedel, *EBi.* 1847–1849; Wellhausen, *Einl.* § 6; Allen, pp. xiii–xxxv; Nicolardot, pp. 1–114, and B. H. Alford, *HJ.*, 1909, 649–661.)

Besides Q (see above, pp. 194 f.), Mk. is the main source of the editor. He has treated it with a mixture of deference and freedom. Thus (*a*) in style, Mt. as a rule improves the rougher or Aramaic language of Mk.; he is fond of inserting δὲ instead of καὶ, omitting ὅτι often after verbs of saying, diminishing the number of imperfects and historic presents, and reducing the use of ἤρξατο (ἤρξαντο) with the infinitive and of compound verbs (cp. 4^{18} 9^{1} 12^{9}). In the matter of chronological arrangement (*b*) Mt.'s procedure exhibits more variations. Up to 4^{22} (from 3^{1}), for all its additional material, the narrative of Mt. follows the exact order of Mk $1^{1\text{-}20}$, but after this it diverges sharply. Mk. brings out the synagogue-ministry of Jesus in Galilee, but Mt. only mentions it vaguely * in his summaries (4^{23} 9^{35}); it is not until $12^{9f.}$ (cp. 13^{34}) that he gives any incident that occurred in a synagogue. The impression created by Jesus on the first occasion of his teaching in the synagogue of Kapharnaum (Mk 1^{22}) is made by Mt. ($7^{28\text{-}29}$) to follow the long Sermon on the Mount † (5^{1}–7^{27}). After transferring Mk $1^{40\text{-}44}$ (cp. Mt $8^{1\text{-}4}$), he then, for the healing of the demoniac in the same synagogue (Mk $1^{23\text{-}28}$), substitutes the healing of a centurion's servant in the town ($8^{5\text{-}13}$). ‡ For a line or two he now reverts to the Marcan order ($8^{14\text{-}16}$ = Mk $1^{29\text{-}34}$), rounding off this triplet § of cures (leprosy, paralysis, and fever) with a prophetic citation (8^{17}). In Mk $1^{35\text{-}39}$ the embarrassing popularity of Jesus as a healer leads

* $4^{23\text{-}25}$ is substituted for Mk 1^{21} and based loosely on Mk 1^{39} + 6^{6a}.

† Cp. Moffatt (*EBi.* 4375–4391), Votaw (*DB.* v. 1–45), Adeney (*DCG.* ii. 607–612), and Salmon (*Human Element in Gospels*, 109 f.).

‡ Probably because it was so placed in Q. The setting of the Sermon is artificially taken from Mk 3^{13}, which Lk. ($6^{12f.}$) retains in its original position.

§ One sufferer asks help; another has it asked for him; the third receives aid without asking (note Mt.'s omission of Mk 1^{30b}).

him to leave Kapharnaum to prosecute his proper work of preaching throughout the synagogues of Galilee; but Mt. merely makes it an occasion for crossing the lake ($8^{18f.}$), and inserts the stories of Mk 4^{35}–5^{20} (= Mt 8^{18-34}), Mk 2^{1-22} (= Mt 9^{1-17}), Mk 5^{21-43} (= Mt 9^{18-26}).* The short account of the choice and commission of the twelve (Mk 3^{13-19} 6^{6-13}) is then expanded characteristically into a long discourse (Mt 10); † but 10^{17-25} is irrelevant (cp. Mk 13^{9-13}), and Mt. omits Mk 6^{12-13}. His commission is not followed by a mission; the disciples do not go forth, and consequently do not return with any report of their work (as in Mk 6^{30}). Hence the connection of $14^{12f.}$ differs entirely from that of Mk 6^{29-31}. The eleventh chapter has no Marcan material, but for the conflicts of ch. 12 Mt. harks back to the substance of Mk 2^{23}–3^{12} (= Mt 12^{1-16}), closing with a characteristic OT citation (12^{17-21}). Mk 3^{20-21} he omits, adds a fresh miracle (12^{22-23}), and then (12^{24-45}) expands Mk 3^{22-30}, following it up with Mk 3^{31-35} (= 12^{46-50}), and an enlarged version of Mk 4 (= Mt 13). The adherence to Mark's order from this point becomes closer than ever; having already used up Mk 4^{35}–5^{43}, Mt. passes at once to Mk 6^{1-6} (= 13^{53-58}), and henceforth never drops the Marcan thread, though he embroiders it often with OT reminiscences, especially in the passion (*e.g.* $27^{34.\ 43}$). A comparison of Mk. and Mt. thus proves that the latter is upon the whole secondary, and that he had no independent chronological tradition or information to guide him in placing either sayings or incidents. His choice and disposition of materials becomes less and less reliable, from a historical standpoint, when he leaves the Marcan record; the Palestinian anecdotes which belong to his *Sondergut* rarely rise above the level of edifying stories to that of historicity. Mt.'s corrections of Mk. are not those of an eye-witness, or of one who had access

* Note how the president of the synagogue (Mk.) becomes simply the president in Mt. For the latter the synagogues had won an evil reputation (10^{17}).

† On reaching 10^{1} he inserts a passage (10^{2-5a} = Mk 3^{16-19}) which he had previously missed, and then expands ($10^{9-10a.\ 11-14}$) Mk 6^{8-11}. The whole section throws valuable light upon the Palestinian missions of the early church; for its literary structure, see B. Weiss (*Quellen d. Lukas-Evglms*, 128 f.), and Schott in *ZNW*. (1906) 140 f.; for its reflection of the apostolic efforts between A.D. 30 and 60, Weizsäcker, *AA*. i. 29–32, ii. 48 f. On the special difficulty of 10^{9-10} (with Mk 6^{8-9}, Lk 10^{4} 22^{35-38}), see P. Méchineau in *Études Relig.* (1896) 303–315, and A. Wright (*ET*. iv. 153–157).

to special, first-hand sources of information. Their origin is almost entirely topical.

The chronological data and the synchronisms are characteristically vague. The mission of John the Baptist is dated roughly 'in the days of Archelaus' (2^{22} 3^{2}); the writer's favourite and loose *τότε* (3^{13} $12^{22.38}$ $15^{1.29}$ 19^{13} 20^{20}) links several paragraphs together, and even the more exact references are as a rule due to the context (3^{5}? $4^{1.23}$ $9^{14.37}$ 11^{20} 14^{22} 15^{12} 18^{21} $19^{23.27}$ etc.). The first saying of the Sabbath is introduced *ἐν ἐκείνῳ τῷ καιρῷ* (12^{1}), without any clue to the period. No hint is given of the return of the disciples from their mission, yet this is assumed to have occurred, and the place (12^{10}, cp. 11^{23}) is evidently Kapharnaum. The remark of Herod (14^{1}) is similarly vague, and the *ἐν ἐκείνῃ τῇ ὥρᾳ* of 18^{1} is at once vaguer and more precise than the setting of Mk 9^{33-34}. The retiral to Galilee (4^{12}) is simply dated after the arrest of John the Baptist, but neither here nor later ($4^{23f.}$ 8^{18} $9^{35f.}$ 11^{1} 12^{16} 16^{1}) is any duration of time indicated. Some of the time notices (*e.g.* 8^{16}) are borrowed directly from Mk.; other chronological notes are more characteristic, *e.g.* 9^{18} (*while he was speaking*), 11^{1} (after instructing the twelve for their mission, Jesus departs on one of his own), 12^{46} (as at 9^{18}), 13^{1} *ἐν τῇ ἡμέρα ἐκείνῃ*), 15^{32} (three days apart with the crowd).

(*c*) The writer's engrossing interest in the sayings of Jesus leads him not only to break up the Marcan narrative with masses of logia, arranged in systematic blocks, but to abbreviate Mark's introductory matter (cp. the omission of Mk 9^{21-24} in 17^{14-21}). Where Luke generally omits, Mt. prefers to condense or compress (statistics in *HS.* 158–160).

It is a further note of Mt. to insert names * where the Marcan source had none (*e.g.* Matthew, 9^{9}; Caiaphas, $26^{3.57}$; Jesus,† 27^{16-17}). This circumstantial trait is counterbalanced by a tendency to allegorise Marcan sayings (cp. Nicolardot, *Les procédés de Rédaction des Trois Premiers Évangélistes*, pp. 37–46). Matthew concludes with a saying of Jesus, and this tallies with his greater emphasis on the Lord's doctrine. Unlike Mk. (1^{22-27}) and even Luke (4^{32-36}), he confines the authority of Jesus to teaching, instead of embracing under it the power of exorcising demons, etc. It is the sayings rather than the narratives of his book which reflect historical traditions; the contents of the latter are sometimes as ambiguous as their connections.

(*d*) The later and more ecclesiastical standpoint of Mt. comes out definitely in his recasting of the Marcan traditions relating to the disciples and Jesus. The former play a more important rôle than in Mk.; thus the saying about the spiritual family of Jesus is confined to them (Mt 12^{49}) instead of being

* On the names in Mk., see Wright (*Some NT Problems*, 57–73), and C. D. Burns (*Contemporary Review*, 1907, 417–424).

† That this reading is preferable to the ordinary text, is shown by Burkitt (*Evang. Da-Meph.* ii. 277–278).

addressed generally to the bystanders (Mk 3^{34}). Mt. minimises * the faults of the disciples (13^{16-18} with Mk 4^{13}, cp. 13^{51}; 14^{33} with Mk 6^{52}; 16^{9-12} with Mk 8^{17-22}; cp. the significant omission of Mk $9^{6.\,10.\,32}$, the smoothing down of Mk $9^{38f.}$ in $18^{1f.}$, the change of Mk 10^{32} in 20^{17} etc.), and endeavours to eliminate or to soften any trait derogatory to the credit of the twelve. A similar † reverence for the character of Jesus appears in his omission of words or passages like Mk 1^{43} 3^{5} 3^{21} (charge of madness) 10^{14} and 11^{3}, and in changes like those of $19^{16f.}$ (Mk $10^{17f.}$) and 26^{59} (cp. Mk 14^{58}); the miraculous power of Jesus is heightened (contrast 8^{16} with Mk 1^{32-33}, 17^{17-18} with Mk 9^{20-26} etc.), and the author shrinks as far as possible from allowing demons to recognise him as the messiah; ‡ the prophetic power of Jesus is also expanded and made more definite (cp. 7^{15} 12^{45} 21^{43} 24^{10} 26^{2} etc.).

§ 3. *Structure.*—The composite nature of Matthew may be explained not only on the hypothesis of the use of earlier sources, but also on the theory that the canonical text represents later glosses, interpolations, and expansions, like that in Sir 49^{14-16}. The three places at which this theory (which depends largely on the use of textual criticism) comes into special prominence are, (*a*) 1–2, (*b*) 16^{17}, and (*c*) 28^{16-20}.

(*a*) The *βίβλος γενέσεως* of 1–2 represents the author's version of a Palestinian tradition which already contained the virgin-birth. None of its three sections (1^{1-17} the genealogy, 1^{18-25} the birth, 2^{1-23} the childhood), not even the first, need be anything else than a free composition; whatever was the basis for the Jewish-Christian belief upon which the writer drew (cp. W. C. Allen, *Interpreter*, 1905, pp. 51 f.; Box, *ibid.*, 1906, 195 f.), the narrative, judged from the standpoint of literary criticism, offers no adequate criteria for distinguishing between a source and an editor, or between an original gospel and an addition. It is a

* But not invariably (cp. 15^{17} and 26^{8}).

† Both the desire to spare the twelve and the reluctance to dwell on the human affectionateness of Jesus appears in his version (19^{13-15}) of Mk 10^{13-16}; the former, together with a characteristic hesitation to record a reproach addressed to Jesus, in 8^{25} (cp. Mk 4^{38}).

‡ This is one of his clearest attempts to improve upon Mark (cp. Bacon, *ZNW.*, 1905, 155 f.); it "is to be viewed in the light of the known accusations of collusion with Beelzebub brought against Jesus and his followers, with the marked silence of the Fourth gospel on this type of mighty works."

piece of early Christian midrashic narrative, drawn up in order to show how the various incidents and features of the nativity were a fulfilment of OT prophecy (virgin-birth $1^{22f.}$, in Bethlehem $2^{5f.}$, flight to Egypt 2^{15}, weeping in Ramah 2^{17-18}, and the name Nazarene 2^{23}).*

Neither the style nor the contents of 1–2 afford valid evidence for suspecting that they are a later insertion in the gospel.† The hypothesis that this section did not originally form part of the gospel was advocated in the eighteenth century by Dr. John Williams (*A Free Enquiry into the Authenticity of the First and Second Chapters of St. Matthew's Gospel*[2], London, 1789), then by Ammon (*Dissertatio de Luca emendatore Matthæi*, 1805), and afterwards by Norton (i. 16–17); it is still urged on the plea that 1^{18}–2^{23} was an afterthought or later interpolation (so, *e.g.*, Keim and Merx), since the connection between 1^{17} and 3^{1} is quite natural. The hypothesis that the editor or final author of the gospel has incorporated an earlier source ‡ in 1–2, working it over for his own purposes, becomes especially plausible (i.) with reference to the genealogy (1^{2-16}), which has often been taken (*e.g.* by de Wette, Olshausen, Sabatier: *ESR.* v. 464, Delitzsch, Meyer, Bacon: *DB.* ii. 137 f., and Loisy) as originally a Jewish Christian document, or even as a later insertion (*c.* A.D. 170; Charles in *Academy*, 1894, 447 f.). The latter theory is improbable; the interest in the Davidic sonship was not paramount at that period. As for the former conjecture, the genealogy is probably the composition of the author himself arranged for mnemonic purposes in three sets of fourteen generations (the double 7 reflecting the author's penchant for that sacred number). In structure and contents it is quite artificial,§ inferior to Luke's, and intended

* The further problem (cp. Feigel, *Der Einfluss des Weissagungsbeweises u. anderer Motive auf d. Leidens geschichte*, 1910) for the historical critic is to determine to what extent the prophetic citations created or moulded the narratives, here as elsewhere in Mt. "The narratives have a basis in fact, or in what is assumed to be or regarded as fact. But in form they have often been assimilated to earlier models, and display unmistakable midrashic features" (Box, *ZNW.*, 1905, 88).

† On 1–2 as an integral part of the gospel, cp. Box (*ZNW.*, 1905, 83 f.).

‡ Or sources; Meyer, *e.g.*, finds three in 1^{1-16} 1^{18-25} and 2.

§ "It is artificial from beginning to end, and meant to be so, as artificial as the lists of the twelve thousand sealed out of every tribe of Israel except Dan in the book of Revelation" (Burkitt, *Evang. Da-Meph.* ii. 260). Halévy (*RS.*, 1902, 221 f.) ingeniously suggests that the forty-two generations of Mt., with the twenty from Adam to Abraham, are designed to make up the 62 'weeks' of years in Dn 9^{25-26}, which were to follow the 7 weeks of Zerubbabel, and to be followed by messiah's tragic death (cp. 24^{15}). But, apart from the exegetical obstacles, there is no adequate proof that the Daniel-tradition was a norm to which any messianic aspirant had to conform, or that Mt. dated the death of Jesus from such a messianic prophecy. If any source of the schematism has to be postulated, the cabbalistic interpretation of דוד, whose three letters are equivalent by gematria to the number 14, is the most probable.

to show that Jesus, as the Christ, was legally descended from David—the primary essential, from a Jewish standpoint, for any messianic claimant. A further apologetic motive is evident in the introduction of the women's names, especially of Rahab, Tamar, and Bathsheba. They reflect the Jewish slanders which the author desired to rebut, not only by stating what he believed to be the truth about Mary, but by arguing that, even on the Jewish level, women of irregular life played an honoured rôle in the history of the Davidic lineage. Mary's character, he proceeds to argue, was not irregular. How much less therefore (the inference is) are Jewish objections to her and to Jesus justified! These data of the genealogy show that the story of $1^{18f.}$ was its natural sequel (cp. Allen, *ET.* xi. 135 f.), and consequently that the case for a source is much weaker here than in Luke. There is no obvious reason why a Jewish Christian who, like the author, was interested in the lore of Judaism, should not have compiled the genealogy for his own special purposes.

The birth-narratives in Matthew and Luke stand thus on a different footing. In the latter, the omission of a word or two (in 1^{34-35}) leaves the narrative fairly consecutive and intelligible. In the former, no hypothesis of literary criticism or textual emendation * can disentangle the conception of a virgin-birth from a story which is wrought together and woven on one loom. †

(ii.) The textual problem of 1^{16} is not yet settled, but the earliest variants (of which that in the Dialogue of Timothy and Aquila—Conybeare, *HJ.* i. 96–102—is not one) show traces, variously phrased, of belief in the virgin-birth (cp. J. R. Wilkinson, *HJ.* i. 354–359). Such modifications as may be due to doctrinal prepossessions are designed to re-set or to sharpen the reference of the original text to the virgin-birth, not to insert the dogma in a passage which was originally free from it. The Syriac variants (cp. Burkitt, *Evangelion da-Mepharreshe*, ii. 262 f.) may be regarded as derived from SS (*Jacob begat Joseph, Joseph, to whom was betrothed Mary the Virgin, begat Jesus who is called the Messiah*),‡ which is connected with the Greek text of the Ferrar group, underlying the old Latin, and the Armenian versions (*i.e.* Ἰακὼβ δὲ ἐγέννησεν τὸν Ἰωσήφ, ᾧ μνηστευθεῖσα παρθένος Μαριὰμ ἐγέννησεν Ἰησοῦν τὸν λεγόμενον Χριστόν). In any case ἐγέννησε refers throughout to legal kinship, not to physical parentage (cp. A. S. Lewis, *Old Syriac Gospels*, 1910, pp. xiv–xvii).

(iii.) The story § of 2^{1-11} in whole or part has been assigned to a period

---

* The deletion of ἐκ πνεύματος ἁγίου (1^{18}) by Venema, Markland, Bakhuyzen, and Vollgraff is quite arbitrary, though Burkitt (*Ev. Da-Meph.* ii. 261) rightly follows SS in omitting οὐκ ἐγίνωσκεν ἕως οὗ (1^{25}) as a later Christian comment introduced to safeguard the physical miracle.

† This tells against the primitive origin of the *euangelium infantiae*, and against all theories of its place in Q or in any pre-canonical source which can be detected in the gospels. Resch's attempt (*Kindheitsevangelium*, 264–276) to prove that Paul was acquainted with it is a complete failure.

‡ Cp. van Manen (*TT.*, 1895, pp. 258–263), who defends this as the original reading in Matt. The textual phenomena are displayed in *EBi.* 2962, as amended in *PM.*, 1902, 85–95.

§ Cp. Beyschlag, *NTTh.* ii. 478: "In the story of the travelling star which pointed the way to the magi, in that of Peter walking on the waves, later than that of the gospel; but on insufficient grounds. In a Syriac tract, attributed to Eusebius, and extant in a sixth century MS (cp. transl. by Wright in *Journal of Sacred Lit.*, April, October, 1866; Nestle, *ZWT.*, 1893, 435–438), an account of the magi and the star is given, whose date purports to be A.D. 118–119. If it could be established (so Conybeare in *Guardian*, April 29, 1903, cp. D. Völter, *TT.*, 1910, 170–213), that the author "had in his hands a pre-canonical Greek source of 119 or 120," this might denote the *terminus a quo* for the incorporation of 2^{1-18} into the canonical text of Mt.; but the inference is hazardous. The text runs thus: "This question [*i.e.* about the Balaam-prophecy of the star and the coming of the magi to Bethlehem in the reign of Pir Shabour] arose in the minds of men who were acquainted with the holy books, and through the efforts of great men in various places this history was sought for, and found, and written in the tongue of those who attended to the matter." The 'holy books' probably include the NT, the 'history' is not the story of Mt 2^{1-11} but the Balaam-legend, and the question related to the verification of the date in Mt. or to the harmonising of the Lucan and Matthæan stories of the infancy (cp. Hilgenfeld, *ZWT.*, 1895, 447 f., and Zahn, *INT.* ii. 527). It is curious that according to astronomical observations an important and rare conjunction of the planets (Jupiter and Saturn) did take place between April 15th and December 27th of 6 B.C., which may have led to acute speculation amongst Babylonian astrologers, who were accustomed to forecast the effects of such phenomena upon Syria.* This may suggest a historical nucleus for the early Christian haggada of Mt 2^{1-11}.

(*b*) 16^{17-20} is also more likely to be organic to a gospel which reflected the later catholic consciousness of Christianity (cp. *HNT.* 646 f.), and particularly Matthew's high estimate of the apostles, than a later interpolation in a very early gospel, much less an integral part of such a gospel (Keim, iv. 266 f.; Stevens, *NTTh.* 136 f.). The original saying † goes back to the Jewish conception of *petra* (פטרא, cp. the rabbinic quotation in Taylor's *Sayings of Jewish Fathers*², 160) as applied by God to Abraham, 'when He saw Abraham who was going to arise, He said, Lo, I have found a *petra* to build and to found the world upon.' Even in the Greek expansion of the evangelist the saying does not presuppose a period of christological development later than that assigned to the gospel as a whole, and the similar passage in Jn 20^{22-23} seems a correction of the specifically Petrine privilege

or of the OT saints rising in the hour of Jesus' death, Mt. has manifestly translated poetic traditions into history. Even Lk. has taken for genuine history the legendary traditions of his introductory chapters."

* The suggestions of Kepler have been recently elaborated, on the basis of a Babylonian demotic papyrus, by Oefele in his essay (*Mittheilungen der Vorderasiat. Gesellschaft*, 1903) on 'das Horoskop der Empfängnis Christi.'

† Cp. Bruston in *RTQR.* (1902) 326–341.

of the Matthæan logion. For this, as well as for other reasons (cp. Zahn's *Forschungen*, i. 163 f., 290 f.), it is unlikely that 16^{17-19} (cp. Schmiedel, *EBi.*, 1876, 1892, 3104–3105) is an interpolation, or that 16^{18-19} represents an insertion made by the church of Rome (Victor), *c.* A.D. 190, in the interests of its catholic authority (so Grill, *Der Primat des Petrus*, 1904, pp. 61–79).

(*c*) While the epilogue (28^{16-20}) naturally does not give the *ipsissima uerba* of Christ (cp. *HNT.* 647–649), it is an organic part of the gospel, which rounds off the narrative;* there is nothing in its phraseology which is inconsistent with the catholic consciousness of the early church during the last quarter of the first century. The only point of dubiety lies in 28^{19}. The theory that the textus receptus of this verse arose between A.D. 130 and 140 in the African old Latin texts, owing to baptismal and liturgical considerations, and that the original text was the shorter Eusebian form (*πορευθέντες μαθητεύσατε πάντα τὰ ἔθνη ἐν τῷ ὀνόματί μου*), was proposed by F. C. Conybeare (*ZNW.*, 1901, 275–280; *HJ.* i. 102–108) and has been accepted by Usener (*Rhein. Museum*, 1902, 39 f.), Kirsopp Lake: *Influence of Text. Criticism on NT Exegesis* (1904), pp. 7 f., Wellhausen, Allen, and Montefiore, amongst others. The opposite side is represented by Riggenbach (*BFT.*, 1903, vii. 1, 'Der trinitarische Taufbefehl Mt 28^{19} nach seiner ursprüngliche Textgestalt und seiner Authentie untersucht') and Chase (*JTS.*, 1905, 483 f.). The phrase *ἐν τῷ ὀνόματί μου* may be a Western harmonising interpolation (so Riggenbach, from Lk 24^{47}; Chase, from Mk 16^{17}), or an insertion of Eusebius himself, independent of any codices in the Cæsarean library. Also, the fact that Eusebius in a number of his works refrains from quoting the verse in its canonical form, and omits all reference to baptism, does not necessarily involve that the canonical form was not in existence, if it can be proved that it was natural for him to omit the baptismal clause as irrelevant to his immediate purpose, quoting only the words which follow and precede it in the canonical text. The occurrence of the latter in the Syriac version of the *Theophania*

* Cp. Norden (*Antike Kunstprosa*, ii. 456): '*Χρῶ τοῖς μὲν Ἕλλησιν ὡς Ἕλλησιν, τοῖς δὲ βαρβάροις ὡς βαρβάροις*, ist die Weisung, die der Griechische Philosoph einer Tradition zufolge seinem die Welt erobernden Schüler Alexander auf den Weg mitgab; *πορευθέντες οὖν μαθητεύσατε πάντα τὰ ἔθνη* sagte der Stifter der christlichen Religion zu seiner Schüler als er sie in die Welt aussandte.'

(iv. 8) shows that some old Syriac MSS must have had the baptism in the name of the Trinity, and Ephraim's comment on the Diatessaron indicates that the latter represented the ordinary text of Mt. at this point (cp. Burkitt's *Evang. Da-Meph.* i. 172 f., ii. 171, 279). Didachê 7, again, shows that the trinitarian formula was possible by the first quarter of the second century, but this does not prove that it was derived from Mt 28^{19}. The question has an obvious bearing not only on the date, but on the ethos of Matthew's gospel. On the whole, the probabilities seem to converge on the likelihood that the trinitarian form was introduced by the author of the gospel himself, as a liturgical expansion of the primitive formula of baptism into the name of Jesus (cp. J. R. Wilkinson, *HJ.* i. 571–575; Stanton, *GHD.* i. 355 f.).

Most of the other structural difficulties can be explained as the result either of the author's work as a compiler and editor, or of later harmonising. The main exception is 5^{18-19}, but even this does not justify the hypothesis of a later revision.

The disruption of the context by Mt 28^{9-10}, whose contents do no more than repeat those of vv.$^{5-7}$, suggests that it is an editorial interpolation or later gloss (so, *e.g.*, Keim, vi. 308 f.; Soltau, Schmiedel). Nothing new is communicated by Jesus; he simply repeats what the angel has already said. Whether it is a reminiscence of the tradition underlying Jn 20^{14-17} (cp. the common use of *brethren*), or borrowed from the lost Marcan ending (see above, pp. 238 f.), it is a plausible conjecture (Rohrbach, Harnack) that its insertion may have taken place early in the second century, when the formation of the gospel-canon led to a certain amount of alteration especially in the resurrection-narrative, in order to level up the synoptic traditions (with their Galilean appearances) to the Johannine (Jerusalem).

This dual character of the resurrection-stories (Galilee, Jerusalem), which becomes a special problem in the historical criticism of Mt. and Lk., has started an ingenious attempt to locate the Galilee-appearances at Jerusalem by means of a harmonising hypothesis which assumes that Galilee here is not the province but a place in the vicinity of Jerusalem (so especially R. Hofmann, "Galiläa auf dem Oelberg," 1896; Zimmermann in *SK.*, 1901, 446 f., and Lepsius, "Die Auferstehungsberichte," in *Reden. u. Abhandlungen*, iv., 1902), and which summons to its aid the conjecture (Resch, *TU.* x. 2. 381 f., x. 3. 765 f., xii. 332 f., 362 f., 586) that περίχωρος (in Mk 1^{28} etc.; cp. Abbott's *Diat.* 438 f., 1232)* is the Gk. equivalent of גְּלִילָה (cp. Ezek 47^{8}), a district east of the temple, surrounding the mount of Olives and including Bethany. There would thus be two Galilees in the NT: one that of northern Palestine, the sphere of the early ministry of Jesus, the other that

* The double sense of גְּלִיל is used both by Chajes (*Markus-Studien*, 13) and Abbott to explain Lk 4^{37}=Mk 1^{28}.

of Jerusalem, the location of Christ's appearances after death. But the evidence for this theory breaks down upon examination. The mediæval pilgrims found a site here and there for Galilee on Olivet or Mount Sion, simply because they already (cp. Zahn, *GK.* ii. 937) felt the difficulty of harmonising the resurrection-narratives. Tertullian's language in *Apol.* 21 does not bear out Resch's contention (cp. Schürer, *TLZ.*, 1897, 187 f.), while the theory is further handicapped by the need of assuming not only that Luke at one place (24^{6}) misread Mk 16^{7}, although elsewhere he (24^{50}, Ac 1^{12}) preserved the real meaning of Galilee, but that, without any warning, the term changes its geographical meaning in the synoptic tradition. The hypothesis therefore falls to the ground (so, *e.g.*, Keim. vi. 380; W. C. Allen, *EBi.* 2987; Gautier, *EBi.* 3498; Schmiedel, *EBi.* 4044; Lake, *Resurrection Narratives*, 208–209; Masterman, *DCG.* ii. 207; A. Meyer, *Auferstehungsberichte*, 95 f.).

§ 4. *Characteristics.*—The main problem of the gospel remains, however, viz. the juxtaposition of Jewish or particularistic (*e.g.* $10^{5f. 23}$ 15^{24} 19^{28} 23^{2}) and catholic (*e.g.* $12^{7f.}$ 24^{14} and $28^{19f.}$) sayings (cp. 16^{12} and 23^{8}). Are the former due to a Judaistic recension of the Logia (Schmiedel, *EBi.* 1842–3, 1870), and were the latter, together with some of the less historical traits, the work of a later editor or editors more friendly to the Gentiles (Hilgenfeld, Ewald, Schwegler: *NZ.* i. 199 f., 241 f.)? The answer to these questions depends upon the critical analysis of the gospel. Keim (i. 86 f.) ascribes, *e.g.*, 1^{17}–2^{23} 3^{14-15} 8^{11-12} 22^{1-14} 25^{1-12} $27^{19. 62-66}$ $28^{15f.}$ to a zealous Jewish-Christian, of liberal sympathies, who wrote after the fall of Jerusalem. Soltau's better theory (*ZNW.*, 1900, 219–248) is that a series of editorial additions to the original Matthew may be found, *e.g.*, in 1–2, 3^{14-15} 4^{14-16} 5^{18-19} 8^{17} 12^{17-21} $13^{14-15. 35}$ 21^{2-5} $26^{15. 53 (56)}$ $27^{(3) 9-10. 34. 43. 57}$ 27^{62}–28^{20}; the original Matthew was compiled from Mk. and the Logia by an opponent of Judaism, but the editor was a strict Jewish Christian of catholic sympathies and dogmatic prepossessions. This is decidedly simpler than the older theory of Scholten (*Het Oudste Evangelie*, 93 f.), which postulated three different editions of Matthew. But the solution lies in the idiosyncrasies of the author rather than in the strata of the gospel. The author of Matthew is unconsciously self-portrayed in 13^{52}; he is *γραμματεὺς μαθητευθεὶς τῇ βασιλείᾳ τῶν οὐρανῶν ὅμοιος ἀνθρώπῳ οἰκοδεσπότῃ ὅστις ἐκβάλλει ἐκ τοῦ θησαυροῦ αὐτοῦ καινὰ καὶ παλαιά.* He is a Jewish Christian, acquainted with rabbinic learning;* the midrashic element is more pronounced in his work than in either

* "Les formules bien frappées, brèves, sentencieuses y abondent; on y sent vraiment le docteur qui parle avec autorité" (Jacquier, *INT.* ii. 383).

Mark or Luke, and it is most conspicuous in the passages which come directly from his own pen. The Jewish Christian traits of his gospel are, however, largely due to the Palestinian traditions which he employed, as well as to the thesis of his own work, viz. that Christianity as the new law and righteousness of God had superseded the old as a revelation of God to men.* He voices the catholic and apostolic consciousness of the early church, which saw in its universal mission to the world a commission of Jesus to his disciples, and in its faith a new and final law of God's messiah. Mt. thus approximates to the standpoint of Luke and of James. He does not show any anti-Pauline tendency; it is forced exegesis to detect a polemic against Paul,† *e.g.* in the description of *the enemy* in 13^{28} or in 5^{19} (cp. 1 Co 15^{9}). If Mt. has any affinities with the great apostle, it is with the Paul of Ro $9^{1f.}$, not of Ro $11^{1f.}$, much less of Gal $2^{6f.}$. His Jewish Christian proclivities are strongly marked even in details (*e.g.* 24^{20}, his fondness for ἡ βασιλεία τῶν οὐρανῶν, the addition of καὶ τὴν δικαιοσύνην in 6^{33} [cp. $3^{15} = 5^{17}$, Gal 4^{4}], etc.), but he sees the real Judaism not in the Israel ‡ which had deliberately (cp. 27^{25}, note the emphatic πᾶς ὁ λαός) rejected Jesus, but in the church. It is not accidental that ἐκκλησία only occurs in Mt., among the evangelists. He reflects an age when the church

* Wellhausen (*Einl.* 70 f.) minimises unduly the catholic and universal traits of the final editor. "Mt. has in view the primitive church of Jerusalem, which sought to hold fast by Judaism in spite of everything. Hostility to the official representatives of the Law is never expressed more bitterly than by him. . . . But this enmity is a rival race for the same goal, viz. for the fulfilment of the Law and for righteousness. This goal is naturally higher for Christians than for Jews; nevertheless, on that very account the former claim to be the true representatives of Judaism and refuse to yield place to the false. They still take part in the cultus at Jerusalem (5^{23-25}), pay the temple-tax, . . . confine their propaganda outside Jerusalem to Jews, exclude pagans and Samaritans, and will not cast their holy pearls before swine (10^{5} 7^{6})." But this is retained, partly for archaic reasons, from the sources; it is not so fundamental for Mt. as the larger atmosphere of catholic feeling. Wellhausen himself (*Einl.* 88 f.) admits the probability of this later on.

† He alone of the evangelists uses ἀνομία, and he is specially opposed to hypocrisy; but the former need not, any more than the latter, be an anti-Pauline touch.

‡ Cp. Wellhausen's remark on 23^{37-39} "Er [*i.e.* Jesus] hat durch seine Apostel immer wieder Versuche gemacht, die Juden in seiner Gemeinde (*k'nischta*) zu sammeln (*k'nasch*) und vor dem drohenden Zorn zuflucht zu gewähren, aber vergebens."

and the kingdom were becoming more closely identified, when the Gentile mission was in full swing, when the initial flush and rush of the faith in Palestine had been succeeded by experiences of false prophets, unworthy members,* and the obstacles which a new organisation creates as well as removes.

Writing for the practical needs of the church, he betrays the vocation of a teacher incidentally in the mnemonic and mathematical arrangements of his material, among other things. Thus there are three divisions in the genealogy ($1^{2\text{-}17}$), three angel-messages to Joseph in dreams (1^{20} $2^{13.\ 19}$), three temptations ($4^{1\text{-}11}$), a triple description of the mission (4^{23} see above), a triple illustration in 5^{22} (cp. $5^{34\text{-}35.\ 39\text{-}41}$), the threefold definition of $6^{1\text{-}4.\ 5\text{-}15.\ 16\text{-}18}$ (cp. also $6^{9\text{-}10}$ $7^{7\text{-}8.\ 22.\ 25.\ 27}$), three miracles of healing ($8^{1\text{-}15}$), three further miracles (8^{23}–9^{9}), three other miracles of healing ($9^{18\text{-}34}$), the triple rhythm of $11^{7\text{-}9}$ (cp. 12^{50}), the threefold attack of the Pharisees ($12^{2f.\ 10f.\ 24f.}$), three parables of sowing ($13^{1\text{-}32}$), three instances of *Verily I say to you* ($18^{3.\ 13.\ 18}$),† three classes of eunuchs (19^{12}), the threefold rhythm of 20^{19} (εἰς τὸ κτλ.) and 21^{9}, three parables (21^{18}–22^{14}), three questions put to Jesus ($22^{15\text{-}40}$), three warnings ($23^{8\text{-}10}$, cp. $23^{20\text{-}22}$ 23^{23} *mint and dill and cummin, justice and mercy and faithfulness*, 23^{34} *prophets and wise men and scribes*), the three men of the parable ($25^{14f.}$), three prayers in Gethsemane ($26^{36\text{-}45}$), three denials of Peter ($26^{69f.}$), three questions of Pilate ($27^{17\text{-}22}$), three mockeries of the crucified ($27^{39\text{-}44}$), three women specially mentioned at the cross (27^{56}), and the threefold rhythm of $28^{19\text{-}20}$. With this numerical trait we may rank the fivefold occurrence of the formula καὶ ἐγένετο ὅτε ἐτέλεσεν κτλ. (7^{28} 11^{1} 13^{53} 19^{1} 26^{1}), the fivefold antithesis of $5^{21\text{-}48}$, and the fivefold rhythm of $10^{7\text{-}8}$ (cp. $10^{9\text{-}10}$); the seven evil spirits of 12^{45}, the sevenfold forgiveness of $18^{21\text{-}22}$ (cp. 22^{25}), the seven loaves and baskets ($15^{34.\ 37}$), and the sevenfold woe of 23. It may be only accidental that there are ten OT citations (1–4^{11}) previous to the beginning of the Galilean mission, and there happen to be ten miracles in 8^{1}–9^{34}. The irregular number of the beatitudes ($5^{1f.}$), where schematism would have been easy, shows that the writer did not work out

* "He seems to move amid a race of backsliders" (Abbott, *EBi.* 1788); but the references are too general to be connected with the retrogression of Jewish converts when the breach between Gentile and Jewish Christians widened *c.* A.D. 70.

† The ἀμὴν in 18^{19} is to be omitted.

numerical schemes * quite regardless of the materials at his disposal, though homiletic influences undoubtedly were responsible for the form as occasionally for the content of the latter.

The character of the OT citations throws a particular ray of light on the heterogeneous strata of the gospel as well as on the specific interests of the compiler or editor. In 2^{6} $4^{15f.}$ 8^{17} 13^{35} and $27^{9f.}$ we have paraphrastic renderings of the Hebrew.† Here, as elsewhere, citations which differ alike from the Hebrew and the LXX may occasionally be the result of the natural looseness with which early Christian writers occasionally cited the OT from memory, or freely adapted texts for purposes of edification. In such cases the differences are immaterial. In others, *e.g.* in $27^{9f.}$ (cp. H. R. Hatch, *Biblical World*, 1893, 345–354, and J. R. Harris, *Exp.*[7], 1905, 161–171), the use of a *florilegium* is the clue to the textual phenomena. The dual nature of the citations remains, however, upon any hypothesis, and it is a watermark of compilation. As a rule Matthew assimilates quotations already found in Mk. more closely to the LXX, or else leaves them as he finds them in that state. The main exceptions to this—in 21^{13}, where, like Lk. (19^{46}), he omits the *πᾶσιν τοῖς ἔθνεσιν* of the LXX (Mk 11^{17}), and in 27^{46}, where the closer approximation of *ἱνατί* to the LXX is balanced by the substitution of the vocative *θεέ μου* for *ὁ θεός μου* (Mk 15^{34} LXX)—are not of any special moment. The same holds true of the non-Marcan allusions to, or citations of, the OT, with the striking exception of twelve passages (1^{23} 2^{15} 2^{18} 2^{23} 4^{6} 12^{18} 21^{5} besides the five noted above),‡ which indicate a recourse to the original with a more or less subordinate use of the LXX. These passages are all connected with the fulfilment of prophecy. Two of them (2^{23} and 27^{9-10}) may have been taken originally from the apocryphal book of Jeremiah (Jerome, cp. Resch's *Parallel-Texte*, ii. 334 f., 369 f.), three come from Micah (2^{6}), Hosea (2^{15}),§ and Jeremiah (2^{18}) respectively, while a couple (4^{6} 13^{35}) are from the Psalter. The rest are drawn from Isaiah (21^{5} being a composite citation of Isaiah and Zechariah).

With regard to the motives underlying Mt.'s account, an apologetic element emerges at the outset in the ascription of the birth to prophecy, as well as in the inclusion of the women in the

* On this cp. Luthardt's paragraphs in his essay, *De Compositione Evangelii Matthaei* (Leipzig, 1861), Plummer (pp. xix f.), and Abbott (*Diat.* 3352 *e*).

† Cp. E. Haupt's *Zur Würdigung der alt. Citationen im Ev. Mt.* (Treptow, 1870) on 8^{17} (pp. 1–7) 13^{35} (pp. 7–10) and 27^{9} (pp. 10–16); Allen in *ET.* xii. 281 f., and Nestle in *ET.* xix. on 2^{23} (pp. 527 f.), and (*ET.* xx. 92–93) on 12^{19}.

‡ The midrashic development in 21^{5} is carried a step further by Justin (*Apol.* i. 32), who binds the foal to a vine.

§ The difference between this forced application (due to the identification of Jesus here, as in the temptation story, with Israel) and the apt citation in 9^{13} (12^{17}), illustrates the composite character of Matthew's gospel (cp. Burkitt's *Transmission*, 202–203).

genealogy. The author aimed at contemporary Jewish insinuations against the honour of Mary. The birth of Jesus was the fulfilment of prophecy; Joseph openly recognised Mary as his wife before the birth; and even in the Davidic genealogy women like Tamar and Rahab, besides Ruth the foreigner, had played a part by Divine commission. It is true that the earliest possible record of the well-known Jewish slander dates from about A.D. 130, while it does not become prominent till the age of Celsus, half a century later (Hilgenfeld in *ZWT.*, 1900, pp. 271 f.); but it must be earlier than its literary records, and some such slander was inevitable in Jewish circles as soon as the dogma of the virgin-birth was marked, particularly when argument was rife over the messianic claims of Jesus. Elsewhere in Mt. a sensitiveness to contemporary Jewish slander is visible, as in the story of 28^{11-15}, and the humble, grateful recognition of Jesus the messiah * at his birth by the foreign magi is thrown into relief against his subsequent reception by the Jews.

Mt. has also his eye upon difficulties felt inside the church, *e.g.* about the relation of Jesus to the Law and the Gentile mission. A certain perplexity had further been felt, by the time he wrote, about the baptism of Jesus, and his account in $3^{13f.}$ attempts to explain how the holy messiah submitted to baptism at the hands of John.† The purpose of John's baptism, εἰς ἄφεσιν ἁμαρτίων (Mk 1^4), is omitted, and there is a tacit contrast between the people (Mt 3^6) and the religious authorities (3^{11} ὑμᾶς . . . εἰς μετάνοιαν) on the one hand, and Jesus ($3^{14f.}$) on the other. The curious story of the Gospel according to the Hebrews (cp. Jerome, *contra Pelag.* iii. 2, and Cyprian, *de rebapt.* xvii.), that Jesus only went ‡ after refusing at first to accompany his father and mother (cp. the motive of John $7^{3f.}$), is accepted by some scholars, *e.g.* by O. Holtzmann (*Leben Jesu*, Eng. tr. 127 f.), as authentic. Both this and the account in Mt. are probably more or less independent attempts to explain the same

* The significant change in 3^{17} (cp. Jub $22^{26.28}$; Halévy, *RS.*, 1903, 32 f., 123 f., 210 f.) substitutes a public proclamation for an inward assurance.

† The passage thus tallies with the ratification of Christian baptism in 28^{19}; the validity of the institution is proved apologetically by the fact that Jesus himself not only enjoined it but submitted to it.

‡ "Dixit autem eis, quid peccaui, ut uadam et baptizer ab eo? nisi forte hoc ipsum, quod dixi, ignorantia est." The fragment breaks off here; but, as the next fragment proves, Jesus did go eventually.

incident. But this opens up the larger question of the relation between the two works.

§ 5. *Mt. and the Euangelium iuxta Hebræos.*—When the Matthæan document is identified with Q (see above, pp. 194 f.), the speculations of early tradition and recent investigation upon the relation of the canonical Mt. to the τὸ Ἰουδαικὸν lose their basis and interest, although the latter document remains one of the problems and enigmas of early Christian literature. Even yet there is no sort of agreement upon the relation of the canonical Matthew, or of Q (= the Matthæan Logia), to what came to be called 'the Gospel according to the Hebrews' (εὐαγγέλιον καθ' Ἑβραίους). The latter, to judge from the Stichometry of Nikephorus, was larger than Mk. and smaller than Mt.; it was the Greek translation of an Aramaic original, used by the Nazarenes and the Ebionites especially, and eventually circulated among the Jewish Christians of Egypt. So much is clear. But its origin is a mystery. Was it (so from Bleek and Frank: *SK.*, 1846, 369 f., to Wernle, *Syn. Frage*, 248 f.; Jülicher, *Einl.* 261; A. F. Findlay, etc.) a second-hand and second-century compilation mainly based on the canonical gospels (especially Mt. and Lk.),* or a source co-ordinate with the canonical Gospels (O. Holtzmann's *Leben Jesu*, Eng. tr. 46–52) and even used by Mt. and Lk. (Handmann, *TU.* v. 3. 127 f.)? These are the two extremes of critical opinion. The latter is modified by those who hold that both Mt. and Heb. gospel were written by the same hand (Nicholson, *The Gospel according to the Hebrews*, 1879), or that both were versions of the Ur-Matthäus (so, *e.g.*, Schneckenburger, Zahn), while there is still support for the traditional view that the Heb. gospel were really the work of Matthew to which the tradition of Papias refers (so, *e.g.*, Hilgenfeld, *Die Evglien*, 43 f.; *ZWT.*, 1863, 345 f., 1889, 280 f., and Barns, cp. A. Meyer, *HNA.* i. 18–19).† Setting aside the latter theory, we may upon the whole feel

* Specifically a second-century Jewish-Christian adaptation of Mt. (Weizsäcker, *Untersuchungen*, 223 f.; Resch, *TU.* v. 4. 322 f.; Hoennicke, *JC.* 98, etc.) or of Lk. (B. Weiss, *Einl.* 494 f.).

† To the literature cited by Ehrhard (*ACL.* 139 f.) and A. Meyer (*HNA*, ii. 21 f.), add Menzies (*DB.* v. 338–342), A. F. Findlay (*DCG.* i. 675 f.), Stanton (*GHD.* i. 250 f.), Adeney (*HJ.* iii. 139–159), and Barnes (*JTS.*, April 1905, 356 f.). The extant fragments are collected in Preuschen's *Antilegomena* (3–8) and Harnack (*ACL.* i. 1. 6 f.), and translated by Nicholson (*op. cit.* pp. 28 f.) and B. Pick (*Paralipomena*, Chicago, 1908).

justified in refusing also to regard the gospel καθ' Ἑβραίους as a derivative compilation. Its use by Hegesippus (cp. *SR.* 270 f.), possibly also by Ignatius and Papias,* throws the date of its composition into the early part of the second century, and the internal evidence suggests an even earlier period (A.D. 70–100, Harnack, *ACL.* ii. 1. 625 f.). The gospel, in its original form,† was probably one of the narratives which preceded Luke (1^1); it was a Jewish Christian διήγησις which assigned special prominence to James as Mt. did to Peter, and which derived part of its material from primitive and fairly authentic sources. The tradition which connected it with Matthew is pure guesswork, started by misinterpretations of the earlier tradition about Matthew's Logia. The gospel καθ' Ἑβραίους was originally anonymous (Handmann, pp. 114 f.); it was a gospel of the twelve, not a gospel of Matthew. Unlike the canonical Mt. it had no *Euangelium infantiæ*, though it may have had a genealogy, since its purpose was to prove the messianic legitimacy of Jesus. It is related, in point of religious aim and literary quality, to the canonical Mt. pretty much as the epistle of Barnabas is to Hebrews.

(D) *LUKE.*

LITERATURE.—(*a*) Editions ‡—Origen's *Homiliæ in Lucam* (mainly on chs. 1–4); Ambrose, *Expositio Evangelica* (fourth century); Beda (eighth century); Theophylact (eleventh century); Cajetan (1543); Cornelius à Lapide (1638, Eng. tr. of Luke, London, 1887); H. Pape (Leipzig, 1778); S F. N. Morus (Leipzig, 1795); Stein (Halle, 1830); F. A. Bornemann's *Scholia* (1830); Glöckler (Frankfort, 1835); Olshausen (1837, Eng. tr. 1863); Baumgarten-Crusius (Jena, 1845); Meyer (1846, Eng. tr. of fifth ed., Edin. 1880); de Wette[3] (1846); Trollope (London, 1847); Diedrich

* Schwegler (*NZ.* i. 197 f.) also heard echoes in Jas 5^{12} and 2 P 1^{17}, since the gospel, like the apocalypse of John, voiced the primitive Jewish Christianity of the early church. Pfleiderer (*Urc.* ii. 160 f.), though regarding it as an independent form of the original Aramaic gospel, admits the presence of later legends.

† The legendary features are cruder than the naive stories, *e.g.*, of Mt 17^{24-27} $21^{18f.}$ and 27^{51-53}; on the other hand, it has preserved a more accurate form of 23^{35}. The latter is more likely to be primitive than the correction of the canonical text of Mt. by a well-informed editor, and it is not the only instance of good primitive tradition in the τὸ Ἰουδαϊκόν.

‡ The Greek comments of Eusebius (Cæs.) and Cyril (Alex.) are extant only in fragments; the latter is translated into English (ed. R. P. Smith, Oxford, 1859).

(1864); J. J. Owen (New York, 1867); Bisping (1868); Burger (1868); A. Carr (1875); Jones and Cook (*Speaker's Comm.* 1878); E. H. Plumptre (Ellicott's *Comm.* 1878); Hofmann (1878); Oosterzee (Lange's *Bibel-Werk*[4], 1880); van Doren (New York, 1881); Fillion (Paris, 1882); Schanz (1883)*; Farrar (*CGT.* 1884); M. F. Sadler (1886); Godet[3] (1888, Eng. tr. of second ed. 1881); T. M. Lindsay (Edin., n. d.); J. Bond (1890); Hahn (Breslau, 1892–4)*; J. Weiss* (— Meyer[8], 1892); Knabenbauer (Paris, 1895); Plummer (*ICC.* 1896 and foll. ed.); Blass, *Evangelium secundum Lucam* (1897); Nösgen[2] (Strack-Zöckler, 1897); Riezler (Brixen, 1900); A. Wright (1900); B. Weiss (— Meyer[9], 1901); Adeney (*CB.* 1901); Girodon (*Commentaire critique et moral*, Paris, 1903); Wellhausen* (1904); V. Rose, *L'évangile selon S. Luc* (Paris, 1904); Merx, *Die Evglien Marcus u. Lukas nach der Syrischen im Sinaikloster gefund. Palimpsest-handschrift erläutert.* (1905)*; J. M. S. Baljon (1908)*; A. S. Walpole (1910).

(*b*) Studies—B. L. Königsmann, *De fontibus commentariorum Lucæ* (1798); Schleiermacher, *über die Schriften des Lucas* (1 Theil, 1817, Eng. tr. 1828, with preface by Thirlwall);[1] Mill, *The Hist. Char. of St. Luke's Gospel* (1841); J. Grimm, *Die Einheit des Lucas-Evglms* (1863); G. Meyer, *Les Sources de l'év. de L.* (Toulouse, 1868); Renan, v. (ch. xiii.); Keim, i. 98 f.; Scholten, *das Paulinische Evglm*, *Kritische Unters. d. Ev. nach Lucas*, etc. (Germ. ed., Redepenning, 1881); Stockmeyer, 'Quellen des Lk-Evglms' (*ZSchw.*, 1884, 117–149); C. Campbell, *Critical Studies in St. Luke's Gospel* (1890, on Ebionitism, demonology, etc.); Feine, *Eine vorkanonische Ueberlieferung des Lukas* (1891)*; Bebb (*DB.* iii. 162–173); Pfleiderer, *Urc.* ii. 98–190, 280 f.); P. C. Sense, *Origin of Third Gospel* (1901); E. C. Selwyn, *Luke the Prophet* (1901); A. B. Bruce, *Kingdom of God*[6] (1904)*; J. Haussleiter, *Die Missionsgedanke im Evglm des Lukas* (1905); B. Weiss, *Die Quellen des Lukasevglms* (1908)*; A. Wright (*DCG.* ii. 84–91).

§ 1. *The Preface.*—Blass (*Philology of Gospels*, 1898, 1–20); Abbott (*EBi.* 1789–90).

Luke's gospel and its sequel are addressed to a certain Theophilus. This is a genuine proper name, not an imaginary *nom de guerre* for the typical catechumen, nor a conventional title for the average Christian reader. Nothing is known of Theophilus, except what may be inferred from Luke's language, viz. that he was not simply an outsider interested in the faith, but (κατηχήθης, cp. Ac 18^{25} 21^{21}) a Christian who desired or required fuller acquaintance with the historic basis of the Christian gospel; also that, as κράτιστε implies (cp. Ac 23^{26} 24^{8} 26^{25}), he was a man of rank. Luke's emphasis on the relation between Christianity and the Roman empire, and his stress upon the hindrances and

[1] Criticised by Planck in an essay, *De Luca evang. analysi critica quam Schleiermacher proposuit* (Göttingen, 1819).

temptations of money,* would tally with the hypothesis that his friend belonged to the upper and official classes; but beyond these inferences lies the land of fancy.†

Luke's method is historical, but his object, like that of John (20[31]), is religious. He makes no claim, however, to be an eye-witness. All he professes is to write a correct, complete, and chronological (in the sense of well-arranged, or logical) account of the primitive παράδοσις as received from the first generation of disciples. This attempt was neither new nor superfluous. Luke had numerous predecessors in the enterprise, but their work did not satisfy his purpose, and he resolved to make a fresh essay. He makes no claim to be inspired (contrast the ἔδοξε κἀμοί with the ἔδοξεν πνεύματι τῷ ἁγίῳ καὶ ἡμῖν of Ac 15[28]); his qualifications are simply the pains he had taken to acquaint himself (ἀκριβῶς) with the contents of the παράδοσις. Whatever his success was, his historical aim and method contrast favourably with the easy-going practice of his pagan contemporary, Q. Curtius Rufus (vii. 8. 11, utcunque sunt tradita incorrupta perferemus; ix. 1. 34, equidem plura transcribo quam credo). Luke did not rest his narrative on unsifted traditions.

(*a*) The dedication proves that the compilers of early Christian gospels, among whom Luke ranks himself, drew upon the παραδόσεις of eye-witnesses and primitive evangelists, but that the latter did not write down their information. The drawing up of narratives, it is implied, followed the oral stage. As Luke's writings show, he availed himself not simply of the written composition of his predecessors (*e.g.* Mk. and Q), but of oral tradition.

(*b*) The preface or dedication not only is modelled on the conventional lines of ancient literature, but shows if not an acquaintance with similar passages in medical treatises, *e.g.* that of Dioskorides περὶ ὕλης ἰατρικῆς (cp. Lagarde's *Mittheilungen*, iii. 355 f.; Hobart, *Medical Language of St. Luke*, 86 f.; J. Weiss, etc.), at any rate a medical flavour.‡ Thus, ἀκριβῶς

* The so-called 'Ebionitism' of Luke arises partly from his sources, several of which apparently reflected the suffering, poor churches of Palestine (A.D. 40–70), and partly from the familiar diatribê-themes of contemporary Stoicism. The tone of the relevant passages (cp. O. Holtzmann's *War Jesus Ekstatiker*, pp. 16 f.) is that of James' epistle, curiously ascetic and more than suspicious of wealth.

† Beck (*Der Prolog des Lukas Evglm*, 1901) *e.g.* argues from ἐν ἡμῖν that Luke was one of the Emmaus-disciples, and Theophilus a rich tax-collector of Antioch who met Luke, Philip, and Paul at Cæsarea, whither he had accompanied Herod and Bernice.

‡ Thumb (*Die Griechische Sprache im Zeitalter des Hellenismus*, 1901, 225–226) contends that the linguistic parallels with Dioskorides and Hippokrates (pref. to Περὶ ἀρχαίης ἰατρικῆς, ὁκόσοι ἐπεχείρησαν περὶ ἰητρικῆς

παρακολουθεῖν is a phrase of Galen (*Prognat.* ii. 13, *Theriac. ad Pisonem*, 2), and in his preface to the latter work he writes, καὶ τοῦτόν σοι τὸν περὶ τῆς θηριακῆς λόγον, ἀκριβῶς ἐξετάσας ἅπαντα, ἄριστε Πίσων σπουδαίως ἐποίησα. Luke's preface therefore hints that the writer is not only composing a literary work, but familiar with medical phraseology. It is the first piece of evidence for the correctness of the tradition (see below) that he was Luke, the Greek physician who was in touch with Paul during his later life.

(*c*) Polybius similarly (iv. 1–2) explains that he begins his main history at 220–216 B.C., since he was thus able "to speak as an eye-witness of several of the events" of the periods, "as well as from the information of those who were eye-witnesses of other events. To go further back and write the report of a report (ὡς ἀκοὴν ἐξ ἀκοῆς γράφειν) seemed to me an insecure basis for conclusions or for assertions." Luke would have also agreed with the further reason of Polybius, "Above all, I started at this point, inasmuch as the whole world's history entered upon a new phase at this period."

§ 2. *Outline and contents.*—After the preface (1^{1-4}), the gospel falls into four sections: (*a*) The first (1^{5}–4^{13}) describes the birth of John and of Jesus (1^{5}–2^{20}), the boyhood of Jesus (2^{21-52}), the preliminary mission of John (3^{1-20}) and his baptism of Jesus ($3^{21f.}$), the genealogy of the latter (3^{23-38}) and his temptation (4^{1-13}).* The second part (4^{14}–9^{50}) is devoted to the Galilean mission.† The third section (9^{51}–19^{27}) brings Jesus to Jerusalem after a series of journeys through Samaria and elsewhere. The closing part (19^{28}–24) covers the same ground as the corresponding sections in Mk. and Mt., though with characteristic omissions and additions.‡

Luke's relation to the Marcan order is of primary significance in an estimate of his work. Between Mk 1^{1-6} and Mk 1^{7-8} he inserts an even fuller account of John's preaching (3^{7-14}) than Mt. (3^{7-10}); §

λέγειν ἢ γράφειν) are too general, and that they only prove a knowledge of medical phraseology. On the coincidences with the prefaces and dedications of Josephus, see Krenkel's *Josephus u. Lukas*, 50 f.

* On the Lucan handling of this tradition, cp. *EBi.* 4960–4961, and B. Weiss, *Quellen d. Lukas Evglms*, 100 f.

† The second and the third sections both open with a rejection of Jesus (4^{16-30} 9^{51-56}).

‡ In the passion-narrative the resemblances with Ac 22–24 are very marked: both Jesus and Paul, according to Luke, were struck on the mouth before the Sanhedrim; both were given up by the Jews to the Roman authorities; both were accused of treason by the Sadducean priesthood, and both were three times pronounced innocent.

§ This is one case in which Mt. keeps much closer to Q than Luke (cp. Salmon's *Human Element in Gospels*, 49 f.); the latter, by changing the Pharisees and Sadducees into a vague *crowd* (cp. 7^{30}), fails to explain the point and sharpness of John's rebuke.

he then follows Mk. down to 4^{15} (= Mk 1^{15}), but proceeds to insert a programmatic and proleptic account of the rejection of Jesus at Nazara (4^{16-30}).* Returning, in 4^{31-44}, to the Marcan scheme (1^{21-39}), he stops at this point to insert a special version of Peter's call (5^{1-11}), in place of the tradition (Mk 1^{16-20}) which he had just omitted. The Marcan thread is followed again till 6^{11} (= Mk 3^{6}), where he reverses the position of the call of the twelve (6^{12-16} = Mk 3^{13-19}, 6^{17-19} = Mk 3^{7-12}). After this, Luke goes his own way for a while. Mk 4^{1-25} is reproduced in 8^{4-18}; 8^{19-21} picks up Mk 3^{31-35} (another instance of reversed order), and 8^{22-56} follows Mk 4^{35}–5^{43}; the parabolic teaching of $4^{26-29. 33-34}$ is entirely omitted, and 4^{30-32} is not used till 13^{18-19}. In 9^{1-9} Luke returns to Mk. (6^{6b-16}), and the thread is on the whole followed in 9^{10-17} (= Mk 6^{30-44}). Then, omitting Mk 6^{45}–8^{26}, with the exception of 8^{11-13} and 8^{14-21}, which are caught up in reverse order later (12^{54-56} 11^{53}–12^{1}); he follows Mk. (8^{27}–9^{8}) in 9^{18-36} (omitting Mk 9^{9-13}), and on the whole in 9^{37-50} (= Mk 9^{14-41}). Mk 9^{42-48} reappears afterwards in 17^{1-2}, the salt-saying of 9^{49-50} (like 10^{1-12}) never appears at all, and it is not till 18^{15-34} that the Marcan scheme (10^{13-34}) is resumed (18^{35-43} = Mk 10^{46-52}).† The narrative of the last days in Jerusalem then follows Mk. pretty closely, though it omits ‡ Mk $11^{12-14. 20-26}$ (fig-tree incident), $13^{21-23. 33-37}$ and 15^{16-20}, reverses the order of Mk 14^{18-21} (= 22^{21-23}) and 14^{22-25} (= 22^{15-20}), and makes a number of significant additions.

Luke's detailed chronology varies between vague notices of time and definite synchronisms which are generally more graphic than historical. Thus the birth of John the Baptist and of Jesus alike fell 'in the days of Herod' (1^{5}, cp. 2^{1} ἐν ταῖς ἡμέραις ἐκείναις); § he is now and then precise upon days (1^{59} $2^{21. 44. 46}$ etc.), months ‖ ($1^{24. 26. 56}$), years (2^{42}, cp. 3^{23}), ¶ or even hours (2^{28}, cp. 10^{21} 22^{59}), and he attempts at one place an elaborate sixfold synchronism (in 3^{1-2}, with which the sixfold date of the Thebans' entry into Platæa, in Thuc. ii. 2, has been compared). He knows that the

* Which Mk. reserves till 6^{1-6a}. Hence the anachronism of Lk 4^{23}.

† On the neglect of the Marcan source in 9^{51}–18^{14}, cp. Sir J. C. Hawkins in *ET.* xiv. 18 f., 90 f., 137 f.

‡ The anointing in Bethany (Mk 14^{8-9}) had been already used in 7^{36-50}.

§ Cp. 1^{39} 6^{12} (ἐν τ. ἡμ. ταύταις).

‖ Apart from the ritual (Gal 4^{10}), the OT (Ja 5^{17}), and the apocalyptic references (in Apoc. Joh.), μήν, in its literal sense, is used only by Lk. of all the NT writers.

¶ This ὡσεί is not uncommon in Luke's chronological notices (cp. 8^{42} $9^{14. 28}$ 22^{59} 23^{44}, Ac 2^{41} and elsewhere).

call of twelve disciples took place* *in the morning* (6^{12-13}) after a night of prayer. On the other hand, his connections are often vague; *e.g.* ἐν τῷ ἑξῆς (7^{11}), ἐν τῷ καθεξῆς (8^{1}), ἐν τῇ ἑξῆς ἡμέρᾳ (9^{37}). As a rule, he follows Mark, *e.g.* in 4^{1} 4^{31-44} $5^{27f.}$ 6^{1} (adding the enigmatic δευτεροπρώτῳ) and 6^{6} (=Mk 3^{1}), though now and then he loosely uses ἐν μιᾷ τῶν ἡμερῶν (5^{17} 8^{22}—where, like Mt 8^{23}, he departs from Mark 4^{35}—20^{1}), or phrases like ἐν αὐτῷ τῷ καιρῷ (13^{1}) and ἐν αὐτῇ τῇ ὥρᾳ (13^{31} 20^{19}).

All through, whenever he leaves Mk., and even sometimes when he follows him, we have therefore to distinguish between a sequence which is apt enough in an edifying homily or in a catechetical manual, but unlikely to be historical.† Thus Lk. arranges the temptation in 4^{1-13} so as to avoid the abrupt change from the desert to the temple, and at the same time in order to produce a climax; he also inserts 7^{11-17} in order to prepare the way for 7^{22} (νεκροὶ ἐγείρονται). His work is full of these deliberate transitions and re-arrangements which were already a feature of the primitive synoptic tradition even in Mk.

§ 3. *Sources and structure.*—Besides Mk. and Q, the sources used by Luke (1^{1-4}) in composing his gospel, so far as they were written, may have provided him with material for 1^{5}–2^{52}, 9^{51}–18^{14}, and some passages elsewhere, especially in the passion-narrative; but he has worked over them so thoroughly that it is rarely possible to distinguish their number or even their nature.

(*a*) 1^{5}–2^{52}, cp. Hillmann (*JPT.*, 1891, 192–261), Badham (*ET.* viii. 116–119, defence of integrity), Zimmermann (*SK.*, 1901, 415–458, *ibid.* 1903, 247–290), Hilgenfeld (*ZWT.*, 1900, 177–235, 1901, 313–318), Schmiedel (*EBi.* 2954 f.), Usener (*EBi.* 3441 f.), Spitta (*ZNW.*, 1906, 281–317, 'Die Chronologischen Notizen und die Hymnen in Lc 1 und 2'), R. J. Knowling (*DCG.* i. 202 f.), Clemen (*Religionsgeschichtliche Erklärung des NT*, 1909, pp. 223 f.), and D. Völter (*TT.*, 1910, 289–334, 'Die Geburt des Taüfers Johannes und Jesu nach Lukas').

The stylistic data of 1^{5}–2^{52} permit of three hypotheses: (i.) the use of a Palestinian Jewish-Christian Greek or Aramaic

* Other morning incidents, peculiar to Luke, are 5^{1-11} (cp. 5^{5}) 21^{37} 22^{66} and 23^{54}.

† J. F. Blair in *The Apostolic Gospel* (pp. 7 f.) rightly notes Luke's arrangement of sayings and stories as an illustration of this; *e.g.* Lk 7^{36-50} is an example of 7^{34}, Lk $10^{25f.}$ (the captious νομοδιδάσκαλος) and $10^{38f.}$ (Mary the receptive) of 10^{21}. For other cases of editorial motive, see Westcott's *Introd. to Study of Gospels*, pp. 393 f.

(Bruce, Zimmermann, Plummer, Wright) source, which Luke has revised and incorporated; * (ii.) the free composition of the section, in archaic style, by Luke himself; or (iii.) its later insertion. The marked change of style and diction, as the gospel passes from 1^{4} to 1^{5} and, though less markedly, from 2^{52} to 3^{1}, and the Hebraistic phenomena of 1^{5}–2^{52}, together with the Lucan characteristics which emerge in $2^{15\text{-}20.\ 41\text{-}52}$ (Harnack, *SBBA.*, 1900, pp. 538–566) and elsewhere (Zimmermann, pp. 250 f.), are best met by the first of the three hypotheses, in its translation-form.

It requires too arbitrary handling of the text to disentangle from 1^{5}–2^{52} and $3^{23f.}$, under a double Christian redaction (*e.g.* in $1^{26\text{-}56}$ and $1^{78f.}$), a Jewish apocalypse of Zechariah (Völter, *TT.*, 1896, 244–269; N. Schmidt, *EBi.* i. 936), which is mentioned in the stichometry of Nikephorus and elsewhere, or to detect a Jewish-Christian interpolation (so Usener, *Das Weihnachtsfest*, 1889, 122 f.; Gercke, *Neue Jahrb. für d. klass. Alterth.*, 1901, 187) in $3^{23\text{-}28}$ as well as in Mt $1^{1\text{-}17}$ (for Lk 1–2, cp. Corssen in *GGA.*, 1899, 326 f.).

The main drawback to (ii.), *i.e.* to the theory that the author himself produced the archaic Semitic style by means of a conscious art (so, *e.g.*, Pfleiderer and Harnack, *BNT.* i. 199 f.), apart from the fact that the so-called Lucan characteristics are almost wholly derived from the LXX, is the difficulty of imagining how a Gentile Christian like Luke could throw himself back, by a supreme effort of the historical imagination, to the standpoint of these chapters (cp. Sanday, *ET.* xiv. 296 f.; Zahn, *INT.* iii. 112 f., and Stanton in *GHD.* ii. 223 f.). When the section is viewed as Luke's translation-Greek, and as embodying some primitive document, not as a piece of free composition, 1^{5}–2^{52} with $3^{23\text{-}28}$ represent an early Palestinian source which Luke has worked over, perhaps inserting, *e.g.*, the references to the decree (2^{1}) † and the virgin-birth ($1^{34\text{-}35}$), with the ὡς ἐνομίζετο of 3^{23}. He probably translated the source himself from Aramaic. In spite of Dalman's scepticism (*Worte Jesu*, Eng. tr. pp. 38 f.) there is no reason why Luke should not have known Aramaic; and here as elsewhere there are fairly evident traces of a Semitic original (Briggs, *Messiah of Gospels*, 41 f.; Wellhausen, *Einl.* 35 f.; Nestle, *ZNW.* vii. 260 f.; Spitta, *ZNW.* vi. 293 f.; Wright, Zimmermann, Jülicher, etc.).

* So J. G. Machen, *Princeton Review* (1906), 48–49.

† The chronological notices cannot claim to be more than vague, popular synchronisms (cp. Spitta, *op. cit.* p. 300).

It is no objection to argue (Hilgenfeld, etc.) that references to the Davidic throne and reign (1^{32-33}), the righteousness of works (1^{6} 2^{25} etc.), and the obligations of the law (2^{22-23}), could not have come from the pen of Luke the Paulinist, but must have been added by a redactor who was responsible for the songs, etc. To be a friend or companion of Paul was not equivalent to sharing all his particular theological opinions (see below under Acts); Luke's historic sense was sufficient to prevent him from suppressing such features in the interests of doctrine; and, even upon Hilgenfeld's peculiar thesis, the redactor was himself a Paulinist!

One object of the source was to represent John the Baptist as emphatically the forerunner and inferior of Jesus—the same motive which re-appears in Ac 18–19 as well as in the Fourth gospel. This tradition, with its juxtaposition of the two births, met the tendency in some circles to aggrandise the prestige of John (cp. J. R. Wilkinson, *A Johannine Document in the First Chapter of S. Luke's Gospel*, 1902). This leads to the first of the three problems of textual and literary criticism in the section. (*a*) Was the virgin-birth originally part of the source, or even of Luke's version? The hypothesis * that 1^{34-35} represents an interpolation in the text (so, *e.g.*, Hillmann, Völter, Holtzmann, Conybeare, Usener, Harnack: *ZNW.*, 1901, 53–57, Schmiedel, Pfleiderer, Grill, N. Schmidt, J. Weiss, Loisy, Montefiore) rests entirely † on internal evidence. When these verses are omitted, it is claimed, the context (*i.e.* to v.^{33}, and from v.^{36}) runs smoothly. Jesus is announced as destined to be born to Joseph, a descendant of David (so *ἐξ οἴκου Δαυείδ* must be taken in 1^{27} in the light of $1^{27. 32}$ and 2^{4}) and Mary. The application of *γονεῖς* to Joseph and Mary, and of *πατήρ* to Joseph, does not give the slightest hint of any merely adoptive relationship between Joseph and Jesus, and such a connection is not suggested by the episode of the Baptist's birth. Mary is a virgin when the angel announces the birth of a son and (a messianic scion) to her (1^{27}); *i.e.* as a betrothed maiden, presently to be married (in less than a year), she is promised this gift of God in her married life. The marriage is taken for granted, as in Is 7^{14}. After this, the sequence of 1^{34} (*How shall this be, since I know not a man?*) is held to be abrupt. Hitherto the angelic promise referred simply to her future as a married woman, and the difficulty of this question, unmotived by what precedes, is not to be explained by her maidenly consciousness or confusion at the announcement. Furthermore, the words are as real an expression of incredulity as those of Zachariah (1^{18}); yet the latter is punished for unbelief, while Mary is praised for her faith (1^{45}). This eulogium is hard to understand ‡

* Häcker's (*ZWT.*, 1906, 18–60) inclusion (so Spitta and Montefiore) of $^{36-37}$ in the interpolation has this in its favour, that it gets rid of the supposed miraculous inference in ^{37}. B. Weiss confines the interpolation to $^{34-35a}$.

† The substitution of ^{38} for ^{34}, and the omission of ^{38} after ^{37}, in *b* is too slender a basis, and may have been accidental, whilst the alleged omission of $^{34-35}$ from the *Protevangelium Jacobi* breaks down upon examination (cp. Headlam's discussion with Conybeare in the *Guardian* for March–April 1903).

‡ On the other hand, it is precarious to argue that Mary's subsequent surprise ($2^{19. 33. 50}$) would be inconsistent with the revelation given her in 1^{34-35}, and that therefore either the latter passage, or the whole of ch. 2, is an interpolation.

in view of 1^{34}, for the question there is surely more than an involuntary cry of surprise, unless we are to resort to conjecture (so W. C. Allen, *Interpreter*, 1905, pp. 121 f.) and assume an unrecorded indication of something unique in the conception. An alternative modification of the interpolation-hypothesis would be simply to omit ἐπεὶ ἄνδρα οὐ γινώσκω from 1^{34} (so Kattenbusch, *Apost. Symbol*, ii. 623; Merx; Weinel, *ZNW.*, 1901, 37 f.; L. Köhler, *ZSchw*, 1902, 220 f.) on the ground that the conception by the Holy Spirit does not necessarily exclude human paternity (Joseph's agency being taken as a matter of course, like that of Zachariah), and also because Mary's cry of surprise then relates to the career of her son, and not to the method of his conception. But it is the latter which is the point of $1^{35f.}$, whereas in the source (*i.e.* up to πῶς ἔσται τοῦτο) the surprise and hesitation are motived by the fact that Mary and Joseph were of humble origin.

The argument therefore is that 1^{34-35} can be removed, not only without impairing, but actually with the result of improving, the context.* If the allusion to virginity (1^{27}) and the absence of any subsequent mention of marriage are taken as implying 1^{34-35}, it is open to the critic either to regard παρθένος as interpolated by the author of 1^{34-35} (so Harnack), or to suppose that the redactor omitted the mention of the marriage and subsequent conception (Usener). The double mention of π., however, and its vital connection with the sentence, render the former hypothesis less probable,† while the latter seems unnecessary in view of 2^{5} (*with Mary his wife*). Here τῇ ἐμνηστευομένῃ αὐτῷ οὔσῃ ἐγκύῳ is correctly interpreted by the early glossarial addition of γυναικί after αὐτῷ (A C² Γ Δ Λ, l, q*, Syr^p, vulg., goth., æth.) ‡ even if one is indisposed to admit γυναικί as the original reading (*e.g.* Häcker, 53–54), on the ground that its alteration into ἐμν. is more likely than the Ebionitic change of ἐμν. into γυναικί. The sole reason for Mary's presence with Joseph was the fact of her marriage to him.

The style of $^{34-35}$ is fairly Lucan, though διό occurs only once in the third gospel and ἐπεί never. If it be an interpolation, it is due either to Luke or to a redactor who wrote ^{35} on the basis of 1^{31-32} and Mt 1^{18-25}, with ^{34} as its prelude. The main difficulty in the way of the Lucan authorship is not so much the silence of Acts on the virgin-birth as the discrepancy between 1^{34-35} and a passage like 3^{22}, where the Lucan reading undoubtedly was υἱός μου εἶ σύ· σήμερον γεγέννηκά σε (so, *e.g.*, Corssen; Usener, *Weihnachtsfest*, 40–50; Harnack, *BNT.* ii. 310–314; cp. Resch, *Agrapha*, 346 f., 365 f., and *Paralleltexte*, iii. 20–24). At all events, the insertion must have been made, for harmonistic purposes, prior to the formation of the gospel-canon. §

---

* Note how the omission, *e.g.*, lessens the gap between the ἰδοὺ συλλήμψῃ of ^{31} and the καὶ ἰδοὺ Ἐ. ἡ συγγ. σ. κ. αὐτὴ συνείληφεν of ^{36}.

† Cp. Bardenhewer, *BZ* (1905), p. 158.

‡ Syr^Sin substitutes γ. for ἐμνηστ. (so *a*, *b*, *c*, *ff*² = *uxore sua*).

§ Zimmermann (*SK.*, 1903, 273 f.) attributes the interpolation to Luke himself, who, in translating his Aramaic Jewish-Christian source of the nativity (which described only a natural birth), added 1^{34-35} (hence the Spirit as masculine, not—as in Semitic—feminine), altered 1^{27} and 2^{5} in order to make Mary merely the betrothed of Joseph, not his wife, inserted the erroneous chronology of 3^{1-2}, the parenthesis of 2^{35a}, the mistranslation in 2^{22} (αὐτῶν),

Against this,* it is argued that the deletion of vv.$^{34-35}$ does not leave the answer of v.^{38} with the same wealth and depth of meaning; such a resigned acceptance of God's will would be much less likely than a glad rejoinder in the case of any Jewish maiden who, after her betrothal, was told that her eldest child would be the messiah. The tremor, in the other case, is natural. It is scarcely fair to find an absolute discrepancy between Elizabeth's praise of Mary's faith (v.^{45}) and the very natural and momentary hesitation of v.^{34}. It is the almost immediate repression of her doubt and the resigned words of ^{38} which justify her cousin's eulogy (cp. Halévy in *RS.*, 1902, 328 f.). On the other hand, the further argument that the omission of the virgin-birth throws the narrative out of balance, by leaving no contrast between Zachariah and Joseph, is partly met by the relegation of the magnificat to Elizabeth, and by the consideration that the story, unlike that of Matthew, is written from Mary's point of view.

If 1^{35} is retained, the term *υἱὸς θεοῦ* there, as in 3^{37}, suggests the idea of Jesus as the second Adam, whose birth or creation renders him *Son of God.* Justin (*Dial.* 100), who employs the Lucan tradition, expands this analogy by contrasting Eve and Mary, pointing out that by Jesus "God destroys the Serpent, and those angels and men who resemble him, whereas he works deliverance from death for those who repent of their evils and believe on him." But, in view of Paul's conception of the second Adam, the independence of human parentage is not necessary.

An Egyptian ostrakon preserves a hymn to Mary, the second part of which, reproducing the matter of Lk 1^{28b-38} presents some variations from the Lucan text, *e.g.*, the absence of 1^{36-37} and the conception of Mary at the moment of the theophany. The text is too corrupt, however, to be relied on, and in any case it has no claim to be regarded as superior (so Reitzenstein, *Zwei religionsgeschichtlichen Fragen*, 1901, 112–131) to the Lucan account. Even in the latter this idea of Mary's conception as due to a divine utterance† has occasionally been found by some critics; this is not Luke's view, but, apart from this altogether, chronologically and intrinsically the Lucan story takes precedence of the Egyptian fragment.

(β) A second equally complex problem is started by the criticism of the songs. Here, also, a number of the characteristic terms of these songs in Lk 1–2 may be shown to come from the LXX, while, on the other hand,

---

and, in fact, the whole of 2^{22b-28}. Zimmermann consequently identifies Luke with Hilgenfeld's 'Pauline interpolator' whose hand is seen in $1^{55b. 76-79}$. He precariously identifies this Aramaic source with the *βίβλος γενεσέως* of Mt 1^{1}.

* The case against the interpolation is stated by Halévy (*RS.*, 1902, 318–330, who holds, however, that Luke's narrative was written to supplant Matthew's), by Hilgenfeld, and by G. H. Box (*ZNW.*, 1905, 91 f., and *DCG.* ii. 804 f.).

† The idea of 1^{35} is Hellenic rather than Jewish. "Quant au fond même de l'idée, il ne s'accorde pas mieux avec la théologie juive en ce qui fait l'originalité propre de celle-ci, à savoir la notion de la transcendance divine, qui ne permet guère de concevoir Dieu comme le principe générateur, physique et immédiat, d'une vie humaine individuelle. En grec et pour l'esprit hellénique, ces embarras n'existent pas" (Loisy, i. 292).

quite a number of them are specifically Lucan. On linguistic grounds alone it is impossible to determine whether the songs were adopted by Luke from some earlier source (so, *e.g.*, Spitta) or whether he composed them himself in the archaic manner (Harnack), but it is best to regard them as part of the Aramaic source.* They are variously taken to echo the psalter and 1 S 2^{1-10} (Hillmann, 201 f.; P. Haupt, *Zeitschrift der d. Morgenl. Gesellschaft*, 1904, 617-632), or Judith (Hilgenfeld), or the psalter of Solomon (cp. Ryle and James, *The Psalms of Solomon*, pp. xci f.). Any one of these derivations is preferable to the intricate hypotheses of Spitta, who holds that the four hymns were originally independent of their present setting; the gloria (2^{14}) and the couplet in 19^{38} are quotations from the same hymn; the magnificat † (cp. Holtzmann's *Festgabe*, 1902, 63 f.) was an Israelitish war-song of triumph; the psalm of Zachariah was composed of two separate pieces, one ($^{68-75}$) on the appearance of Messiah, one ($^{76f.}$) a prophetic outburst of Zachariah over his child; while Luke took the songs of Mary, Zachariah, and Simeon from an early Christian collection. But this theory fails to account for the gloria, and the structure, *e.g.*, of Zachariah's song is, as Spitta himself (p. 309) admits, unexampled.

It is the magnificat which presents the greatest difficulty. As the original text of 1^{46} was καὶ εἶπεν (cp. Burkitt, *Evang. Da-Meph.* ii. 286), the problem is whether Μαριάμ or Ἐλισάβετ was the correct addition. The latter is read by three old Latin MSS (*a*, *b*, *rhe*), and represents an early tradition vouched for by Niceta of Remesiana (who assumes in his *De Psalmodiæ Bono* that Elizabeth spoke the magnificat), which is apparently pre-Origenic (cp. Lommatzsch, v. 108 f., 'non enim ignoramus quod secundum alios codices et hæc uerba Elisabet uaticinetur') and even prior to Irenæus (cp. iv. 7. 1, 'sed et Elisabet ait, Magnificat anima mea dominum,' *ZNW.*, 1906, 191–192). The internal evidence, it is argued, corroborates this early tradition. It is Elizabeth, not Mary, who is filled with the ecstatic spirit (1^{41}), and Luke was 'fond of inserting εἶπεν δὲ or καὶ εἶπεν between the speeches of his characters without a change of speaker' (Burkitt). Furthermore, the σὺν αὐτῇ of 1^{56} suits Elizabeth as the previous speaker better than Mary, otherwise the reference would be to the mention of her in v.[4]. Then a phrase like ἐπέβλεψεν ἐπὶ τὴν ταπείνωσιν τῆς δούλης αὐτοῦ is more congruous with Elizabeth's release from long barrenness than with Mary's situation. The whole question has been fully discussed, in favour of Elizabeth, by F. Jacobé (Loisy?) in *RHLR.* (1897) 424–432; Harnack (*SBBA.*, 1900, 538–556), Völter, Conrady (*Quelle der kan. Kindheitsgeschichte*, 48–51), H. A. Köstlin (*ZNW.*, 1902, 142–145), Loisy (i. 303 f.), Schmiedel (*EBi.* 2956–2957), F. C. Burkitt (in A. E. Burn's *Niceta of Remesiana*, 1905, pp. cliii–cliv; *JTS.* vii. 220 f.),

---

* Cp. *e.g.* F. Zorell's study of the Hebrew or Aramaic rhythmical structure of the magnificat, in *Zeitschrift für kath. Theologie* (1905), 754–758. For the connection of the Lucan canticles with the prayers of the Jewish synagogue, see Chase, *TS.* i. 3. 147–151. See, further, W. Steinführer: *Das Magnificat Luc. 1 identisch mit Ps. 103* (1908), and J. F. Wood (*JBL.*, 1902, 48–50).

† According to Hilgenfeld, the magnificat was inserted like Lk 1^{68-79} by the second Paulinist, who prefixed the birth-stories to the gospel.

and Montefiore; in favour of Mary, by A. Durand (*RB.*, 1898, 74–77), O. Bardenhewer (*Biblische Studien*, vi. 1–2, 1901), Nilles (*Zeits. f. kirchl. Theol.* 1903, 375 f.), Ladeuze (*Revue d'historie ecclés.*, 1903, 623 f.), F. Jubaru, *Le Magnificat expression réelle de l'âme de Marie* (Rome, 1905); F. P. Parisi, *Il Magnificat*[2] (1905); Wordsworth (in Burn's *Niceta*, pp. clv–clviii), A. E. Burn (*DCG.* ii. 101–103), and C. W. Emmet (*Exp.*[7] viii. 521–529), in addition to Spitta and Wernle (*GGA.*, 1904, 516 f.).

(γ) The genealogy of Jesus in Lk 3^{23-28}, unlike the theocratic and Jewish-Christian list of Mt $1^{1f.}$, ascends from Jesus to Adam, quite in the universalist spirit of Ac 17^{26}, though, like that list, it is a genealogy of Josephus artifically drawn up. The concluding editorial touch (*Son of God*) refers back * to 2^{22}, especially when 1^{34-35} are regarded as subsequent interpolations. Whether Luke translated it or not, a touch like the Kainan of 3^{36} is taken from the LXX of Gn 10^{24}.

(iii.) The third hypothesis (Hilgenfeld, Usener), that 1^{5}–2^{52} are a subsequent addition to the gospel, is based on the argument that the ἄνωθεν of the prologue excludes the birth-stories. The primitive apostolic tradition upon Jesus certainly started with an account of his baptism by John (Ac 1^{21-22}); and, if the prologue were interpreted in this light, it would usher in, not 1^{5}–2^{52} but $3^{1f.}$, at which point the *eye-witnesses* of 1^{2} could first vouch for the facts. On the other hand, τῶν πεπληροφορουμένων ἐν ἡμῖν πραγμάτων need not be restricted to facts; *matters of conviction among us* would be as fair a rendering. No great stress can be put on the introduction of John as the son of Zachariah in 3^{2} as if for the first time (see 5^{10}); this may be naturally explained as a sententious impressive allusion.† Nothing hangs on the addition to the two twelfth-century MSS of the Armenian version of Efraim's commentary on the Diatessaron (*Lucas autem initium fecit a baptismo Joannis*, cp. Conybeare in *ZNW.*, 1902, 192–197); for, apart from the lateness and obscurity of the fragment in question, Efraim must have read Lk 1–2 in his copy of the Diatessaron. The elaborate chronological data of 3^{1-2} indeed seem more in keeping with the beginning (1^{3}) of a story than as the introduction even to an important epoch, and the presumption in favour of the baptism as the starting-point of the gospel is corroborated by

* This explains why Luke has placed the genealogy so late; he reserved this part of his source till he could prepare for it by the baptism at which Jesus, according to the primitive view, became *Son of God.* But ἀρχόμενος does not refer to the beginning of this divine sonship (Spitta).

† Similarly the repetition of Joseph, Mary, and Nazareth in $2^{4f.}$ simply resumes 1^{26-27}; it does not imply that two sources lie side by side.

Ac 1^{1}, which defines it as an account of *all that Jesus began both to do and to teach.* It suggests, especially in view of 1^{22}, that the original tradition opened (as in Mk.) with the baptism, but it does not necessarily exclude such introductory matter as the poetical birth-narratives of 1–2; the latter were cognate tc the subject and scope of $3^{1f.}$, they were preliminary notices leading up to (cp. 1^{80} with 3^{2}) the historical traditions.*

(*b*) 9^{51}–18^{34} is not a travel-narrative; although it contains some incidents of travel ($9^{51-56.\ 57-62}$ $10^{38f.}$ $13^{22f.}$ $14^{25f.}$ $17^{11f.}$), these do not dominate the general situation. It is not a Perean source; there is a certain thread in the stories of the Samaritan village (9^{51-56}), the good Samaritan (10^{30-37}), and the Samaritan leper (17^{11-19}), but no geographical connection is visible. Although it may be inferred from Mk 10^{1} and Mt 19^{1} that Luke meant to locate some of this material in Perea, the setting and the juxtaposition of the contents are topical and literary, not chronological. He begins with a mirror for Christian missionaries (9^{51}–10^{42} centring round the mission of the 70): how they are to behave towards incivil people ($9^{51f.}$), how they must be whole-hearted ($9^{57f.}$), how they are to carry out their mission ($10^{1f.}$), and how they are to be received ($10^{38f.}$).† Then follows a little group of sayings on prayer (11^{1-13}). The next groups, with any unity, occur in 12^{1-53} (duties of fearlessness, disinterestedness and unworldliness, and watchfulness in the Christian mission) and in 12^{54}–13^{35} (addressed to ὄχλοι, on repentance). Another ($11^{37f.}$) group of dinner-sayings follows (14^{1-24});‡ $14^{25f.}$ recalls $9^{57f.}$; 15 (cp. Hilgenfeld, *ZWT.*, 1902, 449–464) defends the graciousness of the gospel against Jewish cavilling (cp. $15^{2.\ 28}$); 16^{1}–17^{10} are a loose§ collection of sayings upon various social

* If λόγος in 1^{2} were not = the Christian preaching, and if ὡσεί in 3^{23} were not = *about*, instead of *as if*, there might be some reason for adopting Corssen's theory (*GGA.*, 1899, pp. 310 f.) that the personal logos appeared at first on earth in the baptism (3^{22}), and that αὐτόπται and ὑπηρέται should be taken together, with τοῦ λόγου in the Johannine sense adumbrated in Ac 10^{36} $13^{26f.\ (37)}$.

† 10^{25-37} has no connection with what precedes and very little with what follows. On the whole arrangement of this section, see Wernle, *Syn. Frage*, 99 f.; Pfleiderer, *Urc.* ii. 138 f.

‡ The transference of 14^{16-24} to a place between 13^{24} and 13^{25} (cp. Blair's *Apostolic Gospel*, pp. 212 f.) has several points in its favour. The table-talk, which is a feature of Luke, reflects the Greek symposium-dialogues.

§ E. Rodenbusch (*ZNW.*, 1903, 243 f., 'Die Komposition von Lucas 16') deletes 16^{17} as a gloss; Soltau (*ZNW.*, 1909, 230–238) restores the original relationships; 17^{20}–18^{8} is on the general theme of the parousia;* and $18^{9\text{-}14}$ would follow ^{15} better than 18^{8}. Thus the section is neither (so Schaarschmidt, *SK.*, 1909, 12–28) a fragment of some independent gospel, which covers (though with more definiteness in its setting) the same ground as Mt 12^{15}–24^{51} = Mk 3^{7}–13^{37}, nor an independent source (P. Ewald, Renan, Burton), nor (Wendt) a block of material from Q which Luke has inserted here (as in 6^{20}–8^{3}), but (cp. Wright, *NT Problems*, 23–29) a collection of sayings and stories, partly drawn from special traditions of the Judean ministry of Jesus, partly from Q, and partly even from Mark. Luke, who elsewhere shows a knowledge of the Judean traditions, was too dependent on the Marcan outline to be able to find any chronological place for them; since he had no independent knowledge, *e.g.*, of the Judean ministry, beyond what came from his Palestinian (Jerusalemite or Bethlehemite) sources here as in 1–2, he inserted them and the rest of his material in the only available gap offered by the Marcan outline.

(*c*) In the passion-narrative, especially at and after the last supper, Luke sits more loose than ever to Mark;† but even when a source may be postulated, it does not follow that it was Q. Luke makes much less of the cleansing of the temple ($19^{45\text{-}46}$) than Mark or even Matthew; it does not excite the authorities to immediate action, and their interference ($20^{1f.}$) is not only separated from it by a vague interval, but motived by his teaching rather than his actions. This is another of the approximations to the standpoint of the Fourth gospel,‡ where the cleansing is removed entirely from the last days at Jerusalem. The same softening of the revolutionary traits in Jesus re-appears in the remarkable addition of 22^{51} to the synoptic account of Peter's attack on the servant of the high priest. No source need

order thus: $15^{1\text{-}32}$ $17^{(1\text{-}2).\ 3\text{-}4.\ (5\text{-}6).\ 7\text{-}10.\ 11\text{-}19.\ 20\text{-}37}$ $16^{1\text{-}8}$ $18^{1\text{-}8}$ $16^{19\text{-}31.\ 9\text{-}15}$ $18^{9\text{-}14}$ with $16^{16\text{-}18}$ and $17^{1\text{-}2.\ 5\text{-}6}$ as insertions from Matthew. But even $16^{19f.}$ is composite; $16^{(26).\ 27f.}$ does not flow from the preceding story (cp. Cölle in *SK.*, 1902, 652 f.)

* Conceived here, as in $11^{49f.}$ and 19^{27}, 'als Tag der Rache an den christusfeindlichen Juden' (Wellhausen).

† Cp. Burkitt's *Transmission*, 134 f., and *DCG.* ii. pp. 750 f.

‡ See also the Satanic suggestion of Judas (22^{3} = Jn $13^{2f.}$). These and other 'Johannine' phenomena of Luke are either due to the use of the latter in the Fourth gospel (see below), or the result of a common use by both authors of an independent source (so Zimmermann, *SK.*, 1903, 586–605).

be postulated for these Lucan touches any more than for the additions in $22^{28f.}$ (talk at supper), 23^{27-31} (on way to Calvary), 23^{39-43} (dying robber), $24^{13f.}$ (Emmaus story, etc.);* for these Luke only required some oral tradition to start him; the Herod-scene (23^{6-12}),† like $13^{31f.}$, probably came from a source or sources connected with Joanna and Chuza (cp. 1^{5} $3^{1.19}$ 8^{3} 9^{7-9}, Ac 13^{1}), but it is hazardous to connect this with the tradition of the virgin-birth.

Accretions are specially numerous in the closing chapters. The most notable are the 'Pauline' interpolations of 22^{19b-20} into the original text ‡ as preserved in D (cp. *HNT.* 653 f.; Burkitt, *Evang. Da-Meph.* ii. 300 f.), and the legendary insertion § of 22^{43-44} (which in some MSS of the Ferrar-group is placed, by conformation, after Mt 26^{39}); 23^{34a} (cp. Harnack, *SBBA.*, 1901, 255 f.; *HNT.* 654; Resch, *TU.* x. 3. 721 f.) is, like Jn 7^{53}–8^{11}, probably a non-Lucan fragment of genuine tradition which has floated in to this section of the gospel, although there are almost as strong arguments for its omission from the original, apart from the difficulty of seeing why neither Mt. nor Mk. received the honour of its addition. 24^{12}, besides being textually suspect, contains two words peculiar to Lk. and Jn. (20^{5}) among the gospel-writers (ὀθόνιον and παρακύπτω); breaks awkwardly into the flow of the story; and, like Jn 20^{6-8}, implies that Peter did not believe although he saw the empty tomb. Furthermore, the emphasis on Peter alone (cp. 24^{11} 24^{12}) contradicts 24^{24}. The insertion of the passage (condensed from Jn 20^{3-10}) is probably to be attributed to some harmonistic editor, or to the Asiatic presbyters, as a reply to the natural objection—why did not some of the apostles go to the

---

* The Emmaus-tale, which does not fit in well with 24^{1-11} and $24^{36f.}$, might be taken from a special source; as it stands, 24^{34} (which Merx deletes) does not tally with the agitation of 24^{37}. The materialising of the resurrection-stories in $24^{39f.}$ (cp. Denney, *Jesus and the Gospel*, 143 f.) is quite Lucan, however (cp. the realism of 3^{22}), though the realism is no mark of veracity (Hoffmann, *ZWT.*, 1909, 332 f.).

† Cp. Verrall (*JTS.*, 1909, 321–353) and Abbott (*Diat.* 3183).

‡ Blass (*SK.*, 1896, 773 f.) and Wellhausen further omit 22^{19a}, which Zahn (*INT.* iii. pp. 39 f.) transfers to a place after v.^{16} and before v.^{17}. The case for the larger reading is best put by Jülicher (*ThA.* 235 f.) and Salmon (*Human Element in Gospels*, 492 f.). According to H. E. D. Blakiston (*JTS.*, 1903, 548–555), 22^{14-23} is a conflation of two distinct stories (L=$22^{14-18.21}$, S=22^{19-20}), the latter existing in two forms (Paul, Luke: Mk. Mt.). "Paul's account is the oldest in its present form and also the simplest. It appears to be a slightly condensed form of S, as quoted from memory; and S may have been in Paul's time not a document at all but an oral narrative incorporated in an inchoate liturgy." Luke conflates L and S, using Mk. who had already absorbed a part of L. This theory simplifies the problem in one direction, but only complicates it in others; it fails, *e.g.*, to explain why Luke omitted the second mention of the bread.

§ Defended as original by Harnack (*SBBA.*, 1901, 251 f.).

tomb and see for themselves? or to a sense that v.^{24} required some such episode. The reasons for its subsequent insertion are upon the whole stronger than those urged (*e.g.* by Blair, *Apostolic Gospel*, 385 f.; E. A. Abbott, *Diat.* 1798–1804, and Merx) for the likelihood that it would be omitted. Similar harmonistic insertions occur in $24^{36a.\ 40.\ 52}$ (καὶ ἀνεφέρετο εἰς τ. οὐρ.) and ^{53} (προσκυν. αὐτόν). The two latter, at any rate, may have belonged to the original text, however, being omitted by a later scribe or editor who wished to bring the gospels more into line (cp. Gräfe, *SK.*, 1888, 524–534), perhaps by the author of D, who also changed the λέγοντας of 34^{34} into λέγοντες, in order to harmonise it with Mk 16^{14}.

Luke is thus a compiler and redactor of previous sources or traditions, though his functions are larger than those of the editors who finally put together the Hexateuch. Allowance must be made for his freedom of composition, as in Acts, but the primary feature of his work is its power of selection and collocation. "If the evangelist can be appropriately described as a painter, according to ancient tradition, on account of the pictorial art displayed in some of his narratives, he may be compared with equal propriety to a gardener on account of his arrangement of the logia. His two digressions [*i.e.* 6^{12}–8^{3}, 9^{51}–18^{14}] are beds of transplanted flowers, arranged with some degree of skill, and fragrant in their beauty; but as no observer can argue from the appearance of a flower to the soil in which at first it grew, so also the desire of the critic to find for the logia their original context appears to be utterly hopeless" (Blair, *The Apostolic Gospel*, 157). For this reason, the attempts to reconstruct a special source, running all through the gospel, whether Ebionitic (so, *e.g.*, Keim, i. 101 f., and Schmiedel, *EBi.* 1855–1856)* or not, are less successful than the hypothesis that Luke, in addition to Q and Mark, drew upon a number of more or less fragmentary sources, written and oral.

Typical theories of a special source are—

(*a*) Feine's (pp. 13–33): his source, Jewish Christian in character (*c.* A.D. 67), emanates from the church of Jerusalem, and contains the narratives of 1^{5}–2^{52} (birth-stories), 3^{23-38} (genealogy), 4^{14-30} (rejection at Nazareth), 5^{1-11} $7^{1-10.\ 11-17.\ 36-50}$ 8^{1-3} 9^{51-56} 10^{38-42} $13^{10-17.\ 31-33}$ 14^{1-6} 17^{11-19} $19^{1-10.\ 39-44}$ $21^{37f.}$ $22^{14-23.\ 31-34.\ 35-38.\ 39-46.\ 47-53.\ 54-62.\ 63-71}$ 23^{1-56} 24^{1-53}. (*b*) Similarly, both G. H. Müller and B. Weiss find a third large source behind Luke's gospel; the former's S, like the latter's L, begins with the birth-stories (1–2) and concludes with the passion, death, and resurrection. B. Weiss' reconstruction (printed in Greek in his *Quellen der Synopt. Überlieferung*, pp. 97 f.) is as follows:—
L = 1–2 $3^{10-14.\ 23-38}$ 4^{16-30} $5^{1-11.\ 33.\ 36.\ 39}$ $6^{13.\ 15-16.\ 20-38.\ 46-49}$ $7^{1-22a.\ 36-50}$ 8^{1-4}

* So recently A. Meyer (*Die Auferstehung Christi*, 1905, pp. 34, 341).

$9^{43-45. 51-56. 61-62}$ $10^{1. 29-42}$ $11^{27-28. 37-54}$ $12^{1a. 33-38. 49-53}$ 13^{1-17} 14^{1-33} $15^{1-3. 11-32}$ $16^{14-15. 19-31}$ 17^{3-19} $18^{9-14. 31-34. 43b\,f.}$ $19^{1-28. 37-44. 47-48}$ $20^{20-26. 34-38}$ $21^{12-19. 20-28. 34-38}$ $22^{1-6. 14-23. 31-34. 39f.}$ 23^{1}–24^{49}. In this case, as in that of the cognate analyses, Luke must have assigned high importance to his source, for which he repeatedly leaves even Mark. But the precision with which L is picked out, and materials assigned to it or to Q, carries very little conviction. 'They see not clearliest who see all things clear.' The linguistic and inward criteria for determining what belongs specially to L are too subjective in the large majority of cases. A similar criticism applies as forcibly to (*c*) J. Weiss' analysis of the gospel into three sources: Q, M (Mark), and S (Luke's special source).

Q 3^{7-9} 16(?). 17 4^{1-13}
M 3^{4} 19-20 (?) 21b-22 4^{14-15} 31-44 $5^{1-2(?). 3f. (?)}$
S 1^{5}–3^{3} 5-6 10-15 18 21a 23-28 4^{16-30} $5^{1-11(?)}$

Q 6^{20-23} 27f. $7^{1f.}$ 18-35 9^{57-60}
M $5^{10-11. 12-38}$ 6^{1-19} 8^{4}–9^{50}
S 5^{39} 6^{24-26} $7^{3. 11-17}$ 36-50 8^{1-3} 9^{51-56} 61-62

Q $10^{2. 13-16}$ 21-24. 25f. (?) 11^{2-3} 9f. 15f. 19f. 29f.
M $11^{16-18 (?)}$ 21 (?)
S $10^{1f.}$ 17-20 28f. (?) 38f. 11^{1-2} 5-8 14 27-28

Q $11^{39f.}$ $12^{1-12 (?)}$ 22-31 33-34 37f. 42f. 51-59
M 11^{38}
S 11^{37-38} 53-54 12^{13-21} 32 35-36 41 47-50 54f. 13^{1-17}

Q 13^{18-21} 23f. 34-35 14^{11} 15-23 26-27 34-35 15^{3-7}
M
S 13^{22-23} 31f. 14^{1-10} 12-14 24-25 28-33 15^{1-2} 8f. 16^{1-12}

Q 16^{13} 16-17 17^{1-6} 23 26-27 31 33f. 18^{14}
M $16^{18 (?)}$ 18^{15-43}
S 16^{14-15} 19-31 17^{7-22} 25 28-30 32 18^{1-13} 19^{1-12}

Q 19^{13} 15-26
M 19^{28-37} 47-48 20^{1-47} $21^{1-4 (?). 5f.}$ 25f. 22^{1-13}
S 19^{14} 27 38f. $21^{20f. (?)}$ 37-38 $22^{14f.}$

Q $22^{21-23 (?)}$
M 22^{39-71} 23^{1-5} 10 18-26 32-33 35-38 44f. 24^{1-12}
S $22^{24f. (?)}$ 23^{6-9} 11-12 27-31 34-35 39-43 24^{13-53}

(*d*) Wright, recognising more truly the composite and heterogeneous character of Luke's *Sondergut*, assigns it to (*a*) a Pauline collection of parables, etc. (cp. his *Synopsis*, pp. 241 f.), (*b*) anonymous fragments, and (*c*) a private source, including 1^{5}–2^{52} 3^{23-28} $4^{16f.}$ $7^{11f.}$. The travel-section ($9^{51f.}$) he regards as an editorial collection of undated material, partly derived from Q and partly from (*a*). This answers better to the facts of the case than with Burton to deny any use of Q or the Matthæan logia, finding the Lucan sources in (*a*) 1^{5}–2^{52}, (*b*) a so-called Perean * document (9^{51}–18^{14} 19^{1-28}), (*c*) a Galilean

* Briggs (*New Light on Gospels*, 64 f.) bases a Perean ministry of Jesus on reliable oral sources possessed by Luke.

document ($3^{7-15.\ 17.\ 18}$ $4^{2b-13.\ (14-15).\ 16-30}$ 5^{1-11} 6^{20-49} 7^{1}–8^{3}), (*d*) Mark, and (*e*) some minor sources or traditions. There are several places in Luke which resemble a passage like Herod. v. 1–27, where two or three various traditions are blended into one narrative, which have come to the writer, "perhaps at different times, and from different sources, and he has combined them, as usual, with such skill as almost to defy detection" (R. W. Macan, *Herodotus*, ii. 57 f.).

§ 4. *Style.*—Special literature: Krenkel (*Josephus und Lukas*, pp. 44 f.), W. H. Simcox (*Writers of NT*, 1890, 16–24), Norden (*Antike Kunstprosa*, ii. 485–492),* Vogel (*Zur Charakteristik des Lukas nach Sprache und Stil*², 1899), J. H. Ropes (*Harvard Studies in Classical Philology*, 1901, xii. 299 f.), Jacquier (*INT.* ii. 450 f.).

The literary finish of the third gospel is evident at the outset in the careful rhythm of the prologue—

> *ἐπειδήπερ πολλοὶ ἐπεχείρησαν ἀνατάξασθαι διήγησιν*
> *περὶ τῶν πεπληροφορημένων ἐν ἡμῖν πραγμάτων,*
> *καθὼς παρέδοσαν ἡμῖν οἱ ἀπ' ἀρχῆς αὐτόπται καὶ ὑπηρέται γενόμενοι τοῦ λόγου,*
> *ἔδοξεν κἀμοὶ παρηκολουθηκότι ἄνωθεν πᾶσιν ἀκριβῶς*
> *καθεξῆς σοι γράψαι, κράτιστε Θεόφιλε,*
> *ἵνα ἐπιγνῷς περὶ ὧν κατηχήθης λόγων τὴν ἀσφάλειαν.*

The succeeding words, *ἐγένετο ἐν ταῖς ἡμέραις Ἡρῴδου κτλ.*, show,† like the passage which they introduce, the writer's versatility, whether he is composing in archaic semi-Biblical style or leaving the rough translation of an Aramaic source practically unchanged for the sake of effect. Luke's Hellenistic style and the popular Hebraistic phraseology which characterises many dialogues of the gospel resemble Arrian's preservation of the colloquialisms in the sayings of Epictetus side by side with his own more polished style (cp. Heinrici, *Litterarische Charakter d. neutest. Schriften*, 46 f.).‡

Luke, true to the Atticist-tradition, prefers *ἀπὸ τοῦ νῦν* ($22^{18.\ 69}$) to *ἀπ' ἄρτι* (Mt $26^{29.\ 64}$) and *βελόνη* (18^{25}) to *ῥαφίς* (Mk 10^{25}, Mt 19^{24}), avoids verbs like *ἐκέρδησα* ($19^{16.\ 18}$ cp. Mt $25^{20.\ 22}$), *ἀγγαρεύειν* (23^{26} cp. Mt 27^{32}), and

* The differences of treatment in Luke's two volumes, and the greater freedom used in the first as compared with the less uniform handling of the sources in the second, do not justify Norden's (p. 482) plea for confining a survey of Luke's style to the third gospel.

† On the Lucan uses of *ἐγένετο*, cp. J. H. Moulton, *Grammar of NT Greek*, i. 16 f.

‡ Four senarii are noted in the gospel, 5^{21} (*τίς ἐστιν οὗτος ὃς λαλεῖ βλασφημίας*), 5^{31} (*ἀλλ' . . . ἐλήλυθα*), 5^{32} (*καλέσαι . . ἁμαρτωλούς*), 5^{39} (*οὐδεὶς πίων παλαιὸν εὐθέως θέλει νέον*).

διεσκόρπισας ($19^{21.\ 22}$ cp. Mt $25^{24.\ 26}$), phrases like ὀψία used substantively (*e.g.* 9^{12}=Mk 6^{35}, Mt 14^{15}, 23^{50}=Mk 15^{42}, Mt 27^{57}), μύλος ὀνικος (17^{2} cp. Mk 9^{42}, Mt 18^{6}) and κοράσιον ($8^{51.\ 54}$ cp. Mk 5^{41-42}, Mt 9^{24-25}), and adopts phrases like the distributive ἀνά (9^{14} cp. Mk 9^{39}) and the alliterative * λιμοὶ καὶ λοιμοί (21^{11}). As Jerome pointed out to Damasus (*ep.* 19), he omitted (19^{38}) the ὡσαννά of Mk 11^{9}, Mt 21^{2}, and Jn 12^{14}, owing to his Greek sense of style (*inter omnes euangelistas græci sermonis eruditissimus*), the term being one of the foreign phrases (βάρβαρος γλῶσσα) which it behoved a good writer to omit (cp. Norden, i. 60–61, ii. 482). There is real significance in the omission of terms like κοδράντης (12^{59} cp. Mt 5^{26}, 21^{2} cp. Mk 12^{42}), ὡσαννά (see above), ῥαββεί (22^{47} cp. Mk 14^{45}, Mt 26^{49}), Γολγοθᾶ (23^{33} cp. Mk 15^{22}, Mt 27^{33}),† and σύνδουλος (12^{45} cp. Mt 24^{49}), the substitution ‡ of φόρος (20^{22}) for κῆνσος (Mk 12^{14}, Mt 22^{17}), of θεραπεία (12^{42}) for οἰκετεία (Mt 24^{45}), of εὖγε (19^{17}) for εὖ (Mt 25^{21}), and of ἐπιβαλεῖν τὰς χεῖρας (20^{19} 22^{53}) for κρατεῖν, the insertion of good stylistic phrases like ὑπάρχων (23^{50} cp. Mk 15^{43}), καθήμενοι (10^{13} cp. Mt 11^{21}), and participial clauses in general (*e.g.* 19^{35} with Mk 11^{7}, $22^{13\ \text{and}\ 58}$ with Mk 14^{16}, Mt 26^{55}). On the other hand, the Hellenistic features are not always in due proportion. "He sometimes gets out of his depth when the effort is long continued, and in trying to be elegant ceases to be correct" (Simcox, p. 22).§

The unity of style is varied, however, by a characteristic freedom of expression and range of vocabulary which prevents any stereotyped uniformity. Luke does not hesitate to vary his language in describing the same incident twice (cp. *e.g.* the two accounts in 10 and 11), and he shows sound literary feeling in variations like ἐπὶ πρόσωπον πάσης τῆς γῆς (Lk 21^{35}) and ἐπὶ παντὸς προσώπου τῆς γῆς (Ac 17^{26}), τοῦ ἐπικαλ. Μάρκου (Ac 12^{12}), τὸν ἐπικληθέντα Μ. (12^{25}), and τὸν καλ. Μ. (15^{37}). It is obvious that in the analysis of the text into source and editorial revision, due weight must be allowed to this element of freedom in Luke's method of composition, to "his fondness for repetition, and his tendency to vary even facts of some importance when rehearsing a story for the second time" (Ropes, *op. cit.* 304). But this consideration only serves as a caution against the abuse, not as a veto against the exercise, of source-criticism in the gospel or in Acts.||

§ 5. *Characteristics.*—(Bruce, *Kingdom of God*, pp. 1–37;

* For the good Greek of this alliteration, see Lobeck's *Paralip. gramm. græc.* i. 53 f.

† Cp. the omission of ἐλωὶ ἐλωὶ λαμὰ σαβαχθανεί in 23^{46}, and of the double negative (19^{30}) in Mk 11^{2}.

‡ So ἐπί with dative (21^{6} cp. Mk 13^{2}, Mt 24^{2}), and τις (9^{57} 10^{25} etc.) for εἷς.

§ *e.g.* in Ac 17^{2} 23^{23-24} and 24^{10}.

|| It is an open question, *e.g.*, how far the two forms (Ἰερουσαλήμ and Ἱεροσόλυμα represent a difference of sources or literary tact upon Luke's part (cp. V. Bartlet in *ET* xiii. 157–158), and how far Luke used them indifferently.

Plummer, pp. xli f.; Abbott, *EBi.* 1789 f.; Nicolardot, *Les Procédés de Rédaction des trois premiers Evangélistes*, pp. 123 f.).

Luke belongs to the class of historians who are "drawn towards the dramatic and personal elements in history, primarily as they appear in the lives of famous individual men."* The biographical note, so prominent in Acts, is more marked in his gospel than in any of the others; he dramatises situations, likes to put a soliloquy into a parable, throws a number of the logia into table-talk, and tries often to create a suitable *mise en scène* in public for others (*e.g.* $15^{1f.}$).† He is fond of using questions in order to provide good connections or to vivify the situation (*e.g.* 3^{10-15} 6^{39} $22^{48.\ 49.\ 51}$), and this feature emerges in the more historical sections as well as in the graceful stories which come from his own pen. This literary device is accompanied by a considerable amount of idealisation,‡ due to the author's religious prepossessions. The omissions, insertions, and alterations in the gospel are sufficiently well marked to bring out several of his predilections, *e.g.* his sense that Gentile readers would not be specially interested in the criticism of the Jewish law, his irenic tendency (as in Ac 15, etc.) to 'spare the twelve,' his emphasis on the Gentile mission as essentially part of the gospel, his heightening of the authority and also of the tenderness of Jesus, the place he assigns to women (cp. Harnack, *BNT.* i. 153 f.), his love of antitheses between different types of character, the prominence given to prayer, to the holy Spirit,§ and to thanksgiving.‖

* Bryce, *Studies in Contemporary Biography* (1903), p. 149.

† Instances are cited by Nicolardot, *op. cit.* pp. 130 f. ('Luc donne, aux introductions qui lui sont propres, un réalisme précis, mais factice, qui symbolise dans un cadre pseudo-historique la verité plus large d'une situation ou d'un état de choses postérieurs'). The tendency is carried on in the Fourth gospel, where the circumstantial details are generally a proof of tradition in its later stages rather than of any eye-witness's testimony.

‡ Cp. Bruce, *With Open Face* (1896), pp. 52 f., 'The Idealised Picture of Luke.'

§ On the case for *ἐλθέτω τὸ πνεῦμα σου ἐφ' ἡμᾶς* as the original reading in 11^2, see Resch, *TU.* v. 4. 398 f., x. 2. 228 f.; Blass, *Ev. sec. Lucam*, pp. xlii f., and Harnack, *SBBA.*, 1904, 195 f.

‖ He might have taken as the motto for his gospel, says Nicolardot (p. 123), the phrase, *ἠγαλλίασεν τὸ πνεῦμα μου ἐπὶ τῷ θεῷ τῷ σωτῆρί μου* (cp. Harnack, *BNT.* i. 63 f.). But Paul's words, *πάντοτε χαίρετε, ἀδιαλείπτως προσεύχεσθε, ἐν παντὶ εὐχαριστεῖτε*, are an even better summary of Luke's message for his age.

It is a literary rather than a religious characteristic which emerges in what has been termed Luke's "law of parsimony" (Storr, *Über den Zweck der evang. Geschichte und der Briefe Johannis*, 1786, pp. 274 f.) *i.e.*, his method of abbreviating, as far as possible, material which already lay before him in another form, or of omitting what had been narrated by earlier writers, when such omissions did not seriously interfere with his own plan. This tendency *summa uestigia sequi* is more marked in the gospel than in Acts, however. A conspicuous instance is the shortening of the Gethsemane-scene by the omission of Mk $14^{39f.}$, even although this abbreviation lessens (cp. 4^{42}) his favourite emphasis on prayer; but an examination of his comparative avoidance of duplicates and his selections from the logia (cp. Resch's *Paulinismus*, 575 f., and *Ausserkan. Paralleltexte*, iii. 838 f.), affords full proof of the law.*

According to Hilgenfeld (*ZWT.*, 1901, 1–11), Theophilus needed to be confirmed in the basis of the Pauline gospel, and the author of the third gospel wrote with that aim in view. This motive cannot be attributed to Luke. One of the most assured results of recent research † is that he was not a Paulinist masquerading as a historian. He substitutes χάρις, *e.g.*, in 6^{32} (cp. Mt 5^{46}), but neither here nor elsewhere in the Pauline sense of the term. There are numerous echoes of Pauline phraseology like 4^{32} = 1 Co 2^{4}, 6^{36} = 2 Co 1^{3}, 8^{12} = 1 Co 1^{21}, 8^{13} = 1 Th 1^{6}, 10^{8} = 1 Co 10^{27}, 10^{16} = 1 Th 4^{8}, 11^{7} = Gal 6^{17}, 12^{42} = 1 Co 4^{2}, 20^{38} = Ro 14^{8}, and 21^{24} = Ro 11^{25}; but in some of these and other cases Paul has genuine logia in mind, and there is no distinct 'Paulinism' audible in the gospel any more than in its sequel. 'Luke made no attempt to introduce a propaganda of Paulinism into the sacred history' (Jülicher). The graciousness and universalism of the gospel are due to Jesus ultimately, not to the apostle. Luke reflects, partly through his sources, several tendencies of the apostolic age, but these do not include Paulinism in the technical sense of the term.

§ 6. *In Tradition.*—The patristic tradition that Marcion abbreviated and altered our canonical third gospel, may be accepted as correct. A critical investigation of the data shows that Luke's gospel, as we have it, must have represented substantially

* Ruegg (*SK.*, 1896, 94–101, 'Die Lukasschriften und der Raumzwang des antiken Buchwesens') uses the restricted size of papyrus-rolls to account for Luke's narrative, *e.g.*, in 24.

† "L'auteur . . . ne s'intéresse pas à la théologie particulière de saint Paul, et l'on disait presque qu'il l'ignore . . . en certain passages très caractéristiques, il néglige les additions pauliniennes de Marc pour s'en tenir aux données primitives" (Loisy, i. p. 173); so Wellhausen (on 7^{48-50}), Schmiedel (*EBi.* 1840–1841), and B. Weiss (*Quellen d. synopt. Ueberlieferung*, 251).

the document which was in his hands (cp. Sanday, *Gospels in Second Century*, 204 f., 362 f.; Zahn, *GK.* i. 585 f., ii. 409 f.).* Within less or little more than half a century after the book was written, it was used by Marcion not only as Lucan, but as a collection of evangelic materials which could be re-shaped for his own purposes. The references in Justin Martyr probably imply not only the existence of Matthew and Luke, but of some fusion of them in a gospel harmony upon which, rather than upon these gospels directly, Justin seems to have drawn. The third chief witness to the existence and estimate of the third gospel in the second century is the Muratorian Canon, whose text, though corrupt to the verge of obscurity, echoes the tradition of the Lucan authorship.

Tertium euangelii librum secundum Lucam Lucas iste medicus, post ascensum Christi cum eum Paulus quasi itineris (sui) socium secum adsumpsisset, nomine suo ex opinione (sc. Pauli) conscripsit. The text is badly preserved. *Ut iuris* must be emended either as above (so, *e.g.*, Bunsen, Hort, Schwartz) † or into *litteris* (Buecheler, Lietzmann). The following words ***studiosum secundum*** are probably a corruption of the original (*sui*) ***socium secum*** (so, *e.g.*, Bunsen, Hort); ***secundum***, at any rate, unless it be due to dittography, was originally ***secum*** (Routh, Schmid, Westcott, Lietzmann, etc.). The difficult words ***ex opinione*** represent not ἐξ ἀκοῆς (Rönsch, Westcott, Lietzmann, etc.), but either *ex ordine* (Routh, Leipoldt, etc.) or as above (so, Schwartz = Παύλου γνώμῃ, a counterpart to *nomine suo*, just as ***recognoscentibus cunctis*** lower down is to ***Johannes suo nomine***) rather than ***ex (omnium) opinione*** (Corssen).

ACTS.

Literature.—(*a*) editions (modern) ‡—S. J. Lorinus (1605); Gaspard Sanchez (1616); Grotius (1644); L. Fromond (Louvain, 1654); G. Benson (1756); Pearce (London, 1777); J. M. Lobstein (unfinished, Strassburg, 1792); S. F. N. Morus (*Versio et explicatio A. A.*, ed. G. J. Dindorf, 1794); Thiess, *Lukas' Apgeschichte neue übersetzt mit Anmerkungen* (1800); Kistenmaker (*Gesch. d. Ap. mit Anmerkungen*, 1822); Kuinoel (*Commentarius in libros NT historicos*, iv.[2], 1827); Biscoe (Oxford, 1829); Hastings Robinson (London, 1830); Olshausen (1832); Meyer (1835); W. Trollope (Cambridge, 1847); W. G. Humphrey (1847); de Wette[3] (1848); Bornemann (1848); Beelen (1851, second ed. 1869); C. M. Du Veil (ed. F. A. Cox, London, 1851); H. B. Hackett[2] (1858); Ebrard

* On the Lucan version and Marcion's account of 4^{16-30}, cp. Hilgenfeld (*ZWT.*, 1902, 127–144).

† Cp. Ac 9^{2} 19^{9} 24^{22}.

‡ The main sixteenth-century contributions were made by Calvin, Erasmus (1516, Basle), Vatable (Paris, 1545), and Gagnæus (*Scholia*, Paris 1552).

(1862); J. A. Alexander[3] (1867); F. X. Patrizi (1867); Alford[6] (1868); Meyer[4] (1870, Eng. tr. 1883); P. J. Gloag (1870); Overbeck (—de Wette[4], 1870); Beelen (1870); Bisping[2] (1871); Ewald (1871); Abbé Crampon (Paris, 1872); W. Denton (1874); Reuss (1876); Cook (1880); H. Conrad (Potsdam, 1882); Nösgen (Leipzig, 1882); Crelier (Paris, 1883); T. E. Page (London, 1886); Wordsworth[4] (1887); Felten (Freiburg, 1892); G. T. Stokes (*Expositor's Bible*, 1893); Zöckler[2] (1894); Lumby (*CGT.* 1894); Blass, *Acta Apost. sive Lucæ ad Theophilum liber alter* (editio philologica, 1895); F. Rendall (1897); Couard (1897); A. Wright (London, 1897); Barde (1898); Wendt (—Meyer[8], 1899)*; Schroeder[2] (Lausanne, 1899); Hilgenfeld (Berlin, 1899)*; Knabenbauer (Paris, 1899); Knowling (*EGT.* 1901); H. J. Holtzmann[3] (*HC.* 1901)*; J. F. Hückesheim (Paderborn, 1902); Schlatter (1902); F. C. Ceulemans (*Commentarius*, 1903); J. M. S. Baljon (1903); V. Bartlet (*CB.* n. d.); V. Rose (Paris, 1905); J. E. Belser (1905); B. Weiss[2] (1907); H. P. Forbes (New York, 1907); R. Knopf (*SNT*[2], 1907); H. T. Andrews (Westminster NT, 1908); G. H. Gilbert (New York, 1908); R. B. Rackham[7] (*WC.* 1909)*.

(*b*) Studies—(i.) general:—J. Lightfoot's *Hebrew and Talmudical Exercitations on the Acts of the Apostles* (1678); Griesbach, *De Concilio quo scriptor in Actis concinnandis ductus fuerit* (Jena, 1798); H. Robinson, *Acta Apost. Variorum Notis* (Cambridge, 1824); Gfrörer, *Die heilige Sage* (1838), i. 383 f. ii. 244 f.; Schneckenburger, *Über den Zweck d. Apgeschichte* (1841); B. Bauer, *die Apgeschichte* (1850); Pearson, *Lectures on Acts* (1851); M. Baumgarten, *die Apgeschichte, oder d. Entwickelungsgang der Kirche von Jerus. bis Rom*[2] (1859, Eng. tr. 1854 of first ed.); Zeller,[1] *die Apgeschichte nach ihrem Inhalt u. Ursprung kritisch untersucht* (1854)*; Trip, *Paulus nach d. Apgeschichte* (1866); Oertel, *Paulus in d. Apgeschichte* (Halle, 1868; Paley's *Horæ Paulinæ* (ed. Birks, 1870); Zimmer, *Galaterbrief u. die Apgeschichte* (1882); H. J. Holtzmann (Schenkel's *BL.* i. 208 f.); Jäger's *Gedanken u. Bemerkungen* (1891 f.); J. B. Lightfoot (Smith's *DB.* i. 25 f.); Reuss, *NTTh.* ii. 296–310; Cone, *The Gospel and its Earliest Interpretations* (1893), pp. 138–150; Pfleiderer, *Urc.* i. 469 f. (Eng. tr. ii. 191 f.); McGiffert (*AA.* 345 f., 433 f.)*; Belser's *Beiträge zur Erklärung d. Apgeschichte* (1897); A. C. Headlam (*DB.* i. 25–35); J. Weiss, *Über die Absicht und den litter. Charakter d. Apgeschichte* (1897); V. Bartlet (*Biblical World*, xix. pp. 260 f.); P. W. Schmiedel (*EBi.* 37–57)*; G. Semeria, *Venticinque anni di storia del Cristianismo nascente* (Rome, 1900); Bumstead (*Biblical World*, 1901, 355 f.); Moffatt (*HNT.* 412 f., 655 f.); F. H. Chase (*The Credibility of Acts*, 1902); Cassel, *SR.* 565–752; Corluy (Vigoroux' *DB.* i. 151–159); R. J. Knowling, *Testimony of St. Paul to Christ* (1905), 148 f., 431 f.; C. Clemen, *die Apgeschichte im Lichte der neueren textquellen und histor.-krit. Forschungen* (1905); W. Hadorn, *die Apgeschichte und ihr geschichtl. Wert* (1906); A. Hilgenfeld (*ZWT.*, 1906, 461–483, 1907, 176–215), and J. E. Belser, *die Apgeschichte* (1908). (ii.) On special points:—Burton, *Chron. of Acts and S. Paul's Epp.* (Oxford, 1830);

---

[1] Overbeck's introduction to Acts and this essay of Zeller occupy pp. 1–84 and pp. 85 f. of the Eng. tr. (London, 1875), entitled, *Contents and Origin of the Acts of the Apostles* (cited as Zeller-Overbeck).

R. Anger, *de temporum in Actis Ap. ratione* (1833); Klostermann's *Probleme im Aposteltexte* (1883); M. W. Jacobus, *A Problem in Criticism* (1900), 105 f.; W. Soltau, 'Inwieweit kann d. Apgeschichte als historische Quelle gelten' (*Beiträge z. alten Geschichte*, v. 117–123); S. Grandjean, 'étude sur la valeur historique du Livre des Actes' (*Liberté Chrétienne*, 1906, 247–260). (iii.) On religious ideas:—J. Weiss, *DCG*. i. 25–28; Shailer Mathews, *Messianic Hope in NT* (1906), 137 f.; Mangenot, 'Jésus, Messie et Fils de Dieu, d'après les Actes des Apôtres' (*Revue de l'Institut catholique de Paris*, 1907, 385–423), and V. Ermoni, 'La Cristologia degli Atti degli Apostoli' (*Rivista delle Scienze teolog.*, 1908, 369–383). (iv.) On the sources:—Konigsmann, *Prolusio de fontibus commentariorum sacrorum qui Lucæ nomen præferunt, deque eorum consilio et ætate* (1798); J. K. Riehm, *dissertatio critico-theologica de fontibus Act. Ap.* (1821); Schwanbeck, *Ueber die Quellen d. Apgeschichte* (1847); Horst, *Essai sur les sources de la deuxième partie des Actes des apôtres* (1849); Lekebusch, *die Composition u. Entstehung der Apgeschichte von neuem untersucht* (1854); Jacobsen, *die Quellen d. Apgeschichte* (Berlin, 1885); van Manen, *Paulus I = de handelingen der Apostelen* (Leiden, 1890); Sorof, *die Entstehung d. Apgeschichte* (1890); Feine, *Eine vorkanonische Ueberlieferung des Lukas im Evglm und Apgeschichte* (1891)*; Spitta, *die Apgeschichte, ihre Quellen und deren Geschichtlicher Wert* (1891)*; J. Weiss (*SK.*, 1893, 480–540); Jüngst, *die Quellen der Apgeschichte* (1895); Zimmermann (*SK.*, 1901, 438 f.); Mallinckrodt, 'Het wij-bericht in de Handelingen, in verband met die Handelingen, en het evangelie van Lucas beschouwd' (*Geloof en Vrijheid*, xxxv. 5); Soltau (*PM.*, 1903, 265 f., 296 f.); Harnack (*BNT.* iii. 162 f.)*; J. Wellhausen's *Noten zur Apgeschichte* (in 'Nachrichten von der königlichen Gesellschaft der Wissenschaften zu Göttingen. Philologisch-Historische Klasse, 1907, Heft i. pp. 1–21), and E. Schwartz, *Zur Chronologie des Paulus* (*ibid.* pp. 263–299); B. W. Bacon (*AJT.* xiii. 59–76, review of Harnack, etc.), P. W. Schmidt (*Die Apgeschichte bei de Wette-Overbeck und bei Adolf Harnack*, 1910). (v.) the speeches:—Kähler (Petrine Speeches, *SK.*, 1873, 492 f.); Bethge (*Die Paulinische Reden der Apgeschichte*, 1887); Cassel (*SR.* 618–637); E. Curtius, 'Paulus in Athen' (*SBBA.*, 1893. 925 f., cp. *Exp.*^{7} iv. 436–455)*; Schulze (*SK.*, 1900, 119–124 on 20^{18-31}); Baljon (*Theol. Studiën*, 1900, 179 f.); W. Soltau, 'Die Herkunft der Reden in der Apgeschichte' (*ZNW.*, 1903, 128–154); P. Gardner (*Cambridge Biblical Essays*, 1909, 378–419)*; M. Jones (*St. Paul the Orator*, 1910).

§ 1. *Outline and contents.*—This sequel to the third gospel is an account of some deeds of *the holy Spirit* ($1^{2.\ 5.\ 8}$) of Jesus Christ, performed through some of the apostles, notably Peter and Paul. The scope and aim of the book is the triumphant extension of the Christian faith from Jerusalem to Rome, through Judæa and Samaria (1^{8}). The first part (1^{1}–6^{6}) describes the origin of the church at Jerusalem, the second (6^{8}–9^{30}) its diffusion throughout Palestine, including Samaria, the third (9^{32}–12^{23}) its expansion from Judæa to Antioch, the fourth its spread throughout Asia Minor (12^{25}–16^{4}), the fifth its extension to Europe or Macedonia and Achaia (16^{6}–19^{19}), culminating in the arrival of Paul as the representative of the Gentile Christian gospel at Rome (= *the uttermost parts of the earth*, 1^{8}, cp. Ps. Sol 8^{16}). Each section is summarised (6^{7} 9^{31} 12^{24} 16^{5} 19^{20} and 28^{31}) by a rubric of progress.

The increased prominence of the Spirit in the third gospel is evident in the δεύτερος λόγος, where the holy Spirit is treated as the inspiring force of the early church's energies (cp. especially characteristic passages like $2^{4f.}$ $5^{9.\,32}$ 7^{55} $8^{15f.\,39}$ $10^{44f.}$ $11^{12.\,28}$ 13^{2} 15^{28} $16^{6\text{-}7}$ $19^{2f.}$ 20^{28} 21^{11}). This serves to explain how Luke could follow up a gospel, narrating the sayings and doings of Jesus, with an account of apostolic activity in the early church, whether the preface of Luke $1^{1\text{-}4}$ is meant to cover the sequel or not. Neither Acts nor the third gospel, at any rate, were written for non-Christian readers (as, *e.g.*, Overbeck, J. Weiss, Nestle, Zahn, and von Soden argue). Theophilus was some distinguished convert, perhaps a Roman official like Sergius Paulus, who needed fuller instruction in the historic basis of the faith (cp. *DCG.* ii. 726–727). Behind him Luke probably saw many like-minded inquirers, and he wrote this δεύτερος λόγος in order to follow up the impression made by the πρῶτος λόγος. The geographical plan adopted in the latter (Galilee, Samaria, etc., Jerusalem) is retained in the former (Jerusalem, Samaria, etc., Rome); but more important is the conception that the work of the church is a continuation of Christ's energy. The Lucan writings in this, as in several other respects (see below), reflect the Christian consciousness of the Fourth gospel, in which the utterances and actions of the church are regarded as the direct outcome of the living Lord (cp. *Exp.*[6] iv. 237 f.).

Πράξεις (τῶν) ἀποστόλων, though not the author's title, must have been prefixed to the book during the second century. For purposes of convenience it is usually quoted by early writers simply as πράξεις (*acta, actus*). The variant πρᾶξις (Nestle, *Einf.* 240) is generally no more than a familiar abbreviation of the *scriptio plena*, but Hilary of Poitiers seems to have taken it as a genuine singular (cp. J. Denk in *ZNW.*, 1906, 92–95).

It has been thought that Luke wrote, or intended to write, a third volume, describing Paul's release, subsequent travels, and death, or the fortunes of Peter and the rest of the apostles. So, *e.g.*, Bleek, Spitta, E. Bertrand (*sur l'authenticité des Épîtres Pastorales*, 1858, 50 f., who feels that "les Actes se terminent avec une brusquerie presque brutale"), Ramsay, Zahn, Balmer, and Burkitt. The arguments for this theory, however, are not sufficient to bear its weight. (*a*) Πρότερον would have been, strictly speaking, more accurate than πρῶτον in 1^{1}, if Luke had meant the first of two volumes; but πρῶτος can quite well denote 'one of two,' and, as Luke never uses πρότερος, the likelihood is that πρῶτος is its equivalent here as in 7^{12}. (*b*) The argument from internal evidence, viz., that the contents and climax point to Luke's purpose of carrying forward the lines of Christian progress which he had dropped in his second volume, depends on *a priori* theories of the historian's aim (cp. McGiffert, *AA.* 418 f.).

§ 2. *Source-criticism.*—Special literature: in addition to works cited above (p. 284), see surveys by B. Weiss (*Einl.* § 50), Zeller-Overbeck (i. 31 f., ii. 291 f.), Heitmüller (*TR.*, 1899, 47–59, 83–95, 127–140), Zöckler (*Greifswalder Studien*, 1895, pp. 129 f.), Rose (*RB.* vii. 325–342), Moffatt (*HNT.* 655 f.), Bludau (*BZ.*, 1907, 166–189, 258–281), and Clemen (*Paulus*, i. pp. 162 f.).

The presumption that in his δεύτερος λόγος, as in its predecessor (Lk 1^{1-4}), Luke employed not only oral traditions but written sources, is borne out by an examination of the gaps, discrepancies, roughnesses, and repetitions which stud the pages of Acts (cp. the list in Harnack's *BNT.* iii. 203 f., and *EBi.* 39 f.). These render it as likely as in the case of John's apocalypse that the earlier sections of the book at least contain strata of different periods and aims. The hypothesis of (i.) a single written source is presented in various forms. Briggs (*New Light on the Life of Jesus*, pp. 135 f.) and Blass (*Acta Apost.* iv f., *Philology of Gospels*, pp. 141 f.), *e.g.*, finds a Jerusalem-source due to John Mark,* who wrote in continuation of his gospel (which originally ended at 16^{8}), a sequel describing (*a*) the appearances of Jesus after his death, and (*b*) the acts of the local disciples. Luke, who had incorporated Mk. in his gospel, is supposed to have made a similar use of this sequel in his second volume. Feine prefers to trace his pre-canonical source of the third gospel through Ac 1–12, *i.e.* a Jewish Christian document of considerable historic value, written *c.* A.D. 67, describing the growth of the Jerusalem-church ($1^{4-5.\ 8.\ 9-12.\ 13-17.\ 20-26}$ $2^{1-4a.\ 12-13.\ 14-42\ (43-47)}$ $3^{1-8a.\ 11-26}$ $4^{4.\ 7b-14.\ 15.\ (21).\ 22.\ (23).\ 24-31.\ 33.\ 36-37}$ $5^{1-11.\ 12-16.\ 24-35.\ 37-42}$ $6^{(8).\ 9-11.\ 15}$ $7^{22-28.\ 35-43.\ 51-56.\ 59-60}$ $8^{1b-2.\ 4-9.\ 11-13}$ 9^{31-43} $10^{1-27.\ 29b-33.\ 36-42a.\ 44-48}$ $11^{2-17.\ 19-30}$ 12^{1-24}). B. Weiss detects editorial additions in $1^{1-11.\ 18-19}$ 2^{43-47} $3^{4-5.\ 8-10}$ $4^{2-3.\ 5.\ 7.\ 15-17.\ 19-20.\ (25.\ 27).\ 31.\ 34-35}$ $5^{(3.\ 9).\ 14.\ 16-20.\ (21).\ 22-24.\ 33.\ 36.\ 42}$ $6^{11-12.\ (15)}$ $7^{58-59.\ 60}$ $8^{1b.\ 3}$ $10^{37.\ 40}$ 11^{1-18} 12^{18-22} $15^{1-4.\ 23-25}$; similarly Clemen, abandoning his former very complicated analysis, now finds a single source in 1–11, with editorial additions. (ii.) The dual-

* Cp. Weiss, *Marcus-Evglm.* p. 511. Schärfe (*die petrinische Strömung in der NT Lit.*, 1893, pp. 53 f., 113 f.) is also an exponent of this view. Ewald's theory of a Petrine and a Pauline source overlapping in 1–12 is restated by Badham (*ET.* xi. 287 f.).

source hypothesis is represented by Sorof, Spitta, and Jüngst. Van Manen and Hilgenfeld combine it with a form of what is substantially (iii.) the triple-source theory advocated by Schwanbeck. Harnack (*BNT.* iii. 162 f.) simply detects a Jerusalem-Antioch source in 6^{1-8} 11^{19-30} 12^{25}–15^{35} (based on the authority of Silas), which probably, but only probably, was written; also a Jerusalem-Cæsarean source (or group of traditions) in 3^{1}–5^{16} 8^{5-40} 9^{31}–11^{18} 12^{1-23}; 9^{1-30} comes from a separate plot of tradition. (B) $2 + 5^{17-42}$ and (A) 3^{1}–5^{16} are double recensions of the same story which follows up the incidents of 1; (A) is mainly derived from men like Philip and Mark, and is much superior to the confused and unreliable (B), which "combines things that

(A)		(B)	
Lk 24^{50-53}, ascension of Jesus			
		[1–3]	
15–17*, 20–26*, election of Matthias	i.	4–14, ascension of Jesus; 18, 19, death of Judas	1–11*
1^a (. . . συμπλήρ.), 4, 12, 13, 14–40, Peter's speech	ii.	1^b–3, 5*–6, 9–11	3^{b*}
41–42, 45–47		43	
whole	iii.*		
1, 3–5, 7–33*	iv.	36–37	
12^b–14	v.	1–12^a (Ananias and Sapphira), 15–39*	
1–6 (the Seven), 9–12^a (. . . γραμμ.)	vi.	7–8, 12^b–15	8*
2–54, 57, 58^a (. . . ἐλιθοβ.), Stephen's speech and death	vii.	1, 55, 56, 58^b–60	
1^b, 2.	viii.	1^a (. . . αὐτοῦ), 3, 5–40^a (Philip-section)	
	ix.	1–3*, 6–31, conversion of Paul; 32–43 (Peter)	1*, 18*
	x.	1–35, 44–48	
19–21, church of Antioch; 27–30*	xi.	1–18, 22*–26	23*
25	xii.	1–24, death of James, etc.	
1–5, 13*–41, Paul's speech; 43, 50, 51	xiii.	6–12, 42, 44*–49, 52	2*
1–2, 4–6, 7*, 21–26, 28	xiv.	3, 8–20	
35–41	xv.	[1–33, the Council]	5–12*
1–19 (22–23*) (35*), 37–40*	xvi.	20, 21* (22, 23*), 24–34 (36*)	
1–4 (5*), 10–34 (Berea and Athens)	xvii.	(5*), 6–9	
1–5^a (. . . Παῦλος), 7–24* (25), 26–28	xviii.		
1^a (. . . Ἔφεσον), 8–10^a (. . . δύο), 21, 22	xix	1^b–7, 10^{b*}–20, 24–41 (riot in Ephesus)	
whole	xx.		1*
1–9, 12–14*, 15–20^a (. . . Θεόν), 27–40	xxi.	10, 11*, 20^b–26*	
1–29*	xxii.	30*	5*
11–35	xxiii.	1–10*	
whole	xxiv.		
whole	xxv.		18*
whole	xxvi.		
whole	xxvii.		
1–16, 30–31	xxviii.	17–23*	

* The redactor's presence is marked by an asterisk (*), and he is responsible for the passages omitted in the above list. For the sake of clearness the references have been arranged in the order of the chapters, but more than once, especially in (B), Spitta transposes whole paragraphs, *e.g.* 9^{3-31} is transferred to a place between 8^{3} and 8^{4}, and $15^{1-4.\ 13-33}$ occurs between 12^{24} and 13^{1}.

have no real connection with one another, omits what is important, and is devoid of all sense of historical development" (p. 194). Harnack lays great stress, however,—though not so much as Ramsay (*Exp.*[7] vii. 172 f., 262 f., 358 f., 450 f.),—on the authority or traditions of men like Philip, Mnason, etc. Both Harnack and Ramsay thus hark back to a position approximating to that of Overbeck who denied any written sources except the We-journal. The data cannot, however, be explained apart from some source or sources, especially in the opening chapters, although most of the hypotheses proposed run to the opposite extreme of over-precision, as the following analyses will show. The main constructive feature of Spitta's analysis—and at the same time its weak point—consists in the comparatively limited and unimportant function which he assigns to the redactor (see p. 287).

Spitta's hypothesis * involves two primary sources. (A), a well-informed source which underlies the third gospel also, is probably from the pen of Luke, contains the most trustworthy passages of the book, and is superior in historical insight to (B). The latter, like (A), contains "supernatural" elements, but these are drawn from popular traditions, and appear to be more highly coloured and less coherent; the stress falls on "wonders" throughout, whereas in (A) the preaching of the apostles is emphasised. Both sources, independent in origin and individually featured, have been combined, arranged, and edited by a redactor (R) before the end of the first century, though (B) was composed by a Jewish-Christian admirer of Peter much earlier—after 70 A.D.

Jüngst also confines himself, like several of the more sober critics, to a bisection of the book. (A), including the we-journal, extends through the whole book, the latter part of which has been interpolated by the final editor (R), who is not Luke but a companion of Paul, writing in the early part of the second century (under Trajan). He has used in the first half of the work an Ebionitic source (B) already employed in the gospel of Luke, but here rearranged to suit (A). The final redaction is supposed to have taken place A.D. 110–125 (cp. 13^{48} 19^{10}, which are taken to imply a wide diffusion of Christianity). (R) is differentiated chiefly by his style and his conception of Paul's work and teaching, (B) is anti-Jewish, and (A) possibly Lucan. Upon the other hand, Hilgenfeld finds three sources used by the final editor (R): like van Manen, he assigns the chief importance to (C) = *πράξεις Παύλου*, an account of Paul's work and person by Luke, to which the final redactor, a Pauline unionist, subordinated his other source (B) = *πράξεις τῶν ἑπτά*, and especially (A) = (Jewish Christian) *πράξεις Πέτρου*, adding passages of his own:

(A) = 1^{15}–5^{42} 9^{31-43} 12^{1-23} [R mainly in 1^{1-14} $2^{39b.\ 41b.\ 43.\ 46}$ $3^{13b.\ 21b.\ 25b}$ $4^{2b,\ 6.\ 12a.\ 27-28.\ 33b-35}$ $5^{14-16.\ 36}$]

(B) = 6–8^{40}.

(C) = 9^{1-30} 11^{17-26}.

---

* Partially modified by J. Weiss (*SK.*, 1893, p. 480 f.; *Die Absicht*, especially p. 38 f.), who finds only (B) in chs. 1–5, only (A) in the second half of the book, and in the middle chapters a blending of material from (A) and (B). Cp. the notices by von Soden (*TLZ.*, 1892, 639 f.) and Wrede (*GGA*, 1895, p. 497 f.), of Spitta's volume.

Schwanbeck.					Sorof.				Jüngst.		
PB (A biography of Peter, including 1–6⁷.)	Special source.	B (A biography of Barnabas, including $4^{36f.}$)	Special source.	S (A memoir by Silas.)	Genuine Lucan source: a sketch of early Christianity developing among the Gentiles—Paul prominent—containing, in addition to 1^{1-2} 2^{46} 4^{33-37} etc.	A Petrine source, somewhat legendary in character (1^{3}–2^{24} 3^{1}–4^{3} 4^{5-31} 5^{1-11}).	The whole supplemented and revised by Timotheus, from a Jewish-Christian standpoint.	Chap.	Analysis of his main source (A) in three parts: (*a*) 1–12 (15), (*b*) 13–21, (*c*) 21–28. (Besides 1^{2}. 3. 6-8. 12a. 13a. 14b 2^{4}. 12-23. 32-33. 36-39. 41a. 43c. 46-47a 3^{1-3a}. 5-8a. 11-13. 14b-17. 19. 20. 25a. 26 4^{1}. 6-14. 18-21b. 22-27a. 30. 32. 33.)	(B), inferior to (A) in point of historicity, an edifying Jewish-Christian narrative of the development of the Palestine churches. (Besides 1^{15-21}. 22b-26 2^{1-2a}. 3. 5-11 3^{25b}. 21-24. 18. 14a 2^{24-31}. 34. 35. 45. 43a. 41b-42 4^{36}. 37 5^{12a}. 14-16. 17-25. 34-38a. 39b. 40a.)	
	7–15				whole			vi.	9–10, 12^{c}–14	1–6, 7^{bc}, 8, 11, 15	
	1–59				1–58^{a}, 59, 60		58^{b}	vii.	1–21, 29–34, 44–50, 58^{b}–60	22–28, 35–43, 51–58^{a}	
1, 3–40	2				1^{b} (except πλ. τ. ἐ.) 2	5–40	1^{a}, b^{*}, 3, 4	viii.	1^{bc}	1^{a}, 2, 3, 5–9^{ac}, 11–13, 19–24^{*}, 26–40^{a}	
3^{1}–43		1–30				32–43	1–31	ix.	1–5, 22^{b}–25, 30^{b}	6–15, 17–20^{a}, 26–28 [32–43	
whole						whole		x.		[1–35, 44–48: after 12^{17}]	
1–18		19–30			19–30	1–17	18	xi.	19–23, 25, 26 [27–28^{a}–30, after 14^{28}]	1–15, 17^{ac}, 24^{a}	
		25			25	3–23	1–2, 24	xii.	[25^{ab} „ „	1–3, 4–6^{*}, 7–14, 15^{*}, 16, 17, 18	
		whole			1–26, 32, 33, 38–52	27–30, 34–37		xiii.	1–8^{*}, 13–23, 26–27^{a}, 28, 30–33, 38, 43, 50, 51	40, 41	R (among other passages) 44–49
		„			1, 2, 4–7, 11^{b}–18	3, 8–11^{a},		xiv.	1, 2^{*}, 6, 7, 21^{b}–27^{b}, 28		8–21^{a}
		2–4	3–13	rest	1–6, 19–33 (except σὺν ὁ.τ. ἐκκ. 22), 35–41	7–18, 22^{a}		xv.	[1–4, 30^{a}, 32–35] 36–41	13^{bc}–18, 20 [9^{21}]	5–13^{a}, 21–29
				whole	6–10, 18^{b}–49	1–5, 10–18^{a}		xvi.	1, 3^{a}, 6^{a}, 7–23^{a}, 35^{*}, 37–40		3^{bc}–5, 23^{b}–34
				„	1–14^{a}, 16^{b}–34	14^{b}–16^{a}		xvii.	1–6, 8–16^{a}, 18^{ab}, 34		18^{cd}–33
				„	1–4, 19 (exc. καὶ . . . αὐτὸς δέ)–23	5–18, 19^{*}, 24–28		xviii.	1–5^{b}, 7, 8, 11, 18^{b}–19^{b}, 21^{c}, 22, 22–24, 26, 27^{a}, 28^{*}		12–17
				„	1^{b}–10, 21–41	1^{a}, 11–20		xix.	1^{ab}, 8–10^{a}, 21, 22		10^{bc}–20, 23–41
				„	1–3, 17–38	4–16		xx.	1^{*}–19^{a} 22, 31, 32, 36, 37, 38^{a}		20^{a}–26
				„	20^{b}–24 26–40	1–20^{a}, 25		xxi.	1–10^{a}–20^{a}, 27–37^{a}, 39, 40		30
				„	1–19, 21–29	20		xxii.	1–4^{a}, 5–10^{a}, 21^{a}–29		1–10
				„	whole			xxiii.	11–27, 30		
				„	„			xxiv.	1–14^{b}, 17–19, 22–27		
				„	„			xxv.	(1–24^{a}), 26		
				„	„			xxvi.	1–5, 9–32		
				„			whole	xxvii.	1–20, 27–44		
				„	16^{b}–31	1–16^{a} besides $2^{43-45.47}$ $4^{4.33}$ 5^{12-42}		xxviii.	1–16, 30, 31 Jüngst dates the Council previous to Ac 13, 14 (like Weizsäcker), and regards the first of his three parts in (A) as inferior to the other two.		17–28

§ 3. *Structure.*—(*a*) In 1–5 (cp. Clemen, *SK.*, 1895, 297–357) it is sometimes difficult to be sure that any written source underlies the narrative; oral tradition of a heterogeneous and even of a legendary character may be held to explain most, if not all, of the data. There is fair ground for conjecturing, however, that Luke used and translated an Aramaic source (or sources; cp. Harnack, *BNT.* i. 118 f.). Once or twice the brush-work of the final artist becomes plain. Thus $1^{21a-22b}$ is an editorial insertion (Spitta, Weiss, J. Weiss, Jüngst, Moffatt, Wellhausen) to emphasise sharply the conditions of the apostolate; 2^{43-47} again, with its proleptic anticipation of the first miracle (2^{43}, cp. $3^{1f.}$ 4^{16}) and its interruption of the connection between 2^{42} and 3^{1}, is probably one of the general summaries which Luke was fond of inserting in order to mark progress. The first real* suggestion of double sources occurs in 4^{1-22} = 5^{17-42}, unless the latter is a free composition based on the former or on some parallel tradition, like the doublets in the synoptic gospels. 4^{4} is an editorial insertion, like 6^{7}, on the lines of 2^{43-47}, but otherwise it is impossible to distinguish the source under the revision, though 4^{27-28} sound like an editor's insertion in the prayer (Hilgenfeld, Weiss). 5^{14} is another editorial parenthesis or insertion, to mark what Luke believed to have been the rapid growth of the church. Here as elsewhere the miraculous powers of Peter are enhanced like those of Jesus (cp. Lk 4^{40} with Mk 1^{34}, Lk 9^{11} with Mk 6^{34}, Lk 7^{21} with Mt $11^{3f.}$). Peter, all through, is the prominent figure, and if the source goes back to any authority, it is to him; the allusions to John may even be editorial (cp. Harnack).

(i.) There is no reason to deny any connection between $1^{6f.}$ and 1^{1-5}, as if the former represented a fresh Jewish-Christian source, and thus to omit 1^{8} (Spitta) or 1^{5} (J. Weiss). The mistake of the disciples (1^{6}) *is* tacitly corrected by the words of 1^{8} which point to the true extra-national vocation of the Christian apostles; besides, the idea of receiving the Holy Spirit would not unnaturally suggest to minds trained in Jewish expectations the near advent of the Israelitish messianic reign.

(ii.) Source-phenomena of a special nature lie not only in the midrashic story of the death of Judas (1^{18-21}), but in the preparation of the disciples during forty days' communion for their task (like Moses on Sinai, Ex. 24^{18}), and the naive expression of the catholicity of the new gospel ($2^{1f.}$), which goes

* Two sources (De Faye, *AA.* 28 f.) for the first part (notably Theologus in *Preuss. Jahrb.*, 1897, 223 f.) and for the latter part (Batiffol: *Études d'histoire et de théologie positive*[3], ii. 39 f.) of 2 have been conjectured.

back* to the midrash (cp. Philo, *De Decal.* 11, *Septen.* 22), that at Sinai all the nations of the world heard God's voice in their own languages (cp. Spitta's *Apgeschichte,* 27 f.; *SR.* 788 f.; Hausrath, ii. 116 f.; Bartlet; Schmiedel, *EBi.* 4785 f.; Pfleiderer's *Urc.* ii. 203, etc.; with the *συναλιζόμενος* of 1^{4} cp. Ex 24^{11}). Even the list of countries and peoples in $2^{10f.}$ is based on rabbinic schemes (cp. von Dobschütz, *ZWT.*, 1902, 407–410). Luke, in short, "views the Pentecostal gift from the standpoint of the Hellenistic litterateur, as a parallel to the giving of the Law, which tradition reported to have taken place at Pentecost" (Bacon, *INT.* 216). The next stratum, which corresponds to this, lies in the speech of Stephen.

(iii.) The mention of the so-called 'communism' (cp. Hicks, *Exp.*[7] i. 21 f.), which in 2^{43-47} leads to nothing, opens up in 4^{32-35} into (*a*) a story of Barnabas (4^{36-37}), and (*b*) the anecdotes of Ananias and Sapphira (5^{1-11}). The latter are introduced as a foil to the conduct of Barnabas, and as an illustration of the apostolic power and the popular dread noted in the context (for the composite nature of 4^{32}–5^{11}, cp. Schmiedel in *EBi.* 878–880). Luke is also careful to bring out the growth (2^{47} 4^{4} 5^{14} $6^{1.7}$) and the popularity (2^{47} 3^{10} 4^{21} $5^{13.26}$) of the local church. The mixture of general and even vague outlines with specific details (which are not always circumstantial) points clearly to the editorial use of some early tradition or sources in this section, and the presence of dual sources is even suggested by the parallelism of $4^{1f.}$ and 5^{17-42}:—

5^{17-42}.	$4^{1f.}$.
(*a*) Annas *καὶ πάντες οἱ σὺν αὐτῷ* arrest the apostles:	(*a*) arrest and arraignment of Peter and John before Annas, etc.:
(*b*) their miraculous release: arraigned before Sanhedrin:	(*b*) Answer . . . *εἰ δίκαιόν ἐστιν ἐνώπιον τοῦ θεοῦ, ὑμῶν ἀκούειν μᾶλλον ἢ τοῦ θεοῦ, κρίνατε.*
(*c*) Speech of Peter and apostles (*πειθαρχεῖν δεῖ θεῷ μᾶλλον ἢ ἀνθρώποις κτλ.*).	(*c*) release.

(*b*) Hitherto (cp. $5^{32.42}$ *ἐν τῷ ἱερῷ καὶ κατ' οἶκον*) the Christian propaganda has been confined to Jerusalem. Now the forward movement begins, but not by any of the apostles. The appointment of the Seven (6^{1-6}) led to three unexpected results: (i.) One of their number became the first Christian martyr, after making a vigorous attack upon the unbelief of Judaism (6^{8}–7^{60}), and the subsequent persecution led to the first Samaritan mission (8^{1-40}) under the leadership of Philip, another of the Seven. (ii.) The conversion of Paul is also linked to the episode of Stephen's martyrdom (7^{58} 8^{1-3} $9^{1f.}$): he is arrested by Jesus on his way to counteract the results of Philip's mission, and from the outset he is set apart for the Gentile mission (9^{15}), though

* The Jewish legend is much closer than the Buddhistic story cited by Seydel (*Die Buddha-Legende und das Leben Jesu nach den Evglien*, 1884, pp. 27 f.), which only describes hearing the word, not speaking with tongues.

his first efforts are devoted to his own countrymen ($9^{20f.}$). Peter is now suddenly introduced again (9^{32}–11^{18}) in a cycle of stories, culminating in his conversion of Cornelius a proselyte, and some other Gentiles at Cæsarea. This carries on the propaganda a stage further than Philip's incidental conversion of a proselyte ($8^{26f.}$), but Peter is able to persuade the suspicious Jewish Christians of Palestine that this unexpected conversion of the Gentiles is the work of God. The third (iii.) effect of the Jewish outburst after Stephen's death is the evangelisation of Gentile Antioch, in which Paul is eventually summoned to take part ($11^{19\text{-}26}$).

The source dropped at 8^4 is resumed in 11^{19} (so, *e.g.*, Wendt, *ZTK.*, 1891, 250 f.; Feine, 207 f.; De Faye, *AA.* pp. 72 f.; Harnack), in order to explain the existence and character of the Gentile Christian community at Antioch from which the mission of $13^{1f.}$ started. Barnabas and Paul are introduced in 13^1, as if no previous allusion had just been made to either. Hence $11^{22f.\ 30}$ 12^{25} are plainly editorial insertions, either from oral tradition or from some other source, in order to emphasise Luke's dominant conception of the Jerusalem-church as the patron and promoter of missionary effort (cp. *EBi.* 908–913). The fifteenth chapter is the watershed of the history, in his view. "Practically all that lies between the sixth and the fifteenth chapters, *i.e.* more than a third part of the book, is devoted to the demonstration of the historical problem, how it came to pass that there was a mission to the Gentiles at all" (Harnack, *BNT.* iii. p. xxvi). After the council, Paul comes to the front as the apostle to the Gentiles, and the rest of the book is occupied with his fortunes (cp. J. Weiss, *Absicht*, pp. 25 f.).

(i.) In 6^1–8^{40} Luke has used (see Appendix M) sources describing the Acts of Stephen and Philip, the leading members of the Seven (6^5). Whether $6^{1\text{-}6}$ comes from a special document (Feine, 184 f.; De Faye, 61 f.) or not, 6^7 is inserted by the editor, to mark progress as usual, and the following account of Stephen (6^8–8^2, cp. *EBi.* 4787–4797) represents a source edited by Luke in $6^{8.\ 11\text{-}12\ (13).\ 15}$, so that what originally recorded an irregular *émeute*, during which Stephen defended himself at some length before an exasperated audience containing some members of the Sanhedrin, has become the story of a trial (as in 4–5). This bisection of the narrative reappears at the close; $7^{58b.}$ $8^{1b.\ 3}$ are all editorial touches which not merely attribute Stephen's death to the testimony of judicial witnesses, instead of to the outburst of the mob, but link on the source to the subsequent story of Paul by proleptic touches which no doubt reflect a genuine tradition (so, *e.g.*, Bleek, *INT.* i. 366 f.; B. Weiss, Sorof, Clemen, Krüger, *TLZ.*, 1895, 299; Wendt, Hilgenfeld, Schmiedel, Moffatt, Bacon). The significance of the Stephen-episode is twofold; it marked one of the crises at which Jewish fanaticism only served to accelerate the extension of the new faith to the Gentile world, and it denoted the awakening of the Christian church to the consciousness of what the universal gospel of Jesus involved (De Faye, *AA.* 143 f.).

(ii.) It is almost arbitrary not only to find, with H. Waitz (*ZNW.*, 1904, 121 f., 1906, 340 f.), editorial additions, *e.g.*, in $8^{10.\ 14\text{-}18a.\ 19b}$, but to regard the entire story of 8 as originally Petrine. In this section, *i.e.* the Acts of Philip ($8^{4\text{-}40}$), the account of his mission to the Samaritans ($8^{5\text{-}25}$) is interwoven with the episode of Simon Magus, which may have come from the same source, written or oral, as 3–5. The second part ($8^{26\text{-}40}$), describing how he converted an Ethiopian eunuch, is much more of a unity; probably it was derived from the Cæsarean cycle of traditions upon the primitive church.

(iii.) The first of the narratives of Paul's conversion ($9^{1\text{-}30}$) is written on the basis of the second (22) or the third (26) or both (cp. Zimmer, *ZWT.*, 1882, 465 f., and on the other side M. Goguel, *L'Apôtre Paul et Jésus-Christ*, 1904, pp. 40–68).

(iv.) For the isolated narrative of $12^{1\text{-}23}$ describing ($^{1\text{-}2}$) the martyrdom of James, Peter's arrest and escape ($^{3\text{-}19}$), and Herod's subsequent death ($^{20\text{-}23}$), it is natural to suppose that John Mark * ($12^{12.\ 25}$) was the ultimate source. Legendary and historical traits blend inextricably; but there are partial parallels in the two Lucan tales of $5^{18\text{-}23}$ and $16^{25\text{-}34}$, and the presence of many Lucan touches (*e.g.* ἐπέβαλεν τὰς χεῖρας and κακῶσαι, ^{1}; the Hebraism προσέθετο συλλαβεῖν, ^{3}; ἐκτενῶς, ^{5} (cp. 12^{7} = Lk 2^{9}); γενόμενος ἐν ἑαυτῷ and προσδοκία, ^{11}; ἦσαν with ptc. ^{12}; ἀπὸ τῆς χαρᾶς, ^{14}; διϊσχυρίζετο, ^{15}; κατασείσας and σιγᾶν and ἀπαγγείλατε, ^{17}; the litotes οὐκ ὀλίγος, ^{18}; ἀνακρίνω, ^{19}; ὁ δῆμος, ^{22}, and ἀνθ' ὧν, ^{23}) shows that in any case Luke must have rewritten his source, adding $12^{1 \text{ and } 24\text{-}25}$ as editorial links. The inconsequent opening and the abrupt allusion in v.^{17} indicate that it was not originally composed for its present position. Like the previous stories of Philip ($8^{4\text{-}40}$) and Peter (9^{32}–10^{48}), it begins at Jerusalem and closes in Cæsarea.

(*c*) The remainder † of the story ($13^{1f.}$) becomes practically a biographical sketch of some phases in Paul's life and work. The unity (especially after 16^{8}) grows more marked. But one or two passages even in the later sections of the book are generally taken to be additions; *e.g.* in $16^{25\text{-}34}$ (so Weiss, Zeller, Weizsäcker, Clemen, Forbes, etc.), in $18^{1\text{-}6.\ 18\text{-}22.\ 25f.}$ (the two latter passages ‡ being confused and loosely written; cp. *HNT.* 672 f.), in $19^{11\text{-}20}$ ("the writer is here rather a picker-up of current gossip, like Herodotus, than a real historian," Ramsay,

* As it happens, two of the words peculiar to Acts and Mark occur in this passage (σανδάλιά, 12^{8} = Mk 6^{9}, and αὐτομάτη, 12^{10} = Mk 4^{28}). Ramsay romantically makes Rhoda the *fons et origo* of the story.

† The recent tendency is to find the second section of Acts from 16^{1} onwards. On the entire composition see Bousset's essay in *ZNW.* (1914) 141 f., and Norden's darting but unreliable paragraphs (pp. 312 f.).

‡ On Apollos, see *JTS.* xvi. 241 f., and Schmiedel in *EBi.* 262–264.

SPT. 273),* in $20^{26-27.\ 33-35}$, in 20^{20b-26}, and in 22^{30}–$23^{10\ (11)}$. The widely accepted excision of 27^{21-26} as a later interpolation (cp. *HNT.* 676 f.) in the original We-source, has led Wellhausen (pp. 17–19) to conjecture boldly that $27^{9-11.\ 31.\ 33-38}$ are also secondary insertions made for the purpose of turning an anonymous piece of seafaring into a Pauline episode, just as he had already taken 19^{23-41} to be an independent account of some riot which Luke assimilated for his biographical sketch of Paul at Ephesus. On the vividness and accuracy of the details in 27, see James Smith (*Voyage and Shipwreck of St. Paul*[4], 1880), Breusing's *Nautik der Alten* (1886, pp. 142–205), Goerne in *NKZ.* (1898) 352–375, Hans Balmer (*Die Romfahrt des Apostels Paulus und die Seefahrtskunde im röm. Kaiseralter*, 1905, pp. 269 f.), and Montgomery (*Exp.*[8] ix. 356 f.). The phenomena of $28^{17f.}$ have suggested dual sources or the loss of the original conclusion (so, *e.g.*, Gercke in *neue Jahrb. für die klass. Alterth.*, 1901, 17), but, although the conclusion is hurried, it is dramatic. 28^{28} is the watchword of the writer's age, and the ringing ἀκωλύτως of 28^{31} echoes the exulting strain of the Lucan writings.

§ 4. *The Journal.*—The main structural feature of the latter half of the book is the presence of four extracts from a diary kept by one of Paul's companions (16^{10-17} $20^{(4).\ 5-15}$ 21^{1-18} 27^{1}–28^{16}). "It was customary for distinguished travellers, princes, and generals of the ancient Hellenic world to have short diaries kept by some companion as an aid to memory, in which the stations of the route and perhaps, here and there, notable experiences were cursorily set down. For instance, according to Hermann Diels, the *Anabasis* of Xenophon is founded on a diary of this description, which Xenophon himself developed into an historical work, inserting all kinds of narratives and speeches" (von Soden, *INT.* p. 243; cp. Deissmann's *St. Paul*, p. 25, and Norden, 316 f.). No features of style or diction in these passages differentiate them from the rest of the Lucan compositions. They contain over fifty words peculiar to, and over seventy specially characteristic of, Luke, and it may be due to accident or to subject-matter that they omit such Lucan

* "The history of Greek literature presents few other instances of the destruction of books, whether for the sake of conscience or for the good of the community, or under the authority of the State" (G. H. Putnam, *Authors and their Public in Ancient Times*[2], 1894, pp. 118 f.; later and Latin instances on pp. 264 f.).

favourites or peculiarities as ἄν with the optative, ἀπὸ τοῦ νῦν, ἀναστάς (-άντες), ἀπόστολος, εἰρήνη, ἐν ταῖς ἡμέραις ταύταις, ἐρωτάω, ἔτος, καθ' ἡμέραν, κριτής, λαός, μετὰ ταῦτα, ὅς in attraction, πίμπλημι, πράσσω, ῥῆμα, τίς with the optative, τοῦτον (= him), ὕψιστος, χάρις, and ὡσεί, while τῇ ἑτέρᾳ (= next day), παραινέω ($27^{9.\ 22}$), and περιαιρέω ($27^{20.\ 40}$) are found here alone, so far as Luke is concerned. These idiosyncrasies of vocabulary only throw into relief the linguistic, stylistic, and mental affinities between the We-journal and the rest of Acts. Such data, it may be held, do not foreclose the question of the authorship. While they bring the We-sections into line with the rest of Acts, they leave it an open question (i.) whether the author may not have dealt here as freely with some source from another hand as he did in the gospel, or (ii.) whether the journal is of his own composition. On the latter hypothesis, the use of ἡμεῖς, not unlike the μέχρις ἐμὲ ἐόν or ἔτι ἐς ἐμὲ ἐόν of Herodotus, is designed to mark indirectly but unmistakably the periods at which the author was a companion of Paul and an eye-witness of what he records, so that the We-sections would represent his own written notes or memoranda of a time when he happened to be associated closely with the apostle. This conclusion, formerly pressed, *e.g.*, by A. Klostermann, *Vindiciæ Lucanæ seu de itinerarii in libro Actorum asservato auctore* (1866), pp. 46 f.; V. H. Stanton (*Exp.*[4] vii. 336 f., *GHD.* ii. 254 f., 312 f.), and Vogel (*Zur Charakteristik des Lukas*[2], 1899), has now been put practically beyond doubt by the exhaustive researches of Hawkins (*HS.* 182 f.) and Harnack (*BNT.* i. 20–87), which support the hypothesis that the diarist was the author of the third Gospel and Acts (cp. Ramsay, *Pauline and other Studies*, 301 f., and Burkitt, *Gospel History and its Transmission*, 115 f.), and that the ἡμεῖς-passages are either bona-fide extracts from his journal or (as is less likely) bona-fide reminiscences.

(*a*) When the hypothesis of a delicate personal reference is set aside, the use of the first person in these sections is held to denote, as in the case of the memoirs incorporated in Ezra (7^{27}–8^{31} 9^{1-15}) and Nehemiah (1^{1}–7^{5} 12^{27-43}), the existence of an earlier document written by some companion of Paul. While the editor must have worked over his source to some extant, as usual, he evidently chose to leave the first person plural intact for the sake, not only of vividness, but of assuring his readers that it denoted a diary, or intercalated passages from the diary, of some early Christian who had been in Paul's company at the time. Instances of this literary practice occur among the mediæval chroniclers (cp. Schwanbeck, 188 f.). Most of those who are sceptical on the Lucan authorship hold, however, that the author left the ἡμεῖς 'in order to designate himself as the companion of Paul' (Zeller, ii. 258 f.; Schmiedel, etc.), while some admit that the journal in question came from Luke—which would explain the Lucan tradition in the early church in the same way as the use of Matthew's Logia connects his name with Matthew's gospel.* When the Lucan authorship of Acts is given up, this is the most reasonable theory of the We-passages. Unless some dislocation of the text in 20^{4-5} be assumed (Weizsäcker), Timotheus (Schleiermacher, Bleek, Sorof, etc.) is ruled out, along with the other six companions who accompanied Paul by the inland route from Greece to Troas.† The introduction of Timotheus (16^{1-3}), not long before the beginning of the journal, does not tell in favour of his authorship; and although after 16^{18} Silas alone is mentioned, Timotheus is soon referred to in $17^{14f.}$. The entire silence of Acts upon Titus does not preclude the hypothesis that Luke might have employed a diary by that companion of Paul (Horst, Krenkel's *Paulus*, 214 f.; Jacobsen, O. Holtzmann, Seufert in *ZWT*, 1885, 367 f.), in which case the genuine notice of 2 Ti 4^{10} cannot refer to the imprisonment of Cæsarea; for, if Titus had left for Dalmatia, he could not have written Ac 27–28.

(*b*) The passages marked by ἡμεῖς need not, however, represent the entire original diary. Luke must have omitted certain parts of it;‡ 16^{17} has no connection with 20^{5} beyond the fact that Philippi is the scene, nor has 21^{18} with 27^{1}; and even if the writer had left Philippi before the final scene between Paul and the slave-girl, it is almost impossible to suppose that, some years later, he resumed his memoranda without a break in the terms of 20^{5-6}. That the We-sections originally belonged to a larger work is fairly certain. Why Luke selected these and only these passages, is another and a very delicate question, which is only partly solved by the hypothesis that traces of this source may be found elsewhere in Acts, in places where Luke has re-written parts of it freely in the third person. Probably the substance of 16^{18-24} 20^{16-38} and 26, at least, belonged to the source, though the diarist may not have been an actual eye-witness of the scenes, and though Luke, perhaps on that account, has worked them over pretty carefully. Spitta, Jüngst, Hilgenfeld, van Manen, and Wendt make the We-passages part of larger, more or less complete sources, which run all through Acts; Soltau finds a We-record of Luke in $16^{6-24\ (35-40)}$ 20^{2-16} $21^{1-20a.\ 27-30}$ 22^{23-29} $23^{11-24.\ 32-35}$ 24^{24}–25^{13} 25^{23-27} 27^{1}–28^{16}; but none of these reconstructions, even (cp. *e.g.* 11^{28}) with the aid of the 'Western' text, is much more than problematical (cp. Weizsäcker, *AA*. i. 242 f.; McGiffert, *AA*. 238 f.).

* The stylistic data (see below) tell against the hypothesis (Sorof, Gercke, Norden, and Soltau) of Acts as the later edition of a Lucan work which already included the We-sections. Bacon's theory (*Story of St. Paul*, 152 f., 193 f.) that they were a report to the churches of Paul's collecting mission, written by the 'brother' of 2 Co 8^{18-21}, is needlessly subtle.

† Mayerhoff (*Historisch-critische Einl. in die petrin. Schriften*, 1835, pp. 1–30) argued that Timotheus was the real author of the 'Lucan' writings, and that Luke's share in them was quite subordinate. This fails to explain how the latter's name ever became associated with the books.

‡ The second and third extracts both close with *on the next day*, though the Greek phrase is different (τῇ δὲ ἐχομένῃ, 20^{15}; τῇ δὲ ἐπιούσῃ, 21^{18}).

§ 5. *Authorship.*—The strong case for identifying the diarist with the historian simplifies the problem of the authorship considerably.

To begin with, (*a*) the third gospel and Acts are by the same author. Each has a special vocabulary of its own (Gospel over 250, Acts over 400 words), due partly to the difference of subject-matter, partly to the versatility and compass of Luke's literary power. On the other hand, while Acts has only about a dozen words peculiar to itself and Matthew (excluding βαρέως, καμμύω, παχύνομαι, and ἐπιβαίνω as occurring in LXX citations), and 14 peculiar to itself and Mk., no fewer than 57 occur in the NT only in the third gospel and in Acts (56, if δούλη, which occurs in a LXX citation, be omitted). Even the words and phrases absent from one and present in the other of the two Lucan books are neither numerous nor weighty. Of about 20, used fairly often in Acts and absent from the gospel, 8 are not used by the other synoptists (ἀναλαμβάνω only in Mk 16^{19}); 7 others occur in Mt. and Mk. (γένος, ἐπαύριον, δραμα, προσκαρτερεῖν, προσλαμβάνομαι, τέρας, and χιλίαρχος) where Lk. has no parallel passage, while χωρίον only occurs in Mt 26^{36} (Mk 14^{32}) apropos of Gethsemane, which Lk. does not mention. Lk., again, often uses about 30 words and phrases (like ἀγαθοποιέω, ἀγαπάω, ἁμαρτωλός, βίος, διαλογίσμος, ἔλεος, νομικός, ὁμοίως. οὐχί . . . ἀλλά πλούσιος, and στραφείς), which are absent from Acts, just as 10 or 11, like κελεύω and συνέρχομαι, are much more common in Acts than in its predecessor. But such variations in diction are of as little cumulative weight as the corresponding differences in style, such as the gospel's entire avoidance of the habit, so common in Acts (*e.g.* 2^{38} 5^{9} $9^{5.\ 11}$ 10^{15} 19^{2} 25^{22} $26^{25.\ 28\text{-}29}$), of omitting *he said* or its equivalents, or of using εἴπας (Ac 7^{37} 22^{24} 24^{22} 27^{35}), or of beginning a sentence with καὶ νῦν (Ac 3^{17} 10^{5} 13^{11} 16^{37} $20^{22.\ 25}$ 22^{16} 23^{21} 26^{6}). The Lucan ἐγένετο . . καί occurs but once in Acts (5^{7}); ἐγένετο with a finite verb, and ἄνθρωπε (Lk 5^{20} etc.) never, whilst the latter book is comparatively sparing in its employment of terms and phrases like ἀπὸ τοῦ νῦν (18^{6}), ἐν τῷ with infin., ἐξέρχομαι ἀπό, καὶ οὗτος (nomin.), ὁ αὐτὸς, ὄνομα (=by name), and πλήν, which are specially characteristic of the gospel. Again, while the greater frequency of πνεῦμα ἅγιον, ἀνακρίνω, and ἀπολογέομαι in Acts may be due in part to the exigencies of the subject, it is noticeable that μὲν οὖν and τε occur far more frequently in the second volume. Yet the resemblances far outnumber such variations. The specially Lucan use of ἄν or τίς with the optative, of ἄρχοντες (Jewish), of ἐγένετο δέ, of εἴη (optat.), of εἶπεν(αν) δέ, of ἐν ταῖς ἡμέραις ταύταις, of καθ' ἡμέραν, of καλούμενος with names or titles, of ὀνόματι (=by name), of πᾶς (ἅπας) ὁ λαός, of πρός with verbs of speaking, of προστίθεναι,* of σύν,† of τις with nouns, of τοῦ with the infinitive, of ὡς (=when), etc., runs through both volumes. They corre-

* "His use of it probably arose from his medical pursuits, as it was a very frequent and necessary word in medical language" (Hobart, p. 104, adding numerous medical citations).

† Again attributed (Hobart, 253 f.), though fancifully, to Luke's medical training, on the ground that the works of Galen show how remarkably often this preposition was in a physician's mouth.

spond so closely in size, in style, and in general spirit (cp. *e.g.* parallels like 1^{1}=Ac 15^{24-25}, 1^{89}=Ac 1^{15}, 1^{66}=Ac 11^{21}, 2^{18}=Ac 7^{42}, 3^{10} etc.=Ac 2^{37} etc. (τί ποιήσωμεν), 4^{25}=Ac 7^{11} (11^{28}), 4^{41}=Ac 18^{20} (5^{42}), 9^{51}=Ac 2^{13}, 12^{14}=Ac 7^{27}, 15^{20}=Ac 20^{37}, 18^{2}=Ac $24^{2.5}$, 20^{1}=Ac 4^{1}, 21^{15}=Ac 6^{10}, 23^{1}=Ac 5^{17}, 24^{14}= Ac 26^{31}) that, although the hypothesis that both works did not come from the same pen still crops up occasionally, *e.g.* in the pages of Sorof, Hilgenfeld, Soltau, Gercke ('Der δεύτερος λόγος des Lukas und die Apgeschichte,' *Hermes*, 1894, 373 f.), and even Norden (*Das antike Kunstprosa*, ii. 483 f.), it should nowadays be decently interred under the epitaph, 'non fui, fui, non sum.' Adequate statements of the case for a single author are given by Zeller (in Zeller-Overbeck, ii. 213 f.), Friedrich (*Das Lukas-Evglm und die Apgeschichte, Werke desselben Verfassers*, 1890), Jacquier (*INT.* iii. 7 f.), Sir J. C. Hawkins (*HS.*² 174–193), and Goodspeed (*JBL.*, 1912, 92 f.).

(*b*) The author was a physician.

The 'medical' element in the language of the third gospel and Acts, though several times noted (cp. *e.g.* J. D. Winckler, *De Luca Evangelista medico*, Leipzig, 1736), was first fully worked out by Dr. W. K. Hobart (*The Medical Language of St. Luke*, 1882), whose materials have recently been sifted with results which converge on the thesis that the author of both works was a Greek physician, and therefore, inferentially, the Luke of the NT. Since the following abstract was written, Harnack's study (*BNT.* i. 175–198; cp. Zahn's *Einl.* § 62; Chase, *Credibility of Acts*, 13 f.; and Plummer's *Luke*, pp. lxiii f.) has proved this pretty conclusively.

Too much stress need not be laid on the fact that in his gospel Luke alone quotes the medical proverb, *Physician, heal thyself* (4^{23}), and omits (8^{43}) the disparaging comment of Mk. on the profession, or employs words like βάτος (6^{44}; the bramble 'was extensively used by the ancient physicians,' Hobart), μανία (Ac 26^{24}), πρηνής * (Ac 1^{18}), and βρύχειν (Ac 7^{54}); but evidence of his early studies and professional training may be discovered in his methods of (*a*) describing the cures of Jesus and others, the choice of the technical terms for convulsions (ῥίπτειν) and damage to the system (βλάπτειν 4^{35}, only elsewhere in NT in Mk 16^{18}) as well as for a doctor's examination (ἐπιβλέπειν, 9^{38}), of πλήρης λέπρας (5^{12}) after the medical use of πλήρης, of the correct medical term παραλελυμένος (5^{18}, Ac 9^{33}) for the popular παραλυτικός, as well as the use of the technical classification of fevers into *great* and *small* (4^{38}, so Galen), of ἐνοχλεῖν (6^{18}) and ὀχλεῖν (Ac 5^{16}), repeatedly used by Hippokrates and Galen for diseased persons, of ἀνακαθίζειν (7^{14}, Ac 9^{40}, the medical expression for a patient sitting up in bed), of ἔκστασις in the sense of a trance (11^{5} 22^{17}, Ac 10^{10}), of ἀνακύπτειν for the straightening of the spine (13^{11}), of a remarkable number of professional terms in $10^{30f.}$ $16^{19f.}$ (Hobart, pp. 26 f.) and Ac 3^{1-8} (pp. 35 f.), of ἀποπίπτειν and λεπίς (Ac 9^{17-19}), ἐπιπίπτειν and ἀχλύς (Ac 13^{11}), and the technical ἀπαλλάσσειν (Ac 19^{12}); (*b*) in his choice of medical terms † to express ordinary ideas or

---

* Chase's theory that πρηνής is a technical medical term for 'swollen' or 'inflamed' (*JTS.*, 1912, pp. 278 f., 415) is discussed by Harnack (*TLZ.*, 1912, 235 f.) and Rendel Harris (*AJT.*, 1914, 127 f.).

† Thrice at least in the We-journal (20^{8-9}=καταφέρεσθαι and ὕπνος βαθύς, 28^{3-8} πίμπρασθαι and καταπίπτειν, πυρετοί plur. of an individual, $27^{9.22}$

events;* *e.g.* the substitution, for other terms, of the medical πλήμμυρα, προσέρρηξεν, συνέπεσε, and ῥῆγμα (Lk 6^{48-49}), of λυσιτελεῖν (17^{2}, so Hippokrates), of παρατήρησις (17^{20}) and παρατηρεῖν, of ἰκμάς (med. = juices) and συμφύεσθαι (Dioskorides) in 8^{6-7}, of πτύσσειν (med. = roll up a bandage) in 4^{20} (never elsewhere in this sense), of βελόνη (= surgical needle) in 18^{25}, of παράδοξα (med. = unexpected recovery, etc.) in 5^{26}, of the common medical terms διανέμειν (Ac 4^{17}), διάστημα (Ac 5^{7}), εὔθετος (9^{62} 14^{35}, cp. Ac 27^{12}), διανυκτερεύειν (6^{12}), διαπραγματεύεσθαι (19^{15}), εὐπορία (Ac 19^{25}, common med. term, so vb.), πιέζειν (6^{38}), ἐκλείπειν (med. = failure of pulse, etc.) in 16^{9} and 22^{32}, of ἀνάπηρος and ζεῦγος in $14^{13.\ 19}$, of δραχμή and μνᾶ in 15^{8} and 19^{13} ('the common weights employed in dispensing medicines and in writing prescriptions'), of φόβητρα (21^{11}, a rare word which Hippokrates uses of the terrifying objects in delirium), of προσδοκία (21^{26}, Ac 12^{11}, med. = expectation of fatal result, so προσδοκᾶν), of σάλος (21^{25}, med. = tossings of sick), of κραιπάλη (21^{34}, med. = drunken nausea), of θεωρία (23^{48}), of λῆρος (24^{11}, med. = raving in delirium), ἀσκεῖν (Ac 24^{16}, med. = practise), περιμένειν (Ac 1^{4}), ἀποκατάστασις (3^{21}), ἀσιτία (in medical sense, cp. J. R. Madan, *JTS.* vi. 116), αὐγή (20^{11}, med. = light), διαπρίειν (5^{33} 7^{54}), ἐκδιηγεῖσθαι (15^{3}, cp. Hobart, p. 229), ἐκπηδᾶν (14^{14}), ἐπακροᾶσθαι (16^{25}, med. = auscultation), ἐπικουρία (26^{22}), ζήτημα (15^{2} etc., med. = a disputed point), καταστέλλειν (19^{35}), τιμωρεῖν (22^{5} 26^{11}), ὑποζώννυμι (27^{17}),† ὑποστέλλειν ($20^{20.\ 27}$, in sense of 'withhold'), χρώς (19^{12}; 'the use of χ., to mean the body, not the skin, continued in medical language from Hippokrates to Galen,' Hobart), and φιλανθρώπως (27^{3});‡ (*c*) in his practice of avoiding Mt.'s use of words like μαλακία or βασανίζειν for sickness (the former = effeminacy or delicacy, the latter = examine, in med.

παραινεῖν, med. = opinion of doctor) a medical flavour is to be detected; even the collocation of ἄσιτος and διατελεῖν (Ac 27^{33}) is found in Galen. Terms like ἐρείδειν, διαφεύγειν, and κολυμβᾶν (in sense of swimming) were also in medical use.

* The eleven compounds or derivatives of βάλλειν, the five of νεύειν, the four of ψύχειν, the three of τρέχειν, and the two of ἐλαύνειν, peculiar to Luke, are all characteristic medical expressions (Hobart, pp. 137–146, 166 f., 191 f., 206 f.); while Luke's preference for terms like ὑπερῷον instead of ὑπερῴη, for ὑπεροpᾶν, συγχέειν and σύγχυσις, συναρπάζειν, μεστοῦσθαι, προσπήγνυμι, διασπείρειν, διάγνωσις and διαγινώσκειν, ἐνέδρα, ἐνεδρεύειν, κατόρθωμα, κατὰ λόγον, ἐπιμελεῖσθαι, ἐπιμελῶς, εὐθυμεῖν(-ως), and the three main medical terms for "stimulating" (ἐπεγείρειν, παροτρύνειν, and προτρέπειν), lies parallel. Hippokrates also, in his epistles (μία πόλεων οὐκ ἄσημος), uses ἄσημος of a city (Ac 21^{39}), and ἀναδιδόναι of a letter being delivered (Ep. 1275, cp. Acts 23^{33}).

† This rare term for undergirding a ship was common in medical parlance, being applied to the membrane or pleura which undergirt and supported the thorax; so that, as Hobart suggests (273), its application in this case may have been natural to Luke, particularly as a ship's sides were called πλευραί. Similarly θέρμη (28^{3}), for θερμότης, is the usual medical term for heat.

‡ Both Hippokrates and Galen (Hobart, 296–297) were strong upon φιλανθρωπία as an essential note of the true physician.

terminology), and the confusion* between συκομορέα and συκάμινος (17[6] 19[4]). "Nearly all the alterations and additions which the third evangelist has made in the Marcan text are most simply and surely explained from the professional interest of a physician" (Harnack, *BNT.* iii. 187). As this 'medical' element is spread over both the third gospel and Acts, instead of being confined to the 'We-sections,' it corroborates the argument, which is also the tradition of the second century (as early as Marcion, for the third gospel) that the author of the third gospel and Acts was the Luke of Col 4[14], Philem [24], and 2 Ti 4[10].

The linguistic data, however, do not support the common inference that Luke was strongly affected by Paul's style and language, and that therefore he was either a Paulinist or acquainted with the Pauline epistles. Out of about 98 words peculiar to Lk. and Paul in the NT, 17 occur only in the Pastoral epistles, and 8 in Ephesians, which reduces the number at once to 73. Of these, Mt. and Mk. had no occasion to use one or two like ἀροτριάω, while διαγγέλλω, μήτρα, στεῖρος, and σωτήριον (in Paul, only in Eph 6[17] and Tit 2[11]) occur in one or the other writer merely as LXX quotations. This leaves about 68 at most, of which we must exclude in all fairness the following 27, viz. ἄδηλος, αἰχμαλωτίζω, ἀναζάω, ἀναλύω, ἀνταπόδομα, ἀνταποκρίνομαι, ἀσφάλεια, ἄτοπος,† διερμηνεύω, δόγμα, ἐγγράφομαι, ἔνδοξος (Lk. of things, Paul of persons), ἐπαναπαύομαι, ἐπέχω, ἐφίστημι, ἡσυχάζω, κυριεύω (Paul, metaph.), οἰκονομία (Paul, metaph.), παγίς, πληροφορέω, σπουδαίως, συγκλείω (Paul, metaph.), συναντιλαμβάνομαι (Paul, relig. sense), συνευδοκέω, συνοχή, ὑπωπιάζω, and ψαλμός (Lk. only of Psalter), of which some (to which ἄρα, καταξιοῦμαι, μεθίστημι, προκόπτω, σκοπέω, and συγχαίρω must be added) are used in different constructions, and all in senses which are very different in the two writers. Even of the remaining 35, quite half are neither favourite nor characteristic terms in either writer, while the numerical preponderance, as compared with Mt. and Paul (about 22) or Mk. and Paul (about 20), is not specially significant. So far as the internal evidence suggests, Luke did not use any of Paul's epistles; his acquaintance with Paul's movements and ideas is drawn from oral tradition or personal reminiscence, not from the reading of his correspondence. Some critics still (*e.g.* Soltau) consider that the Pauline speeches as well as the narratives are drawn from materials provided by the Epistles (so formerly Jacobsen, *op. cit.* pp. 8 f.), but there is no real evidence to render this a necessary hypothesis (cp. Sabatier's essay in *Bibliothèque de l'école des hautes études*, i. 1889, 202 f.; Moffatt, *HNT.* 416 f.; Jacquier, *INT.* iii. 96 f., and Zahn, *INT.* iii. 118 f.). The juxtaposition of Acts and the Pauline epistles in the Canon is apt to produce an optical illusion, until it is remembered that Acts was not written to be read alongside of the apostle's correspondence, and that it really contains nothing which Luke could not have obtained elsewhere.

---

* Noted by Dioskorides. The distinction was familiar to physicians, who had occasion to use both in their prescriptions.

† Add perhaps δεκτός, in Lk. of persons only, in Paul (Phil 4[18]) of things, 2 Co 6[2] and Lk 4[24] being LXX citations. It is uncertain whether ἐφυλίδιος (WH) should be read, instead of αἰφνίδιος, in Lk 21[34].

§ 6. *Characteristics and aim.*—(*a*) It is no longer necessary to controvert the theory that, when Luke wrote, Jewish and Gentile Christianity required to be reconciled, or that the parallelism between Peter and Paul is wholly due to the historian's pragmatism. Luke's position is that of the later church, as reflected, *e.g.*, in Mt 28^{18-20}; the Gentile mission was carried out by the twelve in obedience to a revelation of Jesus (cp. *HD.* i. 158 f., 213 f.). According to Acts, Peter, as the leader of the apostles, not only took the first step in this direction ($10^{1f.}$), but claimed that this was his commission (Ac 15^7); also, between the twelve and Paul there was no vital difference on the burning question of Gentile Christianity. Luke smoothes over the crucial antagonism which Gal 1–2 reveals. He prefers to emphasise the common loyalty of both sides to the gospel of Jesus; "trop loyal pour condamner son maître Paul, trop orthodoxe pour ne pas se ranger à l'opinion officielle qui prévalait, il effaça les différences de doctrines pour laisser voir seulement le but commun que tous ces grands fondateurs poursuivirent" (Renan, ii. p. xxiii). His whole treatment of the question breathes the air of an age when the rights of Gentile Christianity had long ago been won, and when even an admirer of Paul, especially in writing for the particular object defined in Lk 1^{1-4}, was more concerned to emphasise the providential development upon which the church looked back than to revive the bitter memories of a bygone phase of controversy.

This irenical attitude, with its idealising spirit, is not inconsistent with the Lucan authorship, even though we assumed that Luke was familiar with the exact course of events as, *e.g.*, Paul describes them in Gal $2^{1f.}$. A man may surely be the friend and physician of a great church-leader, without necessarily sharing or even understanding all his religious opinions and without assenting to his ecclesiastical policy in every respect. Luke had more in his mind than to be a protagonist of Paul, and we have no right to demand that consciously or unconsciously he must come into line with the apostle. In spite of the arguments or rather the assumptions to the contrary,*

* This idea underlies the criticisms passed by Schürer (*TLZ.*, 1906, 405–408), Bousset (*TR.*, 1908, 185–205), Clemen (*TR.*, 1907, 97–113, and *HJ.*, 1910, 780 f.), and Lake (*DAC.* i. 719 f.) on the Lucan hypothesis as argued by Harnack (*BNT.* i. 121 f., *TLZ.*, 1906, 466–468) and Stanton (*GHD.* ii. 241–255). The 'theological' attitude of Acts, when it is not isolated and exaggerated, does not seem incompatible with the Lucan authorship, for which the literary evidence is fairly conclusive, provided that it is not mixed up with extravagant claims for Luke as a historian, or with harmonising, conservative expedients.

on the part of conservative and radical critics alike, it does not follow that Acts, if written by Luke, must tally, historically and theologically, with Paul, or that Luke's statements must invariably exhibit (cp. p. 268) agreement with the apostle's epistles. Luke's object was neither to correct nor to elucidate these epistles. He was not a Paulinist (cp. Harnack, *BNT.* i. 139 f., iv. 30–89), and even had he been an eye-witness of certain events, that would not necessarily prevent him from describing them years afterwards in semi-historic fashion. To a modern reader it does appear difficult to understand how any one who had shared in the Pauline mission could describe the relation of baptism and the Spirit, the glossolalia, and above all the relation between Paul and the pillar-apostles, as Luke has done; but once allowance is made for the time at which and the purpose for which Luke wrote, once the idea that he was a Paulinist is abandoned, and once we recognise the freedom with which he treated the sources and traditions at his disposal for Acts as for his gospel, the admitted difficulties can no longer break through the strong thicket of linguistic evidence in favour of the Lucan authorship.

Luke's idealisation of the primitive council at Jerusalem does not prevent him from mentioning the fate of Ananias and Sapphira. Nor, although he ignores the scene at Antioch, does he hesitate to tell how Paul lost his temper twice. There were physicians and physicians among the historians of the ancient world. One of them, Kallimorphos, is pilloried by Lucian (*de hist. conscrib.* 16) for having written a *προοίμιον ὑπέρψυχρον* to his history of the Parthians, in which he vaunted: *οἰκεῖον εἶναι ἰατρῷ ἱστορίαν συγγράφειν, εἴ γε ὁ 'Ασκληπιὸς μὲν 'Απόλλωνος υἱὸς, 'Απόλλων δὲ Μουσηγέτης καὶ πάσης παιδείας ἄρχων.* In Acts there is no empty rhetoric. There are no eulogies of the early Christians, not even of Paul. Luke knew, better even than the author of the *Vita Agricolæ*, what Lucian meant when he spoke of the broad gulf between history and panegyric (*de hist. conscrib.* 7, *οὐ στενῷ τῷ ἰσθμῷ διώρισται καὶ διατετείχισται ἡ ἱστορία πρὸς τὸ ἐγκώμιον*); his literary taste, as well as his religious feeling, prevented him from painting the great apostle of the Gentiles with a halo.

(*b*) A similar consideration bears upon Luke's treatment of the supernatural. On the one hand, the presence of miraculous anecdotes (cp. Harnack, *BNT.* iii. 133–161) is no proof that they are unprimitive. A comparison, *e.g.*, of the historical traditions gathering round figures like St. Patrick or even Thomas à Becket will show that it is the most natural thing in the world for such stories to spring up within a man's lifetime, and the mushroom of legend appeared under certain conditions as rapidly in the East as in the West. This applies in some degree to the miracles in Acts as well as to those in the gospels. On the other hand, their presence in Acts is no disproof of Luke's authorship.* He took most of them from his available sources

* Luke's three defects as a historian, according to Harnack (*BNT.* iii. p. xxxix), are credulity, a tendency to be careless and inaccurate, and a tendency to work up important situations. Still, he adds, "ich halte ihn

and inserted them for the sake of bringing out a point vividly. It is psychologically accurate to hold that even the special class of tales about demoniac possession, which as an educated physician he might be supposed to have disbelieved, were accepted by him on the score of his Christian beliefs (cp. J. Naylor in *HJ.*, 1909, 28–46: "it is certain that the phenomena he witnessed in Christian circles made it easy for him to believe in demoniac causes of diseases"; "he was led to believe in the power of faith in the sick, and of personality in Paul and Christ, to work marvellous cures and do mighty works"). The supernaturalism of stories like $2^{1f.}$ 5^{1-11} $12^{1f.}$ $16^{25f.}$ $19^{11f.}$ and $20^{9f.}$, which are near the level of popular Oriental tales, does not tell against either the likelihood that in some cases a nucleus of historic fact underlies the moral apologue, or the probability that the writer (or editor) was an educated man who, like Luke, must have been familiar with, *e.g.*, the real glossolalia of the Pauline churches. We know so little about Luke that it is impossible to determine how far he worked in the spirit of the advice given by Lucian (*de hist. conscrib.* 60) to his friend Philo: *καὶ μὴν καὶ μῦθος εἴ τις παρεμπέσοι, λεκτέος μέν, οὐ μὴν πιστωτέος πάντως, ἀλλ' ἐν μεσῳ θετέος τοῖς ὅπως ἂν ἐθέλωσιν εἰκάσουσι περὶ αὐτοῦ· σὺ δ' ἀκίνδυνος καὶ πρὸς οὐδέτερον ἐπιρρεπέστερος.* Probably, his attitude to the miraculous stories of Acts was more naive. There is no hint of any Blougram-like reserve in his method of narrating these episodes; on the contrary, we can feel the same realistic and materialising tendency which appears in his recasting of the resurrection stories. There is little force, therefore, in the argument that his version of the glossolalia in $2^{1f.}$ could not have come from an eye-witness of the phenomena, *e.g.*, at Corinth. Even if Luke knew the latter, this would not have prevented him from repeating the embellished and circumstantial miracle which he found in his source. "That it involved a miracle attracted rather than repelled him. . . . He loves a good miracle" (P. Gardner in *Cambridge Biblical Essays*, p. 390).

(*c*) A subordinate aim is to exhibit the political inoffensiveness of Christianity. Paul is never formally condemned by the Roman authorities (cp. the conduct of the proconsuls in 13^{12} 18^{12} etc., and of the Asiarchs in 19^{31}); Luke skilfully omits any

innerhalb der griechischen Historik trotz seiner offenkundigen Gebrechen und Leichtgläubigkeiten für einen respektablen Berichterstatter, Schriftsteller und Zeugen" (*TLZ.*, 1906, 467; cp. Wendland, *HBNT.* i. 2. 324 f., 330 f.).

allusion to the three occasions when he had been flogged by lictors (2 Co 11[25]), and emphasises his Roman citizenship. As in the third gospel (cp. *e.g.* 20[20-26]), so in its sequel, the historian points out that Christians were admittedly loyal (cp. 18[14f.] 19[37] 23[29] 25[18f. 25] 26[31]), though it is hardly fanciful to detect in his references to ἐξουσία or the authority of civil powers (in his gospel 4[6-7] ‖ Mt 4[9], 12[4-5] ‖ Mt 10[28], 22[25] ‖ Mk 10[42] and Mt 20[25]) a less favourable view than that of Acts (cp. E. A. Abbott, *Diat.* 1565–1571), where the allusions to Roman officials are upon the whole respectful and intended to be irenical. He is careful to expose the hollowness of the charge of sedition brought against Christians especially by malevolent Jews, and such passages further contain an implicit plea for the toleration by Rome of Christianity as a *religio licita* no less than of the Judaism from which it sprang and of which, as Luke is careful to point out, it forms the true consummation.

Some (*e.g.* D. Plooij, *Exp.*[8] viii. 511 f., xiii. 108 f.; cp. P. I. Melle in *Theol. Studiën*, 1915, 111 f.) even hold that Acts was the defence entered by Luke at Paul's trial before Nero on the charges of 24[5]; J. Weiss (*Absicht*, 54 f.) more moderately brings out the author's desire to portray the innocent character of Christianity in view of suspicions aroused in part by the charges levelled at it by Jews (cp. *e.g.* p. 31, *à propos* of 16[20f. 37] "Die hochmütig-geringschätzige Anschauung, die in der Denunciation zum Ausdruck kommt, wird nachträglich glänzend zurückgewiesen. Die apostel sind nicht hergelaufene Agenten einer orientalischen Nation, in deren Dienste sie eine staatlich nicht unbedenkliche Propaganda treiben, sie sind Römer so gut wie die Richter auch und wollen nach römischen Recht beurteilt werden. Was aber hier von den Aposteln gesagt ist, das gilt im Sinne des Verf. vom Christenthum überhaupt"). So far as this bears on the problem of the date, it leaves any period open after Nero. The motive would be as relevant shortly after Domitian's persecution as before it, since the vehement anti-Roman tone of the Apocalypse was by no means normal.

(*d*) For Luke's remarkable degree of accuracy in geographical, political, and social data, it is sufficient to refer to the essays of Lightfoot (*Essays on 'Supernatural Religion,'* 1889, 291–302) and Vigouroux (*Le Nouveau Testament et les découvertes archéologiques modernes*, Paris, 1896, pp. 183–332), and to the epoch-making researches of Sir W. M. Ramsay (*CRE.*, chs. ii.–viii. etc.). Still, he must be judged by the canons of his age, and in the light of his opportunities. Not only as regards the origins of the Palestinian church and mission, but even on the earlier part of Paul's career, he is plainly writing at second-hand. As the book proceeds, the level of historicity rises on the whole. The nearer Luke comes to his own period, the less liable he is to discrepancies and errors, although even here the ordinary conditions of the period must be taken into account in an evaluation of his testimony as an eye-witness. For the first part of the story, however, he had to rely upon such information of primitive Christians as may have been available, or upon certain written sources, *e.g.*, for Stephen and Philip. Thus in the circles to which he had access it is altogether likely that the crisis at Antioch and Jerusalem would sometimes be viewed very differently from what Paul considered to be its real inwardness,* and the lapse of nearly half a century was certain to alter not only the standpoint of his own judgment, but also the memories upon which he drew. Owing to distance from the time and place, he was imperfectly acquainted with much that transpired in Palestine during the early decades of the Christian movement. But here as elsewhere he knew more than he chose to put down. His omissions are not invariably due to lack of available knowledge; they are sometimes intentional. The choice of episodes, the relative scope assigned to them, the passing over of years either silently or in a sentence, the ignoring of a figure like Titus, the indifference towards such movements of Christianity in the East as Peter's evangelisation of Asia Minor and Paul's mission in North Galatia,—all these phenomena show that Luke had no intention of writing the history of early Christianity, and that even his reconstruction of that history requires to be reset at more points than one (cp. Wendt in *HJ.* xii. 141–161).

The speeches in the earlier part may represent not untrustworthily the primitive Jewish-Christian preaching of the period (Peter, 1^{15-22} 2^{14-36} 3^{12-26} 4^{8-12} 5^{29-32}; Gamaliel,† 5^{35-39}). "To the doctrinal discourses of Peter we may in a certain sense grant that they faithfully represent the primitive preaching of the messiah by the apostles, and that so far they possess a certain originality" (Overbeck).‡ This is due, not to any verbatim reports or Hellenistic versions being available, but to the

* Cp. Franke in *SK.* (1890) 668 f., J. Warschauer in *New World* (1898), pp. 722–749, and Watkins in *St. Paul's Fight for Galatia* (pp. 94 f.).

† Chase, *Credibility*, pp. 122–159 (pp. 167 f., on Paul's speeches).

‡ So especially Riehm, *op. cit.* pp. 126 f.; Chase, *op. cit.* 105 f.; W. Lock (*Exp.*[4] vii. 178–190); and E. F. Scott's *The Beginnings of the Church* (1914). Mayerhoff (*Einl. in die petrin. Schriften*, 218–233) makes them, as well as Stephen's and Paul's, free compositions of the author.

excellent historical sense of the author, who, while following the ordinary methods of ancient historiography in the composition of such speeches, was careful to avoid moulding and shaping his materials with a freedom which should obliterate the special cast of their aim and temper. These materials were probably furnished in the main by oral tradition. Preaching so continuous as we know that of Peter to have been, would leave definite reminiscences of its general type and tenor. A skilful writer, having access to circles where such Jewish Christian ideas had been cherished and still lingered (*e.g.* John Mark), would find little difficulty in composing discourses such as these, which would harmonise satisfactorily with the period he was engaged in depicting. Of the later speeches, that at Miletus is probably nearest to a summary of the original words of Paul; the others, for the most part, reflect in the main Luke's historic sense of what was appropriate to the speaker and situation. Stephen's speech is the most notable exception; it obviously was derived from a special source.

The letter of Claudius Lysias to Felix (Ac 23^{25-30}) might have been verbally copied from the original, if Luke had had access to the archives or private papers of Felix. Instances of this are not unknown (*e.g.* Sallust, *Catil.* 34, 3; 44, 5), but they are extremely rare, and the more probable hypothesis is that the letter, like the speeches of the history, must be ascribed to Luke himself, in common with the universal practice of his age. The same holds true of the letter in 15^{23-29} (cp. Harnack, *BNT.* i. 219–223), though this document probably embodies a source as its nucleus (see above, pp. 42–43).

The last-named passage opens up a cluster of textual, literary, and historical problems which have a profound bearing upon the authorship and authority of Acts. The problem was, what are the conditions upon which Gentile Christians can be saved, *i.e.* participate in the messianic reign of Jesus the Christ? The strict Jewish Christians of the capital (*τινες τῶν ἀπὸ τῆς αἱρέσεως τῶν Φαρισαίων πεπιστευκότες*) insisted on circumcision and the complete observance of the Mosaic law. A keen controversy took place among the apostles and elders. Finally, Peter repudiated this claim on the score of practice. Facts had already proved that Gentiles could believe in Jesus Christ and receive the Spirit which guaranteed membership in his kingdom, without submitting to the law. Barnabas and Paul corroborate this from their own experience in the mission-field, while James clinches it by an appeal to messianic prophecy, and proposes that, though the claim for legal submission should be repudiated, the Gentile Christians should be enjoined to abstain from εἰδωλόθυτα, αἷμα, πνικτά, and πορνεία.* A formal decree (ἔδοξεν τῷ πνεύματι τῷ ἁγίῳ καὶ ἡμῖν) to this effect, in the shape of a pastoral epistle, is dispatched to the Gentile Christians of Antioch, Syria, and Cilicia. The course of events is not so clear, however, as at first sight appears. No proper motive is given for the sudden interference of the narrower Palestinian Christians with the church at Antioch (15^{1}). Psychologically, the reaction would come better after 11^{21-22}; it is difficult to see how such a recrudescence of legalism could take place after Peter had settled, as he is said to have done, the question of the rights of uncircumcised Gentiles to membership in the church (11^{1-18}). Furthermore, the decrees of $15^{23f.}$ are sent not to the Pauline churches in Lystra, Iconium, etc., but to the Gentile Christians of Antioch, Syria, and Cilicia; and if they were merely meant to meet a local emergency, this is hardly Luke's conception of their place and purpose (see Appendix N).

The silence of Paul in Gal 2 upon the decree of Ac 15 tells against the historicity of the latter, if the fourfold prohibition was its main message, and if it was promulgated at the Jerusalem council. It is conceivable that Paul might have agreed to a number of concessions for the sake of peace and harmony, but "that he consented to, or was party to, a *demand* that his converts should observe these four legal conditions is not only disproven by his own clear words, but by the absence of any such precept in his letters to Gentile churches on this matter" (Forbes, p. 54). If he had distributed the decrees as Luke says he did (16^{4}), it may be questioned if he could or would have treated them in his epistles as a *quantité négligeable* (cp. *EBi.* 916 f.; Bacon, *Story of St. Paul*, 138 f., 151 f.). Unless, therefore, the authenticity of the decree or the Lucan authorship is to be abandoned, the alternatives apparently are (i.) to adopt the Western reading of Ac 15, as has been done recently by Hilgenfeld (*ZWT.*, 1899, 138 f.), G. Resch in a careful monograph *TU.* xiii. 3, 1905; cp. *Exp.*[7] iii. 564 f.), R. Steinmetz, *Das Aposteldekret* (1911), and with vigour by Harnack (*BNT.* iii. 248 f.); or (ii.) adhering to the ordinary text, to conjecture that Luke has antedated a decree† which only came into existence at a later period in the history of the Jerusalem church, viz. some time between Paul's composition of Galatians

* Halévy (*RS.*, 1902, 228 f.), like Bentley, proposes to read πορκείας or χοιρείας, on the ground that the change of this into πορνείας would be more intelligible than *vice versa*, and that this reading is in line with the other allusions to food.

† Achelis, *Urc.* pp. 60 f. The Western form is rejected after careful scrutiny by Diehl, Coppieters (*RB.*, 1907, 34–54), and A. Seeberg (*Die beiden Wege und das Aposteldekret*, 1906).

and Corinthians on the one hand and his arrival (21^{25}) at Jerusalem on the other (so, especially, Weizsäcker, *AA.* i. 313 f.; Grimm, *SK.*, 1880, 622 f.; McGiffert, *AA.* 215 f.; Pfleiderer, *Urc.* ii. 241 f.; von Dobschütz, *Urc.* 152 f.; R. Knopf, *SNT.* i. 2. 65; Bousset; Diehl, *ZNW.*, 1909, 277–296), in any case prior to the composition of the Apocalypse (2^{14}). The decree would thus be the work of James and his party, whether brought down to Antioch by the emissaries of the former (McGiffert, Bacon) or, more probably, promulgated at some later period. It is noticeable that in 21^{25} James tells Paul about it, as if the latter had not heard of it before. This tells in favour of the second hypothesis, as against either the former or the bolder conjecture that Gal 2^{1-10} did not refer to the scene of Ac 15 at all (see above, pp. 100 f.).

The shorter Western form of 15^{29}, which omits (so Wellhausen and Lake) *καὶ πνικτῶν* and inserts, between *πορνείας* and *ὧν*, the words *καὶ ὅσα μὴ θέλετε ἑαυτοῖς γίνεσθαι ἑτέρῳ μὴ ποιεῖν, ἀφ'*, with *φερόμενοι ἐν τῷ ἁγίῳ πνεύματι* between *πράξετε* and *ἔρρωσθε*, cannot have arisen later than the middle of the second century, as it is guaranteed not only in D but in Irenæus (iii. 12, 14), Tertullian (*de pudic.* 12), and Cyprian (*Testim.* iii. 119). On the other hand, it resembles a moral catechism rather than the decree in its historical setting, and its secondary character, as compared with the canonical text, is fairly obvious. Its protest against the exaggeration of the ceremonial law, at the expense of its ethical elements, was both timely (cp. 4 Mac 5^{19-20}; Schürer, *GJV.* ii. 464 f.) and in accord with the principles of Jesus; but, instead of the ambiguous *εἰδωλόθυτον*, *εἰδωλολατρεία* would have been more apposite. The 'Western' reading avoids the difficulty of the superfluous *πνικτῶν* after *αἷμα* (in sense of 'tasting blood'), and also of understanding how Paul could be silent on the decree in Gal 2. Such injunctions would only be the obvious ethical maxims of the Christian catechism (*αἷμα* = murder). But, on the other hand, this neutral interpretation blunts the point of the council, and makes it hard to see how the controversy could have attained the proportions of Gal $2^{1f.}$.

This difficulty is bound up with another, relating to the visit of Paul to Jerusalem in 11^{30}–12^{25}. The omission of this visit in Gal 1^{17}–2^{10} has caused keen perplexity to editors of Acts and of that epistle. Why did Paul pass it over? Not because it was too hurried and short (Usteri), nor because he* was prevented from going, perhaps at the last moment (so, *e.g.*, Neander, Meyer), nor because the envoys prudently stopped in Judæa (so, *e.g.*, Credner, Bleek, in contradiction to 12^{25}). Such harmonistic expedients are not satisfactory. It would be fairer to argue that Paul, in writing Galatians, aimed not at giving any complete chronicle of his visits to Jerusalem, but only at mentioning those which affected his claim to a divine commission independent of the twelve. The two visits at which this was called, or might be supposed to have been called, in question, were his first (Gal 1^{18}) and his third (Gal $2^{1f.}$). The second visit, recorded in Ac 11^{30} 12^{25}, afforded no chance of misconception; his character and doctrine were not in dispute then, and the Galatians needed no explicit description of that journey. Hence he could pass it over, in his rapid survey, as having no bearing on the authority and independence of his gospel (so, *e.g.*, Godet, Hort, Light-

---

* Renan thinks that Barnabas alone conveyed the *chaluka*, and Zimmermann deletes *καὶ Σαύλου* (*SK.*, 1901, 454).

foot, Blass, G. H. Gilbert, Watkins (pp. 170 f.), Steinmann's *Abfassungszeit d. Galaterbriefes*, 127 f.). This is a legitimate hypothesis. Paul is not writing a protocol in Gal 1–2, which would be falsified were he to omit any visit to the Jewish capital; all his argument requires is a note of the occasions when he was brought into contact with the apostles at Jerusalem, and of this there is no mention in Ac 11^{30}, which seems even to exclude (by the reference to *the elders*) any communication between them and the Cilician evangelist.

Those who are dissatisfied with this have the choice of three alternatives. (*a*) They may delete the visit of Ac 11^{30} 12^{25} as unhistorical (so, *e.g.*, Zeller, Overbeck, Hilgenfeld, Weizsäcker, Sabatier, B. Weiss, Jülicher, Clemen's *Paulus*, i. 215 f.; Forbes), whether the historian confused (H. J. Holtzmann) the visit of Gal 2^{1} with the collection visit of 1 Co 16^{4} (which is therefore passed over at Ac 19^{21}), or whether he inserted 11^{30} and 12^{25} (with 11^{22-26a}) erroneously in the source which lay before him (Wendt, *SK.*, 1892, 270 f.). Others, *e.g.* Spitta (179 f.), Pfleiderer, Schwartz, Wellhausen, Wendland, and McGiffert (*AA.* 170 f.) improve upon this by supposing (*b*) that the visit of 11^{30} 12^{25} was the same as that of $15^{1f.}$, and that Luke, finding these two narratives of what was the same event, supposed them to refer to different incidents. This is not impossible, but the two narratives are hardly parallel enough. The object of the one visit is the conveyance of funds; the object of the other (as of Gal $2^{1f.}$) is a question of religious principle. This consideration rules out with equal certainty (*c*) the bolder and even less probable hypothesis which indentifies 11^{30} 12^{25} (not $15^{1f.}$) with Gal 2^{1-10} (so, *e.g.*, Belser, *Einl.* 168 f.; Ramsay, Weber, Gutjahr, after Fritzsche's *Opuscula*, 233 f.). Luke (in 11^{20}–12^{25}) never alludes to the circumcision-problem or to any trouble over Gentile Christians; there is not a syllable about the presence of John, Peter, and James (as in Gal $2^{4f.}$); the relative prominence of Paul in the two passages is too different to admit of both referring to the same event, even when due allowance is made for the natural emphasis on his own personality in the epistle; and it is unlikely that the circumcision-question could again emerge and be decided (as in Ac 15), after it had been once settled (as in Gal 2^{1-10}; see above, pp. 100 f.). (*d*) It is enough to mention * the identification of Paul's visit (in Gal $2^{1f.}$) with the fourth recorded by Luke (viz. in Ac 18^{22}). The visit of Ac $15^{1f.}$ would then be passed over by Paul—an omission which may be described as incredible.

§ 7. *The text.*—The remarkable phenomena of the 'Western' text had been already noted by earlier NT critics like Simon, Hug, and Credner (*Einl.* i. 452–519 f.), as well as by Lagarde in his monograph *de NT ad versionum orientalium fidem edendo* (1857), and the problem of their origin and value has been investigated by A. Resch (*Agrapha*, pp. 30 f.), J. R. Harris (*A Study of Codex Bezæ*, 1891; *Four Lectures on the Western Text*,

* So, *e.g.*, Köhler, *Versuch über die Abfassungszeit der epist. Schriften im NT u. der Apocalypse* (1830), pp. 7 f.; Wieseler's *Chronologie* (pp. 184 f.), and Bertheau, *Einige Bemerkungen über die Stelle Gal 2 u. ihr Verhältniss zur Apgeschichte* (1854), pp. 3 f. Cp. Baur's critique of Wieseler in *Theol. Jahrb.* (1849) 457–480, and M. Meinertz on Ac 15^{24} and Gal 2^{11} (*BZ.*, 1907, 392–402).

1894), F. H. Chase (*The Old Syriac Element in the text of Codex Bezæ*), and Ramsay (*CRE.*, ch. viii.), amongst others (cp. *HNT.* 611 f.). The bearing of the question upon the third gospel and Acts was brought to the front specially by F. Blass, who in a series of monographs (*SK.*, 1894, 86–119; *NKZ.*, 1895, 712 f.; *Hermathena*, ix. 121 f., 291 f.; *SK.*, 1896, 436 f., 1898, 539 f., 1900, 5 f.) argued that Luke, like several ancient authors, re-edited his works, and that the Western text represents the church-edition of the gospel and the first draft of Acts. The theory won the support, more or less, of Hilgenfeld (*ZWT.*, 1896, 625 f., 1899, 138 f., and in his edition of Acts), Belser (*TQ.*, 1897, 303 f. etc.), Haussleiter (*Theol. Lit. Blatt.*, 1896, pp. 105 f.), Dräseke (*ZWT.*, 1894, 192 f.), Zöckler (in *Greifswalder Studien*, 1895, pp. 129 f.), and Nestle (*Christliche Welt*, 1895, pp. 304 f.; *SK.*, 1896, pp. 103 f.; *Einf.* pp. 56 f., 186 f.); it is rejected by Ramsay (*Exp.*[5] i. pp. 129 f., 212 f., vi. pp. 460 f.), Chase (*Critical Review*, 1894, 303–305), Page (*Class. Rev.*, 1897, 217), Bebb (*DB.* iii. 164–165), Schmiedel (*EBi.* i. 50–56), Jülicher (*Einl.* § 32), and Jacquier (*INT.* iii. 178–184), amongst others, mainly on the ground that (i.) the phenomena of the 'Western' text are not confined to the Lucan writings; that (ii.) they are not homogeneous, but represent different strata; that (iii.) the 'original' text of Acts and the 'revised' text of the third gospel cannot be reconstructed with certainty (compare the differences between Hilgenfeld's text and that of Blass' *Acta Apostolorum secundum formam quæ videtur romanam*); and that (iv.) the later origin of the 'Western' text appears in several places (*e.g.* 5^{39} addition of *kings and tyrants*). These and other reasons for maintaining the secondary character of the Western text are put especially by Harnack (*SBBA.*, 1899, pp. 150 f., 1900, pp. 2 f.), Bousset (*TR.*, 1898, 410–414), Corssen (*GGA.*, 1896, pp. 425 f., 1901, pp. 1 f., in reviewing Hilg.'s edition of Acts), B. Weiss (*TU.* xvii. 1. pp. 52–107), Kenyon (*Textual Criticism of NT*[2], pp. 341 f.), H. Coppieters (*De Historia Textus Actorum Apostolorum dissertatio*, 1902), and Schmiedel (*EBi.* 54–56), from the standpoint of textual criticism. D may have occasionally (cp. Zahn's *Einl.* § 59) preserved the original reading,* but as a whole it cannot be ascribed to the author of Acts (see Harnack's

* According to A. Pott (*Der abendländische Text der Apgeschichte und ihr Wir-quelle*, 1900), because the editor had access to the We-source or Acta Pauli which underlies the canonical Acts.

final reply in *TLZ.* (1907) 396–401, based on a fresh examination of the D text in Ac 1–7).

If the Western text of 11^{27-28} be the original draft (ἦν δὲ πολλὴ ἀγαλλίασις. συνεστραμμένων δὲ ἡμῶν ἔφη εἷς ἐξ αὐτῶν ὀνόματι Ἄγαβος σημαίνων κτλ.; so Blass, Pfleiderer, Hilgenfeld, Zahn, F. Dibelius, J. Weiss, etc.), a strong light is thrown upon the personality of the writer. Here the *we* is not Paul's companions, but the Christian community of Antioch. Consequently, if this isolated occurrence of ἡμεῖς is to be taken along with the others, as is most natural, the writer plainly conveys the impression that he himself was a Christian of Antioch, which is not improbable (cp. Harnack, *BNT.* i. 21 f.) for other reasons (cp. the tradition in Eus. *H. E.* iii. 4, and Jerome, *uir. inlust.* 7, 'Lucas, medicus antiochensis,' etc.). But the latter fact is not bound up with this reading, which may be due to a reviser who wished to emphasise the tradition in question (cp. *ET.* xxii. 479).

One or two cases of displacement, due to copyists, may be noted. Thus 4^{33}, which is an erratic block as it lies, originally came after 4^{31}; 5^{12a} has been displaced (cp. Laurent, *NT Studien,* 138–139) from between 5^{14} and 5^{15}; there is quite a case for Cramer's (*Exegetica et Critica,* v., 1896, 34–40) suggestion that 19^{21-22} originally followed 18^{18-23}; 14^{3}, unless it is an early gloss, lay before 14^{2} (Wendt, cp. *HNT.* 671); and 26^{8} has been displaced from its site between 26^{22} and 26^{23} (Nestle, *Philologica Sacra,* 54; Wendt; Moffatt, *HNT.* 676). Such phenomena, taken together with the fact that by the middle of the second century (*i.e.* within fifty years of its composition) divergent recensions of the text were current, might suggest that Luke did not publish the book himself, while the roughnesses of the extant text, which have set correctors early at work, prompt the conjecture that the author did not manage to revise his δεύτερος λόγος for purposes of publication.

§ 8. *Date.*—(Harnack, *BNT.* iv. 90–116; J. A. Cross, *ET.* xii. 334–336, 423–425, xiii. 43–46). As Acts is a sequel to the third gospel, and as the latter was written after A.D. 70, the *terminus a quo* for the composition of the δεύτερος λόγος is determined without further ado. The time which elapsed between the two has been variously calculated (nine or ten years, Renan), but it is impossible to draw any safe inferences on this point from the more developed phase, *e.g.*, of the resurrection-stories. If Luke used Josephus (see above, pp. 29–31), the *terminus a quo* of both his works could not be earlier than A.D. 94. On other grounds the older Tübingen school relegated

Acts to the reign of Trajan or Hadrian (so Zeller-Overbeck: ii. 267–284; Schwegler, Hausrath, followed by Krenkel, Rovers: *INT.* 205 f., Schmiedel in *EBi.* 49–50, and Baljon); Pfleiderer, S. Davidson (*INT.* ii. 76–176), and Martineau (*Seat of Authority*, 267) condescend on A.D. 110–120; but others fix on the beginning of the second (so, *e.g.*, Volkmar, Weizsäcker, Holtzmann, Jacobsen, Renan: iv. ch. xix.; Jülicher, Wrede, Burkitt), or the close of the first century (so Wendt, J. Weiss, Peake, Lake). It is impossible to go earlier than *c.* A.D. 100, if it is allowed that Luke knew Josephus (*Jewish Wars* before A.D. 80; *Antiq.*, A.D. 93–94). In this event he must have been about seventy when he wrote Acts, which is by no means impossible or even improbable. When the dependence on Josephus is given up, Acts falls to be dated within the Domitianic period (so, *e.g.*, Schleiermacher, Mangold, Keim, i. 63; Hilgenfeld, Reuss, McGiffert, Löning's *Gemeindeverfassung*, 62; J. Réville, *Les origines de l'épiscopat*, 43–44; Bacon; Ramsay's *SPT.* 386 f.; Spitta, Knopf, Feine), perhaps as early as *c.* A.D. 80 (Ewald, Bleek, Hoennicke, Sanday's *Inspiration*[2], 1894, 318–330; Gilbert) or the eighth decade of the century (Bartlet, Furneaux, Headlam, Zahn). We may reconstruct Luke's literary activity roughly as follows: Between A.D. (50) 55 and 65 he wrote his memoranda of Paul's travels; later, between A.D. 80 and 60, the third gospel; finally, *c.* A.D. 100, he worked up his memoranda into the book of Acts. Unless the Josephus-references, however, in the gospel are subsequent additions, the first of his works may also need to be placed towards the end of the first century.

The notion that Acts was written immediately after the events recorded at its close, *i.e.* prior to A.D. 70, which sprang up early (cp. Eus. *H. E.* ii. 22. 6), through Jerome (*uir. inlustr.* 7: edidit uolumen egregium, quod titulo apostolicarum πράξεων prænotatur. Cuius historia usque ad biennium Romæ commorantis Pauli peruenit, id est usque ad quartum Neronis annum. Ex quo intelligimus in eadem urbe librum esse compositum), lingers still, *e.g.*, in Godet, Salmon, Alford (A.D. 63), Rendall, Koch, Barde (*Comm.* 508–583), Gloag (A.D. 62–64), Belser (A.D. 63), Bisping, Cornely, R. B. Rackham (*JTS.*, 1899, 76–87), Dawson Walker (*Gift of Tongues*, etc., A.D. 68–70), Corluy (A.D. 64), Blass, Edmundson (*Urc.* 32 f.), and Jacquier; while Harnack (*BNT.* iv. 90 f., 114 f.) concludes that Acts must have been written before the fall of Jerusalem, even before Paul's death (see above, p. 304). The most plausible argument in its favour is drawn from the last verse of the book Luke, it is held, wrote no more because he knew no more; when he wrote, Paul was still in his two years' detention, or at least still alive. This becomes more arguable, if he is supposed to have planned a third volume; but, when such a hypothesis is regarded as untenable, critics fall back on the position that he brought Acts up to date and issued it as it was. This plea, that if he had known of Paul's martyrdom or release, he must have mentioned it, does not flow from the structure of the book, however. As a matter of fact, Paul was not released. Both Luke and his readers probably knew that the apostle had perished at the end of the two years' residence in Rome; the historian had as little interest in mentioning it as in suppressing it; he closes on the ringing chord of ἀκωλύτως, because he had now depicted the establishment of Gentile Christianity in Rome under the auspices of his hero. Paul's martyrdom was as irrelevant to him as Peter's. Acts is not a biography of Paul, but a sketch of the early church written from a special standpoint and for a special object; the omission of any reference to Paul's subsequent fortunes only becomes perplexing to those who persist in reading into Acts an aim which the author never contemplated (cp. J. Weiss, *Urc.* 293). From the standpoint of modern realism it would no doubt be more satisfactory to have the book rounded off by an account of Paul's death; but to expect such a finale is to misread the currents of the narrative. Even if the evidence for the post A.D. 70 date of the third gospel and for Luke's use of Josephus could be set aside, there would not be sufficient internal evidence to establish a seventh-decade date for Acts.

The other argument, that if Luke had written later he would have been sure to know and use Paul's epistles, and in this way would have avoided some of the discrepancies between these and his own work, is equally insecure. Even if the epistles were widely circulated by the opening of the second century, Luke seems to have had no interest in Paul as a letter-writer (cp. Menzies, *Interpreter*, 1914, 254 f.). So far as Acts is concerned, the apostle might never have written an epistle at all: it was the churches who were to Luke Paul's epistles (2 Co 3[2]). Nor was Luke careful even in his own works (cp. Lk 24 and Ac 1) to avoid apparent (cp. Bacon, *Exp.*[7] vii. 254–261) discrepancies. "There are stranger things in the Acts than the appearance of contradicting St. Paul's epistles. There are the contradictions (apparent or real) of the OT, of the writer's own gospel, and of the book of Acts itself" (Cross).

§ 9. *Traces in early Christian literature.*—(*SR.* 567–584; Zeller, i. 93–164; Leipoldt, *GK.* i. 197 f.) As Luke's two volumes were dedicated to Theophilus, evidently a man of position and means, it is more than probable that the latter would arrange for their circulation. This was the recognised practice of the time. The *patronus libri* often undertook to have copies of the book made by *librarii* at his own expense, and thus its introduction to wider circles was facilitated (cp. *e.g.* Mart. iii. 2. 16, vii. 97. 13; Cic. *ad Att.* xii. 40. 1). No traces of Acts are visible, however, until at least the second decade of the second century.

Clem. Rom. 2[1] (ἥδιον διδόντες ἢ λαμβάνοντες) is merely an allusion * to an *agraphon* circulating through primitive Christianity, which chances to be cited

* So Did. 1[2] = Ac 15[20. 29], and the use, attributed by Hegesippus to James the Just, of the logion preserved in our canonical Lk 23[34] (Ac 7[60]).

in Ac 20^{35}; Clem. 18^{1}=Ac 13^{22} reflects the use of a common source, and slight coincidences like Clem. $5^{4.7}$=Ac 1^{25}, Clem. 59^{2}=Ac 26^{18} are quite fortuitous.* In view of the rabbinical use of the phrase *to go to his own place*, the echo of Ac 1^{25} in Ign. *Magn.* 5^{1} becomes more apparent than real. Upon the other hand, Ac 2^{24} does appear to have been in the mind of the writer of Polyk. 1^{2} (*ὃν ἤγειρεν ὁ Θεὸς λύσας τὰς ὠδῖνας τοῦ ᾅδου*); it is not easy to suppose that the striking mistranslation of חבלי was made independently. If so, lesser references or reminiscences may be seen in Polyk. 2^{1} (*judge of living and dead*)=Ac 10^{42} perhaps, and in Polyk. 6^{3}=Ac 7^{52}, as well as (probably) in Polyk. 12^{2}=Ac 2^{5} 8^{21} 26^{18}. Similarly Ac $17^{24f.}$ is echoed in Diogn. 3, Tatian (*Orat. ad Gr.* 4), and Athenagoras (*Leg.* 13); while Ac 7^{60} seems reproduced, like Lk 1^{6}, in the epistle of the Vienne and Lyons churches —which throws back the composition of the book into the first half or even the first quarter of the second century. Irenæus and the Muratorian Canon attest its repute as scripture in the Western church, like Tertullian in the church of Africa, and Clement in Alexandria. Its history in the Alexandrian church, together with the fact that its text could be so freely altered as in the D revision, shows that in some quarters, however, Acts was not considered *γραφή* by the middle of the second century. What helped eventually to popularise it † and to win canonical prestige was its ecclesiastical emphasis on the apostles and Paul as leaders of the catholic church—a trait which became particularly grateful in the controversy with Marcion. "The book was canonised first of all as a supplement to the catholic epistles,—to make up for the fact that many of the apostles had left no writings behind them,—and, in the second place, as a link between the Pauline and the catholic epistles, by way of documentary proof that Paul and the twelve were at one" (Leipoldt, *GK.* i. 205). Hence probably the third and fourth words in the description of the Muratorian Canon: "Acta autem omnium apostolorum sub uno libro scripta sunt. Lucas optimo Theophilo comprehendit, quæ sub præsentia eius singula gerebantur, sicut et semota passione Petri euidenter declarat, sed et profectione Pauli ab urbe ad Spaniam proficiscentis." This ambiguous reference is connected by Dr. M. R. James (cp. *TS.* v. ii., 1897, pp. 10 f.) with the Leucian *Actus Petri Vercellenses*, which begin with the *profectio Pauli ab urbe in Spaniam*, and close with the *passio Petri*—a coincidence which seems to imply that these Acts were known to the compiler of the Murat. Canon, who confused Luke with Leucius or took the Leucian Acts (where the first person is also used anonymously, cp. *JTS.* xvi. 505) to be written, as Leucius may have intended his readers to suppose, by Luke.

---

* As are Herm. *Sim.* 9^{28}=Ac 5^{41} and *Vis.* 4^{2}=Ac 4^{12}; Ign. *Smyrn.* 3^{3}=Ac 10^{41}, and Barn. 7^{2}=Ac 10^{42}, with perhaps Just. *Dial.* 36, 76=Ac 26^{22-23}.

† The apocryphal Acta draw upon it and embellish its hints by fantastic embroideries of their own (cp. *HNA.* i. 347 f.). In his opening homily, Chrysostom observes that (*πολλοῖς τοῦτο τὸ βιβλίον οὔτ᾽ ὅτι ἔστι γνώριμόν ἐστιν οὔτε ὁ γράψας αὐτὸ καὶ συνθείς*) many Christians were ignorant alike of its existence and of its authorship: some said Clement of Rome, others Barnabas, others again Luke. The authenticity of the homily has been questioned, but, even so, it throws light on the indifference towards Acts which was felt in some quarters of the early church during the fourth or fifth century.

CHAPTER III.

HOMILIES AND PASTORALS.

It is with a sense of baffled curiosity, which almost deepens into despair at some points, that one leaves the literary criticism of the following fragments of the primitive Christian literature which have been gathered into the NT. In Greek and Roman literature there are also several writings which present unsolved, if not insoluble, problems of authorship and date, but, between the death of Paul and the journey of Ignatius to Rome, a mist lies over the early church, which is hardly dissipated by the recognition of Luke as the author of the third gospel and Acts, or of a John in Asia Minor towards the close of the first century, with whom some of the 'Johannine' writings may be connected. The former approximates more closely than any other early Christian writer to the literary figures of the contemporary ancient world; the latter remains a more or less shadowy figure, round whom later traditions throw conflicting rays of light. The result is that in these pastorals and homilies we are left face to face with a number of writings which are obviously sub-Pauline, which must have been composed during the last thirty years of the first century and the opening decades of the second, which can be approximately grouped and in some cases dated, but which elude any attempt to fix them down to a definite author. No contemporary tradition enables us to place them. Even the traditions of the next century, such as they are, yield little or no data upon the problems raised by literary criticism; it is seldom certain whether such traditions are much more than imaginative deductions from the writings themselves.

This is one of the perplexing differences between the Christian literature of the first and that of the second century. The latter reveals a series of striking personalities, while the NT literature, which is practically synonymous with the literature of the church during the first century, has only one writer whose personality is well marked, *i.e.* the apostle Paul. Luke, the historian, is known to us mainly from his writings, and these, from their very nature, are objective rather than subjective. The John of Asia Minor whom we can detect behind the Johannine literature, must have been a commanding figure, but we cannot feel him breathe and move, as we can feel Paul. On the other hand, the second century and its literature reveal strong and varied personalities, from Ignatius to Irenæus, from Polykarp to Tertullian, from Marcion and even Papias and Hegesippus to Justin, Tatian, and Clement of Alexandria. One result of this contrast is that, while these writers and others reflect the existence of the earlier NT literature, it is more difficult to fix down the latter. When the NT canon begins to emerge, in the second and third centuries, we find it composed of writings which may, on independent grounds, in a large majority of cases, be assigned to A.D. 70–120; but it is a task beyond the resources of criticism—at least beyond such resources as are at present available—to locate a number of these writings with any sort of precision. They come to us out of that misty half-century; they are found to be in use throughout the later church in certain quarters; echoes of them in later writers help to prove their period within certain limits, and internal evidence determines their relative order now and then. But beyond this we can seldom go with very much security. The questions of their authorship, object, and structure may be discussed with the aid of hypotheses, but these hypotheses are almost wholly derived from internal evidence, and this evidence in its turn is vitiated by our comparative ignorance of the literary conditions in which these compositions originated.

One reason for this was that such problems were irrelevant to the interests of the later church. *Nihil de titulis interest*, said Tertullian (see below, p. 390); and this abjuring of interest in questions which pertain to literary criticism fairly represents the general temper of the age immediately following the origin of the NT documents. Their religious validity was the only thing that mattered. Since that seemed to involve a claim for apostolic authorship or authority, evidence was led, in the shape of tradition usually, on behalf of the claim; otherwise the morphology of the documents usually excited no interest in the devout or the ecclesiastical mind.

This feeling went back further. These documents were not composed as pieces of literature. Luke is the only writer who reminds us, in style and treatment, of an ancient Greek or Roman author: the dedication of his works to an individual, their prefaces, and their general ethos, offer a certain parallel to contemporary pagan literature. Otherwise, the NT literature, and especially that of the pastorals and homilies, may be described as communal in origin; it approximates to the Hebrew rather than to the Greek or Roman literature. The pastorals and homilies, like the gospels, were not written with any literary object; their authors voice various sides of a movement, even when their idiosyncrasies are most evident; and, on the whole, in passing from Paul's correspondence through the contemporary gospels to this group of pastorals and homilies, we touch more and more the catholic spirit of the early church, rather than any great personality. Tradition in the case of 1 Peter and of 2–3 John brings figures within reach which may be more or less securely connected with these homilies, but otherwise most of the later traditions upon their origin are derivative and secondary. The writings are all post-Pauline. In several, *e.g.*, Hebrews, 1 Peter, and James, vibrations of the Pauline theology are audible; Ephesians, Timotheus, and Titus are associated explicitly with the apostle's name, and this drew them, together with Hebrews (usually), into the Pauline canon. But it is not possible to classify them chronologically, or even according to types of thought, and while they are grouped in the following pages it is principally for the sake of convenience (cp. above, p. 20).

None of these epistolary writings contains any narrative. The epistolary form of literature was devoted mainly to the interests of edification. Several writings have been preserved which, while epistolary in form, are practically narratives, and narratives of martyrdom, of which the most significant are the so-called 'Martyrdom of the holy Polykarp,' an epistle written by the church of Smyrna to that of Philomelium, and the epistle of the church at Vienne and Lyons, about twenty years later, describing the persecution which had broken out in Gaul under Antoninus Verus. These, however, are both later. 2 Peter may not be earlier than the Smyrniote epistle, but with this partial exception the homilies and pastorals which have been grouped in the NT canon are not only prior to this epistolary narrative, but closer to exposition and exhortation. Even in form * they vary. Hebrews has no address, and 1 John has no definite address; while neither James nor 1 John has any epistolary conclusion. The more important of them show how Paul had popularised the epistolary form in primitive Christianity, but it is as homilies rather than as epistles that they are to be ranked (pp. 48–50).

The so-called 'catholic' or 'canonical' (cp. *ZNW.*, 1913, 266 f.) epistles are best connected with the anonymous apostles and prophets who

---

* Cp. Deissmann, *Bible Studies*, pp. 50 f.; Heinrici, *Der Litter. Character d. neutest. Schriften*, 73 f.; Bacon, *Making of NT*, 107 f.

belonged to Christendom as a whole, not to any particular community (cp. Harnack, *MAC.* i. 341 f.). But Harnack's further hypothesis (cp. *TU.* ii. 2. pp. 106 f., *ACL.* ii. 1. 455 f.), that 1 Peter, Judas, and James were originally the work of such unknown teachers and prophets, and that the later tendency of the church to run back its doctrine and institutions to apostles led to the insertion of apostolic names in these homilies, does not work out well in detail.

Editions by the French scholar Jacques Le Fèvre d'Etaples (Basle, 1527), J. Ferus the Franciscan (Paris, 1536 f.), N. Serarius (Mayence, 1612), S. J. Justinianus (Lyons, 1621), Fromond (Paris, 1670), G. Schlegel (1783), J. B. Carpzov (1790), J. C. W. Augusti (1801), J. W. Grashof (1830), K. R. Jachmann (1838), de Wette (1847), Brückner (— de Wette[3], 1865), H. Ewald (1870), A. Bisping (1871), Hofmann (1875–6), E. Reuss (1878), J. M. S. Baljon (1903), B. Weiss (vol. iii. of his *NT. Handausgabe*), T. Calmes (Paris, 1905), F. Weidner (*Annotations*, New York, 1906), van Steenkiste (*Epp. Cath. Explicatæ*[4], 1907), and Windisch (*HBNT.* 1911). Special studies by G. C. Storr, *de catholicarum epistolarum occasione et consilio* (Tübingen, 1789), C. F. Stäudlin, *de fontibus epistolarum catholicarum* (Göttingen, 1790), P. J. Gloag (*Introd. to Cath. Epp.*, Edin. 1877), S. D. F. Salmond (*DB.* i. 359–362), and W. Bauer (*Die Katholischen Briefe des NT*, Tübingen, 1910); they are also translated and annotated by F. W. Farrar in his *Early Days of Christianity*. On their canonical place, see Leipoldt (*GK.* i. 232 f.), and Lietzmann's *Wie wurden die Bücher des NT. heilige Schrift?* (1907) pp. 99–110.

(A) *THE (FIRST) EPISTLE OF PETER.*

LITERATURE.—(*a*) Editions[1]—Erasmus (1516); Luther (1523); H. Bullinger (1534); Bibliander (1536); Calvin (1551); Hemming (1555); F. Feuardent (Paris, 1600); N. Byfield (London, 1637); Gerhard (Jena, 1641); John Rogers (London, 1650); Grotius (*Annotat.* 1650); A. Nisbet (London, 1658); David Dickson (1659); Benson, *Paraphrase and Notes* (1756); J. S. Semler's *Paraphrasis* (Halle, 1781); Morus (Leipzig, 1794); Roos, *Brief explanation of the Two Epp. of P.* (1798); Pott (1810); C. G. Hensler (Sulzbach, 1813); Hottinger (Leipzig, 1815); Eisenschmidt (1824); W. Steiger (Berlin, 1832, Eng. tr. 1836); J. D. Schlichthorst (1836); Windischmann (*Vindiciæ Petrinæ*, 1836)*; de Wette (1847); J. E. Riddle (1849); J. F. Demarest (New York, 1851); A. Wiesinger, *Briefes d. Jakobus, Petrus, und Judas* (Königsberg, 1854); Olshausen (1856); T. Schott (Erlangen, 1861); B. Brückner* (1865[3]); J. Brown[3] (Edin. 1868); Alford[4] (1871); Wordsworth (1872); Hundhausen (Mainz, 1873, 1878); Hofmann, *der Erste Brief Petri* (Nördlingen, 1875); Reuss (1878); E. H. Plumptre (*Camb. Bible*, 1879); F. C. Cook (*Speaker's Comm.* 1881); Huther (— Meyer, Eng. tr. 1881); C. A. Witz (Vienna, 1881); Keil, *Briefe d. Petrus und Judas* (Leipzig, 1883); S. D. F. Salmond (Schaff's *Comm.* 1883)*; A. J. Mason (Ellicott's *Comm.* 1883); J. M. Usteri* (Zürich, 1887); R. Johnstone (Edin. 1888); B. C. Caffin (*Pulpit Comm.* 1889); Fronmüller (Lange's

[1] In addition to the patristic notes of Didymus (ed. F. Zoepfl, 1914), Oecumenius, and Theophylact.

Bibel-Werk[4], 1890, Eng. tr. 1872); J. R. Lumby (*Expositor's Bible*, 1893); Goebel (1893); J. T. Beck, *Erklärung d. Briefe Petri* (1895); K. Burger[2] (1895); H. Couard (1895); E. Kühl (— Meyer[6], 1897); F. J. A. Hort* (posthumous and incomplete [1^{1}–2^{17}], 1898); H. von Soden[3] (*HC.* 1896); Monnier (1900)*; J. H. B. Masterman (1900); C. Bigg[2] (*ICC.* 1902)*; Bugge, *Apostlerne Peters og Judas's Breve* (1902); Gunkel (*SNT.*[2] 1907); Hart (*EGT.* 1910); Windisch (*HBNT.* 1911), van Kasteren (Utrecht, 1911), R. Knopf (— Meyer[7], 1912); G. Wohlenberg (*ZK.* 1915).

(*b*) Studies—Cludius, *Uransichten des Christenthums* (Altona, 1808), 296–311; Augusti, *Nova hypothesis, quæ primæ Petri epistolæ αὐθεντίαν impugnat, sub examen voc.* (Jena, 1808); J. D. Schulze, *Der schriftstellerische Charakter u. Werth des Petrus, Judas, u. Jakobus* (Leipzig, 1811); Seyler (*SK.*, 1832, 44 f.); Mayerhoff, *Einleit. in die Petrin. Schriften* (Hamburg, 1835)*; Lecoultre's *Thèses* (Geneva, 1839); A. L. Pölmann, *Theologia Petrina* (Gröningen, 1850); J. C. Zaalberg's *Disquisitio* (1851); B. Weiss, *Petrin. Lehrbegriff* (1855), and in *SK.* (1865, pp. 619–657, 1873, pp. 539 f.); Baur (*Theol. Jahrb.*, 1856, 193–240, in reply to Weiss; also *Church History*, Eng. tr. i. pp. 150 f.); Schmid, *Biblical Theology of the NT* (ii. pp. 374 f.); Sabatier (*ESR.* x. 619 f.); Davaine, *Étude dogmatique sur 1 P.* (1867); Grimm (*SK.*, 1872, pp. 657–694); Holtzmann (*BL.* iv. 494–502); C. H. van Rhijn, *de jougste bezwaren tegen de echtheid vaan d. eersten brief van Petrus getoest* (1875); Gloag, *Introd. to Catholic Epistles* (Edin. 1887), pp. 109–203; E. Scharfe, *die petrinische Strömung in d. NT Literatur* (1893)*; R. H. Drijber (*Geloof en Vrijheid*, 1895, 28–60); Ramsay, *CRE.* (ch. xiii.) and *Exp.*[4] viii. 282–296; Seeberg, *der Tod Christi* (1895), 288 f.; McGiffert. *AA.* pp. 482 f., 593 f.; Dalmer, 'Zu 1 P 1^{18-19}' (*BFT.*, 1898, 6); Harmon, 'Peter—The man and the epistle' (*JBL.*, 1898, 31–39); F. H. Chase (*DB.* iii. 779–796)*; van Manen, *Handleiding voor de ondchristelijke Letterkunde* (1900), pp. 64–67; Pfleiderer, *Urc.* iv. 243 f.; Sieffert (*PRE.* xv. 186–212)*; Moffatt, *HNT.* pp. 242–257; Kögel, 'die Gedankeneinheit des ersten Briefes Petri' (*BFT.*, 1902, 5–6); L. Goutard, 'Essai critique et historique sur la prem. épître de S. Pierre' (Lyons, 1905); Orello Cone (*EBi.* iii. 3677–3685); B. Weiss, 'Der erste Petrusbrief u. die neuere Kritik' (1906); P. Schmidt, 'Zwei Fragen zum ersten Petrusbrief' (*ZWT.*, 1907, 28–52); R. Scott, *The Pauline Epistles* (1909), 208–211; J. C. Granbery, 'Christological Peculiarities in 1 Pt.' (*AJT.*, 1910, 62–81); K. Lake (*EB.*[11] xxi. 295 f.); S. J. Case (*DAC.* ii. 201 f.); Edmundson (*Urc.* 119 f.).

§ 1. *Characteristics of the pastoral.*—After a brief address[1] (1^{1-2}), Peter thanks God for the living hope of salvation possessed by his readers—a salvation which their present trials only serve to guarantee to them (1^{3-9}), as the long-promised messianic heritage (1^{10-12}). This hopeful[2] prospect is a source of joy. It involves, however, a reverent and godly conduct in the present

[1] Cp. W. Alexander (*Exp.*[3] iv. 1–13).

[2] The temper inculcated by Peter, in view of suffering, is not a grey, close-lipped stoicism, but a glow of exultation such as Jesus (Mt 5^{11-12}) and Paul (Ro $5^{3f.}$) had already counselled. Christians can only be patient under their trials by being more than patient.

life ($1^{13\text{-}21}$), particularly brotherly love ($1^{22f.}$) as the vital expression towards one another of the mercy which all, as the true and new Israel, had received in Christ from God.* The appeal then, as in He 13^{1}, widens ($2^{11f.}$) into a variety of social duties incumbent on Christians as citizens (2^{12}), subjects ($2^{13f.}$), slaves † ($2^{18f.}$), wives ($3^{1\text{-}6}$), and husbands (3^{7}), and the closing general exhortation ($3^{8f.}$) to mutual duties passes back into the cardinal question of a Christian's right behaviour under trial and unjust punishment. Christ's example of patience and innocence, and the imminence of the final deluge ($3^{18f.}$), are adduced as the main motives for Christians keeping themselves free from pagan vice and ($4^{8f.}$) from lovelessness within the church.‡ A final paragraph ($4^{12\text{-}19}$), warning them against repining, gathers up these admonitions, after which Peter ($5^{1\text{-}4}$) appeals § to the elders for considerate and faithful supervision of the churches, and to the younger members ($5^{5f.}$) for a humility towards men and God which is the normal Christian safeguard. The blessing ($5^{10\text{-}11}$), as ‖ in He $13^{20f.}$, is followed by some brief personal notices, with which the epistle closes. Its keynote is steady

* Cp. the striking parallel, 1 P $2^{6f.}$ = Mk $12^{10\text{-}11}$; also the similarity of argument in 1 P 4^{7} = Mk $13^{29\text{-}33}$.

† The association of advice to these *οἰκέται* with an exposition of Christ's death is partly due to the fact that crucifixion was a punishment for slaves in the Roman world. The large place given to the duties of slaves and wives, as contrasted with the lack of any regulations for masters and the slight counsel for husbands, is remarkable. 3^{3} is one of the rare sumptuary directions in primitive Christian literature.

‡ Two points may be noted to show how the strange legendary reference of $3^{19f.}$ would possess a certain aptness as a local allusion. (*a*) Marcion, the Pontic Christian, is known at a later stage to have caught up a similar idea (*Iren.* i. 27. 3); and (*b*) Apamea was one of the places where the Noah-legend, like the Enoch-legend, had been localised (cp. Babelon in *RHR.*, 1891, pp. 174–183), though Parthia and Phrygia competed for the honour of having been the ark's resting-place (see Schürer, *GJV.* iii. 18–20).

§ Cp. W. Alexander (*Exp.*[3] iv. 184–193).

‖ Both 1 P. and Heb. are brief exhortations (5^{12} = He 13^{22}) to exiles of heaven (1^{1} 2^{11} = He 11^{13}, Mk 13^{27}), written in view of penultimate persecution ($4^{7.\ 17\text{-}19}$ = He 10^{37}). See, further, 1^{2} = He 12^{24}, 2^{2} = He $5^{12f.}$, 2^{5} = He 3^{6}, 3^{9} = He 12^{17}, 3^{21} (*ἀντίτυπον*) = He 9^{24}, with the use of *φανεροῦσθαι* (1^{20} = He 9^{26}) and the emphasis on *ἅπαξ* (3^{18} = He 7^{27} $9^{7.\ 26f.}$) and the common exaltation of hope. But Heb. implies a longer period of Christian experience in its audience than 1 P. In view of Col $4^{15\text{-}17}$ and 2 Co 1^{1} it cannot be argued that (von Soden) the circulation of an encyclical like this implied that the churches had been organised for some time.

encouragement (5^{11} = Lk 22^{32}) to endurance in conduct and innocence in character.

The dominant note of the epistle is hope (1^{13} etc., cp. Seyler, *SK.*, 1832, pp. 44 f.; Weiss, *NTTh.* ii. 243 f.), but it would be unsafe to argue freely from the tone of a practical letter, written under special circumstances, to the character of the writer, any more than to his theological temper, as if the letter represented a divergence from orthodox Paulinism (Holtzmann, *NTTh.* ii. 308–311), or as if the virtue of hope was specially prominent in his personality. Probably the author wrote about hope, because hope was what his readers needed. The line of argument and application pursued must have been congenial to him, for it is worked out with sagacity and insight; but its employment at this particular crisis does not permit us to infer that it was normal to the writer, except in the general sense in which the messianic outlook of the early Christians tended to develop it. The emphasis put upon it here is due to the emergency of the moment rather than to any idiosyncrasy or dogmatic prepossession on the part of the author (so, rightly, Reuss, pp. 156–157, and Wrede, *Ueber Aufgabe d. sogen. NT Theologie*, 18–19). Many other Christians might have written similarly, and as a matter of fact hope is also prominent in Titus (cp. 3^7 etc.), an epistle with which 1 P. has some traits in common (*e.g.* *λυτροῦσθαι* 1^{18} = Tit 2^{14}, 2^1 = Tit 3^3, 2^9 = Tit 2^{14}, 2^{11} = Tit 2^{12}, 2^{13} = Tit 3^1; regeneration in baptism, 1^3 3^{21} = Tit 3^5 etc.).

At the same time, a writing like this reveals a man's personality in several aspects, and one of these aspects is a warm,* kindly spirit which is allied to a certain grace of style. The plastic language and love of metaphor † (cp. the frequent use of ὡς, $1^{14.19}$ $2^{2.5.16}$ $4^{10.11.15.16}$ 5^8) shows an easy and natural temperament, with a vivid outlook upon the concrete surroundings of human life. The sequence of ideas is not marked by any rhetorical devices, though there is a deftness in the linking of clause to clause (*e.g.* $1^{6.18}$ 2^{10}), and although a clause like *ὁ ἔξωθεν ἐμπλοκῆς τριχῶν καὶ περιθέσεως χρυσίων ἢ ἐνδύσεως ἱματίων κόσμος* has been pronounced 'quite Thucydidean' (Bigg). On

* "Das Eigenthumliche des Briefes ist eine durchgehende Wärme" (Mayerhoff, p. 102).

† Cp. Scharfe (*SK.*, 1889, pp. 633–670), Chase (pp. 781–782), and Bigg (pp. 2–5). The style is "more varied, more nearly classical, but less eloquent and of less literary power" (Simcox) than that of James.

the other hand, the writer never uses ἄν, and he rarely employs connecting particles. The correlation of the paragraphs denotes the preacher, with his eye on an audience, rather than the composer of a literary epistle. He is fond, it should be noted, of developing a thought first negatively, then positively (*not . . . but*, $1^{14-15.\ 18-19.\ 23a-23b}$ $3^{6a-6b.\ 21a-21b}$ $5^{2a-2b.\ 2c-3}$), and of presenting an idea by means of sharp contrasts ($1^{6.\ 8.\ 11.\ 15-16}$ $2^{4.\ 7.\ 10.\ 16.\ 23-25}$ $3^{1.\ 8.\ 9.\ 11-12.\ 17-18}$ $4^{2.\ 6.\ 14-15.\ 17-18}$ $5^{1.\ 8}$), five times with the idiomatic μέν . . . δέ, whose use in 1 P. of all the NT writings "is freest and contributes most to the sense" (Simcox, *Language of NT*, p. 167). He likes compounds of συν-, and verbs compounded of ἀνα- ($1^{3.\ 13.\ 15.\ 17.\ 23}$ $2^{5.\ 24}$ $4^{4.\ 14}$). His favourite formula for introducing OT quotations is διότι (1^{24}), with γέγραπται (1^{16}) or περιέχει ἐν τῇ γραφῇ (2^{6}), but just as often an OT phrase is woven into the texture of the epistle without any comment, or several are twisted together.

The beautiful spirit of the pastoral shines through any translation of the Greek text. "Affectionate, loving, lowly, humble," are Izaak Walton's quaternion of adjectives for the epistles of James, John, and Peter, but it is 1 P. which deserves them pre-eminently. To this writer Christians in the present age seem exiles (1^{1} 2^{11}, cp. also 1^{17}),* or pilgrims (contrast Eph 2^{19}), whose inheritance is in heaven (1^{4}), but who possess here a sure footing in the true grace of God (5^{12} a reminiscence of Col 1^{6}?). This *grace*, which is the core and heart of the epistle, is described in historical retrospect as the subject † of OT prophecy (1^{10}), and in prospect as the final boon to be fully bestowed at the second coming of Jesus Christ (1^{13}). By a remarkable turn (cf. Phil 1^{29}), the suffering of innocent Christians is described as a χάρις in God's sight (2^{19-20}). *The grace of life* is Peter's equivalent for Christianity (3^{7}); God is to him *the god of all grace* (5^{10}), and Christians are to be stewards of God's ποικίλη χάρις (4^{10}), or bounty bestowed on them for various ends of service. The epistle is a blend of παράκλησις and ἐπιμαρτυρία (5^{12}), the latter testifying ταύτην εἶναι ἀληθῆ χάριν τοῦ θεοῦ, εἰς ἣν στῆτε (cp. 4^{14}). Here Peter uses χάρις where Paul had used εὐαγγέλιον (1 Co 15^{1}), and the unsettling tendencies are due to suffering, not to wrong views (as at Corinth).

---

* This disposes of one of Harnack's arguments (see p. 342). He pleads that the address does not lie on the same plane as the rest of the epistle, whereas this conception of Christians as exiled colonists of heaven is intimately bound up with the conception of their sufferings. But it is simpler to suppose that the address came from the same source as the bulk of the letter, than to conjecture that a later scribe studied the letter and wrote the address so as to be in line with what followed. Cp. also the use of ὑπακοή ($1^{2.\ 14.\ 22}$).

† This is in keeping with its associations in Paul and in Acts (cp. J. A. Robinson, *Ephes.* pp. 221 f.), where χάρις is generally tinged with colours drawn from the admission of the Gentiles into the prerogatives and privileges of Israel.

§ 2. *The situation.*—It is this hostile pressure, with the perplexities and pains which ensue, that differentiates 1 P. from the preceding correspondence of Paul. The relations between Christians and the authorities have entered on a phase of strain, which marks a new epoch in the story of the primitive church, and the date, as well as inferentially the authorship, of the epistle may be said to depend largely upon the view adopted of the disturbance under which the readers were suffering. They are not to be taken aback at the *burning trial* (4^{12}) which has befallen them; for (i.) it is not purposeless, but a furnace where the genuine elements of their Christian character are being tested and tempered ($1^{6f.}$); (ii.) it is not abnormal, but the natural order of experience exemplified as well as ordained by Jesus himself ($4^{13f.}$); (iii.) it is not permanent, but merely the short, sharp prelude to eternal glory; and (iv.) it is not uncommon (5^{9}), but the contemporary lot of their fellow-Christians throughout the world. The detailed allusions to this untoward environment are often held to indicate an organised persecution, when Christians were hunted out and hunted down as Christians; and it is argued strongly that this extension of persecution from the capital to the provinces, together with the fact of suffering for the Name, must point to the reign of Trajan, or at least to that of Domitian. It would be no valid objection to the latter date, that a contemporary Asiatic writing, the apocalypse of John, reflects quite a different attitude towards the State; for John represents a special phase of Asiatic Christianity in hot protest against the local Imperial cultus (see below, ch. iv.), whereas Clem. Rom., like 1 Peter, would voice the more patriotic temper consonant with the Christianity of the capital. But the internal evidence does not appear to carry us beyond the seventh decade of the first century, as reflected, *e.g.*, in a contemporary passage like Mk $13^{9\text{-}11}$. Here, as there, Christians are liable to official interference as well as to social annoyance on the score of their religion; they are dragged before ἡγεμόνες and royalty (cp. 1 P 2^{13}), ἕνεκεν ἐμοῦ (= ὡς Χριστιανός, 4^{16}), and have to answer for themselves. Mk. does not specify the charges; he merely makes Jesus describe the trials as incurred (13^{13}) διὰ τὸ ὄνομα μου. This tallies fairly with the evidence of 1 P. and the Roman historians alike in pointing to a period as early as the seventh decade when, not only at Rome but throughout the provinces, the popular belief that Christianity was bound up with such *flagitia* as Thyestean δεῖπνα and Οἰδοπόδειοι μίξεις (Arnold, *op. cit.* below, pp. 22 f., *FFG.* iv. 398 f.), besides anti-imperial tendencies, exposed any adherent of that religion, against whom information was laid, to arrest and even execution.

When Nero cleverly shifted the suspicion of arson from himself to "quos per flagitia inuisos uulgus Chrestianos appellabat," the pestilential superstition of Christianity, Tacitus (*Annal.* xv. 44) continues, had spread already in Rome, "quo cuncta undique atrocia aut pudenda confluunt celebranturque." Originally the Romans may have scarcely taken the trouble to distinguish between Christianity and its parent-stock Judaism, but before the seventh decade * it must have been the interest of the Jews, especially at Rome, where they enjoyed the favour of Poppæa, to differentiate themselves from the Nazarenes; and it was inevitable that the occurrence of legal proceedings such as happened in Paul's career (*e.g.* Ac 18^{15}) should make the distinction fairly plain to most of the authorities. It was in all likelihood the Jews who, out of ζῆλος or spiteful malice (cp. Clem. Rom. 6), instigated Nero's *émeute*, or at least suggested his victims and scapegoats (cp. Harnack in *TU.*, 1905, 2, pp. 1–9). In any case this outburst presupposes that the general public had become accustomed, by the seventh decade of the first century, to single out Christians from Jews, even when levelling against the former some of the charges (*e.g.* hatred of the human race) which were current against the latter. The accounts of Tacitus and Suetonius (*Ner.* 16) further show that while Nero's attack was short if sharp, it must have rendered the general situation more perilous for Christians throughout the empire. The former writes: 'in the first place some were denounced (or put on trial) and made to confess.† Thereupon, thanks to their information, a vast multitude was associated with them (reading *conjuncti* for the MS *convicti*) on the charge not so much of arson as of enmity to the human race.' In line with this, "Suetonius' sober statement shows that Nero's government did not confine itself in its measures of repression against the Christians to those accused of arson. We may safely assume that they began under Nero partly in defence of the public gods, partly against the excesses said (and probably not in all cases unjustly) to reign among them" (Mommsen, *Exp.*[4] viii. 6). This second stage of imperial procedure against Christians as hostile to the

* It is therefore arbitrary, as I have elsewhere shown (*DCG.* i. 316–318, *HJ.* vi. 704–707), to find a *hysteron proteron* either in Luke's or in the classical historians' use of the name 'Christian.' So F. C. Arnold, *die Neronische Christenverfolgung* (1888), pp. 52 f., and E. Klette, *die Christenkatastrophe unter Nero* (1907), pp. 16 f., 40 f. Klette's monograph summarises the wide results of recent research upon the problem, especially the novel views of Profumo and Pascal.

† To confess what? probably not the fact that they were Christians, but their guilt as incendiaries (so Schiller, F. C. Arnold, Duruy, Henderson, Klette), in spite of the innocence of Christians on this count. Either they turned traitors and for sectarian ends gave incriminating testimony falsely, or they were tortured into bearing false witness, or else they were fanatical enthusiasts.

human race, inaugurated under Nero,* prevailed during the Flavian dynasty, and invested the mere name of Christian with perilous and compromising associations. No adequate evidence of any change under Vespasian has been adduced. Christians, as Mommsen put it, were persecuted just as robbers were exterminated; it was a standing order, one of the permanent police measures, so Suetonius implies.† When the correspondence of Trajan and Pliny unveils the proceedings of the latter as governor of Bithynia, he is found to be acting instinctively on the principle that he has a perfect right to execute those who persist in calling themselves Christians. No question of crime is raised. The profession of this *religio illicita* is assumed to be a capital offence. Trajan's answer to his lieutenant neither disputes nor authorises this mode of action; the emperor simply sanctions it as an admitted feature of the State policy towards such dissenters.‡

In the light of these historical data, the language of 1 P. becomes more intelligible. Not only does it contain no definite or necessary allusion to the second-century persecution for the Name, but the very terms employed are satisfactorily explained by the position of Christians under the Empire during the third quarter of the first century, especially subsequent to A.D. 64. Thus, while κακοποιός has its general meaning of 'wrong-doer' in $2^{12.14}$, its position between murderer and thief and ἀλλοτριοεπίσκοπος in 4^{15}, shows that here it is specially (cp. *malus* in Hor. *Sat.* I. i. 77, iii. 59, etc.) equivalent to *maleficus* in the contemporary usage of Suetonius, *i.e.* wizard or magician, —magic, in the sense of possessing supernatural powers and of wielding undue influence over others,§ being a common charge against Christians, and one which, like arson, rendered the people liable to the penalties of the *Lex Cornelia de sicariis* (cp. Arnold, *op. cit.* pp. 64 f.). Hence ἀλλοτριοεπίσκοπος would mean not so much seditious or inconsistent as either a busybody—one

* Cp. Sanday (*Exp.*[4] vii. 407 f.); E. G. Hardy, *Christianity and the Roman Empire* (1894), pp. 70 f., 80 f., 125 f.; and Klette, *op. cit.* 54 f. "Die Möglichkeit, dass die Verhältnisse, welche der Brief voraussetzt, schon unter Vespasian, ja selbst unter Nero, begonnen haben und je nach Einsicht und Temperament christlicherseits mit mehr oder weniger Sorge und Befürchtung beurtheilt worden sind, lässt sich nicht abweisen" (Harnack, *ACL.* ii. 1. 454).

† "Only," as Mommsen adds (*Provinces*, ii. p. 199 n.), "such regulations were put into practice at times more gently or even negligently, at other times more strictly, and were doubtless on occasion specially enforced from high quarters."

‡ The further questions arising out of this important correspondence, including that of Trajan's rescript, do not bear on the NT literature. Cp. Neumann's *der röm. Staat u. die allgemeine Kirche*, i. [1890] pp. 9 f., and Knopf (*NZ.* 96 f.).

§ For Christians who were actually *mathematici*, cp. Tert. *de Idol.* ix.

who, like the Cynics, interfered (cp. Zeller in *SBBA.*, 1893, pp. 129 f.) rudely and indiscreetly with ordinary practices and the social order, by a propaganda of divisive principles—or actually a 'delator,'* like some of the Christians who informed against their fellows under Nero.† This kind of persecution would be spasmodic and sporadic (5^9). Evidently it had but recently broken upon these Asiatic Christians; and while there was always a danger of the capital punishment being inflicted, it is clear that suffering of a less arduous character (calumny, annoyance, social ostracism, etc.) is contemplated in the main (cp. 4^{1-2} *τὸν ἐπίλοιπον ἐν σαρκὶ βιῶσαι χρόνον*, the expression *μὴ αἰσχυνέσθω*, 4^{16}, and *οἱ πάσχοντες πιστῷ κτίστῃ παρατιθέσθωσαν τὰς ψυχὰς αὐτῶν ἐν ἀγαθοποιΐᾳ*). Furthermore, while the epistle has judicial proceedings in view now and again, it does not exclude the hardships due to exasperated popular feeling; indeed, the two cannot be kept apart, as the action of governors was usually stimulated by private information laid by angry citizens, and the language of the epistle cannot fairly be held to imply that the authorities were taking the initiative regularly against Christians simply and solely because the latter confessed the name and faith of Christ. "L'ennemi, ce n'est pas encore le pouvoir, ce sont les gens ignorants, débauchés, c'est la foule aveugle, qui n'admet pas un culte et une morale par lesquels elle se sent condamnée" (Monnier, p. 325). After the Neronic wave had passed over the capital, the wash of it was felt on the far shores of the provinces (cp. 4^{12}); ‡ the dramatic publicity of the punishment must have spread the name of Christian *urbi et orbi*, far and wide over the empire; the provincials would soon hear of it,

* It tells against this explanation, however, that Tertullian deliberately renders the word, not by *delator*, but by *speculator alieni* (*Scorp.* 12). P. Schmidt (*ZWT.*, 1907, 28 f.) compares the oath taken by the Christians of Pliny's provinces to abstain from misappropriation of trust funds (ne fidem fallerent, ne depositum appellati abnegarent); but the ὡς before ἀλλ. separates it from the preceding adjectives.

† A. Bischoff (*ZNW.*, 1906, 271–274) prefers to think of Christians exposing themselves to the *lex maiestatis* by imprudent, if generous, resentment against the authorities on behalf of some ill-used fellow-citizen; but this interpretation, suggested long ago by Bengel, hardly seems broad enough by itself to explain the warning of the text. For the danger caused by *delatores* within Judaism after A.D. 70, cp. Joseph. *B. J.* vii. 3. 3, etc.

‡ Barth (*Einl.* p. 127) compares the effects produced throughout the French provinces by the massacre of St. Bartholomew.

and, when they desired a similar outburst at the expense of local Christians, all that was needed was a proconsul to gratify their wishes, and some outstanding disciple like Antipas or Polykarp to serve as a victim.

§ 3. *Destination and origin.*—The epistle is addressed to the Christian churches (cp. 5^{13}) in Pontus, Galatia, Cappadocia, Asia, and Bithynia. The order, from NE. to S. and W. (cp. p. 94), reflects the road followed by the bearer of the letter, who was to take the trade-route by sea to Amisus or Heraclea or Sinope, and thence make a circuit through the four * provinces in question, returning finally to Bithynia (so Ewald and Hort, cp. *EBi.* iii. 3806–3807). Why these particular districts are mentioned, to the exclusion of Cilicia, Pamphylia, and Lycia, it is as difficult to explain as to account satisfactorily for the selection of the seven Asiatic cities in Apoc 2–3; in any case their order is natural, upon the presupposition that the bearer sailed from Rome to Pontus. As a glance at the map is enough to show, "the order Pontus, Galatia, Cappadocia is an exact inversion of the order which would present itself to a writer looking mentally towards Asia Minor from Babylon." † The facilities of travel throughout the empire, and the habit of exchanging copies of such letters between the churches, would render the dissemination of the epistle quite possible, even if we supposed that the bearer had only a single copy to begin with. The explicit mention of neighbouring provinces in the title puts the pastoral on a different footing from, *e.g.*, James, Judas, and 2 Peter.

This assumes that Βαβυλών in 5^{13} is a symbolic term for Rome—an interpretation which accords with the figurative language upon Israel (1^1 $2^{4\text{-}10}$),

---

* *i.e.* (i.) Bithynia and Pontus, (ii.) Galatia, (iii.) Cappadocia, and (iv.) Asia. Bithynia (Ac 16^7) and Cappadocia, so far as we know, were never evangelised by Paul, but (cp. p. 53) their Christianity may be explained by Ac 2^9 (where Hemsterhuis and Valckenaer conj. Βιθυνίαν for Ἰουδαίαν), which would also throw light on the Pontus and Cappadocia of 1 P 1^1. Galatia was a Pauline sphere (2 Ti 4^{10}), as was Asia in part, but the tone of Galatians suggests that there must have been some local interest in Peter. Whether Peter ever travelled in these districts, it is impossible to say. At all events the Gentile Christians must have largely outnumbered the Jewish Christians by the time that 1 Peter was written (cp. *ET.* xxviii. 411 f.).

† So Hort (p. 168), after Bengel. Cilicia is omitted because it belonged to Syria till about A.D. 74, whilst Pamphylia and Lycia might roughly be regarded as "outside the Taurus."

the early patristic tradition (Eus. *H. E.* ii. 15, quoting Papias and Clem. Alex. as his authorities, so Jerome), which knew of no Christian church at Babylon nor of any visit of Peter to that region, the association of Mark (see above) with the apostle, and the allusion in 2^{14} (*εἴτε βασιλεῖ . . . εἴτε ἡγεμόσιν*). Erbes (*ZKG.*, 1901, pp. 16 f.), in his attempt to disprove Peter's death at Rome (so van Manen), denies the mystical sense of Babylon,* and, like Solger (following Grimm and Hase), supposes that Peter went to the Assyrian † Babylon itself (in 58, Solger). The presence of Jews in the latter district may be granted, but persecution and plague had reduced them sadly in the fifth and sixth decades of the century; the Syriac tradition is strangely silent upon any such mission; and Thomas, not Peter, is associated with the evangelisation of Parthia. Besides, the figurative description of Mark in 5^{13b} as *my son*, tells in favour of the spiritual interpretation of Βαβυλών in the immediately preceding words, no less than against the theory which would see in ἡ ἐν Βαβυλῶνι συνεκλεκτή an allusion to Peter's wife (so Bengel, Mayerhoff, Jachmann, Alford, Stanley, and Bigg), who accompanied her husband on his mission-tours (1 Co 9^{5}) and was not unknown to later tradition. Apart from the fact that the phrase is an extremely singular description of an individual, it would be very awkward to follow it up with a reference, which was not literal (though some, *e.g.* Bengel and Stanley, would take it literally), to *my son Marcus*. The combination of 'the church in Babylon' (especially in greeting a series of churches) 'and my spiritual son' is much more likely than 'my wife and my spiritual son,' particularly as Peter is said to have been a father (Eus. *H. E.* iii. 30. 1; Clem. Alex. *Strom.* iii. 6. 52). His mission at Rome is probably historical.

There is no hint in the epistle of any trouble between Jewish and Gentile Christians, and no allusion to the vexed question of the Law. The audience present to the writer's mind is composed of Christians regarded as the true Israel (ἐκλεκτοῖς παρεπιδήμοις διασπορᾶς), who were aliens in a world of suffering and persecution. Their pre-Christian condition was one of religious ignorance (1^{14} ἄγνοια, cp. Eph 4^{18}, Ac 17^{30}), in which they were no *people of God* ($2^{9.\,10}$), but the long destined purpose of God's salvation had been achieved in them ($1^{8\text{-}12}$),

* So after Calvin, Alford, Dean Stanley (*Sermons and Essays on Apost. Age*, p. 68), Johnstone (*op. cit.* pp. 23–28), and Kühl (pp. 264 f.) among modern critics. The arguments for Rome, as against the Mesopotamian Babylon, are best put by Windischmann (pp. 130–133), Seufert (*ZWT.*, 1885, 146–156), Salmon (*INT.* pp. 440 f.), Lightfoot (*Clement*, ii. pp. 491 f.), Zahn (*Einl.* ii. 19 f.), and Burger (pp. 154 f.).

† The tradition connecting Mark with Alexandria, and the possibility of the *Preaching of Peter* having an Egyptian origin, might tell in favour of the Egyptian Babylon, a Roman fortress in Old Cairo (cp. Cone, *EBi.* 3681), whose claims were advocated by Le Clerc, Mill, Pearson, Pott, and Greswell. Michaelis thought of Seleucia, Semler (following Pearson, Harduin, and some others) of Jerusalem.

and they were now the true and the new People (2^{10}). All this points to Gentile Christians as the preponderating and characteristic element in the churches addressed. Since there were Jewish settlements throughout these provinces, the local churches in all likelihood included members of Jewish birth, probably also some who had been proselytes.* This would account in part for the familiarity with the LXX which the writer presupposes; besides, it adds point to several of his appeals. But of the Gentile Christian character of the main body (Cassiodorus: 'Petri ad gentes') there can be no doubt (cp. Grimm, pp. 657 f., and Hoennicke, *JC.* pp. 113–117). Even a phrase like πατροπαράδοτος in connection with ἀναστροφή (1^{18}), which might imply Jewish converts, would well apply to the strong yoke of hereditary pagan custom "built up and sanctioned by the accumulated instincts and habits of past centuries of ancestors."† Finally, the tone of 4^{3-4} puts it beyond doubt that the readers had been pagans prior to their conversion; such a description would not apply to Jewish Christians.

§ 4. *Relation to Paul and Paulinism.*—1 P. is therefore a pastoral addressed to the Gentile Christians north of the Taurus in Asia Minor. The writer evidently did not belong to the evangelists who had founded the local churches (1^{12}), for the tradition reported by Origen (*apud* Eus. *H. E.* iii. 1), that Peter evangelised the Jews in Pontus, Galatia, Bithynia, Cappadocia, and Asia, is little more than an inference from 1 P 1^{1}. The writer neither refers to any previous visit, nor promises a visit. His knowledge of the conditions of his readers does not imply any close personal relationship such as that presupposed in Paul's letter to the churches of Galatia, and there is no hint

* The idea, at one time advocated by some critics (*e.g.* Michaelis, *Einl.* § 246), that the epistle was meant for proselytes of the gate (cp. 2^{4}) has no basis in facts. The other view, which limited the epistle to Jewish Christians (so, *e.g.*, Augusti, Pott, de Wette, and Bertholdt), is mainly advocated to-day by Weiss and Kühl, partly on their peculiar and untenable theory of the date of the epistle, partly on erroneous exegetical grounds. Thus, even had Paul not written Ro 9^{25}, it would be daring to argue that because Hosea's words, cited in 1 P. 2^{10}, originally referred to the Jews, they must bear the same reference in this connexion.

† So Hort (p. 76), who refers to Gataker's note on M. Aurel. iv. 6; cp. Denney, *The Death of Christ*, pp. 93 f. The Jewish Christian character of the readers of 1 P. is assumed by Shailer Mathews, *Messianic Hope in NT* (1906), pp. 150 f.; but this hypothesis is almost entirely abandoned.

of what title he had to address these Asiatic believers.* He simply writes as *an apostle of Jesus Christ.* This impression of indefiniteness, however, is due to the scanty records of the evangelisation of Asia Minor during the first century, even within Paul's lifetime. The difficulty is really not removed by the pseudonymous hypothesis, for even it assumes that readers of the epistle were meant to understand that Peter had had some connection with these provinces.

The internal evidence of the epistle reveals an interesting affinity (which Semler was one of the first to bring out) which is almost equally difficult, viz., with the writings as well as with the religious ideas of Paul. The echoes of Romans, if not of Galatians, are unmistakable. The language of 1^{5} (*φρουρουμένους διὰ πίστεως εἰς σωτηρίαν ἑτοίμην ἀποκαλυφθῆναι ἐν καιρῷ ἐσχάτῳ*) echoes Gal 3^{23} (*ἐφρουρούμεθα εἰς τὴν πίστιν ἀποκαλυφθῆναι*), though the ideas differ; and 2^{16} closely parallels Gal 5^{13}. More clearly, however, 1^{22} answers to Ro $12^{9f.}$, and 2^{11} (*τῶν σαρκικῶν ἐπιθυμιῶν, αἵτινες στρατεύονται κατὰ τῆς ψυχῆς ὑμῶν*) recalls Ro 7^{23} (*ἕτερον νόμον ἐν τοῖς μέλεσίν μου ἀντιστρατευόμενον τ. ν.*); while 2^{13-14} is an obvious reminiscence of the thought in Ro 13^{1-4}, just as 2^{5} is of Ro 12^{1}, or 1^{14} of Ro 12^{2}, or 3^{9} of Ro 12^{17}. The quotation in 2^{6-8} need not necessarily † have been moulded by Paul's language in Ro 9^{32-33}; but a comparison of both epistles, in the order and expression of thought, reveals a relationship which is not explicable except on the hypothesis that the one was written by a man who knew the other (cp. *e.g.* 2^{10} = Ro 9^{25}, 4^{7-11} = Ro 12^{3-6}). The dependence is naturally on the side of 1 Peter.‡ Apart altogether from the other evidence which places 1 Peter not earlier than the seventh decade, Paul's originality of thought and style is too well marked to admit of the hypothesis that he was the borrower.

But while an acquaintance not only with the general conceptions, but also with one or two of the epistles of Paul (*e.g.* 1 Co $3^{1f.\ 10f.}$ = 1 P $2^{1f.}$ = Col 3^{8}, 1 Co 16^{20} = 1 P 5^{14}) is indubitable, the writer is by no means a Paulinist. His attitude is rather that of the common practical consciousness pervading the

* If Paul wrote to the Roman and the Colossian churches, which he had not founded, and which contained a proportion at least of Jewish Christians, there is no great reason to hesitate about the probability of Peter having sent a pastoral to the Gentile Christians of Northern Asia Minor.

† The common use of a non-Septuagintal version of Is 28^{16} might be due to a *florilegium* (see above, p. 24); but the context suggests that the writer of 1 P. was not independent of Paul at this point, and this is corroborated by other data of the epistle.

‡ This is now admitted on almost all hands; for the evidence in detail, see especially Brückner's *Chron.* pp. 13–31; S. Davidson, *INT.* i. 538 f.; Sanday and Headlam, *Romans* (*ICC.*), pp. lxxiv–lxxvi; Usteri (*op. cit.* pp. 279 f.), and Völter (see below), pp. 28–31, with Seufert's elaborate article in *ZWT.* (1874) pp. 360–388.

churches,—a consciousness which was prior to Paul, and in which Paulinism, for the most part, operated merely as a ferment. The proper appreciation of this central popular Christianity in the apostolic age is vital to the proper focus for viewing the early Christian literature. Instead of 1 Peter representing a diluted and faded Paulinism, it denotes an attitude influenced, but essentially uncontrolled, by the special ideas of Paul's theology. The latter's faith-mysticism, his conception of justification, and his eschatology, are absent from this writer's pages, which reflect the outlook of a primitive Christian who had breathed the messianic atmosphere of the better Judaism. He criticises neither the Law nor the ritual of the OT. He has only two distinctive 'theological' ideas ($1^{10f.}$ $3^{19f.}$), and each is used practically (cp. *ERE.* v. 655 f., and Denney's *Death of Christ*, p. 86).

On the hypothesis that Peter wrote the epistle, this 'Pauline' feature might be accounted for by the fact that when Peter reached Rome, he must have found Romans a treasured possession in the archives of the local church. Already he must have been fairly familiar with the central ideas of Paul's preaching; the difference between them, which emerged at Antioch, was practical in the main, and their general conception of the gospel and its obligations was fairly alike, so far as we have any evidence on the point. Like Paul, he was not averse to consorting with Gentile Christians (Gal 2^{12-16}), and he, too, believed in justification, not by the law, but by faith in Jesus Christ. This would explain in part the "marriage of true minds" which is involved in the relation of 1 P. to the earlier Pauline gospel. On the other hand, Peter's nature was not speculative.* He was much more receptive and much less original than Paul. Hence his untheological temperament would naturally lead him to use phrases like ἐν Χριστῷ (3^{16} $5^{10.\ 14}$), and conceptions such as that of regeneration, for his own purposes of practical exhortation; cp. Maurenbrecher's *Von Jerusalem nach Rom* (1910), 247 f., and Kennedy in *ET.* (1916) 264 f.

§ 5. *The authorship.*—The Pauline cast of the epistle need not, however, be wholly attributed to Peter himself. Silvanus, his amanuensis,† had been associated with Paul in the Macedonian mission (1 Th 1^1, 2 Th 1^1) and at Corinth (2 Co 1^{19}), after which (Ac 18^5) he disappears from view. It cannot be too often and too emphatically denied that because an early Christian formed one of Paul's côterie, he must therefore have

* This consideration is brought out by Renan (ii. ch. v.) and Wernle (*Synoptische Frage*, pp. 199 f.); see also Rapp's essay in *PM.* (1898) pp. 323–337.

† Mark (5^{13}) and Glaukias (Clem. Alex. *Strom.* vii. 17) were the other interpreters or secretaries whose names have been preserved.

assimilated the apostle's entire theological system. At the same time, the probability is that Silvanus, during this early association with Paul, naturally acquired a sympathy or familiarity with his characteristic modes of thought and expression, and that as naturally these emerged when he wrote out what Peter had in substance dictated.

It does not follow that because Peter apparently did not write down his reminiscences of Jesus, he could not have written an epistle in Greek. And the Greek of this epistle, which is fairly correct and even idiomatic in style, is mainly drawn from the vocabulary of the LXX; in fact,* from certain sections of the LXX (*e.g.* $1^{8f.}$ with Dt 10–12, 2^{2}=Dt 11^{9}, 3^{9}=$11^{26f.}$ $12^{15f.}$, 5^{8}=11^{6} etc.). But the numerous reminiscences of the LXX, together with traces of an acquaintance with Philo (cp. Salmon, *INT.* 506), the book of Wisdom,† and 2 Maccabees, a large proportion of classical words, and a general style which 'shows that the writer within certain limits had a very considerable appreciation of, and power over, the characteristic usages of Greek' (Chase, p. 782), suggest the likelihood that the conceptions of the apostle owe something of their characteristic setting to his amanuensis. According to Papias, Peter needed Mark as his ἑρμηνευτής even in the work of preaching. As a native of Galilee, he cannot have been wholly unfamiliar with colloquial Greek, but even the power of speaking in a language does not imply skill in composition, and without denying Peter's ability to address audiences in Greek—which was essential to his mission-work—or his acquaintance not simply with the LXX but with the religious traditions circulated by books like Enoch, we are entitled to conclude that he required the services of a man like Silvanus‡ to compose such an epistle as the present, just as he needed Mark, if his reminiscences of Jesus were to be committed to writing. "Tradition tells us that St. Peter employed more than one interpreter; it is indeed hard not to think that we have the work of one in the First Ep. Is it credible that a Galilean fisherman who left out his H's (that, we are told, is what Mt 26^{73} implies) § should after middle life, and in the midst of absorbing occupations, have learnt to write

---

* Cp. Scharfe (*SK.*, 1889, pp. 650 f.). The writer's fondness for Isaiah (*e.g.* $1^{24f.}$=Is $40^{6f.}$, $2^{6f.}$=Is 8^{14} 28^{16}, $2^{9f.}$=Is $43^{20f.}$, $2^{22f.}$=Is $53^{5.\ 9.\ 12}$; also 1^{11b}=Is 53^{7-8}, 1^{18}=Is 53^{3b}, 2^{25b}=Is 40^{11}, 3^{15}=Is 8^{13} 29^{23}, 4^{14}=Is 11^{2}, 4^{17}= Is 25^{29}) may have been one reason why he followed the symbolic method of alluding to Rome as Babylon (cp. Is 47^{1} etc.). But that reference is earlier than the first literary evidence for it, *e.g.*, in Sib. Or. $5^{159f.}$ (cp. *DB.* i. 214–215).

† Cp. 2^{25}=Sap. 1^{6} 3^{13}, 3^{20}=Sap $14^{6f.}$ etc.

‡ Eichhorn thought of John Mark as the writer who worked up Peter's ideas, or (according to Baronius) translated them from Hebrew into Greek. But the translation-hypothesis (so Jerome: from Aramaic) is untenable in view of the style.

§ Not necessarily a mark of illiteracy, however (cp. C. F. Hogg, *ET.* iii. 426–427).

scholarly Greek like this?"* The query cannot but be answered in the negative.

The recognition of the share of Silvanus in writing the epistle (Ewald, Grimm) has spread in recent years; it is advocated in different forms by Zahn, Usteri, Bacon, Bigg, Monnier, and Hart. In this event Peter either dictated the letter, the phrase διὰ Σιλουανοῦ ἔγραψα (5^{12}) being equivalent practically † to expressions like Ac $15^{22\text{-}23}$, Ro 16^{22}; Polyk. *ad Phil.* 14; Ign. *Rom.* 10, etc. (cp. Link, *SK.*, 1896, pp. 405–436), or entrusted its composition (Zahn, Feine, Wohlenberg) to Silvanus, revising and sanctioning his work. As the latter was in all likelihood the bearer, there was no need of his inserting a special salutation from himself (as from Tertius in Ro 16^{22}); 5^{12} not only accredits him as an apostolic delegate, but possibly implies that he will supplement by means of oral teaching and information what the apostle has briefly incorporated in the epistle.‡ This may stamp the epistle, if one choose to say so, as semi-pseudonymous. At any rate it serves to account fairly for the data of the letter, the primitive and even Petrine cast of the ideas on the one hand, and the power of handling Greek upon the other.§ That the general tone and standpoint are Peter's, need not be doubted, in view of the coincidences between the epistle and the speeches of Peter in Acts.

The responsibility of Silvanus for the epistle's form and contents is pushed a step further by those who, like Seufert, Baljon, von Soden, Spitta, and R. Scott (*The Pauline Epistles*, 208 f.), make him its author after Peter's death. But, while Silvanus was undoubtedly an apostle (1 Th 2^{6}) and prophet (Ac 15^{32}) himself, and while this or almost any form of the pseudonym-hypothesis is legitimate and indeed deserving of

* Simcox, *The Writers of the NT.* (p. 68). "En tout cas, la langue de l'épître ne peut guère être la sienne. . . . On ne voit guère l'ardent Galiléen équilibrant ses phrases, s'appliquant à enchaîner exactement ses propositions" (Monnier, pp. 315 f.).

† Dionysius of Corinth (*apud* Eus. *H. E.* iv. 23. 11), writing to the Roman church, refers to the epistle of Clem. Rom. as a previous communication from Rome, τὴν προτέραν ἡμῖν διὰ Κλήμεντος γραφεῖσαν, *i.e.* the author is regarded as the mouthpiece of the Roman church.

‡ Erasmus misread the verse as a reference to some previous epistle composed by Silvanus.

§ When Josephus wrote his history of the Jewish war, "after all my materials were prepared for the work, I employed some *collaborateurs* to be quite *au fait* in the Greek idioms" (*Apion*, i. 9, tr. Shilleto).

serious consideration in view of the enigmatic data of the writing, the self-praise of 5^{12} becomes offensive on such a view. Besides, the age and authority of Silvanus would not have required any extraneous aid, in order to address the Asiatic Christians then, and the theory fails to explain why he chose Peter instead of Paul as his mouthpiece.

The lack of detailed personal reference to the life and words of Jesus has also been felt to tell heavily against the conception that the epistle could have been written by an apostle, and especially by so intimate an apostle and disciple as Simon Peter. This objection, however, is less serious than it seems. For one thing, the criterion presupposed is unhistorical; the supreme interests of the first generation of disciples were not biographical. For another thing, we have no evidence to establish a standard of what or how a disciple of Jesus would have written of him in a letter of exhortation addressed to a Christian church or group of churches. The so-called first epistle of John, on the supposition that it was composed by the son of Zebedee, has less biographical detail than First Peter; and even those who hold that the epistle of James * was written by the son of Alphæus, will admit that, for all its wealth of apparent allusions to the sayings of Jesus, it is practically devoid of any explicit allusion to his earthly career. Peter was accustomed to give reminiscences of the Lord's acts and words in his preaching. A transcript of these forms the basis of Mark's gospel; and although the latter was not yet published, any early Christian churches would be in possession of a certain catechetical summary of the Lord's chief sayings and of the main events of his career. The existence and circulation of such evangelic manuals in the primitive churches is highly probable, from the historical standpoint; the Christian confession, *Jesus is the Christ*, would have lacked meaning, had not catechumens learnt authoritatively to put some content into the term *Jesus*. Consequently any apostle like Peter might presuppose an elementary acquaintance with the historical outline of the Lord's life, so far as that was essential to the purposes of vital Christianity. First Peter not only does presuppose it, especially in connection

* James has more of the letter but less of the spirit of the gospels. 1 Peter contains much fewer reminiscences (cp. Scharfe, 138 f.) of the sayings of Jesus, in their synoptic form, but it is superior to Jas. in its intuitions of the genuinely Christian spirit.

with the messianic hopes of the OT, but also conveys unobtrusively certain allusions to Christ's life which harmonise with Peter's discipleship (1^{8} whom, having not seen, *ye* love; 2$^{22f.}$ 5^{1}). If the epistle lacked the opening word (*Peter*), says Jülicher (*Einl.* p. 178), no one would have conjectured that Peter wrote it. But this is as valid an argument—so far as it is valid—in favour of its Petrine origin. A writer who desired to write under Peter's name would probably have emphasised his figure. As a matter of fact, we have in 2 P (1^{1} etc.) an illustration of how a later writer would go to work who desired to lend *vraisemblance* to an epistle purporting to come from Peter; the apostle is made to speak prophetically of a future age, stress is laid on his qualifications as an eye-witness of Jesus, and an irenical allusion to Paul occurs. The absence of such traits in 1 P. is really a point in its favour.

A supplementary point is the consonance between the religious ideas of the epistle and those of the Petrine speeches in Acts: *e.g.* God no respecter of persons (1^{17}=Ac 10^{34}), the cleansing of the soul through faith (1^{22}=Ac 15^{9}), the rejoicing in shame (4$^{13.16}$=Ac 5^{41}), etc. These data are not decisive. They might (i.) point to the use of the earlier traditions by a later writer, who had access to them either in Acts or in their original shape. Or, (ii.) they might in some cases be no more than illustrations of the common fund of ideas and expressions within the primitive church. But when one makes allowance for the difference of circumstances (as, *e.g.*, Mayerhoff, pp. 218 f., fails to do), there is enough to indicate that the tradition underlying the speeches reflects the same mind as the epistle.*

§ 6. *Traces in early Christian literature.*—The evidence for the existence and authority of the epistle in the church is both ample and early. As Eusebius pointed out (*H. E.* iv. 14. 9, *ὅ γέ τοι Πολύκαρπος ἐν τῇ δηλωθείσῃ πρὸς Φιλιππησίους αὐτοῦ γραφῇ φερομένῃ εἰς δεῦρο, κέχρηταί τισι μαρτυρίαις ἀπὸ τῆς Πέτρου προτέρας ἐπιστολῆς*), the epistle was familiar to Polykarp); † this is

* For this primitive type of early Christian thought, especially in connection with the Petrine tradition preserved by Luke in Acts 1–5, cp. Ritschl's *Entstehung*², pp. 116 f., 285; Reuss, *NTTh.* ii. pp. 262 f.; P. Ewald, *das Hauptproblem d. Evglnfrage*, pp. 68–75; Mangold (*INT.* pp. 659 f.), Jacoby (*NT Ethik*, pp. 220 f.), Stevens (*NTTh.* pp. 258 f.), with B. Riggenbach (*ZSchw.*, 1890, 185–195), and De Faye (*AA.* 164 f.).

† While the allusions to 1 Peter in Polykarp, though introduced by no explicit formula of quotation, render it beyond question that the bishop knew the epistle, he never mentions Peter as the author, although he frequently cites Paul by name. This feature is employed by Harnack (*TLZ.*, 1887, p. 218) to show that the epistle or homily was as yet destitute of its Petrine address and conclusion (see below, § 8). But the inference is not conclusive. Paul had been at Philippi, to which Polykarp was writing; Peter, so far as we know, had not (contrast the case of Corinth in Clem. Rom.).

evident from echoes so distinct as, *e.g.*, i. 3 (εἰς ὃν οὐκ ἰδόντες πιστεύετε χαρᾷ ἀνεκλαλήτῳ καὶ δεδοξασμένῃ εἰς ἣν πολλοὶ ἐπιθυμοῦσιν εἰσελθεῖν) = $1^{8.12}$, ii. 1 (διὸ ἀναζωσάμενοι τὰς ὀσφύας δουλεύσατε τῷ Θεῷ . . . πιστεύσαντες εἰς τὸν ἐγείραντα τὸν Κύριον ἡμῶν Ἰησοῦν Χριστὸν ἐκ νεκρῶν καὶ δόντα αὐτῷ δόξαν) = $1^{13.21}$, ii. 2 (μὴ ἀποδιδόντες κακὸν ἀντὶ κακοῦ ἢ λοιδορίαν ἀντὶ λοιδορίας) = 3^{9}, v. 3 = 2^{11} (cp. Gal 5^{27}), vi. 3 (ζηλωταὶ περὶ τὸ καλόν) = 3^{13}, vii. 2 (νήφοντες πρὸς τὰς εὐχάς) = 4^{7}, viii. 1–2 = 2^{21}, amongst others (*GK.* i. 957 f., *NTA.* pp. 86–89). The use of the epistle in Clem. Rom. is less copious and clear, but on the whole visible in passages like vii. 2 f., where, after exhorting the Corinthians to abandon idle and *vain* thoughts (1^{18}), Clement bids them fix their eyes on 'the blood of Christ and know ὡς ἔστιν τίμιον τῷ Θεῷ τῷ πατρὶ αὐτοῦ' (= 1^{18-19}), following this up with an allusion to its redeeming power and to Noah's preaching of repentance (3^{20}); or in lix. 2 (ἐκάλεσεν ἡμᾶς ἀπὸ σκότους εἰς φῶς, ἀπὸ ἀγνωσίας εἰς ἐπίγνωσιν δόξης ὀνόματος αὐτοῦ) = $2^{9.15}$. The parallel of xxxvi. 2, ἀναθάλλει εἰς τὸ θαυμαστὸν αὐτοῦ φῶς (= 2^{9}), is dubious, owing to the textual uncertainty about θαυμαστόν (= om. Syr. Clem. Alex.). But the hypothesis of an agraphon (Resch, *Agrapha*, p. 248) must not be allowed to affect the force of the argument* from xlix. 5, where Pr 10^{12} is quoted in a form which, differing from the Hebrew text and the LXX alike, occurs in 1 P 4^{8}. Here, as elsewhere, it is possible (p. 24) that both passages independently derive from some common source, either a manual of citations or a Greek version of Proverbs; but this supposition is needless in view of the other evidence,† *e.g.* the occurrence in Clem. as in 1 P. alone of ἀδελφότης (ii. 4, 2^{17} 5^{9}) in the sense of brotherhood, ἀγαθοποιΐα (ii. 2, 4^{19}), and ὑπογραμμός (2^{21}, cp. xvi. where it is also used, with a citation from Is 53, of Christ's lowly patience). In *Eph.* v. 2–3, Ignatius uses ποιμήν and ἐπίσκοπος together (1 P $5^{2f.}$) in a context where he also quotes Pr 3^{34} (1 P 5^{5}) to enforce the duty of submission on the part of members towards their superiors in the church; but neither this nor any other resemblances (e.g. *Magn.* xiii. 2 = 5^{5}, *ad Polyk.* iv. 3 = 2^{6}) can be said to prove that the epistle was known to Ignatius, or at least used by him. In Barn. iv. 11 f. (μελετῶμεν τὸν φόβον τοῦ Θεοῦ . . . ὁ Κύριος ἀπροσωπολήμπτως κρινεῖ τὸν κόσμον· ἕκαστος καθὼς ἐποίησεν κομιεῖται) the

---

Besides, Polykarp more than once adopts silently the words of Paul (*e.g.* iii. 3 = Gal 4^{26}, iv. 1 = 1 Ti 6^{10}, vi. 2 = Ro $14^{10.12}$) as he does those of 1 Peter; and even the quotations from the former, introduced by εἰδότες ὅτι, are epigrammatic and axiomatic statements, 'while the phrases quoted from 1 Peter are rather of a hortatory type' (Chase, p. 781*a*).

* The quotation in Ja 5^{20} is slightly different. As Pr 3^{34} is quoted not only in 1 P 5^{5} but in Ja 4^{6}, its occurrence in Clem. xxx. 2 cannot safely be drawn upon in this connexion.

† The greeting (p. 352) goes back in part to the LXX (εἰρήνη ὑμῖν πληθυνθείη, Dn 3^{98} 6^{25}), though its Christian expansion and stamp were probably due to 1 P 1^{2}. A contemporary Jewish phrase is the שלומכן יסגא in the address of the official letters sent by R. Gamaliel of Jerusalem to the Jews of the Dispersion (cp. Derenbourg's *L'Histoire et la Géographie de la Palestine*, i. pp. 242 f.). These letters were dictated to John, his secretary (cp. 1 P 5^{12}).

ideas and language of 1 P 1^{17} recur, just as the conception of the OT prophets having been inspired to anticipate Christ's suffering (1 P $1^{10f.}$) is reproduced in v. 5–6; but no stress can be laid on this, while the only other parallels (πάσης χάριτος, of God: xxi. 9 = 5^{10}; *a spiritual temple built up unto the Lord*, xvi. 10 cp. 2^5) of moment are indecisive.

The lonely echoes in the Didachê (i. 4, ἀπέχου τῶν σαρκικῶν καὶ σωματικῶν ἐπιθυμιῶν = 2^{11} ἀπέχεσθαι τῶν σαρκικῶν ἐπιθυμιῶν) and Diognetus (ix. 2 = 3^{18}) contrast with the more numerous coincidences* between Hermas and 1 Peter. But none of these seems quite decisive, and their cumulative force does not involve any literary relation between the two writings. The same holds true of 2 Clement (xiv. 2 = 1^{20}, xvi. 4 = 4^8), and even of Justin Martyr. On the other hand, Papias knew and used the epistle (Eus. *H. E.* iii. 39. 17), as did οἱ πάλαι πρεσβύτεροι (iii. 3. 1), and the echoes of it in the epistle from Lyons and Vienne show (Eus. *H. E.* v. 1–2) that it was one of the scriptures current in Gaul by the middle of the second century. By the time of Tertullian (Rönsch, *das NT Tert.* pp. 556 f.), Irenæus, Origen, and Clement of Alexandria (Zahn's *Forschungen*, iii. 79 f.), it was freely quoted as Petrine; but 'the actual traces of the early use of 1 Peter in the Latin churches are very scanty. There is not the least evidence to show that its authority was ever disputed, but, on the other hand, it does not seem to have been much read' (Westcott, *Canon*, p. 263). Thus, while included in the Peshiṭta, it is not mentioned in the Muratorian Canon, though the Apocalypse of Peter is canonized. The omission may have been accidental, as in the case of Hebrews, and, as the document in question is mutilated, it may have been really mentioned, although none of the attempts to find a place for it in the extant text possesses any critical significance. Nevertheless by this time the epistle was elsewhere known, and known as Petrine. From Clem. Alex. (*Strom.* iv. 12. 81) it is possible to infer that Basilides, and, from a fragment of Theodotus (12), that the Valentinian school of the East, may also have read the epistle (for the *Hypotyposeis*, see Zahn's *Forschungen*, iii. 133 f.), but its character was not likely to commend it to the Gnostics in general.

On the other hand, the simpler and more direct character of the epistle appears to indicate its priority to Ephesians.† The fact that both encyclicals to the Asiatic churches open with the same formula (*Blessed be the God and Father of our Lord Jesus Christ, who*, etc.) is not robbed of its significance by the occurrence of *Blessed be God, who created heaven and earth*, at the opening of the king of Tyre's letter quoted by Eusebius (*Præp. Euang.* ix. 34) from Eupolemus; for, although Paul (2 Co 1^3) partially adapted the Jewish formula, its Petrine form is unique. The following paragraph (1^{3-12}) is carried

* Cp. Zahn's *Hirten des Hermas* (pp. 423 f.), *NTA.* 115–117, and Spitta, *Urc.* ii. 391–399 (where the dependence is assigned to 1 Peter). For echoes in the Odes of Solomon, see *JTS.* xv. 47–52.

† So Schwegler, Ewald (*Sieben Sendschreiben*, pp. 156 f.), Davidson, Hönig, but especially Hilgenfeld (*ZWT.*, 1873, 465–498, *Einl.* 624 f.), Clemen (*Paulus*, i. 139 f.), and W. Brückner (*Chron.* pp. 41 f.), with B. Weiss (*Petr. Lehrbegriff*, 426 f.) and Kühl, of course, as against Koster (pp. 207 f.), P. Ewald (*op. cit.* 28 f.), Klöpper (pp. 33 f.), and particularly Holtzmann (*Kritik. der Eph. u. Col. Briefe*, pp. 260 f.).

on with ἐν ᾧ and participles, as in Eph 1^{5-15}, whilst in Eph 1^{18-20} ἐλπίς and κληρονομία are correlated, on the basis of human faith supported by the divine δύναμις, as in 1 P 1^{3-5}. Further parallels of thought and language occur in 1 P 1^{10-12} = Eph $3^{5.\,10}$, 1 P 1^{13} = Eph 6^{14}, 1 P 1^{13-15} = Eph 2^{3}, 1 P 1^{18} = Eph 4^{17}, 1 P 1^{20}=Eph $1^{4.\,9}$, 1 P 1^{23}=Eph 1^{13}, 1 P 2^{1-2}=Eph 4^{22-25}, 1 P 2^{4-6} = Eph $2^{18-20.\,21-22}$, 1 P 2^{13} = Eph 5^{21}, 1 P 2^{18} = Eph 6^{5}, 1 P 3^{22}=Eph 1^{20-22} (a specially striking coincidence), 1 P $3^{1.\,5}$=Eph 5^{21-22}, 1 P 3^{4}=Eph 3^{16}, 1 P 3^{7}=Eph 5^{25}, 1 P 4^{2-3}=Eph $2^{3f.}$, 1 P 4^{10}=Eph 3^{2}. Both use διάβολος, not σατανᾶς, both reproduce the 'descensus ad inferos' (1 P 3^{19}= Eph 4^{8-9}); the predominance of *hope* in 1 P. corresponds to its prominence in Eph. (cp. 1^{18} 2^{12} 4^{4}), and common to both are terms like ἀκρογωνιαῖος and εὔσπλαγχνος. The affinities between the two, not only in phraseology but in structure and conception, involve a literary relationship which implies that the one drew upon the other, unless we admit, with Seufert and R. Scott, that both were written by Silvanus. Either Peter knew Ephesians, or, if the latter is post-Pauline, the author of Ephesians more probably was acquainted with the Petrine pastoral.

The connection with James is practically of the same nature. Both 1 P. and Jas. use διασπορά in a derived sense in their addresses, both emphasise τὸ δοκίμιον τῆς πίστεως (1^{7}=Ja 1^{3}) under the fire of trial and temptation (1^{6}= Ja 1^{2}), both employ a special rendering of Pr 10^{12} (4^{8}=Ja 5^{20}; cp. Field's *Notes on Tr. of NT.* 239), and both follow up the citation from Pr 3^{34} by an admonition to submit to God and to resist the devil ($5^{6f.}$=Ja $4^{6f.}$); common to both, among the NT writers, are ἀνυπόκριτος, ἄσπιλος, παρακύπτω, and στηρίζω, and there are further parallelisms in 1^{3}=Ja 1^{18}, 1^{23}=Ja 1^{18}, $2^{1f.}$ =Ja $1^{20f.}$, 2^{11}=Ja 4^{1}, 2^{25}=Ja 5^{19}, 3^{15-16}=Ja 3^{13}, 5^{4}=Jas 1^{12}, 5^{6}=Ja 4^{10} (see Spitta's *Urc.* ii. 184 f.). The dependence of Jas. on 1 P. is argued by Brückner (*ZWT.*, 1874, pp. 533 f.; *Chron.* pp. 60-65), Holtzmann (*ZWT.*, 1882, pp. 292–310), Wrede (*LC.*, 1896, 450–451), Grimm, Usteri (pp. 292 f.), von Soden, and Bigg, as against Sabatier (*ESR.* x. 620 f.), Mayor, and Zahn. Both handle, from different sides, the same theme, *i.e.* the Christian under suffering. It is possible that in some cases, at any rate, the coincidences may be fortuitous, either because the same or a similar topic suggested similar language to writers familiar, *e.g.*, with the LXX, or because a certain community of style and conception prevailed among early Christian writers of this class (so Mayerhoff, pp. 115 f., and Windisch). But probabilities converge on the conclusion that the one writing echoes the other, and, if 1 P. is on other grounds put early, the dependence of Jas. naturally follows.

§ 7. *The date.*—Within these limits, the theories of the date fall into two main classes, pre-Neronic or post-Neronic. The former includes the impossible hypothesis of Weiss and Kühl (*S.K.*, 1865, 619–657), that the epistle was written (*c.* A.D. 54) prior to Romans; but * its leading statement is that which assigns the composition of the letter to the period immediately or almost immediately preceding A.D. 64 (so, *e.g.*, Hofmann,

* B. Brückner dates it previous to Paul's imprisonment at Jerusalem, while Gloag chooses A.D. 59–60.

Bleek ± 62;* Burger 63; Bartlet *c.* 63; Renan, Cook, Feine, and Belser, 63–64; Zahn and Wohlenberg, spring of 64; Lightfoot, Monnier, and Chase). But not until the Neronic outburst took place was the mere name of Christian enough to expose believers to interference and suffering (cp. Workman's *Persecution in the Early Church*, 1906, pp. 52 f.); and, on the supposition that the epistle is connected directly with Peter, the balance of probability is strongly in favour of a date subsequent to the massacre of 64. Such post-Neronic hypotheses may be conveniently subdivided into (i.) those which assign the epistle to a date not long after that crisis, *i.e.* between 64 and 67 (so Eichhorn, Grimm, Hug, de Wette, Thiersch, Huther, Ewald, Neander, Mayerhoff, L. Schultze's *Hdbuch der theol. Wissensch.* i. 2. pp. 106–109; Reithmayr, Beyschlag's *NTTh.* i. 377–382; Allard's *Histoire des persécut.* i. pp. 61 f.; Farrar, *Early Days of Christianity*, pp. 67–85; Plumptre, Salmon, Bovon's *NTTh.* ii. 440 f.; Schäfer, *Einl.* 319–329; Hatch, Hort, Bacon, Sieffert, and Barth), and (ii.) those which, abandoning the traditional date of Peter's martyrdom, feel that the references to persecution demand the eighth decade (Swete [*Mark*, pp. xvii f.] = 70–75; F. J. Briggs [*Critical Review*, 1897, pp. 449–454]; and particularly Ramsay [*Exp.*[4] viii. pp. 8 f., 110 f., 282 f.] = 75–80). The former position seems to fit most if not all of the internal evidence of the epistle. The latter involves the abandonment of A.D. 67 as the traditional *terminus ad quem* of Peter's life; were the countervailing arguments decisive, this might conceivably be yielded, but, as has been already urged, their weight is not heavy enough to tell in favour of so drastic a measure. The lack of any reference to Paul,† alive or dead, is at first sight surprising, upon the post-Neronic hypothesis. But the

* This date, during Paul's imprisonment in the capital, is advocated generally by Keil, Steiger, Guericke, Wieseler (*Chronologie*, pp. 564 f.), and Jacquier. Alford thinks of some date 'between 63 and 67'; Bigg fixes on 58–64; and B. W. Henderson (*Life and Principate of Nero*, 438–439) decides for 64. Neither Mr. Henderson nor Dr. Klette (see above), both of whom come to the study of this document from the side of classical investigation, find any serious objection to the setting of 1 P. in connection with the Roman situation of the seventh decade.

† F. W. Lewis (*Exp.*[6] x. 319–320) argues that the epistle must have been written after Paul's death, since the absence of any allusion to him in $5^{12\text{-}13}$ indicates that Mark and Silvanus had been deprived by death of their former leader.

critic of ancient as well as of modern literature is well accustomed to instances in which a person or event is ignored by a contemporary, although some allusion might more or less reasonably be expected.

The epistle is assigned to Domitian's reign by A. H. Blom (*de Brief van Jac.* pp. 241 f.), Scholten (*Bijdragen*, 1882, pp. 79 f.), von Soden (*JPT.*, 1883, 461 f.), Wrede (*ZNW.*, 1900, pp. 75–85), J. Réville (*Les Origines de l'épiscopat*, i. pp. 358 f.), and McGiffert (*AA.* pp. 482 f., 593 f.), as well as by Harnack (in its original form, A.D. 83–93 or even earlier), Soltau (see below), Völter (in its original form, before A.D. 96), and Knopf (*NZ.* 90 f.). The objections to this date are (i.) that the allusions to any so-called persecution do not necessarily (see above) point to the Domitianic period; (ii.) that on such a hypothesis it is not any easier to understand the geographical address of 1^1 than on the hypothesis that the epistle was written by Silvanus for Peter; and (iii.) that the pseudonymous theory fails (see above) to account adequately for the lack of emphasis on Peter's prestige and apostolic qualifications. It is true that an author who wrote under an apostolic name would feel less inclination to emphasise his *nom de guerre* if he wrote merely for hortatory purposes than if he had any polemical or theological aim (so Wrede). Still, this consideration hardly meets the data of 1 P. It is the apparent absence of definite motive which tells against the pseudonymous hypothesis most heavily. Once the 'mediating' tendency of the epistle is abandoned, it becomes more difficult than ever to find any satisfactory place for it after Peter's death, and the further down we go, the object of the writing becomes less and less obvious. Any writer, producing a work under Peter's name, towards the end of the first century, would almost certainly have coloured the personality of the apostle to suit not only the tradition (cp. Mt $16^{18f.}$; Clem. Rom. 40–41), but the contemporary status of his office. Volkmar's hypothesis, that it was composed under Antoninus, *c.* A.D. 140 (*ZWT.*, 1861, pp. 427 f.), drops with his idea that Enoch (quoted in 3^{19}) was not written till A.D. 132, and in any case the use of the epistle by Polykarp rules such a view out of court, as well as that of Zeller (*ZWT.*, 1876, pp. 35 f.), Steck (*JPT.*, 1891, pp. 561 f.), and van Manen, who adhere to Hadrian's reign. The choice really lies between the age of Trajan and that of Domitian. The former view was at one time almost dominant (Cludius, Schwegler's *NZ.* ii. 14 f.; Hilgenfeld, *Einl.* 624 f.; Baur, Mangold, Lipsius, Keim, Weizsäcker's *AA.* ii. 160; W. Brückner, Hausrath, and S. Davidson, *INT.* i. 529–563), and is still maintained by Holtzmann (*GGA*, 1894, pp. 27 f.), Schmiedel (*EBi.* 761–762), Baljon, Kreyenbühl (*Evglm der Wahrheit*, i. 97 f.), Pfleiderer (*Urc.* iv. 250–251), and P. Schmidt (*ZWT.*, 1907, pp. 24 f.). Recently there has been a disposition, however, to retreat towards the beginning of the second century,* in the direction of a date *c.* A.D. 100 rather than A.D. 112–117, as in the case of Cone (*Gospel and its Interpretations*, pp. 260 f.), Jülicher (*GGA.*, 1884, pp. 549 f.), and Gunkel, partly to allow time for the epistle's use by Papias and Polykarp, partly because the alleged traces of the Trajanic persecution under Pliny no longer seem decisive (indeed, when the imperial cultus was in force, an unqualified phrase like that of 2^{17} becomes almost incredible), and partly owing to a general retreat from the Tübingen † idea (*e.g.* Schwegler, *NZ.* ii. 22) that the epistle represents a second-century attempt, from the Jewish Christian side, to come to some understanding with the Pauline opposition. The last-named conception is no longer defensible or defended, though two romantic attempts have been made recently to combine part of it with a defence of the Petrine authorship, Zahn (*Einl.* § 41) suggesting that Gentile Christians would feel in-

* One unresolved difficulty in the path of this hypothesis lies in the relaxation of the imperial régime after Domitian's assassination in 96. There is nothing to account for the sense of pressure about A.D. 100, when there was rather a lull in the storm.

† Even Mayerhoff (pp. 103 f.) and Reuss (*NTTh.* ii. pp. 262 f.) at one time detected a mediating tendency in the epistle, while some (*e.g.* Alford) detect in 5^{12} a ratification of the Pauline type of doctrine originally taught in these churches. Schmiedel still takes $5^{12f.}$ as an expression of ecclesiastical tendency, although in the same breath he avers that "the remaining contents of the epistle show little of that tendency to bring about a reconciliation between Paulinism and Jewish Christianity which the Tübingen school attributed to it" (*EBi.* 4521). For "little," "nothing" ought to be substituted. But, even apart from that, the interpretation is inconsistent and inadequate. The coherence and point of the writing are lost, if a special and subtle motive is introduced at the very close. Whichever way the epistle moves, it must move all together, like Wordsworth's cloud, if it moves at all. Cp. Pfleiderer's *Paulinismus* (Eng. tr.), ii. pp. 149 f., and Hilgenfield (*ZWT.*, 1873, pp. 465 f.). The arguments against the Trajanic date are best put by Usteri (pp. 239 f.).

spirited and consoled by receiving such counsels of faith from one who had been the leader of the circumcision (Gal 2^7), whilst Chase conjectures (p. 790) that Paul actually summoned Peter to Rome in order that their co-operation might be an object-lesson of unity, and that Silvanus, though the bearer of Peter's letter, was primarily Paul's messenger to the Asiatic Christians.

§ 8. *Literary structure.*—Four endeavours have been made, from different sides, to show that the writing is of more or less composite origin. (*a*) Harnack's view (*TU.* ii. 2. 106–109, *ACL.* ii. 1. 451–465), partly anticipated by Cludius, that 1^{1-2} and 5^{12-14} represent second-century additions* (A.D. 150–175) to an earlier, anonymous homily, in order to guarantee its apostolic rights to a place in the rising canon of Christian scriptures, is due to his perception of the insuperable difficulties that beset any form of the pseudonymous hypothesis; but it is liable to the crucial objections that (i.) it fails to explain why a homily which is *ex hypothesi* so devoid of Petrine and so full of Pauline Christianity should be attributed to Peter; (ii.) that it implies the tract or homily began with *Blessed be the God and Father*, etc. ($1^{3f.}$)—an opening which is otherwise known to us (cp. 2 Co 1^3, Eph 1^3) only as the sequel to the address of an epistle; † (iii.) that the difficulties in 1^{1-2} 5^{12-14} are at least as explicable on the hypothesis of these verses being original as on that of their addition by a later scribe; (iv.) that Harnack frankly abandons all attempts to explain why in a so-called 'catholic' epistle a definite selection of provinces, and, indeed, of such provinces as those of 1^1, should be introduced; (v.) that *the true grace of God* (5^{12}) bears directly, though not exclusively, on the main thought of the epistle (cp. 5^{10} *after you have suffered a little the God of all grace shall*, etc.), namely, that the reality of God's grace and the genuineness of his calling are not to be doubted on account of the suffering to which they expose the Christian; (vi.) that this view involves the unlikelihood of one corrected copy having supplanted the numerous uninterpolated copies which must have been in circulation throughout the churches before the particular scribe began his work; and (vii.) that the self-designation in 5^1 (*a witness of the sufferings of Christ*) points naturally to Peter,‡ whether the epistle is pseudonymous or not, rather than to some unknown Roman confessor, just as the following allusion

* Possibly made by the author of 2 Peter (3^1). This is as precarious as the alternative idea that the writing had originally another address, but it is more plausible than the hypothesis that Peter's name was added by some irresponsible scribe, "who had no idea of giving the epistle canonical authority, but thought he saw good reason for regarding it as the work of Peter" (McGiffert, *AA.* p. 596). If the data of the writing afford no sufficient motive for pseudonymity, they are still less likely to have suggested Peter to any scribe or copyist.

† Similarly, on the analogy of the other early Christian epistles, 5^{10-11} suggests the close of a letter or epistle, not of a homily, and an allusion like that of 5^1 confirms this idea.

‡ The similar phrase in 1 Co 15^{15} is not quite parallel, and does not fix the sense of the term here.

to shepherding the flock of God (5^{2-3}) echoes the tradition afterwards voiced in Jn 21^{15-17}. For these reasons, drawn from internal and external evidence alike, this ingenious theory cannot be held to have hit the ford exactly.*

(*b*) Soltau's essay (*SK*, 1905, 302 f.; 1906, 456–460),† starting from the erroneous literary criterion that an original writer will eschew verbal repetitions, disentangles an early Christian tract or homily, written during Domitian's reign, from a series of interpolations (1^{1-2} 3^{14-22} 4^{5-6} $5^{1-5a.\ 12-14}$, with smaller insertions, *e.g.*, in 1^{22b} 2^{5} 3^{12b}) which transformed it into a Petrine epistle. The proofs of literary dependence (5^{2} on Tit 2^{7}, 5^{4} on He 13^{20}, 5^{5b} on Ja 4^{6}, and 3^{19-22} on Col 2^{11-15} 3^{1}), however, are most hazardous; the evidence for a difference of tone and style between the original and the later additions is not convincing (*e.g.* 2^{9} explains 5^{13} quite as well as 1^{1}, while the conceptions of 1^{1-2} are not different from those of the body of the writing); and if 5^{1-5} does appear slightly disconnected in its present setting, instead of regarding it as an interpolation (for which the contents afford no justification), I should prefer to regard 5^{1-9} as a misplaced section which originally lay between 3^{7} and 3^{8}.

(*c*) Völter's independent attempt (*Der Erste Petrusbrief, seine Entstehung und Stellung in der Geschichte des Urchristentums*, 1906) distinguishes a pseudonymous Petrine epistle, written at Rome previous to the Domitianic persecution, from a series of later interpolations (Ἰησοῦ Χριστοῦ, Πόντου . . . Βιθυνίας, 1^{1}; καὶ ῥ. . . . πληθυνθείη, 1^{2}; τοῦ κυρίου . . . Χριστοῦ, δι' ἀναστάσεως Ἰ. Χ. ἐκ νεκρῶν, 1^{3}; ἐν ἀποκ. Ἰ. Χ., 1^{7}; ὃν . . . πιστεύοντες δὲ, 1^{8}; 1^{11}; ἐν πνεύματι ἁγίῳ ἀποστ. ἀπ' οὐρανοῦ, 1^{12}; ἐν ἀποκ. Ἰ. Χ., 1^{13}; 1^{18-21} 2^{4b}; διὰ Ἰ. Χ., 2^{5}; ἐπ' αὐτῷ, 2^{6}; 2^{21-25}; τὸν Χριστόν, 3^{15}; ἐν Χριστῷ, 3^{16}; 3^{18}–4^{6}; διὰ Ἰ. Χ., 4^{11}; 4^{12-19}; καὶ μάρτυς . . . κοινωνός, 5^{1}; εἰδότες . . . ἐπιτελεῖσθαι, 5^{9}; ὀλίγον παθόντας, ἐν Χριστῷ, 5^{10}; ἐν β., 5^{13}; τοῖς ἐν Χριστῷ, 5^{14}) added ‡ *c.* 115 A.D. dur-

---

* McGiffert (*AA.* 598 f.) ingeniously suggests Barnabas as the author of the anonymous original. Certainly, so far as we can judge, Paul, Barnabas, and Peter were the only three men who stood in the relationship indicated by 5^{11-14} to Mark and Silvanus. Barnabas had been in touch with Paul and Asia Minor; he was a Hellenist, also, who would know the LXX. But 2^{6-9} need not have come from a Levite, and Barnabas had no special call to remain anonymous as an author.

† Cp. Clemen's adverse discussion (*SK.*, 1905, 619–628).

‡ 3^{19-21} and 4^{6}, the passages on the descent and mission to the underworld, are no doubt parenthetical; but this does not involve their interpolation at a later date, as Cramer (*Nieuwe bijdragen*, vii. 4. 73 f., 126 f.) and A. Meyer (*die moderne Forschung über die Gesch. d. Urc.*, 1898, p. 43) propose (cp. Baljon, *Theol. Stud.*, 1891, 429–431), followed recently by P. Schmidt (*ZWT.*, 1907, 42 f.), who assigns $3^{19f.}$ and 4^{6} to various hands, the latter interpolation being made by one who either did not know of $3^{19f.}$ or wished to emphasise a simpler and more orthodox idea of the descensus. In any case, the interpolation must have been inserted during the earlier part of the second century, as Origen found it in his text. Hart (*EGT.* v. 2 f.) suggests that 4^{12}–5^{11} is a postscript intended for some of the community who were exposed to special trial; but the allusions to persecution in 2–3 are sufficient to show that the situation of the churches addressed was probably homogeneous in this respect.

ing the Asiatic persecution under Trajan. This hypothesis is beset, however, with insuperable difficulties, literary and historical. It is improbable that any writing towards the close of the first century would be circulated as Petrine which explicitly avoided all mention of Jesus Christ (p. 27; by way of protest against Paul's Christology!) and contented itself with religious conceptions which added nothing specifically Christian to the OT. piety.

(*d*) Perdelwitz (*Die Mysterienreligion und das Problem des I Petrusbriefes*, 1911) regards 1^{3}–4^{11} as a baptismal address, added to a homily for the general church of these neophytes, a church composed mainly of people who had once been members of a mystery-cult like that of Cybele. But even to this Wendland's verdict applies: "hier, wie bei Col Jac II Petr Barnabas halte ich alle Zerstückelungshypothesen für Spielerei" (*HBNT*. i. 2. 368). Perdelwitz's proofs of a literary fusion in 1 Pt are less attractive than his evidence for a background of 'mystery-religion.'

Any theory of the writing thus turns out to involve a fairly speculative reconstruction of the historical data requisite for its setting. If, as Harnack insists, the alternative lies between some form of his own theory and a Petrine origin, the latter probably will carry the day. An early date is favoured by the absence of any heretical tendencies among the readers, the naïve outlook on the imminent end ($4^{17f.}$), and the exercise of charismatic gifts (4^{10}); ἀποκάλυψις and ἀναστροφή are favourite words of the epistle, and by common consent it has the stamp of primitive Christianity more clearly than any other, not only of the writings in the Petrine New Testament (Gospel, Acts, Epp., Apoc.), but of the post-Pauline writings. The hypothesis of Silvanus' share in its composition is not illegitimate, and since it meets the difficulty of the style as well as—in part—that of the religious outlook, while the problem of the "persecution"-allusions is not insuperable, there is some reason to accept the pastoral as the earliest literary memento of the primitive apostolic mission, a writing which voices not so much a personality as a great cause. The fact that it is practically the sole witness of its class, is intelligible in the light of the mission itself. If tradition is to be credited, attention to literary composition was precluded, as a rule, not simply by natural inaptitude, but by the more pressing concerns of practical organisation and propaganda (cp. Eus. *H. E.* iii. 24. 3: τῆς τῶν οὐρανῶν βασιλείας τὴν γνῶσιν ἐπὶ πᾶσαν κατήγγελλον τὴν οἰκουμένην, σπουδῆς τῆς περὶ τὸ λογογραφεῖν μικρὰν ποιούμενοι φροντίδα· καὶ τοῦτ' ἔπραττον ἅτε μείζονι καὶ ὑπὲρ ἄνθρωπον ἐξυπηρετούμενοι διακονίᾳ).

THE EPISTLE OF JUDAS.

LITERATURE.—(*a*) Editions—Luther (1523); Calvin (1551); R. Turnbull (London, 1606); Grotius, *Annotationes* (1650); Manton (1658); J. C. Wolf (1735); Witsius (Basel, 1739); C. F. Schmid (Leipzig, 1768); Semler (Halle, 1784); Hasse (Jena, 1786); Hartmann (1793); L. Morus (1794); H. C. A. Haenlein (Erlangen, 1799); M. T. Laurman (Gröningen, 1818); Schneckenburger (Stuttgart, 1832); K. R. Jachmann (1838); C. A. Scharling (1841); de Wette (1847); R. Stier (Berlin, 1850); E. Arnauld (*Recherches critiques sur l'épître de Jude, avec commentaire*, 1851; Eng. tr in 'British and Foreign Evang. Review,' July 1859)*; M. F. Rampf (Salzburg, 1854)*; John Lillie (New York, 1854); F. Gardiner (Boston, 1856); Fronmüller (Lange's *Bibel-Werk*[4], Eng. tr., New York, 1867); Wiesinger (Olshausen's *Comm.* 1862); Th. Schott (Erlangen, 1863); M. F. Roos (1864); B. Brückner[3] (Leipzig, 1865); Ewald (1870); Bisping (1871); Alford[4] (1871); Hofmann (1875); Huther (— Meyer[4], 1877, Eng. tr. 1881); Reuss (1878; Plumptre (*Cambridge Bible*, 1880); Lumby (*Speaker's Comm.* 1881); Angus (Schaff's *Comm.* 1883); Keil (Leipzig, 1883); Salmond (*Pulpit Comm.* 1889); F. Spitta, *Der 2 Brief des Petrus und der Brief des Judas* (1885)*; Burger[2] (*Kurzgefasster Comm.* 1895); Kühl (— Meyer[6], 1897)*; G. Wandel, *Der Brief Judas* (Leipzig, 1898); von Soden[3] (*HC.* 1899); Basil Gheorghiu (Czernowitz, 1901)*; C. Bigg[2] (*ICC.* 1902)*; Calmes (Paris, 1905); F. Weidner (New York, 1906); J. B. Mayor, *The Epistle of St. Jude and the Second Epistle of St. Peter* (1907)*; G. Hollmann (*SNT*[2], 1907); J. de Zwaan (*Tweede Petrus en Judas*, 1909)*; J. B. Mayor (*EGT.* 1910); Windisch (*HBNT.* 1911); R. Knopf (— Meyer[7], 1912); M. R. James (*CGT.* 1912); G. Wohlenberg (*ZK.* 1915).

(*b*) Studies—Adam Sasbouth, *In Epist. Judæ* (1500); C. Sibelius, *In divinam J. apostoli epistolam conciones sacræ* (Amsterdam, 1631); Antoine-Nicolas du Bois, *Catholica Judæ epistola . . . explicata* (Paris, 1644); Dahl, *De Authent. Epp. Petri post. et Judæ* (Rostock, 1807); J. D. Schulze, *Der schriftstellerische Charakter u. Werth des Petrus, Judas, und Jakobus* (Leipzig, 1811); A. Jessieu, *De authentia ep. Judæ* (1821); L. A. Arnauld's *Essai Critique sur l'authent. de Jude* (1835); Mayerhoff's *Petrinische Schriften*, pp. 171–182 (1835)*; F. Brun's *Essai d'une introd. critique à l'épître de Jude* (1842); E. Arnauld, *Examen de l'objection faite à l'épître de J. au sujet de ses citat. apocryphes* (1849); Ritschl (*SK.*, 1861, pp. 103 f., on the errorists); Schenkel (*BL.* iii. 433 f.); Schwegler's *NZ.* i. 518–522; Straatman (*TT.*, 1879, pp. 100 f.); Venables (Smith's *DB.* i. 1164–1167); Sabatier (*ESR.* vii. 476–478); Farrar, *Early Days of Christianity* (ch. xi.); A. Vieljeux, *Introd. à l'épître de Jude* (Montauban, 1894); Moffatt (*HNT.* 589 f.); Cone (*EBi.* 2630–2632); Sieffert (*PRE.* ix. 589–592); Chase (*DB.* ii. 799–806)*; V. Ermoni (Vigouroux' *DB.* iii. 1807 f.); Zahn (*Einl.* § 43); F. Maier (*Biblische Studien*, xi. 1906, 1–2)*; T. Barns, 'The Epistle of Jude, A Study in the Marcosian Heresy' (*JTS.*, 1905, 391–411, answered by Mayor, *ibid.* pp. 569–577); Maier (*Zeitschrift für kath. Theologie*, 1906, 693–729); Bacon (*EB.*[11] xv. 537–538); Werdermann's *Die Irrlehrer d. Judas u. 2 Petrusbriefe* (1913).

§ 1. *Contents.*—After the address (vv.[1-2]) the writer explains that his reason for communicating with his friends (vv.[3f.]) is to warn them against a body of errorists within the church, a set of loud, arrogant, and poisonous characters,[1] whose doom (τοῦτο τὸ κρίμα, proleptic) is violently and vividly described as that of their older angelic and human prototypes (vv.[5-11]) in vice. The writer especially recalls a prediction of their fate in the book of

[1] The phrase τινες here (v.[4]), as, *e.g.*, in Gal 2[12] (see above, p. 85), has 'quelque chose de méprisant' (Arnauld).

Enoch (vv.$^{12f.}$),* and urges his readers to adhere (vv.$^{17-18. 20f.}$) steadfastly to the primitive, apostolic tradition of the faith against plausible innovations (cp. v.^{8} τῇ ἅπαξ παραδοθείσῃ). With a brief doxology (vv.$^{24-25}$) the letter closes. Religious conservatism † is its keynote. The pretensions of the ἀσεβεῖς are contrasted with the fixed and final Christian tradition (cp. 1 Jn $2^{20f.}$ $4^{1f.}$ $5^{6f.}$). Their very methods and fate are no new thing; long ago (πάλαι) this had been foreseen by prophets and apostles alike. The writer disclaims originality even for his own warnings; all he requires to do is to remind orthodox Christians (vv.$^{5. 17}$) of the principles and prophecies of that faith which they already know (cp. 1 Jn 2^{20-21}),—a plea for orthodoxy which is curiously bound up with belief in several superstitions drawn from what the author of Titus (1^{14}) would have sharply denounced as 'Jewish myths.'

Conservatism involves retrospect, and the epistle looks back upon the apostolic age as (vv.$^{3. 17}$) ‡ distant and authoritative. These allusions are not to be explained away as if they meant no more than that the apostles were scattered (and therefore out of reach), or that the primitive Palestinian apostles alone are conceived of as dead. Neither does the ἔλεγον ὑμῖν necessarily imply that the readers had at one time been hearers of the apostles. On the other hand, it is a forced interpretation of v.^{5} which finds in it an allusion to the Lord's punishment of unbelieving Israel at the fall of Jerusalem (so, *e.g.*, Hofmann, Zahn); for, apart from other reasons (cp. F. Maier's essay in *BZ.*, 1904, 377–397), τὸ δεύτερον refers not to two separate events, but to a stage later than the σώσας (cp. 1 Co $10^{1f.}$, He $3^{12f.}$), and it would be irregular to introduce a symbolic modern (contrast πάλαι, v.^{4}) example in the midst of historical ones. The order of $^{5-7}$ is no doubt unchronological, but the anticlimax is not bettered by shifting v.^{5} into the NT period. The reverse attempt (*e.g.* Credner, Rampf, Bleek, Gutjahr) to argue from J.'s silence that he must have written prior to the disaster of A.D. 70, is as unconvincing here as in the case of Hebrews. It is doubtful if the destruction of Jerusalem would have seemed to him an instance of divine

* On the Enochic background of the epistle, cp. Lods, *Le livre d'Hénoch* (pp. 98–100), M. R. James (pp. xli f.), and Chase (*DB.* ii. 801–802).

† "Jude's language about the Faith is highly dogmatic, highly orthodox, highly zealous. His tone is that of a bishop of the fourth century" (Bigg, p. 325).

‡ While πίστις by itself was used objectively by Paul now and then (cp. Gal 1^{23}, Phil 1^{27}, cp. Ac 6^{7}), the context and the form of v.^{3} (*the faith once for all delivered*, not to you, but *to the saints*), taken with v.^{17} (*your most holy faith*), show unmistakably the sub-apostolic atmosphere (cp. *e.g.* Polykarp, who speaks of being 'built up εἰς τὴν δοθεῖσαν ὑμῖν πίστιν' [iii. 2, iv. 2]). But there is no allusion to any formula of faith transmitted to the disciples, as A. Seeberg contends (*Der Katechismus d. Urchristenheit*, 1903, pp. 195–196); πίστις is simply the body of Christian belief.

judgment on sceptical antinomianism, and in any case his choice of instances is dictated by special motives, *e.g.* the desire to adduce the prototypes of error in ancient prophecy, particularly from apocalyptic sources.

§ 2. *Characteristics.*—The writer and his circle are at home within the (pp. 32 f.) literature and legends * of Judaism, as the allusions to the book of Enoch and (vv.$^{9.\ 16}$) the Assumption of Moses (cp. R. H. Charles, *Assumption of Moses*, pp. 105 f.) show; but this is no clue to the epistle's date or *milieu*, since both were written by the time of Jesus, and since the former was widely read and honoured in early Christianity, if we may judge from the allusions and citations of the first and second centuries (cp. F. Martin, *Le livre d'Hénoch*, 1906, pp. cxii f.; Lawlor in *Journal of Philology*, 1897, 164–225). The latter "represents that tendency in Jewish thought which was most nearly allied to primitive Christianity" (Burkitt, *DB.* iii. 449), and its opposition to the antinomian tendencies of the Sadducees may have recommended it to J. in view of his contemporary errorists. His familiarity with apocalyptic literature is probably responsible for the *οὗτοί εἰσιν* rubric, cp. vv.$^{(8)\ 10.\ 12.\ 16.\ 19}$, a favourite expression with such writers (cp. *e.g.* Zec $1^{9f.}$, Apoc 7^{14} etc., En 46^{3}, Slav. En 7^{3} etc.), as well as for the Hebraistic colouring of his periods.† "Die ganze Redeweise ist über aus lebhaft und gedrängt, plastisch und konkret, mit einem Wort: echt orientalisch" (F. Maier, p. 168). The fondness for triple grouping (vv.$^{2.\ 4.\ 5\text{-}7.\ 8.\ 11f.\ 23.\ 25c}$) is more outstanding than the three instances where a fivefold arrangement (vv.$^{12\text{-}13.\ 16.\ 25}$) can be observed, and there is a certain balance and even rhythm of structure (cp. Cladder in *JTS.*, 1904, 598–603) visible in the antithetical poise of various sentences and paragraphs, which smacks of the older Jewish writings. These features, however, do not stamp the work as late or early. The epistle shares with Luke's writings in the NT collection, words like *ἀγαλλίασις* (He 1^{9} LXX), *ἄλογος*, the Hellenistic *χάριτα* for *χάριν* (v.^{4} = Ac 24^{27} 25^{9}), *ἐνυπνιαζόμενοι* (Ac 2^{17} LXX), and the dative in v.^{14} = Lk 18^{31}: with Hebrews,‡

* On the Michael-myth, see J. T. Marshall (*ET.* xi. 390–391) and Lueken's *Erzengel Michael* (1898), with Cheyne's *Bible Problems* (226 f.).

† That he was a Jewish Christian does not necessarily follow, much less that his audience were Jewish Christians (Hoennicke, *JC.* 92–93), though the former inference is plausible on broader grounds.

‡ Cp. the collocation of three participles with a finite vb. (v.$^{21f.}$ = He $12^{1\text{-}3}$).

ἀντιλογία, ζόφος, μεγαλωσύνη; and with Paul one or two terms, such as *ἀΐδιος, κυριότης, οἰκητήριον*, and *προγράφειν*, besides *ἅγιοι* and *κλητοί*. But these are either too casual or too diverse in meaning to prove any literary relationship. Apart from the allusion in v.^{19} to language which the later Gnostics had adopted from Paul (cp. 1 Co 2^{14}), and the resemblances of the address (cp. 1 Th 1^{4}, 2 Th 2^{13}) and the doxology (v.$^{24f.}$ = Ro $16^{25\text{-}27}$, see above, p. 135), there is little or nothing to indicate any use or even reminiscences of the genuine Pauline correspondence. The impression of a similarity of atmosphere between the epistle and the Pauline pastorals is heightened, however, by a series of coincidences in thought and expression ($^{5\text{-}11}$ = 2 Ti 3^{8}, the use of *πίστις* and of *θέος σωτήρ*), particularly in v.^{17} which implies the circulation of a prophecy such as has been preserved in these pastorals. It is therefore highly probable that the latter were known to this writer, though there is no clear evidence that he used them.

§ 3. *Relation to 2 Peter.*—Special literature: E. A. Richter, *De origine epist. P. posterioris ex epist. Judæ repetenda* (1810); E. Moutier, *La seconde épître de Pierre et celle de Jude* (Strassburg, 1829), Mayerhoff's *Einleitung in die petrinischen Schriften* (1835), pp. 171–182; B. Weiss (*SK.*, 1866, 256 f.); O. Michael in *Festschrift für Ficke* (Leipzig, 1897); H. Schwienhorst, *Das Verhältniss des Judasbriefes zum zweiten Petrusbrief untersucht* (Münster, 1904); A. Maier (*TQ.*, 1905, 547–580); J. B. Mayor in *EGT.* v. 303–317.

The similarities between Judas and 2 P. are not altogether confined to $^{4f.}$ of the former and the second chapter of the latter (cp. *e.g.* Jud ^{3} = 2 P 2^{21}, Jud $^{6\text{-}7}$ = 2 P 3^{7}, Jud $^{17\text{-}18}$ = 2 P $3^{1f.}$, Jud $^{21.\ 23}$ = 2 P 3^{14}, Jud ^{24} = 2 P 3^{17}, Jud ^{25} = 2 P 3^{18}), but in that chapter they mount up to an exceptional height, as may be seen from the following summary:

JUDAS	2 P 2
(^{4}) For certain men have slipped in by stealth (*παρεισέδυσαν*), those who were long ago (*πάλαι*) predestined (*εἰς τοῦτο τὸ κρίμα*) to this doom—impious men, perverting our God's grace into **ἀσέλγειαν**, and denying	(^{1}) False teachers, men who shall stealthily introduce (*παρεισάξουσι*) destructive heresies . . . denying the Master who bought them (*τὸν ἀγοράσαντα αὐτοὺς δεσπότην ἀρνούμενοι*).*

* The contrast of *ἀγοράσαντα* is with the extortionate demands of the errorists for remuneration (2^{3}, cp. Tit 1^{11}; Iren. i. 13. 3; Eus. *H. E.* v. 18. 2).

the only Master and our Lord Jesus Christ (*καὶ τὸν μόνον δεσπότην καὶ κύριον ἡμῶν Ἰ. Χ. ἀρνούμενοι*).

(2) And many still follow their **ἀσελγείας**

(3) *οἷς τὸ κρίμα ἔκπαλαι οὐκ ἀργεῖ.*

(6) And angels which kept not their office but abandoned their own habitation, he has kept under the nether blackness in fetters everlasting (*δεσμοῖς ἀϊδίοις ὑπὸ ζόφον τετήρηκεν*) for the judgment (*εἰς κρίσιν*) of the great day.

(4) God spared not angels when they sinned, but thrusting them down to Tartarus, to pits of nether blackness (*σειροῖς ζόφου*), delivered them to be kept for judgment (*παρέδωκεν εἰς κρίσιν τηρουμένους*).

(7) Even as * Sodom and Gomorrha, with the surrounding cities . . . are exhibited as a warning (*δεῖγμα*), undergoing the penalty of fire eternal.

(6) Reducing the cities of Sodom and Gomorrha to ashes . . . making an example of them (*ὑπόδειγμα τεθεικώς*).

(8) These men † with their sensual dreams pollute the flesh (*σάρκα μιαίνουσιν*), contemn the Lordship (*κυριότητα ἀθετοῦσιν*), and abuse Majesties (*δόξας βλασφημοῦσιν*).

(10) Those who walk after the flesh in the lust of pollution (*ὀπίσω σαρκὸς* [=Jud ^{7} *ὀπίσω σαρκὸς*] *ἐν ἐπιθυμίᾳ μιασμοῦ*), and despise the Lordship (*κυριότητος*). Daring (*τολμηταί*, cp. Jud ^{9}), . . . they tremble not when they abuse Majesties (*δόξας βλασφημοῦντες*).

(9) Now when Michael the archangel was disputing with the devil in controversy over the body of Moses, he dared not (*οὐκ ἐτόλμησεν*) bring an abusive accusation against him (*κρίσιν ἐπενεγκεῖν βλασφημίας*).

(11) Whereas angels . . .† do not bring an abusive accusation against them (*φέρουσιν βλάσφημον κρίσιν*).

(10) But these men heap abuse on whatever they are ignorant of (*οὗτοι δέ, ὅσα μὲν οὐκ οἴδασιν βλασφημοῦσιν*),

(12) But these men, like irrational brutes (*οὗτοι δέ, ὡς ἄλογα ζῷα*) by nature born (*φυσικά*) for capture and

---

* The region of the Dead Sea, with its volcanic features, is associated in En 17^{6} with the subterranean burning of the fallen angels. In 2 P. the deluge is inserted between the fall of the angels and the destruction of Sodom and Gomorrha (cp. 3^{6}), whereas Cain and Korah fall out. By the omission of the apostasy of the Israelites, 2 P. straightens out the chronology of Jud. On the other hand, 2 P.'s insertion of God's rescuing mercy ($2^{5.7.9}$), when contrasted with Jud $^{21-23}$, shows that the situation has become more serious. 2 P.'s start with the fallen angels is motived by the fact that they were the instructors of mankind in malpractices, according to Jewish tradition (cp. En. ix. 5–6, x. 7, etc.), and consequently the natural prototype of false teachers ($2^{1f.}$); his insertion anticipates the milder thought of 3^{9}, and is suggested by the allusion of 1 P 3^{20} to Noah. J.'s reference to the sin of the angels in connection with Sodom echoes the tradition preserved in Test. Napth. iii.

† Peter's generalising version is less clear than J.'s; indeed, were it not for the latter, it would be fair to call it "the most enigmatical sentence in the N.T." (Alford).

and whatever they do understand by nature (φυσικῶς), like the irrational brutes (ὡς τὰ ἄλογα ζῷα), through that are they corrupted (φθείρονται).	corruption (φθοράν), uttering abuse about things they are ignorant of (ἐν οἷς ἀγνοοῦσιν βλασφημοῦντες), shall also perish in their corruption (ἐν τῇ φθορᾷ αὐτῶν φθαρήσονται).
(11) They went the road of (τῇ ὁδῷ) Kain, rushed headlong for wages (μισθοῦ) in the error of Balaam.	(15) They followed the road (τῇ ὁδῷ) of Balaam the son of Bosor,* who loved the wages (μισθόν) of malpractice.
(12) These men are the sunken rocks (σπιλάδες) in your love-feasts (ἐν ταῖς ἀγάπαις ὑμῶν), feasting with you (συνευωχούμενοι).	(13) Spots and blots (σπίλοι καὶ μῶμοι) . . . ἐν ταῖς ἀπάταις † (v.l. ἀγάπαις) αὐτῶν . . . feasting with you (συνευωχούμενοι ὑμῖν).
(12-13) Rainless clouds (νεφέλαι ἄνυδροι), swept along by winds . . . for whom the nether blackness of darkness has been for ever reserved (οἷς ὁ ζόφος τοῦ σκότους εἰς αἰῶνα τετήρηται).	(17) These men are waterless fountains (πηγαὶ ἄνυδροι) and mists driven by a squall . . . for whom the nether blackness of darkness has been reserved (οἷς ὁ ζόφος τοῦ σκότους εἰς αἰῶνα τετήρηται).
(16) Their mouth speaks extravagantly (ὑπέρογκα).	(18) Uttering futile extravagances (ὑπέρογκα).
(17) Remember the words (μνήσθητε τῶν ῥημάτων) spoken beforehand by the apostles of our Lord Jesus (τῶν προειρημένων ὑπὸ τῶν ἀποστόλων).	(3^2) Remember the words spoken beforehand (μνησθῆναι τῶν προειρημένων) by the holy prophets and the commandment of the apostles sent you from the Lord and Saviour ; ‡
(18) how they told you : at the end of the time (ἐπ' ἐσχάτου τοῦ χρόνου) there shall be (ἔσονται, v.l. ἐλεύσονται) scoffers (ἐμπαῖκται), walking after their own impious lusts (κατὰ τὰς ἑαυτῶν ἐπιθυμίας πορευόμενοι τῶν ἀσεβειῶν).	3^3 knowing this first of all, that in the last days (ἐπ' ἐσχάτων τῶν ἡμερῶν) scoffers (ἐμπαῖκται) shall come (ἐλεύσονται) scoffing, walking after their own lusts (κατὰ τὰς ἰδίας ἐπιθυμίας αὐτῶν πορευόμενοι).

These phenomena imply either (*a*) the common use of some earlier document, or (*b*) a literary relationship between the two epistles. The former theory fails to explain anything except the legendary elements, which can satisfactorily be accounted for, especially since the discovery of the book of Enoch, without conjecturing (with older critics like Herder and Hasse) some Persian original, or § some Aramaic document containing Noachic and

* *Bosor* is a blunder for Beor (cp. ℵ B), unless, with A. Sanda (*BZ.*, 1904, 188 f.), it is to be taken geographically.

† For this use of ἀπάτη, see Nägeli's *Der Wortschätz d. Paulus*, p. 15.

‡ Spitta and Baljon omit καὶ τῆς . . . σωτῆρος as a gloss ; Blass inserts διὰ between τῆς and τῶν (as in the title of the Didachê).

§ Cp. Sherlock's *Dissertation concerning the Authority of the Second Epistle of Peter* ; Kaiser's *Commentarius, quo linguæ aramaicæ usus ad judicanda et interpretanda plure N.T. loca . . . defenditur* (1831), pp. 77 f., and Lumby in *Exp.*[1] iv. 461.

Enochic prophecies upon the deluge, or, finally, a Jewish or Jewish Christian 'Strafpredigt.'* The alternative hypothesis (*b*) is rather to be accepted in the form of a dependence of 2 P. upon Judas (so most critics, especially Credner, Alford, Ewald, Hilgenfeld, Holtzmann, Abbott, Weiss, Baljon, James, Chase, F. Maier, Jülicher, Salmon, Mayor, and Belser, as against Luther's opinion, which was supported by Dietlein, Lumby, Mansel, Hofmann, Plummer, Spitta, Zahn, Wohlenberg, and Bigg). (i.) It is more likely that a later writer should incorporate practically the bulk of a brief note like that of Judas, than that the author of the latter should select only the middle portion of 2 Pet. To this it is not enough to reply that he chose only the section which suited his purpose, for if his purpose (as Spitta urges) was to emphasise the apostolic warnings against libertines, he would have made it more clear that he was using Peter's *ipsissima uerba*, and in any case a section like that of $3^{2f.}$ would have been as apt to his aim. Furthermore (ii.) Judas has the notes of an original writer. The style is sententious, forcible, and terse, as compared with the cloudy and rhetorical language of 2 P. (cp. Jud ^{4} with 2 P 2^{3}, Jud ^{6} with 2 P 2^{4}, Jud ^{7} with 2 P 2^{6}, Jud ^{8} with 2 P 2^{10}, Jud ^{9} with 2 P 2^{11}, Jud ^{10} with 2 P 2^{12}); thus—to quote one instance—the more popular *σπουδὴν παρεισφέρειν* of the later writer (1^{5}) is a relapse from the correct *σπουδὴν ποιεῖσθαι* of Jud ^{3}. Again, (iii.) 2 P. has exaggerated the habit of iteration which crops up now and again in Jud. (cp. *τηρεῖν* and *ζόφος* in $^{6. 13}$ *κρίσις* in $^{6. 9. 15}$, and *βλασφημ.* in $^{8-10}$, also ^{16} and ^{18}) despite the latter's skill in devising synonyms. In the later writer, partly owing to an imitation of 1 P., where this literary trait occasionally recurs (cp. *σωτηρία* in 1^{9-10}; *κακοποιός*, $2^{12. 14}$; *ἀγαθοπ.*, $2^{14-15. 20}$), the iteration of insignificant terms becomes almost wearisome (cp. *ἐπιχορηγεῖν*, $1^{5. 11}$; *ἐνεχθ.*, 1^{17-18}; *ἀποφεύγειν*, $1^{4. 11. 18. 20}$; *προφητεία*, $1^{20. 21}$; *φθέγγεσθαι*, $2^{16. 18}$; *δελεάζειν*, $2^{14. 18}$; *μισθὸς ἀδικίας*, $2^{13. 15}$; *στοιχεῖα καυσούμενα*, $3^{10. 12}$ etc. etc.). Finally, (iv.) at several points the language of 2 P. is only intelligible from that of Judas; *e.g.* the generalised allusion to angels in 2 P 2^{10-11} becomes clear from Jud ^{9} with its specific reference to Michael. The haste and vehemence of Judas the zealot lead him now and then into a certain confused tone of denunciation, which is at once softened and straightened out in the later epistle. 2 P. has not the urgency which dictated the composition of Judas; it is more derivative than the latter. "The impression which they leave on my mind is that in J. we have the first thought, in P. the second thought; that we can generally see a reason why P. should have altered J., but very rarely a reason why what we read in P. should have been altered to what we find in J. P. is more reflective, J. more spontaneous" (Mayor, p. xxv). "Es ist eine absurde Vorstellung, dass der kleine, an Vorstellungen viel reichere Jud aus einzelnen, da und dort herausgerissenen, über eine grössere Fläche zerstreuten, an sich meist ganz nebensächlichen, fast armseligen Wörtern und Sätzen des grossen 2 Petr zusammengestoppelt ist" (Maier, *Der Judasbrief*, 107–108). "Begreiflich ist, dass ein Mann, der seinen Lesern noch mehr zu sagen hatte, den Inhalt des Judasbriefes in seinem grösseren Briefe verarbeitete; dass aber Judas, wenn er vor den von Petrus geschilderten Irrlehrern warnen will, statt sich ausdrücklich auf diese grosse Autorität zu berufen, einfach ein Stück

---

* Cp. Heinrici, *Urc.* 112, and *Lit. Charakter d. NT Schriften*, 78–79.

des Petrusbriefes neu herausgibt unter seinem Namen, ist undenkbar" (Haupt in *SK.*, 1904, 149).

§ 4. *Literary connections.*—While the earliest trace of the epistle is in 2 Pet., its brevity, limited circulation, and lack of significant ideas prevented it from being used by other writers in the second century; almost the only document which presents any resemblance to it is the Didachê, where 2^{7} (οὐ μισήσεις πάντα ἄνθρωπον, ἀλλὰ οὓς μὲν ἐλέγξεις, περὶ δὲ ὧν προσεύξῃ, οὓς δὲ ἀγαπήσεις ὑπὲρ τὴν ψυχήν σου) recalls the similar triple sentence of Jud $^{22-23}$ (καὶ οὓς μὲν ἐλέγχετε διακρινομένους, οὓς δὲ σώζετε . . . οὓς δὲ ἐλεᾶτε),* whilst J.'s assertion that the errorists' κυριότητα ἀθετοῦσιν (v.^{8}) is explained by the counsel of Did. 4^{1} (τιμήσεις αὐτὸν—*i.e.* him who speaks the word of God—ὡς Κύριον· ὅθεν γὰρ ἡ κυριότης λαλεῖται, ἐκεῖ Κύριός ἐστιν). The connection between murmuring and blasphemy is not striking enough to justify stress being laid (as, *e.g.*, by Spitta, 534–535, and F. Maier, p. 65) on 3^{6-8} as a possible instance of the use of Jud $^{8-10}$, and even were the text of Jud $^{22-23}$ (cp. WH. ii. 106 f.) and of Did 2^{7} more certain than it is, it would be imprudent to base any conclusions of literary filiation upon so lonely and precarious a piece of evidence. "On other grounds it seems likely that the two documents had their origin within the same circle of Christian thought, and it is conceivable that parts of the Didachê are *ultimately* the work of the author of the epistle" (Chase, 795). Be this as it may, the Didachê on the whole fails to furnish any *terminus ad quem* for Judas, and still less do Barnabas (2^{10} 4^{9}, against Jud $^{3-4}$), 2 Clem. (20^{4} = Jud ^{6}, cp. *NTA.* 129), and Hermas (*Sim.* v. 7. 2 = Jud ^{8}, *Sim.* ix. 9. 13 against Jud ^{21}), though the coincidence between Mart. Polyk. (address ἔλεος καὶ εἰρήνη καὶ ἀγάπη . . . πληθυνθείη) = Jud ^{2} (ἔλεος ὑμῖν καὶ εἰρήνη καὶ ἀγάπη πληθυνθείη) is remarkable enough (see above, p. 336).

By the end of the second century the homily was accepted as canonical and apostolic in Alexandria (Clement, Origen), Africa (Tertullian), and Rome (Murat. Canon); but the very terms and context in which it is mentioned in the Mur. Canon and even in Origen (*in Matt.* t. xvii. 30) indicate that its reception was far from being unanimous; † and this is corroborated by its

* A case for the omission (with C* Syr. hl.) of οὓς δὲ ἐλεᾶτε is presented by R. A. Falconer (*Exp.*^{6} iv. 200–207); see, further, Souter (*GK.* 61).

† Besides, Tertullian not only mistakes J. for an apostle, but is chiefly interested in his epistle because it guarantees the authority of the book of Enoch (*de cultu fem.* i. 3); while Clem. Alex.'s opinion is weakened by the fact that he attributes Hebrews to Paul.

absence subsequently from the writings of the Antioch school and the Syriac vulgate. The suspicions (Eus. *H. E.* ii. 23. 25) which thus hindered its entrance into certain circles of the church, as one of the ἀντιλεγόμενα, were due not to critical scruples so much as to the hesitation aroused by the source and character of its apocryphal citations (so Jerome, *de uir. illustr.* cx.). Its unpopularity in the African churches, to judge from Cyprian's lack of reference to it and from other data, and its failure to win acceptance in the school of Antioch, rendered its ecclesiastical career as precarious and chequered as that of several of the other 'catholic epistles.' Its disrepute in many quarters, particularly throughout the West, was only partially counterbalanced by the fact that Clement of Alexandria (in his *Hypotoposeis*, cp. Westcott's *Canon*, pp. 355 f.) and Didymus of the same city (in the fourth century) wrote comments on it, the latter with especial regard to its compromising employment of apocryphal writings.

§ 5. *Object.*—The writer is not interested in the ἀσεβεῖς, as the apologists of the second century are in the principles of the errorists whom they controvert. He attempts no refutation of their theories, nor does he go into any detail in exposing their aberrations. He is a plain, honest leader of the church, who knows when round indignation is more telling than argument. His interest is purely practical. Alarmed at the possibility of his friends being contaminated by these intruders, he writes this brief, forcible warning, full of what Origen called ἐρρωμένοι λόγοι. It denounces * rather than describes the objects of its attack, and there is a note of exaggerated severity in it, 'a certain hastiness and tendency to take things at the worst' (Bigg). When the news of the movement's spread reached him (v.[3]), he was in the act of composing an epistle or treatise for his friends περὶ τῆς κοινῆς σωτηρίας: this he laid aside at once in order to lose no time in putting them on their guard. His practical object, together with the fact that the readers were well acquainted with the errorists, naturally gave no occasion for a minute transcript of the latter's aims; one or two hints emerge which indicate their general physiognomy, but these glimpses are neither unambiguous nor coherent, *i.e.* they do not point to any one of the regular gnostic circles of which we have any knowledge. The note of dualism (v.[4] τὸν μόνον δεσπότην ἀρνούμενοι, v.[25] μόνῳ θεῷ) † was common to most Gnostics, including, of course, the Carpokratians (so for Judas, Grotius and Mangold, *Einl.* 723 f., with

* "To a modern reader it is curious rather than edifying, with the exception of the beginning and end" (Mayor, p. clii).

† The phrase is not so much liturgical as a polemical reference to gnostic theosophies (cp. Jn 5[44] 17[3], and E. A. Abbott's *Diat.*, 1895, 2664).

Schenkel, *Christusbild*, 161 f.; Cone, *Gospel and its Earliest Interpretations*, 338–341; and Pfleiderer, *Urc.* iv. 251 f.) and the Cainites (v.[11]), who (according to Irenæus, i. 31. 1) claimed kinship with the Sodomites (v.[7]) and Korah (v.[11]); though the allusion to Cain, in the light of [13f.], seems to voice the Jewish tradition, as old as Philo (cp. Siegfried's *Philo*, pp. 150 f.), that Cain was the first sceptic, who denied any future rewards for the good or punishment for the wicked (Targ. Jerus. on Gn 4[7]). Again, the abuse of love-feasts (v.[12]), flattery of the rich (v.[16]), and antinomian tendencies, are common to these errorists and to the followers of Marcus in Asia Minor, *c.* A.D. 160 (Iren. i. 13–21); but Judas never alludes to the women over whom Marcus exercised extraordinary power, and the above traits are not peculiar to the Marcosians. The combination of *denying Christ* (v.[4]) with immorality would harmonise either with Tit 1[16] or with the Nikolaitans * (Apoc 2[6. 15] cp. 2[13] οὐκ ἠρνήσω τὴν πίστιν μου). There is no evidence to connect it with any theoretical error, such as that of Cerinthus (cp. 1 Jn 2[22f.]), on the person of Christ, but the libertine conduct of J.'s errorists was plainly justified in their own opinion by their views (cp. v.[8]); just as the Carpokratians (*c.* A.D. 140), whose heresy Clem. Alex. (*Strom.* iii. 2. 6–10) found prophetically described in this epistle, advocated promiscuous sexual indulgence on the ground that the sexual impulse was a God-given instinct. Cain and Korah (v.[11]) were honoured by the Ophites, of whom the Cainites were an offshoot, and the adherents of Simon Magus and of Carpokrates are said by Irenæus (i. 25. 1) to have scoffed at the angels who were responsible for the creation.

Whoever they were, they were charged by Judas with sodomy (v.[7]) and sexual abuses (v.[10b]),† as well as with covetousness—

* So Thiersch, Ewald, Schott, Huther, Wiesinger, Mansel, Sieffert, Bartlet, and recently Knopf (*NZ.* 320–322), who argues that J.'s errorists not only were libertines and spiritualists like the N., but shared the same attitude towards the devil, holding that the true Christian could scoff at his power and safely practise immorality. This involves the identification of the angelic powers in v.[8] with evil spirits (so, *e.g.*, Weiss and Schott). A cognate view (E. P. Gould, *NTTh.* pp. 157–158) makes J. point to the summary fate of the wicked angels as a proof that angels in general need not be reviled, and that the errorists had better not justify their sensual indulgence by appealing 'more or less cynically to' the 'roving propensities' of these aerial beings.

† For which the ἀγάπαι (v.[12]) would give opportunity to the unscrupulous, as in the case, *e.g.*, of the Carpokratians. This lust, combined with insub-

the latter (v.[11], v.[12] ἑαυτοὺς ποιμαίνοντες, v.[16] ὠφελείας χάριν) pointing to a familiar type of the prophet or mystagogue, who traded on the generosity and credulity of his dupes. On being checked by the authorities of the churches, they became rebellious and discontented (8b. 11c. 16a) like Korah; while, like Balaam (v.[11]), they were pseudo-prophets (this is the force of ἐνυπνιαζόμενοι, v.[8]) as well as selfish. Furthermore, they made loud pretensions (v.[18a], v.[16] τὸ στόμα αὐτῶν λαλεῖ ὑπέρογκα), evidently on the score of superiority to the rank and file of ordinary Christians. Like most of the Gnostics, they appear to have called themselves πνευματικοί, in contrast to the inferior ψυχικοί of the church (this is the point of J.'s retort in v.[19]); the exclusiveness (vv.[19. 22]) and lack of brotherly love (v.[12] νεφέλαι ἄνυδροι, δένδρα ἄκαρπα), which this ostentation developed, are a constant source of reproach in the writings of this period (cp. 1 John, Ignatius). Such traits belong to the incipient phases of some local, possibly syncretistic, development of libertinism upon gnostic lines,* rather than to any definite school; they cannot be fairly explained (Spitta, 503 f., after Neander) as natural to some ultra-Paulinists, or to errorists of a purely practical bent, resembling those attacked by Paul at Corinth or Colossæ, or to Jewish Christian heretics (so, *e.g.*, Credner and Salmon).

§ 6. *Period and authorship.*—In view of Eph 2^{20} 3^{5} and Apoc 18^{20} 21^{14}, the allusion to the apostles in v.[17] would not necessarily fix the *terminus a quo* for the epistle beyond the last quarter of the first century; but neither would the evidence just adduced from the incipient gnostic tendencies which it controverts, converge upon a date for its composition in the early decades of the second century. If there is an allusion in ver. 17 to 2 Ti $3^{1f.}$ and 1 Ti $4^{1f.}$, it would be hard (cp. Jacoby, *NT Ethik*, 455 f.) to attribute the authorship either (*a*) to Judas,

ordination, is the point made by J. (v.[6]) in comparing the errorists to the fallen angels (cp. Justin, *Apol.* ii. 5; Jub iv. 15 f.), who in Jewish legend (cp. Volz, *Jüd. Eschatologie*, pp. 273 f., and Bousset, *die Religion des Judentums*, 326 f., for the evidence from Enoch, etc.) were guilty of both these sins.

* So Harnack (early representatives of the Archontikoi, Kainites, Nikolaitans, etc.) and Belser: "man wird sonach in diesen 'Gottlosen' Anhänger des Simon Magus, eines Menander und Nikolaus (Iren. *adv. haer.* i. 23; Tert. *de anima*, 50; Apoc $2^{6. 15}$) erblicken dürfen; Gesinnungsgenossen des Thebutis und Dositheus, von welchen ersterer zunächst ein Schisma veranlasste und dasselbe bald zur Häresie weiterbildete (Eus. *H. E.* iv. 22)" (*Einl.* 661–662).

the brother of James (Mk 6^{3}, Mt 13^{55}), who is supposed (Clem. Alex.) to have described himself as the servant, not the brother, of the Lord, owing to reverent humility (so the large majority of edd.); or (*b*) to the apostolic* Judas of Lk 6^{16}, Ac 1^{13} (so, *e.g.*, Bertholdt, Schneckenburger, Hofmann, Lange, Keil, Belser, Wordsworth); or (*c*) even to Judas Barsabas (Ac 15^{22-23}), the prominent prophet of the Jerusalem-church (so Schott, Welcker, Dr. John Lightfoot, *Works*, viii. 38–39; Selwyn, and Plumptre). (*b*) is weakened by the dubiety clinging to Ἰούδας Ἰακώβου (which may mean 'son of James' rather than 'brother'), and like (*a*) is handicapped by the difficulty of seeing how Judas could have lived long enough to write the epistle. The well-known story about the grandsons of Judas, the brother of James of Jerusalem, being brought before Domitian, suggests that the grandfather could hardly have survived till *c.* A.D. 85. Apart from this, it must be admitted, a fair case can be made out for his authorship, and many scholars find themselves able to read the allusions to the errorists in such a way as to place them in the third quarter of the first century, thus interpreting the title literally.† Renan (iii. ch. x.) is alone in relegating it to *c.* A.D. 54 as a covert and rancorous pamphlet against Paul, but a date within the seventh decade of the first century (Arnauld, Weiss) is upheld by many scholars, *e.g.* 60–64 (Bigg), 63 f. (Bisping, F. Maier, Gheorghiu), 64–66 (Rampf, Henkel, Schäfer, pp. 314 f.; Gutjahr, Belser, Kaulen, Trenkle), or predominantly 66 f. (Reithmayr, Valroger, Fronmüller, Eichhorn, Bleek, Schulze, Weiss, Wandel, Burger, Arnauld, Guericke, Stier, Langen, Salmond in *Pulpit Commentary*; Selwyn, *The Christian Prophets*, pp. 146 f. etc.). Others, like Kühl (65–80), fix it somewhat later, *e.g.*, in the eighth decade, so Zahn and Wohlenberg (70–75), Barth (after 70), Mayor, Sieffert

* Tertullian and Origen (Lat.) both make the author an apostle; the similar assertion of the *Decretum Gelasianum* (see above, p. 17) only points to N. Italy or Gaul as the *provenance* of that document (*JTS.* xiv. 471). The writer himself does not claim to be one of the apostles, and indeed he dissociates himself from them.

† If Ἰησοῦς (A B etc., cp. WH. ii. 106; *EBi.* 2632) is read (so, *e.g.*, Alford and Zwaan) in v.[5] instead of κύριος, the difficulty of supposing that a brother of Jesus could have written thus (or, for the matter of that, have meant Jesus by ὁ κύριος), is well-nigh insuperable. Even Paul used ὁ Χριστός (1 Co 10^{4}). Nor would it ease matters to take Ἰησοῦς as equivalent to Joshua (E. E. Kellett, *ET.* xv. 381).

(70–80), and Bartlet, *AA.* 344–351; *c.* A.D. 80, favoured by Credner, Reuss, Lumby, Schott (80–90), Ewald, Hofmann, Spitta, Keil, Knopf, Werdermann, and von Soden.* The latter period has most in its favour, if the manifesto could be connected with the Judas of the early church. Otherwise, criticism is pushed into the first quarter of the second century (so, *e.g.*, Harnack, McGiffert, Jülicher, Hollmann), slightly later by Schenkel (A.D. 130–140) and Straatman (pp. 102 f.), and later still by Volkmar, Mangold, Davidson, Pfleiderer, N. Schmidt in *The Prophet of Nazareth*, p. 192 (after A.D. 150), and Barns (*c.* A.D. 160), as formerly by Semler (A.D. 150–200).

On any form of the latter hypothesis, some explanation of the title (Ἰούδας Ἰ. Χ. δοῦλος, ἀδελφὸς δὲ Ἰακώβου) becomes imperative. (*a*) The main objection to the pseudonym-hypothesis (Schwegler, Pfleiderer, Reuss, etc.), which makes the writer take the brother of Jesus as his mouthpiece, is that J. was far from important enough, that he would probably have been made an apostle (as by Tertullian afterwards), and that no attempt is made to develop his personality, as would have been natural under the circumstances.† (*b*) More plausibly Harnack (*ACL.* i. 1, pp. 465 f.) would modify this by conjecturing that some unknown Judas‡ of the second century (A.D. 100–130) wrote the homily against a contemporary phase of Syro-Palestinian gnosticism, and that the words ἀδελφὸς δὲ Ἰακώβου were added later (A.D. 150–180) when it became desirable, in the light of the rampant gnosticism of the age, to guarantee the writing's authority. Such a theory (so McGiffert, *AA.* 585–588; Bacon, Barns) in one form or another at once does some justice to the contents of the writing, which does not appear to come from one who either belonged to or survived the first generation, and to the title itself; it would not be difficult for a second-century scribe or editor, finding the words Ἰούδας Ἰ. Χ. δοῦλος at the head of an earlier ('not far from A.D. 90,' Bacon, p. 170) manifesto against antinomian errorists, to amplify them with ἀδελφὸς δὲ Ἰακώβου, supposing or wishing it to be supposed that the writer was the brother of the notable James of Jerusalem, whose rigid attitude towards pagan

* *i.e.* in his commentary. The hurried and superficial paragraph at the close of his *Introduction* (pp. 470–472) seems to abandon both the authorship of Judas and the first century date.

† Jülicher (*Einl.* p. 200) now thinks that the author belonged to a circle where James was held in honour, but that he chose Judas as his pseudonym because he perhaps outlived the other Palestinian apostles, and therefore was a suitable mouthpiece for warnings against the rising peril.

‡ Grotius thought of Judas, a Jewish Christian bishop of Jerusalem in the second century, as the actual author; but ἀδελφὸς δὲ Ἰακώβου could hardly be taken as an episcopal Jerusalemite title, and the very personality of this Judas is in dispute (cp. Zahn's *Forschungen*, vi. 293 f., and Turner, *JTS.* i. 529 f., against Schlatter, *TU.* xii. 25 f., *BFT.* xii. 3, 1898, 'die Kirche Jerusalems vom Jahre 70–130,' pp. 29 f.). Otherwise one might think of some presbyter called Judas (Dahl).

antinomian tendencies was so notorious. This, at any rate, seems upon the whole a more feasible line of conjecture than to suppose that the writing was originally an anonymous epistle or a manifesto.

The destination of the pastoral, whether Syro-Palestine (de Wette, Bartlet), Antioch and its neighbourhood (Chase), Corinth* or, as some have more plausibly argued, Egypt (Mayerhoff, Schenkel, Mangold, etc.), cannot be precisely ascertained from the contents, and tradition is silent. If a Judas of the first century wrote it, Palestine or Antioch is a natural suggestion. The resemblances between the gnostic phenomena of J.'s opponents and those of John's apocalypse, the Pauline pastorals, and Ignatius, might suggest Asia Minor (so von Soden and Bacon, the latter conjecturing that the local destination of the epistle has disappeared from the title), but more or less analogous phenomena can be shown to have emerged in several quarters. As a matter of fact, we are absolutely in the dark as to the relation between the writer and his audience. The pastoral resembles 1 John in its general outlook and adaptation to some definite situation or circle of churches whose oversight belonged to the writer. How Judas learnt of the peril, whether by observation or by information, why he wrote instead of visiting the churches in person, and what was the outcome of his manifesto—on these topics the epistle itself and the subsequent tradition of the church yield no information whatsoever. Possibly he meant his tract to be a sort of fiery cross, to rouse the churches. Instead of showing its readers how to contend for the apostolic faith (v.^{3}), it is so engrossed with the invaders that not until the very close is any instruction given as to the behaviour of true Christians in the crisis. To be forewarned was evidently, in J.'s view, to be forearmed. Were any tradition extant, connecting Judas with some lost treatise or epistle, it would be tempting to read v.^{3} in the light of Tit 1^{5}, 1 Ti $3^{14f.}$ as a piece of literary *vraisemblance* on the part of the pseudonymous author, in order to justify the object and size of the writing, and its lack of positive religious teaching. The obscurity of the whole situation unfortunately prevents us from discovering, except in a general sense, what that religious teaching could have been.†

2 PETER.‡

LITERATURE.—(*a*) Editions—Besides most editions of 1 Peter and Judas (*q.v.*), the following special commentaries: C. Ullmann (*Der zweite Brief P. kritisch untersucht*, 1821); W. O. Dietlein (1851); F. Steinfass (1863); Harms (1873); J. F. Demarest (New York, 1865); L. J. Hundhausen, *Das zweite Pontifikalschreiben des Apostelfürsten Petrus* (1878); Lumby

---

* On the slender ground that the evils denounced by J. resemble those attacked by Paul in Corinth.

† "Many of the phrases packed together in Jude's epistle might each be the head of a discourse; so that I could easily believe that we had in this epistle heads of topics enlarged on, either in a larger document, or by the apostle himself in *viva voce* addresses" (Salmon, *INT.* p. 477).

‡ On the latest book in the NT canon, English scholarship is easily first; Chase's article and Mayor's edition throw all previous work into the shade.

(*Speaker's Comm.* 1881); Plummer (Ellicott's *Comm.* 1883); Weidner's *Annotations* (New York, 1897); R. H. Strachan (*EGT.* 1910).

(*b*) Studies—F. A. S. Nietzsche's *Epistola Petri posterior uindicata* (1785); J. F. Flatt, *Genuina sec. P. Epistolæ origo defenditur* (Tübingen, 1806); P. E. Picot, *Recherches sur la deux épître de Pierre* (Geneva, 1829); F. H. Kern, *de secunda Petri epistola* (Tübingen, 1829); C. N. de Graaff, *Analecta in ep. P. alteram* (1833); A. Delille, *L'authenticité de la seconde épître de Pierre* (Strassburg, 1835); J. H. Magnus, *Examen de l'authent. de la sec. ép. de S. Pierre* (1835); L. Heydenreich, *Ein Wort zur Vertheidigung*, etc. (1837); L. Audemars, *Seconde épître de Pierre* (Geneva, 1838); A. L. Daumas, *Introd. critique à la deux. épître de Pierre* (Strassburg, 1845); F. Ollier, *Essai d'introduction critique à la sec. épître de S. Pierre* (Toulouse, 1852); E. G. King, *Did S. Peter write in Gk.? Thoughts and criticisms intended to prove the Aramaic origin of Second Peter* (Cambridge, 1871); Grosch, *die Echtheit des 2. Briefes Petrus* (1889, sec. ed. 1911); F. H. Chase (*DB.* iii. 796–818)*; Schenkel (*BL.* iv. 502–506); Sanday, *Inspiration* (1893); 346 f., 382 f.; McGiffert, *AA.* 600 f.; O. Cone (*EBi.* 3682 f.); Moffatt *HNT.*² 596 f., 707 f.); Pfleiderer (*Urc.* iv. 255 f.); Abbott (*Diat.* 1116 f.); K. Henkel, *Der zweite Brief des Apostelfürsten Petrus geprüft auf seine Echtheit* (1904*); A. Camerlynck (*Collectiones Brugenses*, 1907, 6–13, 'quæritur utrum demonstrari possit, sec. epist. S. Petri a principe Apostolorum fuisse conscriptam'); Dillenseger (*Mélanges de la Faculté Orientale*, Beyrout, ii. 173–212, 1907, 'l'authenticité de la deux. ép. P.'); S. J. Case (*DAC.* ii. 207 f.).

§ 1. *Contents and characteristics.*—The salutation (1^{1-2}) passes over into an exhortation (1^{2-11}) to attain, by means of a pure and diligent life, that ἐπίγνωσις of the divine nature which is at once the privilege and goal of Christianity. Such a reminder ($1^{12f.}$) comes with special aptness from one whose apostolic relation to Jesus guarantees his witness to the historic voice of God. Furthermore, Christians ($1^{19f.}$) have OT prophecy to be their light in this darkling world until the second advent of Jesus. The mention of the OT prophets, however, reminds the writer that there were false prophets as well, and this leads him ($2^{1f.}$) to denounce in round terms the false teachers of his own day as vicious, greedy, and insubordinate characters who will share the doom of their prototypes, viz. the fallen angels, the contemporaries of Noah, and the men of Sodom and Gomorrha. The prediction of the doom awaiting these apostates is followed ($2^{10f.}$) by a pungent description of their malpractices. In writing thus, the author is only reminding his readers once more of the OT prophecies and the apostolic injunctions (3^{1-2}). They must remember that the appearance of those who idly scoff at the second advent is one mark of the latter days (3^{3-7}),[1] whereas the

[1] Cf. Clem. Rom. xxiii. 3, 2 Clem. xi. 2. 3^{6} = En 83^{3-4}.

coming of the Lord's day is sure ($3^{8f.}$). This great hope of a new world implies that Christians must keep themselves pure and steadfast, to be worthy of it ($3^{11f.}$). With an appeal to Paul's authority * for the view of a gracious purpose in the delay of the end ($3^{15f.}$), and a final exhortation to growth in the grace and *γνῶσις* of Christ, the pastoral ends in a brief doxology (3^{18}).

The Hellenistic colouring of the tract is noticeable. Terms like *θεία δύναμις* (1^{3}) and *θεία φύσις* (1^{4}) were, indeed, current during the first century, but their application to Jesus Christ is strange, and their point is missed unless the writing is placed in the second century, when a diffused Stoicism was predominant throughout the empire, whose keynotes were participation in the divine nature and advance (*προκοπή*, cp. 1^{5-7}) in the scale of ethical virtue (*ἐπιχορηγεῖν*, see below), and when a type of *γνῶσις* was popular which was compatible with an inadequate conception of the *χάρις* in Christ's person and with a defective morality. Beside these lie late Greek terms like *ἔκπαλαι*, *ὑπόδειγμα*, *γεγυμνασμένην* (2^{14}),† (? *ὑποζύγιον*=ass), *ὀλίγως*, *ἐξεράω* (=vomit), the use of active for middle in 3^{18}, splinters of Hellenistic Greek like *λήθην λαβών* (Josephus) and *μυωπάζων* (1^{9}),‡ the dramatic background of *ἐπιχορηγηθήσεται* (1^{11}), the technical term *ἐπόπτης* (1^{16}=initiate), unique semi-philosophical formations like *αἰώνιος βασιλεία* (1^{11}) and *εἰλικρινὴς διάνοια* (properly=pure reason, Plato's *Phæd.* 66 A), grandiloquent periphrases like *ἡ μεγαλοπρεπὴς δόξα* (1^{17}), *eyes full of an adulteress* (2^{14}), and *ὁ ζόφος τοῦ σκότους τετήρηται* (2^{17} as the doom of wells and mists !), the awkward abstract plurals in 3^{11} etc. etc. Similarly, an examination of the linguistic data shows that the writer's characteristic vocabulary is often allied to the Greek versions of the OT or of extra-canonical volumes (*e.g.* *ἄπταιστος*, 3 Mac 6^{39}; *γογγυστής*, Theod. Pr 26^{20}, Symm. Pr 26^{22}, Is 29^{24}; *ἐκπορνεύειν*, *ἐμπαικτής*, Theod. Is 3^{4}; *ἐνυπνιάζεσθαι* without *ἐνύπνιον*, and *ἀΐδιος*, *ἄλογα*, *ζῷα*, *σπιλοῦν* from the Book of Wisdom).§ These indications of provenance need not be pressed, however. Thus the occasional resemblances to iambic rhythm which have been noted (Bigg refers to $2^{1. 3. 4}$) are no more than the accidental cadences that recur in many of the imaginative reaches of prose literature, from Livy and Tacitus to Dickens. Even the *παροιμία* of 2^{22} need not be referred to the influence of such writers as Ezekiel of Alexandria; the second part, at any rate, echoes (p. 35) the traditional reproach upon Nadan preserved in the Syriac and Armenian texts of Ahiḳar (cp. J. Rendel Harris in *The Story of Ahiḳar*², pp. lxviii f.), "My son, thou hast behaved like the swine which went to the bath (*λουσαμένη*, 2 P.) with people of quality, and when he came out saw a stinking drain and went and rolled himself in it." At the same time, there is signifi-

* Echoing perhaps Polyk. iii. 8 (*τῇ σοφίᾳ τοῦ μακαρίου καὶ ἐνδόξου Παύλου, ὃς . . . ἔγραψεν ἐπιστολάς*).

† The genitive with this, like the description of the mists in 2^{17}, is one trace of the Homerisms frequent in second-century rhetoric.

‡ "There can be little doubt that the writer of 2 P. is here guilty of a rhetorical bathos" (Chase, 808).

§ For some traces of the Apocalypse of Baruch, see M. R. James' edition, pp. lviii–lix.

cance in the pagan and Philonic * conception of inspiration as a state in which men were simply mouthpieces of the divine spirit (1^{21}, so φθεγξάμενον in 2^{16}); in classical borrowings like the second proverb of 2^{22} and στηριγμός (3^{17}), and especially in the exploitation of the idea, familiar to Jews (cp. Joseph. *Ant.* i. 2. 3: "Adam's prediction that the world would be destroyed one day by the force of fire, and at another time by the force of water") † and to Christians of the second century, but promulgated especially by contemporary Stoicism (cp. Zeller's *Stoics*, *Epicureans*, and *Sceptics*, Eng. tr. pp. 155 f.), that the universe was to be destroyed by fire; no less than in solecisms like βλέμμα, which the author uses as = *seeing*, instead of *ocular expression* (2^{8}), παραφρονία (2^{16}), κύλισμα (2^{22}, properly = a cylinder), ἐμπαιγμονῇ (3^{3}), the genitive after βραδύνει (cp. Blass, *Gramm.* § 36. 9), the use of σπεύδειν (3^{12}), the present for the future in 3^{12} (τήκεται), and καυσοῦσθαι ($3^{10. 12}$).

This Hellenistic colouring is mediated by Alexandrian influences, however, and is associated with a strong predilection for the midrashic tendencies of the later Judaism (see above, p. 23). There (cp. Kalisch, *Bible Studies*, i. 24 f.), while some characters like Lot acquired an unwonted halo of respect (cp. 2^{7} after legends in Bereschith Rabba), others, like Cain, Korah, Balaam, and Jezebel, became blackened with the growth of evil associations. Even Philo turns Balaam into a juggling, disloyal impostor; while in *Targ. Jon.* on Ex 7^{11} he is the teacher of Jannes and Jambres (2 Ti 3^{8}), those masters of witchcraft and divination who rivalled Moses in his feats of magic (see below, p. 399). Thus the allusion to his covetousness in Jud. [14] is probably to be seconded by a reference in v.[8], where the *sensual dreams* reflect Balaam's Targumic reputation as an exponent of corrupt dreams. Similarly Noah (2^{5}) became in Jewish tradition (Jos. *Ant* i. 3. 1; Sib. Or. i. 128; Jub. vii. 20 f.) a preacher of righteousness to his corrupt age.

There is a strange parallel (cp. Franke, *Deutsche Litteraturzeitung*, 1901, 2760 f., and van den Bergh van Eysinga's *Indische Einflüsse auf Evang. Erzählungen* 53 f.) between $3^{8. 10f.}$ and the early Buddhist Nidânakathâ (cp. Rhys Davids, *Buddhist Birth-Stories*, i. 58): "Friends, one hundred thousand years from now there will be a new dispensation; this system of worlds will be destroyed; even the mighty ocean will dry up; this great earth will be burned up and destroyed; and the whole world, up to the realms of the immaterial angels, will pass away. Therefore, O friends, do mercy, live in kindness, and sympathy, and peace."

§ 2. *Object.*—It is as difficult as in the case of Judas, to make out the physiognomy of the errorists from any comparison of the homily with the traits of the second-century errorists preserved for us in Irenæus and his fellow-apologists. But whether their gnosticism was that of Carpokrates (so Grotius, Schenkel, Mangold, Völter, Holtzmann, etc.) or the earlier Nikolaitans

* Josephus (*Ant.* iv. 6. 5) applies it to Balaam.

† See above, p. 28. The final burning of the star-spirits or στοιχεῖα (3^{10}, cp. Spitta, 265 f.) is another relic of later Jewish tradition (cp. En 60^{12} 69^{22} etc.; Wendland, *HBNT.* i. 2. 369).

(Mansel),* its traits are too distinctive to be explained simply from the practical libertinism or the incipient scepticism which Paul or even the prophet John had encountered within the first century, much less from Sadducean Christians (Bertholdt, *Einl.* § 672 f.).

The Gnostics objected to any proof from the Scriptures, on the ground that truth was delivered *viva voce*, not by means of written documents. This at first sight appears to harmonise with the catholic position, that tradition is the supreme standard; but the Gnostics rejected the catholic apostolic tradition, preferring their own construction, as Irenæus bitterly complains (iii. 2 f.), and claiming to be wiser "not only than the presbyters, but even than the apostles." This claim in turn led them to twist the scriptures into consonance with their own views (παρατρέποντες τὰς ἑρμηνείας καὶ ῥᾳδιουργοῦντες τὰς ἐξηγήσεις, Iren. i. 3. 6), and both features of their teaching are antagonised by the author of 2 Peter. The false γνῶσις promulgated successfully ($2^{18f.}$) in several circles of contemporary Christianity by these teachers (2^{1}) appears to have developed much the same results in conduct as those denounced by Judas—so much so that all the author thinks he requires to do is to reproduce the incisive exposure of their greed, sensuality, and arrogance, given in the earlier letter. The colours are heightened, the terms become more extravagant and excited, but the errorists here represent a full-blown development of the tendencies opposed by Judas in his pamphlet. The special burden of this homily is, however, the rehabilitation of belief in the second advent ($1^{11.\ 16.\ 19}$ $3^{3f.}$), as against the scoffers (ἐμπαῖκται). To controvert these teachers the writer brings forward four pleas: (i.) the primitive apostolic witness of the second advent ($1^{16f.}$), (ii.) the messianic prophecies of the ($1^{19f.}$) OT which that witness corroborates, (iii.) an explanation of the delay (based on a current Jewish piece of exegesis), as really due ($3^{8f.}$) to the long-suffering and consideration of God,† and (iv.) an assertion that belief and disbelief in the second advent were

* "There may have been shades of difference between them; some, perhaps, had a philosophy, and some had not; but in the eyes of the Christian preacher, judging the party as a whole by its practical results, they would all seem to wear the same livery" (Bigg, *ICC.* p. 239).

† To infer from the absence of any allusion to chiliasm that the epistle must be very old, is doubly erroneous; for (i.) chiliasm was not universal in the second century, (ii.) nor was the quotation from Ps 90^{4} its starting-point, as Apoc $20^{4f.}$ is enough to show.

bound up with pure and vicious lines of conduct respectively ($3^{8.\ 11f.}$). Incidentally, he asserts towards the close the complete harmony of Paul's teaching on this point with his own, with a view to discredit the appeal made by the errorists to certain sayings of the great apostle.

The errorists who are thus denounced in 2 P. belonged probably to circles where spiritualistic views of the universe were promulgated,* as if it were immutable; but while Philo defends this line of speculation against the Stoic theory of a final conflagration (*de incorrupt. mundi*, 18 f.), our author uses the latter, which was popular among ordinary Christians of the time (cp. Origen, *adv. Cels.* iv. 11. 79), to rebut the former. If one could be sure that their *sophistical myths* (1^{16}) represented an allegorising interpretation of the life of Jesus, it might be possible to see in them an exaggerated expression of the spiritualising movement which, as the Fourth gospel indicates, had already begun in Asia Minor to resolve difficulties in the literal statement of such ideas as that of the second advent. In denouncing them, the writer, like the author of the Pauline pastorals (2 Ti 3^{1-6}), passes from the future to the present; in the heat of his denunciation he forgets that he has begun by putting his counsels into the form of a prediction, couched against apprehensions of a danger in the days to come (cp. Henkel, *op. cit.* 37 f.), and speaks of the errorists naturally as they lived and moved before his eyes.

§ 3. *Period and origin.*—Even apart from the use of a pastoral (Judas) which was not composed till long after Peter had died, the late origin of the epistle, involving its pseudonymous character, would be revealed by the character of (*a*) its allusion to Paul's epistles (3^{16}, where αἱ γραφαί cannot be non-technical). These are apparently viewed as the subject of varied interpretations and even of serious misunderstandings. Furthermore, they are ranked on a level with *the other scriptures*, *i.e.* the OT primarily; and evidently a collection of them is presupposed (cp. Gutjahr, pp. 49 f.), for the reference of 3^{15} can hardly be confined to Romans (2^{4} 9^{22}, so Grotius, Huther, and Dietlein)† or Ephesians (with its conception of σοφία, so Hofmann, Belser, von Soden), or Thessalonians (Alford), or Galatians (Augusti), much less Hebrews (Cramer, Bengel, Horne, Forster, *Apost. Authority of Hebrews*, pp. 625 f. etc.), or some Pauline letter no longer extant (so, *e.g.*, Pott, Kühl, Spitta, Zahn, Bigg). This allusion (cp. Spitta, 286 f.) to a collection of Pauline

* Cp. Irenæus, *adv. haer.* v. 19. 2: substantiam [mundi] a semetipsa floruisse et esse ex se natam . . . alii aduentum Domini contemnunt, incarnationem eius non recipientes.

† This is used by those who, like Mayor recently, argue for the Roman destination of the writing.

epistles is therefore an anachronism which forms an indubitable water-mark of the second century, and which is corroborated by the allusion to *your apostles* in 3^2, where the context, with its collocation of prophets and apostles, reflects the second-century division of scripture into these two classes. The general period is further indicated by (*b*) the dependence of the homily upon 1 Peter. Early in the church the differences of style between 2 Peter and 1 Peter led many to suspect that the former was not written by the author of the latter. "Simon Petrus . . . scripsit duas epistolas, quæ catholicæ nominantur; quarum secunda a plerisque eius negatur propter stili cum priore dissonantiam" (Jerome, *uir. inlust.* 1). The differences of style and diction are exactly those which denote an individual writer, who is composing his work with 1 Peter, if not with the Petrine speeches in Acts, before his mind (cp. Simcox, *Writers of NT*, 63–69, with the older works of Olshausen and Mayerhoff, *Einleitung in die petrinischen Schriften*, 158–170). 2 Peter is more periodic and ambitious* than 1 Peter, but its linguistic and stylistic efforts only reveal by their cumbrous obscurity a decided inferiority of conception, which marks it off from 1 Peter. Thus—to mention only one or two characteristics in the vocabulary—ἐπιχορηγεῖν is used, not as χορηγεῖν in 1 P 4^{11} (and Paul) in a religious application, but in its ethical sense current among philosophic moralists (1^5); the groups of words compounded with ἀγαθός and κακός, which recur in 1 Peter, are entirely absent from the later writing; the predilection for compounds with σύν disappears in 2 Peter, while in the latter ἐπόπτης replaces μάρτυς, ἡγέομαι displaces λογίζομαι, the gospel becomes an ἐντολή, and the expectation of the near end (1 P 4^7) is prolonged indefinitely (2 P $3^{4.8}$). 1 Peter never uses words like ἐκεῖνος or ὅσος, εὐσέβεια or εὐσεβής, κρίσις or μισθός, ὑπάρχω or ὑπομονή, whereas, on the contrary, 2 Peter uses δὲ καί but never μέν . . . δέ, or ἀλλήλων, ἀπειθέω, ἐλπίς, ἔθνος, κληρονομία, ζάω, μένω, the sing. of ὀλίγος, φόβος, and the ideas of joy and sojourning; unlike 1 Peter, the writer also is fond of using σωτήρ (and that of Christ), ἀποφεύγω, ἐπίγνωσις, ὁδός, and παρουσία (for ἀποκάλυψις), though the end is not the appearance

* "Neither style nor matter can be called simple. It is not altogether without eloquence, but the eloquence is elaborate and often artificial, as in the octave of virtues (1^{5-8}). In many passages the thought is too subtle to be easily followed" (Mayor, cxiii).

of Christ but the day of terrible judgment. Even after all allowance is made for difference of subject, *e.g.*, such considerations fail to account for the discrepancies of thought and expression, except upon the hypothesis of a dual authorship. "No change of circumstances can account for the change of tone of which we are conscious on passing from the one epistle to the other" (Mayor, p. lxxx).

This difference of tone and style involves the pseudonymous character of 2 Peter. The writer is at pains to invest his writing with verisimilitude. Symeon Peter is made to refer to his own mission and death, foretold by Jesus ($1^{13f.}$), to (1^{15}, cp. above, pp. 15, 191 f.) the Petrine tradition under Mark's gospel, to the transfiguration of which he was a witness ($1^{16f.}$), and to the First epistle (3^{1}), evidently widely circulated by this time.

The recent attempt of Spitta and Zahn to explain 3^{1} as referring to some lost epistle and not to 1 Peter, is based on the erroneous idea that 2 Peter is addressed to Jewish Christians (and therefore that the audience of 2 P 3^{1} could not be that of 1 Peter), and on the assertion that 3^{1} is not an accurate description of 1 Peter. But the latter contains teaching on the prophetic witness to Christ and on the second coming, besides at least one (5^{1}) allusion to the apostolic witness. Other features corroborate the late date. Thus, the mount of transfiguration is referred to as *the holy mount* (1^{18}) quite in the sub-apostolic fashion of investing sacred scenes with a halo of pious associations. Jesus is explicitly called θεός (1^{1}, cp. 3^{18}), as in the later strata of the early Christian literature (Jn 1^{1} 20^{28}, cp. Ign. pref. *ad Eph.*). Christianity is viewed as *the* (*holy*, 2^{21}) *commandment* (3^{2}) transmitted through the apostles to the churches. *The fathers*, too, have died (3^{4}), *i.e.* the founders of the church, the first generation, have passed away.* In short, even more definitely than in Judas, we are in the atmosphere which reappears not long afterwards in Tertullian's familiar sentence (*de praescr. haeret.* vi.): apostolos domini habemus auctores, qui nec ipsi quicquam ex suo arbitrio quod inducerent elegerunt, sed acceptam a Christo disciplinam fideliter nationibus assignauerunt. One outcome of this feeling is shown in the fact that the author, finding an allusion in Jud $^{17\text{-}18}$ to what he conceived a written apostolic prophecy of licentious mockers in the last days, puts into the lips of Peter (2 P 3^{3}) words which might serve as a basis for that

* It is sometimes argued that the pseudonymous writer would not have given himself away by thus introducing an anachronism. But, as his use of the present tense ($2^{10.\ 12.\ 17\text{-}18}$) already shows, he had to introduce some contemporary allusions in order to lend point to his words; whether he was conscious of the slip or not, cannot be determined. At all events, the reference is a water-mark of the date, since it is not possible to read οἱ πατέρες in this connection as a term for the OT saints.

prophecy.* Similarly, it is another method of adding *vraisemblance* to the writing when the author alludes to Peter's part in the tradition preserved by Jn $21^{15f.}$.

The author thus reveals himself as the composer of a pseudepigraphon under the honoured name of Peter (see above, pp. 40 f.). What authority he had for writing thus we do not know. "Capit autem magistrorum uideri quæ discipuli promulgarint," says Tertullian (*adv. Marc.* iv. 5); and if the writer felt himself a true disciple of the apostles he probably chose this literary artifice, with its self-effacing spirit, for the purpose of conveying a message which he believed to be timely and inspired. The prestige of Peter, owing to the circulation of the first epistle and the tradition of the churches, would naturally suggest the use of his name for this encyclical.

The hypothesis that the phenomena of style and expression may be accounted for by a difference of amanuensis, is as old as Jerome (*ep. Hedib.* 120, *Quæst.* xi., 'duæ epistolæ quæ feruntur Petri stilo inter se et charactere discrepant structuraque uerborum. Ex quo intelligimus pro necessitate rerum diuersis eum usum interpretibus'); after being revived by Calvin, who thought a follower of Peter might have written at his command, it has been more recently defended by Farrar, Cook, W. H. Simcox, and Selwyn (*St. Luke the Prophet*, 157 f., Luke as amanuensis). But there is no allusion to an amanuensis in the epistle, and the theory that 1 Peter and 2 Peter were dictated to different secretaries is a mere makeshift. The linguistic data of the epistle do not bear out the view that Aramaic oral teaching has been translated into Greek, and the ideas of the two Petrine letters are too different to permit a common authorship for both epistles. The idiosyncrasies of the writer of 2 Peter are not less striking than his dependence upon earlier authors; it is hardly too much to say that not another sentence in the extant early Christian literature can be shown to have come from his pen. 1 Peter has its own charm and beauty, but of the pages of 2 Peter we might almost say, as Quintilian said of the verses of Ennius, that they are more impressive than beautiful (*non tantam habent speciem quantam religionem*)—with this reservation, that their impressiveness is due not to the weighty Christian truths they convey (of the incarnation, the sufferings of Jesus, the resurrection, the Spirit in the Christian, and prayer, they contain not a single syllable) but to the moral vigour and earnest feeling of the writer's protest against the lax tendencies of contemporary gnosticising innovations.

Besides the use of Judas (pp. 348 f.), 1 Peter, and Josephus (pp. 28–29), the occasional and remarkable coincidences between 2 P. and the *Apocalypse of Peter* (cp. Chase, *DB.* iii. 814–816; M. R. James, xxvi f.) have been held to

---

* This is inherently more probable than Kühl's idea that Jud $^{17-18}$ is a quotation from 2 P 3^{3}. The author of 2 Peter draws on Judas, as Eusebius in the ninth chapter of his *Præparatio Euangelica* (bk. ix.) lifts material, without acknowledgment, from Joseph. *Apion*, i. 22.

involve a literary relationship. Those who feel that (*a*) the origin of the two within the same school of religious thought is inadequate to explain the data satisfactorily, argue for (*b*) a use of the apocalypse in 2 P. (so, *e.g.*, Harnack, *ACL.* ii. 1. 470f., and Weinel in *HNA.* i. 211 f. ii. 285 f.; (*c*) a use of 2 P. in the apocalypse (so, *e.g.*, Bigg; Zahn's *GK.* ii. 810 f.; Belser, *INT.* 870–871; Mayor, cxxx–cxxxiv), or even (*d*) the possibility of a common authorship for both (so, *e.g.*, hesitatingly Kühl and Sanday's *Inspiration*, 347). The popularity of the Petrine apocalypse in many churches during the second century, together with the fact that it is attested earlier than 2 P., may be held to favour (*b*), especially as the occurrence and sequence of the phrases in question * are more natural in the apocalypse than in the epistle; but a decision on the relationship of the two is handicapped by (i.) our ignorance of the conditions in which the Petrine literature of the second century originated, (ii.) the possibility that both † drew on common sources of a syncretistic nature, and (iii.) the fragmentary state of the extant apocalypse. The alternative lies between (*a*) and (*b*); in the present state of our knowledge, the probabilities upon the whole incline to (*b*). It is more likely, at any rate, that the existence of the apocalypse was one of the motives which inspired the composition of 2 P. (in its apocalyptic outlook) than that 2 P 2–3 led to the fabrication of the apocalypse. The origin of the Petrine canon (gospel, acts, and epistles) during the first two centuries is one of the most enigmatic problems in the early Christian literature; but, while 1 P. was certainly the earliest and the Acts are certainly the latest of the group, 2 P. is linked somehow to the κήρυγμα and the ἀποκάλυψις not later than the middle of the second century.

The determination of the epistle's relation to the Petrine apocalypse is practically the only clue to the period of its composition in the second century. Most critics suggest *c.* A.D. 150 (*e.g.* Hilgenfeld, Bleek, Mangold, Renan, S. Davidson, R. Knopf, Holtzmann, von Soden, Chase, Jacoby in *NT Ethik*, 459 f., and Brückner), though some go earlier (before A.D. 130, Ramsay, Simcox, Strachan) and others later (*e.g.* Semler [in *Paraphrasis*: 'alteram uero epistolam seculo demum secundo tribuere audeo et quidem fere labenti'], Keim, Sabatier, Pfleiderer, Schenkel, Schwegler, van Manen, and Harnack). The *terminus ad quem* is furnished by the fact of the epistle being known to Origen (Eus. *H. E.* vi. 25), and possibly to Clement of Alexandria. This renders it impossible to descend later than *c.* A.D. 170. How

* The two writings would be brought closer together, if 2 P $1^{16f.}$ (= Apoc. Pet. § 2) were taken, as by Hofmann, to denote a post-resurrection appearance of Jesus to the twelve; but this interpretation is improbable (cp. Spitta, 89 f., *ZNW.*, 1911, 237–242).

† The parallel between the apocalypse (1) and 2 P $2^{1f.}$ is hardly closer than that between Justin's *Dial.* lxxxii. For the Jewish traits of the apocalypse, see M. Gaster in *Journal of Royal Asiatic Society*, 1893, 571 f., and A. Marmorstein in *ZNW.* (1909) 297–300.

much earlier one can mount, depends upon the view taken of its relations to the apocalypse of Peter and Justin Martyr (see below). When the epistle is considered to have been written by Peter, the *terminus ad quem* of its composition is naturally the latter's death, *i.e.* within the seventh decade of the first century. But the historical reconstructions involved in such theories are more or less hypothetical. The Petrine authorship still finds one or two defenders (*e.g.* Henkel, Camerlynck, and Dillenseger, in the Roman church); R. A. Falconer (*Exp.*[6] v. 459 f., vi. 47 f., 117 f., 218 f.) regards it as a genuine circular epistle addressed by Peter to the churches of Samaria, while others conjecture that it was prompted by the disorder at Corinth and written, previous to 1 P., either from Antioch to the Jewish Christians of Palestine before the seventh decade (Zahn and Wohlenberg), or to Asiatic churches troubled by stragglers from the main body of the Corinthian errorists (Bigg). But, apart from the insuperable internal difficulties and the absence of all primitive tradition, even the ingenious attempt of Zahn and Spitta to regard it as more Petrine than 1 P. is shipwrecked on the linguistic data, and the defence of B. Weiss and Grosch falls with their impossible date for 1 P. It (*a*) is incredible that a manifesto issued by Peter during the seventh decade of the first century should only appear in tradition at a very late period, and even then be received with considerable suspicion; and (*b*) it is worse than paradoxical to sacrifice the priority and even the authenticity of 1 P. in order to avoid the conclusion that a pseudepigraphon like 2 P. could be admitted into the canon.

To sum up: in the strictest sense of the term, 2 Peter is a catholic epistle, addressed to Christendom in general (1^1 3^{16}); it may be defined as a homily thrown into epistolary guise, or a pastoral letter of warning and appeal. Unlike 1 P. (1^{1-2}), it is directed to no church or group of churches; the references in $1^{12f.}$ and $3^{1f.}$ belong to the literary drapery of the writing, and there is an entire absence of any personal relation between the writer and the church or churches. No evidence points to Gentile much less to Jewish Christians as the audience specially in the writer's mind. The problem of the Jewish Law does not exist for him and his readers.

The origin of the pastoral has been usually given as Egyptian (Mayerhoff, *op. cit.* pp. 193 f.; Harnack, Chase); but the *Apocalypse of Peter* was circulated far beyond Egypt, even if it was written there; Philonic traits do not prove any local origin for an early Christian writing; and the evidence is too insecure to point decisively to Egypt rather than to Syro-Palestine or even Asia Minor (cp. Deissmann's *Bible Studies*, 360 f., for parallels from an early decree of Stratonicea). Indications of its date and soil are not to be expected in the case of this or of any pseudepigraphon. "The real author of any such work had to keep himself altogether out of sight, and its entry upon circulation had to be surrounded with a certain mystery, in order that the strangeness of its appearance at a more or less considerable interval after the putative author's death might be concealed" (Stanton, *JTS.* ii. 19).

§ 4. *Integrity.*—Some critics * who feel the sub-apostolic atmosphere, but who are reluctant to admit that the epistle is pseudonymous, have attempted to clear up the literary problems by recourse to the hypotheses of (*a*) interpolation, and (*b*) transposition. The most plausible statement of the former (*a*) is Kühl's theory that 2^{1}–3^{2} is an interpolation from the epistle of Judas, dovetailed into 2 Peter. On this view, the original form of the letter is to be found in 1^{1-21} 3^{2-18}, the allusion to prophecy in 1^{20-21} being immediately followed by the exhortation ($3^{2f.}$) to remember the words of the prophets. But (i.) the debt to Judas is not confined to 2^{1}–3^{2}. Echoes of the earlier writing are audible in 1^{1-21}, so that the connection between Jud. and 2 P 2^{1}–3^{2} is not of itself sufficient to justify the excision (Bertholdt, *Einl.* 3157 f.; Kühl, and Weiffenbach in *TLZ.*, 1898, 364 f.) of the latter passage † as a later interpolation, much less of 1^{20b}–3^{3a} (Gess, *Das Apost. Zeugniss von Christi Person*, ii. 2. pp. 414 f.), or even of 2^{1}–$3^{7\,(18)}$ (Bartlet, *AA.* pp. 518–521); such attempts are usually dictated by a desire to conserve the rest of the epistle as an original Petrine writing, the canonical epistle being a later edition of the original brought up to date by the incorporation of the bulk of the epistle of Judas. (ii.) There are no differences of style in 2^{1}–3^{1} and in the rest of the epistle sufficiently decisive to warrant their separation on the score of

* According to E. I. Robson (*Studies in Sec. Ep. of St. Peter*, Cambridge, 1915), four catechetical flyleaves (1^{5b-11} 1^{16-18} 1^{20}–2^{19} 3^{8-13}) with apostolic imprimatur were reset *c.* 130 A.D., after being used by Jud.

† Ullmann's suggestion, that ch. 1 is the fragment of a lost original epistle of Peter, is not more convincing than Bunsen's theory that $1^{1-12}+3^{18}$ represents the original writing (*Ignatius u. seine Zeit*, pp. 175 f.).

internal evidence; cp. the use of *ἀπώλεια* ($2^{1.3}$ $3^{7.16}$), *τηρεῖν* ($2^{4.9.17}$ 3^{7}), *ἐντολή* (2^{21} 3^{2}), *ἡμέρα κρίσεως* (2^{9} 3^{7}), *ἴδιος* ($1^{3.20}$ $2^{16.22}$ $3^{3.16\text{-}17}$), and the occurrence of *ἐπίγνωσις* (1^{2} 2^{20}), etc. The mockers of $3^{3f.}$ are not different from the libertines of $2^{1f.}$. (iii.) This argument is corroborated by the fact that in chs. 1–2 alike there are uniform traces of Apoc. Pet., which militates against the theory of two separate authors, though not against the cognate view of Grotius,* who held that 1–2 and 3 were different epistles (3^{1} alluding to 1–2) by Symeon, the Jewish Christian successor of James in the bishopric of Jerusalem (*Πέτρος* and *ὁ ἀπόστολος* in 1^{1} being interpolated, as well as *ὁ ἀγαπητὸς ἡμῶν ἀδελφός* in 3^{15}, by those 'qui spectabiliorem et uendibiliorem uoluerunt facere hanc epistolam'). Finally, (iv.) the transition between $1^{20\text{-}21}$ and 2^{1} is not artificial. The allusion to true prophecy leads the writer to digress into a warning against the false prophets of his own age, and to find parallels between the propaganda of the future and the past.

The last-named argument tells equally against (*b*) P. Ladeuze's ingenious conjecture that $3^{1\text{-}16}$ has been displaced, by a scribe's error, from its original position after 2^{3a} (*RB.*, 1905, 543–552). Such a rearrangement, it is claimed, smoothes out the roughness of connection between the prophetic future of $2^{1\text{-}3a}$ and the present of 2^{3b}, since this change of outlook is mediated by $3^{1\text{-}3.4f.}$; it also acquits the author of the awkward digression of ch. 2, where he seems to forget the question of the advent with which he had started, for on this rearrangement the warnings against errors on the advent precede the negative section (3^{16} $2^{3b\text{-}22}$), which warns the faithful against the seductive arguments of the errorists. But it seems too elaborate to suppose that some copyist of the archetype, who was interrupted at 2^{3a}, began again by mistake at 2^{3b} and only added the omitted passage at the close, perhaps marking the error by a note on the margin which has disappeared. This implies that the archetype was in roll form; but even were it otherwise, the transposition of a leaf would be a possible accident; and in a palimpsest of the eighth or ninth century it is pointed out that $2^{3b\text{-}22}$ (75 lines) is almost equal in length to $3^{1\text{-}16}$ (72 lines). On the other hand, the object of the

* So Weber, *De numero epistolarum ad Corinthios rectius constituendo*, pp. 153 f., laying undue stress on the tense of *γράφω* (3^{1}). Grosch takes 2 $3^{15b\text{-}18}$ as a subsequent insertion by Peter in his own epistle.

transposition is unnecessary, as the interchange of futures and presents is explicable otherwise; the collocation of 3^{16} and 2^{8b} is unduly harsh; and 3^{17} (ὑμεῖς οὖν) falls abruptly after 2^{20-22}.

§ 5. *Setting and history in early church.*—No clear trace of the epistle's existence can be found till comparatively late in the second century. The allusions to Noah's preaching of repentance in Clem. Rom. (vii. 6, ix. 4, xi. 1, cp. 2 P 2^5) imply no more than an acquaintance with the Jewish haggada already current in earlier Jewish literature (see above, p. 25). Μεγαλοπρεπής, besides being associated (in substantival form) with the divine δόξα in the Psalter (LXX), is one of Clem.'s favourite adjectives,* so that the phrase τῇ μεγαλοπρεπεῖ δόξῃ αὐτοῦ (ix. 2) is as likely a proof that 2 P. (1^{17}) used Clem. as that Clem. used 2 P. No literary relation need be postulated, however, for the phrase may be liturgical (cp. Chase, p. 799), and any other coincidences (e.g. *the way of truth,*† xxxv. 5=2 P 2^2, xxxiv. 4 and 2 Clem. v. 5=2 P 1^4) are slight. The description of those who were sceptical of the second advent (xxiii. 2, *miserable are the double-minded which doubt in their soul and say, We heard that even in the time of our fathers, but, lo! we have grown old, and nothing of it has befallen us*) recalls 2 P 3^4; but Clem. expressly quotes it ‡ from some γραφή, perhaps Eldad and Modad (see above, p. 32); he would probably have cited the phrase more definitely had he had 2 P. before his mind. The scanty verbal coincidences (noted especially by Mayerhoff and Spitta) in 2 Clem. are due ultimately to a common acquaintance with the LXX, while the description of the final conflagration (xvi. 3) draws on the same myth as that employed in 2 P $3^{7f.}$, just as Barn. xv. 4, with 2 P 3^8, Justin (*Dial.* lxxxi.), and Irenæus (v. 23. 2), independently reflect the Jewish tradition, preserved, *e.g.*, in Jub iv. 30 and Slav. En xxxiii. 1. Either or both of these causes, *i.e.* use of older Jewish Greek scriptures and indebtedness to Jewish traditions, may reasonably be held to explain any parallels between the epistle and Test. XII. Patr., or Hermas,§ or Melito (cp. Westcott's *Canon*, pp. 222–223). There is nothing to show that it was known to Irenæus, who quotes (iv. 9. 2, Petrus ait in epistola sua) 1 Peter, while the apparent reminiscences in Clem. Alex., who must have known it if he commented on all the catholic epistles (Eus. *H. E.* vi. 14), are neither clear nor definite. The apparent echoes in the Latin version of *Actus Petri cum Simone* may be interpolated.

---

* Similarly he loves to speak of God's glorious and marvellous gifts (*e.g.* xix. 2, xxxv. 1, cp. 2 P 1^3).

† Cp. Herm. *Vis.* iii. 7. 1, and Clem. Alex. *Protrept.* § 106.

‡ In 2 Clem. xi. 2 it is again loosely cited as ὁ προφητικὸς λόγος, which throws light on the atmosphere in which 2 P. (cp. 1^{19}) was composed. See, further, 2 Clem. xi.=2 P 3^{3-4}.

§ Spitta's (*Urc.* ii. 399–409) discussion is convincing as against the use (Warfield, Zahn) of 2 P. by Hermas; but his argument that 2 P. depends on the Jewish original of Hermas, partakes too much of special pleading.

On the other hand, there are some threads of evidence which suggest that, like the apocalypse of Peter, with which it was associated in some circles of the early church, the epistle must have been composed by *c.* A.D. 150. The use of ἔξοδος=martyrdom (cp. 1^{15}) in the epistle of Lyons and Vienne would not itself be decisive (cp. *DB.* iii. 770), but another phrase (ὁ δὲ διαμέσου καιρὸς οὐκ ἀργὸς αὐτοῖς οὐδὲ ἄκαρπος ἐγίνετο, Eus. *H. E.* v. 145) is too unique to be almost anything than a reminiscence of 2 P 1^{8} (οὐκ ἀργοὺς οὐδὲ ἀκάρπους); cp. also the description of the apostates * as 'sons of perdition βλασφημοῦντες τὴν ὁδόν' (2 P 2^{2} δι' οὓς ἡ ὁδὸς τῆς ἀληθείας βλασφημεῖται), and of Alexander the physician as οὐκ ἄμοιρος ἀποστολικοῦ χαρίσματος (2 P 1^{1}, where ἡμῖν=the apostles). Secondly, although ψευδοδιδάσκαλος could easily be formed on the analogy of terms like ψευδοπροφῆται and ψευδαπόστολοι, still its use in Justin's *Dial.* lxxxii. ('as there were also false prophets in the time of the holy prophets who arose among you [*i.e.* Jews], so, too, are there in the present day many *false teachers*, of whom our Lord forewarned us'), especially in view of 2 P 2^{1} ('false prophets also appeared among the People [*i.e.* the Jews], as among you also there shall be *false teachers* . . αἱρέσεις ἀπωλείας), seems more than an accidental coincidence. As the context shows, Justin is referring loosely to Mt $24^{9f.}$ when he speaks of the Lord's warning; but this does not exclude the Petrine reference in the preceding words, particularly as αἱρέσεις and false prophets are conjoined in *Dial.* li.; cp., too, *Apol.* i. 28 (καὶ γὰρ ἡ ἐπιμονὴ τοῦ μηδέπω τοῦτο πρᾶξαι τὸν Θεὸν διὰ τὸ ἀνθρώπινον γένος γεγένηται· προγινώσκει γάρ τινας ἐκ μετανοίας σωθήσεσθαι) † with 3^{9}. Thirdly, Theophilus of Antioch some years later appears to have 2 P 1^{21} in mind when he writes of οἱ δὲ τοῦ Θεοῦ ἄνθρωποι πνευματόφοροι πνεύματος ἁγίου καὶ προφῆται γενόμενοι (*ad Autol.* ii. 9), though πνευματόφορος does occur in the LXX (Hos 9^{7}, Zeph 3^{4}); and he is as likely to have derived the idea of *ad Aut.* ii. 13 (ὁ λόγος αὐτοῦ, φαίνων ὥσπερ λύχνος ἐν οἰκήματι συνεχομένῳ, ἐφώτισεν τὴν ὑπ' οὐρανόν) from 2 P 1^{19} as from 4 Es 12^{42}, whence the author of 2 P. drew it (cp. Schott, pp. 278 f.). Here as elsewhere such verbal echoes do not necessarily imply literary filiation. All they denote may be the existence of the book which first gave currency to the particular phrase or phrases; the latter would often pass into the Christian parlance and be used by those who knew little or nothing of their origin. Thus with regard to 2 Peter, "the church of Vienne, for example, may have quoted one of its phrases, and yet never have read the epistle itself. Indeed, there is reason for thinking that the epistle did not enjoy a wide circulation. Otherwise it would be difficult to account for the extremely bad state of the text" (Bigg, p. 211; cp. Vansittart in *Journal of Philology*, iii. 537). Even in the fourth century it was not only rejected by the Syrian canon but regarded with suspicion, and more than suspicion, in most circles of the Western church.

---

* Were it alone, this might be referred to the Apoc. Petri, 22, 28 (βλασφημοῦντες τὴν ὁδὸν τῆς δικαιοσύνης).

† His failure to cite 2 P 3 when (*Apol.* i. 20) proving belief in the world-conflagration is significant, but it should not be pressed too far. Origen's similar silence (*c. Cels.* iv. 11. 79) is probably due to his suspicion of the epistle, whose conception of the fire differed from his own.

(B) *EPHESIANS.*

Literature.—(*a*) Editions—Launcelot Ridley, *Comm. on Ephesians* (London, 1540); J. Nacchiante, *Enarrationes in Eph.* (Venice, 1554); Musculus, *Comment. in epp. ad Galatas et Ephesios* (1561); M. Bucer, *Prælectiones in Ephes.* (1562); Binemann's *Expositio* (London, 1581); Robert Rollock's *Commentarius* (Edinburgh, 1590); B. Battus (1619); P. Bayne (London, 1643); D. Dickson's *Expositio Analytica* (Glasgow, 1645); Principal R. Boyd (London, 1652); Fergusson of Kilwinning (Edinburgh, 1659); G. Calixtus (*Expositio litt. in epistolas ad Eph. Col.*, etc., 1664–1666); Locke (London, 1707); P. J. Spener (1707); P. Dinant, *de Brief aan die Efese* (1711); M. Harmeken (1731); A. Royaards, *Paulus' brief aan de Ephesen schriftm. verklaart* (Amsterdam, 1735–8); J. D. Michaelis (1750); Schulz (Leipzig, 1778); J. A. Cramer, *neue Uebersetzung des Briefs an die Epheser, nebst eine Auslegung* (Hamburg, 1782); F. A. W. Krause (1789); Müller (Heidelberg, 1793); S. F. N. Morus (Leipzig, 1795); G. C. Popp, *Uebersetzung u. Erklärung der drei ersten Kapital des Briefs an die Eph.* (Rostock, 1799); J. F. von Flatt's *Vorlesungen* (1828); K. R. Hagenbach (1829); F. Holzhausen (Hanover, 1833); L. J. Rückert (Leipzig, 1834); G. C. A. Harless (1834); F. K. Meier (Berlin, 1834); C. S. Matthies (1834); T. Passavant, *Versuch einer prakt. Auslegung*, etc. (Basel, 1836); Baumgarten-Crusius (Jena, 1847); De Wette[2] (1847); Stier (Berlin, 1848); C. Kähler (Kiel, 1854); C. Hodge (New York, 1856); S. H. Turner (New York, 1856); Harless[2] (Stuttgart, 1858); R. E. Pattison (Boston, 1859); Newland (Oxford and London, 1860); Olshausen (1860); Bleek's *Vorlesungen* (Berlin, 1865); Schenkel[2] (1867, Lange's *Bibel-Werk*); Braune[2] (*ibid.* 1875, Eng. tr. of first ed. New York, 1870); Ewald (*Sendschreiben*, 1870); Hofmann (Nördlingen, 1870); Koster (1877); Hahn[4] (1878); Reuss (1878); Meyrick (*Speaker's Comm.* 1881); Eadie[3] (*Comm. on Gk. Text of Epistle of Paul to Eph.*, Edinburgh, 1883); J. Ll. Davies[2] (London, 1884); Ellicott[5] (1884)*; Schnedermann (*Kurzgef. Comm.* 1888); M. F. Sadler (London, 1889); J. Agar Beet (1890 f.); J. T. Beck's *Erklärung d. Briefes P. an die Eph.* (Gütersloh, 1891); A. Klöpper (Göttingen, 1891)*; H. Oltramare (Paris, 1891); J. Macpherson (Edinburgh, 1892); von Soden[2] (*HC.* 1893)*; J. S. Candlish (Edinburgh, 1895); G. Wohlenberg (Strack-Zöckler, 1895); B. Weiss (1896); T. K. Abbott (*ICC.* 1897, 'primarily philological'); Haupt[8] (— Meyer, 1902)*; J. A. Robinson* (1903); S. D. F. Salmond (*EGT.* 1903); Krukenberg (Gütersloh, 1903); W. Lueken[2] (*SNT.* 1907); Baljon (1907); Westcott[2] (1907); F. A. Henle[2] (1908); J. E. Belser (1908); Gross Alexander (New York, 1910); P. Ewald[2] (*ZK.* 1910)*; Knabenbauer (Paris, 1912); M. Dibelius (*HBNT.* 1912); J. O. F. Murray (*CGT.* 1914).

(*b*) Studies—(i.) general:—J. F. Burg, *Analysis logica*, etc. (1708); F. Coulin, *Recherches critiques sur l'ép. aux Ephésiens* (1851); E. Coquerel, *Études dogmatiques sur l'épître aux Ephésiens* (1852); Chottin, *étude sur l'épître aux Eph.* (1858); R. Stier, *Die Gemeinde in Christo Jesu. Auslegung des Briefes an die Epheser* (Berlin, 1848–9); R. W. Dale (*The Epistle to the Ephesians*[6], 1892); G. G. Findlay (*Expos. Bible*, 1892); Gore (*A Practical Exposition*, 1898); Jülicher (*EBi.* i. 866 f.). (ii.) specially against Paul's authorship:—Baur's *Paul* (Eng. tr. ii. pp. 1–44); Hoekstra

(*TT.*, 1868, pp. 599 f.); Schwegler, *NZ.* ii. 330 f., 375 f.; Planck (*Theol. Jahrb.*, 1847, 461 f.); Hitzig, *zur Paul. Briefe* (1870), 22 f.; Weizsäcker (*AA.* ii. 240 f.); Renan, iii., xii. f.; Hönig (*ZWT.*, 1872, 63 f.); Brückner (*Chron.* 257 f.); S. Davidson (*INT.* ii. 261–300); von Soden (*JPT.*, 1887, 103 f., 432 f., and *INT.* 284–305); von Dobschütz (*Urc.* 175 f.); Pfleiderer's *Urc.* iii. 300 f.; Clemen, *Paulus*, i. pp. 138 f.; R. Scott, *The Pauline Epistles* (1909), 180–208; Freitag (*ZNW.*, 1912, 91 f.); Wendland (*HBNT.* i. 2. 361 f.). (iii.) for Paul's authorship:—Lünemann, *de epist. ad Eph. authentia, lectoribus, consilio* (Göttingen, 1842); W. F. Rinck, *disputatio ad authent. ep. P. ad Ephes. probandam* (1848); Räbiger, *de Christologia Pauli contra Baurium Commentatio* (1852); Schenkel (*BL.* ii. 120–127); Sabatier (*ESR.* iv. 439–442, and in his *Paul*, pp. 225 f.); McGiffert (*AA.* 378–385); Hort (*Romans and Ephesians*, 1895, 65–184); A. Robertson (Smith's *DB.*[2] i. 947 f.); Lock (*DB.* i. 714 f.); Brunet, *L'authenticité de l'épître aux Ephésiens* (1897); Bartlet (*AA.* 189 f.); Shaw, *Pauline Epistles*[3] (331 f.); B. W. Bacon, *Story of St. Paul* (1905, 299 f.); R. J. Knowling, *Testimony of St. Paul to Christ*, 94 f.; Grenstedt (*DAC.* i. 343 f.). (iv.) on special points:—Haenlein, *de lectoribus Epist. ad Ephesios* (Erlangen, 1797); van Bemmelen, *Epistolæ ad Eph. et Coloss. collatæ* (1803); W. C. Perry (*de rebus Ephesiorum*, Göttingen, 1837); Méritan (*RB.*, 1898, 343–369, 'L'ecclésiologie . . .'); J. Albani, 'die Metaphern . . .' (*ZWT.*, 1902, 420–446); M. Dibelius, *Geisterwelt im Glauben des Paulus* (1909), 155–169; Harnack, *Adresse des Epheserbriefes des Paulus* (from *SBBA.*, 1910, 696–709); Coppieters (*RB.*, 1912, 361–390); Moffatt (*Exp.*[8] x. 89 f.).

§ 1. *Outline and contents.*—After an extremely brief address (1^{1-2}), the pastoral opens into the first of its two large sections (1^{3}–3^{19}); this is divided by a brief doxology (3^{20-21}) from the second (4^{1}–6^{20}), which concludes with a few lines of personal detail (6^{21-24}). 1^{3-14} is a glowing paragraph of praise, in rhythmical strophes (Innitzer, *ZTK.*, 1904, 612–621, and Coppieters in *RB.*, 1908, 74–88), to God for his complete and gracious revelation to men in Christ, followed by a prayer that the readers may have a perfect knowledge of this open secret in Christ as the head of the church (1^{15-23}). Their personal experience of such a salvation is due to grace alone (2^{1-10}), and as Gentile Christians they should especially realise the gracious union effected by Christ between themselves and the Jewish Christians (2^{11-22}). Of this gospel for Gentile Christians, Paul is the chosen herald (3^{1-13}), and the section closes with an impressive prayer for their attainments in the Christian experience (3^{14-21}, resuming the ideas of 1^{15-19}). The second section ($4^{1} = 2^{10}$) expounds the ethical obligations of this privilege, unity (4^{1-16}) being set in the forefront.[1] Then follows (4^{17} resuming the thought of 4^{1}) a series of

[1] On $4^{8f.}$ cp. Dalmer in *SK.* (1890) pp. 579 f.

counsels on purity of conduct (4^{17-24}, $4^{24} = 2^{10}$), and the general morals of the new life (4^{25}–5^{2} $5^{3-5.\ 6-21}$), concluding with a household table of maxims for wives and husbands ($5^{22-24.\ 25-33}$), parents and children (6^{1-4}), and slaves and masters (6^{5-9}). A final word of exhortation on the spiritual conflict (6^{10-18}) drifts into a brief request for prayer on Paul's behalf (6^{19-20}).

§ 2. *Relation to Colossians.*—The most obvious feature of Eph. consists of its resemblances to and differences from Colossians. The relationship between the two writings forms an intricate problem of literary criticism, which is almost decisive upon the larger question of the period and authorship of Ephesians. In striking a balance between the competing probabilities, the weight of the arguments (such as they are) inclines upon the whole to favour the authenticity of Colossians and the sub-Pauline origin of Ephesians (so, *e.g.*, Ewald, Mangold, von Soden, Klöpper, Heinrici, von Dobschütz, Clemen, Lueken, Wrede, Wendland), and the basis for this hypothesis—at best only a working hypothesis—lies in a comparative analysis of the two writings. That there is a connection between them is admitted on all hands. Those who hold that both were written by the same author either place them together in the second century or attribute them both to Paul. On the latter hypothesis, he read over Colossians (or a copy of it) before writing Ephesians, or else composed the letter when his mind was still full of what he had just addressed to the church of Colossæ. The relationship in this event would resemble that of the Thessalonian letters, when 2 Thess. is accepted as genuine. As against the hypothesis that a Paulinist wrote Eph. on the basis of Colossians, it is argued that so original a genius as this writer would not need to reproduce so much of Colossians,* and that the relationship is psychologically more credible if Paul wrote both. But—leaving out of account the relationship of 2 P. to 1 P., since Eph. is far superior in massiveness and height to the former—the synoptic problem is enough to show that the deliberate employment of a source was not incompatible with original work on the part of an early Christian writer, and Eph. may be fairly regarded as a set of variations played by a master hand upon one or two themes suggested by Colossians.

The literary phenomena, in outline, are as follows:—

Col.	Eph.
(1^{1-2}) Paul, an apostle of Christ Jesus through the will of God, and Timotheus our brother, to the saints and faithful brothers in Christ which are at Colossæ: Grace to you and peace from God our Father.	(1^{1-2}) Paul, an apostle of Christ Jesus through the will of God, to the saints which are [at Ephesus.] also the faithful brothers in Christ Jesus: Grace to you and peace from God our Father and the Lord Jesus Christ.
	(1^{3} Blessed be the God and Father of our Lord Jesus Christ.)

* "Imitators do not pour out their thoughts in the free and fervid style of this epistle" (Davies, *op. cit.* p. 9).

(1^{3}) We *give thanks* to God the Father of our Lord Jesus Christ, *praying* always *for you,* (1^{4}) having heard of your faith in Christ Jesus, and of the love which you have toward all the saints * . . . (1^{9}) FOR THIS CAUSE WE ALSO, since the day we heard it, DO NOT CEASE to pray and make request for you, that you may be filled with the knowledge of his will in all spiritual wisdom and understanding.	(1^{15}) FOR THIS CAUSE I ALSO, having heard of the faith in the Lord Jesus which is among you and of your love toward all the saints, (1^{16}) CEASE NOT to *give thanks for you, making mention of you in my prayers,* (1^{17}) that the God of our Lord Jesus Christ . . . may give unto you a spirit of wisdom and revelation in the knowledge of him.
(1^{10}) to walk worthily of the Lord . . . †	(4^{1}) I beseech you to walk worthily of the calling wherewith you were called.
($1^{13f.}$) The son of his love, in whom we have our redemption, the forgiveness of our sins . . .	($1^{6f.}$) in the Beloved, in whom we have our redemption through his blood, the forgiveness of our trespasses . . . ‡
(1^{16}) *in him* were *all things* created, *in the heavens and upon the earth,* things visible and things invisible, *εἴτε θρόνοι εἴτε κυριότητες εἴτε ἀρχαὶ εἴτε ἐξουσίαι.*	(1^{21}) far above all ἀρχῆς καὶ ἐξουσίας καὶ δυνάμεως καὶ κυριότητος. (1^{10} *all things in him, things in the heavens and things upon the earth.*)
(1^{18-19}) and he is the head § of THE BODY, THE CHURCH . . . that in all things he might have the preeminence, *ὅτι ἐν αὐτῷ εὐδόκησεν πᾶν τὸ πλήρωμα* ‖ *κατοικῆσαι.*	(1^{22-23}) And he put all things in subjection under his feet, and gave him to be the head over all things to THE CHURCH, WHICH IS HIS BODY, *τὸ πλήρωμα τοῦ τὰ πάντα ἐν πᾶσιν πληρωμένου.*
(1^{20}) *καὶ δι' αὐτοῦ ἀποκαταλλάξαι τὰ πάντα εἰς αὐτὸν, εἰρηνοποιήσας* διὰ *τοῦ αἵματος* τοῦ σταυροῦ *αὐτοῦ,* whether THINGS UPON THE	(1^{10}) *ἀνακεφαλαιώσασθαι τὰ πάντα ἐν τῷ* Χριστῷ, THINGS IN (ἐπὶ) THE HEAVENS AND THINGS UPON THE EARTH . . . ($2^{15f.}$) that he

---

* Also minor parallels in Col 1^{6} = Eph 1^{12-13}, Col 1^{8} = Eph. 4^{2-3} (love and the Spirit). On *ἀγάπην* in Eph 1^{15} cp. *Exp.*[8] ii. 136 f., 193 f., 321 f.

† Also Col 1^{11} = Eph 1^{19} 3^{16}, Col 1^{12} = Eph 5^{20} (*εὐχαριστοῦντες τῷ* Πατρί).

‡ Except 2^{16} (cross = means of amalgamating Jewish and Gentile Christians), this is the only allusion to Christ's death in Eph.—an advance upon the Pauline view in the direction of the Johannine. The sacrifice of Jesus (5^{2}) is simply adduced as an example of love for Christians (cp. 1 P $2^{21f.}$ in another aspect of imitation).

§ In Col. = headship over supernatural spirits and the church alike, in Eph. = (primarily) headship over the church. See below, p. 379.

‖ Cp. Eph. 3^{19} (*ἵνα πληρωθῆτε εἰς πᾶν τὸ πλήρωμα τοῦ θεοῦ*). Note different use of *κατοικῆσαι* in Col 1^{19} and Eph 3^{17}.

EARTH OR THINGS IN (ἐν) THE HEAVENS.	might create in himself of the twain one new man, ποιῶν εἰρήνην, καὶ ἀποκαταλλάξῃ both in one body unto God διὰ τοῦ σταυροῦ.
(1^{21}) And you ποτὲ ὄντας ἀπηλλοτριωμένους καὶ ἐχθροὺς τῇ διανοίᾳ,	(2^{1}) And you . . . (2^{3}) ποιοῦντες τὰ θελήματα τῆς σαρκὸς καὶ τῶν διανοιῶν . . . (2^{12}) ἀπηλλοτριωμένοι . . . (2^{16}) having slain τὴν ἔχθραν in him . . . (4^{18}) ἐσκοτωμένοι τῇ διανοίᾳ ὄντες, ἀπηλλοτριωμένοι . . .
(1^{22}) yet now* has he reconciled (ἀποκατήλλαξεν)† in the body of his flesh through death, to present you holy and without blemish and unreprovable before him:	($2^{15\text{-}16}$) having abolished in his flesh the enmity . . . might reconcile (ἀποκαταλλάξῃ) them both in one body . . . (1^{4}) to be holy and without blemish before him . . . ‡ (5^{27}) that he might present the church to himself . . . holy and without blemish . . .
(1^{23}) if so be § that you continue in the faith τεθεμελιωμένοι and steadfast, and not moved away from the hope of the gospel which you heard, which was preached in all creation under heaven; whereof I Paul was made a minister.	(3^{17}) rooted and τεθεμελιωμένοι in love . . . (3^{7}) by the gospel, whereof I was made a minister.
(1^{24}) Now I rejoice in my sufferings for your sake, and fill up on my part that which is lacking of τῶν θλίψεων τοῦ Χριστοῦ in my flesh ὑπὲρ τοῦ σώματος αὐτοῦ, which is the church;	(3^{1}) For this cause I Paul, the prisoner of Christ Jesus in behalf of you Gentiles . . . (3^{13}) I ask that you faint not at ἐν ταῖς θλίψεσίν μου ὑπὲρ ὑμῶν. ($1^{22\text{-}23}$, the church which is τὸ σῶμα αὐτοῦ.) 3^{9} ἡ οἰκονομία τοῦ μυστηρίου τοῦ ἀποκεκρυμμένου
(1^{25}) whereof I was made a minister κατὰ τὴν οἰκονομίαν τοῦ θεοῦ τὴν δοθεῖσάν μοι εἰς ὑμᾶς, to fulfil the word of God,	(3^{9}) ἀπὸ τῶν αἰώνων . . . (3^{2}) τὴν οἰκονομίαν τῆς χάριτος τοῦ θεοῦ τῆς δοθείσης μοι εἰς ὑμᾶς, (3^{3}) how that by revelation ἐγνωρίσθη to me τὸ

* So Eph 2^{13} (yet now).

† In Col. = reconciliation of supernatural powers and of sinners to God, in Eph = reconciliation of Jews and Gentiles together ($2^{11f.}$) to God; hence the change in the conceptions of the *Body*, *making peace*, and *the enmity*. The function of reconciliation, which in 2 Co $5^{18f.}$ and even in Col. is attributed to God, is transferred in the higher Christology of Eph. to Christ; a similar instance occurs in 1 Co 12^{28} = Eph 4^{11} (authorship of gifts).

‡ The addition of ἐν ἀγάπῃ (a frequent phrase), as the form in which the spotless character manifests itself, is an un-Pauline touch.

§ εἴ γε as in Eph 4^{21}.

(1^{26}) even τὸ μυστήριον* τὸ ἀποκεκρυμμένον ἀπὸ τῶν αἰώνων καὶ ἀπὸ τῶν γενεῶν—but has now† been manifested **τοῖς ἁγίοις αὐτοῦ**,	μυστήριον . . . (3^{5}) ὃ ἑτέραις γενεαῖς οὐκ ἐγνωρίσθη to the sons of men, as it has now been revealed **τοῖς ἁγίοις** ἀποστόλοις **αὐτοῦ** καὶ προφήταις ἐν πνεύματι. . . .
(1^{27}) οἷς ἠθέλησεν ὁ θεὸς **γνωρίσαι** τί τὸ πλοῦτος τῆς δόξης ‡ τοῦ μυστηρίου τούτου ἐν τοῖς ἔθνεσιν, which is Christ in you, ἡ ἐλπὶς τῆς δόξης.	(1^{9}) **γνωρίσας** ἡμῖν τὸ μυστήριον τοῦ θελήματος αὐτοῦ . . . (1^{18}) εἰς τὸ εἰδέναι ὑμᾶς τίς ἐστιν ἡ ἐλπὶς τῆς κλήσεως αὐτοῦ, τίς ὁ πλοῦτος τῆς δόξης of his inheritance . . . (3^{8}) τοῖς ἔθνεσιν εὐαγγελίσασθαι the unsearchable πλοῦτος τοῦ Χριστοῦ. . . .
(1^{28}) . . . that we may present § every man τέλειον ἐν Χριστῷ.	(4^{13}) [the object of the ministry being the attainment of all] εἰς ἄνδρα τέλειον, to the measure of the stature τοῦ πληρώματος τοῦ Χριστοῦ.
(2^{2}) συμβιβασθέντες ἐν ἀγάπῃ . . . εἰς ἐπίγνωσιν τοῦ μυστηρίου τοῦ θεοῦ, Χριστοῦ.	(4^{16}) συμβιβαζόμενον . . . ἐν ἀγάπῃ. . . . (4^{13}) τῆς ἐπιγνώσεως τοῦ υἱοῦ τοῦ θεοῦ.
(2^{4}) τοῦτο λέγω.	(4^{17}) τοῦτο οὖν λέγω.
(2^{6}) παρελάβετε τὸν Χριστόν. . . .	(4^{20}) ἐμάθετε τὸν Χριστόν.
(2^{7}) rooted and built up in him, καὶ βεβαιούμενοι τῇ πίστει καθὼς ἐδιδάχθητε.‖	(2^{22}) in whom you also are built up together . . . (3^{17}) rooted and grounded in love . . . (4^{21}) ἐν αὐτῷ ἐδιδάχθητε καθώς ἐστιν ἀλήθεια.
(2^{9}) For in him dwells πᾶν τὸ πλήρωμα τῆς θεότητος σωματικῶς,	(3^{19}) and to know the love of Christ, ἵνα πληρωθῆτε εἰς πᾶν τὸ πλήρωμα τοῦ θεοῦ [see also 4^{13} above].
(2^{10}) and you are ἐν αὐτῷ πεπληρωμένοι, who is the head πάσης ἀρχῆς καὶ ἐξουσίας,	cp. $1^{21\text{-}23}$ above.
(2^{11}) in whom you were also circumcised with a circumcision not made with hands . . .	(2^{11}) you, Gentiles in the flesh, who are termed Uncircumcision by that which is termed Circumcision, in the flesh, made with hands.
(2^{12}) you were also raised with him διὰ τῆς πίστεως τῆς ἐνεργείας τοῦ θεοῦ who raised him from the dead.	($^{19\text{-}20}$) the exceeding greatness of his power εἰς ἡμᾶς τοὺς πιστεύοντας κατὰ τὴν ἐνέργειαν of the strength of his might which he wrought in Christ, raising him from the dead.
($2^{13\text{-}14}$) And you, being dead through your trespasses and the uncircumcision of your flesh, συνεζωοποιήσεν σὺν	(2^{1}) And you, being dead through your trespasses and sins . . . (2^{5}) even when we were dead through our

* In Col. = Χριστὸς ἐν ὑμῖν, ἡ ἐλπὶς τῆς δόξης (2^{2} 4^{3}), in Eph. = the participation of Gentiles ; a difference of emphasis.

† Cp. Eph 3^{10} (ἵνα γνωρισθῇ νῦν ταῖς ἀρχαῖς κτλ.).

‡ = Eph 3^{16}. § = Eph 5^{27}. ‖ Also Col 2^{8} = Eph 5^{6}.

αὐτῷ, χαρισάμενος ἡμῖν πάντα τὰ παραπτώματα, having blotted out τὸ καθ' ἡμῶν χειρόγραφον τοῖς δόγμασιν ὃ ἦν ὑπεναντίον ἡμῖν, and took it out of the way, nailing it to the cross.	trespasses, συνεζωοποίησεν τῷ Χριστῷ —χάριτί ἐστε σεσωσμένοι—. . . (2^{15}) having abolished τὸν νόμον τῶν ἐντολῶν ἐν δόγμασιν. . . .
(2^{19}) the Head,* ἐξ οὗ πᾶν τὸ σῶμα διὰ τῶν ἁφῶν καὶ συνδέσμων ἐπιχορηγούμενον καὶ συμβιβαζόμενον αὔξει τὴν αὔξησιν τοῦ θεοῦ.†	$(4^{15\text{-}16})$ the Head, Χριστός, ἐξ οὗ πᾶν τὸ σῶμα συναρμολογούμενον καὶ συμβιβαζόμενον διὰ πάσης ἁφῆς τῆς ἐπιχορηγίας κατ' ἐνέργειαν ἐν μέτρῳ ἑνὸς ἑκάστου μέρους τὴν αὔξησιν τοῦ σώματος ποιεῖται εἰς οἰκοδομὴν ἑαυτοῦ ἐν ἀγάπῃ.
(3^{1}) If then you were raised with Christ, seek the things that are above, where Christ is, seated at the right hand of God . . . (3^{3}) For you died, and your life is hid with Christ in God.	(1^{20}) He raised him from the dead and seated him at his right hand ἐν τοῖς ἐπουρανίοις . . . (2^{6}) raised us with him, and made us to sit with him ἐν τοῖς ἐπουρανίοις in Christ Jesus.
(3^{5}) πορνείαν, ἀκαθαρσίαν, πάθος, ἐπιθυμίαν κακήν, καὶ τὴν πλεονεξίαν ἥτις ἐστὶν εἰδωλολατρεία.	(4^{19}) εἰς ἐργασίαν ἀκαθαρσίας πάσης ἐν πλεονεξίᾳ . . . (5^{3}) πορνεία δὲ καὶ ἀκαθαρσία πᾶσα ἢ πλεονεξία . . . (5^{5}) πᾶς πόρνος ἢ ἀκάθαρτος ἢ πλεονέκτης, ὅ ἐστιν εἰδωλολάτρης . . .
(3^{6}) δι' ἃ ἔρχεται ἡ ὀργὴ τοῦ θεοῦ.	(5^{6}) διὰ ταῦτα γὰρ ἔρχεται ἡ ὀργὴ τοῦ θεοῦ ἐπὶ τοὺς υἱοὺς τῆς ἀπειθείας.
$(3^{7f.})$ ἐν οἷς καὶ ὑμεῖς περιεπατήσατέ ποτε, when you lived in them; but now do you also put off all these: ὀργήν, θυμόν, κακίαν, βλασφημίαν, αἰσχρολογίαν ἐκ τοῦ στόματος ὑμῶν· lie not one to another, seeing that you have PUT OFF THE OLD MAN	$(2^{2\text{-}3})$ ἐν αἷς ποτὲ περιεπατήσατε . . . καὶ ἡμεῖς πάντες ἀνεστράφημέν ποτε . . . (4^{22}) PUT OFF THE OLD MAN . . . $(4^{25f.})$ Putting off falsehood, speak the truth each with his neighbour . . . be angry and sin not . . . let no corrupt speech issue ἐκ τοῦ στόματος ὑμῶν . . . (4^{31}) let all bitterness καὶ θυμὸς καὶ ὀργὴ καὶ κραυγὴ καὶ βλασφημία be put away from you σὺν πάσῃ κακίᾳ.
with his doings, and have put on the new man, who is ἀνακαινούμενον εἰς ἐπίγνωσιν κατ' εἰκόνα τοῦ κτίσαντος αὐτόν. . . .	(4^{24}) and put on the new man τὸν κατὰ θεὸν κτισθέντα ἐν δικαιοσύνῃ καὶ ὁσιότητι τῆς ἀληθείας.
$(3^{12\text{-}13})$ Put on therefore, *as ἐκλεκτοὶ τοῦ θεοῦ*,‡ holy and *beloved*, σπλάγχνα οἰκτιρμοῦ, χρηστότητα, ταπεινοφροσύνην, πραΰτητα, μακροθυμίαν, FORBEARING ONE ANOTHER, AND FORGIVING	(4^{2}) with all ταπεινοφροσύνης καὶ πραΰτητος, with μακροθυμίας, FORBEARING ONE ANOTHER in love . . . (4^{32}) be χρηστοί one to another, εὔσπλαγχνοι, FORGIVING ONE ANOTHER,

* In Col., as opposed to supernatural media; in Eph., as opposed to schism. See Weinel's *NTTh.* p. 352.

† Also Col 2^{22} = Eph $4^{14.\ 22}$ (verbal parallels).

‡ Cp. Eph 1^{4} (καθὼς ἐξελέξατο ἡμᾶς . . . εἶναι ἁγίους κτλ.).

ONE ANOTHER, if any man have a complaint against another; EVEN AS THE LORD FORGAVE YOU, so do you:

(3^{14-15}) and above all these things put on love, *ὅ ἐστιν σύνδεσμος τῆς τελειότητος.* And let the peace of Christ* rule in your hearts, to the which also you were called in one body.

(3^{16-17}) Let the word of Christ dwell in you *πλουσίως, ἐν πάσῃ σοφίᾳ,* teaching and admonishing yourselves with psalms and hymns and spiritual songs, singing with grace in your hearts unto God. And whatsoever you do, in word or in deed, do all in the name of the Lord Jesus, giving thanks to God the Father through him.

(3^{18-19}) Wives, be subject to your husbands, *ὡς ἀνῆκεν ἐν κυρίῳ.* Husbands, love your wives, and be not bitter ‡ to them.

(3^{20}) Children, obey parents in all things, *τοῦτο γὰρ εὐάρεστόν ἐστιν ἐν κυρίῳ.*‖

(3^{21}) Fathers, irritate not your children, that they be not discouraged.

(3^{22-25}) Slaves, obey in all things those who are your masters *κατὰ σάρκα,* not with *eye-service, as men-pleasers,* but in singleness of heart, fearing the Lord.** Whatsoever ye

EVEN AS GOD IN CHRIST FORGAVE YOU. (5^{1}) *γίνεσθε οὖν μιμηταὶ τοῦ θεοῦ, as beloved* children.

(4^{3-4}) giving diligence to preserve the unity of the Spirit *ἐν τῷ συνδέσμῳ τῆς εἰρήνης*: one body and one Spirit, even as also you were called in one hope of your calling.†

(1^{8} *τὸ πλοῦτος τῆς χάριτος αὐτοῦ ἧς ἐπερίσσευσεν εἰς ἡμᾶς ἐν πάσῃ σοφίᾳ κτλ.*) (5^{19-20}) speaking to yourselves with psalms and hymns and spiritual songs, singing and making melody with your heart to the Lord; giving thanks always for all things in the name of our Lord Jesus Christ to God, even the Father.

($5^{22f.}$) Wives, be subject to your own husbands, *ὡς τῷ κυρίῳ . . . ἐν παντί.* ($5^{25f.}$) Husbands, love your wives, even as Christ loved the church.

(6^{1}) Children, obey your parents in all things, *τοῦτο γάρ ἐστιν δίκαιον* § [then follows the fifth commandment ¶].

(6^{4}) And you fathers, provoke not your children to anger: but nurture them in the chastening and admonition of the Lord.

(6^{5-8}) Slaves, obey those who are your masters *κατὰ σάρκα,* with fear and trembling, with singleness of your heart, as to Christ; not by way of *eye-service as men-pleasers*; but as

---

* Cp. Eph 2^{14} (*αὐτὸς γάρ ἐστιν ἡ εἰρήνη ἡμῶν*).

† Eph. proclaims the spiritual unity of Jewish and Gentile Christians, not as Paul did on the score of arguments drawn from the Law and promises, but from the essential and eternal purpose of God. This is a distinct development beyond the position of Rom., which neither Col. nor Phil. anticipates.

‡ Broadened out in Eph 4^{31} (*πᾶσα πικρία . . . ἀρθήτω ἀφ' ὑμῶν*).

§ *τὸ δίκαιον* applied to masters in Col 4^{1}.

‖ Broadened out in Eph 5^{10} (*δοκιμάζοντες τί ἐστιν εὐάρεστον τῷ Κυρίῳ*).

¶ The *εὖ γένηται* of 6^{3}, unprecedented in Paul, is a LXX quotation.

** Broadened out in Eph 5^{21} into *ὑποτασσόμενοι ἀλλήλοις ἐν φόβῳ Χριστοῦ* (the latter an un-Pauline phrase). In the table of domestic duties in Eph. "we miss the brevity and clearness, the insistence on the things of great practical significance, which distinguishes Paul" (von Dobschütz, *op. cit.* 182).

do, ἐκ ψυχῆς ἐργάζεσθε as to the Lord and not to men; knowing that from the Lord you shall receive the inheritance that is your due: you serve the Lord Christ. For the wicked shall be paid back for his wickedness, *and there is no respect of persons.*	slaves of Christ, doing the will of God ἐκ ψυχῆς; doing service with goodwill as to the Lord, and not to men: knowing that each shall be paid back from the Lord for whatever good he does, whether he be slave or free man.
(4^{1}) Masters, render to your slaves what is just and fair; knowing that you also have a Master in heaven.	(6^{9}) And you masters, act in the same way to them, refraining from threats, knowing that their Master and yours is in the heavens, *and there is no respect of persons* with him.
(4^{2-4}) Continue steadfastly in prayer, watching therein with thanksgiving; praying at the same time for us also, that God may open us a door for the word, to declare τὸ μυστήριον τοῦ Χριστοῦ (for which also I am in bonds); that I may utter it as I should declare it.	(6^{18-20}) praying at all seasons in the Spirit, and attentive thereto with all constancy and entreaty for all the saints, and for me, that word may be given me whenever I open my mouth, to make known with confidence τὸ μυστήριον τοῦ εὐαγγελίου (for which I am an ambassador in chains); that I may have confidence therein, as I should declare it.
(4^{5-6}) Walk wisely towards those outside, making the very most of your time. Let your speech always be ἐν χάριτι, ἅλατι ἠρτυμένος know how ye ought to answer each person.	(5^{15-16}) Be careful then how you walk, not as unwise but as wise, making the very most of your time, because the days are evil. (4^{29}) Let no foul speech issue from your mouth, but only such as is good for improving the occasion, that it may bring χάριν to the hearers.
(4^{7-8}) Τὰ κατ' ἐμὲ πάντα γνωρίσει ὑμῖν Tychicus, the beloved brother and faithful minister and fellow-servant in the Lord: whom I send to you for this very purpose, that you may know τὰ περὶ ἡμῶν, and that he may encourage your hearts.	(6^{21-22}) Now that you also* may know τὰ κατ' ἐμέ, τί πράσσω, πάντα γνωρίσει ὑμῖν Tychicus, the beloved brother and faithful minister in the Lord: whom I send to you for this very purpose, that you may know τὰ περὶ ἡμῶν, and that he may encourage your hearts.

§ 3. *Relation to* 1 *Peter* (see above, p. 338).—The affinities of thought and structure between Eph. and 1 P. begin with the opening doxology, and include the connection of hope with the κληρονομία, the conception of the spiritual House (with Christ as the corner-stone), of the descent into

* The insertion of this καί means that the writer, with his eye on Col 4^{7}, intends to present the apostle as having just composed Colossians. The situation intended for the epistle (cp. 3^{13}) is that of Colossians.

Hades * (4^{9} = 1 P 3^{19} 4^{6}), of the Christian προσαγωγή as the object of Christ's death, of ἄγνοια (4^{18} = 1 P 1^{14}) as the pre-Christian condition, and of redemption by the blood of Christ; they conclude with the parallels in $6^{10f.}$ = 1 P 5^{8-9} (warfare against ὁ διάβολος), 6^{23} = 1 P 5^{14} (peace). Both homilies are addressed to Gentile Christians (of Asia Minor), but 2^{19} (no longer strangers and sojourners, cp. Odes of Solomon 3^{7}) differs from 1 P 2^{11}; and the ethical admonitions ($5^{21f.}$) are not linked so naturally to what precedes as in 1 P $2^{18f.}$, which the *auctor ad Ephesios* is reproducing in his own way. Even after allowance has been made for the coincidences due to the common store of early Christian thought, critics either differ on the question of literary priority or hesitate to pronounce definitely. Unless both are to be assigned to the same author, the probabilities on the whole point to an acquaintance on the part of the *auctor ad Ephesios* with the simpler 1 P., if on other grounds the latter is attributed to Peter and Ephesians assigned to a Paulinist. The salient parallels are (cp. Selwyn, *St. Luke the Prophet*, 183 f.):—

1 PET.	EPH.
(1^{3}) Blessed be the God and Father of our Lord Jesus Christ. . . .	(1^{3}) Blessed be the God and Father of our Lord Jesus Christ. . . .
($1^{10f.}$) προφῆται † . . . οἷς ἀπεκαλύφθη ὅτι οὐχ ἑαυτοῖς ὑμῖν δὲ διηκόνουν αὐτά, ἃ νῦν ἀνηγγέλη ὑμῖν διὰ τῶν εὐαγγελισαμένων ὑμᾶς πνεύματι ἁγίῳ. . . .	($3^{5f.}$) οὐκ ἐγνωρίσθη τοῖς υἱοῖς τῶν ἀνθρώπων ὡς νῦν ἀπεκαλύφθη τοῖς ἁγίοις ἀποστόλοις αὐτοῦ καὶ προφήταις ἐν πνεύματι. . . .
(1^{14}) ὡς τέκνα ὑπακοῆς μὴ συσχηματιζόμενοι ταῖς πρότερον ἐν ἀγνοίᾳ ὑμῶν ἐπιθυμίαις, ἀλλὰ κατὰ τὸν καλέσαντα ὑμᾶς ἅγιον καὶ αὐτοὶ ἅγιοι ἐν πάσῃ ἀναστροφῇ γενήθητε. . . .	(2^{2-3}) . . . ἐν τοῖς υἱοῖς τῆς ἀπειθείας, ἐν οἷς καὶ ἡμεῖς πάντες ἀνεστράφημέν ποτε ἐν ταῖς ἐπιθυμίαις τῆς σαρκὸς ἡμῶν.
(2^{11} ἀπέχεσθαι τῶν σαρκικῶν ἐπιθυμιῶν.)	

* The Ephesians-passage is influenced, according to Bacon (*Story of St. Paul*, 361 f.), by the sayings of Jesus preserved in Mt 12^{24-29}. See, further, Eph 5^{1} = Mt $5^{44.\ 48}$.

† The *auctor ad Ephesios* changes the OT. prophets into Christian prophets, and fails to connect the reference so aptly as 1 P. His estimate of prophecy from the standpoint of fulfilment is, as Weiss notes, "based entirely on the view developed in 1 P 1^{10-12}, where, as in Eph 3^{10}, the contemplative share of angels in the work of redemption is also mentioned" (*INT.* i. 355).

(1^{19-20}) Χριστοῦ προεγνωσμένου πρὸ καταβολῆς κόσμου. . . .	(1^{4}) Chose us ἐν αὐτῷ πρὸ καταβολῆς κόσμου (cp. 3^{9}).
(2^{2}) ἵνα ἐν αὐτῷ αὐξηθῆτε εἰς σωτηρίαν.	(2^{21}) ἐν ᾧ πᾶσα οἰκοδομὴ . . . αὔξει εἰς ναὸν ἅγιον ἐν κυρίῳ.
(2^{4}) πρὸς ὃν προσερχόμενοι . . . οἰκοδομεῖσθε οἶκος πνευματικὸς εἰς ἱεράτευμα ἅγιον. . . . (2^{6}) λίθον ἀκρογωνιαῖον.	(2^{18}) δι' αὐτοῦ ἔχομεν τὴν προσαγωγὴν* . . . ἐν ἑνὶ πνεύματι πρὸς τὸν πατέρα . . . (2^{20}) ἐποικοδομηθέντες . . . ὄντος ἀκρογωνιαίου αὐτοῦ Χριστοῦ Ἰησοῦ.
(2^{9}) λαὸς εἰς περιποίησιν, ὅπως τὰς ἀρέτας ἐξαγγείλητε τοῦ ἐκ σκότους ὑμᾶς καλέσαντος εἰς τὸ θαυμαστὸν αὐτοῦ φῶς.	(1^{14}) εἰς ἀπολύτρωσιν τῆς περιποιήσεως,† εἰς ἔπαινον τῆς δόξης αὐτοῦ . . . ($5^{8f.}$) ἦτε γάρ ποτε σκότος, νῦν δὲ φῶς ἐν κυρίῳ· ὡς τέκνα φωτὸς περιπατεῖτε.
(2^{18}) οἱ οἰκέται ὑποτασσόμενοι ἐν παντὶ φόβῳ τοῖς δεσπόταις.	(6^{5}) οἱ δοῦλοι, ὑπακούετε τοῖς κατὰ σάρκα κυρίοις μετὰ φόβου καὶ τρόμου.
(3^{1}) ὁμοίως γυναῖκες ὑποτασσόμεναι τοῖς ἰδίοις ἀνδράσιν.	(5^{22}) αἱ γυναῖκες (ὑποτασσόμεναι) τοῖς ἰδίοις ‡ ἀνδράσιν ὡς τῷ κυρίῳ.
(3^{7}) οἱ ἄνδρες § ὁμοίως. . . .	(5^{25}) οἱ ἄνδρες. . . .
(3^{8}) εὔσπλαγχνοι.‖	(4^{32}) γίνεσθε δὲ εἰς ἀλλήλους χρηστοί, εὔσπλαγχνοι.
(3^{22}) (Jesus Christ) who is on God's right hand, πορευθεὶς εἰς οὐρανόν, ὑποταγέντων αὐτῷ ἀγγέλων καὶ ἐξουσιῶν καὶ δυνάμεων.	($1^{20f.}$) (God) seated him on his right hand ἐν τοῖς ἐπουρανίοις ὑπεράνω πάσης ἀρχῆς καὶ ἐξουσίας καὶ δυνάμεως . . . καὶ πάντα ὑπέταξεν ὑπὸ τοὺς πόδας αὐτῷ.

§ 4. *Relation to Lucan and Johannine writings.*—(Cp. Holtzmann's *Kritik der Epheser und Colosserbriefe*, 250 f.) As in Luke, men are the objects of the divine εὐδοκία (Lk 2^{14} = Eph 1^{5}), the ascension is emphasised (Eph 1^{20} $4^{8.\ 10}$ = Lk 24^{51}),

* Cp. 1 P 3^{18} (ἵνα ἡμᾶς προσαγάγῃ τῷ θεῷ).

† The passive sense of περιποίησις here (=hæreditas acquisita) differs from the Pauline active sense (1 Th 5^{9}, 2 Th 2^{14}), evidently under the influence of the Petrine passage.

‡ This remarkable ἰδίοις in Eph. is one of several traits which show a reminiscence of 1 P. in the passage.

§ In both the duties of husbands, though differently defined, are comparatively brief, whereas the duties of wives are elaborated (in contrast to Col 3^{18}). The description of the latter shows a Biblicising of the Christian ideal (1 P $3^{5f.\ 10-12}$ = Eph. $5^{31f.}$).

‖ εὔσπλαγχνος only here in NT (except 1 P 3^{8}).

and there are further affinities * in 2^{5} = Lk 15^{24}, 5^{18} = Lk 15^{18}, 5^{17} (6^{6}) = Lk 12^{47}, and 6^{14} = Lk 12^{35}. Resch (*Paulinismus*, 273–274) gives a long list of parallels between Eph 2^{1-19} and Lk 15^{11-32}, though it is an exaggeration to say that Paul saw Pharisaic Judaism in the older son of the parable. There are also several affinities between Eph. and Paul's address at Miletus, *e.g.* the βουλή of God (1^{11} = Ac 20^{27}), the commission of Paul ($3^{2.\ 17}$ 4^{11} = Ac 20^{24}), the purchasing of the church (1^{14} = Ac 20^{28}), the κληρονομία of Christians (1^{14} = Ac 20^{32}), and the shepherding of the church (4^{11} = Ac 20^{28}). The common use of the 'building'-metaphor for the church is not peculiar to Ac $20^{18f.}$ or to Eph., but significance attaches to certain traits of phraseology (Ac 20^{19} = Eph 4^{2} 6^{7}, Ac 20^{20} = Eph 1^{15}, Ac 20^{29} = Eph 1^{7}, Ac 20^{32} = Eph 1^{18}).

The Lucan parallels touch a smaller group in the same neighbourhood, viz. the Pauline pastorals; cp. *e.g.* the conception of the πρεσβύτεροι or ἐπίσκοποι being under apostolic direction, the warnings against insidious errorists, the divine χρηστότης ($2^{7f.}$ = Tit 3^{1-4}) and unity (4^{5} = 1 Ti 2^{4}), the word of the truth (1^{13} = 2 Ti 2^{15}), the devil's devices (6^{11} = 1 Ti 3^{7}, 2 Ti 2^{26}), evangelists (4^{11} = 2 Ti 4^{5}), the House of God ($2^{19f.}$ = 1 Ti 3^{5}, 2 Ti 2^{19}); cp., further, 1^{15} = 1 Ti 3^{13} and 2 Ti 3^{9}, $4^{11f.}$ = 2 Ti 3^{16}, 4^{13} = 1 Ti 2^{4} (coming to a knowledge of the truth), $5^{2.\ 25f.}$ = Tit $2^{13f.}$ and 1 Ti 2^{6}, 5^{27} = 1 Ti 5^{14}, and λουτρόν (5^{26} = Tit 3^{5}). But beyond suggesting a sub-Pauline *milieu* of thought and language, these coincidences amount to very little.

The interpretation of Christ's relation to the universe already bears traces of the Philonic conception of the Logos which afterwards blossomed out in the christology of the Fourth gospel, and this opens up the relationship between Eph. and the instrumentum Johanneum. The bridal conception of the church, which in the Apocalypse (except in 22^{17}) is eschatological, is applied (*e.g.* $5^{25.\ 29.\ 32}$) to the church on earth (cp. 2 Co 11^{2}, an epistle with which Eph. has notable affinities); a similar process has taken place in the conception of the resurrection (2^{5-6} = Jn $5^{21.\ 25}$), and in Eph. (where the παρουσία falls into the background) as in the Fourth gospel the general eschatology is spiritualised, in a fashion which is unexampled in Paul, while at the same time the writer contemplates a vista of the ages.

* One or two words are peculiar to Eph. and Lk.'s vocabulary, *e.g.* ἀνιέναι (exc. He 13^{5} LXX quotation), ἀπειλή, ἐργασία, ὁσιότης (4^{24}, as in Lk 1^{75}, with δικαιοσύνη), πανοπλία, πατριά, πολιτεία, συγκαθίζειν, σωτήριον, φρόνησις, and χαριτοῦν. βουλή (=divine counsel) might almost be added to this list, for, outside Lk. and Eph., it is only used in this sense in He 6^{17}; Paul's solitary use is in the plural, meaning human devices (1 Co 4^{5}).

The unity of the church, including Gentiles as well as Jews, is the divine object of Christ's death (cp. Jn 10^{16} 17^{20}); the church is the πλήρωμα of Christ and of God (1^{23} etc., cp. Jn 14^{20} $15^{4.\ 8}$ $17^{11f.}$); exceptional stress is laid on the functions of the Spirit, the word, and baptism, the unity of the church as the result of the divine unity between Christ and God and as the means of advancing the gospel, Christ as beloved (1^{4}), the idea of μέτρον (Eph 4^{17}, cp. Jn 3^{31}), the description of God in 1^{17} (= Jn 20^{17}), the collocation of Christ and God as indwelling (Eph 2^{22} 3^{17} = Jn $14^{20.\ 23}$), etc.; see also $4^{9f.}$ = Jn 3^{13}, 5^{6} = 1 Jn $3^{7f.}$ and Jn 3^{36}, $5^{8f.}$ = 1 Jn $1^{6f.}$ and Jn 12^{35}, 5^{13} = Jn $3^{19f.}$, besides the αὐτός-passages (Eph 2^{14} = 1 Jn 2^{2}), the use of λύσας (2^{14} = Jn 2^{19}), the emphasis on ἁγιάζειν and cleansing (5^{26} = Jn $17^{17.\ 19}$, 1 Jn $1^{7.\ 9}$), on ψεῦδος as opposed to ἀλήθεια, on the danger of doketism (Eph 4^{21}), on the spiritual advent of Jesus (2^{17} = Jn 14^{18}), on the duty of Christian love (Eph 4^{15} etc.), etc. These links of thought and language have led one critic to remark that "it would be a tenable view that the writer was the author of the Fourth gospel, writing in the name of St. Paul" (Lock, *DB.* i. 717), but the likelihood is that the unknown *auctor ad Ephesios* was a Paulinist who breathed the atmosphere in which the Johannine literature afterwards took shape. None of the parallels, however, between the Apocalypse of John and Eph. is of much weight; the idea that the latter employed the former is quite untenable. Like Hebrews, another sub-Pauline writing which has also its affinities with the Lucan as well as with the Johannine circle, Eph. emphasises the blood of Christ (1^{7} = He 9^{12}), his sanctifying influence ($5^{25\text{-}26}$ = He 10^{10} 13^{12}), his session on God's right hand (1^{20} = He 1^{3} 8^{1} 10^{12}), and his gift of παρρησία to Christians (3^{12} = He 4^{16}); some linguistic parallels also occur (*e.g.* αἷμα καὶ σάρξ, ἀγρυπνεῖν, κραυγή, ὑπεράνω π. τ. οὐρανῶν, εἰς ἀπολύτρωσιν, αἰὼν μέλλων, προσφορὰ καὶ θυσία), but neither these nor stray coincidences like 2^{18} = He 7^{18} prove more than a common atmosphere of religious feeling and phraseology.

§ 5. *Vocabulary and style.*—The literary relations with Col., Lk., and the Johannine literature, besides 1 P. and the pastorals, thus indicate a period subsequent to that of Paul. This is further corroborated by the evidence of the language and style, which are on the whole favourable to the hypothesis that another mind than that of the apostle is at work in Eph. It contains (*a*) thirty-eight words which are not elsewhere used in the NT literature :—ἄθεος, αἰσχρότης, αἰχμαλωτεύω, ἀνανεόω,* ἄνοιξις, ἀπαλγεῖν, ἄσοφος, βέλος, ἑνότης, ἐξισχύειν, ἐπιδύειν, ἐπιφαύσκειν, ἑτοιμασία, εὐτραπελία, θυρεός, καταρτισμός, κατώτερος, κληρόω, κλυδωνίζεσθαι, κοσμοκράτωρ, κρυφῇ, κυβεία, μέγεθος, μεθοδεία, μεσότοιχον, μωρολογία, πάλη, παροργισμός, (τὰ) πνευματικά,† πολυποίκιλος, προελπίζειν, προσκαρτέρησις, ῥυτίς, συμμέτοχος, συμπολίτης, συναρμολογεῖν, συνοικοδομεῖν, σύσσωμος (cp. Preuschen in *ZNW.* i. 85–86). In addition to these, there are (*b*) no fewer than 44 words which, while employed elsewhere in the NT, are never used by Paul:— ἄγνοια (Lucan), ἀγρυπνεῖν,‡ ἀκρογωνιαῖος (1 P), ἅλυσις, τὰ ἀμφότερα (Ac 23^{8}), ἄνεμος,§ ἀνιέναι,‖ ἅπαντα, ἀπατάω (Ja 1^{26}, 1 Ti 2^{14}),¶ ἀπειλή (Ac 9^{1}), ἀσωτία (1 P 4^{4}, Tit 1^{6}), διάβολος, ἐπέρχομαι, (τὰ) ἐπουράνια, ἐργασία, εὐαγγελιστής, εὔσπλαγχνος (1 P 3^{8}), καταβολή (πρὸ κ. κόσμου, 1 P 1^{20}, Jn 17^{24}), λέγω εἰς, μακράν, ὀργίζω, ὁσιότης (Lk 1^{75}), ὀσφύς, παιδεία,** πανοπλία, πάροικος,†† πατριά, περιζώννυμι,‡‡ πλάτος,§§ ποιμήν,‖‖ πολιτεία,¶¶ σαπρός,*** σπίλος (2 P 2^{13}), συγκαθίζω (Lk 22^{55}),††† σωτήριον, τιμᾶν, ὕδωρ, ὑπεράνω (He 9^{5}), ὑποδεῖσθαι, ὕψος, φραγμός,‡‡‡ φρόνησις (Lk 1^{17}),§§§ χαριτοῦν (Lk 1^{28}), χειροποίητος. The absence of some of these from the extant letters may be accidental (*e.g.* ἄγνοια, ὀργίζω), but real significance attaches to the (4^{27} 6^{11}) substitution of διάβολος (as in 1 Ti 3^{6}, 2 Ti 2^{26}) for the Pauline σατανᾶς, and the use of ἐν τοῖς ἐπουρανίοις (five times). The collective and objective allusion to *the holy apostles and prophets* (3^{5}), and to *the apostles and prophets* (2^{20}) as the foundation of the church (cp. Apoc 21^{14}), are partly, but only partly, eased by passages like 1 Co 9^{5} 12^{28} and Ro 16^{7}; probably they too are best viewed as water-marks of a later age, which looks back upon the primitive, apostolic propaganda. The indirect and rather awkward appeal in 3^{2-4} (πρὸς ὃ δύνασθε ἀναγινώσκοντες νοῆσαι τὴν σύνεσίν μου κτλ.) corroborates this impression; the phrase sounds more characteristic of a Pauline disciple than of Paul himself.‖‖‖ These indications are followed up by other un-Pauline

---

* Instead of the Pauline ἀνακαινοῦν.

† Only in Eph 6^{12} of spiritual beings.

‡ Only in Eph 6^{18} with εἰς. Paul invariably uses γρηγορεῖν (1 Th 5^{6}, 1 Co 16^{13}, Col 4^{2}).

§ Only in Eph 4^{14} metaphorically.

‖ ,, ,, 6^{9} ,, (He 13^{6} being a quotation from the LXX).

¶ ,, ,, 5^{6} with τινά τινι.

** ,, ,, 6^{4} in literal sense of moral and mental education.

†† ,, ,, 2^{19} and 1 P 2^{11} metaphorically.

‡‡ ,, ,, 6^{14} metaphorically.

§§ ,, ,, 3^{18} ,,

‖‖ ,, ,, 4^{11} ecclesiastically.

¶¶ ,, ,, 2^{12} metaphorically.

*** ,, ,, 4^{29} ,, , with λόγος.

††† ,, ,, 2^{6} ,,

‡‡‡ ,, ,, 2^{14} ,,

§§§ ,, ,, 1^{8} of man.

‖‖‖ Hort (*op. cit.* 149 f.) ingeniously but unconvincingly takes ἀναγινώσκοντες as = reading the OT. Like 6^{21} it is probably meant to allude to Col. rather than to Eph $1^{9f.}$ 2^{11-22}, or to some lost letter.

touches, such as *ἴστε γινώσκοντες* (5^{5}), *the Father of Glory* (1^{17}), *before the foundation of the world* (1^{4}=Jn 17^{24}), the novel use of *μυστήριον* (5^{32}) and *οἰκονομία* (in providential aspect), the application of *φωτίζειν* (3^{9}), *πνεῦμα τοῦ νοός* (4^{23}), etc., besides the predilection for the *oratio pendens*, an unparalleled number of genitival formations (95 in all, out of 155 verses) which occur in almost every second verse, including such strange compounds as *ἁφὴ τῆς ἐπιχορηγίας* (4^{16}), *ἐπιθυμία τῆς ἀπάτης* (4^{22}), etc., and some redundant epexegetic formations (*e.g. βουλὴ τοῦ θελήματος, κράτος τῆς ἰσχύος*).

The last-named feature runs through the general style of the writing, with its wealth of synonyms, which often add little or nothing to the thought, its unique employment of prepositions like *ἐν* (115 times) and *κατά*, and the unusual length to which the sentences are occasionally spun out, one period passing into another through relatival and participial constructions whose logical bearing it is frequently almost impossible to determine. The linguistic data may be allowed to leave the problem of the authorship fairly open.* But the idiosyncrasies of the style are by no means so easily explained. Thus 1^{3-14} 1^{15-23} 2^{1-7} 2^{11-13} 2^{14-16} 2^{19-22} 3^{1-7} 3^{8-12} 3^{14-19} 4^{1-6} 4^{11-16} 4^{17-19} 4^{20-24} 5^{3-5} 5^{18-23} 5^{25-27} 5^{28-30} 6^{1-3} 6^{5-8} 6^{14-20}, are all lengthy sentences which are often cumbrous in their internal construction and beset by ambiguities in the juxtaposition of clauses and the collocation of separate words. They are at once elaborate and irregular. 3^{2-13} is a long parenthesis or digression, after which $3^{14f.}$ resumes 3^{1}; similarly the subject is repeated in 2^{13}, after the break. Such rhetorical anacoloutha are not paralleled by an impassioned irregularity like that in Gal 2^{6-9}. The latter is natural, as the abrupt language of a man dictating under the strong emotion of an indignant memory. The Ephesian instances, on the other hand, show the deliberate indifference of the writer to the niceties of literary symmetry, and thus fall into a class by themselves. "If we may regard this epistle as our best example of that *σοφία* which, according to 1 Co 2^{6}, *was* to be found in Paul's teaching, we may see in its style something like a *ὑπεροχὴ λόγου* (*ibid.* v.[1]), corresponding to the *ὑπεροχὴ σοφίας*. . . . It would be less inappropriate than elsewhere to call the language elaborate; and it is at the same time apt oftener than elsewhere to stray beyond the bounds of symmetry and regularity" (Simcox, *Writers of NT.* p. 32).

It is unfair to characterise the temper thus mirrored in the style of the epistle as phlegmatic;† lyric would be a fitter term for the opening chapters in especial, with their soaring, subtle movement of thought and at the same time

"With many a winding bout
Of linked sweetness long drawn out."

Upon the other hand, these features of serenity and profundity only serve to bring out more decisively the difference between Ephesians and the letters of

* Nägeli (*Wortschatz des Paulus*, 85) goes even further, "im ganzen scheint mir der Wortschatz dieses Briefes . . . eher eine Instanz für als gegen die Echtheit zu sein."

† So von Soden (*HC.* iii. 1. 90); cp. the criticisms of Jacquier, i. 306, and Hort (pp. 152 f.). Von Soden himself, however, subsequently speaks of the 'lyrical' passages in 4–6 (*INT.* 287–288).

Paul. It is often urged that the acceptance of Colossians as written by Paul renders the acceptance of Ephesians more easy, but in some respects it only adds to the difficulties felt by the literary critic. The nearer the two are brought together, the more distinctive is the impression made by the conceptions as well as the style of Ephesians; particularly as regards the latter, it becomes increasingly hard to understand the unparalleled phenomena which the Greek presents. Granted that 'the lofty calm which undeniably does pervade it may in part be due to the mellowing effect of years, but doubtless much more to the sense of dangers surmounted, aspirations satisfied, and a vantage-ground gained for the world-wide harmonious action of the Christian community under the government of God' (Hort, *op. cit.* 152–153); the problem remains, however, how can such tones be psychologically harmonised with what we know of Paul's mind and style a few months before and after he wrote thus? Philippians, his swan-song, cannot have been written very long after this; Colossians was composed very little before. Yet Ephesians stands apart from both, in style and conceptions alike. The separate items of difficulty in the thought and expression may be explained, but the cumulative impression which they make is that of a writer who occupies a later standpoint of his own; and this is more than corroborated by the style, which makes it extremely difficult to believe that Paul suddenly dropped into this method of writing and as suddenly abandoned it. "The old vivacity appears to be lost. The sentences and paragraphs become larger and more involved. The tone of challenge dies out. Even the affectionateness seems buried in weighty but almost laboured disquisitions" (Sanday in *St. Margaret's Lectt. on Crit. of NT*, 1902, p. 22). This may be partly due to the fact that the direct controversy of Colossians is absent from Ephesians, but the larger explanation of the latter's general tone is that the writer, unlike Paul, is not writing with any particular communities in view.

To sum up. The cumulative force of the arguments already noted is in favour of a Paulinist, imbued with his master's spirit, who composed this homily in his name as Luke composed the Pauline speeches in Acts (either from a sense of what Paul would have said under the circumstances or from some basis in tradition). From the writing of such speeches to the composition of an epistolary homily on the basis of an epistle like Colossians it was an easy step (cp. pp. 42, 47). The writer designed his work to be read (3^4) by the church as a manifesto of Paul's mind upon the situation; it was a pamphlet or tract for the times, insisting on the irenical needs of the church (like Acts) and on the duty of transcending the older schisms which had embittered the two sections of Christendom.

Schleiermacher (*Einl.* 165 f.), who was the first to detect the internal problems of the epistle, suggested its composition by Tychicus under Paul's directions—a theory advocated by Usteri and Renan ("Que Paul ait écrit ou dicté cette lettre, il est à peu près impossible de l'admettre; mais qu'on l'ait composée de son vivant, sous ses yeux, en son nom, c'est a qu'on ne saurait déclarer improbable," iii. p. xx). The Tübingen view of Colossians carried Ephesians also into the second century, but the recent recognition of the former as Pauline has left the problem of Ephesians more of an open question, resembling, *e.g.*, the problem of the exact connection between Aristotle and the recently discovered treatise upon the Athenian Constitution. A number of critics (so especially, in addition to those named on p. 374, B. Weiss, *AJT.* i. 377 f.; Godet, *INT.* 475–490; Salmon, *INT.* 388 f.; Zahn, *Einl.* § 29; Oltramare, and Baljon) attribute it to Paul; Jülicher and others content themselves with a *non liquet* verdict; while some (see p. 375) attempt to do justice to the combination of specifically Pauline elements and absolute novelties in thought and language by postulating, as in the case of the Pauline pastoral epp., a Paulinist who is reproducing Paul's ideas, on the basis of Colossians, in view of later interests within the neo-catholicism of the church. This does not involve the assumption that Paul was not original enough to advance even beyond the circle of ideas reflected in Colossians, or that he lacked constructive and broad ideas of the Christian brotherhood. It is quite possible to hold that he was a fresh and advancing thinker, and yet to conclude, from the internal evidence of Ephesians, that he did not cut the channel for this prose of the spiritual centre. In Paul's letters there is always something of the cascade; in Eph. we have a slow, bright stream which brims its high banks.

One of the indirect traits of the sub-Pauline period is the significant omission of the Lord's supper in 4^{5} (one Lord, one faith, one baptism). This is all the more striking as Paul's treatment of the eucharist in 1 Co 10^{17} (*εἷς ἄρτος, ἓν σῶμα οἱ πολλοί ἐσμεν, οἱ γὰρ πάντες ἐκ τοῦ ἑνὸς ἄρτου μετέχομεν*) naturally pointed to its use as a symbol and proof of the unity of Christians with one another and their Lord (cp. Didachê, 9^{4}). But the Fourth gospel voices a feeling of protest against a popular view of the Lord's supper which was tinged by pagan sacramentalism (cp. E. F. Scott, *The Fourth Gospel*, pp. 122 f.); Hebrews (13^{7-17}) also opposes the idea that the *σῶμα Χριστοῦ* could be partaken of, as in several of the contemporary pagan cults (cp. below, p. 455; O. Holtzmann, *ZNW.*, 1909, 251–260); Ephesians, we may conjecture, shows a like indifference to this growing conception of the supper (whether due to Paul, or developed from his language in 1 Cor.), and therefore omits the supper entirely.

§ 6. *Destination and object.*—The ὑμεῖς of the homily, which first appears in 1^{13}, is defined in 2^{11} (cp. 2^{1} and 3^{1}) as Gentile Christians. The writer has these primarily in view; but the situation is no longer one in which they are exposed to any Jewish Christian propaganda of legalism. In fact, it is assumed that the Gentile Christians are now in the majority; it is their predominance which forms the starting-point for the broad survey of history which Ephesians outlines. The ἡμεῖς of 1^{11-12} certainly represents Jewish Christians. Paul here voices that section of the church in its historical relation to the gospel. But the language is general, and neither here nor in $2^{1f.}$ (cp. Hoennicke, *JC.* 125 f.) is there any real justification for the view that Jewish Christians were contemplated as a definite part of the writer's audience.

The author addressed his homily in Paul's name τοῖς ἁγίοις

τοῖς οὖσιν καὶ πιστοῖς ἐν Χριστῷ Ἰησοῦ, omitting the place-name of Col 1[1] and adding τοῖς οὖσιν (cp. Ro 8[28] τοῖς κατὰ πρόθεσιν κλητοῖς οὖσιν) in order to amplify the following phrase, which further defines the ἅγιοι whom the writer has in mind (cp. 2[21] ἅγιον ἐν κυρίῳ, and 5[3]). Those who defend ἐν Ἐφέσῳ as original, explain its early omission in some copies by urging either (i.) that this was due to Paul himself, who ordered Tychicus to leave a space blank in some copies for other churches (so, *e.g.*, Schott); or (ii.) that it was the result of a transcriber's error; or (iii.) that it sprang from a feeling that passages like 1[15] 3[1-4] 4[21] involved readers who were not, like the Christians of Ephesus, personally known to the apostle. None of these hypotheses is convincing.* A number of early copies in the second century evidently lacked the words, as Origen and Basil after him remark; traces of this form of the text are still present in the first hand of ℵ and B,† and the likelihood is that Marcion must have received the epistle in this shape. Tertullian charges him with changing the title (*adv. Marc.* v. 17: titulum aliquando interpolare gestiit, quasi et in isto diligentissimus explorator, nihil autem de titulis interest, cum ad omnes apostolus scripserit, dum ad quosdam); but this merely means that the title of 'Ephesians' in Tertullian's Canon (as in the Muratorian) already contained the Ephesian designation, whereas Marcion's differed (cp. *adv. Marc.* v. 11: prætereo hic et de alia epistola quam nos ad Ephesios præscriptam habemus, hæretici uero ad Laodicenos), and Tertullian naturally supposed the canonical title to be the original. He falls back on the *ueritas ecclesiæ* or church-tradition of the title, not upon the text, from which any place-name was apparently absent.

There would be a partial analogy to the insertion of a place-name if the original text of Ro 1[7] were (as in G) τοῖς οὖσιν ἐν ἀγάπῃ θεοῦ κλητοῖς ἁγίοις

* Jacquier (i. 290) dismisses (i.) as "une supposition toute gratuitè et assez ridicule." Harnack (*Die Adresse*, 704 f.), who now identifies Eph. with the Laodicean epistle (see above, pp. 159–161), suggests *speciosius quam uerius* that it was the degeneration of the local church (Apoc 3[14f.]) which led to the substitution of Ephesus for Laodicea in the title and address (by the first decade of the second century), in order to punish a community which no longer deserved to possess a Pauline epistle (cp. *Exp.*[8] ii. 197 f.).

† Also in "the corrector of a later MS (67), whose corrections are evidently taken from another quite different MS of great excellence, now lost" (Hort). Basil (*contr. Eunomium*, ii. 19) explicitly writes: οὕτω γὰρ (*i.e.* the reading of Eph 1[1] without ἐν Ἐφέσῳ) καὶ οἱ πρὸ ἡμῶν παραδεδώκασι (*i.e.* Origen and others), καὶ ἡμεῖς ἐν τοῖς παλαιοῖς τῶν ἀντιγράφων εὑρήκαμεν.

(so Zahn, *INT.* i. 378 f., 394 f.), for which, at a subsequent period, *τοῖς οὖσιν ἐν Ῥώμῃ ἀγαπητοῖς θ. κ. ἁ.* was substituted; but the former reading is probably due to a revision of the text for liturgical purposes (see above, p. 141). It is not certain whether Tertullian's words imply that Marcion's text or his own text had a place-name after *οὖσιν*, since 'titulus' might here, as in the case of Galatians (*adv. Marc.* v. 5) include the address. The probabilities on the whole are in favour of an inference to the contrary. The canonical Ephesians in this case would be originally a general pastoral addressed in Paul's name to Gentile Christians, which Marcion evidently identified with the epistle to the Laodiceans. The title *πρὸς Ἐφεσίους* first appears in the Muratorian Canon; when it was appended to the epistle previously, and whether this addition was derived from the presence of *ἐν Ἐφέσῳ* in 1^1, remains uncertain.

If ἐν Ἐφέσῳ in 1^1 was the original reading, the epistle cannot have been written by Paul. Its tone presupposes that the church (or rather, the Christian recipients) was personally unknown to him (1^{15} 3^2 4^{21}); there is not the slightest reference to his long mission among them; and while Paul could write letters without sending greetings, the Thessalonian epistles, *e.g.*, contain definite allusions to the apostle's relations with the church which are conspicuous by their absence from Ephesians. In spite of all arguments to the contrary (*e.g.* by Cornely, Henle, Schmidt, Rinck in *SK.*, 1849, 948 f.; Alford, and A. Kolbe in his *Theol. Comm. über das erste Capital des Briefes an die Epheser*, Stettin, 1869), there is no internal evidence to prove that Ephesus was the church (or even one of the churches) addressed, and much to the contrary. Some Greek commentators, beginning with Theodore of Mopsuestia, ingeniously got over the difficulty by arguing that Eph. was written before Paul had reached Ephesus —a desperate hypothesis which need not be seriously refuted. Even when the epistle is attributed to a Pauline disciple, it is not probable that ἐν Ἐφέσῳ (so, *e.g.*, Klöpper, 34 f.; and Holtzmann, cp. Corssen in *ZNW.*, 1909, 35 f.) was an integral part of the address. Paul's intimate connection with the church of Ephesus was notorious, and any one writing in his name must have known better than to make him address the Ephesian Christians as if he and they had no personal acquaintance (cp. 1^{15} 3^2). To defend its originality by postulating the writer's ignorance of the relation between Paul and Ephesus is a *tour de force* of criticism, which contradicts, *inter alia*, the affinities of the writing with Luke.

The same considerations tell against the circular-hypothesis which regards Ephesus as merely one of the communities for which the epistle was designed. Paul would have made some distinction in the body of the epistle between readers well known to him and others to whom he was a stranger (as in Col 2^1); he would hardly have grouped the church of Ephesus, or even the adjoining churches (to many of which he was personally known, cp. Ac 19^{10} 20^{25}), with communities who had no personal connection with himself. This notion, that Eph. was designed for a wider circle of churches than Ephesus, originated with Beza ('sed suspicor non tam ad Ephesios ipsos proprie missam epistolam, quam Ephesum ut ad ceteras Asiaticas ecclesias transmitteretur'), and was worked up by Ussher into the hypothesis of a circular letter, which has been practically the dominant view, ever since, of those who hold to the Pauline authorship (so, most recently, J. Rutherford, *St. Paul's Epp. to Colossæ and Laodicea*, 1908; S. J. Case, *Biblical World*, 1911, 315 f.; G. S. Hitchcock, *Ephesians an Encyclical of St. Paul*, 1913). The further identification of Eph. in this form with the letter mentioned in Col 4^{16} (Laodicea being one of its recipients) is generally held along with the circular-hypothesis. The latter, however, is not free from difficulties. Primitive Christian epistles designed for a wide circle of churches were composed otherwise (cp. 1 Co $1^{1\text{-}2}$, Gal 1^1); the notion of copies with blanks for the local address is not true to ancient methods of epistolography; besides, we should expect traces of several readings, and at best the retention of ἐν. If ἐν Λαοδικίᾳ had been the original reading in 1^1, the change to ἐν Ἐφέσῳ becomes unintelligible; and, *vice versa*, if ἐν Ἐφέσῳ was in the autograph, Marcion's change becomes almost inexplicable. As none of the conjectural emendations, such as κατ' Ἶριν for καὶ πιστοῖς (Ladeuze in *RB.*, 1902, 573–580), or ἔθνεσιν for Ἐφέσω (R. Scott), is probable,* the alternatives are: (*a*) that the place-name was lost at an early period from copies of the autograph; or (*b*) that 1^1 originally ran τοῖς ἁγίοις τοῖς οὖσιν καὶ πιστοῖς ἐν Χριστῷ Ἰησοῦ. When the sub-Pauline date of the writing is assumed, the latter theory becomes decidedly superior, in spite of the difficulties which attach to the interpretation of the words. It is preferable on the whole to take πιστοῖς in the sense of *faithful* rather than of *believing*; the latter interpretation

* Shearer (*ET.* iv. 129) reads τ. ἁ. τοῖς Ἴωσι (the Ionians), and P. Ewald, (*NKZ.*, 1904, 560–568) conjectures ἀγαπητοῖς for ἁγίοις τοῖς (*i.e.* 'to those who are beloved and believing'), while D omits τοῖς (so Zahn); but the difficult οὖσιν was in Origen's text, and there is no reason to suspect its originality.

would most naturally imply Jews who were also Christians, and the tenor of the homily tells against this characterisation of its audience.

The advance on Paul's idea of unity is that Eph. correlates the two conceptions of Christ's supremacy and the unity of Christians by running back the latter, *i.e.* the ideal church's unity,* to the supremacy of Christ as the cosmic and religious head of the universe. In this way the epistle represents the climax of the Pauline development; its theme is "not simply the unity of the church, but the unity of the church in Jesus Christ supreme. This Paul had not preached before" (M. W. Jacobus, *A Problem in NT Criticism*, 275). The former division of Jew and Gentile is for ever abolished by Jesus Christ, whose church constitutes the final relationship of man to God; this *μυστήριον* or open secret is hailed as the climax of revelation, and Paul is the chosen herald of the message. The writer correctly regards Paul's work as the presupposition of the catholic church. The *ἑνοτης* ($4^{3.\ 13}$, here only) and the *εἰρήνη* of the church, attained as the result of Paul's propaganda, were due, however, not to any diplomatic adjustment of the two parties, but to the full and deep apprehension of the meaning of the gospel which Paul proclaimed. The author does not disparage (cp. 3^{5}) the other apostles, any more than Luke does; on the contrary, he expressly associates the apostles with Paul in the promulgation of the church's universality and unity; but he insists on Paul's importance for the divine unfolding of that catholic unity which in the Fourth gospel is run back to the original teaching of Jesus. Similarly the problems of freewill and election, which were raised in Romans, are ignored in Eph., not because Paul felt now dissatisfied with the answers he had given (so Davies, *JTS.*, 1907, 460), but because this Paulinist moved in a region of thought where such idiosyncrasies of the apostle were transcended.

It seems probable, therefore, so far as probability can be reached in a matter of this kind, that the epistle, or rather homily in epistolary form, originally had no notice of any church. It was a catholicised version of Colossians, written in Paul's name to Gentile Christendom (2^{11} 3^{1}); the solitary reference to concrete conditions (6^{21-22}) is adapted from Colossians, in order to lend *vraisemblance* to the writing, and the general traits of the homily rank it among the catholic epistles or pastorals of the early church. Marcion evidently conjectured that the epistle must be that referred to in Col 4^{16}, and therefore included it in his Pauline canon under the title of πρὸς Λαοδικέας. The title πρὸς Ἐφέσιους, with the insertion ἐν Ἐφέσῳ in 1^{1}, was either (*a*) due to the fact that the Pauline canon of the church was drawn up at Ephesus,

* Cp. Schmiedel in *EBi.* 3120–3121 ("From the divine predestination of the church in Eph 1^{10} $3^{2-6.\ 9-11}$, there is but a single step further to that of its pre-existence, which is accepted in Hermas, *Vis.* ii. 4. 1 and in 2 Clem. 14^{1}").

where possibly a copy of Ephesians was preserved, and from which it was circulated (hence the title; so, *e.g.*, Haupt and Zahn); or (*b*), as Baur suggested, to an editorial combination of 6^{21} with 2 Ti 4^{12} (Τυχικὸν δὲ ἀπέστειλα εἰς Ἔφεσον). The latter hypothesis does not seem too artificial, especially in view of the fact that Ephesus has other links to the circle of Pauline traditions in which the epistle to Timotheus and Titus originated.

§ 7. *Period.*—The *terminus ad quem* may be roughly fixed by the echoes of the epistle in the later Christian literature. The *darkened understanding* of Clem. Rom. 36^{2} may have been suggested by Eph 4^{18}, just as *the eyes of your heart* (Clem. Rom. 59^{3}) seems to echo Eph 1^{18}, while Eph 4^{4-6} is reflected in Clem. Rom. 46^{6} (*have we not one God and one Christ and one Spirit of grace shed forth upon us? and one calling in Christ?*). If these (cp. also Eph 1^{3-4}=Cl. Rom. 64) are, as it seems to the present writer, more than coincidences, Ephesians must have been composed some time previous to A.D. 96. Twenty years later the existence of the epistle becomes still more plain, through the glimpses of it in Ignatius* (*e.g.* 5^{25} with Polyk. 5^{1} *love your wives, even as the Lord the church*; 1^{23} 2^{16} with Smyrn. 1^{1} *in one body of his church*, embracing Jews and Gentiles; 4^{2-3} with Polyk. 1^{2} *Take heed to unity—bear with all in love*; 5^{1} with *Eph.* 1^{1} 10^{3} *let us be zealous to be imitators of God* in forgiveness and forbearance; also 3^{9} with *Eph.* 19, and $6^{13f.}$ with Polyk. 6^{2}). As distinct, if not more so, is its use by Polykarp (cp. Eph 2^{8} with Pol. 1^{3} *knowing that by grace you are saved, not of works, but by the will of God through Jesus Christ*; Eph 4^{26} with Pol. 12^{1} modo, ut his scripturis dictum est, Irascimini et nolite peccare, et Sol non occidat super iracundiam uestram, etc.). Beyond this it is needless to go down into the second century, except to notice the reminiscences (cp. Zahn's *Hirt des Hermas*, 412 f.) in Hermas (*e.g. Mand.* iii. 1, 4, *Sim.* ix. 13, 17), its use by the Valentinians (cp. Iren. i. 8. 4–5; Hipp. vi. 3), and the likelihood that the use of 4^{14} $5^{6f.}$ in Epiph. 26^{13} and 34^{22} proves that Eph. as well as Judas was known to Marcus, the gnostic founder of the Marcosians, *c.* A.D. 160. To judge from Hippolytus (*e.g.* v. 7 f., vii. 25), it was a favourite among several early gnostic sects.

A second-century date for the composition of the homily (so, formerly, *e.g.*, Baur, Holtzmann, Mangold, Pfleiderer, Cone, S. Davidson, Rovers' *INT.* pp. 65 f., Brückner) is therefore ruled out; besides, no polemic against either Montanism (so, *e.g.*, Schwegler, arguing from the emphasis on the Spirit, the prophets, etc.) or any phase of gnosticism (so, *e.g.*, Hilgenfeld, *Einl.* 669 f.)

---

* Ignatius describes the Ephesian Christians as 'initiated together into the mysteries with Paul' (12=Eph $3^{4.9}$ etc.), 'who makes mention of you in every epistle'—a hyperbole based on 1 Co 16^{8}, 2 Ti 1^{16}, 1 Ti 1^{3} etc. But it is a fair inference that he did not know 'Ephesians' with its canonical address and title. While his letter to Ephesus has traces of 'Ephesians,' it never suggests that the latter had special Ephesian associations (cp. Zahn's *Ignatius von Antiochien*, 607 f.); he does not remind the Ephesians of Paul's letter to them, as Clemens Rom. does the Corinthian church.

is audible.[1] The *terminus a quo* is fixed by Colossians, which was certainly, and 1 Peter which was probably, used by the anonymous *autor ad Ephesios.* Ewald, who regarded Colossians as written by Timotheus under Paul's supervision, held that Ephesians was composed by a Paulinist between A.D. 75 and 80, and if the *terminus ad quem* is extended to *c.* A.D. 85, this conjecture may serve as a working hypothesis for the general period of the writing.

While the literary relationships fix approximately the date, they throw no light on the place of the homily's composition, except that the traces of its circulation in Asia Minor suggest the latter province as its locus.

PAUL: TO TIMOTHEUS AND TITUS.

LITERATURE. — (*a*) Editions — After the fifth century homilies of Chrysostom (ed. Field, 1849–1855) and the commentary of Theodore of Mopsuestia (ed. H. B. Swete, Cambridge, 1882), no special edition of any significance appeared till the Reformation, when Calvin (1549, 1556) published his Genevan treatises, and Luther wrote his *Annotationes* (ed. Bruns, Lübeck, 1797); see, further, C. Magalianus (*Operis hierarchici libri iii.* etc., Lyons, 1609); Louis de Sotomayor (Paris, 1610); Charles Rapine (Paris, 1622); Grotius (*Annotationes*, Paris, 1641); J. D. Michaelis (Göttingen, 1750); Mosheim (1755); Bengel's *Gnomon* (1759); Heydenreich, *die Pastoralbriefe P. erlautert* (1826–1828) *; Flatt's *Vorlesungen* (ed. Kling, 1831); C. S. Matthies (1840); Mack[2] (1841); A. S. Paterson (1848); Wiesinger (in Olshausen's *Kommentar*, vol. v. 1850, Eng. tr., New York, 1858); Oosterzee (Bielefeld, 1861); Huther[3] (Göttingen, 1866); Bisping's *Erklärung* (1866); Ewald (1870); Plitt, *die Pastoralbriefe praktisch ausgelegt* (1872); Hofmann (1874); P. Fairbairn (*The Pastoral Epistles*, Edin. 1874); J. T. Beck, *Erklärung der 2. Briefe P. an Tim.* (ed. Lindenmeyer, 1879); Ellicott[5] (1883) *; Wace and Jackson (*Speaker's Comm.* 1881); Knoke (1887–1889); Reuss (1888); Kübel (in Strack-Zöckler's *Komm.* 1888); von Soden[2] (*HC.* 1893) *; Knoke[4] (Lange's *Bibel-Werk*, 1894); Riggenbach (— Zöckler, 1897); A. E. Humphreys (*Cambridge Bible*, 1897); J. H. Bernard (*CGT.* 1899) *; Stellhorn (1900); Horton (*CB.* 1901); R. M. Pope (London, 1901); J. P. Lilley (Edin. 1901); Krukenberg (1901); Cone (*Intern. Hdbks. to NT.* 1901); Weiss[7] (— Meyer, 1902) *; Koehler (*SNT.*[2] 1907); J. E. Belser (Freiburg im Breisgau, 1907) *; N. J. D. White (*EGT.* 1910); Wohlenberg[2] (*ZK.* 1911); E. Bosio (Florence, 1911); M. Meinertz (1913); J. Knabenbauer (Paris, 1913); M. Dibelius (*HBNT.* 1913); E. F. Brown (*WC.* 1917).

Also Jerome (fourth century), J. Willichius (*Expositio brevis et familiaris*, 1542); D. N. Berdotus (1703); Mosheim (*Erklärung des Briefe an d. Titum*, 1779); Kuinoel (*Explicatio ep. Pauli ad Titum*, 1812); and J. S. Howson (Smith's *DB.* iii. 1520–1521) on Titus; Caspar Cruciger (1542); C. Espencaeus (*In priorem ep. ad Tim. commentarius et digressiones*, Paris,

---

[1] Baur's contention was that Eph. voices, instead of opposing, gnosticism, and that it dates from a time "when the gnostic ideas were just coming into circulation, and still wore the garb of innocent speculation" (*Paul*, Eng. tr. ii. 22).

1561); Melanchthon (*Enarratio epist. P. ad Tim. et duorum capitum secundæ*, 1561); Tilemann Heshusius (*comm. in priorem epist. P. ad Tim.* 1582); Gerhard (*adnotationes in I P. ad Tim. epistolam*, 1643); A. C. Fleischmann (1791); J. A. L. Wegscheider (1810); M. G. E. Leo (*Pauli epist. I ad Tim. cum comm. perpetuo*, Leipzig, 1837); Kölling (*Der I Brief P. an Tim. aufs neue untersucht und ausgelegt*, 1882–7); Liddon (1897); and Sir W. M. Ramsay (*Exp.*[7] 1908 f.) on 1 Tim.; C. Espencaeus (Paris, 1564); J. B. Rembowski (1752); M. G. E. Leo (1850); Bahnsen, *die sog. Pastoralbriefe, I. der II Tim.* (1876)* on 2 Tim.; with Mosheim (*Erklärung der beyden Briefe des Ap. Pauli an den Timotheum*, Hamburg, 1755), and Plumptre (Smith's *DB.* iii. 1507–1572) on 1 and 2 Tim.

(*b*) Studies—(i.) general:—P. Anton (*Exegetische Abhandlungen der Pastoralbriefe*, 1753);[1] van den Es (*Pauli ad Titum epistola cum eiusdem ad Tim. epp. composita*, Leyden, 1819); L. R. Rolle (*De authentia epist. pastoralium*, 1841); Scharling (*Die neuesten Untersuchungen über die sog. Pastoralbriefe*, 1846); A. Saintes, *Études critiques sur les trois lettres past. attribuées à S. Paul* (1852); Schenkel (*BL.* iv. 393–402); Sabatier (*ESR.* x. 250–259); Ginella, *De authentia epist. pastoralium* (Breslau, 1865); Pfleiderer's *Paulinismus* (Eng. tr. ii. 196–214); J. R. Boise, *The epp. of Paul written after he became a prisoner* (New York, 1887); Plummer (*Expositor's Bible*, 1888); Hesse, *Die Entstehung d. NT Hirtenbriefe* (1889); Bourquin, *étude critique sur les past. épîtres* (1890); Hatch (*EB.*[9], 'Pastorals'); Harnack (*ACL.* ii. 1. 480–485, 710–711); Moffatt (*EBi.* 5079–5096); W. Lock (*DB.* iv. 768 f.); Jacquier (*INT.* i. 353, 414); R. Scott, *The Pauline Epistles* (1909), pp. 128 f., 329 f.; R. A. Falconer (*DAC.* ii. 583 f.). (ii.) specially against the Pauline authorship of one or all:—Schleiermacher (*über den sog. ersten Brief des P. an den Tim., Ein krit. Sendschreiben an Gass*, Berlin, 1807; cp. his *Werke zu Theol.* ii. 221–230); Baur, *die sogen. Pastoralbriefe* (1835)*; Schenkel, *Christusbild d. Apostel* (162 f.); Schwegler (*NZ.* ii. 138–153); H. J. Holtzmann, *die Pastoralbriefe kritisch. u. exegetisch behandelt* (1880)*; Renan, iii. pp. xxiii–liii, v. (ch. vi.); Pfleiderer (*Urc.* iii. 373 f.); W. Brückner, *Chron.* 277–286; Weizsäcker, *AA.* ii. 163 f., 259 f.; M. A. Rovers, *Nieuw-test. Letterkunde*[2] (1888), 66–78; J. Réville, *Les origines de l'episcopat*, i. 262 f.; E. Y. Hincks, *JBL.* (1897) 94–117; von Soden (*INT.* 305 f.); Gould (*NTTh.* 142 f.); McGiffert (*AA.* 398, 423); E. Vischer (*Die Paulusbriefe*, 1904, 74–80); Knopf, *NZ.* 32, 300 f.; Baljon, *INT.* pp. 150–174; A. S. Peake, (*INT.* 68–71); Wendland (*HBNT.* i. 2. 364 f.); H. H. Mayer, *Ueber d. Pastoralbriefe* (1913); F. Koehler (*Die Pastoralbriefe*, 1914). (iii.) Schleiermacher was answered by Planck (*Bemerkungen über den ersten Brief an Tim.* 1808); Baur by M. Baumgarten (*die Echtheit d. Pastoralbriefe*, Berlin, 1837) and Matthies (1840); the traditional view was maintained by Good, *Authent. des épîtres past.* (Montauban, 1848); Dubois, *étude critique sur l'authent. de la première ép. à Tim.* (1856); and Doumergue (*l'authenticité 1 Tim.* 1856); but especially by T. Rudow, *de argum. hist. quibus epp. past. origo Paulina impugnata est* (1852); C. W. Otto, *die geschichtlichen Verhältnisse der*

---

[1] Said to be the first German work where the name 'pastorals' can be found applied to these epistles.

Pastoralbriefe, 1860); M. J. Cramer (*JBL.*, 1887, pp. 3 f.); Bertrand, *essai critique sur l'authenticité des ép. Past.* (1888); G. G. Findlay * (Appendix to Eng, tr. of Sabatier's *L'apôtre Paul*, pp. 341–402); Hort, *Christian Ecclesia* (1898), 189–217, and A. Ruegg (*Aus Schrift u. Geschichte*, 1898, pp. 59–108) *; followed by Roos, *die Briefe des apost. Paulus u. die Reden des Herrn Jesu* (156–202); G. H. Gilbert, *Student's Life of Paul* (1899), 225–232; J. W. Falconer, *From Apostle to Priest* (1900), 109–146; W. E. Bowen (*Dates of Past. Letters*, 1900); G. G. Findlay (Hastings' *DB.* iii. 714 f.); W. M. Ramsay (*CRE.* pp. 248 f., *Exp.*[4] viii. 110 f. etc.); R. D. Shaw (*Pauline epp.*[3] pp. 423 f.); T. C. Laughlin (*The Pastoral Epp. in the Light of one Roman Imprisonment*, California, 1905); R. J. Knowling (*Testimony of St. Paul to Christ*[3], 1906, pp. 121–147); J. D. James (*Genuineness and Authorship of Past. Epp.*, 1906); *CQR.* (1907) 63–86, 344–358; Barth (*INT.* § 14); Zahn (*INT.* §§ 33–37) *; A. Maier (*Hauptprobleme d. P.-Briefe*, 1911); C. Bruston (*RTQR.* xxii. 248 f., 441 f.); V. Bartlet (*Exp.*[8] . 28 ff.); Edmundson (*Urc.* 160 f.). (iv.) on special points:—Beckhaus, *Specimen observationum de vocabulis ἁπαξ λεγ. et rarioribus dicendi formulis in prima epistola Paulina ad Tim.* (1810); Ad. Curtius, *de tempore quo prior epist. Tim. exarata sit* (1828); G. Böhl, *über die Zeit der Abfassung und die Paulin. Charakter der Briefe an Tim. u. Tit.* (Berlin, 1829, conservative); W. Mangold (*Die Irrlehrer der Pastoralbriefe*, Marburg, 1856); Eylau, *Zur Chronologie der Pastoralbriefe* (1888); E. Belin, *étude sur les tend. hérétiques combattues dans les ép. past.* (1865); Hilgenfeld (*ZWT.*, 1880, 448–464); Havet, *le Christianisme et ses origines*, iv. 376–380 (1884); Henri Bois, *JPT.* (1888) 145–160; Clemen, *Einheitlichkeit d. Paulin. Briefe* (1894), 142–176; A. Klöpper, *ZWT.* (1902) 339–361 ('*Zur Christologie der Pastoralbriefe*'); W. Lutgert, *Die Irrlehrer d. Pastoralbriefe* (*BFT.* xiii. 3, 1909); Moffatt (*EB.*[11] xxvi. 991 f.).

§ 1. *Order.*—In addition to πρὸς Ἐφεσίους, three epistles addressed to Timotheus (πρὸς Τιμόθεον Ā, B̄) and Titus (πρὸς Τίτον) appear in the canon under the name of Paul. As these titles did not form part of the original autographs, the early church, which took them as written within Paul's lifetime, naturally argued from the internal evidence that 2 Tim., with its richer individual references, reflected the last phase of the apostle's career, and that 1 Tim. was earlier. When the epistles are recognised to belong to a sub-Pauline period,[1] a comparative study of their contents indicates that 2 Tim. is the earliest of the three, and 1 Tim. the furthest from Paul (so, *e.g.*, Mangold, de Wette, Reuss, *La Bible*, vii. 243 f., 703 f.; Baur, Holtzmann, von Soden, Harnack, Pfleiderer, Rovers, Bourquin, Brückner, S. Davidson, Beyschlag, McGiffert, Clemen, Schmiedel, Jülicher, R. Scott,

[1] Cp. Lock, *DB.* iv. 784: "On this latter supposition the priority of Titus to 1 Tim. would seem almost certain, as there would be so little reason for the same writer composing it if 1 Tim. were in existence, and intended as a general treatise."

and Koehler); cp. *HNT.* 559–561. The more advanced situation of 1 Tim. is betrayed by its sharper emphasis on ecclesiastical procedure; *e.g.* πίστις in its objective sense occurs four times in 1 Tim., once in Titus, never in 2 Tim.; σωτήρ of God* only occurs in 1 Tim.; the ὑγιαίνουσα διδασκαλία is elevated to an extraordinary position † in 1 Ti 1^{10}, and τινὲς ἄνθρωποι or τινες is confined to 1 Tim. (seven times). 2 Ti $2^{17\text{-}20}$ is presupposed in 1 Ti 1^{20}, and there is a heightening scale in 2 Ti 2^{23} = Tit 3^{9} = 1 Ti 1^{4}, 2 Ti 1^{11} = 1 Ti 2^{7}, 2 Ti 3^{1} = 1 Ti $4^{1f.}$, and Tit 1^{7} = 1 Ti 3^{2}. When the author wrote 2 Tim., he must have had some Pauline materials or sources at his command; this preponderates to a lesser degree in Titus; but in 1 Tim., where he is more of an author and less of an editor, the Pauline background of reminiscences and traditions recedes before the tendency of the writer to emphasise the authority rather than the personality of the apostle, to become more severe towards the errorists, and to elaborate the details of ecclesiastical organisation and discipline. In this respect the superiority of 2 Tim. is fairly obvious, and the probability is that superiority here is equivalent to priority.

1 Tim. was the first to rouse the suspicions of critics (J. E. C. Schmidt, *Einl.* i. 257 f.; Schleiermacher), and it is assigned to a post-Pauline date even by some who incline to accept 2 Tim. as a composition of Paul (so, *e.g.*, Löffler, *Kleine Schriften*, ii. 216 f.; Neander, Bleek, and Heinrici, *Der litt. Charakter d. neutest. Schriften*, 1908, 64).‡ Were it not for 1 Tim., it might be plausible to seek room for the other two within the lifetime of Paul, but all three hang together, and they hang outside the historical career of the apostle. The critical position underlying the following pages is that while the three epistles are, in Coleridge's phrase, ἐπιστολαὶ Παυλοειδεῖς, they are pseudonymous compositions of a Paulinist who wrote during the period of transition into the neo-catholic church of the second century, with the aim of safeguarding the common Christianity of the age in terms of the great Pauline tradition. He knew Paul's epistles and venerated his gospel, but

---

* In contrast to the gnostic antithesis between God the Creator and God the Saviour.

† As an antithesis to parricide, matricide, and other abnormal vices. "This is so unnatural an application of the term that we can hardly believe that Paul himself used it in such a connection, but rather another writer who imitated the Pauline expression" (Bleek, *INT.* ii. 85–86).

‡ Heinrici writes: "der zweite Timotheusbrief wohl von Paulus selbst verfasst ist, während dem Titus und dem ersten Timotheusbrief Weisungen des Paulus über Gemeindeorganisation, Gottesdienst, Lehre und sittliche Pflichten der Gemeindeleiter zugrunde liegen, welche in Briefform gefasst sind." Bruston also makes Paul write 2 Tim. first.

he had also access to some Pauline *reliquiæ* as well as to traditions which are not represented in Luke's history. The pastorals, especially 2 Tim., are composite, and they show further traces of subsequent accretion. It is unlikely that these writings were nothing more than the products of a later Paulinist's inventive imagination, working on the book of Acts and the Pauline letters. Many of the details, *e.g.* the references to Paul's cloak and books (2 Tim 4^{12-13}), are too circumstantial and concrete to be explained upon any such hypothesis (cp. Conybeare's *Myth, Magic, and Religion*, p. xvi). No theory of verisimilitude accounts for them, any more than for the numerous allusions to apostolic figures, which place them in a different light from that of the earlier traditions. Furthermore, as has often been urged (cp. Lemme, pp. 7 f., and Krenkel, pp. 449 f.) with true historical insight, the very discrepancies and roughness in the various situations presupposed throughout the epistles, especially in 2 Tim., are enough to indicate that the writer had not a free hand. He was not sketching a purely imaginary set of circumstances, but working up materials which were not always quite tractable.

The apocryphal reference in 2 Ti 3^8 (cp. *EBi.* 2327 f., Charles' *Apocrypha and Pseud.* ii. 811) threw suspicions on that epistle at an early date: 'item quod ait *sicut Iannes et Mambres restiterunt Mosi* non inuenitur in publicis scripturis sed in libro secreto qui suprascribitur Iannes et Mambres liber. Unde ausi sunt quidam epistolam ad Timotheum repellere, quasi habentem in se textam alicuius secreti; sed non potuerunt' (Origen, *in Matth.* ser. 117). This, however, was a passing curiosity of early criticism. The reasons for the widespread reaction (since Eichhorn) against the traditional hypothesis of the pastorals are based on their diction, theological and ecclesiastical standpoint, and ecclesiastical tendencies. The sub-Pauline elements are decisive for a date later than any in Paul's lifetime. But any arguments in favour of the hypothesis that Paul wrote these letters will be best met indirectly, in the course of a positive statement of the other position.

§ 2. *Contents.*—(*a*) In the first part of 2 Tim. (1^1–2^{13}) the emphasis falls on suffering with and for the gospel as a note of genuine Christianity. The greeting (1^{1-2}) is followed by a thanksgiving for Timotheus' unfeigned faith, and an exhortation against being ashamed of Paul and the Pauline gospel in their hour of adversity. Paul urges his own example to the contrary ($1^{12f.}$), together with the example of a brave Asiatic Christian, Onesiphorus (1^{15-18}). This Pauline gospel, of which endurance is a leading feature, Timotheus as Paul's deputy is to teach (2^{1-2}) to his subordinate agents, and to practise himself ($2^{3f.}$), with the certainty of ultimate success and reward (2^{4-13}). The second section of the epistle lays stress on the wordy, bitter, and barren controversies which endanger this trust and tradition ($2^{14f.}$). Their immoral consequences and methods are hotly exposed (3^{1-9}); then Timotheus is warned, by Paul's own example ($3^{10f.}$), that suffering not ease is the mark of the true gospel, and that innovations ($3^{13f.}$) are to be eschewed. After solemnly laying this charge on him (4^{1-5}), Paul speaks of his own position ($4^{6f.}$), and the letter closes with a number of private and personal data.

The author evidently means the epistle to be taken as sent by Paul from his Roman imprisonment (cp. 4^{6} = Ph 1^{23} 2^{17}) to Timotheus at some unknown place (perhaps in Asia Minor, 1^{15-18}). For an attempt to explain $4^{16f.}$ as an allusion to Paul's defence before Felix, see Krenkel's *Beiträge*, pp. 424 f., 442 f.; Kreyenbühl's *Evglm d. Wahrheit* (1900), i. 213 f., and (see above, p. 138) Erbes in *ZNW.*, 1909, 128 f., 195 f., with Spitta's *Urc.* i. 37 f. But (see above, p. 169) the reference is obviously to the first stage of the Roman trial (cp. Ph $1^{12f.}$): in any case it does not imply acquittal and release (Zahn). Dr. T. C. Laughlin (see below) is obliged to refer the first defence to a supposed trial of Paul before the Ephesian courts (Ac 19^{38}), which is even more improbable.

Bahnsen ingeniously analyses the epistle thus: 2^{8-13} develops 2^{6}, 2^{14-16} develops 2^{4}, and $3^{1-4\,(8)}$ develops 2^{5}. Otto's classification attempts to arrange the contents under the three notes of the πνεῦμα in 1^{7}.

For a textual discussion of 2^{19}, cp. Resch's *Paulinismus*, pp. 258–259. The μεμβράναι of 4^{13} were probably *pugillares membranei* or sheets for private memoranda. The βιβλία may have included the Logia or evangelic scriptures from which 1 Ti 5^{18} is quoted (so Resch); but this is a mere conjecture. See, generally, Birt's *Das Antike Buchwesen*, pp. 50 f., 88 f.; Nestle's *Einf.* 39 f., and Zahn's *GK.* ii. 938–942.

(*b*) The construction of the epistle to Titus is simpler and more lucid than that of the other two pastorals. After the greeting (1^{1-4}), Paul discusses the rules for the conduct of presbyters or bishops in Crete, in view of current errors and local vices (1^{5-16}). He then sketches 'the sound doctrine' which Titus is to inculcate on aged men (2^{1-2}) and women (2^{3-5}), younger men (2^{6-8}) and slaves (2^{9-10}), in the light of what God's grace demands (2^{11-15}) from all Christians. This is enlarged and enforced (3^{1-11}),* in view of the position of Christians towards the outside world; instead of worldliness or wrangling, ethical superiority is to be the aim of all believers. Then, with a brief personal message (3^{12-15}), the epistle ends.

The literary setting goes back to some early tradition which associated a Pauline mission, under Titus, with Crete; the island, owing to its position, was a favourite wintering-place for vessels (cp. Ramsay, *Pauline and other Studies*, 1907, 76), and, in the absence of all information about

---

* On the sub-Pauline tone of 3^{5}, cp. Sokolowski's *Geist und Leben bei Paulus* (1903), 108 f.; on 3^{10-11}, *Exp.*[8] xi. 137 f.

the origin of Cretan Christianity, it is a reasonable conjecture that Paul may have touched at Crete during one of his voyages even prior (cp. 3^{12-13} with Ac 20^{3}) to Ac $27^{8f.}$. There was a strong Jewish element in the population, which seems to explain the local allusions in $1^{13f.}$ 3^{9}. On the original basis, in Epimenides, for the harsh attack upon the Cretan character, cp. Rendel Harris in *Exp.*[7] iii. 332 f., *Exp.*[8] ix. 29 f., and above, p. 35.

(*c*) 1 Tim. is more discursive and miscellaneous than 2 Tim., but the practical, ecclesiastical motive of the epistle (3^{15} *ταῦτά σοι γράφω . . . ἵνα εἰδῇς πῶς δεῖ ἐν οἴκῳ θεοῦ ἀναστρέφεσθαι*) is fairly obvious throughout its somewhat desultory contents. After the greeting (1^{1-2}), Paul contrasts (1^{3-17}) the methods and aims of some contemporary antinomians at Ephesus with 'the sound doctrine' of his own gospel, of which Timotheus (1^{18-20}) is the natural heir. The writing then passes forward into the first (2–3) of its two sections. Regulations are given for various sides of church-life: (*a*) for whom ($2^{1f.}$) and by whom ($2^{8f.}$) prayer is to be offered—the latter direction drifting* into a word on the subordination of women; and (*b*) the qualifications of *ἐπίσκοποι* (3^{2-8}), deacons and deaconesses (3^{9-13}). The closing words of the section (3^{14-16}) imply that such care for the worship and organisation of the church as a pillar and prop of the truth cannot wholly prevent moral aberrations and heresies; hence the second section (4–6) deals with Timotheus' attitude towards such ascetic errors ($4^{1-5. 6-10. 11-16}$)† as well as towards individual members of the church (5^{1-2}), particularly widows (5^{3-16}),‡ presbyters ($5^{17f.}$), and slaves (6^{1-2}). A sharp word follows (6^{3-10}) on the errorists who made their religion a profitable trade, and with a solemn charge to the 'man of God,' the epistle closes in a doxology (6^{11-16}). The postscript contains a charge for wealthy Christians (6^{17-19}), and a warning for Timotheus himself against contemporary *γνῶσις* (6^{20-21}).

In 5^{18}, where an OT quotation lies side by side with a NT saying, the latter must be taken as equally from *ἡ γραφή*. It is artificial to conjecture that a logion of Jesus has been loosely appended to the former. By the time the author of the pastorals wrote, either Luke's gospel or some evan-

---

* The inner connection, such as it is, between $3^{2f.}$ and what precedes, probably is to be found in the thought of worship suggesting the qualifications of those who presided over it.

† On 4^{13} (*τῇ ἀναγνώσει*), see Glaue, *Die Vorlesung heiligen Schriften im Gottesdienste* (1907), pp. 35–38.

‡ Könnecke (*BFT.* xii. 1. 31–32) proposes to rearrange $5^{4f.}$ thus: $5^{3. 4. 8. 5. 6. 7}$.

gelic collection containing Lk 10^7 was reckoned as γραφή. This would be partially, but only partially, explained if Luke were the author, in whole or part, of the pastorals (see below, p. 414).

§ 3. *Structure.*—The more or less loose connection of the three epistles and the frequent abruptness or awkwardness of transition between successive passages, naturally suggest a recourse in the first instance to the hypothesis of transposition or redaction. The results, however, do not of themselves point to any satisfactory solution of the literary problem.

Tit 1^{7-9} certainly appears to be a marginal gloss (so O. Ritschl, *TLZ.*, 1885, 609; Knoke, pp. 227 f.; Harnack, *ACL.* 710 f., and McGiffert, cp. *EBi.* 5091), breaking the connection between 1^6 (*ἀνυπότακτα*) and 1^{10} (*εἰσὶν γὰρ πολλοὶ ἀνυπότακτοι*); it may have been added subsequently by the author himself (cp. 1 Ti $3^{2f.}$) or inserted by a later editor interested in the monarchical episcopate.* Similarly 1 Ti 5^{23} has probably got displaced (cp. *EBi.* 5080) from between 4^3 and 4^4 (Holtzmann), or 4^{12} and 4^{13} (Bois, Könnecke), the motive of the change (unless it was accidental) being the desire of some copyist to qualify *ἁγνόν*. It is scarcely adequate to treat it merely as parenthetical, or (with Owen) to place it after 5^{25}. Knatchbull and Bakhuyzen prefer to omit it entirely as a later gloss, while Calvin and Heydenreich suggested that 5^{22c-23} was written on the margin originally. More drastically P. Ewald (*Probabilia betr. den Texte des 1 Tim.* 1901) conjectures that by an accidental displacement of the *plagulæ* or leaves in the original copy 1 Ti 1^{12-17} has been displaced from between 1^2 and 1^3, and 3^{14}–4^{10} from after 6^2; which certainly smoothes out the roughness of the transition † at various points. The awkward transitions in 3^{10-13} have also suggested a textual irregularity which has been variously cured, *e.g.* by the deletion of 3^{12} (Naber, *Mnemosyne*, 1878, 371), or its removal to a place between 3^9 and 3^{10} (Knoke omitting 3^{11}, Hesse putting 3^{13} between 3^{10} and 3^{11}). 4^9 is also awkward in its present site, but it need not be an interpolation (Bois, Baljon), though "it is very probable that the Pastoral Epistles [especially 1 Tim.] contain many interpolations in which statements about errors and even directions about discipline have been somewhat altered to suit the requirements of the middle of the second century. This is what would naturally happen to a document which was used, as we know these epistles were used, for a manual of ecclesiastical procedure" (Lindsay, *Church and Ministry in Early Centuries*², 141).

---

* Clemen (*Einheitlichkeit*, pp. 157 f.) and Hesse (pp. 148 f., who begins at 1^6) extend the interpolation to the close of v.^{11}, on inadequate grounds. The connection between vv.^{11} and ^{12} is quite good, and there is no real difficulty about Epimenides being styled a prophet loosely after v.^{11}.

† Better than the transposition of 1^{18-20} to a place between 1^8 and 1^9 (Bois), which leaves too large a gap between *νομοδιδάσκαλοι* (1^8) and the allusions to the law in 1^9, although it gives a good connection between the *charge* of $1^{5f.}$ and 1^{18}.

On a closer examination into their literary unity, the epistles, and especially 2 Tim., at once reveal different strata. Thus in 2 Tim., 1^{15-18} and 3^{10-12} are plainly erratic boulders as they lie; both interrupt the context, and both contain material * which is genuinely Pauline. The same holds true of 4^{9-22a}, possibly even of 4^{6-22a} in the main, within which 1^{15-18} is sometimes held to have originally lain (after 4^{10} McGiffert, after 4^{13} Knoke). But even $4^{(6).\ 9-22a}$ is not homogeneous, although it is easier to feel differences of time and temper within its contents than to disentangle and place the various elements of which it is composed.† Thus v.^{11a} (*Luke alone is with me*) hardly seems consonant with v.^{21b} (*Eubulus salutes thee, and so do Pudens and Linus, and Claudia, and all the brothers*); if Timotheus was to rejoin Paul at once (vv.$^{9.\ 21}$), it is not easy to see how he could devote himself to the local discharge of the duties laid on him in 1^{6}–4^{5} (cp. Simcox, *ET.* x. 430–432, on the unlikelihood that the commissions and cautions of $4^{13-15.\ 21-22a}$ could have come from a dying man). Such phenomena ‡ have led to schemes of reconstruction which attempt to solve the complexity of the epistles' structure by recourse to partition-methods, especially in the case of 2 Tim. The presumably authentic material is analysed, *e.g.*, as follows. (*a*) von Soden: $1^{1f.\ 3-5a.\ 7f.\ 15-18}$ ($2^{1.\ 3-12a}$?) $4^{6-19.\ 21-22}$ = a genuine letter written from the close of the Roman imprisonment. (*b*) McGiffert: 1^{1-18} (except $1^{6b.\ 12-14}$) ($2^{1.\ 3-13}$?) $4^{1-2.\ 5-8.\ 16-19.\ 21b.\ 10}$ written towards the end of his imprisonment and life, a complete epistle, 'his dying testament' to the favourite disciple who was to carry on his work at Ephesus. (*c*) Dr. T. C. Laughlin: 4^{9-21a} (a note written from Macedonia, shortly after Ac 20^{1}), the rest of 2 Tim. written after Philippians from Rome. (*d*) Hausrath (iv. 162 f.): $1^{15-18}+4^{9-18}$, like Phil 3^{1}–4, written soon after his arrival in Rome, the former after his first trial. Other analysists find incorporated in 2 Tim. a fragment written from the Cæsarean imprisonment: *e.g.* (*a*) Hitzig (*Ueber Johannes Marcus*, 1843, 154 f.), who distinguishes

* Lemme (*Das echte Ermahnungsschreiben des Ap. Paulus an Tim.* 1882), Hesse, and Krenkel needlessly omit $1^{15b.\ 18a}$.

† Ewald assigned vv.$^{9-12}$ and $^{19-22}$ to Rome, vv.$^{13-15}$ to Macedonia, during Paul's third tour from Ephesus.

‡ It is more natural, in the majority of cases, to explain these internal discrepancies as the result of accretion, when different notes (see above, p. 41) have been fused together, than as *lapsus memoriæ* or *calami*.

such a note (1^{15} $4^{13-16.\ 20-22a}$) from another written during the Roman captivity ($4^{6-12.\ 19.}$ 1^{16-18} 4^{22b} *c.* A.D. 63); (*b*) Bacon (*Story of St. Paul*, 196 f.), who regards $4^{9.\ 11-18.\ 20-21a}$ as probably composed during the two years at Cæsarea;* (*c*) Clemen (*Paulus*, i. 405 f.), who places 4^{9-18}, together with Colossians and Philemon (A.D. 59–60), in this period (A.D. 61), 1^{15-18} falling in the Roman captivity (A.D. 62) previous to Philippians, whilst 4^{19-22a} was written after 1 Cor. from Corinth in A.D. 57 (*op. cit.* p. 354); and (*d*) Krenkel (*Beiträge zur Aufhellung der Geschichte u. der Briefe des Apostel Paulus*, 1890, pp. 395–468), who addresses 4^{9-18} from Cæsarea to Timotheus at or near Troas, subsequently to Colossians and Philemon, $4^{19}+1^{16-17.\ 18b}+4^{21}$ being written from the Roman imprisonment.

The net result of such investigations is tentative. Beyond the general fact that the author had some *reliquia Paulinæ* † at his disposal, and that the internal evidence here and there suggests the incorporation of such notes by one who felt justified in working up such materials, we can hardly go with very much confidence. One of the most elaborate and least convincing recent reconstructions is proposed by Hilgenfeld (*ZWT.*, 1897, 1–86), *viz.* that 2 Tim. has been worked over by an anti-Marcionite redactor, who also edited Titus in the interests of orthodox doctrine (in $1^{1-2.\ 12-13a}$ 2^{13} 3^{10-11}), and revised (pp. 32 f.) later in the second century the post-Pauline original of 1 Tim. (= $1^{1-2.\ 12-17}$ $2^{1-6a.\ 8-15}$ 3^{1-16} 4^{9-11} 4^{12}–5^{18a} $5^{19-22.\ 24-25}$) which had sought to commend the monarchical episcopate.

Titus, on the other hand, presents less difficulty. It is probably sub-Pauline, and the alternatives seem to be (*a*) either a genuine note of Paul worked up by a later disciple, who was responsible for 1 Tim. at least, or (*b*) an epistle based on

* The rest of 2 Tim., with some interpolations (*e.g.* 1^{13} 2^{20-26}), is regarded as written subsequently to Philippians (pp. 375 f.). Böttger dated the whole epistle from the Cæsarean period of imprisonment, with 1 Tim. from Patara (Ac 21^{1}) or Miletus (Ac 20^{27}). The change of Μιλήτῳ into Μελίτῃ (so, *e.g.*, Baronius, Beza, Grotius, Knoke, Bahnsen) would date 2 Tim. or this part of it from the Roman imprisonment (cp. Ac 28^{1-10}); but the textual evidence is slight, and Trophimus is not mentioned by Luke (Ac 27^{2}) in this connection.

† The preservation of such private notes, as, *e.g.* in the cases of the correspondence between Vergil and Augustus, Cicero and Atticus (cp. Peters, *Der Brief in der römischen Literatur*, 1901, 27 f., 78 f.), was all the more likely, since Paul was the first 'man of letters' in the primitive church, and since the extant canonical collection represented only part of his actual correspondence. Private notes would be more apt to remain overlooked than others, unless, like the letter of recommendation to Phœbe, they were attached by later editors to some larger epistle (p. 139).

one or two genuine fragments of the apostle's correspondence. The former class of theories is represented by Hesse (pp. 150 f.), who finds $1^{1f.\ 5\text{-}6.\ 12\text{-}13a.\ 16}$ $3^{1\text{-}7.\ 12\text{-}13.\ 15}$ a genuinely Pauline note, written shortly after he left Crete, and worked up by a Paulinist who inserted the warnings against heresy; by von Soden ($1^{1.\ 4.}$ $3^{12\text{-}15}$), and by McGiffert ($1^{1\text{-}6}$ $3^{1\text{-}7.\ 12\text{-}13}$, written before Paul's stay of three months at Corinth, Ac 20^{3}). The alternative, which seems more probable (so nearly all the critical editors), is that the writer was drawing upon some ancient and even authentic tradition connecting Titus with Crete during Paul's lifetime, and that $3^{12f.}$, which is likely to be genuine (so Weisse, Hase, Ewald, etc.), has been preserved from that tradition. Most allow that the historical site for such a fragment and tradition lies in the neighbourhood of Ac 20^{3}, Krenkel, *e.g.*, dating it (*i.e.* Tit 3^{12}, 2 Ti 4^{20}, Tit 3^{13}) perhaps from Illyria during the apostle's second journey to Corinth (Ac $20^{1\text{-}3}$), Clemen (*Paulus*, i. 399 f., ii. 233–234) similarly from Macedonia after 2 Co 10–13, 1–9, and previous to Romans (A.D. 59).

1 Tim., again, yields even less to the partition-theories. No fragment can be referred with any confidence to the apostle. The incidental allusions to Paul's personality ($3^{14f.}$ 4^{13}) merely betray the writer's consciousness that there was a certain awkwardness in such elaborate commissions and instructions upon the commonplace regulations of a Christian community being addressed to one who was not merely himself in mature life, but *ex hypothesi* separated only for a time from his superintendent. In such touches we can feel the author's literary conscience and his tactful attempt to preserve the *vraisemblance* of the situation, but there is nothing to indicate the presence of any definite note from the apostle. As it stands, the ep. is a unity, though $2^{11\text{-}15}$ reads like a gloss (Hesse, Knoke), $4^{1\text{-}8}$ parts easily from its context, and the οὖν of 2^{1} is a loose transition. More than the other two epistles, it breathes from first to last the atmosphere in which the editor or author of all the three lived and moved. It is a free and fairly homogeneous composition, not constructed (as Schleiermacher suggested) simply out of the two previous epistles, but with a content and *cachet* of its own. On the other hand, the literary structure of its paragraphs shows that it has suffered accretion after it was originally composed, *e.g.* in $6^{17\text{-}21a}$, possibly also in $3^{1\text{-}13}$ $5^{17\text{-}20\ (22a)}$, besides the marginal glosses in 3^{11} and 5^{23}. When $6^{17f.}$ is thus taken as a later

addition (Harnack, Knopf in *NZ.* 305–306), the allusion in ἀντιθέσεις τῆς ψευδωνύμου γνώσεως may be to Marcion's well-known volume. Otherwise the use of 1 Tim. in Polykarp (see below), besides the inappropriateness of 1^{7} (Tit. 1^{10}) to the Marcionites, rule out the Tübingen view that the pastorals were directly anti-Marcionite pamphlets. Thus Hort (*JC.* 113 f.) prefers, with several recent critics, to explain the ἀντιθέσεις as Jewish casuistical decisions, the γενεαλογίαι of 1^{4} and Tit 3^{9} being the legendary pedigrees of Jewish heroes, such as swarm in the book of Jubilees and elsewhere (cp. Wohlenberg, pp. 31 f.).

Hesse (*op. cit.*), assuming that the Ignatian epistles were written under Marcus Aurelius, finds a genuine Pauline letter in $1^{1-10.\ 18-20}$ 4^{1-16} $6^{3-16.\ 20f.}$. Knoke (*op. cit.*) similarly disentangles an epistle to Tim. from Corinth ($1^{3f.\ 18-20}$ 2^{1-10} 4^{12} $5^{1-3.\ 4c-6.\ 11-15.\ 19-23.\ 24f.}$) and one from Cæsarea ($1^{12-17}$ 3^{14-16} $4^{1-11.\ 13-16}$ 2^{12-15} $5^{7f.}$ 6^{17-19} 1^{5-11} $6^{2c-16.\ 20f.}$) from editorial work of a second-century redactor. But the comparative evenness of the style is almost enough (*EBi.* 5093) to invalidate such hypotheses.

§ 4. *Literary characteristics.*—(*a*) The pastorals contain a number of terms which are common to them and to the other Pauline epistles; but some of these cannot be described as distinctively Pauline, while others are due to the fact that the writer was composing in Paul's name. The significant feature of the terminology, as of the thought, is its difference from Paul's. The similarities are neither so numerous nor so primary as the variations, and the latter point to a writer who betrays the later milieu of his period in expression as well as in conception.*

A study of the Greek vocabulary shows not only that the very greeting is un-Pauline, but that there is a significant absence of many characteristically Pauline terms, *e.g.* ἄδικος, ἀκαθαρσία, ἀποκαλύπτειν, διαθήκη, δικαίωμα, ἐλεύθερος, ἐνεργεῖν, κατεργάζεσθαι, καυχᾶσθαι, μείζων, μικρός, μωρία, παράδοσις, πατὴρ ἡμῶν, πείθειν, περιπατεῖν (for which, as for στοιχεῖν, ἀναστρέφειν is substituted), περισσεύειν, πράσσειν (for which the author substitutes ποιεῖν), σῶμα, υἱοθεσία, τέλειος, and χαρίζεσθαι. Furthermore, the author has a favourite vocabulary of his own, full of compounds and Latinisms, with new groups of words (cp. those in ἀ privative, διδασκ-, εὐσεβ-, οἰκο-, σωφρ-, φιλο-, etc.) and an unwonted predilection for others (*e.g.* those in

---

* So especially the philologist, Th. Nägeli (*Der Wortschätz des Apostels Paulus*, 1905, 85 f.), whose evidence is all the more important as this is the only point where he admits that the linguistic phenomena are adverse to the Pauline authorship of any of the canonical epistles.

καλο-).* As compared with Paul, he employs the definite article less frequently; unlike the apostle, he uses μήποτε and δι' ἣν αἰτίαν (thrice), and eschews ἀντί, ἄρα, ἄχρι, διό, διότι, ἔμπροσθεν, ἔπειτα, ἔτι, ἰδού, παρά (accus.), σύν, and ὥστε. The difference in the use of the particles is one of the most decisive proofs of the difference between Paul and this Paulinist (cp. *CQR.*, 1903, 428 f., and Bonhöffer's *Epiktet und NT.* 201 f.).

(*b*) These characteristics of the writer's diction are corroborated by the qualities of his style. It is hardly too much to say that upon the whole, when the total reach and range of the epistles are taken into consideration, the comparative absence of rugged fervour, the smoother flow of words, and the heaping up of epithets, all point to another sign-manual than that of Paul. Even more than in Ephesians, the Pauline impetuousness and incisiveness are missing. "Le style des pastorales . . . est lent, monotone, pésant, diffus, décousu: en certaines parties, terne et incolore" (Jacquier, *INT.* i. 366). "The syntax is stiffer and more regular . . . the clauses are marshalled together, and there is a tendency to parallelism" (Lightfoot, *Biblical Essays*, p. 402). "Die rhetorischen Mängel von Eph. sind den Briefen fremd. Die Bilder sind correct. Doch zeigt sich in der Bilder mancherlei Umbiegung und Abstumpfung der paulinischen Theologie nach dem Nomistischen und Intellekualistischen. Ethik und Glaube treiben auseinander" (J. Albani, *ZWT.*, 1902, 57, in an essay on 'Die Bildersprache der Pastoralbriefe'). "On ne peut nier que le style de notres épîtres ait quelque chose de lâche et de diffus" (Bertrand, *op. cit.* 62). There are Pauline echoes, it is true, but anacoloutha and paronomasiæ were not specifically Pauline, and even these features fail to outweigh the impression made by the style as a whole.

(*c*) The force of these linguistic considerations cannot be turned by the assertion that Paul's style would vary in private letters; the pastorals are not private letters (see below), and in Philemon, the only extant example of such from Paul's pen, such traits do not appear. Nor can it be argued that in writing on questions of church-order and discipline he would necessarily adopt such a style, for in the Corinthian correspondence he deals with similar phenomena, and here again the treatment differs materially

* Καλός, which Paul uses only as a predicate or a neuter substantive, is employed repeatedly by this author as an attribute. Δεσπότης supplants the Pauline κύριος as a human term, and ἐπιφάνεια (see above, p. 79) replaces the Pauline παρουσία.

from that of the pastorals. Still less can we ascribe the peculiar phraseology to the fact that Paul quotes from the vocabulary of his opponents (Otto, *op. cit.* 8–9), or that he is now, in contrast to his former letters, dealing with the duties of a holy life instead of with controversial topics (Lock, *Paul the Master-Builder*, 117–121). If it is contended that some of these differences in vocabulary may be due to difference of subject-matter, this fails to explain the appearance of ἀρνεῖσθαι, ἀποτρέπεσθαι, βέβηλος, διαβεβαιοῦσθαι, ὑγιαίνειν, etc. etc. Besides, an examination of the topics handled in these pastorals, and of their method of treatment, reveals fresh proof that they belong to a sub-Pauline period, and that the ἅπαξ εὑρημένα (amounting to the large total of nearly 180) cannot fairly be attributed to such factors as change of amanuensis, lapse of time, fresh topics, literary versatility, or senile weakness (cp. *EBi.* 5087).

§ 5. *Object.*—The aim of the pastorals, which were composed (as Tertullian observes) to expound church affairs, is to enforce the continuity of apostolic doctrine and discipline against speculations which were threatening the deposit of the faith and the organisation of the churches. (*a*) These speculations (cp. E. F. Scott, *The Apologetic of the NT.*, 1907, 152 f.) were due to a blend of incipient Gnosticism and Judaism which is indistinct, partly because the writer's method (see p. 409) is to denounce vaguely and somewhat indiscriminately, partly because his desire of avoiding anachronisms led him to avoid being explicit about the details of error which had not risen till after Paul's death, and partly owing to our ignorance of the budding forms of Christian gnosticism.

The dualism and favouritism inherent in gnostic theosophy are explicitly opposed in Tit $2^{11f.}$ (*for all men*), as in 1 Ti 2^{1-4}, and the denial of the resurrection, combated in 2 Ti 2^{18}, was a gnostic inference from the dualism which opposed the flesh and the spirit. The 'myths and interminable genealogies' of 1 Ti 1^{4} are not wholly explained (see above, p. 406) by the haggadic embroidery of Jewish biographies, which would hardly be classed among 'novelties'; they must include some reference to the gnosticism which constructed out of ample mythological materials long series of æons or spiritual powers, arranged in pairs. Here and elsewhere gnostic traits are visible, some of which recall the Ophite gnostics who, starting from an antithesis between the supreme God and the creator, held that the fall of Adam (1 Ti 2^{13-14}) was really his emancipation from the latter's authority, and that therefore the serpent symbolised the γνῶσις which raised man to the life of the God who was above the creator. The place assigned to the serpent naturally varied, however. The Naassenes, one of the earliest branches of this movement, are said by Hippolytus to have been the first to assume the name 'gnostic' (ἐπεκάλεσαν ἑαυτοὺς γνωστικούς, φάσκοντες μόνοι τὰ βάθη γινώσκειν, cp. Apoc 2^{24}), and it is some of their views * which are controverted not only by the prophet John but by this Paulinist, viz. the prohibition of marriage, the assertion that the resurrection was spiritual, and the exploitation of myths. One recommendation of this Ophite hypothesis (Schmiedel, Lightfoot, etc.) is that it does justice to the Jewish substratum of the errorists, especially in Titus and 1 Tim. It is plain that the errorists in Crete include Jewish Christians (μάλιστα οἱ ἐκ τῆς περιτομῆς), † who are promulgating Ἰουδαϊκοὶ μῦθοι (*i.e.* probably haggadic traditions like those in Jubilees and the pseudo-Philonic *de biblicis antiquitatibus*) and ἐντολαὶ ἀνθρώπων, which (as the next words indicate) relate to ceremonial and ritual distinctions between clean and unclean foods. The Jewish character of these speculations, which attempted a fusion of the gospel with their own theosophy, is borne out by the contemptuous allusion (3^9) to silly discussions and γενεαλογίαι (part of the aforesaid μῦθοι with which they are grouped in 1 Ti 1^4) and wrangles about the Law (cp. Zenas ὁ νομικός in 3^{13}). There is no trace, however, of any direct attack upon the Pauline gospel or upon Paul himself; the ἡμᾶς of 3^{15} is too incidental to be pressed into any proof of such a local antagonism. The writer felt that Paul was essentially anti-gnostic, and that such tenets would have been repugnant to the man who had waged war upon the precursors of the movement at Colossæ. But his own practical bent prevents him from developing in reply Paul's special theory of gnosis as a special endowment superior to faith and mediated by the Spirit. His method is denunciation rather than argument or the presentation of some higher truth, and this is one of the reasons which leave the physiognomy of the errorists so largely in the shadow.‡ The exhaustive investigations on the precise character of these errorists (cp. *e.g.* Bourquin, *op. cit.* 55 f.; *EBi.* 5083–5084) have generally led to the negative conclusion that no single system of second-century gnosticism is before the writer's mind. He is not antagonising any one phase of contemporary heresy, allied to the Naassenes (Lightfoot, *Biblical Essays*, 411 f.), the Essenes (Credner, Mangold), the Valentinian Ophites (Lipsius, Pfleiderer), etc. He simply makes Paul predict, vaguely of course, the tendencies of an incipient syncretistic gnosticism (cp. von Dobschütz, *Urc.* 253 f.; Klöpper in *ZWT.*, 1904, 57 f.) which was

* "The first appearance of the Ophite heresy in connection with Christian doctrines can hardly be placed later than the latter part of the first century," Mansel, *Gnostic Heresies*, 1875, pp. 104 f. (cp. *ERE.* ix. 499–501).

† Possibly the connection of Titus with the controversy over circumcision (Gal $2^{1f.}$) may have been one of the reasons which led the author to compose the epistle from Paul to him.

‡ It also is one of the numerous and decisive proofs that Paul did not write the pastorals. "Such indiscriminate denunciations are certainly not what we should expect from a man like Paul, who was an uncommonly clear-headed dialectician, accustomed to draw fine distinctions, and whose penetration and ability to discover and display the vital point of difference between himself and an antagonist have never been surpassed. Those who ascribe to Paul the references to false teaching which occur in the pastoral epistles do him a serious injustice" (McGiffert, *AA.* 402).

evaporating the Pauline gospel. Traits of the physiognomy of these errorists or innovators can be found here and there in the Ophites and the Encratites, Cerinthus, Saturninus of Antioch, and even Marcion; more than once, *e.g.* in the references to the resurrection and to marriage, it is possible to detect distortions or exaggerations of Paul's own teaching, which this Paulinist wishes to correct. But he is writing a pastoral manifesto, and naturally he does not trouble to draw fine distinctions between the various phases of unsettling doctrine which confront the church.

(*b*) These traits of the author's controversial temper open up into further traces of his sub-Pauline environment. Thus the polemic against the legalists in 1 Ti $1^{9f.}$ is no longer that of Paul, but the outcome of the neo-catholic position which, now that the Pauline controversy was over, sought to retain the moral code of the law for the ethical needs of the church. The Paulinist who writes under his master's name pleads for the *usus legis politicus*. Certainly, he replies to those who uphold the validity of the law, we are well aware that the law, as you say, is an excellent thing—for ἄδικοι. The Law is a useful code of morals, in short, exactly as the rising spirit of the sub-apostolic period was accustomed to insist.

To note only two other minor points out of many. The conception of Christ as mediator (1 Ti 2^{5}) is closer to the standpoint of Hebrews than of Paul. Also, the language of 1 Ti 1^{15}, even more than of Eph 3^{8}, is really more natural in a Paulinist than in Paul himself; the motive of the whole section ($1^{12\text{-}17}$) is to throw the glorious gospel into relief against the unworthiness and weakness of its original agents—precisely as in Barn 5^{9} (cp. Wrede, *Das Messias-geheimnis*, 107 f.). From Paul the language of depreciation about himself would be as exaggerated as the description of privilege in 'the disciple whom Jesus loved' would have been from John himself. As a matter of fact, 1 Ti 1^{13} (ἀλλὰ ἠλεήθην, ὅτι ἀγνοῶν ἐποίησα ἐν ἀπιστίᾳ) is almost a verbal echo of Test. Jud. 19 (ἀλλ' ὁ θεὸς τῶν πατέρων μου ἠλέησέ με ὅτι ἐν ἀγνωσίᾳ ἐποίησα), where the context is a warning against ἡ φιλαργυρία (cp. 1 Ti $6^{9f.}$).

The sub-Pauline atmosphere is further felt unmistakably in the details of the ecclesiastical structure which is designed to oppose these errorists. The stage is less advanced than that of the Ignatian epistles, but the monarchical episcopate is beginning (cp. Knopf, *NZ.* 196 f.), and, even apart from this, the unwonted attention paid to the official organisation of the church marks a development from that freer use of spiritual gifts by the members which Paul never ignored. The χαρίσματα had by no means died out; but they are not congenial to this writer, and he deals with the situation very differently from his great master.

One crucial instance of this may be seen in the ascetic regulations for the organised register of *widows*. The χήρα, like the ἐπίσκοπος and the διάκονος, is forbidden, *e.g.*, to contract a second marriage. This antipathy to second marriages (cp. Jacoby's *NT Ethik*, 378 f.) is quite in keeping with sub-apostolic practice; Athenagoras called them 'respectable adultery'; but the ethical standpoint is almost as un-Pauline as the assumption that every ἐπίσκοπος must be married.

On this whole subject, see Hilgenfeld (*ZWT.*, 1886, 456 f.) and Schmiedel (*EBi.* 3113 f.), as against the view advocated by Hort (*Christian Ecclesia*, 1898, 189 f.) and Lindsay (*HJ.* i. 166 f., *Church and Ministry in the Early Centuries*[2], pp. 139 f.). The alternative explanation of 1 Ti 3^2 (δεῖ οὖν τὸν ἐπίσκοπον . . . εἶναι μιᾶς γυναικὸς ἄνδρα), as a prohibition of clerical celibacy ("To interpret the words as a prohibition of second marriage—the 'bigamy' of the canonists—is to go behind the text, and, indeed, involves an anachronism. The obvious meaning is that he to whom so responsible a charge as that of the ἐπισκοπή is committed, must be no untried, perhaps susceptible youth, without family ties and domestic duties, but a grave, elderly Christian, with a reputation and permanent residence in the community, a sober married man," *Edinburgh Review*, 1903, p. 63), is almost equally decisive against the Pauline authorship (cp. Paul's view of marriage in 1 Co 7^{17}).

The strict emphasis on ecclesiastical order tallies with the fact that the church has now behind her a body of religious truth which it is her business to enforce. Paul, too, had his definite dogmas, but this writer presents the nucleus of the creed in technical, crystallised phrases, partly (see p. 58) rhythmical, partly stereotyped in prose aphorisms (cp. A. Seeberg's *Der Katechismus der Urchristenheit*, 1903, pp. 172 f.), and the outcome is a piety nourished on 'good works,' with conceptions of reward, a good conscience and reputation, which are stated with more emphasis than Paul would have allowed. The later conception of πίστις as *fides quæ creditur* predominates in the pastorals, where the objective sense has overgrown the subjective, as in the homily of Judas ([3] and [20]).* Similarly (cp. Holtzmann, *op. cit.* 175 f.), δικαιοσύνη has no longer its technical Pauline content; it has become an ethical quality

* Cp. Gross, *der Begriff der πίστις im NT* (Spandow, 1875), pp. 7–9: "Could the age of a writing be determined simply from the peculiar usage of some such significant term, Judas must be described as the latest of the NT writings. . . . Even a church-father could hardly have expressed himself otherwise [than v.[3]], had he been speaking of the Christian confession of faith." See above, p. 346.

rather than a religious relation (cp. 2 Ti 2^{22}, 1 Ti 6^{11}). The conception of the Spirit has passed through a corresponding process. "L'inspiration de l'Esprit est escamotée au profit d'une orthodoxie ecclésiastique. Au lieu d'être un ferment de vie et de renouvellement, la doctrine de l'Esprit devient un moyen de défendre les formules du passé" (M. Goguel, *La notion Johannique de L'Esprit et ses antécédents historiques*, 1902, p. 69). The Spirit, as in 2 Peter and the Apocalypse of John, is essentially prophetic; its functions in the faith-mysticism of Paul have dropped into the background.

The trinity of the pastorals therefore corresponds to that of John's apocalypse, *i.e.* God, Jesus, and the (elect) angels. For the sub-Pauline tone of the references to angels, spirits, etc., cp. Everling, *die Paul. Angelologie und Dämonologie* (1888), 112–117, and M. Dibelius, *Die Geisterwelt im Glauben des Paulus* (1909), 175–180. The conception of God brings out his absoluteness, his unity, his awe, his eternal purpose of salvation, but not his fatherhood.

No possible change of circumstances or rise of fresh problems could have made Paul thus indifferent to such cardinal truths of his gospel as the fatherhood of God, the believing man's union with Jesus Christ, the power and witness of the Spirit, the spiritual resurrection from the death of sin, the freedom from the law, and reconciliation. Throughout his epistles we can see Paul already counteracting mischievous speculations and church-disorders, but his method is not that of the pastorals; his way of enforcing ethical requirements and the duties of organisation is characterised by a force of inspired intuition which differs from the shrewd attitude of this Paulinist. The latter handles the problems of his period with admirable sagacity, but not with the insight and creative vigour of an original thinker like Paul. He has the intuition of authority rather than the authority of intuition.

"The general impression one gets from the pastoral epistles is, that as a doctrine Christianity was now complete and could be taken for granted . . . there is nothing creative in the statement of it; and it is the combination of fulness and of something not unlike formalism that raises doubts as to the authorship. St. Paul was inspired, but the writer of these epistles is sometimes only orthodox. . . . St. Paul could no doubt have said all this [Tit $3^{4f.}$], but probably he would have said it otherwise, and not all at a time" (Denney, *The Death of Christ*, 1902, 202 f.).

To sum up. The three epistles are not private or even open letters to Timotheus or Titus, but general treatises (cp.

e.g. 1 Ti 2^{8} ἐν παντὶ τόπῳ) addressed to an age or a circle which was inclined to doubt the validity or to misconceive and misapply the principles of the Pauline gospel. It is incredible that the Ephesian church, much less Timotheus, should require solemn reminders of Paul's apostolate such as 2 Ti $1^{11f.}$ $2^{9f.}$, Tit 1^{3}, 1 Ti $1^{12f.}$; the real audience appears in the greetings of 2 Ti 4^{22} (ἡ χάρις μεθ' ὑμῶν), Tit 3^{15}, and 1 Ti 6^{21}. 1 Tim., especially, is a practical assertion and application of the Pauline standard, in the literary form of an address written by the apostle to his lieutenant, Timotheus. The author, wishing to convey Paul's protests against error and his ideals of church-life, naturally adopted the *mise en scène* of a temporary absence. The drawback was that, if Paul was soon to see his colleagues again (Tit 1^{5}, 1 Ti 1^{3}), there was no need of conveying such detailed injunctions (contrast 2 Jn ^{12}, 3 Jn $^{13-14}$). This imperfection, however, was inevitable. A further weakness lay in the form of the injunctions themselves, which were in many cases at once far too fundamental and elementary to have been required by men of the experience and age of Timotheus and Titus. As literally meant for them, the counsels often seem inappropriate, but when these men are viewed as typical figures of the later ἐπίσκοποι, the point of the regulations becomes plain;* they outline the qualifications of the church-officers in question, especially of the ἐπίσκοποι, though not so finely as the epistle of Ignatius to Polykarp. Their primary concern is for these officials as responsible (cp. Schmiedel, *EBi.* 3124, 3145 f.) for the maintenance of the Pauline tradition and teaching (2 Ti 1^{6} 2^{1-8}). Christianity is becoming consolidated into an organisation, with orthodox teaching embodied in a baptismal formula (2 Ti 2^{2-8} 4^{1}, 1 Ti 6^{12-16}), and the church is called upon to defend this with might and main. The author thus falls into line with the attitude taken up by the prophet John (Apoc $2^{1f.}$) and afterwards by Ignatius to the church of Ephesus; both of these teachers acknowledge heartily its alertness in detecting erroneous doctrine, and this Paulinist seeks to stimulate the same orthodox feeling by recalling the Pauline warrant for it. The same motives indeed

* "An Gemeinden wagte er angesichts der fertigen Sammlung der Gemeindebriefe des P. den Apostel nicht mehr schreiben zu lassen; ein neuer Gemeindebrief des P. hätte bereits schweres Misstrauen herausgefordert" (Jülicher, *INT.* 169). Thus Ephesians was probably a catholic pastoral originally, not addressed to Ephesus or any specific church (see above, p. 393).

vibrate through the pastorals as are audible in the farewell address to the presbyters of Ephesus (Ac 20^{17-35}), where the historian makes Paul predict perversions of the faith, both from outside and inside the church, and enforce on the officials the duty of supervision, besides appealing to his own example.

§ 6. *Authorship.*—The internal evidence does not justify any hypothesis of a plurality of authors. The pastorals in all likelihood came originally from one pen, but it is not possible to ascertain who the author was. Tradition has not preserved any clue to his personality, as was not unnatural, since his pious aim was to sink himself in the greater personality of the apostle whose spirit he sought to reproduce. That the epistles were composed by Timotheus and Titus themselves, on the basis of notes addressed to them by Paul (so Grau, *Entwickelungsgeschichte des neutest. Schriftthums*, ii. pp. 185 f., 208 f.), is more improbable than that Luke was their author or amanuensis (so, after Schott's *Isagoge*, pp. 324 f.; R. Scott, and J. D. James, *op cit.* pp. 154 f.; Laughlin).

The remarkable affinities between the pastorals and the Lucan writings are displayed by Holtzmann (*Pastoral-Briefe*. 92 f.), von Soden (*ThA*. 133–135), and R. Scott (*The Pauline Epistles*, 333–366). They have been used to prove either that Luke acted as Paul's secretary, or that he composed the epistles himself at a later period. It would be no argument against the latter that they differ from the Third gospel and Acts; a literary man of Luke's capacity must not be measured by one or two writings. But the parallels of thought and language need not mean more than a common milieu of Christian feeling during the sub-Pauline age in the Pauline circles of Asia Minor. It is, *e.g.*, not easy to understand why Luke should deliberately ignore Titus in his history and at the same time make him the central figure of a Pauline epistle.

The pastorals really present not the personality of their author, but a tendency of early Christianity (cp. Wrede's *Ueber Aufgabe und Methode der sogen. NT Theologie*, 1897, 357); like Barnabas, James, Judas, and 2 Peter, they do not yield materials for determining the cast of the writer's thought, and little more can fairly be deduced from their pages than the communal feeling which they voice and the general stage in the early Christian development which they mark. All we can say of their author is that he betrays wider affinities to Greek literature, *e.g.* to Plutarch (cp. J. Albani in *ZWT*., 1902, 40 f.), than Paul, and that there are traces of an acquaintance not only with second but with fourth Maccabees. This is not enough, however, to justify us in urging that he was a pagan by birth. The affinities with 1 Peter (cp. 1 Ti 2^{9-11} = 1 P 3^{1-6}, Tit 1^{5-19} = 1 P 5^{1-4}, Tit 3^{4-7} = 1 P 1^{3-5}, and 1 Ti 3^{16} = 1 P 3^{19}) are barely strong enough to prove that the writer was acquainted (so, *e.g.*, Bigg, Holtzmann, and Brückner's *Chron.* 57 f., 277 f.) with Peter's letter, although the circulation of the latter in Asia Minor renders this hypothesis *a priori* probable, if the pastorals are assigned to an Asiatic Paulinist instead of (so, *e.g.*, Baur, Schenkel, Holtzmann, Renan) to a Roman.

It is not necessary to spend words upon the reasons which justified him in composing these Pauline pseudepigrapha (cp. *HNT.* 597 f., 619 f.; *EBi.* 1324 f., 3126 f., 5095). The pastorals are a Christian form of *suasoriæ*, treatises or pamphlets in the form of letters (cp. p. 49), which were widely employed by jurists; they represent not only a natural extension of the letters and speeches, *e.g.*, in Luke's history, but a further and inoffensive development of the principle which sought to claim apostolic sanction for the expanding institutions and doctrines of the early church. It is curious that half a century later an Asiatic presbyter composed the *Acts of Paul and Thekla* from much the same motives, but was checked apparently for having illegitimately introduced ideas incompatible with the church's creed (cp. Rolffs in *HNA.* i. 366 f.).

Quodsi quæ Pauli perperam inscripta sunt, exemplum Theklæ ad licentiam mulierum docendi tinquendique defendunt, sciant in Asia presbyterum qui eam scripturam construxit quasi titulo Pauli de suo cumulans conuictum atque confessum id se amore Pauli fecisse loco decessisse (Tertullian, *de bapt.* 17). Jerome repeats the story (*de uir. inlust.* 7): Tertullianus refert presbyterum quendam in Asia σπουδαστὴν apostoli Pauli conuictum apud Johannem quod auctor esset libri at confessum se hoc Pauli amore fecisse loco excidisse. For our present purpose it is irrelevant to discuss the historicity or valuelessness (cp. Corssen, *GGA.*, 1904, pp. 719 f.) of the statement. In either case it illustrates a process of literary morphology within the second century, which might be abused but which was open to devout disciples of a master (cp. p. 40), a recognised method of literary impersonation which chose epistolary as well as historical expression in order to gain religious ends. "To a writer of this period, it would seem as legitimate an artifice to compose a letter as to compose a speech in the name of a great man whose sentiments it was desired to reproduce and record; the question which seems so important to us, whether the words and even the sentiments are the great man's own, or only his historian's, seems then hardly to have occurred either to writers or to readers" (Simcox, *Writers of the New Testament*, 38).

§ 7. *Period.*—The *terminus ad quem* is fixed by the evident familiarity of Ignatius and Polykarp with the pastorals (see below). The ambiguous data of Clem. Romanus might further be interpreted in such a way as either to throw the pastorals into the ninth decade of the first century, or into the first decade of the second. In general, a date between 90 and 115 (120) is usually fixed by modern critics, though some do not go down later than A.D. 100 (Kattenbusch, *Das Apost. Symbol,* ii. 344; so von Soden for 2 Tim.), while a few (*e.g.* Cone, *The Gospel and its earliest Interpretations,* 327 f.) still descend as far as A.D. 118–140. The internal evidence yields no fixed point for the date. The allusions to persecution and suffering are quite general, and it is no longer possible to find in the plural of *βασιλέων* (without any *τῶν*!) a water-mark of the age of the Antonines. The *terminus a quo* is the death of Paul, and probably the date of 1 Peter's composition. Between that and the limit already noted the period of the pastorals must lie.

Those who still are able to believe that Paul wrote these letters generally admit that they must have been composed during a missionary enterprise which is supposed to have followed Paul's release from the captivity of Ac 28^{30}. The chief exceptions are W. E. Bowen, V. Bartlet, Lisco (*Vincula Sanctorum,* 1900), Bruston, and Laughlin, whose conjectural schemes are mutually destructive and exegetically untenable; the utter impossibility of dating them within the period covered by Acts is stated clearly by Hatch, Holtzmann (*op. cit.* 15–27), Bourquin (pp. 10–25), Bertrand (23–47), and Renan (iii. pp. xxviii–xlviii).

The denial of the Pauline authorship is not bound up with the rejection of the tradition about the release; the two positions may be held separately, as, *e.g.*, by Harnack. For attempts to rehabilitate the hypothesis of the release, see especially Steinmetz (*Der zweite röm. Gefangenschaft des Apostels Paulus,* 1897), Belser (*TQ.*, 1894, 40 f.), Hesse (*op. cit.* 244 f.), Frey (*die zweimalige röm. Gefangenschaft u. das Todesjahr des Ap. Paulus,* 1900), and Resch, *Der Paulinismus* (*TU.* xii. 493 f., journey to Spain adumbrated in Ac 1^8 = Ro 15^{19}). Macpherson (*AJT.*, 1900, 23–48), like Otto and Knoke, giving up the hypothesis (cp. Pfister in *ZNW.*, 1913, pp. 216–221, for a disproof of this hypothesis) of a second imprisonment, holds to the authenticity of the pastorals.

The outline of Paul's career as given in Acts, even when ample allowance is made for the *lacunæ* of Luke's narrative, does not leave any place for the composition of these pastorals.

Their style and aim render it impracticable to disperse them over a term of years, during which Paul was writing his other letters. They must be taken as a group, and in this event the only alternative to a sub-Pauline origin is to date them subsequent to a supposed release of Paul from his imprisoment in Rome. The evidence for this release, followed by a tour in the Western Mediterranean, is not adequate, however; such as it is (*Actus Petri cum Simone*, Murat. Canon),* it is probably due to an imaginative expansion of Ro $15^{24. 28}$. The devout fancy of the later church believed that because Paul proposed such a visit to Spain, he must have carried it out; but no such tradition lingered in Spain itself, and the express statements of Ac $20^{25. 38}$, together with the significant silence of Clemens Romanus, imply that the first-century tradition knew of no return to Asia Minor. The Pauline pastorals themselves say nothing of a visit to Spain prior to the return to the East, or of a proposed tour to Spain (see, however, Dubowy's essay in Bardenhewer's *Bibl. Studien*, xix. 3).

The rhetorical passage in Clem. Rom. 5^{6-7} describes how Paul, *κῆρυξ γενόμενος ἔν τε τῇ ἀνατολῇ καὶ ἐν τῇ δύσει, τὸ γενναῖον τῆς πίστεως αὐτοῦ κλέος ἔλαβεν. δικαιοσύνην διδάξας ὅλον τὸν κόσμον καὶ ἐπὶ τὸ τέρμα τῆς δύσεως ἐλθὼν καὶ μαρτυρήσας ἐπὶ τῶν ἡγουμένων, οὕτως ἀπηλλάγη τοῦ κόσμου.* The writer is portraying the sweep of Paul's career from Jerusalem to Rome (Ro 15^{19}), where his sun had ended its course. To a Roman *τὸ τέρμα τῆς δύσεως* would probably denote the Western Mediterranean, but Clement was writing for Eastern readers and adopting their standpoint. Thus *ἀνατολῆς* and *δύσιν* are used of Syria and Rome respectively in Ignat. *Rom.* 2. This interpretation is corroborated by the close collocation of *ἐλθὼν* and *μαρτυρήσας κτλ.* in Clement (implying that Paul bore his testimony at *τὸ τέρμα τῆς δύσεως*), and clinched by the context which dates the death of Paul and Peter prior to the Neronic persecution. Otherwise, it might be taken as an inference, like the later allusions, from Ro 15^{24} (cp. Moffatt, *EBi.* 5088; Schmiedel, *EBi.* 4599–4600; Workman, *Persecution in the Early Church*, 1906, 36 f.).

§ 8. *Traces in early Christian literature.*—The coincidences of thought and expression between Barnabas and the pastorals are too general to prove literary dependence either way. Phrases like *μέλλων κρίνειν ζῶντας καὶ νεκροὺς* (vii = 2 Ti 4^{1}), *φανεροῦσθαι ἐν σαρκί* (vi, xii, cp. 1 Ti 3^{16}) and *ἐλπὶς ζωῆς* (i = Tit 1^{2} 3^{7}) probably belonged to 'the common atmosphere of the church' (Holtzmann, von Soden, Bernard), liturgical or catechetical, and the same consideration would fairly cover v.^{6} = 2 Ti 1^{10}, xix = 1 Ti 5^{17}, although the manifestation of Christ's grace in choos-

* For the *Acta Pauli*, see Rolffs in *HNA*. ii. 368 f., and Lake in *DAC*. i. 32 f.

ing apostles *ὄντας ὑπὲρ πᾶσαν ἁμαρτίαν ἀνομωτέρους* (v.^{9}) is a striking parallel to 1 Ti 1^{13}. Not much stress could be put upon the occurrence in Ignatius of some terms characteristic of the pastorals (*e.g.* *αἰχμαλωτίζειν* of errorists, *ἀναζωπυρήσαντες*, *ἑτεροδιδασκαλεῖν*, *καλοδιδασκαλία*, *κατάστημα*, and *πραϋπάθεια*), did such phenomena stand alone, but further traces of the epistles being familiar to Ignatius (cp. Inge in *NTA.* 71–73) occur in *Magn.* xi. etc. (Jesus Christ our hope) = 1 Ti 1^{1}, *Polyk.* iv. 3 = 1 Ti 6^{2}, *Polyk.* vi. 2 (*ἀρέσκετε ᾧ στρατεύεσθε*) = 2 Ti 2^{4}, *Magn.* viii. 1 = 1 Ti 4^{7}, Tit 1^{14} 3^{9}, possibly also in the use of *ἀναψύξαι* (*Eph.* ii. 1, cp. *Smyrn.* x. 2 = 2 Ti 1^{16}), *τέλος δὲ ἀγάπη* (*Eph.* xiv. 1 = 1 Ti 1^{5}), and *οἰκονομία* (*Eph.* xx. 1 = 1 Ti 1^{4}, cp. *Polyk.* vi. = Tit 1^{7}). The case of Clem. Rom. is not quite so clear. A phrase like *lifting holy hands* (xxix. 1, cp. 1 Ti 2^{8}) is too current, as Lightfoot shows, to count as evidence of literary filiation, while *βασιλεῦ τῶν αἰώνων* (lxi. 2, cp. Apoc 15^{8} א C, 1 Ti 1^{17}) goes back to Jewish liturgical terminology; but these would gain significance if other parallels like ii. 7 (*ἕτοιμοι εἰς πᾶν ἔργον ἀγαθόν*, cp. xxiv. 4) = Tit 3^{1} (*πρὸς πᾶν ἔργον ἀγαθὸν ἑτοίμους εἶναι*, cp. 2 Ti 2^{21} 3^{17}), vii. 3 (*καὶ ἴδωμεν τί καλὸν καὶ τί τερπνὸν καὶ τί προσδεκτὸν ἐνώπιον τοῦ ποιήσαντος ἡμᾶς*) = 1 Ti 2^{8} (*τοῦτο καλὸν καὶ ἀπόδεκτον ἐνώπιον τοῦ σωτῆρος ἡμῶν θεοῦ*), xxvii. 1–2 (*ταύτῃ οὖν τῇ ἐλπίδι προσδεδέσθωσιν αἱ ψυχαὶ ἡμῶν τῷ πιστῷ ἐν ταῖς ἐπαγγελίαις . . . οὐδὲν γὰρ ἀδύνατον παρὰ τῷ θεῷ εἰ μὴ τὸ ψεύσασθαι*) = Tit 1^{2} (*ἐπ᾽ ἐλπίδι ζωῆς αἰωνίου, ἣν ἐπηγγείλατο ὁ ἀψευδὴς θεός*), xlv. 7 (*ἐν καθαρᾷ συνειδήσει λατρευόντων*) = 2 Ti 1^{3} (*λατρεύω ἐν καθαρᾷ συνειδήσει*), and liv. 3 = 1 Ti 3^{13} (*περιποιεῖσθαι* in connection with the ministry), were allowed to indicate some literary relationship.* That they do so, is suggested further by a series of coincidences, including ii. 1 (*τοῖς ἐφοδίοις τοῦ Θεοῦ ἀρκούμενοι*) = 1 Ti 6^{8}, and xxxii. 3 = 2 Ti 1^{9}, Tit 3^{5-7}. In this event, unless we attribute all these phenomena to a common milieu of church feeling, a literary dependence must be postulated on the side of the pastorals, or of Clement. The former is not impossible. It is erroneous to assume, in the case

* The possibility of a common source, in the shape of some catechetical manual (A. J. Carlyle in *NTA.* pp. 50–51) might explain the correspondence between i. 3 and Tit 2^{4-5} (where *οἰκουργούς* has a v.l. *οἰκουρούς*). *Πίστις ἀγαθή* occurs in xxvi. 1 = Tit 2^{10}, but in different senses, and a common atmosphere might account for the frequent use of *εὐσέβεια* in both, and allied ecclesiastical conceptions, as, *e.g.*, i. 3, xliv. 4 = 1 Ti 5^{17}, xlii. 4 = 1 Ti 3^{10}.

of a NT writing and an extra-canonical document, that the literary filiation must *ipso facto* be in favour of the former as prior; this is a misconception due to the surreptitious introduction of the canon-idea into the criticism of early Christian literature (p. 10). If an examination of the pastorals in other aspects points to the first decade of the second century as their period, there can be no objection to the view that Clem. Rom. is used by their author just as by Polykarp. The deep and wide influence speedily won by Clem. Rom. is otherwise shown by its incorporation in the Muratorian Canon. But the hypothesis of the use of the pastorals in Clement has also a fair case, which would involve their composition not much later than A.D. 80. The latter date is not impossible, particularly if the presence of later glosses and accretions is admitted.

The most assured traces of the pastorals in early Christian literature occur in Polykarp's epistle; for although Titus cannot be shown to have been before Polykarp's mind (vi. $3 = 2^{14}$), both 1 Tim. (iv. $1 = 6^{7.10}$, iv. $3 = 5^{5}$, v. $2 = 3^{8}$, viii. $1 = 1^{1}$, xi. $2 = 3^{5}$, xii. $3 = 2^{1}\ 4^{15}$) and 2 Tim. (v. $2 = 2^{11}$, ix. $2 = 4^{10}$, xi. $4 = 2^{25}$, xii. $1 = 1^{5}$) are evidently familiar to him, as indeed is generally acknowledged. There are only two or three allusions in Justin Martyr's *Dialogue* (vii. 7 and xxxv. $3 = 1$ Ti 4^{1}, better still xlvii. $15 =$ Tit 3^{4}); but, as the second century advances, the evidences for the circulation of the pastorals multiply on all sides, from Theophilus of Antioch (*ad Autolyk.*, quoting as θεῖος λόγος Tit $3^{1.5}$, 1 Ti 2^{2}) and Hegesippus (if Eus. *H. E.* iii. 32 may be taken as conveying his exact words) in the East, to Athenagoras of Athens, the churches of Lyons and Vienne (Eus. *H. E.* v. 1–3), and 2 Clement in the West. 2 Tim. seems to be presupposed in the Acts of Paul, as is 1 Tim. in the *Apost. Constitutions* (cp. Harnack in *TU.* iii. 5, 49 f.); and all three are authoritative to Irenæus, Tertullian, and Clem. Alex. They appear in the Muratorian Canon as private letters ('pro affectu et dilectione'), yet like Philemon honoured and accepted by the church catholic. Cp., generally, Zahn's *GK.* i. 634 f.; Steinmetz, *Die zweite röm. Gefangenschaft des Apostels Paulus*, (1897) 104 f.

According to Tertullian (*adv. Marc.* v. 21), Marcion excluded them from his canon on the ground that they were private letters, and therefore unsuitable for purposes of general edification (contrast the protest of the Muratorian Canon). But, as his admission of Philemon proves, this was probably no more than a pretext; his real reason was either that he suspected their authenticity, or that the epistles struck at conceptions which were allied to his own, and that no process of excision, such as he practised in the case, *e.g.*, of Galatians and Romans, could adapt these pastorals to his own use. The gnostic errorists of the second century felt the same objection to them. Ὑπὸ ταύτης ἐλεγχόμενοι τῆς φωνῆς (1 Ti $6^{20f.}$) οἱ ἀπὸ τῶν αἱρέσεων τὰς πρὸς Τιμόθεον ἀθετοῦσιν ἐπιστολάς (Clem. Alex. *Strom.* ii. 11. 52). Jerome, in his preface to Titus, notes that Basilides and other teachers, as well as Marcion, rejected the Pauline pastorals together with Hebrews, as savouring too much of the OT, although Tatian, 'Encratitarum patriarches,' made an exception in favour of Titus, and the Valentinians seem to have read the epistles to Timotheus.

(C) *HEBREWS.*

LITERATURE.—(*a*) Editions[1]—Erasmus (*Paraphrasis*, 1521); J. B. Pomeranus (*Annotationes*, Nuremberg, 1525 f.); Cajetan, *Litteralis expositio* (Rome, 1529); Bullinger (1532); Oecolampadius (1534); Calvin (1549)*; Beza (1582); N. Hemming (1586); J. J. Grynæus (Basle, 1586); J. A. Delfini (Rome, 1587); de Ribeira (Salamanca, 1598); Salmeron (Cologne, 1602); R. Rollock, *Analysis Logica* (Edinbnrgh, 1605); F. Balduinus (*Disputationes*, 1608); de Tena (Toledo, 1611); Lushington (1646); Alting (1652); Lawson (1662); I. Owen (London, 1668–1674); Sebastian Schmidt (1680, third edition, 1722); Wittichen's *Investigatio* (1691); S. S. Nemethus (1695); Braunius (1705); Rambach (1742); Pierce and Benson (Lat. ed. by Michaelis, Halle, 1747); Carpzow, *Sacræ exercitationes in St. Pauli epist. ad Hebræos* (1750)*; Sykes (1755); J. A. Cramer (1757); Baumgarten (Halle, 1763); Moldenhawen (1762–1770, Leipzig); G. T. Zachariä (Göttingen, 1771); S. F. N. Morus (1781); Abresch, *Paraphrasis et annot.* (1786 f.); F. W. Hezel (1795); J. Ernesti, *Prælectiones Academicæ* (1795); G. C. Storr (Stuttgart, 1809); Walckenauer, *Selecta e Scholis* (1817); D. Schulz, *der Brief an die Heb.*, *Einleitung*, *Uebersetzung. und Anmerkungen* (Breslau, 1818)*; A. M'Lean (London, 1820); C. F. Boehme (1825)*; S. T. Blomfield (London, 1826–7); F. Bleek (1828–40)*; C. T. Kuinoel (1831); H. E. G. Paulus (1833); H. Klee's *Auslegung* (Mayence, 1833); C. W. Stein (1838); R. Stier (1842); Lombard (1843); de Wette[2] (1847); Thiersch (Marburg, 1848); Stengel's *Erklärung* (1849); Ebrard (1850, Eng. tr. 1853); Tholuck[3] (1850); S. H. Turner (New York, 1855); A. S. Patterson (Edinburgh, 1856); Delitzsch[3] (1857, Eng. tr. 1868)*; Moses Stuart[4] (1860); E. Reuss (1860 and 1878); A. Maier (Freiburg, 1861); C. Schweighauser's *Paraphrase* (Paris, 1862); John Brown (Edin. 1862); Alford[2] (1862); A. Bisping (1863); Kluge (*Auslegung u. Lehrbegriff*, 1863); Lünemann[3] (1867, Eng. tr. of fourth ed. 1882); W. Lindsay (Edinburgh, 1867); Ripley (Boston, 1862); J. H. Kurtz (1869); Ewald, *Sendschreiben an die Heb.* (1870); J. B. M'Caul (London, 1871); L. Harms (1871); Hofmann* (1873); Wörner (1876); Moll (in Lange's *Bibel-Werk*[3], 1877);

---

[1] For the Latin commentaries, from the sixth century onwards, cp. E. Riggenbach's "Die ältesten lateinischen Kommentare zum Heb." (1907, in Zahn's *Forschungen zur Gesch. d. neutest. Kanons*, viii. 1).

Biesenthal (*Epistola Pauli ad Heb. cum rabbinico commentario*, Leipzig, 1878); L. Zill (Mayence, 1879); Kay (*Speaker's Commentary*, 1881); Panek (1882); A. B. Davidson (1882)*; Angus (Schaff's *Comm.* 1882); O. Holtzheuer (Berlin, 1883); Keil (Leipzig, 1885); J. Barmby (*Pulpit Comm.*[2] 1887); F. Rendall (1888, London); Schlatter (1888); Kähler[2] (1890); C. J. Vaughan (London, 1890); W. F. Moulton (Ellicott's *Comm.* n. d.); Farrar (*CGT.* 1893); A. Schäfer (Münster, 1893); Padovani (Paris, 1897); Weiss[6] (— Meyer, 1897)*; Kübel (1898); von Soden[3] (*HC.* 1899); C. Huyghe (Gand, 1901); Cone (1901, New York); Westcott[3] (1903)*; F. Blass, *Brief an die Hebräer, Text mit Angabe der Rhythmen* (1903); J. van Andel, *De Brief aan de Hebräer* (1906); A. S. Peake (*CB.* n. d.)*; Hollmann (*SNT.*[2] 1907); E. J. Goodspeed (New York, 1908); Dods (*EGT.* 1910)*; E. C. Wickham (*WC.* 1910); A. Seeberg (Leipzig, 1912); Riggenbach (*ZK.* 1913)*; Windisch (*HBNT.* 1913); A. Nairne (*CGT.* 1918).

(*b*) Studies—(i.) on the religious ideas:—D. Dickson (1635); J. D. Michaelis[2] (*Erklärung*, 1780); C. G. Tittmann (*de notione sacerdotis in Ep. ad Heb.* 1783); Planck (*Negatur philos. platonicæ vestigia exstare in epist. ad Heb.*, Göttingen, 1810); de Wette (*Theol. Jahrb.*, 1822, 1–51); A. Gügler, *Privat-Vorträge* (Sarmenstorf, 1837); C. C. Meyer, *Essai sur la doctrine de l'ép. aux H.* (1845); van den Ham, *Doctrina ep. ad H.* (1847); C. C. Moll, *Christologia in ep. ad Heb. proposita* (1854–9, Halle);[1] Ritschl, *Altkatholischen Kirche*[2] (pp. 159 f.); J. A. Haldane (1860); Riehm, *der Lehrbegriff des Hebräerbriefs*[2] (1867)*; Baur's *Vorlesungen über NT-liche Theologie* (pp. 230 f.); H. W. Williams (*Exposition*, 1872); Baur, *Church History of First Three Centuries* (Eng. tr. 1878, i. 114–121); J. E. Field, *The Apost. Liturgy and the Epist. to Heb.* (1882); T. C. Edwards (*Expositor's Bible*, 1888); Reuss (*NTTh.* ii. 265 f.); Klostermann, *zur Theorie der bibl. Weissagung u. z. Charakteristik des Hebräerbriefs* (1889); Cone, *The Gospel and its Earliest Interpret.* (1893) 233–249; Ménégoz, *Théologie de l'ép. aux H.* (1894)*; Farrar, *Early Days of Christianity* (bk. iii.); Holtzmann, *NTTh.* ii. 261–308; Wendt (*ZWT.*, 1895, 157–160); A. B. Bruce (in Hastings' *DB.* ii. 327–338, and *The Epistle to the Hebrews*, 1899)*; Milligan, *Theology of the Epistle to the Hebrews* (1899)*; G. H. Gilbert, *First Interpreters of Jesus* (1901), 259–297; G. Hoennicke (*ZWT.*, 1902, 24–40); G. Bailey, *Leading Ideas of Ep. to Hebrews* (1907); Bruston (*RTQR.*, 1907, 39–66); A. Nairne, *The Epistle of Priesthood* (1913); H. L. MacNeill, *Christology of the Epistle to the Hebrews* (1914)*; G. Vos (*Princeton Theol. Review*, 1915, 587 f., 1916, 1–61); Moffatt (*ET.* xxviii–xxix, 'Christology of Hebrews'). (ii.) general:—W. C. L. Ziegler's *Einleitung* (Göttingen, 1791); A. Réville, *De ep. ad Heb. authentia* (Geneva, 1817); Seyffarth, *De indole peculiari* . . . (1821); F. Vidal, *De l'authenticité de l'ép. aux Heb.* (Geneva, 1829); Laharpe, *Essai critique sur l'auth.* (Toulouse, 1832); Grossmann, *De philos. Jud. sacræ vestigiis in ep. ad Heb. conspicuis*

---

[1] Superior, on the whole, to Zimmermann's *La personne et l'œuvre de Christ d'après l'ép. aux H.* (Strassburg, 1858); Sarrus' *Jésus Christ, d'après l'auteur de l'ép. aux H.* (Strassburg, 1861), and Capillery's *Christ et son œuvre d'après l'ép. aux H.* (Toulouse, 1866); but not to G. E. Steuer's *die Lehre des H. vom Hohenpriestenthum Christi* (Berlin, 1865).

(Paris, 1833); Duke of Manchester (*Horæ Hebraicæ*, 1835; on 1^1–4^{11}); K. R. Köstlin, *Theol. Jahrb.* (1853) 410f., (1854) 366f., 465f.; W. Tait, *Meditationes Hebraicæ* (London, 1855); Wieseler's *Untersuchung* (1861); Guers, *Étude sur l'épître aux H.* (Paris, 1862); Schneckenburger's *Beiträge* (1861–1862); Renan, iv. (ch. ix.); W. Grimm (*ZWT.*, 1870, pp. 19f.)*; G. Steward, *Argument of the Epistle to the Hebrews* (Edinburgh, 1872); Hilgenfeld (*ZWT.*, 1873, 1–54); G. Meyer (*ESR.* vi. 113f.); Overbeck (*Zur Gesch. der Kanons*, pp. 1f., 1880); von Soden (*JPT.*, 1884, pp. 435f., 627f.)*; W. T. Bullock (Smith's *DB.* i. 771–777); Reuss, *NTTh.* ii. 238–261; Godet (*Exp.*[3] vii. 241–265); G. G. Findlay, *Epistles of Paul the Apostle* (1895), pp. 257–287; H. B. Ayles, *Destination, Date, and Authorship of the Ep. to the Hebrews* (1899); Moffatt (*HNT.* 344f.); Jacquier (Vigouroux' *DB.* iii. 515–551); W. Wrede, *Das literarische Rätsel des Hebräerbriefs* (1906)*; E. Burggaller (*ZNW.*, 1908, 110–131, critique of Wrede); J. R. Willis (Hastings' *DB.*, 1909, 335–340); B. Weiss, *Der Hebräerbrief in zeitgeschichtlicher Beleuchtung* (*TU.* xxxv. 3, 1910); R. Perdelwitz (*ZNW.*, 1910, 59–78, 105–123; cp. M. Jones, *Exp.*[8] xii. 426f.); V. Monod, *De titulo epistulæ vulgo ad Hebræos inscriptæ* (Montauban, 1910); Burggaller (*TR.*, 1910, 369f., 409f.); F. S. Marsh (*DAC.* i. pp. 534f.); J. W. Slot, *De letterkundige vorm v. den Brief aan de Hebräer* (Groningen, 1912); J. Quentel (*RB.*, 1912, 50f.). (iii.) on the authorship:—C. A. Clewberg (*De auctore ep. ad Heb.* 1753); C. F. Schmid (*Super orig. epist. ad Heb.* 1765); G. Bratt (*De argumento et auctore*, . . . 1806); Baumgarten-Crusius (*De origine epistolæ ad Heb. conjecturæ*, Jena, 1829); F. C. Gelpe (*Vindiciae orig. paul. ep. ad Heb.* 1832); C. Jundt (*Examen critique sur l'auteur de l'ép. aux Hébreux*, Strassburg, 1834); H. Monod (*L'épître aux Héb. n'est pas de S. Paul*, Strassburg, 1838); E. G. Parrot (*Appréciation des preuves pour et contre l'orig. paul.*, Toulouse, 1852); J. Kroecher (*De auctore Ep. ad Hebræos*, Jena, 1872); G. H. Rouse (*Thinker*, 1895, 210–213); A. Wright, *Some NT Problems* (1898), pp. 331f.; Harnack (*ZNW.*, 1900, 16–41)*; F. M. Schiele (*AJT.*, 1905, 290–308); K. Endelmann (*NKZ.*, 1910, 102–126); F. Dibelius (*Der Verfasser d. Hebräerbriefes, Eine Untersuchung zur Geschichte des Urchristentums*, Strassburg, 1911). (iv.) on the destination:—E. M. Röth, *Epist. vulgo ad Hebræos inscriptam ad . . . christianos genere gentiles et quidem ad Ephesios datam esse demonstrare conatur* (Frankfurt, 1836)*; M. J. Mack (*über die ursprunglichen Leser d. Brief an die Hebräer*, Tübingen, 1836); G. C. A. Lünemann (*De lit. quæ ad Heb. inscribuntur primis lectoribus*, Göttingen, 1853); B. Heigl (*Verfasser und Adresse des Briefes an die Hebräer*, 1905)*.

§ 1. *Contents and outline.*—(Cp. Thien, *RB.*, 1902, 74–86). The writer opens, in a stately paragraph, by describing the superiority of Jesus Christ, as God's Son, to the angels (1^1–2^{18});[1]

[1] The so-called logion (Resch, *Paulinismus*, 454f.), quoted four times by Epiphanius (ὁ λαλῶν ἐν τοῖς προφήταις, ἰδοὺ πάρειμι), is simply taken from Is 52^6 (LXX). It is equally precarious to connect (so Resch, *Paulinismus*, 456–457) 4^{15} with the logion preserved by Origen (*In Matt.* tom. xiii. 2): καὶ Ἰησοῦς γοῦν φησιν· διὰ τοὺς ἀσθενοῦντας ἠσθένουν καὶ διὰ τοὺς πεινῶντας ἐπείνων καὶ διὰ τοὺς διψῶντας ἐδίψων.

lordship over the world to come is the prerogative of Jesus alone. He is superior also, as God's Son, to Moses (3^{1}–4^{13}), and assures his people of a perfect Rest in the world to come. Finally, as God's Son, he is superior to Aaron and the Levitical priesthood ($4^{14f.}$), as the high priest of the good things to come (9^{11}), *after the order of Melchizedek.* Here the writer grapples with the matter which is really at issue between himself and his friends (cp. A. Schmidt, *Heb. iv. 14–v. 10: Eine exegetische Studie*, 1900). Reproaching them for their immaturity and backwardness in the theology of their faith (5^{11}–6^{20}),* he proceeds to instruct them in the higher doctrine of Christ's heavenly priesthood. This, with all its far-reaching consequences for religion, is the heart and height of the author's message. Since he conceives religion under the aspect of a covenant or διαθήκη, which must be determined by a priesthood of some sort, the introduction of the final and perfect covenant implies the revelation of a corresponding priesthood in the person of Jesus Christ the Son of God, which is held to be only the fulfilment of the Melchizedek sacerdotal order; and, as the latter was prior to the Levitical, the supersession of the Levitical order by the eternal, heavenly priesthood of God's Son, Jesus Christ, is quite natural, even apart from the fact that a change of priesthood involved a change of the law or the religious economy (7). The climax or crown of the argument† is now reached (8^{1}). Whereas the divine revelation in Judaism had been given through angels (2^{2}), established by Moses ($3^{8f.}$) and perpetuated by the Aaronic priesthood ($5^{1f.}$), Jesus is superior to all, especially to the third as the embodiment of the two former. The superiority of Christ's priestly ministry over that of the Levitical order, as a means of access to, and fellowship with, God, is the fulfilment‡ of Jeremiah's famous oracle ($8^{6f.}$) which promised such a valid and absolute covenant as Christ has inaugurated at his ascension; and (9^{1-14}) it is a superiority § (a διαφορωτέρα λειτουργία) which is exemplified in the sanctuary, the offering, and the consequent

* Cp. J. Albani's essay (*ZWT.*, 1904, 86–93) on 'Heb 5^{11}–6^{8}, ein Wort zur Verfasserschaft des Apollos.'

† For this use of κεφάλαιον, see F. Field's *Notes on Tr. of NT.* (1899), pp. 227 f., and Musonius' κεφάλαιον γάμου (*Musonius*, ed. Hense, pp. 67 f.).

‡ This makes it all the more remarkable that, unlike Paul (1 Co $11^{23f.}$), he never alludes to Christ's words upon the διαθήκη at the Last Supper.

§ For the depreciatory nuance in 9^{11}, cp. Field (*op. cit.* p. 229).

fellowship of the Son's ministry for men. His sacrifice of himself for them, being spiritual, is final (9^{15}–10^{18}); it attains the end vainly sought by previous sacrifices, and therefore supersedes the latter. Having elucidated this central truth, the writer advances to make it the basis of an earnest appeal for religious confidence and steadfastness ($10^{19f.}$). With a brief warning against the danger of carelessness and apostasy (10^{26-31}), he rallies his suffering readers by inciting them to be worthy of their past faith ($10^{32f.}$). This leads him to kindle their imagination and conscience by a magnificent roll-call of the sorely tried heroes and heroines of Israel who had believed and pleased God (11), closing with the example of Christ as the leader and perfecter of faith in this world (12^{1-3}). The example of the Son's suffering and loyalty proves that trouble is a mark of the Father's education of men, and therefore that it should be borne patiently, for the sake of its uses ($12^{4f.}$), all the more so that the privileges thus opened to the faith of the new covenant involve a fearful penalty for those who reject them. A choice must be made between the two dispensations, and the author rounds off his exhortation with a moving antithesis between the terrors and punishment of the one and the eternal hope and reverent confidence of the other (12^{18-29}). The thought of the break with the old order that is needful for any adhesion to true Christianity follows the writer even into his postscript, where, after a short table of ethical duties (13^{1-7}), the mention of the former teachers, from whom his readers had received their faith, prompts him (in a digression) to emphasise the need of loyalty to such principles (13^{8-16}) and to their present faithful leaders (13^{17}). A request for prayer (13^{18}) and a word of prayer (13^{19-21}), followed by some personal greetings, end the epistle (13^{22-25}).

§ 2. *Characteristics and style.*—A closer examination of the writing reveals traces of Greek rhetorical prose, but not, strictly speaking, in its arrangement upon the lines of a *προοίμιον πρὸς εὔνοιαν* (1^{1}–4^{13}) and a *πρόθεσις*, followed by a *διήγησις πρὸς πιθανότητα* (4^{14}–6^{20}), an *ἀπόδειξις πρὸς πειθώ* (7^{1}–10^{18}), and an *ἐπίλογος* (10^{19}–13^{21}). None of these terms exactly corresponds to the relative sections of the epistle (Wrede, p. 37). Where the literary skill of the author comes out is in the deft adjustment of the argumentative to the hortatory sections (Dibelius, pp. 6 f.). The superiority (cp. *Diat.* § 2998, xxiv) of Jesus Christ to all angels first suggests the enhanced danger of neglecting the revelation of God in his

Son (2^{1-4}, contrast 1^{2} and 2^{2}). Then the mention of σωτηρία (2^{3}) opens out into a paragraph upon the objects of that salvation (men, not angels, 2^{16}), and their moral unity through suffering with Christ as the strong and sympathetic high priest of humanity. Here the leading note of the epistle is struck by anticipation (2^{17} 3^{1} *wherefore . . . consider Jesus the apostle and high priest of our confession*). Before pursuing this theme, however, the author resumes the idea of Christ as the ἀπόστολος or herald and agent of God's final salvation (1^{1} 2^{3}), superior as God's Son to Moses, who was only God's servant (3^{1-6}); this passes into a reiterated warning against unbelief ($3^{7f.\ 12}$ $4^{1-11f.}$, cp. $2^{1f.}$), after which the author reverts to encouragement ($4^{14f.}$), in view of Jesus (God's Son) as *the great high priest* of Christians, considerate and sympathetic (as in 2^{14-18}). Once this theme is under way ($7^{1f.}$), its progress is hardly interrupted. The gathered momentum of the argument finally breaks out ($10^{19f.}$) into the long appeal with which the writing ends, an appeal directly addressed to the situation of the readers. The second personal pronoun is more frequently used ($10^{32f.}$ $12^{3f.}$ $13^{1f.}$, cp. $3^{1.\ 12-13}$ $5^{12f.}$), though not to the exclusion of the first ($10^{19f.\ 39}$ 11^{40}–12^{2} 12^{9-10}, cp. 12^{25}). Still, the redeeming sacrifice of Christ continues to reappear ($10^{19f.\ 29}$ 12^{24} $13^{10f.\ 20f.}$), even amid the practical counsels of the epilogue. Hebrews has a sense of the centre; there is a constant return to the permanent and vital religion of Jesus Christ, amid all the arguments on ancient ritual and history.

On the strophic character of the earlier part (1^{4-14} 2^{1}–3^{2} 3^{3}–4^{13} 4^{14}–5^{10} 5^{11}–6^{8} 6^{9-20} 7^{1}–8^{2} 8^{3-13} 9^{1-12} 9^{13-22} 9^{23}–10^{7} 10^{8-25} 10^{26-39}), see H. J. Cladder in *Zeitschrift für kath. Theologie* (1905), pp. 1–27, 500–524; the rhythmical prose of the epistle is discussed by Thackeray (*JTS.* vi. 232 f.) in relation to the Wisdom of Solomon, and by Blass in *SK.*, 1902, 420–461, and in *Die Rhythmen der asianischen und röm. Kunstprosa* (1905), pp. 41–42, 78 f., 87 f., where attempts are made to find rhythm right and left (cp. above, p. 57).

The style corresponds to these phenomena. It is literary and even classical in parts. "Si Paul est un dialecticien incomparable, le rédacteur de l'épître aux Hébreux a plutôt les qualités d'un orateur, riche et profond assurément, mais qui ne néglige pas non plus les affets du style et la recherche du beau language" (Bovon, *NTTh.* ii. 391). Thus—to note only one or two salient points—the predilection for the perfect tense may sometimes be explained from the author's desire to emphasise the permanent and contemporary value of some remote action (as, *e.g.*, in 7^{6-14} 8^{13}, see Westcott's note on 7^{6}); sometimes it is natural enough, as may be gathered from the context (*e.g.* 10^{14}), but occasionally the perfect seems used, neither for the present nor as the perfect of recorded action (cp. Abbott's *Diat.* 2758), but either for the sake of literary variety, to break a line of aorists ($11^{17.28}$), or (1^{13}, cp. 1^{5}) as a result of the movement which afterwards, in Byzantine Greek, substituted the perfect often for the aorist (Burton, *Moods and Tenses*, 88; Jannaris, *Hist. Gk. Gramm.* 439). Besides the rare use of the aor. ptc. in 2^{10}, and the sparing use of the definite article, other traces of Greek culture * are visible in the use of *μέν . . . δέ* (seven times, *e.g.*, in ch. 7; cp. Norden's *Das antike Kunstprosa*, i. 25–26), in the oratorical imperatives of 7^{4} (cp. *θεωρεῖτε*, 4 Mac 14^{13}), in the assonances and composite phrases which dignify his style, and in the application of *αὐτός* to God the speaker (13^{6}), as in the Pythagorean school's phrase *αὐτὸς ἔφα* (*thus spake the Master*, cp. Ac 20^{35}). The epistle shows generally a striving after rhetorical effect; the author is not a litterateur, but, for all his religious aims, he is now and then a conscious stylist. There is also a notable predilection for technical philosophical terms, or for words and phrases which were specially employed by earlier philosophical writers from Plato and Aristotle to Philo, *e.g.* *αἰσθητήριον*, *δημιουργός* (of God), *θέλησις*, *μετριοπαθεῖν*, *τιμωρία*, and *ὑπόδειγμα* (cp. A. R. Eagar, *Hermathena*, xi. 263–287, G. H. Gilbert, *AJT.*, 1910, 521 f., and H. T. Andrews, *Exp.*[8] xiv. 348 f.). Such idiosyncrasies of his style and diction are thrown into relief against those of Paul's (cp. Rendall's *Hebrews*, Appendix, pp. 26 f.). Unlike Paul, he uses *ἐάνπερ*, *καθ' ὅσον*, *ὅθεν*, *ὡς ἔπος εἰπεῖν*, and studiously avoids *ἄρα οὖν*, *εἴ τις*, *εἴγε*, *εἶτε*, *μὴ γένοιτο*, *μήπως*, *μηκέτι*, *πάντοτε*, *τί οὖν*, etc. (see, further, below). His grammatical use of *κοινωνεῖν* and *κρατεῖν* also differs from that of Paul, and other terms, like *τελειόω*, are employed in different senses. The last-named word is one indication of the distinctive mental

* There are, of course, traces of vernacular Greek as well as of idiomatic Greek, but it is surely rash to argue that the sole occurrence of the optative mood in 13^{21} (*καταρτίσαι*) "is presumptive proof that an Alexandrian did not write this epistle, as it is not likely that the use of this word in but one instance would have satisfied his fine Greek taste" (Harmon, *JBL.*, Dec. 1886, p. 10). Robinson Crusoe, as Huxley once put it, did not feel obliged to infer, from the single footstep in the sand, that the man who made the impression possessed only one leg.

cast of the *autor ad Hebræos*. He employs and adopts the Aristotelian idea of the τέλος or final end, with its τελείωσις or sequence of growth, in order to exhibit the historical evolution of Christianity from Judaism, the development of Christian doctrine from its ἀρχή to its τελειότης, the perfecting of Christ himself through suffering (2^{10} $5^{8f.}$), and the growth of the Christian after Christ in the discipline and experience of life. At the same time, he combines this with the more congenial view, derived by Alexandrian Judaism from Plato, of the contrast between the transitory shows or shadows of this world and the genuine, ideal realities of the heavenly sphere.* This is one of the genuinely Philonic antitheses in the epistle. The shadow is opposed to the substance, the earthly to the heavenly, the present to the future, the ἀντίτυπα (9^{24}) to the ἀληθινά. As the sensuous and passing is thus set against the spiritual and absolute, there is a tendency to identify the latter with the future sphere. The ethical feeling of the writer occasionally breaks through this speculative and futuristic view (cp. *e.g.* $4^{3.\ 10}$ 6^{5}); but, owing to his philosophical category of the antithesis between the phenomenal and the archetypal realities in heaven, the epistle seldom does more than hover "on the verge of that deeper truth for which its theological scheme allows no room—that the world of the eternal is already ours, in so far as we have entered into the spirit of Christ" (E. F. Scott, *The Apologetic of the NT*, 1907, p. 206). Hebrews thus represents a less developed stage in the application of Alexandrian Judaism to Christianity than the Fourth gospel, while at the same time it works out the Logos-predicates with regard to the person of Christ independently of Paul or even of the *autor ad Ephesios*.

The world in which this author lived is revealed further by his knowledge of Philo (see above, p. 27), and also by his use of the Wisdom of Solomon

---

* "Actual Judaism is merely the copy, the shadow, the reflection, of an archetypal religion standing above it, from which such primary types as the high priest Melchizedek project into it. What Christianity is in its true essence, what distinguishes it from Judaism, is ideally and essentially present in those archetypes" (Baur, *Church History*, i. 117). "The author of Hebrews . . . says that Christianity is eternal, just as it shall be everlasting, and that the true heavenly things of which it consists thrust themselves forward on to this bank and shoal of time and took cosmical embodiment, in order to suggest their coming, everlasting manifestation. The whole apostolic exegesis of the OT is but an application of the principle of finding the end in the beginning" (A. B. Davidson, *Biblical and Literary Essays*, 317).

(cp. Rendall, *Theology of Hebrew Christians*, 53–58), whose terminology is often applied to the definitely Christian conception of the epistle, as is evident from several passages, *e.g.* (besides those noted on p. 26), 5^{9} (=Wisd 4^{13} of Enoch), 6^{6} (=Wisd 6^{9}), $8^{2f.}$ (=Wisd 9^{8}, Apoc. Bar 4^{5}), 11^{3} (=Wisd 9^{1} 13^{7}), 11^{5} (=Wisd $4^{10f.\ 13f.}$), 11^{6} (=Wisd 1^{1-2}), 11^{28} (=Wisd 18^{9}), 11^{29} (=Wisd $10^{18f.}$ 19^{4-8}), 12^{14} (=Wisd 6^{19}), 12^{17} (=Wisd $12^{10.\ 20}$), and 13^{7} (=Wisd 2^{17}). In this respect, the writer resembled Paul (see above, p. 26), but his employment of these Hellenistic Jewish categories is much more thoroughgoing. For his use (see pp. 25–26) of Sirach, compare 2^{5}=Sir 17^{17} (4 Es. $8^{21f.}$ etc.), 2^{14}=Sir 14^{18} (17^{31}), 2^{16}=Sir 4^{11} (ἐπιλαμβ. of σοφία), 4^{13}=Sir $17^{19f.}$ (23^{19}), 11^{5}=Sir 44^{16} (49^{14}), 11^{17}=Sir 44^{20} (1 Mac 2^{52}), 12^{12}=Sir 25^{23}, and 13^{16}=Sir 32^{4}.

These data converge on the conclusion that Paul had nothing to do with the epistle; the style and religious characteristics put his direct authorship out of the question, and even the mediating hypotheses which associate Apollos or Philip or Luke with him are shattered upon the non-Pauline cast of speculation which determines the theology. But it is superfluous to labour this point. As Professor Saintsbury puts it, in dealing with another equally obvious result of literary criticism, "one need not take sledge-hammers to doors that are open."

The hypothesis of Paul's authorship, once ardently defended by editors like Forster (*Apostolical Authority of the Ep. to the Hebrews*), Moses Stuart, Wordsworth, and Hofmann, still lingers in one or two quarters, especially among Roman Catholic scholars (cp. Jacquier, i. 486), who feel bound by the luckless decision of the Council of Trent. Heigl's recent essay is the most thoroughgoing presentation of this view. It would be ungenerous even to mention the hypothesis nowadays, except in order to throw the idiosyncrasies of the *auctor ad Hebræos* into relief, and to determine approximately his relation to the earlier Pauline standpoint.

§ 3. *Structure.*—Hebrews is, like James, a homily in epistolary form; but while the latter possesses an introduction and no conclusion, Heb. has a conclusion, without any introductory greeting. This is the problem which meets the literary critic on the threshold. Two solutions have been proposed. Either (*a*) the original paragraph of greeting has been omitted, deliberately or accidentally, or (*b*) the writing never possessed any.

(*a*) An accident was always possible (cp. p. 52) to the opening of a document, whether treatise or letter, and this hypothesis explains the phenomenon of He 1^{1} (so, *e.g.*, Barth, V. Monod) at any rate less unsatisfactorily than the conjectures * that the original address was omitted because it contained severe

* "Unter allem Vorbehalt wage ich die Vermutung, dass—wenn nicht gar eine Deckadresse gebraucht worden war—die Adresse vorsichtshalber fortge-

blame (Kurtz), or the name of some church too insignificant for the inclusion of the writing as a semi-catholic epistle in the Canon. Harnack's conjecture, that it was suppressed for the further reason that a prejudice existed against women as composers of scripture, falls with his ingenious idea that Prisca was the authoress (see p. 441). On the hypothesis that Hebrews was written by some non-apostolic early Christian like Barnabas or Apollos, it might be possible to explain the deletion of the address as due to canonical interests (so, *e.g.*, Overbeck, *op. cit.* 9–18). But some trace of the original would surely have survived; besides, had it been felt necessary (as Overbeck pleads) to claim the writing for Paul, an alteration would have been more natural than a total excision (cp. Zahn's *GK.* i. 300 f.).

(*b*) Unless an accident is supposed to have happened (as, *e.g.*, in the case of 3 Mac.), the likelihood, therefore, is that Hebrews never had any address. 1 Jn 1^{1-4} is hardly a parallel, for there the epistolary aim is definitely expressed at the close of the opening sentence (*καὶ ταῦτα γράφομεν ἡμεῖς ἵνα ἡ χαρὰ ἡμῶν ᾖ πεπληρωμένη*), whereas the word *write* never occurs in Hebrews, and it is not until 3^{1} that the author definitely addresses his readers, not until $5^{11f.}$ that he puts himself into any direct relation to them. Even Barnabas and 2 Clement get sooner into touch with their readers. The former at least has a short, vague greeting, and intrinsically He 1^{1} might have followed a greeting like Ja 1^{1}, Barn 1^{1}, or Eph 1^{1-2}. Still, there is no decisive reason why the writing should not originally have begun as it does in its canonical form, except the natural hesitation whether an admission of this kind, which attributes an unexampled opening to the epistle, does not conflict with the data of the conclusion. The latter, taken together with the sonorous, impersonal opening, raises the further problem, whether Hebrews was originally an epistle or a treatise (cp. M'Neile, *Interpreter*, 1913, 156–160).

Down to 12^{29} and indeed to 13^{17}, there is nothing which might not have been originally spoken by a preacher to his audience.* The contents are certainly not impersonal, as if the writer were merely addressing an ideal public (Wrede) or writing a treatise for Christendom, but they are not strictly epistolary. The author never names his audience directly, but passages like 5^{11}–6^{12} $10^{32f.}$ $12^{4f.}$ 13^{1-9} show that he was intimately acquainted with their local situation and religious

lassen worden ist, vielleicht weil man die Uebermittlung Heiden anvertrauen musste und denen nicht sagen wollte, welche Art von 'Rede' sie beförderten, vielleicht, weil dem Briefschreiber aller Verkehr nach aussen untersagt war und er die Aufmerksamkeit nicht durch zu deutliche Angaben an der Spitze des Briefs erregen durfte" (Julicher, *Einl.* 132). Diogenes Laertius' history of the philosophers also begins without any address, and yet (cp. 3^{47} and 10^{29}) it must have had some address or *Epistola dedicatoria* originally prefixed to it.

* "Beginning with a rhetorical introduction, it resembles in general a letter as little as the oration *pro lege Manilia*. As far as the doxology in 13^{21} it is entirely a rhetorical production" (Hug, *Einl.* ii. 421).

needs, and it is impossible to explain away such allusions as rhetorical abstractions. The *we* and *you* may be the speech of a Christian addressing a congregation,—some parts of Hebrews in all likelihood represent homilies or the substance of homilies written out,*—but the evangelist or preacher knew whom he was counselling. Hebrews is not a διατριβή in the form of an epistle, as 4 Maccabees is in the form of an address. While it probably represents a homily or sermon written out (like 2 Clement) by its author, its epistolary form is neither (Deissmann, *Bible Studies*, 49–50) a piece of literary fiction nor added by a later hand (Overbeck, Lipsius in *GGA.*, 1881, 359 f.). The author had his church or community in view all along, and the difficulty of explaining why Hebrews lacks any address is not sufficient to compel a recourse to any theory (so, *e.g.*, Reuss) which would treat the epistolary conclusion ($13^{18(22)-25}$) as irrelevant to the main purpose of the writing (see Appendix O).

Perdelwitz, who regards even 13^{19} as spoken by the preacher to his audience, takes 13^{22-25} as a postscript added *breui manu* by some bearer of the λόγος παρακλήσεως who wrote out a copy and forwarded it to some Italian church (in Rome ?); but neither the style nor the contents bear out this hypothesis. If a bearer or scribe could append such a note, why not the author himself? G. A. Simcox (*ET.* x. 430–432), taking 13 as an ἐπιστολὴ συστατική (to which alone, not to 1–12, the words of 13^{22} apply) appended to the homily, argues from the double reference to the ἡγούμενοι in $13^{7.\ 17}$ that it contains in whole or part two commendatory notes, perhaps from Paul or some other apostle. "If the work in the oldest form known had one or more letters of commendation (or excerpts from such) attached to it, tradition would ascribe the whole to the higher authority." But 13^{22} (καὶ γὰρ διὰ βραχέων ἐπέστειλα ὑμῖν) refers back to passages like 5^{11} (περὶ οὗ πολὺς ἡμῖν ὁ λόγος κτλ.) and 11^{32} (καὶ τί ἔτι λέγω; ἐπιλείψει με γὰρ διηγούμενον ὁ χρόνος κτλ.). To judge from 1 P 5^{12} and Barn 1^5 (ἐσπούδασα κατὰ μικρὸν ὑμῖν πέμπειν, cp. 1^8 ὑποδείξω ὀλίγα), it seems to have been almost a conventional mode of expression in early Christian epistolography.

§ 4. *Traces in later literature.*—(Leipoldt, *GK.* § 29.) The first traces of Hebrews in the early Christian literature occur in Clem. Rom., who quotes tacitly (and with his usual freedom) from 1^{3-4} in xxxiv. 2–5, citing also Ps 104^4 as in He 1^7. Similarly 2^{18} 3^1 are echoed in xxxiv. 1, and 12^1 in xix. 2, whilst xxi. 9 (ἐρευνητὴς γάρ ἐστιν ἐννοιῶν καὶ ἐνθυμήσεων· οὗ ἡ πνοὴ αὐτοῦ ἐν ἡμῖν ἐστίν, καὶ ὅταν θέλῃ ἀνελεῖ αὐτήν) recalls 4^{12} (cp. xxvii. 1 = 10^{23} 11^{11}, and xxvii. 2 = 6^{18}). Other coincidences may go back either to an independent use of the LXX (*e.g.* xvii. 5 = 3^2, xliii. 1 = 3^5) or to some common apocryphal

---

* Cp. Clemen (*Exp.*[5] iii. 392 f.) for 3–4, one of the sections which might have been originally a λόγος παρακλήσεως (Ac 4^{36} 13^{15}) or part of a synagogal address (Perdelwitz; M. Jones, *Exp.*[8] xii. 426 f.).

source (*e.g.* xvii. 1 = $11^{37.\ 39}$), just as the common order of LXX citations occasionally may indicate an independent use of some messianic *florilegium*; but there can be no hesitation in admitting that reminiscences of Hebrews occur in the later Roman writing. Almost equally clear is the use of the epistle in Barnabas* (cp. Bartlet's careful statement in *NTA*. 6–11). Possibly, if one may judge from *Magn*. 3^{2} and *Philad*. 9^{1}, Ignatius also 'had the epistle to the Hebrews in his mind' (Lgft.); but the evidence does not raise this above the level of probability, while the occurrence of *sempiternus pontifex dei filius* (He 6^{20} 7^{3}) in 12^{2} and of *εὐλαβεία* in 6^{3} (cp. He 12^{28}, Ps 2^{11}) hardly suffices to prove that Polykarp knew the epistle, any more than Did. 4^{1} can be regarded as an echo of He 13^{7}. Upon the other hand, 2 Clem. (i. 6 = 12^{1}, xi. 6 = 10^{23}, xvi. 4 = 13^{18}, xx. 2 = 10^{32-37}) appears to presuppose it, and, as might be expected in a Roman writing, Hermas evidently was acquainted with it; cp. *e.g. Vis*. II. iii. 2 (*τὸ μὴ ἀποστῆναι* or *ἀπὸ Θεοῦ ζῶντος* = 3^{12}, also III. vii. 2), *Sim*. I. i.–ii. (= 11^{13-16} 13^{14}),† IX. ii. 2 (= $10^{19f.}$), etc. (cp. Zahn's ed. pp. 439–452). Justin Martyr also seems to have known it (cp. Engelhardt's *das Christenthum Just*. pp. 367 f.); he calls Jesus 'the Son and Apostle of God' (*Apol*. i. 12, 63, cp. 3^{1}).‡ Like 1 Peter and James, it was omitted in Marcion's Canon and the Muratorian, but it was read by Clem. Alex.,—who indeed quotes 'the blessed presbyter' (Pantænus?) as believing in its Pauline authorship,—Irenæus possibly, and Tertullian, besides Pinytus, the Cretan bishop of Gnossus (Eus. *H. E*. iv. 23. 8 = He 5^{12-14}), and Theophilus of Antioch. The circulation of it as an edifying treatise, however, was wider than its recognition as a canonical scripture, which was slow and fitful, especially in the West. It was eventually included in the Syrian canon of Paul's epistles (Gwilliam, *ET*. iii. 154–156; Salmon, *INT*. 605–607; W. Bauer, *Der Apostolos der Syrer*, 24 f.), and accepted even at Rome as Pauline and therefore canonical (or, as canonical and therefore Pauline). The early fluctuation of opinion and the hesitation about its right to such a place are reflected in the remark of Amphilochius of Ikonium, the Cappadocian scholar (end of fourth century), *τινὲς δέ φασιν τὴν πρὸς Ἑβραίους νόθον | οὐκ εὖ λέγοντες· γνησία γὰρ ἡ χάρις*.

It was in the course of its canonisation that the epistle probably received its present title, to correspond with those of the Pauline epistles alongside of which it was now ranked. We can only conjecture whether or not the addition of such a title

* For the materials, cp. van Veldhuizen, *de Brief van Barnabas* (1901, Gröningen), pp. 74 f., 104 f. J. Weiss's scepticism (*der Barnabasbrief kritisch untersucht*, 1888, pp. 117 f.) is unjustified.

† "One might almost say that He 13^{14} is the text of this discourse in *Sim*. I." So Spitta (*Urc*. ii. 413), whose peculiar theory of the latter book obliges him, however, to explain away these coincidences.

‡ Cp. also *Dial*. 33 (Christ defined as 'he who, according to the order of Melchizedek, is king of Salem and eternal priest of the Most High') = He 5^{9-10}. There are even traces in the Jewish rabbis of the second century of a polemic against the Christian use of the Melchizedek-legend (cp. Bacher's *Agada d. Tannaiten*[2], i. 259).

implied a theory of its Pauline authorship (or origin). In any case πρὸς Ἑβραίους (see p. 448) could not have been the original title of an epistle which presupposes a definite community (*e.g.* 13^{23}). No author, who wrote with such a specific community in view, could have described his work as addressed 'to Jewish (Palestinian) Christians' in general, as if it were an encyclical. Furthermore, the title is not even accurate, since the readers were not Jewish Christians. On the other hand, it is not known to have borne any other title. The idea (so from Semler, Ziegler, and Storr to Schleiermacher, Hilgenfeld, Köstlin, and Hofmann) that it was the epistle *ad Alexandrinos* included in the Muratorian Canon ('fertur etiam ad Laodicenses, alia ad Alexandrinos, Pauli nomine finctæ ad hæresem Marcionis') is untenable, whatever view be taken of the words *ad hæresem* (=πρὸς τὴν αἵρεσιν). If the latter mean 'against, or bearing on, M.'s heresy,' Hebrews shows no traces of so direct a purpose. If they mean 'in favour of M.,' as is more probable, they describe Hebrews even less aptly; whatever that epistle is, it is out of line with Marcion's views of the OT religion. Besides, Hebrews (in its extant form) is not composed in Paul's name.

Ἑβραῖοι does not necessarily involve Palestinian origin (cp. 2 Co 11^{22}, Phil 3^{5}), but, as used by Christians of the second century, it would very naturally denote Jewish Christians of Palestine (cp. *e.g.* Eus. *H. E.* iv. 5, vi. 14). Ποῦ δὲ οὖσιν ἐπέστελλεν; Chrysostom asks in the preface to his commentary, and his answer is, ἐμοὶ δοκεῖ ἐν Ἱεροσολύμοις καὶ Παλαιστίνῃ. This interpretation, however, is derived from the title itself, not from any independent tradition, and the title itself was, like πρὸς Ἐφεσίους, an editorial inaccuracy which originated at the time of the homily's incorporation in the Pauline canon. The fact that, on emerging from its local obscurity into the canon, it received so vague a title, shows that by this time, *i.e.* about half a century after its composition, the circumstances of its origin had been entirely lost sight of. In the absence of any other evidence, the early use of Hebrews by Clement of Rome may be allowed to tell in favour of its Roman destination. From Rome it would circulate to Alexandria. But even the scholars of the latter church had no idea of its origin or audience. So far as the authorship is concerned, the writing was evidently anonymous by the time that it rose into the light of the canon, though it is not so certain as Zahn (*Einl.* § 45) contends, that Irenæus and Hippolytus knew it as such. Had it been originally connected *e.g.* with the name either of Paul or of Barnabas, however, it is impossible to explain how the one tradition could have risen out of the other. The scholars of the Alexandrian church, where it first gained a canonical position, felt obvious difficulties in the Pauline authorship which was bound up with its claim to canonicity. Pantænus (cp. Eus. *H. E.* vi. 14. 4) is said by Clement to have explained the absence of

Paul's name by conjecturing that the apostle of the Gentiles considerately (διὰ μετριότητα) refrained from naming himself in an epistle addressed to Jewish Christians. Clement himself met the more serious difficulty of the style by supposing that Luke translated Paul into Greek; the omission of Paul's name he prefers to ascribe to tact on the part of the latter, in view of the suspicions felt by Jewish Christians (Eus. *H. E.* vi. 14. 2 f.). Origen also felt the discrepancy between the style of Paul and the style of Hebrews, but he contented himself with referring it to some unknown amanuensis (Eus. *H. E.* vi. 25. 11).

§ 5. *The Pauline hypothesis.*—The earliest hint of a Pauline authorship occurs towards the close of the second century, when Clement of Alexandria, who quotes it often as Pauline, reports a saying of "the blessed presbyter," probably Pantænus, to the effect that "since the Lord, being the apostle of the Almighty, was sent to the Hebrews, Paul, as if sent to the Gentiles, did not subscribe himself as an apostle of the Hebrews, owing to his modesty; but subscribed himself, out of reverence to the Lord, and since he wrote to the Hebrews out of his abundance, merely the herald and apostle of the Gentiles" (Eus. *H. E.* vi. 14). This belief in Paul's authorship was natural, as Paul was the supreme letter-writer of the early church; but it was far from being unanimous even in Alexandria, where the beginning of the third century reveals divergent traditions attributing it to Paul, Clement of Rome, or Luke; while Origen, sensitive to the stylistic features of the epistle, refuses to connect it with Paul except by the medium of a Greek editor or (Ro 16^{22}) amanuensis. Τίς δὲ ὁ γράψας τὴν ἐπιστολήν, τὸ μὲν ἀληθὲς θεὸς οἶδεν. The Pauline authorship was denied also by many in the Roman church (Eus. *H. E.* iii. 3, vi. 20),* till ecclesiastical considerations during the fourth century brought it into line with the Eastern church, where the epistle had been widely received as Pauline.

The very church in which the first traces of the epistle occur was therefore opposed to Paul's authorship, and later research has vindicated this position. For one thing, as Luther and Calvin clearly saw, Paul could never have described his religious position in the terms of 2^3; his religious message and experience were mediated by no human agent (Gal 1^{1-12}), and no explanation of 2^3 can avail to reconcile the strong language of the apostle with this later writer's admission of his indebtedness to apostolic preachers (cp. Bleek i. 285–295). Furthermore, the style and the vocabulary are alike decisive

* As the v.l. τοῖς δεσμοῖς μου in 10^{34} was apparently known to Clem. Alex., it must have been an early correction of the text in view of the Pauline hypothesis.

The careful syntax, purged of anacolouthа, the regular succession of periods, and the elaborate rhetorical structure of the whole writing, show no trace of Paul's rugged, broken style. We might contrast the *auctor ad Hebræos* and Paul, in fact, as Johnson contrasted Dryden and Pope. Paul occasionally uses allegories and types; but these are the characteristic atmosphere of Hebrews, which also prefers (except in 2^{6}), in its OT citations (see Bleek, i. 338 f., and Büchel, *SK.*, 1906, 506–591), the formula *the holy Spirit saith* or *God saith* to the Pauline methods of introducing such quotations (γέγραπται, λέγει ἡ γραφή, etc.). Both form and formula differentiate the two writers. Their conceptions of faith, the Law, and the Spirit are equally dissimilar, and these reach their height in the view of Christ's priesthood, which has no analogy in the early Christian literature until the Fourth gospel (cp. Jn 17^{19}). It follows that the vocabulary is distinctive, marked by groups of words ending in -ίζειν (ἀνακαιν., ἐνυβρ., καταρτ., μερ., προσοχθ., πρίζειν, τυμπανίζειν) and -σις (*e.g.* ἀθέτη., ἄθλη., αἶνε., ἀπόλαυ., μετάθε., τελειώ., ὑπόστασις), and by the absence of Pauline phrases like Χριστὸς Ἰησοῦς. The author's interest, *e.g.*, in Leviticalism as a poor and temporary proviso for the religious τελείωσις of Christianity, leads him to view the result of Christ's redeeming death as sanctifying (ἁγιάζειν), not as justifying (δικαιοῦν); and such radical differences of thought partly account for the differences in terminology between him and his great predecessor. In short, as Origen candidly allowed, "the style of the epistle to the Hebrews has not the apostle's roughness of utterance (τὸ ἐν λόγῳ ἰδιωτικόν); . . . that it is more Hellenic in its composition (συνθέσει τῆς λέξεως), will be admitted by every one who is able to discern differences of style. . . . I should say that the thoughts are the apostle's, while the style and diction belong to some one who wrote down what the apostle said, and thus, as it were, gave an exposition of (σχολιογραφήσαντος) his master's utterances" (Eus. *H. E.* vi. 25).

Even this secondary Paulinism of Hebrews is indefensible, however, although the Alexandrian critics' hypothesis has been variously worked out by later scholars, who regard Hebrews as (*a*) pseudonymous, (*b*) a translation, or (*c*) a joint-production. None of these theories is satisfactory.

(*a*) The older view (cp. Schwegler, *NZ.* ii. 304 f.), that Hebrews was written by a Paulinist who wished to pass off his work as Paul's, has been revived in a modified form by Wrede (so Wendland). He argues that the anonymous author, on coming towards the end of his treatise, suddenly determined to throw it into the shape of an epistle written by Paul in prison; hence the allusions in $13^{22f.}$ which are a cento of Pauline phrases (especially from Philippians). But, apart from other reasons (cp. Knopf in *TLZ.*, 1906, 168 f.; Burggaller, pp. 111 f.), it is difficult to see why he did not insert more allusions in the body of the writing; the bare references at the close are too ambiguous and incidental to serve the purpose of putting the epistle under Paul's ægis. Had a Paulinist desired to create a situation for the epistle in Paul's lifetime (like that, *e.g.*, of 1 Co 16^{10}, Philem ^{22}, Ph $2^{19.\ 23f.}$), he would have written more simply, as, *e.g.*, the author of 1 Tim. (1^{3}). 'Freilich bleibt uns manches undurchsichtig; aber das ist doch nur der klarste Beweis, dass dasselbe nicht, wie man annehmen wollte, erst später angefugt ist, da sonst der Interpolator doch wohl nur allgemein verständliche Dinge in ihm angebracht hätte' (Weiss, *TU.* xxxv. 3. 109).

(*b*) The hypothesis (J. Hallet in Wolf's *Curæ Philologicæ*, iv. 806–837; J. D. Michaelis, Biesenthal) that the epistle represents the translation by Luke or some other disciple of Paul's original Hebrew, arose from the discrepancies of style which were early felt between it and the Pauline epistles (so from Clement of Alex. to Thomas Aquinas), but it never had any basis in the internal evidence of the epistle, and may be dismissed as a curiosity of criticism. No Hebrew (Aramaic) original has ever been heard of in connection with the epistle. The whole argument swings from the language of the LXX (see especially 1^{6} 10^{5}) as opposed to the Hebrew text; the special Gk. sense of *διαθήκη*=testament ($9^{15\text{-}20}$)* was unknown to Hebrew usage; and it would be difficult in a version to account, not only for the rhetorical finish, but also for paronomasiæ and verbal assonances like those of 1^{1} $5^{8.\ 14}$ 8^{7} $10^{29.\ 39}$ 13^{14} etc.

(*c*) The joint-authorship theory, in its later forms, tends more and more to refer the ideas as well as the diction to the Paulinist who co-operated with Paul, and may therefore be discussed conveniently under the question of the authorship.

§ 6. *Authorship.*—(*a*) The combination of Paul and Luke, suggested by Clem. Alex. (cp. Eus. *H. E.* vi. 14. 2–3, *καὶ τὴν πρὸς Ἑβραίους δὲ ἐπιστολὴν Παύλου μὲν εἶναί φησι, γεγράφθαι δὲ Ἑβραίους ἑβραϊκῇ φωνῇ, Λουκᾶν δὲ φιλοτίμως αὐτὴν μεθερμηνεύσαντα ἐκδοῦναι τοῖς Ἕλλησιν, ὅθεν τὸν αὐτὸν χρῶτα εὑρίσκεσθαι κατὰ τὴν ἑρμηνείαν ταύτης τε τῆς ἐπιστολῆς καὶ τῶν πράξεων*, also vi. 25), has attracted many scholars from Eusebius (*H. E.* iii. 38) to Calvin, Hug, Ebrard, Delitzsch, Field, Zill, and Huyghe. Some (*e.g.* Grotius, and recently W. M. Lewis, *Biblical World*, August 1898, April 1899, with A. R. Eagar, *Exp.*[6] x. 74–80, 110–123, 'The authorship of the Epistle to the Hebrews') attribute practically the entire authorship to him, mainly† on the score of the undoubted affinities of language and style between Hebrews and the Lucan writings. These affinities present a curious problem, but they are quite inadequate to prove that Luke wrote all three works.

Some (*e.g.* *ἄγκυρα* 6^{19}=Ac $27^{29\text{-}30}$, *ἀναδέχομαι* 11^{17}=Ac 28^{7}, *ἀναθεώρεω* 13^{7} =Ac 17^{23}, *ἀνώτερον* 10^{8}=Lk 14^{10}, *ἀπαλλάσσω* 2^{15}=Lk 12^{58}, *ἀπογράφεσθαι* 12^{23}=Lk $2^{1\text{-}5}$, *βοηθεία* 4^{16}=Ac 27^{17}, *ἱλάσκεσθαι* 2^{17}=Lk 18^{13}, *καταφεύγω* 6^{18}=

* This interpretation of *διαθήκη* (which, as Calvin saw, was itself fatal to the translation theory) is preferable on many counts to the more usual one of *covenant*. "In the papyri, from the end of cent. iv. B.C. down to the Byzantine period, the word denotes *testament* and that alone, in many scores of documents. We possess a veritable Somerset House on a small scale in our papyrus collections, and there is no other word than *διαθήκη* used" (Moulton in *Cambridge Biblical Essays*, 1909, p. 497).

† "He certainly could not have been the author. The striking contrast between his account of the agony in the garden and that given in the Epistle is sufficient to settle that question" (A. B. Bruce, *DB*. ii. 338).

Ac 14^6, κεφάλαιον 8^1=Ac 22^{28}, and παροξυσμός 10^{24}=Ac 15^{39}) are used in a different sense. In Ac 7^{20} and He 11^{23} ἀστεῖος is a reminiscence of Ex 2^2, which may have been independent in each case, while ἔντρομος (Ac 7^{32} 16^{29}= He 12^{21}) is probably,* in Heb., an emendation of ἔκτρομος. Similarly ἐκλείπω does not count, for in He 1^{12} it occurs in an OT citation; and the same fact rules out ἄστρον (11^{12}), ἐνοχλέω (12^{15}), ἐσώτερον (6^{19}), ἦχος (12^{19}), μετόχοι† (1^9), ὀρθός (12^{13}), παραλύομαι (12^{12}), παρίημι (12^{12}), πολίτης (8^{11}), συναντάω (7^1), and φύω (12^{15}); while παλαιοῦσθαι, which in 1^{11} is also part of a citation, is differently applied in 8^{13} and Lk 12^{33}, κατάπαυσις in Ac 7^{49} occurs in an OT quotation, καταπαύω in Ac 14^{18} has a different sense and construction from those of Heb., and παροικέω (11^9=Lk 24^{18}) is also employed in a different construction. No stress can be laid on the further coincidence that both writers mention the Red Sea (11^{29}=Ac 7^{36}), or use πατριάρχης (Ac 2^{29} etc. =He 7^4). Thus an examination of the language reveals only‡ about (*a*) 6 words peculiar in the NT to Hebrews and the Gospel of Luke, with (*b*) 6 peculiar to Acts and Hebrews, and two (διαβαίνω and διατίθεμαι) which occur in all three. Of (*a*), three (ἱερατεία, λύτρωσις, and τελείωσις) are plainly due, as is the specially frequent use of λαός, to a common use of the LXX by writers who treat of the same or similar subjects, while εἰς τὸ παντελές is too frequent in the Hellenistic literature to make its preservation in Heb. and Lk.'s gospel more than an accidental coincidence. This leaves merely πόρρωθεν and εὔθετος in this class, while ἀρχηγός§ and εἴσειμι in (*b*), with καίτοι and σχεδόν and ὕπαρξις, cannot be said to denote any special or striking affinities between Acts and Heb. (ἀσάλευτος being employed in quite a different sense) in point of vocabulary.‖ This verdict is corroborated by the absence from Heb. of several characteristically Lucan words and phrases, *e.g.*, ἄν or τίς with the optative, ἀπὸ τοῦ νῦν, γε, δὲ καί, ἐγένετο in its various constructions, εἴη, ἔχω with infin., ὀνόματι, παραχρῆμα, πράσσω, and ὡς (=when). An examination of the style and vocabulary of Heb. and Luke hardly tends to indicate even a special amount of material common to both; it certainly discourages any attempt to ascribe the epistle to the author of the third gospel and of Acts. Luke 'could report a speech after the manner of a Hebrew rabbi or of a Greek rhetorician; and it may be rash to say that he *could* not have written a hortatory work in the style of Hebrews. But when we compare Ac $13^{38\text{-}41}$ $28^{17\text{-}28}$ with He 3^{12}–4^{13}, not to say with $6^{4\text{-}12}$, we see that

---

* The variant in Ac 21^{25} also lowers the force of the use of ἐπιστέλλειν here and in He 13^{22}, while the construction in Ac 15^{20} is different.

† The solitary Lucan use (5^7) is, moreover, quite different in sense.

‡ Heb. has about four words really peculiar to itself and Mt., and the same number in common with Mk.

§ With 'salvation' in the context of Ac 5^{31} and He 2^{10}.

‖ The same holds true of such phrases as καὶ αὐτός, κυκλοῦσθαι (of cities), μάστιξ (literally, He 11^{36}=Ac 22^{24}), ἐν τῷ with infin., περικεῖσθαι with accus., and the use in Heb. of πάσχειν by itself for the sufferings of Jesus. On the other hand, Heb. avoids σύν, except in compounds, and omits several distinctly Lucan phrases and expressions like προσεύχομαι, while a passage like He 2^{14} shows affinities rather with Mt. (28^{10}, cp Jn 20^{17}). Heb. once (6^5) uses γεύομαι with the accus. (cp. Jn 2^{10}); Luke never does.

St. Luke *did* not in fact write like Hebrews, even in hortatory passages' (W. H. Simcox, *Writers of the NT*, 1890, p. 48).* Community of atmosphere is all that can fairly be postulated.

The claims of (*b*) Barnabas, which have been advocated, *e.g.*, by Schmidt (*Einl.* 289 f.), Hefele (*Apostolic Fathers*, pp. xi–xiv), Ullmann (*SK.*, 1828, 377 f.), Wieseler (*Chronologie*, 478 f.; *SK.*, 1867, pp. 665 f.), Maier, Twesten, Grau, Volkmar, Thiersch (joint-authorship of Paul), Ritschl (*SK.*, 1866, 89 f.), Renan (iv. pp. 210 f.), Kübel, Salmon (*INT.* 424 f.), B. Weiss, Gardiner, Ayles, Blass, Walker (*ET.* xv. 142–144), Edmundson, Riggenbach, Prat (*Théologie de S. Paul*^{3}, 502), Barth, Gregory (*Canon and Text of NT*, 1908, 223–224), Heinrici (*Der litt. Charakter d. neutest. Schriften*, 1908, 71–73), Dibelius and Endelmann, have the support of an early tradition (cp. Tertullian's *de pudicitia*, 20: exstat enim et Barnabæ titulus ad Hebræos), unless Tertullian confused Barnabas with Hebrews—which is unlikely, as he explicitly quotes He 6^{1-8}. The quotation is only given as a proof 'ex redundantia'; still, the tradition probably reflected not only the North African church's view or a Montanist's opinion, but some Roman tradition. In the *Tractatus Origenis de libris ss. Scripturarum* (ed. Batiffol, Paris, 1900, p. 108), as by Philastrius, He 13^{15} is quoted as a word of 'sanctissimus Barnabas.' It may be admitted that Barnabas, as a Levite of the Levant, with gifts of edification (υἱὸς παρακλήσεως, Ac 4^{36}), would suit several characteristics of the epistle. As the inaccuracies with regard to the worship refer not to the temple but to the tabernacle, it is hardly fair to press them against the likelihood of his authorship, on the ground that he would have been well informed about the temple-cultus at Jerusalem. On the other hand, his relation to the original gospel was probably closer than that implied in 2^{3}, and the rise of the Pauline tradition is inexplicable if Barnabas (or indeed any other name) had been attached to the epistle from the first. His reputed connection with the temple (Ac 4^{36}), the existence of the epistle of Barnabas with its similar Judaistic themes, and perhaps the coincidence of Ac 4^{36} † and He 13^{22}, may quite well have

* Cp. a paper by the same writer in *Exp.*^{3} viii. 180–192 on 'The Pauline Antilegomena.' The differences of the Lucan style and that of Heb. are discussed excellently by Dr. F. Gardiner (*JBL.*, 1887, pp. 1–27).

† A similar instance is pointed out in the attribution of Ps 127 to Solomon on the score of 127^{2} = 2 S $12^{24f.}$.

led to the guess that he was the author of this anonymous scripture.

Both of the inaccuracies are due to the later Jewish traditions which the author used for his description of the Levitical cultus. The daily sin-offering of the high priests (7^{27}) is a fusion of their yearly sin-offering on the day of atonement and of the daily sacrifice which, according to Philo (*de Special. Legibus*, iii. 23, οὕτως καὶ τοῦ σύμπαντος ἔθνους συγγενὴς καὶ ἀγχιστεὺς κοινὸς ὁ ἀρχιερεύς ἐστι . . . εὐχὰς δὲ καὶ θυσίας τελῶν καθ' ἑκάστην ἡμέραν κτλ.; rabbinic evidence collected by Delitzsch in *Zeitschrift für die Luther. Theol. und Kirche*, 1860, 593 f., cp. also Schürer, *GJV.*[4] ii. 347 f.), they offered. The golden altar of incense (9^4) is placed inside the holy of holies, instead of the holy place, by a similar reliance upon later Jewish tradition (*e.g.* Apoc. Bar 6^7: et uidi eum descendisse in sancta sanctorum et sumsisse inde uelum . . . et propitiatorium et duas tabulas . . . et thuribulum, etc.), just as the author turns the pot of manna into gold after the precedent of the LXX (Ex 16^{33}), which Philo had already followed (*De Congressu eruditionis gratia*, 23: ἐν στάμνῳ χρυσῷ). The two passages bring out (*a*) the dependence of the author on the LXX and on rabbinic traditions mediated by Josephus * and Philo, with (*b*) his total indifference to the second temple of Judaism.

(*c*) Clement of Rome (Erasmus, Reithmayr, Bisping, Cornely) has also early traditional support; † but the marked differences of style alone are sufficient to refute any such hypothesis, which probably arose from the fact that his epistle contains several indubitable allusions to Hebrews.

Outside the pale of tradition, the imagination of later editors has turned to (i.) Apollos, (ii.) Silas (Silvanus), (iii.) Peter, (iv.) Aristion, (v.) Philip, and (vi.) Prisca. The claims of (i.) Apollos have been favoured more or less confidently, after Luther, ‡ by Semler (doubtfully), Osiander, Ziegler, Bleek, Reuss, de Wette,

* Thus 9^{21} echoes the tradition preserved in Josephus, *Ant.* iii. 8. 6. Dibelius argues that Mark (cp. 15^{38}; Zahn, *NKZ.*, 1902, 729–756) could only have derived the symbolical trait of the rent veil from Hebrews (cp. 6^{19-20} 9^8 10^{19-20}), *i.e.*, from his relative and teacher, Barnabas (Col 4^{10}), the author. But it is not certain that this conception was peculiar to Hebrews.

† Cp. Jerome, *de uir. inlustr.* 5, epistola autem quæ fertur ad Hebræos non eius [*i.e.* Pauli] creditur propter stili sermonisque dissonantiam, sed uel Barnabæ iuxta Tertullianum uel Lucæ euangelistæ iuxta quosdam uel Clementis Romanæ postea ecclesiæ episcopi, quem aiunt sententias Pauli proprio ordinasse et ornasse sermone. Cp. Eus. *H. E.* iii. 38. 2–3. Jerome consoles himself by reflecting (ep. 129) that, although the majority assign it either to Barnabas or to Clement, 'nihil interesse, cuius sit, cum ecclesiastici uiri sit et quotidie ecclesiarum lectione celebretur.'

‡ The conjecture of Apollos' authorship was not first made by Luther; he was only the first, so far as we can ascertain, to mention it ('etliche meinen, sie sei St. Lucas, etliche St. Apollo,' cp. Leipoldt's *GK.* ii. 77).

Kurtz, Schott, Lütterbeck (*NT Lehrbegriffe*, ii. 101 f.), Lünemann, Tholuck, Credner, Riehm (doubtfully), Feilmoser (*Einl.* 359 f.), Alford,* Moulton, G. Meyer, Hilgenfeld (*Urc.* 76 f.), Plumptre (*Exp.*[1] i. 329 f., 409 f.),† Bartlet (*EB.*[11] xiii. 191), Pfleiderer (*Urc.* iii. 282), Albani, Büchel, Farrar, Selwyn, and (?) von Soden ("This Apollos—or whoever he may be—has the noble distinction of having been the first to lead Alexandria to Bethlehem," *EBi.* 2000). Belser (*Einl.* 600 f.), though obliged by the Council of Trent to defend Paul's authorship in some shape or form, believes, like Lütterbeck, that Apollos wrote the epistle, but that Paul added the closing paragraphs. Klostermann (*op. cit.* 55 f.), conjecturing πρὸς Βεροιαίους as the original form of the title, supposes that the epistle was written by Apollos to the Jewish-Christian community of Berea (Ac 17^{10}), while Schütze (*Magazin für Evang. Theol. u. Kirche*, 1904, 112 f., 275 f.) holds that Apollos wrote it to some Jewish-Christian house-church in Rome (cp. Ro $16^{8\,f.}$). The biblical learning of Apollos, his Alexandrian training, and his relation to Paul and the Pauline circle (He 13^{19} = 1 Co $16^{10\text{-}12}$), are all adduced as arguments why this teacher might have written Hebrews. "Paul laid the foundation; the author of Hebrews built on it, not with wood or hay or stubble, but with gold, silver, precious stones. Should it have been Apollos to whom we owe this epistle, then would that saying be true: Paul planted, Apollos watered" (Resch, *Paulinismus*, p. 506, echoing the similar remarks of Luther and Tindale). But the entire absence of any early tradition tells strongly against this, the most plausible of all conjectures drawn from purely internal evidence. (ii.) Silas (Silvanus) was no doubt a member of the Pauline circle, who was also associated with Timotheus, and connected somehow with the composition of 1 Peter (a writing allied to Hebrews); but these data are too slight to support the weight of any hypothesis (Mynster, Boehme, Riehm, Godet doubtfully, Wohlenberg in *NKZ.*, 1913, 752 f.) which would attribute Hebrews to a man of whom so little is known. (iii.) The resemblances

* Alford (pp. 71–72) ingeniously pleads that Apollos modestly shrank from putting his own name forward, to avoid suspicion of rivalry with Paul, and that Clement similarly refrained from quoting the epistle by the author's name in writing to a church where there had been a danger of "rivalry between the fautors of the two teachers."

† Plumptre credited Apollos not only with Hebrews but with the Wisdom of Solomon, the latter being written, of course, before his conversion.

(Rendall, *Theology of Heb. Christians*, 42–45), between Hebrews and 1 Peter, which cover the thoughts no less than the style of both epistles, are not insignificant. Both describe Christ as *the Shepherd* (He 13^{20} = 1 P 2^{25} 5^{3}), and use the phrase *the blood of sprinkling* (12^{24} = 1 P 1^{2});* both conceive faith as steadfast reliance on the unseen God under stress of trial, hold up Christ's example under sufferings, and attach the same disciplinary value to human suffering; both use αἷμα ἄμωμον, ἀντίτυπος, ξένοι καὶ παρεπίδημοι, etc., and there are further parallels in 1 P 2^{25} = He 5^{2}, 1 P 3^{9} = He 12^{17}, 1 P 3^{11} = He 12^{14}, 1 P 3^{18} = He 7^{27}, 1 P 4^{14} = He 11^{26}, 1 P 5^{10-11} = He 13^{20-22} etc. But such correspondences cannot be mixed up with a supposed allusion in 2^{3} to the incidents of Jn 1^{35-42}, in order to support the hypothesis that Peter actually wrote Hebrews (A. Welch, *The Authorship of the Epistle to the Hebrews*, 1899, pp. 1–33). At most they suggest a dependence of the one writing upon the other, possibly no more than a common milieu of Christian feeling. "The natural inference from them is that the author was either a personal disciple of St. Peter or a diligent student of his epistle" (Rendall). The claims of (iv.) Aristion, the supposed author of Mk 16^{9-20}, have been recently proposed by J. Chapman (*Revue Bénédictine*, 1905, 50–62) and argued by R. Perdelwitz (*ZNW.*, 1910, 105–110) on the ground that the sharp tone of He 6^{4-6} and 10^{26-27} agrees with the trend of the teaching quoted by Irenæus from the presbyter-circles (*adv. haer.* iv. 28. 1, iv. 40), and also with that of the newly discovered fragment of Mk 16^{9-20} (see pp. 240 f.), where ἄλλα δεινά are supposed to refer to the fate of apostates. Hence all three converge on the same author. But even if Aristion were the author of the Mark-ending, these conceptions are far too general and incidental to be made the basis of any such argument. (v.) Philip the deacon (cp. W. M. Ramsay, *Exp.*[5] ix. 407–422, *Luke the Physician and other Studies*, 1908, pp. 301–308) is also conjectured to have written the epistle from the church of Cæsarea (spring of A.D. 59) after discussions with Paul on topics raised by the local leaders, to reconcile the Jewish party in the Jerusalem church to Paulinism (Paul adding the last verse or two). E. L. Hicks (*The Interpreter*, 1909, pp. 245 f.), denying the Pauline postscript, argues for the same origin,

* Ἀρχηγός is common to Hebrews (2^{10} 12^{2}) and Peter's speech in Ac 3^{15} 5^{31} (see above, p. 436).

mainly on the ground of linguistic analogy between Hebrews and Col-Eph.

Those who (*e.g.* Lewis, Ramsay, and Hicks) make Cæsarea the locus of the epistle's composition, argue that Italian Jewish pilgrims would be there *en route* to or from Jerusalem (see below, § 7).

(vi.) Did Lady Pembroke collaborate with her brother in the composition of the *Arcadia*? The problem which rises for the student of English literature has been raised in connection with the NT by those who conjecture that Prisca and Aquila, Paul's devoted and intelligent συνεργοί, composed the epistle to the Hebrews. Their claims are urged tentatively by Harnack (see above, p. 422, and his essay in *SBBA.* 1900, "über die beiden Recensionen d. Gesch. der Prisca u. des Aquila in Ac. Ap. 18^{1-27}"), Schiele, Peake, and Rendel Harris (*Sidelights on NT Research*, pp. 148–176). Aquila's name had been more than once suggested (*e.g.* by Bleek and Alford), but Prisca is supposed, on this theory, to have been mainly responsible for the epistle, and traces of the wife rather than of the husband are sought for. The hypothesis certainly might account for the loss of the name, as canonical authority could hardly be claimed for a woman's writing. But the positive arguments are not substantial. Paul had forbidden a woman even to teach in church (1 Co $14^{34f.}$), and the action described in Ac 18^{26} does not prove that any exception would be made in favour of a gifted lady like Prisca, for the instruction of Apollos was private, not public. The supposed signs of femininity in Hebrews are extremely dubious; as a matter of fact, one would have expected a reference to Deborah instead of Barak in 11^{32}, if a woman had written the epistle. The stylistic argument, that now a single now a plural authorship is implied, can hardly be maintained; *our* brother (in 13^{23}) means not our colleague, but the brother known to you and to me (the writer, cp. *I will see you*); phrases like those in 11^{32} and 13^{19} imply a single author, and the *we* which elsewhere occurs is either editorial or due to the figure of συγκατάβασις. The association of Aquila and Prisca with a house-church in Rome depends on a view of Ro 16 which is not tenable (see above, pp. 135 f.). Finally, the masculine διηγούμενον in 11^{32} (cp. Deissmann, *TR.* v. 64) rather tells against the feminine hypothesis than otherwise; and, had any exception been taken to Prisca, the deletion of her name from the address (leaving that of

Aquila) would have been simpler than the excision of the address *en bloc* (cp. Wrede, 82–83). One has therefore (cp. Heigl, 149 f.) reluctantly to forego the romance which this hypothesis would introduce into the primitive Christian literature.

All such attempts (cp. the summary in Heigl, *op. cit.* pp. 125–156) to identify the author start from the assumption that he (or she) must be found among the figures which the Acts of the Apostles reveals in a relation to Timotheus corresponding to that of 13^{24}, and (perhaps) in a more or less close connection with Paul. Neither of these postulates is necessary. Acts does not give any exhaustive list of the διδάσκαλοι in the first century of Christianity who were capable of writing such an epistle, and Timotheus, especially after Paul's death, must have had a wider acquaintance than history records. In the absence of better evidence, we must resign ourselves to the fact that the author cannot be identified with any figure already known to us from tradition. He was probably a highly trained Hellenistic Jewish Christian, a διδάσκαλος of repute, with speculative gifts and literary culture; but to us he is a voice and no more. He left great prose to some little clan of early Christians, but who he was, and who they were, it is not possible, with such materials as are at our disposal, to determine. No conjecture rises above the level of plausibility. We cannot say that if the *auctor ad Hebræos* had never lived or written, the course of early Christianity would have been materially altered. He was not a personality of Paul's commanding genius. He did not make history or mark any epoch. He did not even, like the anonymous authors of Matthew's gospel and the Fourth gospel, succeed in stamping his writing on the mind of the early church at large. But the later church was right in claiming a canonical position for this unique specimen of Alexandrine thought playing upon the primitive gospel, although the reasons upon which the claim was based were generally erroneous.

The Jewish origin of the writer cannot, however, be deduced simply from his frequent citations of the OT—a feature which is as marked in Gentile Christians like Justin and Clement of Alexandria. Nor does the divergence of some of these quotations necessarily imply his employment of the Hebrew text as distinguished from the LXX. He may have had access to a different Greek version of the OT. Nor again does his acquaintance with Jewish customs and beliefs point inevitably to Jewish birth. Opportunities of familiarising oneself with Judaism abounded in the first century. The influx of Jews into the Christian church, the widespread diffusion of the synagogues, and the knowledge of the LXX, opened ample channels of information to an interested inquirer.

§ 7. *Object and destination.*—This anonymous epistle, like the Melchizedek whom it describes and allegorises, is ἀγενεαλόγητος, a lonely and impressive phenomenon in the literature of the first century, which bears even fewer traces of its aim than of its author. The Christians to whom it was addressed had been evangelised by disciples of Jesus (2^{3}), and had passed through severe suffering on account of their faith shortly afterwards ($10^{32f.}$). A considerable time had elapsed since then, during which the early leaders of the church had died (13^{7}). This internal trial, together with a contemporary pressure from the outside, threatened to prove dangerous to them on account of their dulness in the faith (5^{11-12}), and it is to this situation that the writer addresses himself. The author of Barnabas writes, ἵνα μετὰ τῆς πίστεως ὑμῶν τελείαν ἔχητε τὴν γνῶσιν. Hebrews is also a λόγος γνώσεως, though more on the lines of Paul's γνῶσις (1 Co 12^{8}), intended to meet the special, practical needs of the church by furnishing the readers with conceptions of christology which will brace them against apostasy and discouragement.

Ignatius, in a passage (*Trall.* 5) which reminds us of He $5^{11f.}$, excuses himself from imparting his deeper conception (τὰ ἐπουράνια γράψαι), on the ground that his readers, being babes, would be unable to digest the stronger food. On the other hand (*Rom.* 3), he praises the Roman church for its propaganda (οὐδέποτε ἐβασκάνατε οὐδενί· ἄλλους ἐδιδάξατε). A generation might, of course, have made a difference in the Roman church; the counsel of the *auctor ad Hebræos* may have been laid to heart. Still, the probability is either that Hebrews was sent to some other church than that of Rome, or that it was addressed to some special circle or group in the Roman church, and not to the Roman Christians as a whole. Whatever was its original destination (Italian, Palestinian, or Alexandrian), the original recipients were in all likelihood not any great church as a whole. The feeling of this 'special' address is widespread in recent criticism of the epistle (see below), and 5^{11-13} is one of the passages which suggests it. At the same time, the words—ὀφείλοντες εἶναι διδάσκαλοι—are to be taken, as Wrede observes (p. 32), *cum grano salis*; they do not necessarily mean more than a reproachful reflection upon the backwardness and immaturity of the church or community which is addressed; at best, they only corroborate the impression, made by other allusions, that a small group or circle of Christians is in the writer's purview.

Much ink has been spilt on the question whether the epistle was meant for Jewish Christians in general (so, *e.g.*, Baumgarten, Heinrichs, Schwegler, *NZ.* ii. 304), or specifically in Asia Minor

(C. F. Schmid),* Galatia (Storr, Mynster in *Kleine Schriften*, 289 f.), Thessalonika (Semler), Corinth (M. Weber), Ravenna (Ewald), Cyprus (Riggenbach), or Rome (so from Wettstein to Kurtz, Renan, Mangold, Schenkel, Alford, etc.). The Alexandrian or Egyptian destination is upheld by J. E. C. Schmidt, Hilgenfeld, Baur (*Einl.* 385 f.), Wieseler (*Chron.* 481 f.), Köstlin (*Theol. Jahrb.*, 1853, 410 f., 1854, 366 f., 465 f.), Plumptre (*Exp.*[1] i. 425 f.), and others; the Palestinian not only by Chrysostom, but recently by Bleek, Schott, de Wette, Delitzsch, Tholuck, Ewald, Bisping, Riehm, Moll, Grimm, Lünemann, Findlay, etc., either as Jerusalem (*e.g.* Langen, *Theol. Quartalschrift*, 1863, 379 f.; Kay, Ayles), or as Cæsarea (Moses Stuart, Bartlet), or Jamnia (Grimm, *ZWT.*, 1870, pp. 19 f.). Others (*e.g.* Kübel and Rendall) fix on Syria, Hofmann on Antioch (written perhaps after Paul's release from the Roman imprisonment at Brundisium).

On the general hypothesis which dominates the Palestinian and Alexandrian theories in particular, the writer has in view Jewish Christians who, like the primitive Palestinian church, clung still to the ritual system (Ac 2^{46}), valued highly the prestige and associations of the older cultus, and were in danger of allowing such fascinations to injure their sense of the finality and supremacy of Jesus and his religion. It is supposed that the imminent disaster of A.D. 70 moved the writer to appeal to them to be done with the old order, which was now breaking up, or that the shock of the temple's overthrow threatened to shake the foundation of faith altogether. This view has no sure foothold either in the epistle itself or in history. "Any positive grounds for such a theory are difficult to find. Such a despair ought to have seized all Hebrews alike, whether Christians or not; but there is no historical evidence of such a thing" (A. B. Davidson, *Hebrews*, 21). The crisis did not shake loyal Jews in their adherence to the old covenant,† and

* Röth thinks of Gentile, Farrar and Bartlet of Jewish Christians at Ephesus; Perdelwitz of Gentile Christians in one of the Asiatic centres.

† "The Priesthood, the Sacrifice, the Temple, as they all went down at one sudden blow, seemed scarcely to leave a gap in the religious life of the nation. The Pharisees had long before undermined these things, or rather transplanted them into the people's homes and hearts. . . . Long before the Temple fell, it had been virtually superseded by hundreds of synagogues, schools, and colleges, where laymen read and expounded the Law and the Prophets" (E. Deutsch, *Literary Remains*, p. 139). See above, p. 3. It was

there is no reason to imagine why it should have shaken Jewish Christians, particularly as this epistle has no thought of detaching its readers from the sacrificial system in vogue at Jerusalem. Its real object is very different. The author, who was well versed in the LXX, "but who only knew the temple-cultus from the OT, addresses himself to Gentile Christians who had become lax during a period of persecution; he essays to bring them back to the right path by proving from the OT the glory of the Christian faith" (Büchel, *SK.*, 1906, 548). "His knowledge of Judaism is apparently not derived from actual contact with it as a living religion; it is book-knowledge, like that of St. Clement of Rome" (*CQR.*, 1903, 428). The LXX is his codex, and it is on the basis of the LXX, not on current politics, that he deploys his arguments. Apparently he is quite unconscious of any division between Jewish and Gentile Christians. The homily is not addressed to the former exclusively; *the seed of Abraham* (2^{16}) means not the Jewish race but human beings who believe (cp. Gal $3^{7f.}$ *γινώσκετε ἄρα ὅτι οἱ ἐκ πίστεως, οὗτοι υἱοί εἰσιν Ἀβραάμ*, Ro 4^{1} 9^{5}); *the People* (2^{17}) are, as in 1 Peter, the elect of God (cp. 2^{9} 7^{27} 13^{12}) from among men; such arguments and descriptions, as Paul's letters and Clem. Rom. show, were more than applicable to Gentile Christians (compare, *e.g.*, that of 3–4 with 1 Co 10), and the tenor of the epistle on the whole indicates Gentile Christians who were perhaps affected by a speculative or theoretical Judaism as well as by the temptation of some cults in the surrounding paganism. The writer (so, *e.g.*, Röth, Weizsäcker, Schürer, Wendt, von Soden, McGiffert, Pfleiderer, Jülicher, Harnack, Barth, Büchel, Wrede, Hollmann, Feine, Perdelwitz) knows no distinction between the two branches of the early church; he is addressing Christians, quite irrespective of their origin.

Some of those who still defend the Jewish Christian nationality* of the readers (*e.g.* Zahn and Peake) now admit that there is no question of any relapse into legal and ceremonial

the collapse of the Jewish worship, in fact, "which compelled Christianity to find what is offered in our epistle—a theory of the disappearance of the old dispensation in the new" (W. Robertson Smith, *EB.*[9] xi. 606).

* Ably restated by G. Hoennicke (*JC.* 93–95), whose arguments, especially that based on the crucial passage in 6^{1-2}, are controverted by Perdelwitz in *ZNW.*, 1910, 113f. B. Weiss's latest monograph is a running critique, on the other hand, of von Soden's arguments.

Judaism. This concession not only removes the need of fixing on a pre-70 A.D. date, but affects the view taken of the destination. Of the three main directions in which the church has been sought, Jerusalem (or even Palestine) is the least appropriate.

(*a*) Even at the eighth or ninth decade of the first century, and (much more) prior to A.D. 70, there must have been many Christians in the local church who had heard the gospel from Jesus himself (contrast 2^{3}). (*b*) The language and argument of the epistle are not likely to have been appropriate to the church of Jerusalem. "It is difficult to suggest any period in the history of the Jerusalem-church during which a liberal-minded Hellenist like the author, who was probably ignorant of Hebrew, and who could in an off-hand way dispose of the whole OT ritual as 'standing on meats and drinks and divers washings' (9^{10}) and 'useless' (7^{18}), could have stood in such relations to this church" (A. B. Davidson, p. 14). The force of this argument may be met by admitting that the circle addressed is not the whole church, but a Hellenistic section of it, but (*c*) the censure of 5^{12} would be singularly inapplicable to any section of the mother-church of Jerusalem at any period, even after A.D. 70. (*d*) Though poverty was not incompatible with generosity (cp. 2 Co 8^{2}), the Jerusalem-church was notoriously rather the object than the source of charity (6^{10} 10^{34} $13^{2,5,16}$). Finally, (*e*) the rigid use of the LXX does not favour an audience of Jewish Christians in Jerusalem or Palestine.

The employment of the LXX and of the Wisdom writings on the other hand, is no decisive argument in favour of Alexandria; neither is the hypothesis (once favoured by Wieseler) that the writer had in mind the Jewish temple (cp. the 4th of the *Odes of Solomon*, ed. J. R. Harris, 1909, p. 91) at Leontopolis; neither again is the Alexandrian tone of the argument, which would be perfectly intelligible in many quarters owing to the widespread diffusion of Hellenistic Judaism. When Jewish Christians of a Hellenistic type are supposed to be the recipients of the epistle, Alexandria is a natural place to think of. Otherwise it has little more in its favour than any other, and the erroneous Pauline tradition which first sprang up there tells against the view that the local church was the original community addressed. Besides, the Alexandrian tradition was that Hebrews was addressed to Palestinian Christians.

The Roman destination has perhaps most in its favour, *e.g.* the reference in 13^{24}, the use of ἡγούμενοι as in Clem. Rom. and Hermas (cp. Harnack's *Constitution and Law of the Church*, 1910, pp. 63 f., 69 f.) for the leaders, and the fact that Clement of Rome is the first to use the epistle.* The modern form of

* This early knowledge of the epistle at Rome might be otherwise explained, though not so naturally *e.g.* if written from Rome, it may

this hypothesis finds that Hebrews was sent not to the whole church, but to some house-church or small circle of it. For this we cannot quote Ro $16^{1f.}$, since the latter refers to Ephesus. But the language of the epistle suggests (so, *e.g.*, Harnack, Zahn, von Dobschütz, Bacon, G. Milligan, *Exp.*[6] iv. 437–448; Peake, Hollmann, M. Jones, Feine, Seeberg, Dickie in *Exp.*[8] v. 371 f.) that, instead of being addressed to any large church as a whole (in which case it is unlikely that the author would have refrained from handling differences of opinion), it was designed for a small community or gathering (10^{25} 13^{24}) which had a history and character of its own within the general church of the city or district. If the readers were Jewish Christians, they might have been drawn from the συναγωγὴ Ἑβραίων in Rome (cp. Nestle, *ET.* x. 422). If they were Gentile Christians, the composition of the Roman church is equally favourable to the existence of such a circle. In any case, the readers, as Zahn rightly contends, were too homogeneous in feeling and position to represent the entire body of the Roman church, and are probably to be identified with one of the household churches in the capital. No groups are mentioned, no parties are singled out, yet a fairly definite and uniform circle is presupposed in such admonitions as those of 5^{12} $10^{32f.}$ 13^{7}, a circle perhaps of experienced Christians from whom greater maturity of conviction might reasonably have been expected.

It is pressing language too far when 5^{12} (ὀφείλοντες εἶναι διδάσκαλοι) is taken to mean that Hebrews was written primarily for a group of διδάσκαλοι or evangelists (Heinrici, *TLZ.*, 1895, 289), as though the error of these Christians was the opposite of that against which the author of James warns his audience (Ja 3^{1}).

Hebrews therefore represents neither Paulinism nor the primitive Jewish Christian theology, but a special development of both, especially of the former, along the speculative lines of Alexandrianism, which may have been addressed to some group in Rome or in Italy.

The phrase οἱ ἀπὸ τῆς Ἰταλίας (13^{24}, cp. Deissmann, *TR.* v. 164) might grammatically mean 'those resident in Italy,' but it is rather more natural to take it as denoting some Italian Christians abroad who happened to be with the writer (cp. Ignat. *Magn.* 15), and who sent greetings to their compatriots. This is the sole clue to the origin of Hebrews, for the allusion

---

have been copied before it was sent off (cp. Gardiner, *Exp.*[8] xiii. 60 f.), unless the phrase in 13^{24} denotes Italians out of their country.

to the imprisonment of Timotheus (13[23]) finds no echo in Acts or in early tradition, and he is as likely to have been imprisoned outside Italy as at Rome. The movements of Timotheus, after his release, are apparently uncertain; the author hopes, however, that his colleague will soon rejoin him, and that they may together revisit the church, as soon as his own way is smoothed (13[19]).* Meantime, he forwards the epistle (13[22]), for which he bespeaks a favourable reception. The writer is evidently not quite sure how his words will be taken.

The wider question of the epistle's object has no light thrown on it by Πρὸς Ἑβραίους the title, which, like the *ad Familiares* of Cicero's correspondence, is one of the erroneous titles of antiquity, and (see p. 432) was probably added to the epistle during the earlier part of the second century as a reflection of the impression made by its apparently Hebrew preoccupation upon the mind of a generation which had lost all direct knowledge of the writing's origin and standpoint.

No explanation of πρὸς Ἑβραίους as a corruption either, *e.g.*, of πρὸς Βερναίους = Βεροιαίους (Klostermann, see above) or of πρὸς τοὺς ἑταίρους (cp. *ZNW.* i. 21) has any plausibility. A more attractive hypothesis, which would explain the title as chosen by the author, is to take Ἑβραῖοι in the symbolic or allegorical sense of the term. On this view, the readers were conceived as *Hebrews* in the light and lineage of Abraham (2[6] 11[18]) the Hebrew *crosser* from the sensible to the spiritual world. To Philo, ὁ Ἑβραῖος is the type of such a believer who migrates (11[8f.] 13[13]) as a pilgrim; and, it is asked, in view of the Philonic etymological parallels elsewhere in the epistle, to say nothing of the typological idiosyncrasies which pervade it, "Can a more appropriate appellation be found for the non-legalistic, yet not antinomian, believers addressed in the epistle to the Hebrews than is derived from Abram *the Hebrew*, in whom, on the one hand, all believers saw their father, and whose act [of bringing tithes to Melchizedek, 7[4]] acknowledges, on the other hand, the superiority of the non-legalistic cult of the θεὸς ὕψιστος to the Levitical cult?" (Schiele, 303 f., V. Monod). This smacks of subtlety, however; besides, we should have expected allusions to the *crossing* of Abraham (in 11[8f.]), whereas the very term Ἑβραῖος is absent from the epistle.

Even the internal evidence of the epistle yields very little material for a decision upon the precise aim which the writer had in mind. As the problem before him was not a relapse into Judaism,—for he never discusses any question of combining the Christian faith with legalism,—there is no obvious need to suppose that the readers were mainly of Jewish birth. The sole suggestion yielded by the course of the epistle is that they

* In spite of Burggaller's caveat (126–127), the words of 13[19] seem to imply the temporary absence of the writer from the readers; they do not naturally suit a preacher speaking to his audience.

may have been exposed to the seductions of a subtle Judaism, and this liability implies no more than the ordinary interest of Gentile Christians in the OT scriptures and institutions. There is no hint of circumcision being a danger, or of ritual formality; and if Christians of Jewish birth formed any serious element in this church, their training must have been that of Hellenistic Judaism such as Stephen was trained under—liberal, biblical, and to a certain extent syncretistic. Evidence for such Jewish communities * is furnished in the East, where independent Hebrew circles sprang up, without any legalistic ties to the synagogues, and yet with a combination of Jewish piety (including reverence for the sacred books) and Hellenic conceptions such as the cult of the *Most High God* (cp. He 7[1], and for Rome, *CIG.* 5929). "This precedent," as Schürer rightly observes, "is instructive for the earliest history of Christianity. Certain symptoms indicate that the formation of Gentile-Christian communities, free from legalism, was not exclusively the work of Paul. In several places, *e.g.* in Rome, it appears to have been prepared for by the fact that the preaching of Christ won acceptance especially in circles of the σεβόμενοι τὸν θεόν" (*op. cit.* p. 225; cp. *EEP.* 37 f.). As the title ὕψιστος only occurs once, however, in an incidental quotation, in Hebrews (7[1], cp. Clemen's *Urc.* pp. 80 f., and MacNeill, p. 114), no stress can be laid on it as evidence for the *milieu* of the epistle. It would be unsafe to identify such a group or association of converted Jews with the Roman ἐπισυναγωγή to which this epistle was probably addressed, or to argue from the prevalence of such a form of religious association in Pontus (Ac 18[1-2]) in favour of Prisca's claim to the authorship. All that can be said with safety is that the situation of this church or company of Christians possibly included certain temptations of a specifically Jewish cast, which might appeal especially to Christians who, from some religious idiosyncrasy, were nourishing their faith upon the Levitical portions of the OT scriptures. It is conceivable that these seductive tendencies were the issue of a speculative Judaism which, allied to certain ritualistic and sacerdotal proclivities (similar, perhaps, to those controverted in Romans or Colossians), was besetting Gentile Christians, or even

* Schürer (*SBBA.*, 1897, 200–225) shows how the σεβόμενοι θεὸν ὕψιστον did not form one large association in Tanais, but rather a number of small groups, each containing about forty members. See also Achelis, *Urc.* 33 f.

Christians who had been thrown into contact with Judaism, during the second decade after the fall of Jerusalem (so Häring. *SK.*, 1891, pp. 589–598, and Bacon, *INT.* 149, after Schürer, *ibid.*, 1876, pp. 776 f.), when rabbinical tendencies revived, and provincial Christianity was often exposed to such apostasy (Wellhausen, *Skizzen u. Vorarbeiten*, iii. pp. 196 f.; Harnack, *TU.* i. 3, pp. 73 f.; *HD.* i. 293, 298). For although Judaism may be reckoned—despite Barkochba's revolt—as a lost cause, subsequent to A.D. 70 it was very far from being a forsaken belief. During the closing quarter of the first century, Jewish propaganda continued to flourish throughout the Empire, nowhere more than at Rome. The morality and monotheism preached by Hellenistic Jews especially must have proved not simply a rival to Christianity in the eyes of many pagans, but a source of dangerous fascination for weaker and less intelligent members of the Christian church, who lay open, through birth or associations, to such Jewish influences. Several hints in this epistle may be held to indicate the presence of the peril (*e.g.* 6^{6} 13^{9-16} etc.; cp. Hort's *JC.* pp. 156 f., and Haupt in *SK.*, 1895, pp. 388–390). *Uiuere more judaico* was evidently a specious watchword. It represented, as we find in Cerinthus afterwards, a distinct and subtle danger, prompting Gentile Christians—especially proselytes—to revert to their old life, and inclining others to favour a heterogeneous syncretism of Jewish and Christian beliefs. The time came, ere long, when Ignatius needed to cry out, 'Better listen to Christianity from a circumcised man than to Judaism from one uncircumcised' (*ad Philad.* 6), 'it is monstrous to talk of Jesus Christ *καὶ ἰουδαΐζειν*, for Christianity did not believe in Judaism, but Judaism in Christianity' (*Magn.* 10, cp. 8–9). In the qualified sense just defined, a Jewish danger may be admitted as a subordinate factor in the situation of the Christians to whom Hebrews was addressed. But the pro-Jewish propaganda was certainly not one of circumcision or of legalism, as in Paul's day, and the presence of other elements, drawn from the cults and worship of paganism, is almost as evident. The time that had elapsed since the primitive flush and freshness of the gospel, together with the severity of the situation, had tended to produce a dissatisfaction in these Christians, which tempted them to abandon the worship and membership of the church (10^{25}), as if it were a philosophic school or a cult whose capacities they had exhausted (cp. *HD.*

i. 151). Whether this temptation was accentuated by any Jewish propaganda (so especially Ménégoz) or by some of the pagan religious cults, or by a fusion of both, it it almost impossible, in the lack of corroborative evidence, to determine.

It does not follow even that such realistic details of the Levitical cultus could not have appealed to certain Gentile Christians. This may be held in view not only of the fact that the allegorical interpretations had carried them far and wide, but also of the further fact that the Greek and Roman world had pieces of ritual not wholly dissimilar to the precise regulations of the Mosaic cultus. A recently discovered inscription (pre-Christian) from Eresos in Lesbos gives rules, *e.g.* for the purification of women, which are analogous to those of Leviticus (cp. W. R. Paton, *Class. Rev.*, 1902, 290–292; also P. Kretschmer in *Jahreshefte des österreich. archäol. Instit.* v. pp. 143 f.).

§ 8. *Date.*—The period of composition is naturally bound up with the particular view taken of the authorship, and especially of the aim and destination. Thus the epistle is placed close to the final crisis of Judaism in Palestine, *i.e.*, in A.D. 68–70, by Grimm, Kübel (A.D. 67–68), Rendall, Riggenbach, Barth, and others. Some, sharing the same general view of its religious purpose, put it earlier, between 64 and 67 or 65 and 70; *e.g.* Bleek, Beyschlag (*NT Theol.* ii. 286–288), Renan, Scholten, Godet, Clemen (*Chron.* 277–279), Ewald, Farrar, Westcott, Roberts (*Greek the Language of Christ and His Apostles*, ch. viii.), S. Davidson, Bovon (*NTTh.* ii. 387–389), Ménégoz, G. G. Findlay (*c.* A.D. 67), G. B. Stevens (*NTTh.* 485 f.), Huyghe, Trenkle (*Einl.* 88 f.), G. Milligan, G. Meyer (A.D. 67–69), Farrar (A.D. 67–68), Edmundson (*Urc.* 153 f.: 66 A.D.), Kay and Heigl (A.D. 65), Ayles (*c.* A.D. 64). It is placed slightly earlier by Hilgenfeld (before A.D. 66), Mill, Bullock, Salmon, and Holtzheuer (A.D. 63), Schäfer (*Einl.* 149–157), and Belser (A.D. 63–64), Bartlet * (A.D. 62), W. M. Lewis,† Nairne, and Ramsay (A.D. 58–60). A second-century date, such as A.D. 95–115 (Pfleiderer) or A.D. 116–118 (Volkmar, *Religion Jesu*, 388 f.; Keim, Brückner, Hausrath), is ruled out of court by the use of Hebrews in Clem. Romanus, and the contrary assertion (Hitzig, *Zur Kritik der Paulinischen Briefe*, 34–36) that Hebrews depends on the Antiquities of Josephus is of no importance. It is needless to be too precise, in condescending, *e.g.*, upon *c.* A.D. 95 (Köstlin), but *c.* A.D. 80, or more generally the Domitianic period, would

* From Brundusium by Paul (Hofmann).

† Joint-production of Paul and Luke from the Cæsarean imprisonment (Ac 23^{35}).

represent the converging opinions of many critics, including Schenkel (*das Christusbild der Apostel*, 1879, 130 f.), Mangold (*Römerbrief*, 1884, pp. 258 f.), Holtzmann (*BL.* ii. 615 f.; *ZWT.*, 1884, pp. 1–10), Weizsäcker (*AA.* ii. 155–160), von Soden, Cone, Jülicher, McGiffert (*AA.* 463 f.), Zahn (*RE.* vii. 492–506), Rovers (*INT.* 80 f.), Bousset (*TR.*, 1897, 9–10), J. Réville (*Les origines de l'épiscopat*, i. 363–366), Pfleiderer (*Urc.* iii. 280 f.), Krüger's *Altchristl. Litteratur*² (1898), p. 11; Bacon, Häring (*SK.*, 1891, 589–598), Ropes (*AA.* 269 f.), Goodspeed, Hollmann, Wrede's *Entstehung der Schriften des NT* (1907), 82 f.; Willis, MacNeill, Windisch, and Perdelwitz. Völter's theory (*TT.*, 1908, 537 f., nucleus written *c.* A.D. 75 to Rome, but reissued twenty years later with additions in $1^{2a-3.\ 5b-13}$ 2^{11-14a} 3^{3-4} 4^{14}–10^{18} $10^{19-23.\ 28f.}$ $11^{9f.\ 13-16.\ 18.\ 26a.\ 39f.}$ 12^{18-28} $13^{8-16.\ 20}$) had been partially anticipated by J. S. F. Chamberlain (*The Epistle to the Hebrews*, 1904), who took Hebrews as addressed to the Jews by a prominent Christian (Paul?), and afterwards edited with additions by another Christian for Gentile Christians.

(*a*) The allusions in the present tense ($7^{8.\ 20}$ 8^{3-5} $9^{6-9.\ 13}$ 13^{10}) to the cultus by no means imply a date prior to A.D. 70. Nothing is more common (Schürer, *HJP.* I. ii. pp. 268 f.), in writings subsequent to that date, Jewish (Josephus, *Antiq.* iii. 6. 7–12, *Apion.* i. 7, ii. 8. 23) and Christian (Clem. Rom. 40–41; Justin, *Dial.* 107, Diognetus 3, and Barnabas), than such references. They denote a literary method, not any contemporary existence of the practices or places mentioned. Besides, the allusions "to the Mosaic ritual are purely ideal and theoretical, and based on the Law in the Pentateuch. . . . The mode of reasoning adopted would have been as valid after the destruction of the Temple as during its existence" (A. B. Davidson, *Hebrews*, p. 15). Hence (*b*) it is no argument for a pre-70 date to hold that the writer implies the existence of the temple-cultus, and that he would have been sure to notice its abolition if he had written after the overthrow of the Jewish capital. The Judaism with which he is dealing is that of the tabernacle, not of the temple. Neither he nor his readers are concerned with the temple-ritual at all; its existence mattered as little to his idealist method of argument as its destruction. Thus the expression in 8^{13} (the old covenant ἐγγὺς ἀφανισμοῦ) means simply that the old régime, superseded by Jesus, was decaying even in Jeremiah's age. If it had lain in his way to cite the Jewish catastrophe of A.D. 70 as a proof of the evanescence of the old order, a more apposite allusion (Jülicher) would have been to the murder of Jesus, the heavenly high priest, at the instance of the earthly high priests. But all such arguments lay outside the circle of his interests. He finds his cogent demonstration of the superiority of the gospel not in contemporary history, but in the sacred pages of the LXX. (*c*) For the same reason the allusion to the *forty years* of Israel's wandering ($3^{17f.}$) is not a covert reference to the time which had elapsed since the resurrection, while (*d*) the reference in 13^7 is too general to refer specifically to the death of James (in Jerusalem) or of Peter and Paul (in Rome). There is no hint in $3^{9.\ 17}$ (*forty years*) of the period of time since the crucifixion, as if the day of Israel's grace were almost ended, or had ended. The writer is not calculating the present from the past. He does not find any typical significance in the number,—which in this case would be merely a round term (cp. Mk 1^{13}, Ac 1^3) for a generation. It is only on one forn of the Palestinian (Jerusalem) hypothesis that any allusion can be found in 13^7 to the death of James; and even on the post-70 A.D. hypothesis, it is unnecesary to find a reference here to the deaths of Peter and Paul.

The surest criteria for fixing the period of composition lie in the literary relationships of the epistle. The *terminus ad quem* is fixed by Clemens Romanus (see above, pp. 430 f.), the *terminus a quo* by the familiarity of the writer with some of Paul's epistles, and probably with 1 Peter (see above, pp. 439 f.). Like the latter, Hebrews, with its indifference to the burning questions of the Law and circumcision, reflects a period when Paul's efforts had settled the problem of Jew and Gentile in the early church.

Of the Pauline epistles (cp. Brückner's *Chron.* 236–241; Holtzmann, *ZWT.*, 1867, pp. 18 f.), Romans is pretty clearly used, as is only natural in an epistle written by a διδάσκαλος who had apparently connections with some Christians in Rome. The similarity of the Deuteronomy-citation in Ro 12^{19} = He 10^{30} might be due to the independent use of a common tradition or *florilegium*; but Ro 4^{17-21} seems to underlie He $11^{11-12.\ 19}$, and further instances of the same dependence may be traced, *e.g.*, in Ro 1^{17} = He 10^{38}, $14^{3f.}$ = He 13^9, Ro 14^{19} = He 12^{14}, Ro 15^{33} = He 13^{20}, 1 Co 2^6 = He 5^{14}, 1 Co 3^2 = He 5^{12}, 1 Co 12^{11} = He 2^4, 1 Co 15^{26} = He 2^{14}, 1 Co 15^{27} = He 2^8, 2 Co 1^{11-12} = He 13^{18-19}, 2 Co 8^4 = He 6^{10}, 2 Co 13^1 = He 10^{28}, and Galatians (3^1 = He 6^6, 3^{19} = He 2^2, $4^{25f.}$ = He 12^{22} 13^{15}), and Phil $2^{9f.}$ = He 1^4, Phil $4^{15.\ 18}$ = He 13^{16}, Phil 4^{21-22} = He 13^{24}. "Der Gedankengang bewegt sich in voller Selbständigkeit, die Anlehnung an Paulus ist daher immer frei und ungefähr, meistens vermutlich rein gedächtnismässig' (Wrede, p. 54). Of the seven words peculiar, in the NT, to Heb. and the Pastorals, ἀπόλαυσις is used in entirely different senses (He 11^{25} = 1 Ti 6^{17}), as is ὀρέγεσθαι (11^{16} = 1 Ti 3^1 6^{10}), while the remainder (ἀφιλάργυρος, βέβηλος, ἐκτρέπεσθαι, ὀνειδισμός, and πρόδηλος) are neither numerous nor significant enough to show any particular affinity between the two, especially in the absence of any common characteristics of style and thought.

The interpretation of 10^{32-34} as an allusion to the theatrical displays (θεατριζόμενοι) which accompanied Nero's outburst against the Roman Christians is not necessary, in view of the use of θέατρον in 1 Co 4^9; the language is too general and even mild; and the reference in 10^{34} is not to legal confiscation of property (cp. on this Klette's *Christenkatastrophe unter Nero*,

1907, 43 f.), but to the results of mob-rioting. The passage cannot therefore be taken as a proof of any particular destination (Roman, or even Palestinian) for Hebrews, and the same holds of the other allusions to suffering and persecution throughout the epistle. They may be fitted into a theory which rests on other grounds, but by themselves they furnish no decisive evidence. It did not lie in the writer's way to be detailed, any more than it occurred to the author of the *Religio Medici* to mention the Star Chamber, the fortunes of the Huguenots, or even the Civil War in England. So far as he has any explicit aim in these allusions, it is rather to prepare his readers for bearing the brunt of some imminent danger, which hitherto (οὔπω μέχρις αἵματος, 12^{4}) they have been spared. This is the point, *e.g.*, of the enigmatic and allegorical passage in $13^{12f.}$, where he summons them, after the example of Jesus (cp. $12^{2\text{-}3}$), not to break with Judaism,—such a realistic use of παρεμβολή would be hopelessly out of keeping with the symbolism of the epistle,—but to be ready to be outcasts from the world in their pursuit of the real religion (cp. 4^{11}). The reproach of Christ which they are to bear is that cheerfully borne by Moses long ago ($11^{25\text{-}26}$), in abjuring the fascinations and advantages of the pagan world.

It is prosaic and untrue to the semi-allegorical cast of the argument, to take $13^{9f.}$ as an appeal to break finally with Judaism. The contrast is between the various pagan cult-feasts, which the readers felt they could indulge in not only with immunity but even with profit, and the Christian religion which dispensed with any such participation. Our altar, says the writer, is one of which the worshippers (λατρεύοντες of Christians, as in 9^{14} 12^{28}) do not partake (in 13^{10} σκηνή is the NT temple, contrasted with that of 9^{8}). The Christian sacrifices are a cheerful confession of God even in suffering, and beneficence towards others; they have nothing whatever to do with participation in any sacramental meal. The latter practices are a foreign novelty, inconsistent with the spirituality and adequacy of the relation which Jesus Christ establishes between God and his people. Such innovations are to be eschewed, in favour of the primitive λόγος τοῦ θεοῦ (13^{7}) or χάρις which alone can establish the heart, however much a religion without a sacrificial meal may be despised and persecuted by the world. Christians have a sacrifice for sins which brings them into full communion with God, but they have no sacrificial meal* (cp. Spitta, *Urc.* i. 325 f.). When θυσιαστήριον is

* The association of φωτισθέντες (10^{32}), especially in connection with a metaphorical allusion to eating, suggests the phraseology of the Greek mysteries (cp. *ERE.* viii. 54 f.; Wobbermin's *Religionsgeschichtliche Studien*, pp. 154 f.), as in Eph 1^{18} 3^{9}, 2 Ti 1^{10}. Similarly, the reference in $12^{16\text{-}17}$,

identified with the Lord's table, it becomes possible to hear (cp. above, p. 389) an early protest against the realistic sacramental view of the Lord's supper which sought to base its efficacy on conceptions of communion popular among the pagan mysteries. The writer controverts these by means of arguments drawn from the Levitical system of Judaism, not because he has the latter directly in view, but because his method of working from the OT enables him to prove that Jesus, as the perfect sin-offering, superseded all such religious devices; the spurious and superstitious tendencies of pagan communion to which these readers were exposed were part and parcel of a system which the sacrifice of Christ had entirely antiquated, by realising the religious instincts latent in pre-Christian and non-Christian sacrifices (cp. P. Gardner, *Historic View of the NT*[2], 1904, 234 f.). There is to be no eating of the *σῶμα Χριστοῦ*. The author of the Fourth gospel's attitude is less uncompromising and unambiguous than that of the author of Hebrews, though, like the significant omission of the Lord's supper in Eph. (see above, p. 389), it marks the same current of tendency flowing through the more spiritual and idealistic circles of the early church towards the close of the first century.

§ 9. *Text.*—The text has suffered early injuries, though seldom in important passages. The difficult and early variant *χωρὶς*, for *χάριτι* in 2[9], which Origen and Jerome already found in some MSS, may have arisen from a transcriptional error; certainly it is much less relevant to the context, whether taken with *ὑπὲρ παντὸς* (Origen) or *γεύσηται* (Zimmer, Weiss). But *χωρὶς* is as likely to have been smoothed out into *χάριτι*, and in this case one must either conjecture that the phrase *χωρὶς θεοῦ* originally lay after (or as a marginal gloss to) *ἀνυπότακτον* in v.[8], or assume that some primitive corruption underlies the text of v.[9] (Baljon, *Theol. Studiën*, 1890, 213–214). Such a corruption is probably visible not only in 10[1] but also in 4[2], where WH (see their note) favour Noesselt's conjecture *τοῖς ἀκούσμασιν* (= 'things heard'). The parenthesis *ὁ λαὸς γὰρ ἐπ' αὐτῆς νενομοθέτηται* (7[11]) would fit in perhaps better at the close of 7[12]; but that is no reason for supposing (so Bakhuyzen) that the present position of the words is due to the transposition of a copyist. On the omission of 8[3] as a gloss by Kuenen, Prins, and Bakhuyzen, see Baljon, *op. cit.* 216 f. The conjecture ΗΔΕΙΟΝΑ for ΠΛΕΙΟΝΑ in 11[4] (so Cobet and Vollgraff; cp. Maynard in *Exp.*[7] vii. 163 f.) is not more than plausible, and the emendation (Blass; cp. C. Könnecke's *Beiträge zur Erklärung des NT*, 1896, p. 15) of 11[5b] into *καὶ οὐχ ηὑρίσκετ' αὐτοῦ θάνατος* (Orig., Clem. Rom. 9[3]) is not even plausible. The same may be said of the proposal to omit *τοῦτ' ἔστι τῆς σαρκὸς αὐτοῦ* as a later gloss (*The Ep. to the Hebrews*, by two Clerks, 1912, p. 40) in 10[20], and of Field's hypothesis (*Notes on Translation of NT*, 233) that *καὶ αὐτὴ Σάρρα* in 11[11] is an interpolated marginal comment. In 11[37] *ἐπειράσθησαν* is either (cp. WH's note) a corruption of some less general term like *ἐπρήσθησαν* or *ἐπυράσθησαν* or *ἐνεπρήσθησαν*, or a dittography of the previous *ἐπρίσθησαν* (Naber, Bakhuyzen), or a marginal gloss which originally (*ἐπειράθησαν*) explained *πεῖραν ἔλαβον* (F. Field).

THE EPISTLE OF JAMES.

LITERATURE.[1]—(*a*) Editions — Althamer (*In epist. Jacobi*[2], 1533); Grynæus (*Explicatio epp. Cathol.*, Basel, 1593); R. Turnbull (London, 1606); Cornelius à Lapide (1648); Estius (1661); Brochmand (1706); Damm (1747); Benson and Michaelis (1756); Seemiller (1783); Rosenmüller (*Der Brief J. übersetzt und erlaütert*, 1787); J. B. Carpzov (Halle. 1790); Morus, *Prælectiones in Jacobi et Petri epistolas* (Leipzig, 1794); Hensler (Hamburg, 1801); Hottinger (Leipzig, 1815); Pott[3] (1816); Schulthess (Zürich, 1824); Gebser (Berlin, 1828, with valuable patristic materials); Schneckenburger's *Annotatio* (1832); Theile's *Commentarius* (Leipzig, 1833); Jachmann (1838); Kern (Tübingen, 1838) *; J. A. Cramer's *Catena in epp. Catholicas* (Oxford, 1840); Scharling (1841); Stier (Barmen, 1845); de Wette (1847); Cellerier (1850); Neander (Eng. tr. 1851); T. W. Peile (1852); Wiesinger (1854); Messmer (Brixen, 1863); H. Bouman (1865); B. Brückner (1865); J. Adam (Edinburgh, 1867); Lange (1862, Eng. tr. 1867); Ewald (1870); Huther[3] (1870, Eng. tr. 1882); A. Bisping (Münster, 1871); Wordsworth (1875); E. G. Punchard (Ellicott's *Comm.* n. d.); Bassett (London, 1876); Plumptre (*Camb. Bible*, 1878); Erdmann (1881); Scott (*Speaker's Comm.* 1881); Gloag (Schaff's *Comm.* 1883); E. C. S. Gibson[2] (*Pulpit Comm.* 1887); Johnstone[2] (1888); Plummer (*Expos. Bible*, 1891); Trenkle, *Der Brief des heiligen Jakobus* (1894); K. Burger[2] (Strack-Zöckler's *Komm.* 1895); Carr (*CGT.* 1896); Beyschlag (— Meyer[6], 1898) *; von Soden[3] (*HC.* 1899); Baljon (1904); H. Wilbers (Amsterdam, 1906); G. Hollmann[2] (*SNT.* 1907); Hort (1909); Belser (1909) *; R. J. Knowling[2] (*WC.* 1910); Oesterley (*EGT.* 1910); Windisch (*HBNT.* 1911); Mayor[4] (London, 1913) *; J. H. Ropes (*ICC.* 1916) *.

(*b*) Studies.—(i.) general: — Heisen's *Novæ Hypotheses interpretandæ epistolæ Jacobi* (1739); Storr's *Dissertatio exegetica* (Tübingen, 1784); J. D. Schulze (see above, p. 319); Gabler, *De Jacobo, epistolæ eidem ascriptæ auctore* (Altdorf, 1787); Bricka, *Réflexions relat. à l'introduction à l'épître de s. Jacques* (1838); F. L. Schaumann's *Origo apostolica et authent. epistolæ Jacobi* (Helsingfors, 1840); Galup's *Essai d'une Introd. critique* . . . (1842); J. Monod's *Introduction* . . . (Montauban, 1846); Loeffler's *Études historiques et dogmatiques sur Jac.* (1850); Ritschl's *Entstehung d. Altkath-kirche*[2] (1857), 108 f.; A. Boon, *De epist. Jacobi cum libro Sirac. conven.* (1866); Wohlwerth (*Sur l' authent.* etc., 1868); A. H. Blom, *De Brief van Jakobus* (1869) *; Sabatier (*ESR.* vii. 125–132); W. Schmidt, *Lehrgehalt des Jakobus-Briefes*[3] (1869); Leo Vèzes, *Dissertatio de epist. Jacobi* (1871); Beyschlag (*SK.*, 1874, pp. 150 f.); Holtzmann (*BL.* iii. 179–189, and in *ZWT.*, 1882, pp. 292 f.); Gloag's *Introd. Cath. Epp.* pp. 23–108; P. Schegg, *Jakobus der Brüder des Herrn und sein Brief* (1883); von Soden (*JPT.*, 1884, pp. 137–192) *; Meyrick (Smith's *DB.*[2] 1520–1522); Zimmer (*ZWT.*, 1893, 481–503); Pfleiderer (*Urc.* iv. pp. 293–311); P. Feine, *Der Jakobusbrief nach Lehranschauungen und Entstehungsverhältnisse*

[1] See Kawerau's study of 'die Schicksale des Jakobusbriefes im 16 Jahrhundert' (*Zeitschrift für kirchl. Wiss. und Leben*, 1889, pp. 359–370), and Leipoldt's paragraphs on Luther's criticism (*GK.* ii. pp. 67–77).

(1893)*; Kühl (*SK.*, 1894, 795–817); van Manen (*TT.*, 1894, 478–496); Holtzmann, *NTTh.* ii. 328–350; Spitta (*Urc.* ii. 1. 1–239)*; Bovon, *NTTh.* ii. 447–462; Vowinckel (*BFT.* vi. 1898); Moffatt (*HNT.* 576 f., 704 f.); Cone (*EBi.* 2321–2326); Sieffert (*PRE.* viii. 581 f.); J. B. Mayor (*DB.* ii. 543–548, and *Further Studies in Ep. of James*, 1913); J. Parry, *A Discussion of the General Epistle of James* (London, 1903); V. Ermoni (Vigouroux' *DB.* iii. 1087–1098); Grafe, *Stellung u. Bedeutung d. Jakobusbriefes*, etc. (Tübingen, 1904)*; B. Weiss, *Der Jakobusbrief und die neueste Kritik* (1904); H. J. Cladder in *Zeitschrift für Kathol. Theologie* (1904, 37–58, 1904, 295–330); M. Meinertz, *Der Jakobusbrief und sein Verfasser in Schrift und Ueberlieferung* (in Bardenhewer's 'Biblische Studien,' x. 1905)*; Zahn's *Skizzen*[3] (1908), 93 f.; Hoennicke (*JC.* pp. 90 f., 191 f.); C. W. Emmet (Hastings' *DB.*, 1909, 424–426); Wendland (*HBNT.* i. 2. 370 f.); Gaugusch (*Lehrgestalt d. Jakobus-Epistel*, 1914); W. Montgomery (*DAC.* i. 629 f.). (ii.) on 2^{14-26} in relation to Paul: Hulsemann's *Harmonia* . . . (1643); C. S. Ruger's *Conciliatio* . . . (1785); Knapp (*Scriptura varii argumenti*[2], 1823, i. pp. 411 f.); Frommann (*SK.*, 1833, pp. 84 f., harmonising); Isenberg, *Die Rechtfertigung durch d. Glauben oder Paulus und Jakobus* (1868); Riggenbach (*SK.*, 1868, 238 f.); Martens, *Geloof en weerken naar den brief van Jakobus* (1871); H. W. Weiffenbach, *Exegetische-theologische Studie über Jakobus*, ii. 14–26 (Giessen, 1871)*; Fritzsch, *Der Glaube, die Werke, und die Rechtfertigung nach der Lehre d. Jakobus* (1875); Schanz (*TQ.*, 1880, pp. 3 f., 247 f.); Kübel, *Ueber das Verhältniss von Glaube und Werken bei Jakobus* (1880); Klöpper (*ZWT.*, 1885, pp. 280 f.); Usteri (*SK.*, 1889, 211–256); C. Schwartz (*SK.*, 1891, 704–737); B. Bartmann, *S. Paulus und S. Jakobus über die Rechtfertigung* (in Bardenhewer's 'Biblische Studien,' 1897, ii. 1); J. Böhmer (*NKZ.*, 1898, 251–256); Ménégoz in *Études d. Théol. et d'Histoire* (Paris, 1901, pp. 121–150); E. Kühl, *Die Stellung des Jakobusbriefes zum alttest. Gesetz*, etc. (1905); F. W. Mozley (*Exp.*[7] x. 481–503); A. Köhler, *Glaube u. Werke in Jak.* (1914).

§ 1. *Contents and outline.*—The brief address (1^1) closes with the (p. 48) Greek salutation χαίρειν, and this is caught up in the first of the following five paragraphs with which the homily opens (πᾶσαν χαρὰν ἡγήσασθε κτλ.). The thread on which these are loosely strung together is the thought of πειρασμός. The first paragraph is a statement of π. as part of the divine discipline for perfecting (τέλειοι) the Christian character (1^{2-4}). This suggests (ἐν μηδενὶ λειπόμενοι. Εἰ δέ τις ὑμῶν λείπεται σοφίας), though not very relevantly,* a word on the need of sincere faith †

* The writer has in mind Sap 9^6: *though a man be perfect* (τέλειος) *among the sons of men, yet if the wisdom* (σοφία) *that is from thee be absent, he shall be reckoned of no account.* The whole section, with its emphasis on God as the liberal giver of wisdom to sincere suppliants, breathes the spirit of the sapiential Hebrew literature and of Philo (cp. H. A. A. Kennedy, *Exp.*[8] ii. 39–52).

† Luther's marginal note on 1^6 (as on 5^{16}) is: "der einzige und beste Ort

in praying for practical guidance in life (1^{5-8}). Then, as the insincere person or ἀνὴρ δίψυχος, a familiar type and figure in the older Jewish literature, was unstable (ἀκατάστατος ἐν πάσαις ταῖς ὁδοῖς αὐτοῦ, 1^{8}, cp. $3^{8.16}$, Sir 1^{25}, En 91^{4}) owing to his half-hearted attachment to the divine σοφία, the writer adds a paragraph (1^{9-11} καυχάσθω δέ κτλ.) on the fate of the rich man who fades ἐν ταῖς πορείαις* αὐτοῦ—the timely loss of wealth thus being in reality a blessing, a πειρασμός for which he should be thankful.† A word on the reward for enduring trial (1^{12}) follows. Logically and strictly it resumes the thought of 1^{4}, but the writer is reproducing the sequence of thought in Sir (34) 31^{8-10} *blessed is the rich man who goeth* (ἐπορεύθη) *not after gold. Who is he? Verily we will call him blessed* (μακαριοῦμεν). . . . *Who hath been tried thereby* (ἐδοκιμάσθη) *and found perfect* (ἐτελειώθη)? *Then let him glory* (ἔστω εἰς καύχησιν). Here, however (μακάριος ἀνὴρ ὃς ὑπομένει πειρασμόν, ὅτι δόκιμος γενόμενος κτλ.), the conception of the sphere of πειρασμός is broadened to cover poor and rich alike, just as its reward is made eschatological (cp. Sap $5^{15f.}$ *the just live for ever . . . they shall receive*—λήψονται—*the diadem of beauty from the hand of the Lord*, Zec 6^{14} LXX). The writer then meets a current objection ($1^{13f.}$; cp. Judas ^{16}) by proving that the origin of πειρασμός lies not in God, whose gifts are only good,‡ but in the lusts of human nature; and the ideas of Gn 3, suggested by the latter thought ($1^{14f.}$), lead him to contrast the birth of sin from lust with the new creative word of the gospel (1^{18}), which is God's supreme gift to mankind. The condition of receiving this gift is threefold. First, meekness (1^{19-21}), the spirit that refuses to resent God's dealings or to flame up (κακία = malice) in irritation against other people. Secondly, while the perfect (τέλειος) Christian must be *quick to hear* (1^{19}), it is the hearing which is

in der ganzen Epistel." For Luther's opinions, see Walther in *SK.* (1893) pp. 595 f., and Meinertz, *op. cit.* pp. 216 f. The liberal criticism of Cardinal Cajetan and some others in that age is outlined by Simon, *Histoire Critique du Texte du NT*, pp. 189 f.

* Corssen (*GGA.*, 1893, pp. 594 f.) prefers to read, with minuscule 30, εὐπορείαις (so Mangey and Bakhuyzen; cp. Baljon, *Theol. Studiën*, 1891, pp. 377 f.).

† The similar Jewish teaching of Akiba is discussed by Bacher in his *Agada d. Tannaiten*², i. (1903) pp. 320 f. Job's sufferings (cp. 5^{11}) were one of Akiba's favourite illustrations of πειρασμός (see above, p. 33).

‡ In 1^{17} it is tempting to place ἢ after τροπῆς instead of before it, especially in view of Sap 7^{17-18} (τροπῶν ἀλλαγὰς καὶ μεταβολὰς καιρῶν); so Koennecke, *Emendationen zu Stellen des NT* (1908, *BFT.* xii.), pp. 12 f.

followed by practical obedience (1^{22-25}). Thirdly, not talk * but charity and chastity form the true worship of God (1^{19} *slow to speak*, 1^{26-27}) the Father (cp. Ps 68^{5}).

The implicit antithesis between pagan and Christian *θρησκεία* then leads the writer † to denounce an abuse within (*συναγωγὴν*) contemporary Christian worship, viz. respect of persons, the worship of social distinctions, the undue deference paid to wealthy people, and the consequent depreciation of the poor (2^{1-5}). Before our *Lord of glory* (or, *the Lord, our Glory*), social and human glories are of no account. Besides, the poor are the chosen of God (2^{5}), and the overbearing un-Christian conduct ‡ of the rich entitles them to no such respect (2^{6-7}); to love rich people as Christian neighbours is one thing, to be servile towards them is quite another (2^{8-9}). Nor can such neighbourly love make up for a failure to keep the command against respect of persons (Lv $19^{15.\ 18}$), for the law is a unity (2^{10-11}). Furthermore, the writer adds, gathering up the thoughts of 1^{19-26} as well as of 2^{1-11}, this law which regulates words and deeds alike is a *law of freedom*, *i.e.* (cp. 1^{25}) one which answers completely to the spontaneous instincts of our true nature (a Philonic touch, cp. *quod omn. probus liber*, 7). And, finally, according to Jewish ethic (cp. Sir 28^{12}, En $98^{12f.}$, Test. Zeb 8^{1-3}), mercilessness is the unpardonable sin, whereas the merciful soul need have no fear of the final judgment (2^{13}).

Having thus put the antithesis between the true Christian faith (2^{1}) and the favouritism which breeds injustice, the writer develops § the idea of hardheartedness (2^{9-13}) in a pungent

* With 1^{19b} and 1^{26} compare the famous saying of R. Simeon (*Pirke Aboth* i. 18; Derenbourg's *L'Histoire et la géogr. de la Palestine*, i. pp. 271 f.), 1^{19b} (*slow to anger*) = *Pirke Aboth* ii. 10 (R. Eliezer b. Hyrcanus). With 1^{26-27} cp. the eighth reason given by R. Eleazar b. Jehuda (*Sabbath*, 326 f.) for trouble in life, viz., filthy speech, which causes widows and orphans to wail (cp. Is 9^{16}); also *Nedarim*, 40a, for the supreme duty of visiting the sick.

† Reversing the sequence of Ps (81) 82^{1-8}, where God's presence *ἐν συναγωγῇ θεῶν* is made a reason for refusing to respect sinners and for being just to orphans and poor folk, just as in Sir (32) 35^{12-15} men are warned against offering sacrifice to God at the expense of practical charity and justice, since *οὐκ ἔστιν παρ' αὐτῷ δόξα προσώπου . . . οὐ λήμψεται πρόσωπον ἐπὶ πτωχοῦ . . . οὐ μὴ ὑπερίδῃ ἱκετίαν ὀρφανοῦ, καὶ χήραν ἐὰν ἐκχέῃ λαλιάν.*

‡ With 2^{6} (*ἕλκουσιν ὑμᾶς εἰς κριτήρια*) compare Deissmann's restoration of the second of the (second series) Oxyrhynchite Logia, *οἱ ἕλκοντες ἡμᾶς [εἰς τὰ κριτήρια] κτλ* (*LA.* 437 f.).

§ Unless (see below, p. 463) $4^{11f.}$ originally lay here.

section (2^{14-26}), criticising all conceptions of faith which regard it as valid apart from its exercise in deeds. Thereupon, passing from lack of deeds to excess of words, he returns to his favourite warning against the abuses of speech ($3^{1f.}$), not as a substitute for true faith (2^{14}), but as a danger to it. Since Christian teachers * by their profession were specially liable to this sin, they are first of all mentioned (3^{1}), but the counsel at once broadens out ($3^{2f.}$ ἅπαντες, cp. 1^{19} πᾶς ἄνθρωπος, 1^{26} εἴ τις κτλ.) into a general philippic against the mischievous power ($3^{3f.}$) and inconsistency ($3^{9f.}$) † of evil words. The connection between this and the following definition of the criteria of true σοφία (3^{13-17}) becomes visible in the light of the author's intimate acquaintance with the Wisdom-literature, where (*e.g.* in Sir $24^{30f.}$) the wisdom of the teacher is compared to a stream. So here the allusion to fresh fountains (3^{11-12}) helps to introduce a contrast between the false σοφία, whose notes are bitterness and factiousness (3^{14-16}), and the true celestial σοφία (3^{17}) with its *good fruits* (contrast 3^{12a}). Carrying on the metaphor as well as the thought of *peace* (3^{17}), the writer then contrasts the future reward of the peaceable (3^{18}) with the wrangling and dissatisfaction evident on all sides among those who practised the false σοφία as their rule of life (4^{1-3}).‡ The outer dispeace springs from an inward trouble, above all from worldly compromise (4^{4-6}); hence the author adds a straight word on the need of purity and penitence (4^{7-10}).

The next brief paragraph against defamation and censoriousness (4^{11-12}), if it is not misplaced (see below), must be an echo and expansion of $4^{1f.}$. Then, rebuking another aspect of overweening presumption, this time against God, he attacks traders

* Irenæus (*adv. Haer.* i. 28, iii. 23. 8) attributes the heresy of Tatian to the fact that he allowed his conceit as a teacher to develop a passion for novelties. For the high repute, as well as for the perils, of διδάσκαλοι, who survived προφῆται in the early church, cp. Harnack, *MAC.* i. 354 f.

† The conception of man as *made in God's likeness* (3^{9}) was a fundamental principle of Akiba's ethic (see, *e.g.*, *Pirke Aboth* iii. 14). R. Simon ben Azzai ranked this even higher than neighbourly love (cp. Bacher's *Agada d. Tannaiten*^{2}, i. 417 f.). For the connection of 3^{6-8} with Herakleitus, see E. Pfleiderer (*JPT.* xiii. 177–218); for Philonic sources, Siegfried's *Philo*, pp. 311 f. In 3^{6} James has used, for his own purpose, an Orphic phrase; for ὁ τῆς μοίρας τροχὸς καὶ τῆς γενέσεως and ὁ κύκλος τῆς γενέσεως, see Rohde's *Psyche*^{2}, ii. 123, Stiglmayr in *BZ.* (1913) 49–52, and Lobeck's *Fragm.* 797 f.

‡ On the duty of generosity among teachers, see *Megilla*, 28a.

(4^{13-17} ἄγε νῦν κτλ.) for ignoring God in their plans for future acquisition, and wealthy landowners ($5^{1f.}$ ἄγε νῦν κτλ.) for their personal selfishness and for defrauding their employés. The closing words of the latter denunciation (5^{5-6}, cp. Sir 34^{22} *as a shedder of blood is he who deprives a hireling of his hire*),* with their picture of the unresisting patience of the poor, strike the keynote of the following exhortation to patience (5^{7-11}) in view of the near approach of the Lord. Above all, Christians must refuse to take an oath (5^{12-13}) even when dragged into court by their oppressors (cp. 5^{6} 2^{6}); otherwise, whether they manage to escape man's condemnation or not, they will fall under God's (so Sir $23^{9f.}$). A general counsel, in gnomic form, on prayer in relation to sickness, then follows (5^{13-18}),† and the homily abruptly ends with an encouragement to the reclaiming of backsliders (5^{19-20}).‡

§ 2. *Structure.*—The homily is neither a loosely knit series of quasi-proverbial passages nor the logical exposition of a single theme. The opening paragraphs contain the three dominant ideas of the writing, viz., πίστις, σοφία, and πειρασμός; but after 4^{11} these recede into the background, and even the earlier part of the writing contains groups of aphorisms with as little cohesion as a handful of pearls. This is largely due to the gnomic style, as in the Wisdom-literature, Epictetus, and Marcus Aurelius. But the pearls are occasionally strung. Like Wordsworth's

* Ὁ δίκαιος in 5^{6} is generic (from Sir $50^{1f.}$ 2^{20}), but it is a curious coincidence that James of Jerusalem had this title from Jews and Christians alike, according to Hegesippus (cp. Eus. *H. E.* ii. 23). Justin (*Dial.* 16) uses almost the same language about the responsibility of the Jews for the murder of Jesus.

† The effect of a pious man's prayer for rain is a commonplace in contemporary Jewish (cp. *e.g.* Taanith, 25b) and Christian (Tert. *ad Scap.* 4, *Vita Polykarpi*, 29, etc.) tradition. Against the Romanists, who twisted Ja $5^{14f.}$ into a warrant for their sacrament of extreme unction, Luther thundered (*De Babyl. Capt. ecclesiæ præludium*): "si uspiam deliratum est, hoc loco præcipue deliratum est. Omitto enim, quod hanc epistolam apostoli Jacobi non esse, nec apostolico spiritu dignam multi ualde probabiliter asserant, licet consuetudine autoritatem, cuiuscunque sit, obtinuerit. Tamen, si etiam esset apostoli Jacobi, dicerem non licet apostolum sua autoritate sacramentum instituere." For the medicinal use of oil by sects in the early church, see Bousset's *Hauptprobleme der Gnosis* (1907), pp. 297 f., and *FFG.* iv. 175 f.

‡ The teaching about forgiveness is not exactly un-Christian, but it falls far short not only of the Pauline gospel, but of the primitive Christian collocation of forgiveness with faith in Jesus Christ.

poems of 1831, though the various paragraphs of this homily are semi-detached, they too

> "Have moved in order, to each other bound
> By a continuous and acknowledged tie,
> Though unapparent"—

unapparent, that is, to those who do not approach them from the Wisdom-literature on which they are so closely modelled in form as well as in spirit. Thus the analogous abruptness with which Sap 19^{22} and Sir 51^{29-30} end, militates against the hypothesis that the original conclusion of Jas. was lost. On the other hand, the analogy of Hermas suggests that Jas. may have been put together from fly-leaves of prophetic addresses, and even that the detached character of one or two paragraphs is to be explained by the hypothesis of interpolations (cp. J. E. Symes, *Interpreter*, 1913, 406 f.); so, *e.g.*, 3^{1-18} (the essay of an Alexandrian scribe, von Soden), 4^{1-10} (Jacoby, *NT Ethik*, pp. 170 f.), 5^{1-6} (Jacoby and Oesterley), or 4^{11}–5^{6} (von Soden), the latter passages being possibly Jewish fragments. The difference in size between Hermas and Jas., however, is against the hypothesis that the latter, like the former, arose by a process of gradual accretion. It is a homily or tract in epistolary form (cp. Deissmann, *Bible Studies*, pp. 52–53), though, like Hebrews, it may have sprung from spoken addresses. Thus, *e.g.*, Feine regards it as the transcript of a homily delivered by James before the church at Jerusalem; while Barth, following a hint of Luther,* refers it to some hearer who had taken notes of James's preaching. But, in any case, neither the Jewish nor the Gentile Christians ἐν τῇ διασπορᾷ (1^{1}) were organised so closely as to render the circulation of such a manifesto practicable, and there is no trace of any concrete relation between the writer and his readers.

Once or twice the text *medicam manum exspectat. e.g.* (*a*) in the obscure passage $2^{18f.}$ (cp. P. Mehlhorn in *PM.*, 1900, 192–194, and G. Karo, *ibid.* pp. 159–160), where Pfleiderer (*Urc.* iv. 304) and Baljon read σὺ ἔργα ἔχεις, κἀγὼ πίστιν ἔχω (after codex Corbeiensis)†—which is unconvincing, since 2^{18b} is the reply of the genuine Christian to 2^{18a} (so, recently, J. H. Ropes,

---

* In his *Tischreden* (quoted by Kawerau, p. 368): "Ich halt, dass sie irgendein Jude gemacht hab, welcher wol hat hören von Christo läuten aber nicht zusammenschlagen."

† On the general problem of the Vulgate text of Jas., cp. Belser's essay in *TQ.*, 1908, 329–339; and, for other emendations of this particular passage, E. Y. Hincks in *JBL.*, 1899, pp. 199–202, with Ropes' note (pp. 208 f.).

Exp.[7] v. 547–556). (*b*) In the equally difficult (cp. Bruston in *RTQR.*, 1896, 433–436, and Pott, *op. cit.* pp. 329–355) passage, 4^{5}, where E. Paret (*SK.*, 1907, 234 f.) takes πρὸς (=περὶ) φθόνον with what precedes, ἐπιποθεῖ (*sc.* φθόνος) beginning the quotation and Gn 4^{7} being the scripture before the writer's mind (referring to Kain, as in 1 Jn 3^{10-12}), Kirn (*SK.*, 1904, 127 f. and 593–604) and Koennecke (pp. 15 f.) read (τὸν) θεὸν for φθόνον, while Baljon would omit πρὸς φθόνον . . . διὸ λέγει as a gloss (Hottinger and Schulthess omit μείζονα . . . χάριν, the latter conjecturing that μείζονα was originally a marginal comment at the end of the verse, as if μ. ἢ τοῖς ὑπερηφάνοις), which is at least better than regarding the words as a parenthesis. One or two minor suggestions of transposition have been made; *e.g.* that 2^{26} originally * came after 2^{23}, or 4^{17} after 1^{17} (2^{26}?), or ἐθησαυρίσατε ἐν ἐσχάταις ἡμέραις (5^{3}) after 5^{1} (Koennecke), as, *e.g.*, *Pirke Aboth* i. 15 should probably follow i. 12. The passage 4^{11-17} (see above, p. 459) seems misplaced; a much better connection with what precedes as well as with what follows is gained if the paragraph is restored to its original position between 2^{13} and 2^{14}; cp. 2^{12-13} with 4^{11-12}, and 4^{17} followed by $2^{14f.}$.

The ordinary interpretation of τὸ τέλος κυρίου in 5^{11} as the final outcome or purpose of the divine discipline seems adequate to the context. But (after Augustine, Beda, Wetstein, and others) it is referred to 'exitus Domini,' in spite of the adjoining OT examples, by Bois (*SK.*, 1886, 365–366) who puts τὴν . . . εἴδετε in brackets and takes ὅτι with μακαρίζομεν, as well as by Bischoff (*ZNW.*, 1906, 274–279), who proposes to put ἰδοὺ . . . ὑπομείναντας after εἴδετε: while Koennecke (pp. 17–18) again regards κυρίου not as a *genitivus auctoris*, but as a primitive corruption of αὐτοῦ (*i.e.* Job). The suspicions cast on 5^{12} by Kühl (*Die Stellung des Jakobusbriefs*, pp. 73 f.) are due to his *a priori* views of the law in Jas. See the note of Schulthess (p. 180: "Bahrdtius censet, quæ vv. 14–16 leguntur, ab illis uerbis ἀλείψαντες αὐτὸν usque ad hic ὅπως ἰαθῆτε manus haud nimium religiosæ additamentum esse; atque sine ullo sententiarum detrimento abesse posse iudicat Hottingerus, cum quæ ante et post leguntur, obliteratis his uerbis apte cohæreant. . . . Haud sufficit ad crimen interpolationis si quid salua συναφείᾳ orationis prætermitti possit"). Jacoby (*NT Ethik*, 153 f., 193 f.) ascribes 5^{12} (p. 174) to a redactor who added γνῶμαι like those of 1^{19b-20} and $4^{13-15\ (16-17)}$.

§ 3. *Situation.*—The author is a Christian διδάσκαλος (compare and contrast 3^{1-2} with He 5^{12}), trained in Hellenistic Judaism, who is keenly alive to the laxity of the moral situation within the church, and who seldom allows his readers to go far from the *agenda* of the faith, repudiating, with the vivid

* Schulthess quaintly confesses: "ut fatear quod res est, admodum lubeat v.[26] qui saluo contextu abesse posset, pro interpolato putare. Nam cuius fides erga Deum mendaci perfidia in ciuitatem suam regemque probatur, mali exempli est populo Christi. Hinc facile colligi posset, infidelibus fidem nullam habendam esse. Ceterum apostolis ignoscendum, si quando dormitabant" (pp. 129–130).

rhetoric of the διατριβή, a Christianity of the head or of the tongue. Of him it might be said, in the words of a modern novelist (G. W. Cable in *Dr. Sevier*, p. 7), that "his inner heart was all of flesh; but his demands for the rectitude of mankind pointed out like the muzzles of cannon through the embrasures of his virtues." In one hundred and eight verses, fifty-four imperatives have been counted; they lie side by side with passages of deep sympathy, but of praise there is not a syllable. He has been dubbed the Jeremiah of the NT, though his affinities are rather with the pungent and stubborn realism of a prophet like Amos. His sympathies clung to an Essene-like character which again resembles the simplicity and winsomeness of Francis the great *Poverello* (cp. von Dobschütz, *TU.* xi. 1. pp. 110 f.).

The address *to the twelve tribes of the dispersion* (1^{1}) denotes, not Christians of Jewish birth, but Christendom in general conceived under the œcumenical symbol of ancient Israel (cp. Gal 6^{16}, Rev $7^{4f.}$ 21^{12}); it is probably an abbreviated form of 1 P 1^{1}. The term for their ecclesiastical organisation is ἐκκλησία (5^{14}); the phrase *εἰς συναγωγὴν ὑμῶν* (2^{2}) means *into your gathering* or *meeting* (cp. He 10^{25}; Ignat. *ad Polyk.* 4^{2} πυκνότερον συναγωγαὶ γινέσθωσαν; Theoph. *ad Autolyk.* 2^{14} δέδωκεν ὁ θεὸς τῷ κοσμῷ . . . τὰς συναγωγάς, λεγομένας δὲ ἐκκλησίας ἁγίας, etc.), not a literal synagogue in which a majority of Jewish Christians had obtained administrative authority.* Abraham is the father of these Christians (2^{21}, cp. Hebrews, Paul, and Clem. Rom.), and Christianity is described as *the perfect law of freedom* (1^{25}), which means not the *Torah* but the λόγος or revelation of God in Jesus Christ as the nascent catholicism of the later church viewed it (cp. Barn 2^{6} ὁ καινὸς νόμος τοῦ κυρίου ἡμῶν Ἰησοῦ Χριστοῦ ἄνευ ζυγοῦ δουλίας; Justin's *Dial.* 12^{4}; etc.). Instead of the freedom from law, which Paul taught, and at which this writer looked askance in the popular Paulinism of his own day, he

* For such an idea there is no evidence, and the probabilities, even during the seventh decade of the first century, are strongly against it. Συναγωγή was a term taken over from Greek worship (=annual gatherings of religious cults) as an equivalent of ἐκκλησία (cp Heinrici in *ZWT.*, 1876, pp. 523 f., and Harnack on the parallel passage in Hermas, *Mand.* xi. 9), though the Ebionites were almost alone in preferring it to the latter term (Epiph. xxx. 18). The absence of ἐπίσκοποι in 5^{14} is no proof of a very primitive period. Here and there churches existed, long after the first century, which had no officials save πρεσβύτεροι and διδάσκαλοι. Dionysius of Alexandria, *e.g.* (Eus. *H. E.* vii. 24. 6), refers to village-churches in Egypt as late as the middle of the third century which were thus organised. The ep. of James in all likelihood originated in some community of this primitive or rather archaic order, off the main line of the general Christian development. The slowness of its recognition and circulation as an œcumenical homily was due to its original *milieu* in a comparatively obscure (Nazarene ?) circle.

proclaims a law of freedom—the correcting motive being much the same as that of a passage like 1 Ti $1^{8f.}$. There is no reference in the epistle which necessarily involves the Jewish Christian character of the readers—not even 2^{19}, which is more apt as the definition of a monotheism which would distinguish a Gentile Christian's faith from his pagan polytheism. Pagan outsiders did occasionally attend the worship of the early Christians (cp. $2^{7f.}$ with 1 Co 14^{23-25}), but, in face of the Christian admonitions in $1^{10f.}$ (cp. 1 Co 6^{1-2}), it is not necessary to suppose that the rich persons of $2^{2f.}$ $4^{13f.}$ 5^{1-6} were Jews, much less pagans. The racial divisions of Jewish and Gentile Christians really do not exist for this writer any more than for the *autor ad Hebræos*; his horizon is œcumenical Christendom, and his period a time when the older parties had become fused.

The writer has either misapprehended Paulinism or he is correcting a popular abuse (in Gentile Christian circles? Sieffert) of Paul's teaching upon faith, which had laid exaggerated stress on faith as the supreme and sole basis of genuine religion, until a certain indifference to morality had sprung up, accompanied by a false view of faith itself, as if it were equivalent to a formal act of assent to this or that article of belief. So far as the Christian praxis of religion is concerned, James and Paul are at one,* but each lays the emphasis on different syllables. The πίστις of Ja 2^{14-26} is an acceptance of the divine νόμος as an impulse and standard of moral conduct; the caricature of it, which he denounces, is a belief which is divorced from good behaviour. Paul could never have used the term *dead faith* (2^{26}),† although he had often in mind the same ethical fruitlessness which roused the indignation of James. Furthermore, what James calls ἔργα, Paul described as *fruits of the Spirit* (Gal 5^{22}); to Paul ἔργα are ἔργα νόμου, and over against them he sets πίστις. The idea that a man was justified by works and faith combined (Ja 2^{24}) is contrary to the genius of Paul's religion, and thus, although both James and he agree in their demand for an ethical faith, the demand is based upon different conceptions of what faith means.

* Modern harmonising discussions have seldom advanced far beyond Augustine's explanation, (Migne, xl. pp. 87 f., 211): "non sunt sibi contrariæ duorum apostolorum sententiæ Pauli et Jacobi, cum dicit unus, justificari hominem per fidem sine operibus, et alius dicit, inanem esse fidem sine operibus: quia ille dicit de operibus, quæ fidem præcedunt, iste de iis, quæ fidem sequuntur; sicut etiam ipse Paulus multis locis ostendit." For the history of opinion, see Bartmann, pp. 2 f.; Reuss, *INT.* § 143, and Holtzmann, *NTTh.* ii. 329 f.

† Luther's indignant comment on this verse is: "Ei Maria, Gottes Mutter, wie eine arme similitudo ist das! Confert fidem corpori, cum potius animæ fuisset comparanda."

That the controversy presupposes the Pauline propaganda is beyond all reasonable doubt. There is not evidence to show that pre-Christian Judaism knew this problem of a contrast between faith and works in relation to justification, or that even pre-Pauline Christianity had any consciousness of such a difficulty. The stamp of Paul is on a phrase like δικαιοῦται ἐκ πίστεως.

§ 4. *Literary connections.*—While no literary connection between Jas. and either Hebrews or the Apocalypse is demonstrable, the dependence of the epistle upon not only 1 P. (see above, p. 338) but some of Paul's epistles (especially Romans, *e.g.* 1^{2-4} = Ro 5^{3-5}, 1^{6} = Ro 4^{20}, 1^{22} = Ro 2^{13}, 2^{11} = Ro 2^{22-25}, 2^{21} = Ro $4^{1f.}$, 2^{24} = Ro 3^{28}, 4^{1} = Ro 7^{23}, $4^{4.7}$ = Ro 8^{7}, 4^{11} = Ro 2^{1}; also 1^{26} = 1 Co 3^{18}, Gal 6^{3}, 2^{5} = 1 Co 1^{27}, 3^{15} = 1 Co 2^{14}, 2^{8-12} = Gal 5^{14}, Ro $13^{8f.}$, 2^{10} = Gal 5^{3}, 4^{4-5} = Gal 5^{17}), is plain. It would be gratuitous scepticism, in view of the polemic in $2^{14f.}$, to doubt that Jas. draws upon the conceptions which Paul had already minted for the primitive church.* On the other hand, the resemblances between Jas. and Ephesians (*e.g.* 1^{4-6} = Eph $4^{13f.}$, $5^{13f.}$ = Eph 5^{19} 6^{18}) are indecisive.

The reminiscences of the synoptic tradition indicate a predilection for their Matthæan form (*e.g.* 1^{22-23} = Mt 7^{24}, 3^{18} = Mt 5^{9}, 5^{12} = Mt 5^{34-37}), although no evidence for the literary use of any canonical gospel is available, not even for Luke, with whose gospel there are several parallels (cp. Feine, *eine vorkanon. Ueberlieferung*, pp. 132–133), *e.g.* in 1^{5} = Lk 11^{9}, 1^{7} = Lk 11^{13}, $1^{22f.}$ = Lk $6^{46f.}$, 2^{5} = 6^{20}, $2^{15f.}$ and $3^{17f.}$ with Lk 3^{11} 12^{33} and 16^{9}, 3^{1} = Lk 12^{48}, 4^{4} = Lk 16^{13}, 4^{13-15} = Lk 12^{16-21}, 4^{17} = Lk 12^{47}, 5^{1} = 6^{24-25}, and 5^{17} = Lk 4^{25}. There is the same fusion of Wisdom-ideas with the tradition and formation of the evangelic logia, and the same attitude † towards wealth which has led many writers to ascribe a sort of Ebionistic sympathy to Luke (cp. *EBi.* ii. 1841). This neighbourhood to the Lucan writings will further explain the apparent coincidences ‡ between Jas and the speech and pastoral letter of Ac 15^{13-33}. Χαίρειν is the common epistolary salutation (used by Lk. in Ac 23^{26}); neither it nor the equally natural ἀκούσατε ἀδελφοί μου points to any characteristic of the speaker or writer. The alternative is to use these data as proof of the Jacobean authorship, or to conjecture that the pseudonymous author of the homily drew upon the Lucan tradition of his prototype.

---

* See, especially, Zimmer's essay; Schwegler, *NZ.* i. 430–438; Reuss, Weiffenbach, and von Soden.

† The treatment of money and its perils, of labour and its rights, of swearing, and so forth, is occasionally parallel to Essenism (cp. pp. 270 f. of Massebieau's essay, cited below).

‡ Noticed, over a century ago, by M. Weber in an essay *De epist. Jacobi cum epist. et orat. eiusdem Actis inserta utiliter comparanda* (1795).

The data provided by Clem. Rom. hardly seem to warrant the conclusion (held, *e.g.*, by Hilgenfeld, Spitta, Hort, Parry: pp. 73–74; Mayor, and Zahn) that Jas. was before the mind of that writer. The citations in 23^{3} (= Ja $1^{6f.}$) and 30^{2} (= Ja 4^{6}) probably go back to a common source in each case (see above, p. 32). Clement does combine faith and works (*e.g.* in 12 and 31), but there is no indication that he was balancing or reconciling (so Mayor and Meinertz) Paul and James—to the latter of whom he never alludes; the allusions to Rahab, Abraham, and Job were commonplaces of Jewish and Christian thought (cp. Hebrews); and the few verbal parallels, which are seldom very close, are probably coincidences (4^{16} = Clem. Rom. 21^{5}; 4^{1} = Clem. Rom. 46^{5}, cp. Plato's *Phæd.* 66 C; 3^{13} = Clem. Rom. 38^{2}, cp. Sir 3^{17-28}; 1^{19-21} = Clem. Rom. 13^{1}) due to community of atmosphere, rather than to borrowing on the part of Clement or of James (Holtzmann).*

The case for dependence becomes clearer in Hermas. Some of the parallels here again may be accounted for by the use of a common source like *Eldad and Modad* (see above, p. 32), or the OT, but others are fairly unambiguous; *e.g.* the repeated collocations of the divine πνεῦμα with κατῴκισεν (4^{5} = *Mand.* iii. 1, *Sim.* v. 6. 5–7, cp. *Mand.* v. 2. 5–7), of διψυχία with prayers (1^{4-8} = *Mand.* ix. *passim*), of bridling (χαλιναγωγεῖν) and taming ($3^{2.4.8}$ = *Mand.* xii. 1. 1–2); 4^{7} = *Mand.* xii. 2. 4, 4. 7, 5. 2; 4^{8} = *Vis.* iii. 2. 2, and a number of minor resemblances like those of 1^{8} = *Mand.* v. 2. 7; $2^{5}+5^{16}$ = *Sim.* ii. 5; $2^{7}+5^{2}$ = *Sim.* viii. 6. 4; 3^{8} = *Sim.* ix. 26. 7, *Mand.* ii. 2. 3; 3^{15} (1^{17}) = *Mand.* ix. 11; 5^{1-4} = *Vis.* iii. 9. 4–6, etc. These data (deployed by Spitta, *op. cit.* 382 f.; Zahn, *Hirt d. Hermas*, 396–409; Dr. C. Taylor in *Journ. of Philology*, xviii. 297 f., and Dr. J. Drummond in *NTA.* 108–113) indicate not simply a common atmosphere (Ropes), much less the dependence of Jas. on Hermas (Pfleiderer), but a strong probability that Jas., like the Tabula of Cebes, was known to the latter author. In this event, Hermas furnishes a *terminus ad quem* for the composition of James. But its circulation must have been limited, possibly to Syrian or Palestinian circles of the church, since it is not until the literature of the third century that any definite allusion occurs to the existence of this writing, and even then the first mention of it (by Origen) shows

* Prof. Bacon (*JBL.*, 1900, 12–22, on "the doctrine of faith in Hebrews, Jas., and Clement of Rome") arranges the documents in that order.

that much hesitation was felt about its right to a place in the apostolic canon. The great Alexandrian scholar once refers to it as ἡ φερομένη Ἰακώβου ἐπιστολή (*In Joann.* tom. xix. 6), and (on Mt 13^{55-56}) elsewhere fails to mention James as its author even when he speaks of Judas as the author of the epistle of Judas. Eusebius also classes it ('the epistle circulating under the name of James') among the disputed books which were familiar to most Christians (*H. E.* iii. 33), and adds, after mentioning the martyrdom of James, that "the first of the so-called catholic epistles is said to be his. But I must observe that it is considered spurious. Certainly not many writers of antiquity have mentioned either it or the epistle of Judas, which is also one of the seven so-called catholic epistles. Still we know that these have been used in public along with the rest of the scriptures in most churches" (*H. E.* ii. 23). Some deemed it pseudonymous (see below, p. 472). Indeed, the external evidence is strongly adverse; not until the end of the fourth century did the homily succeed in gaining the official sanction of the canon. This hesitation may have been due, in part, to an uncertainty about the apostolic rank of James, or to the comparatively obscure origin of the writing; but it is more intelligible upon the hypothesis that Jas. was of late origin, than on the view that it was a product of the primitive church, prior to A.D. 70.

§ 5. *Date.*—The hypothesis of Jas. as a pre-Pauline document, the product of a Christianity whose theology was still undeveloped, has been advocated, *e.g.* by Neander, Theile, Bunsen, Ritschl, Hofmann, Schegg, Mangold, Lechler, Erdmann, Alford (*c.* A.D. 45), Bassett, Huther, Weiss, Beyschlag, Blanc-Milsand (*Étude sur l'origine et le développement de la Théol. Apostolique*, 1884, pp. 36–57), Salmon (*INT.* 448–468), Carr, Gibson, F. H. Krüger (*Revue Chrét.*, 1887, 605 f., 686 f.), Meyrick (Smith's *DB.*² 1520–1522), Bartlet (*AA.* 217–250), Stevens (*NTTh.* 249–252), A. van Heeren (*Collationes Brugenses*, xvii. 316 f.), Patrick, Mayor, Zahn, Belser, and Meinertz. The salient objections to this hypothesis are: (*a*) The total absence of any early tradition, even in Jewish Christian circles, which associates James with the composition of an epistle like this, or indeed of any epistle. Had the revered head of the Jerusalem church written such a manifesto, it is difficult to understand its comparative oblivion for two centuries. (*b*) While it would be naively uncritical to assume that the vices denounced by the homily must have taken nearly a century to develop in early Christianity, on the other hand they are not specifically Jewish. Their soil is human nature, not Jewish. (*c*) While the range of education open to Galileans is not to be underrated—Jesus himself may have known some of the Wisdom writings (see above, p. 26),—it is hardly conceivable that a man like James should possess the wide culture, the acquaintance with classical as well as Jewish writings (LXX., not Hebrew), the rhetorical and idiomatic Greek style,* and the power of literary expression and allusion which characterise this writing. (*d*) The entire absence of allusions to the proofs of the resurrection (after 1 Co 15^{7}) and the messianic claims of Jesus, even where (*e.g.* at $2^{14f.}$ $4^{7f.}$ $5^{14f.}$) they would have been to the point. To suppose that these could be taken for granted at this period of Christianity, especially among Jews or Jewish Christians of the diaspora, is to violate historical probabilities even more seriously than to posit such an attitude to the moral and ceremonial Law on the part of the rigid James † prior to Paul's propaganda.

A final difficulty (*e*), that the epistle presupposes a knowledge of the Pauline gospel and epistles, is obviated by the hypothesis which would relegate the composition of the epistle to the seventh decade, though still adhering to the authorship of James. This view, which was formerly held by Mill (*Prolegomena*, p. 7) and Hug, is championed by Schäfer (*Einl.* 304 f.), Trenkle (*Einl.* 210 f.), Scholten, Cornely, Weiffenbach, Bleek, Farrar (*Early Days of Christianity*, 309–311), Sabatier, Hort (*JC.* 148), Felten, Jacoby (*NT Ethik*, 200 f.), T. A. Gurney (*ET.* xiv. 320 f.), Parry (A.D. 62, or a few years later), Bartmann, and Barth, mainly on the ground that the matter-of-fact and even cursory tone in which the Christian principles are mentioned shows that "these have been thoroughly assimilated by the minds and consciences both of the writer and of his readers. We are at a late stage rather than an early stage in the development of the Christian conscience, social and individual" (Parry,

* Some, *e.g.* Sabatier (pp. 132 f.), get over this by suggesting that he used a secretary; but there is no hint of this in the epistle, and the further difficulty of the wide culture remains.

† It is usually assumed that James of Jerusalem was the author, not James the brother of John (Ac 12^{2}). The tradition of the church has never been quite unanimous on the relationship between James the brother of Jesus and James the son of Alphæus.

op. cit. p. 31). On this view the epistle might be written by James (partly before his conversion, Symes?) to Paul's Jewish Christian converts in Syria and Cilicia (Gal 1[12]: so, *e.g.*, Kühl and Hoennicke); but a more plausible form of this hypothesis would be that of Renan (iv. ch. iii.), who regards the homily as an anti-Pauline invective against the rich and overbearing Sadducees of Jerusalem. In favour of this date it may be urged that James, as represented even in Acts, stood for an attitude of Jewish Christian aloofness towards Paul, while in Gal 2[12] Paul himself distinctly conveys the impression that the intruders from Jerusalem were emissaries of James (τινες ἀπὸ Ἰακώβου) who claimed his authority for acting on behalf of rigorous Jewish Christians. Unless, however, we assume a modification of James' position, under the influence of Paul,* or attribute to him a fairly liberal view of the situation, the seventh-decade date presents more psychological and historical difficulties than even the earlier date.

Several of the objections, moreover, which are valid against the latter (*a*, *b*, *c*, and in part *d*), still operate against this hypothesis, and the additional drawback emerges, that no reference occurs to questions like circumcision and the general problem of the Law, which were organic to the controversy between Paul and James over the relations of Jewish and Gentile Christians. It is such considerations which have suggested a later period for the composition of this pastoral. "Nous ne serons donc pas étonnés de voir la critique contemporaine pencher de plus en plus vers l'opinion que cette épître de Jacques date du second âge et a été en partie écrite pour réagir contre une tendance, peut-être mal appréciée, laquelle elle-même n'appartenait pas aux débuts de l'enseignement apostolique" (Reuss, *Les épîtres catholiques*, p. 117).

A later date, prior to the end of the first century, is advocated generally by Hilgenfeld (*Einl.* 537–542), Klöpper, S. Davidson (doubtfully), McGiffert (*AA.* 579–585), J. Réville (*Les origines de l'épiscopat*, pp. 230 f.), A. H. Blom ('de achtergrond van den Jakobusbrief,' *TT.*, 1881, 439–449), Bacon (*INT.* 158–165), von Soden (doubtfully), and Rovers (*Einl.* 93). A date *c.* A.D. 100 is favoured by Knopf (*NZ.* 34–35), while others (*e.g.* Baur, *Church History*, Eng. tr. i. 128–130; Schwegler, *NZ.* i. 413 f., 441 f., and Volkmar, *ZWT.*, 1861, p. 427) fix generally

* So, *e.g.*, Gould (*NTTh.* 102 f.), who notes that "the mind of Christ, but not his personal spell, is exhibited here in many essential matters." Yet it is just this personal impression which we would expect in James, whether he was the son of Alphæus (Meinertz) or the son of Joseph and Mary, at least as much as in Peter (see above, p. 334).

on the period of the pastoral epistles or on that of Hermas (*e.g.* Holtzmann and Pfleiderer's *Urc.* iv. 293 f., regarding Jas. as a protest against the secularising tendencies of contemporary Christianity).* Brückner (*Chron.* 60 f., 287 f.) assigns it to a conventicle of Jewish Christian Essenism, during the reign of Hadrian; Jülicher (*Einl.* § 16), like Usteri (*SK.*, 1889, 211–256) and Grafe, thinks of the period A.D. 125–150; Peake (*INT.* 87) assigns 'a date comparatively early in the second century,' owing to the lack of any anti-gnostic references; N. Schmidt (*Prophet of Nazareth*, p. 191) conjectures *c.* A.D. 150, Ropes, A.D. 75–125, and W. Wrede (*Entstehung der Schriften des NT*, 91–92), A.D. 110–140. This hypothesis, in a general form, has the merit of explaining more of the internal data, and of explaining them more satisfactorily, than any other. The so-called primitiveness of the epistle, with its undogmatic or rather anti-dogmatic bias, is explicable, not against any imaginary † background of a nascent elementary stage in Christianity, at which the appreciation of Jesus was still meagre, but in the light of such moralistic tendencies and features as emerged in certain circles of Christianity towards the opening of the second century, when for various reasons, as Klöpper puts it, the moral deficiencies of Christian conduct were being covered by the withered fig-leaves of an intellectual belief, and a higher legalism was promulgated as an antidote. The atmosphere and situation resemble the moralism of the Didachê; the distinctively religious tenets are assumed (cp. He $6^{1f.}$) rather than proclaimed. Upon the other hand, any idea of anti-gnostic polemic or of allusions to persecutions must be given up. The range of the homily does not include such hints of its environment.

The blanched Christology of the Didachê and Diognetus throws light also upon the scanty allusions to Jesus which, in a primitive apostle, are almost incomprehensible. One of the most vital and central ideas of the primitive Christian preaching, in all its phases, was the relation of Christ's death to the forgiveness of sins. But James refers to the latter in a Jewish manner (5^{20}), devoid of any specifically Christian background. It is not possible

---

* Cp. Steck (*ZSchw.*, 1889, xv. 3), J. H. Wilkinson (*AJT.* ii. 120–123), and Cone (*EBi.* 2321 f.). Those who are satisfied with the proofs of the epistle's use by Clem. Rom. are naturally able to place it within the first century. Otherwise, Hermas furnishes the *terminus ad quem*, just as Romans or 1 Peter the *terminus a quo*.

† Ac $15^{23f.}$ is no argument to the contrary, for it was written for a specific purpose; James is a general homily.

to explain this away by pleading that the homily has a practical bent. As if the forgiveness of sins, owing to Christ's death, was not intensely practical to the early Christian! On the other hand, while no pre-occupation with OT conceptions can be supposed to have excluded from an apostle's purview the belief in forgiveness through the death of Christ, this and other phenomena become intelligible in the neighbourhood of writings like Hermas. Luther's comment on 2^{19}—"und nicht viel von Christo"—applies to the greater part of the homily; it is unnatural (with Parry, 23–24) to take τὴν πίστιν τοῦ κυρίου ἡμῶν Ἰησοῦ Χριστοῦ τῆς δόξης as a summary of the preceding paragraphs, as if *the Lord Jesus Christ* here were an embodiment of ὁ ἔμφυτος λόγος, and *our Glory* a description of Christ as the ideal embodiment of human nature's glory, nor is there any allusion to the death of Jesus even where we would expect it, in 5^{11} (see above). It is possible to deduce from the homily characteristics which may fit into a view of James' character towards the end of his life, but such reconstructions are at best fanciful; although a certain amount of ambiguity attaches to any view of the writing, there is perhaps less violence done to the probabilities of the evidence, internal and external, upon the later hypothesis than upon any other.

§ 6. *Authorship.*—The main problem, upon this view, is to explain the authorship in the light of 1^1. (*a*) The pseudonymous hypothesis arose early (see the early prologue to the cath. epp. discussed in *Revue Bénéd.*, 1906, 82 f.; and Jerome, *uir. inlustr.* 2: "Jacobus, qui appellatur frater Domini, unam tantum scripsit epistolam, quæ de septem catholicis est; quæ et ipsa ab alio quodam sub nomine eius edita asseritur, licet paulatim tempore procedente obtinuerit auctoritatem"). But the lack of any emphasis upon the apostle's personality and authority (no ἀπόστολος in 1^1, as in 1 P 1^1, 2 P 1^1) tells against this theory. If a second-century writer, who wished to counteract some ultra-Paulinists (cp. 2 P 3^{16}), had chosen the name of the revered head of the Jerusalem church (so, *e.g.*, S. Davidson, Grafe, Jülicher), why did he not make more of Paul's opponent? To argue that he refrained from introducing such traits, lest his writing should incur suspicion as a literary fiction, is to attribute too modern and subtle motives to him. At the same time, the practical motive of the writer, and the conviction that he was in sympathy with James, may have been felt to justify such a literary method (see above, p. 340). (*b*) A variant hypothesis argues that, while it was erroneously ascribed in the course of tradition to James the apostle, it was really written by some other James (so, *e.g.*, Erasmus, "fieri potest ut nomen commune cum apostolo præbuerit occasionem ut hæc epistola Iacobo apostolo ascriberetur, cum fuerit alterius cuiusdam Iacobi," Pfleiderer, etc.). The interpretation of the title as the self-designation of the Lord's brother would be natural in an age when no Christian writing could hope to secure canonical prestige or to retain its place in ecclesiastical use, if it had not some link with the apostles. (*c*) Finally, 1^1 may be taken in whole or part as an addition of the early church (so Harnack, *TU.* ii. 2. 106 f., and *ACL.* ii. 1. 485–491; Bacon, *INT.* pp. 158–165; McGiffert*), or a Jacobean nucleus (Oesterley), to which later excerpts from other writings were added, may be postulated. The conjecture (G. C. Martin, *Exp.*[7] iii. 174–184) that the writing was originally a collection of logia with comments made by James the brother of Jesus, and issued in his name after A.D. 70 as a treatise on practical Christianity, helps to reconcile the late circulation of the book with its primitive character, and clears up the address; but it does not explain 2^{14-26}, and it lies open to most of the objections valid against any theory of apostolic authorship, though it is better than Weizsäcker's (*AA.* ii. 27 f.) similar hypothesis of an Ebionitic anti-Pauline tract, containing glosses and expansions of Matthæan logia, written not by James but by some one after A.D. 70.

The question of the date thus depends upon the crucial problem of the authorship, and that in turn falls to be decided primarily upon two internal features, the religious colour and the style. Each of these features has set literary criticism recently in motion towards and away from the apostolic authorship. The comparative lack of any definitely Christian traits and the strangely Jewish colouring of the homily as a whole have started two hypotheses: (i.) One is represented by the independent attempts of Spitta and Massebieau ('L'épître de Jacques, est-elle l'œuvre d'un Chrétien?' *RHR.*, 1895, pp. 249–283) to prove that the writing was originally the work of a Jewish writer ('un juif, helléniste, lettré, atteint par la philosophie grecque, universaliste, connaissant le milieu théologique de la Dispersion,' Massebieau, pp. 270 f.) which has been edited and adopted (in 1^1 2^1) for the uses of the Christian church. But, even apart from the lack of allusions to any ritual or legal

* "It is possible that the phrase, 'James, a servant of God and of the Lord Jesus Christ,' was added to the anonymous epistle under the influence of the parallel words in the epistle of Jude" (p. 585). The tradition which associates the ep. of Judas with Judas the brother of Jesus is much earlier and stronger than the Jacobean.

usages, which would be natural in a Jewish original, the Christian sense of passages like 1^{18} (=the regenerating word, not the word of creation), 2^{7} (τὸ καλὸν ὄνομα), and 5^{7-8} (ἡ παρουσία τοῦ κυρίου), is unmistakable; a Christian interpolator would scarcely have contented himself with inserting so little, when he could have added references to Christ's life, *e.g.*, at 5^{11}; and he would probably have left 2^{1} clearer.* (ii.) The ingenious suggestion that the epistle was composed by James of Jerusalem for the benefit of Jews, not of Christians (J. H. Moulton, *Exp.*[7] iv. 45–55), is liable to the same objections which invalidate the Jewish hypothesis or that of James the apostle's authorship, viz. the absence of any specific allusion to the burning questions of the law (with regard to circumcision especially) and of the messianic claims of Jesus, which agitated Jewish Christendom at that early period. Can we suppose that a Christian, especially one of James's position, suppressed his distinctively Christian beliefs in order to recommend Christian morals to Jews? The hypothesis fails to provide adequate motives for such a procedure, and the difficulty of $2^{14f.}$ is practically as great on this view as on that of Spitta and Massebieau.

The conviction that so rich and idiomatic a Greek style—to say nothing of the culture (cp. Hilgenfeld, *Einl.* 539 f.)—could not have been at the command of a man like James of Jerusalem,† has tempted several critics (*e.g.* Faber, *observ. in epistolam Jacobi ex Syro*, 1770; Schmidt, Bertholdt, and Wordsworth, *SB.* i. pp. 144 f.) to conjecture that the epistle was originally written in Aramaic. But the Corbey old Latin version, with all its peculiarities, does not hark back to a Greek text which was, like the canonical text, a version of any Aramaic original. The epistle has assonances and idioms which preclude any idea of its being a translation; most of it is as distinctively and independently Greek as a page of Marcus Aurelius (cp. Mayor's ed. ch. x. and Jacquier's *INT.* iii. 228–230). Besides, it is

---

* For adverse discussions, see especially Mayor (*Exp.*[5] vi. 1–14, 321–338 and in pp. cliv–clxxviii of his edition), van Manen (*TT.*, 1897, 398–427: 'Jacobus geen Christen?'), Wrede (*LC.*, 1896, 450–451), von Soden (*TLZ.*, 1897, 581–584), Adeney (*Critical Review*, 1896, 277–283), Haupt (*SK.*, 1896, 747–777), Steck (*ZSchw.*, 1898, pp. 169–188); Harnack (*ACL.* ii. 1. pp. 485–491), R. P. Rose (*RB.* v. 519–534), and Patrick (*James the Lord's Brother*, 1906, 337–343). His companion hypothesis of a Jewish original for Hermas has met with equal disfavour (cp. Réville in *RHR.*, 1897, 117–122, and Stahl's *Patrist. Studien*, 1901, pp. 299–356).

† The best statement of the case for the bi-lingual attainments (Aramaic and Greek) of most Palestinians is given by Dr. James Hadley in *Essays Philological and Critical* (1873), pp. 403 f.

highly improbable that any epistle, intended *ex hypothesi* for circulation throughout the diaspora, would be written in Aramaic. Whatever bearing the fact has upon the origin of the writing, it should be acknowledged frankly that the author, like the *auctor ad Hebræos*, was thinking, as well as composing, in Greek.

The wide differences of critical opinion upon James are not unparalleled in other departments of literary inquiry. Thus a very different writing, the *Ciris*, was not only attributed to Vergil himself, but has been placed either before him or after him, as a work which either influenced, or was influenced by, his language. An almost equally large range has been covered by the efforts of classical scholars to place the *Aetna* of the Vergilian appendix, and the *Nux* of Ovid presents similarly baffling features. The phenomena of criticism upon the Jacobean homily are perplexing, but they are not to be taken as discrediting the science of NT literary research.

(D) *TWO LETTERS OF JOHN THE PRESBYTER (2 AND 3 JOHN).*

LITERATURE.—In addition to the editions and studies cited below (p. 582) under "The First Epistle of John":—(*a*) 2 John: Ritmeier (*de Electa Domina*, 1706); C. A. Krigele (*de Κυρίᾳ Joannis*, 1758); Carpzov (*Theologica Exegetica*, pp. 105–208); H. G. B. Müller (*Comm. in Secundam epistolam Ioannis*, 1783); C. Klug (*De authentia*, etc., 1823); F. L. Gachon (*Authenticité de la 2e et 3e épp. de Jean*, 1851); Knauer (*SK*, 1833, 452 f.); Poggel (*Der 2 und 3 Briefe d. Apostel Johannes*, 1896)*; Belser (*TQ.*, 1897, 150 f., review of Poggel); J. Rendel Harris (*Exp.*[6] iii. pp. 194 f.); W. M. Ramsay (*ibid.* pp. 354 f.); Gibbins (*Exp.*[6] xii. 228–236, 2 John a prophetic epistle); J. Chapman (*JTS*, 1904, 357 f., 517 f., 'The Historical Setting of the Second and Third Epistles of St. John'); V. Bartlet (*JTS.*, 1905, 204–216). (*b*) 3 John (generally in connection with 2 John): Heumann's *Commentatio in Joan. ep. III.* (1778); Harnack (*TU.* xv. 3)*; E. C. Selwyn (*The Christian Prophets and the Prophetic Apocalypse*, 1900, 133 f.); B. Bresky (*Das Verhältniss d. zweiten Johannesbriefes zum dritten*, 1906); U. von Wilamowitz-Moellendorff (*Hermes*, 1898, 529 f.); G. G. Findlay, *Fellowship in the Life Eternal* (1909), pp. 1–46.

§ 1. *2 John.*—This note is written by a certain πρεσβύτερος to a Christian community, figuratively described as *the Elect Lady*, some of whose members he had met (4) and valued for their integrity of Christian character. Owing perhaps to information supplied by them, he sends this warning against the indiscriminate entertainment of itinerant teachers * who promulgate progressive or 'advanced' docetic views (7) upon the person of Christ. The note is merely designed to serve (12) till the writer arrives in person. He sends greetings to his correspondents from some community in which he is resident (13) at present, and with which they had evidently a close connection.

That ἐκλεκτῇ κυρίᾳ denotes a church is clear, in spite of recent arguments to the contrary (Poggel, *op. cit.* 127 f.; Harris), from (*a*) a comparison of v.[13] with 1[1] and 5[13] of 1 Peter (an earlier writing circulated in Asia Minor); and (*b*) from the plurals of [6. 8. 10], and [12]. The origin of this semi-poetic personification of the church (cp. Rev 22[17] and Hermas) or of a community (cp. 2 Co 11[2]) as Κυρία, may lie in the conception of a Bride of the κύριος (Eph 5[21. 32] cp. Jn 3[29]).

In the absence of any tradition upon the origin and destination of the epistle, Baur and Schwegler set to work upon a remark of Clemens Alexandrinus (*Adumbrationes*, iv. 437: secunda Johannis epistola, quæ ad uirgines scripta est, simplicissima est; scripta uero est ad quandam Babyloniam Electam nomine, significat autem electionem ecclesiæ sanctæ). It is building too much on the term *Babyloniam* in this blundering † fragment (in connection with 1 P 5[13]) to identify the church addressed in 2 John with a section of the Roman church, however, as though the Diotrephes of 3 John were a symbolical expression for the bishop of Rome (Soter or Eleutherus), and the later note a controversial missive against the pretensions of the hierarchy. No hint of Montanist sympathies is visible in the letter, and there is nothing specifically Montanist about a term like ἐκλέκτη.

When all trace of its original destination had been lost, it was natural to suppose that it would suit any church, and therefore that it was addressed to the church at large (so Jerome,

* As in Did. 11[1-2] 'Whosoever then shall come and teach you all these things aforesaid, receive him. But if the teacher himself be perverted and teach a different doctrine to the undoing thereof, hear him not; yet if he teaches to the increase of righteousness and the knowledge of the Lord, receive him as the Lord.' See above, p. 460.

† Clement's error in regarding 'Eklekta' as a Babylonian Christian led him (as Zahn ingeniously argues, *Forschungen*, iii. 92 f., 99 f., *INT.* iii. 383) to consider her and her children as Parthians. Hence the erroneous title πρὸς Πάρθους (v.l. παρθένους) prefixed to 2 John and afterwards to the group of the 'Johannine' letters. This solution had been already proposed by C. Wordsworth, though, unlike Zahn, he imagined the title to be correct.

Ep. 123^{11-12} ad Ageruchiam, after Clem. Alex.), by a process of inference similar to that of the Muratorian Canon on Paul. This was a particularly likely interpretation, in view of its position among the 'catholic' epistles of the Canon. But the note must have originally been meant for some definite community, most probably for one of those in Asia Minor, though it is superfluous to chronicle the endless conjectures.

§ 2. *3 John.*—3 John is another note from the presbyter—this time a private note, addressed to Gaius, evidently a convert and disciple of the author ([4]), and a member of the same community or house-church ([9]) as that to which 2 John had been written. The immediate occasion of the note is the welcome news ([8]) of Gaius's adherence to the true faith, and of his hospitality ([5-8]) to itinerant preachers who are, it is implied, of sound character and doctrine. The duty of hospitality is pressed upon him, instead of, as usual (cp. He 13^{2}), upon the local church as a whole or its heads (cp. 1 Ti 3^{2}, Tit 1^{8}; Herm. *Sim.* ix. 27, etc.), since one of its leaders, a certain Diotrephes ([9-10]), had repudiated the authority and suppressed some previous church-epistles of the presbyter, besides denying hospitality to his representatives. He would even carry his hostility the length of excommunicating their hosts, including Gaius, from the local community (cp. Abbott, *Diat.* 2258). With this opponent the writer promises to deal sharply when he comes in person ([10]). Meanwhile he dispatches the present note ([14]), in appreciation of his correspondent's attitude; Gaius is to continue his hospitality to the evangelists in question ([6]), who now bring this note to him. He must have preserved it among his papers, but there is no tradition upon his residence. The name was so common * that it is precarious to argue from 1 Co 1^{14} or Ac 20^{4} that his church was that of Corinth (Michaelis, Alexander, Coenen in *ZWT.*, 1872, 264–271), or Pergamos (Wolf, Hilgenfeld, Thoma, Findlay), where John is said to have ordained him bishop (*Ap. Const.* 7^{46}), Thessalonika (another traditional site for his bishopric, Chapman), or Thyatira (Bartlet).

The present note may be a letter of introduction for Demetrius ([12]) and its other bearers ([5-8]); although such letters were usually addressed to a community or church, not to

* "The coincidence of name [with the Gaius of 1 Co 1^{14}] is as little surprising as it would be to find two hospitable *Smiths* in distant counties of England" (Findlay, p. 37).

an individual (cp. 2 Co 3^1 $8^{23f.}$; Polyk. *Phil.* 14), the circumstances were peculiar in this case (see above). If ἐκκλησίας could be read in v.[12] (cp. Gwynn, *Hermathena*, 1890, 304), Demetrius would be a presbyter. The name is too common to make it likely that he is to be identified with the Demas of 2 Ti 4^{10} (Chapman),—as though the writer wished to prevent his bad reputation from discrediting him,—or with the Demetrius of Ac 19^{24} (so recently Selwyn and Bartlet); and there is no reason to suppose (with Harnack and others) that the note of v.[9] was written to him, or that he was the sole bearer of 3 John.

The note is set in a new light by the hypothesis of Harnack (*op. cit.*, also *HD.* i. pp. 213 f., and *The Constitution and Law of the Church in First Two Centuries*, 100 f.; cp. Schmiedel in *EBi.* 3146–3147), followed by von Dobschütz (*Urc.* 220–222), Windisch, and Knopf (*NZ.* pp. 206 f.), that the presbyter, who had already (2 Jn [10]) put the* church on its guard against itinerant preachers, is here opposed as an intruder by Diotrephes, the head of some local church, who feels that the interests of the organisation are no longer compatible with the outside supervision exercised over the Asiatic communities by the presbyter himself. The territorial authority of the latter is repudiated. On this view, the presbyter would be making a conservative protest against the first of the monarchical bishops. It was unsuccessful. By the time Ignatius came to write, the monarchical episcopate was fairly settled in Asia Minor; the action of Diotrephes was ratified by history, and John the presbyter's reputation rested on his writings, not on his ecclesiastical policy. The theory, however, involves some speculative treatment of 2 John, *e.g.* the assumption that κυρία practically admits the church's independence; also the assumption that Diotrephes was a bishop, and that he represented the monarchical episcopate, whereas he may have been on quite the opposite side; and finally, the assumption that his fault was ecclesiastical rather than doctrinal (cp. Krüger, *ZWT.*, 1898, 307–311; Hilgenfeld, *ibid.* 316–320; and Belser, *TQ.*, 1897, 150 f.).

§ 3. *Traces of 2 and 3 John in sub-apostolic literature.*—No clear allusion to either note occurs in the apostolic fathers; 3 Jn [12] need not lie behind the phrase of Papias in Eus. *H. E.* iii. 39. 3 (ἀπ' αὐτῆς παραγινομένας ἀληθείας), and Ignatius did not require to have read 2 Jn [10] in order to write *ad Smyrn.* 4^1. The existence of the pair is plain, however. The allusion in the Muratorian Canon ('epistula sane Judæ et superscripti [supra-

* Harnack considers 2 John to have been written, however, to another church, and refuses, on inadequate grounds, to see 2 John in 3 John [9]. But this allusion in [9] (ἔγραψα) refers in all likelihood to 2 John rather than to 1 John or to some lost epistle; it was in order to avoid the last-named suggestion that ἄν was added at an early stage in the textual history of the letter.

scripti?] Ioannis duæ in catholica habentur') is certainly to 2 and 3 John (cp. Lightfoot's *Biblical Essays*, 99–100); the fragment has already referred to 1 John, which went with the Fourth gospel. Irenæus (iii. 16. 8, cp. i. 16. 3) quotes 2 Jn [7-8] as if it came from 1 John, with a laxity which is not unexampled in subsequent writers. Both were known to Clement and Dionysius of Alexandria. For their earliest appearance, at a later date, in the Syrian church, see Gwynn (*Hermathena*, 1890, 281 f.). Codex Bezæ originally had 3 John (and therefore, probably, 2 John and 1 John) immediately before Acts, the 'Johannine' epistles thus following the Fourth gospel. 2 and 3 John could only have survived on account of their traditional connection with their author, and when the later development of the Johannine tradition obliterated John the presbyter in favour of his apostolic namesake, 2 and 3 John, like the Apocalypse, usually passed into the canon (so far as they passed in at all) as compositions of John the apostle.

It was probably the fugitive character and the doctrinal insignificance of the notes which not only prevented their wide circulation but started doubts upon their canonicity. Origen (quoted in Eus. *H. E.* vi. 25. 10: ['Ιωάννης] *καταλέλοιπεν καὶ ἐπιστολὴν πάνυ ὀλίγων στίχων, ἔστω δὲ καὶ δευτέραν καὶ τρίτην· ἐπεὶ οὐ πάντες φασὶν γνησίους εἶναι ταύτας· πλὴν οὐκ εἰσιν στίχων ἀμφότεραι ἑκατόν*) and his pupil Dionysius (in *H. E.* vii. 25. 10) both reflect these suspicions. Eusebius (*H. E.* iii. 25. 3), in mentioning the notes among the NT *ἀντιλεγόμενα*, alludes to the possibility that they were by a namesake of the apostle; this early tradition, which is definitely chronicled by Jerome (*de uir. inlustr.* 9: 'reliquæ autem duæ . . . Iohannis presbyteri adseruntur, 18: . . . superiorem opinionem, qua a plerisque rettulimus traditum duas posteriores epistulas Iohannis non apostoli esse, sed presbyteri'), and which reappears elsewhere (cp. p. 17 and *JTS*. i. 534 f.), has been largely ratified by modern research.

§ 4. *Authorship.*—The *πρεσβύτερος* is unnamed. Even on the theory that John the apostle survived till the beginning of the second century in Asia Minor and wrote one or both of the larger 'Johannine' books, it would not follow that he composed these notes. There is no claim to apostolic authority, even in 3 John where it would have been relevant on discipline and doctrine; and although Peter is termed a presbyter in 1 P 5[1], this is in an epistle which had already explicitly called him an apostle (1 P 1[1]), so that the former passage is not a parallel to the supposed apostolic origin of notes like 2 and 3 John, where the writer simply calls himself ὁ *πρεσβύτερος*. The only important figure of that age who is known to us as 'the presbyter' κατ' ἐξοχήν is John the presbyter, to whom Papias refers in exactly this fashion (cp. *H. E.* iii. 39. 15, καὶ τοῦτο ὁ πρεσβύτερος ἔλεγε). The early tradition of his authorship has therefore won wide acceptance since Jerome's day; so, *e.g.*, Erasmus, Grotius, Fritzsche, Bretschneider, Wieseler, Credner, Jachmann, Ebrard, Renan (iv. pp. 78 f.), Forbes, Harnack, Selwyn, von Dobschütz (*Urc.* 218 f.), von Soden (*INT.* 445 f.), Heinrici (*Urc.* 129 f.), J. Weiss, Peake, and R. Knopf (*NZ.* 32 f.). The πρεσβύτερος of the letters has an antipathy to gnostic speculation and an authority over the local churches similar to those reflected in Apoc 2–3. It is true that 2 and 3 John do not reproduce the distinctive eschatological or chronological tenets of the larger work, but in such small notes, written for a special purpose, there was no occasion to develop chiliastic opinions or any of the specific views promulgated in the Apocalypse. Furthermore, it must be noted that in Apoc 2–3 the presbyter is giving each church ἐπιταγὴν κυρίου (1 Co 7^{25}) in the name of the Lord, or rather ἐν λόγῳ κυρίου (1 Th 4^{15} cp. 1 Co 7^{10} οὐκ ἐγὼ ἀλλὰ ὁ κύριος), while in 2 and 3 John he writes κατὰ τὴν ἐμὴν γνώμην (in the sense of 1 Co 7^{40}). When allowance is made for a certain flexibility and versatility, there is little more difficulty in regarding 2 and 3 John as written by the author of the Apocalypse than in believing that Philemon and Colossians were almost contemporary products of Paul's pen. On the other hand, there is no reason to suppose (Schleiermacher, *Einl.* 400; Clemen) that 2 and 3 John were written by different hands (2 John after 3 John, according to Clemen).

The contents and characteristics of the two notes are too occasional to support the rival theory that they were pseudonymous, written under the name of John the apostle (Baumgarten) or the presbyter (Schmiedel) in order to correct the description of him by Papias (Lüdemann, *JPT.*, 1879, 565–676). Schwartz (*Der Tod d. Söhne Zebedæi*, 42 f., 47 f.), who, like Harnack, rightly sees that they are genuine notes from the same hand of an Asiatic presbyter, conjectures (so Wendland) that the author's name was left out in order that his title of ὁ πρεσβύτερος might connect the notes with the more famous presbyter John. This would have been a roundabout way of reaching such an end. Bacon (*Fourth Gospel in Research*, 1910, 184 f.) regards all the three 'Johannine epistles' as a piece of editorial framework or epistolary commendation written by the author of John 1–20 in order to give currency to the latter, and afterwards used by R, the author of John 21, who finally edited the Fourth gospel in its present form. But if any hypothesis along these lines had to be worked out, it would be better to connect the author of 1 John with the appendix and the final revision of the gospel (see below). At all events, the common phraseology of 3 Jn ^{12} and Jn 21^{24} might as well be a reminiscence in the case of the latter (where the application is less natural) or the independent use of a catch-word of the 'Johannine' circle. For similar reasons, the parallels between 2 and 3 John and the longer homily (1 Jn.) do not necessarily involve the literary dependence of the former on the latter. In the case of a school or group, like the Asiatic 'Johannine' circle, the currency of phrases and ideas renders it not impossible that the smaller notes were written earlier and independently.

When the theory that all five 'Johannine' writings came from John the apostle or John the presbyter is abandoned, and the gospel assigned to a different author from the apocalypse, the problem of the three epistles remains. *Prima facie* 1 Jn. goes with the Fourth gospel, either as written by the Fourth evangelist or by some like-minded Christian of the same group. 2 and 3 John, on the other hand, go more naturally with the apocalypse, when the latter is assigned to John the presbyter, in spite of traits like the doctrinal antichrist-conception of 2 Jn ^{7} = 1 Jn 2^{18} $4^{1f.}$ The alternative would be to group them with 1 John, assuming that the latter was not written by the author of the Fourth gospel. In a problem like this, where the data are almost entirely drawn from the internal evidence of the literature, no result can claim more than a high degree of probability, but the scale appears to turn, upon the whole, in favour of the hypothesis that 2 and 3 John were written by John the presbyter,—whether before or after he wrote the Apocalypse it is not possible to say,—and that they diverge from 1 Jn. The latter position is more than defensible.* The two notes have a distinctiveness of form and even of language which justifies the hypothesis that their origin is not that of 1 Jn. and the Fourth gospel. Thus we find idiosyncrasies like *εἴ τις* for the Johannine *ἐάν τις*, *ἐρχόμενος*† *ἐν σαρκί* for *ἐληλυθὼς ἐν σαρκί*, *κοινωνεῖν* for *κοινωνίαν ἔχειν*, *εἰς οἰκίαν* for *εἰς τὰ ἴδια*, etc. The collocation of *χάρις*, *ἔλεος*, *εἰρήνη* is not Johannine, and there are other resemblances to Pauline language, apart from the apparent acquaintance with 1 Peter which 2 John betrays. The common denominator of language and style between 1 John and 2–3 John is patent. But "not even all these resemblances are conclusive. They are in no case very remarkable idioms or phrases. Current peculiarities and turns of language at Ephesus might account for them all, so far as they need to be accounted for" (Selwyn, p. 133).

§ 5. *Characteristics and style.*—The notes reveal the presbyter journeying (so Clem. Alex. *quis diues salu.* 42) to and fro among his churches, and writing letters, now and then, to serve as temporary guides till he could arrive in person. He has a coterie of like-minded Christians (this is the force of the *we* in $^{9\text{-}10.\ 12}$, cp. 1 Jn $1^{1\text{-}4}$ $4^{6.\ 14}$), in whose name as well as in his

* The difference of authorship between 1 Jn and 2–3 Jn is recognised by Credner (*Einl.* i. 692 f.), Ebrard (359 f.), Selwyn (135 f.), J. Réville (*le quatr. Évangile*, 49 f.), Schwartz, and Jülicher (*Einl.* 218–216), especially.

† Cp. Apoc 1^{8} = 2 Jn ^{7}. The contrast between this and 1 Jn 4^{2} is equalled by the difference between 3 Jn ^{11} and 1 Jn $4^{12b.\ 20}$.

own he speaks with authority, and *the truth* (3 Jn $^{3-5}$) is simply a life answering to the apostolic standard laid down by these authorities. Thus 2 John is a specimen of the excommunicating letters occasionally dispatched by early Christian leaders to a community (cp. 1 Co 5^{9}), while 3 John is nearer to ἐπιστολαὶ συστατικαί (cp. 2 Co 3^{1}) like Ro $16^{1f.}$.

In 3 Jn [1], as the use of ἀγαπητὸς for φίλτατος might be thought "Schönrednerei und nicht vom besten Geschmacke," the writer added ὃν . . . ἀληθείᾳ (U. von W. Moellendorff, pp. 529 f.). In v.[2] Rendel Harris (*Exp.*[5] viii. 167) proposes to correct περὶ to πρὸ, after the common formula in the papyri. The latter bring out the epistolary character of the notes. Thus, *e.g.*, for κυρία as a term of affectionate courtesy, cp. *e.g. Oxyrhynchus Papyri*, iv. 243 f. (Βεροῦτι τῇ κυρίᾳ μου); for καλῶς ποιεῖν and the idea of 3 Jn [2],* the papyrus-note quoted in Witkowski's *Epistulæ Privatæ Græcæ* (1906), 5 f. (καλῶς ποιεῖς εἰ ἔρρωσαι καὶ τὰ λοιπά σοι κατὰ γνώμην ἐστίν) and the second-century letter (*Berliner Griechische Urkunden*, ii. 84 f., πρὸ μὲν πάντων εὔχομαι σε ὑγιαίνειν κτλ.). The phrase in the fourth-century Christian letter of Justinus to Papnuthius (cp. Deissmann's *Licht vom Osten*, 151 f.), ἵνα οὖν μὴ πολλὰ γράφω καὶ φλυαρήσω, may be an unconscious reminiscence of 3 Jn [13] (cp. [10]).

§ 6. *Date.*—Those who ascribe the notes to John the apostle date them anywhere between 80 and 100, or even earlier (after Neronic persecution, Chapman). Otherwise, on the hypothesis of their composition by John the presbyter or some anonymous 'Johannine' disciple, they may fall later, before 110 (Harnack), between A.D. 125 and 130 (Pfleiderer, *Urc.* ii. 450), between 130 and 140 (Holtzmann, Hilgenfeld, *Einl.* 682–694; Weizsäcker's *AA.* ii. 239, and Brückner, *Chron.* 302 f.), or even *c.* A.D. 155 (Kreyenbühl, *Evglm der Wahrheit*, i. 131 f.). Their lack of definite allusions to the gnostic systems and their attitude towards the ecclesiastical organisation of the church, however, are best met by a date not later than the opening decades of the second century (cp. J. Réville, *Les origines de l'épiscopat*, i. 204–208), when the organisation was being consolidated. A period somewhat earlier than the Didachê and Ignatius would suit most of the requirements of these letters. Their similarity of tone suggests that they were written shortly after one another, but they stir rather than satisfy the curiosity of the historian. In the dark, wide bay of early Christian life, they glimmer like two adjacent specks of light, indicating some place where Asiatics dwell and work, unknown to passers-by upon the high seas.

* J. R. Harris (*Exp.*[5] viii. 166 f.).

CHAPTER IV.

THE APOCALYPSE OF JOHN.

LITERATURE.—(*a*) Editions—although the earliest Greek commentaries (*e.g.* by Melito and Hippolytus) have been lost, those of Oecumenius (cp. Diekamp in *SBBA.*, 1901, 1046 f.), Andreas (ed. Sylburg, 1596), and Arethas survive, as well as Latin commentaries by Victorinus of Pettau (cp. Ehrhard, *ACL.* 484 f.), Tyconius, Primasius, Apringius (ed. Férotin, Paris, 1900), Beatus (cp. H. L. Ramsay, *Le Commentaire de l'apoc. par Beatus*, 1900), etc., and the Syriac work of Barṣalibi (cp. Gwynn in *Hermathena*, vi.-vii.). Haymo, Joachim, and Rupert of Deutz are the best representatives of the mediæval school. The sixteenth century threw up the *Annotationes* of Erasmus (1516), with the commentaries of T. Bibliander (Basle, 1569), F. Ribeira (Salamanca, 1591), and J. Winckelmann (Frankfort, 1590); the seventeenth added A. Salmeron's *Prœludia* (Cologne, 1614), De Dieu's *Animadversiones* (1646), and the *Cogitationes* of Cocceius (Amsterdam, 1673), with the commentaries of Brightman (London, 1616), D. Paraeus (Heidelberg, 1618), Mariana (1619), Cornelius à Lapide (1627), H. Grotius (*Annotationes*, Paris, 1644), and Hammond (London, 1653); while the eighteenth[1] produced Vitringa's Ἀνάκρισις (1721)[2], Abauzit's *Discourse, Hist. and Critical* (London and Geneva, 1730), and the commentaries of Schlurmann (1722), Bengel (1740), Wetstein (Amsterdam, 1752), and Eichhorn (Göttingen, 1791). The literature of the nineteenth century includes the editions of Woodhouse (London, 1805); P. J. S. Vogel (*Commentationes VII. de apoc. Joh.*, Erlangen, 1811-6); Ewald (*Commentarius . . . exegeticus et criticus*, 1828); A. L. Matthaei (Göttingen, 1828); Züllig (Stuttgart, 1834-40); S. P. Tregelles (1844); Moses Stuart[2] (1845)*; de Wette (1848); Ebrard (— Olshausen, 1853); C. Stern (1854); C. Wordsworth (London, 1860); E. W. Hengstenberg[2] (Berlin, 1861-2); J. Glasgow (Edinburgh, 1862); G. Volkmar (Zürich, 1862); Alford[2] (1862); Wolf (Innsbruck, 1870); H. Kienlen (1870); Kliefoth (1874); J. L. Fuller (1874); Hofmann (1874); A. Bisping (Münster, 1876); C. H. A. Burger (1877); J. P. Lange[2] (1878, Eng. tr. 1874); E. Reuss (1878); Garrat[2] (1878); S. Lee (*Speaker's Comm.* 1881); Waller (Freiburg, 1882); Ph. Krementz (Freiburg, 1883); Beck (1885); Düsterdieck[4] (— Meyer, 1887); Kübel (— Zöckler, 1888); W. Milligan (London, 1889); Randall (*Pulpit Comm.* 1890); F. S. Tiefenthal (1892); W. H. Simcox (*CGT.* 1893), and Lindenbein[2] (1895). More recent works include the editions of

[1] For the cloud of homiletical and prophetical books, see Elliott's *Horæ Apocalypticæ*, iv. 275 f.

E. W. Benson (London, 1900); B. Weiss[2] (1902); C. A. Scott (*CB.* 1902); A. Crampon (*L'Apocalypse de S. Jean, traduite et annotée*, Tournai, 1904); Th. Calmes (Paris, 1905)*; F. Weidner (*Annotations*, New York, 1906); W. Bousset[2] (— Meyer, 1906); H. B. Swete[2] (1907)*; H. P. Forbes (New York, 1907); F. J. A. Hort (posthumous fragment, 1907); J. Weiss[2] (*SNT.* 1907); Holtzmann-Bauer (*HC.*[3] 1908)*; J. M. S. Baljon (Utrecht, 1908); Moffatt (*EGT.* 1910); E. C. S. Gibson (London, 1910); A. Ramsay (*Westminster NT*, 1910).

(*b*) Studies—(i.) general:—Semler's *Neue Untersuchungen* (Halle, 1776); A. Tilloch's *Dissertations Introductory to Study of the Language, Structure, and Contents of the Apocalypse* (London, 1823); Lücke's *Versuch einer vollständigen Einleitung in die Offenbarung Johannis*[2] (1852)*; E. Boehmer, *über Verfasser und Abfassungszeit d. johan. Apokalypse und zur bibl. Typik* (1855); H. J. Gräber, *Versuch einer histor. Erklärung . . .* (Heidelberg, 1857); Meijboom, *De Openbaring* (1863); Manchot, *Die Offenbarung Johannes* (1869); Farrar, *Early Days of Christianity* (1882, ch. xxviii.); E. Havet, *Le Christianisme et ses origines* (1888, iv. pp. 314 f.); Chauffard, *L'apocalypse et son interprétation historique* (1888); Löhr, *die Offenbarung Johannes* (1890); Milligan, *Discussions on the Apocalypse* (London, 1893); S. Davidson, *Outlines of a Comm. on Revelation* (1894); H. Berg, *The Drama of the Apocalypse* (London, 1894); W. Bousset (*EBi.* 194–212); Schmiedel (*EBi.* 2514–2518); F. C. Porter (Hastings' *DB.* iv. 239–266)*; E. C. Selwyn, *The Christian Prophets and the Prophetic Apocalypse* (1900); Baljon (*INT.* pp. 241–265); Wernle's *Urc.* i. (Eng. tr.) pp. 360 f.; G. H. Gilbert, *The First Interpreters of Jesus* (1901), pp. 332 f.; F. C. Porter, *Messages of Apoc. Writers** (1901), pp. 169–296; W. M. Ramsay, *Letters to the Seven Churches** (1904); G. Linder, *die Offenbarung des Johannes aufgeschlossen* (1905); Calmes, *L'apoc. devant la tradition et devant la critique*[2] (1907); E. A. Abbott (*Diat.* 2942, 2998, § 11)*; J. Bonnet's *Eclaircissement de l'apocalypse* (1908); A. Reymond's *Explication* (Lausanne, 1908); C. W. Votaw (*Bibl. World*, 1907, 32–40, 290–299, 1908, 39–50, 314–328); J. J. Scott, *Lectures on the Apocalypse* (1909); A. V. Green, *The Ephesian Canonical Writings* (1910), pp. 164–246; G. T. Jowett, *The Apocalypse of St. John* (1910). (ii.) on special points: (*a*) religious ideas:—Herder's *Maran Atha* (Riga, 1779); A. Schneider's *Essai sur les idées de l'apocalypse touchant la personne de Christ* (Strassburg, 1855); Bleek's *Vorlesungen* (ed. Hossbach, 1862; Eng. tr. 1874); Gebhardt's *Lehrbegriff der Apocalypse* (1873, Eng. tr.); Hoekstra's 'de Christologie d. Apok.' (*TT.*, 1869, 363–402); Briggs, *Messiah of the Apostles* (pp. 285–461); Cone, *The Gospel and its earliest Interpreters* (1893), pp. 346–361; M. S. Terry (*JBL.*, 1895, 91–100); Hofmann's *Vorlesungen* (ed. Lorenz, 1896); Trench, *Comm. on Epp. to Seven Churches*[7] (1897)*; J. O. Michael, *Die Gottesherrschaft als leitender Grundgedanke in der Offenbarung des Johannes* (Leipzig, 1903); V. Ermoni, 'la cristologia dell' Apocalisse' (*Riv. d. Scienz. Teol.*, 1908, 538–552); A. S. Peake, 'The Person of Christ in the Revelation of John' (*Mansefield College Essays*, 1909, 89–109)*. (*b*) text, etc.:—C. F. Matthaei's *Apocalypsis Joh. græce et latine ex codicibus nunquam antea examinatis* (Riga, 1785); A. Birch, *Variæ lectiones ad textum Apoc.* (Copenhagen, 1800); F.

Delitzsch, *Handschrifte Funde*, i. ('die erasmischen Entstellungen des Textes d. Apokalypse nachgewiesen aus dem verloren geglaubten codex Reuchlins') 1861; Haussleiter's ed. of Primasius in Zahn's *Forschungen zur Gesch. d. NTlichen Kanons* (iv. 1–224)*; B. Weiss, 'die Joh.-Apokalypse, textkritische Unterschungen und Textherstell.' (*TU.* vii. 1, 1891)*; Goussen's *Theolog. Studia* (fasciculus i., 'Apoc. S. Joh. apostoli versio sahidica'); G. H. Gilbert (*Bibl. World*, 1895, 29f., 114f., 'The Originality of the Apocalypse'); Gwynn, *The Apocalypse of S. John in Syriac* (1897)*; J. H. Barbour (*Bibl. World*, 1899, 316–325, 'The structure and teaching of the Apocalypse'); T. C. Laughlin, *The Solecisms of the Apocalypse* (Princeton, 1902); F. Palmer, *The Drama of the Apocalypse* (1903); Delaporte, *Fragments Sahidiques du NT Apokalypse* (Paris, 1906); F. C. Conybeare, *The Armenian Text of Revelation* (London, 1907; Text and Translation Society).

§ 1. *Outline and contents.*—(Cp. F. Palmer, *The Drama of the Apocalypse*, 1905, and Swete, pp. xxix–xli.)

$1^{1-3.\ 4-8}$ prologue.

1^{9-20} vision of heaven, with John's commission to write to seven Asiatic churches[1] at

2^{1}–3^{22} Ephesus, Smyrna, Pergamos, Thyatira, Sardis, Philadelphia, and Laodicea.

4^{1}–5^{14} vision of heaven, introducing

6^{1-17} the plagues of the seven seals—

(1) the white horse (Parthian raid),
(2) the red horse (war and bloodshed),
(3) the black horse (famine),
(4) the livid horse (pestilence),
(5) the souls of the slain,
(6) the earthquake and eclipse (the last Day, panic of kings, etc.).

Intermezzo:—

7^{1-8} sealing of redeemed on earth,

7^{9-17} bliss of redeemed in heaven.

8^{1} (7) the silence (ominous pause for half an hour).

8^{2-5} vision of heaven, an episode of angels, introducing

8^{6}–9^{21} the plagues of the seven trumpets—

(1) earth (shower of bloody hail and fire),
(2) sea (volcanic bomb),
(3) streams and springs (poisoned by torch-like meteor),
(4) eclipse (partial),
(5) demonic locusts,
(6) demonic cavalry (Parthian invasion).

Intermezzo:—

10^{1-11} episode of angels and a booklet,

11^{1-14} the apocalypse of the two μαρτύρες.

[1] Cp. G. Lampakis, Οἱ ἑπτὰ ἀστέρες τῆς ἀποκαλύψεως, ἤτοι ἱστορία, ἐρείπια, μνημαῖα καὶ νῦν κατάστασις τῶν ἑπτὰ ἐκκλησιῶν τῆς Ἀσίας (Athens, 1909).

11^{15-19} (7) voices and visions in heaven, introducing
12^{1-17} the dragon or Satan, war in heaven,
$13^{1-10.\ 11-18}$ {the Beast from the sea, the dragon's vice-regent / the Beast from the land, the vice-regent's ally.} war on earth.

Intermezzo:—

14^{1-5} bliss of redeemed in heaven,
14^{6-20} episode of angels and doom on earth
15^{1-8} vision of heaven, an episode of angels, introducing
16^{1-21} the plagues of the seven bowls—on
(1) earth (adherents of Cæsar-cult punished by noisome ulcers),
(2) sea (poisoned by coagulated blood)
(3) streams and springs (turned into blood),
(4) sun (scorching heat),
(5) throne of the Beast (darkness),
(6) Euphrates (dried up to facilitate Parthian invasion),
(7) air (storm and cosmic collapse).

visions of doom on
17^{1-18} (*a*) the realm of the Beast (Rome)—
18^{1-24} a taunt-song of doom on earth *
19^{1-10} a triumph-song in heaven—
19^{11-21} (*b*) the Beast and his allies,
20^{1-10} (*c*) the dragon or Satan and his adherents. †

visions of
20^{11-15} (*a*) the great white throne,
21^{1-8} (*b*) the new heaven and earth,
$21^{9}-22^{5}$ (*c*) the new Jerusalem.
22^{6-21} epilogue.

The outcome of the opening vision ($1^{9f.}$) is a commission to write charges to seven churches of Western Asia Minor (2–3). As the Roman emperors addressed letters to the Asiatic cities or corporations (the inscriptions mention at least six to Ephesus, seven to Pergamos, three to Smyrna, etc.; cp. Deissmann's *Licht vom Osten*, pp. 274 f.), so Jesus the heavenly *κύριος* communicates through John his instructions to these Christian

* This magnificent dramatic lyric, after a short prelude (vv.$^{1-3}$), and a stanza of triumph over the oppressor's fall (vv.$^{4-8}$), describes the wail of kings (vv.$^{9-10}$), merchants (vv.$^{11-16}$), and seafaring men (vv.$^{17-19}$), like Ezekiel's well-known doom-song over the fall of Tyre. The closing lines (vv.$^{21-23}$) vividly portray the sudden, violent, and irrevocable doom of the grandeur that was Rome.

† The author welds together here the two mythological traditions of (*a*) a temporary restraint of the evil power, and (*b*) a temporary messianic reign, using the latter in order to provide a special reward for the martyrs. This re-arrangement obliges him to connect, though vaguely, the Gog and Magog legend with the recrudescence of Satan, and also to postpone the resurrection till after the messianic interval.

communities.* The scene then changes (4^{1}). The churches and their angels give place to a fresh tableau of the heavenly penetralia (4–5). The prophet is admitted to the celestial presence-chamber, where Christ as the redeemer of his people receives the book of Doom,† which he alone can open and read. At the breaking of each of the seven seals of this roll, some fresh woe is chronicled (6), the sixth being the great day of God's wrath. Here the writer relieves the strain by a consoling rhapsody ($7^{1-8.\ 9-17}$), which lifts the eyes of the faithful over the foam and rocks of the rapids in which they were tossing to the quiet, sunlit pool of heavenly bliss beyond. The seventh woe drifts over, however, into a fresh cycle of catastrophes, introduced by trumpet-peals from seven angels (8–9). The sixth of these is also followed by an *entr'acte* (10^{1}–11^{13}) of considerable length, in which the personality of the seer emerges on earth instead of (since 4^{1}) in heaven. A colossal jin, bestriding earth and sea, gives him a *βιβλαρίδιον* whose enigmatic contents he has to digest. The fresh series of visions which now opens is concerned with the two protagonists of the final struggle, the messiah of Satan or the Beast and the messiah of God. The former is introduced in a foiled attack of antichrist on messiah's forerunners ($11^{1f.}$), and then in an equally futile onset of the dragon or Satan on messiah himself (12). The Roman empire, as Satan's delegate on earth, then appears on the scene (13).‡ Here is the crisis of the world! The imperial power, with its demand for worship, is confronted by an undaunted nucleus of Christians, and the prophet breaks off, in characteristically proleptic fashion, to paint their final bliss (14^{1-5}) and the corre-

* The epistolary form into which the Apocalypse is thrown is merely intended (cp. Zahn, *INT.* iii. 300) to show that it was meant for circulation primarily in the churches of Asia Minor.

† In the form of a papyrus-roll or *ὀπισθόγραφον* (cp. Blau's *Studien zur Alt-Heb. Buchwesen*, 36 f.; E. Maude Thompson's *Palæography*, 56–60, and E. J. Goodspeed, *JBL.*, 1903, 70–74), not of a codex in book-form (so recently Zahn).

‡ Even here the first Beast (*i.e.* the Roman empire) is identified with one of its heads (or emperors), *i.e.* Nero, who is a travesty ($13^{3a} = 5^{6}$) of the Lamb (his resurrection heralding the final conflict of God and the pagan power). Hence, whatever the number 666 originally meant as a naïve parody of the sacred number seven, the prophet cryptically and cabbalistically identifies it with the human personality of Nero (cp. the recent discussion by Corssen, *ZNW.*, 1902, 236 f., 1903, 264 f., and E. Vischer, *ibid.*, 1903, 167 f., 1904, 74 f.), using the favourite methods of gematria and isopsephia.

sponding tortures reserved for their impious opponents (14^{6-20}). At this point the kaleidoscope of the visions again shifts abruptly. In a cycle of horrors, in which the element of fantasy becomes more ornate than ever, seven angels drench the world of men and nature with the anger of God, which can no longer be repressed (15–16). The impenitence of the world reaches its climax in the policy of the Roman city and empire, and the prophet describes in rapid succession the doom of Rome (17–18) at the hands of the Beast and his allies, the horrible fate of the latter (19), and finally the overthrow of the Satan who had instigated both (20^{1-10}). The general resurrection and judgment which follow (20^{11-15}) usher in the closing description of the heavenly bliss rescued for the saints (21^{1}–22^{5}), which the poet describes in genuine Semitic fashion. From the smoke and pain and heat of the preceding scenes it is a relief to pass into the clear, clean atmosphere of the eternal morning where the breath of heaven is sweet and the vast city of God sparkles like a diamond in the radiance of his presence. The epilogue (22^{6-21}) sounds the two characteristic *motifs* of the book, viz. its vital importance as an inspired scripture, and the nearness of the end which it predicts.

Underneath this general unity of conception and aim, however, there are incongruities and vacillations in the symbolism, isolated allusions, unrelated predictions left side by side, and episodical passages, which in several cases denote planes of religious feeling and atmospheres of historical outlook, differing not simply from their context but from one another. These features, together with the absence or comparative absence of distinctively Christian traits from one or two sections, the variations of christological climate, the juxtaposition of disparate materials, and the awkward transitions at one point after another, show that source-criticism of some kind is necessary in order to account for the literary and psychological data. John's apocalypse, like most of its class, is composite (see above, p. 40).

§ 2. *Source-criticism.* — Surveys by H. J. Holtzmann (*JPT.*, 1891, 520 f.), Baldensperger (*ZTK.*, 1894, 232–250), A. Hirscht (*Die Apokalypse und ihre neueste Kritik*, 1895), Barton (*AJT.*, 1898, 776–801), Moffatt (*HNT.* pp. 677–689, and *Exp.* 1909, March), A. Meyer (*TR.*, 1897, 47 f., 91 f., 1907, 126 f., 182 f.), Porter (Hastings' *DB.* iv. 242 f.), Bousset (pp. 108–129); Holtzmann-Bauer (*HC.*^{2} iv. 390–394); adverse discussions by Bovon (*Revue de théologie et philosophie*, 1887, 329–362), Beyschlag (*SK.*, 1888, 102–138), Düsterdieck (*GGA.*, 1889, 554 f.), E. C. Moore (*JBL*

1891, 20–43), Milligan (*Discussions on the Apocalypse*, 1893, 27–74), M. S. Terry (*JBL.*, 1894, 91–100), M. Kohlhofer (*Die Einheit des Apokalypse*, 1902), and Jacquier (*INT.* iv. 362–376).

The main analyses of the book may be classified as follows:—

(*a*) The compilation-hypothesis posits several fairly independent sources, which have been pieced together by a redactor or by successive redactors. Most critics of this school find two Jewish sources. So, *e.g.*, G. J. Weyland (*TT.*, 1886, 454–470; *Omwerkings en compilatie-hypothesen*, etc., 1888) saw Christian additions (*c.* A.D. 100) in $1^{1-3.\ 11.\ 18.\ 20}$ 2–3, 5^{6-14} ($6^{1.\ 16}$) 9^{18} 10^{7} $11^{8b.\ 19}$ $12^{11.\ 17c}$ 14^{1-5} $15^{1.\ 6-8}$ $16^{1-12.\ 15.\ 17a.\ 21}$ 17^{14} $19^{7-10.\ 13b}$ $22^{7a.\ 12-13.\ 16-21}$, and two sources in א (A.D. 81) = 1, 4^{1}–5^{5} 6–8, 9, 11^{14-18} 14^{2-3} 15^{5} 16^{17b-20} 14^{14-20} 17–18, 19^{1-6} 21^{9-27} $22^{1-11.\ 14-15}$; ב (A.D. 69) = 10^{2}–11^{13} 12–13, 14^{6-11} 15^{2-4} $16^{13-14\ \text{etc.}}$ 19^{11-21} 20^{1}–21^{8}; Ménégoz (*Annales de Bibliogr. Théologie*, 1888, pp. 41–45), and O. Holtzmann (in Stade's *Geschichte Israels*, ii. 658 f.), like K. Kohler (*Jewish Encyclopædia*, x. 390 f.), also postulate two Jewish sources; but after Weyland this view has been best put by Eugen de Faye (*les Apocalypse Juives*, 1892, pp. 171 f.), who, working along the lines indicated by Spitta, distinguishes an anonymous Jewish apocalypse in 7^{1-8} 8^{2}–9^{21} $10^{1a.\ 2b-7}$ $11^{14-15a.\ 19}$ 12–13, $14^{(1-5)\ 6-11}$ 16^{13-20} $19^{11-16.\ 17-21}$ $20^{1-3.\ 7-15}$ 21^{1-6}, written during the stormy reign of Caligula; and another, also of Jewish origin, in $10^{1b.\ 2a.\ 8-11}$ $11^{1-13.\ 15b-18}$ 14^{14-20} 15–$16^{12.\ 17a.\ 21}$ 17–19^{8} 21^{9-27} 22^{15}, written close to A.D. 70. He correctly sees that 4–6 are inseparable from 1–3, containing several allusions to the latter and partaking of the same Christian spirit and style. Three * Jewish sources are postulated by P. W. Schmidt (*Anmerkungen über die Komposition der Offenbarung Johannes*, 1891); one in 4^{1}–7^{8}, another in 8^{2}–11^{15} (10^{1}–11^{13} being an insertion), and a third in 11^{16}–19^{5} 21^{1}–22^{5}, with an anti-Pauline Christian author in 2–3 and subsequent (Trajanic) editorial work in 1 and 22^{6-21}. This complicated scheme was no improvement upon Spitta's triple division (*Die Offenbarung des Johannes untersucht*, 1889); into an original apocalypse of John Mark, *c.* A.D. 62 (= $1^{4-6.\ 9-19}$ 2–3, 4^{1-11} 5^{1-14} 6^{1-17} 8^{1} 7^{9-18} 19^{9b-10} $22^{8.\ 10f.\ 20-21}$), in which the Christian redactor under Trajan, besides numerous additions (*e.g.* $1^{1-3.\ 7-8.\ 20}$ $2^{7.\ 11.\ 17.\ 26-29}$ $3^{5-6.\ 12-13.\ 21f.}$ 13^{9-10} $14^{2b-3.\ 11b-12}$ 17^{7-18} 20^{4-7} $21^{2-4.\ 6b-8}$ $22^{9.\ 14-15.\ 18b-20a}$), incorporated not only an apocalypse of 63 B.C. (= bulk of 10–11, $14^{14-16.\ 18-20}$ $15^{2-6.\ 8}$ $16^{1-12.\ 17.\ 21}$ 17^{1-6} 18^{1-23} $19^{1-3.\ 5-8}$ 21^{9-27} $22^{1-3.\ 15}$), but a Caligula-apocalypse of A.D. 40 (= 7^{1-8} 8^{2-13} 9^{1-21} $10^{1-3.\ 5-7}$ $11^{15.\ 19}$ $12^{1-5.\ 7-10.\ 12-18}$ $13^{1-8.\ 11-18}$ $14^{1-2.\ 4-7.\ 9-11a}$ $16^{13-14.\ 16-17b.\ 18-20}$ $19^{11-14.\ 16-21}$ $20^{1-3.\ 8-15}$ $21^{1.\ 5-6}$). J. Weiss (*Die Offenbarung des Johannes*, 1904) makes one of his two sources Jewish, viz., a composite prophetic work (*c.* A.D. 70) = 10, 11^{1-13} $12^{1-6.\ 14-17}$ (13^{1-7}) 15–19, 21^{4-27}; this was incorporated with the original apocalypse of John the presbyter (A.D. 65–70) = $1^{4-6.\ (7-8).\ 9-19}$ 2–3, 4–5, 6–7, 9, 12^{7-12} 13^{11-18} (14^{1-5}) 14^{6-20} $20^{1-10.\ 11-15}$ 21^{1-4} $22^{3-5.\ 8f.}$, by a Domitianic redactor or editor, who desired to rally the Asiatic churches during the Flavian crisis. Bruston

---

* W. Brückner (*Protest. Kirchenzeitung*, 1896, 653 f., 680 f., 703 f., 733 f.) went one better; the Lamb, in one of his four Jewish sources, is even held to have denoted the people of Israel. C. Rauch (*die Offenbarung des Johannes*, Haarlem, 1894) had already discovered five behind a Jewish apocalypse of A.D. 62.

again (*Études sur Daniel et l'Apocalypse*, 1908, summarising his previous studies) holds that both of his (Hebrew) sources were Christian, the one (Neronic) = $10^{1-2.\ 8-11}$ $11^{1-13.\ 19a}$ 12^{1}–14^{1} $14^{4f.}$ 15^{2-4} $16^{13-16.\ 19b}$ 17^{1}–19^{3} 19^{11}–20^{15}, the other (cp. *RTQR.*, 1908, 171–187; a posthumous work of John the apostle, composed by a disciple) = $1^{4f.}$ 2–3, 4^{1}–10^{1} 10^{2b-7} 11^{14-19} $14^{2-3.\ 12-13}$ 19^{4-10} 21^{1-8} $22^{6-13.\ 16-17.\ 20-21}$; the editor dove-tailed the one into the other and made alterations in both as well as additions. Völter's latest analysis (*Die Offenbarung des Johannis, neu untersucht und erklärt*, 1904) approximates to this type of criticism, by postulating a Christian apocalypse of John Mark (*c.* A.D. 65), and an apocalypse of Cerinthus (as early as A.D. 70, = 10^{1-11} 17^{1-18} 11^{1-13} 12^{1-16} $15^{5-6.\ 8}$ 16^{1-21} 19^{11}–22^{6}), which were successively edited under Trajan and Hadrian.

(*b*) A simplified variant of the compilation-theory is the Jewish and Christian hypothesis which posits only one Jewish original. Thus Vischer ('Die Offenbarung Johannes eine jüdische Apk. in christlicher Bearbeitung,' *TU.* ii. 3, 1886, second ed. 1895) traced a Christian editor's hand (*e.g.* in 1^{1}–3^{22} 5^{9-14} 7^{9-17} 11^{8b} 12^{11} 13^{9-10} $14^{1-5.\ 8-13}$ 16^{15} 17^{14} 19^{9-10} $20^{4b-5a.\ 6}$ $21^{5b-8.\ 14b}$ 22^{6-21}, and the Lamb-passages) working on an earlier Aramaic Jewish apocalypse of the seventh decade; similarly Harnack, Rovers (*TT.*, 1887, 616–634), Martineau (*Seat of Authority*, 217–227), an anonymous writer in *Zeitschrift für alt. Wiss.* (1887), 167 f.; S. Davidson (*INT.* ii. 126 f.; Aramaic Jewish apocalypse translated and edited), and von Soden (*INT.* 338 f.: Jewish apocalypse, 'written between May and August of the year A.D. 70.' = 8^{1}–22^{5}, edited and altered by John the presbyter under Domitian, with a few later editorial notes from another hand in 1^{1-3} etc.).

(*c*) According to the incorporation-theory, the Apoc. is substantially a literary unity, but it incorporates several earlier fragments of Jewish or Jewish Christian origin. These are variously disentangled, but there is a substantial agreement upon most. According to Weizsäcker (*AA.* ii. 173 f.), who first propounded the hypothesis, they lie in 7^{1-8} 11^{1-13} 12–13, and 17. Sabatier (*Les origines littéraires et la composition de l'Apocalypse*, 1888) found Jewish fragments in 11^{1-13} 12–13, 14^{6-20} $16^{13-14.\ 16}$ 17^{1}–19^{2} 19^{11}–20^{10} 21^{9}–22^{5}; Schön (*L'origine de l'Apocalypse*, 1887), less extensively in 11^{1-13} $12^{1-9.\ 13-17}$ and ^{18}; and Pfleiderer (*Urc.* ii. 281 f.) in 11–14, 17–18, and 21^{10}–22^{5}. This line of criticism is followed by Bousset, Jülicher (*Einl.* § 22), C. A. Scott, F. C. Porter, McGiffert (*AA.* 633 f.), A. Meyer, E. A. Abbott, Baljon (*INT.* 241–265), Wrede (*Entstehung der Schriften des NT*, 103–104), Schmiedel, and Calmes, amongst others; of all the theories it does most justice to the linguistic unity on the one hand, and to the disparate phenomena of the text upon the other.

C. A. Briggs (*Messiah of the Apostles*, 285–461) detects a fourfold editing, with redactional matter, *e.g.*, in 1^{1-3} and 22^{18-19}, of earlier (mainly Hebrew) apocalypses, written prior to A.D. 70, the latest being a special source written by the apostle John (including 1^{10}–3). According to a more recent theory (B. W. Bacon, *Fourth Gospel in Research and Debate*, 1910, 157 f.), 1–3 and 22^{8-21} are simply a prologue and epilogue added by some Ephesian editor to invest the Palestinian apocalypse with apostolic authority; but they do not claim apostolic authority, and their links with 4–22^{7} are not broken so easily. Nor is the theory that John's early martyrdom underlies 11^{7-12} at all plausible

The seven cities or their churches disappear with $4^{1f.}$, and the bulk of the apocalypse is certainly a tale of two cities, Babylon and Jerusalem; but these are not played off against one another, and the special phenomena of 4^{1}–22^{7} are not sufficient to disprove identity of authorship in 1–3 + $22^{8\text{-}13}$ and 4^{1}–22^{7}. Bacon finds traces of the Ephesian editor in 4^{5} 5^{6} $7^{9\text{-}17}$ 9^{11} $11^{4.\ 8}$ 12^{9} 15^{3} $17^{6.\ 14}$ 19^{13} etc.

Barth (*Einl.* 250–276) explains the different time-allusions in the book by the simpler expedient (after Grotius) of conjecturing that John revised and reissued, under Domitian, an apocalypse which he had already (shortly before 70) composed for the smaller audience of the Asiatic churches. H. B. Workman (*Persecution in the Early Church*, p. 46, cp. pp. 355–358) more ingeniously proposes to reconcile the conflicting evidence for the date by suggesting that "while the apocalypse was mainly written in or about 69 (certainly before 70), the opportunities for a convict in Patmos to transmit such a work to the mainland were few,—the letters to the seven churches would be short notes sent separately, easily concealed,—and consequently the publication of the work as a whole in Asia was not until 95 or so."

Wellhausen's analysis (*Analyse der Offenbarung Johannis*, 1907) is more complex. The Domitianic author, he argues, edited even the letters to the seven churches (*e.g.* in the promises of 2^{7b} etc. and $2^{10c.\ 23\text{-}28}$ $3^{8b.\ 10\text{-}12.\ 20\text{-}21}$), as well as the seven seals (inserting, *e.g.*, 7, $8^{2b\text{-}4}$, $7^{1\text{-}8}$ being a separate fragment) and the seven trumpets (in $9^{13f.\ 20\text{-}21}$), changed the original Christ of $10^{1\text{-}4}$ into an angel, and incorporated two Jewish fragments from A.D. 70 in $11^{1\text{-}2}$ (oracle of Zealots) and 12 (Pharisaic, editorial touches in $12^{10\text{-}12}$ and elsewhere), besides doubling the original single witness (= Elijah) of the Jewish source in $11^{3\text{-}13}$, and the original single Beast of the Jewish source in 13. Further editorial touches are detected in $15^{2\text{-}3}$ and in the present text of the seven bowls source (*e.g.* in $16^{5\text{-}17.\ 13\text{-}16}$); in 17, as in 12, two separate Jewish sources have been pieced together; the brushwork of editorial Christian touches is found in $18^{20.\ 24}$ $19^{12\text{-}13}$; the Jewish source in $20^{1\text{-}15}$ has been coloured by the Christian editor in $20^{4\text{-}6.\ 10.\ 12.\ 14}$; 21^{1}–22^{5} is certainly composed by the apocalyptist himself, but $22^{18\text{-}19}$, like $1^{1\text{-}3}$, must be the work of some further redactor, for whom the fourth evangelist was the apocalyptist. The latter wrote under Domitian.

Overprecision and arbitrary canons of literary analysis have handicapped most of these theories. "Differences of style undoubtedly exist, in different portions of Revelation, but not a tenth part of such differences as separate *The Tempest* from *Richard II.* In contrast with all the other books of the NT, the Apocalypse of John is written in a language of its own, a blend of Hebraic Greek and vernacular Greek, defiant of grammar. Its peculiarities stamp the whole work—barring a few phrases—as not only conceived by one mind but also written by one hand" (E. A. Abbott, *Diat.* 2942,* xxiii.; cp. Gallois, *RB.*, 1894, 357–374). This sense of stylistic unity tells against most forms of the compilation-hypothesis, for example, but it does not rule out the view that, while the Apocalypse is neither a literary conglomerate nor a mechanical blend of earlier shreds and patches, it contains not simply divergent traditions but earlier sources which have been worked over for the prophet's own purpose. He has wrought as an editor no less than as a transcriber of personal visions. In some parts the Apocalypse is not a vision at all. It represents not only the literary embellishment of what the writer remembered he had seen in moments of ecstasy, but the re-setting of fragments which were current and honoured in the circle where he moved.

One further consideration falls to be noted at this point. The unsatisfactory results of the source-criticism of the Apocalypse have not simply been due, as in the case of Acts, to a prosaic Western and ultra-rigid conception of what an early Oriental author could have written. There are other causes. (i.) The criterion of Jewish or Christian is hazardous in a book which deals with eschatology, where no primitive Christian could work without drawing upon Jewish traditions, in themselves neither stereotyped nor homogeneous. Though a given passage may not be couched in Christian language, it does not necessarily come from a Jewish pen. The Jewish nucleus of the Apocalypse, *e.g.*, cannot be disentangled by the naive expedient of cutting out all references to the Lamb, etc. A closer examination of its contents reveals omissions which prove unmistakably a non-Jewish origin; *e.g.* the lack of any reference to the prevalent category of the *two æons*, the return of the ten tribes, the contemporary Jewish wail over the cessation of sacrifice after A.D. 70 (cp. Apoc. Bar 10^{10}), the expiatory function of the martyrs' death, and the law (cp. Charles' note on Apoc. Bar 15^{5}). (ii.) Inconsequence of a certain kind is one of the psychological phenomena of visions, and (iii.) any transcript of these, especially by a poetic nature, is certain to reflect the changes which come over the spirit of religious as well as of other dreams. (iv.) Many of the inconsistencies and incongruities were due to the fact that the author, as an apocalyptist, inherited old traditions which not only had passed through various phases before they reached him, but had to be re-adapted to a later situation. The last-named consideration was first stated by Gunkel in his epoch-making *Schöpfung und Chaos* (1895), and ever since then the principles of the *religionsgeschichtliche* school have been recognised in the best literary criticism of the Apocalypse with excellent results. Gunkel's work did not supersede analytic literary criticism here any more than in the case of Genesis; it rather corrected an ultra-literary bias. He himself failed to allow enough for the references to contemporary history (cp. Wellhausen's critique in *Skizzen und Vorarbeiten*, vi. 215 f.); he made extravagant claims for the Babylonian origin of the traditions (especially in ch. 12); and, at first, he failed to allow enough for the element of genuine prophetic vision and experiences in the book. But it is only in the light of the principles which he laid bare that a due estimate can be formed of the seer's method in dealing with his material.

The traditions employed in the book reach back primarily to OT prophecies like those of Daniel, Ezekiel, and Zechariah; several of the visions imply that the seer had been brooding over such scriptures. But neither their shape nor their content is explicable apart from a wider use of such traditions as were current in pseudepigrapha like Enoch and books of the later Judaism like Tobit and the Psalter of Solomon. There are also elements akin to Zoroastrian, Babylonian, Greek, and Egyptian eschatology and cosmology which were not altogether derived indirectly from the apocalyptic channels of the later Judaism. For the mythological background, *e.g.*, of $6^{1f.}$, cp. H. Gressmann in *Deutsche Literaturzeitung* (1907), 2252 f., and M. W. Müller in *ZNW.* (1907) 290–316; for the astrological basis of the Parthian tradition in $9^{15f.}$, Fries in *Jahrb. für die klass. Alterthum.* (1902) 705 f.; for the mythological basis of 12, Calmes (*RB.*, 1903, 52–68) and B. Allo (*RB.*, 1910, 509–554), Cheyne's *Bible Problems* (195–207), and Pfleiderer's *Early Christian Conceptions of Christ*, 56 f.; for 19^{17-21} see Gressmann's *Ursprung d. Isr.-jüd. Eschatologie*, 136 f.; and for $20^{1f.}$, see *ERE.* i. 203 f., and Klausner's *Messian. Vorstellungen d. jüd. Volkes im Zeit d. Tannaiten*, 61 f.

§ 3. *Structure.*—The first passage where a source becomes visible is 7^{1-8}. Ch. 7 is not a literary unit with editorial touches (Weyland, Erbes, Bruston, Rauch), but the combination of a Jewish (Jewish Christian: Völter, J. Weiss) fragment (7^{1-8}: so, *e.g.*, Vischer, Schmidt, Pfleiderer, Porter, Bousset, von Soden, Scott, Wellhausen) with an original delineation in 7^{9-17}. The scenery of the former (cp. 14^{1}) is not organic to the prophet's outlook. The winds are never loosed, the sealing is not described, and the sealed are not seen. The collocation of the fragment with what precedes (winds = 6^{13}, numbering = 6^{11}, seals = $6^{1f.}$, standing = 6^{9}) is editorial. Its connection with what follows depends on whether 7^{1-8} and 7^{9-17} are meant to represent the same group viewed from a different standpoint—as if John applied the Jewish oracle to the real Jews, God's Israel of faithful Christians—or different persons, the 144,000 being Jewish Christians as opposed to the numberless multitude of Gentile Christian martyrs. Upon the whole, the tenor of the Apocalypse tells in favour of the hypothesis that 7^{9-17} represents 7^{1-8} read in the light of 5^{9} (so, *e.g.*, de Wette, Bruston, Porter, Wellhausen, Hoennicke's *JC.* 194 f.) with a specific application to the *candidatus martyrum exercitus.*

In 10^{1-11} the author drops the figure of a roll of Doom being opened, and describes the subsequent oracles as a *βιβλαρίδιον* of prophecy *ἐπὶ λαοῖς καὶ ἔθνεσιν καὶ γλώσσαις καὶ βασιλεῦσι πολλοῖς*, whose contents he had digested. For some reason, perhaps to make room for this new source, he omitted a seven-thunders cycle. The following oracles (11–13, perhaps even 11–19) incorporate, in whole or part, this *βιβλαρίδιον* (so, *e.g.*, Sabatier, Weyland, Spitta, Pfleiderer, and J. Weiss), although its origin (Jewish or Christian), date (Neronic or Vespasianic), and exact outline can no longer be determined with any precision, owing to the freedom with which the composer has worked over his source. Thus 11^{1-2} is commonly taken as a scrap of the Zealots' prophecies, just before A.D. 70 (so, *e.g.*, Bousset, Wellhausen, Baljon, J. Weiss), but the whole of 11^{1-13} is more probably a Jewish (or Jewish Christian) oracle of that period.* In 11^{14-18} the prophet leaves his source in order to herald the final crisis by noting the seventh trumpet and the third woe, in an overture which leads up to two sagas drawn from the mythological background of messianism. 12^{1-17} represent a Jewish source edited and probably translated by the writer, but the real problem of the passage lies not in its literary analysis but in the determination of the precise form of the sun-myth (Greek, Egyptian, or Babylonian) which the Jewish original adapted for messianic purposes. 13^{1-10} is one of the passages in which a Caligula-source has been more than once detected, either Jewish (Spitta, Pfleiderer, de Faye, O. Holtzmann, Rauch) or Christian (Erbes, Bruston, Briggs), mainly because 'Caligula' in Greek and Hebrew answers to the early variant (616) of the Beast's number; but the source might as readily be Neronic or Vespasianic (Kohler, J. Weiss, etc.). The ghastly scene in 14^{14-20}, with its abrupt allusion to *the city* (v.[20]), belongs to the same cycle of tradition as 11^{1-13}, but it is not quite

* Abbott, however, points out that in Ezekiel and Zechariah, two of the main models for John, the measuring of the temple does not take place till after the old temple has fallen. He is right in contending that John's attitude to such items of history is that of a poet, not of an exact historian.

certain whether it is a fragment, Jewish (Sabatier, Pfleiderer, Rauch) or Jewish Christian (Schön, Erbes, Bruston, J. Weiss, etc.), or simply an original sketch on the basis of tradition. The twofold thread of tradition in $16^{12f.}$ is obvious, but again the author may have twisted together the ideas of (*a*) a last conflict between God and the world-powers, and (*b*) Rome's ruin at the hands of Nero redivivus and the Parthians, without using written sources. The latter idea proleptically introduces 17 (see p. 505), where the main difficulty is to ascertain whether there are two sources or one, whether both are Jewish, and whether the revision indicates one hand or two (cp. Peake, *INT.* 161 f.). 17^{14} is an abrupt proleptic allusion to 19^{11-21}, but the writer first of all edits (in $18^{20.\ 24}$) an earlier doom-song over the fall of Babylon-Rome which voices, like the source underlying 17, the exultation as well as the indignation of a Jewish apocalyptist over the guilty, glorious empire. In 19^{11-21}, and especially in its horrible finâle, one would be almost relieved to discover a Jewish source (so, *e.g.*, Vischer, Sabatier, de Faye, Weyland, Spitta, von Soden); but neither here nor even in 20 are the results of the literary analysis convincing. More plausibility attaches to the analysis of 21^{9}–22^{5}, which is the imaginative delineation of a Christian ideal (11^{15-17}) in terms of a Jewish tradition originally describing an earthly Jerusalem surrounded by the respectful nations of the world. Several traits in the sketch (*e.g.* $21^{12.\ 16}$ 21^{24-27a} $22^{2c.\ 3a.\ 5}$) are plainly inappropriate in the new settting to which they have been transferred, but they are retained not only for the sake of their archaic association, but in order to round off the pictorial description of the eternal city. They do not necessarily prove the existence of the Jewish source which most critics find in the whole passage, and some prefer to trace under the repetitions and parallelisms a dual Christian ending (so, *e.g.*, Erbes and Selwyn).

The comparatively well-marked unity of the apocalypse does not exclude upon the one hand the possibility that it embraced sources of an earlier date which the author worked up for his own purpose, to meet the requirements of a later age. Even on the hypothesis that no sources were employed, it cannot have been the product of a single vision, much less composed or dictated at a sitting. The truer hypothesis, that earlier leaflets or fragments of tradition were re-set, although their date and shape and aim can no longer be ascertained with precision, simply involves that the writer as a poet and a practical religious seer attached primary importance to the new sense which he found in the inherited materials. Upon the other hand, there may be traces (pp. 37 f.) of subsequent editing, during the Trajanic period or later. (i.) The use of the book in Christian worship * (cp. 1^8 2^7 etc.) probably accounts for prose glosses like ἅ εἰσιν . . θεοῦ (4^5), οἵ εἰσιν . . . γῆν (5^6), ἅ εἰσιν . . . ἁγίων (5^8), τὸ γὰρ . . . ἐστίν (19^8), ἡ γὰρ . . . προφητείας (19^{10}), καὶ κέκληται . . . θεοῦ (19^{13}), and οὗτος . . . πυρός (20^{14}), as well as for the references to the Lamb, *e.g.*, in 13^9 and $14^{4.10}$. (ii.) Several cases of transposition or misplacement also occur within the traditional text. Thus (*a*) 16^{15} is an interpolation or a gloss misplaced perhaps from 3^{18} or 3^3. (*b*) 18^{14} has been displaced from its original position between the last ἔτι and the first ὅτι of 18^{23} (so Beza, Vitringa, Volkmar, Baljon, Weiss, and Könnecke, *BFT.* xii. 1. 37–38) by a copyist whose eye confused ὅτι οἱ ἔμποροί σου with οἱ ἔμποροι τούτων. (*c*) Probably 19^{9b-10} also has been disturbed from its original site at the close of 17, where the hierophant angel is speaking (cp. $17^{17} = 19^{9b}$ *words of God*). The displacement in this case was not accidental, but due to a scribe who saw that the similar assurance in 21^5 22^6 related primarily to future bliss rather than to judgment, and who took the first λέγει not as a divine saying (cp. 21^5), but as angelic (22^6). (*d*) 20^{14b}, which is textually suspect in any case, is either a marginal gloss (so, Krüger: *GGA.*, 1897, 34, von Soden, Wellhausen) or, more probably (cp. Haussleiter, 212–213), displaced from its original position after 20^{15}, where it would suit the context better, since there is no question of any second death except for human beings. The misplacement was due to the attraction of θάνατος in 20^{14a}. (*e*) The loose contexture of the epilogue (22^{6-21}) is improved (cp. *EGT.* v. 580–581) if vv.$^{6-7}$ are placed between ^{9} and ^{10}, and $^{18-12}$ interpolated between ^{16} and ^{17}.

If the apocalypse, like the Fourth gospel, was edited prior to (or, in view of) its reception into the canon, the most likely traces of the process would be found in 1^{1-3} and 22^{18-19}. The former passage, however, might conceivably have been added by the author, like the προοίμιον of Thucydides, after he had

* The liturgical element is naturally more prominent than in Ephesians; cp. the antiphonal bursts of song (*EBi.* 2138–2140, 3242) in the congregation, the responsive amen in 5^{14} 7^{12} etc.

finished the book as a whole. The change from the third person to the first (1^9) is not unexampled in such cases, and a certain sententious objectivity is not unnatural at the commencement of an ancient writing when the author is introducing himself. A similar uncertainty besets the uncompromising claim in 22^{18-19} (cp. En $104^{10f.}$), which might be taken as part of the apocalyptic literary tradition (cp. *e.g.* Slav. Enoch 48^{7-9}). The likelihood, however, is that it represents an editorial note (so Jn 21^{24-25}) designed to authenticate the writing as in the direct succession of the OT prophecies (cp. Jos. *Ant.* xx. 11. 2), possibly also to warn wilful or careless copyists (so Eus. *HE.* v. 20). Whether written by the author or appended by an editor, it definitely asserts that the apocalypse is entitled to the canonical privilege of the OT scriptures.

This latter passage has been used, in recent developments of criticism upon the NT canon, to support the paradoxical thesis that the Apocalypse was the first NT scripture to become canonical (cp. Leipoldt, *GK.* i. 28 f., Hans Windisch, 'Der Apokalyptiker Johannes als Begründer der NT Kanons,' *ZNW.*, 1909, 148–174, with Harnack's *Reden u. Aufsätze*, ii. 239 f.), and that this claim of a book which contained sayings of the Lord, descriptions of God's kingdom on earth, and church-epistles, paved the way for the subsequent canonization of the gospels, Acts, and epistles.

§ 4. *Traces in early Christian literature.*—From an allusion like that of *Philad.* vi. 1 (στηλαί εἰσιν καὶ τάφοι νεκρῶν, ἐφ' οἷς γέγραπται μόνον ὀνόματα ἀνθρώπων) = Apoc 3^{12} (to Christians of Philadelphia, ποιήσω αὐτὸν στύλον . . . καὶ γράψω ἐπ' αὐτὸν τὸ ὄνομα τοῦ θεοῦ μου κτλ.), it is possible that Ignatius had read the apocalypse, but the occasional similarities of language between it and Barnabas (*e.g.* $1^{7.18}$ = Barn vii. 9, 21^5 = Barn vi. 13, $22^{10.12}$ = Barn xxi. 3, cp. Clem. Rom. xxxiv. 3) are insufficient to prove any literary filiation. If the testimony of Andreas is reliable, Papias knew the apocalypse; which is intrinsically likely, since its chiliasm would appeal to the bishop of Hierapolis as it did to Justin Martyr (*Apol.* i. 28, ὄφις καλεῖται καὶ σατανᾶς καὶ διάβολος, ὡς ἐκ τῶν ἡμετέρων συγγραμμάτων ἐρευνήσαντες μαθεῖν δύνασθε, *Dial.* 81). Like the Fourth gospel, it became speedily popular in some gnostic circles. Cerdon and Marcion naturally would have nothing to do with it, but it circulated among the Marcosians and Valentinians as a sacred book, and the Montanists in particular, if we may judge from their opponents (Eus. *H. E.* v. 18) and from the scanty traces of their own opinions (cp. Zahn's *GK.* i. 205 f.), exploited it in the interests of their propaganda.

The repeated echoes in the epistle from the churches at Vienne and Lyons (Eus. *H. E.* v. 1) prove that it must have reached Gaul by about the middle of the second century. Indeed, Irenæus (v. 30. 1) could appeal not only to those who had seen John, but to πᾶσι τοῖς σπουδαίοις καὶ ἀρχαίοις ἀντιγράφοις. If the language of Hermas (*Vis.* ii. 2. 7, iv. 3. 1) could be interpreted as referring to our apocalypse, it must have been known to the Roman church even prior to Justin Martyr. By the end of the second century, it was circulated not only at Alexandria (Clemens Alex.), but in the African churches (Tertullian).

The use of the book by the Montanists especially led, by a curious phase of revulsion, to the earliest serious criticism which was levelled at it by any party within the church. It is significant that the first explicit reference to the apocalypse occurs in Justin Martyr's *Dial.* 81. He tells Trypho that, like all other orthodox Christians, he believed that there was to be not only a resurrection of the flesh but "a thousand years in Jerusalem, which will then be rebuilt, adorned, and enlarged, as the prophets Ezekiel, Isaiah, and others declare." In proof of this he interprets Is 65^{22b} as a mystical reference to the thousand years of Ps 90^{8}, and then proceeds, καὶ ἔτι δὴ καὶ παρ' ἡμῖν ἀνήρ τις, ᾧ ὄνομα Ἰωάννης, εἷς τῶν ἀποστόλων τοῦ Χριστοῦ, ἐν ἀποκαλύψει γενομένῃ χίλια ἔτη ποιήσειν ἐν Ἱερουσαλὴμ τοὺς τῷ ἡμετέρῳ Χριστῷ πιστεύσαντας προεφήτευσεν. Justin evidently ranks John, as the author of the apocalypse, in the prophetic succession. Παρὰ γὰρ ἡμῖν, he continues (82), καὶ μέχρι νῦν προφητικὰ χαρίσματά ἐστιν. Justin values the apocalypse because its evidence for the chiliastic eschatology was conveyed through prophetic ecstasy. Chiliasm, however, was not at all so popular in the Western church, and the Montanist movement tended to draw suspicion upon persons or books which claimed the prophetic spirit of ecstasy. This reaction was one of the influences which told against the reception of John's apocalypse. Thus, in the anti-Montanist Muratorian Canon, the reference runs: 'apocalypses etiam Iohannis et Petri tantum recipimus, quam quidam ex nostris legi in ecclesia nolunt.' Here John's apocalypse has risen above Hermas, but not yet above the Petrine apocalypse. Among the most prominent critics who rejected its authority was Gaius, the Roman churchman at the opening of the third century. Prior to him the church-party who were afterwards dubbed the Alogi, had demurred to the symbolism of the book as unedifying, and to some of its prophecies as fantastic and ridiculous; but Gaius, who evidently attributed its composition to Cerinthus (cp. Schwartz's *Ueber der Tod d. Söhne Zebedæi*, 1904, 33–45), took particular objection to its inconsistencies with the rest of the NT; *e.g.* 8^{7-11} contradicted 1 Th 5^{2}, $9^{3f.}$ was out of keeping with 2 Ti 3^{12-13}, and Satan (20^{2}) was already bound (Mt 18^{29}). All this distaste for the book formed part and parcel of a strong antipathy in certain circles of the early church. "In the course of the third century the reaction in the East against the book was in full swing. The rise of Greek Christian scholarship during the 'long peace' after Severus (A.D. 211–249) made men more conscious of the critical difficulties of common authorship of Apocalypse and gospel. The slackening of persecution set free the natural recoil of the Hellenic spirit against the apparent materialism with which the rewards of the blessed and the glories of the heavenly Jerusalem are portrayed" (C. H. Turner, *JTS*. x. 372). The fortunes of the apocalypse, after this point, form a chapter in church history. Though its unpopularity in the Syrian and Greek churches (cp. Gwynn, *op. cit.* civ.) did not prevail in the end over the acceptance of it by the Latin churches of the West, yet this movement of antipathy threw up the first piece of serious literary criticism upon the book. "Between 350 and 450, Greek texts of Revelation were rare in the Eastern half of the empire. The best minds of the Greek church, men such as Eusebius Pamphili, and Dionysius of Alexandria, denied its Johannine authorship. Living in an age when old Greek was still the language of everyday life, they were too conscious of the contrasts of style which separate it from the Fourth gospel to accept the view that a single author wrote both. Having to accept John the apostle as author of one or the other, they decided in favour of the gospel. In the West, on the other hand, where both documents circulated only in a Latin dress, men were unconscious of these contrasts of style, and so found no difficulty in accepting both as writings of the apostle John" (F. C. Conybeare, *The Armenian Text of Revelation*, pp. 161 f.).

Dionysius grounds his objections to the apocalypse not on the score of its millenarian teaching, although he had been in controversy with an Egyptian bishop called Nepos on that very point, nor on the score of its obscurity, but on other grounds. In the second volume of his work περὶ ἐπαγγελιῶν (as cited by Eus. *H. E.* vii. 25) he refers to earlier Christians who had rejected the book entirely, after a careful and critical examination; *τινὲς μὲν οὖν τῶν πρὸ ἡμῶν ἠθέτησαν καὶ ἀνεσκεύασαν πάντῃ τὸ βιβλίον, καθ' ἕκαστον κεφάλαιον διευθύνοντες ἄγνωστόν τε καὶ ἀσυλλόγιστον ἀποφαίνοντες ψεύδεσθαί τε τὴν ἐπιγραφήν. Ἰωάννου γὰρ οὐκ εἶναι λέγουσιν, ἀλλ' οὐδ' ἀποκάλυψιν εἶναι τὴν σφόδρα καὶ παχεῖ κεκαλυμμένην τῷ τῆς ἀγνοίας παραπετάσματι.* These views, together with the attribution of the book to Cerinthus, plainly refer to the second-century criticisms passed by the so-called Alogi and Gaius. Dionysius, however, hesitates to follow this radical lead. He thinks that the apocalypse is the work of "a holy and inspired person" called John, but, he adds, "I would be slow to admit (*οὐ μὴν ῥᾳδίως ἂν συνθείμην*) that he was the apostle, the son of Zebedee, the brother of James," the author of the Fourth gospel and the First epistle. The evidence he leads is purely internal. (1) The John of the apocalypse expressly mentions himself by name, unlike the author of the gospel and the epistle. Who this John was, is not certain (*ποῖος δὲ οὗτος, ἄδηλον*). Had he been the beloved disciple, he would have indicated this. Perhaps, of the many Johns, he was John Mark or another John of Asia Minor. *Ἄλλον δέ τινα οἶμαι τῶν ἐν Ἀσίᾳ γενομένων, ἐπεὶ καὶ δύο φασὶν ἐν Ἐφέσῳ γενέσθαι μνήματα καὶ ἑκάτερον Ἰωάννου λέγεσθαι.* With this conjecture on the authorship, he then passes on (2) to differentiate the apocalypse from the Fourth gospel (and First epistle) in style and conception. Compared with the latter, he premises, the apocalypse has a distinctly foreign look (*ἀλλοιοτάτη δὲ καὶ ξένη, μήτε ἐφαπτομένη μήτε γειτνιῶσα τούτων μηδενί, σχεδόν, ὡς εἰπεῖν, μηδὲ συλλαβὴν πρὸς αὐτὰ κοινὴν ἔχουσα*). This general impression of an alien origin is borne out by a scrutiny of the language (*τῆς φράσεως*). The gospel and epistle "are composed not only in faultless Greek (*ἀπταίστως κατὰ τὴν τῶν Ἑλλήνων φωνήν*), but with great skill in their expressions, their arguments, and the arrangement of their expositions (*πολλοῦ γε δεῖ βαρβαρόν τινα φθόγγον ἢ σολοικισμὸν ἢ ὅλως ἰδιωτισμὸν ἐν αὐτοῖς εὑρεθῆναι*)"; the author had the double gift of knowledge and of expression. As for the author of the apocalyse, says Dionysius, "I will not deny that he had seen revelations and received knowledge and prophecy, but I notice that his dialect and language are not correct Greek (*οὐκ ἀκριβῶς ἑλληνίζουσαν*); he makes use of barbarous constructions (*ἰδιώμασιν βαρβαρικοῖς*), and sometimes of actual solecisms (*καί που καὶ σολοικίζοντα*)."

The solecisms are patent. The only question is how far they are due to lack of culture or to the influence of Semitic idiom. The Hebraistic colouring is evident in anomalous phrases like διδάσκειν with dat. (2^{14}, after למד ל), the variation in the gender of ληνός (4^{19-20} after Is 63^{3}), the collocation of fem. substantives and mascul. adjectives or participles (*e.g.* 4^{1} 11^{4} 17^{3}), or of nominatives and accusatives (10^{8} 11^{3}, also 5^{6} $14^{6-7.14}$ etc.), or of nominatives in apposition to genitives (1^{5} 3^{12}), datives (9^{14}), and accusatives (2^{20} 20^{2}), and mannerisms of style such as the nomin. pendens placed at the opening of a sentence for emphasis (*e.g.* 3^{12} 6^{8} etc.), and the redundant αὐτός in relative clauses (3^{8} $7^{2.9}$ etc.). These are due in part to the translation of Hebrew or Aramaic sources, in part to the influence of the LXX, which is more marked than in the Fourth gospel—*e.g.* in the use of phrases like *the temple of the tent of testimony* (cp. Ex 40^{34} etc.), ἐνώπιον (= לפני), the repetition of prepositions ($7^{1.9}$ 16^{13} etc., cp. Zec 6^{10}), and of special words (see σάρκας in 19^{18}, with 16^{18} and Zec 8^{12}).

The criticism of Dionysius thus opens up the problem of the relation between the apocalypse and the Fourth gospel, including the authorship and (inferentially) the date of the former.

§ 5. *The Apocalypse and the Fourth Gospel.*—The relationship of the two books is best solved by attributing them to the same school or circle in Asia Minor but to different authors. Such affinities of thought and style as are evident in both writings (*e.g.*, the relation of God, Christ and the believer; keeping God's word or commandments; the use of parentheses and of the antithetical method), imply no more than the use of a common religious dialect which contemporary writers of the same group might fairly be expected to share, for all their idiosyncrasies. It is the latter which are decisive. The apocalypse ignores many of the most characteristic and favourite terms of the Fourth gospel, *e.g.* ἀλήθεια, ἀλήθης, ἀληθῶς, ἀντί, ἀπεκρίθη καὶ εἶπεν, ἀφίεναι τὰς ἁμαρτίας, θεᾶσθαι, ἴδε, ἴδιος, καθὼς, μέντοι, πάντοτε, παρρησία, πώποτε, ὑπό (accus.), and χάρα. Furthermore, it often uses the language of the gospel in a way of its own; the αἰώνιος of the latter it employs only once (14^{6}), and it never connotes it with ζωή; ἄξιος takes the infinitive, not ἵνα; ἔρχου replaces ἐλθέ; φῶς and ὁ κόσμος are invariably physical, not spiritual; ἐκεῖνος is never substantival, νικᾶν never transitive; Ἱερουσαλήμ is substituted for Ἱεροσόλυμα, and οὖν is never used of historical transition. These instances might be multiplied (cp. Bretschneider's *Probabilia*, 150–161; Lücke, pp. 660 f.; J. Réville, *Le quatrième évangile*, 26–47, 333 f.; Selwyn's *Christian Prophets*, pp. 81 f., 222 f.).* It must suffice here to point out that the apoc. reserves *τὸ ἀρνίον* for Christ, while the gospel confines *ἀρνίον* to Christians and uses *ὁ ἀμνὸς τοῦ θεοῦ* for Christ. Their common use of the redemptive function of the Lamb is not distinctive; it was widespread in primitive Christendom. The apparent coincidence of the Logos is still less real; the applications of *ὁ λόγος* in Jn $1^{1f.}$ and of *ὁ λόγος τοῦ θεοῦ* in Apoc 19^{13} are drawn from totally different soils in pre-Christian Judaism and turned to alien ends. Affinities of style like the use of *ἵνα* or of *ἐκ* (after *σώζειν, τηρεῖν*) are unimportant.† In several cases, as in that of the Logos, the presence of similar or identical phrases only betrays the radical difference of standpoint between the two books; *e.g.* *σκηνόω* in Jn 1^{14} and Apoc 7^{15}, and Jesus receiving from the Father (Jn 10^{18} and Apoc 2^{28}).

The strong linguistic presumption against the theory that the relationship of the two books is one of common authorship, is amply corroborated by the differences of religious thought, christological, spiritual, and eschatological. Christians in the apocalypse are never bidden love God or Christ (the *ἀγάπη* of $2^{4.19}$ is mutual affection between members of the church); on the contrary, they are ranked as *δοῦλοι*, which in Jn 15^{15} is explicitly described as an inferior relationship from which Jesus has raised his disciples. Similarly, the conception of believers as children or sons of God is wholly absent from the apocalypse; the solitary allusion (21^7) in the latter is eschatological, and even so it is an OT quotation. All this tallies with the remarkable difference of emphasis in the idea of God. He is a dazzling, silent, enthroned figure of majesty, not a Father in direct touch with his children on earth. God's love ‡ is only once mentioned, and that casually in an eschatological prediction (20^9 *τὴν πόλιν τὴν ἠγαπημένην*); the fatherhood of God (for Christ's sonship, cp.

* Selwyn, like Thoma (*ZWT.*, 1877, 289–341), regards the gospel as a correction of the Apocalypse.

† "So far as these tests [*i.e.* of language and style] can go, they strengthen the criticism of Dionysius, who (we must remember) was a Greek, weighing stylistic and grammatical differences found in books written in his own language" (J. H. Moulton, *Cambridge Biblical Essays*, p. 490).

‡ Christ's love is rather more prominent (1^5 3^9, cp. 3^{19}), but this is not a specifically 'Johannine' trait.

1^6 2^{27} $3^{5.21}$ 14^1) is ignored entirely (even in 21^7 θεός is substituted for the OT εἰς πατέρα), and the conception of the Spirit is purely prophetic,* in as sharp contrast to the Fourth gospel as the concrete, realistic eschatology. It is not too much to say that such idiosyncrasies decisively outweigh any affinities of language or conception which may be urged to the contrary.

Bruston (*Études sur Daniel et l'Apocalypse*, pp. 74 f.) surmounts the difficulty of the style by conjecturing that while John the apostle composed the gospel and epistles, the apocalypse (or rather, Bruston's second source for it) was not written till after his death by one of his disciples, 'peut-être sur la recommendation que le vieillard lui en avait faite avant sa morte et d'après le récit qu'il lui avait fait oralement de la révélation et des visions qu'il avait eues à Patmos.' This, however, fails to meet the crucial discrepancy of religious outlook † (especially in eschatology) between the apocalypse and the Fourth gospel. The same objection is valid against Zahn's (*INT.* § 74) view that while the gospel and epistles were revised by friends of John, who knew more about Greek than he did, the apocalypse was left unpolished. The reason alleged for this ("the more important the contents, the less important the form"), that a prophet transcribing his visions is less inclined than a historian or teacher to embellish the first draft, involves the extraordinary assumptions that the contents of a gospel are less important than those of a prophetic ecstasy, and that the apocalypse is no more than the transcript of ecstatic visions.

§ 6. *Date.*—The Neronic date (*i.e.* prior to the fall of Jerusalem and after Nero's massacre of the Roman Christians) appeals especially to those who feel the dramatic situation of passages like $11^{1f.}$, and who decline to admit the use of any sources. It is handicapped, however, by (*a*) the phase of the Nero-redivivus myth which the apocalypse represents, and above all by (*b*) the fact that no worship of the emperor, which is adequate to the data of the apocalypse, was enforced until Domitian's reign. The hypothesis of a date during Vespasian's reign (so, *e.g.*, B. Weiss, Düsterdieck, Bartlet: *AA.*, 388 f., C. A. Scott) evades (*a*) but not (*b*). Vespasian did not take his official divinity very seriously. There is no record of any persecution during his reign; such might conceivably have

* We even get the *angelus interpres* of the apocalyptic tradition and *the seven spirits* of the older Babylonian or Persian mythology.

† "The writer of the Fourth gospel has a very definite conception of how the Lord spoke on earth; it is difficult to think that the same writer at any period should have represented Him as speaking after the manner—the quite distinct and sustained manner—in which He speaks in the Apocalypse. The earlier date does not help us out of this difficulty" (J. A. Robinson, *JTS.*, 1908, p. 9).

taken place, but Christians seem to have enjoyed a comparative immunity under him, and our available knowledge * of the period renders it unlikely (cp. Linsenmayer's *Bekämpfung des Christentums durch den römischen Staat*, 1905, 66 f.) that anything occurred either under him or under Titus to call forth language so intense as that of the apocalypse. Some parts of the book (*e.g.* in 13 and 17) may be referred to (Jewish ?) sources of this period, but the manifesto as a whole demands a concrete situation for which the relations of the empire and the church during the eighth decade of the first century do not furnish anything like sufficient evidence. The most probable solution is that, when John wrote, Christians were being persecuted here and there in Asia Minor for what Domitian regarded as the cardinal offence of refusing to acknowledge him as the divine head of the empire. It is not necessary to assume that any widespread 'persecution' in the later and technical sense of the term was before the prophet's mind. He himself (1^9) had been only banished or imprisoned like some of his friends (2^{10}, cp. Clem. Rom. 9). But from the position of matters he argued the worst. The few cases of hardship and martyrdom in Asia Minor and elsewhere were drops of rain, which warned him that a storm was rolling up the sky. Eusebius probably exaggerates when he speaks of "many others" along with Clemens and Domitilla (*H. E.* iii. 18), and the period of terror was admittedly short (*H. E.* xx. 9–11, cp. Tert. *Apol.* 5), but it dinted the tradition of the second century deeply, and in any case the crisis opened John's mind to the fundamental issues at stake. It is this sense of the irreconcilable antagonism between the imperial cultus and Christianity, rather than any specific number of martyrdoms, which accounts for the origin of the apocalypse during the latter years of Domitian. Its language and spirit reveal a situation at once more serious and definite than any caused by earlier allusions to persecution for *The Name* or *My Name* which obtained more or less widely after the Neronic outburst (see p. 323). John sees another name set up against the name of Christ, and he stamps it as the essence of blasphemy to recognise any such title. The Domitianic demand for what John dubbed the worship of the Beast is to be met by

* The alleged evidence from Suetonius (*Vesp.* 15) and Hilary of Poitiers (*c. Arian.* 3) for a persecution under Vespasian is not worth the trouble of weighing. On the title *μάρτυς*, see Kattenbusch (*ZNW.*, 1903, 111–127).

passive resistance on the part of those who put loyalty to Christ above any other loyalty.

The Domitianic date thus offers a fair explanation of this apocalypse's references to the worship of the Beast, in the light of contemporary history during the latter part of the first century. It is also (*a*) in line with the earliest tradition, and (*b*) corroborated by the internal evidence of the document itself.

(*a*) Wherever Epiphanius derived his information that John's exile and release took place during the reign of Claudius (*haer.* li. 12, 233), it is palpably a wrong tradition, unless the tradition meant Nero, whom Epiphanius carelessly calls by his second name. So far as the early church had any tradition on the subject, it referred the banishment to Domitian's reign.

The tradition emerges first in Irenæus, whose remark on the name of antichrist is quoted (in Eus. *H. E.* iii. 18) as follows: *εἰ δὲ ἀναφανδὸν ἐν τῷ νῦν καιρῷ κηρύττεσθαι τοὔνομα αὐτοῦ, δι' ἐκείνου ἂν ἐρρέθη τοῦ καὶ τὴν ἀποκάλυψιν ἑορακότος. οὐδὲ γὰρ πρὸ πολλοῦ χρόνου ἑωράθη, ἀλλὰ σχεδὸν ἐπὶ τῆς ἡμετέρας γενεᾶς, πρὸς τῷ τέλει τῆς Δομετιανοῦ ἀρχῆς.* It is not possible to turn the force of this passage by pleading (so, *e.g.*, Simcox, Selwyn) that Irenæus confused the reign of Domitian with his (cp. Tac. *Hist.* iv. 2. 11) temporary regency in A.D. 70 (January to October), or by referring *ἑωράθη* to ὁ Ἰωάννης instead of to ἡ ἀποκάλυψις (so, *e.g.*, Wetstein, MacDonald's *Life and Writings of St. John*, New York, 1880, 169, E. Böhmer: *Über Verfasser und Abfassungszeit des Apokalypse*, pp. 30 f., Bovon,* and Chase, *JTS.* viii. 431–435). The latter is particularly unsuccessful (cp. Abbott, *Diat.* 2977a); the subject of *ἑωράθη* is plainly the apocalypse just mentioned, and, as Irenæus elsewhere (*e.g.* ii. 22. 5) declares that John lived till the reign of Trajan, there would be no sense in saying that he was seen during Domitian's régime.

(*b*) Ch. 17 discloses a plurality, or at least a duality, of literary strata as well as of traditions. Those who postulate a Jewish source (so, *e.g.*, Vischer, Weyland, Charles, Schmidt, Sabatier, Ménégoz, von Soden) usually make it a Vespasianic oracle, prophesying doom for Rome as the persecutor of God's people. When the source is taken to be Christian, the Domitianic editor's hand is found especially in 17^{11} (so Harnack: *TU.* ii. 3. 134 f.; *ACL.* ii. 1. 245–246, Briggs, Gunkel, J. Weiss, etc.). But neither on these hypotheses, nor on those of two sources (*e.g.* Wellhausen), are the data of the passage quite clear. The strata of tradition can be seen overlapping more clearly than the editorial processes of revision or combination. Thus, in

* Cp. Hort's ed. pp. 41–42, and Jacquier, *INT.* iv. 317–318.

vv.[8. 12f.] the Beast is the infernal Nero redivivus, while v.[11] identifies Domitian with Nero the Beast; and it is hard to believe that one and the same writer could simultaneously regard Domitian as a second Nero and expect Nero redivivus as a semi-supernatural power. Upon the whole, one of the least unsatisfactory solutions is to take [11] as a Domitianic gloss by the Christian editor, who also added [6b] (if not all of [6]) and [14] to a Vespasianic (Jewish?) oracle in 17[4f.] which anticipated the downfall of Rome at the hands of Nero redivivus and his Eastern allies. The reckoning of the seven Roman kings, which resembles the calculations of 4 Esdras and Barnabas (4), begins with Augustus* (so Tacitus) and passes over the three usurpers (Galba, Otho, and Vitellius; cp. Suet. *Vespas.* 1), as provincials would naturally do, to whom the struggle of the trio was no more than a passing nightmare. The sixth and reigning emperor (*ὁ εἷ ἔστιν*) is Vespasian, with whom the Flavian dynasty took up the imperial succession after Nero's death, which ended the Julian dynasty, had well-nigh broken up the empire (13[8f.]). Vespasian's successor, Titus, is to have only a brief reign. As a matter of fact, it did not last more than a couple of years. After him, the deluge! Nero redivivus (*τὸ θηρίον*), who had already reigned (*ὃ ἦν*), but who meanwhile was invisible (*καὶ οὐκ ἔστιν*), is to reappear from the abyss, only to be crushed finally (*καὶ εἰς ἀπώλειαν ὑπάγει*). Thus the downfall of the persecuting empire is to be heralded by the advent after Titus of one belonging to the seven (*ἐκ τῶν ἑπτά ἐστιν*) emperors who, on the traditional reckoning of the *heads*, were to see the rise and fall of Rome. The author of v.[11], living under Domitian, is obliged to identify the latter with Nero (as in another sense some of his own pagan subjects did);† but he still anticipates the imminent crisis predicted by his source. It is plain, therefore, that a Vespasianic oracle has been brought up to date in v.[11]; the course of actual history had broken through the eschatological scheme at one point, but, while the prophet seeks (in the contemporary and

* Augustus = *σεβαστός*, a word which had (especially in Asia Minor) the distinctly religious connotation of worshipful, was one of the *ὀνόματα βλασφημίας* (13[1]) which horrified the prophet John.

† The *caluus Nero* gibe of the Romans had a sterner replica in early Christianity (cp. Eus. *H. E.* iii. 17: *ὁ Δομετιανὸς . . . τελευτῶν τῆς Νέρωνος θεοεχθρίας τε καὶ θεομαχίας διάδοχον ἑαυτὸν κατεστήσατο. δεύτερος δῆτα τὸν καθ' ἡμῶν ἀνεκίνει διωγμόν, καίπερ τοῦ πατρὸς αὐτῷ Οὐεσπασιανοῦ μηδὲν καθ' ἡμῶν ἄτοπον ἐπινοήσαντος*).

historical note of v.[11]) * to repair the latter, he adheres firmly to his belief in it.

No literary filiation can be established between the apocalypse and any other NT writing which throws light upon its date. But one incidental water-mark of the Domitianic period, first pointed out by S. Reinach, occurs in 6[6] (cp. the present writer's study in *Exp.* 1908, Oct., 359–369), where the immunity of wine may be a local allusion to Domitian's futile attempt (in A.D. 92) to check the cultivation of the vine in the Ionian provinces.

The post-Neronic period is indicated by two other minor traits. (i.) The language, *e.g.*, of 13[1f.] is sometimes used to prove that the apocalypse breathes the atmosphere of the wild commotion and anarchy between A.D. 70. This interpretation is certainly truer to the data than that which finds an allusion to the murder of Julius Cæsar (so, *e.g.*, Gunkel, Porter, and Bruston), or to Caligula (Spitta). But the point of the oracle is that this weltering chaos had passed, leaving the empire stronger than ever, under the Flavians. The apocalyptist looks back upon the bloody interregnum which followed Nero's death. The collapse of the Julian dynasty, so far from proving fatal to the State, had simply aggrandised its influence; the tradition of the wounded head (Dn 8[8]) had been fulfilled. This retrospective attitude, together with the belief in Nero redivivus, points away from the Neronic period. (ii.) A further proof that the apocalypse could not have been written earlier than the eighth decade of the first century is furnished by the evidence of Polykarp (*ad Phil.* 11[3], cp. Zahn's *Forschungen*, iv. 252 f.), which shows that the church at Smyrna could hardly have had, by A.D. 70, the history presupposed in 2[8-11].

Several reasons contributed to the popularity of the seventh decade date. (i.) The Tübingen school required it for their thesis that the Balaamites and Nicolaitans were Pauline Christians whom the narrower faith of John the apostle attacked (cp. Hausrath, iv. 256 f., and Baur's *Church History of First Three Centuries*, i. pp. 84–87). Soon after Paul left Asia Minor, John settled there and wrote this vigorous pamphet in which he congratulated the metropolitan church of Ephesus for having detected false apostles like Paul, and for having resisted the subtle encroachment of the latter's Gentile Christian propaganda. It is no longer necessary to refute this theory, except to point out that, when the Neronic date and the Johannine authorship are maintained, there is a much more plausible case for it than several conservative critics appear to realise. (ii.) Those who

* John's revisal of the seven heads is paralleled by the author of Daniel's addition of the eleventh horn to the traditional ten, under similar historical exigencies. Bruston, Zahn, and Clemen (*ZNW.* ii. 109 f., xi. 204 f.) are among the few critics who still refuse to see any reference to Nero the infernal *revenant*.

ascribed both the apocalypse and the Fourth gospel to the apostle, naturally required a long period during which his thought and style were supposed to mature.* (iii.) The allusions in $11^{1f.}$ and elsewhere were taken to imply the period prior to the final destruction of Jerusalem, upon the view that the apocalypse reflected the contemporary situation in Palestine —a view not dissimilar to that which placed Hebrews in the same decade. The recognition of Palestinian traditions and sources removes any difficulty about the later date which may be felt on this ground.

For recent defences of the Neronic date, see Hort (cp. *JC.* 160 f.), Simcox, Selwyn (*op. cit.* pp. 215 f.), and B. W. Henderson (*Life and Principate of Nero*, 439 f.). The Domitianic date is argued, in addition to older critics like Mill, Hug, and Eichhorn, by Hofmann, Lee, Havet, Milligan (*Discussions*, 75–148), Alford, Gloag (*Introd. Joh. Writings*), Salmon (*INT.* 221–245), Schäfer (*Einl.* 347–355), Godet, Holtzmann, Cornely, Belser, Jülicher, Weizsäcker, Harnack (*ACL.* ii. 1. pp. 245 f.), McGiffert (*AA.* 634 f.), Zahn, Wernle, von Soden, Adeney (*INT.* 464 f.), Bousset, von Dobschütz, Wellhausen, Porter, R. Knopf (*NZ.* 38 f.), Abbott, Kreyenbühl (*Das Evglm der Wahrheit*, ii. 730 f.), Forbes, Swete, A. V. Green (*Ephesian Canonical Writings*, 182 f.), and A. S. Peake (*INT.* 164 f.), as well as †, from outlying fields, by J. Réville (*Origines de l'episcopat*, i. 209 f.), F. C. Arnold (*Die Neronische Christenverfolgung*, 1888), Neumann (*LC.*, 1888, 842–843, reviewing Arnold), Ramsay (*CRE.* pp. 268–302, *ET.* xvi. 171–174, *Seven Letters*, 93–127), S. Gsell (*Règne de l'empereur Domitien*, 1895, pp. 307 f.), Matthaei (*Preussische Jahrb.*, 1905, 402–479), and E. T. Klette (*Die Christenkatastrophe unter Nero*, 1907, 46–48).

§ 7. *Object.*—Over two centuries earlier the great exemplar of apocalyptic literature had been published in order to nerve the faithful who were persecuted for refusing to admit the presumptuous divine claims of Antiochus Epiphanes. John's apocalypse is a latter-day pamphlet thrown up by a similar crisis. The prophet believed that the old conflict had revived in its final form; Daniel's predictions were on the way to be fulfilled when a Roman emperor blasphemously claimed the title of ***dominus et deus***, and insisted on the rites of the Cæsar-

* Cp. Hort (*Apocalypse*, p. xl), "Without the long lapse of time and the change made by the fall of Jerusalem the transition cannot be accounted for. Thus date and authorship hang together. It would be easier to believe that the Apocalypse was written by an unknown John, than that both books belong alike to St. John's extreme old age." See below, § 8.

† Several critics who assign parts to an earlier date agree also that the final shaping of the book took place under Domitian (so, *e.g.*, Erbes, Barth, and J. Weiss).

cultus as a test of loyalty.* This popular deification of the emperor, with the corresponding recognition of *dea Roma*, were particularly rampant in Asia Minor, and the apocalypse is a vigorous summons to the church to repudiate the cultus at all costs. Hence its emphasis upon the virtues of martyrdom and upon the speedy downfall of the Roman empire.

> "Rome shall perish! write that word
> In the blood that she has spilt."

The loyalist attitude of Paul, and even of the author of First Peter or of Clemens Romanus, is exchanged for a passionate belief that the empire is the incarnation of anti-divine power; the prophet's aim is to rally the faith of the church by heralding the imminent downfall of her oppressor. The imperial cultus is taken to mean the last iniquity on earth, and Rome's downfall means the downfall of the world.

§ 8. *Authorship.*—The internal evidence thus shows a writer who was (or, was represented to be) an ardent Jewish Christian prophet named John, steeped in apocalyptic traditions, and in close touch with some of the Western Asiatic churches. The disjunctive canon which we owe primarily to the critical insight of Dionysius, Origen's thoughtful scholar, further proves that he was not the author of the Fourth gospel (or, inferentially, of the First Epistle of John).

(*a*) The hypothesis of John the apostle's authorship † is ruled out by the acceptance of the tradition of his early martyrdom (see below, Chap. V. (C.)), and, even apart from this, it is improbable, especially as presented by those who maintain that the Fourth gospel (with the Epistles) and the apocalypse were both written by him at the very end of his life. The acceptance of the Domitianic date, which throws the apocalypse close to the Fourth gospel, renders it quite impossible to maintain the common authorship of both works, as though, *e.g.*, a short exile at Patmos temporarily transformed (Ramsay, *Seven Letters*, 87) 'the head of the Hellenic churches in Asia Minor' into a

* For the literature, cp. Lindsay, *Church and Ministry in Early Centuries*[2] (1903), 341, and *EGT.* v. 400.

† So, recently, B. Weiss, W. H. Simcox, C. A. Scott, Zahn, Batiffol (*Leçons sur les évangiles*[8], 1907, 106 f.), Stanton (*GHD.* i. 171 f.), Lepin (*L'origine du quatr. évangile*, 1907, 257 f.), Jacquier (*INT.* iv. 321 f.), and Abbott.

Hebrew seer. Even the relegation of the apocalypse to the earlier date, and the inference that twenty or twenty-five years' residence in a Greek city like Ephesus improved John's style and broadened his outlook into a more spiritual range, do not suffice to meet the facts of the case. As Lücke and Alford* have pointed out, the Greek of the Fourth Gospel and of the first Epistle of John is not that of the apocalypse in an improved and maturer state. "The difference," as Swete rightly observes (pp. clxxviii–clxxix), "is due to personal character rather than to relative familiarity with Greek. And when style expresses individual character it undergoes little material change even in a long life of literary activity, especially after the age which St. John must have reached in A.D. 69 or 70." The fundamental difference in the use of language is corroborated, as the same writer adds, by an equally decisive difference in the attitude of both writers to Christianity, which is not fairly explained by making the apocalypse the expression of a rudimentary faith. "Even conceding the priority of the Apocalypse, can we explain the difference of standpoint by development? Is the relation of the apocalyptic to the evangelical teaching that which exists between rudimentary knowledge and the maturity of thought? And is it to be maintained that St. John's conceptions of Christian truths were still rudimentary forty years after the ascension, and reached maturity only in extreme old age?" The answer to these searching questions must be in the negative.

Even those who give up John's authorship of the Fourth gospel fail to make out a good case independently for his authorship of the apocalypse. Thus the vindictive, passionate tone of the latter is connected with the temper displayed in the incident of Mk $9^{38f.}$ (Lk 9^{55}); but in that case we should have to assume that the rebuke of Jesus produced no impression on one of the two disciples, and that forty years later he was unaffected by what he had heard his Master say. If it is hard to fit the personality of the beloved disciple or the mystical genius who wrote the Fourth gospel to the personality of the apocalyptic seer, there are almost as great psychological difficulties in the path of those who would associate him with

* Milligan (*Discussions on the Apocalypse*, 185–186) also dismisses this theory (held, *e.g.*, by Lightfoot, *Galatians*, 337, etc.) as "highly unsatisfactory."

the son of Zebedee. These would not be insuperable if the apocalypse showed other evidence of apostolic (Johannine) authorship, but the reverse is the case. Thus, in 3^{21} (δώσω αὐτῷ καθίσαι μετ' ἐμοῦ ἐν τῷ θρόνῳ μου) the writer attributes to Jesus the very prerogative which the Lord disclaimed (Mk 10^{40}). In 11^{1-2} the inviolability of the Jerusalem-ναός is assumed, in contrast to the explicit logion of Mk 13^{1-2} (cp. Ac 6^{14}). The general scheme of the apocalypse, with its calculations of the end, is more in keeping with the eschatological methods of the later Judaism than with the spirit, *e.g.*, of Mk 12^{15-17}, Mk 13^{32}, Ac 1^{6-8}, and 7^{1-8} (where the safeguarding of the elect precedes instead of following the crisis, where the four winds are agents of destruction instead of being geographical, and where the rôle of messiah is entirely omitted) differs from the synoptic scheme (Mk 13^{24-27}) as 9^{15} does from Mt 24^{7} (so Gaius). These features suggest that the author was some early Christian prophet who sat looser to the synoptic tradition than one of the twelve would have done. This is borne out by the fact that he claims no apostolic authority, nor is there any evidence * that he had been an eye-witness of Jesus on earth. An apocalypse is not a gospel; still, a personal friend is a personal friend, and the apocalyptic categories of $1^{9f.}$ are not such as might have been expected from one who had been numbered among the inner circle of the Galilean disciples. Finally, though 18^{20} does not absolutely exclude the possibility that an apostle wrote it,—since *apostles* as well as *prophets* might describe objectively the order to which the prophet belonged,—the objective and retrospective tinge of 21^{14} (*the twelve apostles of the Lamb*) suits a non-apostolic writer upon the whole better than an apostle.

"One may wisely hesitate to define the area of the impossible, but it is surely in the highest degree unlikely . . . that an unlettered Galilean peasant should, in the stress of the Parousia expectation of those earliest years, have turned to literary investigation and Oriental learning, . . . and that, above all, one who had sat at the feet of Jesus could put forth a work in which the great teachings of the divine Fatherhood, the universal brotherhood, the spiritual kingdom scarcely appear, but in their place we hear hoarse cries for the day of vengeance, and see the warrior Christ coming to deluge the earth with blood" (Forbes, *Intern. Hdbks to NT.* iv. 96).

---

* "That the writer of Rev. need not have known Jesus, remains a strong indication that he did not know Him" (Porter, *DB.* iv. 265); cp. Hoekstra, *op. cit.* 366 f.

(*b*) When the hypothesis of an apostolic authorship is set aside, the choice lies between the two figures suggested by Dionysius of Alexandria, each of whom has advocates in modern criticism. (i.) Some Asiatic prophet of that name (so, *e.g.*, J. Réville and Jülicher). This is quite possible, as the name was common enough. (ii.) John Mark, however, is a more authoritative personality (Ac $13^{5.13}$) than any unknown John, and his claims have been urged especially by Hitzig (*Ueber Johannes Marcus und seine Schriften*, 1843, pp. 11 f., 67–116), Weisse (*Evangelien-Frage*, 1856, pp. 91 f., 140, 180), and Hausrath (iii. 268),* as well as by those who (like Spitta and Völter) make him responsible for one of the sources underlying the book (see above, pp. 489 f.). Dionysius, who does not connect John Mark with the second gospel, brings forward no stylistic argument from that quarter; he simply dismisses the suggestion on the ground that John Mark (Ac 13^{13}) did not accompany Paul into Asia Minor. This would be no valid argument against the theory, for John Mark may have settled subsequently there quite as well as John the apostle. Acts is as silent on the one as on the other, in this connection. Still, the share of Mark in the second gospel, if it does not absolutely exclude his composition of the apocalypse, does not favour it; and, as the John-Mark hypothesis is a pure deduction from one or two statements and a large amount of silence in the early Christian literature, it has never commanded very much support.

(*c*) The possibility that this apocalypse, like most of its class, may be pseudonymous ("qui hoc opus negabant esse Ioannis euangelistæ, aut alium fuisse Ioannem ab euangelista credebant, quemadmodum duas posteriores epistolas adscribebant Ioanni non euangelistæ sed presbytero, aut eum qui conscripsit librum id egisse, ut ab euangelista scriptus uideretur eoque locum suo instituto commodum affinxisse," Erasmus) has also to be taken into account (so, *e.g.*, Volkmar, S. Davidson, Weizsäcker, Forbes, Wernle: *Urc.* i. 363, cp. Bacon in *Exp.*, 1907, 233 f., and *Fourth Gospel in Research and Debate*, pp. 160 f.), particularly in the form of a literary fiction under the name of John the apostle. *A priori*, the hypothesis is legitimate. On the other hand, an

* Hausrath, however, will not decide between John Mark and some other John. In any case, the apocalyptist, he holds, was a Palestinian Christian who strongly objected to the liberal practices of Pauline adherents in the Asiatic churches.

early Christian apocalypse was not necessarily pseudonymous. Hermas is not. It is true that the apocalypse of Peter, which ranked along with John's apocalypse in some circles of the early church, belongs to the pseudepigrapha; but here the apostolic characteristics are definitely drawn by the author, whereas John's apocalypse contains no specific traits which would lead the reader to imagine that the seer was an apostle.* Another *raison-d'être* for pseudonymity is absent, viz. the consciousness that the prophetic spirit was no longer present in the church. Though the contents of the apocalypse are sometimes no more than a secondary product of the prophetic inspiration, some of its cardinal passages represent direct personal visions; the ante-dated predictions in the apocalypse (*e.g.* in 13 and 17) are too subordinate to necessitate a recourse to pseudonymity here as in the older Jewish pseudepigrapha. On the other hand, if John the apostle was martyred early, it becomes more possible to conceive how the apocalypse was written under his name towards the close of the century, and modifications of the pseudonymous theory in this direction are upheld by those who find in it earlier fragments or traditions either of John the son of Zebedee (so, *e.g.*, Erbes and Bruston), or of John Mark, or of John the presbyter (see above, p. 489).

(*d*) The last-named figure, however, may well have been the real author of the book. He suits the requirements at least better than any other contemporary who is known to us, and, unless we are content to share the pious agnosticism of Dionysius upon the apocalypse, as of Origen on Hebrews, or to adopt some form of the pseudonymous hypothesis, the balance of probability inclines to John the presbyter, who must have shared the prophetic and even the chiliastic aptitudes of the Asiatic circle to which he belonged,—this is a fair inference from his relation to Papias and the presbyter-traditions of Irenæus,—who was a μαθητὴς τοῦ κυρίου in the wider sense of the term (*i.e.* a primitive Palestinian Christian), and who was one of the most important authorities in touch with the earlier apostolic tradition. It is more feasible to credit him with the rabbinic erudition and the eschatological lore of the apocalypse than one who was ἀγράμματος καὶ ἰδιώτης (Ac 4^{13}).

* The seer is simply the *brother* of his readers (1^{9} ὁ ἀδελφὸς ὑμῶν καὶ συγκοινωνός). Paul in 2 P 3^{15} is no more (ὁ ἀγαπητὸς ἡμῶν ἀδελφός), it is true, but there one apostle is supposed to be referring to another.

This hypothesis, which goes back to Eusebius (basing on the hint of Dionysius), was suggested afresh by Vogel * and Heinrichs (in Koppe's *NT.* 1818), and worked out from different standpoints by Eichhorn, Rettig (*Das erweislich älteste Zeit f. d. Apocalypse*, 1831), Bleek (cp. his *Beiträge zur Ev. Kritik*, 184–200), Lücke (*SK.*, 1836, 654 f.), de Wette, Schenkel, Ewald, Wittichen, Wieseler, Mangold, Credner, Neander, Keim, Havet, O. Holtzmann, Mejjboom, Düsterdieck, Selwyn, Erbes, Harnack, Bousset, Kohler, Lindenbein, von Soden, Heinrici (*Urc.* 1902, 126 f.), A. Meyer (*TR.*, 1907, 138), and von Dobschütz (*Probleme d. apost. Zeitalters*, 1904, 91 f.). Grotius threw out a conjecture to explain it ('credo autem presbytero, apostoli discipulo, custoditum hunc librum; inde factum ut eius esse opus a quibusdam per errorem crederetur'), but it is favoured more or less tentatively by recent critics like Loisy (*Le Quatr. Évangile*, 134), Swete, McGiffert, Pfleiderer (*Urc.* ii. 420 f.), Jacoby (*Neutest. Ethik*, 1899, 444–455), and Peake (*INT.* 152 f.).

---

* Vogel's idea was that 4^{1}–11^{19} and 1^{9}–3^{22} were (Neronic) fragments, written by the apostle and subsequently edited by the presbyter, who (under Galba) was responsible for the apocalypse as a whole.

CHAPTER V.

(A) *THE FOURTH GOSPEL*.[1]

LITERATURE. — (*a*) Modern editions — G. Hutcheson (London, 1657); Lampe's *Comm. Analytico-Exegeticus* (1724); Semler's *Paraphrasis* (1771); S. G. Lange (Weimar, 1797); H. E. G. Paulus (*Philologisch-kritisch und historische Commentar über den Evglm Joh.* 1812); Kuinoel[2] (Leipzig, 1817); L. Usteri's *Commentatio Critica* (Zürich, 1823); J. Munter's *Symbolæ ad interpret. Evang. Joh. ex marmoribus et nummis maxime græcis* (1826); Klee (1829); H. A. W. Meyer (1834, Eng. tr. 1875); Lassus, *Commentaire philosophique* (Paris, 1838); Lucke[3] (1840)*; A. Maier (1843 f.); Baumgarten-Crusius (1844–5); De Wette[3] (1846); Tholuck[7] (1857, Eng. tr. 1874); J. P. Lange (1860, Eng. tr. 1872 f.); L. Klofutar (1862); Olshausen[3] (1862, Eng. tr. 1855); Ewald, *Die Johan. Schriften* (1862); W. Bäumlein (Stuttgart, 1863); D. Brown (Glasgow, 1863); J. J. Astié (*Explication de l'év. selon S. Jean*, 1864); A. Bisping (1865); Hengstenberg[2] (1867 f., Eng. tr. 1879–80); Burger (1868); Luthardt[2] (1875–6, Eng. tr. 1876); Schaff (ed. of Lange; New York, 1872); H. W. Watkins (Ellicott's *Comm.* 1879); Milligan and Moulton (Schaff's *Comm.*, vol. ii.); Westcott (*Speaker's Comm.* 1880)*; C. F. Keil (1881); H. Conrad (Potsdam, 1882); P. Schanz (1885)*; Fillion (1887); Reynolds (*Pulpit Comm.* 1887–8); Whitelaw (1888); Wahle (1888); Godet[4] (1903, Eng. tr. of third ed., Edin. 1888–9)*; K. Schneider (1889); G. Reith (Edin. 1889); Wohlfart (1891); Plummer (*CGT.* 1893); Bugge (Germ. tr. by Bestmann, 1894); M. Dods (*EGT.* 1897); Knabenbauer (1897); A. Schroeder (Lausanne, 1899); M'Clymont (*CB.* 1901); Ceulemans (Malines-Dessain, 1901); Schlatter[2] (1902); J. M. S. Baljon (1902); Petersen (1902); Blass, *Evglm sec. Joh. cum var. lect. delectu* (1902); B. Weiss (— Meyer[9], 1902)*; Loisy (1903)*; Calmes (1904); Gutjahr (1905); A. Carr (Cambridge, 1905); Belser (1905): Heitmuller[2]

---

[1] For periodic surveys of the literature and detailed bibliographies, see, in addition to the works of Luthardt, Schürer, Watkins, and Sanday, Pfitzenmeier's *Aperçu des controverses sur le quatrième Évangile* (Thèse de Strasbourg, 1850); H. J. Holtzmann in Bunsen's *Bibel-Werk*, viii. (1866) pp. 56 f.; Pfleiderer (*PM.*, 1902, 57–74); Conybeare (*TT.*, 1906, 39–62); A. Meyer (*TR.*, 1906, 302 f., 339 f., 387 f.); and H. L. Jackson, *The Fourth Gospel and some recent German Criticism* (1906).

(*SNT.* 1907); H. P. Forbes (*Intern. Hdbks NT.* iv. 1907); Westcott (Greek text and notes, 1908); Holtzmann-Bauer * (*HC.*[3] 1908); Wellhausen * (1908); Zahn[3] (*ZK.* 1909) *.

(*b*) Studies.—(i.) against Johannine authorship :—Edward Evanson (*The Dissonance of the Four generally received Evangelists and the Evidence of their Authenticity examined*, Ipswich, 1792);[1] Vogel, *Evglm Johannes und seine Ausleger*, etc. (1801); Horst in Henke's *Museum für Religionswissen*, i. 47 f.; H. H. Cludius, *Uransichten* (1808), pp. 50 f., 350 f.; Ballenstedt, *Philo und Johannes* (1812); Bretschneider, *Probabilia de Evang. et epistolarum Johannis apostoli indole et origine* (1820) *; H. C. M. Rettig, *De quattuor Evang. Canonicorum origine* (1824); Lützelberger, *Die Kirchl. Tradition über d. Apostel Johannes*, etc. (1840); B. Bauer, *Kritik d. Evang. Geschichte d. Johannis* (1840); A. Schweitzer, *Das Evglm Johannis* (1841); Zeller (*Theol. Jahrb.*, 1845, 577 f., on internal evidence); Schwegler (*NZ.* ii. 346 f.); Baur, *Die Kanonischen Evglien* (1847); also in *Theol. Jahrb.* (1848), pp. 264 f. (on paschal controversy); Hilgenfeld, *Das Evglm und die Briefe Johannis nach ihrem Lehrbegriff* (1849) *, and *Die Evglien nach ihrer Stellung und geschicht. Bedeutung* (1854); Volkmar, *Die Religion Jesu* (1857); J. R. Tobler, *Die Evglienfrage im allgem. und die Johannisfrage insbesondere* (1858); Weizsäcker (*Jahrb. deutsche Theologie*, 1859, 685 f., on 'Beiträge zur Charakter d. Johan. Evglms'); M. Nicolas, *Études critiques sur la Bible*, pp. 127 f. (1864); Scholten, *Het evangelië naar Johan.* (1864, Germ. tr. 1867); J. J. Tayler, *An attempt to ascertain the Character of the Fourth Gospel* . . . (1867, second ed. 1870); J. C. Matthes, *De ouderdom van het Johannes-evangelië* (Leyden, 1867); E. V. Neale (*Theological Review*, 1867, 445–472); Schenkel, *Das Charakterbild Jesu*[4] (1873); W. Cassels (*SR.* 1874); Thoma, *Die Genesis des Joh.-Evglms* (1882) *; Jacobsen, *Untersuchungen über das Joh.-Evglm* (1884); M. Schwalb, *Unsere vier Evglien erklärt und kritisch geprüft* (1885); O. Holtzmann, *Das Johannes-Evglm* (1887) *; Brückner, *Die vier Evglien* (1887); R. Mariano (*Urc.* iv. 45–110) *; Cone (*Gospel and its Earliest Interpret.*, 1893, 267–317, also in *New World*, 1893, 1–28); van Manen, *OCL.* §§ 32–40; J. Réville, *Le quatrième évangile, son origine et sa valeur* (1901); E. A. Abbott (*EBi.* 1761 f.) *; P. W. Schmiedel (*EBi.* 2503 f.); Loisy, *Autour d'un petit livre* (1903, pp. 85–108); Wrede, *Charakter und Tendenz des Joh.-Evglms* (1903) *; Kreyenbühl, *Das Evglm der Wahrheit. Neue Lösung der Joh.-Frage* (i. 1900, ii. 1905). (ii.) in favour of Johannine authorship :—L. Bertholdt, *Verisimilia de origine Evangelii Johannis* (Erlangen, 1805: gospel orig. = Aramaic notes); J. A. L. Wegschneider, *Versuch einer vollständigen Einleitung in das Evglm Joh.* (Göttingen, 1806); J. T. Hemsen, *Die Authentie d. Schriften d. Evang. Joh. untersucht* (1823, reply to Bretschneider);[2] K. Frommann (*SK.*, 1840, 853–930, against Weisse); Ebrard, *Das Evglm Joh. und die neueste Hypothese über seine Entstehung*

---

[1] Cp. a reply by Thos. Falconer: Certain Principles in Evanson's Dissonance, etc., examined (Oxford, 1811); also the English reply to Strauss by Andrews Norton (*Genuineness of Four Gospels*, 1837 f.).

[2] Other replies to Bretschneider by Olshausen (*Die Echtheit d. vier kanon. Evglien*, 1823) and Crome (*Probabilia hand Probabalia*, 1824).

(1845, against Baur); Bleek's *Beiträge zur Evglienkritik* (1846); A. Norton, *Evidences of Genuineness of Gospels*[2] (1846–8, Cambridge, U.S.A.); Ebrard's *Wissensch. Kritik*[2] (1850, third ed. 1868, pp. 828 f.); A. Ritschl (*Theol. Jahrb.*, 1851, pp. 500 f.); G. K. Mayer, *Die Echtheit des Evglms nach Joh.* (Schafthausen, 1854); O. Thenius, *Das Evglm d. Evglien* (an open letter to Strauss, 1865); Hase, *Vom Evglm des Johannis* (Leipzig, 1866); Riggenbach, *Die Zeugnisse für das Evglm Joh.* (1866, external evidence); Jas. Orr, *The Authenticity of John's Gospel* (London, 1870, reply to J. J Tayler and S. Davidson); S. Leathes, *The Witness of St. John to Christ* (1870); Sanday, *Authorship and Historical Character of Fourth Gospel* (1872)*; Witting, *Das Evglm S. Joh. die Schrift eines Augenzeugen und zwar d. Apost. Johannis* (1874); C. E. Luthardt, *St. John the author of the Fourth Gospel* (Eng. tr. by Gregory, Edin. 1875, with valuable bibliography)*; Beyschlag (*SK.*, 1874, 607 f., 1875, 413 f.); Sanday, *The Gospels in the Second Century* (1876); J. M. M'Donald, *Life and Writings of St. John* (New York, 1880, pp. 268 f.); H. H. Evans, *St. John the author of the Fourth Gospel* (1888); Watkins (Bampton Lectures, 1890); Wetzel, *Die Echtheit u. Glaubwürdigkeit d. Evang. Joh.* (1899); Camerlynck, *De quarti euangelii auctore* (1899–1900, also in *BLE.*, 1900, 201–211, 419 f., 633 f.); T. B. Strong and H. R. Reynolds in *DB.* ii. 680–728; Mangenot (Vigoroux' *DB.* iii. 1167–1203); Hoonacker (*RB.*, 1900, 226–247); J. Drummond, *An Enquiry into the Character and Authorship of the Fourth Gospel* (1903)*; Haussleiter (*Theol. Litteraturblatt*, 1903, 1–6, 17–21, and *Die Geschichtlichkeit des Joh.-Evglms* (Leipzig, 1903); C. Fouard, *S. Jean et la fin de l'âge apostolique* (Paris, 1904, Eng. tr.); R. Seeberg (*NKZ.*, 1905, 51–64); Sanday, *The Criticism of the Fourth Gospel* (1905); R. H. Strachan (*DCG.* i. 869–885); *CQR.* (1905) 84–107, 387–412, (1906) 106–134; Lepin,[1] *L'origine du quatrième Évangile* (1907)*; C. E. Scott-Moncrieff, *St. John, Apostle, Evangelist, and Prophet* (1909). (iii.) on special points:—G. C. Storr, *ueber den Zweck d. evang. Geschichte und der Briefe Johannis*[2] (1810); K. F. Ranke, *Plan und Bau des Joh.-Evglms* (Berlin, 1824); Weizsäcker (*Jahrb. deutsche Theologie*, 1857, 154 f., 1859, 685 f., 'das Selbstzeugniss d. Joh. Christus'); H. Spaeth (*ZWT.*, 1868, 168 f., 309 f., 'Nathanael, ein Beitrag zum Verständniss der Composition d. Logos-Evglms'); R. H. Hutton, *Essays Theol. and Literary* (1871, 'Historical Problems of the Fourth gospel')*; G. W. Pieritz, *The Gospels from the rabbinical point of view, showing the perfect harmony between the Four Evangelists on the subject of the Lord's Last Supper* (1873); F. von Uechtritz, *Studien über den Ursprung, die Beschaffenheit, und Bedeutung des Evang. Joh.* (1876); A. H. Franke, *Das AT bei Johannes* (1885); Resch, *Paralleltexte zu Johannes* (1896); Schlatter, 'die Parallelen in den Worten Jesu bei Johannes und Matthäus' (*BFT.*, 1898, v.); Rollins (*Bibliotheca Sacra*, 1905, 484–499, written by John, edited by Apollos);[2] J. H. A. Hart (*Exp.*[7] v. 361 f., vi.

---

[1] Lepin's volume, like the essays by A. Nouvelle (*L'authenticité du quatr. Évangile et la thèse du M. Loisy*, Paris, 1905) and C. Chauvin (*Les idées de Loisy sur le quatr. Evangile*, 1906), is specially directed against Loisy.

[2] Tobler (see above) had already conjectured that Apollos composed the Fourth gospel on the basis of Johannine traditions.

42 f., 'plea for recognition of historical authority of Fourth gospel'); C. Gleiss (*NKZ.*, 1907, 470 f., 548 f., 632 f., 673 f., 'Beiträge zu der Frage nach der Entstehung und d. Zweck des Joh.-Evglms'); R. H. Strachan (*Exp.*[7] viii.-ix., 'The Christ of the Fourth Gospel'); P. Ewald (*NKZ.*, 1908, 824–853, 'die subjective Form der Johann. Christus-Reden'); van Eysinga (*PM.*, 1909, 143–150, 'zum richtigen Verständniss d. Johann. Prolog'); O. Zurhellen, *Die Heimat des vierten Evglms** (1909); D. H. Müller (*SBAW.*, 1909, 'Das Joh.-Evglm im Lichte d. Strophentheorie'); A. Merx, *Die vier Kanonischen Evglien nach ihrem ält. bekannten Texte . . . ii. 3. Johannes* (Berlin, 1910)*; M. Goguel, *Les Sources du récit Johannique de la Passion* (Paris, 1910); Lepin, *La Valeur Historique du Quatrième Évangile* (Paris, 1910)*; E. H. Askwith, *The Historical Value of the Fourth Gospel* (1910). (iv.) on the Logos-conception:—W. Baumlein's *Versuch die Bedeutung des Johannischen Logos aus dem Religionssystemen des Orients zu entwickeln* (1828); Anathon Aal, *Geschichte d. Logosidee* (i. 1896, ii. 1899): E. Bréhier, *Les idées philosophiques et religieuses de Philon d'Alexandrie* (Paris, 1908)*; J. S. Johnston, *The Philosophy of the Fourth Gospel* (*A Study of the Logos-Doctrine, its Sources and Significance*), 1909. (v.) general:—R. Shepherd, *Notes Crit. and Diss. on the Gospel and Epp. of St. John* (London 1796); J. G. Herder, *Von Gottes Sohn der Welt Heiland. Nach Joh.-Evglm* (Riga, 1797); C. C. Tittmann, *Meletemata Sacra* (1816, Eng tr. 1844); Köstlin, *Lehrbegriffe des Evglm u. der Briefe Johannis* (1843); C. Niese, *Die Grundgedanken des Joh. Evglms* (Naumburg, 1850); C. P. Tiele, *Het evang. van Johannes* (1855); M. Aberle (*Theol. Quartalschrift*, 1861, 37 f.); B. Weiss, *Der Joh. Lehrbegriff* (1862); Nolte (*Theol. Quartalschrift*, 1862, 464 f.); Schwalb (*Revue de Théol.*, 1863, 113 f., 249 f., 'Notes sur l'évangile de Jean'); Weissäcker's *Untersuchungen über die Evang. Geschichte* (1864, second ed. 1901)*; Sabatier (*ESR.* vii. 181–193); Renan, i. pp. 477–541; M. Wolf, *Das Evglm Johannis in seiner Bedeutung für Wiss. u. Glauben* (1870); H. Delff, *Entwickelungsgeschichte d. Religion* (1883, pp. 264 f., 284 f., 329 f.); F. D. Maurice, *The Gospel of St. John* (1888); H. Delff, *Geschichte d. rabbi Jesus von Nazareth* (1889, 67–206);[1] Reuss, *NTTh.* ii. 331 f.; H. Köhler, *Das Evglm Joh., Darstellung des Lehrbegriffs* (1892); C. Montefiore (*JQR.*, 1894, 24–74); G. B. Stevens, *The Johannine Theology* (New York, 1894); Baldensperger, *Der Prolog des Vierten Evglm* (1898)*; A. Titius, *Die Joh. Anschauung unter d. Gesichtspunkt der Seligkeit* (1900)*; Purchas, *Johannine Problems and Modern Needs* (1901); Schlatter (*BFT.*, 1902, iv. 'die Sprache u. Heimat des vierten Evglms'); J. Grill, *Untersuchungen über die Entstehung d. Vierten Evglms* i. (1902)*; J. L. Nuelsen, *Die Bedeutung des Evglm Joh. für d. Christliche Lehre* (1903); Inge (*DCG.* i. 885–895, also in *Cambridge Biblical Essays*, 1909, 251–288); H. A. Leenmans (*Theol. Studiën*, 1905, 377–412); J. d'Alma, *La Controverse du Quatrième Évangile* (1908); E. F Scott, *The Fourth Gospel, its Purpose and Theology*[2] (1909)*; A. E. Brooke

---

[1] Delff's further works included *Das Vierte Evglm, ein Authentischer Bericht über Jesus von Nazareth* (1890); *Neue Beiträge zur Kritik und Erklärung d. vierten Evglms* (1890); and an essay in *SK.* (1892) pp. 72 f.

'Historical Value of Fourth Gospel' (*Cambridge Biblical Essays*, 1909, 289–328); B. W. Bacon, *The Fourth Gospel in Research and Debate* * (New York, 1910); A. V. Green, *The Ephesian Canonical Writings* (London, 1910).

§ 1. *Outline and contents.*—Special literature: K. Meyer, *der Prolog des Joh.-Evglms* (1902); Lattey (*Exp.*^{7}, May 1906, 424–434), Hitchcock (*Exp.*^{7}, Sept. 1907, 266–279), Walther, *Inhalt u. Gedankengang des Evglm nach Joh.* (1907).

The analysis of the gospel, as it stands (leaving out ch. 21), depends upon its bisection into two parts (1–12, 13–20) or three (1–6, 7–12, 13–20). The latter suits the data better. The earlier ministry oscillates between Galilee and Jerusalem (2^1–6^{71}, Samaritan city = $4^{5\text{-}42}$ followed by a σημεῖον of resurrection); the later (7^1–12^{43}) is confined to Judea, with two retreats ($10^{40\text{-}42}$ and $11^{54\text{-}57}$), the former (πέραν τοῦ Ἰορδάνου) of which is followed by a σημεῖον of resurrection ($4^{39.\ 41}$ = 10^{42} belief of many), the latter being εἰς Ἐφραὶμ λεγομένην πόλιν. The third part (13^1–20^{31}) describes the conversation of Jesus at the last supper (13^1–17^{26}), the arrest, trial, and death (18^1–19^{42}), and the appearances after death ($20^{1\text{-}31}$).

The prologue illustrates Pindar's comparison of an opening lyric to a stately *façade*: ἀρχομένου δ' ἔργου χρὴ πρόσωπον θέμεν τηλαυγές.

> Quod initium sancti euangelii cui nomen est secundum Iohannem, quidem Platonicus . . . aureis litteris conscribendum et per omnes ecclesias in locis eminentissimis proponendum esse dicebat (Aug. *Ciuit. Dei*, x. 29).

The Logos is the divine principle of creation ($1^{1\text{-}3}$), apart from which the universe is unintelligible; no δημιοῦργος has any place or function in creation, beside the active Logos. Neither here nor elsewhere, however, does the author dwell upon the general creative energy of the Logos; it is the specific function of revealing the divine nature to men ($1^{4\text{-}5}$) which immediately absorbs his attention. *The life was the light of men.* The opposition encountered by the pre-Christian revelation is so characteristic of human nature in all ages that the writer drops into the present tense in v.^{5}. Hurrying on to the final revelation, for which John the Baptist was merely a witness ($1^{6\text{-}8}$), he explains that, when John was testifying, the Light was already coming into the world. In spite of John's testimony and his own revelation, however, only an elect minority of believers* ($1^{12c} = 20^{31}$) welcomed the Logos (1^{9-13}). To them the incarnate Logos (no phantom of docetic gnosticism), in virtue of his divine sonship,† manifests and imparts the real nature of God the Father (1^{14-18}).

The introduction (1^{19-51}) develops the witness of John the baptizer to Jesus as the Christ ($1^{25f.}$), the Son of God (1^{34}, cp. 20^{31}). This witness is borne in a triple fashion: (*a*) before sceptical Judaism (= οἱ Ἰουδαῖοι, 1^{19-28}), (*b*) in a soliloquy ‡ (1^{29-34}), and (*c*) before two of his own disciples ($1^{35f.}$). The third testimony starts a movement towards Christian discipleship: (*a*) two of John's disciples join Jesus (1^{37-39}), (*b*) they bring over others (1^{40-42}), and (*c*) finally (*τῇ ἐπαύριον*, as in $1^{29.35}$), Jesus himself calls a third set ($1^{43f.}$).§ The genuine Israelite is he who (1^{47-49}) comes to Jesus through sceptical prejudice and confesses him to be the Son of God.

The religion of Jesus is now under way. The three following stories bring out its superiority to the older Judaism ($2^{1f.}$ $2^{13f.}$ 3^{1-21}) from various points of view. The activity of the disciples in baptizing throughout Judea leads up (note the loose *μετὰ ταῦτα*) to John's final witness ($3^{22f.}$) and incidentally to a mission at Sychar ($4^{1f.}$) as Jesus and his disciples make their way north to Galilee ($4^{43f.}$). Here the second *σημεῖον* rounds off the opening cycle which began with the first *σημεῖον* (both at Kana: petition for help, eliciting of trust $2^{5} = 4^{50}$, mysterious aid). The faith of the *μαθηταί* (2^{11}) has now widened into the faith of those benefited (4^{53}); for this faith in the word ($3^{32f.}$) of Jesus, see already 4^{41}, as contrasted with faith in his *σημεῖα* (2^{23} 4^{48}).

The second cycle contains two controversies with the Jews occasioned by three *σημεῖα*, one at Jerusalem (5) and two in Galilee (6). The second of the latter *σημεῖα* (6^{16-21}) is really a pendant, as in the synoptic tradition, to the former (6^{1-13}), and does not appear to have any independent significance. The narrative of the period closes with a messianic confession of

* Note the climax of ^{10a} (humanity), ^{11a} (Judaism), and ^{14a} (Christians).

† A Philonic touch: to see God was the mark of primogeniture (*De post. Caini*, 18). The phrase *χάριν ἀντὶ χάριτος* is another reminiscence and adaptation of Philonic language (cp. *de post. Caini*, 43).

‡ At any rate, no audience is mentioned.

§ Note in this paragraph the interweaving of (*b*) and (*c*) in $1^{45f.}$ and 1^{49}.

faith on the part of the eleven disciples (6^{69}); the secret disloyalty of the twelfth (6^{70-71}) is noted by way of dramatic anticipation.

The mystical revelations and claims of Jesus have now not only driven many of his *μαθηταί* away from him ($6^{60f.\ 66f.}$), but provoked the deadly antipathy of Judaism ($5^{16.\ 18}$ 7^{1}). The controversies of 5–6 have led to nothing; they have evoked only perplexity and irritation, even in Galilee. The second part of the ministry (7–12) includes the deepening conflict with Judaism, in a series of discussions at Jerusalem during the feast of tabernacles (7–10^{21}) and the feast of dedication (*τὰ ἐγκαίνια*, 10^{22-39}). A partial sympathy is elicited ($7^{43} = 10^{19}$), but it is a resurrection-*σημεῖον* (11^{1-44}, after 10^{27-28}) which first converts many of the Jews (11^{45} 12^{11}), though it also brings the mortal hatred of the Jews as a whole to a head ($11^{46f.}$). The subsequent entry into Jerusalem (12^{1-19}) is followed by an episode (12^{20-23}) which is the third anticipation of Christ's death and resurrection as prefigured in the *σημεῖον* of 11^{1-44}, the two others being the prophetic word of Kaiaphas (11^{47-53}) and the action of Mary (12^{1-8}). A final summary of the results achieved by the public mission of Jesus is appended, the general unbelief of Judaism being accounted for on the theory of predestination.

The third section of the gospel opens with the actions ($13^{1f.}$), the instructions (13–16), and the last prayer of Jesus at a private supper with his disciples. After death he appears thrice: to Mary of Magdala (20^{1-18}), to the ten disciples (20^{19-23} in the evening), and, a week later, to the eleven, including Thomas (20^{24-29}).

The oscillation between Galilee and Judea is strongly marked. Jesus appears in the vicinity of John the Baptist *πέραν τοῦ Ἰορδάνου* ($1^{29f.}$); he then moves into Galilee (1^{43}, no reason given), from which the approach of the passover recalls him to Jerusalem ($2^{13f.}$); he departs *εἰς τὴν Ἰουδαίαν γῆν* (3^{22}, no reason given), returns to Galilee *viâ* Samaria (for enigmatic reason given in 4^{1}), and again goes up to Jerusalem to attend a Jewish festival (5^{1}). The next chapter (6^{1}) places him in Galilee (no reason given for his return), and in $7^{2f.}$ he goes back upon his own initiative to the capital for the *σκηνοπηγία*. He is still here in $10^{22f.}$, but retires (10^{40-42}) *πέραν τοῦ Ἰορδάνου* ($= 1^{29f.}$) to avoid being arrested for blasphemy. After a brief visit to Bethany ($11^{2f.}$), for the purpose of raising Lazarus, he again retires in order to avoid arrest, this time not north into Galilee, but to the town of Ephraim (11^{54}). Finally, the approach of the passover brings him back to Jerusalem ($11^{1f.}$ $^{12f.}$), where all the resurrection-appearances take place (pp. 254–255).

§ 2. *Sources.*—Apart from the OT, the main currents which flow through the gospel are those of (*a*) Paulinism,* (*b*) the Jewish Alexandrian philosophy, and (*c*) Stoicism. Though not mutually exclusive, for practical purposes they may be noted separately. (*a*) The author has worked in the Pauline antithesis of grace and law (1^{17} cp. Ro 6^{14}),† and Pauline ideas like God's sending of his Son (3^{17} = Gal 4^{4-5}) and God's love (ἠγάπησεν, 3^{16}, cp. Eph 2^{4}). On the other hand, a conception like that of Phil 2^{7-11} is different from that of Jn 3^{24-25}; the idea of the Spirit as a factor in the glorified nature of Christ (Ro 1^{4}) lies outside the special view of the Fourth evangelist, who tends to confine the operations of the Spirit to believers; and both the Pauline conceptions of sin and faith fall into the background before other interests. These differences, however, do not affect the general impression that on such cardinal topics as union with Christ, freedom ($8^{33f.}$), and life in relation to the glorified Christ, the writer has developed his theology from Pauline germs. Even the specific sense attached to Ἰουδαῖοι in the Fourth gospel may be but the development of Paul's usage in his epistles, where the synoptic Φαρισαῖοι tends to be dropped for Ἰουδαῖοι as the opponents of Christ and Christianity (cp. Resch, *Paulinismus*, 194–196, 540).

(*b*) Alexandrian Judaism had already blended with Paulinism in Hebrews, which lies midway between Paul and the Fourth gospel; cp. the parallels with the latter in creation διὰ Χριστοῦ (1^{2} 2^{10} cp. Jn 1^{3}), absence of self-glorification on Christ's part (5^{4} cp. Jn 8^{54}), Christ as man's access to God (7^{25} cp. Jn 14^{6}), Christ the shepherd (13^{20} cp. 10^{11}), the unity of the ἁγιάζων and the ἁγιαζόμενοι (2^{11} = Jn $17^{19.\ 21}$), and 3^{1} = Jn 20^{21}, 10^{20} = Jn 14^{6}, 11^{16} = Jn 14^{2}. The conception of Jesus in Hebrews is closer (5^{7-9}) to the synoptic tradition at some essential points, however, than to the Johannine, which tends to omit such features of crying and infirmity as derogatory to the Logos-Christ on earth.

* Cp. Reuss, *NTTh.* ii. 513 f.; A. Titius, pp. 11 f., 15 f., 32 f., 70 f., 115 f., etc.

† The phrase incidentally shows how far the old controversy over the law lay behind the writer and his readers. As Reuss (*op. cit.* 533) observes, "he seems almost to have forgotten that this was a point around which controversy had raged long and passionately."

The helpful idea that even Jesus required to win his way into the higher reaches of thought and feeling towards God is vividly present to the mind of the Alexandrian genius who wrote Hebrews, but it is not congenial to the temperament of the Fourth evangelist.

The most noticeable channel for this Alexandrian influence on the Fourth gospel, however, is Philonism. "The reader of Milton," said Coleridge, "must be always on his duty; he is surrounded by sense; it rises in every line; every word is to the purpose." This canon answers to the critical spirit in which the Fourth gospel has to be read. Symbolic or semi-allegorical meanings are not to be expected or detected in every phrase or touch, however incidental; allowance must be made for the introduction of circumstantial details such as an imaginative and dramatic writer is accustomed to employ for the purpose of heightening the effect at certain points. Generally, however, the reader of the gospel is surrounded by allusions which are not always obvious upon the surface. There is often a blend of subtlety and simplicity in which the significance of some expression is apt to be missed, unless the reader is upon the outlook, or, as Coleridge put it, upon his duty. The brooding fulness of thought and the inner unity of religious purpose which fill the book demand for its interpretation a constant sensitiveness, especially to the deeper meaning which prompted the methods of contemporary religious speculation along the lines of the Alexandrian Jewish philosophy (cp. p. 27) as represented by Philo. Τὸ *μὴ ἐκ φαινομένων τὸ βλεπόμενον γεγονέναι.*

The differences between Philo and John only bring out the latter's familiarity with the Philonic methods and materials which he uses for higher ends. Thus the numerous *δυνάμεις* or *λόγοι* of the speculative religious world, which were expressions or agents of one divine Power,* were swept aside by this author, just as Paul had already done along a different line; there is but one Logos, and that is Jesus Christ. John's Logos is historical and personal. In the very act of setting aside such speculations,† however, the writer uses many of their phrases. Thus 1^{18} is a thought characteristic of Philo, who protests earnestly against the idea that God can be seen (*de mut. nomin.* 2), and adds, *à propos* of Gn 17^{1}, that such allusions

---

* Cp. Usener's *Götternamen*, pp. 339 f.

† Cp. the sentence of Cornutus, *τυγχάνει δὲ ὁ Ἑρμῆς ὁ λόγος ὤν, ὃν ἀπέστειλαν πρὸς ἡμᾶς ἐξ οὐρανοῦ οἱ θεοί.*

to the vision of God imply the manifestation of one of his powers (*ibid.* 3, ὡς μιᾶς τῶν περὶ αὐτὸ δυνάμεων, τῆς βασιλικῆς, προφαινομένης). Similarly, the changing of the name, in order to express a deeper significance in the bearer's new relation to God (1^{42}), is in Philo also (*de mut. nom.* 13) a function of the Logos (in the case of Jacob, not of Abram), where it is associated with being 'born of God' (cp. *de gig.* 14, 'when Abram became improved and was about to have his name changed, he then became a man of God'). John's habit of using phrases of mysterious and symbolic significance* for apparently simple actions and events, is illustrated not only by the rabbinic *come and see* (1^{46}), which was commonly employed as the prelude to some deep truth,† but, *e.g.*, by Philo, who, commenting on the τί ζητεῖς of Gn 37^{15} (*quod det. potiori*, 8, cp. Jn 1^{38} τί ζητεῖτε), explains it as the utterance of the Elenchos (or convicting Logos) to the wandering homeless soul. A further Alexandrian trait occurs in 2^{1-11} where the Logos-Christ not only opens his ministry by supplying mankind with the new wine of the gospel, but fulfils the rôle of Philo's Melchizedek, the prototype of the Logos, who ἀντὶ ὕδατος οἶνον προσφερέτω καὶ ποτιζέτω καὶ ἀκρατιζέτω ψυχάς (*leg. alleg.* iii. 26). The Logos-Christ is also omniscient (cp. 1^{48} 2^{24}, He 4^{12-13}, Philo, *leg. alleg.* iii. 59), and a διδάσκαλος (3^{2} 13^{13}: Philo, *quod deus sit immutabilis*, 28). Furthermore, the *six* ὑδρίαι (2^{6}) from which the wine is produced, correspond to the Philonic principle that "six is the most productive of numbers" (ἑξάδι τῇ γονιμωτάτῃ, *Decalogo*, 30). There is also a remarkable parallel to 3^{34} in Philo's comment on Nu 11^{17} (*gigant.* 6), while the *five husbands*‡ of 4^{18} are the five earlier deities of the Samaritan cultus (2 K $17^{24f.}$; Jos. *Ant.* ix. 14. 3),§ and *he whom thou now hast is not thy husband*, is either Yahweh, who really belongs to Israel, or else Simon Magus (Ac $8^{9f.}$, Justin's *Apol.* i. 26), the contemporary idol of the Samaritans. Similarly, $4^{39.\,42}$ reflect the Philonic idea (deduced from Ex 32^{2}) that χειρόκμητος οὐδείς ἐστιν ὄψει καὶ πρὸς ἀλήθειαν θεός, ἀλλ' ἀκοῇ καὶ τῷ νομίζεσθαι, καὶ ἀκοῇ μέντοι γυναικός, οὐκ ἀνδρός (*de post. Caini*, 48), while the conception in 5^{17} echoes the Alexandrian doctrine of God's unresting activity (Philo,

---

* Cp. Abbott, *Diat.* 1119–1120 ("He is always mystical, always fraught with a twofold or manifold meaning, as though he said, 'You shall not go a step with me unless you will think for yourselves.' Sometimes he seems to meander in long discourses or dialogues. . . . In some respects the style is complicated as a sonnet; and we feel beneath it the influence of the allegorising school of Philo and of the Jewish canons about the methods of stating terrestrial and celestial doctrine").

† On the Philonic element and influence, see especially E. F. Scott, *The Fourth Gospel*, 53 f., and Feine, *NTTh.* 638 f.

‡ Cp. Philo, *de fuga et inuentione*, 14, τὸ δὲ πολυμιγὲς καὶ πολύανδρον καὶ πολύθεον κτλ., also *de mutat. nominum*, 37.

§ Josephus writes that the Cuthæans, "according to their nations, which were five, introduced their own gods into Samaria," and that, after being plagued to death for their idolatry, they "learned by an oracle that they must worship Almighty God." He adds, "when they see the Jews in adversity, they say they are in no way related to them, and that the Jews have no right to expect any kindness from them" (cp. Jn 4^{9}). See above, p. 29.

leg alleg. i. 3, παύεται γὰρ οὐδέποτε ποιῶν ὁ θεὸς κτλ., adding in 7, ἅτε οὐ τεχνίτης μόνον ἀλλὰ καὶ πατὴρ ὢν τῶν γινομένων).* The identification of the Logos-Christ with the bread of life or manna in $6^{35f.}$ is reproduced from Philo's well-known identification of the manna (Ex $16^{4.\,15}$) with the Logos (e.g. *de profug.* 25). With 15^{15} we may also compare the Philonic original in the comment on Gn 18^{17} in *de sobrietate*, 11 (οὐχὶ δεσπότης ἢ κύριος· φίλον γὰρ τὸ σοφὸν θεῷ μᾶλλον ἢ δοῦλον), and the equally striking anticipation in *migrat. Abrah.* 9. These instances will suffice to show that in literary methods, no less than in religious speculation, the Fourth evangelist had been trained in the Philonic spirit.

(*c*) The Stoic ring of some sentences in the prologue is natural, in view of the fact that Ephesus had been the head-quarters of the Logos-idea as developed by the philosophy of Herakleitus, himself a well-known and revered author in Asiatic Christian circles (Justin, *Apol.* i. 64, cp. Orig. *c. Cels.* i. 5). Though the Logos-idea was mediated and moulded for the author by the speculations of Alexandrian Judaism, and though the fusion of Stoicism with the latter had blended several characteristic traits, there are (see below) elements in the Fourth gospel which point to a fairly direct contact with the Stoic propaganda. Thus the sentence, *in the beginning was the Logos, and the Logos was* θεός, might have been written literally by a Stoic, as Norden argues (ii. 472 f.); it was written by one acquainted with the writings of Herakleitus, though the un-Stoic sentence, *and the Logos was with God.* at once betrays a Jewish current.

§ 3. *Object and christology.*—The dominant feature of any gospel is its conception of Jesus, and the Fourth gospel is a study or interpretation of his life, written in order to bring out his permanent significance as the Logos-Christ for faith. The author does not find Jesus in the Logos; he finds the Logos in the Jesus of the church, and the starting-point of his work is a deep religious experience of Jesus as the revelation of the Father. At the same time, even as a historical writer he is to be judged by the fact that his account of Jesus is introduced by a sketch of what he understood to be an adequate philosophy of the Christian religion.†

* The activity of the Logos-Christ on the sabbath answers to Philos' identification of God's rest on the seventh day (Gn $2^{2.\,4}$) with his higher activity in creating through the Logos natures of divine capacity (*leg. alleg.* i. 6. 8). With 5^{19} cp. Philo, *de confus. ling.* 14, and G. Klein's *Der Aelteste Christliche Katechismus* (1909), pp. 53 f.

† The prologue is organic to the conceptions of the book; for an opposite view, see Harnack, *ZTK.* ii. 213 f.

One result of this Logos-category is that the human career of Jesus tends to become an episode in the eternal existence of the Logos, through which he passes comparatively unhampered and unruffled. There is an aversion, on the writer's part, to admit any outside impact upon Jesus and a corresponding tendency, as far as possible, to dissociate his course of action from the natural suggestions and motives which might be supposed to have rippled on his personality. This emphasis on the self-determining authority of Jesus may be illustrated by a reference to 2^{1-11} 7^{1-11} 10^{15-18} and 18^{4-7}; from first to last he is master of his course. It is consonant with this attitude that he alone speaks from the cross (19^{26-30}); no one ventures to address him there (as in the synoptic gospels). The same pragmatism recurs in 11^{1-16}, where the action of Jesus is studiously removed from the sphere of human influence or appeal, and where the tendency to emphasise his mysterious wisdom is as marked as the desire to bring out the greatness of the miracle. The omniscience * of Jesus in this gospel is full-orbed from the very beginning; it requires neither to be sustained nor to be matured by new accesses of experience, and in fact represents a dramatic expansion of the Logos-idea in Col 2^{9} or He 4^{12-13}. The Jesus of this writer anticipates human insight. He is first, with men, even with the keenest ($1^{38.\ 42.\ 47-48}$). He forms his own plans, knows where to hold aloof from human nature, and rarely (4^{1} 11^{3-6}) requires any information as to the temper and attitude of his contemporaries (contrast 2^{24-25} with Mk 8^{27}, cp. also 9^{35} 11^{42} 15^{16}). Not even his relatives can fathom or forecast his intentions (2^{3} 6^{6} 13^{7}). He takes the initiative (contrast 6^{5} with Mk 6^{36} 8^{4}), and, even when initiative is impossible, shows himself serenely conscious of all that is transpiring ($6^{61.\ 71}$ $13^{1.\ 3}$). The Passion is no drift but an open-eyed choice, exhibiting marks of a royal advance ($14^{2f.\ 12.\ 22}$ $16^{5.\ 7.\ 22-23}$). Jesus is not swept into the power of death (10^{18}); up to the very last he takes the lead, and after the resurrection he is too holy for human endearment (note the correction in 20^{7} of Mt 28^{9}). Similarly, during his lifetime on earth he hardly requires to pray (11^{47}); on the contrary, he is prayed to by the church (note the significant omission in 6^{15} as compared with Mk 6^{46}, Mt 14^{23}; not prayer, but the need of avoiding pressure from the

* He is *αὐτοδιδάκτος* (1^{48} $4^{17-18.\ 36}$ 5^{42} $6^{15.\ 61.\ 64}$ 8^{40} etc.), and entitled to the divine name of *καρδιογνώστης*. "Nothing to him falls early or too late."

side of men is the motive for his retirement). He also carries his own cross (19^{17}, as against Mk 15^{21}).

The desire to minimise anything like suggestion or influence from without is part of the Logos-motive in the delineation of Jesus, which tended to emphasise the transcendental and inviolate freedom of the Logos-Christ on earth. The Jesus of the Fourth gospel really never acts upon the direct initiative of others, and it is this abstract tendency in the book which accounts for such features as his attitude to his mother (in 2^{4}) and his brothers (in 7), as well as for the conception of the σημεῖα. To a greater degree than the synoptic Jesus, the Jesus of this evangelist possesses a knowledge of his own career and fate which invests him with a unique detachment and independence of spirit. The writer has too much artistic taste and historical sense to represent his Jesus on earth as a mere symbol of the Logos-idea; the latter is dexterously confined to the prologue, although its essential contents underlie the subsequent stories and speeches which are interpenetrated by its spirit. But its exploitation led to a new representation of the Lord's character on earth. To graft it upon the synoptic tradition meant a problem of extreme delicacy; to harmonise the human Jesus and the mysterious Logos involved a reaction of the latter idea upon the data of the former, and the success of the writer is to be measured by the comparative skill with which he has retained the impression of psychological reality and human feeling in the description of Jesus as the Logos-Christ. He is too Christian to have committed the error of depicting an entirely superhuman or docetic Jesus; his Christ is still subject to the natural laws of the world (11^{15}), to space and time (4^{1-4}), to weariness and thirst, to motives like prudence (7^{1} 8^{59} 10^{40} 11^{54}), grief (11^{35}), joy, and indignation (18^{20}). But the tendency to obliterate the features of surprise, ignorance, mistake, and disappointment reaches its climax in the Fourth gospel, and one result is that the unspeakable gains in our conception of Christ are accompanied by a certain lack of the homeliness and definite human charm with which the earlier synoptists invest his person. To the writer Jesus is more than ever the head of the church, a community standing over against Judaism, the representative of divine light amid darkness, the final source of truth amid error The surprising thing is that, writing under so dominant a tendency, he has managed to delineate a character and at the same time to develop abstract antitheses and dogmatic ideas, in such a way that the Logos-idea has not overwhelmed historic circumstantiality or led to serious contradictions. This bears out the conclusion that he "is not dramatising a metaphysical abstraction, but idealising (showing the highest significance of) a historical figure." *

This emphasis upon the self-possession of Jesus, as I have elsewhere shown (*Exp.*[6] iv. pp. 127 f., 221 f.), is due to the influence of contemporary Stoicism, mediated in part by the conception of the divine σοφία in the *Wisdom of Solomon*, where autonomy is predicated of the highest life. As this independent volition and self-contained power was regarded, *e.g.*, by the best Stoics as the crowning excellence of human life, it is likely that this element contributed more or less unconsciously to a portrait of Jesus in which the writer aimed at bringing out as far as possible his absolute authority in action and his superiority to human pressure. While the employment of the Logos-category in itself involved a free handling of the synoptic tradition and at the same time encouraged any tendency to heighten the majestic self-possession of Jesus in the interests of reverence and faith, this does not suffice to explain the distinctive quality of the Fourth gospel; the latter is intelligible in the light of the contemporary Stoic bias and of its affinity to the author's speculative bent, though he is far from the extreme standpoint of Clement of Alexandria, and indeed makes statements which may be regarded now and then as implicit criticisms of the Stoic ideal (cp. *e.g.* Abbott's *Diat.* 1705–1706, 1727 c.).

This subordination of humane compassion to divine authority comes out specially in the σημεῖα. Neither here nor elsewhere is Jesus viewed as an embodiment of the divine χάρις. He says, "I am ἡ ἀλήθεια," but not "I am ἡ χάρις," and the omission of words like ἐλεέω, οἰκτιρμός, σπλαγχνίζομαι, and ἔλεος is significant. The σημεῖα retain a human element, but it is subordinate, if not accidental.† "The miraculous power, which in St. Matthew, St. Mark, and St. Luke is mainly the organ of a divine compassion for human misery and pain, is in this gospel—primarily at least—the revealing medium of a mighty spiritual presence, and intended more as a solemn parting in the clouds of Providence, to enable man to gaze up into the light of divine mystery, than as a grateful temporary shower of blessing to a parched and blighted earth" (R. H Hutton, *Theological Essays*, p. 178).

* Inge in *Cambridge Biblical Essays*, 281–282.

† Cp. Bruce, *The Miraculous Element in the Gospels*[2] (1886), p. 151, "the synoptical miracles are, in the main, miracles of *humanity*; the Johannine miracles are, so to speak, miracles of *state*. They are wrought for the purpose of glorifying the worker."

This is one of the numerous points at which the Fourth gospel represents the climax of a development which may be traced already in the synoptic tradition of Mk. as employed by Mt. especially—a development which heightened the thaumaturgic character of the σημεῖα, and also began to view them not so much as incidental acts of mercy and love, but as repeated and general demonstrations of Christ's messianic power. These traits are predominant in the Fourth gospel, where the σημεῖα are moulded into proofs of mysterious power and immanent glory resident in the personality of Jesus.

The monotones of the Fourth gospel thus relate to the life and teaching of Jesus. The synoptic distinction between the periods before and after the messianic confession at Cæsarea Philippi (Mk $8^{27\text{-}30}$) is omitted in a writing which from the outset presents both Jesus and his adherents as fully conscious of his messianic dignity; the variety and practical bearings of his teaching in the synoptic record are replaced in the Fourth gospel by an unvarying series of modulations upon the theme of his own person in relation to the Father, believers, and the world in general. The synoptic Jesus also alluded to the unique significance of his person, but only occasionally (Mt $11^{2f.}$, Lk $7^{18f.}$), and exalted personal claims were elicited from him by the carping criticism and suspicion of the Jewish opposition, but these flashes of unfolding self-revelation are neither so numerous nor so spontaneous as the sustained personal discourses of the Fourth gospel;* the latter suggest the work of a writer whose religious presuppositions have led him to isolate and expand what was at most a subordinate feature in the synoptic tradition of Jesus.

The influence of this tendency upon the writer's schematism will be clear from a comparison of the following passages:—

Jesus refers the Samaritan woman to the water of eternal life ($4^{10.\ 13f.}$ οὐ μὴ διψήσει).	Jesus refers the Jews to the heavenly bread of eternal life ($6^{27\text{-}35}$ οὐ μὴ διψήσει).
She refers to the ancestral well from which her fathers had drunk (4^{12}).	They refer to the manna which their fathers had eaten (6^{31}).
But the true water of life comes from Jesus ($4^{13f.}$).	But the true bread of life is Jesus himself ($6^{32f.}$).

* Dr. Rush Rhees, on the other hand, finds the striking monotony of the Fourth gospel already present in the conflict-stories of the synoptists (*JBL.*, 1898, 87–152).

She asks for it (4^{15} δός μοι κτλ.).	They ask for it (6^{34} δὸς ἡμῖν κτλ.).
The food of Jesus=obedience to will of the Father (4^{34}), who has sent him.	The object of Jesus to execute the will of the Father who has sent him (6^{38}).
question of disciples (9^{2} ῥαββεί).	question of disciples (11^{8} ῥαββεί).
divine object in disease (9^{3} ἵνα φανερωθῇ τὰ ἔργα τοῦ θεοῦ ἐν αὐτῷ).	divine object in sickness (11^{4} ἵνα δοξασθῇ ὁ υἱὸς τοῦ θεοῦ δι' αὐτῆς).
need of working during the day (9^{4}).	need of walking during the day (11^{9}).
intervention of Pharisees ($9^{13f.}$).	intervention of Pharisees ($11^{46f.}$).

Such coincidences (cp. Kreyenbühl, ii. 39 f.) reveal the dialectic of the author, as he brings out the leading themes of his gospel; he also represents Jesus baffling his opponents and playing on the inward meaning until even his sympathetic hearers were often puzzled. "Jesus uero euangelii quarti dialectice disputat, ambigue loquitur, stylo mystico utitur, obscura profert, adeo ut uel doctissimi de uero multorum effatorum eius sensu dubii hæreant" (Bretschneider, *Probabilia*, 2).*

§ 4. *Polemical aims.*†—(*a*) One note of the gospel is the attempt to correct misapprehensions and exaggerated views of John the Baptizer which were current in the Asiatic circles (Ac 18^{24}–19^{7}) of primitive Christianity,‡ views which placed him in competition with the Lord as a religious authority. John, the writer significantly remarks, *was not the light* (1^{8}). His function was merely that of a witness or harbinger. He is represented as

* Bretschneider (p. 25) comments severely upon 2^{20}: "si intelligis de templo uisibili, est uaniloquentia; si intelligis de templo inuisibili, ecclesia, est argumentum ineptum, cum ea tum temporis non adesset; si intelligis de resurrectione, etiam hæc futura erat; si omnino intelligis allegorice, uanum et incommodum manet argumentum, quia partim sensus allegoriæ Judæis non poterat esse liquidus, partim eadem multo maiori effectu propriis dici potuissent verbis, non uero ambiguis, uarium sensum admittentibus, igitur ineptis ad conuincendum."

† 'Answers to questions' put by contemporaries would be a more suitable term. In the Fourth gospel we overhear the writer, in the name of the church, replying to such questions as these: Is Jesus only one of the æons? Is he a vice-god or a higher Logos? Why was Judas admitted to the circle of the twelve? Why did not Jesus predict his own resurrection? Was the crucifixion foretold in the OT? What is the meaning of eating Christ's flesh and drinking his blood? Why were not the Greeks evangelised by Jesus? Why were not the Samaritans evangelised by him? Some of these questions suggest cavillers, and others imply puzzled Christians.

‡ This trait, already noted by Grotius, Russwurm (*Johannes der Donnerer*, 1806), Storr, and others, has been worked out speculatively by Baldensperger, followed partly by Wrede (*GGA.*, 1900, 1–26), the latter of whom refers to the theory noticed in Siouffi's *Études sur la religion des Soubbas ou Sabéens, leurs dogmes, leurs mœurs* (Paris, 1880, pp. 179 f.), that the prologue is directed against Sabæan views of the Baptizer.

explicitly disavowing all messianic claims ($1^{20f.}$ $3^{20f.}$, cp. 4^{1} 10^{41}), and even his witness was not the final or highest (5^{36}). This polemic, however, is at best subordinate, and it is more likely to form part of the general anti-Jewish tendency of the gospel than to represent a direct allusion to some contemporary sect of John's disciples. (*b*) Another feature is the traditional antithesis of the gospel to Cerinthus, the Jewish gnostic of Alexandria, who held that the world was created not by God but by "a certain Power far separate from him, distant from that Principality who is over the universe, and ignorant of the God who is over all" (Iren. *adv. Haer.* i. 26. 1, contrast Jn 1^{3} etc.), and who taught that Christ, the spiritual and unsuffering One, descended upon Jesus in the form of a dove at the baptism, wrought miracles and proclaimed the unknown Father, and then ere the crucifixion withdrew (contrast Jn 1^{14} etc.). The attribution of the Fourth gospel to Cerinthus was not such a groundless conjecture as modern critics of the Alogi have sometimes made out, for the Fourth gospel ignores the birth of Jesus (although 1^{18} was soon altered into an allusion to the virgin-birth), and lays stress on the Spirit remaining upon him at his baptism (1^{32-33}). But this conjecture was even more impossible than the modern idea that it was written by (Kreyenbühl) or for gnostics.* Naturally it was more congenial to the latter than the synoptic gospels. It was, in fact, its early popularity among gnostic Christians which, together with its repudiation by the Alogi, distressed the good Irenæus. But the aversion to gnosticism, which begins with the prologue, continues through the whole book, and is only thrown into relief by the author's use of gnostic phrases and formulæ.† The gnostic tendencies which were operating at the time when this writing was composed, tended to resolve revelation into a process of æons, semi-mythological and semi-metaphysical, by means of which God and the world came into relations; they further developed an ethical barrenness by their intellectualism. Against both of these tendencies the author of the gospel seeks

* "Prorsus igitur adsentior Eichhornio (*Introd. in NT.* pt. ii. p. 191) profitenti, euangelistam non quidem adversus gnosticos sed in eorum usum scripsisse" (Bretschneider, *Probabilia*, p. 7). On this and on the recent attempt of Fries to prove that Cerinthus has interpolated the Fourth gospel, as written by John the presbyter originally, see *EBi.* 4737–4738.

† Cp. Feine, *NTTh.* 645 f. On the Hermetic mysticism of the prologue, see Reitzenstein's *Zwei religionsgesch. Fragen* (71 f.) and *Poimandres* (244 f.).

specially to safeguard his readers. He is also (cp. *e.g.* 16^{13-14}, and above, pp. 187–188) sensitive to the gnostic claim that their secret tradition was derived from the apostles themselves, or that their teaching was an improvement and a legitimate advance upon that of the apostles, who had not always correctly understood the Lord (cp. *e.g.* Iren. *adv. haer.* ii. 2, aduersantur traditioni dicentes se non solum presbyteris sed etiam apostolis exsistentes sapientiores sinceram inuenisse ueritatem: apostolos enim admiscuisse ea quæ sunt legalia, saluatoris uerbis; also iii. 1).

(i.) The Alogi may have been Monarchians in christology, but their general spirit was that of the conservative commonsense people,* who suspected any adoption of semi-gnostic ideas and expressions such as the Fourth gospel furnished. The simple synoptic account of Jesus was enough for them, and their objections to the Fourth gospel were on the score of its theosophical traits rather than on account of its historical discrepancies with the earlier records, though the latter were not ignored. In spite of the uncertainties attaching to the whole question (cp. *GHD.* i. 239 f.), the likelihood is that Hippolytus' *Defence of the Gospel according to John and the Apocalypse* was the source from which the five *Heads against Gaius* were drawn, and that Gaius rejected not only the apocalypse but the Fourth gospel (cp. J. R. Harris, *Hermas in Arcadia and other Essays*, 1896; Bacon, *Fourth Gospel*, 231 f. The Montanist † exploitation of the Fourth gospel would naturally lead Gaius in the ardour of his polemic against Proklus to cut away the feet from under the Montanists by denying the apostolic claim of the only gospel to which they could appeal.

(ii.) The dualism between light and darkness is regarded as a cosmic antithesis, whose origin the writer never attempts to investigate. His interests are not philosophic. The evil one is the prince of darkness, but evil-doers (3^{19} 8^{44}) are none the less responsible for their actions. It is pressing the language of 1^{3} (*all things were made by him*) to an unreal extreme, to infer from it that the Logos originated the natural darkness; the language of the book is permeated by the practical aim of showing how the world can be brought from darkness into the light of Christ (so Corssen, *GGA.*, 1904, pp. 166 f., in opposition to Grill), not by any attempt to prove how the darkness originated.

---

* In one sense there has been a Johannine problem in the church from the beginning; as soon as the Fourth gospel was placed alongside of the synoptists, the divergences were felt. In another sense, the piety of Christians has solved the problem; in spite of these divergences, it has been sensitive to the real unity between the synoptic and the Johannine Jesus. But, as Godet (Eng. tr. i. 159) observes, "philosophy still seeks the synthesis of the two Sokrates; theology searches, and will for a long period still continue to search, for that of the two images of the Christ."

† But ch. 21 is not a Montanist appendix (Barns, *Exp.*[7] iv. 533–542).

§ 5. *Relation to the Synoptic Gospels.*—Special literature: * A. W. P. Möller (*de genii et indolis Ev. Joh. et priorum evv. diversa ratione rite definienda*, 1816); Baur, *Krit. Untersuch. über die kanon. Evglien* (1847), pp. 239 f.; Freytag's *Symphonie der Evglien* (1863); E. Delon, *Le récit de S. Jean dans ses rapports avec la narration synoptique* (1868); Holtzmann (*ZWT.*, 1869, pp. 62 f., 155 f., 1875, pp. 448 f.); Keim, i. 164 f.; J. J. Taylor, *An attempt to ascertain the character of the Fourth gospel, especially in its relation to the first Three* (1870)[2]; P. Ewald, *das Hauptproblem der Evglienfrage* (1890); T. R. Birks, *Horæ Evangelicæ* (1892), pp. 180 f; Schlatter ('die Parallelen in den Worten Jesu bei Joh. u. Matthäus,' *BFT.* ii. 5); Wernle, *die Synoptische Frage* (1899), pp. 234–248; R. Mariano, *Urc.* iv. pp. 81–92 ('Relazione coi Sinottici'); Loisy, *Le quatrième Évangile* (1903), pp. 56–76; P. Féret ('Le problème synoptico-Johannique,' *Annal. d. Philos. Chrét.*, 1903, pp. 24–42); O. Holtzmann, *Leben Jesu* (Eng. tr. 1904, pp. 32–46); *CQR.* (1905), 106–134; Barth, *das Johannesevglm u. die Syn. Evglien* (1905); E. A. Abbott, *Diat.* 1665–1874 (invaluable); Monnier, *La mission hist. de Jésus* (1906), 354 f.; Zahn, *INT.* § 67; W. Richmond, *The Gospel of the Rejection* (*a study in the relation of the Fourth gospel to the three*), 1906; P. W. Schmiedel, *das vierte Evglm gegenüber den drei ersten* (1906, Eng. tr. 1908); F. W. Worsley, *The Fourth gospel and the Synoptists* (1909); Bacon, *Fourth gospel in Research and Debate* (1910), 332–384.

(1) That the Fourth gospel presupposes the general synoptic tradition may be taken for granted; the real problem of literary criticism is to determine whether it can be shown to have used any or all of the synoptic gospels.

The omissions of synoptic phrases and ideas by John † include the casting out of devils, diseases like leprosy and paralysis (hence om. of terms like καθαρίζω, δαιμονία, λεπρός, etc.), Sadducees, publicans, and scribes, with repentance, forgiveness, watchfulness and prayer, sun, cloud, generation, hypocrite (hypocrisy), market-place, rich, substance or possessions, vineyard, and woe. One class of such omissions is not particularly significant, *i.e.* the synoptic adverbs for *exceedingly* (ἐκπερισσῶς, λίαν, περισσῶς, and σφόδρα), *adultery* and *adulteress*, γυνή (= wife), *precede* (προ-άγω, -έρχομαι, πορεύομαι), ἱκανός and πόσος,

* Historical sketches of opinion (foreign) on this problem, in Schweitzer's *Von Reimarus zu Wrede*, pp. 114–117, 124–126, 217 f., etc. In speaking of J. Weiss' *Die Predigt Jesu vom Reiche Gottes*, he divides and defines the course of investigation into the life of Jesus thus: the period inaugurated by Strauss, 'purely historical or purely supernatural?'—the period represented by the Tübingen school, 'synoptic or Johannine?'—the period inaugurated by J. Weiss, 'eschatological or non-eschatological?'

† See a carefully annotated and classified list of synoptic terms (*i.e.* terms used by all three, as a rule) rarely, if ever, used by John, in *Diat.* 1672–1696.

καταλείπω (=leave), and ἀναγινώσκω (of scripture). More important is the substitution, *e.g.*, of σημεῖα for δυνάμεις, and of παροιμία for παραβολή. This is one outcome of that pragmatism which also explains the absence of any allusion to the virgin-birth, the temptation, the transfiguration, the agony in Gethsemane, etc., as inconsistent with what the writer aimed at in delineating the character of Jesus the Logos-Christ.

The similarities of language between Mk. and Jn. alone are both few and, on the whole, insignificant; the occurrence, in parallel passages in both, of terms like διακόσιοι and τριακόσιοι, θερμαίνομαι, νάρδος πιστικός, (πτύω?), ῥάπισμα, and ὠτάριον, in the same sense (cp. also *the great multitude*, Mk 12^{37} = Jn $12^{9.12}$, Mt. and Lk. omitting the ὁ), is hardly of weight enough to float the thesis that these indicate a sustained and subtle intention on the part of the fourth evangelist to support Mk. against the omissions and deviations of Mt. and Lk. (*Diat.* 1739 f.).* Apart from Mt 28^{10} = Jn 20^{17} (*my brothers*, see above, p. 254), the coincidences between Mt. and Jn. are still less remarkable (*Diat.* 1745–1757). Mk. breaks off before the narrative reaches the point where Jesus calls the disciples *my brothers*, and John's agreements with Mt. probably go back to Mk. In short, the real connection of the Fourth gospel with its predecessors lies not in vocabulary but in ideas, and falls to be tested, not on stylistic so much as on historical and doctrinal grounds. These upon the whole support the hypothesis that the author of the Fourth gospel is frequently concerned to balance one of the synoptists against another as well as to correct all three. At almost every point where the orbit of the Fourth gospel coincides with that of the synoptic tradition, the former can be shown to represent a more developed stage of Christian reflection upon the facts, even where traces of a development can already be noted within the synoptic gospels themselves (see, *e.g.*, detailed proofs in Wendt, pp. 14–48, and E. A. Abbott in *New World*, 1895, pp. 459–483, or in *EBi.* 1773 f.).

The only gospel about which there need be any hesitation is that of Lk. Here the repeated similarities of style and statement render it a fair question whether both gospels do not go back independently to common traditions (or sources), or whether the Fourth gospel simply represents in one aspect

* I cannot see any adequate basis for the idea that (*Diat.* 1744 f.) John intends to convey, by his allusions to the beloved disciple, a tacit contrast to the disappointing adherent of Mk 10^{21} (*Jesus loved him*).

the climax of a development which can be traced from Mk. tc Lk.* The solution lies in a combination of both hypotheses. The Lucan affinities of the Fourth gospel do not necessarily imply Syrian Antioch † as the locus of the latter (so Zurhellen recently); traditions are not confined by geographical boundaries, and the later affinities of Ignatius and Justin Martyr are as explicable on the ordinary Ephesian hypothesis. But some of the currents of the Lucan and 'Johannine' traditions flowed in all probability from Syrian Antioch. This may be admitted, without abandoning the use of Luke's gospel by the author of the Fourth evangelist. The two gospels are almost contemporary; they breathe often the same atmosphere of religious thought and tendency. But John corrects Luke; his gospel is not a complete account of Jesus, he admits, but he seeks to lay a deeper and more mystical basis for faith. Both have a remarkable common element in their vocabulary (cp. Gaussen in *JTS.* ix. 562–568); *e.g.* *ἀπόκρισις*, of Jesus (Lk 2^{47} 20^{26}, cp. Jn 19^{9}); *βάπτειν* (Lk 16^{24}, Jn 13^{26}); ‡ *γείτων* (Lk 14^{12} $15^{6, 9}$, Jn 9^{8}); *διατρίβειν* (intrans. = stay, Ac 12^{19}, 15^{35}, Jn 3^{22}); *ἐκμάσσειν* (Lk $7^{38, 44}$, Jn 11^{2} 12^{3} 13^{5}); *ἐνθάδε* = hither (Ac 25^{17}, Jn $4^{15f.}$); *κῆπος* (Lk 13^{19}, Jn 18^{1} etc.); *κόλπος* = bosom or breast (Lk 16^{23}, Jn 1^{18} 13^{23}); *νεύειν* (Ac 24^{10}, Jn 13^{24}); *ὁμοῦ* (Ac 2^{1}, Jn 4^{36} etc.); *προδραμεῖν* (Lk 19^{4}, Jn 20^{4}); *πώποτε* (Lk 19^{30}, Jn 1^{18} etc.); *στόα* (Ac 3^{11} 5^{12}, Jn 5^{2} 10^{23}), and *φρέαρ* (Lk 14^{5}, Jn 4^{11-12}).§

In one class of passages some special trait of Lk. has been adopted and adapted by the Fourth evangelist; *e.g.* 3^{15} = Jn $1^{19f.}$ (is John the Christ?), 4^{6} = Jn 16^{30} (the devil ruler of this world), 4^{29-30} = Jn 8^{59} (Jesus eluding a crowd), 6^{8} = Jn 2^{25} (the divine insight of Jesus), 7^{2} = Jn 4^{47}, 16^{30-31} = Jn $5^{39f. 47}$ 12^{10-11}, 19^{38-39} = Jn 12^{19}, $21^{36f.}$ = Jn $8^{1f.}$, 22^{3} = Jn $13^{2, 27}$, 22^{32} = Jn 21^{15-17}, 22^{50} = Jn 18^{10}, 23^{49} = Jn $19^{25f.}$; both use *ὁ κύριος* of Jesus in narrative; both apply the phrase *son of Joseph* to Jesus (4^{22} = Jn 1^{45} 6^{42}); both separate the idea of Mt 10^{24} from that of Mt 10^{25-28} (cp. Lk 6^{40} and 12^{4} = Jn 13^{16-17} and $15^{14-15, 20}$ where *friends* is applied by Jesus in Lk. and Jn. alone to the disciples). There is an increasing tendency in both to describe the relation of Jesus to God as that of the Son to the Father, to limit God's fatherhood to Christians, to emphasise the Spirit, and to speak of Jesus as *ὁ σωτήρ* who brings

---

* See especially Holtzmann and Jacobsen (*op. cit.* pp. 46 f.) on this point, with P. Feine's *Vorkanonische Ueberlieferung*, pp. 133–136, and above, pp. 268, 274.

† Kreyenbühl uses these and other traits to further his hypothesis that the Fourth gospel was written by Menander of Antioch and afterwards rescued from the gnostics by the church, which re-edited it for ecclesiastical purposes. But Menandei as an author is otherwise unknown; Kreyenbühl's estimate of gnosticism is too ideal, and the theory involves a recourse to arbitrary exegesis in general.

‡ The sense in Apoc 19^{13} is different (= 'dyed'), as is the case with *φρέαρ* also (9^{1-2}).

§ *ἑλκύειν*, *ἐξηγεῖσθαι*, *σύρειν*, and *σχοινίον* are used in totally different senses by both writers, and *συντίθεσθαι* in different constructions; terms like *πλευρά*, Ἑλληνιστί, *ἀριστᾶν*, and *ζωννύναι* (both latter in Jn 21) are too casual and minor to deserve notice, while the uncertainty about Lk 24^{12} prevents *ὀθόνια* (Jn 19^{40} etc.) being reckoned.

τὴν σωτηρίαν. Both have Samaritan-stories and stories about Martha and Mary; both agree, in opposition to Mk. and Mt., in placing the prediction of Peter's denial during the last supper, and the denial itself previous to the violence done to Jesus in the judgment-hall; both also note a triple (Lk $23^{4.14.22}$ τὸ τρίτον = Jo 18^{38} $19^{4.6}$) vindication of Jesus by Pilate.

There are further traces of more or less conscious correction on the part of the Fourth evangelist: thus 13^2 is a correction * of Lk 22^3; the discourse on humble, mutual service corresponds to the Lucan narrative, and some references in the passion narrative (*e.g.* Annas and Kaiaphas) betray the same atmosphere, but in the latter narrative and in the resurrection-stories the motive of correction is more audible. Thus the appearance on the evening of the resurrection-day in the Fourth gospel (20^{19-23}) tallies with that recorded by Lk 24^{36-49} in three points: † (*a*) the sudden appearance in the midst, (*b*) the showing of the body (hands and feet, Lk.; hands and side, Jn.), and (*c*) the reference to forgiveness. John, however, changes the superstitious terror of the audience (the ten disciples, not, as in Lk., the eleven disciples and their companions) into a glad ($16^{20.22}$) recognition, and makes them receive the Spirit at once instead of waiting for it. This latter point is significant. ‡ In the Fourth gospel the ascension takes place on the day of the resurrection; Jesus then comes (20^{19}), as he had promised, back to his disciples, and breathes on them (not sends to them) the holy Spirit, which he had also promised (15^{26} 16^7). This is the real παρουσία of the Fourth gospel, and after 20^{24-29} there is no word of any subsequent departure any more than in Mt 28. According to Lk 24 and Jn 20, the disciples never leave Jerusalem; Galilean appearances of the risen Jesus are definitely excluded. The redactor of Jn 21 seeks to harmonise the two lines of tradition by appending a final Galilean vision, drawn either from the Lucan 5^{1-11} or from a common tradition. The revelation or recognition of Jesus ἐν τῇ κλάσει τοῦ ἄρτου (Lk $24^{30f.}$), and the eating of fish by Jesus in presence of the disciples (Lk $24^{36f.}$), reappear in Jn 21^{1-13} in altered form; here Jesus is recognised before the meal (of which he does not partake), and the meal consists of bread and fish. This suggests "that there may have been various traditions combining a literal and a symbolical meaning (1) about the catching of fish, (2) about a Eucharistic meal (after the resurrection)

---

* Bacon (*Fourth Gospel*, pp. 376 f.) even takes 8^{57} as a repudiation of Lk 3^2 and as representing the older Palestinian view, which has a better chance of being historical. Westberg (*Biblische Chronologie nach Flavius Josephus und das Todesjahr Jesus*, 1910, pp. 86 f.) also defends this tradition on the ground that Jesus was really born in 12 B.C., and that Luke confused the consulate of Quirinius with his governorship over Judea.

† Four, if καὶ λέγει αὐτοῖς· εἰρήνη ὑμῖν is inserted after αὐτῶν in Lk 24^{36}.

‡ The characteristic standpoint of the Fourth gospel is not the yearning for a return of Jesus the messiah to finish his work: *It is finished* (Jn 19^{30}). The prophetic and eschatological element in the last supper is obliterated, in order to make it a feast of love and love's duties among Christians. It is the intensity of present communion with the living Lord in the Spirit which dominates the Fourth gospel and determines many of its departures from the Synoptic tradition (see below).

in which fish formed a part" (*Dial.* 2483*a*).* In the Lucan story of $24^{39f.}$ the general permission to handle (ψηλαφήσατέ με καὶ ἴδετε) precedes the further proof (eating) of the reality of the resurrection-body; whereas in the Fourth gospel, where the same order occurs ($20^{24f.}$ $21^{10f.}$), only Thomas is bidden handle the body of Jesus; and Jesus, in the sequel, distributes the food instead of eating it (see above, p. 275).

The apocalyptic element, which almost disappears in the Fourth gospel, had already been diminished in Lk. (note, *e.g.*, the significant change in 22^{69} from Mk 14^{62} = Mt 26^{64}; the Jewish authorities, unlike Simeon, $2^{26.\ 30}$, are to die without seeing the Christ), but the Fourth evangelist transcends it as part and parcel of the Jewish messianism which he and his age felt to be no longer adequate to the Christian consciousness of the day. Traces of it still occur, *e.g.*, in 5^{28-29} (which cannot be eliminated as a later interpolation), just as the older view of Jesus' redemptive function incidentally recurs in 1^{29}, but such features do little more than denote the transition from the old to the new, and the characteristic aims of the author lie elsewhere, in a conception of Jesus for which he found the Logos-idea, not the messianic idea, to be the most effective category. This process had been already anticipated not only by Paul, but by the authors of Ephesians and Hebrews in their own way, without detriment to the supreme significance of Jesus Christ to the Christian. The Fourth evangelist, however, is less interested in the cosmological or typological significance of Jesus than his predecessors on this line, and generally he develops an independent view of his own, which is more thoroughly dominated by the set and spirit of the Logos-idea.

(2) Not merely on the content but on the position of the Baptist's ministry, the Fourth gospel is at issue with the synoptic tradition. The latter consistently defers the beginning of Christ's public ministry till the Baptist had been arrested (Mk 1^{14-15}, Lk 3^{18-21} = Mt 4^{12}), as is the case with Ac 10^{37} $12^{24f.}$ 19^{4}. The Fourth gospel makes the two ministries overlap (Jn 3^{22-30} 4^{1-2}), and does so, not from any naive forgetfulness of memory on the part of an old disciple, but in order to emphasise the superiority of Jesus to John; the latter recognises and confesses publicly the messianic claim of Jesus from the very outset. The development of the synoptic tradition in Mt. and Lk., which tends to heighten and ante-date the Baptist's consciousness of Jesus' significance, is thus brought to a climax. It is in keeping with this view, which knows (in contrast to the original tradition) of no secrecy upon the messianic authority of Jesus, that his full authority as God's messiah is seen from the outset by his

* There is no mysterious significance in the ἔρχεται of v.[13], however; it goes with the following verb, as in 6^{15} and 12^{22}. The insertion of εὐχαριστήσας by Syr[Sin] and D in Jn 21^{13}, if not a restoration of the original text, at least points to the early prevalence of this eucharistic conception of the scene.

disciples and by others. Here, again, the tendency already present, *e.g.*, in Mt. (pp. 252, 259), is fully operative.

Some further instances of this principle may be noted. (*a*) The first two σημεῖα * are followed by no address; the fourth and fifth, which complete the Galilean cycle, lead up to a discussion which, however, attaches only to the fourth. The two Jerusalem-σημεῖα, on the other hand, furnish the situation for long harangues, while the seventh (in Judea) not only is accompanied by an announcement of religious truth, but forms the pivot for the closing scenes in Jerusalem. Thus the only Galilean teaching is in $6^{27f.}$; but although part of it is placed in the synagogue at Kapharnaum, even this is a debate with the Jews which might as well have occurred at Jerusalem; there is barely a trace of the characteristic Galilean gospel as that is preserved in the synoptic gospels.

(*b*) An equally secondary trait lies in 2^{13-22}, where an original saying is placed in a setting which has been transposed (so, *e.g.*, among most recent writers, J. Réville, pp. 137 f.; Drummond, 61; J. Weiss, Loisy, and Oesterley in *DCG.* ii. 712 f.) from its historical site † in the synoptic tradition and recast for special reasons. According to the Fourth gospel, the cleansing of the temple took place on the occasion of the first and early visit paid by Jesus to Jerusalem, and was the act not of messianic authority but of a prophetic or reforming zeal ‡ (so, *e.g.*, recently Wernle, *Syn. Frage*, 240; Stanton, *DB.* ii. 245; and Sanday, *ibid.* 613; after Beyschlag, *zur Johann. Frage*, 83 f.; R. H. Hutton, *Theological Essays*, 222 f.; A. B. Bruce, *Kingdom of God*, 306 f.). In the synoptic tradition it brings the enmity of the scribes and priests to a head (Mk $11^{15-18. 27}$); it is the natural climax of his ministry, a supreme effort to assert the rights of God in the headquarters of the nation, and his subsequent fate is the natural outcome of the deed. In the Fourth gospel the act is at once ante-dated and minimised. The saying connected with it is rightly reproduced, as is the connection of the incident with the passover. But the daring assertion of authority produces no impression beyond a mild remonstrance (2^{18}, reproduced from the synoptic tradition, Mk 11^{28} = Mt 21^{23}, which also connected this with a defence of its legitimacy); the authorities do not take action. Possibly, however, the writer simply introduced the incident at this point in order to emphasise the saying as a proof that Jesus foresaw his death and resurrection from the very beginning. He has thus reset the incident, under the influence of his pragmatism. On the one hand, he found sufficient occasion in the Lazarus-miracle for the arrest of Jesus and the enmity of the authorities; on the other hand, he considered that the first public visit of Jesus to Jerusalem must have been marked by an open assertion of his divine authority.

(*c*) Another case of a synoptic saying being misplaced occurs in 4^{44}, but

* Even in the second, which is a variant of Mt 8^{5-13} = Lk 7^{1-10}, faith is (as usual in this gospel) the result of the miracle, not, as in the synoptic tradition, the indispensable condition of help or healing.

† Tatian also follows the synoptic order.

‡ This is usually associated with the admission that the act might have been repeated; but if not, that the Johannine chronology is preferable.

the allusion in 4^{54} refers back to 2^{11} not to Mt 8^{5-13} = Lk 7^{2-10} as the second miracle; the story (4^{46-54}) is a heightened form of the Matthæan narrative, just as $5^{1f.}$ and $6^{1-13. 16-21}$ are of the synoptic originals. 6^{42} is a fresh instance of misplacement (cp. Mk 6^{3} = Mt 13^{55} = Lk 4^{22}; for Marcion's treatment of the story, see Hilgenfeld in *ZWT.*, 1902, 127–144), while in 6^{70-71}, as in 12^{4-6}, there is a distinct tendency to exculpate the twelve or Peter (see the synoptic parallels) at the expense of Judas Iskariot.

(*d*) The Lazarus-miracle ($11^{1f.}$) is exceptional in several respects. In the synoptic stories of people being raised by Jesus from the dead, the miracle takes place naturally; the opportunity is furnished, and Jesus takes advantage of it. Here he consciously delays his arrival not only until the dead person is buried, but until the process of physical corruption has set in. The miracle is thus rendered more wonderful, in comparison with the synoptic stories, where Jesus only raises the unburied (and indeed those who have just died), and where he never arranges for any heightening of the effect. It is an illustration of the profound truth that Jesus is the source of life eternal in a dead world, and that the resurrection is not, as the popular faith of the church imagined (11^{24}), something which takes place at the last day, but the reception of Christ's living Spirit: *I am the resurrection and the life, he who believes on me, though he were dead, shall live, and no one who lives and believes on me shall ever die.* Faith in the living Christ, as Paul had taught in his own way, meant a risen life independent of physical changes in the future. Whether more than this religious motive, operating on the Lucan material, is necessary to explain the story, remains one of the historical problems of the gospel (cp. A. E. Brooke in *Cambridge Biblical Essays*, 313 f.). It is just conceivable that the incident failed for some reason to be included by the synoptic gospels; their silence would not by itself be absolutely conclusive against the historicity. The difficulty is to give any adequate psychological reason why so stupendous and critical an episode (witnessed *ex hypothesi* by all the disciples) should have failed to win a place in the synoptic tradition, even when that tradition is admitted to be incomplete at certain points, and this difficulty is heightened by the obvious motives of the writer, who makes this miracle the pivot of the final Jewish attack on Jesus, instead of the purging of the temple, which he transfers to the beginning of the ministry. "The whole evidence points strongly to the conclusion that the evangelist, using some tradition to us unknown and the synoptic material mentioned, elaborated them freely into a narrative designed to be at once: (*a*) an astounding manifestation of the Logos-Christ, (*b*) a pictorial setting forth of the spiritual truth of Christ as Life, (*c*) a prophetic prefiguration of the death and resurrection of Jesus, as shown by the facts that the names Jesus and Lazarus have the same meaning, and that the narrative forms a transition to the final struggle and to death" (Forbes, p. 273). It may be a miracle which like that of Mk $11^{12f.}$ (see pp. 225, 236) has grown up * mainly out of a parable—in this case the parable of Lazarus (Lk $16^{19f.}$), which closes (16^{27-31}) with a passage (irrelevant to the original motive of the story) asserting that not even the witness of one risen

* With hints from other synoptic traditions, *e.g.* the raising of the widow's son at Nain (Lk 7^{11-17}, performed, like the raising of Lazarus, before a large crowd).

from the dead would avail to produce repentance and faith in those who reject the testimony of the OT revelation (Lk 16^{30}=Jn 5^{46}). What historical nucleus lies behind the story, it is no longer possible to ascertain. The allegorical or symbolical ends of the writer are the outstanding feature (cp. Bretschneider's *Probabilia*, p. 79, "tota igitur narratio conscripta est ut consilio dogmatico inseruiret, scl. ut doceret exemplo clarissimo, in Iesu habitasse λόγον diuinum. Dogmaticum igitur potius hic egit scriptor, quam historicum"). They indicate that the story may be another instance of what Origen in his commentary called the preservation of spiritual truth in bodily inaccuracy (σωζομένου πολλάκις τοῦ ἀληθοῦς πνευματικοῦ ἐν τῷ σωματικῷ ὡς ἂν εἴποι τις ψευδεῖ); so, *e.g.*, Abbott* (*Ebi.*, 1804 f., 2744–2751), Loisy, Burkitt (*Transmission*, pp. 221 f.), Forbes, E. F. Scott (*op. cit.* 37 f.), Heitmüller, and Bacon (*The Fourth Gospel*, 345 f.).

(*e*) The story in 12^{1-8} has been changed from after (Mk., Mt.) to before the entry, but the further question of its relation to Lk 7^{36-50}, or even of the relation between the latter and the Marcan (Matthæan) parallel, remains another of the enigmas of gospel-criticism, which can hardly be solved along the lines of purely literary investigation.†

(3) The day is now over, or almost over, when the Fourth gospel and the synoptists could be played off against each other in a series of rigid antitheses, as though the one were a matter-of-fact and homogeneous chronicle and the other a spiritual reading of the earlier tradition. The problem is too delicate and complex for such crude methods. Recent criticism of the synoptic gospels has brought them nearer to the Fourth gospel. It has revealed not simply variant traditions, some of which reappear in the Fourth gospel, but chronological gaps, and above all the operation of tendencies which exercise a creative as well as a moulding pressure upon the tradition. The Fourth gospel presents, in one aspect, a further and special phase of the tendency to interpret and reflect upon the evangelic traditions in the light of the later Christian conciousness. The synoptic gospels are not objective chronicles, relating the incidents and sayings of which the Fourth gospel provides the spiritual interpretation. In Mark, especially, the presence of such an interpretation has now been proved (pp. 226 f.); and this is all the more significant, since the Fourth gospel is recognised upon all hands to go back ultimately to the Marcan tradition rather than

* Cp. also *Diat.* 1528 f. ("even though we may be obliged to reject some of the details of the Raising of Lazarus as unhistorical, we may be able to accept the fact that our Lord did occasionally restore to life those who would ordinarily be described as 'dead'").

† "Der Weg von Mk. und Lk. aus zu Joh. erscheint fast unmöglich lang ohne Zuhilfnahme einer Sondertradition" (Wernle, p. 241).

to the Matthæan or to the Lucan. The synoptics, as well as the Fourth gospel, were written ἐκ πίστεως εἰς πίστιν. The motto of Jn 20^{31} would apply to all the three, but in a special sense to Mark; for, in spite of the difference of angle from which Mark and John view the messianic dignity of Jesus, both aim at demonstrating that he was *the Son of God* (see p. 234).

The most important aspect of this relationship is historical. There is good evidence to show that Jesus had a ministry in Judea, during which he visited Jerusalem, prior to his final visit, and that the narrative of the Fourth gospel on this point goes back to a nucleus of primitive tradition from which they have been worked up.* The synoptic tradition really is derived from Mk.'s scheme, which is admittedly far from exhaustive, and even in it there are traces which corroborate the view elaborated in the Fourth gospel. Thus the temptation-stories clearly presuppose a Jerusalem and Judean mission larger than the synoptists themselves suggest; and even if Mt $23^{37f.}$ = Lk $13^{34f.}$ is a quotation, still the fact that it was attributed to Jesus seems to imply more than a mere willingness or desire to have come to Jerusalem previously. Similarly the journey through Samaria to Jerusalem in Lk 9^{51-56}, though editorially relegated to the last visit on the Marcan scheme (10^1), is followed by a number of incidents which suggest that it could not have originally belonged to that visit. On any view of the ministry of Jesus, his public mission must have lasted more than twelve months, so that ample room is left for at least one visit to celebrate the passover. It is needless to postulate that he must have been accompanied by his disciples on such an occasion, and their absence may account for the early apostolic silence on the Judean ministry. No stress can be laid on the fact that when Jesus finally reached Jerusalem, he was well-known to a number of people not only in Bethany but in the capital; this does not necessarily imply more than visits to the passover prior to his public ministry. Nor do the discussions with the scribes and Pharisees involve a Jerusalemite *locus*. The significant data, which seem to indicate that the tradition of at least one intermediate visit to Jerusalem has been almost obliterated in the synoptic tradition, occur in (i.) the temptation-story, which requires no comment, and (ii.) in Lk $9^{51ff.}$, the contents of which (pp. 273 f.) cannot be arranged within the limits of the last journey to Jerusalem. Thus 10^1 (dispatch of the seventy, or the seventy-two, εἰς πᾶσαν πόλιν καὶ τόπον οὗ ἤμελλεν αὐτὸς ἔρχεσθαι), when taken with 10^{17}, cannot denote the dispatch of the disciples as harbingers of Jesus on the route (as in $9^{51f.}$). The subsequent incidents are for the most part undated or vaguely set; some imply Jerusalem (11^{51} etc.), others Galilee (13^{31} etc.), others Samaria.

* Cp. *e.g.* Bleek (*INT.* § 71), Wendt (p. 12): "there is nothing to justify us in refusing to acknowledge that Jesus may really have made several visits to Jerusalem," and J. Weiss in his review of Spitta's *Streitfragen* (*TLZ.*, 1909, 460 f.) and in *die Aufgaben d. NT Wissenschaft* (p. 44): "Was lässt sich sachlich gegen eine längere Wirksamkeit, gegen ein Wirken auch in Jerusalem einwenden?" Compare the discussion by A. E. Brooke in *Cambridge Biblical Essays* (1909), pp. 296 f.

But in 17^{12-19} the incident presupposes a journey from Jerusalem,* as is still clear from 17^{11}, where Luke has overlaid the original (*καὶ αὐτὸς διήρχετο διὰ μέσον Σαμαρείας καὶ Γαλιλαίας*) with the pragmatic heading, *καὶ ἐγένετο ἐν τῷ πορεύεσθαι εἰς Ἱερουσαλήμ* (9^{51} 13^{22}).

(iii.) The lament over Jerusalem.

Mt $23^{37f.}$	Lk $13^{34f.}$
Ἱερουσαλὴμ Ἱερουσαλήμ, ἡ ἀποκτείνουσα τοὺς προφήτας καὶ λιθοβολοῦσα τοὺς ἀπεσταλμένους πρὸς αὐτήν, ποσάκις ἠθέλησα ἐπισυναγαγεῖν τὰ τέκνα σου, ὃν τρόπον ὄρνις ἐπισυνάγει τὰ νοσσία αὐτῆς ὑπὸ τὰς πτέρυγας, καὶ οὐκ ἠθελήσατε· ἰδοὺ ἀφίεται ὑμῖν ὁ οἶκος ὑμῶν [ἔρημος]· λέγω γὰρ ὑμῖν, οὐ μή με ἴδητε ἀπ᾿ ἄρτι ἕως ἂν εἴπητε, εὐλογημένος ὁ ἐρχόμενος ἐν ὀνόματι κυρίου.	*Ἱερουσαλὴμ Ἱερουσαλήμ, ἡ ἀποκτείνουσα τοὺς προφήτας καὶ λιθοβολοῦσα τοὺς ἀπεσταλμένους πρὸς αὐτήν, ποσάκις ἠθέλησα ἐπισυνάξαι τὰ τέκνα σου, ὃν τρόπον ὄρνιξ τὴν ἑαυτῆς νοσσιὰν ὑπὸ τὰς πτέρυγας, καὶ οὐκ ἠθελήσατε· ἰδοὺ ἀφίεται ὑμῖν ὁ οἶκος ὑμῶν· λέγω [δὲ] ὑμῖν [ὅτι] οὐ μὴ ἴδητέ με ἕως ἥξει ὅτε εἴπητε, εὐλογημένος ὁ ἐρχόμενος ἐν ὀνόματι κυρίου.*

The two versions are practically identical,† whereas Luke departs from Mt. emphatically in the context. This confirms the view (p. 197) that the saying belonged to Q or the apostolic source, which therefore reflected a tradition that Jesus had appealed to Jerusalem prior to his last visit. The latter interpretation implies that Jesus either spoke the words as they stand, or, at any rate, the nucleus (so Merx) of the quotation (see above, pp. 26, 33); and, in spite of scepticism to the contrary, this hypothesis has much in its favour. Unless on *a priori* grounds one is prepared to defend the synoptic chronology at all costs, a saying like this must be fairly allowed to have some weight in deciding the question of the visits paid by Jesus to the capital. The plain inference to be drawn from the passage is either (*a*) that it was spoken as a farewell word after some visit (or, visits) to the capital during which Jesus had vainly endeavoured to win over the citizens to his gospel,‡ or (*b*) that Mt. has correctly placed it (see above, p. 195). In either case, it betrays the fact that Jesus had exercised a ministry of some kind in Jerusalem prior to his final entry. "The words have no meaning whatever in Luke, who puts them into the mouth of Jesus before he had even seen Jerusalem during his public ministry (13^{34}); and even from the better arrangement of Matthew (23^{37}) it is unintelligible how Jesus, after a single residence of a few days in Jerusalem, could found his reproaches on multiplied efforts to win over its inhabitants to his cause. This whole apostrophe of Jesus has so original a

* To Nazareth, where he was rejected (J. F. Blair, *Apostolic Gospel*, pp. 108 f.)?

† Ἱερουσαλήμ occurs only here in Mt. The significance of the variant forms Ἱερουσαλήμ and Ἱεροσόλυμα, especially in Lk., is discussed by R. Schütz in *ZNW.*, 1910, 169–187.

‡ So, *e.g.*, Spitta (*Streitfragen*, pp. 63 f.) and Allen (*Matthew*, p. 251): "The words seem to be a fragment belonging to an earlier period of the ministry, when Christ was leaving Jerusalem for the last time before His triumphal entry. We must imagine a controversy with the Jews similar to that recorded in S. John 10^{22-39}."

character, that it is difficult to believe it incorrectly assigned to him; hence, to explain its existence, we must suppose a series of earlier residences in Jerusalem, such as those recorded by the fourth Evangelist" (Strauss, p. 271).* This supposition has several items in its favour. Whatever be the reason for the synoptic silence on a Judean ministry (or, for the matter of that, on the mission to Chorazin and Bethsaida, Mt 11^{21} = Lk 10^{13}),† once the erroneous idea of a ministry limited to twelve months is abandoned, the general probability is that during his ministry to the lost sheep of the house of Israel, Jesus would not ignore the capital. Unless the accuracy and adequacy of synoptic chronology are to be made a critical dogma,—and few will admit this, at the present day,—there is an *a priori* likelihood that the Fourth gospel may after all represent an aspect of the activity of Jesus which was overlooked in the Marcan scheme. This does not imply that the festivals-programme of the Fourth gospel is superior to the outline of the synoptic tradition, or even that the two can be harmonised. The author of the Fourth gospel, with his predilection for displaying the religion of Jesus in contrast to Jewish theories and objections, naturally chose Jerusalem as the locus for his debates; the simpler Galilean preaching did not interest him. But, in view of the general probabilities and of the occasional indications preserved in the synoptic tradition itself,‡ it is arbitrary to deny outright that he may have had some traditional justification on which to rear his superstructure. The synoptic scheme rests ultimately upon a single line of historical tradition, and the synoptists themselves, especially Mt. and Lk., not only amplify the earlier scheme by material which is assigned in part to extra-Galilean situations, but even contain indications of a Judean mission. Furthermore, as Weizsäcker § points out (p. 174), had the Fourth evangelist possessed simply the synoptic tradition, and had he had no other aim than to set forth his own idea of Jesus, there was no obvious reason why he should

---

* The rather forced alternative is to conjecture (*a*) that Jesus spoke, or was simply made by the evangelists to speak, in the name of the divine Sophia, so that the πόσακις κτλ. would be read in the sense of the preceding Mt $23^{34f.}$ (*i.e.* attempts through the disciples or apostles), or (*b*) that τέκνα Ἱερ. is equivalent to Jews in general.

† Bethsaida falls within the purview of the Fourth gospel.

‡ The reception of Jesus in Mk 11^{1-10} and the saying in Mk 14^{49} may both imply a longer connection between Jesus and Jerusalem than the synoptic scheme allows for. Cp. also Mk 12^{35}, Lk 19^{47} 20^{1} 21^{37} 22^{53}. Wellhausen (on Mk 11^{1-10}) recognises that the data of the last visit imply a longer connection with Jerusalem than the Marcan week accounts for; but, as he refuses to admit any prior connection with Jerusalem, he feels obliged to throw over the Marcan schematism.

§ "Wenn er aber auch schon früher Jesus in Jerusalem auftreten lässt, so lag dafür überall keine Nothigung in seiner Tendenz. Es kann dies kaum aus einem anderen Grunde, als dem einer eigenen Kunde geschehen sein. Ebenso verhält es sich mit den eigenthümlichen Wandererzählungen des Evglms . . . Wenn er Geschichten berichtet, die nicht aus den Synoptikern genommen sind, so liegt auch hier die Erklärung am nächsten, dass er dieselben aus eigener Ueberlieferung hatte" (*Untersuchungen*, 174 f., cp. 328 f.).

introduce earlier Judean visits; the mere desire to exhibit Jesus on the prophetic stage of messiah's activity does not adequately account for the particular form of the Fourth gospel's tradition. The conclusion * therefore is that the material incorporated by Matthew, and especially by Luke, presupposed at least one visit to Jerusalem prior to the final entry, but that both Matthew and Luke, adhering to the Marcan chronology, fused the incidents of this visit with the final visit.

(iv.) *The date of the Crucifixion.*—The primary tradition (Mk 14^{1-2} = Mt 26^{3-5}) expressly dates the arrest and crucifixion of Jesus *μὴ ἐν τῇ ἑορτῇ*, from which it follows (cp. Mt 27^{62}) that Jesus was crucified before the passover. This is the standpoint of the Fourth gospel (*e.g.* 13^{1} 18^{28}) and of the gospel of Peter (1^{5} crucifixion *πρὸ μιᾶς τῶν ἀζύμων, τῆς ἑορτῆς αὐτῶν*), possibly even of Paul (1 Co 5^{7-8} 15^{20}): it was adopted independently by the Quartodecimans during the controversy which broke out in the second century (cp. Drummond, pp. 444 f.; Zahn's *Forschungen*, iv. 283 f.; *GHD.* i. 173 f.; Preuschen in *PRE.* xiv. 725 f., and Bacon, *Fourth Gospel in Research and Debate*, 1910, 413 f.). In the synoptic gospels,† however, this tradition has been overlaid by another (Mk $14^{12f.}$ = Mt $26^{17f.}$ = Lk $22^{7f.}$), which made the last supper synchronous with, instead of prior to, the Jewish passover. But that Jesus died on Nisan 15, the feast day, is unlikely, as work was going on (Mk 15^{21}, Lk 23^{56}) and arms were being carried (Mk 14^{47} etc.), both of which, as well as a meeting of the Sandedrin, were strictly prohibited on the feast day. Some of the details preserved by the synoptic gospels about what happened on the day of the crucifixion and the day after tally, in fact, with the primary tradition, and are inconsistent with the special identification of the last supper and the passover. The improbabilities of the latter view have led to a widespread agreement among modern critics that the former tradition is the older and more reliable; so, *e.g.*, C. H. Turner (*DB.* i. 411), Sanday (*DB.* ii. 633 f.), Wellhausen (on Mk 12^{1} "man hat richtig erkannt, das die hier vorliegende Zeitrechnung der gewöhnlichen synoptischen widerspreche, und richtig geurteilt, dass sie die alte sei und noch im vierten Evangelium befolgt werde"),‡ O. Holtzmann (*Leben Jesu*, ch. xiii.; *ZNW.*, 1904, 89–120), Spitta (*die Urchrist. Trad. über Ursprung und Sinn des Abendm.*, 1893, 205–237), J. Weiss, Kattenbusch (*Christliche Welt*, 1895, 317 f., 331 f.), Wendt, von Dobschütz (*Probleme*, 17), Preuschen (*ZNW.*, 1904, pp. 14 f.), Bousset (*Jesus*, Eng. tr. 19), Heitmüller, Bacon, F. M. Hitchcock (*DCG.* i. 414 f.), Westberg (*op. cit.* 130 f.), etc. On this view, the synoptic gospels are inconsistent with themselves, and the Fourth gospel intervenes in support of the better tradition. The recognition of this has important bearings on the whole question of early Christian tradition, for if, in one case, the typological significance of an event is proved to be

---

* This has been urged from Schleiermacher downwards.

† Later Jewish writers, who seem to contradict the synoptic chronology, were often tempted to idealise the past by reading back into this period later customs and ideas (cp. N. Schmidt, *JBL.*, 1891, pp. 6 f.).

‡ Also on John $19^{31f.}$ ('Wenn Jesus nach Joa wirklich am Tage vor dem Pascha gestorben ist, so kann das nicht auf Tendenz beruhen, sondern nur auf den alten Tradition, die auch bei Markus noch durchschimmert').

derived from the event, there is a probability that in other cases an incident is not to be dismissed as unhistorical simply because it lends itself to a religious application or moral. The correctness of the Johannine tradition is corroborated * by the likelihood that Luke (22^{15-16}) preserves a saying which seems to show that when Jesus ate his last meal with the disciples, he knew that he would not live to celebrate the passover that year with them. He had earnestly hoped to do so; *ἐπιθυμίᾳ ἐπεθύμησα τοῦτο τὸ πάσχα* (*i.e.* this year's festival) *φαγεῖν μεθ' ὑμῶν πρὸ τοῦ με παθεῖν*. But he now knew this hope was to be disappointed. He was to die ere then. *Λέγω γὰρ ὑμῖν, ὅτι οὐ μὴ φάγω αὐτὸ ἕως ὅτου πληρωθῇ ἐν τῇ βασιλείᾳ τοῦ θεοῦ.* This implies that the Lord's supper was eaten prior to the passover; the words are not a paschal reference.

Repeated efforts have been made (*a*) to harmonise the synoptic and Johannine traditions as they lie before us,† or (*b*) to explain the origin of the synoptic technical error; the former by identifying, *e.g.*, the supper of Jesus with the *Chagigah* or the *Kiddusch* (G. H. Box, *JTS.*, 1902, 357 f.), the latter by assuming a primitive confusion (due originally to the editor of the second gospel?) ‡ in the Marcan chronology of $14^{12.17}$ which underlies Mt. and Lk., or elsewhere (good summary in *DCG.* i. 414 f.; cp. also Abbott's *Diat.* 1289 f.). Chwolson, the rabbinic expert, in the second edition (1908) of his *Letzte Passamahl Christi* (cp. *Monatsschrift für Gesch. u. Wiss. d. Judentums*, 1893, 537 f., and *ZWT.*, 1895, 335–378), holding that Jesus was crucified on Nisan 14, explains that, as the passover fell on a Friday, the lamb could be slain and eaten on Nisan 13, and that the synoptic error is due to a misinterpretation of ביומא קמי דפסחא in the Aramaic original of Mt 26^{17}, which could be rendered (1) rightly, "day before paschal day," *i.e.* Nisan 13, (2) 'day before paschal-feast,' *i.e.* Nisan 14, or (3) 'first day of paschal feast,' *i.e.* of unleavened bread. If this explanation can be transferred to Mk 14^{12} (cp. Lambert in *JTS.*, 1903, 184 f., and Allen's *Matthew*, pp. 269–274), the preliminary error is explicable. Whether or not the last supper was meant to be a sort of (anticipated?) paschal meal, it was probably not celebrated on the regular day, though the inferior tradition of the synoptists arose from the idea that it was the paschal supper. Another reconstruction of the original source would be מקדם הפסח (=before the passover) read as בקדם הפסח (=on the first day of the passover) in the Hebrew primitive gospel (Resch, *Paralleltexte zu L.* 615 f., cp. Briggs, *New Light*, pp. 56–63).

(v.) The argument from some minor points is significant, but is not to be pressed, in the present state of our knowledge. Thus (*a*) Mk 1^{14} = Mt 4^{12} implies an earlier ministry in Judea, but it could not have been of the character described in the Fourth gospel. (*b*) The strongly attested v.l. Ἰουδαίας in Lk 4^{44}, which has every appearance of being original, might be taken in its Lucan sense as an equivalent for Palestine, *i.e.* including, not

---

* Cp. G. H. Box (*Critical Review*, 1903, 32–34), Brooke and Burkitt in *JTS.*, 1908, 569–571, Askwith, and Harnack in *TLZ.*, 1909, 49–50.

† So, recently, A. Wright (*New Testament Problems*, pp. 159 f.), Zahn (*INT.* iii. 273 f.), Gwilliam (*DCG.* ii. 5 f.), and Belser (*INT.* 292–295).

‡ So, *e.g.*, Bacon (*Beginnings of Gospel Story*, pp. 195 f.) and Spitta, with special force.

excluding, Galilee; it need not necessarily by itself include any visit to Jerusalem. (*c*) The elimination of the words τὸ πάσχα in 6^4 (Hort in *WH.* 77–81; van Bebber in *Zur Chronologie des Lebens Jesu*, 1898, pp. 33 f., after Jacobsen and others), which rests on their neglect by the Alogi, Irenæus, Origen, etc., and on the possibility of assimilation with 2^{13}, would reduce the chronological discrepancy between the Fourth gospel and the synoptists; but the evidence does not yet seem strong enough for this hypothesis (cp. Burkitt's *Ev. da-Mepharr.* ii. 313), unless, with Schwartz, Wellhausen, R. Schütz, and others, the whole verse is deleted as one of the editorial insertions.*

(4) The Fourth evangelist, like his two immediate predecessors, thus bases on Mk.'s narrative, but diverges from it repeatedly; these divergencies are in some cases accidental, in others due to a preference for Mt. or Lk., or for both combined, and in other cases, again, the result of some independent tradition. Their motive cannot always be explained from his pragmatism, but the important point is that his method and its results do not suggest invariably the instinct of an eye-witness who sifts earlier traditions of differing value. The details are in the main the circumstantial minutiæ of a vivid or symbolic (Philonic) imagination, when they are not borrowed from the synoptic narratives. The use made of these narratives by the Fourth evangelist really illustrates the derivative and secondary character of his work, judged from the historical standpoint, and this conclusion is not affected by the admission that on two points in particular, *e.g.*, the date of the death and the previous connection with Judea, the tradition of the Fourth gospel has substantially reproduced elements which later phases of the synoptic tradition tended to obliterate.

(*a*) It would tell strongly against an eye-witness or a Palestinian Jewish Christian as the author of, or one of the authorities for, the gospel, if the description of Kaiaphas as ἀρχιερεὺς ὢν τοῦ ἐνιαυτοῦ ἐκείνου ($11^{49.51}$ 18^{13}) meant that the writer really believed the Jewish high priests were appointed annually, like the Asiarchs (so from Bretschneider and Baur to Martineau and Forbes). But this argument is not valid. The phrase might either mean *in that fateful year* (so, *e.g.*, Keim, Godet, Zahn, Peake, amongst others), or that the writer simply adapted his description to the local customs with which his readers were familiar (so, *e.g.*, Holtzmann and Loisy). The former

* The widespread admission, that a historical nucleus underlies the Johannine traditions about the Judean ministry, is opposed to the predominant view which has been recently argued with exceptional ability by Dr. James Drummond (pp. 41 f.), whose critical position generally is as favourable to the external evidence for the Johannine authorship as it is unfavourable to the historicity of the gospel's contents.

explanation is preferable, upon the whole. "The year of which the evangelist speaks was the year of all years; the acceptable year of the Lord, as it is elsewhere called; the year in which the great sacrifice, the one atonement, was made, the atonement which annulled once and for ever the annual repetitions. It so happened that it was the duty of Caiaphas, as high priest, to enter the holy of holies and offer the atonement for *that* year. The evangelist sees, if we may use the phrase without irreverence, a dramatic propriety in the fact that he of all men should make this declaration. By a divine irony he is made unconsciously to declare the truth, proclaiming Jesus to be the great atoning sacrifice, and himself to be instrumental in offering the victim. This irony of circumstances is illustrated in the case of Pilate, as in the case of Caiaphas" (Lightfoot, *Exp.*[4] i. 88–89).

(*b*) A similar verdict may be passed upon the discourses, where the creative genius of the author is at its height. Even here, in spite of the dialectic which pervades the debates of Jesus and the Jews, in spite also of the later standpoint of the Christian consciousness which reads itself back at several points into the sayings, there is good evidence of an accurate acquaintance, on the part of the author or of his sources, with the Palestinian situation. "One of the most remarkable facts about the writings of recent Jewish critics of the New Testament has been that they have tended upon the whole to confirm the gospel picture of external Jewish life, and where there is a discrepancy these critics tend to prove that the blame lies not with the New Testament originals, but with their interpreters. Dr. Güdemann, Dr. Bücheler, Dr. Schechter, Dr. Chwolsohn, Dr. Marmorstein, have all shown that the Talmud makes credible details which many Christian expositors have been rather inclined to doubt. Most remarkable of all has been the cumulative strength of the arguments adduced by Jewish writers favourable to the authenticity of the discourses in the Fourth gospel, especially in relation to the circumstances under which they are reported to have been spoken." *

§ 6. *Topography.*—Nearly forty years ago, Matthew Arnold, in *God and the Bible* (ch. v.), observed that the Fourth evangelist's "Palestinian geography is so vague, it has for him so little of the reality and necessity which it would have for a native, that when he wants a name for a locality he takes the first village that comes into his remembrance, without troubling himself to think whether it suits or no." This hasty verdict had been rejected by anticipation in Keim (i. 179), and subsequent research has shown that whoever the author was, he must have had a first-hand acquaintance with the topography of Palestine prior to A.D. 70. Summaries of the evidence may be seen in K. Furrer's article on 'das Geographische im Evglm nach Johannes' (*ZNW.*, 1902, 257–265), Drummond (pp. 366–374), Löhr's essay on 'Wie stellt sich die neuere Palästinaforschung zu den geographischen Angaben des Johannesevglms' (*Deutsch-Evang. Blätter*, 1906,

* Dr. Abrahams in *Cambridge Biblical Essays* (1909), 181.

795 f.), and Bacon, *The Fourth Gospel in Research and Debate* (1910), ch. xv.

In most cases the difficulty resolves itself into our ignorance of the local geography, not into the writer's. Thus, the Bethany πέραν τοῦ Ἰορδάνου (cp. 10^{40}) which was the scene of John's mission (1^{28}) may be identified either with the Betonim (Betâne) of Jos 13^{26} (so Zahn, *NKZ.*, 1907, 266 f., and Furrer), or, if the inferior reading *Bethabara* be adopted, with Bashan (Batanea, so Henderson's *Palestine*, 154, and Conder, *Tent-Work*, 230; the latter identifying the spot with ford *'Abarah*). But the *Bethabara* of Origen * and the *Evang. da-Meph* (cp. Mrs. Lewis, *The Old Syriac Gospel*, 1910, p. xxviii, and Burkitt's ed. ii. 308 f.) seems due to local tradition, which identified the scene with a pre-Christian holy place which became, at any rate, a sacred spot for Christians before the end of the second century. Others (*e.g.* Mommert, *Aenon u. Bethania*, 1903, and Löhr) suggest that both names refer to the same spot, Bethany being a ford nearly opposite Jericho (=Bethabara), 'house of the ford,' while some (from Sir George Grove and Sir C. W. Wilson to Cheyne, *EBi.* 548; and Rix, *Tent and Testament*, 175 f.) variously explain the names as corruptions of an original Βηθαναβρά, *i.e.* Beth-Nimrah (cp. Βαιθαναβρά, Jos 13^{27}) over thirteen miles east of the Jordan (cp. Abbott, *Diat.* 13–14, 610–616). This is, at any rate, better than the identification of Bethabarah with the Βαιθηρά or Beth-barah of Jg 7^{24} (Sanday, *Sacred Sites*, 23).

The other scene of John's mission, Αἰνὼν ἐγγὺς τοῦ Σαλείμ (3^{23}), is either Ainûn, seven miles from Salim (Conder's *Tent-Work*, i. 91 f.), or 'Ain-Fâra, about two hours N.N.E. of Jerusalem (Furrer, Moore in *DCG.* i. 35; Sanday's *Sacred Sites of Gospel*, 1903, 33 f.), or 'Ain Dschirm da (Mommert), eight miles S. of Scythopolis (for other identifications, see Lagrange in *RB.*, 1895, 509 f.; Hastings' *DB.* iv. 354; *EBi.* 4242, and Nestle in *DCG.* ii. 550–551). In any case the actuality of the place is not affected, even if the name † is supposed to carry a certain allegorical significance (e.g. *Fountains near to Peace*, the Baptist preparing for the higher purification by Christ the king of Salem = Melchizedek; so Abbott in *Diat.* 615–616, and *EBi.* 1796; Pfleiderer, Loisy, Kreyenbühl: i. 589, ii. 378). This possibility of a symbolic allusion recurs in the case of the Samaritan town Συχάρ (4^{5}), which the majority of recent geographers (notably Sir Charles Wilson in Hastings' *DB.* iv. 635; Conder, G. A. Smith's *Hist. Geography*, ch. xviii.; A. W. Cooke, *DCG.* ii. 685–687; Furrer, Löhr, and Rix's *Tent and Testament*, 26 f.) continue to identify with 'Askar. The term is hardly, as Jerome thought, a transcriptional error for Συχέμ, but it might be a play on it, either as *Sheker* =false (of idols, Hab 2^{18}, so Hengstenberg and others), or *Shikkor* = drunken

* On the variant Βηθαρά in the MSS of Origen, see Brooke (*JTS.* i. 65). Origen's explanation of it as = οἶκος κατασκευῆς suggests to him a play upon the name as appropriate to the mission of one who *prepared* (Mt 11^{10}) the Lord's way. "Fortasse primum scriptum fuit Βηθσαν, quæ urbs in campo ad Iordanem ad ripam parui fluminis erat" (Bretschneider, 96).

† An error (Bretschneider, 96–97), due to the writer mistaking עֵינָן (= *fontes, aquæ*) for עֵינָן, the name of a town.

(Is 28^1, of the Samaritans). The latter has been widely held, *e.g.*, among recent editors by Abbott (*EBi.* 1796, 1801), Loisy, and Calmes; Kreyenbühl (ii. 396–397) modifies it into an identification of Sychar with שִׁכּוֹר = a drinker—here of water *i.e.*, Samaria, personified in the woman, lives on a religious knowledge which is inferior to the true water or knowledge of Christianity.

The pool ἐπιλεγομένη Ἑβραϊστὶ Βηθζαθά, πέντε στοὰς ἔχουσα (5^2) is still a vexed problem in the topography of Jerusalem (best summary by G. A. Smith, *Jerusalem*, ii. 564 f.; cp. Moore in *DCG.* i. 193–195); even the name is uncertain, though *Bethzatha* or *Bezatha* seems the original form (cp. Keim, iii. 215 f.; WH. ii. 76; Nestle in *ZNW.*, 1902, 171–172) either as *Bezetha* (so Josephus for the north quarter of the city) or Βηθζαιθά = 'the house of the olive.' But again the local touch is not affected by the symbolic meaning of the five porches as the five books of the Mosaic law (which has been obvious since Augustine) with its intermittent purification, and of the thirty-eight years in v.[5] (= Israel's thirty-eight years in the wilderness, Dt 2^{14}). The inferior reading *Bethesda* (= בֵּית חֶסְדָּה, house of mercy or grace) probably was substituted for the original on this account.

In 6^1 (as in 21^1) τῆς Τιβεριάδος is a water-mark of the second century, or, at any rate, of the end of the first century (cp. Josephus, *Bell.* iv. 8. 2). 'Alle Schriftsteller im ersten Jahr. n. Chr. den Ausdruck See von Tiberias noch nicht haben; Strabo, Plinius, Josephus brauchen die Form See Gennesar oder Gennesaritis, auch die Targumim haben diese Form. Vom 2 Jahrh. an scheint der name Tiberiassee mehr und mehr officiell geworden zu sein' (Furrer, *ZNW.*, 1902, 261).* It is needless to suppose (so, *e.g.*, Dods, Wellhausen, Cheyne: *EBi.* 1632, Drummond, and Furrer) that τῆς T. is a later gloss in 6^1 (cp. Abbott, *Diat.* 2045).

The symbolic touch in 9^7 (Σιλωάμ, ὃ ἑρμηνεύεται ἀπεσταλμένος) † is enigmatic. The meaning of the original *Shiloah* (= sent or conducted) is evidently, in the light of the symbolism which shimmers through the whole story, applied to Jesus as the one sent by God (on this favourite Johannine phrase, cp. Abbott's *Diat.* 2277, etc.), who came by water (*i.e.* in the Spirit conferred at baptism). If Siloam is identified here with the mysterious messianic Shiloh of Gn 49^{10} (so Grotius), then there is a mystic reference (Abbott, *EBi.* 1803) to the supersession of the Law by him who was sent from God. In any case, baptism is the true illumination of the soul. The other interpretations (the pool as a second messenger of God, the apostles, the blind man himself) are highly speculative (cp. Kreyenbühl, ii. 115 f.).

Βηθσαϊδὰ τῆς Γαλιλαίας (12^{21}) is regarded by Furrer as another water-mark of the second century, since Claudius Ptolemæus (*c.* A.D. 140) is the first

* Any one acquainted with the local landscape, he adds, will recognise that the topographical details of the following story are strikingly vivid and exact.

† Lücke takes the last three words as a gloss; but the play (שִׁילוֹחַ and שָׁלוּחַ = ἀπεσταλμένος) is quite characteristic of the author, and there is no MS evidence for their omission. The pool "is one of the few undisputed sites in the topography of Jerusalem" (Rix, *Tent and Testament*, 213 f., precariously identifying Bethesda and Siloam).

writer who reckons Julias (*i.e.* Bethsaida) to Galilee. But as "the province of Galilee ran right round the lake, and included most of the level coast-land on the East" (G. A. Smith, *Hist. Geography*, p. 458), and as the latter was definitely included in Galilee by A.D. 84, it is needless (see the proofs in Rix, *op. cit.* 265 f.) to posit two Bethsaidas, or to date the expression of the Fourth gospel later than at least the last decade of the first century.

Only two points of topography in the passion-narrative present any difficulty. (*a*) τοῦ Κέδρων (the original reading in 18^{1}) is the ravine or winter-brook dividing Gethsemane and the Mount of Olives from the city proper. The original meaning of the term (=black, קִדְרוֹן) may have been in the writer's mind, as well as a recollection of David's retreat from the treachery of Absalom (2 S 15^{23}). The extremely difficult (cp. Nestle in Hastings' *DB.* ii. 74–75) expression (*b*) in 19^{13}, describing the tribunal in Herod's palace as set upon a spot called Λιθόστρωτον, Ἑβραϊστὶ δὲ Γαββαθᾶ, is at least as likely to be a correct trait (so Keim, vi. 85 f.), derived either from good tradition or from personal knowledge, as a misunderstanding of some notice about the meeting-place of the Sanhedrin (Brandt, *Evang. Gesch.* 133), although the lack of any other evidence leaves its meaning almost hopelessly obscure. Beyond the general agreement that Gabbatha, perhaps a Gk. equivalent for the Aramaic גַּבְּתָא (=ridge or height), is not a translation for λιθόστρωτον (mosaic or pavement), but another description of the place on which the βῆμα stood, we can hardly go. The variant Καπφαθα (I, cp. Burkitt's *Evang. da-Meph.* ii. 251) and Dalman's (*Worte Jesu*, i. 6, Eng. tr. 7) derivation of Gabbatha are both set aside by Wellhausen (p. 86). The attempt of Hönig (*ZWT.* xiv. 564) and Hausrath to connect λ. with Mk 14^{15} is futile; Jesus the Lamb of God is not slain by Pilate, and the terms in question are incongruous. The theory that the whole phrase is an artificial and meaningless invention (M. A. Canney, *EBi.* 3638–3640) is inconsistent with the symbolic predilections of the writer (cp. G. A. Smith's *Jerusalem*, ii. 575, who tentatively refers to גבב=to rake or put together little things—a possible source of the 'mosaic' meaning, which Zahn unhesitatingly adopts).

The Fourth gospel ignores the Lucan tradition (24^{50}) that the ascension took place in the vicinity of Bethany, about a mile and three-quarters from Jerusalem, on the Mount of Olives, but ($11^{1f.}$) assigns the resurrection of Lazarus to this village, and, following Mk. and Mt., makes Jesus reside there prior to his entry into the capital ($12^{1f.}$). Even were the meaning of the name (=בֵּית עֲנְיָא, house of affliction or misery?) plainer than it is, there would be no reason to regard it in $11^{1f.}$ as an allegorical invention of the Fourth evangelist. Consequently, while one or two place-names are invested with symbolic meaning, it cannot be said that topographical investigation lends any support upon the whole to the theory that the writer invented geographical allusions for the sake of his own purposes or mistook earlier traditions.

§ 7. *Structure.*—Special literature (in addition to works cited below)—(*a*) in favour of literary reconstruction: Burton (*BW.*, 1899, 16–41), Bacon (*AJT.*, 1900, 770–795, *INT.* 272 f., *Fourth Gospel in Research and Debate*, chs. xviii.–xix.), Moffatt (*HNT.* 689–694), Briggs (*New Light on Life of Jesus*, 1904,

140–158), Wellhausen's *Erweiterungen und Aenderungen im vierten Evglm* (1907)* and *Das Evglm Johannis* (1908), R. Schütz (*ZNW.* viii. 243 f.), Schwartz ('Aporien im vierten Evglm,' *Gott. Gelehrte Nachrichten*, 1907, 342 f., 1908, 116 f., 149 f., 497 f.), Bousset (*TR.* xii. 1–12, 39–64), F. J. Paul (*HJ.*, 1909, 662–668), F. W. Lewis (*Disarrangements in Fourth Gospel*, 1910).

(*b*) adverse = Holtzmann (*ZNW.* iii. 50–60) and C. R. Gregory, *Wellhausen und Johannes* (1910).

The further question is whether all this local knowledge and circumstantial detail of the Fourth gospel can suffice to prove that the author had been a Palestinian apostle. The inference is not necessary. Literary annals abound with cases of an imaginative historical reconstruction, where the author is known to have had no direct acquaintance with the countries in which his scenes are laid. *Gil Blas de Santillane*, for all its masterly delineation of Spanish manners, was composed by a man who had never been in Spain. And Shakespeare was like Le Sage in this. His Italian plays reveal a wonderfully wide and intimate acquaintance with Italy, which was due, not to local knowledge, but to "the power to grasp some trifling indication, some fugitive hint, and from it to reconstruct a whole scheme of things which shall, in all essentials, correspond to fact." † Besides, circumstantial detail is not an infallible note of historical veracity, as Defoe alone is enough to prove. Geographical precision is often accompanied by a varying level of historical accuracy, and minute touches are as likely to prove a later age as a contemporary witness (see above, p. 280). The 'Johannine' deviations from the synoptic traditions are to be referred partly to the freedom of the writer's imagination, working under the influence of certain religious preconceptions, and partly—when they are accurate—to an independent historical tradition mediated orally *or in writing*. But, is the latter hypothesis tenable? In answering this question, we premise that the gospel cannot any longer be assumed by the literary critic to be a seamless robe. Two sets of theories prevail upon its structure: (*a*) the partition-theories, which disentangle a more or less genuine Grundschrift from the subsequent editorial

* Adverse reviews of this pamphlet by Corssen (*ZNW.* viii. 125–142) and Moffatt (*Exp.*[7], 1907, 56–69).

† H. F. Brown, *Studies in Venetian History* (1907), ii. pp. 159 f.

additions, apostolic (so especially Wendt and Spitta) or not (Wellhausen); and (*b*) the revision-theories, which explain the phenomena of the canonical gospel by positing an editor who has not only in the appendix but elsewhere recast the gospel for purposes which originally it was not meant to serve (so variously Kreyenbühl, Harnack, Bousset, Heitmüller, Völter, Schwartz, Bacon). Either set of theories may be combined with the further hypothesis (*c*) of dislocations in the text, which are not always to be accounted for on the score of the writer's preference for association of ideas rather than chronological sequence.

The besetting danger of such hypotheses is their tendency to assume a logical or chronological sequence in the gospel, which may not have been present to the author's mind, and especially to harmonise the relative sections with the synoptic order. On the other hand, it is equally illegitimate to attribute a schematism to the gospel which would rule out at all costs any application of the transposition-theory. The author certainly had a pragmatism of his own, which often admits of unevennesses* in order to gain its end; he thought more of the religious ideas than of the historical setting which he could provide for them, and his adjustment of the latter between Judea and Galilee was partly controlled by the need of adhering in some degree to the synoptic outline; chronological affinities are repeatedly sacrificed to the needs of dialectic, and the opponents of Jesus form a unity rather than any series of different people in Galilee and Judea. But these considerations only suggest that most of the transpositions and interpolations are more probably due to copyists and later editors than to the author himself.

(*a*) The attempts to rearrange the prologue start mainly from the parenthetical v.^{15}, which breaks the sequence of ^{14} and ^{16}; if any change is to be made, the verse lies better after ^{18} (so, Markland, Bakhuyzen, and Ritschl, *SK.*, 1875, 576 f., who conjectures the original order to have been $1^{1-5.\ 10-13.\ 6-9.\ 14.\ 16-18.\ 15}$) than after ^{8} ($1^{1-5.\ 9-14.\ 16-18.\ 6-8.\ 15}$, so Wagenmann in *Jahrb. für deutsche Theologie*, 1875, 441 f.). 1^{6-8} and ^{15} are thus editorial additions (so, *e.g.*, Wendt and Bacon, *Fourth Gospel*, 477 f.); the latter verse is probably a marginal gloss† (based on 1^{30}), incorporated in order to emphasise John's witness to the Logos (as to the Light, $1^{7f.}$).

---

* Cp. Gregory, *op. cit.* 50, "Mir ist es durchaus nicht auffallend das Alles nicht völlig klar ist. Kein Literarkritiker kann die feine Arbeit eines Sainte-Beuve im NT suchen."

† Here as throughout the gospel it is a question whether such apparent displacements or interpolations are due to the accidental disarrangement of

(*b*) A minor case of interpolation has been also found in 3^{5}, where ἐξ ὕδατος καὶ (omitted in the best text of v.^{5}) is taken by several scholars, from Dieffenbach * (in Bertholdt's *Krit. Journ.* v. 1–16) to van Manen (*TT.*, 1891, pp. 189 f. 'Het Misverstand in het vierde Evangelie'), Wendt, Kirsopp Lake (*Influence of Textual Criticism on Exegesis of NT*, 1904, 15 f.), K. Andresen (*Ideen zu einer jesuzentrischen Welt-Religion*, 1904, pp. 324 f.), Tolstoy, Wellhausen, and others, to be a catholicising addition or interpretative gloss. The variants of the Syriac versions (cp. Burkitt, *Evang. da-Meph.* ii. 309 f.) are explicable if such an abbreviated text is assumed to have underlain them. In any case, the reference is to the Christian sacrament of baptism, as in $3^{22f.}$, not to John's baptism (Usteri, *SK.*, 1890, 517 f.).†

(*c*) 4^{43} *μετὰ δὲ τὰς δύο ἡμέρας ἐξῆλθεν ἐκεῖθεν εἰς τὴν Γαλιλαίαν.* ^{44} *αὐτὸς γὰρ Ἰησοῦς ἐμαρτύρησεν ὅτι προφήτης ἐν τῇ ἰδίᾳ πατρίδι τιμὴν οὐκ ἔχει.* ^{45} *ὅτε οὖν ἦλθεν εἰς τὴν Γαλιλαίαν, ἐδέξαντο αὐτὸν οἱ Γαλιλαῖοι, πάντα ἑωρακότες ἃ ἐποίησεν ἐν Ἰεροσολύμοις ἐν τῇ ἑορτῇ· καὶ αὐτοὶ γὰρ ἦλθον εἰς τὴν ἑορτήν.* ^{46} *ἦλθεν οὖν πάλιν εἰς τὴν Κανᾶ τῆς Γαλιλαίας, ὅπου ἐποίησεν τὸ ὕδωρ οἶνον.* After the Samaritan interlude, v.^{43} picks up the thread of v.^{3} (*ἀφῆκεν τὴν Ἰουδαίαν καὶ ἀπῆλθεν πάλιν εἰς τὴν Γαλιλαίαν*), but the synoptic material is broken up as well as re-set. The writer reserves the synagogue question, *Is not this the son of Joseph?* till 6^{42}, giving it a sceptical turn and transferring it from the citizens of Nazareth to the Jews of Kapharnaum. He also makes the companion proverb apply not to a town but to a country—for *πατρίς* in v.^{44} (as it stands) cannot denote Nazareth, much less Jerusalem. But is this country Galilee or Judea? The following words seem to indicate the latter upon the whole, for the explanations of *πατρίς* as Galilee are more ingenious than convincing. But then the Fourth gospel assumes the Galilean origin of Jesus ($2^{46f.}$ 7^{41-52}), and Judea could hardly be called the *πατρίς* of Jesus because it was the *πατρίς* of the prophets in general, or because it included Bethlehem (which the Fourth gospel ignores as the birthplace of Jesus). The question thus arises, does v.^{44} stand in its proper place? It is not enough (with Wellhausen) to dismiss it as an insertion, without accounting for its present position, and if the exegetical difficulties drive us to the hypothesis of a gloss, it is better to conjecture some misplacement in the text, and to put the verse either after ^{45} (so Blass, changing γὰρ to δὲ) or, better, after ^{46} (so Cramer, and Könnecke, *Emendationen zu Stellen des NT*, 1908, pp. 10–11). In the latter case, *πατρίς* has its synoptic sense of "native place," and explains why (in the scheme of the Fourth gospel) Cana was preferred to Nazareth.

---

leaves in the original, or to editorial revision. Some instances suggest accident, others a scribe's error, others again a more conscious purpose (see above, p. 39).

* He anticipates Kreyenbühl in regarding 17^{3c} as another gloss.

† Bacon (*Fourth Gospel*, 518 f.) thinks Tatian has preserved the original order by placing 3^{1-21} after 7^{30}. Like Delff and Wellhausen, he recognises the abruptness of $2^{13f.}$ after 2^{1-12}, but the transposition (so, *e.g.*, Lewis) of 3^{22-30} to its original position after 2^{12} probably solves most of the difficulties (cp. *e.g.* $2^{6}=3^{25}$, $2^{2.9}=3^{29}$, $2^{12}=3^{22}$) and restores the original connection between 3^{11-21} and 3^{31-36} (cp. *e.g.* $3^{19}=3^{32}$, $3^{16-17}=3^{35}$, $3^{18}=3^{36}$).

(*d*) Anticipated by a fourteenth-century writer, Ludolphus de Saxonia,* J. P. Norris (*Journ. Philol.*, 1871, 107–112), Lewis, and Burton transpose 5 and 6, the latter being (like 21) a Galilean episode which was added after the gospel had been finished, and placed too late. The connection of 4^{54} and 6^{1} is certainly good, while 7^{1} echoes 5^{18} and 7^{19-20} (when 7^{15-24} is restored to its original position after 5^{47}). Becker (*SK.*, 1889, 117–140) holds that the episodical chapters 5, 7, and 15–16 were added to the gospel by the author, after he had finished his first draft of the work, while Burton puts 7^{37-44} after 7^{52}, 8^{12-20} after 10^{21} (a specially good setting, since 8^{12} presupposes, not the audience of 7^{52}, but one like that of 10^{19-21}, while 8^{21} follows $7^{35f.}$ very aptly), and 10^{1-18} after 10^{29} (which also brings 10^{19} nearer to 9^{16} and gives a better opening for $10^{1f.}$).

(*e*) Various attempts have been made to break up the speech in 6. Besides those of Wendt, Wellhausen, and Spitta (*Urc.* i. 216–221: 6^{51-59} a eucharistic addition), which are improbable (cp. Schmiedel, *EBi.* 2523 f., and Kreyenbühl, ii. 34 f.), Chastand (*L'apôtre Jean et le quatrième évangile*, pp. 241 f.) distinguishes a speech in the synagogue ($6^{28-30.\ 36-40.\ 43-46}$) from one by the seaside ($6^{26-27.\ 31-35.\ 41-42.\ 47-58}$). The unexpected ἐν συναγωγῇ of 6^{59}, coming after 6^{25}, and 6^{30} after 6^{14}, suggest a conflation of two traditions. This is, at any rate, better than to regard 6^{1-26} as an interpolation (so Schweitzer, *Das Ev. Johannes*, 1841, pp. 80 f.).

(*f*) One of the clearest instances of misplacement is the removal of 7^{15-24} from its original position after 5^{47} (Bertling, *SK.*, 1880, 351 f., unconvincingly† puts 7^{19-24} before 5^{17}); its themes—faith in Christ's teaching, his authority and relation to Moses, his healing on the Sabbath—fit in closely to the argument of 5 (cp. $5^{39.\ 46}=7^{15}$, $5^{44}=7^{18}$, $5^{18}=7^{19}$, $5^{5-7}=7^{21}$, $5^{16-18}=7^{20-23}$, $5^{30}=7^{24}$). This hypothesis (Wendt, J. Weiss: *TLZ.*, 1893, 397, Burton, Blass, Spitta, Moffatt, F. J. Paul) further leaves the original course of 7^{14} and $7^{25f.}$ open; Jesus enters the temple and teaches in public, which sets some of the Jerusalemites talking, *not* upon the subject of 7^{15-24}, but on his openness (7^{14}) and unhindered action. Whether the displacement was accidental, or part of a redactor's work, the case for the restoration of 7^{15-24} to its original site is extremely strong. Thus—to quote only one or two items of proof—the question of 7^{25} becomes pointless if Jesus had just spoken 7^{19-21}, and 7^{20-21} requires a much closer connection with $5^{15f.}$ than the traditional arrangement provides; the murderous attitude of the crowd (7^{19-23}) contradicts 7^{12} but is organic to the situation created in 5^{16-18}. The question of the Sabbath is certainly dropped at 5^{17} (Schmiedel, *EBi.* 2529), but it leads naturally to the question of Moses, and by as natural a transition (in the Johannine dialectic) to the original topic in dispute (7^{22}). The replacement of the passage in its proper setting clears up some of the arguments which Wellhausen (p. 37)‡ raises against its unity; others (*e.g.* οἱ Ἰουδαῖοι, 7^{15-18},

* Bacon (*Fourth Gospel*, 505) plausibly suggests that Ludolphus was influenced by the Tatianic *Diatessaron* which "circulated in an ancient High German and Latin bilingual translation as early as the ninth century."

† Cp. Waitz in *SK.* (1881) 145–160.

‡ He admits, however, the identity of situation and theme in 5 and 7–8. "Dass das bloss auf Oscitanz des Schriftstellers beruhe, dass dieser an die

but ὁ ὄχλος, $7^{20f.}$) are not serious (cp. $6^{22.\ 24f.}$ and $6^{41f.}$). It was perhaps the allusions in 7^{1} and 7^{25} which led an early copyist to mistake this site for the true one. Displacement is, at any rate, preferable to the idea that v.^{39} (Scholten), or vv.$^{37-39}$ (Bacon), or $^{37-44}$ (Wellhausen), are editorial additions.

(*g*) The pericopê adulteræ (7^{53}–8^{11}), though occasionally defended by critics of opposite schools (*e.g.* Burgon and Miller, *Causes of Corruption in the Trad. Text of the Holy Gospels*, 1896, 232 f.; A. Syski, *De authentia loci . . . dissertatio critica* [Warsaw, 1905], Bretschneider, Thoma, Jacobsen, and Kreyenbühl, ii. 162 f.) as an integral part of the gospel, betrays by its un-Johannine tone and style an outside origin, either in the gospel of the Hebrews * (Bleek, Pfleiderer), or in the gospel of Peter (Volkmar, cp. Harnack in *TU.* xiii. 2. 50 f.), the Aramaic original of Matthew (Resch, *Agrapha*, 36 f., *Paulinismus*, 419 f.), the original synoptic tradition (Holtzmann), or, as most critics are content to imagine, the collected materials of Papias (*i.e.* the traditions of John the presbyter). The textual evidence is conclusive (cp. Westcott, ii. 380 f.; Gregory's *Canon and Text*, 379, 513 f., and Zahn's *INT.* iii. 346 f.). A number of MSS read it here, as early as Jerome's day,—which in any case is an impossible position,—but the majority of MSS and versions ignored it. The internal evidence points to a source nearer the synoptic traditions, and to a site for the story (which is undoubtedly authentic †) during the last days of Jesus in Jerusalem. Its original position may have been somewhere between Mk 12^{17} and 13^{1} (O. Holtzmann, perh. before 12^{35}, cp. ἐν τῷ ἱερῷ with εἰς τὸ ἱερόν, Jn 8^{2}; Keim, v. 165 f.; Wittichen, *JPT.*, 1881, 366 f.; and Hitzig, between 12^{17} and 12^{18}), or (the Ferrar group) after Lk 21 (so Blass: *op. cit.* 155 f., Bacon, Westcott, Harnack, *SBBA.*, 1904, 193; cp. 8^{2}=Lk 21^{38}), if not between Lk 20^{26} and 20^{27} (Holtzmann, *TLZ.*, 1898, 536 f.). Whether the textual form in D is original (cp. von Soden's *Schriften des NT.* i. 486–524; *ZNW.*, 1907, 110–124) or not (Lietzmann, *ZNW.*, 1907, 34–37), the synoptic colour of the passage points to some such locus rather than any position, *e.g.*, after 7^{30} or 7^{44} (so some later MSS), or between 5 and 6 (Rendel Harris, *New Testament Autographs*, pp. 10 f.). If it was inserted after 7^{52} in order to fill up a vacant place originally occupied by another story (Hausrath, Spitta, *Urc.* i. 194 f.), the early uncials betray as little knowledge of either pericopê as the versions. The probability is that this floating passage of primitive tradition

---

Leser seines Buches denke, für die das Kap. 5 wenige Seiten vorher stand, nicht aber an die Hörer der Rede, die durch anderthalb Jahre von dem in Kap. 5 Geschehenen getrennt waren, ist eine verzweifelte Auskunft, welche die Rückständigkeit der modernen theologischen Exegese kennzeichnet."

* In which, according to Eusebius (*H. E.* iii. 39. 18), there was a *ἱστορία περὶ γυναικὸς ἐπὶ πολλαῖς ἁμαρτίαις διαβληθείσης ἐπὶ τοῦ κυρίου* included in the book of Papias. It is uncertain, however, whether this *ἱστορία* refers to Lk 7^{36-50} or to Jn 7^{53}–8^{11}.

† Halévy (*RS.*, 1901, 244–257) objects to a lack of the gratitude and affection which fallen women in the synoptic tradition show to Jesus, and argues that the writing on the dust (cp. Jer 17^{13}) was to condemn the Pharisees as false witnesses. But there are only quasi-reasons for supposing that she was another Susanna (cp. 8^{11} and Herm. *Mand.* iv. 1. 4).

(cp. Burkitt's *Two Lectures on the Gospels*, 81 f.; C. Taylor in *JTS.* iv. 129-130, and Weiss in *ZWT.*, 1903, 141–158) drifted as a marginal note into some MSS of John at this point (perhaps as an illustration of 7^{51} or 8^{15}), and finally was settled in the text during the third or the fourth century. If it was at one time written (as there is some textual evidence to believe that it was) at the end of the gospel-canon, it would be natural to find a place for it somewhere in the Fourth gospel; but this could not have been its early or original position (cp. Loisy, 541).

(*h*) $10^{22f.}$, which interrupts 10^{1-21} and 10^{24-42}, may have originally lain before 8^{12} (cp. *JTS.* ii. 137–140), or (Bacon, *Fourth Gospel*, 493 f.) may have been added, editorially, along with 2^{13-25} to fill up the five festal revelations of Jesus (cp. Wellhausen, 49–50).

(*i*) The traditional position of 12^{44-50} is isolated. There is an awkwardness in ^{44} coming after ^{36b} (the cry does not suit the secrecy), and indeed after $^{40f.}$. When the passage is restored (cp. Wendt, Moffatt's *HNT.* 692) to what may be conjectured to have been its original site between ^{36a} and ^{36b}, the ideas of light and faith (which it is far-fetched to view as a recapitulation of 8^{12} etc.) are carried on without any interruption, and Christ's public utterances receive a sonorous climax. Earlier in the chapter, 12^{27-30} (a Johannine reproduction of Lk 22^{43-44}) has been placed after 11^{41} by Fries (*ZNW.*, 1900, 300); but this breaks the symmetry of the latter passage.

(*j*) The hypothesis that chs. 15–16 represent a later addition, either by the author himself (Becker, *SK.*, 1889, 132 f.; Lattey, *Exp.*[7], May 1906, 433–434) or by a redactor (so, for 15–17, Wellhausen, Heitmüller), allows 14^{31} to lie in its original connection with 18^{1} (ch. 17 being spoken by Jesus standing in the attitude of prayer before leaving the room). The data in favour of another author are hardly adequate, however (cp. Corssen, *ZNW.*, 1907, pp. 138 f., and Moffatt, *Exp.*[7], July 1907, 63 f.), except on the extremely precarious hypothesis that the gospel as a whole underwent a process of accretion which was largely due to theological tendencies. To strike out *ἐγείρεσθε, ἄγωμεν ἐντεῦθεν* (Corssen) is to cut the Gordian knot, and the only alternative is to follow the internal evidence, which points to the conclusion that, by some dislocation, 14 has been displaced from its original position immediately before 17. The canonical arrangement leaves some awkward sequences, *e.g.* in the fact of a long discourse following 14^{30} (*hereafter I will not talk much with you*),* the contradiction between 16^{5} and 13^{36} or 14^{5-6} (when the latter are put earlier), and the incongruity of $16^{17f.}$ after declarations like 13^{33} 14^{18} etc. The climax and final tone of 14^{31} (*Arise, let us go hence*) has always been felt to be strange, in view of the unexpected sequence of 15–16 and 17; and though more or less forced psychological explanations are possible, it is a fair hypothesis to regard this parallel to Mk 14^{42} as indicating some break or (to use geological language) some fault in the strata of the literary record. Three theories of the place originally occupied by 15–16 have been suggested; either (i.) to set them between 13^{35} and 13^{36} (Wendt, F. J. Paul), or (ii.) to interpolate them between 13^{20} and 13^{21} (Bacon,

* In the subsequent narrative only two brief words (18^{11} 19^{27}) are addressed to disciples.

JBL., 1894, pp. 64–76),* or (iii.) to restore them to their original position between 13^{31a} and 13^{31b} (Spitta, *Urc.* i. pp. 168–193; Moffatt, *HNT.* 522 f., 692 f.). (i.) interrupts the evident sequence of 13^{33} and 13^{36}, and reduces 16^{29-33} and 13^{36-38} to the level of mere episodes between 14^{1-2} and 16^{27-28}. (ii.) also has the drawback of breaking the connection between 13^{1-11} and 13^{21-30}. (iii.) is, of all the variants of this hypothesis, the most attractive and intelligible. After the withdrawal of Judas, Jesus, in view of the wine at table (Mk 14^{25}, Lk 22^{18}, Did. 9^{2}), utters the parable of the Vine ($15^{1f.}$) beginning with a special and warning allusion to the recent apostasy of his friend (an unfruitful branch, $15^{2}=13^{30-31}$, $15^{6}=13^{27}$), and urging brotherly love as the bond of life ($15^{9f.}$ carrying on $13^{14f.}$; cp. also 13^{10-11} echoed in 15^{2-3}, 13^{17-18} in 15^{4-5}, 13^{18} in 15^{16}, and 13^{16} in 15^{20}). The connection of thought between 13^{1-30} and 15 grows in fact more vivid as the two passages are set in juxtaposition; thus the love of the disciples suggests to Jesus ($15^{18f.}$) the hatred shown them by the outside world, whose persecution forms the next topic (15^{18}–16^{3}), passing over into the compensations for the bodily absence of Jesus from his afflicted followers (16^{4}–16^{33}). This stream of counsel and warning closes with a word of triumph, ($16^{33}=13^{31b-32}$), which runs out into a renewed appeal for mutual love among the disciples. Then follows Peter's protest (13^{36-38}), exactly as in the synoptic tradition (Mt 26^{31-35}), after Christ's mournful anticipation (16^{32}). The final discourse of 14 ends in the prayer of 17 (cp. $14^{30}=17^{1}$, $14^{6f.}=17^{2f.}$, $14^{13}=17^{4}$). In the solemn pause before the exit—a pause too short for such a discourse as that of 15 and 16—Jesus utters this sublime rhapsody of faith, and then (18^{1}) leads the disciples out to face the end. Note that on this rearrangement 13^{34-35} is not further from $15^{12.\ 17}$ than on the traditional, that $14^{15.\ 21}$ echoes 13^{34-35}, and that 14^{19} is more natural after 16^{16} (where the same statement, made for the first time, rouses wonder).

(*k*) The difficulties of 18^{13-28} require some hypothesis of transposition or dislocation. (*a*) The order of Syr^{sin} ($^{13.\ 24.\ 14-15.\ 19-23.\ 16-18.\ 25b-28}$), unless it was due to early harmonising tendencies,† yields a coherent outline (so, *e.g.*, Mrs. A. S. Lewis, *ET.* xii. 518–519, and *Old Syriac Gospels*, 1910, p. xxxiv; Blass, *Philology of Gospels*, 57 f.; Loisy, *Études Bibliques*, 142 f.; Calmes, 420 f.), though the separation of ^{15} and ^{16} is unlikely. (*b*) Spitta's proposal (*Urc.* i. 158–168) is $^{13.\ 19-24.\ 14-18.\ 25b-28}$, v.^{25a} being a copyist's repetition of ^{18b} for the sake of the narrative. This, however, still involves among other things the awkward separation of ^{13} and ^{14}, and, unless we read (*c*) $^{13-14.\ 24.\ 15-23.\ 25-28}$ (with J. N. Farquhar, *ET.* vi. 284–288), the alternative is (*d*) $^{13-14.\ 19-24.\ 15-18.\ 25b-28}$ (G. G. Findlay, *ET.* vi. 335 f., 478 f.; Moffatt, *HNT.* 528 f., 693), which straightens out the narrative, requires little textual change, and arose from quite a credible slip on the part of a copyist, who passed from ^{14} to ^{15} in the exemplar and only discovered his mistake in time to insert $^{19-24}$ after

---

* 13^{36-38} being also restored to their original position after $16^{31f.}$. The revisionists prefer to omit 13^{36-38} (Corssen) or 13^{34-35} (Wellhausen, Heitmüller), to which Schwartz adds 13^{23-26}, Wellhausen 13^{27-29}.

† It is doubtful whether Tatian can be cited in favour of this order; cp. Hjelt's *Die syrische Evangelienuebersetzung u. Tatian's Diatessaron*, 1901, pp. 128 f.

^{18}, catching up the last words of ^{18} in order to ease the transition in ^{25a} and thus recover the thread of the narrative. On this rearrangement the εἶπον of ^{25} gets a satisfactory subject, the high priest is Kaiaphas (as 11^{49-51}), and the dispatch of Jesus to the latter ceases to be purposeless, as it is in the traditional order.

The slightest change would be to take ^{24} as a parenthesis or intercalated remark (so from Erasmus to Edersheim). Otherwise it might be placed after ^{14} (so from Cyril of Alexandria to Luther) or ^{13} (Strauss). Wellhausen omits it with ἀπὸ τοῦ Καιαφᾶ (^{28}), and πρῶτον and ἀρχιερεὺς ὢν τοῦ ἐνιαυτοῦ ἐκείνου (^{13}), believing, with Schwartz (adding $^{25-27}$) and Bousset, that the references to Kaiaphas are interpolated (after Mt $26^{3.57}$); Bacon (*Fourth Gospel*, 485 f.) omits $^{14(15)-18}$ and $^{24-27}$ as interpolated by an editor, but his thesis that the Tatianic order reflects the order in the original of the Fourth gospel (see *AJT.* iv. 770–795), implies (*a*) that the Diatessaron follows the chronological outline of the Fourth gospel—which is not the case, as the feasts, *e.g.*, are rearranged (cp. the excellent statement by Hobson in *The Diatessaron of Tatian and the Synoptic Problem*, pp. 33 f.)—and (*b*) that the Tatianic order of the Johannine material is free from the abruptness occasionally evident in the canonical text—which, again, is not the case, since 4^{45b} forms but a poor bridge between 5^{47} and 7^{1}, while, *e.g.*, 6^{71} is hardly a natural prelude to 4^{4}.

Turning back, with these data, to the larger problem of the gospel's structure, we still lack a sure clue to any process of extensive editing. Upon the one hand, the Fourth gospel has been composed in such a way that any earlier documents can no longer be disentangled without recourse to highly arbitrary canons of literary procedure and speculative reconstructions of the text. On the other hand, any original* details and sayings which may be assumed to lie embedded in its pages do not require more than some primitive witness upon whom the author draws, either in the way of reproducing them from oral tradition or by direct reminiscence. These reminiscences are more easily felt than defined. But while the recognition of a good tradition under, *e.g.*, some of the Judean passages and Jewish allusions in the Fourth gospel may imply an eye-witness as their ultimate source, it need not have been John the apostle. The disciples who accompanied Jesus on any of his visits to Judea and Jerusalem must have included those familiar to us in the synoptic gospels,

* Original, *i.e.* in the sense of being independent of the synoptic traditions. The speeches are not condensed summaries, but expansions of such sayings or variations upon homiletic themes suggested more than once by OT passages upon which midrashic interpretation had been playing (cp. G. Klein's *Der älteste Christliche Katechismus*, 1909, pp. 49 f.). For the Fourth gospel as an inspired Targum, freely rendering the sense of Christ's teaching for a later age, cp. Abbott's *Diat.* 3374 A.

but it is only on the last visit to Jerusalem that the beloved disciple appears in the rôle of pre-eminence; this rôle at one point (18^{15}) suggests not a Galilean fisherman, but a Jerusalemite; it is significant that the beloved disciple is not claimed as an authority for the characteristic episodes in the earlier portion of the gospel, at some of which, indeed (*e.g.* $3^{1f.}$ and $4^{6f.}$), he could not have been present, and the sole trait for which his authority is cited (19^{35}) is one of the most doubtful statements in the whole narrative.

Little or no result has flowed from the repeated attempts to postulate a Johannine document or substratum, which have been made for a century and a quarter by critics from Bertholdt (*INT.* iii. 1302 f.), who argued that John took down the Aramaic sayings of Jesus on the spot and afterwards wrote them out from his notes, to Wendt, Briggs,* and Spitta † (*Das Johannes-Evglm als Quelle der Geschichte Jesu,* 1910). Since John the apostle was martyred early, the only available hypotheses of this kind are those which make the historical narrative come from a disciple of John, and merely the discourses from the apostle himself (so, *e.g.*, Eckermann originally in *Theologische Beiträge*, 1796; C. H. Weisse, *die Evglienfrage*, 1856); or those which more cautiously make John only the witness or guarantee of the tradition, the authorship being relegated to a later hand (so, *e.g.*, Paulus, in the Heidelberg *Jahrbücher der Literatur*, 1821, pp. 112 f.; J. R. Tobler, *ZWT.*, 1860, pp. 169 f., ascribing composition to Apollos; Karl von Hase's *Geschichte Jesu*, 1876; Reuss, *La Bible*, vi., 1879; Sabatier, *ESR.* vii. 181 f.; Ewald, Renan, and Weizsäcker). It is one thing to postulate a general historical basis underlying some of the logia and perhaps the incidents in the gospel, and quite another thing to work out in detail a theory of literary partition by means of which the Johannine tradition is disengaged from the later editorial expansion (so variously Schweitzer, *das Evglm Joh. nach seinem inneren Werth u. seiner Bedeutung*, 1841; Tobler's *die Evglienfrage*, 1858; Delff, Soltau, Wendt, and Spitta).

Delff's ‡ earlier nucleus of the gospel consists mainly of the following passages:—$1^{6-8.\ 19-51}$ $2^{12-16.\ 18-20.\ 23-25}$ 3^{1}–4^{43} 4^{45} $5^{1-16.\ 30-47}$ $6^{30-36.\ 41-58.\ 60-71}$ $7^{1-36.\ 45-52.\ 37-38.\ 40-44}$ 8^{12}–11^{57} $12^{1-15.\ 17-24.\ 31-32.\ 34-37.\ 42-50}$ $13^{1-19.\ 21-38}$ 14^{1}–18^{40} $19^{1-34.\ 39-42}$ $20^{1-8.\ 19-31}$. Wendt's apostolic source, or Johannine logia, may be traced

---

* Cp. *New Light on Life of Jesus* (1904), pp. 140–158.

† Spitta's exhaustive analysis, with its Johannine *Grundschrift* (A) and its second and secondary source (B), both edited by the redactor, is no advance on its predecessors; its extra complexity is not warranted by the complexity of the data.

‡ Criticisms of Delff by Sanday (*Exp.*[4] iv. 328 f., v. 375 f.), A. Meyer (*TR.*, 1899, 255 f., 295 f.), and Holtzmann (*TLZ.*, 1890, 588 f.). The most permanent suggestion of Delff's was that the author was a Jerusalemite disciple of Jesus, of priestly lineage, who after writing the gospel in Jerusalem worked in Ephesus as a διδάσκαλος and then re-edited his gospel (adding, *e.g.*, ch. 21) for Asia Minor. This stands better than his linguistic analysis.

for the most part in—$1^{1-5.\ 9-14.\ 16-18}$ $2^{13-16\ (\text{substance}).\ 18-20}$ $3^{1-2a.\ 3-21}$ $4^{4-12\ (\text{substance}).\ 13-15.\ 19-25\ 27.\ (?).\ 31-38}$ $5^{1-3.\ 5-7.\ 16-27.\ 30-32.\ 34a.\ 36b-47}$ $7^{15-19.\ 21b-24}$ $6^{27-58\ (\text{substance}).\ 60-61.\ 63-64a.\ 65-69}$ $7^{1-7\ (?).\ 10-14\ (\text{substance}).\ 25-27\ (\text{substance}).\ 28-29.\ 33-43\ (?)}$ $8^{12-20a.\ 21-29.\ 31b-59}$ $9^{1.\ 4-5.\ 39-41}$ $10^{1-18.\ 19-21a\ (\text{substance}).\ 23-38.\ 40\ (?)}$ $11^{1.\ 3.\ 5-6\ (?).\ 7-10.\ 16.\ 17-22\ (\text{substance}).\ 23-27.\ 28-35\ (\text{substance}).\ 38}$ $12^{20-28a.\ 31-32.\ 34-36a.\ 44-47a.\ 48-50}$ $13^{1-10.\ 12-17.\ 20.\ 31b-35}$ 15–16, 13^{37-38} 14, 17, 18^{33-38a} 19^{9-11a}. Similarly Soltau (*ZNW.*, 1901, 140–149; *SK.*, 1908, 177–202), after putting on one side the material derived from the synoptic tradition (*e.g.* $1^{19-28.\ 31-34\ (35-42)}$ $2^{13-17.\ 19.\ 22}$ 4^{43-54} $6^{1-25.\ 66-71}$ $9^{1.\ 6-23}$ $11^{47-55\ (57).}$ $12^{3-8.\ 12-16}$ 13^{26-27} 18, $19^{1-24.\ 38-42}$ $20^{1-2.\ 11-18.\ 19-23}$), finds the original Johannine Logia (*i.e.* sayings with a historical introduction) in $1^{1\ (35-42).\ 43-51}$ 2^{9-11} $3^{1-12.\ 22-31a}$ $4^{1-9\ (16-19).\ 29-30.\ 39-42}$ $5^{1-16\ (18)}$ 7^{1}–8^{1} 8^{2-11} 9^{23-41} $12^{20-33\ (37-43)}$ $13^{2-15\ (16-20).\ (31-36)}$ 19^{25-37} $20^{14-18.\ 25-29}$. Even the attractive shape into which Wendt has thrown the hypothesis of C. H. Weisse breaks down;* the distinguishing data of the two sources are inadequate; it is just in the discourses of Jesus that some of the least historical features of the gospel recur, and these cannot be eliminated without an arbitrary treatment of the text. The distinction, moreover, between the narratives (with their emphasis on σημεῖα) and the speeches (with ἔργα = ῥήματα) cannot be carried through, for in the latter the ἔργα of Jesus are not severed entirely from the σημεῖα (cp. $6^{26.\ 30}$), whereas once at least in the narrative Jesus does not lay stress on his σημεῖα (20^{29}), and in 7^{3} (narrative) *works* are equivalent to signs and wonders.† The *work* of Jesus (17^{4}) was to manifest the glory of God (17^{3}), and this surely included the manifestation of the divine life in the σημεῖα as well as in the words of the Son. In the light of 5^{17-27} etc., it is not possible to confine *work* and *working* in the Fourth gospel to any specific line of activity such as that of preaching and teaching. The *work* to which Jesus refers in 7^{21} is a miracle, and when *the works* of himself (5^{36}) and God (5^{37}) are ranked objectively with the testimony of the Baptist (5^{33-34}) and the Scriptures (5^{39}), those ἔργα, especially in the light of an allusion like that of 10^{37}, cannot be what Wendt's theory demands.

More help is to be secured by recognising that the addition of 21 to the gospel must have been accompanied by some further process of editing in the text of 1–20. The extent to which this was carried depends on the view taken of the 'beloved disciple' and of the putative authorship, as well as on the theory adopted with regard to the First epistle. The author of the latter—it is a fair hypothesis—may have edited Jn 1–20 (Zurhellen adds the Apocalypse in 1–3, 21–22); but even this conjecture leaves us in

* Cp. the critiques by Holtzmann (*TLZ.*, 1886, 197–200), Haupt (*SK.* 1893, 217 f.), Lock (*JTS.*, 1903, 194–205), G. W. Stewart (*Exp.*, 1903, 65–80, 135–146), Corssen (*GGA.*, 1901, 645–656), Bacon (*AJT.*, 1901, 146–148), Hitchcock (*AJT.*, 1901, 146–148), Howlett (*Dublin Review*, 1904, 314–335), J. A. Cross (*ET.*, 1903, 331–333), Swete (*Exp.*, 1903, 267–282), Hargrove (*HJ.* i. 410–412), and Schmiedel (*EBi.* 2554–2556).

† There is no evidence in the context that Jesus corrects this idea of his brothers. He simply protests against their eagerness for a manifestation of power in Judea.

the dark as to the precise extent and motives of the editorial revision which added 21^{1-24}, and which has been traced in 12^{33} and 18^{32} as well as in 19^{35}, in 5^{28-29} (Scholten, Wendt, Zurhellen), $6^{40.\ 44.\ 54}$ $11^{25f.}$ $14^{3.\ 18b.\ 28b}$ (Zurhellen), and in the editorial additions or marginal glosses already noted, *i.e.* especially in the more eschatological and popular traits which distinguish the First epistle from the bulk of the gospel. A further application of this hypothesis attributes to it the beloved-disciple passages (Schwartz), while Schütz, Wellhausen, and F. Westberg (*Die Biblische Chronologie nach Flavius Josephus und das Todesjahr Jesu*, 1910, 83 f.), agree that the festival-journeys of Jesus have been interpolated in the original gospel, in order to lengthen out the ministry to three or four years. Wellhausen postulates a Galilean *Grundschrift* (A), with no speeches, composed by some anonymous author; but its resemblances to Mark do not serve to throw much light upon it, if the anonymous author (*Ev. Joh.* pp. 102 f.) dealt freely with his prototype; and its Marcan character is not obvious, if it lacked teaching and stories of the healing ministry. It has also been worked over by a redactor (B), who draws especially on Matthew and Luke,[*] and reproduces dialogues and discourses of Jesus. The criteria for this are not more convincing than in the case of Wendt's partition-theory.

The outcome of our investigation is therefore negative and tentative on the whole. The central problems of the gospel lie beyond the reach of purely literary criticism, and no reconstruction of a supposed apostolic source does justice to the dual characteristics of the book. "In many sections," as even Zahn admits (*INT.* iii. p. 337), "the narrative lacks the clearness and definiteness which we should expect from an eye-witness." "The whole nature of his employment of the synoptic literature is symptomatic of the secondary character of his history. An independent witness might, of course, have been acquainted with earlier presentations of the same history: his own might have coincided with them in its main features; but, writing in the light of his own recollections and the impressions made on himself, he must have preserved some originality of detail. The fourth evangelist, on the other

[*] Bousset regards the *Grundschrift* as Lucan in tone, and ascribes to the redactor a predilection for Matthew. Thus, "im übrigen charakterisiert sich die Perikope 1^{19-27} als eine freie Bearbeitung von Apg 13^{25} und dem lukanischen Bericht über den Täufer, dem auch der Wortlaut $1^{26f.}$ am nächsten steht" (*TR.* xii. 55).

hand, is dependent, even in minute details, on the earlier narrative" (Wendt, p. 48). This feature of a later age is even more marked in passages which have no synoptic parallels. Thus the dialogues, beginning with the introduction of some figure, pass over into a disquisition or monologue, in which the author voices, through Jesus, his own or rather the church's consciousness, usually upon some aspect of the christology which is the dominant theme of the whole book. The original figure is forgotten; Nicodemus, the Samaritan woman, or the Greeks serve as the *point d'appui*, and presently the so-called conversation drifts over into a doctrinal meditation upon some aspect of Christ's person, leaving the figure or figures in question without any record of Christ's final attitude, or of the effect which he produced.* This method recurs even in the description of John's cross-examination by the deputation from Jerusalem ($1^{19f.}$). It precludes the idea that the author could have been an eye-witness of these scenes, or that he is reproducing such debates from memory. The interests of the writer lie in the dialectic of his faith rather than in the situation which he provides for its successive movements.

The objection taken to this view of the Fourth gospel, viz. that there was no *milieu* for such controversial discussions, falls to the ground in presence of writings like Justin's dialogue with Trypho, where the obscure origin of the Christ (viii., cx., cp. Jn 7^{27}), his birthplace (cviii., cp. Jn $7^{41f.}$), the question of Sabbath observance (xxiii., xxvi. f., xlvii. etc., cp. Jn $8^{10f.}$ $7^{19f.}$), the coming of Elijah (xlix. f., cp. Jn 1^{21}), Jews and Samaritans (lxxviii., cp. Jn 4, 8^{5}), etc., are among the topics of contemporary interest (see above, p. 531).

Over against these traits lie the indications already mentioned, which suggest that the author had access to some reliable historical traditions for his work. In view of such dual phenomena, the least objectionable hypothesis lies among those which postulate not only the influence of Alexandrian thought in the Asiatic church and the development of Pauline and post-Pauline conceptions, but a certain oral tradition (Johannine or not) upon the life of Jesus which had hitherto flowed apart from the ordinary channels of evangelic composition.† The logia of this tradition

* An instance of this, in epistolary literature, occurs in Gal $2^{1ff.}$.

† So, after Wendt and others, Cone (*Gospel Criticism and Historical Christianity*, 1891, pp. 251 f.: "While on any hypothesis of its origin many critical problems remain unsolved, there is at least a strong probability for a Johannine nucleus in the book, for frequent 'words of the Lord

cannot often be disentangled from their setting. The discourses in which they are embodied represent the genius of a single writer, voicing the faith of his circle as well the ideas of his own mind. Nor is it possible to ascertain the exact literary channel by means of which these sayings and traditions have flowed into their present position through the homilies of the early church, any more than to estimate precisely the extent to which their original shape and colour have been altered, previous to their incorporation in this gospel, or during their passage through the rich, devout mind of the author (see pp. 43–44). But their gnomic character, their outstanding originality, and their profound depth, prove that the dramatic and creative genius of the author had materials to draw upon * in composing the meditations and illustrations of Jesus which distinguish this gospel from the synoptists.

§ 8. *The Beloved disciple and others.* — The mixture of adherence to the synoptic tradition and imaginative freedom in its treatment comes out (*a*) in the author's references to the disciples, and (*b*) in his allusions to the family of Jesus.

Peter, in accordance with the dominant tradition, still occupies a certain position of primacy among the disciples. Alluded to before he comes on the scene ($1^{40f.}$), he is still their spokesman upon occasion, plays a prominent rôle at the last supper ($13^{6-10. 24f. 36f.}$) and in the closing scenes (18^{10-27}), and, in accordance with primitive tradition (1 Co 15^{5}, cp. Lk 24^{4}), has his own access to the risen Lord (Jn 21^{7-8}).† Andrew is *Simon Peter's brother* ($1^{41f.}$ 6^{8}), and Jesus calls him *Kephas* from the outset—a proof not only of divine prescience but of Peter's pre-eminence as the bulwark of the church, of which he is the

---

(κυριακὰ λόγια) handed down from the apostle without connection, probably, and without a historical setting. . . . The attentive reader finds on almost every page of the Gospel words which are probably genuine Johannine logia of Jesus"), and O. Holtzmann (*Leben Jesu*, Eng. tr. p. 46: "At the time that he composed his work the traditions of the life of Christ had not yet become crystallised in the church's faith. Hence the current of the evangelic narrative was still able to carry along with it much material that had not been utilised by the synoptists").

* "It may be said with certainty that a literary artist capable of inventing the most striking sayings of Jesus to Nicodemus or to the woman of Samaria would have made his composition as a whole more flawless, more artistically perfect than the Fourth gospel actually is. Judged from an artist's point of view, it has blots and awkwardnesses which a master of imaginative invention would never have suffered his work to exhibit" (M. Arnold).

† In 20^{6-8}, however, it is suggested that while *the other disciple* entered the tomb and believed, Peter had entered without believing (on the early attempts in Syr^{sin} to correct 20^{8} into the plural, cp. *Diat.* 1556 f.).

spokesman ($6^{67f.}$). The author thus not only throws back Mt 16^{18} so as to cover Peter's career from the beginning, but omits the subsequent rebuke (*thou Satan!*) of Mt 16^{23}, and associates the devil not with Peter, but with Judas Iskariot (6^{71} $13^{2.\,27}$).

The remarkable prominence of Andrew, as compared with his position in the synoptic tradition (where he stands second to Peter in the apostolic lists of Mt. and Lk.), appears in three places, $1^{40f.}$ $6^{8f.}$ and $12^{21f.}$. (*a*) He is not only one of the first two disciples (of John the Baptist) who joined Jesus, but is the first disciple named in the gospel; he brings his brother Peter to Jesus, and Bethsaida is expressly called *the city of Andrew and Peter.* (*b*) He volunteers information to Jesus about the food-supply—another detail which the synoptic tradition omits. (*c*) Finally, he acts as intermediary between the Greek inquirers and Jesus. These allusions, corroborated by the traditions (*e.g.* Papias, Gospel of Peter, Gospel of the Twelve) of the second century,* indicate that Andrew, like Philip, was an important figure for the (Asiatic) circle in which the Fourth gospel circulated. The latter is the first disciple whom Jesus *finds* (1^{43}). Andrew's confession of faith is the first in the gospel, *We have found the messiah*, but Philip's is more explicit: *We have found him of whom Moses wrote in the law and of whom the prophets wrote, Jesus the son of Joseph, from Nazareth.* He is prominent at the feeding of the multitude near his native place ($6^{5f.}$), and it is he to whom the Greek inquirers first apply (12^{21}). On all these occasions he is associated more or less closely with his fellow-townsman, Andrew; in his request for a theophany (14^{8}) he is alone, but it is possible that he and Andrew are the anonymous pair of disciples in 21^{2}.

Thomas, who has no independent rôle in the synoptic tradition, comes into prominence in the final Judean cycle of stories in the Fourth gospel, at 11^{16} 14^{5} and $20^{24\text{-}29}$; in the appendix he is mentioned, next to Peter (21^{2}), among the disciples to whom Jesus appeared after death in Galilee. It is curious that John only mentions 'the twelve' four times, and always 'in connection with some mention of treachery, possible desertion, or unbelief'; he significantly widens (13^{20}) the saying recorded in Mt 10^{40}=Lk 10^{16}, and apparently ranks Nathanael almost on a level with the twelve, some of whom he entirely ignores (cp. *Diat.* 1671, 1695). The absence of N. from the synoptic lists of the twelve, together with the fact that Philip in the latter is followed by Bartholomew, has suggested that B. and N. represent the same person, B. being the patronymic name (so, *e.g.*, Keim, Renan, Calmes, and Zahn); the similarity of the name has led others (*e.g.*, Resch, *TU.* x. 3. 829 f.; Rohrbach, *Berichte auf d. Auferstehung*, 51 f.; Weizsäcker) to identify him with Matthew Levi, which has the merit of reproducing the Papias-list; the details † in $1^{45f.}$ have led others again to see in him a symbolical figure of

---

* In one Coptic (Akhmim) fragment of a second century (A.D. 150–180) anti-gnostic gospel (ed. Schmidt, *SBBA.*, 1895, 705–711), Andrew appears with Peter and Thomas in a scene corresponding to that of Jn $20^{25f.}$, while in another gnostic fragment (ed. Schmidt, *SBBA.*, 1896, pp. 839 f.) he plays a similar rôle of incredulity.

† Abbott (*Diat.* 3375–3377) regards the story as a version of the story of Zacchæus in the sycamore tree.

Paul or Paulinism (Hönig, *ZWT.*, 1884, 110 f.; Holtzmann, *BL.* iv. 294 f; O. Schmiedel, *Hauptprobleme d. Leben-Jesu*², 22 f., 117 f.; Kreyenbühl, ii. 353 f.; E. F. Scott, pp. 47 f. etc.), the Paul who, a genuine Israelite, worshipping under the unsatisfactory fig-tree of Judaism, was called by Christ (Ac 22^{8}=Jn 1^{48}), and broke through the prejudices of his early environment to win personal intercourse with Jesus and to utter a greater confession of faith in the divine Son than his predecessors in the apostolate. But in view of Gal $1^{1.\,15\,f.}$, a later writer would hardly have described Paul's approach to Jesus as mediated by any human agency (Jn $1^{45.\,48}$), and even the desire of emphasising the apostolic prestige would not have made the agency apostolic; he would rather have chosen terms like those of 1^{43}. Besides, visions were not a special feature of Paul's apostolate (2 Co 11^{21} 12^{1}), and the call of Paul was not motived as in Jn 1^{48} (note εἶδον, not ἐκάλεσα or ἐφώνησα). It would be more plausible to identify him with the beloved disciple John (so, *e.g.*, Spaeth, *ZWT.*, 1868, 168 f., 309 f., and Rovers, *TT.*, 1869, 653–661). This would imply that the references in Jn 21 are from another plane of thought, though, if the note in 21^{2} is correct, it helps to fill out the connection between $1^{44f.}$ and $2^{1f.}$.[*]

It is often argued that by the πρῶτον or πρῶτος of 1^{41} the writer subtly suggests that after Andrew found his brother Peter, the other disciple of 1^{35-40} found *his* brother; consequently, as the sons of Zebedee were the only other pair of brothers who (according to the synoptic tradition) were among the earliest disciples of Jesus, and as the Fourth gospel never mentions them by name, their calling is implied here (so, *e.g.*, Westcott, Godet, Zahn, Calmes; cp. Abbott, *Diat.* 1720, 1901). The Fourth gospel is full of subtle touches, but this is hyper-subtle John plays no independent or special rôle in the synoptic tradition; he and his brother James are called (Mk 1^{19-20}) after Peter and Andrew; in the lists of the twelve he comes fourth (except in Mk 3^{16-18} where Andrew falls from the second to the fifth place, as in Mk 13^{3} to the fourth); the only occasion on which he acts as spokesman for the twelve (Mk 9^{38-41}=Lk 9^{49-50}) exposes him to a rebuke for having failed to appreciate the generous temper of Jesus, and the presumptuous claim advanced by himself and his brother (Mk $10^{35f.}$, softened by Mt $20^{20f.}$) betrays an equal misconception. He is third in the group of the four disciples who draw from Jesus (Mk $13^{3f.}$) his prophecy of the future, and in the group of three who fail Jesus in Gethsemane (Mk $14^{32f.}$=Mt $26^{36f.}$); but neither at the last supper, nor during the trial, nor after the death of Jesus, does he appear. On the other hand, there are slight traces in Lk. of a higher place (contrast 8^{51} with Mk 5^{37}, 9^{28}=Mk 9^{2} and Mt 17^{1}) next to Peter in the only two scenes (raising of daughter of Jairus, and the transfiguration) where Peter and the sons of Zebedee appear as a trio of intimates, before the vigil in Gethsemane. Furthermore, Lk. omits the claim of Mk $10^{35f.}$, though he was aware of it (cp. 12^{49-50} $22^{24f.}$=Mt $20^{25f.}$), identifies the two confidential disciples of Mk 14^{13} (Mt $26^{17f.}$ simply οἱ μαθηταί) with Peter and John (22^{7-14}), omits the fact (Mk $14^{33f.}$=Mt $26^{37f.}$) that Peter and the two sons of Zebedee

---

[*] To Loisy (246 f.), N. is a composite figure, idealised out of Matthew, Zacchæus, and Paul. The identity of N. with Matthew and Zacchæus was first suggested by Strauss.

slept in Gethsemane and were rebuked by Jesus (22^{39-46}), and that all the disciples fled after their Master was arrested (Mk 14^{50} = Mt 26^{56}), and adds to the women at the cross (Mk 15^{40-41} = Mt 27^{55-56}) πάντες οἱ γνωστοὶ αὐτῷ standing at a distance (22^{49}). This is carried forward in Acts, where John is closely associated with Peter (1^{13} $3^{1f.}$ $4^{13f.}$ 8^{14-15}) during the early Jerusalemite period (cp. Gal 2^{9}) in the leadership of the church. He then drops into oblivion; the control of the Jerusalemite church passes into the hands of James, the brother of Jesus. He is absent from the Fourth gospel, unless he is *the beloved* (or, *other*) *disciple*. Comparatively little is made of the latter figure, except to hint at his pre-eminence in one or two scenes (adapted from the synoptic tradition) where Peter is prominent.* At the last supper ($13^{23f.}$) this favourite disciple is assumed to be in the secret of Jesus, as none of the others is. During the trial ($18^{15f.}$) Peter again requires his intervention, this time to gain entrance to the palace of the high priest. At the cross ($19^{25f.}$) he receives charge of the mother of Jesus (mission to Jewish Christians?) † and witnesses the *humor effusus*; at the grave ($20^{2f.}$) he is the first to see the empty tomb and then believe, *i.e.* without requiring to see the risen Christ. The empty tomb was enough for him; all else, OT proofs and even the witness of the women, was secondary.

The possibility of a mystical reference in all (except $18^{25f.}$) of these passages does not exclude—in fact it would rather point to—a literal basis. If by the disciple whom Jesus loved (ὃν ἠγάπα ὁ Ἰησοῦς) the author means to suggest the typical or ideal Christian, a permanent witness to Christ's love (*till I come*, 21), the ideal is in part a Pauline ideal (= Gal 2^{20}); so, *e.g.*, Bacon (*Exp.*[7] iv. 324 f., *Fourth Gospel in Research and Debate*, 301 f.),‡ who declares that "the heart of the Fourth Gospel is Paul's confession of his faith in Gal 2^{20}" (p. 326), and that "when we can be satisfied to take this Gospel for what it is, the richest, choicest flower of the spiritual life of the Pauline churches a half century after Paul's death . . . a new era will begin in the appreciation of this great Gospel." The choice lies between identifying the beloved disciple with John the apostle § or John a Jerusalemite (Delff, Bousset, etc.), and regarding him as ideal. The chief objections to the latter

---

* He is never contrasted with sceptical Jews or imperfect Christians.

† Völter (*Mater Dolorosa und der Lieblingsjünger des Johannes Evglms, Mit einem Anhang über die Komposition dieses Evglm*, 1907) makes the beloved disciple in 1–20 the John Mark of Ac 12^{12}; the gospel is to prove that he was not a mere interpreter of Peter, but superior to him. In 21, however, the beloved disciple is the Ephesian presbyter. This is great honour done to John Mark (see above, p. 512).

‡ "The artist who paints an ideal figure has a model, but what he aims to delineate is not *the* model." While the beloved disciple originally was an ideal figure (according to Bacon), partially drawn from Paul, the editor of the appendix identified him with the apostle.

§ An idealised figure of the historical John (Scholten, *op. cit.* 397 f.) is as adequate an explanation as perhaps any other; the title is a play upon the meaning of the name. Similarly we may feel the inwardness of Nikodemus and the Samaritan woman as types of Judaism uniting belief and the love of wonders, and the more susceptible paganism of the age.

view are the psychological difficulty of conceiving how an abstract figure could be put side by side with the other disciples, and the fact that, in the Jerusalem-scenes, Delff's hypothesis has considerable plausibility.

(*b*) The sisters of Jesus are ignored, but his brothers are introduced as different from his disciples (2^{12}) and sceptical of his claims (7^{1-10}), a practical illustration of 1^{11-13}. The coolness of the relations between them and the Logos-Christ is developed in the case of his mother, whose earthly relationship is carefully detached from the higher interests of the Logos-Christ on the only two occasions on which she is mentioned (2^4 19^{25-27}). The symbolic significance of the mother is evident in both places. Taken literally, the two passages may be held not only to conflict with historical probability, but to reveal an aloofness which it is psychologically difficult to associate with Jesus. The presence of Mary at the cross may be a deduction from Ac 1^{14}, and both scenes possibly reflect a dramatised variant of Mk 3^{31-35} etc., introduced for the purpose of differentiating the new religion from its parent stock. In the former, the Logos-Christ denies that he has anything in common with his family; in the latter he finally loosens the nearest tie of earthly relationship. It is only when the narratives are taken as symbolic rather than as a mere record of fact that their full meaning emerges.

§ 9. *The authorship.*—The fourth gospel makes no statement about its author. It ends with the remark, ταῦτα δὲ γέγραπται ἵνα πιστεύητε, but it is silent upon ὁ γράψας. The appendix, however, after describing the destiny of the μαθητὴς ὃν ἠγάπα ὁ Ἰησοῦς, adds in an editorial note (21^{24}): οὗτός ἐστιν ὁ μαθητὴς ὁ μαρτυρῶν περὶ τούτων καὶ ὁ γράψας ταῦτα. Unless the last four words are to be regarded as an interpolation (so, *e.g.*, von Soden), the beloved disciple, who only appears definitely in the closing days of Christ's life, is claimed not simply as the authority for the whole gospel (to which ταῦτα here refers), but as its author. But *quis custodiet custodes?* This claim is not made by himself;* it comes from the anonymous circle who endorse the gospel (καὶ οἴδαμεν ὅτι ἀληθὴς αὐτοῦ ἡ μαρτυρία ἐστίν), and who have added the two closing notes (21^{24-25}), both of which indicate that the gospel had been, or might be expected to be, criticised for its unique contents (so different, *e.g.*, from the synoptic tradition) and for its incompleteness. The latter criticism has been already met by anticipation in 20^{30-31}; the former is to be felt at 19^{35}, the only passage in the gospel which definitely connects the author with an eye-witness. Here, after the soldier has pierced the side of Jesus with a lance, causing blood and water to pour out of the wound, the narrative continues: *and he who saw it has borne witness* (καὶ ὁ ἑωρακὼς

* For attempts to preserve part of these verses for John, cp. Wetzel (*op. cit.* pp. 15 f.).

μεμαρτύρηκεν), *and his witness is true,—yea, he knows that he is telling the truth* (καὶ ἐκεῖνος οἶδεν ὅτι ἀληθῆ λέγει),—*that you also may believe.* Is ἐκεῖνος, in this enigmatic protest, a human authority or, by a strong asseveration (cp. 2 Co 11[11. 31]), the exalted Christ (so, *e.g.*, Dechent, *SK.*, 1899, 448 f.; Abbott, *EBi.* 1809; Zahn, *Kommentar*, 658 f.; Peake, *London Quart. Review*, 1905, 275; Forbes, Haussleiter's *Zwei Apost. Zeugen*, 26–28)? When the mystic or symbolic sense of αἷμα καὶ ὕδωρ is connected in any way with 1 Jn 5[6], the divine reference of ἐκεῖνος becomes rather more probable, since in 1 Jn. the pronoun always means the exalted Christ. Still, the connection is different here, and upon the whole ἐκεῖνος may be reasonably regarded as equivalent to ὁ ἑωρακὼς, the beloved disciple of 19[26]. This would imply (*a*) that the writer was or wished to be taken for (so, *e.g.* Renan, Jülicher, Loisy) the said eye-witness, or (*b*) that he appeals to this earlier authority in order to corroborate a statement which he anticipates will rouse suspicion (so, *e.g.*, Hilgenfeld, Weisse, Harnack, Weizsäcker, von Soden, Wendt, Pfleiderer, J. Réville, Calmes, Schmiedel, Wellhausen).

Physiologically, it is possible that water mixed with blood issued from some wheal or bleb on the surface of the body, which the lance pierced, "but blood and water from an internal source are a mystery" (Dr. C. Creighton, *EBi.* 960–961), or, as Origen called it, τὸ παράδοξον (*c. Cels.* ii. 36). The main point, however, is that the writer's religious interpretation of the phenomenon which he records is not anti-doketic (as in 1 Jn 5[6]),—the effusion of blood would have sufficed for that purpose,—but symbolical. The object of 19[31-37] is to clinch the proof that Jesus died as the true paschal Lamb, of which no bone was to be broken. This rounds off the isolated testimony of 1[29], and explains the symbolism of *the blood and water* as the evidence of spiritual life issuing from the death of the Christ; the effusion of blood signifies the removal of sins, the effusion of water the impartation of life eternal, and the collocation of both indicates that these are vitally connected in the work of Christ.

This would be confirmed if ὁ πιστεύων εἰς ἐμέ in 7[38] were taken with καὶ πινέτω of 7[37] (cp. Nestle, *ZNW.*, 1909, 323), and αὐτοῦ referred not to the individual believer but to the Christ (so, *e.g.*, Grill, 16; Loisy, Calmes, Forbes, Westcott), as was apparently the view of the Gallic Christians *c.* A.D. 570 (Eus. *H. E.* v. 1. 22) and possibly Cyprian amongst others.* The author makes

* All three points, Christ as the source of living water, believers not only as the recipients but transmitters of it, and the identification of it with the Spirit, are represented in the third ode of Solomon in the *Pistis Sophia*, an ode which (cp. Ryle and James, *The Psalms of Solomon*, pp. 157 f.: R. Harris, *The Odes and Psalms of Solomon*, 12–13) is tinged with Johannine rather than specifically gnostic colours, and is probably to be dated not later than the first half of the second century A.D.

Jesus refer to himself as αὐτοῦ, because the passage (see p. 33) is a prophetic quotation, with a proleptic allusion to the Spirit which was not to be poured out upon believers until Jesus was glorified ($7^{39} = 20^{22}$). On the other hand, when 7^{38} is read with ὁ πιστεύων εἰς ἐμέ as equivalent to the following αὐτοῦ, the conception of the believer as a source of spiritual blessing for others tallies with 20^{22-23}, especially if the μαθηταί of the latter scene are not restricted to the apostles.

19^{35} is therefore, as Blass warned critics (*SK.*, 1902, 128 f.), a foundation of sand upon which to build any critical theory of this gospel's origin, whether the verse should be relegated to the margin (*e*, fuld. om.) or not. Its use is to prove not the presence of an eye-witness, but the spiritual testimony or interpretation which is the essential aim of the writer. Furthermore, the verse is so closely connected with 21^{24}, that either the editor of the appendix must have moulded his words on the former passage, or inserted the latter (so, *e.g.*, Bacon, *Fourth Gospel in Research and Debate*, 171 f.) * as a paraphrase of 3 Jn ^{12} and 1 Jn $5^{6f.}$ The latter alternative is preferable. If $19^{34-35.\,37}$ are omitted (with the opening and un-Johannine ἐγένετο γὰρ ταῦτα of v.^{36}), the sense is clear: οὐ κατέαξαν αὐτοῦ τὰ σκέλη, ἵνα ἡ γραφὴ πληρωθῇ· ὀστοῦν οὐ συντριβήσεται αὐτοῦ (so, *e.g.*, Schwartz, Wellhausen, Heitmüller). The interpolation in vv.$^{34-35}$ tallies substantially with 21^{24}, the main difference being the substitution of ἐκεῖνος οἶδεν for οἴδαμεν. V.^{37}, with its un-Johannine ἑτέρα γραφή, points to the circle from which Apoc 1^{7} (cp. Mt 24^{30}) originated, though the quotation is differently applied (there eschatological, here historical). On the other hand, it must be allowed that the mere omission of v.^{35} (with καὶ ἐξῆλθεν εὐθὺς αἷμα καὶ ὕδωρ in ^{34}, and ἐγένετο γὰρ ταῦτα in ^{36}) gives an equally good sense, and at the same time avoids the necessity of regarding 20^{27} as another interpolation (or part of one).

Unless John the presbyter is brought in (cp. besides Harnack, etc., S. Eck in *Preuss. Jahrb.*, 1898, 25–45), the author of Jn 1–20 and the editor who revised it and added the

* According to Bacon, R. (the Ephesian editor) identified the nameless elder who composed the Fourth gospel and the epistles with the beloved disciple. It is too drastic to regard (so, *e.g.*, Schwartz and Bousset) the 'beloved disciple' passages as editorial insertions—an analysis which, among other results, would leave Judas with little else than the bag, in the original draft of the gospel. On the other hand, no theory of an apostolic *Grundschrift*, or even of a 'Johannine' source for narratives or logia, has yet been worked out with any approach to probability.

appendix are both unknown. The former, like the writer of Matthew, was one of the anonymous early Christian authors, probably of Jewish origin, who were content to sink their names in their great cause and subject. All we can discover is the general traits and tendencies of his mind, as these may be supposed to come out in his work. It is not a paradox to say that nothing in his pages necessarily implies, while several features practically forbid the conjecture that he was an eye-witness. "His mastery of midrashic method, especially that of a 'spiritualising' Alexandrian type, reminds us of an Apollos; his attitude towards Stoic conceptions and to some of the commonplaces of Greek philosophy recalls the venerable Ephesian teacher of Justin Martyr. All reasonable inferences of this kind have value in proportion as they help us to understand the author, his task and his times" (Bacon, *Fourth Gospel*, 464). It may be a convincing proof of the superiority of Christianity, that, "when the exquisite Greek word-science, the brilliant dialectic, the dramatic colouring, of the alluring life, the exalted death, the perfect self-sacrifice, of the Platonic Socrates had failed altogether to influence the masses of mankind, the religion of Jesus, springing from a despised unlettered people, triumphed over the world"; but, in view of writings like Hebrews, the writings of Luke, the epistle of Diognetus, the Apology of Aristides, and above all the Fourth gospel, it is incorrect to describe the religion of Jesus, in its initial approach to the ancient world, as "dressed in nothing that made it attractive to the cultured intellect." * The Fourth gospel represents the first serious attempt to re-state the primitive faith for some wider circles who were susceptible to Hellenic influences, and the author, in translating the gospel of Jesus for their benefit, shows himself a master not only in his selection of the matter he had to convey, but in his grasp of the language in which he had to reproduce his beliefs.

§ 10. *The appendix.*†—The epilogue or appendix (ch. 21)

* J. H. Shorthouse, *Literary Remains* (1905), p. 229.

† Special literature: Hoekstra (*TT.*, 1867, 407–424, 'het laatste Hoofdstuk van het vierde Evangelië'); Eberhardt, *Evang. Joh.* c. 21 (1897); Klöpper (*ZWT.*, 1899, 337–381); Zahn, *INT.* (§ 66); Wendt (pp. 248–253); J. Réville (305–320); Moffatt, *HNT.* 694 f.; Horn, *Abfassungszeit, Geschichtlichkeit, und Zweck von Ev. Joh Kap. 21* (1904); Bacon, *Fourth Gospel in Research and Debate* (1910), 190 f., 211 f. (due to revision at Rome).

describes a Galilean appearance of the risen Jesus to seven of his disciples, which falls into two parts. In the former (21^{1-14}), Jesus enables the disciples to secure, with unbroken net, an astonishing take of fish, and then provides them with a meal upon the beach. In the second part (21^{15-23}), which describes the conversation after the meal (cp. Merx, *PM.*, 1898, 154–160), Peter is restored to his vocation, while the destinies of Peter and the beloved disciple are contrasted. Finally, an editorial note (vv.$^{24-25}$) vouches for the beloved disciple as the authority and author of the gospel, and also apologises for its lack of completeness (cp. *Diat.* 2414–2416, and Lucretius, i. 410 f.). The naive hyperbole of the latter verse is quite consonant with contemporary rabbinism (see Bacher's *Agada d. Tannaiten*², i. 24 f., for a striking parallel from Jochanan b. Zakkai). The former opens up at a stroke the problem of the gospel's origin and authorship.

The true climax to the gospel is 20^{30-31}, which Tertullian (*adv. Prax.* 25) called its "clausula." Had the author originally meant to add the contents of 21, he would have transferred the "clausula" to a place after 21^{14} or $21^{23\ (24)}$ (Zahn), as indeed Dr. Rendel Harris (*New Testament Autographs*, pp. 14 f.) once proposed to do, on the ground that v.^{30} implies an insufficient amount of writing material (cp. 2 Jn ^{12}, 3 Jn ^{13}). After 20^{30-31} anything further is almost an anti-climax. The seven σημεῖα are complete. Jesus has appeared thrice after death. The disciples have all received their commission (not to baptize, cp. Mt 28^{19} above, p. 253, and *ERE.* ii. 380).

(*a*) Was the gospel edited posthumously, like Vergil's *Aeneid*, by some friend or friends of the author (*summatim emendata*)? On this hypothesis (Weiss, Reuss, Eberhardt, Bovon, etc.), the epilogue might be the work of Philip and Andrew (21^2 cp. $1^{40f.}$ 6^{51} $12^{30f.}$, so Haussleiter *), or of Andrew alone (Chastand). (*b*) Or, was the appendix added by John himself † as a deliberate

* Both Haussleiter and Horn, however, hold that the appendix was written during the lifetime and with the sanction of John, so that their views really approximate to (*b*). Kenyon (*Hdbk to Text. Crit. of NT*, pp. 27 f.) represents a popular opinion in concluding that the gospel, after being dictated by the apostle, "seems to have been finally issued by a Committee of the church of Ephesus."

† As a curiosity of criticism, one may record the hypothesis of P. F. Vigelius (*Hist. krit. Onderzoek naar den Schrijver von Joh. xxi.*, Leiden. 1871), that the epilogue, but not the gospel, came from the hand of John.

finalê to his gospel (so, *e.g.*, Luthardt, Godet, Westcott, Lightfoot, Plummer, Schanz, Becker, Drummond, Lepin, Sanday)? Or (*c*) was it added by the unknown and anonymous author of the gospel to a work which he had already finished (so, *e.g.*, Renan, Hilgenfeld, Thoma, Baljon, Jacobsen, Jülicher)? The view that it was not written by the author of the gospel is upon the whole more probable than any of these theories, even than the last. As the writer belonged to the "Johannine circle," and as he was composing an appendix to the gospel, his style naturally approximates to that of the work which he is editing, but, even within the brief space of the appendix, idiosyncrasies of language and style appear which are practically sufficient to indicate another hand:* *e.g.* δεξιός, ἐκτείνω χεῖρας, ἐκ τρίτου, ἐπιστρέφω, ἐξετάζω, ἰσχύω, τολμάω, τρίτον (adv.), οἱ ἀδελφοί, ὑπάγω with infinitive, παιδία for τεκνία, πρωία for πρωΐ, ἐγερθείς for ἀναστάς, and φέρειν for ἄγειν (v.[18]); ἐπὶ in v.[1] is different from the ἐπὶ of 6^{19-21} (cp. *Diat.* 2340–2342); φανερόω (vv.[1. 14]) is unusually employed to describe a resurrection appearance (cp. Mk $16^{12.\,14}$); the ἐαν after ὅστις in v.[25] also corresponds to the use in 1 Jn 3^{20} rather than to Jn 2^{5} 14^{13} 15^{16}, and the disciples are described in synoptic rather than Johannine style (Peter a fisherman, the sons of Zebedee). The date of the passage—if appreciably different from that of the gospel—must have been early enough to allow of its incorporation into the archetype of all existing texts (not before A.D. 180, Krenkel; not before A.D. 155, Erbes in *ZKG.*, 1901, 10–11, as unknown to Irenæus). Several of those who insist that it formed an integral part † of the gospel, however, use this conclusion in order to bring the whole work down pretty far into the second century (particularly Thoma and Jacobsen), and Keim dates its composition *c.* A.D. 160, previous to 2 P 1^{14}, in the age when the cult of John was rising in Asia Minor. Probably it is to be dated not long after the Fourth gospel itself, in the first half of the second century.

* So, *e.g.*, Baur, Schwegler (*NZ.* ii. 355 f.), Scholten, Keim, Klöpper, Pfleiderer, Chastand (*L'Apôtre Jean*, 98–104), J. Réville, Loisy, Weiss, J. Weiss, Bacon, Loofs, Schwartz, Schmiedel, Bruston (*Revue de Théol. et de Philos.*, 1906, 501 f.), Heitmüller, etc.

† Especially when its contents are interpreted allegorically as representations of the latter church and its experiences, as, *e.g.*, by Keim (vi. pp. 313–318) and Pfleiderer. Chastand (*L'Apôtre Jean*, pp. 98–104) regards it as the work of a later hand, but a fruit of the apostle's oral teaching: "Nous en faisons comme le codicille qui accompagne le testament de l'apôtre."

The appendix falls into three parts (21^{1-14} 21^{15-23} 21^{24-25}), which are more or less closely linked together.

(i.) The failure of the disciples to recognise Jesus, which comes in awkwardly after $20^{24f.}$, shows that originally the story of 21^{1-14} was the first * of a Galilean series of appearances. The abrupt and unmotived change of place, from Jerusalem to Galilee, suggests that the writer or editor desired to harmonise the two lines of tradition upon the resurrection-appearances of Jesus, but it is more easy to feel this motive than to trace its mode of operation.

Loofs (*die Auferstehungsberichte und ihr Wert*, pp. 31f.) regards 21^{1-14} as based originally on a pre-resurrection story, which has been misplaced and combined with a (non-Galilean) post-resurrection appearance to Peter (21^{15-19}; cp. Resch, *TU.* x. 4, pp. 47 f., 195 f.). The main theories of 21^{1-19}, however, associate it either (*a*) with the lost conclusion of Mark's gospel, or (*b*) with Lk 5^{1-11}. (*a*) Upon the former hypothesis, it is argued that the passage represents a more or less freely edited form of the lost ending to Mk.'s gospel (Rohrbach, pp. 52 f.; Harnack, *ACL.* ii. 1. 696 f., and *BNT.* i. 227 f.; Eberhardt, 81–83; Loisy; † von Dobschütz, *Probleme d. ap. Zeitalter*, 14 f.; H. Schmidt, *SK.*, 1907, 487), or, more probably, a variant of the same tradition (Wendt, Kirsopp Lake, pp. 143 f.; Heitmüller). If Mk.'s gospel was ever finished, it must have included a Galilean vision (16^7) in which Peter played a prominent (perhaps an exclusive) rôle; but even if this were equivalent (cp. Meltzer, *PM.*, 1902, 147–156) to 1 Co 15^5=Lk 24^{34}, it would not correspond with the narrative of Jn 21^{1-19} (where Peter is not the first or the only one to see the Lord, and where it is not the eleven disciples who are present). If Mk.'s original conclusion is to be felt anywhere, it is (see pp. 239 f.) in Mt 28 rather than in Jn 21 (so especially, against Rohrbach, Schmiedel, *EBi.* 4054–4055). (*b*) But possibly the story is based on the tradition of Lk 5^{1-11} (so many editors and critics, from Strauss and Weisse to Brandt, *Evang. Geschichte*, 401 f.; Klöpper, Pfleiderer, *Urc.* ii. 390; A. Meyer, Wellhausen, Forbes, etc.). The ordinary view of the Lucan story is to find a symbolic representation of Peter undertaking the mission

* The rehabilitation of Peter also is more tardy than might be expected, "One is inclined to sacrifice the historical accuracy of the writer of this appendix to the Fourth gospel, so that one may identify this meeting of Jesus and Peter with that mentioned in Luke's gospel (24^{34}). One may ask, would Peter unpardoned have been found in the apostolic company? Could the loving heart of Jesus have left him so long uncomforted? The incident loses much of its significance if placed at a later date and after another meeting with Jesus; surely the restoration to apostleship must have taken place at the first and not the second meeting" (Garvie, *Exp.*[7], July 1907, p. 18).

† Loisy (*Syn. Évang.* i. 444 f.) explains its presence here as due to Luke's deliberate omission of the Galilean appearances and at the same time to his desire to conserve the story on account of its symbolic value. He conserved it by using it not for the rehabilitation, but for the original call of Peter.

to the Gentiles only at the express command of Jesus (cp. Ac 10^{14}) and requiring Paul or the other apostles to assist him (5^{7}), while the broken net is supposed to imply the rupture between the Jewish and the Gentile Christians, and so forth (v.^{9}=Gal 2^{9}). Loisy, who recognises the improbability of a definite symbolism in details, agrees with Holtzmann and others that the unsuccessful night's fishing is "sans doute une allusion à l'insuccès de la prédiction apostolique auprès les Juifs"—a strange allusion in face of Ac $2^{41f.}$! The mission to the Gentiles, which shines through both Lk 5^{1-11} and Jn 21^{1-14} is, however, as unmistakable as the fact of some connection between the two stories or traditions, particularly when that of Jn 21^{1-14} is recognised (as, *e.g.*, by Loofs) to have originally represented a pre-resurrection incident which had no connection with Jn $21^{15f.}$. It is noticeable that Luke (5^{1-11}) substitutes for Mk 1^{16-20}=Mt 4^{18-22} a call which not only puts Peter first (before James and John), but makes a miraculous draught of fishes the occasion for a confession of sinfulness on the part of Peter which Jesus turns into an assurance of his apostolic vocation. This was probably the theme which suggested the tradition of the following story in $21^{15f.}$.

It is doubtful if even 21^{1-14} is a unity as it stands, though the analyses of its composite character have not yet reached any measure of agreement; cp. Soltau, who finds two strata in $21^{1-8.\ 11}$ and $21^{9.\ 12-14}$, H. Schmidt (*SK.*, 1907, 487–512), who traces the dual background in Lk 5^{4-11} and Lk $24^{41f.}$, and Völter (*Die Entstehung des Glaubens an die Auferstehung Jesu*, 1910, pp. 52) who detects the redactor's hand in $21^{6-8.\ 10-11}$ and the source in $21^{1-5.\ 9.\ 12a.\ 13.\ 12b}$.

(ii.) The rehabilitation of Peter, with the prediction of his death and of that of the beloved disciple (21^{15-23}), is a symbolic fragment which has no synoptic analogue,* but $21^{20f.}$ may be interpreted in the light of a synoptic logion.

The fact that the words in 21^{22} *If I choose that he should survive till I come*, are immediately followed by an allusion to authorship (v.^{24}) has suggested the hypothesis that they refer to the latter form of activity and influence. (*a*) Thus Irenæus took the words as a reference to the apocalypse, with its reiterated allusions to the Lord's coming; on this form of the theory (so variously Bengel, Ebrard, and Luthardt), John survived to see the Lord's coming at the fall of Jerusalem. (*b*) Strauss even less probably suggests that *μένειν* meant the permanence of John's teaching, which was to outlive the Petrine tradition.† This is the idea of 21^{24}, where the witness (*μαρτυρῶν*) is the permanent function fulfilled by the gospel once written (*γράψας*); the disciple, though dead, yet speaketh. It is just conceivable that the terms

* Schwartz's (*ZNW.*, 1910, 96 f.) theory that 21^{15-17} is a doublet to Mt $16^{17f.}$ sounds far-fetched.

† Schwartz (48 f.) fantastically refers *μένειν* in v.^{22} to the later legend of John lying incorruptible in the grave (cp. Corssen's ed. of the third century *Monarchian Prologues*, p. 102), and makes v.^{23} the later addition of a scribe who mistook it for a reference to the Parousia. The *ἀκολουθεῖν* of Peter is no proper antithesis to this, however, and the legend is not mentioned in the Leucian Acta.

might apply to him when still alive, though in this case we should have one authority being certificated by a lesser. But the natural impression made by 21[20f.] is that the beloved disciple has died. Jesus did *not* will that he should survive till the second coming.

The ordinary interpretation is that one object of the story was to remove an erroneous impression created by John's longevity. It is obvious that this would exclude the identification of the beloved disciple with John the son of Zebedee, if the early martyr-death of the latter is accepted as historical. If it is not, the figure of the beloved disciple may be (*a*) identified either with that John or with John the presbyter, or else (*b*) he may be regarded as the ideal Christian. When (*a*) is followed, those who regard ch. 21 as from a different hand may still take the beloved disciple of 1–20 as originally modelled on the apostle John; in which case ch. 21 betrays the conscious or unconscious confusion of the apostle with the presbyter. But it is even possible to interpret 21[20f.] in such a way as to permit its reference to John the apostle, in the light of his early martyrdom. The starting-point of this interpretation is the mysterious saying of Jesus preserved in Mk 9[1] = Mt 16[28] = Lk 9[27] that some (*τινες*) of the disciples (not simply of his contemporaries) would survive until he returned in messianic glory.* Whether Mt. has expanded eschatologically, and Lk. abbreviated, the original Marcan form (cp. 1 Co 4[20]; Resch, *Parallel-Texte*, iii. 156 f.), or whether Mt. is closer to the original, matters nothing for our present purpose. The Fourth evangelist has already generalised and spiritualised the saying (8[51-52]) in characteristic fashion; in 21[23] it is at once applied specifically to the beloved disciple and also cleared of popular misconceptions. What the writer means is that the beloved disciple did not stay where he was, but followed Jesus in his own way, *i.e.* that John outlived Peter, and, although he too died as a martyr, did not die in the same way as his fellow-disciple. Whatever was the original context of the saying (cp. Mk.'s *καὶ ἔλεγεν αὐτοῖς*), it follows in the synoptic tradition Christ's claim that the true disciple must take up his cross and follow the Lord (*ἀράτω τὸν σταυρὸν αὐτοῦ καὶ ἀκολουθείτω μοι*, Mk 8[34] = Mt 16[24] = Lk 9[23]). This connexion underlies the association of Peter's death on the cross and his following of Jesus in Jn 21[18-22], and also the suggestion in 21[20. 21-23] that, as in the case of the beloved disciple, there was a following which did not involve such a death and yet did not, on the other hand, imply survival till the return of Jesus. The beloved disciple did not suffer martyrdom on the cross, but he did taste of death before the Lord returned. The point of 21[20f.] therefore lies in the contrast between *ἀκολουθοῦντα* and *μένειν*. The beloved disciple also *follows* Jesus; he too goes forward to a martyr-death. Peter's question in v.[21] expresses curiosity about the particular form of that death. Is it to be the same as his own, or what? The reply in v.[22] is that whatever be the fate of the other disciple, his own

* It is improbable (i.) that this saying is to be connected (so, *e.g.*, O. Holtzmann) with Mk 10[39] = Mt 20[23], as if Jesus expected that some, including James and John, would share his martyrdom at Jerusalem, or (ii.) that it is to be read, in the light of Ac 7[55-56], along with the following transfiguration-story (Abbott, *Diat.* 2998, xxv.a), as if Peter, James, and John in their lifetime enjoyed the martyr's privilege of a vision of the heavenly Son of Man

duty and destiny are plain; σύ μοι ἀκολούθει. Of the other disciple, who is already following Jesus, it is said, ἐὰν αὐτὸν θέλω μένειν ἕως ἔρχομαι, τί πρὸς σέ; here μένειν ἕως ἔρχομαι means survival till the second coming of Jesus, but the fact that the words are spoken about one who was already following (*i.e.* in the pregnant and fateful sense of the term, on the way to martyrdom) shows that μένειν in this context denotes a Christian life which did not *follow*, a life which stayed where it was (cp. 11^{6}) without moving. "Even if I choose that he should not follow at all, but remain where he is, it is no concern of yours." The passage thus corrects the idea (21^{23} = Mk 9^{1}) that John's early martyrdom was less notable than that of Peter's or out of accord with the will and word of Jesus. I suggest this interpretation with some diffidence; but it seems to me the only way of fitting in the logion (as applied to John) to the early martyrdom-hypothesis.

(iii.) It is obvious, as Zahn admits, that v.[24] was not written by the author of the gospel. "The *we* includes the *I* [of v.[25] οἶμαι] and excludes the *he* [*i.e.* the μαθήτης of v.[24]]." Whether the *we* represents the Ephesian presbyters, or a local church, or the apostles (as in the legend of the Muratorian Canon), or a small group of apostles (Haussleiter), the whole of ch. 21, and not merely the imprimatur of vv.[24-25], was probably composed by the editor who wrote in their name. 21^{24-25} is a postscript, but it is closely connected with what precedes. The narrative could never have left off at 21^{23}, though it might have been rounded off with 21^{24}, v.[25] being subsequently added with a sort of rhetorical flourish to signalise the position of the book at the close of the gospel-canon. How apt a remark, for all its naive hyperbole, to be made by a scribe or editor as the finalê of the last scripture in the collection of evangelic narratives! But although more hands than one may have touched the gospel editorially, v.[25] in all likelihood came from the same pen as the preceding passage. The external evidence against the verse is of the slenderest; Dr. Gwynn, after an examination of the textual phenomena (*Hermathena*, viii. pp. 368–384), even pronounces it non-existent. Whether or not its "real service to the scholar is to illustrate the morbid disposition of editors and scribes towards a species of appendicitis," it seems to have formed part of the canonical text as early as that text can be verified. The atmosphere of 21^{24-25} is local patriotism and reverence felt by the Asia Minor communities for the memory of their distinguished head.* (V.[25] "seems an inflated version of 20^{30},"

* If this was John the apostle, he must have been martyred in Asia Minor, or after work there. This theory in any case renders the confusion between him and his namesake in Asia more probable. If the beloved disciple was John

Dods, *EGT.* i. p. 867. The same idea is more moderately put in 1 Mac 9^{22}.) An instance of this habit of adding notes to a volume is afforded by Ec $13^{9. (13)-14}$, although the spirit of that epilogue is corrective rather than confirmatory. Thoma, who attributes 21^{1-23} to the author of the gospel (*i.e.* the presbyter of 2 and 3 John), gives $21^{24. 25}$ to the author of 1 John as being a later insertion; while Chastand attributes ch. 21, like 7^{53}–8^{11} $1^{1-5. 13-18}$, to a pupil of John who wrote after his death. But when the whole chapter is taken as a unity, it falls into the age and spirit (Klöpper) of vv.$^{24. 25}$, and as the gospel could not have ended with 21^{23}, there is no reason to take vv.$^{24. 25}$ as notes added before publication (O. Holtzmann).

§ 11. *Traces in second-century literature.*—The earliest traces * of the Fourth gospel occur in (*a*) Papias, (*b*) Ignatius, (*c*) the Marcan appendix (16^{9-20}), and (*d*) Justin Martyr; the alleged traces in Polykarp, Barnabas, and Hermas are quite indecisive.

(*a*) Where Papias criticises, or rather reports the criticism of John the presbyter upon, Mk. for not writing his account of Jesus τάξει, he is tacitly contrasting the synoptic manner (see above, pp. 187 f.) with that of the Fourth gospel (so, *e.g.*, Zahn, Schwartz, Corssen in *ZNW.*, 1901, 212 f.). This is borne out by the fact that Irenæus quotes a fantastic exegesis of Jn 14^{2} from the presbyters, evidently the presbyters of Papias; this logion might have been current apart from the Fourth gospel (as has been recently argued by Kreyenbühl, i. 64 f.), but the probability is that the presbyters knew it in its present context and embroidered it with passages like Slav. En 61^{2} etc.

(*b*) The conceptions of Ignatius have been held to imply rather an acquaintance with the general ideas which reappear in special guise in the Fourth gospel and the First epistle of John, than any literary relationship.

---

the presbyter, the same motive operates, viz. the desire of the Asiatic Christians to uphold their chief against the Roman claims of Peter; but, again, this tendency is more explicable if the confusion between the two Johns was already accomplished, unless the present chapter is a deliberate attempt to promote it.

* On the general external evidence for the circulation and reception of the Fourth gospel in the churches of the second century, see Ezra Abbot's essay in the volume (1891) by A. Peabody, Lightfoot, and himself; E. A. Abbott (*EBi.* 1813 f.); Lepin, *L'Origine*, pp. 19 f.; Sanday, *Criticism of Fourth Gospel*, 236 f.; Zahn (*INT.* § 64); H. L. Jackson (*Fourth Gospel*, 38-61); Stanton (*GHD.* i. part 1), and Bacon's *Fourth Gospel in Research and Debate* (1910) 17 f.

This conclusion, argued especially by von der Goltz in 'Ignatius von Antiochien als Christ u. Theologe' (*TU.* xii. 3, pp. 118–144, 197–206), is shared by Abbott (*EBi.* 1829–1830), J. Réville, Harnack (*ACL.* ii. 1, pp. 396 f., 674), Schmiedel (*EBi.* 2547), and Bacon (*Fourth Gospel in Research and Debate*, 64). The dependence of Ignatius is argued, not only by Dietze (*SK.*, 1905, 563–603),* but by Lightfoot (*Biblical Essays*, pp. 81 f.), Zahn (*GK.* ii. 903 f.), Resch (pp. 11–12), Drummond, Loisy, and Sanday. The evidence for the latter view is "somewhat indeterminate" to Stanton (*GHD.* i. 19 f.), and highly probable, though short of certainty, to Inge (*NTA.* 81–83). In the Johannine circle of thought, and in the Ignatian epistles alike, the great contrasts of *life* and *death*, God and *the ruler of this world*, appear, together with a predilection for the same conceptions of γνῶσις and πίστις, ἀλήθεια and ἀγάπη. But it is the christocentric tendency, so strongly marked in Ephesians, which reappears characteristically in the Fourth gospel and the Ignatian epistles, where the entire value of Christianity is identified with the person of Christ, and where the communication of the divine knowledge and redemption to mankind depends essentially upon the historical reality of Jesus (cp. Jn 6^{53}), who really lived, really died, and really rose again (*Smyrn.* 3^1 etc., *Trall.* 9). The complete manhood of Jesus, from birth (1^{45} 6^{42} 7^{27} 8^{46}) to death (*Smyrn.* 9), is the historic guarantee of God's manifestation to men, and to deny this denotes the spirit of antichrist or blasphemy (*Smyrn.* 5^2). Apart from the σάρξ of Christ (*Trall.* 7^1), faith is vain. On the other hand, so far from impairing the divine uniqueness of Christ, this essential humanity only serves to bring out his deity, and Ignatius, while distinguishing him from the Father (*e.g. Magn.* 6^1 8^2), goes so far as to call him θεός, and to speak of αἷμα θεοῦ (*Eph.* 1^1).

As in Hebrews so in Ignatius and the Fourth gospel, the absolute and unique character of the Christian revelation does not exclude, but rather implies, that among the Hebrews this culminating epoch had been practically anticipated. The prophets of old (cp. *Magn.* 8^{1-2}) had been inspired by grace to speak and suffer; their life had been κατὰ Χριστόν, and consequently they had still a significance and authority for Christians (*Smyrn.* 7, cp. Jn 5^{39} 12^{41}). Even the Mosaic law, properly regarded, was a step towards faith in Christ (Jn 5^{46} 7^{19} etc., cp. *Smyrn.* 5^1).† But the latter, as final, supersedes all previous revelations.

In Ignatius, however (cp. Ro 8^2, *Magn.* 8^2), as opposed to the Fourth gospel, the Logos is associated, by a play on its etymological significance, with the self-utterance of God, connected with στόμα and γνώμη, and contrasted with the silence of the divine nature. Furthermore, the emphasis on

* The fact that Ignatius develops the Logos-idea on naive religious lines, and not on the semi-philosophic line of the Fourth gospel, must not be taken (as by Dietze, p. 587) as determining the character of the latter. The affinities of the Logos-idea in the Fourth gospel, with their undoubted echoes of Philonic speculation, simply show that the idea, as we see from Hebrews and John's apocalypse, was capable of varied application in the hands of varied writers.

† Jn 4^{22-24} and Ign. *Magn.* 10^3 both regard Judaism as the prelude to the universal and spiritual religion of the Christ.

the birth and death of Christ (*Eph.* 19^1) as the cardinal moments of his saving work suggests a development of the Pauline ideas in popular combination with the later synoptic tradition, rather than a reflection of the Johannine thought. Ignatius also reflects the Pauline conception in the emphasis which he attaches to the death of Christ as summing up the significance of his *παρουσία* (*Eph.* 7^2, *Smyrn.* 5^3, *Phil.* 8^2 9^2). In collocating the virgin-birth with this, he assimilates Paul's thought to the later synoptic tradition of Mt 1–2 and Lk 1–3. But, as in Paul the death of Jesus set free the redeeming powers of the risen life, so in Ignatius the death of Christ stands in relation to the semi-physical conception of *ζωή* as equivalent to *ἀφθαρσία*, the latter state of immortality being conditioned by that triumph over sin * and death which Jesus achieved by his sinless birth and redemptive death.

The thought and even the language of *Smyrn.* 1^2 are almost as Pauline as Johannine ($12^{20\text{-}24}$). The passage follows a sentence where Ignatius echoes Ro 1^4 and the synoptic tradition of the virgin-birth and baptism (Mt 3^{15}). He then proceeds to describe Christ as *truly nailed up* (*καθηλωμένον*) *for our sakes in the flesh ἐπὶ* Ποντίου Πιλάτου (1 Ti 6^{13}) *καὶ* Ἡρώδου *τετράρχου* . . . *that he might set up an ensign* (Is 5^{26} 49^{22}) *to all ages through the resurrection, for his saints and faithful ones* (cp. Eph 1^1), *whether among Jesus or among Gentiles, in one body of his church.* The underlying thought is no more than a popular adaptation of that in Eph $1^{20\text{f.}}$ $2^{14\text{f.}}$, where the death *ἐν σαρκὶ* and resurrection of Jesus are the divine means of uniting Jew and Gentile *in one body.* The influence of Paulinism, however, does not explain satisfactorily the resemblance between Ignatius and the Fourth gospel. As Ignatius uses, but inexactly cites, the epistles of Paul without any formal citation or reproduction of their contents in any given passage (cp. *e.g.* 1 Co 12^{12} with *Trall.* 11, *Smyrn.* 1), why may not he have dealt with the text of the Fourth gospel similarly? May not the sovereign freedom of a writer who uses earlier writings to help out his characteristic ideas, neglecting the form but conserving so much of the spirit as he found congenial, be held to explain the one problem as well as the other?

(*c*) As Mk $16^{9\text{-}20}$ (pp. 239 f.) presupposes the Fourth gospel (cp. *e.g.* Sanday, *Criticism of Fourth Gospel*, p. 244, and Bacon, *Fourth Gospel in Research and Debate*, 213 f.), this dates the latter, or, at any rate, 1–20 (Bacon), prior to the middle of the second century.

(*d*) Justin Martyr: cp. Schwegler (*NZ.* i. 216 f., 359 f.), Hilgenfeld (*ZWT.*, 1879, 492 f., J.'s relation to Paul and Fourth gospel), Bousset, *Die Evgliencitate Justins der Märtyrers* (1890), and Zahn, *GK.* i. 463 f.

The only question with regard to Justin is whether he attributed the gospel to John the apostle, as he did the apocalypse. The gospel was certainly in circulation when he wrote, and therefore it is probable that echoes are to be heard

* A point at which the affinities of Ignatius with 1 John are noticeable.

in places like *Apol.* i. 61 (=Jn 3^{3-5}) and *Dial.* 88 (=Jn $1^{20.23}$ though Ac 13^{25} is as probable a source), though not in *Apol.* 1^{35} (=Jn 19^{13}, ἐκάθισεν misunderstood as in *Gospel of Peter*).*

The independent character of Justin's Logos-doctrine, and the scantiness of any definite allusions in his writings to the Fourth gospel, render it highly probable that, like Ignatius, he did not assign it any authoritative position as an apostolic or Johannine work,—it is doubtful if he even ranked it among the ἀπομνημονεύματα τῶν ἀποστόλων,—but the evidence, such as it is, indicates that it was known to him. This conclusion, which is practically that arrived at by Keim, Thoma, Hilgenfeld, Harnack, J. Réville, Kreyenbühl, Loisy, and Bousset, does not go so far as that of scholars like Ezra Abbot (*Authorship of Fourth Gospel*, 20 f.), Resch (*Paralleltexte zu Joh.* 17 f.), and Drummond (pp. 86–162), who think that Justin believed in the Johannine authorship, but it is an advance upon the older attitude of scepticism which could not find any secure trace of the Fourth gospel in Justin at all, and much more upon the view of those who argued that Justin represented a stage of Logos-speculation prior to the Fourth gospel.

The inferences from such uses of the Fourth gospel are inconclusive, and even unfavourable (see below), so far as the Johannine authorship is concerned, but they converge upon a proof that it was in circulation from the second decade onwards of the second century in Asia Minor at least; the Johannine teaching and the Johannine epistles (with the apocalypse), whose existence is verified for that period, are not sufficient to account by themselves for the phenomena of the so-called "echoes" of the Fourth gospel, *e.g.* in Papias, Ignatius, and Justin. They do not suggest that the gospel was reckoned as the work of John the apostle, but they are sufficient to prove its diffusion as early as the first quarter of the second century.

§ 11. *The date.*—The various dates to which the gospel has been assigned cover a period of about one hundred years. It has been placed between 70 and 85 (Wittichen, Alford, Reithmayr, Bleek), between 80 and 90 (Ewald, Godet, Bisping, Westcott, Calmes, Zahn), between 90 and 100 (Mangenot, Batiffol, B. Weiss, Camerlynck=85–95), *c.* A.D. 100 (Lightfoot, Weizsäcker, Reynolds, Harnack=after 95, Cornely, Lepin=before 100), between 100 and 110 (Renan, Schenkel), in 100–125 (O. Holtzmann, J. Réville, Jülicher, Loisy), in 130–140 (Hilgenfeld, Keim, Thoma, Lützelberger, A. Réville), in 140–155

* Both the *Gospel of Peter* and Justin apparently go back to the *Acta Pilati* at this point. It is superfluous to assume a misreading of the Fourth gospel (cp. *DCG.* i. 678, ii. 758).

(Bretschneider = *c.* 150, Schwegler, Zeller, Volkmar, Taylor, Pfleiderer, van Manen, Kreyenbühl, Schmiedel, Schwartz = *c.* 150), and in 160–170 (Baur, Scholten, Bruno Bauer). Recent criticism, however, has lopped off several branches on both sides. It is now recognised generally that the use of the gospel in the circles of Valentinian gnosis* rules out any date after *c.* 130; again, if Justin, Ignatius, and Papias in all likelihood were acquainted with it, this excludes any *terminus ad quem* for its composition much later than A.D. 110. The *terminus a quo*, on the other hand, is determined approximately by the date of the synoptic gospels, all of which, as we have already seen, were probably known to the writer.

(*a*) One question has indeed been raised which would leave a later date open. Does 5^{43} (ἐὰν ἄλλος ἔλθῃ ἐν τῷ ὀνόματι τῷ ἰδίῳ, ἐκεῖνον λήμψεσθε) allude to the movement headed by Bar Kochba, the pseudo-messiah, under Hadrian? This interpretation, which has been urged especially by Hilgenfeld (*Einl.* 738 f.), Erbes, Pfleiderer, and Schmiedel (*EBi.* 2551), would prevent the composition of the gospel from being earlier than A.D. 135, unless with Wellhausen we regard the saying as an interpolation (see above, p. 37)—much as the allusion in the *Politics* (v. 10. 16) to Philip's murder proves that Aristotle wrote this passage or the entire treatise after 336 B.C. The reference is not to any historical personality, however, but to the belief (cp. 2 Th 2) that antichrist would arise out of Judaism (so, *e.g.*, Bousset and Loisy). (*b*) Upon the opposite side, the dependence of the gospel upon the synoptic writers has been challenged in favour of a much earlier date. Repeated attempts have been made, mainly on the ground of 5^{2} (ἔστιν κτλ., on which Bengel comments, *scripsit Johannes ante uastationem urbis*), to put John prior to A.D. 70 (*c.* 70, Resch, Michaelis), and, indeed, to the synoptic gospels, which are supposed to correct and amplify its traditions. See especially the recent essays (after Lampe, Hahneberg, J. T. Beck, and Cassel) of Wüttig, *Das Joh. Evglm und seine Abfassungszeit*, 1897 (reviewed by H. A. A. Kennedy, *Crit. Rev.*, 1897, 254–356; Blass, *Philol. Gospels*, 241 f., and Holtzmann, *TLZ.*, 1897, 379 f.); W. Küppers, *neue Untersuchungen über den Quellenwert der vier Evglien*, 1902; Wilms, *der Ursprung des Joh. Evglms*, 1904, and H. Gebhardt, *die Abfassungszeit des Johannes Evglms*, 1906, with Halcombe's independent theory in *The Historic Relation of the Gospels, An*

* If the *Exegetica* of Basilides based on the Fourth gospel, this would more than corroborate a date earlier than Hadrian; but possibly (cp. Windisch in *ZNW.*, 1906, 236–246) Basilides commented on an edition of Luke (see above, p. 187). The anti-gnostic aim is carried to unreal extremes by Schwartz, who regards some of the editorial additions as anti-Valentinian; *e.g.* 8^{57} (2^{20}, see above, p. 536) in order to controvert their thirty (cp. Lk 3^{23}) æons, and the festal journeys in order to upset their one-year ministry of Jesus, with the omission of Simon the Cyrenian on account of the gnostic, doketic abuse of this figure in the passion-story.

Essay toward re-establishing Tertullian's account (1891), and in *ET.* iv. pp. 77 f., 215 f., 268 f., 313 f., 404 f., v. 224 f. The hypothesis takes various forms. Thus W. Küppers puts Mk. last (64 f.) and Lk. (pp. 52–57) immediately after John; while Halcombe puts Lk. last and Mk. second. But it is almost superfluous to add that, in any form, the theory will not bear examination. The use of the present tense (along with the past, cp. 4^5 11^8 18^1) is no evidence for the contemporary existence of a building or institution, as Hebrews and Josephus are sufficient to prove; the absence of any allusion in the Fourth gospel[1] to the fall of Jerusalem is no serious plea against its composition after A.D. 70; the external evidence of tradition (cp. Wright in *ET.* iv. 358 f.) upon the order of the gospels is neither unanimous nor of primary importance (see above, pp. 14–16); and, finally, the order of the synoptic gospels, necessitated by this theory, is absolutely impossible (cp. Wright in *ET.* iv. 497–501, v. 126 f., 168 f.).

(B) *A JOHANNINE TRACT (1 JOHN)*.[2]

LITERATURE.—(*a*) Editions—(i.) (of three 'Johannine' epistles):—Grotius (1550); Calvin (1565); Aeg Hunnius (1566); Calovius (1650); W. Whiston (1719); Zachariae (1776); S. F. N. Morus (1786); S. G. Lange (1797); H. E. G. Paulus (1829); de Wette (1837 f.); Jachmann (1838); Lücke[3] (1840; third ed., Bertheau, 1856)*; J. E. F. Sanders (Elberfeld, 1851); G. K. Mayer (1851); Düsterdieck (Göttingen, 1856); C. Wordsworth (London, 1860); Ewald, *Die Joh. Briefe übersetzt und erklärt* (Göttingen, 1861–2); Morgan (Edin. 1865); B. Brückner (— de Wette[5], 1867); F. D. Maurice (1867); Bisping (1874); Reuss (1878); Huther (— Meyer[4], 1880; Eng. tr. 1882); Alexander (*Speaker's Comm.* 1881)*; Pope (Schaff's *Comm.* 1883); Braune (— Lange[3], 1885; Eng. tr. 1887); C. A. Wolf[2] (1885); Plummer (*CGT.* 1886); B. F. Westcott[3] (1892)*; Luthardt[2] (— Zöckler, 1895); B. Weiss (— Meyer[6], 1900)*; W. H. Bennett (*CB.* n. d.); J. E. Belser (1906); Baumgarten (*SNT.*[2] 1907); H. P. Forbes (*Intern. Hdbks to NT*, iv. 1907); Holtzmann-Bauer* (*HC.*[3] 1908); D. Smith (*EGT.* 1910); A. Ramsay (*Westminster NT*, 1910). (ii.) (of '1 John' alone):—John Cotton (*A Practical Commentary*, London, 1655); C. Rickli (1828); Neander (1851; Eng. tr., Conant, New York, 1853); E. Haupt (1869, Eng. tr. 1879); Rothe (1878, Eng. tr. in *ET.* iii.–v.)*; Lias (1887); C. Watson (1891, second ed. 1909).

(*b*) Studies—(i.) of 1 Jn.:—Oporinus, *Paraenesis Joannis ad primos Christianos*, etc. (Göttingen, 1741); J. C. F. Löffler (*Epistola prima Joh.*

---

[1] Written in Ephesus (Gebhardt) or in Jerusalem (Wüttig, Wilms, Küppers, Halcombe). Dräseke (*NKZ.*, 1898, 139–155: 'das Joh-Evglm bei Celsus'), who agreed with Delff that the author was the priestly John of Jerusalem, and that Celsus knew the Fourth gospel minus $6^{1-29. 58}$, agreed with Wüttig in dating the original prior to A.D. 70.

[2] The so-called 'epistles of John,' especially the first, are discussed in most monographs on the Fourth gospel (see above, pp. 516 f.) and often edited in the special commentaries on the 'Catholic epistles' (see p. 318).

gnosticos impugnare negatur, 1784); C. F. Wunder (*Utrum prima epistola Joh. cœtui e Iudæis et judæo-Christianis mixto scripta est*, 1799); C. C. Flatt (*De Antichristis et pseudo-prophetis in epist. Joh.*, Tübingen, 1809); M. Weber (*Authentia epist. primæ Ioannis vindicata*, Halle, 1823); F. H. Kern (*De epistolæ Joh. consilio*, Tübingen, 1830); Schlagenhaufen's, *Étude sur la Ie Jean* (1854); D. Erdmann (*Primæ Johannis epistolæ argumentum, nexus et consilium*, Berlin, 1855); C. E. Luthardt (*De primæ Ioannis epistolæ compositione*, 1860); Stricker's *Introd. analytique* (Strassburg, 1862); Joh. Riemms (*De Beteekenis van den ersten Brief van Joh. in het historisch-kritisch Onderzoek naar den Oorsprung van het Vierde Evangelie*, Utrecht, 1869: epistle and gospel by apostle); J. Stockmeyer (*Die Structur des ersten Joh. Briefes*, Basle, 1873); Holtzmann* in *JPT.* (1881) 690 f., (1882) 128 f., 136 f., 460 f.; E. Mangenot (Vigoroux' *DB.* ii. 1191–1291); Karl, *Johann. Studien I* (1898)*; Wohlenberg (*NKZ.*, 1902, 233 f., 632 f., 'Glossen zum ersten Johannisbrief'); M. Goguel, *La notion Johannique de l'Esprit*, 1902 (pp. 147–153, 'sur la théologie de la première épître'); Wurm, *Die Irrlehrer im ersten Johannisbrief* (1904, in 'Biblische Studien,' viii.); G. G. Findlay (*Fellowship in the Life Eternal*, 1909, 59 f.)*; R. Law, *The Tests of Life*[2] (1909). (ii.) of all three:—Holtzmann (*BL.* iii. 342–352); Sabatier (*ESR.* vii. 177 f.); Henle, *Der Evglist Joh. und die Antichristen seiner zeit* (1884); Farrar, *Early Days of Christianity* (ch. xxxi. f.); Cox, *Private Letters of St. Paul and St. John* (1887); Gloag, *Introd. to Cath. Epp.* (1887), 264–350; Cone, *The Gospel and its earliest Interpret.* (1893) 320–327; S. D. F. Salmond (*DB.* ii. 728–742); McGiffert (*AA.* 617 f.); Bartlet (*AA.* 418 f.); Pfleiderer (*Urc.* ii. 390 f., 441 f.); Moffatt (*HNT.* 534 f.); G. H Gilbert, *The First Interpreters of Jesus* (1901, 301–332); Clemen (*ZNW.*, 1905, 271–281); von Soden (*INT.* 374 f.); Schmiedel (*EBi.* 2556–2562 and *Evang. Briefe u. Offenbarung des Johannes*, 1906, Eng. tr. 1908); A. V. Green, *Ephesian Canonical Writings* (1910, 128–163).

§ 1. *Structure and outline.*—Special literature: Erdmann (*op. cit.* pp. 6–45), Haupt (*op. cit.* 348 f.), Wiesinger (*SK.*, 1899, 575 f.), Häring (*ThA.* 171–200), Westcott and Hort (*Exp.*[7] iii. 481–493).

This encyclica or pastoral manifesto was written neither at the request of its readers nor in reply to any communication on their part. What moved the author (1^4) to compose it was anxiety about the effects produced on the church by certain contemporary phases of semi-gnostic teaching. The early connection of the document with the Fourth gospel suggests that the church may have been that of Asia Minor, in the first instance, but the absence of any local or individual traits renders even that a matter of inference. In any case, the author plainly meant his words to have a wider range. His trait or manifesto, which is thrown into a vague epistolary form (1^4 $2^{1. 7-8. 12-14. 26}$

5^{18}), is a 'catholic' homily,* in the original sense of the term. "Substitute the word 'say' for 'write' . . . and one might imagine the whole discourse delivered in speech to the assembled church" (Findlay, 59). "Non uidetur peregre misisse, sed coram impertiisse auditoribus" (Bengel).

The plan of it is unstudied and unpremeditated; it resembles a series of meditations or variations on one or two simple themes rather than a carefully constructed melody; and little success has attended the attempts to analyse it into a double (*God is Light, God is Love*: Plummer; 1^{5}–2^{27} 2^{28}–5^{5}: Findlay),† triple (1^{1}–2^{11} 2^{12}–4^{6} 4^{7}–5^{21}: Ewald; *God is Light, God is Righteous, God is Love*: Farrar),‡ fourfold (1^{5}–2^{11} $2^{12\text{-}28}$ 2^{29}–3^{22} 3^{23}–5^{17}: Huther), or fivefold (1^{5}–2^{11} $2^{12\text{-}27}$ 2^{28}–3^{24a} 3^{24b}–4^{21} $5^{1\text{-}21}$: Hofmann) arrangement.§ After defining the Christian κοινωνία which forms his subject ($1^{1f.}$), the author proceeds to outline its conditions (1^{5}–2^{17}) under the category of an antithesis between light and darkness. The first of these is a due sense of sin (cp. Karl, *op. cit.* 97 f.), leading to a sense of forgiveness through Jesus Christ. The second is obedience to the supreme law of brotherly love (cp. Ignat. *Smyrn.* 6). Unless these conditions are fulfilled, a fatal darkness falls upon the soul. Hence the writer passes to the dangers of κοινωνία ($2^{18\text{-}29}$), under the further category of an antithesis between truth and falsehood; the pressing peril is a recent heretical view of Christ's person which threatens the existence of any κοινωνία with God or man. He then develops the characteristics of the κοινωνία ($3^{1\text{-}12}$) as sinlessness and brotherly love, under the category of an antithesis between God's children (cp. 2^{29} *born of him*) and the devil's children. This mutual love bulks so largely in his mind that he enlarges on three of its elements, viz., confidence towards God ($3^{18\text{-}24}$), moral discernment ($4^{1\text{-}6}$), and assurance of union with the God of love ($4^{7\text{-}21}$), all these being bound up with a true faith in Jesus

* This was seen long ago by Heidegger and Bengel, amongst others, and is now generally accepted.

† Düsterdieck and Alford (*God is Light*, 1^{5}–2^{28}; *God is Righteous*, 2^{29}–5^{5}).

‡ De Wette (1^{5}–2^{28} 2^{29}–4^{6} 4^{7}–5^{21}), Hort (1^{1}–2^{17} 2^{18}–3^{24} 4^{1}–5^{21}), Erdmann (1^{5}–2^{14} 2^{15}–3^{18} 3^{19}–5^{12}), Haupt (1^{5}–2^{17} 2^{18}–5^{5} $5^{6\text{-}12}$), F. H. Krüger in *Revue Chrétienne*, 1895, 27 f., 100 f. (1^{5}–2^{17} 2^{18}–4^{6} 4^{7}–5^{12}), Pfleiderer (1^{5}–2^{29} $3^{1\text{-}24}$ 4^{1}–5^{13}), etc. Bengel and Sander divide it artificially on a trinitarian plan.

§ "Like the doublings of the Mæander near which he lived, the progress of the apostle at times looks more like retrogression than advance; but the progress is unmistakable, when the whole field is surveyed" (Plummer).

Christ (5^{1-12}). A brief epilogue, which is for tne most part (cp. Klöpper, *ZWT.*, 1900, 585 f.) a resumé of the ideas already discussed, closes the homily (5^{13-21}), with a reiteration of eternal life as experienced by the Christian within 'the wide world and all her fading sweets.' The postscript (after 5^{13}=Jn 20^{31}) specially, however, notes the danger of lapsing and the treatment of the *lapsi* (cp. He $6^{4f.}$).

A closer examination of the context often reveals a subtle connection, as in the case of James (though for different reasons), between paragraphs or even cycles of thought which at first sight appear unlinked. Thus the thought of the world *passing away* (in 2^{17}) suggests the following sentences ($2^{18f.}$) upon the nearness of the Parousia; the signs of the latter are carefully noted, in order to reassure and warn believers, and its moral demands are emphasised (2^{28}–3^{3}). Inside this paragraph,* even the apparently abrupt mention of the *χρίσμα* has its place (2^{20}). The heretical *ἀντιχρίστοι*, it is implied, have no *χρίσμα* from God; Christians have (note the emphasis on *ὑμεῖς*), owing to their union with the true Χρίστος. Again, the genetic relation of $3^{4f.}$ to what precedes becomes evident in the light of the fact that the norm of Christian purity (3^{3}) is the keeping of the divine commandments, or conduct like Christ's on earth (3^{3}=2^{4-6}), so that the gnostic breach of this law not only puts a man out of all touch with Christ ($3^{6f.}$), but defeats the very end of Christ's work *i.e.* the abolition of sin and its effects (3^{8}). 3^{7-10} thus resumes and expands the thought of 2^{29}, the gnostic being shown to be out of touch with the righteous God, partly because he will not share the brotherly love which is the expression of that righteousness, and partly because his claims to sinlessness render God's righteous (1^{9}) forgiveness superfluous. Similarly, the mention of the Spirit in 3^{24} opens out naturally into a discussion of the decisive test to be applied to the false claims of the heretics to spiritual powers and gifts ($4^{1f.}$); and, as this test of the genuine Spirit is the confession of Jesus Christ as really human and incarnate, the writer, on returning (in $4^{7f.}$) to his cardinal idea of brotherly love, expresses it in the light of the incarnate Son (4^{9}), whose mission furnishes at once the proof of God's love and the example as well as the energy of ours ($4^{10f.}$). The same idea of Christ's real humanity as essential to faith's being and well-being is worked out in the succeeding section (5^{1-12}), while the mention of eternal life (5^{11-12}) leads to a recapitulation (5^{13-21}) of the main ideas of the epistle under this special category.

5^{7-8} reads like a later gloss (so Scholten, Baljon, pp. 249 f.); but there is not the textual evidence for its deletion that is available for the adjacent Comma Johanneum of the three witnesses. An attempt has been made by K. Künstle (*Das Comma Johanneum*, 1905) to locate the origin of this

---

* For an attempt to prove, on the basis of 2^{28}–3^{12}, that paraphrastic marginal glosses have entered the writing and so produced the repeated phenomena of abrupt transition, cp. von Dobschütz (*ZNW.*, 1907, 1–8). Cludius (*Uransichten des Christentums*, Altona, 1808) had already conjectured that a gnostic editor must have worked over the Jewish Christian nucleus of the document—a creeping estimate of the tract.

notorious interpolation in Spain during the first half of the fourth century, and to find the earliest trace of it in Priscillian's *Liber Apologeticus* (A.D. 380), where it occurs in an expanded, heretical form (with *in Christo Jesu*). Künstle's theory, however, has not won unanimous assent;* cp. Jülicher's review in *GGA.*, 1905, 930–935; Mangenot (*Le Comma Johanneum*, 1907); and Babut (*Priscillien et le Priscillianisme*, 1909, pp. 267 f.). The probability is that the Comma was prior to Priscillian, wherever it may have originated.

§ 2. *Object.*—The polemic is directed against some contemporary phases of a dualistic gnosticism, which developed theoretically into docetic views of Christ's person (2^{22} 4^{2} etc.) and practically into libertinism (2^{4} etc.). The former aspect marked the idealism or ultra-spiritualism of teachers like Cerinthus, who held that the divine Spirit or heavenly æon (= Christ) only entered Jesus at his baptism and left him before his passion and death, a theory which amounted to a denial of the identity of Jesus and Christ the Son of God. Hence the emphasis in 5^{20}, as opposed to the gnostic idea that the real God was too spiritual to touch human flesh or become incarnate. Hence, too, the stress laid on the blood. The denial of the virgin-birth, which also formed part of the system of Cerinthus, had been met by anticipation in the stories of Mt. and Lk., which pushed back the reception of the Spirit from the baptism to the birth; the Johannine school, on the other hand, preferred to answer this heresy by developing the theory of the Logos, with its implicate of pre-existence. Ignatius combines both.

On its practical side, this docetic christology produced a set of gnostic *illuminati*, whose watchword was *I know him* (2^{4}, cp. Tit 1^{16}, Apoc 2^{24}). The superior theosophic insight to which they laid claim led naturally to a sense of pride in themselves as the *élite* of Christendom, which fostered an unbrotherly contempt for the unenlightened members of the church. The writer retorts that this is not a true enlightenment (2^{9}). He is equally unsparing upon the other feature of this docetic teaching, viz., its tendency to the antinomianism which besets all perfectionist claims (note the catchwords, *we have no sin*, *we have not sinned*, cited in $1^{8.\ 10}$). An indifference to the flesh and to material vices was the outcome of an overstrained spiritualism. To this lowered ethical demand (4^{5}) the writer bluntly attributes the popularity of these errorists, while their perfectionist views rendered the atoning death of Jesus superfluous. In fact, this erroneous view

* On the general question, see Gregory's article in *AJT.* xi. 131–138.

of the death of Jesus involves, according to the homily, three cardinal flaws: (*a*) an inadequate conception of Jesus as the Christ, (*b*) an antinomian attitude towards sin, and (*c*) an inability to love one another (2^{7-11} $3^{10b-18.\ 23}$ 4^{7}–5^{3}) truly, since genuine brotherly love among Christians must be the outcome of God's redeeming love as manifested in the person and work of Jesus Christ.

The author's method of polemic is to present a positive view of (*a*) the historic character and continuity of revelation in the church (1^{1-3} $2^{13-14.\ 24}$ 3^{5-8} 4^{14} $5^{6.\ 11.\ 20}$), a view which, so far from being an innovation (like gnostic ideas), is a recall to the basis of the Christian gospel already familiar ($2^{7.\ 18}$) to the readers. In the historical Jesus, the Christ of God, the churches possess a revelation of God and life which is absolute, and at all costs this must be adhered to (cp. Denney, *The Death of Christ*, 1902, 269–281, *Jesus and the Gospel*, 1908, 83 f.). (*b*) The second line of defence is the adequacy and finality of the Christian experience, which rests upon this correct historical estimate of Jesus as the Christ. Such is the true γνῶσις ($2^{20.\ 27}$ 4^{2}), an assurance of the truth which is mediated by a strict ethical obedience to Christianity as the law of God (3^{22-23} 5^{2} 2^{3-4}), *i.e.* above all by the exercise of a brotherly love, which is more than theoretical, to the members of the Christian community.

The evident care and caution displayed by the writer in rejecting these semi-gnostic views is thrown into relief by the fact that he and his fellow-Christians were themselves breathing and enjoying an atmosphere of such mystical conceptions. Christianity involves the historical Jesus, but none the less is it a γνῶσις ($2^{20.\ 27}$ $3^{6f.}$ 4^{7} etc.). The gnostics held that a spiritual seed was implanted in man, as the germ of his higher development into the divine life (Iren. *adv. haer.* i. 6. 4, on the Valentinian idea that οὐ πρᾶξις εἰς πλήρωμα εἰσάγει, ἀλλὰ τὸ σπέρμα τὸ ἐκεῖθεν νήπιον ἐκπεμπόμενον, ἐνθάδε δὲ τελειούμενον, and Tert. *de anima*, 11, [hæretici] nescio quod spiritale semen infulciunt animæ). The writer takes over this idea for his own purposes. But also, *e.g.*, in 3^{1} (note the emphatic ἡμῖν) especially, a side-reference to Jewish rivalry lies embedded. Contemporary Jews made exactly the same claim on their own behalf (cp. R. Akiba's saying in Aboth iii. 22, חביבין ישראל שנקרא בנים למקום חבה יתרה נודעת להם שנקראו בנים למקום). There is further an implicit contrast here to the Philonic idea that "even if as yet we are not fit to be reckoned θεοῦ παῖδες, still we may be παῖδες of his image (ἀειδοῦς εἰκόνος), the most sacred Logos; θεοῦ γὰρ εἰκὼν λόγος ὁ πρεσβύτατος" (*de confus. ling.* 28). Another phrase in the homily (5^{19} καὶ ὁ κόσμος ὅλος ἐν τῷ πονηρῷ κεῖται) is illustrated by the tradition in Baba bathra, 16a, where Eliezer ben Hyrkanus, who took exception to Job 9^{24a} (*the earth is given into the hand of the wicked*) as blasphemy, s corrected by Joshua ben Chananja. The latter rabbi points out that Job had Satan in view when he uttered these words. For instances of the Palestinian idioms underlying the Greek of the homily, cp. Schlatter in *BFT.* vi. 4. 144–151. The errorists, however, are not to be regarded as simply Judaistic (so recently Wurm and Belser, partly Clemen). The author's definition of sin as *ἀνομία* springs from his conception of Christianity as the divine *νόμος*, and the traces of a docetic movement (which is never connected with Judaism) are too plain to be explained away (cp. Hoennicke, *JC.* 137 f.); they require the incipient phases of a movement like that headed by Cerinthus, not simply a Jewish Christian retrogression. Behind the language we hear vibrations of the gnostic tendencies which set up a dual personality in the historical human Jesus and the divine Christ, the latter descending upon Jesus only at the baptism and withdrawing from him ere the crucifixion. It is plain that some elements of this docetism, such as Cerinthus represented,* were present in the situation presupposed by this homily, whereas the errorists controverted, *e.g.*, in Apoc 2–3, show no definitely christological traits. We can also catch echoes of such gnostic speculations as that the divine Being must include *σκοτία* as well as *φῶς* (1^{8}), that participation in cults and mysteries is essential to moral purification (1^{7}), that only the initiated and *illuminati* can be redeemed (2^{2}), and that the rank and file of believers possessed *πίστις* but not *γνῶσις* (2^{20-21}). Traces of specifically antinomian gnosticism are obvious in the errorists who lay claim to the 'knowledge of God' (2^{4}) apart from a good moral life (cp. *Clem. Recogn.* ii. 22, qui deum se nosse profitentur; Clem. Alex. *Strom.* iii. 4. 31, *τοῖς ἀδίκοις καὶ ἀκρατέσι καὶ πλεονέκταις καὶ μοιχοῖς τὰ αὐτὰ πράσσοντες θεὸν ἐγνωκέναι μόνοι λέγουσιν*). The later Valentinians, according to Irenæus (*adv. Haer.* i. 6. 2), held that while *ἀγαθὴ πρᾶξις* was an essential of salvation for the catholic *ψύχικοι*, they themselves *μὴ διὰ πράξεως, ἀλλὰ διὰ τὸ φύσει πνευματικοὺς εἶναι πάντῃ τε καὶ πάντως σωθήσεσθαι.*

The sort of docetic fantasy that was beginning to play round the evangelic tradition may be illustrated from the Leucian Acts of John, where Jesus appears to John on the Mount of Olives during the crucifixion, saying, "John, to the multitude down there in Jerusalem I am being crucified, and pierced with lances and reeds, and drinking gall and vinegar; but unto thee am I speaking, and do thou hearken to what I say" (xii.). Similarly John recounts how (vii.) "sometimes, desiring to grasp him, I came upon a material, solid body, while at other times, when I handled him (*ψηλαφῶντος*, cp. 1 Jn 1^{1}), the substance was immaterial, bodiless, and as if it did not exist."

The agents of this gnosticising propaganda had evidently been itinerant (2 Jn$^{7.10}$) prophets, laying claim to visions and revelations (4^{1-6}) in support of their teaching. Although some had withdrawn (2^{18}) or been excommunicated (4^{4}), the church must remain on its guard (4^{1}). The poison of their bad example

* The antithesis of John and Cerinthus, unlike that of Paul and Cerinthus (Epiph. *Haer.* xxviii.), is too well based in the tradition of the early church about the Hinterland of the 'Johannine' literature, to be dismissed as a later dogmatic reflection, due to the desire of obtaining apostolic and canonical repudiation of that errorist.

still worked,* and Christians were in danger not merely of being deceived by others, but of deceiving themselves (1^8). Their Christianity apparently was of long standing (2^7), but it was not due to the writer. He addresses them as τεκνία, παιδία, ἀγαπητοί, and ἀδελφοί, but the authority which breathes through his counsels is that of their spiritual director, as one in touch with the historical tradition and experience of the faith, not that of their founder or of an apostle.

§ 3. *Relation to the Fourth Gospel.*—The close affinities of this writing and the Fourth gospel start the problem not only of their chronological order but of their authorship. These common features are too striking to require any systematic or detailed treatment. Less obvious, but not less vital, are the differences between the two writings, and the problem is to determine whether such variations denote duality of authorship or whether they are compatible with a theory which would account for them by pointing to differences of aim and period within the career of a single writer, whose theme in the one case is that 'Jesus is the Christ,' and in the other that 'the Christ is Jesus.' Identity of authorship by no means follows necessarily from a proof that two writings closely resemble one another in style, vocabulary, and ideas. In the Fourth gospel and in 1 John we have, *e.g.*, the same combination of negative and positive statements, the use of contrast, the aphoristic tone, the playing on ideas, etc. Those who hold that these are outweighed by the distinctive characteristics of each writing, are not shut up to argue either that the one writer cleverly imitated the peculiarities and managed to catch the flavour of his predecessor, or that the one wrote (Kreyenbühl) to counteract the other. Their relationship on the disjunctive hypothesis is accounted for by the common language of a group or school in Asia Minor; the affinities are partly conscious perhaps, but mainly unconscious. This general position has been advocated by S. G. Lange, Horst, Cludius, Baur (*Theol. Jahrb.*, 1848, 293 f., 1857, 315–331), Weisse, Planck, Volkmar, Zeller, Strauss, Holtzmann (*JPT.*, 1881, 690 f., 1882, 128 f., 316 f., 460 f.), S. Davidson, Hoekstra, Keim, Scholten, O. Holtzmann (169 f.), W. Brückner (*Chron.* 305 f.), Lüdemann, Matthew Arnold (*God and Bible*, ed. 1891,

* The Essenic Ebionitic traits discovered by Wittichen (*op. cit.* pp. 68 f.) are, for the most part, either traits of human nature or inadequately verified; *e.g.* the separatism, claims to perfection, etc.

175, 228 f.), Pfleiderer (*ZWT.*, 1869, 394–421, and *Urc.* ii. 446 f.), Cone, Grill (*Untersuchungen*, pp. 305–308), N. Schmidt (*Prophet of Nazareth*, p. 192), Schmiedel, Martineau (*Seat of Authority*, 509–512), Kreyenbühl (*Evglm des Wahrheit*, i. 138–144), E. F. Scott (*The Fourth Gospel*, 88 f., 94), Wellhausen, Wendt, and Soltau (see below). The arguments in favour of a single author are stated by Grimm (*SK.*, 1847, 171 f.), B. Weiss (— Meyer, pp. 4–9), Jülicher (*Einl.* 212–215), Lepin (*L'origine du quatrième évangile*, 1907, 250 f.), Jacquier (*INT.* iv. 1–10), and R. Law (*Tests of Life*[2], 1909, pp. 339 f.), and accepted not only by advocates of the apostolic authorship, but, *e.g.*, by Harnack, E. A. Abbott (*EBi.* 1818), Clemen (*ZNW.*, 1905, 278), Wernle, Forbes, and Baumgarten.

(*a*) The salient linguistic data are as follow. Peculiar to the ep. are: ἀγάπη τετελειωμένη, ἀγγελία, ἀνομία, ἀντίχριστος, ἀρνεῖσθαι τὸν υἱόν, διάνοια, ἐκ τινος γινώσκειν, ἐλπίς, ἐπαγγελία, ἔχειν τὸν πατέρα (υἱόν), ἱλασμός, κοινωνία (=ἐν εἶναι of gospel?), ὁμολογεῖν τὸν θεόν,* παλαίος, παρουσία, ποιεῖν τὴν δικαιόσυνην, σπέρμα τοῦ θεοῦ, χρίσμα, and ψευδοπροφῆται. While the ep. omits δόξα † and δοξάζειν, εἶναι ἐκ τῶν ἄνω (κάτω), οὐράνος and ἐπουράνιος, πέμπω, τὸ πνεῦμα τὸ ἅγιον, ἡ ὀργὴ τοῦ θεοῦ, and 'the Father in the Son, The Son in the Father'—all of which are characteristic expressions of the Gospel—it also uses ἀπὸ instead of παρὰ with verbs like αἰτεῖν, ἀκούειν, and λαμβάνειν, omits entirely the favourite οὖν of the gospel, never uses μὲν . . . δὲ, employs particles like γὰρ and δὲ with singular rarity, preferring the monotonous καὶ where any particle of connection is used at all, and, *e.g.*, refrains from using οἶδα with a personal object (cp. Jn 6^{42} 7^{27} 15^{21} etc.). Such traits of style are far from unimportant in literary criticism. Note, further, that the phrase ἡ ἀγάπη τοῦ θεοῦ, which is fairly frequent in the epistle (2^{5} 3^{17} 4^{9} etc.) as an expression for God's love to man, only occurs once in the gospel (5^{42}), and that in the opposite sense of man's love to God.‡ Also, the perfect ἠγάπηκα, absent from the gospel, occurs once in the epistle (4^{10}, s.v.l.), as does ἐὰν with the indicative (5^{15}). It is of minor significance that while the gospel uses the adv. imper. μείνατε 'in the Lord's mouth, the present is used by the writer of the epistle' (2^{28}, cp. *Diat.* 2437). As for conceptions, (*b*) the epistle never cites the OT, and with one exception (3^{12}) refrains from using OT history or prophecy as a witness to the truths of Christianity.

* Ὁμολογεῖν is never used in the gospel of confessing sin (as Ep. 1^{9}), but always of confessing Christ (9^{22} 12^{42}).

† Perhaps in keeping with its subordination of the metaphysical element to the ethical, throughout. So Grill, who points out also (312–313) how *light* in the epistle invariably and primarily denotes an ethical conception, in contrast to the gospel's use of it to denote knowledge of the divine truth.

‡ Dr. Abbott's arguments to the contrary (*Diat.* 2032–2040) do not seem quite convincing, but he proves incidentally that even in 1 Jn 5^{2-3} the genitive may be taken fairly as subjective.

Whether this was owing to the gnostic animus against the OT, or to the feeling that such evidence was superfluous (the Christian revelation being final in itself),* it is noticeable that the gospel adopts an entirely different outlook upon the sacred books of the Jews. The general ideas (*c*) of the two writings also present diverging lines of interest. Thus (i.) while in the gospel Christians are related to God the Father through the medium of Christ (*e.g.* $10^{7.9}$ 14^{6} 15^{5}), God being to Christ as Christ is to his people, the relationship becomes more direct in the Ep., where Christians are in God, or God in them (2^{5} 3^{21} 4^{4} 5^{14}), without any specific mention being made of Christ's person as the essential means of communion. This feature might be explained † by the consideration that such a conception of Christ would be a foregone conclusion; the writer might well assume it in addressing Christians, and especially Christians within a circle affected by a type of thought like that represented in the Fourth gospel. Only, he was addressing Christians also in the Fourth gospel, and, once again, this conception of Christ's person is not isolated. There are other indications of a transference to God, in the ep., of functions which the gospel reserves for Christ (*e.g.*, the hearing of prayer, 3^{22} $5^{14f.}$, cp. Jn $14^{13f.}$), while *light* ($1^{5f.}$) is expressly presented as an attribute not of the Logos (as in the gospel), but of God. The full significance of the latter feature emerges into view when we pass on to a second series (ii.) of ideas. For all the similarities between the two writings on the conception of *life* or *life eternal*, the development of the latter idea (*e.g.* in 1 Jn 1^{2} 5^{20}) tends to correlate it in the epistle, not with the soteriological cycle of beliefs (as in the gospel), but with the person of Christ, in a theological sense (Grill, pp. 301 f.). In 1 Jn 1^{1-4} the cardinal idea is that of Life as the absolute divine reality: "it is of the Word or Logos which is Life that we are speaking (*sc.* λαλοῦμεν, as Jn 7^{13} etc.). And the Life was manifested." Here the prologue's special conception of the Logos as personal to Christ is eliminated, in the interests of Christian monotheism, the writer meeting by anticipation, and upon a christological basis, the difficulty which afterwards led to Monarchianism,‡ viz., the fear of suggesting that certain divine æons, like the Logos, intervened between God and man. It is not, as in the gospel, the Logos, but the Life Eternal which is identified with the person of Christ. The latter idea subordinates the metaphysical to the ethical, whereas in the gospel the reverse is the case. (iii.) A modification of the idea of faith is also noticeable. While in the gospel faith is equivalent to the coming of man to the truth and light of God in Christ, or to a reception of the words of Jesus in the heart, the writer of the epistle, though far from being an intellectualist (cp. 1^{7} 2^{4} etc.), tends to resolve faith into a confession

---

* So Wendt, who shows that, in spite of the absence of any reference to the sayings of Jesus, no other early Christian writing voices so frequently and so impressively the *αὐτὸς ἔφα* of the Lord (*e.g.* $2^{25.27}$ 3^{23} 4^{21} 5^{20}).

† In the light of what follows, the concentration of emphasis upon obedience to the commandments of God as the ground of assurance, instead of upon the name or mediation of Jesus as in the Gospel (yet see 7^{17} 14^{21} etc.), is probably to be referred (with Pfleiderer) to the larger prominence assigned throughout the epistle to the ethical elements of the Johannine mysticism.

‡ So Holtzmann, Pfleiderer, and Häring.

of Jesus as the Son of God (2^{23} $4^{15.\,23}$ 5^{1}); "C'est professer une christologie orthodoxe" (Goguel, p. 148). The epistle, again, (iv.) although ignoring the χάρις of Jn 1^{16} assigns more prominence than the gospel to the idea of sin, and this again carries with it an emphasis upon the propitiatory element in the death of Jesus which is absent from the gospel, where the expiatory value of Christ's death (1^{29} 11^{50} 17^{19}) is secondary (cp. E. F. Scott, *op. cit.* 218 f.). The signs of Jesus (v.) are not adduced by the epistle in proof of his real position as the Christ in whom men are to believe. Such a proof would have been entirely consonant with the object of the writing, which aims (1^{1-4} 5^{10-13}), as does the gospel (20^{30-31}), at laying a basis for faith in the historical Jesus. Yet the one writing ignores what to the other is essential evidence for the messiahship of Jesus (cp. Wendt, Eng. tr. pp. 172 f.). Less weight attaches to (vi.) the eschatological view of the two writings; for, though *the last hour* and the plurality of antichrists are a special feature of the epistle, these, and the more spiritual view of the future which marks the gospel, do not constitute any radical difference (Reuss). At the same time the epistle (4^{17}) uses *the day of judgment*, a synoptic phrase carefully avoided by the gospel, and describe the second advent as a παρουσία (2^{28}). There is, however, a real difference (vii.) in the conception of the Παράκλητος, who is identified in the epistle (2^{1}) with *Jesus Christ* as *the Righteous One*, whereas, in the gospel, Jesus either sends the Paraclete or is at most *a* Paraclete himself. In the gospel the Spirit as the Παράκλητος is the *alter ego* of Jesus, but in the epistle this function is wholly ignored. Here the conception of the Spirit as a whole undergoes a striking change. 'La maîtrisse de l'Esprit est asservie au joug d'une confession de foi' (Goguel, p. 152).* No longer the supreme principle which judges all and is judged by none, the Spirit in the epistle requires to be tested by certain criterions (4^{1-3}, cp. 1 Co 12^{3}). Indeed, with the transference of Παράκλητος to Christ, the allusions to the Spirit are entirely impersonal and neuter (2^{20} 4^{13}). Instead of the Son (Jn 14^{6}), the Spirit = ἀλήθεια (5^{6}); and while Christians *have a* Παράκλητος, it is *with the Father*, as an intercessor (cp. Ro 8^{34} and Ro 3^{26} with 1 Jn 2^{1-2}, He 7^{25} 9^{24}), rather than as an indwelling Presence in the hearts of Christians. "In the later theology, the Spirit was regarded almost solely as the supreme witness to the orthodox belief and the guide to its correct interpretation. John himself does not share in this restricted view, which is already traceable in the later writings of his school (cp. 1 Jn $2^{21.\,27}$ $4^{1f.}$ $5^{6f.}$). The Spirit, as he conceives it, is a principle of inner development by which the traditional form of belief may from time to time be broken up, in order to reveal more perfectly their essential content" (E. F. Scott, 340). This brief outline will serve to show the delicacy of the problem. *Res lubrica, opinio incerta.* Upon the whole, however, the lines of evidence appear to indicate that the epistle came from a writer who, while belonging to the general 'Johannine' school of thought and feeling, occupied slightly different ground from that of the author of the Fourth gospel. It is true that differences between two writings may be due to difference of standpoint and

---

* Though it is too strong to add, 'par là, la doctrine de l'Esprit cesse d'être féconde, elle est énervée et perd toute sa originalité propre et sa valeur décisive, nous dirions volontiers, toute sa raison d'être.'

purpose; it would be uncritical to insist that a writer must adhere to identical forms of expression under varying circumstances, or that he expressed his full mind in one writing. Such canons of literary criticism are mere ropes of sand. But the characteristic traits of the Fourth gospel and the First epistle betray a difference beneath their unity which is best accounted for by the supposition that while the writer of the epistle lived and moved within the circle in which the Fourth gospel originated, he had an individuality and purpose of his own.

§ 4. *Period.*—The relative position of the tract depends upon the answer given to the debated question whether it was composed before or after the gospel. And if so, was it a preface or a postscript? The usual tendency, especially among those who attribute the two writings to different authors, is to regard 1 John as a more popular re-statement of the main Johannine conceptions, as though the writer was conscious of carrying on, from his own point of view, the propaganda of the larger work, developing some ideas hinted at in the gospel (*e.g.* expiation) and adding others, but all with the more or less deliberate aim of reproducing his master's position.* These threads of filiation are gossamer-webs. It is difficult, *e.g.*, to see how the epistle could produce any alteration of attitude towards the gospel. The parallels adduced between the two (*e.g.* 1^{1-2} = Jn $1^{1.\ 2.\ 4.\ 14}$ 20^{27}, 1^{4} = Jn 15^{11}, 2^{1} = Jn 14^{16}, 2^{2} = Jn 11^{51-52}, 2^{8} = Jn 13^{34} 15^{10-12}, 2^{10-11} = Jn 11^{9-10} 12^{35}, 2^{23} = Jn 15^{23-24}, 2^{27} = Jn 14^{26} 16^{13}, $3^{8.\ 15}$ = Jn 8^{44}, $3^{11.\ 16}$ = Jn 15^{12-13}, 4^{6} = Jn 8^{47}, 5^{6} = Jn 19^{34-35}, 5^{9} = Jn $5^{32.\ 34.\ 36}$ 8^{17-18}, 5^{12} = Jn 3^{36}, 5^{13} = Jn 20^{31}, 5^{14} = Jn 14^{13-14} 16^{23}, 5^{20} = Jn 17^{3}) do not necessarily prove more than an acquaintance with the substance of the 'Johannine' doctrine which was current before the Fourth gospel crystallised it into written shape, and the motive for the composition of the homily is not to be found in any supposed relation to the gospel. Both works rise from the same plot of early Christian soil; both aim at developing the faith of the church and (especially the homily) at safeguarding it against current errors; both lay stress on the evangelic historical tradition; but, beyond the general fact that the homily pre-

* Cp. Pfleiderer, *Urc.* ii. 448: "Der Briefsteller war ein dem Evangelisten nahestehender Mann, sein Schüler vielleicht, der sich an dem Geist der Theologie seines Meisters gebildet hatte. Aber so ging ihm ähnlich wie in unserer Zeit den meisten Schülern Schleiermachers: in dem eifrigen Bestreben, die grossen Gedanken des Meisters für die gesamte Kirche nutzbar und brauchbar zu machen, wurde er konservativer als der Meister selbst gewesen."

supposes the teaching and spirit of the gospel, their mutual connection remains obscure. The homily was addressed to people familiar with the doctrine of the gospel, and possibly with the gospel itself. That it was intended to circulate along with it seems a hypothesis suggested by the early juxtaposition of the two writings in the canon rather than by any internal evidence.

A good deal depends on whether the triple ἔγραψα, following the triple γράφω in the *tergemina allocutio* of 2^{12-14}, is a rhetorical variation, or a specific allusion to the Fourth gospel. The latter view is less probable than the reference to what precedes (1^{1}–2^{11}), or to a lost epistle (so, *e.g.*, Michaelis, Baljon, Karl); but even these hypotheses are as unnecessary as the conjecture that 1^{1-4} is an implicit allusion to the prologue of the Fourth gospel. It does not mend matters, from this point of view, to regard v.[14] as an interpolation (Calvin and others, cp. Koennecke in *BFT.* xii. 1. 19–20).

§ 5. *Authorship.*—The Homeric hymns, it has been said, are neither hymns nor Homer's. The so-called 'first epistle of John' is neither an epistle nor is it John's—if by John is meant the son of Zebedee. The homily is anonymous, and all subsequent conjectures about its authorship, either in tradition or in modern investigation, are derived from the internal evidence of its connection with the Fourth gospel (see above). The most attractive form of the latter hypothesis is the semi-pseudonymous theory (so, *e.g.*, Hausrath, Scholten, *Das Evglm nach Johannes*, 68; Thoma, *op. cit.* pp. 807 f.; Soltau,* *ZNW.*, 1901, 140 f.; Pfleiderer, *Urc.* ii. 448 f.; Wellhausen, Heitmüller, Zurhellen), that some Asiatic Christian wrote the epistle, as he revised the Fourth gospel (especially adding ch. 21), in the interests of the beloved disciple; but the obscurity of the whole problem and the linguistic data prevent this from rising to more than a level of approximate probability. Lord Hailes once pointed out to Boswell his additions to a legal paper originally drawn up by Dr. Johnson. The writer of 'First John' had, in all likelihood, some share in the editorial process through which the Fourth gospel reached its final form, but the extent of this share is still uncertain.

Whether the author belonged, or wished to represent himself as belonging, to the original disciples of Jesus (not necessarily the twelve), depends on the

* Soltau makes John the presbyter write 1 John and also (*Unsere Evglien*, 1910, pp. 110 f.) edit the Fourth gospel out of Johannine logia, etc According to Schwartz, both epistle and gospel were edited with the same 'apostolic' motive, by the same editor.

interpretation of 1^{1-4}. The spiritual and semi-mystical sense* (cp. Abbott, *Diat.* 1615–1620; Clemen, *ZNW.*, 1905, 277 f.), is borne out by a comparison of 4^{14}; but it is probably to be combined with the view that the paragraph, with its anti-docetic reference, voices the testimony of the apostolic church, as represented by the circle of μαθηταὶ τοῦ κυρίου in Asia Minor to which the writer belonged. The church stands on the definite incarnation of Jesus Christ the Logos, and the apostolic experience of the latter is the experience of the church, on which her testimony is based.† The writer is the spokesman of this testimony. He uses realistic language which is capable easily of a spiritual and ideal interpretation. Even the phrase *our hands handled* (ἐψηλάφησαν, cp. Ac 17^{27}) is not unparalleled.‡ "No one," says Origen (*c. Cels.* 7^{34}),§ "is so foolish as not to see that the word *hands* is taken figuratively, as when John says, *our hands have handled.*" Irenæus (*adv. haer.* v. 1) observes that the only way we can learn of God and have communion with his Son is by 'magistrum nostrum uidentes et per auditum nostrum uocem eius percipientes.'

§ 6. *Traces in the subsequent literature* (cp. Zahn's *GK.* i. 209 f., 374 f., 905 f., ii. 48 f., 88 f.).

It is unsafe to attach much weight to the apparent reminiscence of $4^{2\text{-}3}$ (or of 2 Jn 7) in Polyk. *ad Phil.* 7 (reading ἐληλυθότα instead of ἐληλυθέναι).‖ Even in Ignatius the alleged traces (cp. Dietze, *SK.*, 1905, 595 f.) are seldom cogent; *e.g.* 3^{14} = *Smyrn.* vii. (συνέφερε δὲ αὐτοῖς ἀγαπᾶν, ἵνα καὶ ἀναστῶσιν), 3^{17} = *Smyrn.* vi. 2, 5^{6} (cp. 3^{17}) = *Eph.* xviii. (ὃς ἐγεννήθη καὶ βαπτίσθη, ἵνα τῷ πάθει τὸ ὕδωρ καθαρίσῃ), $4^{2f.}$ = *Eph.* vii. (ἐν σαρκὶ γενόμενος). Still, if Ignatius knew the Fourth gospel, it is *a priori* likely that he also knew 1 Jn. Papias, at any rate, is said by Eusebius (iii. 39) to have used ἡ Ἰωαννοῦ προτέρα (= ἡ Ἰ. πρώτη, v. 8?), *i.e.* the anonymous tract which, by the time of Eusebius, had come to be known as 'First John'; and there is not the slightest reason to suspect or reject this statement. Justin Martyr also (*Dial.* 123, where the κληθῶμεν καὶ ἐσμέν of 3^{1} is echoed in καὶ θεοῦ τέκνα ἀληθινὰ καλούμεθα καὶ ἐσμέν, if we keep his commandments = 2^{3}) presupposes the homily, so that, although the reminiscences

* So, *e.g.*, Karl, Harnack, J. Réville, 55–56; von Soden, Holtzmann-Bauer, Green (137 f.), and Bacon (*Fourth Gospel in Research*, etc., 189 f.).

† "The vision and witness of the immediate disciples . . . remains as an abiding endowment of the living body" (Westcott, p. 153).

‡ Tacit. *Agricola*, 45, mox nostræ duxere Heluidium in carcerem manus.

§ Cp. also *Clem. Recogn.* i. 17, "He set forth so openly who that prophet was, that I seemed to have before my eyes, and to handle with my hand, the proofs which he adduced."

‖ Some, *e.g.* Volkmar (*Ursprung d. Evglien*, 47 f.), even hold that it is Polykarp who is quoted.

in Clem. Rom. (49^5 $50^3 = 4^{18}$) and even Hermas (*Mand.* $3^1 = 2^{27}$) and the Didachê ($10^5 = 4^{18}$) * are too slight to prove more than the existence of current 'Johannine' terminology, the writing must have been circulated in Asia Minor, at any rate, before the end of the first quarter of the second century. The *terminus a quo* is approximately the general period of the Fourth gospel's composition; but there is no decisive ground for the priority of either, even upon the hypothesis that both were written by the same author. The aim of each is too special to admit of the conjecture that the epistle was intended to accompany, much less to introduce, the larger work. By the end of the second century the epistle seems to have been fairly well known (Clem. Alex. *Strom.* ii. 15. 66; Tert. *de Pudic.* 19; Iren. iii. 16. 8), and in the Muratorian Canon it appears to be reckoned as an appendix or sequel to the Fourth gospel. There is no evidence for the position taken up by the Alogi to the epistle; the statement of Epiphanius, that they rejected all the Johannine epistles together with the gospel and apocalypse (*hær.* 57^{34}, τάχα δὲ καὶ τὰς ἐπιστολάς· συνᾴδουσι γὰρ καὶ αὗται τῷ εὐαγγελίῳ καὶ τῇ ἀποκαλύψει) is a pure guess, unsupported by any early tradition.

On the curious title *ad Parthos* (Aug. *Quæst. Evang.* ii. 39), see above, p. 476. An actual Parthian or Persian destination for 1 John was once defended by Paulus and Michaelis (vi. 399–400), on the ground that the writer's allusions to the dualism of light and darkness were designed to correct the Zoroastrian philosophy of religion!

(C) *THE JOHANNINE TRADITION.*

The rearrangement of the so-called 'Johannine' literature, outlined above, is a tentative hypothesis which involves some resetting of the traditional data upon John the son of Zebedee and John the presbyter. It has been assumed provisionally that the tradition is correct which witnesses to an early martyrdom of John the son of Zebedee as well as of his brother; that

* As in Diognet. 10^3 πρὸς οὓς ἀπέστειλε τὸν υἱὸν αὐτοῦ τὸν μονογενῆ $= 4^9$, or $10^3 = 4^{19}$. If the prayers of the Didachê represent the sacramental prayers of the Palestinian and Syrian churches (cp. Andresen, *ZNW.* iii. 135 f.; Kreyenbühl, i. 706 f.), they may have been known to the author of the Fourth gospel, *e.g.* in chs. 6 and 17; but the former passage, at any rate, resembles a midrashic discourse on Ps 78 (cp. Klein's *Der älteste christliche Katechismus*, pp. 220 f.).

while the former may conceivably be identified with the beloved disciple of the Fourth gospel and the original authority for some of its special traditions upon sayings and (to a lesser degree) the deeds of Jesus, he was not its author; that the apocalypse probably, and 2 and 3 John certainly, were written by John the presbyter in Asia Minor towards the end of the first century; and that the anonymous author of the Fourth gospel may have also composed (though probably he did not) the homily or tract which has come down to us under the canonical title of 1 John. The internal evidence of the literature upon the three latter points has been already discussed. It now remains to give an outline* of the more salient features in the later tradition of the second and third centuries which bear out these conclusions.

The modern investigator of the Johannine problem resembles the woodman in Theokritus; he is bewildered by the rich variety of topics presented to him, and hardly able to decide where he would do best to begin his operations.

> Ἴδαν ἐς πολύδενδρον ἀνὴρ ὑλατόμος ἐλθὼν
> παπταίνει, παρεόντος ἅδην, πόθεν ἄρξεται ἔργου·
> τί πρῶτον καταλέξω; ἐπεὶ πάρα μυρία εἰπεῖν.

The five writings in the NT canon which were eventually grouped together as *instrumentum Johanneum* are surrounded by a thick undergrowth of traditions during the second and third centuries, which is neither homogeneous nor lucid. In order to clear a path, it is necessary to begin, as we have done, with the internal evidence of the writings themselves. The further problem now remains, how to account satisfactorily for the rise and variations of the later tradition, which associated these writings with the personality of a Christian disciple, John, who lived in Asia Minor towards the close of the first century.

§ 1. *The Papias-traditions.*—The earliest data are again, as in the case of the synoptic problem, furnished by Papias; his writings are only extant in the shape of fragmentary quotations in Eusebius and other writers of a later age, but fortunately they preserve a tradition which is prior to any other.

* The following paragraphs make no attempt to survey the dusty and misty history of opinion upon the subject, or to summarise the ramified details of the problem. Their aim is simply to state one or two of the cardinal results of historical investigation, which justify, in the opinion of the present writer, the hypothesis underlying the above literary criticism of the Johannine writings.

The importance of the evidence of Papias on this matter is shown by the fact that he is, as is admitted on almost all hands (*e.g.* by Lightfoot and Gutjahr, no less than by Harnack, Réville, Schwartz, Mommsen, and Corssen), the source for the presbyter-traditions of Irenæus in the second and fifth books of the *adv. Haer.*, by the possibility that the appeal of Irenæus to the Asiatic elders who had known John and some other apostles goes back primarily at least to the elders of the Papias-tradition, and by the probability that the Muratorian Canon (or Hippolytus, its author) borrowed to some extent from the bishop of Hierapolis (Lightfoot).

The first fragment* quoted by Eusebius (*H. E.* iii. 39) is as follows:—

οὐκ ὀκνήσω δὲ σοι καὶ ὅσα ποτε παρὰ τῶν πρεσβυτέρων καλῶς ἔμαθον καὶ καλῶς ἐμνημόνευσα, συγκατατάξαι ταῖς ἑρμηνείαις, διαβεβαιούμενος ὑπὲρ αὐτῶν ἀλήθειαν. οὐ γὰρ τοῖς τὰ πολλὰ λέγουσιν ἔχαιρον ὥσπερ οἱ πολλοί, ἀλλὰ τοῖς τἀληθῆ διδάσκουσιν, οὐδὲ τοῖς τὰς ἀλλοτρίας ἐντολὰς μνημονεύουσιν, ἀλλὰ τοῖς τὰς παρὰ τοῦ Κυρίου τῇ πίστει δεδομένας καὶ ἀπ' αὐτῆς παραγινομένας τῆς ἀληθείας. εἰ δὲ που καὶ παρακολουθηκώς τις τοῖς πρεσβυτέροις ἔλθοι, τοὺς τῶν πρεσβυτέρων ἀνέκρινον† λόγους·‡ τί Ἀνδρέας ἢ τί Πέτρος εἶπεν ἢ τί Φίλιππος ἢ τί Θωμᾶς ἢ Ἰάκωβος ἢ τί Ἰωάννης ἢ Ματθαῖος ἢ τις ἕτερος τῶν τοῦ Κυρίου μαθητῶν, ἅ τε Ἀριστίων καὶ ὁ πρεσβύτερος Ἰωάννης, οἱ τοῦ Κυρίου μαθηταί, λέγουσιν. οὐ γὰρ τὰ ἐκ τῶν βιβλίων τοσοῦτόν με ὠφελεῖν ὑπελάμβανον, ὅσον τὰ παρὰ ζώσης φωνῆς καὶ μενούσης.

Nor shall I hesitate, along with my own interpretations, to set down for thee whatsoever I learnt with care and remembered (or recounted) with care from the elders, guaranteeing its truth. For, unlike the many, I did not take pleasure in those who have much to say, but in those who teach what is true; not in those who recall foreign commandments, but in those who recall the commandments given by the Lord to faith and reaching us from the truth itself. Furthermore, if any one chanced to arrive who had been really (καί) a follower of the elders, I would inquire as to the sayings of the elders—as to what Andrew or Peter said, or Philip, or Thomas or James, or John or Matthew or any other of the Lord's disciples, also as to what Aristion and the presbyter John, the Lord's disciples, say. For I supposed that things out of books would not be of such use to me as the utterances of a living voice which was still with us.

---

* Critical discussions by H. J. Holtzmann (*BL.* iii. 352–360), Schwartz (*Der Tod d. Söhne Zebed.* 9 f.), B. W. Bacon, *Fourth Gospel in Research and Debate*, pp. 101 f.

† The Syriac version presupposes συνέκρινον (so Gutjahr). It is an open question whether ἅ τε . . . λέγουσιν depends, like τί Ἀνδρέας . . . μαθητῶν, on λόγους or directly (so, *e.g.*, Harnack, Corssen, Schmiedel) on ἀνέκρινον λόγους. In the latter case, Aristion and the presbyter John would be singled out from the rest of the πρεσβύτεροι. The visitor would only be able to report what the presbyters knew of the apostles, but he would be able to speak, from personal intercourse, about the other two

‡ Grammatically, this might mean either (so, *e.g.*, Zahn) that Andrew,

As the opening words indicate, the excerpt is taken from the preface to the (five books of) *ἐξηγήσεις λογίων κυριακῶν*, which consisted of interpretations or expositions of *λόγια κυριακά*, together with *διηγήσεις* (explanations) of the sayings of Jesus, such as Aristion furnished, and *παραδόσεις* such as those of John the presbyter (*H. E.* iii. 39. 14). These *ἐξηγήσεις* of Papias may have been directed against gnostic commentaries like the lengthy *Exegetica* of Basilides; if so, his language is carefully chosen (pp. 187–188). These verbose writers also made their appeal to an apostolic tradition (cp. *e.g.* Tert. *de præscr. haer.* 25), which was supposed to have been secret and esoteric: Papias therefore claims that his apostolic traditions are sifted and direct. For the 'foreign commandments,' see 1 Jn $2^{7.24}$.

The first problem of the passage (*a*) is to ascertain the exact relation between Papias and his authorities. Writing probably between A.D. 140 and 150, he is recalling inquiries made in his earlier life (*i.e.* during the first quarter, perhaps even the first decade of the second century). But are the 'sayings of the elders' equivalent to what follows, or does the phrase mean their reports of what the following disciples of the Lord had said? The latter is more probable. These *πρεσβύτεροι* were not apostles; their *λόγοι* related what the apostles or primitive disciples had said.* As Eusebius assumed, the *πρεσβύτεροι* of Papias were simply pupils or successors (*γνώριμοι = μαθηταὶ τῶν ἀποστόλων*) of the primitive disciples. We get three stages, therefore: (i.) the apostles or disciples of the Lord, then (ii.) the *πρεσβύτεροι* who preserved their traditions, and finally (iii.) followers of the *πρεσβύτεροι*. Papias had never known any of the original apostles. For information about their teaching he depended on men whom Irenæus (*adv. Haer.* v. 5. 1) described as *οἱ πρεσβύτεροι τῶν ἀποστόλων μαθηταί*. Even with these he could not maintain any continuous intercourse; he had to fall back upon casual visitors to his parish or diocese who were in a position to report their oral teaching. The alternative is to put (i.) and (ii.) together and regard *οἱ πρεσβύτεροι* as including, if not equivalent to, the personal disciples of Jesus mentioned by name. This exegesis has the advantage of giving an apparently lucid sense to the third sentence; what the elders told their followers was

etc., *were* the elders in question, or (so, *e.g.*, Schwartz, Corssen, Kreyenbühl: ii. 735 f., Abbott) that the *λόγοι* of the elders related to what Andrew and the rest said. The latter view interposes more space between Papias and the disciples than the former.

* This is now admitted by Belser (*INT.* 33 f.), who agrees that the interpretation of Eusebius is correct on this point.

what they (*i.e.* Andrew, etc.) knew of Jesus. But 1 P 5^1 is a slender peg on which to hang the assertion that the (twelve) apostles could be called πρεσβύτεροι by a man in the period of Papias, even if πρεσβύτεροι were rendered "ancient worthies." Besides, οἱ πρεσβύτεροι cannot be identified with Andrew, etc., for Peter and James at least had died before Papias was born; and if οἱ π. merely included Andrew, etc., he would naturally have written παρὰ τινων τῶν πρεσβυτέρων instead of referring twice to οἱ π. as a homogeneous group. Finally, there is an implicit distinction between οἱ π. and οἱ τοῦ Κυρίου μαθηταί.

This opens up the second (*b*) problem. Why are Aristion and John the presbyter called οἱ τ. κ. μαθηταί? Unless it is in the general sense of Christian (Ac 9^1), the words are probably either a primitive corruption or an interpolation (Abbott, *EBi.* 1815; Mommsen in *ZNW.*, 1902, 156–159). For the latter hypothesis there is some textual evidence (*e.g.* the Armenian and Syriac versions); on the former, we may either add μαθητῶν after κυρίου (Renan, iv. pp. xxiii f., vi. 48, and Abbott, *Exp.*[4] iii. 245 f.), or, better still, read (Bacon, *JBL.*, 1898, 176–183) τούτων (by a natural corruption, ΤΟΥΤω̄ passed into ΤΟΥΚῩ).

The (*c*) third problem relates to the change of tense in εἶπεν and λέγουσιν. The natural sense of the distinction, unless it is a rhetorical variation (so, *e.g.*, Lightfoot and Abbott), is that Aristion and John the presbyter were still alive at the period to which Papias refers. So far as the text is concerned, they may have been among the πρεσβύτεροι from whom Papias had once (ποτέ) learnt. Eusebius says that Papias claimed to be one of their hearers (Παπίας . . . Ἀριστίωνος καὶ τοῦ πρεσβυτέρου Ἰωάννου αὐτήκοον ἑαυτόν φησι γενέσθαι); 'at least,' he adds, 'Papias often mentions them and inserts traditions of theirs in his own pages.' The reason given by the historian is obviously too slight to bear the weight of his inference, for Papias might have derived these traditions indirectly. Nevertheless, there is no reason why he should not have come into personal touch at one time in his life with Aristion and John the presbyter. The chronological difficulty is not insuperable. Even if they had been personal disciples of the Lord, they might have survived till the last decade of the first century—which, on a fair estimate of the age of Papias, would permit him to have met them in his youth. If they had not been personal disciples of Jesus, the likelihood that Papias had once been in close touch with them is increased.

although at Hierapolis he seems to have only been able to get information about them. This does not necessarily imply that they were not in Asia Minor at the time. Had they been stationed at Ephesus it is difficult to account for Papias' lack of access to them; but, as Keim (i. 222) observes, "Asia Minor is a wide word, even without Ephesus," and it is not a necessary deduction from Papias to argue that these witnesses to the Palestinian tradition must have been in Palestine (Bacon).* Nor does it follow that they were dead, and that λέγουσιν refers to their writings (Drummond, 199 f.), or at least to writings incorporating their traditions. This would allow them still to be reckoned as personal disciples of Jesus, but it is not easy to see why Eusebius in that case did not allude to their works; besides, the context of Papias (with its immediate praise of oral tradition in preference to written) rather discourages this view.

Finally, as Eusebius proceeds to indicate in commenting on the passage, (*d*) Papias distinguishes between the apostle John, who is simply ranked among the apostolic figures of a bygone age, and the presbyter John, who belongs to a different and later group. This is a most important result for the criticism of the Johannine tradition. Haussleiter (*Theol. Lit.-Blatt*, 1896, 465–468) and Hjelt, expanding a suggestion of Renan (iv. 568), propose to omit ἤ τι Ἰωάννης, on the ground that the omission leaves the text more symmetrical (cp. Camerlynck, 125 f.). Zahn, who (*INT.* § 51) rules out this conjecture as daring, reaches the same end by making Papias refer clumsily to the apostle John in both connections (so Jacquier, iv. pp. 99 f., and Lepin, pp. 133 f.). But neither theory is justifiable. John the presbyter is not to be emended out of existence in the interests of John the apostle.

The second fragment of Papias, which refers to John the apostle, corroborates the first by proving not only that he did not survive to a late age, but that he died early as a martyr. The setting of this fragment is less clear than that of the former, but it has the compensating advantage of being in line with a

* Aristion and Ariston, as we know from Plutarch and Aristotle, could be used of the same person (the latter variant occurs here in Syr. and Arm. versions), but the Aristion of Papias was not the Ariston of Pella to whom Eusebius elsewhere refers (cp. Bacon, *DCG.* i. 114–118, against Resch, *TU.* x. 2. 453 f.). There is more, though not enough, to be said for the identification of John the presbyter (supposing he was not a personal disciple of Jesus) with John the seventh head of the church at Jerusalem (Schlatter).

piece of evidence from the synoptic tradition. The evidence for the early martyrdom of John the son of Zebedee is, in fact, threefold: (*a*) a prophecy of Jesus preserved in Mk 10^{39} = Mt 20^{23}, (*b*) the witness of Papias, and (*c*) the calendars of the church.

The tradition is accepted and defended, on various grounds, by Schwartz (*op. cit.*), Erbes (see below), Bousset (*TR.*, 1905, 225 f., 277 f.), Pfleiderer (*Urc.* ii. 411), Kreyenbühl (i. 366 f.), Badham (*AJT.* iii. 729–740, viii. 539–554), Menzies and Wellhausen and J. Weiss (on Mk 10^{39}), Bacon (*Exp.*[7], 1907, 236 f., and on Mk 10^{39}), Jülicher (*INT.* 377 f.), Loisy (*RHR.*, 1904, 568 f.), Schmiedel (*EBi.* 2509–2510), Burkitt (*Gospel History and its Transmission*, pp. 250 f.), Holtzmann-Bauer (pp. 19 f.), Forbes (pp. 165 f.), and Heitmüller.

MARK.	MATTHEW.
τὸ ποτήριον ὃ ἐγὼ πίνω πίεσθε,	τὸ μὲν ποτήριόν μου πίεσθε
καὶ τὸ βάπτισμα ὃ ἐγὼ βαπτίζομαι βαπτισθήσεσθε,	
τὸ δὲ καθίσαι ἐκ δεξιῶν μου ἢ ἐξ εὐωνύμων	τὸ δὲ καθίσαι ἐκ δεξιῶν μου καὶ ἐξ εὐωνύμων,
οὐκ ἔστιν ἐμὸν δοῦναι,	οὐκ ἔστιν ἐμὸν τοῦτο δοῦναι,
ἀλλ' οἷς ἡτοίμασται.	ἀλλ' οἷς ἡτοίμασται ὑπὸ τοῦ πατρός μου.

Mt. as usual omits the parallel clause (cp. 22^{17} = Mk 12^{14} etc.) and adds the last four words (cp. 25^{34} and ^{41}, where, in the latter passage, ὃ ἡτοίμασεν ὁ πατήρ μου, as read by Iren. Orig. Hil. D and some old Latin MSS, has been altered into τὸ ἡτοιμασμένον). Whether Luke omitted the whole scene * because it appeared to limit the authority of Jesus or because it disparaged the apostles, it is difficult to say. In any case the primitive character of the saying is as patent as its meaning, viz., that both James and John were to suffer martyrdom. "À quelque point de vue qu'on se place, clairvoyance miraculeuse de Jésus ou prédiction mise dans sa bouche *post eventum*, Jean et Jacques ont bu la même 'coupe' et subi le même 'baptême' que lui" (A. Réville, *Jésus de Nazareth*, i. 354). What drinking the cup of Jesus meant, is evident from passages like Mk 14^{36} and *Mart. Polyk.* 14 (ἐν ἀριθμῷ τῶν μαρτύρων ἐν τῷ ποτηρίῳ τοῦ Χριστοῦ). The hypothesis that Jesus was simply referring in general terms to persecution and hardship does not do justice to the specific and definite character of the prediction. Unless it is assumed (as, *e.g.*, by O. Holtzmann) that this anticipation of

* Spitta's attempt to prove that his favourite Luke was correct (*ZNW.*, 1910, 39–58), and that the passage, a later synoptic addition, did not originally refer to death, is rightly set aside by Schwartz (*ibid.* 89–104).

Jesus was not fulfilled, we must admit that he foretold a martyr-death for the two men, and also that this had come to pass by the time Mark's gospel was published. James was beheaded in the beginning of the fifth decade by Herod Agrippa I. (Ac 12^2), although Luke fails to chronicle his death any more than that of Peter. It is possible that other names * originally lay in the isolated tradition or source which is incorporated in Ac $12^{1f.}$, but it is not necessary to assume that the two brothers died simultaneously at this early date (so, *e.g.*, Schwartz and Badham), and it is extremely improbable that John's name was subsequently omitted under stress of the dominant Ephesian legend (Schwartz), after A.D. 150. This involves a tissue of historical difficulties,† including the identification of John Mark with the John of Gal 1–2. It is unlikely that the former would be ranked alongside of Peter, the pillar-apostle. If the death of John the son of Zebedee fell within the subsequent period covered by Acts, the lack of any allusion to it is simply another of the many gaps which are visible in Luke's narrative.

The fact of the martyrdom of John is, however, corroborated very soon by (*b*) a statement of Papias, in the second book of his expositions of *Λόγια κυριακά*, that John "was killed by the Jews, thus plainly fulfilling along with his brother the prophecy of Christ regarding them and their own confession and common agreement concerning him" (*ὑπὸ Ἰουδαίων ἀνῃρέθη, πληρώσας δηλαδὴ μετὰ τοῦ ἀδελφοῦ τὴν τοῦ Χριστοῦ περὶ αὐτῶν πρόρρησιν κνὶ τὴν ἑαυτῶν ὁμολογίαν περὶ τούτου καὶ συγκατάθεσιν*).‡ The evidence for this important quotation (of which the first three words alone belong to Papias) goes back to the best MS (codex Coislinianus, 305) of Georgios Hamartolos (ninth century), who,

* "Etliche andere, die ebenfalls den Zeugentod erlitten, werden nicht einmal mit Namen genannt, als wären sie eine nicht der Rede werte Beilage . . . Man kann sich kaum des Verdachtes erwehren, dass Lukas hier gewisse Namen unterdrückt hat. Vielleicht auch nur einen einzigen" (Wellhausen, *Noten zur Apgeschichte*, 9).

† Schwartz (see p. 284, and *ZNW.*, 1910, 100 f.) tries a chronological hypothesis, by placing Paul's journey (Ac 13–14) after, not before, the events of Ac 15, and taking 11^{27-30} and 15^1–16^4 as versions of the same event, in order to allow Paul's conflict with the pillar-apostles at Jerusalem (Gal 1^{18} 2^1) to precede A.D. 43–44, the date of the martyrdom of the son of Zebedee; but the chronology is highly speculative (see above, p. 309), involving the conversion of Paul in A.D. 28–29 and the crucifixion a year or two earlier.

‡ Then follows Mk 10^{39}. It is impossible, with Godet, Gutjahr, and others, to minimise *ἀνῃρέθη*, here or in Georgios, into injury or exile.

à propos of the synoptic logion (Mk $10^{38f.}$), declares in his *Chronicle* that John the apostle after writing his gospel did suffer martyrdom (*Chron.* iii. 134. 1), buttressing the statement upon Papias and Origen. The former is miscalled **αὐτόπτης τούτου γενόμενος**, and the reference to the latter* seems erroneous. But the recent publication (*TU.*, 1888, v. 2, 170) of the de Boor fragment of what is evidently an epitome (7th to 8th cent.), based on the **Χριστιανικὴ ἱστορία** or *Chronicle* of Philip Sidetes (5th cent.), removes all doubts as to whether Papias really wrote something to this effect. This chronicler incidentally lends a powerful support to the former allusion, by quoting thus: 'Papias in his second book says that John the divine (ὁ θεολόγος) and James his brother were killed by the Jews' (ὑπὸ Ἰουδαίων ἀνῃρέθησαν). While this quotation cannot be verbally exact, as θεολόγος is not known to have been applied to John earlier than the close of the fourth century (cp. Bousset, p. 227, as against Schwartz), it is indubitable that the work of Papias must have contained some statement of this nature about the two sons of Zebedee.† The excerpts are both late; the later of the two may be taken from the epitome of Philip (cp. Funk's *Patres Apost.* i. 368 f.), and Philip's reputation as an independent historian is not particularly high (cp. Socrates, *H. E.* vii. 27; Photius, *Cod.* 35); but, although absolute certainty is unattainable, our deduction is that there are no very valid reasons for conjecturing that they both mistook the sense of some passage in Papias,‡ which either (so Drummond) referred to John as μάρτυς (not in the tragic but in the ordinary sense of the term), or described the martyrdom of John (*i.e.* the

* Origen, *in Mt.* t. xvi. 6. already explains the synoptic saying, with regard to John, by means of the tradition which identified him with the John of the apocalypse.

† On the extreme improbability of the conjectures (cp. Gutjahr, pp. 107 f.) by which Lightfoot (*Essays on Supernat. Religion*, pp. 211 f.), Zahn, Schlatter (*BFT.* ii. 3. pp. 50 f.), and Harnack would eliminate the son of Zebedee from the text of Georgios, see Schmiedel (*EBi.* 2509 f.) and Clemen (*AJT.*, 1905, 648 f.).

‡ Still less, that Papias himself, an ἀρχαῖος ἀνήρ, was in error if he made such a statement. "If Papias made it, the question remains whether he made it under some misapprehension, or merely by way of expressing his conviction that the prophecy of Mk. x. 39 had found a literal fulfilment. Neither explanation is very probable in view of the early date of Papias." Swete, *Apocalypse of St. John*, p. clxxv.

Baptist) and James the Lord's brother (so Bernard, conjecturing that ΟΑΔΕΛΦΟϹΑΥΤΟΥΚΑΙΙΑΚΩΒΟϹ is a corruption of ΟΑΔΕΛΦΟϹΤΟΥΚΥΙΑΚΩΒΟϹ). These conjectures are ingenious but unnecessary. As to the former theory, the whole trend of the later ecclesiastical tradition was in the opposite direction, to regard the witness of John as non-tragic. As to the latter, while the two Jameses were repeatedly confused in later tradition, it is no argument against James the son of Zebedee to say that he was not literally killed by the Jews, for the same expression is applied to Jesus (*e.g.* Ac 2[23] *τοῦτον . . . ἀνείλατε*), though Herod in the one case and Pilate in the other were responsible for an act which pleased or was prompted by the Jews. Furthermore, the collocation of John the Baptist and James the Lord's brother is much less natural than that of the two sons of Zebedee.

Upon the whole, then, there does not appear to be any particularly strong ground for the rejection of the Papias-tradition, *e.g.* by Harnack (*ACL.* ii. 1. 662 f.; *TLZ.*, 1909, 10–12, in a review of Bernard), Drummond (pp. 227 f.), Stanton (*GHD.* i. 166 f.), Zahn (*Forschungen*, vi. 147 f.), H. B. Workman (*Persecution in the Early Church*, 1906, 358–361), Lepin (*L'origine du quatr. évangile*, pp. 108 f.), Abbott (*Diat.* 2935–2941), J. H. Bernard (*Irish Church Quarterly*, 1908, 51–66), and J. Armitage Robinson (*The Historical Character of St. John's Gospel*, 1908, pp. 64–80), if it can be connected organically with the subsequent and divergent traditions of the church. Before proceeding to demonstrate this connection, however, we must weigh the fact that (*c*) the evidence of some ancient calendars (Egli, *ZWT.*, 1891, pp. 279 f.; Erbes, *ZKG.*, 1901, pp. 200 f.) favours indirectly the existence of such a tradition. In the fourth century Syriac,* "John and James, the apostles in Jerusalem," are commemorated together as martyrs there on Dec. 27 between Stephen (Dec. 26) and Paul and Peter (in Rome, Dec. 28); the Armenian and Gothico-Gallic agree, and possibly the original form of the sixth century Carthaginian † (corrobor-

* Edited by W. Wright, *Journ. Sacred Lit.* (1865) 36 f., 423 f.; cp. H. Achelis, *die Martyrologien* (1900), pp. 30–71. In view of ordinary usage and the mention of Rome in connection with Paul and Peter, it is not probable that Jerusalem here denotes (so Gutjahr) merely the place of the festival's celebration, and not the locality of the martyrdom.

† Where a scribe in the extant text has wrongly put John the Baptist

ated by the North African *De Rebaptismate*, *c.* A.D. 250, which contains this sentence: "He said to the sons of Zebedee, 'Are ye able?' For he knew the men had to be baptized, not only in water but also in their own blood"). Two calendars, from the East and the West respectively, thus reflect a belief that John the apostle suffered a martyr-death. The former tallies with the evidence of a Syriac homily of Aphrahat (A.D. 344), *de persecutione*, which (§ 23) bids its hearers listen to "these names of martyrs, of confessors, and of the persecuted," and, after reciting the stories of OT worthies, proceeds, "Great and excellent is the martyrdom of Jesus. He surpassed in affliction and in confession all who were before or after. And after him was the faithful martyr Stephen whom the Jews stoned. Simon also and Paul were perfect martyrs. And James and John walked in the footsteps of Christ their master." Plainly these are all examples of the first of the classes mentioned, viz. the martyrs. Aphrahat then adds examples of confessors. "Also, others of the apostles thereafter in diverse places confessed and proved true martyrs." Finally, he notes the persecuted. "And also concerning our brethren who are in the West, in the days of Diocletian there came great affliction and persecution," etc. Upon the whole, then, the evidence of the early catholic calendars, though not on the same footing as that of the two other blocks of evidence, serves to corroborate substantially the tradition which they embody.

Further confirmation * of this, the earliest tradition upon John the apostle, is furnished incidentally by Herakleon, the early gnostic commentator on the fourth gospel (cp. Clem. *Strom.* iv. 9), who mentions, in connection with Lk 12^{11-12}, those who had escaped martyrdom, "Matthew, Philip, Thomas, Levi, and many others." John's name is significantly omitted from the list, for in view of his contemporary importance it is hardly possible that he could have been included among the "many others." As time went on, the dominant Ephesian legend of

(who is commemorated on June 24th) instead of John the apostle, possibly owing to the mention of Herod (confusing the Herod of Ac 12^{2} with him of Mk 6^{14}); cp. Achelis, *op. cit.* pp. 18–29. Zahn (*Forsch.* vi. 147 f.) and some others even propose to read John the Baptist for John the apostle in the Papias-fragment (see above).

* Cp. Keim, v. 53 f., who already recognised, with Volkmar, that the tradition represented by Georgios Hamartolos must apply to John the apostle. His arguments were not fully met by Grimm in *ZWT.*, 1874, 121 f.

the long-lived apostle, due in part to deductions from the Fourth gospel and the apocalypse, in part to the confusion of John the presbyter and John the apostle, tended to obliterate not only John the presbyter's figure, but the far-away tradition of John the apostle's early death. It is remarkable, however, to find the latter vibrating still at one or two places. Thus, while Clement of Alexandria tells the story * of John and the robber, which implied his long life, he also (*Strom.* vii. 17, *ἡ δὲ ἀποστόλων αὐτοῦ, i.e.* Christ, *μέχρι γε τῆς Παύλου λειτουργίας ἐπὶ Νέρωνος τελειοῦται*) assumes that all the teaching apostles had closed their careers before A.D. 70. Similarly Chrysostom in one homily (lxxvi.) says that John the apostle "lived for a long while after the capture of Jerusalem," while in another (lxv.) he expounds Mt 20^{23} upon the lines of the earlier tradition as a prophecy of martyr-death for the sons of Zebedee. Even Gregory of Nyssa may be cited as one of the later, perhaps unconscious, witnesses to the accuracy of the Papias-tradition, since in his *Laudatio Stephani*, as well as in his *de Basilio magno*, he groups Peter, James, and John as martyred apostles, and places them between Stephen and Paul. The Muratorian canon, which already vindicates the canonicity of the Johannine writings by means of the apostolic authorship, had also reflected indirectly the Papias-tradition by assuming that the Fourth gospel was composed while the apostles were still together (*i.e.* before A.D. 70), and by asserting that in writing to seven churches Paul was simply "sequens prodecessoris sui Iohannis ordinem." The unchronological nature of the latter remark was due not simply to the canonical prestige of the Johannine writings, but to the vague influence of the tradition which in one form associated John's literary exploits and experiences of persecution with Claudius and Nero. A similar fluctuation between the tradition of the martyrdom and that of the banishment occurs in the enigmatic passage, Tert. *de præscr. hæret.* 36 (the apostrophe to the church of Rome, "ubi Petrus passioni dominicæ adæquatur; ubi Paulus Iohannis exitu coronatur [cp. the Muratorian canon's order of John and Paul]; ubi apostolus Iohannes, posteaquam in oleum igneum demersus nihil passus est, in insulam relegatur"). The story of his scatheless immersion in a cauldron of boiling oil, which apparently goes back to the *Acta Johannis*

* It is late and pretty and doubtful, like the tale of Sir Walter Ralegh and his cloak.

(cp. Zahn's ed. pp. cxvi f.), was a rejuvenating touch introduced in order to harmonise the older tradition of his martyrdom with his legendary longevity. His 'baptism' was thus made harmless. He became a *μάρτυς* in the double sense of the term. The original setting of the story was probably in Nero's reign (cp. Jerome, *adv. Jovin.* i. 26, reporting Tertullian); afterwards, when he was identified with John the seer and witness of the apocalypse, the Domitianic period of the latter led to the subsequent transference of the tale from Nero to Domitian. The other legend, that he drank a cup of poison unharmed, betrays the same tendency to evade the literal implication of the synoptic prophecy; but in this case the feat was readily transferred to him from Justus Barsabbas (so Papias quoted in Eus. *H. E.* iii. 39. 9)—which would be all the more easy, as Badham ingeniously points out, since the Encratite phraseology made Christ remove from John "the serpent's poison," *i.e.* sexual desire. Another legend, that of John and Cerinthus in the bathhouse (Eus. *H. E.* iii. 28. 6), is also told of Ebion (Epiph. xxx. 24) and of a Jewish rabbi during Hadrian's reign.

§ 2. *The Irenæus-tradition.*—If these deductions from the Papias-traditions are correct, the later testimony of Irenæus * must be erroneous. Irenæus, in his letter to Florinus (Eus. *H. E.* v. 20), warns him against certain *δόγματα*. *Ταῦτα τὰ δόγματα οἱ πρὸ ἡμῶν πρεσβύτεροι, οἱ καὶ τοῖς ἀποστόλοις συμφοιτήσαντες, οὐ παρέδωκάν σοι.* Then he reminds Florinus of one of these *πρεσβύτεροι*, viz. *ὁ μακάριος καὶ ἀποστολικὸς πρεσβύτερος*, Polykarp, in whose company he (Irenæus) *παῖς ἔτι ὢν* (*i.e.* in his teens) *ἐν τῇ κάτω* Ἀσίᾳ had seen Florinus. Irenæus says he can remember how Polykarp used to describe his intercourse with John and also with the rest who had seen the Lord, and how he used to repeat their sayings and traditions about Jesus (*πάντα σύμφωνα ταῖς γραφαῖς*). Polykarp was thus one

* Defences of its trustworthiness by Stanton (*GHD.* i. 213 f.), V. Rose (*RB.*, 1897, 516–524), and Gwatkin (*Contemp. Review*, 1897, 222–226). According to F. G. Lewis (*The Irenæus Testimony to the Fourth Gospel, Its Extent, Meaning, and Value*, Chicago, 1908), the *γραφαί* of Eus. *H. E.* v. 20. 6 were separate booklets of Johannine reminiscences of the life and words of Jesus, circulating in the churches, which were compiled, perhaps by Polykarp himself, into the Fourth gospel. It is more than probable that the gospel originated in homilies and addresses which had originally a separate existence, but the ordinary sense of *γραφαί* here (=Scriptures) is more relevant to the context.

of the πρεσβύτεροι upon whom Irenæus and Florinus, like Papias, were dependent for their information about the eye-witnesses of Jesus. He was an older man than Papias, though he probably died before him. Consequently, if Irenæus is correct, his testimony to John the apostle is of first-rate importance.

But, while any wholesale depreciation of Irenæus is uncritical (see Preuschen on Schwartz in *Berliner Philol. Wochenschrift*, 1906, 101–105), and while his letter to Florinus is not to be brushed aside as a piece of unauthentic partisanship (Scholten, *Der Apostel Johannes in Klein-Asien*, 1872, pp. 63 f.), he must be held to have mistaken what Polykarp * said, and to have confused John the presbyter with John the apostle. Like Benjamin Franklin, he had 'ever a pleasure in obtaining any little anecdotes' of his spiritual ancestors; but his memory, partly owing to his desire to safeguard the apostolic authority of the Fourth gospel, misled him here as elsewhere. Thus he confuses Peter and Jesus, as if Ac 5^{15} applied to the latter (cp. *TU.* xxxi. 1, p. 40), as well as James the son of Zebedee and the James of Ac 15 = Gal 2 (*adv. Haer.* iii. 12. 15). He also infers (*adv. Haer.* ii. 22, *TU.* xxxi. 1. 42, 62 f.), either from the Fourth gospel 2^{20} 8^{57}) or from the Asiatic presbyters who claimed to represent John's tradition, that Jesus did not die till the reign of Claudius (*i.e.* not till after A.D. 41).

This inference has an important bearing on the whole subject. Whatever was the meaning † attached to the forty-six years of 2^{20}—whether it represents the period between the initiation of Herod the Great's building scheme (20 B.C.) and the date at which the scene of this discussion is laid (*i.e.* A.D. 27–28), or alludes to Ezra's temple (*Diat.* 2023–2024),—neither it nor the allusion in 8^{57} (where Blass, Schwartz, Wellhausen follow ℵ* Syr^{Sin} sah. in reading the more logical but less pungent ἑώρακέ σε, ЄΟΡΑΚЄϹЄ for ЄΟΡΑΚЄϹ) is responsible for the extraordinary exegetical blunder of Irenæus or of his authorities, the Johannine presbyters, that from twelve to twenty years elapsed between the baptism and the death of Jesus. If this tradition was picked up by Irenæus from the book of Papias, it richly confirms the impression of uncritical credulity which the other traditions of this school or circle make upon the modern reader. Neither Papias nor his

* Polykarp himself never calls the apostle John his teacher; indeed, he never alludes to him at all.

† Later tradition took it literally (cp. the pseudo-Cyprianic *De montibus Sina et Sion*, 4), and Loisy (293) has recently revived the allegorical-literal interpretation. For the anti-Valentinian, anti-Lucan motive of the passage, see above, pp. 530, 581, and Bacon's *Fourth Gospel* (pp. 394 f.).

informants can have had any accurate acquaintance with the John whom they claim as their apostolic authority. Their traditions are simply fantastic inferences drawn from the Johannine literature itself; whether Papias was primarily responsible for their circulation or not, they could never have come from a disciple who had been a member of the twelve (cp. Schwartz, pp. 7 f.; Clemen in *AJT.* ix. 661–663, and Corssen in *ZNW.*, 1901, 202–227). Similarly, anything else Irenæus quotes from the presbyters who are claimed to have been in touch with the apostle John, is of a singularly unapostolic character; not only this tradition that Jesus died when he was in his *ætas senior*, i.e. over forty or fifty, but the exegesis of Rev 13[18] (v. 30. 1), and the grotesque saying (p. 23) about the fruitful vines of the messianic era (v. 33. 3), if they do not militate decisively against an apostolic source, certainly do not presuppose it. There is nothing in Irenæus' tradition of the elders which points to any ultimate Johannine apostolic source, and a good deal which invalidates any such reference.

Irenæus was also mistaken, as Eusebius points out (*H. E.* iii. 39. 2), in making Papias a hearer of the apostle John. There is other evidence to show that he used *discipulus apostolorum* in a careless and loose sense. Once at least he inadvertently converts a presbyter *qui audierat ab his qui apostolos uiderant* (iv. 27. 1) into a *discipulus apostolorum* (iv. 32. 1); and this significant instance, all the more significant that it is incidental, corroborates the conclusion that, in his reminiscences of his boyhood beside Polykarp, he mistook similarly the presbyter John for the apostle. The date of Polykarp's death is uncertain, though *c.* 155 is approximately accurate (cp. Corssen in *ZNW.*, 1902, 61 f.). On any fair rendering of the chronological data, Irenæus could not have been more than a boy when he heard or met him (*Haer.* iii. 3. 4, ὃν καὶ ἡμεῖς ἑωράκαμεν ἐν τῇ πρώτῃ ἡμῶν ἡλικίᾳ), and his letter to Florinus (*H. E.* v. 20. 5 f.) does not imply, even if it does not exclude, the supposition that his acquaintance with the aged bishop of Smyrna extended beyond the days of his early youth. We are justified, therefore, in refusing to set aside the Papias-traditions in favour of a claim which rests upon such precarious grounds and which is otherwise open to serious doubts.

The force of this argument some critics attempt to turn, by pointing out the improbability of an error; Irenæus must have many opportunities, in Asia Minor and Rome and Gaul, of acquainting himself with the facts; others, who were contemporaries of Polykarp, must have been alive; and, therefore, Irenæus could not have written down an error which they would have instantly detected (cp. Drummond, pp. 347 f.; Sanday, *Criticism of Fourth Gospel*, 60 f.; Lepin, pp. 161 f.; Gregory, *Canon and Text*, pp. 159 f.). That Irenæus had many links with the far past and opportunities of learning about it, may be admitted freely. But the bearing of all this upon the question of the accuracy of his memory is another matter. There were hundreds of his readers who must have known that Jesus was not crucified in the reign of Claudius, for example; even the pagan historian Tacitus knew better. But this did not prevent Irenæus from committing his blunder, and it does not entitle us to argue that, because so many contemporaries could have corrected him if he had been wrong, therefore he must have been right. The wholesale application of this kind of argument could be used to guarantee many of the most patent inaccuracies in ancient literature, classical and Christian. As a protest against ultra-literary methods of handling early tradition it has some value, but it is only within narrow limits that it can operate legitimately as a positive criterion, and the Johannine witness of Irenæus does not fall within these limits.

Such confusion, owing to identity of names, was not unexampled. The case of the two Philips is a parallel. The Philip of Acts is one of 'the seven' (6^5), who is not one of the twelve (8^{5-40}), but nevertheless is an evangelist who does active work in Samaria and elsewhere. His Greek name, his connection with the Hellenists (Ac 6^1) in Jerusalem, and his efforts outside Judea, tally with the reference in Jn 12^{20-22}, where, as elsewhere in the Fourth gospel, Philip the apostle (*i.e.* one of the synoptic twelve) seems to be meant. Does this entitle us to infer that the confusion between the two Philips began as early as the Fourth gospel (so Stölten, *JPT.*, 1891, 150 f.; Loisy, 30, 683 f.; Holtzmann-Bauer on Jn 12^{22}), or that the Philip of the Fourth gospel is an imaginative figure constructed out of the traditions about the evangelist (so, recently, Thoma, 764 f.; Kreyenbühl, ii. 347 f.; Weizsäcker, and Schmiedel, *EBi.* 3700–3701)? A third alternative, that there was only one Philip, and that the early fathers were right in thinking of Philip as both deacon and apostle (so, recently, Purchas, *Johannine Problems*, 56–67), is negatived by the evidence of Ac 8^{5-40} which assumes that Philip the evangelist had not the apostolic power ($8^{14f.}$) of laying hands on converts and imparting the Spirit. The significant fact that the evangelist, whom Luke met at Cæsarea (Ac $21^{8f.}$), had θυγατέρες τέσσαρες παρθένοι προφητεύουσαι, is the starting-point of any discussion on this problem, unless Ac 21^9 is held, as I now think unlikely, to be an interpolation (cp. *HNT.* 675). The evidence of Papias would be conclusive if only it were clear whether the Philip whom he mentions (see pp. 598, 603) was the apostle or the evangelist. In any case, he derived information at first-hand, not from this Philip but from the daughters of Philip (Eus.

H. E. iii. 39. 9–10, ὡς δὲ κατὰ τοὺς αὐτοὺς ὁ Παπίας γενόμενος, where Harnack and Corssen * rightly understand χρόνους after αὐτοὺς). The probability is that his Philip was the apostle (of the Fourth gospel); but, even so, it does not follow that the daughters of Philip belonged to this Philip's family.† Eusebius, who declares that they furnished Papias with some of his fantastic legends, assumes that they were; but this may be due to the fact that he confused both Philips, and it may be that only ‡ Philip the evangelist had daughters, that they prophesied at Hierapolis, and that they represent the figures to which the Montanists appealed, and about which the later stories gathered. Whether the Fourth gospel or Papias already confused the two Philips or not, Polykrates and Proklus did, and after them the later church. The apostle in the second-century traditions fell heir to the prophetic and ascetic daughters of his namesake (cp. Salmon, *INT.* 313–315; Wendt on Ac 21[9], and McGiffert's excellent note in his edition of Eusebius, on iii. 31). Polykrates, bishop of Ephesus (before the end of the second century), testifies that Philip the apostle, one of the great lights who had died in Asia, was buried in Hierapolis along with 'his two aged virgin daughters,' while 'ἡ ἑτέρα αὐτοῦ θυγάτηρ ἐν ἁγίῳ πνεύματι πολιτευσαμένη now rests at Ephesus' (Eus. *H. E.* iii. 31 = v. 24). Clement of Alexandria (*Strom.* iii. 6. 52; Eus. *H. E.* iii. 30. 1) not only reckons Philip § with Peter among the married apostles, but adds, τὰς θυγατέρας ἀνδράσιν ἐξέδωκεν. In *the dialogue of Gaius and Proklus* (quoted in Eus. *H. E.* iii. 31. 4), the four prophetic daughters of Philip are recorded to have been buried with their father at Hierapolis. Eusebius, who quotes all these passages, evidently identified the two Philips, as Tertullian had done before him, since (as is plain from the use of ἀπόστολους in

* *ZNW.*, 1902, 289–299 ('die Töchter des Philippus').

† The atmosphere of the marvellous in Ac 8 (cp. vv.[7. 13. 39]) is certainly "in entire harmony with the stories which Papias gleaned at a later date from the daughters of Philip" (Purchas, 60–61).

‡ It is just possible that Philip the apostle had also daughters, and that Clement of Alexandria preserves an independent tradition with regard to them; but this leaves the confusion unaffected. The uncertainty of the text in Eusebius, as Schwartz points out (16 f.), prevents us from laying too much stress on the variation in numbers between Polykrates and the other witnessses.

§ He also declares (*Strom.* iii. 25) that the words in Lk 9[60] were spoken to Philip.

iii. 39. 10 = Ac 1[26]) his description of Philip as **τὸν ἀπόστολον** (iii. 39. 9) refers to the narrower, not to the wider (Zahn, *Forschungen*, vi. 162 f.; Drummond, 226), sense of the title. Did Polykrates and Proklus the Montanist already share this confusion? In all likelihood they did.* The Asiatic tendency to trace church origins and traditions directly to members of the twelve must have led at an early period to the substitution of Philip the apostle for his namesake the evangelist.†

§ 3. *The argument from silence.*—Leaving aside, for the moment, the evidence for John the apostle's early martyrdom, and confining ourselves to the tradition of his longevity and residence in Asia Minor, we find the statements of Irenæus, who is the first and chief witness for this tradition, confronted by a significant silence on the part of previous writers. Not merely is the entire early Christian literature down to Irenaeus silent upon any sojourn of the apostle John in Asia Minor,‡ but in one or two cases it is hardly possible that such a silence could have been preserved, had such a long residence been known to the writers. The silence of Clemens Romanus upon the alleged contemporary sojourn of John the apostle in Asia Minor is of minor importance; there was no particular occasion for him to mention the apostle, and his evidence hardly tells either way.§ Much more significant is the silence of Ignatius, especially when it is admitted

* Lightfoot (*Colossians*, 45–47) and Drummond (pp. 226–227) especially hold that the Philip of Polykrates was the apostle. On the other side, cp. (in English) Selwyn's *Christian Prophets*, 247 f.

† Schwartz (p. 17), who declines to follow Schmiedel in regarding the Philip of the Fourth gospel as imaginary, takes his own way: "Der antike Heroencult treibt auf christlichen Boden neue Blüthen; die Kleinasiaten haben den Apostel Philippus mit seinen Töchtern lange nach ihrem Tode, ja nach Papias, schwerlich vor 150, von Cæsarea nach Hierapolis und Ephesus geschafft, wie in früheren Zeiten sich die Städte ihre Heroen in späteren ihre Heiligen holten."

‡ The tradition was first examined and rejected by Vogel (1801), Reuterdahl (*de fontibus hist. eccl. Eusebianæ*, 1826), Lützelberger (*die kirch. Trad. über den apost. Joh.*, 1840), and especially Keim (i. 211 f.).

§ He implies, however, that the apostolic age is over (42, 44), and there would be a certain awkwardness in his retrospective allusions to the apostles if one of the latter was still alive; "I confess I find it hard to believe that one of the greatest apostles was still living, and residing in the very city from which Paul addressed his first letter to the Corinthians" (Drummond, p. 216). This cuts on the whole against the hypothesis of the long-lived apostle in Asia Minor, and it would at least fit in with the early-martyrdom tradition; but, at best, it is corroborative evidence.

that he knew the Fourth gospel (see pp. 577 f.). Even in writing to the church of Ephesus, less than twenty years after John the apostle is supposed not only to have written the apocalypse and the Fourth gospel, but to have exercised ecclesiastical authority in the province, he never alludes to him.* Paul is the one apostle mentioned (*ad. Eph.* xii. 2, Παύλου συμμύσται). The description of the Ephesian Christians (xi. 2) as οἳ καὶ τοῖς ἀποστόλοις πάντοτε συνῄνεσαν ἐν δυνάμει Ἰησοῦ Χριστοῦ, would be incredibly vague if John the apostle had occupied the local position which later tradition assigned to him; and in view of the prestige which, on this hypothesis, he enjoyed as the author of the apocalypse, it is out of the question to turn the evidence from the silence of Ignatius by conjecturing that John's reputation had not yet risen to such a height as would have justified Ignatius in mentioning him along with Paul. The argument from silence requires very careful handling, but in the present case it is quite valid. No serious argument can stand against the conclusion that while Ignatius, like Papias, may have known the Fourth gospel, he did not know of any residence of John the apostle, as its author, in Ephesus. Even Hegesippus does not appear to have known of John's longevity in Asia Minor; in describing the latter's Ephesian career, Eusebius goes away from Hegesippus to ὁ τῶν παρ' ἡμῖν ἀρχαίων λόγος (*H. E.* iii. 20. 9), which he would hardly have done if Hegesippus, who lay before him, had continued the tale in question. In short, the silence of Clemens Romanus, Ignatius, and Hegesippus cannot fairly be called accidental; no satisfactory explanation of it is forthcoming, except the admission that none of them knew of John the apostle as a resident authority and author in Asia Minor towards the close of the first century. The John of Asia Minor at this period (cp. in addition to the authorities already cited, von Dobschütz's *Probleme*, 91 f.) is John the presbyter, a Jewish Christian disciple, originally a Jerusalemite, who taught and ruled with strictness in the local churches. His authority and influence created a 'Johannine' school or circle. He wrote the apocalypse (see pp. 513 f.), and two notes of his (see pp. 475 f.) have survived, all written before the year 96 A.D. Later on, the church looked back to see in him, however, and in his earlier apostolic namesake, not two stars but one.

* "Some personal reference to St. John would have been natural in writing to the church at Ephesus" (*GHD.* i. 166).

§ 4. *Growth of the Johannine tradition.*—The first clue to the mazes of this later Johannine tradition lies in the strong tendency, felt as soon as the canon began to be formed, to connect any gospel or epistle with the apostles, directly or indirectly. The apocalypse was probably the first of the "Johannine" writings to be associated with the name of the apostle. It claimed to be written by a certain John, and the casual remark of Justin, only half a century after its composition, shows how soon and how naturally the primitive tradition, even in Ephesus, had begun to substitute John the apostle for his namesake the presbyter. Since the apocalypse and the Fourth gospel came from the same school, and since their language had certain resemblances, it was natural that the uncritical piety of the second century should extend the apostolic authorship to the gospel as well, especially if its final edition had paved the way for this view of its origin; the first epistle naturally followed in the wake of the gospel, while the second and third epistles were drawn after the apocalypse or the larger epistle. Once the Domitianic date of the apocalypse was granted,—and this is practically unchallenged during the second century,—the identification of John the seer with John the apostle went on apace, to cover the rest of the anonymous Johannine writings. His earlier sufferings did not amount to a red martyrdom; he was banished by Domitian to Patmos, where he composed the apocalypse 'de statu ecclesiæ' (Ps.-Aug. *Serm.* clxix. 2, Ps.-Isidore, Jerome, Primas. = metallo damnatus); after Domitian's death he returned to Asia Minor under Nerva, where he wrote the Fourth gospel against Cerinthus; finally (68 years after the death of Jesus according to Jerome, quoting "historia ecclesiastica"; 70 years, Ps. Isid.), he survived till Trajan's reign. The last item in the tradition is commonly admitted to be more or less an inference. "We may observe that the tradition that John survived till the time of Trajan can hardly claim the same degree of certainty as that of his residence in Asia" (Drummond, p. 216).

These deductions or inductions, under the influence of the apostolising tendency, would not have developed so rapidly, however, had there not been a tendency to confuse John the apostle and John the presbyter. This error, due to or fostered by the mistake of Irenæus, threw practically the whole of the subsequent tradition out of focus. When all the ecclesiastical interests were running so strongly in this direction through an age which was primarily interested in tradition for the sake of its utility in safeguarding the canonical authority of the New Testament writings and the apostolic authority of the twelve, it becomes less surprising that Irenæus ignored the casual remark of Papias about John's martyrdom, or that Eusebius in a later generation passed over it, perhaps as one of the *παράδοξα* or *μυθικώτερα* which he professed to find in the writings of the worthy bishop of Hierapolis. The remarkable thing really is that any traces of the early martyrdom should have been preserved at all. The early criticisms passed on the Fourth gospel for its discrepancies with the synoptic narrative led to the legends of its composition after them as a "spiritual gospel," written to supplement them (Schwartz, 44 f.), and this helps to explain how the tradition of John's early martyrdom * faded almost entirely from the church before that rival tradition of his long life in Ephesus, which made room for the composition of his gospel subsequent to the synoptists, by taking over item after item from the traditions of the presbyter. For the rise and growth of the second-century Christian tradition of the Ephesian John cannot be explained by recourse to fantasy and imagination. To account for the tradition, a definite historical figure must be assumed, one who lived to a great age in Asia Minor, and became an authority there, a John whose name and prestige counted highly in Asiatic circles. Thus, among the great lights who had fallen asleep in Asia, Polykrates numbers not only Philip but also *Ἰωάννης, ὁ ἐπὶ τὸ στῆθος τοῦ κυρίου ἀναπεσών, ὃς ἐγενήθη ἱερεὺς τὸ πέταλον πεφορεκὼς καὶ μάρτυς καὶ διδάσκαλος* (Eus. *H. E.* iii. 31. 3, v. 24. 2). The *πέταλον* phrase, unless it is an unauthentic interpolation (cp. Heinichen's note and Lücke, 20 f.), is either due to the fanciful play of legend—Epiphanius (*haer.* xxix. lxxviii., following Hegesippus ?) decorates James also with it—or else furnishes a proof that the John in question had belonged to the sacerdotal order in Jeru-

* One vague and confused echo of it may be heard in the occasional tradition that the apocalypse (see above, p. 505) was written very early. The remark of Epiphanius (li. 33: *τοῦ ἁγίου Ἰωάννου πρὸ κοιμήσεως αὐτοῦ προφητεύσαντος ἐν χρόνοις* Κλαυδίου Καίσαρος καὶ ἀνωτέρω [ἀνωτάτω, MSS], *ὅτε εἰς τὴν Πάτμον νῆσον ὑπῆρχεν*) is a piece of evidence which is all the more striking since the Domitianic tradition was well known by that period. Schwartz (*op. cit.* 29 f., 39 f.) suggests that this Claudius-tradition may explain the well-known objection of Gaius, that when the apocalypse was written (*i.e.* in fourth year of Claudius), there was no Christian church at Thyatira.

salem. In any case it is as incompatible with John the apostle as the title * διδάσκαλος, which could hardly have been used of an apostle. Polykrates, indeed, calls Philip an apostle, but not John, and as he uses *μάρτυς* immediately afterwards of Polykarp, Thraseas, and Sagaris, it is probably employed here in the light of Apoc 1^{5}. Thus all the indications point to John the presbyter, who is further identified with the beloved disciple of the Fourth gospel. If this identification is right, it tallies with the hypothesis of Delff,† Harnack, and Bousset. If it is wrong, it is a fresh witness to the fusion of John the presbyter with John the apostle (*i.e.* as the bosom-disciple, and perhaps as *μάρτυς* in the tragic sense). Since Polykrates in all likelihood meant to describe John the apostle, the confusion is similar to that in the case of Philip whom he has just mentioned. The really doubtful point is to determine how far the last chapter of the Fourth gospel contributed to this result. Was this appendix (or, at any rate, 21^{24-25}) a deliberate attempt by the Ephesian circle to claim for John the presbyter a gospel of John the beloved apostle, or *vice versa*? Or was the identification of the two men due to the misreading of the text by a later age? In short, does the appendix merely witness to a fusion already present, or was it one of the primary sources of the fusion? Either theory is tenable, and it depends upon the view taken of the gospel's aim and original character which falls to be adopted. The former seems to me slightly preferable, but here as elsewhere in the literary criticism of the Fourth gospel one has to jump for conclusions,—if one is eager for them,—and that is usually to land in a bog of confusion.

(*a*) The probability of Irenæus having confused the son of Zebedee with the presbyter John depends not only upon the fact that the latter really existed,—a fact which it should be no longer necessary to prove,—but on the presbyter's authority and residence in Asia Minor. The latter point is still disputed, on the ground that Papias does not expressly state it; and some critics, who admit the existence of the presbyter John, place him not in Asia Minor but in Syria or Palestine, partly on the grounds of supposed internal evidence drawn from the book of Revelation, partly because he is identified with some former priest called John (*e.g.* that of Ac 4^{6}, cp. Ac 6^{7}), partly because thereby the Judean tradition of the Fourth gospel is accounted for

* It is a different thing when Polykarp is called διδάσκαλος ἀποστολικὸς καὶ προφητικός (*Mart. Polyk.* 16).

† John (the priest of Ac 4^{6}?), a man of priestly rank, composed the Fourth gospel before the fall of Jerusalem (*SK.*, 1892, 83 f.). See above, p. 566.

(so recently A. Meyer and Zurhellen). But when the apocalypse is assigned to John the presbyter, his Asiatic connection follows. There is certainly nothing in Papias to show that John was an Asiatic, or that he had even met him. Still, though *μαθηταί* was the earliest title assumed by the Christian Jews of Palestine, it does not follow that its application to Aristion and John the presbyter denotes their Palestinian *locus*, and the Ephesian *locus* of the Fourth gospel in its present form is indicated, not only by the external evidence of tradition, but by converging lines of internal evidence, *e.g.* the fact that it springs from the same circle or school as the apocalypse (itself an undoubtedly Asiatic document), the presence of the Ephesian Logos ideas, and of the controversy with the Baptist's followers.

(*b*) If the Fourth gospel was ranked by Papias as a standard for measuring the others (see above, p. 187), why did not Eusebius record his evidence? Was it because (Schwartz, 23 f.) the historian could not agree with the bishop's tradition of the origin of the gospel as prior to Luke and Mark? Eusebius, on this hypothesis, would pass over the testimony of Papias because the latter, holding the early martyrdom of John, did not maintain the Ephesian residence and longevity of the apostle which, since Irenæus and Clement, had become the dominant belief of the church. If so, this would also account for the puzzling failure of Irenæus to employ such witness from Papias. The acquaintance of the latter with the Fourth gospel reappears in a curious argumentum of Codex Vatic. Alex. (quoted and discussed by Lightfoot, *Essays on Supern. Relig.* p. 210, and Burkitt, *Two Lectt. on Gospels*, 1901, Appendix ii.): euangelium Johannis manifestatum et datum est ecclesiis ab Johanne adhuc in corpore constituto, sicut Papias nomine Hierapolitanus, discipulus Johannis carus, in exotericis—id est in extremis [*i.e.* externis or extraneis] quinque libris retulit. This argumentum is obviously translated from the Greek, and its origin is pre-Hieronymian. It seems to cite Papias as the authority for a theory of the Fourth gospel's origin which is allied to that of the Muratorian canon; both probably go back to the Leucian *Acta*, or to an independent tradition playing on Jn 21^{24-25}. The paragraph in the Muratorian canon, though mutilated or abbreviated, gives a clear sense: Cohortantibus condiscipulis et episcopis suis dixit: conieiunate mihi hodie triduum, et quid cuique fuerit reuelatum alterutrum nobis enarremus. Eadem nocte reuelatum Andreæ ex apostolis, ut recognoscentibus cunctis Johannes suo nomine cuncta describeret ("when his fellow-disciples and bishops exhorted him [to write a gospel-narrative?], he said: Fast with me for three days from to-day [cp. Ac 13^2, Tert. *de ieiun.* 6] and let us tell one another what may be revealed to any one of us. That very night it was revealed to Andrew, one of the apostles, that John was to narrate all in his own name, while they were all to revise (or collate) it [ἀναγινωσκόντων πάντων]"). If the words *et episcopis* were deleted, as a mere accommodation to the popular legend (so Schwartz), it would be possible to regard this paragraph as a claim for the collective and catholic authority of the twelve behind the gospel of John, or at least for the authority of a certain circle of disciples who were able personally to guarantee traditions of Jesus. The evolution of a tradition like the 'Johannine' is never entirely deliberate and literary; motives of which men are seldom conscious combine to forward a tendency, once it has set in. Still, it throws up written statements which in their turn became factors in the process of ecclesiastical definition or pious fancy. The naive testimony of the Muratorian canon belongs to this class, though intrinsically it is no more than a legendary amplification of Jn 21^{24-25}, interpreted in the light of the rising claim for the apostolic authorship of a gospel which is attributed to special inspiration and possibly credited, as the context implies, with completeness no less than chronological order.

INDEX

(*A*) SUBJECTS AND REFERENCES

(*B*) AUTHORS AND AUTHORITIES.

(*C*) PASSAGES FROM NT.*

* In order to facilitate reference, these passages are printed in the order in which they occur in the ordinary English Bible.

(*D*) PASSAGES FROM EARLY CHRISTIAN LITERATURE.

(*E*) GREEK AND LATIN WORDS

WITHDRAWN

Printed in the United States
41657LVS00001B/13

9 781417 900596